Weiss Ratings' Guide to Property and Casualty Insurers

Weiss Ratings' Guide to Property and Casualty Insurers

A Quarterly Compilation of Insurance Company Ratings and Analyses

Fall 2017

GREY HOUSE PUBLISHING

Weiss Ratings
4400 Northcorp Parkway
Palm Beach Gardens, FL 33410
561-627-3300

Independent. Unbiased. Accurate. Trusted.

Published by Grey House Publishing, Inc., located at 4919 Route 22, Amenia, NY 12501; telephone 518-789-8700. Grey House Publishing neither guarantees the accuracy of the data contained herein nor assumes any responsibility for errors, omissions or discrepancies. Grey House Publishing accepts no payment for listing; inclusion in the publication of any organization, agency, institution, publication, service or individual does not imply endorsement of the publisher.

Grey House
Publishing
4919 Route 22
PO Box 56
Amenia, NY 12501-0056

Edition No. 94, Fall 2017

ISBN: 978-1-68217-433-3
ISSN: 2158-5989

Contents

Terms and Conditions

This document is prepared strictly for the confidential use of our customer(s). It has been provided to you at your specific request. It is not directed to, or intended for distribution to or use by, any person or entity who is a citizen or resident of or located in any locality, state, country or other jurisdiction where such distribution, publication, availability or use would be contrary to law or regulation or which would subject Weiss Ratings or its affiliates to any registration or licensing requirement within such jurisdiction.

No part of the analysts' compensation was, is, or will be, directly or indirectly, related to the specific recommendations or views expressed in this research report.

This document is not intended for the direct or indirect solicitation of business. Weiss Ratings and its affiliates disclaims any and all liability to any person or entity for any loss or damage caused, in whole or in part, by any error (negligent or otherwise) or other circumstances involved in, resulting from or relating to the procurement, compilation, analysis, interpretation, editing, transcribing, publishing and/or dissemination or transmittal of any information contained herein.

Weiss Ratings has not taken any steps to ensure that the securities or investment vehicle referred to in this report are suitable for any particular investor. The investment or services contained or referred to in this report may not be suitable for you and it is recommended that you consult an independent investment advisor if you are in doubt about such investments or investment services. Nothing in this report constitutes investment, legal, accounting or tax advice or a representation that any investment or strategy is suitable or appropriate to your individual circumstances or otherwise constitutes a personal recommendation to you.

The ratings and other opinions contained in this document must be construed solely as statements of opinion from Weiss Ratings, and not statements of fact. Each rating or opinion must be weighed solely as a factor in your choice of an institution and should not be construed as a recommendation to buy, sell or otherwise act with respect to the particular product or company involved.

Past performance should not be taken as an indication or guarantee of future performance, and no representation or warranty, expressed or implied, is made regarding future performance. Information, opinions and estimates contained in this report reflect a judgment at its original date of publication and are subject to change without notice. Weiss Ratings offers a notification service for rating changes on companies you specify. For more information visit WeissRatings.com or call 1-877-934-7778. The price, value and income from any of the securities or financial instruments mentioned in this report can fall as well as rise.

This document and the information contained herein is copyrighted by Weiss Ratings, LLC. Any copying, displaying, selling, distributing or otherwise reproducing or delivering this information or any part of this document to any other person entity is prohibited without the express written consent of Weiss Ratings, LLC, with the exception of a reviewer or editor who may quote brief passages in connection with a review or a news story, is prohibited.

Message To Insurers

All survey data received on or before July 17, 2017 has been considered or incorporated into this edition of the Directory. If there are particular circumstances which you believe could affect your rating, please use the online survey (**http://weissratings.com/survey/**) or e-mail Weiss Ratings, LLC (**insurancesurvey@weissinc.com**) with documentation to support your request. If warranted, we will make every effort to incorporate the changes in our next edition.

Welcome to Weiss Ratings'

Guide to Property and Casualty Insurers

Most people automatically assume their insurance company will survive, year after year. However, prudent consumers and professionals realize that in this world of shifting risks, the solvency of insurance companies can't be taken for granted.

If you are looking for accurate, unbiased ratings and data to help you choose property and casualty insurance for yourself, your family, your company or your clients, Weiss Ratings' *Guide to Property and Casualty Insurers* gives you precisely what you need.

In fact, it's the only source that currently provides ratings and analyses on over 2,000 property and casualty insurers.

Weiss Ratings' Mission Statement

Weiss Ratings' mission is to empower consumers, professionals, and institutions with high quality advisory information for selecting or monitoring a financial services company or financial investment.

In doing so, Weiss Ratings will adhere to the highest ethical standards by maintaining our independent, unbiased outlook and approach to advising our customers.

Why rely on Weiss Ratings?

Weiss Ratings provides fair, objective ratings to help professionals and consumers alike make educated purchasing decisions.

At Weiss Ratings, integrity is number one. Weiss Ratings never takes a penny from insurance companies for issuing a rating. We publish Weiss Safety Ratings without regard for insurers' preferences. However, other rating agencies like A.M. Best, Fitch, Moody's and Standard & Poor's are paid by insurance companies for their ratings and may even suppress unfavorable ratings at an insurer's request.

Our ratings are reviewed and updated more frequently than the other agencies' ratings. You can be sure that the information you receive is accurate and current, providing you with advance warning of financial vulnerability early enough to do something about it.

Other rating agencies focus primarily on a company's current claims paying ability and consider only mild economic adversity. Weiss Ratings also considers these issues, but our analysis also covers a company's ability to deal with severe economic adversity and a sharp increase in claims.

Our use of more rigorous standards stems from the viewpoint that an insurance company's obligations to its policyholders should not depend on favorable business conditions. An insurer must be able to honor its policy commitments in bad times as well as good.

Our rating scale, from A to F, is easy to understand. Only a few outstanding companies receive an A (Excellent) rating, although there are many to choose from within the B (Good) category. An even larger group falls into the broad average range which receives C (Fair) ratings. Companies that demonstrate marked vulnerabilities receive either D (Weak) or E (Very Weak) ratings.

How to Use This Guide

The purpose of the *Guide to Property and Casualty Insurers* is to provide policyholders and prospective policy purchasers with a reliable source of insurance company ratings and analyses on a timely basis. We realize that the financial strength of an insurer is an important factor to consider when making the decision to purchase a policy or change companies. The ratings and analyses in this Guide can make that evaluation easier when you are considering:

- Homeowners insurance

- Business insurance

- Auto insurance

- Workers' compensation insurance

- Product liability insurance

- Medical malpractice and other professional liability insurance

This Guide does not include companies that strictly provide life and health insurance or annuities. For information on those companies, please refer to our *Guide to Life and Annuity Insurers*. Also, only a few of the property and casualty companies in this Guide provide any form of health insurance. For a complete listing of health insurance providers, please refer to our *Guide to Health Insurers*.

The rating for a particular company indicates our opinion regarding that company's ability to meet its commitments to the policyholder – not only under current economic conditions, but also during a declining economy or in the event of a sharp increase in claims. Such an increase in claims and related expenses may be triggered by any number of occurrences including a strong earthquake or hurricane, rising medical or legal costs, or large court awards. The safest companies, however, should be prepared to deal with harsh and unforeseen circumstances.

To use this Guide most effectively, we recommend you follow the steps outlined below:

Step 1   To ensure you evaluate the correct company, verify the company's exact name and state of domicile as it was given to you or appears on your policy. Many companies have similar names but are not related to one another, so you want to make sure the company you look up is really the one you are interested in evaluating.

Step 2   Turn to Section I, the Index of Companies, and locate the company you are evaluating. This section contains all companies analyzed by Weiss Ratings including those that did not receive a Safety Rating. It is sorted alphabetically by the name of the company and shows the state of domicile following the name for additional verification. Once you have located your specific company, the first column after the state of domicile shows its Weiss Safety Rating. Turn to *About Weiss Safety Ratings* for information about what this rating means. If the rating has changed since the last issue of this Guide, a downgrade will be indicated with a down triangle ▼ to the left of the company name; an upgrade will be indicated with an up triangle ▲.

Step 3   Following Weiss Safety Rating are some of the various indexes that our analysts used in rating the company. Refer to the Critical Ranges in our Indexes table for an interpretation of which index values are considered strong, good, fair or weak. You can also turn to the introduction of Section I to see what each of these factors measures. In most cases, lower-rated companies will have a low index value in one or more of the factors shown. Bear in mind, however, that a Safety Rating is the result of a complex propriatary quantitative and qualitative analysis which cannot be reproduced using only the data provided here.

Step 4   Our analysts evaluate a great number of ratios and performance measures when assigning a rating. The right hand page of Section I shows you some of the key financial ratios we consider. Again, refer to the introduction of Section I for a description of each ratio.

Step 5   Some insurers have a bullet ● preceding the company name on the right hand page of Section I. This means that more detailed information about the company is available in Section II. If the company you are evaluating is identified with a bullet, turn to Section II, the Analysis of Largest Companies, and locate it there (otherwise skip to step 8). Section II contains the largest insurers rated by Weiss Ratings, regardless of rating. It too is sorted alphabetically by the name of the company.

Step 6   Once you have identified your company in Section II, you will find its Safety Rating and a description of the rating immediately to the right of the company name. Then, below the company name is a description of the various rating factors that were considered in assigning the company's rating. These factors and the information below them are designed to give you a better feel for the company and its strengths and weaknesses. See the Section II introduction to get a better understanding of what each of these factors means.

Step 7   To the right, you will find a five-year summary of the company's Safety Rating, capitalization and income. Look for positive or negative trends in these data. Below the five-year summary, we have included a graphic illustration of the most critical factor or factors impacting the company's rating. Again, the Section II introduction provides an overview of the content of each graph or table.

Step 8   If the company you are evaluating is not highly rated and you want to find an insurer with a higher rating, turn to the page in Section V that has your state's name at the top. This section contains those Recommended Companies (rating of A+, A, A- or B+) that are licensed to underwrite insurance in your state, sorted by rating. Then turn to the page in Section IV that shows the type of insurance you are interested in at the top. Insurers appearing on both lists will be those Recomended Companies which are licensed to sell that particular type of insurance in your state. From here you can select a company and then refer back to Sections I and II to analyze it.

Step 9   If you decide that you would like to contact one of Weiss Recommended Companies about obtaining a policy or for additional information, refer to Section III. Following each company's name is its address and phone number to assist you in making contact.

Step 10   In order to use Weiss Safety Ratings most effectively, we strongly recommend you consult the Important Warnings and Cautions listed. These are more than just "standard disclaimers"; they are very important factors you should be aware of before using this Guide. If you have any questions regarding the precise meaning of specific terms used in the Guide, refer to the Glossary.

Step 11   The Appendix contains information about State Guaranty Associations and the types of coverage they provide to policyholders when an insurance company fails. Keep in mind that while guaranty funds have now been established in all states, many do not cover all types of insurance. Furthermore, all of these funds have limits on their amount of coverage. Use the table to determine whether the level of coverage is applicable to your policy and the limits are adequate for your needs. You should pay particular attention to the notes regarding coverage limitations.

Step 12   If you want more information on your state's guaranty fund, call the State Commissioner's Office directly.

Step 13   Keep in mind that good coverage from a state guaranty association is no substitute for dealing with a financially strong company. Weiss Ratings only recommends those companies which we feel are most able to stand on their own, even in a recession or downturn in the economy .

Step 14   Make sure you stay up to date with the latest information available since the publication of this Guide. For information on how to set up a rating change notification service, acquire follow-up reports, or receive a more in-depth analysis of an individual company, call 1-877-934-7778 or visit www.weissratings.com.

Data Sources: Annual and quarterly statutory statements filed with state insurance commissioners and data provided by the insurance companies being rated. The National Association of Insurance Commissioners has provided some of the raw data. Any analyses or conclusions are not provided or endorsed by the NAIC.

Date of data analyzed March 31, 2017 unless otherwise noted.

About Weiss Safety Ratings

The Weiss Ratings of insurers are based upon the annual and quarterly financial statements filed with state insurance commissioners. This data may be supplemented by information that we request from the insurance companies themselves. However, if a company chooses not to provide supplemental data, we reserve the right to rate the company based exclusively on publicly available data.

The Weiss Ratings are based on a complex analysis of hundreds of factors that are synthesized into a series of indexes: capitalization, investment safety (life, health and annuity companies only), reserve adequacy (property and casualty companies only), profitability, liquidity, and stability. These indexes are then used to arrive at a letter grade rating. A weak score on any one index can result in a low rating, as financial problems can be caused by any one of a number of factors, such as inadequate capital, unpredictable claims experience, poor liquidity, speculative investments, inadequate reserving, or consistent operating losses.

Our **Capital Index** gauges capital adequacy in terms of each insurer's ability to handle a variety of business and economic scenarios as they may impact investment performance, claims experience, persistency, and market position. The index combines two Risk-Adjusted Capital ratios as well as a leverage test that examines pricing risk.

Our **Investment Safety Index** measures the exposure of the company's investment portfolio to loss of principal and/or income due to default and market risks. Each investment area is rated by a factor that takes into consideration both quality and liquidity. (This factor is measured as a separate index only for life, health, and annuity insurers.)

Our **Reserve Adequacy Index** measures the adequacy of the company's reserves and its ability to accurately anticipate the level of claims it will receive. (This factor is measured as a separate index only for property and casualty insurers.)

Our **Profitability Index** measures the soundness of the company's operations and the contribution of profits to the company's financial strength. The profitability index is a composite of five sub-factors: 1) gain or loss on operations; 2) consistency of operating results; 3) impact of operating results on surplus; 4) adequacy of investment income as compared to the needs of policy reserves (life, health and annuity companies only); and 5) expenses in relation to industry norms for the types of policies that the company offers.

Our **Liquidity Index** evaluates a company's ability to raise the necessary cash to settle claims and honor cash withdrawal obligations. We model various cash flow scenarios, applying liquidity tests to determine how the company might fare in the event of an unexpected spike in claims and/or a run on policy surrenders.

Our **Stability Index** integrates a number of sub-factors that affect consistency (or lack thereof) in maintaining financial strength over time. These sub-factors will vary depending on the type of insurance company being evaluated but may include such things as 1) risk diversification in terms of company size, group size, number of policies in force, types of policies written, and use of reinsurance; 2) deterioration of operations as reported in critical asset, liability, income and expense items, such as surrender rates and premium volume; 3) years in operation; 4) former problem areas where, despite recent improvement, the company has yet to establish a record of stable performance over a suitable period of time; 5) a substantial shift in the company's operations; 6) potential instabilities such as reinsurance quality, asset/liability matching, and sources of capital; and 7) relationships with holding companies and affiliates.

In order to help guarantee our objectivity, we reserve the right to publish ratings expressing our opinion of a company's financial stability based exclusively on publicly available data and our own proprietary standards for safety.

Each of these indexes is measured according to the following range of values.

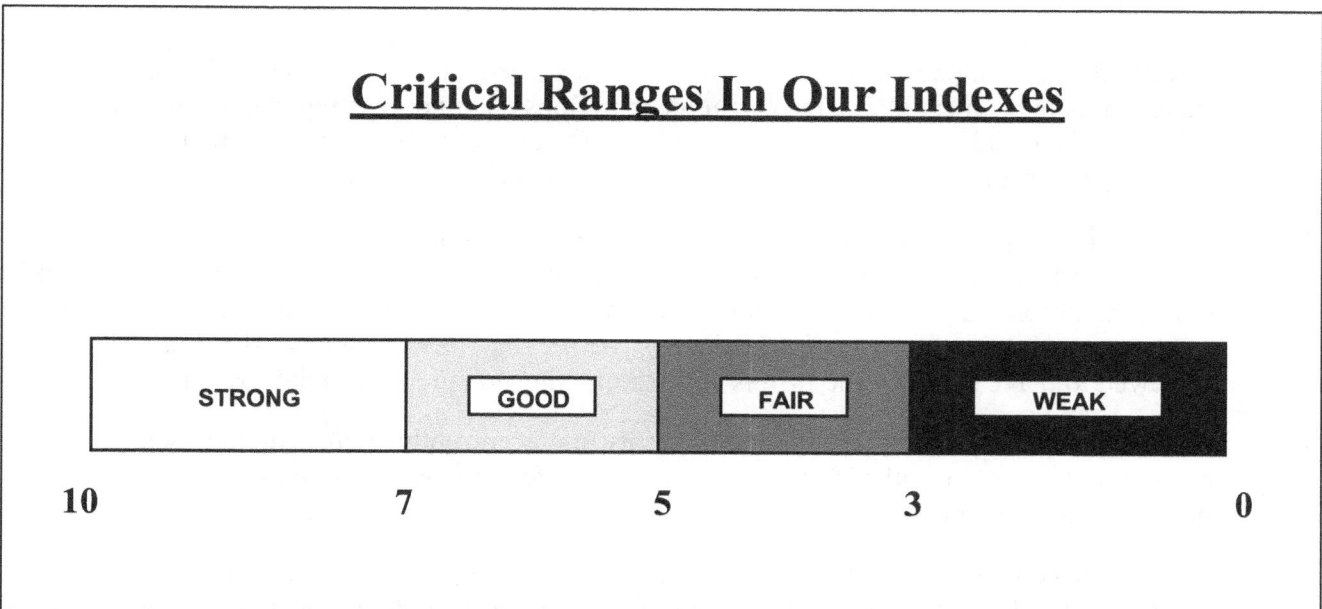

What Our Ratings Mean

A   **Excellent.** The company offers excellent financial security. It has maintained a conservative stance in its investment strategies, business operations and underwriting commitments. While the financial position of any company is subject to change, we believe that this company has the resources necessary to deal with severe economic conditions.

B   **Good.** The company offers good financial security and has the resources to deal with a variety of adverse economic conditions. It comfortably exceeds the minimum levels for all of our rating criteria, and is likely to remain healthy for the near future. However, in the event of a severe recession or major financial crisis, we feel that this assessment should be reviewed to make sure that the firm is still maintaining adequate financial strength.

C   **Fair.** The company offers fair financial security and is currently stable. But during an economic downturn or other financial pressures, we feel it may encounter difficulties in maintaining its financial stability.

D   **Weak.** The company currently demonstrates what, in our opinion, we consider to be significant weaknesses which could negatively impact policyholders. In an unfavorable economic environment, these weaknesses could be magnified.

E   **Very Weak.** The company currently demonstrates what we consider to be significant weaknesses and has also failed some of the basic tests that we use to identify fiscal stability. Therefore, even in a favorable economic environment, it is our opinion that policyholders could incur significant risks.

F   **Failed.** The company is deemed failed if it is either 1) under supervision of an insurance regulatory authority; 2) in the process of rehabilitation; 3) in the process of liquidation; or 4) voluntarily dissolved after disciplinary or other regulatory action by an insurance regulatory authority.

+   The **plus sign** is an indication that the company is in the upper third of the letter grade.

-   The **minus sign** is an indication that the company is in the lower third of the letter grade.

U   **Unrated.** The company is unrated for one or more of the following reasons: (1) total assets are less than $1 million; (2) premium income for the current year was less than $100,000; (3) the company functions almost exclusively as a holding company rather than as an underwriter; (4) in our opinion, we do not have enough information to reliably issue a rating.

How Our Ratings Differ From Those of Other Services

Weiss Safety Ratings are conservative and consumer-oriented. We use tougher standards than other rating agencies because our system is specifically designed to inform risk-averse consumers about the safety of property and casualty insurers.

Our rating scale (A to F) is easy to understand by the general public. Users can intuitively understand that an A+ rating is at the top of the scale rather than in the middle like some of the other rating agencies.

Other rating agencies give top ratings more generously so that most companies receive excellent ratings.

More importantly, other rating agencies focus primarily on a company's *current* claims paying ability or consider only relatively mild economic adversity. We also consider these scenarios but extend our analyses to cover a company's ability to deal with severe economic adversity and potential liquidity problems. This stems from the viewpoint that an insurance company's obligations to its policyholders should not be contingent upon a healthy economy. The company must be capable of honoring its policy commitments in bad times as well.

Looking at the insurance industry as a whole, we note that several major rating firms have poor historical track records in identifying troubled companies. The 1980s saw a persistent decline in capital ratios, increased holdings of risky investments in the life and health industry as well as recurring long-term claims liabilities in the property and casualty industry. The insurance industry experienced similar issues before and during the Great Recession of 2007-2009. Despite these clear signs that insolvency risk was rising, other rating firms failed to downgrade at-risk insurance companies. Instead, they often rated companies by shades of excellence, understating the gravity of potential problems.

Other ratings agencies have not issued clear warnings that the ordinary consumer can understand. Few, if any, companies receive "weak" or "poor" ratings. Surely, weak companies do exist. However, the other rating agencies apparently do not view themselves as consumer advocates with the responsibility of warning the public about the risks involved in doing business with such companies.

Additionally, these firms will at times agree *not* to issue a rating if a company denies them permission to do so. In short, too often insurance rating agencies work hand-in-glove with the companies they rate.

At Weiss Ratings, although we seek to maintain good relationships with the firms, we owe our primary obligation to the consumer, not the industry. We reserve the right to rate companies based on publicly available data and make the necessary conservative assumptions when companies choose not to provide additional data we might request.

Comparison of Insurance Company Rating Agency Scales				
Weiss Ratings [a]	**Best** [a]	**S&P**	**Moody's**	**Fitch**
A+, A, A-	A++, A+	AAA	Aaa	AAA
B+, B, B-	A, A-	AA+, AA AA-	Aa1, Aa2, Aa3	AA+, AA, AA-
C+, C, C-	B++, B+,	A+, A, A-, BBB+, BBB, BBB-	A1, A2, A3, Baa1, Baa2, Baa3	A+, A, A-, BBB+, BBB, BBB-
D+, D, D-	B, B- C++, C+, C, C-	BB+, BB, BB-, B+, B, B-	Ba1, Ba2, Ba3, B1, B2, B3	BB+, BB, BB-, B+, B, B-
E+, E, E- F	D E, F	CCC R	Caa, Ca, C	CCC+, CCC, CCC- DD

[a] Weiss Ratings and Best use additional symbols to designate that they recognize an insurer's existence but do not provide a rating. These symbols are not included in this table.

Rate of Insurance Company Failures

Weiss Ratings provides quarterly Safety Ratings for thousands of insurance companies each year. Weiss Ratings strives for fairness and objectivity in its ratings and analyses, ensuring that each company receives the rating that most accurately depicts its current financial status, and more importantly, its ability to deal with severe economic adversity and a sharp increase in claims. Weiss Ratings has every confidence that its Safety Ratings provide an accurate representation of a company's stability.

In order for these ratings to be of any true value, it is important that they prove accurate over time. One way to determine the accuracy of a rating is to examine those insurance companies that have failed, and their respective Weiss Safety Ratings. A high percentage of failed companies with "A" ratings would indicate that Weiss Ratings is not being conservative enough with its "secure" ratings, while conversely, a low percentage of failures with "vulnerable" ratings would show that Weiss Ratings is overly conservative.

Over the past 28 years (1989–2016) Weiss Ratings has rated 627 insurance companies, for all industries, that subsequently failed. The chart below shows the number of failed companies in each rating category, the average number of companies rated in each category per year, and the percentage of annual failures for each letter grade.

	Safety Rating	Number of Failed Companies	Average Number of Companies Rated per year	Percentage of Failed Companies per year (by ratings category)*
Secure	A	1	154	0.02%
	B	6	1,105	0.02%
	C	70	1,613	0.16%
Vulnerable	D	276	751	1.31%
	E	274	217	4.50%

A=Excellent, B=Good, C=Fair, D=Weak, E=Very Weak

On average, only 0.10% of the companies Weiss Ratings rates as "secure" fail each year. On the other hand, an average of 2.03% of the companies Weiss Ratings rates as "vulnerable" fail annually. That means that a company rated by Weiss Ratings as "Vulnerable" is 21.2 times more likely to fail than a company rated as "Secure".

When considering a Weiss Safety Rating, one can be sure that they are getting the most fair, objective, and accurate safety rating available anywhere.

*Percentage of Failed Companies per year = (Number of Failed Companies) / [(Average Number of Companies Rated per year) x (years in study)]

Data as of December 2016 for Life and Annuity Insurers and Property & Casualty Insurers and Health Insurers

What Does Average Mean?

At Weiss Ratings, we consider the words average and fair to mean just that – average and fair. So when we assign our ratings to insurers, the largest percentage of companies receives an average C rating. That way, you can be sure that a company receiving Weiss B or A rating is truly above average. Likewise, you can feel confident that companies with D or E ratings are truly below average.

Percentage for Property and Casualty Insurers in Each Rating Category

Current Weiss Ratings Distribution

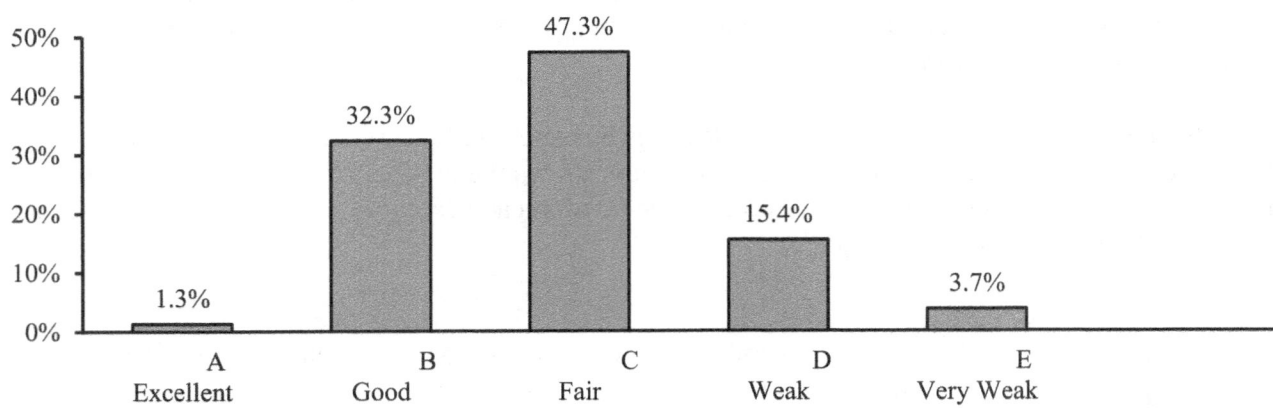

Important Warnings and Cautions

1. A rating alone cannot tell the whole story. Please read the explanatory information contained in this publication. It is provided in order to give you an understanding of our rating philosophy, as well as paint a more complete picture of how we arrive at our opinion of a company's strengths and weaknesses.

2. Weiss Safety Ratings represent our opinion of a company's insolvency risk. As such, a high rating means we feel that the company has less chance of running into financial difficulties. A high rating is not a guarantee of solvency nor is a low rating a prediction of insolvency. Weiss Safety Ratings are not deemed to be a recommendation concerning the purchase or sale of the securities of any insurance company that is publicly owned.

3. Company performance is only one factor in determining a rating. Conditions in the marketplace and overall economic conditions are additional factors that may affect the company's financial strength. Therefore, a rating upgrade or downgrade does not necessarily reflect changes in the company's profits, capital or other financial measures, but may be due to external factors. Likewise, changes in Weiss indexes may reflect changes in our risk assessment of business or economic conditions as well as changes in company performance.

4. All firms that have the same Safety Rating should be considered to be essentially equal in strength. This is true regardless of any differences in the underlying numbers which might appear to indicate greater strengths. Weiss Safety Rating already takes into account a number of lesser factors which, due to space limitations, cannot be included in this publication.

5. A good rating requires consistency. If a company is excellent on four indicators and fair on one, the company may receive a fair rating. This requirement is necessary due to the fact that fiscal problems can arise from any *one* of several causes including speculative investments, inadequate capital resources or operating losses.

6. We are an independent rating agency and do not depend on the cooperation of the companies we rate. Our data are derived, from annual and quarterly financial statements that we obtain from federal regulators and filings with state insurance commissioners. The latter may be supplemented by information insurance companies voluntarily provide upon request. Although we seek to maintain an open line of communication with the companies, we do not grant them the right to stop or influence publication of the ratings. This policy stems from the fact that this publication is designed for the protection of the consumer.

7. Affiliated companies do not automatically receive the same rating. We recognize that a troubled company may expect financial support from its parent or affiliates. Weiss Safety Ratings reflect our opinion of the measure of support that may become available to a subsidiary, if the subsidiary were to experience serious financial difficulties. In the case of a strong parent and a weaker subsidiary, the affiliate relationship will generally result in a higher rating for the subsidiary than it would have on a stand-alone basis. Seldom, however, would the rating be brought up to the level of the parent. This treatment is appropriate because we do not assume the parent would have either the resources or the will to "bail out" a troubled subsidiary during a severe economic crisis. Even when there is a binding legal obligation for a parent corporation to honor the policy obligations of its subsidiaries, the possibility exists that the subsidiary could be sold and lose its parental support. Therefore, it is quite common for one affiliate to have a higher rating than another. This is another reason why it is especially important that you have the precise name of the company you are evaluating.

Section I

Index of Companies

An analysis of all rated and unrated

U.S. Property and Casualty Insurers.

Companies are listed in alphabetical order.

Section I Contents

This section contains the key rating factors and performance measures for all rated and unrated insurers analyzed by Weiss Ratings. An explanation of each of the footnotes and stability factors appears at the end of this section.

Left Pages

1. **Insurance Company Name**

The legally registered name, which can sometimes differ from the name that the company uses for advertising. If you cannot find the company you are interested in, or if you have any doubts regarding the precise name, verify the information with the company before looking the name up in this Guide. Also, determine the domicile state for confirmation. (See column 2.)

2. **Domicile State**

The state which has primary regulatory responsibility for the company. It may differ from the location of the company's corporate headquarters. You do not have to be living in the domicile state to purchase insurance from this firm, provided it is licensed to do business in your state.

3. **Safety Rating**

Our rating is measured on a scale from A to F and considers a wide range of factors. Please see *What Our Ratings Mean* for specific descriptions of each letter grade. Also, refer to how our ratings differ from those of other rating agencies. Most important, when using this rating, please be sure to consider the warnings regarding the ratings' limitations and the underlying assumptions. Notes in this column refer to the date of the data included in the rating evaluation and are explained.

4. **Total Assets**

All assets admitted by state insurance regulators in millions of dollars through the most recent quarter available. This includes investments and current business assets such as receivables from agents and reinsurers.

The overall size is an important factor which affects the ability of a company to manage risk. Generally speaking, risks can be more effectively diversified by large companies. Because the insurance business is based on probability, the number of policies must be large enough so that actuarial statistics are valid. The larger the number of policyholders, the more reliable the actuarial projections will be. A large company with a correspondingly large policy base can spread its risk and minimize the effects of claims experience that exceeds actuarial expectations.

5. **Capital and Surplus**

The company's statutory net worth in millions of dollars through the most recent quarter available. Consumers may wish to limit the size of any policy so that the policyholder's maximum potential claims do not exceed approximately 1% of the company's capital and surplus. For example, when buying a policy from a company with capital and surplus of $10,000,000, the 1% limit would be $100,000. (When performing this calculation, do not forget that figures in this column are expressed in millions of dollars.)

6. Net Premium   The amount of insurance premiums received from policyholders less any premiums that have been transferred to other companies through reinsurance agreements. This figure is updated through the most recent annual report available.

Generally speaking, companies with large net premium volume generally have more predictable claims experience.

Critical Ranges In Our Indexes and Ratios

Indicators	Strong	Good	Fair	Weak
Risk-Adjusted Capital Ratio #1	—	1.0 or more	0.75 - 0.99	0.74 or less
Risk-Adjusted Capital Ratio #2	1.0 or more	0.75 - 0.99	0.5 - 0.74	0.49 or less
Capitalization Index	6.9 – 10	4.9 - 6.8	2.9 - 4.8	Less than 2.9
Reserve Adequacy Index	6.9 – 10	4.9 - 6.8	2.9 - 4.8	Less than 2.9
Profitability Index	6.9 – 10	4.9 - 6.8	2.9 - 4.8	Less than 2.9
Liquidity Index	6.9 – 10	4.9 - 6.8	2.9 - 4.8	Less than 2.9
Stability Index	6.9 – 10	4.9 - 6.8	2.9 - 4.8	Less than 2.9

---

7. Net Income   The company's profit for the period. Profit is defined as revenues minus expenses. In the case of an insurance company, revenues include premiums and investment income, and expenses include claims payments and underwriting expenses.

8. Capitalization Index   An index that measures the adequacy of the company's capital resources to deal with a variety of business and economic scenarios. It combines Risk-Adjusted Capital Ratios #1 and #2 as well as a leverage test that examines pricing risk. (See the table above for the ranges which we believe are critical.)

| 9. **Reserve Adequacy Index** | An index that uses annual and quarterly data to measure the adequacy of the company's reserves. Reserves are funds the company sets aside to cover unsettled claims it estimates each year. Included are claims that the company has already received but have not yet been settled and claims that they expect to receive, but which have not yet been reported. |

If a company consistently estimates its claims accurately, that is good. Or if it errs on the side of being conservative and overestimates its claims from time to time, that is even better. Either case will cause this index to move higher.

On the other hand, some companies may have trouble accurately predicting the claims they will have to pay. Others may intentionally underestimate their claims to inflate their profits for stockholders or to make their capital appear higher than it really is. In either case, inadequate reserve levels will result in a low Reserve Adequacy Index.

If a company has chronically deficient reserves, it calls into question the company's ability to manage its policy risk effectively.

| 10. **Profitability Index** | An index that uses annual and quarterly data to measure the soundness of the company's operations and the contribution of profits to the company's fiscal strength. The Profitability Index is a composite of five factors: (1) gain or loss on underwriting; (2) gain or loss on overall operations; (3) consistency of operating results; (4) impact of operating results on surplus; and (5) expenses in relation to industry averages for the types of policies that the company offers. |

| 11. **Liquidity Index** | An index which uses annual and quarterly data to measure the company's ability to raise the necessary cash to settle claims. Sometimes a company may appear to have the necessary resources to pay claims on paper, but in reality, it may be unable to raise the necessary cash. This can occur, for example, when a company is owed a great deal of money from its agents or reinsurers, or when it cannot sell its investments at the prices at which they are valued in the company's financial statements. |

We look at various cash flow scenarios. Then we apply liquidity tests which tell us how the company might fare in each of those circumstances.

| 12. **Stability Index** | An index which uses annual and quarterly data to integrate a number of factors such as: (1) risk diversification in terms of company size, number of policies in force, use of reinsurance, and single largest risk exposure; (2) deterioration of operations as reported in critical asset, liability, income, or expense items such as premium volume and/or surplus (See the table prior page for the levels which we believe are critical.) |

| 13. **Stability Factors** | Indicates those specific areas that have negatively impacted the company's Stability Index. |

Right Pages

1. Risk-Adjusted Capital Ratio #1

This ratio examines the adequacy of the company's capital base and whether the company has sufficient capital resources to cover potential losses which might occur in an average recession or other moderate loss scenario. Specifically, the figure, calculated from annual and quarterly data, answers the question: For every dollar of capital that we feel would be needed, how many dollars in capital resources does the company actually have?

You may find that some companies have unusually high levels of capital. This often reflects special circumstances related to the small size or unusual operations of the company.

See the table prior page for the levels which we believe are critical. See the Appendix for more details on how this ratio is calculated.

2. Risk-Adjusted Capital Ratio #2

This is similar to the Risk-Adjusted Capital Ratio #1. But in this case, the question relates to whether the company has enough capital cushion to withstand a *severe* recession or other severe loss scenario.

See the table prior page for the levels which we believe are critical. See the Appendix for more details on how this ratio is calculated.

3. Premium to Surplus

The ratio of net premiums written compared to the company's capital and surplus level. This ratio, calculated from the company's annual report, answers the question: For every dollar of capital and surplus, how many dollars of premium does the company take in? Results of over 300% are considered perilous and could indicate that the insurer does not have adequate capital to support the volume of business that it is underwriting. A large figure could also help explain why a company has poor results on its risk-adjusted capital tests.

4. Reserves to Surplus

The ratio of reserves for expected claims compared to the company's capital and surplus level. If a company does not set aside enough reserves, it may have to withdraw capital to pay claims. This ratio, calculated from the annual report, is a rough measure of how much capital cushion the company has against claims reserves. The industry average is around 180%.

High ratios signify that reserve deficiencies would have a strong impact on capital and could help explain why a company has poor risk-adjusted capital results.

5. One-Year Reserve Development

The percentage increase or decrease in the company's annual reserve estimate compared to the previous year. If last year's estimate is below that of this year, this will result in a positive ratio meaning that the company underestimated its future claims and set aside insufficient reserves. Making this error consistently is viewed negatively because it means the company is inflating its income and capital.

6. Two-Year Reserve Development

This ratio is similar to the One-Year Reserve Development ratio. However, instead of comparing the latest estimates with those from the prior year, it compares them to the estimates from two years ago.

Again, a positive ratio means the company underestimated its reserve needs while a negative ratio indicates that reserve needs were overestimated.

7. Loss Ratio

The ratio of claims paid to premiums collected, calculated from the annual report, measures the company's underwriting profits. Needless to say, if an insurer pays out a very high percentage of what it collects, there may not be enough left over for other expenses, let alone enough to build the company's capital and financial strength over time.

8. Expense Ratio

The ratio of overhead expenses to premiums collected, calculated from the annual report, and answers the question: How many cents is the company paying out in executive salaries, agents' commissions, and other administrative expenses for every dollar in premiums that it collects from policyholders? A low Expense Ratio is good for both the company and its policyholders because it means that the company is efficient and can utilize more of each premium dollar to pay claims. A high Expense Ratio is a bad sign because it signals that too much of the company's premiums are being used for things which do not directly benefit its policyholders.

9. Combined Ratio

The sum of the Loss Ratio and the Expense Ratio. The Combined Ratio shows how much the company is paying out in administrative expenses and claims for every dollar of premium collected.

Values over 100% indicate that the company is losing money on its underwriting. This is very common in the industry, but it's still a sign of possible weakness.

Underwriting losses can often be offset by income the company realizes on its investments. This is especially true for companies that issue policies on which they do not have to pay claims for several years (long-tail policies). With these policies, the premiums can be invested in order to earn income for the company until the claims are paid.

10. Cash from Underwriting

The ratio of cash received from premiums (net of reinsurance) to cash outlays for claims and underwriting expenses, compiled from the annual report. A figure under 100% indicates that the company is paying out more in claims and expenses than it is receiving in premiums, whereas a figure over 100% indicates a positive cash flow. A negative figure generally indicates that the company has sold more business to a reinsurance company than it has taken in during the current year.

When a company has a positive net cash flow from its underwriting, it can generate additional funds for investing. On the other hand, if net cash flow is negative, the company may have to rely on its investment income to make up the shortfall. And if that isn't enough, it may even have to sell assets to meet its obligations.

11. Net Premium Growth

The annual percentage change in net premiums compared to the previous year. A company can increase its premium volume by: (1) issuing more new policies; (2) raising its rates; or (3) selling less of its insurance to other insurance companies. Slow and steady growth is healthy but rapid growth is often an indicator of trouble ahead. It may mean that the company is underpricing as a means of gaining market share. Indeed, a high percentage of insurance company failures are related to rapid growth. Regulators consider a fluctuation of more than 33% as a cautionary flag.

A rapid decline in premium volume is also a negative sign. It indicates that the company is losing its customer base. However, if the decline is the result of premium redistribution among a group of affiliates, the significance of the decline is minimal.

12. Investments In Affiliates

The percentage of the company's investment portfolio from the annual report dedicated to investments in affiliates. These investments can be bonds, preferred and common stocks, as well as other vehicles which many insurance companies use to invest in – and establish a corporate link with – affiliated companies. Large investments of this type can pose problems as these investments often produce no income and can be difficult to sell.

Footnotes:

(1) Data items shown are from the company's 2016 annual statutory statement. Other more recent data may have been factored into the rating when available.

(2) Data items shown are from the company's 2015 annual statutory statement except for Risk-Adjusted Capital Indexes 1 and 2, Profitability Index, Investment Safety Index, Liquidity Index and Stability Index which have been updated using the company's September 2016 quarterly statutory statement. Other more recent data may have been factored into the rating when available.

(3) Data items shown are from the company's 2015 annual statutory statement except for Risk-Adjusted Capital Indexes 1 and 2, Profitability Index, Investment Safety Index, Liquidity Index and Stability Index which have been updated using the company's June 2016 quarterly statutory statement. Other more recent data may have been factored into the rating when available.

(4) Data items shown are from the company's 2015 annual statutory statement except for Risk-Adjusted Capital Indexes 1 and 2, Profitability Index, Investment Safety Index, Liquidity Index and Stability Index which have been updated using the company's March 2016 quarterly statutory statement. Other more recent data may have been factored into the rating when available.

(5) These companies have data items that are older than December 31, 2015. They will be unrated (U) if they are not failed companies (F).

Stability Factors

(A) Stability Index was negatively impacted by the financial problems or weaknesses of a parent or **affiliate** company.

(C) Stability Index was negatively impacted by past results on our Risk-Adjusted **Capital** tests. In general, the Stability Index of any company can be affected by past results even if current results show improvement. While such improvement is a plus, the improved results must be maintained for a period of time to assure that the improvement is not a temporary fluctuation. During a five-year period, the impact of poor past results on the Stability Index gradually diminishes.

(D) Stability Index was negatively impacted by limited **diversification** of general business, policy, and/or investment risk. This factor especially affects smaller companies that do not issue as many policies as larger firms. It can also affect firms that specialize in only one line of business.

(E) Stability Index was negatively impacted due to a lack of operating **experience**. The company has been in operation for less than five years. Consequently, it has not been able to establish the kind of stable track record that we believe is needed to demonstrate financial permanence and strength.

(F) Stability Index was negatively impacted by negative cash **flow**. In other words, the company paid out more in claims and expenses than it received in premiums and investment income.

(G) Stability Index was negatively impacted by fast asset or premium **growth**. Fast growth can pose a serious problem for insurers. It is generally achieved by offering policies with premiums that are too low, benefits that are too costly, or agents commissions that are too high. Due to the highly competitive nature of the insurance marketplace, rapid growth has been a factor in many insurance insolvencies.

(L) Stability Index was negatively impacted by results on our **liquidity** tests. While the company may have sufficient cash flow to meet its current obligations, it could encounter difficulties under adverse scenarios, such as a dramatic increase in claims.

(O) Stability Index was negatively impacted by significant changes in the company's business **operations**. These changes can include shifts in the kinds of insurance offered by the company, a temporary or permanent freeze on the sale of new policies, or recent release from conservatorship. In these circumstances, past performance cannot be a reliable indicator of future financial strength.

(R) Stability Index was negatively impacted by concerns about the financial strength of its **reinsurers**.

(T) Stability Index was negatively impacted by significant **trends** in critical asset, liability, income or expense items. Examples include fluctuations in premium volume, changes in the types of investments the company makes, and changes in the types of policies the company writes.

(Z)   This company is unrated due to data, as received by Weiss Ratings, that are either incomplete in substantial ways or contains items that, in the opinion of Weiss Ratings analysts, may not be reliable.

INSURANCE COMPANY NAME	DOM. STATE	RATING	TOTAL ASSETS ($MIL)	CAPITAL & SURPLUS ($MIL)	ANNUAL NET PREMIUM ($MIL)	NET INCOME ($MIL)	CAPITAL-IZATION INDEX (PTS)	RESERVE ADQ INDEX (PTS)	PROFIT-ABILITY INDEX (PTS)	LIQUIDITY INDEX (PTS)	STAB. INDEX (PTS)	STABILITY FACTORS
1ST ATLANTIC SURETY CO	NC	D+	4.0	2.0	1.3	0.0	7.1	4.3	3.0	9.2	1.7	DGT
1ST AUTO & CASUALTY INS CO	WI	C	28.4	11.1	22.6	-0.1	7.1	6.3	3.1	5.3	3.0	DFGR
1ST CHOICE AUTO INS CO	PA	C	20.8	7.5	13.0	0.2	7.2	5.8	2.5	5.1	3.6	DGRT
21ST CENTURY ADVANTAGE INS CO	MN	B	32.5	29.4	0.0	0.1	10.0	4.6	6.2	10.0	4.2	GT
21ST CENTURY ASR CO	DE	B	73.4	69.9	0.0	0.2	10.0	4.6	5.9	10.0	4.3	T
21ST CENTURY AUTO INS CO OF NJ	NJ	U	--	--	--	--	N/A	--	--	--	--	Z
21ST CENTURY CASUALTY CO	CA	B	14.0	13.9	0.0	1.6	10.0	4.6	6.4	10.0	4.3	DGT
21ST CENTURY CENTENNIAL INS CO	PA	B	611.0	592.0	0.0	1.4	8.3	4.6	6.9	10.0	4.8	T
21ST CENTURY INDEMNITY INS CO	PA	B	74.4	68.0	0.0	0.4	10.0	4.6	6.9	10.0	4.1	T
21ST CENTURY INS CO	CA	B	956.7	939.7	0.0	4.5	10.0	4.6	6.6	10.0	6.0	T
21ST CENTURY INS CO OF THE SW	TX	U	--	--	--	--	N/A	--	--	--	--	Z
21ST CENTURY NATIONAL INS CO INC	NY	B	26.6	24.4	0.0	0.1	10.0	4.6	5.7	10.0	4.1	DGT
21ST CENTURY NORTH AMERICA INS	NY	B	600.1	565.6	0.0	1.4	10.0	4.6	6.1	10.0	4.7	RT
21ST CENTURY PACIFIC INS	CO	B	47.6	44.1	0.0	0.1	10.0	4.6	5.7	10.0	4.2	DT
21ST CENTURY PINNACLE INS CO	NJ	B	45.9	42.5	0.0	0.1	10.0	4.6	5.6	10.0	5.6	DT
21ST CENTURY PREFERRED INS CO	PA	B	43.4	41.9	0.0	0.2	10.0	4.6	6.0	10.0	4.0	DT
21ST CENTURY PREMIER INS CO	PA	B-	302.2	284.6	0.0	1.2	10.0	4.6	6.9	10.0	4.6	T
21ST CENTURY SECURITY INS CO	PA	B	222.0	198.1	0.0	0.5	10.0	4.6	5.9	10.0	4.6	DT
21ST CENTURY SUPERIOR INS CO	CA	U	--	--	--	--	N/A	--	--	--	--	Z
360 INS CO	WY	B-	30.6	22.7	6.7	-0.8	10.0	5.3	4.0	7.8	3.8	DGOT
7710 INS CO	SC	D+	12.9	6.1	5.6	-0.3	5.2	3.6	2.1	9.3	2.2	DFGT
A CENTRAL INS CO	NY	C-	113.6	41.7	49.9	-0.6	8.8	7.3	6.0	6.2	3.3	T
A-ONE COMM INS RRG GROUP INC	TN	D	13.6	3.1	5.9	0.0	0.6	3.6	3.5	7.2	1.9	CDGT
ACA FINANCIAL GUARANTY CORP	MD	U	--	--	--	--	N/A	--	--	--	--	Z
ACADEMIC HLTH PROFESSIONALS INS	NY	E-	325.1	-75.7	64.5	5.0	0.0	4.1	0.9	7.0	0.0	CDRT
▲ACADEMIC MEDICAL PROFESSIONALS RRG	VT	D-	4.7	3.2	0.8	0.1	6.8	6.9	6.7	9.3	1.0	DGT
ACADIA INS CO	NH	C	159.5	53.0	0.0	0.2	10.0	N/A	6.1	7.0	4.0	FT
ACCC INS CO	TX	D	303.4	46.0	293.6	-3.6	2.0	1.8	1.9	0.0	2.0	CFLT
ACCEPTANCE CASUALTY INS CO	NE	D	120.2	57.8	48.4	1.6	7.1	5.8	5.2	6.7	2.3	GRT
ACCEPTANCE INDEMNITY INS CO	NE	C-	301.7	146.0	70.7	4.8	5.7	4.4	4.8	5.9	2.7	RT
ACCEPTANCE INS CO	NE	F	15.1	3.3	0.0	-0.3	4.4	0.3	0.1	10.0	0.0	DFGR
ACCESS HOME INS CO	LA	C	37.9	11.8	14.5	0.0	5.2	5.9	8.5	7.6	2.5	DFGT
ACCESS INS CO	TX	C	202.1	33.6	46.1	0.2	4.8	2.4	2.9	6.6	3.5	CFRT
ACCIDENT FUND GENERAL INS CO	MI	B	216.7	74.3	48.4	5.2	8.0	4.3	8.9	7.0	5.9	T
ACCIDENT FUND INS CO OF AMERICA	MI	B-	3,785.0	926.6	925.0	5.6	7.0	4.2	8.7	6.8	4.6	RT
ACCIDENT FUND NATIONAL INS CO	MI	B	167.4	86.1	72.6	8.2	7.9	4.3	8.5	6.7	5.9	T
ACCIDENT INS CO	NM	E	89.8	14.2	14.1	2.6	0.0	0.3	0.9	5.4	0.1	CDFR
ACCREDITED SURETY & CAS CO INC	FL	C+	48.5	26.7	9.2	0.3	7.3	6.1	8.6	7.0	3.3	DGRT
ACE AMERICAN INS CO	PA	B-	13,190.9	2,916.9	1,848.6	95.1	7.2	6.3	7.0	6.6	3.9	RT
ACE FIRE UNDERWRITERS INS CO	PA	C	113.9	77.5	10.0	0.7	10.0	6.1	7.2	7.8	3.9	RT
ACE INS CO OF THE MIDWEST	IN	C	98.1	66.8	-2.9	0.2	10.0	6.0	7.7	7.0	3.9	FT
ACE P&C INS CO	PA	B-	9,120.3	2,222.5	1,748.7	77.4	8.4	6.3	7.9	6.9	3.9	RT
ACIG INS CO	IL	D+	455.9	139.9	69.6	1.2	7.1	7.0	6.6	6.7	2.2	RT
ACSTAR INS CO	IL	C+	57.3	27.4	1.1	0.4	9.2	8.8	4.9	9.7	3.3	DGRT
ACUITY A MUTUAL INS CO	WI	B+	3,686.4	1,668.5	1,316.3	33.8	9.3	9.1	8.9	6.7	5.1	T
ADDISON INS CO	IA	C+	123.1	47.9	38.6	0.8	9.0	8.4	8.5	6.7	4.8	T
ADIRONDACK INS EXCHANGE	NY	C	295.8	99.2	108.0	-0.7	7.7	4.8	4.5	5.8	4.0	RT
ADM INS CO	AZ	C	633.5	23.8	0.0	-0.1	7.9	N/A	5.5	7.0	3.6	T
ADMIRAL INDEMNITY CO	DE	C	56.2	42.0	0.0	0.2	10.0	3.7	7.7	10.0	3.9	RT
ADMIRAL INS CO	DE	C	744.4	655.8	0.0	2.0	8.3	3.8	3.9	10.0	4.1	ART
ADRIATIC INS CO	ND	C	90.4	70.5	24.7	0.9	10.0	7.8	8.6	7.9	3.6	DRT
ADVANCED PHYSICIANS INS RRG INC	AZ	D	1.6	1.4	0.2	0.0	10.0	3.9	2.9	10.0	1.3	DFGT

See Page 27 for explanation of footnotes and Page 28 for explanation of stability factors.
Arrows denote recent upgrades ▲ or downgrades ▼ (see Section VII for explanations)

30

www.weissratings.com

RISK ADJ. RATIO #1	CAPITAL RATIO #2	PREMIUM TO SURPLUS (%)	RESV. TO SURPLUS (%)	RESV. DEVELOP. 1 YEAR (%)	RESV. DEVELOP. 2 YEAR (%)	LOSS RATIO (%)	EXP. RATIO (%)	COMB RATIO (%)	CASH FROM UNDER-WRITING (%)	NET PREMIUM GROWTH (%)	INVEST. IN AFFIL (%)	INSURANCE COMPANY NAME
1.3	1.1	64.0	7.2	-0.8	8.5	4.7	78.2	82.9	133.9	15.3	0.0	1ST ATLANTIC SURETY CO
1.4	1.1	201.1	88.7	-2.1	0.8	77.1	32.2	109.3	93.5	7.1	0.0	1ST AUTO & CASUALTY INS CO
1.7	1.1	180.5	65.8	9.1	5.4	89.6	25.3	114.9	97.1	10.7	0.0	1ST CHOICE AUTO INS CO
29.2	26.2	N/A	0.7	0.2	N/A	N/A	N/A	N/A	-80.4	0.0	0.0	21ST CENTURY ADVANTAGE INS CO
61.3	55.2	N/A	0.6	0.1	N/A	N/A	N/A	N/A	N/A	0.0	0.0	21ST CENTURY ASR CO
N/A	N/A	--	--	--	--	--	--	--	--	--	--	21ST CENTURY AUTO INS CO OF NJ
354.5	177.3	N/A	0.4	0.1	N/A	N/A	N/A	N/A	N/A	0.0	0.0	21ST CENTURY CASUALTY CO
1.8	1.8	N/A	0.7	0.2	N/A	N/A	N/A	N/A	-44.7	0.0	59.4 ●	21ST CENTURY CENTENNIAL INS CO
37.9	34.1	N/A	0.6	0.1	N/A	N/A	N/A	N/A	N/A	0.0	0.0	21ST CENTURY INDEMNITY INS CO
106.7	48.1	N/A	0.4	0.1	N/A	N/A	N/A	N/A	N/A	0.0	0.0 ●	21ST CENTURY INS CO
N/A	N/A	--	--	--	--	--	--	--	--	--	--	21ST CENTURY INS CO OF THE SW
31.3	28.2	N/A	0.9	0.2	N/A	N/A	N/A	N/A	N/A	0.0	0.0	21ST CENTURY NATIONAL INS CO INC
5.8	5.6	N/A	0.9	0.2	N/A	N/A	N/A	N/A	-2.5	0.0	18.0 ●	21ST CENTURY NORTH AMERICA INS
39.4	35.5	N/A	0.9	0.2	N/A	N/A	N/A	N/A	N/A	0.0	0.0	21ST CENTURY PACIFIC INS
38.4	34.6	N/A	0.9	0.2	N/A	N/A	N/A	N/A	N/A	0.0	0.0	21ST CENTURY PINNACLE INS CO
71.4	64.2	N/A	1.0	0.2	N/A	N/A	N/A	N/A	N/A	0.0	0.0	21ST CENTURY PREFERRED INS CO
4.6	4.5	N/A	0.7	0.2	N/A	N/A	N/A	N/A	6.1	0.0	23.8 ●	21ST CENTURY PREMIER INS CO
8.7	8.4	N/A	0.8	0.2	N/A	N/A	N/A	N/A	N/A	0.0	12.3 ●	21ST CENTURY SECURITY INS CO
N/A	N/A	--	--	--	--	--	--	--	--	--	--	21ST CENTURY SUPERIOR INS CO
8.9	5.9	28.4	9.6	-0.4	-0.3	95.4	18.1	113.5	127.0	161.2	0.0	360 INS CO
1.0	0.6	83.4	25.1	-0.8	N/A	56.6	44.8	101.4	19.6	N/A	0.0	7710 INS CO
3.2	2.4	118.4	74.5	1.8	-0.7	66.4	31.2	97.6	106.1	6.3	0.0	A CENTRAL INS CO
0.2	0.2	192.4	207.3	-7.1	1.0	78.6	28.8	107.4	110.8	-23.3	0.0	A-ONE COMM INS RRG GROUP INC
N/A	N/A	--	--	--	--	--	--	--	--	--	--	ACA FINANCIAL GUARANTY CORP
-0.1	-0.1	-79.1	-453.6	9.4	68.3	107.2	20.7	127.9	101.6	-9.8	-0.1	ACADEMIC HLTH PROFESSIONALS INS
1.6	1.0	25.1	28.4	-3.2	-7.4	38.6	28.2	66.8	236.8	38.9	0.0	ACADEMIC MEDICAL PROFESSIONALS
5.8	5.2	N/A	N/A	N/A	N/A	N/A	N/A	N/A	136.0	0.0	0.0	ACADIA INS CO
0.4	0.3	603.4	306.8	61.5	59.0	90.3	17.8	108.1	88.4	-11.8	0.0	ACCC INS CO
1.8	1.1	86.9	46.2	1.6	2.3	64.2	35.3	99.5	149.2	314.9	0.0	ACCEPTANCE CASUALTY INS CO
1.2	0.9	50.5	46.2	1.3	5.3	64.9	34.8	99.7	106.1	6.5	20.4	ACCEPTANCE INDEMNITY INS CO
1.0	0.4	N/A	215.5	-14.6	45.2	N/A	N/A	N/A	N/A	0.0	0.0	ACCEPTANCE INS CO
1.6	1.0	121.1	9.4	-1.4	-0.3	34.7	57.6	92.3	94.4	-6.3	0.0	ACCESS HOME INS CO
0.9	0.8	138.4	88.9	40.3	22.6	102.0	15.9	117.9	87.7	-16.4	0.0	ACCESS INS CO
4.8	4.2	69.2	79.5	-1.4	-0.4	62.9	22.2	85.1	132.1	13.8	0.0	ACCIDENT FUND GENERAL INS CO
1.1	0.9	103.1	118.5	-2.2	-0.5	63.0	22.9	85.9	147.0	13.8	17.2 ●	ACCIDENT FUND INS CO OF AMERICA
3.8	3.5	89.7	103.1	-1.9	-0.5	62.9	18.8	81.7	124.8	13.8	0.0	ACCIDENT FUND NATIONAL INS CO
0.1	0.0	108.2	406.5	201.2	113.3	103.2	51.4	154.6	64.0	-55.2	0.0	ACCIDENT INS CO
2.0	1.4	39.9	64.2	N/A	0.5	0.1	82.6	82.7	-136.8	-1.0	0.0	ACCREDITED SURETY & CAS CO INC
1.4	1.1	65.7	120.0	0.9	0.5	76.5	22.6	99.1	122.7	5.0	18.8 ●	ACE AMERICAN INS CO
14.7	11.1	13.0	23.7	0.2	0.1	76.5	17.9	94.4	103.4	5.0	0.0	ACE FIRE UNDERWRITERS INS CO
14.1	12.7	-4.3	3.9	N/A	0.1	N/A	193.5	N/A	-55.9	-157.3	0.0	ACE INS CO OF THE MIDWEST
2.9	1.9	81.0	148.0	1.1	0.7	76.5	19.5	96.0	118.8	5.0	3.3 ●	ACE P&C INS CO
1.8	1.1	52.1	182.0	-37.8	-36.3	55.8	41.0	96.8	115.2	-25.2	0.0	ACIG INS CO
4.7	3.0	4.1	45.2	-3.4	-9.0	-20.5	98.1	77.6	85.1	-35.2	0.0	ACSTAR INS CO
4.5	2.6	81.9	76.8	-3.8	-7.4	61.3	30.1	91.4	115.6	3.6	0.0 ●	ACUITY A MUTUAL INS CO
4.4	2.9	82.1	90.2	-0.9	-2.9	69.8	30.0	99.8	114.0	8.7	0.0	ADDISON INS CO
2.4	1.9	107.7	59.0	-11.4	10.5	58.5	24.9	83.4	90.8	20.2	11.0	ADIRONDACK INS EXCHANGE
1.7	1.3	N/A	N/A	N/A	N/A	N/A	N/A	N/A	109.1	0.0	0.0	ADM INS CO
14.5	13.0	N/A	N/A	N/A	N/A	N/A	N/A	N/A	169.6	0.0	0.0	ADMIRAL INDEMNITY CO
1.5	1.5	N/A	N/A	N/A	N/A	N/A	N/A	N/A	N/A	0.0	50.0 ●	ADMIRAL INS CO
9.9	6.2	35.5	8.4	-5.0	-4.3	45.3	27.7	73.0	146.6	2.4	0.0	ADRIATIC INS CO
6.8	6.0	11.1	1.7	-3.8	N/A	-33.0	92.6	59.6	67.0	-13.5	0.0	ADVANCED PHYSICIANS INS RRG INC

999 + Denotes number greater than 999.9%
999 - Denotes number less than -999.99%
● Bullets denote a more detailed analysis is available in Section II.

INSURANCE COMPANY NAME	DOM. STATE	RATING	TOTAL ASSETS ($MIL)	CAPITAL & SURPLUS ($MIL)	ANNUAL NET PREMIUM ($MIL)	NET INCOME ($MIL)	CAPITAL- IZATION INDEX (PTS)	RESERVE ADQ INDEX (PTS)	PROFIT- ABILITY INDEX (PTS)	LIQUIDITY INDEX (PTS)	STAB. INDEX (PTS)	STABILITY FACTORS
ADVANTAGE WORKERS COMP INS CO	IN	B-	497.8	209.5	70.6	-1.1	7.0	4.6	4.0	7.0	4.0	GT
AEGIS HEALTHCARE RRG INC	DC	D	6.1	2.4	0.9	0.0	7.5	9.7	3.0	6.4	1.9	DFGR
AEGIS SECURITY INS CO	PA	B-	129.4	56.4	75.7	0.3	4.0	8.4	5.6	2.8	3.7	CLRT
AETNA INS CO OF CT	CT	U	--	--	--	--	N/A	--	--	--	--	Z
AF&L INS CO	PA	E- (2)	139.2	8.8	21.1	8.7	0.0	0.1	1.9	0.0	0.0	CDFL
AFFILIATED FM INS CO	RI	C	2,969.7	1,676.6	423.6	38.8	9.3	6.2	8.8	7.1	3.5	RT
AFFILIATES INS CO	IN	U	--	--	--	--	N/A	--	--	--	--	Z
AFFILIATES INS RECIPROCAL A RRG	VT	B-	8.2	5.4	0.4	0.1	10.0	4.9	4.6	7.0	3.5	DGT
AFFINITY MUTUAL INS CO	OH	C-	14.0	7.7	4.3	-0.5	8.0	6.4	2.4	8.2	2.2	DFGR
AFFIRMATIVE CASUALTY INS CO	LA	F (5)	35.4	28.0	0.0	0.0	10.0	4.6	3.9	7.0	0.0	FGRT
AFFIRMATIVE DIRECT INS CO	NY	F	5.1	5.0	0.0	0.0	10.0	N/A	3.3	7.0	0.0	DFGT
AFFIRMATIVE INS CO OF MI	MI	F (1)	9.5	7.0	0.0	-0.5	10.0	N/A	3.0	9.4	0.0	FRT
AGCS MARINE INS CO	IL	D+	325.2	190.5	0.0	1.4	10.0	3.9	6.4	0.0	2.8	LRT
AGENCY INS CO OF MD INC	MD	C+	153.6	40.4	112.7	-0.2	7.1	5.8	6.2	5.2	3.4	RT
AGENT ALLIANCE INS CO	AL	C	60.0	50.2	0.0	0.3	10.0	2.7	7.9	10.0	3.7	DFT
AGENTS MUTUAL INS CO	AR	D	4.0	2.4	1.6	0.0	3.3	7.0	6.8	3.0	1.9	DGLR
AGIC INC	FL	U	--	--	--	--	N/A	--	--	--	--	Z
AGRI GENERAL INS CO	IA	C-	130.3	123.0	0.0	0.5	10.0	4.6	2.2	10.0	3.1	RT
AGRI INS EXCHANGE RRG	IN	C	18.4	14.6	1.0	0.3	7.4	8.8	8.2	9.8	2.7	DGT
AGRICULTURAL WORKERS MUT AUTO INS	TX	B- (1)	83.9	35.3	38.7	-1.8	6.0	5.9	4.6	6.1	3.5	FRT
AGRINATIONAL INS CO	VT	D (2)	971.1	244.2	287.3	15.2	4.0	9.6	5.7	5.4	1.2	DFRT
AGSECURITY INS CO	OK	C+	60.2	31.7	14.6	-0.1	10.0	9.3	4.9	7.7	3.6	FT
AIG ASR CO	IL	B-	38.5	33.5	0.0	0.5	10.0	N/A	3.9	7.0	3.8	DGT
AIG INS CO - PR	PR	B-	152.2	93.4	14.8	1.1	10.0	7.7	3.8	8.7	4.4	T
AIG PROPERTY CASUALTY CO	PA	C	2,027.7	344.1	806.2	136.2	7.3	3.3	1.9	6.3	2.8	AFT
AIG SPECIALTY INS CO	IL	C+	106.5	47.0	0.0	0.3	10.0	3.7	2.8	6.9	3.9	AT
AIMCO MUTUAL INS CO	NC	U	--	--	--	--	N/A	--	--	--	--	Z
AIOI NISSAY DOWA INS CO LTD	GU	D+	32.5	12.5	9.2	0.0	7.3	9.4	8.7	9.1	1.3	DGT
AIOI NISSAY DOWA INS CO OF AMERICA	NY	C+	138.6	62.1	24.9	-0.1	10.0	8.8	5.3	8.5	3.4	RT
AIU INS CO	NY	C+	88.7	74.7	0.0	13.6	10.0	5.0	1.9	7.0	4.1	ADRT
AIX SPECIALTY INS CO	DE	B-	55.6	46.3	0.0	0.3	10.0	N/A	4.4	7.0	5.3	
ALABAMA MUNICIPAL INS CORP	AL	C+	121.6	48.6	32.8	-0.3	8.3	9.4	6.9	6.9	3.4	RT
ALAMANCE FARMERS MUTUAL INS CO	NC	B-	8.5	5.6	3.2	0.1	7.3	6.4	3.9	6.1	3.5	DFGT
ALAMANCE INS CO	IL	C-	476.9	375.2	27.9	0.6	7.7	7.8	6.1	8.0	2.6	RT
ALASKA NATIONAL INS CO	AK	B	976.4	447.5	221.5	15.5	9.1	9.4	8.8	7.1	4.7	T
ALASKA TIMBER INS EXCHANGE	AK	C	15.0	7.3	3.9	-0.7	8.2	9.5	2.9	7.1	2.2	DFGR
ALEA NORTH AMERICA INS CO	NY	U	--	--	--	--	N/A	--	--	--	--	Z
ALFA ALLIANCE INS CORP	VA	B	39.0	20.8	12.3	-0.2	9.2	7.7	4.7	7.8	4.9	DGT
ALFA GENERAL INS CORP	AL	B	100.3	49.6	49.2	0.4	8.7	7.9	3.6	6.4	4.6	T
ALFA INS CORP	AL	B	99.6	47.1	36.9	-0.5	10.0	7.8	3.4	6.8	4.6	T
ALFA MUTUAL FIRE INS CO	AL	B	768.8	425.4	368.8	-3.3	8.2	7.7	5.0	6.2	4.9	T
ALFA MUTUAL GENERAL INS CO	AL	B+	111.8	58.3	49.2	-0.1	8.4	7.6	5.9	6.7	5.0	T
ALFA MUTUAL INS CO	AL	B	1,307.1	446.3	639.3	-9.3	7.1	7.7	3.0	4.1	4.5	LT
ALFA SPECIALTY INS CORP	VA	B+	57.1	28.1	24.6	-0.4	8.1	7.8	5.3	7.0	6.5	DT
ALFA VISION INS CORP	VA	B	110.9	50.9	49.2	-0.3	9.0	7.7	5.4	7.0	6.3	T
ALINSCO INS CO	TX	C	89.7	13.2	0.0	0.9	7.9	N/A	9.9	10.0	2.5	DGT
ALL AMERICA INS CO	OH	B+	285.9	153.8	98.8	1.1	10.0	9.1	8.4	6.8	5.0	T
ALLEGANY CO-OP INS CO	NY	C+	53.6	34.7	13.5	0.6	9.2	5.4	8.0	7.0	3.4	DRT
ALLEGHENY CASUALTY CO	NJ	C	36.3	22.9	31.9	0.1	4.0	6.1	6.4	6.9	3.1	CDGT
ALLEGHENY SURETY CO	PA	D	4.3	2.3	1.5	-0.2	7.2	3.2	2.4	6.7	1.9	DFGR
ALLEGIANT INS CO INC A RRG	HI	E+	27.2	10.4	6.3	0.6	1.4	0.5	4.8	8.3	0.5	DGT
ALLIANCE INDEMNITY CO	KS	C+	10.5	7.0	3.8	0.1	10.0	7.8	7.8	7.0	3.3	DGRT

See Page 27 for explanation of footnotes and
Page 28 for explanation of stability factors.
Arrows denote recent upgrades ▲ or downgrades ▼   (see Section VII for explanations)

32

www.weissratings.com

RISK ADJ. RATIO #1	CAPITAL RATIO #2	PREMIUM TO SURPLUS (%)	RESV. TO SURPLUS (%)	RESV. DEVELOP. 1 YEAR (%)	RESV. DEVELOP. 2 YEAR (%)	LOSS RATIO (%)	EXP. RATIO (%)	COMB RATIO (%)	CASH FROM UNDER-WRITING (%)	NET PREMIUM GROWTH (%)	INVEST. IN AFFIL (%)	INSURANCE COMPANY NAME
1.8	1.3	33.5	124.7	-4.0	-12.1	71.5	25.3	96.8	-45.2	399.5	0.0 ●	ADVANTAGE WORKERS COMP INS CO
1.5	1.2	38.4	72.1	-8.1	-6.2	118.2	47.0	165.2	61.1	0.6	0.0	AEGIS HEALTHCARE RRG INC
0.8	0.6	136.3	41.9	-0.6	-2.0	49.1	49.4	98.5	101.9	18.3	18.2	AEGIS SECURITY INS CO
N/A	N/A	--	--	--	--	--	--	--	--	--	--	AETNA INS CO OF CT
0.3	0.2	999 +	999 +	999 +	999 +	145.3	-7.8	137.5	53.8	-8.5	0.0	AF&L INS CO
4.3	2.6	26.2	39.8	-1.0	1.1	56.9	26.8	83.7	231.5	0.7	0.0 ●	AFFILIATED FM INS CO
N/A	N/A	--	--	--	--	--	--	--	--	--	--	AFFILIATES INS CO
4.4	2.6	7.0	13.7	-0.6	0.6	73.4	20.4	93.8	-85.6	-0.6	0.0	AFFILIATES INS RECIPROCAL A RRG
2.6	1.7	52.9	21.8	-7.7	-7.7	41.3	61.8	103.1	92.4	1.6	0.0	AFFINITY MUTUAL INS CO
4.8	4.2	N/A	-0.1	N/A	N/A	N/A	N/A	N/A	193.2	0.0	29.1	AFFIRMATIVE CASUALTY INS CO
106.6	48.5	N/A	N/A	N/A	N/A	N/A	N/A	N/A	N/A	0.0	0.0	AFFIRMATIVE DIRECT INS CO
8.3	7.5	N/A	N/A	N/A	N/A	N/A	N/A	N/A	21.9	0.0	0.0	AFFIRMATIVE INS CO OF MI
21.3	19.2	N/A	N/A	N/A	N/A	N/A	N/A	N/A	131.9	0.0	0.8	AGCS MARINE INS CO
1.2	1.0	280.8	108.4	-9.0	-13.4	70.5	23.6	94.1	114.7	31.2	0.0	AGENCY INS CO OF MD INC
21.0	18.8	N/A	N/A	N/A	N/A	N/A	N/A	N/A	999 +	0.0	0.0	AGENT ALLIANCE INS CO
0.7	0.5	68.6	4.6	2.0	8.2	50.8	22.0	72.8	125.9	2.7	0.0	AGENTS MUTUAL INS CO
N/A	N/A	--	--	--	--	--	--	--	--	--	--	AGIC INC
42.6	20.4	N/A	2.6	N/A	N/A	N/A	N/A	N/A	-38.1	0.0	0.0	AGRI GENERAL INS CO
2.1	1.2	6.8	17.8	-3.7	-8.4	9.3	34.1	43.4	999 +	1.9	0.0	AGRI INS EXCHANGE RRG
1.2	0.8	109.6	24.7	1.6	2.1	72.5	23.6	96.1	107.9	3.9	13.6	AGRICULTURAL WORKERS MUT AUTO
0.9	0.7	113.0	101.9	-9.0	-32.6	72.3	14.5	86.8	100.1	35.5	53.2	AGRINATIONAL INS CO
7.2	4.8	45.9	28.1	0.9	-7.7	81.2	27.5	108.7	92.6	5.4	0.0	AGSECURITY INS CO
21.8	19.6	N/A	N/A	N/A	N/A	N/A	N/A	N/A	N/A	0.0	0.0	AIG ASR CO
11.3	6.9	16.2	12.6	-1.9	-3.7	8.5	48.7	57.2	145.6	-7.2	1.4	AIG INS CO - PR
2.1	1.3	84.7	237.9	18.4	21.2	99.8	26.7	126.5	85.6	-13.1	0.1 ●	AIG PROPERTY CASUALTY CO
8.1	7.2	N/A	N/A	N/A	N/A	N/A	N/A	N/A	N/A	0.0	0.0	AIG SPECIALTY INS CO
N/A	N/A	--	--	--	--	--	--	--	--	--	--	AIMCO MUTUAL INS CO
2.6	1.5	71.1	19.8	-6.4	-11.6	34.4	41.0	75.4	154.7	-11.1	0.0	AIOI NISSAY DOWA INS CO LTD
5.9	3.8	40.1	83.5	-3.9	-7.8	66.5	28.0	94.5	106.6	-22.0	0.0	AIOI NISSAY DOWA INS CO OF AMERICA
6.8	6.5	N/A	N/A	N/A	N/A	N/A	N/A	N/A	N/A	0.0	18.9	AIU INS CO
20.1	18.0	N/A	N/A	N/A	N/A	N/A	N/A	N/A	N/A	0.0	0.0	AIX SPECIALTY INS CO
2.4	2.0	67.0	91.2	3.5	-4.2	71.1	23.4	94.5	96.4	2.5	0.0	ALABAMA MUNICIPAL INS CORP
1.9	1.2	58.6	10.0	-2.1	-0.1	45.0	63.5	108.5	88.5	13.0	0.0	ALAMANCE FARMERS MUTUAL INS CO
1.4	1.4	7.5	21.7	-1.4	-2.4	47.9	54.6	102.5	73.5	-14.9	59.1 ●	ALAMANCE INS CO
3.8	2.6	50.6	87.0	-10.1	-14.4	56.7	27.3	84.0	128.9	-3.1	0.0 ●	ALASKA NATIONAL INS CO
2.1	1.6	48.6	90.6	-4.8	-17.8	70.2	24.3	94.5	89.5	-21.3	0.0	ALASKA TIMBER INS EXCHANGE
N/A	N/A	--	--	--	--	--	--	--	--	--	--	ALEA NORTH AMERICA INS CO
4.6	3.1	59.2	23.7	-2.0	-2.6	72.2	30.5	102.7	94.3	8.0	0.0	ALFA ALLIANCE INS CORP
3.4	2.3	100.6	36.4	-2.8	-3.3	71.2	28.6	99.8	98.4	8.0	0.0	ALFA GENERAL INS CORP
4.4	3.0	78.7	28.6	-2.4	-2.9	70.9	26.6	97.5	96.8	8.0	0.0	ALFA INS CORP
2.4	1.9	87.8	31.5	-1.8	-2.6	72.1	28.9	101.0	99.0	8.0	25.6 ●	ALFA MUTUAL FIRE INS CO
3.8	2.5	86.1	30.9	-1.7	-2.4	72.1	29.0	101.1	99.7	8.0	0.7 ●	ALFA MUTUAL GENERAL INS CO
1.2	1.0	141.5	54.4	-2.4	-3.5	72.3	28.5	100.8	96.2	8.0	37.3 ●	ALFA MUTUAL INS CO
3.1	2.1	88.0	31.6	-1.8	-2.6	72.1	28.8	100.9	103.1	8.0	0.0 ●	ALFA SPECIALTY INS CORP
3.8	2.6	97.0	34.8	-2.2	-3.0	72.1	28.9	101.0	99.4	8.0	0.0	ALFA VISION INS CORP
1.6	1.4	N/A	0.6	N/A	N/A	N/A	N/A	N/A	N/A	0.0	0.0	ALINSCO INS CO
6.4	4.3	64.8	44.4	-4.5	-7.9	64.0	33.3	97.3	101.8	6.3	0.1 ●	ALL AMERICA INS CO
4.1	2.7	39.5	29.5	10.3	8.2	72.9	37.8	110.7	116.8	1.4	0.0	ALLEGANY CO-OP INS CO
0.6	0.6	139.6	N/A	-0.1	-0.4	-0.1	98.5	98.4	104.4	5.6	0.0	ALLEGHENY CASUALTY CO
1.2	1.0	58.7	42.4	10.5	21.4	22.0	85.6	107.6	86.6	0.7	0.0	ALLEGHENY SURETY CO
0.5	0.3	66.2	106.2	20.1	46.5	44.6	14.0	58.6	388.4	30.7	0.0	ALLEGIANT INS CO INC A RRG
5.8	4.6	55.1	19.7	-1.1	-3.4	70.8	30.6	101.4	98.0	1.0	0.0	ALLIANCE INDEMNITY CO

999 + Denotes number greater than 999.9%
999 - Denotes number less than -999.99%
● Bullets denote a more detailed analysis is available in Section II.

INSURANCE COMPANY NAME	DOM. STATE	RATING	TOTAL ASSETS ($MIL)	CAPITAL & SURPLUS ($MIL)	ANNUAL NET PREMIUM ($MIL)	NET INCOME ($MIL)	CAPITAL-IZATION INDEX (PTS)	RESERVE ADQ INDEX (PTS)	PROFIT-ABILITY INDEX (PTS)	LIQUIDITY INDEX (PTS)	STAB. INDEX (PTS)	STABILITY FACTORS
ALLIANCE INS CO	KS	C	25.9	12.0	15.3	0.3	7.9	8.7	5.9	6.4	3.0	DGRT
ALLIANCE NATIONAL INS CO	NY	E (2)	48.2	7.0	8.1	-0.4	0.0	5.1	2.9	3.8	0.1	CDFL
ALLIANCE OF NONPROFITS FOR INS RRG	VT	C	97.8	35.8	30.0	0.5	7.2	6.2	6.9	7.2	4.0	RT
ALLIANCE UNITED INS CO	CA	C	596.6	162.1	519.3	7.0	4.4	3.5	2.8	0.0	3.5	LT
ALLIANZ GLOBAL RISKS US INS CO	IL	C	7,630.3	1,989.9	2,124.9	52.0	5.0	9.7	3.7	6.8	3.8	FGRT
ALLIANZ UNDERWRITERS INS CO	IL	C-	104.1	71.1	0.0	0.7	10.0	N/A	7.5	6.8	3.1	RT
ALLIED EASTERN INDEMNITY CO	PA	B-	90.3	17.1	20.9	0.4	6.3	4.5	8.9	6.7	5.3	DT
ALLIED INS CO OF AMERICA	OH	C+	57.2	14.2	0.0	0.0	9.2	N/A	7.1	6.7	3.2	DGT
ALLIED P&C INS CO	IA	B	397.5	59.3	0.0	0.1	10.0	N/A	6.1	8.8	4.1	T
ALLIED PREMIER INS A RRG	CT	E	3.6	0.9	-0.3	0.3	3.3	3.6	0.4	8.0	0.0	DFGT
ALLIED PROFESSIONALS INS CO RRG	AZ	C-	48.6	20.5	13.1	0.5	6.4	1.8	6.0	7.9	2.9	DFRT
ALLIED SERVICES RRG	SC	E	6.3	4.1	1.0	-0.1	5.8	6.0	5.3	7.0	0.0	DG
ALLIED TRUST INS CO	TX	C-	13.5	8.7	2.0	-0.7	9.2	N/A	2.0	9.2	2.3	DGT
ALLIED WORLD ASR CO (US) INC	DE	B-	335.3	141.0	44.3	0.3	10.0	6.2	6.0	7.4	4.5	ART
ALLIED WORLD INS CO	NH	C	1,787.4	1,026.7	199.4	1.0	7.8	6.1	5.3	7.2	3.4	ART
ALLIED WORLD NATL ASR CO	NH	B-	311.8	153.7	44.3	0.3	10.0	6.2	6.9	7.0	4.6	ART
ALLIED WORLD SPECIALTY INS CO	DE	B	808.2	416.2	110.8	0.1	9.3	6.2	6.9	7.0	4.7	RT
ALLIED WORLD SURPLUS LINES INS	AR	C	265.3	97.6	44.3	0.4	9.1	6.5	6.8	6.9	4.2	RT
ALLMERICA FINANCIAL ALLIANCE INS CO	NH	C+	20.4	20.3	0.0	0.1	10.0	N/A	7.1	7.0	4.4	DGR
ALLMERICA FINANCIAL BENEFIT INS CO	MI	C+	40.8	40.7	0.0	0.2	10.0	N/A	7.4	7.0	3.9	RT
ALLSTATE COUNTY MUTUAL INS CO	TX	B	14.7	14.7	0.0	0.0	10.0	N/A	6.2	7.0	4.9	DGT
ALLSTATE F&C INS CO	IL	C+	267.7	259.7	0.0	0.9	10.0	N/A	7.2	10.0	4.6	T
ALLSTATE INDEMNITY CO	IL	B	121.0	111.3	0.0	0.4	10.0	N/A	3.3	8.4	4.5	T
ALLSTATE INS CO	IL	B	46,626.9	16,259.2	28,491.4	874.9	7.7	6.1	4.5	4.2	5.1	LT
ALLSTATE NJ INS CO	IL	B+	2,557.8	849.5	1,164.9	41.2	8.2	6.8	5.2	6.3	6.7	T
ALLSTATE NJ P&C INS CO	IL	C+	75.8	74.3	0.0	0.2	10.0	N/A	7.3	7.0	4.8	T
ALLSTATE NORTH AMERICAN INS CO	IL	U	--	--	--	--	N/A	--	--	--	--	Z
ALLSTATE NORTHBROOK INDEMNITY CO	IL	B-	58.5	58.1	0.0	0.2	10.0	N/A	7.4	7.0	4.1	GT
ALLSTATE P&C INS CO	IL	B	257.5	237.3	0.0	0.8	10.0	N/A	7.3	10.0	4.7	T
ALLSTATE TEXAS LLOYDS	TX	B	17.4	17.1	0.0	0.0	10.0	N/A	6.3	7.0	4.9	DGT
ALLSTATE VEHICLE & PROPERTY INS CO	IL	B	56.5	54.9	0.0	0.2	10.0	N/A	7.4	10.0	4.7	T
ALPHA P&C INS CO	WI	B	31.4	13.5	0.0	0.1	10.0	N/A	5.9	10.0	4.0	DGRT
ALPS PROPERTY & CASUALTY INS CO	MT	C+	115.1	39.2	30.6	0.4	8.0	8.4	6.8	7.4	3.4	RT
ALTERRA AMERICA INS CO	DE	B-	424.0	197.8	73.8	6.0	5.9	6.9	5.4	6.8	3.6	CFGT
AMALGAMATED CASUALTY INS CO	DC	B-	57.7	42.9	11.5	-0.1	10.0	7.9	4.8	7.2	4.2	DT
AMBAC ASR CORP SEGREGATED ACCT	WI	U	--	--	--	--	N/A	--	--	--	--	Z
AMBAC ASSURANCE CORP	WI	E	5,496.2	944.8	45.2	176.5	2.6	2.7	4.2	6.8	-0.5	CRT
AMCO INS CO	IA	C+	989.3	203.3	0.0	1.0	10.0	N/A	3.2	8.1	4.5	T
AMERICA FIRST INS CO	NH	C+	14.8	14.7	0.0	0.1	10.0	N/A	6.9	7.0	4.7	DGR
AMERICA FIRST LLOYD'S INS CO	TX	C+	6.5	6.4	0.0	0.0	10.0	N/A	6.3	7.0	3.8	DGRT
AMERICAN ACCESS CASUALTY CO	IL	D+	371.4	58.4	296.2	-2.5	2.7	2.0	4.1	2.1	2.8	CLT
AMERICAN AGRI BUSINESS INS CO	TX	C+	1,014.4	30.6	0.0	0.4	7.4	N/A	8.9	7.0	4.4	RT
AMERICAN AGRICULTURAL INS CO	IN	B	1,309.2	584.2	340.6	6.0	7.9	7.0	8.8	7.0	6.3	T
AMERICAN ALLIANCE CASUALTY CO	IL	D	30.1	6.1	17.0	-0.3	1.1	1.6	3.1	7.2	1.4	CDGT
AMERICAN ALTERNATIVE INS CORP	DE	C	521.1	178.9	0.0	8.5	10.0	N/A	8.7	10.0	3.7	RT
AMERICAN ASSOC OF ORTHODONTIST RRG	AZ	C	46.1	15.1	6.9	0.2	6.8	10.0	8.0	7.6	3.6	DRT
AMERICAN AUTOMOBILE INS CO	MO	C	109.7	76.4	0.0	0.5	10.0	3.6	2.2	10.0	3.4	RT
AMERICAN BANKERS INS CO OF FL	FL	B	2,070.3	588.0	915.1	55.0	7.7	6.7	6.2	6.1	5.8	AT
AMERICAN BUILDERS INS CO	DE	C	137.3	41.0	22.2	-0.4	9.2	9.1	6.2	7.2	3.5	RT
AMERICAN BUILDERS INS CO RRG INC	AL	U	--	--	--	--	N/A	--	--	--	--	Z
▲ AMERICAN BUS & MERCANTILE INS MUT	DE	C	65.9	32.3	3.6	-0.1	1.8	3.0	3.5	7.3	3.4	CDFG
AMERICAN CAPITAL ASR CORP	FL	B	117.4	64.2	38.3	-0.8	10.0	9.4	3.5	7.4	5.5	FT

See Page 27 for explanation of footnotes and
Page 28 for explanation of stability factors.

34

www.weissratings.com

Arrows denote recent upgrades ▲ or downgrades ▼   (see Section VII for explanations)

RISK ADJ. RATIO #1	CAPITAL RATIO #2	PREMIUM TO SURPLUS (%)	RESV. TO SURPLUS (%)	RESV. DEVELOP. 1 YEAR (%)	RESV. DEVELOP. 2 YEAR (%)	LOSS RATIO (%)	EXP. RATIO (%)	COMB RATIO (%)	CASH FROM UNDER- WRITING (%)	NET PREMIUM GROWTH (%)	INVEST. IN AFFIL (%)	INSURANCE COMPANY NAME
2.5	2.0	131.1	46.9	-2.9	-8.9	70.8	30.6	101.4	98.0	1.0	0.0	ALLIANCE INS CO
0.0	0.0	120.0	391.2	29.1	-96.0	90.4	27.5	117.9	42.9	-20.7	0.0	ALLIANCE NATIONAL INS CO
1.5	1.2	85.2	128.7	-1.1	-4.3	68.1	30.3	98.4	151.8	1.4	0.0	ALLIANCE OF NONPROFITS FOR INS
1.0	0.8	349.1	200.5	3.0	23.8	94.1	22.7	116.8	102.6	17.1	0.0	ALLIANCE UNITED INS CO
0.9	0.7	110.0	190.9	-38.5	-392.8	73.3	38.9	112.2	39.3	94.3	31.9 ●	ALLIANZ GLOBAL RISKS US INS CO
14.4	13.0	N/A	N/A	N/A	N/A	N/A	N/A	N/A	175.8	0.0	0.0	ALLIANZ UNDERWRITERS INS CO
1.1	0.8	124.0	123.5	-1.3	1.1	69.0	27.6	96.6	118.5	-0.9	0.0	ALLIED EASTERN INDEMNITY CO
2.3	2.1	N/A	N/A	N/A	N/A	N/A	N/A	N/A	249.1	0.0	0.0	ALLIED INS CO OF AMERICA
5.3	4.7	N/A	N/A	N/A	N/A	N/A	N/A	N/A	4.0	0.0	4.4	ALLIED P&C INS CO
1.2	1.1	-38.8	322.2	-198.9	N/A	103.8	-918.7	-814.9	-6.9	-106.0	0.0	ALLIED PREMIER INS A RRG
1.3	0.9	65.9	99.2	9.2	24.3	63.3	38.2	101.5	90.5	-8.2	0.0	ALLIED PROFESSIONALS INS CO RRG
1.2	1.0	24.8	38.0	-16.8	-5.3	26.3	25.9	52.2	128.0	0.0	0.0	ALLIED SERVICES RRG
2.5	1.7	21.7	2.3	N/A	N/A	108.7	59.3	168.0	162.9	0.0	0.0	ALLIED TRUST INS CO
5.5	3.6	31.5	63.3	1.5	1.6	74.7	33.9	108.6	100.3	-7.1	0.0	ALLIED WORLD ASR CO (US) INC
1.7	1.7	19.3	38.9	0.9	0.9	74.7	33.9	108.6	99.8	-7.1	46.4 ●	ALLIED WORLD INS CO
6.1	4.0	28.5	57.3	1.6	1.7	74.7	33.9	108.6	112.2	-7.1	0.0	ALLIED WORLD NATL ASR CO
3.2	2.7	26.8	53.9	1.3	1.4	74.7	34.0	108.7	100.1	-7.1	20.6 ●	ALLIED WORLD SPECIALTY INS CO
3.8	2.5	45.6	91.7	2.2	2.4	74.7	33.9	108.6	99.4	-7.1	0.0	ALLIED WORLD SURPLUS LINES INS
86.0	39.5	N/A	N/A	N/A	N/A	N/A	N/A	N/A	N/A	0.0	0.0	ALLMERICA FINANCIAL ALLIANCE INS CO
87.2	40.9	N/A	N/A	N/A	N/A	N/A	N/A	N/A	N/A	0.0	0.0	ALLMERICA FINANCIAL BENEFIT INS CO
98.7	49.3	N/A	N/A	N/A	N/A	N/A	N/A	N/A	N/A	0.0	0.0	ALLSTATE COUNTY MUTUAL INS CO
125.8	58.7	N/A	N/A	N/A	N/A	N/A	N/A	N/A	-455.7	0.0	0.0 ●	ALLSTATE F&C INS CO
46.7	41.3	N/A	N/A	N/A	N/A	N/A	N/A	N/A	98.0	0.0	0.0	ALLSTATE INDEMNITY CO
1.9	1.5	183.1	105.6	0.3	0.8	71.9	24.7	96.6	107.0	2.6	12.7 ●	ALLSTATE INS CO
2.4	1.9	144.3	153.3	-2.6	-2.4	65.6	23.3	88.9	114.2	0.6	5.0 ●	ALLSTATE NJ INS CO
123.1	58.8	N/A	N/A	N/A	N/A	N/A	N/A	N/A	245.3	0.0	0.0	ALLSTATE NJ P&C INS CO
N/A	N/A	--	--	--	--	--	--	--	--	--	--	ALLSTATE NORTH AMERICAN INS CO
174.2	87.1	N/A	N/A	N/A	N/A	N/A	N/A	N/A	999 +	0.0	0.0	ALLSTATE NORTHBROOK INDEMNITY CO
67.1	55.7	N/A	N/A	N/A	N/A	N/A	N/A	N/A	999 +	0.0	0.0 ●	ALLSTATE P&C INS CO
108.0	54.0	N/A	N/A	N/A	N/A	N/A	N/A	N/A	N/A	0.0	0.0	ALLSTATE TEXAS LLOYDS
91.8	57.4	N/A	N/A	N/A	N/A	N/A	N/A	N/A	999 +	0.0	0.0	ALLSTATE VEHICLE & PROPERTY INS CO
4.1	3.7	N/A	N/A	N/A	N/A	N/A	N/A	N/A	-34.2	0.0	0.0	ALPHA P&C INS CO
2.7	1.8	80.0	137.6	1.2	-1.1	67.8	31.5	99.3	109.2	0.6	0.0	ALPS PROPERTY & CASUALTY INS CO
1.3	0.9	38.2	99.9	-19.0	-14.2	44.7	45.3	90.0	65.6	-28.8	0.0	ALTERRA AMERICA INS CO
7.2	4.3	26.8	14.5	-0.3	-2.9	70.8	28.8	99.6	101.6	27.8	0.0	AMALGAMATED CASUALTY INS CO
N/A	N/A	--	--	--	--	--	--	--	--	--	--	AMBAC ASR CORP SEGREGATED ACCT
0.9	0.4	4.6	250.0	-83.6	999 +	1.1	280.8	281.9	-5.1	-15.0	8.3 ●	AMBAC ASSURANCE CORP
5.4	4.5	N/A	N/A	N/A	N/A	N/A	N/A	N/A	10.9	0.0	15.8 ●	AMCO INS CO
120.3	60.1	N/A	N/A	N/A	N/A	N/A	N/A	N/A	N/A	0.0	0.0	AMERICA FIRST INS CO
129.0	108.3	N/A	N/A	N/A	N/A	N/A	N/A	N/A	N/A	0.0	0.0	AMERICA FIRST LLOYD'S INS CO
0.4	0.4	486.7	238.4	5.0	25.1	68.5	26.4	94.9	104.0	21.7	0.0	AMERICAN ACCESS CASUALTY CO
1.7	0.8	N/A	N/A	N/A	N/A	N/A	N/A	N/A	N/A	0.0	0.0	AMERICAN AGRI BUSINESS INS CO
2.4	1.7	59.1	91.3	-8.0	-9.0	73.8	19.2	93.0	110.3	11.7	0.1 ●	AMERICAN AGRICULTURAL INS CO
0.4	0.3	299.4	140.2	18.1	35.8	70.1	28.8	98.9	122.9	52.6	0.0	AMERICAN ALLIANCE CASUALTY CO
16.0	12.0	N/A	N/A	N/A	N/A	N/A	N/A	N/A	12.3	0.0	0.0 ●	AMERICAN ALTERNATIVE INS CORP
1.3	1.0	47.4	170.4	-63.5	-60.9	34.4	36.6	71.0	122.1	2.7	0.0	AMERICAN ASSOC OF ORTHODONTIST
16.4	14.7	N/A	N/A	N/A	N/A	N/A	N/A	N/A	-70.6	0.0	0.0	AMERICAN AUTOMOBILE INS CO
2.8	1.7	173.1	28.4	-4.8	-3.7	45.2	34.4	79.6	124.1	5.5	0.9 ●	AMERICAN BANKERS INS CO OF FL
4.1	2.8	54.7	75.6	-4.7	-11.6	59.5	21.4	80.9	179.4	9.9	0.0	AMERICAN BUILDERS INS CO
N/A	N/A	--	--	--	--	--	--	--	--	--	--	AMERICAN BUILDERS INS CO RRG INC
0.5	0.3	11.8	100.0	N/A	10.8	129.0	40.7	169.7	54.1	27.6	38.0	AMERICAN BUS & MERCANTILE INS MUT
4.9	4.4	58.6	21.8	-7.2	-21.8	19.6	57.8	77.4	103.3	-43.0	0.0	AMERICAN CAPITAL ASR CORP

999 + Denotes number greater than 999.9%
999 - Denotes number less than -999.99%
● Bullets denote a more detailed analysis is available in Section II.

INSURANCE COMPANY NAME	DOM. STATE	RATING	TOTAL ASSETS ($MIL)	CAPITAL & SURPLUS ($MIL)	ANNUAL NET PREMIUM ($MIL)	NET INCOME ($MIL)	CAPITAL-IZATION INDEX (PTS)	RESERVE ADQ INDEX (PTS)	PROFIT-ABILITY INDEX (PTS)	LIQUIDITY INDEX (PTS)	STAB. INDEX (PTS)	STABILITY FACTORS
AMERICAN CASUALTY CO OF READING	PA	C	141.1	140.7	0.0	0.5	8.7	N/A	5.0	8.4	3.8	ART
▲AMERICAN COASTAL INS CO	FL	B-	333.2	183.6	132.3	6.1	9.3	6.3	6.5	7.4	5.0	T
AMERICAN COMMERCE INS CO	OH	B-	349.6	108.4	193.4	-0.2	8.5	4.0	3.6	2.3	4.0	LT
AMERICAN COMPENSATION INS CO	MN	D	71.3	53.8	0.0	0.1	10.0	N/A	6.0	7.2	2.1	RT
AMERICAN CONTRACTORS INDEMNITY CO	CA	B	319.8	118.9	19.3	1.8	10.0	9.6	8.4	9.5	5.5	T
AMERICAN CONTRACTORS INS CO RISK	TX	D-	19.8	9.7	0.0	-0.1	10.0	N/A	6.5	9.3	1.2	DGRT
AMERICAN COUNTRY INS CO	IL	C	131.9	24.6	43.2	0.1	5.1	2.3	5.3	5.1	3.5	FRT
AMERICAN ECONOMY INS CO	IN	B-	70.8	67.2	0.0	-0.3	10.0	4.0	3.7	7.0	4.1	ART
AMERICAN EMPIRE INS CO	OH	C	20.4	20.4	9.2	1.1	5.9	3.8	3.4	8.7	3.4	DRT
AMERICAN EMPIRE SURPLUS LINES INS CO	DE	C	466.8	147.1	83.1	1.4	6.6	3.1	5.0	7.2	4.0	RT
AMERICAN EQUITY INS CO	AZ	U	--	--	--	--	N/A	--	--	--	--	Z
AMERICAN EQUITY SPECIALTY INS CO	CT	B	79.3	29.1	21.8	0.6	8.1	8.1	5.9	7.1	5.8	DT
AMERICAN EUROPEAN INS CO	NH	B-	130.3	59.6	26.6	-2.0	8.4	6.3	2.7	7.0	3.6	FRT
AMERICAN EXCESS INS EXCHANGE RRG	VT	C-	305.6	177.5	21.8	4.6	8.4	6.8	3.0	7.1	2.7	DFRT
AMERICAN FAMILY HOME INS CO	FL	C+	384.1	183.4	187.0	-2.0	8.0	8.0	6.0	6.8	4.4	T
AMERICAN FAMILY INS CO	WI	B	50.8	23.8	0.0	0.2	10.0	N/A	7.9	6.2	4.8	DGT
AMERICAN FAMILY MUTL INS CO SI	WI	B+	16,206.4	6,884.7	7,291.3	177.2	8.1	8.3	7.7	6.3	5.2	T
AMERICAN FARMERS & RANCHERS INS CO	OK	U	--	--	--	--	N/A	--	--	--	--	Z
AMERICAN FARMERS & RANCHERS	OK	C	159.4	72.5	119.1	3.9	7.8	9.6	7.0	5.8	3.5	RT
AMERICAN FEDERATED INS CO	MS	C+	46.8	22.9	18.4	2.0	6.9	7.7	9.2	7.0	4.3	DT
AMERICAN FEED INDUSTRY INS CO RRG	IA	U (5)	--	--	--	--	N/A	--	--	--	--	Z
AMERICAN FIRE & CASUALTY CO	NH	C-	41.5	40.2	0.0	0.1	10.0	3.8	5.7	7.0	3.1	ART
AMERICAN FOREST CASUALTY CO RRG	VT	D+	8.9	4.5	1.9	0.0	7.3	9.5	6.1	6.8	2.3	DGR
AMERICAN FREEDOM INS CO	IL	B-	61.4	20.7	35.8	0.5	7.2	7.0	8.8	6.4	5.3	DT
AMERICAN GUARANTEE & LIABILITY INS	NY	C+	277.4	179.3	0.0	0.5	10.0	N/A	5.7	7.0	4.6	RT
AMERICAN HALLMARK INS CO OF TX	TX	B	425.0	142.7	123.0	2.9	7.7	4.9	6.9	7.0	4.2	RT
AMERICAN HEALTHCARE INDEMNITY CO	OK	U	--	--	--	--	N/A	--	--	--	--	Z
AMERICAN HEARTLAND INS CO	IL	D	18.0	3.0	8.1	-0.1	2.7	7.1	2.9	6.7	2.0	CDGT
AMERICAN HOME ASR CO	NY	C	26,144.8	6,979.5	6,267.6	418.4	7.8	3.0	4.9	5.7	2.8	AT
▼AMERICAN INDEPENDENT INS CO	PA	D+	133.8	9.0	15.8	-0.6	5.6	1.8	1.2	0.0	2.4	DFGL
AMERICAN INS CO	OH	C-	132.1	64.0	0.0	-0.4	10.0	3.6	1.9	7.0	3.1	RT
AMERICAN INTEGRITY INS CO OF FL	FL	C+	219.2	75.0	113.6	1.3	7.5	3.5	8.9	5.9	4.7	T
AMERICAN INTER FIDELITY EXCHANGE	IN	C+	91.6	25.4	36.3	0.6	5.0	6.8	8.8	7.1	3.2	DRT
AMERICAN INTERSTATE INS CO	NE	B-	1,247.4	408.3	291.9	11.1	7.7	9.4	8.6	7.2	4.3	RT
AMERICAN INTERSTATE INS CO OF TEXAS	TX	B	70.3	29.5	17.7	0.8	7.3	9.3	8.9	7.7	6.0	DT
AMERICAN LIBERTY INS CO	UT	E	14.5	2.8	6.6	0.1	0.2	0.2	2.4	3.3	0.3	CDFG
AMERICAN MEDICAL ASR CO	IL	U	--	--	--	--	N/A	--	--	--	--	Z
AMERICAN MERCURY INS CO	OK	B	349.2	151.6	177.1	4.5	8.4	5.7	5.4	6.6	4.1	RT
AMERICAN MERCURY LLOYDS INS CO	TX	B	6.4	5.3	0.0	0.0	10.0	N/A	6.5	10.0	4.9	DFGT
AMERICAN MILLENNIUM INS CO	NJ	D	34.8	8.6	10.2	0.2	1.1	1.9	6.4	6.0	1.5	CDGR
AMERICAN MINING INS CO	IA	B-	37.4	26.2	0.0	0.1	10.0	N/A	7.2	10.0	3.7	GT
AMERICAN MODERN HOME INS CO	OH	C+	1,044.3	419.6	329.0	-5.9	7.8	7.8	5.4	6.4	4.3	RT
AMERICAN MODERN INS CO OF FLORIDA	FL	B-	32.6	9.8	13.9	-0.4	5.7	8.4	5.1	4.0	4.4	CDGL
AMERICAN MODERN LLOYDS INS CO	TX	C	6.7	4.1	0.0	0.0	9.2	N/A	4.4	6.1	2.5	DFGT
AMERICAN MODERN PROPERTY &	OH	B	23.7	16.9	3.5	0.0	10.0	7.5	7.2	7.6	4.0	DGT
AMERICAN MODERN SELECT INS CO	OH	C	289.4	58.0	34.6	0.8	9.5	7.8	8.3	6.2	3.9	FT
AMERICAN MODERN SURPLUS LINES INS	OH	B	62.9	29.2	34.6	-0.5	7.1	8.1	5.3	6.0	6.0	CDT
AMERICAN MUTUAL SHARE INS CORP	OH	C-	267.3	239.7	0.2	-0.8	10.0	7.0	4.6	10.0	1.5	DFGT
AMERICAN NATIONAL GENERAL INS CO	MO	B	103.9	66.2	34.9	-0.8	10.0	8.2	5.2	6.7	4.2	FRT
AMERICAN NATIONAL LLOYDS INS CO	TX	B	87.7	66.1	21.1	-1.8	10.0	5.9	5.6	6.9	6.1	T
AMERICAN NATIONAL PROPERTY & CAS CO	MO	B	1,339.7	632.8	542.6	5.9	8.1	8.4	6.8	6.0	4.9	T
AMERICAN NATL COUNTY MUT INS CO	TX	B	24.3	9.9	0.0	0.0	8.2	N/A	5.3	7.0	4.7	DFGT

See Page 27 for explanation of footnotes and
Page 28 for explanation of stability factors.
Arrows denote recent upgrades ▲ or downgrades ▼   (see Section VII for explanations)

36

www.weissratings.com

RISK ADJ. RATIO #1	CAPITAL RATIO #2	PREMIUM TO SURPLUS (%)	RESV. TO SURPLUS (%)	RESV. 1 YEAR (%)	DEVELOP. 2 YEAR (%)	LOSS RATIO (%)	EXP. RATIO (%)	COMB RATIO (%)	CASH FROM UNDER- WRITING (%)	NET PREMIUM GROWTH (%)	INVEST. IN AFFIL (%)	INSURANCE COMPANY NAME
2.1	2.1	N/A	N/A	N/A	N/A	N/A	N/A	N/A	N/A	0.0	51.4	AMERICAN CASUALTY CO OF READING
3.9	3.6	74.8	20.4	-0.2	0.7	34.2	34.8	69.0	161.9	-15.6	0.0	AMERICAN COASTAL INS CO
2.4	2.0	178.7	84.6	3.2	4.6	78.1	23.6	101.7	95.0	1.9	0.0	AMERICAN COMMERCE INS CO
4.1	4.0	N/A	N/A	N/A	N/A	N/A	N/A	N/A	-968.8	0.0	28.4	AMERICAN COMPENSATION INS CO
9.2	6.6	16.5	19.2	-12.6	-32.2	-25.9	52.9	27.0	119.3	24.4	0.0	AMERICAN CONTRACTORS INDEMNITY
3.9	3.5	N/A	N/A	N/A	N/A	N/A	N/A	N/A	245.7	0.0	0.0	AMERICAN CONTRACTORS INS CO RISK
1.3	0.8	172.3	99.8	27.9	49.7	78.5	26.6	105.1	97.5	2.1	0.0	AMERICAN COUNTRY INS CO
7.9	7.6	N/A	N/A	N/A	N/A	N/A	N/A	N/A	N/A	0.0	17.7	AMERICAN ECONOMY INS CO
6.2	5.6	46.8	127.0	19.2	18.1	120.2	15.4	135.6	124.3	-8.8	0.0	AMERICAN EMPIRE INS CO
1.3	0.8	58.0	157.4	29.2	30.7	120.2	15.4	135.6	113.5	-8.8	5.2	AMERICAN EMPIRE SURPLUS LINES INS
N/A	N/A	--	--	--	--	--	--	--	--	--	--	AMERICAN EQUITY INS CO
2.7	1.7	76.5	126.9	-1.5	-3.9	63.4	29.9	93.3	109.7	4.8	0.0	AMERICAN EQUITY SPECIALTY INS CO
2.2	1.8	42.8	78.1	0.3	-0.5	66.6	40.4	107.0	72.7	-7.7	16.8	AMERICAN EUROPEAN INS CO
2.9	2.0	12.8	76.8	1.5	4.3	112.0	17.6	129.6	50.5	-2.1	0.0	AMERICAN EXCESS INS EXCHANGE RRG
2.8	1.7	100.2	24.4	-2.8	-4.5	54.8	47.9	102.7	76.9	-11.1	9.3	AMERICAN FAMILY HOME INS CO
5.5	5.0	N/A	N/A	N/A	N/A	N/A	N/A	N/A	-331.7	0.0	0.0	AMERICAN FAMILY INS CO
2.1	1.7	106.2	55.9	-2.3	-6.9	68.2	31.4	99.6	106.0	6.4	16.2 ●	AMERICAN FAMILY MUTL INS CO SI
N/A	N/A	--	--	--	--	--	--	--	--	--	--	AMERICAN FARMERS & RANCHERS INS
2.5	1.8	173.3	33.4	-4.1	-22.1	59.8	27.4	87.2	115.1	7.8	8.8	AMERICAN FARMERS & RANCHERS
1.5	1.4	88.0	2.1	-0.9	-1.9	4.9	78.0	82.9	120.0	3.6	0.0	AMERICAN FEDERATED INS CO
N/A	N/A	--	--	--	--	--	--	--	--	--	--	AMERICAN FEED INDUSTRY INS CO RRG
80.7	72.6	N/A	N/A	N/A	N/A	N/A	N/A	N/A	N/A	0.0	0.0	AMERICAN FIRE & CASUALTY CO
1.9	1.4	42.5	67.8	-13.4	-16.8	43.5	35.1	78.6	141.5	16.0	0.0	AMERICAN FOREST CASUALTY CO RRG
1.7	1.4	173.9	78.9	-6.2	-10.4	45.5	41.2	86.7	126.4	14.0	0.0	AMERICAN FREEDOM INS CO
20.1	18.1	N/A	N/A	N/A	N/A	N/A	N/A	N/A	-20.3	0.0	0.0	AMERICAN GUARANTEE & LIABILITY INS
1.8	1.5	88.4	87.2	1.4	1.0	71.3	27.3	98.6	124.1	-3.4	25.2	AMERICAN HALLMARK INS CO OF TX
N/A	N/A	--	--	--	--	--	--	--	--	--	--	AMERICAN HEALTHCARE INDEMNITY CO
0.6	0.5	271.5	346.3	-25.2	-41.3	53.1	45.4	98.5	102.2	-22.3	0.0	AMERICAN HEARTLAND INS CO
2.5	1.6	97.2	189.4	12.2	22.3	90.5	30.8	121.3	117.4	9.8	0.9 ●	AMERICAN HOME ASR CO
0.7	0.5	136.5	109.0	19.7	29.1	106.4	23.8	130.2	194.7	-8.2	21.6	AMERICAN INDEPENDENT INS CO
11.2	10.1	N/A	N/A	N/A	N/A	N/A	N/A	N/A	49.7	0.0	0.0	AMERICAN INS CO
2.3	2.0	155.9	48.7	8.0	15.1	60.4	32.3	92.7	109.4	4.7	0.0	AMERICAN INTEGRITY INS CO OF FL
1.2	0.7	152.5	128.8	10.0	7.0	72.6	22.0	94.6	117.1	21.1	0.0	AMERICAN INTER FIDELITY EXCHANGE
1.9	1.5	74.1	135.9	-11.0	-21.4	54.0	21.8	75.8	136.6	-3.3	12.2 ●	AMERICAN INTERSTATE INS CO
2.0	1.5	61.7	105.2	-10.0	-22.3	54.2	22.0	76.2	136.6	-3.6	0.0	AMERICAN INTERSTATE INS CO OF
0.2	0.1	246.2	289.3	124.7	84.9	101.2	29.8	131.0	88.6	-10.8	0.0	AMERICAN LIBERTY INS CO
N/A	N/A	--	--	--	--	--	--	--	--	--	--	AMERICAN MEDICAL ASR CO
2.3	1.6	109.5	40.0	2.1	4.6	77.4	27.6	105.0	96.7	4.0	10.3	AMERICAN MERCURY INS CO
10.9	9.8	N/A	N/A	N/A	N/A	N/A	N/A	N/A	-38.2	0.0	0.0	AMERICAN MERCURY LLOYDS INS CO
0.3	0.2	123.5	123.4	16.7	29.6	99.3	0.3	99.6	148.8	63.4	0.0	AMERICAN MILLENNIUM INS CO
10.2	9.2	N/A	N/A	N/A	N/A	N/A	N/A	N/A	999 +	0.0	0.0	AMERICAN MINING INS CO
1.9	1.5	80.8	19.7	-2.1	-3.3	54.8	47.6	102.4	111.2	-11.1	38.5 ●	AMERICAN MODERN HOME INS CO
1.5	0.9	133.6	32.5	-4.0	-6.7	54.8	48.3	103.1	81.0	-11.1	0.0	AMERICAN MODERN INS CO OF FLORIDA
4.6	4.1	N/A	N/A	N/A	N/A	N/A	N/A	N/A	55.4	0.0	0.0	AMERICAN MODERN LLOYDS INS CO
9.0	6.0	20.5	5.0	-0.6	-0.8	54.8	48.3	103.1	85.3	-11.1	0.0	AMERICAN MODERN PROPERTY &
5.1	2.9	60.2	14.7	-1.8	-2.9	54.8	39.0	93.8	15.5	-11.1	0.0	AMERICAN MODERN SELECT INS CO
1.8	1.0	115.2	28.0	-3.1	-4.9	54.8	48.7	103.5	94.2	-11.1	0.0	AMERICAN MODERN SURPLUS LINES
9.9	8.8	0.1	8.3	-8.2	-17.6	999 +	999 +	999 +	2.4	10.3	8.7 ●	AMERICAN MUTUAL SHARE INS CORP
5.5	3.8	51.9	24.9	-4.0	-5.4	78.2	24.5	102.7	88.0	11.1	0.0	AMERICAN NATIONAL GENERAL INS CO
8.2	6.7	31.2	8.1	-0.6	-0.1	84.3	24.1	108.4	96.8	9.9	0.0	AMERICAN NATIONAL LLOYDS INS CO
2.1	1.7	86.5	44.4	-2.3	-5.8	77.2	27.6	104.8	100.9	9.3	20.5 ●	AMERICAN NATIONAL PROPERTY & CAS
2.9	1.7	N/A	N/A	N/A	N/A	N/A	999 +	999 +	404.0	13.3	0.0	AMERICAN NATL COUNTY MUT INS CO

999 + Denotes number greater than 999.9%
999 - Denotes number less than -999.99%
● Bullets denote a more detailed analysis is available in Section II.

INSURANCE COMPANY NAME	DOM. STATE	RATING	TOTAL ASSETS ($MIL)	CAPITAL & SURPLUS ($MIL)	ANNUAL NET PREMIUM ($MIL)	NET INCOME ($MIL)	CAPITAL-IZATION INDEX (PTS)	RESERVE ADQ INDEX (PTS)	PROFIT-ABILITY INDEX (PTS)	LIQUIDITY INDEX (PTS)	STAB. INDEX (PTS)	STABILITY FACTORS
AMERICAN PACIFIC INS CO	HI	U	--	--	--	--	N/A	--	--	--	--	Z
▲AMERICAN PET INS CO	NY	C-	61.2	31.8	154.2	1.7	2.8	6.0	8.9	0.0	3.0	LT
AMERICAN PHYSICIANS ASR CORP	MI	U	--	--	--	--	N/A	--	--	--	--	Z
AMERICAN PLATINUM PROP & CAS INS CO	FL	C+	22.8	17.4	3.8	0.1	10.0	5.1	4.6	8.8	3.4	DGT
AMERICAN PROPERTY INS	NJ	D+	23.6	7.9	10.7	0.4	2.5	7.0	3.3	7.4	2.2	CDGR
AMERICAN RELIABLE INS CO	AZ	B	237.5	92.0	67.3	0.3	8.8	5.4	5.4	6.8	4.2	RT
AMERICAN RESOURCES INS CO INC	OK	D	26.0	6.3	11.7	-0.4	1.2	9.3	1.2	6.0	1.6	CDFG
AMERICAN RISK INS CO	TX	D+	32.5	12.7	16.2	0.7	5.1	2.2	6.6	0.7	2.7	DGLT
AMERICAN RISK MGMT RRG INC	TN	D	4.0	1.6	2.7	0.1	5.3	N/A	4.3	9.1	1.2	DGT
AMERICAN ROAD INS CO	MI	C+	711.3	248.7	157.6	1.2	10.0	6.1	6.4	7.4	3.0	FRT
AMERICAN SAFETY INS CO	GA	C	17.6	17.0	0.0	0.1	10.0	N/A	4.1	7.0	3.3	DGRT
AMERICAN SAFETY RRG INC	VT	D+	8.0	5.6	0.3	-0.1	5.3	9.6	1.7	6.9	2.1	DFGR
AMERICAN SECURITY INS CO	DE	B-	1,531.8	594.3	945.8	35.2	7.7	6.3	3.5	6.0	4.7	AT
AMERICAN SELECT INS CO	OH	C	257.0	117.3	90.5	1.8	9.0	8.7	8.6	6.7	3.8	T
AMERICAN SENTINEL INS CO	PA	C-	39.5	17.2	25.2	0.1	2.8	8.5	8.0	5.6	3.1	CDGT
AMERICAN SERVICE INS CO	IL	D	208.0	53.5	72.0	0.4	7.4	2.5	5.7	6.4	1.8	RT
AMERICAN SOUTHERN HOME INS CO	FL	C	149.3	46.9	27.7	0.0	9.0	7.7	8.1	6.4	3.8	FT
AMERICAN SOUTHERN INS CO	KS	C+	103.6	42.3	51.5	1.9	7.9	8.4	8.0	6.4	4.5	RT
AMERICAN SPECIAL RISK INS CO	DE	U	--	--	--	--	N/A	--	--	--	--	Z
AMERICAN STANDARD INS CO OF OH	WI	B	9.6	8.3	0.0	0.1	10.0	N/A	7.9	9.5	4.7	DFG
AMERICAN STANDARD INS CO OF WI	WI	B+	401.3	343.9	0.0	0.7	10.0	N/A	7.2	10.0	5.0	FT
AMERICAN STATES INS CO	IN	B-	144.6	131.5	0.0	-1.0	10.0	3.9	4.8	7.0	4.5	ART
AMERICAN STATES INS CO OF TX	TX	B	12.9	12.1	0.0	0.1	10.0	N/A	3.9	7.0	4.0	DGRT
AMERICAN STATES LLOYDS INS CO	TX	B	3.6	3.6	0.0	0.0	10.0	N/A	6.7	7.0	4.1	DGRT
AMERICAN STATES PREFERRED INS CO	IN	B-	22.1	22.0	0.0	0.0	10.0	3.9	5.5	7.0	3.8	ADGR
AMERICAN STEAMSHIP O M PROT & IND AS	NY	D+	308.0	72.8	85.0	6.1	6.4	5.2	3.9	5.9	2.3	DFRT
AMERICAN STRATEGIC INS CO	FL	C	1,100.4	505.1	618.3	14.2	8.6	9.4	6.2	6.5	3.9	T
AMERICAN SUMMIT INS CO	TX	C+	50.5	31.4	26.6	0.8	8.9	6.6	8.3	6.9	3.6	RT
AMERICAN SURETY CO	IN	C	14.1	10.5	10.8	-0.3	6.7	9.1	5.1	6.9	2.4	DGT
AMERICAN TRADITIONS INS CO	FL	C+	54.0	19.3	28.4	-1.0	7.1	4.9	4.8	6.9	4.5	DRT
AMERICAN TRANSIT INS CO	NY	E+	473.1	64.2	287.1	0.4	0.8	0.1	3.9	5.3	0.4	CGRT
AMERICAN TRUCKING & TRANSP INS RRG	MT	E+	36.7	6.8	12.8	-0.3	0.5	5.7	1.8	7.0	0.7	CDGR
AMERICAN UNDERWRITERS INS CO	AR	D+	7.0	5.0	0.0	0.0	10.0	N/A	3.1	10.0	2.5	DGR
AMERICAN WEST INS CO	ND	C	15.9	12.3	9.7	0.1	7.0	5.7	6.9	5.9	3.0	DGT
AMERICAN WESTERN HOME INS CO	OK	C	148.3	72.9	62.3	-0.7	8.5	7.9	6.0	6.5	3.9	T
AMERICAN ZURICH INS CO	IL	C+	319.1	231.4	0.0	0.5	10.0	N/A	7.5	10.0	4.6	RT
AMERICAS INS CO	DC	C	17.4	7.1	6.9	-0.6	7.4	6.0	2.4	7.4	2.3	DGRT
▲AMERIGUARD RRG INC	VT	C-	15.1	8.3	2.7	0.0	7.1	7.0	5.4	9.9	2.8	DGT
AMERIHEALTH CASUALTY INS CO	DE	B-	322.1	70.9	111.0	4.3	4.7	5.9	6.3	6.5	5.1	CT
AMERIPRISE INS CO	WI	B	49.3	47.5	0.0	0.2	10.0	N/A	6.8	10.0	5.4	
AMERISURE INS CO	MI	B-	968.8	245.8	244.0	1.3	8.2	5.9	7.5	6.8	4.4	RT
AMERISURE MUTUAL INS CO	MI	B-	2,397.2	945.7	545.0	9.0	8.2	6.0	8.3	6.8	4.7	T
AMERISURE PARTNERS INS CO	MI	C+	93.9	24.4	24.4	0.1	7.5	6.0	4.7	6.9	4.5	DT
AMERITRUST INS CORP	MI	D+	41.2	30.2	0.0	0.1	10.0	1.9	4.1	0.9	2.7	DFLR
AMEX ASSURANCE CO	IL	B	244.5	194.9	177.4	13.5	10.0	8.6	4.2	7.0	4.5	RT
▲AMFED CASUALTY INS CO	MS	C-	5.7	5.1	0.0	0.0	10.0	N/A	7.1	10.0	2.4	DFGR
AMFED NATIONAL INS CO	MS	D-	68.9	32.9	10.6	0.6	1.4	0.8	8.4	7.4	0.9	CDFT
AMFIRST SPECIALTY INS CO	MS	D	2.6	2.4	1.5	0.0	9.2	N/A	5.9	9.1	0.6	DGT
AMGUARD INS CO	PA	C	681.0	149.6	160.8	3.9	4.9	9.5	8.3	6.9	3.4	GRT
AMICA MUTUAL INS CO	RI	B+	5,140.7	2,600.1	2,086.5	7.5	8.2	8.2	5.2	5.6	5.4	T
▲AMICA P&C INS CO	RI	B-	82.6	79.2	0.0	0.1	10.0	7.0	3.8	10.0	5.0	DT
AMSHIELD INS CO	MO	U	--	--	--	--	N/A	--	--	--	--	Z

See Page 27 for explanation of footnotes and   38   www.weissratings.com
Page 28 for explanation of stability factors.
Arrows denote recent upgrades ▲ or downgrades ▼   (see Section VII for explanations)

RISK RATIO #1	ADJ. CAPITAL RATIO #2	PREMIUM TO SURPLUS (%)	RESV. TO SURPLUS (%)	RESV. DEVELOP. 1 YEAR (%)	RESV. DEVELOP. 2 YEAR (%)	LOSS RATIO (%)	EXP. RATIO (%)	COMB RATIO (%)	CASH FROM UNDER- WRITING (%)	NET PREMIUM GROWTH (%)	INVEST. IN AFFIL (%)	INSURANCE COMPANY NAME
N/A	N/A	--	--	--	--	--	--	--	--	--	--	AMERICAN PACIFIC INS CO
1.7	0.9	506.4	27.7	2.3	1.3	72.2	23.1	95.3	108.8	32.2	0.0	AMERICAN PET INS CO
N/A	N/A	--	--	--	--	--	--	--	--	--	--	AMERICAN PHYSICIANS ASR CORP
6.5	4.5	21.8	3.9	-0.4	-0.9	29.9	54.7	84.6	111.7	8.0	0.0	AMERICAN PLATINUM PROP & CAS INS
0.6	0.4	143.3	37.4	-0.9	-2.8	49.7	30.7	80.4	159.1	55.1	0.0	AMERICAN PROPERTY INS
3.3	2.1	73.5	73.5	-4.8	-11.7	67.1	37.3	104.4	116.3	607.5	1.7	AMERICAN RELIABLE INS CO
0.6	0.3	232.1	193.3	6.5	-8.7	65.1	45.4	110.5	93.9	18.1	0.0	AMERICAN RESOURCES INS CO INC
1.1	0.8	134.8	39.5	-4.5	4.2	52.0	39.6	91.6	105.9	17.7	0.0	AMERICAN RISK INS CO
1.3	0.8	173.5	32.2	N/A	N/A	60.8	17.1	77.9	235.4	0.0	0.0	AMERICAN RISK MGMT RRG INC
7.7	5.1	63.6	1.2	1.0	0.6	99.0	0.3	99.3	89.2	17.1	0.0 ●	AMERICAN ROAD INS CO
31.8	12.1	N/A	N/A	N/A	N/A	N/A	N/A	N/A	N/A	0.0	0.0	AMERICAN SAFETY INS CO
1.0	0.8	5.2	36.5	4.7	-16.3	168.4	194.7	363.1	36.4	-37.2	0.0	AMERICAN SAFETY RRG INC
2.0	1.6	170.4	38.2	-3.6	-3.9	49.0	47.3	96.3	96.7	-9.7	11.5 ●	AMERICAN SECURITY INS CO
3.8	2.4	78.8	70.7	-3.0	-4.4	62.3	35.0	97.3	106.4	2.3	0.0	AMERICAN SELECT INS CO
0.6	0.4	148.9	45.8	-0.6	-2.3	49.1	49.5	98.6	115.7	18.3	0.0	AMERICAN SENTINEL INS CO
3.0	1.8	142.6	82.6	25.5	48.1	78.5	26.6	105.1	106.1	2.1	0.0	AMERICAN SERVICE INS CO
3.4	2.4	58.3	14.2	-1.7	-2.7	54.8	47.0	101.8	37.2	-11.1	9.0	AMERICAN SOUTHERN HOME INS CO
2.2	1.7	124.1	95.8	-6.7	-3.6	64.0	30.6	94.6	103.4	-7.4	16.9	AMERICAN SOUTHERN INS CO
N/A	N/A	--	--	--	--	--	--	--	--	--	--	AMERICAN SPECIAL RISK INS CO
15.9	14.3	N/A	N/A	N/A	N/A	N/A	N/A	N/A	999 +	0.0	0.0	AMERICAN STANDARD INS CO OF OH
48.5	43.6	N/A	N/A	N/A	N/A	N/A	N/A	N/A	999 +	0.0	0.0 ●	AMERICAN STANDARD INS CO OF WI
59.0	53.1	N/A	N/A	N/A	N/A	N/A	N/A	N/A	N/A	0.0	0.0	AMERICAN STATES INS CO
35.3	31.8	N/A	N/A	N/A	N/A	N/A	N/A	N/A	N/A	0.0	0.0	AMERICAN STATES INS CO OF TX
162.6	81.3	N/A	N/A	N/A	N/A	N/A	N/A	N/A	N/A	0.0	0.0	AMERICAN STATES LLOYDS INS CO
214.5	107.2	N/A	N/A	N/A	N/A	N/A	N/A	N/A	N/A	0.0	0.0	AMERICAN STATES PREFERRED INS CO
1.3	1.0	128.1	244.9	9.2	20.2	84.1	27.0	111.1	67.0	9.2	5.5	AMERICAN STEAMSHIP O M PROT & IND
2.7	2.4	126.3	29.6	-9.4	-14.2	64.5	31.6	96.1	104.5	7.3	1.7 ●	AMERICAN STRATEGIC INS CO
3.1	2.7	87.3	12.5	-0.9	-3.0	59.1	31.0	90.1	109.1	1.3	0.0	AMERICAN SUMMIT INS CO
1.0	0.9	98.6	11.7	-11.0	-11.7	2.0	87.7	89.7	100.6	5.7	0.0	AMERICAN SURETY CO
1.4	1.2	141.7	41.4	-4.5	-2.0	69.3	35.8	105.1	98.0	5.1	0.0	AMERICAN TRADITIONS INS CO
0.2	0.2	452.1	146.5	188.8	384.0	66.1	29.2	95.3	120.2	26.2	0.0	AMERICAN TRANSIT INS CO
0.2	0.1	188.4	279.2	-22.2	15.7	81.3	17.2	98.5	128.3	95.5	0.0	AMERICAN TRUCKING & TRANSP INS
6.7	6.1	N/A	N/A	N/A	N/A	N/A	N/A	N/A	43.1	0.0	0.0	AMERICAN UNDERWRITERS INS CO
1.2	1.0	82.0	13.5	-4.0	-4.8	63.5	25.1	88.6	123.1	40.8	0.0	AMERICAN WEST INS CO
3.4	2.0	84.9	20.7	-2.4	-3.7	54.8	48.4	103.2	95.5	-11.1	0.0	AMERICAN WESTERN HOME INS CO
7.1	6.7	N/A	N/A	N/A	N/A	N/A	N/A	N/A	-185.4	0.0	14.8 ●	AMERICAN ZURICH INS CO
2.1	1.5	89.3	39.2	5.7	2.8	77.0	41.1	118.1	110.8	-14.0	5.9	AMERICAS INS CO
1.3	1.1	31.8	62.3	-2.6	-15.8	63.6	8.7	72.3	230.5	-2.0	0.0	AMERIGUARD RRG INC
1.1	0.8	161.0	237.3	3.6	-12.0	66.8	32.9	99.7	107.7	0.6	0.0	AMERIHEALTH CASUALTY INS CO
69.2	31.7	N/A	N/A	N/A	N/A	N/A	N/A	N/A	N/A	0.0	0.0	AMERIPRISE INS CO
2.4	1.7	99.3	162.3	3.7	4.9	69.5	30.0	99.5	105.8	4.8	0.0 ●	AMERISURE INS CO
2.3	1.8	58.1	95.0	2.3	2.9	69.5	30.5	100.0	107.2	4.8	14.3 ●	AMERISURE MUTUAL INS CO
1.7	1.2	99.6	162.9	3.7	4.8	69.5	30.0	99.5	111.3	4.8	0.0	AMERISURE PARTNERS INS CO
11.3	10.1	N/A	N/A	N/A	N/A	N/A	N/A	N/A	-17.6	-100.0	0.0	AMERITRUST INS CORP
11.2	6.4	97.8	14.7	-1.4	-3.9	39.0	17.3	56.3	176.6	-5.7	0.0	AMEX ASSURANCE CO
18.5	16.7	N/A	N/A	N/A	N/A	N/A	N/A	N/A	999 +	0.0	0.0	AMFED CASUALTY INS CO
0.5	0.3	32.9	88.0	-13.6	2.8	54.0	33.1	87.1	76.0	-53.2	8.6	AMFED NATIONAL INS CO
5.3	3.3	63.0	N/A	N/A	N/A	N/A	2.2	2.2	999 +	0.0	0.0	AMFIRST SPECIALTY INS CO
0.9	0.7	114.1	127.6	-3.8	-20.3	59.1	23.6	82.7	145.8	65.8	0.0	AMGUARD INS CO
2.6	1.7	80.8	45.6	-2.6	-5.4	77.9	23.9	101.8	102.7	7.4	8.2 ●	AMICA MUTUAL INS CO
73.8	46.6	N/A	N/A	N/A	-0.8	N/A	N/A	N/A	171.7	100.0	0.0	AMICA P&C INS CO
N/A	N/A	--	--	--	--	--	--	--	--	--	--	AMSHIELD INS CO

999 + Denotes number greater than 999.9%
999 - Denotes number less than -999.99%
● Bullets denote a more detailed analysis is available in Section II.

INSURANCE COMPANY NAME	DOM. STATE	RATING	TOTAL ASSETS ($MIL)	CAPITAL & SURPLUS ($MIL)	ANNUAL NET PREMIUM ($MIL)	NET INCOME ($MIL)	CAPITAL-IZATION INDEX (PTS)	RESERVE ADQ INDEX (PTS)	PROFIT-ABILITY INDEX (PTS)	LIQUIDITY INDEX (PTS)	STAB. INDEX (PTS)	STABILITY FACTORS
AMTRUST INS CO OF KANSAS INC	KS	B-	206.3	38.5	62.7	5.3	5.1	6.2	9.9	6.9	3.9	CFGR
ANCHOR GENERAL INS CO	CA	C	103.5	21.9	50.0	-0.3	6.5	5.8	3.6	1.3	3.1	DLRT
ANCHOR P&C INS CO	FL	D	67.2	25.8	24.9	-1.9	1.8	3.6	1.8	6.1	1.6	CDT
ANCHOR SPECIALTY INS CO	TX	C	16.5	9.1	4.3	0.0	6.4	4.1	2.6	6.4	3.5	DFGR
ANPAC LOUISIANA INS CO	LA	B	126.1	66.2	53.9	-0.1	8.9	8.0	3.7	5.9	6.0	FT
ANSUR AMERICA INS CO	MI	B	115.8	44.2	48.0	1.0	9.8	9.3	8.8	6.7	4.7	T
ANTHRACITE MUTUAL FIRE INS CO	PA	C-	4.1	4.0	0.4	0.0	10.0	5.0	7.9	9.0	2.5	DGT
ANTILLES INS CO	PR	C	59.7	43.8	26.0	0.6	5.0	7.7	2.9	5.5	3.7	RT
▲APOLLO CASUALTY CO	IL	E	13.8	1.7	8.8	-0.3	0.7	1.3	0.5	0.0	0.1	CDFG
APOLLO MUTUAL FIRE INS CO	PA	C- (1)	4.0	3.9	0.1	0.1	10.0	5.0	6.3	10.0	2.0	DT
APPALACHIAN INS CO	RI	C	330.5	217.2	66.1	-0.2	9.7	3.1	8.4	8.4	3.1	RT
APPLIED MEDICO LEGAL SOLUTIONS RRG	AZ	C	136.7	41.4	30.2	0.4	7.3	5.8	6.7	7.6	4.0	RT
▲APPLIED UNDERWRITERS CAPTIVE RISK	IA	C-	928.7	58.3	0.0	-1.2	7.4	4.9	5.4	7.0	3.0	T
ARAG INS CO	IA	B-	83.1	60.9	76.6	3.7	9.8	8.7	9.4	6.3	3.7	RT
ARBELLA INDEMNITY INS CO	MA	C	51.4	16.6	24.4	0.5	7.6	7.9	4.6	6.3	3.4	DRT
ARBELLA MUTUAL INS CO	MA	C+	1,376.4	576.7	619.2	14.7	8.4	7.7	5.0	6.2	4.3	RT
ARBELLA PROTECTION INS CO	MA	C+	316.4	100.6	130.4	3.0	8.9	8.0	5.3	6.1	4.2	RT
ARCH EXCESS & SURPLUS INS CO	MO	U	--	--	--	--	N/A	--	--	--	--	Z
ARCH INDEMNITY INS CO	MO	B-	103.0	29.5	0.0	0.0	10.0	N/A	4.6	10.0	3.7	RT
ARCH INS CO	MO	C	3,951.7	890.3	793.2	3.6	7.3	7.5	5.8	6.9	3.4	RT
ARCH MORTGAGE ASR CO	WI	U	--	--	--	--	N/A	--	--	--	--	Z
ARCH MORTGAGE GUARANTY CO	WI	B	51.4	49.7	0.3	0.1	10.0	3.6	6.6	9.6	4.6	DGT
ARCH MORTGAGE INS CO	WI	B-	550.5	153.9	88.4	-1.5	7.1	5.0	2.7	5.9	4.5	RT
▲ARCH MORTGAGE REINS CO	WI	C+	20.2	15.5	0.2	-0.1	10.0	5.7	4.7	10.0	3.3	DFGT
ARCH REINS CO	DE	C-	2,016.7	1,245.4	215.7	9.4	7.9	8.2	7.7	7.3	2.7	RT
ARCH SPECIALTY INS CO	MO	B	496.9	297.4	0.1	-4.4	10.0	6.0	4.8	9.1	4.7	FGRT
ARCH STRUCTURED MRTG INS CO	NC	U	--	--	--	--	N/A	--	--	--	--	Z
ARCHITECTS & ENGINEERS INS CO RRG	DE	C	22.0	10.1	1.5	0.2	9.3	7.6	7.8	10.0	2.3	DGRT
ARCOA RRG INC	NV	E+	15.8	7.1	10.4	0.3	0.7	3.8	2.9	6.3	0.6	CDGT
ARECA INS EXCHANGE	AK	C+	27.6	20.1	4.3	0.2	9.7	5.8	3.9	6.9	3.1	DFGR
ARGONAUT GREAT CENTRAL INS CO	IL	D+	37.1	25.9	0.0	0.1	10.0	N/A	6.5	7.0	2.4	GRT
ARGONAUT INS CO	IL	C	1,695.6	817.0	223.7	3.7	7.2	3.3	6.2	7.2	3.3	GRT
ARGONAUT LTD RISK INS CO	IL	U	--	--	--	--	N/A	--	--	--	--	Z
ARGONAUT-MIDWEST INS CO	IL	D	19.0	17.6	0.0	0.1	10.0	N/A	7.4	7.0	2.3	DGRT
ARGONAUT-SOUTHWEST INS CO	IL	D	18.3	18.3	0.0	0.1	10.0	N/A	6.3	10.0	2.3	DGRT
ARGUS FIRE & CASUALTY INS CO	FL	F	3.5	3.1	0.0	0.0	10.0	4.6	2.9	10.0	0.0	DFGT
ARI CASUALTY CO	NJ	U	--	--	--	--	N/A	--	--	--	--	Z
ARI INS CO	PA	D	99.1	21.2	26.9	0.7	0.9	0.8	1.7	3.0	1.6	CDGL
ARISE BOILER INSPECT & INS CO RRG	KY	B-	4.2	3.4	0.9	0.1	10.0	8.6	8.6	7.7	3.5	DGT
ARIZONA AUTOMOBILE INS CO	AZ	C	25.3	9.6	9.3	0.0	9.3	8.3	5.4	6.2	2.9	DFGR
ARIZONA HOME INS CO	AZ	D	27.9	18.0	9.5	0.2	6.8	8.2	8.5	6.7	2.1	DGRT
ARKANSAS MUTUAL INS CO	AR	D	3.4	2.0	-1.9	-0.2	9.2	7.1	0.5	7.0	1.9	DFGT
ARMED FORCES INS EXCHANGE	KS	B-	139.0	65.8	68.8	-1.8	8.7	8.7	4.2	6.1	3.8	FRT
ARROW MUTUAL LIABILITY INS CO	MA	B-	50.7	30.1	6.3	-0.3	8.7	8.3	3.8	7.3	5.1	DFT
ARROWOOD INDEMNITY CO	DE	D	1,284.4	220.7	0.0	-4.8	0.4	4.4	1.6	7.0	2.0	CFGR
ARROWOOD SURPLUS LINES INS CO	DE	U	--	--	--	--	N/A	--	--	--	--	Z
ARTISAN & TRUCKERS CASUALTY CO	WI	C	320.4	64.7	48.2	2.1	10.0	6.0	8.9	7.1	3.6	RT
ASCENDANT COMMERCIAL INS INC	FL	D-	62.2	10.7	18.6	0.0	1.8	0.9	7.6	6.8	1.0	CDFT
ASCENT INSURANCE CO	IL	U	--	--	--	--	N/A	--	--	--	--	Z
ASHLAND MUTUAL FIRE INS CO OF PA	PA	U	--	--	--	--	N/A	--	--	--	--	Z
ASHMERE INS CO	FL	U	--	--	--	--	N/A	--	--	--	--	Z
ASI ASR CORP	FL	B	133.1	52.5	75.5	3.5	9.1	9.5	3.8	7.1	5.6	T

See Page 27 for explanation of footnotes and
Page 28 for explanation of stability factors.

Arrows denote recent upgrades ▲ or downgrades ▼   (see Section VII for explanations)

40

www.weissratings.com

RISK ADJ. RATIO #1	CAPITAL RATIO #2	PREMIUM TO SURPLUS (%)	RESV. TO SURPLUS (%)	RESV. DEVELOP. 1 YEAR (%)	RESV. DEVELOP. 2 YEAR (%)	LOSS RATIO (%)	EXP. RATIO (%)	COMB RATIO (%)	CASH FROM UNDER-WRITING (%)	NET PREMIUM GROWTH (%)	INVEST. IN AFFIL (%)	INSURANCE COMPANY NAME
1.0	0.7	192.5	80.3	5.8	0.3	69.6	-7.1	62.5	89.4	192.5	2.3	AMTRUST INS CO OF KANSAS INC
1.0	0.9	225.3	108.4	10.7	6.9	80.5	26.6	107.1	100.3	-0.8	25.2	ANCHOR GENERAL INS CO
0.7	0.5	107.3	74.9	20.8	N/A	97.5	42.9	140.4	102.5	-53.9	0.0	ANCHOR P&C INS CO
1.8	1.2	47.7	33.7	1.4	4.0	140.5	17.9	158.4	63.2	-55.3	0.0	ANCHOR SPECIALTY INS CO
3.8	2.5	80.4	43.7	2.0	-0.6	98.5	22.4	120.9	83.2	6.8	0.0	ANPAC LOUISIANA INS CO
4.7	3.4	111.0	80.0	-7.9	-12.2	63.3	29.4	92.7	116.3	3.8	0.0	ANSUR AMERICA INS CO
11.4	6.7	9.6	1.3	0.3	0.2	41.8	41.0	82.8	149.7	8.7	0.0	ANTHRACITE MUTUAL FIRE INS CO
1.6	1.0	60.9	6.9	-0.7	-1.3	51.2	71.2	122.4	94.9	-15.5	0.0	ANTILLES INS CO
0.1	0.1	450.9	330.1	33.2	48.7	110.1	28.9	139.0	107.7	66.6	0.0	APOLLO CASUALTY CO
8.0	5.3	3.5	0.1	-0.1	-0.1	1.9	88.8	90.7	117.3	-30.7	0.0	APOLLO MUTUAL FIRE INS CO
4.6	2.8	30.4	32.9	-3.3	3.7	54.8	28.6	83.4	129.6	1.4	0.0 ●	APPALACHIAN INS CO
1.9	1.3	76.8	169.8	8.0	10.9	75.1	37.7	112.8	124.2	-28.1	0.0	APPLIED MEDICO LEGAL SOLUTIONS
1.3	0.7	N/A	34.8	-13.4	-33.8	N/A	N/A	N/A	19.0	0.0	0.0	APPLIED UNDERWRITERS CAPTIVE RISK
4.8	3.0	134.1	28.7	-1.4	-4.4	45.6	31.1	76.7	132.5	10.6	0.0	ARAG INS CO
2.1	1.4	152.0	83.4	-6.0	-3.3	64.1	32.3	96.4	105.5	1.7	0.0	ARBELLA INDEMNITY INS CO
2.5	1.9	111.0	60.9	-4.4	-2.4	64.1	31.4	95.5	107.8	1.7	13.8 ●	ARBELLA MUTUAL INS CO
3.6	2.3	133.2	73.1	-5.2	-2.9	64.1	32.3	96.4	106.0	1.7	0.0	ARBELLA PROTECTION INS CO
N/A	N/A	--	--	--	--	--	--	--	--	--	--	ARCH EXCESS & SURPLUS INS CO
3.7	3.4	N/A	3.3	N/A	N/A	N/A	N/A	N/A	34.5	0.0	0.0	ARCH INDEMNITY INS CO
1.6	1.3	89.3	179.7	-0.2	-1.7	71.5	23.8	95.3	124.9	2.6	14.6 ●	ARCH INS CO
N/A	N/A	--	--	--	--	--	--	--	--	--	--	ARCH MORTGAGE ASR CO
47.6	37.4	0.5	0.1	N/A	N/A	28.7	220.0	248.7	69.0	475.7	0.0	ARCH MORTGAGE GUARANTY CO
1.0	0.9	56.8	23.4	-9.4	-10.2	3.7	124.9	128.6	104.3	45.6	5.2	ARCH MORTGAGE INS CO
11.0	8.1	1.3	16.9	-10.3	-13.6	-321.8	-535.9	-857.7	9.5	-16.0	0.0	ARCH MORTGAGE REINS CO
1.5	1.5	16.8	30.1	-2.1	-4.7	46.9	36.2	83.1	160.1	-1.5	49.5 ●	ARCH REINS CO
5.8	4.6	N/A	14.2	-0.1	0.2	999 +	999 +	872.6	4.7	-62.1	0.0 ●	ARCH SPECIALTY INS CO
N/A	N/A	--	--	--	--	--	--	--	--	--	--	ARCH STRUCTURED MRTG INS CO
3.9	2.4	15.7	41.4	0.4	-0.3	70.0	-2.6	67.4	-283.0	12.9	0.0	ARCHITECTS & ENGINEERS INS CO RRG
0.3	0.2	153.4	119.3	-9.5	-21.1	38.1	43.5	81.6	120.9	1.9	0.0	ARCOA RRG INC
6.4	3.6	21.0	27.3	-4.1	-9.1	45.0	41.1	86.1	72.7	11.5	0.0	ARECA INS EXCHANGE
10.1	9.1	N/A	N/A	N/A	N/A	N/A	N/A	N/A	438.2	0.0	2.6	ARGONAUT GREAT CENTRAL INS CO
1.4	1.2	28.0	57.4	1.9	2.9	61.8	35.6	97.4	101.5	16.4	32.7 ●	ARGONAUT INS CO
N/A	N/A	--	--	--	--	--	--	--	--	--	--	ARGONAUT LTD RISK INS CO
31.4	28.3	N/A	N/A	N/A	N/A	N/A	N/A	N/A	N/A	0.0	0.0	ARGONAUT-MIDWEST INS CO
91.9	44.6	N/A	N/A	N/A	N/A	N/A	N/A	N/A	999 +	0.0	0.0	ARGONAUT-SOUTHWEST INS CO
16.6	15.0	N/A	4.8	0.1	3.7	N/A	N/A	N/A	N/A	0.0	0.0	ARGUS FIRE & CASUALTY INS CO
N/A	N/A	--	--	--	--	--	--	--	--	--	--	ARI CASUALTY CO
0.3	0.2	139.6	320.0	103.9	81.7	142.3	18.7	161.0	132.3	298.0	10.4	ARI INS CO
5.1	4.3	27.0	4.6	-5.2	-6.0	N/A	59.8	59.8	215.6	5.7	0.0	ARISE BOILER INSPECT & INS CO RRG
3.1	2.3	95.9	73.8	-2.9	-6.3	65.5	33.7	99.2	69.7	2.5	0.0	ARIZONA AUTOMOBILE INS CO
1.7	1.0	54.0	15.7	-3.1	-4.6	71.2	21.0	92.2	110.3	1.9	0.0	ARIZONA HOME INS CO
4.3	3.9	-87.3	N/A	N/A	-99.3	N/A	-55.5	-55.5	-160.9	53.1	0.0	ARKANSAS MUTUAL INS CO
2.8	2.0	103.3	29.0	-0.4	-3.6	81.6	37.3	118.9	88.3	-1.6	4.4	ARMED FORCES INS EXCHANGE
3.4	2.2	21.2	39.1	-5.0	-3.8	93.2	11.5	104.7	84.6	-7.8	0.0	ARROW MUTUAL LIABILITY INS CO
0.3	0.1	N/A	443.0	7.6	4.5	999 +	999 +	999 +	6.3	97.8	7.3 ●	ARROWOOD INDEMNITY CO
N/A	N/A	--	--	--	--	--	--	--	--	--	--	ARROWOOD SURPLUS LINES INS CO
6.3	4.6	76.8	46.5	-2.7	-3.0	70.2	17.3	87.5	117.9	8.1	0.0	ARTISAN & TRUCKERS CASUALTY CO
0.5	0.3	174.8	224.4	-5.0	26.5	60.9	34.6	95.5	34.4	-36.2	0.0	ASCENDANT COMMERCIAL INS INC
N/A	N/A	--	--	--	--	--	--	--	--	--	--	ASCENT INSURANCE CO
N/A	N/A	--	--	--	--	--	--	--	--	--	--	ASHLAND MUTUAL FIRE INS CO OF PA
N/A	N/A	--	--	--	--	--	--	--	--	--	--	ASHMERE INS CO
2.9	2.4	152.1	36.3	-10.2	-22.2	47.7	35.4	83.1	137.7	28.8	0.0	ASI ASR CORP

999 + Denotes number greater than 999.9%
999 - Denotes number less than -999.99%
● Bullets denote a more detailed analysis is available in Section II.

INSURANCE COMPANY NAME	DOM. STATE	RATING	TOTAL ASSETS ($MIL)	CAPITAL & SURPLUS ($MIL)	ANNUAL NET PREMIUM ($MIL)	NET INCOME ($MIL)	CAPITAL-IZATION INDEX (PTS)	RESERVE ADQ INDEX (PTS)	PROFIT-ABILITY INDEX (PTS)	LIQUIDITY INDEX (PTS)	STAB. INDEX (PTS)	STABILITY FACTORS
ASI HOME INS CORP	FL	B-	19.2	16.8	2.0	-0.2	10.0	3.6	4.2	8.9	4.6	DGR
ASI LLOYDS	TX	D+	219.1	95.1	120.7	-0.8	9.1	8.9	5.0	6.5	2.7	FRT
ASI PREFERRED INS CORP	FL	B	98.8	42.7	53.1	-0.2	7.0	9.2	6.0	6.1	6.0	GT
▲ASI SELECT INS CORP	DE	C-	24.3	21.5	1.9	0.2	10.0	5.6	4.9	9.0	3.0	DGT
ASOC DE SUSCRIPCION CONJUNTA DEL	PR	C	159.2	102.3	62.4	-0.4	10.0	7.7	3.2	6.7	4.3	FT
ASPEN AMERICAN INS CO	TX	B	791.5	464.8	89.7	8.7	7.9	4.8	4.2	7.1	4.3	GRT
ASPEN SPECIALTY INS CO	ND	C	403.3	144.5	62.8	-1.4	3.5	6.2	3.8	7.2	4.0	CFRT
ASPEN SPECIALTY RRG INC	DC	U	--	--	--	--	N/A	--	--	--	--	Z
ASPIRE GENERAL INS CO	CA	C-	17.4	7.7	6.3	-0.4	6.2	3.6	1.9	6.1	2.3	DFGT
ASSET PROTECTION PROGRAM RRG INC	SC	U	--	--	--	--	N/A	--	--	--	--	Z
ASSN CASUALTY INS CO	TX	C	48.5	19.4	19.6	0.3	8.4	6.3	5.9	6.7	3.4	DT
ASSN OF CERTIFIED MTG ORIG RRG	NV	D	3.1	1.1	0.2	0.0	7.9	3.6	6.0	8.8	1.1	DGT
ASSOCIATED EMPLOYERS INS CO	MA	C	5.5	4.5	0.0	0.0	10.0	N/A	6.4	10.0	3.5	DFGR
ASSOCIATED INDEMNITY CORP	CA	C	108.1	88.7	0.0	0.1	10.0	3.6	7.0	9.8	4.2	FRT
ASSOCIATED INDUSTRIES INS CO INC	FL	C	397.8	111.3	87.7	1.1	7.5	7.0	7.2	7.4	4.0	GRT
ASSOCIATED INDUSTRIES OF MA MUT INS	MA	B-	615.2	218.0	137.3	2.3	8.1	9.4	8.7	6.8	4.1	RT
ASSOCIATED LOGGERS EXCHANGE	ID	C	35.5	14.2	11.9	0.2	5.5	9.2	8.5	6.6	2.6	DGRT
ASSOCIATED MUTUAL INS CO	NY	C	27.2	9.4	8.3	-0.1	4.9	4.1	2.7	7.3	2.3	CDGR
ASSURANCEAMERICA INS CO	NE	D+	74.5	14.4	25.3	1.0	6.5	4.7	5.7	6.9	2.4	DFRT
ASSURED GUARANTY CORP	MD	C-	3,281.8	1,872.8	58.1	-31.9	9.8	1.0	5.5	10.0	2.4	AFRT
ASSURED GUARANTY MUNICIPAL CORP	NY	D+	5,395.9	2,203.8	143.5	32.4	8.1	3.9	7.2	8.5	1.9	ACFR
ASURE WORLDWIDE INS CO	MI	B-	42.4	17.8	18.0	0.4	9.1	9.3	8.8	6.7	5.3	DT
ATAIN INS CO	TX	C	88.3	50.8	13.9	0.4	9.2	6.4	8.1	7.4	3.5	DRT
ATAIN SPECIALTY INS CO	MI	C	378.4	182.1	78.6	2.5	7.6	6.5	8.4	6.9	3.8	RT
ATLANTA INTERNATIONAL INS CO	NY	U	--	--	--	--	N/A	--	--	--	--	Z
▼ATLANTIC BONDING CO	MD	D-	7.9	7.4	0.6	0.2	8.0	6.0	3.7	9.4	0.8	DGT
ATLANTIC CASUALTY INS CO	NC	B-	267.2	101.1	74.2	0.3	7.7	9.3	8.3	7.2	4.5	RT
ATLANTIC CHARTER INS CO	MA	B-	206.4	55.7	61.2	3.4	5.7	9.8	9.0	6.9	3.6	RT
ATLANTIC SPECIALTY INS CO	NY	B-	2,210.6	637.9	552.8	0.0	7.3	4.4	3.2	6.9	4.5	FRT
ATLANTIC STATES INS CO	PA	B-	780.1	228.9	426.3	1.5	8.7	5.8	8.2	6.2	4.3	RT
ATRADIUS TRADE CREDIT INS CO	MD	C	114.3	62.5	18.2	-0.2	10.0	4.7	3.2	7.5	2.9	RT
ATRIUM INS CORP	NY	U	--	--	--	--	N/A	--	--	--	--	Z
ATTORNEYS INS MUTUAL	DC	C-	11.5	6.3	2.4	-0.1	8.3	9.4	1.9	7.5	2.1	DFGR
▲ATTORNEYS INS MUTUAL RRG	HI	C-	15.3	8.9	3.1	0.1	4.4	5.8	6.6	8.9	2.3	DFGR
ATTORNEYS LIAB ASR SOCIETY INC RRG	VT	D	2,203.2	629.0	206.2	12.7	2.0	1.7	5.4	7.0	1.9	CRT
ATTPRO RRG RECIPROCAL RRG	DC	D	3.2	1.1	0.1	0.0	7.6	4.6	1.9	9.5	1.2	DFGT
AUSTIN MUTUAL INS CO	MN	D	59.4	47.2	0.0	1.1	10.0	3.2	8.4	10.0	2.0	R
AUTO CLUB CASUALTY CO	TX	U	--	--	--	--	N/A	--	--	--	--	Z
AUTO CLUB COUNTY MUTUAL INS CO	TX	D+	105.1	8.3	0.0	0.0	6.0	N/A	6.2	9.8	2.7	DT
AUTO CLUB FAMILY INS CO	MO	C	117.4	45.6	34.3	-0.3	8.6	7.4	4.9	6.4	3.8	FT
AUTO CLUB GROUP INS CO	MI	C+	361.7	126.1	141.1	-0.3	9.4	4.6	5.2	6.7	4.5	T
AUTO CLUB INDEMNITY CO	TX	B+	25.9	5.4	0.0	0.0	7.8	N/A	6.5	9.5	5.0	DFG
AUTO CLUB INS ASSN	MI	B	4,174.1	1,817.5	1,492.1	-5.1	7.8	4.7	5.8	6.6	4.9	RT
AUTO CLUB INS CO OF FL	FL	B	383.4	177.7	186.1	3.5	9.1	7.0	8.9	6.5	6.0	T
AUTO CLUB PROPERTY & CASUALTY INS	MI	C	89.2	32.4	40.3	-0.2	8.3	4.4	5.9	6.6	3.9	T
AUTO CLUB SOUTH INS CO	FL	B-	127.0	56.9	58.0	1.1	9.3	6.2	6.9	6.3	3.6	T
AUTO-OWNERS INS CO	MI	A-	14,502.3	9,939.5	3,219.4	106.5	8.6	6.1	8.2	6.9	5.7	T
AUTO-OWNERS SPECIALTY INS CO	DE	U	--	--	--	--	N/A	--	--	--	--	Z
AUTOMOBILE CLUB INTERINSURANCE	MO	C	445.8	228.7	137.3	-2.2	8.6	7.3	4.2	6.3	4.2	T
AUTOMOBILE INS CO OF HARTFORD CT	CT	B	1,021.0	323.7	298.3	7.2	8.3	8.4	6.1	6.7	4.7	T
AVATAR P&C INS CO	FL	B-	49.2	24.7	19.9	0.1	5.2	4.4	8.1	6.5	3.6	CDT
AVEMCO INS CO	MD	B-	83.1	53.5	26.3	0.9	9.8	9.3	3.6	6.8	4.5	RT

See Page 27 for explanation of footnotes and
Page 28 for explanation of stability factors.
Arrows denote recent upgrades ▲ or downgrades ▼   (see Section VII for explanations)

42

www.weissratings.com

RISK ADJ. RATIO #1	CAPITAL RATIO #2	PREMIUM TO SURPLUS (%)	RESV. TO SURPLUS (%)	RESV. DEVELOP. 1 YEAR (%)	RESV. DEVELOP. 2 YEAR (%)	LOSS RATIO (%)	EXP. RATIO (%)	COMB RATIO (%)	CASH FROM UNDER- WRITING (%)	NET PREMIUM GROWTH (%)	INVEST. IN AFFIL (%)	INSURANCE COMPANY NAME
15.8	13.9	12.1	3.4	-0.3	N/A	66.7	38.2	104.9	124.8	173.9	0.0	ASI HOME INS CORP
2.6	2.3	124.3	24.3	-3.8	-9.3	78.7	33.5	112.2	84.2	11.2	0.0	ASI LLOYDS
1.8	1.2	123.4	30.2	-5.0	-15.8	48.2	56.5	104.7	102.9	2.4	0.0	ASI PREFERRED INS CORP
18.9	14.9	8.8	1.3	-0.1	-0.6	76.1	16.4	92.5	232.9	273.3	0.0	ASI SELECT INS CORP
12.4	7.3	61.1	9.1	-4.9	-0.6	74.7	25.1	99.8	77.9	-38.4	0.0	ASOC DE SUSCRIPCION CONJUNTA DEL
2.2	1.7	19.7	34.2	17.5	13.5	69.2	25.3	94.5	146.9	29.2	26.7 ●	ASPEN AMERICAN INS CO
0.7	0.5	43.6	65.3	-5.0	-2.7	80.1	48.0	128.1	67.5	-2.4	0.0	ASPEN SPECIALTY INS CO
N/A	N/A	--	--	--	--	--	--	--	--	--	--	ASPEN SPECIALTY RRG INC
1.3	0.9	75.6	31.8	-1.9	-0.9	92.9	22.1	115.0	92.2	5.5	0.0	ASPIRE GENERAL INS CO
N/A	N/A	--	--	--	--	--	--	--	--	--	--	ASSET PROTECTION PROGRAM RRG INC
2.6	1.9	100.9	71.4	-1.1	-4.5	68.2	29.9	98.1	104.1	13.7	0.0	ASSN CASUALTY INS CO
1.5	1.3	17.5	4.6	0.7	-0.3	22.2	23.5	45.7	388.3	73.8	0.0	ASSN OF CERTIFIED MTG ORIG RRG
10.4	9.4	N/A	N/A	N/A	N/A	N/A	N/A	N/A	-62.5	0.0	0.0	ASSOCIATED EMPLOYERS INS CO
26.3	23.6	N/A	N/A	N/A	N/A	N/A	N/A	N/A	31.1	0.0	0.0	ASSOCIATED INDEMNITY CORP
2.0	1.1	73.5	123.6	-6.8	-12.7	41.2	23.7	64.9	446.4	140.2	6.5	ASSOCIATED INDUSTRIES INS CO INC
2.4	1.8	63.9	128.1	-7.4	-16.2	71.6	21.6	93.2	117.2	3.4	2.2 ●	ASSOCIATED INDUSTRIES OF MA MUT
1.3	0.7	84.6	139.3	3.2	-7.6	76.8	19.9	96.7	113.2	1.7	1.4	ASSOCIATED LOGGERS EXCHANGE
0.9	0.6	88.1	120.5	14.3	15.7	68.8	35.8	104.6	103.0	10.3	0.0	ASSOCIATED MUTUAL INS CO
1.2	1.1	191.3	92.6	0.6	-7.1	73.2	27.6	100.8	94.4	-22.2	0.0	ASSURANCEAMERICA INS CO
3.9	2.9	3.1	6.8	-12.0	133.5	38.1	121.3	159.4	20.6	28.4	11.4 ●	ASSURED GUARANTY CORP
3.1	1.9	6.2	17.7	4.2	6.3	34.8	38.5	73.3	46.5	1.2	10.5 ●	ASSURED GUARANTY MUNICIPAL CORP
3.6	2.6	103.8	74.8	-7.3	-11.4	63.3	29.4	92.7	116.9	3.8	0.0	ASURE WORLDWIDE INS CO
3.4	2.4	28.0	45.4	1.6	2.1	84.0	25.0	109.0	134.3	-4.0	0.0	ATAIN INS CO
1.8	1.4	45.1	73.1	2.7	3.6	83.9	23.8	107.7	117.2	-4.0	15.2	ATAIN SPECIALTY INS CO
N/A	N/A	--	--	--	--	--	--	--	--	--	--	ATLANTA INTERNATIONAL INS CO
2.1	1.3	6.8	1.9	-0.8	0.3	-9.6	68.9	59.3	96.3	-21.0	0.0	ATLANTIC BONDING CO
1.8	1.5	74.6	121.7	-8.1	-13.9	48.8	37.7	86.5	115.3	2.9	0.0	ATLANTIC CASUALTY INS CO
1.4	0.9	113.6	193.8	-13.5	-42.5	60.6	25.9	86.5	119.1	2.3	0.0	ATLANTIC CHARTER INS CO
1.9	1.4	88.5	133.1	4.4	6.6	68.9	34.3	103.2	79.1	-6.3	12.6 ●	ATLANTIC SPECIALTY INS CO
2.9	2.0	187.1	101.4	-1.3	0.6	64.1	32.5	96.6	106.4	8.4	0.0 ●	ATLANTIC STATES INS CO
4.8	3.7	28.9	18.6	3.3	N/A	74.9	54.9	129.8	104.0	0.5	0.0	ATRADIUS TRADE CREDIT INS CO
N/A	N/A	--	--	--	--	--	--	--	--	--	--	ATRIUM INS CORP
2.4	1.8	37.9	41.9	-4.5	-13.8	53.5	74.6	128.1	80.4	11.6	0.0	ATTORNEYS INS MUTUAL
1.0	0.8	35.6	62.3	-7.5	-3.6	68.3	46.4	114.7	84.9	-12.9	0.0	ATTORNEYS INS MUTUAL RRG
0.4	0.3	34.1	166.3	-7.1	-5.8	79.0	17.0	96.0	110.4	-7.5	31.9 ●	ATTORNEYS LIAB ASR SOCIETY INC
1.4	1.2	6.3	7.3	-0.2	1.1	99.1	378.0	477.1	87.5	N/A	0.0	ATTPRO RRG RECIPROCAL RRG
12.4	5.4	N/A	N/A	N/A	N/A	N/A	N/A	N/A	N/A	0.0	0.0	AUSTIN MUTUAL INS CO
N/A	N/A	--	--	--	--	--	--	--	--	--	--	AUTO CLUB CASUALTY CO
0.9	0.8	N/A	N/A	N/A	N/A	N/A	N/A	N/A	89.0	0.0	0.0	AUTO CLUB COUNTY MUTUAL INS CO
3.1	2.0	76.3	27.3	1.3	-0.4	79.4	21.2	100.6	95.2	8.1	0.0	AUTO CLUB FAMILY INS CO
3.4	2.6	111.7	92.6	0.4	-0.2	69.4	28.3	97.7	106.6	4.1	0.0	AUTO CLUB GROUP INS CO
1.5	1.3	N/A	N/A	N/A	N/A	N/A	N/A	N/A	-9.2	0.0	0.0 ●	AUTO CLUB INDEMNITY CO
2.0	1.6	82.5	69.3	0.2	-0.3	69.4	28.3	97.7	106.0	4.1	17.6 ●	AUTO CLUB INS ASSN
3.8	2.8	107.4	50.4	-6.1	-11.2	65.7	22.6	88.3	115.2	5.8	0.0	AUTO CLUB INS CO OF FL
2.5	1.9	123.8	92.4	1.1	1.0	69.2	28.4	97.6	107.1	4.1	0.0	AUTO CLUB PROPERTY & CASUALTY INS
2.8	2.4	103.3	52.1	-0.4	-0.1	79.3	21.4	100.7	108.4	27.5	0.0	AUTO CLUB SOUTH INS CO
2.3	2.0	33.2	23.3	-1.2	-1.4	52.3	31.0	83.3	125.0	12.1	28.7 ●	AUTO-OWNERS INS CO
N/A	N/A	--	--	--	--	--	--	--	--	--	--	AUTO-OWNERS SPECIALTY INS CO
2.7	2.0	60.7	21.7	1.1	-0.3	79.4	21.2	100.6	100.5	8.1	14.2 ●	AUTOMOBILE CLUB INTERINSURANCE
2.8	1.8	94.3	156.4	-1.9	-4.8	63.4	30.1	93.5	105.9	4.8	0.0 ●	AUTOMOBILE INS CO OF HARTFORD CT
1.3	0.9	81.6	33.3	3.0	3.1	44.4	49.6	94.0	109.6	-7.6	0.0	AVATAR P&C INS CO
3.0	2.8	50.0	21.2	-14.6	-10.9	31.0	34.8	65.8	135.5	-5.8	22.8	AVEMCO INS CO

999 + Denotes number greater than 999.9%
999 - Denotes number less than -999.99%
● Bullets denote a more detailed analysis is available in Section II.

INSURANCE COMPANY NAME	DOM. STATE	RATING	TOTAL ASSETS ($MIL)	CAPITAL & SURPLUS ($MIL)	ANNUAL NET PREMIUM ($MIL)	NET INCOME ($MIL)	CAPITAL-IZATION INDEX (PTS)	RESERVE ADQ INDEX (PTS)	PROFIT-ABILITY INDEX (PTS)	LIQUIDITY INDEX (PTS)	STAB. INDEX (PTS)	STABILITY FACTORS
▼AVIATION ALLIANCE INS RRG INC	MT	E-	3.0	0.8	1.2	-0.2	0.0	1.6	1.3	7.5	0.0	CDFG
AVIVA INS CO OF CANADA (US BR)	NY	U	--	--	--	--	N/A	--	--	--	--	Z
AWBURY INS CO	DE	U	--	--	--	--	N/A	--	--	--	--	Z
AXA ART INS CORP	NY	C	15.0	9.7	0.9	0.0	10.0	7.9	1.9	7.0	2.3	DGRT
AXA INS CO	NY	C-	251.9	134.7	52.1	8.4	8.7	6.0	7.9	7.9	3.3	RT
AXIS INS CO	IL	B	1,508.9	567.4	313.7	-7.9	7.6	6.9	4.1	6.9	4.2	ART
AXIS REINS CO	NY	C+	3,236.5	900.1	531.8	-3.0	7.9	9.3	5.2	7.0	4.2	ART
AXIS SPECIALTY INS CO	CT	U	--	--	--	--	N/A	--	--	--	--	Z
AXIS SURPLUS INS CO	IL	C+	436.7	178.1	43.0	0.9	10.0	8.2	3.6	8.0	4.1	FRT
BADGER MUTUAL INS CO	WI	C+	176.5	68.6	87.5	1.1	8.2	3.2	6.4	6.3	4.6	RT
BALBOA INS CO	CA	C-	86.6	77.9	-0.1	0.0	10.0	5.9	1.9	7.0	3.1	DFRT
▲BALDWIN MUTUAL INS CO	AL	C-	12.4	9.6	4.0	0.2	10.0	9.5	8.6	8.2	2.3	DGT
BALTIMORE EQUITABLE SOCIETY	MD	U	--	--	--	--	N/A	--	--	--	--	Z
BANKERS INDEPENDENT INS CO	PA	C (1)	24.3	4.4	11.6	-3.6	2.3	1.3	1.0	0.0	3.7	CDFL
BANKERS INS CO	FL	C	153.1	87.3	35.7	1.8	7.1	5.2	6.5	7.5	3.9	FRT
▲BANKERS SPECIALTY INS CO	LA	B-	59.8	49.0	9.4	0.0	6.3	8.0	3.9	6.1	5.0	DT
BANKERS STANDARD INS CO	PA	C	628.2	171.9	149.9	5.9	7.8	6.3	8.4	6.8	3.7	FGRT
BAR PLAN MUTUAL INS CO	MO	C	44.5	16.9	10.0	-1.2	4.9	5.9	2.9	6.7	2.9	DRT
BAR PLAN SURETY & FIDELITY CO	MO	C	5.3	4.4	0.4	0.1	10.0	7.8	7.4	10.0	3.3	DGOR
BAR VERMONT RRG INC	VT	D+	27.9	18.6	2.0	0.7	7.9	8.6	6.8	10.0	2.3	DGR
BARNSTABLE COUNTY INS CO	MA	C	23.8	21.5	1.8	0.4	10.0	6.1	7.4	9.2	3.5	DGRT
BARNSTABLE COUNTY MUTUAL INS CO	MA	B	106.2	85.6	17.6	1.9	9.0	7.5	7.1	7.4	5.0	T
BATTLE CREEK MUTUAL INS CO	NE	C	9.0	5.8	0.0	0.1	10.0	3.6	6.6	8.9	2.6	DGRT
BAY INS RRG INC	SC	U	--	--	--	--	N/A	--	--	--	--	Z
BAY STATE INS CO	MA	B-	493.9	317.6	80.9	11.6	8.3	6.4	8.1	7.3	4.5	T
BCS INS CO	OH	B	286.3	161.7	101.8	5.6	10.0	6.9	5.7	6.4	4.3	FRT
BEACONHARBOR MUTUAL RRG	ME	U	--	--	--	--	N/A	--	--	--	--	Z
BEAR RIVER MUTUAL INS CO	UT	B	263.4	118.6	138.1	2.6	8.4	8.0	3.4	5.4	6.2	FLT
BEARING MIDWEST CASUALTY CO	KS	C	6.7	5.8	0.0	0.0	10.0	N/A	6.1	7.0	2.7	DGT
BEAZLEY INS CO	CT	B-	285.6	120.4	74.4	-1.6	9.2	8.0	3.8	7.0	3.7	RT
BEDFORD GRANGE MUTUAL INS CO	PA	C-	10.4	5.4	4.7	0.2	7.2	6.7	7.2	7.0	2.1	DGT
BEDFORD PHYSICIANS RRG INC	VT	C-	62.7	9.0	10.7	0.1	3.4	9.5	4.3	9.0	2.8	DGRT
BEDIVERE INS CO	PA	D+	256.8	109.1	0.1	2.1	1.7	4.4	2.1	9.8	2.4	CFGR
BELL UNITED INS CO	NV	C+	35.6	22.1	4.2	-0.4	10.0	9.6	6.0	9.3	3.1	DFGT
BENCHMARK INS CO	KS	B-	296.0	90.6	45.7	2.2	8.5	6.7	8.9	8.4	3.9	GRT
BENEFIT SECURITY INS CO	IL	B-	8.6	4.1	1.6	0.0	7.4	6.0	6.8	7.0	3.5	DG
BERKLEY ASR CO	IA	C-	74.9	54.1	0.0	0.3	10.0	N/A	6.4	10.0	2.9	RT
BERKLEY INS CO	DE	B	17,896.8	5,028.8	5,711.5	121.8	7.3	8.0	7.7	6.9	5.1	AT
BERKLEY NATIONAL INS CO	IA	C	137.0	52.0	0.0	0.2	10.0	3.6	6.3	7.0	4.0	GT
BERKLEY REGIONAL INS CO	DE	C+	755.9	714.3	0.0	2.8	8.2	3.8	6.9	7.0	4.5	ART
BERKLEY REGIONAL SPECIALTY INS CO	DE	C	62.3	56.5	0.0	0.4	10.0	N/A	7.6	10.0	4.0	DT
BERKSHIRE HATHATWAY DIRECT INS CO	NE	C	135.6	120.6	0.3	0.7	9.1	4.1	3.9	10.0	3.9	DGT
BERKSHIRE HATHAWAY ASR CORP	NY	A+	2,454.3	1,869.2	2.9	4.7	9.5	4.6	8.6	10.0	7.6	GT
BERKSHIRE HATHAWAY HOMESTATE INS	NE	C+	2,541.9	1,310.1	441.4	21.4	7.5	6.1	8.0	7.7	4.1	RT
BERKSHIRE HATHAWAY SPECIALTY INS CO	NE	C+	4,330.5	3,399.6	267.4	10.6	9.1	4.9	3.9	9.3	3.5	GRT
BITCO GENERAL INS CORP	IL	B	886.0	291.8	231.5	-0.5	8.4	8.7	6.8	6.8	4.8	AT
BITCO NATIONAL INS CO	IL	B	484.1	155.4	148.0	12.6	7.6	7.0	4.8	6.7	4.5	AT
BLACK DIAMOND INS CO	NV	U (5)	--	--	--	--	N/A	--	--	--	--	Z
BLOOMFIELD MUTUAL INS CO	MN	C-	12.0	9.2	3.9	0.1	10.0	7.8	8.3	6.7	2.9	DGT
BLOOMINGTON COMP INS CO	MN	C+	17.7	14.0	0.0	0.0	10.0	N/A	6.3	7.0	3.3	DGRT
BLUE HILL SPECIALTY INS CO	IL	U	--	--	--	--	N/A	--	--	--	--	Z
BLUE RIDGE INDEMNITY CO	WI	C	6.8	6.8	-2.5	0.0	10.0	3.8	4.0	7.7	2.7	FGRT

See Page 27 for explanation of footnotes and
Page 28 for explanation of stability factors.
Arrows denote recent upgrades ▲ or downgrades ▼   (see Section VII for explanations)

44

www.weissratings.com

RISK ADJ. RATIO #1	CAPITAL RATIO #2	PREMIUM TO SURPLUS (%)	RESV. TO SURPLUS (%)	RESV. DEVELOP. 1 YEAR (%)	RESV. DEVELOP. 2 YEAR (%)	LOSS RATIO (%)	EXP. RATIO (%)	COMB RATIO (%)	CASH FROM UNDER-WRITING (%)	NET PREMIUM GROWTH (%)	INVEST. IN AFFIL (%)	INSURANCE COMPANY NAME
0.0	0.0	114.5	155.2	66.1	79.4	92.0	50.7	142.7	47.9	-0.1	0.0	AVIATION ALLIANCE INS RRG INC
N/A	N/A	--	--	--	--	--	--	--	--	--	--	AVIVA INS CO OF CANADA (US BR)
N/A	N/A	--	--	--	--	--	--	--	--	--	--	AWBURY INS CO
5.0	4.4	9.7	7.3	-2.0	-3.4	-0.8	135.0	134.2	-153.0	36.9	0.0	AXA ART INS CORP
3.1	2.2	40.6	22.7	-2.3	-1.3	37.1	64.1	101.2	116.6	6.2	0.0	AXA INS CO
2.0	1.5	54.6	99.1	-4.2	-6.3	68.0	39.7	107.7	88.0	2.0	18.6 ●	AXIS INS CO
2.6	1.6	59.3	160.8	-5.2	-8.9	71.3	35.6	106.9	103.6	3.6	0.0 ●	AXIS REINS CO
N/A	N/A	--	--	--	--	--	--	--	--	--	--	AXIS SPECIALTY INS CO
6.5	4.2	24.3	43.9	-2.0	-2.6	60.5	39.9	100.4	76.0	4.0	0.0	AXIS SURPLUS INS CO
3.0	1.8	130.6	80.4	8.2	15.6	70.1	29.0	99.1	99.9	-3.8	0.0	BADGER MUTUAL INS CO
3.4	3.3	-0.2	4.4	0.6	1.9	-327.8	74.1	-253.7	466.4	74.0	31.4	BALBOA INS CO
6.2	4.9	43.0	3.2	-0.8	-2.6	25.8	50.6	76.4	126.5	-10.9	0.0	BALDWIN MUTUAL INS CO
N/A	N/A	--	--	--	--	--	--	--	--	--	--	BALTIMORE EQUITABLE SOCIETY
0.4	0.4	261.7	194.6	33.1	50.1	109.3	26.7	136.0	102.3	45.8	0.0	BANKERS INDEPENDENT INS CO
1.7	1.5	42.4	48.0	6.5	4.1	46.9	64.4	111.3	86.2	-20.7	35.0	BANKERS INS CO
1.1	0.9	19.4	4.8	-0.6	-1.9	50.4	51.5	101.9	103.9	-3.7	71.2	BANKERS SPECIALTY INS CO
2.6	1.7	90.2	164.7	1.2	0.9	76.5	17.3	93.8	93.6	50.0	0.0	BANKERS STANDARD INS CO
0.9	0.7	56.8	107.7	-13.7	-19.9	59.5	42.9	102.4	96.9	-3.4	13.6	BAR PLAN MUTUAL INS CO
10.3	9.2	9.9	8.3	-5.9	-3.6	-5.3	37.7	32.4	474.6	0.2	0.0	BAR PLAN SURETY & FIDELITY CO
2.4	1.5	11.3	22.0	-2.0	-6.9	42.7	76.8	119.5	199.5	9.8	0.0	BAR VERMONT RRG INC
8.4	5.1	8.4	2.0	-0.3	-0.5	54.6	48.4	103.0	102.4	8.5	0.0	BARNSTABLE COUNTY INS CO
3.2	2.6	21.1	4.6	-1.1	-1.5	42.7	51.2	93.9	107.1	2.5	21.7	BARNSTABLE COUNTY MUTUAL INS CO
5.2	4.7	N/A	N/A	N/A	N/A	N/A	N/A	N/A	160.7	0.0	0.0	BATTLE CREEK MUTUAL INS CO
N/A	N/A	--	--	--	--	--	--	--	--	--	--	BAY INS RRG INC
3.1	1.9	27.0	14.5	-0.3	-1.9	50.8	38.3	89.1	118.3	4.0	0.0 ●	BAY STATE INS CO
10.1	5.7	65.6	24.0	-5.6	-10.9	64.9	25.7	90.6	91.2	6.8	1.0	BCS INS CO
N/A	N/A	--	--	--	--	--	--	--	--	--	--	BEACONHARBOR MUTUAL RRG
2.8	1.9	116.2	49.2	-5.0	-3.1	90.9	25.3	116.2	94.4	15.1	0.0	BEAR RIVER MUTUAL INS CO
14.3	12.9	N/A	N/A	N/A	N/A	N/A	N/A	N/A	N/A	0.0	0.0	BEARING MIDWEST CASUALTY CO
3.5	2.3	60.9	69.8	-3.8	-0.2	55.8	41.7	97.5	139.5	14.9	0.0	BEAZLEY INS CO
2.0	1.4	93.9	16.4	2.4	-5.0	34.6	46.0	80.6	133.9	5.2	8.8	BEDFORD GRANGE MUTUAL INS CO
0.7	0.6	120.8	335.8	26.2	-23.0	96.2	5.8	102.0	206.7	75.2	0.0	BEDFORD PHYSICIANS RRG INC
0.6	0.3	0.1	116.7	-9.8	9.4	999 +	848.3	999 +	1.1	-29.1	15.9	BEDIVERE INS CO
6.8	4.2	18.7	49.5	-1.1	-18.3	69.4	24.2	93.6	80.7	-28.5	0.0	BELL UNITED INS CO
3.4	2.5	51.8	56.5	-5.4	-9.5	59.2	17.7	76.9	156.3	41.9	0.0	BENCHMARK INS CO
1.7	1.2	39.7	56.4	-18.1	-32.3	26.4	67.8	94.2	103.7	2.7	0.0	BENEFIT SECURITY INS CO
15.0	13.5	N/A	N/A	N/A	N/A	N/A	N/A	N/A	N/A	0.0	0.0	BERKLEY ASR CO
1.3	1.1	104.0	166.6	-2.2	-3.0	60.6	32.7	93.3	116.5	7.0	20.3 ●	BERKLEY INS CO
6.2	5.5	N/A	N/A	N/A	N/A	N/A	N/A	N/A	53.0	0.0	0.0	BERKLEY NATIONAL INS CO
1.4	1.4	N/A	N/A	N/A	N/A	N/A	N/A	N/A	75.2	0.0	48.4 ●	BERKLEY REGIONAL INS CO
33.6	30.3	N/A	N/A	N/A	N/A	N/A	N/A	N/A	N/A	0.0	0.0	BERKLEY REGIONAL SPECIALTY INS CO
6.1	3.6	0.3	0.1	N/A	-261.0	250.8	189.4	440.2	-185.5	100.9	0.0	BERKSHIRE HATHATWAY DIRECT INS
4.9	2.9	0.2	1.2	N/A	-0.8	9.7	36.1	45.8	98.5	-77.1	0.0 ●	BERKSHIRE HATHAWAY ASR CORP
2.4	1.4	35.1	57.3	-3.4	-3.6	87.4	23.2	110.6	132.9	-4.3	0.0 ●	BERKSHIRE HATHAWAY HOMESTATE
5.1	3.0	8.0	7.1	0.1	0.1	70.5	24.5	95.0	282.4	180.0	0.0 ●	BERKSHIRE HATHAWAY SPECIALTY INS
2.8	1.7	78.3	147.1	-3.0	-4.0	72.4	24.5	96.9	105.8	-2.5	0.0 ●	BITCO GENERAL INS CORP
2.5	1.5	101.8	213.6	2.3	2.7	73.9	32.1	106.0	105.8	-0.9	0.0	BITCO NATIONAL INS CO
N/A	N/A	--	--	--	--	--	--	--	--	--	--	BLACK DIAMOND INS CO
8.9	5.3	43.5	8.3	-1.6	-4.8	65.5	33.4	98.9	115.0	16.3	0.0	BLOOMFIELD MUTUAL INS CO
11.6	10.5	N/A	N/A	N/A	N/A	N/A	N/A	N/A	999 +	0.0	0.0	BLOOMINGTON COMP INS CO
N/A	N/A	--	--	--	--	--	--	--	--	--	--	BLUE HILL SPECIALTY INS CO
200.5	180.4	-37.4	N/A	N/A	N/A	N/A	N/A	N/A	-21.1	-136.3	0.0	BLUE RIDGE INDEMNITY CO

999 + Denotes number greater than 999.9%
999 - Denotes number less than -999.99%
● Bullets denote a more detailed analysis is available in Section II.

INSURANCE COMPANY NAME	DOM. STATE	RATING	TOTAL ASSETS ($MIL)	CAPITAL & SURPLUS ($MIL)	ANNUAL NET PREMIUM ($MIL)	NET INCOME ($MIL)	CAPITAL-IZATION INDEX (PTS)	RESERVE ADQ INDEX (PTS)	PROFIT-ABILITY INDEX (PTS)	LIQUIDITY INDEX (PTS)	STAB. INDEX (PTS)	STABILITY FACTORS
BLUESHORE INS CO	CO	C	74.1	17.5	14.1	0.5	8.8	3.6	4.2	8.2	3.0	DGT
▲BOND SAFEGUARD INS CO	SD	C-	80.7	35.6	45.4	2.1	7.1	2.9	5.8	7.3	2.3	RT
BONDED BUILDERS INS CO RRG	NV	D+	3.3	1.8	0.8	0.0	7.1	6.9	8.6	7.0	2.3	DGT
BONDEX INS CO	NJ	B-	6.9	3.3	1.3	-0.1	7.7	9.0	5.3	7.6	3.5	DGT
BOSTON INDEMNITY CO INC	SD	D+	6.7	5.0	2.0	-0.1	7.4	6.3	4.6	7.7	2.2	DFGT
BREMEN FARMERS MUTUAL INS CO	KS	C	44.4	21.4	25.9	0.3	7.7	7.0	8.3	5.9	2.9	DRT
BRETHREN MUTUAL INS CO	MD	B	259.4	126.7	114.2	-1.0	9.6	4.6	5.6	6.8	6.3	T
BRIAR CREEK MUTUAL INS CO	PA	C	14.2	11.1	2.3	0.0	10.0	6.1	8.1	8.0	2.4	DGRT
▲BRICKSTREET MUTUAL INS CO	WV	B-	2,228.6	769.5	337.9	8.1	7.9	9.5	8.6	7.1	5.0	T
BRIDGEFIELD CASUALTY INS CO	FL	C	55.8	46.1	0.0	0.2	10.0	N/A	4.5	9.6	4.3	R
BRIDGEFIELD EMPLOYERS INS CO	FL	B-	121.3	114.2	0.0	0.4	9.4	N/A	5.1	10.0	4.9	RT
BRIERFIELD INS CO	MS	C-	13.3	9.0	0.0	0.0	10.0	N/A	6.7	9.1	3.2	DGR
BRISTOL WEST CASUALTY INS CO	OH	D+	17.3	8.8	0.0	0.0	10.0	5.0	5.6	7.0	2.5	DGR
BRISTOL WEST INS CO	OH	D+	153.5	46.5	0.0	-0.6	10.0	5.7	4.3	10.0	2.6	RT
BRISTOL WEST PREFERRED INS CO	MI	C	27.7	11.7	0.0	0.0	10.0	5.9	6.0	10.0	4.0	DFGR
BRITISH AMERICAN INS CO	TX	C+	56.3	33.9	3.8	0.2	5.4	4.5	6.4	8.6	3.4	DRT
BROADLINE RRG INC	VT	C+	94.0	33.8	18.6	0.0	7.5	9.4	3.5	5.6	3.4	DT
BROADWAY INS & SURETY CO	NJ	D (1)	2.7	1.7	0.8	0.2	9.2	3.6	8.6	9.6	1.3	DT
BROOKWOOD INS CO	IA	U	--	--	--	--	N/A	--	--	--	--	Z
BROOME CO OPERATIVE INS CO	NY	C	21.7	13.9	6.6	-0.2	9.8	6.6	5.4	6.9	3.5	DGT
BROTHERHOOD MUTUAL INS CO	IN	B+	591.8	242.2	341.1	-7.1	8.0	5.0	5.7	5.6	6.5	LT
BTTS INS RRG GROUP INC	SC	U	--	--	--	--	N/A	--	--	--	--	Z
BUCKEYE STATE MUTUAL INS CO	OH	C+	62.4	22.2	41.0	0.6	7.2	9.3	3.5	3.2	3.2	DFLR
BUCKS COUNTY CONTRIBUTIONSHIP	PA	U	--	--	--	--	N/A	--	--	--	--	Z
BUILD AMERICA MUTUAL ASR CO	NY	D+	504.2	432.7	11.4	-5.6	10.0	N/A	2.3	10.0	1.1	DFGT
BUILDERS INS (A MUTUAL CAPTIVE CO)	GA	C	592.6	260.8	154.8	1.7	8.0	9.3	8.5	6.9	3.5	RT
BUILDERS MUTUAL INS CO	NC	A-	803.9	319.8	284.3	5.4	7.9	8.5	8.7	6.7	7.3	T
BUILDERS PREMIER INS CO	NC	C+	12.0	11.9	0.0	0.0	10.0	N/A	6.9	10.0	4.6	DG
BUILDING INDUSTRY INS ASSN INC	VA	E	21.8	5.1	13.8	0.3	0.1	0.3	2.9	0.4	0.3	CDGL
BUNKER HILL INS CAS CO	MA	C	13.4	5.4	5.8	0.2	6.8	6.9	3.6	6.5	2.5	DGT
BUNKER HILL INS CO	MA	C	62.0	29.6	18.4	1.0	7.1	6.9	6.5	6.9	4.2	RT
BUNKER HILL PREFERRED INS CO	MA	U	--	--	--	--	N/A	--	--	--	--	Z
BUNKER HILL PROPERTY INS CO	MA	U	--	--	--	--	N/A	--	--	--	--	Z
BUNKER HILL SECURITY INS CO	MA	U	--	--	--	--	N/A	--	--	--	--	Z
BURLINGTON INS CO	IL	C-	354.9	181.5	39.4	0.2	9.6	8.8	5.9	7.6	2.6	FRT
BUS ALLIANCE INS CO	CA	C+	25.0	17.9	5.7	0.1	9.0	4.1	5.4	9.0	4.0	DFGR
▲BUSINESSFIRST INS CO	FL	B-	35.4	16.6	12.3	0.2	7.6	6.6	8.1	6.7	5.0	DGT
CA CASUALTY COMP INS CO	CA	C+	73.0	71.0	0.5	0.1	7.3	5.8	5.6	10.0	4.6	DGRT
CALIFORNIA AUTOMOBILE INS CO	CA	B	745.8	190.7	600.2	-16.8	7.2	4.2	2.9	2.6	4.0	LT
CALIFORNIA CAPITAL INS CO	CA	B-	567.4	293.4	223.8	-2.4	7.9	5.6	3.5	6.5	4.7	RT
CALIFORNIA CAS GEN INS CO OF OREGON	OR	C	111.1	23.6	41.5	-0.7	7.4	6.3	1.9	6.0	3.3	DFRT
CALIFORNIA CASUALTY & FIRE INS CO	CA	C	67.6	19.8	34.6	-0.6	7.4	6.3	1.9	5.7	3.3	DRT
CALIFORNIA CASUALTY INDEMNITY EXCH	CA	C+	581.9	271.4	242.1	-3.0	7.9	6.2	2.4	6.1	3.9	FRT
CALIFORNIA CASUALTY INS CO	OR	C+	101.0	66.2	27.7	-0.4	7.9	6.1	2.6	6.8	3.9	FRT
CALIFORNIA GENERAL UNDERWRITERS INS	CA	B	21.2	20.9	0.4	0.1	10.0	5.7	6.7	9.3	4.9	DGT
CALIFORNIA HEALTHCARE INS CO INC RRG	HI	C+	128.6	56.3	14.0	0.4	10.0	9.6	8.2	8.1	3.5	DRT
CALIFORNIA INS CO	CA	B	889.6	558.4	255.0	18.5	9.4	7.9	8.9	7.9	4.7	RT
CALIFORNIA MEDICAL GROUP INS CO RRG	AZ	E	15.3	4.3	5.2	-0.1	5.7	10.0	3.4	7.7	0.0	DGRT
▲CALIFORNIA MUTUAL INS CO	CA	C-	14.7	11.0	4.0	-0.1	9.2	6.4	4.1	6.8	2.4	DFGR
CALLICOON CO-OPERATIVE INS CO	NY	C+	31.6	26.0	5.1	0.7	10.0	7.6	8.5	7.1	3.2	DGRT
CAMBRIA COUNTY MUTUAL INS CO	PA	U (1)	--	--	--	--	N/A	--	--	--	--	Z
CAMBRIDGE MUTUAL FIRE INS CO	MA	B-	896.4	536.1	188.8	5.3	8.6	6.6	6.0	7.6	4.6	T

See Page 27 for explanation of footnotes and   46   www.weissratings.com
Page 28 for explanation of stability factors.

Arrows denote recent upgrades ▲ or downgrades ▼   (see Section VII for explanations)

RISK ADJ. RATIO #1	CAPITAL RATIO #2	PREMIUM TO SURPLUS (%)	RESV. TO SURPLUS (%)	RESV. DEVELOP. 1 YEAR (%)	RESV. DEVELOP. 2 YEAR (%)	LOSS RATIO (%)	EXP. RATIO (%)	COMB RATIO (%)	CASH FROM UNDER-WRITING (%)	NET PREMIUM GROWTH (%)	INVEST. IN AFFIL (%)	INSURANCE COMPANY NAME
2.4	2.2	81.9	4.2	N/A	0.4	69.8	21.9	91.7	151.4	23.1	0.0	BLUESHORE INS CO
1.6	1.2	111.6	38.3	-13.4	-10.1	24.6	49.5	74.1	129.2	7.3	0.0	BOND SAFEGUARD INS CO
1.9	1.1	45.8	11.6	-2.8	-6.9	7.6	73.8	81.4	128.3	6.3	0.0	BONDED BUILDERS INS CO RRG
2.0	1.7	37.1	18.9	-2.9	-11.0	24.3	90.8	115.1	99.9	-23.4	0.0	BONDEX INS CO
1.7	1.5	39.0	17.5	-4.1	-3.3	10.1	118.6	128.7	83.9	0.0	0.0	BOSTON INDEMNITY CO INC
2.0	1.8	123.2	15.8	-5.0	-9.2	53.4	27.2	80.6	118.6	2.8	0.0	BREMEN FARMERS MUTUAL INS CO
4.3	2.7	89.7	40.1	1.4	3.5	64.9	33.7	98.6	105.9	4.4	0.0	BRETHREN MUTUAL INS CO
5.7	3.5	20.9	6.8	-0.8	-0.7	29.4	28.6	58.0	138.3	3.0	0.0	BRIAR CREEK MUTUAL INS CO
2.7	1.9	44.7	140.6	-9.2	-21.3	69.6	26.0	95.6	120.9	37.9	1.8 ●	BRICKSTREET MUTUAL INS CO
19.3	17.4	N/A	N/A	N/A	N/A	N/A	N/A	N/A	999 +	0.0	0.0	BRIDGEFIELD CASUALTY INS CO
2.7	2.6	N/A	N/A	N/A	N/A	N/A	N/A	N/A	-33.4	0.0	37.6	BRIDGEFIELD EMPLOYERS INS CO
6.6	5.9	N/A	N/A	N/A	N/A	N/A	N/A	N/A	77.5	0.0	0.0	BRIERFIELD INS CO
4.0	3.6	N/A	N/A	-0.1	0.1	N/A	N/A	N/A	92.3	0.0	0.0	BRISTOL WEST CASUALTY INS CO
5.1	4.6	N/A	3.5	0.2	-0.3	N/A	N/A	N/A	110.2	0.0	0.0	BRISTOL WEST INS CO
3.7	3.4	N/A	1.8	-1.0	-1.1	N/A	N/A	N/A	-18.4	0.0	0.0	BRISTOL WEST PREFERRED INS CO
1.0	0.7	11.4	65.0	1.0	-1.4	65.9	28.1	94.0	95.1	-14.8	0.0	BRITISH AMERICAN INS CO
2.1	1.4	58.2	161.3	1.0	-8.5	104.9	7.3	112.2	103.8	0.3	0.0	BROADLINE RRG INC
3.9	3.4	45.4	7.6	N/A	N/A	-1.5	48.9	47.4	189.2	-0.7	0.0	BROADWAY INS & SURETY CO
N/A	N/A	--	--	--	--	--	--	--	--	--	--	BROOKWOOD INS CO
4.1	2.7	47.6	18.4	-3.2	-2.8	46.9	34.5	81.4	129.4	5.0	0.0	BROOME CO OPERATIVE INS CO
2.0	1.5	139.4	50.5	7.2	8.0	62.1	32.9	95.0	114.7	11.9	0.0 ●	BROTHERHOOD MUTUAL INS CO
N/A	N/A	--	--	--	--	--	--	--	--	--	--	BTTS INS RRG GROUP INC
1.5	1.2	194.8	44.9	-2.3	-7.8	70.3	34.4	104.7	95.2	12.3	16.7	BUCKEYE STATE MUTUAL INS CO
N/A	N/A	--	--	--	--	--	--	--	--	--	--	BUCKS COUNTY CONTRIBUTIONSHIP
9.5	9.2	2.6	N/A	N/A	N/A	N/A	357.4	357.4	30.4	79.5	0.0 ●	BUILD AMERICA MUTUAL ASR CO
2.3	1.8	60.7	95.9	-6.2	-15.1	59.5	30.1	89.6	126.9	7.0	13.0 ●	BUILDERS INS (A MUTUAL CAPTIVE CO)
2.2	1.6	91.7	113.2	-0.6	-2.2	63.9	30.0	93.9	126.0	15.2	1.8 ●	BUILDERS MUTUAL INS CO
102.9	51.4	N/A	N/A	N/A	N/A	N/A	N/A	N/A	N/A	0.0	0.0	BUILDERS PREMIER INS CO
0.1	0.1	270.6	155.0	65.0	101.1	58.8	39.4	98.2	107.8	26.8	0.0	BUILDING INDUSTRY INS ASSN INC
1.4	1.0	109.4	43.4	1.9	1.3	54.4	26.6	81.0	160.4	13.1	0.0	BUNKER HILL INS CAS CO
1.3	1.1	63.2	25.1	1.5	1.1	54.4	25.9	80.3	232.8	13.1	42.8	BUNKER HILL INS CO
N/A	N/A	--	--	--	--	--	--	--	--	--	--	BUNKER HILL PREFERRED INS CO
N/A	N/A	--	--	--	--	--	--	--	--	--	--	BUNKER HILL PROPERTY INS CO
N/A	N/A	--	--	--	--	--	--	--	--	--	--	BUNKER HILL SECURITY INS CO
3.8	3.1	22.0	63.8	-3.5	-6.5	47.9	62.0	109.9	69.8	-15.1	0.0	BURLINGTON INS CO
3.0	2.2	32.1	19.1	8.4	10.2	55.9	36.6	92.5	90.3	2.5	0.0	BUS ALLIANCE INS CO
1.7	1.3	74.2	91.6	-3.8	-4.7	69.9	27.4	97.3	114.2	10.4	0.0	BUSINESSFIRST INS CO
2.3	1.4	0.7	31.4	-0.2	0.1	26.6	21.1	47.7	24.7	4.0	0.0	CA CASUALTY COMP INS CO
1.2	0.9	290.5	98.3	11.5	12.5	76.0	22.9	98.9	102.5	-5.4	3.2 ●	CALIFORNIA AUTOMOBILE INS CO
1.9	1.5	75.2	56.2	7.0	7.4	76.1	34.2	110.3	96.7	2.6	26.0 ●	CALIFORNIA CAPITAL INS CO
1.7	1.1	170.5	70.7	0.8	0.8	81.6	26.3	107.9	94.7	1.5	0.0	CALIFORNIA CAS GEN INS CO OF
1.7	1.2	170.3	70.7	0.8	0.8	81.6	26.3	107.9	96.7	1.5	0.0	CALIFORNIA CASUALTY & FIRE INS CO
1.8	1.5	88.7	36.8	0.5	0.5	81.6	26.3	107.9	96.0	1.5	32.6 ●	CALIFORNIA CASUALTY INDEMNITY
1.5	1.5	40.8	16.9	0.2	0.2	81.6	26.3	107.9	93.5	1.5	53.6	CALIFORNIA CASUALTY INS CO
23.2	10.9	1.9	0.9	0.4	3.5	49.9	27.7	77.6	35.0	-3.4	0.0	CALIFORNIA GENERAL UNDERWRITERS
4.3	3.0	25.3	90.8	-13.7	-22.0	85.7	13.0	98.7	94.3	-16.2	0.4	CALIFORNIA HEALTHCARE INS CO INC
3.6	2.8	48.2	45.9	3.0	-1.0	43.6	28.9	72.5	180.3	-0.1	0.0 ●	CALIFORNIA INS CO
1.1	0.7	115.8	193.6	-2.5	-53.9	67.4	15.3	82.7	207.1	38.4	0.0	CALIFORNIA MEDICAL GROUP INS CO
3.7	2.3	36.3	6.0	-3.9	-2.3	51.4	53.9	105.3	85.9	-1.2	2.4	CALIFORNIA MUTUAL INS CO
12.7	8.9	20.1	7.4	-1.4	-2.3	38.8	38.3	77.1	147.8	-2.8	0.0	CALLICOON CO-OPERATIVE INS CO
N/A	N/A	--	--	--	--	--	--	--	--	--	--	CAMBRIA COUNTY MUTUAL INS CO
3.1	1.9	36.8	19.8	-0.4	-2.6	50.8	38.3	89.1	114.4	4.0	0.0 ●	CAMBRIDGE MUTUAL FIRE INS CO

999 + Denotes number greater than 999.9%
999 - Denotes number less than -999.99%
● Bullets denote a more detailed analysis is available in Section II.

INSURANCE COMPANY NAME	DOM. STATE	RATING	TOTAL ASSETS ($MIL)	CAPITAL & SURPLUS ($MIL)	ANNUAL NET PREMIUM ($MIL)	NET INCOME ($MIL)	CAPITAL-IZATION INDEX (PTS)	RESERVE ADQ INDEX (PTS)	PROFIT-ABILITY INDEX (PTS)	LIQUIDITY INDEX (PTS)	STAB. INDEX (PTS)	STABILITY FACTORS
CAMERON MUTUAL INS CO	MO	C+	83.1	36.6	57.5	-0.7	7.4	6.5	4.6	5.6	3.3	RT
CAMERON NATIONAL INS CO	MO	C-	12.5	10.8	0.0	0.3	10.0	N/A	6.1	7.7	2.9	DGRT
CAMICO MUTUAL INS CO	CA	C	95.8	40.1	30.8	-0.1	8.0	4.3	5.9	7.0	2.9	RT
CAMPMED CAS & INDEM CO INC OF MD	NH	C+	21.1	20.9	0.0	0.1	10.0	N/A	6.7	7.0	4.8	DGR
CANAL INDEMNITY CO	SC	B	47.8	44.4	0.0	0.2	10.0	N/A	6.9	10.0	4.9	DT
CANAL INS CO	SC	B	823.5	444.5	210.0	6.5	8.5	5.3	5.0	7.3	5.8	T
CANOPIUS US INS INC	DE	B	202.1	116.2	29.4	1.5	8.2	5.5	2.9	6.9	5.5	FT
CAPACITY INS CO	FL	D	22.3	10.2	8.9	0.1	1.8	3.8	8.0	5.5	2.1	CDGT
CAPITOL CASUALTY CO	NE	C+	29.8	26.5	0.5	0.3	8.2	7.3	6.8	9.2	3.2	DFGT
CAPITOL COUNTY MUTUAL FIRE INS CO	TX	C	10.5	6.8	0.0	0.0	7.5	4.6	1.3	9.1	2.7	DFGR
CAPITOL INDEMNITY CORP	WI	C	535.5	243.8	175.0	4.3	7.3	4.3	5.6	6.8	4.0	RT
CAPITOL INS CO	PA	E+	17.7	2.0	7.7	0.3	0.3	0.4	0.8	6.4	0.5	CDFG
CAPITOL PREFERRED INS CO	FL	C	55.5	27.0	13.2	0.0	7.9	6.3	8.9	7.5	4.0	RT
CAPITOL SPECIALTY INS CORP	WI	C+	140.4	56.5	37.5	0.4	9.0	4.3	4.5	6.8	4.6	RT
CAPSON PHYSICIANS INS CO	TX	D	25.7	5.2	12.5	0.0	2.4	3.9	1.4	5.1	1.8	CDFG
CAR RRG INC	TN	D	1.4	1.1	0.4	0.0	7.8	N/A	2.8	6.1	0.9	DGT
CARE RRG INC	DC	D+	18.5	4.8	7.0	0.0	4.8	7.0	3.9	7.5	2.3	DGRT
▲ CARE WEST INS CO	CA	C-	132.6	34.1	28.4	0.8	5.1	3.8	2.9	6.5	3.0	RT
CARECONCEPTS INS INC A RRG	MT	F (4)	3.8	0.4	1.3	-0.3	0.7	3.9	0.9	4.1	0.0	CDFG
▲ CAREGIVERS UNITED LIAB INS CO RRG	SC	C-	44.9	27.0	5.1	0.5	9.2	9.4	6.4	9.1	3.0	DRT
CARIBBEAN AMERICAN PROPERTY INS CO	PR	C	40.5	18.9	30.3	1.7	2.5	9.2	3.7	2.4	2.9	CDGL
▲ CARING COMMUNITIES RECIP RRG	DC	B-	96.3	51.5	9.4	0.4	8.5	8.3	8.9	8.2	5.0	T
CAROLINA CASUALTY INS CO	IA	C	170.5	102.2	0.0	0.7	10.0	N/A	3.9	10.0	4.3	RT
CAROLINA FARMERS MUTUAL INS CO	NC	C-	8.8	6.5	3.2	0.2	7.8	7.5	4.3	6.8	2.5	DFGR
CAROLINA MUTUAL INS INC	NC	B-	93.1	45.7	32.8	1.0	8.1	9.7	8.9	7.2	3.5	T
CASCO INDEMNITY CO	ME	C+	30.8	13.7	16.7	0.3	8.6	9.3	8.6	6.6	3.2	DGRT
CASSATT RISK RETENTION GROUP INC	VT	D+	12.1	3.7	0.1	0.0	7.6	6.8	2.8	9.7	2.2	DFGR
CASTLE KEY INDEMNITY CO	IL	B	12.0	11.2	0.0	0.0	10.0	N/A	7.5	10.0	4.9	DG
CASTLE KEY INS CO	IL	B	372.8	218.9	122.7	4.3	9.3	6.4	8.8	6.8	4.3	T
▼ CASTLEPOINT FLORIDA INS	FL	F (5)	10.0	7.3	-1.0	0.0	7.3	3.5	2.3	0.0	0.0	DFGL
▼ CASTLEPOINT INS CO	NY	F (5)	178.4	17.4	-33.8	0.0	2.0	0.9	0.1	3.0	0.0	CDFL
CASUALTY CORP OF AMERICA	OK	D-	12.2	3.1	11.6	0.5	1.6	0.5	3.7	1.0	1.2	CDGL
CASUALTY UNDERWRITERS INS CO	UT	D+	4.7	4.4	0.2	0.0	8.8	4.6	3.4	9.3	2.0	DGRT
▲ CATASTROPHE REINS CO	TX	C-	1,886.3	1,800.4	148.2	37.3	10.0	5.3	8.6	9.1	3.0	T
CATAWBA INS CO	SC	U	--	--	--	--	N/A	--	--	--	--	Z
CATERPILLAR INS CO	MO	B	701.1	326.7	180.7	1.6	9.5	6.6	8.9	7.1	6.3	T
CATLIN INDEMNITY CO	DE	C	144.5	71.3	4.2	0.1	7.4	5.9	3.3	7.7	3.6	FT
CATLIN INS CO	TX	C	226.9	59.2	29.3	1.0	6.0	3.3	2.8	8.4	3.3	FRT
CATLIN SPECIALTY INS CO	DE	C+	728.2	235.2	50.3	1.9	8.0	4.0	4.2	7.2	4.1	RT
CATTLEMANS INS CO A RRG	MT	U (5)	--	--	--	--	N/A	--	--	--	--	Z
CBIA COMP SERVICES INC	CT	C-	25.2	9.1	5.0	-0.2	5.2	9.9	5.9	6.8	2.9	DGRT
CELINA MUTUAL INS CO	OH	C	74.5	34.0	39.6	0.4	8.0	8.2	8.3	6.1	3.5	RT
CEM INS CO	IL	D+	40.9	11.7	14.3	0.4	6.7	2.1	5.9	5.7	2.7	DGRT
CENSTAT CASUALTY CO	NE	C+	24.8	17.7	2.6	0.2	10.0	7.6	7.8	8.1	3.3	DGRT
CENTAURI SPECIALTY INS CO	FL	C	134.8	36.0	79.3	-2.8	4.5	5.4	2.9	6.4	3.3	CGOR
CENTENNIAL CASUALTY CO	AL	B-	118.1	74.2	10.3	1.0	8.2	7.4	8.9	8.1	3.8	DRT
CENTER MUTUAL INS CO	ND	C+	53.5	28.8	26.4	1.1	9.0	8.6	5.8	6.0	3.3	FRT
CENTER VALLEY MUTUAL FIRE INS CO	PA	D+ (1)	2.5	2.4	0.2	0.0	10.0	N/A	5.2	10.0	1.9	DT
CENTRAL CO-OPERATIVE INS CO	NY	C	17.7	10.9	6.9	0.2	8.7	6.5	8.5	7.2	2.4	DGRT
CENTRAL MUTUAL INS CO	OH	B	1,538.9	765.7	518.8	5.0	8.7	9.3	8.4	6.6	4.7	RT
CENTRAL PA PHYSICIANS RRG INC	SC	C	56.2	22.2	11.6	-0.4	7.3	4.4	4.4	7.2	4.0	DFT
CENTRAL STATES INDEMNITY CO OF	NE	C+	468.7	388.8	59.6	-1.0	9.1	7.4	5.0	8.1	4.5	RT

See Page 27 for explanation of footnotes and
Page 28 for explanation of stability factors.
Arrows denote recent upgrades ▲ or downgrades ▼   (see Section VII for explanations)

48

www.weissratings.com

RISK ADJ. RATIO #1	CAPITAL RATIO #2	PREMIUM TO SURPLUS (%)	RESV. TO SURPLUS (%)	RESV. DEVELOP. 1 YEAR (%)	RESV. DEVELOP. 2 YEAR (%)	LOSS RATIO (%)	EXP. RATIO (%)	COMB RATIO (%)	CASH FROM UNDER-WRITING (%)	NET PREMIUM GROWTH (%)	INVEST. IN AFFIL (%)	INSURANCE COMPANY NAME
1.8	1.3	157.3	56.3	-3.7	-1.5	65.9	34.2	100.1	103.2	16.6	15.2	CAMERON MUTUAL INS CO
17.2	15.5	N/A	N/A	N/A	N/A	N/A	N/A	N/A	19.5	0.0	0.0	CAMERON NATIONAL INS CO
2.6	1.7	76.7	81.9	5.2	11.4	68.6	30.9	99.5	119.0	1.3	1.5	CAMICO MUTUAL INS CO
75.4	33.9	N/A	N/A	N/A	N/A	N/A	N/A	N/A	N/A	0.0	0.0	CAMPMED CAS & INDEM CO INC OF MD
5.5	3.2	N/A	N/A	N/A	N/A	N/A	N/A	N/A	24.3	0.0	0.0	CANAL INDEMNITY CO
2.9	1.9	47.8	53.0	5.9	8.1	82.9	31.5	114.4	94.6	13.2	6.0 ●	CANAL INS CO
4.8	2.2	25.6	62.3	-13.5	1.4	46.1	51.1	97.2	66.3	-47.0	0.0	CANOPIUS US INS INC
0.4	0.3	88.4	47.3	3.3	12.9	49.0	46.5	95.5	107.9	4.1	0.0	CAPACITY INS CO
3.2	1.8	2.0	0.7	-0.7	-0.7	27.4	90.3	117.7	80.6	16.3	0.0	CAPITOL CASUALTY CO
1.4	1.3	N/A	N/A	1.6	2.3	N/A	N/A	N/A	-8.3	0.0	49.7	CAPITOL COUNTY MUTUAL FIRE INS CO
1.7	1.3	74.7	71.0	-1.0	-0.4	53.1	44.8	97.9	126.7	13.5	21.1 ●	CAPITOL INDEMNITY CORP
0.1	0.1	416.5	402.0	136.3	103.4	110.4	3.4	113.8	66.2	-21.2	0.0	CAPITOL INS CO
2.2	1.5	48.9	24.9	-7.7	-2.2	111.7	-25.6	86.1	128.0	1.8	0.0	CAPITOL PREFERRED INS CO
4.1	2.4	67.6	61.8	N/A	0.6	54.5	44.2	98.7	108.5	13.5	0.0	CAPITOL SPECIALTY INS CORP
0.6	0.4	242.7	258.5	30.0	14.3	73.3	41.0	114.3	86.6	-5.7	0.0	CAPSON PHYSICIANS INS CO
2.2	1.6	35.4	20.6	N/A	N/A	96.6	46.3	142.9	144.4	0.0	0.0	CAR RRG INC
0.9	0.7	150.3	284.7	-26.3	7.0	73.4	28.9	102.3	120.3	-13.0	0.0	CARE RRG INC
1.5	1.0	85.5	218.8	-18.1	-38.0	58.4	21.8	80.2	112.4	3.5	0.0	CARE WEST INS CO
0.1	0.1	202.6	370.2	28.7	-7.5	73.4	65.4	138.8	82.2	-9.5	0.0	CARECONCEPTS INS INC A RRG
3.7	2.3	19.2	44.3	-9.1	-15.9	36.3	15.5	51.8	184.5	-0.1	0.0	CAREGIVERS UNITED LIAB INS CO RRG
0.6	0.4	153.8	22.2	0.8	-9.2	42.2	36.1	78.3	126.0	10.7	0.0	CARIBBEAN AMERICAN PROPERTY INS
2.2	1.9	18.4	28.5	-2.7	-6.0	44.2	20.3	64.5	195.7	14.8	29.7	CARING COMMUNITIES RECIP RRG
13.5	12.1	N/A	N/A	N/A	N/A	N/A	N/A	N/A	41.1	0.0	0.0	CAROLINA CASUALTY INS CO
2.6	1.6	52.6	7.6	-0.6	-0.6	76.1	32.7	108.8	87.4	-2.9	0.0	CAROLINA FARMERS MUTUAL INS CO
2.6	2.1	73.7	65.6	-19.3	-35.9	41.5	28.9	70.4	124.8	9.7	0.0	CAROLINA MUTUAL INS INC
3.2	2.3	124.4	61.8	-3.9	-5.2	61.7	33.1	94.8	108.7	5.3	0.0	CASCO INDEMNITY CO
1.7	1.5	2.7	1.6	N/A	-0.1	97.8	102.3	200.1	-126.5	0.0	0.0	CASSATT RISK RETENTION GROUP INC
30.3	27.3	N/A	N/A	N/A	N/A	N/A	N/A	N/A	N/A	0.0	0.0	CASTLE KEY INDEMNITY CO
4.4	3.9	57.2	25.1	0.2	0.7	71.0	26.0	97.0	104.0	-0.3	6.4 ●	CASTLE KEY INS CO
7.8	7.0	-14.3	N/A	-7.0	9.7	13.1	-156.6	-143.5	46.3	-119.4	0.0	CASTLEPOINT FLORIDA INS
1.2	0.8	-418.8	N/A	253.5	71.5	108.5	-15.2	93.3	-35.1	-122.8	9.4	CASTLEPOINT INS CO
0.5	0.3	467.8	133.8	-9.2	36.0	78.4	17.9	96.3	108.8	-5.9	0.0	CASUALTY CORP OF AMERICA
3.0	2.2	5.2	2.5	N/A	N/A	87.3	59.5	146.8	65.9	N/A	18.1	CASUALTY UNDERWRITERS INS CO
15.2	8.7	8.5	N/A	-1.7	-1.9	-19.2	0.4	-18.8	999 +	-10.4	0.0 ●	CATASTROPHE REINS CO
N/A	N/A	--	--	--	--	--	--	--	--	--	--	CATAWBA INS CO
3.7	2.6	57.1	4.3	0.2	-0.8	72.4	14.3	86.7	126.6	26.8	0.0 ●	CATERPILLAR INS CO
1.3	1.2	6.1	17.8	1.2	2.2	86.8	26.2	113.0	78.6	-34.5	65.7	CATLIN INDEMNITY CO
1.4	0.9	51.8	151.0	10.1	19.0	86.8	26.3	113.1	50.4	-34.5	0.0	CATLIN INS CO
2.4	1.8	21.5	62.6	4.2	10.2	86.8	26.8	113.6	117.5	-34.5	14.8 ●	CATLIN SPECIALTY INS CO
N/A	N/A	--	--	--	--	--	--	--	--	--	--	CATTLEMANS INS CO A RRG
1.5	0.9	52.4	144.3	-23.1	-58.5	37.6	24.8	62.4	103.4	-2.3	0.0	CBIA COMP SERVICES INC
2.9	1.8	118.2	36.7	-6.3	-5.9	59.4	32.4	91.8	112.5	4.3	0.0	CELINA MUTUAL INS CO
1.6	1.3	128.7	35.6	2.8	5.4	66.0	28.4	94.4	109.2	25.9	0.0	CEM INS CO
5.6	4.5	14.9	8.0	-1.3	-1.4	54.0	37.4	91.4	196.1	28.8	0.0	CENSTAT CASUALTY CO
1.0	0.6	210.1	46.2	0.9	-1.3	71.9	37.1	109.0	112.5	28.1	0.0	CENTAURI SPECIALTY INS CO
3.4	2.0	14.4	5.1	0.2	-0.5	67.2	20.1	87.3	151.3	-6.3	0.0	CENTENNIAL CASUALTY CO
3.7	2.6	96.8	29.5	-4.1	-6.2	81.5	27.7	109.2	91.9	-2.8	0.0	CENTER MUTUAL INS CO
33.4	28.7	6.3	N/A	N/A	N/A	56.9	58.2	115.1	95.0	37.9	0.0	CENTER VALLEY MUTUAL FIRE INS CO
3.2	2.1	64.7	14.0	0.1	-2.3	38.7	37.1	75.8	145.6	18.6	0.0	CENTRAL CO-OPERATIVE INS CO
2.9	2.1	69.8	47.9	-4.9	-8.7	64.0	33.2	97.2	102.3	6.3	11.9 ●	CENTRAL MUTUAL INS CO
1.7	1.2	52.7	114.0	-1.3	6.7	79.4	32.2	111.6	76.4	-6.6	0.0	CENTRAL PA PHYSICIANS RRG INC
3.8	2.4	15.8	1.4	-0.1	-0.3	60.2	45.9	106.1	89.4	8.2	3.2 ●	CENTRAL STATES INDEMNITY CO OF

999 + Denotes number greater than 999.9%
999 - Denotes number less than -999.99%
● Bullets denote a more detailed analysis is available in Section II.

INSURANCE COMPANY NAME	DOM. STATE	RATING	TOTAL ASSETS ($MIL)	CAPITAL & SURPLUS ($MIL)	ANNUAL NET PREMIUM ($MIL)	NET INCOME ($MIL)	CAPITAL-IZATION INDEX (PTS)	RESERVE ADQ INDEX (PTS)	PROFIT-ABILITY INDEX (PTS)	LIQUIDITY INDEX (PTS)	STAB. INDEX (PTS)	STABILITY FACTORS
CENTRE COUNTY MUTUAL FIRE INS CO	PA	D+	6.3	3.6	2.8	-0.1	6.5	6.9	5.4	5.9	2.0	DGT
CENTRE INS CO	DE	U	--	--	--	--	N/A	--	--	--	--	Z
CENTURION CASUALTY CO	IA	B-	36.5	35.4	10.3	1.5	10.0	7.2	1.9	9.0	3.7	DGT
▲CENTURION MEDICAL LIAB PROTECT RRG	AZ	C-	21.2	12.6	6.6	0.1	10.0	9.6	8.6	9.1	3.0	DGRT
CENTURY CASUALTY CO	GA	D+	4.9	2.2	0.0	-0.4	8.2	5.5	1.2	6.9	2.0	DFGR
CENTURY INDEMNITY CO	PA	U	--	--	--	--	N/A	--	--	--	--	Z
CENTURY INS CO GUAM LTD	GU	D	26.9	15.1	7.6	0.8	7.7	3.7	7.7	7.1	2.0	DGT
CENTURY MUTUAL INS CO	NC	C-	9.8	8.1	2.2	0.3	7.2	6.1	4.7	7.1	2.2	DGT
CENTURY SURETY CO	OH	C	172.3	164.6	0.0	1.9	10.0	2.6	4.4	0.1	3.5	FLRT
CENTURY-NATIONAL INS CO	CA	C	544.4	251.4	210.5	4.5	7.9	6.5	2.8	6.0	4.0	T
CGB INS CO	IN	D	378.2	152.1	0.0	0.3	10.0	4.6	8.1	7.0	2.0	FT
CHARITABLE SERVICE PROVIDERS RRG	AZ	U (5)	--	--	--	--	N/A	--	--	--	--	Z
CHARTER INDEMNITY CO	TX	B	12.4	7.8	0.0	0.1	10.0	N/A	5.9	7.0	4.1	DGRT
CHARTER OAK FIRE INS CO	CT	B	950.9	249.5	276.5	6.1	7.9	8.7	5.3	6.7	4.6	T
CHAUTAUQUA PATRONS INS CO	NY	C	21.6	11.5	8.4	0.2	8.1	6.4	5.2	6.8	3.2	DGRT
CHEROKEE GUARANTEE CO INC A RRG	AZ	E	23.2	4.1	3.5	0.2	3.2	6.0	3.9	7.3	0.0	DGT
▲CHEROKEE INS CO	MI	B-	523.9	181.3	190.3	5.2	7.6	4.3	6.7	5.4	5.0	T
CHERRY VALLEY COOPERATIVE INS CO	NY	D	1.7	1.6	0.4	0.1	10.0	7.7	4.8	7.9	1.9	DFGR
CHESAPEAKE EMPLOYERS INS CO	MD	B	2,252.8	579.2	237.4	21.5	7.0	9.4	6.5	6.9	4.4	T
CHICAGO INS CO	IL	C	87.2	65.7	0.0	0.0	10.0	3.6	8.1	7.0	4.1	DRT
CHUBB CUSTOM INS CO	NJ	B-	370.4	217.5	31.7	2.7	10.0	7.9	8.7	7.2	3.9	T
CHUBB INDEMNITY INS CO	NY	B	379.4	165.9	31.7	2.1	10.0	8.0	8.8	7.1	6.0	T
CHUBB INS CO OF NJ	NJ	B (1)	78.9	35.2	0.0	0.7	10.0	N/A	7.1	10.0	4.0	T
CHUBB INS CO OF PR	PR	B	137.8	51.9	63.8	1.3	7.3	9.5	7.3	7.0	4.3	T
CHUBB LLOYDS INS CO OF TX	TX	B	51.3	5.4	0.0	0.0	6.8	N/A	6.7	7.0	4.9	CDGT
CHUBB NATIONAL INS CO	IN	B	379.4	165.0	31.7	2.0	10.0	8.0	8.8	7.0	6.0	T
CHUNG KUO INS CO LTD GUAM BRANCH	GU	C+	40.8	24.1	16.5	0.8	7.8	9.1	8.3	9.0	3.2	DGT
CHURCH INS CO	NY	U	--	--	--	--	N/A	--	--	--	--	Z
CHURCH MUTUAL INS CO	WI	B	1,701.0	688.3	645.8	12.2	8.4	8.3	6.8	6.5	4.9	T
CIM INS CORP	MI	C	17.7	17.3	0.0	0.0	10.0	N/A	6.0	10.0	3.3	DGRT
CINCINNATI CASUALTY CO	OH	B	424.0	365.5	0.0	11.6	10.0	N/A	8.1	10.0	4.7	T
CINCINNATI EQUITABLE INS CO	OH	U	--	--	--	--	N/A	--	--	--	--	Z
CINCINNATI INDEMNITY CO	OH	A-	132.7	94.4	0.0	1.5	10.0	N/A	8.0	9.1	5.5	FT
CINCINNATI INS CO	OH	A	12,253.3	4,763.3	4,393.9	147.5	8.1	8.4	8.5	6.4	7.5	T
▲CINCINNATI SPECIALTY UNDERWRITER	DE	A-	744.7	381.1	189.8	18.3	7.8	9.4	8.7	6.9	7.0	T
CIRCLE STAR INS CO A RRG	VT	D	10.4	2.0	0.5	0.1	10.0	6.9	9.8	9.9	1.6	DGT
CITATION INS CO (MA)	MA	C+	253.1	74.3	159.9	0.2	8.0	4.2	2.7	4.3	3.7	LT
CITIES & VILLAGES MUTUAL INS CO	WI	C+	55.3	29.1	13.9	0.0	7.8	8.0	5.7	6.9	3.3	DT
CITIZENS INS CO OF AM	MI	B	1,541.6	717.8	714.0	9.1	9.9	8.0	8.1	6.2	4.8	RT
CITIZENS INS CO OF IL	IL	C+	5.3	5.3	0.0	0.0	10.0	N/A	7.7	7.0	3.6	DGR
CITIZENS INS CO OF OHIO	OH	C	16.1	15.9	0.0	0.1	10.0	N/A	7.2	7.0	4.2	DG
CITIZENS INS CO OF THE MIDWEST	IN	C	54.1	53.7	0.0	0.2	10.0	N/A	7.4	7.0	4.3	
CITIZENS PROPERTY INS CORP	FL	A+(1)	12,268.8	7,401.8	552.6	-27.1	10.0	5.8	6.4	9.3	8.4	F
CITIZENS UNITED RECIP EXCH	NJ	D	73.3	17.8	37.8	-1.3	2.3	1.4	1.5	4.9	2.2	CDFL
CITY NATIONAL INS CO	TX	C	19.5	11.5	1.3	-0.7	9.7	4.6	1.9	0.9	3.0	DFGL
CIVIC PROPERTY & CASUALTY CO INC	CA	C+	287.4	116.7	147.6	-0.3	9.5	5.9	5.9	6.7	4.7	FRT
CIVIL SERVICE EMPLOYEES INS CO	CA	B-	211.6	103.1	101.2	-5.7	8.6	6.1	3.2	6.2	4.6	FRT
CLAIM PROFESSIONALS LIAB INS CO RRG	VT	D+	4.4	2.6	0.6	0.0	8.0	7.0	8.9	9.6	2.0	DGR
CLARENDON NATIONAL INS CO	IL	C	661.5	168.9	0.4	2.9	8.0	10.0	2.6	7.9	3.8	FRT
CLAVERACK CO-OPERATIVE INS CO	NY	D	2.9	1.6	0.0	0.1	7.9	9.3	3.0	6.9	1.8	DFGT
CLEAR BLUE INS CO	IL	C	30.0	27.9	0.0	0.1	10.0	7.2	2.9	9.3	3.4	FGT
CLEAR BLUE SPECIALTY INS CO	NC	C+	64.3	63.9	0.0	0.1	8.6	3.4	5.9	10.0	3.5	DGRT

See Page 27 for explanation of footnotes and Page 28 for explanation of stability factors.
Arrows denote recent upgrades ▲ or downgrades ▼ (see Section VII for explanations)

50

www.weissratings.com

RISK ADJ. CAPITAL RATIO #1	CAPITAL RATIO #2	PREMIUM TO SURPLUS (%)	RESV. TO SURPLUS (%)	RESV. DEVELOP. 1 YEAR (%)	RESV. DEVELOP. 2 YEAR (%)	LOSS RATIO (%)	EXP. RATIO (%)	COMB RATIO (%)	CASH FROM UNDER-WRITING (%)	NET PREMIUM GROWTH (%)	INVEST. IN AFFIL (%)	INSURANCE COMPANY NAME
1.5	0.9	79.5	15.3	-0.7	1.2	54.5	34.1	88.6	118.2	10.1	0.0	CENTRE COUNTY MUTUAL FIRE INS CO
N/A	N/A	--	--	--	--	--	--	--	--	--	--	CENTRE INS CO
12.3	9.9	30.2	1.1	-0.1	-0.2	4.6	18.4	23.0	412.6	-12.2	0.0	CENTURION CASUALTY CO
6.1	4.9	53.0	22.1	-6.5	-9.8	14.8	23.6	38.4	219.2	55.4	0.0	CENTURION MEDICAL LIAB PROTECT
2.3	1.7	1.2	65.1	2.3	9.9	999 +	654.4	999 +	16.6	-96.0	0.0	CENTURY CASUALTY CO
N/A	N/A	--	--	--	--	--	--	--	--	--	--	CENTURY INDEMNITY CO
3.0	1.8	52.9	21.0	1.4	-2.2	39.6	35.8	75.4	147.4	4.5	0.0	CENTURY INS CO GUAM LTD
1.6	1.1	28.2	3.5	0.1	-0.5	61.6	46.0	107.6	94.8	6.7	0.0	CENTURY MUTUAL INS CO
2.8	2.4	N/A	N/A	N/A	N/A	N/A	N/A	N/A	3.9	-100.0	39.6	CENTURY SURETY CO
2.1	1.5	84.9	52.0	-3.6	-3.6	70.8	18.1	88.9	115.4	27.4	0.0 ●	CENTURY-NATIONAL INS CO
11.2	5.6	N/A	N/A	N/A	N/A	N/A	N/A	N/A	N/A	0.0	0.0	CGB INS CO
N/A	N/A	--	--	--	--	--	--	--	--	--	--	CHARITABLE SERVICE PROVIDERS RRG
5.4	4.9	N/A	N/A	N/A	N/A	N/A	N/A	N/A	5.2	0.0	0.0	CHARTER INDEMNITY CO
2.4	1.5	113.8	188.9	-2.2	-5.6	63.4	30.3	93.7	109.6	4.8	0.0 ●	CHARTER OAK FIRE INS CO
2.4	1.5	74.0	33.6	2.2	1.3	67.6	39.3	106.9	100.1	5.0	0.0	CHAUTAUQUA PATRONS INS CO
0.7	0.4	100.6	324.9	44.8	6.5	93.7	10.5	104.2	252.2	-30.0	0.0	CHEROKEE GUARANTEE CO INC A RRG
2.4	1.4	105.3	130.5	1.9	5.8	91.5	8.0	99.5	108.0	4.7	0.0	CHEROKEE INS CO
4.4	3.0	29.6	4.7	-8.1	-4.5	34.0	24.1	58.1	81.5	52.5	0.0	CHERRY VALLEY COOPERATIVE INS CO
2.0	1.2	43.7	242.1	-5.6	-18.6	81.4	25.8	107.2	86.1	2.7	0.0 ●	CHESAPEAKE EMPLOYERS INS CO
18.6	16.8	N/A	N/A	N/A	N/A	N/A	N/A	N/A	68.0	0.0	0.0	CHICAGO INS CO
11.5	7.2	14.7	36.0	-1.7	-3.4	53.5	34.2	87.7	92.2	-35.2	0.0 ●	CHUBB CUSTOM INS CO
9.3	5.8	19.4	47.3	-2.2	-4.1	53.5	34.1	87.6	80.0	-35.2	0.0	CHUBB INDEMNITY INS CO
5.8	5.2	N/A	N/A	N/A	N/A	N/A	N/A	N/A	N/A	0.0	0.0	CHUBB INS CO OF NJ
1.5	1.2	125.7	122.5	-5.5	-13.9	30.9	68.6	99.5	114.3	0.0	0.0	CHUBB INS CO OF PR
0.8	0.7	N/A	N/A	N/A	N/A	N/A	N/A	N/A	N/A	0.0	0.0	CHUBB LLOYDS INS CO OF TX
9.3	5.8	19.4	47.5	-2.2	-4.1	53.5	34.2	87.7	96.1	-35.2	0.0	CHUBB NATIONAL INS CO
3.2	2.1	70.7	13.0	-10.6	-11.5	29.4	40.6	70.0	113.3	3.8	0.0	CHUNG KUO INS CO LTD GUAM BRANCH
N/A	N/A	--	--	--	--	--	--	--	--	--	--	CHURCH INS CO
2.8	1.9	97.3	67.7	-1.5	-2.2	55.9	35.0	90.9	111.4	4.9	6.7 ●	CHURCH MUTUAL INS CO
112.8	101.5	N/A	N/A	N/A	N/A	N/A	N/A	N/A	42.1	0.0	0.0	CIM INS CORP
9.9	5.7	N/A	N/A	N/A	N/A	N/A	N/A	N/A	940.7	0.0	0.0 ●	CINCINNATI CASUALTY CO
N/A	N/A	--	--	--	--	--	--	--	--	--	--	CINCINNATI EQUITABLE INS CO
11.1	6.4	N/A	N/A	N/A	N/A	N/A	N/A	N/A	-0.7	0.0	0.0 ●	CINCINNATI INDEMNITY CO
2.2	1.6	93.8	96.2	-3.1	-4.5	64.9	30.2	95.1	116.4	4.9	9.9 ●	CINCINNATI INS CO
3.2	1.6	51.0	63.4	-11.1	-20.2	37.6	30.5	68.1	170.2	8.6	0.0 ●	CINCINNATI SPECIALTY UNDERWRITER
0.9	0.8	24.0	30.8	-8.0	-9.7	31.4	-149.1	-117.7	-83.8	3.0	0.0	CIRCLE STAR INS CO A RRG
2.0	1.6	221.3	104.8	3.7	4.7	78.1	25.2	103.3	102.8	1.2	0.0	CITATION INS CO (MA)
2.3	1.4	49.0	56.6	-2.9	-4.2	57.3	27.0	84.3	140.1	2.3	5.9	CITIES & VILLAGES MUTUAL INS CO
4.6	3.0	101.2	58.6	-1.8	-6.6	57.7	27.0	84.7	119.4	4.9	0.0 ●	CITIZENS INS CO OF AM
216.0	108.0	N/A	N/A	N/A	N/A	N/A	N/A	N/A	N/A	0.0	0.0	CITIZENS INS CO OF IL
68.9	30.8	N/A	N/A	N/A	N/A	N/A	N/A	N/A	N/A	0.0	0.0	CITIZENS INS CO OF OHIO
73.5	32.8	N/A	N/A	N/A	N/A	N/A	N/A	N/A	N/A	0.0	0.0	CITIZENS INS CO OF THE MIDWEST
30.9	16.1	7.5	9.7	1.0	1.4	82.0	43.3	125.3	71.8	-4.4	0.0	CITIZENS PROPERTY INS CORP
0.5	0.4	210.2	194.4	19.4	30.8	97.1	27.9	125.0	71.7	-9.2	0.0	CITIZENS UNITED RECIP EXCH
5.6	5.0	11.4	N/A	N/A	N/A	66.2	44.4	110.6	14.4	-93.8	0.0	CITY NATIONAL INS CO
3.9	2.8	125.8	75.5	1.1	2.3	71.2	32.4	103.6	94.5	-1.1	0.0	CIVIC PROPERTY & CASUALTY CO INC
2.3	1.9	90.8	36.2	-0.1	-0.3	71.7	32.8	104.5	87.6	1.3	21.3	CIVIL SERVICE EMPLOYEES INS CO
3.5	2.3	24.4	26.6	-4.7	-8.2	44.5	-7.3	37.2	244.9	4.7	0.0	CLAIM PROFESSIONALS LIAB INS CO
1.2	1.2	0.2	34.3	-0.3	-96.8	-569.7	999 +	999 +	48.2	100.2	0.0	CLARENDON NATIONAL INS CO
3.2	2.5	N/A	17.9	-39.2	-2.1	41.0	999 +	999 +	72.3	-100.0	0.0	CLAVERACK CO-OPERATIVE INS CO
36.1	32.5	N/A	N/A	N/A	-0.2	N/A	N/A	N/A	N/A	100.0	0.0	CLEAR BLUE INS CO
2.3	2.1	N/A	9.5	6.5	8.5	999 +	N/A	N/A	N/A	-100.0	43.3	CLEAR BLUE SPECIALTY INS CO

999 + Denotes number greater than 999.9%
999 - Denotes number less than -999.99%
● Bullets denote a more detailed analysis is available in Section II.

INSURANCE COMPANY NAME	DOM. STATE	RATING	TOTAL ASSETS ($MIL)	CAPITAL & SURPLUS ($MIL)	ANNUAL NET PREMIUM ($MIL)	NET INCOME ($MIL)	CAPITAL-IZATION INDEX (PTS)	RESERVE ADQ INDEX (PTS)	PROFIT-ABILITY INDEX (PTS)	LIQUIDITY INDEX (PTS)	STAB. INDEX (PTS)	STABILITY FACTORS
CLEARFIELD CTY GRNGE MUT FIRE INS CO	PA	C-	2.9	2.2	0.7	-0.1	9.2	5.1	1.6	7.8	1.8	DFGT
CLEARWATER SELECT INS CO	CT	D	1,239.0	494.2	196.7	11.7	7.2	1.9	8.6	8.7	1.7	RT
CLERMONT INS CO	IA	C	26.0	22.8	0.0	0.1	10.0	N/A	7.1	7.0	3.6	DGRT
CLINIC MUTUAL INS CO RRG	HI	U (5)	--	--	--	--	N/A	--	--	--	--	Z
CLOISTER MUTL CAS INS CO	PA	C	9.7	9.7	0.1	0.0	10.0	7.2	3.9	10.0	2.9	DGT
▲CM REGENT INS CO	PA	B-	179.2	71.5	37.8	2.5	8.4	7.0	6.8	7.5	5.0	FT
CM VANTAGE SPECIALTY INS CO	WI	B	58.8	52.6	0.0	0.1	10.0	N/A	4.9	10.0	4.3	DT
CMIC RRG	DC	C+	7.1	2.8	0.3	0.0	8.1	4.9	4.0	9.2	3.3	DGT
CO-OPERATIVE INS COS	VT	B-	134.1	74.7	64.7	3.2	10.0	8.1	7.9	6.7	3.8	RT
COAST NATIONAL INS CO	CA	D+	598.4	429.0	0.0	2.0	10.0	6.0	6.7	10.0	2.7	RT
COASTAL AMERICAN INS CO	MS	C-	8.9	4.4	4.5	-0.5	5.9	6.2	2.9	6.6	2.1	DGT
COASTAL SELECT INS CO	CA	D+	112.6	38.2	39.9	1.8	1.1	7.7	3.6	0.3	2.4	CLRT
CODAN INS CO LTD	NY	U	--	--	--	--	N/A	--	--	--	--	Z
COFACE NORTH AMERICA INS CO	MA	C	165.9	48.0	53.0	2.1	7.1	7.0	2.8	8.0	2.6	RT
COLISEUM REINS CO	DE	U	--	--	--	--	N/A	--	--	--	--	Z
COLLEGE LIAB INS CO LTD RRG	HI	D	14.6	6.2	3.4	-0.5	1.8	6.9	1.7	6.9	1.5	CDGT
COLLEGE RRG INC	VT	C	26.0	10.0	5.8	0.1	7.0	6.8	8.0	7.1	2.3	DGT
COLONIAL AMERICAN CAS & SURETY CO	MD	C+	25.4	22.9	0.0	0.1	10.0	N/A	6.5	9.4	3.6	DGRT
COLONIAL COUNTY MUTUAL INS CO	TX	B	157.5	13.9	0.0	0.0	7.5	N/A	3.9	7.0	4.3	DT
COLONIAL LLOYDS	TX	C-	9.1	6.4	0.5	0.0	10.0	4.3	3.9	9.0	2.6	DFGT
COLONIAL MORTGAGE INS CO	TX	D+	3.0	2.1	0.2	-0.1	9.6	2.3	3.7	10.0	2.2	DGT
▲COLONIAL SURETY CO	PA	B-	59.6	37.1	9.8	0.9	9.9	9.3	8.8	9.1	5.0	DT
COLONY INS CO	VA	C	1,554.7	386.9	261.8	6.0	7.3	9.3	8.5	7.3	3.3	RT
COLONY SPECIALTY INS CO	OH	D+	62.4	21.6	0.0	0.2	9.2	N/A	4.3	10.0	2.4	DRT
COLORADO CASUALTY INS CO	NH	C+	25.7	24.6	0.0	0.1	10.0	N/A	6.7	7.0	3.7	DGRT
COLORADO FARM BUREAU MUTUAL INS CO	CO	C	82.5	35.3	26.0	0.0	8.5	9.4	3.8	6.2	3.3	FT
COLUMBIA CASUALTY CO	IL	C	240.6	240.1	0.0	1.6	10.0	N/A	5.7	10.0	3.9	ART
COLUMBIA FEDERAL INS CO	DC	D+	3.5	2.3	0.8	0.0	7.1	9.2	5.5	6.7	1.8	DFGT
COLUMBIA INS CO	NE	U	--	--	--	--	N/A	--	--	--	--	Z
COLUMBIA LLOYDS INS CO	TX	C+	50.8	24.9	22.1	0.6	4.8	5.9	5.4	6.6	3.3	RT
COLUMBIA MUTUAL INS CO	MO	B-	393.8	189.1	143.6	2.1	8.1	6.3	5.9	6.5	4.1	RT
COLUMBIA NATIONAL INS CO	NE	C+	93.3	38.6	37.0	0.4	9.2	6.3	6.2	6.6	3.7	T
COLUMBIA NATIONAL RRG INC	VT	E	1.9	1.2	0.3	0.0	10.0	N/A	8.3	10.0	0.0	DGT
COMCARE PRO INS RECIPROCAL RRG	VT	D+	5.1	3.2	2.1	-0.1	5.7	4.1	3.0	6.3	2.1	DFG
COMMERCE & INDUSTRY INS CO	NY	C	403.2	394.2	-521.1	9.1	10.0	4.0	1.9	0.0	4.2	AFLT
COMMERCE INS CO	MA	C+	2,144.7	630.5	1,285.1	5.7	8.1	4.2	3.4	3.0	4.6	FLT
COMMERCE WEST INS CO	CA	C	182.3	53.7	106.6	1.1	8.3	4.1	3.2	4.5	4.3	LT
COMMERCIAL ALLIANCE INS CO	TX	C	85.3	41.4	34.9	1.0	5.8	3.6	6.0	6.6	3.7	RT
COMMERCIAL CASUALTY INS CO	IN	U	--	--	--	--	N/A	--	--	--	--	Z
COMMERCIAL HIRECAR INS CO RRG	TN	D	4.0	1.6	1.5	0.0	7.4	N/A	3.6	7.3	1.2	DGT
COMMERCIAL MUT INS CO	GA	F (5)	0.0	0.0	7.9	0.0	0.0	2.3	0.1	0.0	0.0	CDFL
COMMONWEALTH CASUALTY CO	AZ	E	25.4	7.9	25.0	-1.0	0.0	3.7	2.1	0.0	0.3	CGLT
COMMONWEALTH INS CO OF AMERICA	DE	U	--	--	--	--	N/A	--	--	--	--	Z
COMMUNITIES OF FAITH RRG INC	SC	C	15.1	12.7	1.1	0.1	9.8	8.0	5.7	9.3	3.3	DGR
COMMUNITY BLOOD CENTERS EXCHANGE	IN	C	18.5	15.1	1.9	0.0	10.0	9.4	7.3	8.5	2.8	DGRT
COMMUNITY CARE RRG INC	DC	D	7.1	2.7	2.5	0.0	7.3	3.6	7.0	7.2	0.6	DGT
COMMUNITY HEALTH ALLIANCE RECIP RRG	VT	U	--	--	--	--	N/A	--	--	--	--	Z
▲COMMUNITY HOSPITAL ALTERNATIVE RRG	VT	B-	276.5	128.2	38.9	2.4	9.2	9.7	8.9	7.0	5.0	T
COMMUNITY INS CORP	WI	C+	7.3	6.0	0.0	0.0	10.0	3.7	6.5	7.0	3.8	DGRT
COMMUNITY MUTUAL INS CO	NY	D+	2.0	1.1	0.0	0.0	9.3	5.1	4.0	8.5	1.3	DGRT
COMPASS INS CO	NY	U	--	--	--	--	N/A	--	--	--	--	Z
COMPASS SPCLTY INS RRG INC	TN	D	1.9	1.2	0.9	0.0	8.2	N/A	3.3	9.3	0.9	DGT

See Page 27 for explanation of footnotes and
Page 28 for explanation of stability factors.
Arrows denote recent upgrades ▲ or downgrades ▼   (see Section VII for explanations)

52

www.weissratings.com

RISK ADJ. RATIO #1	CAPITAL RATIO #2	PREMIUM TO SURPLUS (%)	RESV. TO SURPLUS (%)	RESV. DEVELOP. 1 YEAR (%)	RESV. DEVELOP. 2 YEAR (%)	LOSS RATIO (%)	EXP. RATIO (%)	COMB RATIO (%)	CASH FROM UNDER-WRITING (%)	NET PREMIUM GROWTH (%)	INVEST. IN AFFIL (%)	INSURANCE COMPANY NAME
3.2	2.3	29.2	4.4	-0.8	-0.9	40.3	80.9	121.2	60.5	-11.0	0.0	CLEARFIELD CTY GRNGE MUT FIRE INS
1.5	1.1	41.6	132.0	-6.9	-9.5	57.6	26.8	84.4	107.7	-1.8	10.8 •	CLEARWATER SELECT INS CO
21.8	19.6	N/A	N/A	N/A	N/A	N/A	N/A	N/A	86.7	0.0	0.0	CLERMONT INS CO
N/A	N/A	--	--	--	--	--	--	--	--	--	--	CLINIC MUTUAL INS CO RRG
17.3	7.4	1.5	0.3	-0.3	-0.1	8.6	158.2	166.8	62.3	2.7	0.0	CLOISTER MUTL CAS INS CO
4.7	3.0	54.2	136.2	-15.5	-24.3	45.8	30.3	76.1	99.8	-7.6	0.0	CM REGENT INS CO
30.1	27.1	N/A	N/A	N/A	N/A	N/A	N/A	N/A	999 +	0.0	0.0	CM VANTAGE SPECIALTY INS CO
2.0	1.8	10.3	20.0	3.0	-0.1	-253.1	-234.9	-488.0	43.2	199.9	0.0	CMIC RRG
4.5	3.1	88.0	25.3	-3.6	-6.9	52.3	31.9	84.2	110.3	5.6	1.0	CO-OPERATIVE INS COS
7.9	7.2	N/A	N/A	N/A	0.2	N/A	N/A	N/A	147.2	0.0	12.2 •	COAST NATIONAL INS CO
1.5	1.0	92.5	9.3	-5.8	-5.2	28.1	48.7	76.8	151.1	7.8	0.0	COASTAL AMERICAN INS CO
0.3	0.2	108.6	24.6	-0.1	-2.4	41.5	30.2	71.7	144.2	21.7	0.0	COASTAL SELECT INS CO
N/A	N/A	--	--	--	--	--	--	--	--	--	--	CODAN INS CO LTD
1.4	1.0	114.9	102.0	8.1	0.1	52.7	62.8	115.5	135.2	1.3	0.0	COFACE NORTH AMERICA INS CO
N/A	N/A	--	--	--	--	--	--	--	--	--	--	COLISEUM REINS CO
0.4	0.3	52.9	107.3	16.8	7.8	152.3	16.9	169.2	109.3	31.2	0.0	COLLEGE LIAB INS CO LTD RRG
1.3	1.1	59.5	105.3	6.0	7.2	83.7	22.5	106.2	105.8	2.6	0.0	COLLEGE RRG INC
26.8	24.1	N/A	N/A	N/A	N/A	N/A	N/A	N/A	72.1	0.0	0.0	COLONIAL AMERICAN CAS & SURETY CO
1.4	1.3	N/A	N/A	N/A	N/A	N/A	N/A	N/A	51.0	0.0	0.0	COLONIAL COUNTY MUTUAL INS CO
7.1	6.4	7.8	3.9	-5.1	2.2	61.1	-77.0	-15.9	60.6	-58.1	0.0	COLONIAL LLOYDS
4.8	3.9	9.1	15.8	5.2	6.3	56.2	30.4	86.6	148.9	-40.8	0.0	COLONIAL MORTGAGE INS CO
5.1	3.6	27.2	31.1	-6.7	-14.6	4.9	40.3	45.2	213.1	2.9	0.0	COLONIAL SURETY CO
1.8	1.2	71.0	120.9	-1.8	-3.2	59.6	32.4	92.0	118.6	-6.1	5.3 •	COLONY INS CO
3.7	2.4	N/A	N/A	N/A	N/A	N/A	N/A	N/A	-16.9	0.0	0.0	COLONY SPECIALTY INS CO
54.0	48.6	N/A	N/A	N/A	N/A	N/A	N/A	N/A	N/A	0.0	0.0	COLORADO CASUALTY INS CO
3.0	2.4	74.1	30.8	-11.9	-15.2	75.9	21.6	97.5	88.6	0.5	2.3	COLORADO FARM BUREAU MUTUAL INS
67.7	28.0	N/A	N/A	N/A	N/A	N/A	N/A	N/A	N/A	0.0	0.0 •	COLUMBIA CASUALTY CO
1.7	1.0	37.2	45.6	6.1	-0.1	78.3	21.4	99.7	96.4	-1.6	0.0	COLUMBIA FEDERAL INS CO
N/A	N/A	--	--	--	--	--	--	--	--	--	--	COLUMBIA INS CO
1.3	1.0	89.0	16.2	-21.0	-3.7	60.7	15.7	76.4	118.0	-1.1	34.9	COLUMBIA LLOYDS INS CO
2.0	1.8	76.3	54.0	-0.5	-3.4	68.2	30.8	99.0	97.4	13.7	26.6	COLUMBIA MUTUAL INS CO
3.4	2.4	95.5	67.6	-0.6	-4.0	68.2	29.7	97.9	112.8	13.7	0.0	COLUMBIA NATIONAL INS CO
4.2	3.8	21.7	N/A	N/A	N/A	N/A	48.8	48.8	191.5	14.7	0.0	COLUMBIA NATIONAL RRG INC
1.1	0.8	68.2	35.7	26.4	5.8	106.0	18.6	124.6	86.2	27.7	0.0	COMCARE PRO INS RECIPROCAL RRG
8.9	8.1	-136.4	N/A	N/A	N/A	N/A	14.2	N/A	-13.1	-156.2	10.4 •	COMMERCE & INDUSTRY INS CO
2.2	1.7	206.8	97.9	3.4	4.7	78.1	22.6	100.7	92.0	11.0	3.8 •	COMMERCE INS CO
2.2	1.8	204.0	96.6	3.6	4.7	78.1	19.9	98.0	94.3	-1.8	0.0	COMMERCE WEST INS CO
1.6	1.0	87.5	62.9	4.1	8.9	67.0	32.7	99.7	130.7	3.3	0.0	COMMERCIAL ALLIANCE INS CO
N/A	N/A	--	--	--	--	--	--	--	--	--	--	COMMERCIAL CASUALTY INS CO
1.9	1.4	101.6	11.7	N/A	N/A	35.5	28.1	63.6	380.0	0.0	0.0	COMMERCIAL HIRECAR INS CO RRG
0.0	0.0	544.6	674.2	9.5	40.7	76.4	80.1	156.5	91.3	-17.7	0.0	COMMERCIAL MUT INS CO
0.0	0.0	279.7	57.7	-0.5	12.7	73.7	30.1	103.8	99.6	498.6	0.0	COMMONWEALTH CASUALTY CO
N/A	N/A	--	--	--	--	--	--	--	--	--	--	COMMONWEALTH INS CO OF AMERICA
4.6	2.8	8.8	10.1	-3.0	-3.4	21.9	46.5	68.4	154.3	18.6	0.0	COMMUNITIES OF FAITH RRG INC
6.8	4.2	12.6	10.8	-1.0	-10.1	6.8	42.5	49.3	209.4	-30.3	0.0	COMMUNITY BLOOD CENTERS
1.6	1.2	96.2	113.1	14.4	N/A	76.1	17.1	93.2	530.6	1.5	0.0	COMMUNITY CARE RRG INC
N/A	N/A	--	--	--	--	--	--	--	--	--	--	COMMUNITY HEALTH ALLIANCE RECIP
3.5	2.6	30.9	88.2	-5.2	-24.4	63.4	15.1	78.5	83.9	-6.2	0.0	COMMUNITY HOSPITAL ALTERNATIVE
11.2	10.1	N/A	N/A	N/A	N/A	N/A	N/A	N/A	92.5	0.0	0.0	COMMUNITY INS CORP
3.1	2.8	N/A	N/A	N/A	N/A	N/A	N/A	N/A	-146.5	0.0	7.7	COMMUNITY MUTUAL INS CO
N/A	N/A	--	--	--	--	--	--	--	--	--	--	COMPASS INS CO
3.4	2.0	76.9	9.4	N/A	N/A	33.4	32.4	65.8	193.1	0.0	0.0	COMPASS SPCLTY INS RRG INC

999 + Denotes number greater than 999.9%
999 - Denotes number less than -999.99%
• Bullets denote a more detailed analysis is available in Section II.

INSURANCE COMPANY NAME	DOM. STATE	RATING	TOTAL ASSETS ($MIL)	CAPITAL & SURPLUS ($MIL)	ANNUAL NET PREMIUM ($MIL)	NET INCOME ($MIL)	CAPITAL-IZATION INDEX (PTS)	RESERVE ADQ INDEX (PTS)	PROFIT-ABILITY INDEX (PTS)	LIQUIDITY INDEX (PTS)	STAB. INDEX (PTS)	STABILITY FACTORS
COMPTRUST AGC MUT CAPTIVE INS CO	GA	C	35.7	15.4	16.1	1.1	4.5	9.4	4.4	6.9	3.6	DGT
COMPUTER INS CO	RI	U	--	--	--	--	N/A	--	--	--	--	Z
▲COMPWEST INS CO	CA	B-	206.3	141.0	48.4	4.9	10.0	5.9	8.7	7.3	5.0	T
CONCORD GENERAL MUTUAL INS CO	NH	B-	473.5	251.5	162.5	3.2	8.1	8.5	6.8	6.8	4.1	T
CONEMAUGH VALLEY MUTUAL INS CO	PA	C	13.9	6.6	3.6	0.0	8.8	8.1	6.9	7.2	2.7	DGRT
CONIFER INS CO	MI	D-	95.8	29.3	57.4	-0.3	0.7	4.7	2.9	5.2	1.0	CT
CONNECTICUT MEDICAL INS CO	CT	B	509.6	298.0	34.1	-1.1	7.3	9.3	5.0	7.8	4.2	RT
CONSOLIDATED INS ASSN	TX	U	--	--	--	--	N/A	--	--	--	--	Z
CONSOLIDATED INS CO	IN	C	13.4	13.1	0.0	0.1	10.0	N/A	3.8	7.0	3.1	DGRT
CONSOLIDATED LLOYDS	TX	U	--	--	--	--	N/A	--	--	--	--	Z
CONSTITUTION INS CO	NY	C	25.2	22.3	5.1	0.7	10.0	3.8	8.3	8.7	3.0	DGT
CONSUMER SPECIALTIES INS CO RRG	VT	D+	4.2	2.5	0.5	0.0	7.6	8.4	1.9	7.2	2.0	DFGR
CONSUMERS COUNTY MUTUAL INS CO	TX	D	228.1	2.3	0.0	0.0	0.7	N/A	6.2	0.0	1.8	CDGL
CONSUMERS INS USA INC	TN	B	71.8	32.4	21.4	-0.3	8.9	5.0	4.6	6.9	5.6	DFT
CONTINENTAL CASUALTY CO	IL	C+	43,255.0	10,414.8	5,997.0	262.5	7.8	6.3	5.3	7.0	3.3	ART
CONTINENTAL DIVIDE INS CO	CO	C+	17.2	13.3	0.0	0.3	10.0	N/A	8.9	10.0	3.3	DGT
CONTINENTAL HERITAGE INS CO	FL	C	21.5	20.5	3.4	0.1	10.0	7.2	8.0	9.5	2.7	DGRT
CONTINENTAL INDEMNITY CO	IA	C	203.6	103.3	54.6	3.9	8.6	8.2	9.0	7.9	3.8	RT
CONTINENTAL INS CO	PA	C	1,694.4	1,519.1	0.0	14.1	10.0	3.7	6.2	7.0	4.2	ART
CONTINENTAL INS CO OF NJ	NJ	C (1)	18.7	18.7	0.0	0.4	10.0	N/A	6.3	10.0	3.3	ADRT
CONTINENTAL MUTUAL INS CO	PA	D	1.7	1.4	1.6	0.0	7.1	6.2	8.4	6.4	1.8	DGRT
CONTINENTAL RISK UNDERWRITERS RRG	NV	U (5)	--	--	--	--	N/A	--	--	--	--	Z
CONTINENTAL WESTERN INS CO	IA	C	220.3	92.7	0.0	0.5	10.0	N/A	7.1	7.0	4.3	T
CONTINUING CARE RRG INC	VT	E	6.3	1.6	4.8	0.2	1.2	2.3	1.0	0.0	0.3	CDFG
CONTRACTORS BONDING & INS CO	IL	B	217.7	117.0	67.7	2.4	10.0	9.4	7.5	7.0	4.0	RT
▲CONTRACTORS INS CO OF NORTH AMER	HI	C-	37.5	27.5	3.2	1.6	8.7	5.0	5.5	7.0	3.0	DGT
CONTROLLED RISK INS CO OF VT RRG	VT	B-	152.1	39.5	20.8	0.6	9.4	6.8	8.2	7.4	5.3	T
CONVENTUS INTER-INS	NJ	B- (1)	92.4	41.4	15.2	2.2	10.0	9.4	7.4	8.0	5.0	D
COOPERATIVA D SEGUROS MULTIPLES D	PR	B-	496.6	151.5	198.4	4.2	8.1	6.2	4.1	7.0	4.0	RT
COPIC A RRG	DC	U (1)	--	--	--	--	N/A	--	--	--	--	Z
▲COPIC INS CO	CO	A-	716.3	417.7	100.4	1.2	10.0	9.4	7.7	8.1	7.0	T
COPPERPOINT AMERICAN INS CO	AZ	C+	6.7	5.4	0.0	-0.1	10.0	N/A	3.5	7.0	3.0	DGT
COPPERPOINT CASUALTY INS CO	AZ	C+	7.1	4.4	0.0	-0.1	10.0	N/A	2.7	6.9	3.5	DG
COPPERPOINT GENERAL INS CO	AZ	B-	15.9	9.8	0.0	-0.1	10.0	N/A	3.3	10.0	4.4	DG
COPPERPOINT INDEMNITY INS CO	AZ	C	10.7	7.5	0.0	-0.1	10.0	N/A	3.5	10.0	2.8	DGT
COPPERPOINT MUTUAL INS CO	AZ	A+	3,655.7	1,385.9	247.6	12.2	8.5	6.9	6.7	7.6	7.7	T
COPPERPOINT NATIONAL INS CO	AZ	C	7.1	4.6	0.0	0.0	10.0	N/A	2.8	6.9	2.6	DGT
COPPERPOINT PREMIER INS CO	AZ	U	--	--	--	--	N/A	--	--	--	--	Z
COPPERPOINT WESTERN INS CO	AZ	B-	8.7	5.0	0.0	-0.1	10.0	N/A	3.6	7.0	3.6	DG
COREPOINTE INS CO	MI	C-	89.1	56.5	10.3	0.4	9.5	9.3	2.3	6.9	2.9	DGRT
CORNERSTONE MUTUAL INS CO	GA	F (5)	0.0	0.0	7.9	0.0	0.3	3.2	0.8	0.1	0.3	CDFL
CORNERSTONE NATIONAL INS CO	MO	C-	31.4	9.1	28.7	-0.7	5.5	6.9	2.0	3.0	3.0	DFGL
COUNTRY CASUALTY INS CO	IL	B+	85.4	69.6	0.0	0.1	10.0	N/A	6.5	10.0	5.0	T
COUNTRY MUTUAL INS CO	IL	A-	4,756.8	2,425.9	2,023.8	2.5	9.9	5.5	6.8	6.2	5.9	T
COUNTRY PREFERRED INS CO	IL	B	255.8	70.8	0.0	0.2	10.0	N/A	7.5	9.5	4.6	T
COUNTRY-WIDE INS CO	NY	D-	247.0	34.4	90.6	0.1	0.9	0.4	2.0	6.0	0.9	CRT
COUNTRYWAY INS CO	NY	C	28.1	24.1	0.0	0.2	10.0	3.7	7.0	9.6	3.9	DFG
COUNTY HALL INS CO INC A RRG	NC	D	6.1	2.0	3.6	-0.2	5.5	N/A	2.8	7.0	0.6	DGT
COURTESY INS CO	FL	B	810.4	384.1	128.8	1.1	10.0	6.0	8.7	7.1	4.2	RT
COVENANT INS CO	CT	C	87.0	27.4	40.7	0.9	7.6	8.0	5.1	6.0	3.7	T
COVENTRY INS CO	RI	U	--	--	--	--	N/A	--	--	--	--	Z
COVERYS RRG INC	DC	C-	33.9	13.5	0.9	-0.3	4.4	4.6	2.5	6.6	2.5	DGT

See Page 27 for explanation of footnotes and
Page 28 for explanation of stability factors.
Arrows denote recent upgrades ▲ or downgrades ▼   (see Section VII for explanations)

54

www.weissratings.com

RISK ADJ. RATIO #1	CAPITAL RATIO #2	PREMIUM TO SURPLUS (%)	RESV. TO SURPLUS (%)	RESV. DEVELOP. 1 YEAR (%)	RESV. DEVELOP. 2 YEAR (%)	LOSS RATIO (%)	EXP. RATIO (%)	COMB RATIO (%)	CASH FROM UNDER- WRITING (%)	NET PREMIUM GROWTH (%)	INVEST. IN AFFIL (%)	INSURANCE COMPANY NAME
1.1	0.9	113.3	96.0	-8.2	-14.7	49.0	42.0	91.0	119.0	28.5	0.0	COMPTRUST AGC MUT CAPTIVE INS CO
N/A	N/A	--	--	--	--	--	--	--	--	--	--	COMPUTER INS CO
7.7	6.6	35.8	41.2	-0.7	-0.2	62.9	17.3	80.2	133.8	13.8	0.0	COMPWEST INS CO
2.6	1.7	66.1	29.1	-4.2	-5.1	60.5	34.6	95.1	104.4	-0.9	5.6 ●	CONCORD GENERAL MUTUAL INS CO
3.1	2.1	54.5	18.7	-1.5	-3.1	47.6	50.1	97.7	107.8	98.3	0.0	CONEMAUGH VALLEY MUTUAL INS CO
0.3	0.2	194.3	102.5	14.0	12.6	65.5	35.4	100.9	102.3	39.5	0.0	CONIFER INS CO
1.3	1.1	11.5	46.3	0.4	-4.1	93.7	31.8	125.5	87.4	7.3	0.0 ●	CONNECTICUT MEDICAL INS CO
N/A	N/A	--	--	--	--	--	--	--	--	--	--	CONSOLIDATED INS ASSN
96.8	87.1	N/A	N/A	N/A	N/A	N/A	N/A	N/A	N/A	0.0	0.0	CONSOLIDATED INS CO
N/A	N/A	--	--	--	--	--	--	--	--	--	--	CONSOLIDATED LLOYDS
9.4	6.0	23.8	9.3	-6.4	-5.9	4.7	49.9	54.6	243.5	-26.5	0.0	CONSTITUTION INS CO
2.0	1.4	19.5	51.4	-5.8	-5.3	82.3	105.0	187.3	44.6	-3.7	0.0	CONSUMER SPECIALTIES INS CO RRG
0.2	0.2	N/A	N/A	N/A	N/A	N/A	N/A	N/A	101.7	0.0	0.0	CONSUMERS COUNTY MUTUAL INS CO
3.8	2.8	66.0	48.7	-0.5	-1.3	64.1	37.9	102.0	85.9	-0.4	0.0	CONSUMERS INS USA INC
1.9	1.4	55.8	167.4	-1.6	-3.5	82.5	32.1	114.6	87.9	-0.7	10.8 ●	CONTINENTAL CASUALTY CO
10.7	9.6	N/A	5.3	N/A	N/A	N/A	N/A	N/A	-26.6	0.0	0.0	CONTINENTAL DIVIDE INS CO
7.5	6.4	20.6	3.1	-0.2	-0.3	14.5	69.1	83.6	146.1	80.1	0.0	CONTINENTAL HERITAGE INS CO
3.1	2.4	56.1	53.4	3.7	-1.1	43.9	28.7	72.6	196.1	-4.6	0.0	CONTINENTAL INDEMNITY CO
6.3	3.4	N/A	56.6	8.1	10.4	N/A	N/A	N/A	-91.7	0.0	9.8 ●	CONTINENTAL INS CO
58.0	25.3	N/A	N/A	N/A	N/A	N/A	N/A	N/A	N/A	0.0	0.0	CONTINENTAL INS CO OF NJ
1.3	1.2	116.8	4.3	-1.8	-6.1	28.5	66.9	95.4	104.4	-2.7	0.0	CONTINENTAL MUTUAL INS CO
N/A	N/A	--	--	--	--	--	--	--	--	--	--	CONTINENTAL RISK UNDERWRITERS
10.0	9.0	N/A	N/A	N/A	N/A	N/A	N/A	N/A	98.2	0.0	0.0	CONTINENTAL WESTERN INS CO
0.4	0.3	363.1	178.2	41.3	72.2	71.3	25.6	96.9	96.7	16.2	0.0	CONTINUING CARE RRG INC
5.4	4.3	57.8	41.2	-7.1	-12.3	30.7	48.0	78.7	134.9	7.4	0.0	CONTRACTORS BONDING & INS CO
5.2	3.8	12.3	38.2	7.7	18.7	155.4	42.2	197.6	-264.8	-10.8	0.0	CONTRACTORS INS CO OF NORTH
2.9	2.4	53.3	39.6	-0.3	0.2	34.3	57.3	91.6	131.1	22.0	0.0	CONTROLLED RISK INS CO OF VT RRG
4.8	3.9	36.7	70.2	-7.5	-11.8	60.8	33.8	94.6	109.2	19.1	0.0	CONVENTUS INTER-INS
2.5	1.6	133.7	24.0	-2.1	-5.0	62.8	36.6	99.4	99.9	12.5	5.9	COOPERATIVA D SEGUROS MULTIPLES
N/A	N/A	--	--	--	--	--	--	--	--	--	--	COPIC A RRG
5.8	3.8	24.5	49.6	-4.3	-12.9	63.6	23.7	87.3	159.4	22.3	0.0 ●	COPIC INS CO
9.9	8.9	N/A	N/A	N/A	N/A	N/A	N/A	N/A	41.5	0.0	0.0	COPPERPOINT AMERICAN INS CO
4.8	4.4	N/A	N/A	N/A	N/A	N/A	N/A	N/A	509.9	0.0	0.0	COPPERPOINT CASUALTY INS CO
5.6	5.1	N/A	N/A	N/A	N/A	N/A	N/A	N/A	649.4	0.0	0.0	COPPERPOINT GENERAL INS CO
7.2	6.5	N/A	N/A	N/A	N/A	N/A	N/A	N/A	-689.7	0.0	0.0	COPPERPOINT INDEMNITY INS CO
3.2	2.0	18.3	152.7	-0.9	-0.4	76.2	33.7	109.9	81.3	2.3	1.7 ●	COPPERPOINT MUTUAL INS CO
5.4	4.9	N/A	N/A	N/A	N/A	N/A	N/A	N/A	242.2	0.0	0.0	COPPERPOINT NATIONAL INS CO
N/A	N/A	--	--	--	--	--	--	--	--	--	--	COPPERPOINT PREMIER INS CO
4.3	3.8	N/A	N/A	N/A	N/A	N/A	N/A	N/A	-59.4	0.0	0.0	COPPERPOINT WESTERN INS CO
3.4	2.8	18.3	20.2	8.0	-17.3	77.5	81.2	158.7	79.3	209.2	11.5	COREPOINTE INS CO
0.1	0.1	172.5	213.5	6.7	29.5	76.4	86.4	162.8	67.9	-17.7	0.0	CORNERSTONE MUTUAL INS CO
0.8	0.7	280.2	119.9	-3.8	-9.0	80.6	29.7	110.3	81.3	9.7	0.0	CORNERSTONE NATIONAL INS CO
22.7	20.4	N/A	N/A	N/A	N/A	N/A	N/A	N/A	130.6	0.0	0.0 ●	COUNTRY CASUALTY INS CO
4.5	3.2	91.7	47.8	0.5	-1.1	71.6	29.0	100.6	98.6	0.0	4.0 ●	COUNTRY MUTUAL INS CO
7.2	5.5	N/A	N/A	N/A	N/A	N/A	N/A	N/A	999 +	0.0	0.0	COUNTRY PREFERRED INS CO
0.2	0.2	266.0	400.7	45.5	60.8	109.4	7.5	116.9	85.8	2.5	1.3	COUNTRY-WIDE INS CO
19.1	17.2	N/A	N/A	N/A	N/A	N/A	N/A	N/A	-251.2	0.0	0.0	COUNTRYWAY INS CO
1.3	0.8	184.6	9.5	N/A	N/A	78.5	2.3	80.8	99.3	0.0	0.0	COUNTY HALL INS CO INC A RRG
9.5	5.4	34.1	6.2	0.7	0.6	85.7	15.2	100.9	106.1	-5.0	0.0 ●	COURTESY INS CO
2.3	1.5	153.2	84.1	-6.1	-3.4	64.1	32.3	96.4	106.8	1.7	0.0	COVENANT INS CO
N/A	N/A	--	--	--	--	--	--	--	--	--	--	COVENTRY INS CO
2.9	2.1	24.0	78.4	1.4	0.8	227.8	-25.8	202.0	999 +	22.2	0.0	COVERYS RRG INC

999 + Denotes number greater than 999.9%
999 - Denotes number less than -999.99%
● Bullets denote a more detailed analysis is available in Section II.

INSURANCE COMPANY NAME	DOM. STATE	RATING	TOTAL ASSETS ($MIL)	CAPITAL & SURPLUS ($MIL)	ANNUAL NET PREMIUM ($MIL)	NET INCOME ($MIL)	CAPITAL- IZATION INDEX (PTS)	RESERVE ADQ INDEX (PTS)	PROFIT- ABILITY INDEX (PTS)	LIQUIDITY INDEX (PTS)	STAB. INDEX (PTS)	STABILITY FACTORS
COVERYS SPECIALTY INS CO	NJ	B	63.9	51.9	0.0	0.3	10.0	N/A	4.9	8.8	4.3	DT
COVINGTON SPECIALTY INS CO	NH	B	98.0	46.8	14.7	0.4	9.6	5.9	4.8	7.6	6.3	T
CPA MUTL INS CO OF AM (A RRG)	VT	C-	16.5	5.8	4.0	0.3	4.6	6.7	1.8	8.0	2.4	DGRT
CRESTBROOK INS CO	OH	B	143.2	83.1	0.0	0.4	10.0	N/A	3.6	7.1	4.5	AT
CRONUS INSURANCE CO	TX	U	--	--	--	--	N/A	--	--	--	--	Z
CROSSFIT RRG INC	MT	C	6.6	2.7	2.5	-0.1	1.7	1.8	5.1	7.0	2.3	CDFG
CROWN CAPTIVE INS CO	GA	D	2.0	1.0	0.6	0.0	7.7	7.0	8.6	9.2	1.4	DGT
CROWN CAPTIVE INS CO INC	DC	D	5.8	2.0	3.7	0.0	4.8	4.0	2.9	5.1	1.7	DGT
CRUDEN BAY RRG INC	VT	D	17.3	7.3	2.0	0.2	7.9	10.0	6.3	9.1	0.9	DGT
CRUM & FORSTER INDEMNITY CO	DE	D+	53.2	17.0	18.0	0.5	7.0	5.9	6.4	8.1	2.7	DRT
CRUM & FORSTER INS CO	NJ	D+(1)	52.4	18.1	18.0	0.3	7.2	5.9	6.7	8.5	2.7	DT
CRUM & FORSTER SPECIALTY INS CO	DE	D+	71.5	50.0	0.0	0.1	10.0	N/A	7.2	10.0	2.7	FRT
CRUSADER INS CO	CA	B-	118.0	57.2	32.6	-1.9	10.0	9.2	3.3	8.0	3.6	FRT
CRYSTAL RUN RECIPROCAL RRG	VT	E	21.3	2.8	5.5	-0.2	0.1	0.6	2.9	9.2	0.2	CDGT
CSAA AFFINITY INS CO	AZ	C	236.4	155.2	52.5	-0.5	10.0	6.1	4.7	6.8	3.5	RT
CSAA FIRE & CASUALTY INS CO	IN	C	145.2	48.3	17.5	0.0	10.0	6.1	6.6	6.8	3.9	T
CSAA GENERAL INS CO	IN	C	349.8	152.4	104.9	-0.3	10.0	6.1	6.4	6.6	3.9	T
CSAA INS EXCHANGE	CA	B-	7,009.7	3,443.4	3,290.5	-20.3	9.0	6.1	2.9	6.1	4.8	RT
CSAA MID-ATLANTIC INS CO	AZ	C-	39.2	24.2	10.5	0.0	10.0	6.1	5.8	6.8	3.2	DGRT
CSAA MID-ATLANTIC INS CO OF NJ	NJ	C-	55.3	24.6	21.0	-0.1	9.7	6.1	3.5	6.5	3.3	DT
CSE SAFEGUARD INS CO	CA	C+	87.9	36.6	50.5	-3.0	9.0	6.2	3.4	6.0	3.7	RT
CUMBERLAND INS CO	NJ	B-	104.5	54.3	22.3	-0.3	10.0	8.3	6.1	6.9	4.8	DFRT
CUMBERLAND MUTUAL FIRE INS CO	NJ	B-	275.4	160.7	95.6	2.8	8.4	6.4	5.4	6.7	4.0	RT
▲CUMIS INS SOCIETY INC	IA	A-	1,894.2	885.4	820.9	13.6	10.0	9.2	8.8	6.3	6.9	T
CUMIS MORTGAGE REINS CO	WI	C+	13.1	9.6	2.7	-0.1	10.0	3.6	3.8	7.5	3.1	DGT
CUMIS SPECIALTY INS CO INC	IA	B	56.7	53.6	0.0	0.4	10.0	4.8	3.6	10.0	4.1	DT
CYPRESS INS CO	CA	C+	1,573.5	397.3	428.9	14.1	5.0	9.3	8.5	9.0	4.4	CGT
CYPRESS P&C INS CO	FL	C	91.9	28.3	35.5	-1.5	7.1	9.5	2.1	6.0	3.7	FT
CYPRESS TEXAS INS CO	TX	D	56.5	11.8	25.5	-2.8	1.6	8.5	2.6	7.2	2.0	CDGT
DAILY UNDERWRITERS OF AMERICA	PA	C+	44.3	33.2	12.6	0.8	8.6	3.3	8.4	7.3	3.2	DT
DAIRYLAND COUNTY MUTUAL INS CO OF TX	TX	B	13.3	12.5	0.0	0.0	10.0	N/A	5.1	9.4	4.9	DGT
DAIRYLAND INS CO	WI	B+	1,297.4	484.6	352.2	4.8	9.6	8.0	5.6	6.8	5.3	T
DAKOTA FIRE INS CO	ND	C	229.9	68.0	100.5	0.7	7.9	8.7	8.4	6.5	4.3	T
DAKOTA TRUCK UNDERWRITERS	SD	C+	115.9	47.2	36.6	1.5	8.0	6.2	8.9	6.7	3.4	RT
DAN RRG INC	SC	D	2.1	1.0	0.0	0.0	7.7	N/A	3.1	9.3	0.8	DGT
DANBURY INS CO	MA	C	12.2	7.6	4.3	0.1	9.1	8.1	5.2	6.8	2.8	DGRT
DANIELSON NATIONAL INS CO	CA	U	--	--	--	--	N/A	--	--	--	--	Z
DE SMET FARM MUTUAL INS CO OF SD	SD	C+	31.5	18.2	12.9	0.9	7.7	5.9	6.7	6.5	3.0	DGRT
DE SMET INS CO OF SD	SD	C	16.1	7.6	10.1	0.5	7.7	8.3	3.6	5.8	2.6	DGRT
DEALERS ASR CO	OH	B-	109.4	62.9	11.3	1.4	10.0	4.6	8.8	9.3	3.6	RT
DEALERS CHOICE MUTUAL INS INC	NC	C-	24.7	7.6	6.7	-0.1	3.7	7.0	3.4	6.4	2.2	DFGT
DELAWARE GRANGE MUTUAL FIRE INS CO	DE	D	1.5	1.3	0.2	0.0	8.6	4.6	5.2	7.8	1.2	DFGR
DELAWARE PROFESSIONAL INS CO	DE	D (5)	5.1	1.4	0.9	-0.5	2.8	10.0	0.7	5.7	1.4	CDFT
DELPHI CASUALTY CO	IL	D (1)	2.7	2.1	-0.6	0.2	9.3	1.2	3.4	2.7	2.2	DFLT
DELTA FIRE & CAS INS CO	GA	C-	7.6	5.8	1.9	0.0	7.9	8.5	4.5	6.7	2.9	DFGR
DELTA LLOYDS INS CO OF HOUSTON	TX	D+	6.5	5.3	0.1	0.0	8.4	4.2	1.5	6.9	2.1	DFGR
DENTISTS BENEFITS INS CO	OR	C	17.6	12.8	4.6	0.4	9.1	8.6	5.8	6.9	2.8	DFGT
DENTISTS INS CO	CA	B	325.8	182.1	63.5	2.7	9.2	8.8	6.1	7.5	4.1	RT
DEPOSITORS INS CO	IA	B-	309.2	37.3	0.0	0.1	10.0	N/A	6.0	6.8	3.8	FT
▼DEVELOPERS SURETY & INDEMNITY CO	CA	D	146.1	101.7	0.1	2.7	2.9	9.0	8.4	10.0	2.1	CFRT
DIAMOND INS CO	IL	D	49.0	8.8	19.7	0.0	1.6	5.9	4.5	6.9	1.5	CDRT
DIAMOND STATE INS CO	IN	B-	126.6	66.2	32.3	-0.2	9.0	6.5	6.2	7.0	3.9	RT

See Page 27 for explanation of footnotes and
Page 28 for explanation of stability factors.
Arrows denote recent upgrades ▲ or downgrades ▼   (see Section VII for explanations)

56

www.weissratings.com

RISK ADJ. CAPITAL RATIO #1	CAPITAL RATIO #2	PREMIUM TO SURPLUS (%)	RESV. TO SURPLUS (%)	RESV. DEVELOP. 1 YEAR (%)	RESV. DEVELOP. 2 YEAR (%)	LOSS RATIO (%)	EXP. RATIO (%)	COMB RATIO (%)	CASH FROM UNDER- WRITING (%)	NET PREMIUM GROWTH (%)	INVEST. IN AFFIL (%)	INSURANCE COMPANY NAME
19.6	17.6	N/A	N/A	N/A	N/A	N/A	N/A	N/A	-240.0	0.0	0.0	COVERYS SPECIALTY INS CO
5.3	2.7	31.8	39.8	0.4	1.7	69.1	28.5	97.6	120.0	-8.8	0.0	COVINGTON SPECIALTY INS CO
1.0	0.8	76.3	131.9	-5.3	-3.2	89.0	23.4	112.4	95.8	6.6	0.0	CPA MUTL INS CO OF AM (A RRG)
11.5	10.3	N/A	N/A	N/A	N/A	N/A	N/A	N/A	102.0	0.0	0.0	CRESTBROOK INS CO
N/A	N/A	--	--	--	--	--	--	--	--	--	--	CRONUS INSURANCE CO
0.5	0.3	90.4	68.6	18.4	24.4	45.7	50.7	96.4	97.5	16.4	0.0	CROSSFIT RRG INC
2.1	1.9	65.7	66.5	-9.9	-13.0	54.0	23.6	77.6	179.8	67.4	0.0	CROWN CAPTIVE INS CO
1.1	0.8	192.3	156.7	-9.3	18.1	60.4	31.6	92.0	98.5	13.6	0.0	CROWN CAPTIVE INS CO INC
2.3	1.7	28.2	113.3	-86.0	-123.8	66.6	11.3	77.9	195.0	-33.3	0.0	CRUDEN BAY RRG INC
1.7	1.0	109.0	153.0	-1.3	-2.0	63.7	34.6	98.3	106.2	8.5	0.0	CRUM & FORSTER INDEMNITY CO
1.8	1.1	99.9	140.3	-1.2	-1.8	63.7	34.5	98.2	110.4	8.5	0.0	CRUM & FORSTER INS CO
13.6	12.2	N/A	N/A	N/A	N/A	N/A	N/A	N/A	151.2	0.0	0.0	CRUM & FORSTER SPECIALTY INS CO
3.2	2.8	55.2	63.5	-0.3	-5.2	72.4	31.2	103.6	94.8	5.1	0.0	CRUSADER INS CO
0.1	0.1	189.1	398.4	80.8	80.3	80.9	17.7	98.6	142.6	77.7	0.0	CRYSTAL RUN RECIPROCAL RRG
3.3	3.1	33.7	16.2	-0.8	-0.4	75.0	28.7	103.7	96.2	5.6	25.0	CSAA AFFINITY INS CO
5.4	4.9	36.7	17.6	-0.8	-0.5	75.0	16.8	91.8	189.6	5.6	0.0	CSAA FIRE & CASUALTY INS CO
6.8	5.0	69.1	33.1	-1.5	-0.9	75.0	25.6	100.6	94.6	5.6	0.0	CSAA GENERAL INS CO
3.4	2.3	97.1	46.6	-2.1	-1.0	75.0	28.8	103.8	101.0	5.6	4.8 ●	CSAA INS EXCHANGE
7.2	5.3	43.3	20.8	-1.0	-0.5	75.0	27.2	102.2	103.5	5.6	0.0	CSAA MID-ATLANTIC INS CO
3.7	2.7	85.2	40.9	-1.8	-1.0	75.0	27.6	102.6	103.8	5.6	0.0	CSAA MID-ATLANTIC INS CO OF NJ
3.3	2.4	128.4	51.2	0.7	-0.5	71.8	32.7	104.5	95.9	1.3	0.0	CSE SAFEGUARD INS CO
6.2	3.8	41.2	66.1	-1.6	-2.0	70.4	31.7	102.1	93.2	-1.2	0.0	CUMBERLAND INS CO
2.4	2.0	60.7	32.1	0.1	1.3	62.7	34.7	97.4	107.9	-0.4	21.2	CUMBERLAND MUTUAL FIRE INS CO
5.2	3.7	94.4	44.7	-6.6	-11.2	64.8	29.8	94.6	107.3	-0.7	4.1 ●	CUMIS INS SOCIETY INC
3.5	3.2	27.9	1.6	-0.3	N/A	4.8	80.5	85.3	246.4	163.7	0.0	CUMIS MORTGAGE REINS CO
54.0	46.4	N/A	N/A	N/A	N/A	N/A	N/A	N/A	999 +	100.0	0.0	CUMIS SPECIALTY INS CO INC
1.0	0.7	117.2	228.6	-16.2	-18.8	68.0	20.3	88.3	191.6	31.2	9.5 ●	CYPRESS INS CO
1.6	1.0	118.8	53.2	0.6	-17.9	69.7	74.2	143.9	69.3	-42.7	0.0	CYPRESS P&C INS CO
0.4	0.3	194.0	76.1	-22.1	-0.4	48.2	45.4	93.6	110.8	75.3	0.0	CYPRESS TEXAS INS CO
3.3	2.4	39.5	13.7	5.8	9.8	51.0	32.3	83.3	118.9	2.5	0.0	DAILY UNDERWRITERS OF AMERICA
36.6	32.9	N/A	N/A	N/A	N/A	N/A	N/A	N/A	21.5	0.0	0.0	DAIRYLAND COUNTY MUTUAL INS CO OF
4.2	2.6	74.1	116.2	-0.9	-2.8	73.9	28.2	102.1	104.2	7.2	0.0 ●	DAIRYLAND INS CO
2.5	1.6	151.2	154.4	-8.5	-9.6	64.6	31.9	96.5	106.9	2.0	0.0	DAKOTA FIRE INS CO
2.1	1.7	80.9	105.2	-3.4	-1.7	67.5	20.8	88.3	123.6	6.4	7.6	DAKOTA TRUCK UNDERWRITERS
1.8	1.7	3.2	1.1	N/A	N/A	555.4	34.2	589.6	999 +	0.0	0.0	DAN RRG INC
3.9	2.6	57.4	20.3	-1.7	-2.1	48.0	46.0	94.0	109.3	0.1	0.0	DANBURY INS CO
N/A	N/A	--	--	--	--	--	--	--	--	--	--	DANIELSON NATIONAL INS CO
1.9	1.7	76.7	22.1	6.0	2.9	66.7	27.3	94.0	115.7	2.3	25.2	DE SMET FARM MUTUAL INS CO OF SD
2.1	1.6	142.8	73.6	-2.5	-5.6	83.7	15.4	99.1	105.4	0.4	0.0	DE SMET INS CO OF SD
9.8	6.5	18.5	0.3	N/A	0.7	11.0	28.5	39.5	285.0	-21.6	0.0	DEALERS ASR CO
0.9	0.6	88.9	213.6	-28.5	-33.7	68.9	30.0	98.9	81.0	6.5	0.0	DEALERS CHOICE MUTUAL INS INC
3.6	2.2	15.3	4.2	-0.6	N/A	68.5	42.7	111.2	67.7	-8.2	0.0	DELAWARE GRANGE MUTUAL FIRE INS
0.5	0.4	63.7	190.5	-60.3	-57.8	58.0	103.7	161.7	36.5	31.8	0.0	DELAWARE PROFESSIONAL INS CO
6.4	5.8	-26.6	N/A	N/A	N/A	76.1	8.1	84.2	32.1	-120.9	0.0	DELPHI CASUALTY CO
1.8	1.5	34.2	5.2	-4.1	-6.3	26.5	100.0	126.5	77.9	0.5	20.1	DELTA FIRE & CAS INS CO
3.1	1.8	2.1	18.7	5.2	15.2	217.4	291.7	509.1	9.5	-89.2	0.0	DELTA LLOYDS INS CO OF HOUSTON
4.9	3.0	37.4	22.2	4.4	-5.7	67.5	40.4	107.9	98.8	-0.7	0.0	DENTISTS BENEFITS INS CO
3.3	2.0	35.5	47.6	-2.0	-4.9	78.5	24.8	103.3	96.9	3.8	0.0	DENTISTS INS CO
3.5	3.1	N/A	N/A	N/A	N/A	N/A	N/A	N/A	7.9	0.0	3.3	DEPOSITORS INS CO
0.5	0.5	0.1	17.3	-19.9	-17.5	408.0	999 +	999 +	-107.3	-99.7	18.6	DEVELOPERS SURETY & INDEMNITY CO
0.5	0.3	228.5	316.2	10.8	10.2	76.0	26.5	102.5	105.1	-10.5	0.0	DIAMOND INS CO
5.1	3.2	50.5	50.5	-3.5	-6.7	67.1	18.5	85.6	103.3	-1.2	0.0	DIAMOND STATE INS CO

999 + Denotes number greater than 999.9%
999 - Denotes number less than -999.99%
● Bullets denote a more detailed analysis is available in Section II.

INSURANCE COMPANY NAME	DOM. STATE	RATING	TOTAL ASSETS ($MIL)	CAPITAL & SURPLUS ($MIL)	ANNUAL NET PREMIUM ($MIL)	NET INCOME ($MIL)	CAPITAL- IZATION INDEX (PTS)	RESERVE ADQ INDEX (PTS)	PROFIT- ABILITY INDEX (PTS)	LIQUIDITY INDEX (PTS)	STAB. INDEX (PTS)	STABILITY FACTORS
DIRECT AUTO INS CO	IL	D	52.7	10.1	28.6	0.1	2.3	10.0	8.7	7.7	2.2	CDT
DIRECT GENERAL INS CO	IN	C+	121.8	116.6	323.4	12.4	6.2	4.2	4.8	0.5	4.2	LRT
DIRECT GENERAL INS CO OF LA	LA	C-	12.4	11.4	9.7	0.8	7.3	4.3	2.4	2.7	2.9	DFGL
DIRECT GENERAL INS CO OF MS	MS	C-	11.9	11.7	28.3	1.0	6.4	6.5	5.1	2.4	3.3	DGLR
DIRECT INS CO	TN	C-	24.8	24.3	67.3	2.9	4.4	6.5	4.1	0.9	3.2	DLRT
DIRECT NATIONAL INS CO	AR	C+	6.9	5.3	11.6	0.2	6.2	6.9	2.2	1.3	3.4	DFGL
DISCOVER P&C INS CO	CT	C+	136.5	64.0	30.5	1.0	10.0	7.8	5.5	7.0	4.1	T
DISCOVER SPECIALTY INS CO	CT	C+	108.3	39.0	30.5	0.8	8.7	8.2	5.6	6.9	4.7	T
DISCOVERY INS CO	NC	C-	29.3	12.2	20.5	0.6	7.1	7.0	5.9	1.9	2.4	DFGL
DIST-CO INS CO INC RRG	HI	E	3.8	2.9	0.4	0.1	10.0	5.2	5.7	10.0	0.0	DFGT
▲DISTRICTS MUTL INS & RISK MGMT	WI	C-	23.2	14.0	5.4	0.3	8.6	9.5	4.9	7.5	3.0	DGT
DOCTORS & SURGEONS NATL RRG IC	VT	F (3)	9.1	1.1	5.4	0.0	1.0	4.3	0.6	7.3	0.0	CFGT
DOCTORS CO AN INTERINS	CA	B-	4,272.9	1,929.6	602.4	-23.1	7.8	8.8	3.7	7.1	4.7	RT
DOCTORS CO RRG A RECIPROCAL	DC	D+	22.2	3.4	1.1	-0.9	6.0	N/A	2.3	7.9	2.5	DGT
DOCTORS DIRECT INS INC	IL	C	14.3	6.6	2.3	0.0	7.9	9.4	6.4	7.2	2.6	DGR
DOCTORS PROF LIAB RRG INC	NC	D	2.4	1.2	0.8	0.0	8.2	N/A	5.7	9.2	0.9	DGT
DONEGAL MUTUAL INS CO	PA	B-	462.3	237.4	118.0	0.3	6.7	5.9	8.3	7.0	4.3	T
DONGBU INS CO LTD	HI	D	263.6	61.3	90.2	0.1	1.8	0.9	2.7	6.5	1.4	CRT
DONGBU INS CO LTD US GUAM BRANCH	GU	B-	61.8	41.9	14.6	0.2	9.7	8.8	8.5	7.5	3.8	T
DORCHESTER INS CO LTD	VI	C	21.1	12.0	3.9	0.1	9.7	9.4	6.4	7.8	3.0	DGRT
DORCHESTER MUTUAL INS CO	MA	C	88.8	43.7	30.0	0.7	8.3	5.9	6.8	6.8	3.7	RT
DORINCO REINS CO	MI	C-	1,538.0	549.5	172.7	11.4	7.1	7.0	6.3	6.7	2.6	T
▲DRIVE NEW JERSEY INS CO	NJ	B-	209.6	37.0	30.7	1.3	9.6	6.3	8.3	6.9	5.0	T
DRYDEN MUTUAL INS CO	NY	B	204.1	134.2	61.0	3.9	10.0	6.3	8.8	7.1	4.1	RT
DTRIC INS CO LTD	HI	C	104.8	26.8	48.1	1.2	5.2	9.3	2.7	6.1	3.5	RT
DTRIC INS UNDERWRITERS LTD	HI	C	12.5	4.7	0.0	0.0	8.8	N/A	7.9	6.5	3.5	DGR
DUBOIS MEDICAL RRG	DC	C	12.8	9.8	1.0	0.2	9.4	9.3	8.7	9.4	2.9	DG
EAGLE BUILDERS INS CO RRG INC	NC	U	--	--	--	--	N/A	--	--	--	--	Z
EAGLE POINT MUTUAL INS CO	WI	D+	5.2	3.6	1.1	0.0	7.4	3.6	8.5	6.9	2.0	DGT
EAGLE WEST INS CO	CA	C+	127.4	50.6	58.7	-0.6	7.8	4.4	4.9	5.8	4.7	T
EAGLESTONE REINS CO	PA	C	6,355.1	1,881.2	4.5	52.0	0.7	1.6	3.6	9.6	3.1	CGT
EASTERN ADVANTAGE ASR CO	PA	B-	58.4	15.2	17.0	0.3	5.3	4.6	8.9	6.2	5.1	CDFT
EASTERN ALLIANCE INS CO	PA	D	321.1	107.2	97.8	2.6	8.1	4.6	8.9	6.7	1.9	RT
EASTERN ATLANTIC INS CO	PA	C-	68.9	32.0	18.1	0.3	7.7	6.6	2.7	6.9	3.2	DFT
▲EASTERN DENTISTS INS CO RRG	VT	B-	55.0	24.8	10.7	0.2	7.8	9.5	8.5	6.9	4.9	DT
EASTERN MUTUAL INS CO	NY	C	25.4	16.4	5.9	0.2	10.0	9.2	8.6	6.9	3.2	DGT
EASTGUARD INS CO	PA	D+	155.0	46.5	45.9	1.3	1.8	9.3	8.7	2.9	2.6	CLRT
ECHELON P&C INS CO	IL	D	14.5	4.2	7.4	-0.1	1.7	2.2	1.6	5.6	2.0	CDGR
ECOLE INS CO	AZ	D	13.9	7.8	4.3	0.2	1.4	6.2	5.3	7.2	2.1	CDGT
ECONOMY FIRE & CAS CO	IL	B-	503.8	384.8	0.0	2.7	10.0	N/A	6.6	7.0	4.7	T
ECONOMY PREFERRED INS CO	IL	B	44.1	11.2	0.0	0.1	8.5	N/A	7.7	7.0	4.9	DT
ECONOMY PREMIER ASR CO	IL	B	82.6	49.5	0.0	0.4	10.0	N/A	7.9	10.0	4.3	T
EDISON INS CO	FL	D+	52.8	21.7	27.7	0.4	1.0	1.9	4.0	1.7	2.6	CDGL
ELECTRIC INS CO	MA	C+	1,577.7	539.7	329.3	7.1	8.7	9.3	6.0	6.7	3.4	RT
ELEMENTS PROPERTY INS CO	FL	D (1)	49.1	15.4	34.1	-13.0	1.5	4.6	1.0	1.5	1.8	CDFL
ELEPHANT INS CO	VA	C	236.2	45.6	67.7	-2.6	5.2	6.0	2.3	6.8	3.5	FGT
ELITE TRANSPORTATION RRG INC	VT	E-	14.4	1.1	6.1	0.1	0.0	0.5	0.7	0.0	0.0	CDGL
ELIZABETHTOWN INS CO	DE	U (5)	--	--	--	--	N/A	--	--	--	--	Z
ELLINGTON MUTUAL INS CO	WI	D+	6.3	3.6	2.5	-0.3	7.4	6.9	3.9	6.8	2.2	DGR
EMC PROPERTY & CASUALTY CO	IA	C	94.3	89.5	-24.0	0.5	10.0	4.7	8.5	9.0	4.2	T
EMC REINS CO	IA	B-	472.2	214.5	131.0	4.3	8.0	9.4	8.8	6.8	3.8	T
EMCASCO INS CO	IA	B-	484.2	147.4	208.7	1.7	8.0	8.6	8.4	6.6	4.5	T

See Page 27 for explanation of footnotes and
Page 28 for explanation of stability factors.
Arrows denote recent upgrades ▲ or downgrades ▼   (see Section VII for explanations)

58   www.weissratings.com

RISK ADJ. RATIO #1	CAPITAL RATIO #2	PREMIUM TO SURPLUS (%)	RESV. TO SURPLUS (%)	RESV. 1 YEAR (%)	DEVELOP. 2 YEAR (%)	LOSS RATIO (%)	EXP. RATIO (%)	COMB RATIO (%)	CASH FROM UNDER-WRITING (%)	NET PREMIUM GROWTH (%)	INVEST. IN AFFIL (%)	INSURANCE COMPANY NAME
0.5	0.4	292.8	302.2	-89.0	-136.2	51.8	39.4	91.2	147.7	10.3	0.0	DIRECT AUTO INS CO
1.1	1.0	286.2	103.8	3.6	-6.4	85.5	19.0	104.5	97.7	-4.8	12.9	DIRECT GENERAL INS CO
3.1	2.7	91.6	71.2	4.5	10.6	101.2	8.9	110.1	61.6	-51.4	0.0	DIRECT GENERAL INS CO OF LA
1.5	1.3	240.3	76.5	3.3	5.6	75.6	22.8	98.4	100.5	4.2	0.0	DIRECT GENERAL INS CO OF MS
1.1	1.0	285.7	92.0	1.9	5.4	79.4	22.2	101.6	95.2	4.6	0.0	DIRECT INS CO
1.5	1.2	211.5	64.2	7.2	4.9	86.9	29.9	116.8	86.8	-10.2	0.0	DIRECT NATIONAL INS CO
5.5	3.5	48.4	80.3	-1.0	-2.4	63.4	30.4	93.8	110.0	4.8	0.0	DISCOVER P&C INS CO
3.2	2.1	79.7	132.2	-1.6	-4.0	63.4	29.9	93.3	108.7	4.8	0.0	DISCOVER SPECIALTY INS CO
3.4	1.8	178.9	36.8	-10.3	-15.8	87.9	12.9	100.8	88.3	17.0	0.0	DISCOVERY INS CO
7.7	4.9	15.6	2.9	-0.6	-0.8	10.0	38.9	48.9	62.7	8.0	0.0	DIST-CO INS CO INC RRG
3.4	2.1	40.4	53.6	-12.2	-17.3	59.6	48.8	108.4	98.0	-1.4	0.0	DISTRICTS MUTL INS & RISK MGMT
0.2	0.2	302.1	366.1	-138.9	-29.6	67.7	32.1	99.8	80.1	44.6	0.0	DOCTORS & SURGEONS NATL RRG IC
1.9	1.5	31.3	77.3	-2.7	-6.8	77.7	25.0	102.7	110.5	-3.3	18.0 •	DOCTORS CO AN INTERINS
0.9	0.6	28.4	65.9	N/A	N/A	193.1	-47.9	145.2	541.7	24.6	0.0	DOCTORS CO RRG A RECIPROCAL
2.2	1.7	34.0	81.4	-3.3	-12.7	67.1	59.2	126.3	97.7	-6.1	0.0	DOCTORS DIRECT INS INC
2.4	2.0	73.2	10.8	N/A	N/A	58.0	9.8	67.8	266.2	0.0	0.0	DOCTORS PROF LIAB RRG INC
1.0	0.9	50.2	26.3	-0.2	0.5	59.1	29.4	88.5	142.0	7.5	65.1 •	DONEGAL MUTUAL INS CO
0.5	0.3	146.2	217.9	51.7	57.4	107.2	28.5	135.7	101.2	0.3	0.0	DONGBU INS CO LTD
6.8	4.1	34.0	9.0	0.4	-9.4	21.4	43.5	64.9	132.8	-9.3	0.0	DONGBU INS CO LTD US GUAM BRANCH
4.1	2.7	33.2	35.6	-4.9	-11.6	24.2	57.2	81.4	120.9	-0.6	0.0	DORCHESTER INS CO LTD
2.6	1.8	70.6	42.0	-2.6	-0.4	52.9	38.2	91.1	120.1	11.5	7.6	DORCHESTER MUTUAL INS CO
1.4	1.1	32.5	152.1	-9.6	-16.3	50.9	17.4	68.3	103.2	12.4	0.0 •	DORINCO REINS CO
3.5	2.7	86.2	65.9	-2.8	-1.5	69.2	19.4	88.6	108.8	7.2	0.0	DRIVE NEW JERSEY INS CO
7.2	5.1	47.1	21.4	-1.8	0.4	32.8	38.4	71.2	134.9	3.8	0.0	DRYDEN MUTUAL INS CO
1.2	0.8	187.2	165.2	-13.9	-16.7	67.3	34.1	101.4	103.8	7.0	5.9	DTRIC INS CO LTD
2.3	2.0	N/A	N/A	N/A	N/A	N/A	N/A	N/A	92.5	0.0	0.0	DTRIC INS UNDERWRITERS LTD
5.9	3.7	10.2	26.5	-1.5	-9.3	75.1	22.6	97.7	226.3	-4.2	0.0	DUBOIS MEDICAL RRG
N/A	N/A	--	--	--	--	--	--	--	--	--	--	EAGLE BUILDERS INS CO RRG INC
2.2	1.3	30.2	3.3	-0.9	1.7	41.8	39.0	80.8	123.3	8.6	0.0	EAGLE POINT MUTUAL INS CO
2.4	1.5	114.5	85.5	11.2	12.6	76.1	34.2	110.3	96.7	2.6	0.0	EAGLE WEST INS CO
0.2	0.2	0.2	326.2	21.8	45.0	766.5	999 +	999 +	0.1	-89.0	0.0 •	EAGLESTONE REINS CO
1.2	0.6	113.8	96.8	1.1	2.1	71.1	24.7	95.8	93.0	1.0	0.0	EASTERN ADVANTAGE ASR CO
2.2	1.7	94.5	81.3	N/A	-0.7	70.1	25.4	95.5	126.1	1.6	0.0	EASTERN ALLIANCE INS CO
2.2	1.4	58.4	76.6	10.8	4.9	90.1	37.1	127.2	86.9	-4.1	0.0	EASTERN ATLANTIC INS CO
1.9	1.6	43.9	90.8	-9.1	-19.2	45.2	42.8	88.0	106.0	-3.2	0.0	EASTERN DENTISTS INS CO RRG
4.3	2.9	37.0	24.9	-4.6	-4.7	44.5	31.4	75.9	110.0	0.1	0.3	EASTERN MUTUAL INS CO
0.3	0.3	105.3	116.4	-3.6	-1.8	59.0	23.6	82.6	143.2	21.4	0.0	EASTGUARD INS CO
0.4	0.3	171.3	122.4	14.3	39.9	85.1	40.5	125.6	105.3	-0.7	1.3	ECHELON P&C INS CO
0.3	0.3	56.1	37.1	-4.6	-3.7	78.0	12.7	90.7	222.9	46.2	0.0	ECOLE INS CO
6.5	6.0	N/A	N/A	N/A	N/A	N/A	N/A	N/A	999 +	0.0	14.8 •	ECONOMY FIRE & CAS CO
2.2	2.0	N/A	N/A	N/A	N/A	N/A	N/A	N/A	999 +	0.0	0.0	ECONOMY PREFERRED INS CO
10.0	9.0	N/A	N/A	N/A	N/A	N/A	N/A	N/A	N/A	0.0	0.0	ECONOMY PREMIER ASR CO
0.2	0.1	130.8	27.0	2.7	-0.1	70.1	9.0	79.1	314.5	278.2	0.0	EDISON INS CO
3.6	2.1	61.7	145.9	-9.9	-11.6	76.0	22.0	98.0	97.2	-5.0	1.9 •	ELECTRIC INS CO
0.4	0.3	221.8	45.4	2.8	0.6	97.5	43.2	140.7	73.8	8.8	0.0	ELEMENTS PROPERTY INS CO
0.9	0.7	125.6	44.7	0.4	0.1	95.1	36.9	132.0	94.7	43.4	0.0	ELEPHANT INS CO
0.0	0.0	672.9	767.3	33.5	33.0	75.2	25.2	100.4	100.2	57.5	0.0	ELITE TRANSPORTATION RRG INC
N/A	N/A	--	--	--	--	--	--	--	--	--	--	ELIZABETHTOWN INS CO
1.8	1.2	65.9	7.0	-2.9	-2.7	44.8	44.6	89.4	103.1	11.7	0.0	ELLINGTON MUTUAL INS CO
60.1	49.3	-27.0	N/A	N/A	N/A	N/A	17.0	N/A	77.6	-145.2	0.0	EMC PROPERTY & CASUALTY CO
2.7	1.8	62.8	96.8	-6.0	-13.9	68.1	23.9	92.0	111.2	5.2	0.0 •	EMC REINS CO
2.6	1.7	144.1	147.1	-8.2	-9.3	64.6	31.9	96.5	106.9	2.0	0.0	EMCASCO INS CO

999 + Denotes number greater than 999.9%
999 - Denotes number less than -999.99%
• Bullets denote a more detailed analysis is available in Section II.

INSURANCE COMPANY NAME	DOM. STATE	RATING	TOTAL ASSETS ($MIL)	CAPITAL & SURPLUS ($MIL)	ANNUAL NET PREMIUM ($MIL)	NET INCOME ($MIL)	CAPITAL-IZATION INDEX (PTS)	RESERVE ADQ INDEX (PTS)	PROFIT-ABILITY INDEX (PTS)	LIQUIDITY INDEX (PTS)	STAB. INDEX (PTS)	STABILITY FACTORS
EMERGENCY CAP MGMT LLC A RRG	VT	D	9.6	2.7	1.4	-0.1	3.5	2.2	2.9	6.9	1.9	DGT
EMERGENCY MEDICINE PROFESSIONAL	NV	C	21.3	8.5	6.0	0.2	7.4	9.4	6.3	7.1	4.0	GRT
EMERGENCY PHYSICIANS INS RRG	VT	C	28.1	9.6	4.0	0.0	4.8	5.9	2.9	6.9	2.9	DFGR
EMPIRE BONDING & INS CO	NY	B-	3.7	2.3	0.9	0.1	10.0	5.5	8.7	9.3	3.5	DGT
EMPIRE FIRE & MARINE INS CO	NE	C+	63.4	38.8	0.0	0.1	10.0	N/A	3.5	6.9	3.9	GRT
EMPIRE INDEMNITY INS CO	OK	C+	55.4	51.6	0.0	0.0	10.0	N/A	6.7	10.0	4.0	FRT
EMPIRE INS CO	NY	U	--	--	--	--	N/A	--	--	--	--	Z
EMPLOYERS ASSURANCE CO	FL	C	482.0	182.7	83.4	2.0	8.6	7.9	4.5	7.1	3.3	FRT
▲EMPLOYERS COMPENSATION INS CO	CA	A-	1,095.5	367.1	243.1	8.9	7.6	8.0	8.6	6.8	6.5	T
EMPLOYERS FIRE INS CO	PA	U	--	--	--	--	N/A	--	--	--	--	Z
EMPLOYERS INS CO OF NV	NV	C-	546.2	162.4	125.0	4.4	6.3	8.4	1.9	6.7	3.1	RT
EMPLOYERS INS OF WAUSAU	WI	B-	5,648.8	1,592.5	2,119.9	-10.6	8.0	5.8	6.0	6.2	3.6	AT
EMPLOYERS MUTUAL CAS CO	IA	B-	3,269.9	1,413.0	1,123.0	11.5	8.0	7.8	8.1	6.5	4.8	RT
EMPLOYERS PREFERRED INS CO	FL	C	933.6	140.1	243.1	4.0	3.6	7.9	2.6	6.3	3.3	CRT
ENCOMPASS FLORIDIAN INDEMNITY CO	IL	U	--	--	--	--	N/A	--	--	--	--	Z
ENCOMPASS FLORIDIAN INS CO	IL	U	--	--	--	--	N/A	--	--	--	--	Z
ENCOMPASS HOME & AUTO INS CO	IL	B-	20.3	19.8	0.0	0.1	10.0	N/A	7.2	10.0	4.9	DG
ENCOMPASS INDEMNITY CO	IL	B	29.8	26.3	0.0	0.1	10.0	N/A	6.4	10.0	4.6	GT
ENCOMPASS INDEPENDENT INS CO	IL	B-	6.7	6.6	0.0	0.0	10.0	N/A	3.7	10.0	3.8	DG
ENCOMPASS INS CO	IL	C+	9.7	9.6	0.0	0.0	10.0	3.6	3.9	10.0	4.3	DG
ENCOMPASS INS CO OF AM	IL	C+	20.7	20.6	0.0	0.1	10.0	N/A	6.4	10.0	4.8	DG
ENCOMPASS INS CO OF MA	MA	C+	6.0	5.9	0.0	0.0	10.0	N/A	3.6	7.0	3.6	DG
ENCOMPASS INS CO OF NJ	IL	C+	27.0	26.8	0.0	0.1	10.0	N/A	3.6	10.0	4.5	GT
ENCOMPASS PROP & CAS INS CO OF NJ	IL	C+	12.2	12.0	0.0	0.1	10.0	N/A	3.6	10.0	4.6	DG
ENCOMPASS PROPERTY & CASUALTY CO	IL	B-	10.8	10.3	0.0	0.1	10.0	N/A	5.4	7.0	4.4	DG
ENDEAVOUR INS CO	MA	C+	6.2	6.2	0.0	0.0	10.0	N/A	7.7	7.0	3.8	DGR
ENDURANCE AMERICAN INS CO	DE	B-	1,717.5	283.1	253.8	-3.7	6.7	6.1	3.6	6.2	5.3	T
ENDURANCE AMERICAN SPECIALTY INS CO	DE	C+	439.6	105.3	129.3	-1.9	5.2	6.1	3.2	6.5	3.7	RT
▲ENDURANCE ASR CORP	DE	A-	1,824.1	792.9	299.0	10.0	8.3	8.6	5.5	7.3	7.0	AT
ENDURANCE RISK SOLUTIONS ASR CO	DE	C+	263.6	72.4	95.8	-1.5	5.1	6.1	3.3	6.1	3.7	CRT
ENUMCLAW P&C INS CO	OR	C+	8.5	8.0	0.0	0.0	10.0	N/A	6.3	7.0	4.1	DG
EQUITABLE LIABILITY INS CO	DC	D	3.0	1.2	1.1	0.1	8.1	9.7	3.4	9.0	1.3	DFGT
EQUITY INS CO	TX	C	86.0	30.3	53.3	0.1	7.4	6.1	4.0	5.6	3.2	RT
ERIE & NIAGARA INS ASSN	NY	B	213.7	145.8	66.4	2.5	10.0	6.1	8.8	6.9	6.0	T
ERIE INS CO	PA	B-	987.1	358.3	312.7	3.7	10.0	7.9	8.3	6.6	4.7	T
ERIE INS CO OF NEW YORK	NY	B	113.0	31.8	31.3	0.1	9.2	8.1	5.2	6.6	4.0	T
ERIE INS EXCHANGE	PA	B	15,885.8	7,924.5	5,910.0	138.8	9.4	7.8	8.4	6.6	5.1	T
ERIE INS P&C CO	PA	B-	102.3	12.4	0.0	0.1	7.4	N/A	7.3	7.0	3.9	DT
ESSENT GUARANTY INC	PA	A-	1,384.2	595.1	340.6	60.8	10.0	5.2	6.5	7.7	5.7	T
ESSENT GUARANTY OF PA INC	PA	B	87.8	43.3	14.8	2.8	10.0	5.2	9.1	8.5	4.0	DT
ESSENTIA INS CO	MO	C	70.4	30.9	26.9	5.4	8.5	3.6	4.1	9.1	3.7	ART
ESURANCE INS CO	WI	C	179.9	164.8	0.0	0.4	10.0	3.6	3.8	7.0	3.9	RT
ESURANCE INS CO OF NJ	WI	C	14.3	11.9	0.0	0.0	10.0	3.7	7.3	7.0	3.0	DGRT
ESURANCE P&C INS CO	WI	C	97.6	42.4	0.0	0.1	10.0	3.7	6.7	6.7	3.7	RT
ETHIO-AMERICAN INS CO	GA	D+	10.7	3.9	6.6	0.2	5.6	3.7	2.9	6.9	2.2	DGT
EULER HERMES NORTH AMERICA INS CO	MD	B	427.4	146.8	81.9	2.5	10.0	9.3	6.4	7.6	4.1	RT
EVANSTON INS CO	IL	C	4,551.2	1,346.5	1,370.0	31.2	7.0	9.5	8.7	6.8	3.8	AGRT
EVER-GREENE MUTUAL INS CO	PA	C	6.1	6.1	0.4	0.1	10.0	7.3	8.9	9.8	2.1	DGT
EVEREST DENALI INSURANCE CO	DE	U	--	--	--	--	N/A	--	--	--	--	Z
EVEREST INDEMNITY INS CO	DE	C	166.5	60.6	0.0	1.5	10.0	3.5	7.5	7.7	3.9	RT
EVEREST NATIONAL INS CO	DE	C+	910.9	137.6	0.0	6.4	10.0	2.9	5.4	2.3	4.5	GLRT
EVEREST PREMIER INSURANCE CO	DE	U	--	--	--	--	N/A	--	--	--	--	Z

See Page 27 for explanation of footnotes and
Page 28 for explanation of stability factors.
Arrows denote recent upgrades ▲ or downgrades ▼   (see Section VII for explanations)

60

www.weissratings.com

RISK ADJ. RATIO #1	CAPITAL RATIO #2	PREMIUM TO SURPLUS (%)	RESV. TO SURPLUS (%)	RESV. DEVELOP. 1 YEAR (%)	RESV. DEVELOP. 2 YEAR (%)	LOSS RATIO (%)	EXP. RATIO (%)	COMB RATIO (%)	CASH FROM UNDER- WRITING (%)	NET PREMIUM GROWTH (%)	INVEST. IN AFFIL (%)	INSURANCE COMPANY NAME
0.6	0.4	53.4	134.1	1.8	35.5	45.6	6.3	51.9	369.9	33.0	0.0	EMERGENCY CAP MGMT LLC A RRG
1.8	1.3	72.8	80.0	-15.5	-0.4	27.2	49.9	77.1	113.3	6.0	0.0	EMERGENCY MEDICINE PROFESSIONAL
0.9	0.7	41.7	137.8	11.1	-4.0	108.7	39.5	148.2	44.2	-5.5	0.0	EMERGENCY PHYSICIANS INS RRG
4.0	3.6	39.1	6.5	-2.3	-2.4	10.6	53.3	63.9	166.1	10.8	0.0	EMPIRE BONDING & INS CO
9.6	8.7	N/A	N/A	N/A	N/A	N/A	N/A	N/A	-384.3	0.0	0.0	EMPIRE FIRE & MARINE INS CO
43.2	38.9	N/A	N/A	N/A	N/A	N/A	N/A	N/A	-124.5	0.0	0.0	EMPIRE INDEMNITY INS CO
N/A	N/A	--	--	--	--	--	--	--	--	--	--	EMPIRE INS CO
3.0	2.0	46.3	114.8	-0.8	-0.9	62.5	29.3	91.8	74.7	-6.0	0.0	EMPLOYERS ASSURANCE CO
2.1	1.4	67.9	168.1	-1.4	-1.7	62.5	29.4	91.9	99.8	-8.3	0.0 ●	EMPLOYERS COMPENSATION INS CO
N/A	N/A	--	--	--	--	--	--	--	--	--	--	EMPLOYERS FIRE INS CO
1.7	1.1	81.1	201.0	-0.6	-0.7	62.5	27.3	89.8	109.3	514.2	0.0	EMPLOYERS INS CO OF NV
2.5	1.7	133.7	173.9	1.1	-0.5	69.8	32.0	101.8	100.7	3.4	3.2 ●	EMPLOYERS INS OF WAUSAU
2.0	1.6	81.5	81.5	-4.3	-4.3	65.2	30.4	95.6	106.7	18.7	19.8 ●	EMPLOYERS MUTUAL CAS CO
0.8	0.5	178.2	441.5	-1.7	-2.0	62.5	29.2	91.7	128.5	-22.9	0.0	EMPLOYERS PREFERRED INS CO
N/A	N/A	--	--	--	--	--	--	--	--	--	--	ENCOMPASS FLORIDIAN INDEMNITY CO
N/A	N/A	--	--	--	--	--	--	--	--	--	--	ENCOMPASS FLORIDIAN INS CO
88.4	79.5	N/A	N/A	N/A	N/A	N/A	N/A	N/A	999 +	0.0	0.0	ENCOMPASS HOME & AUTO INS CO
23.5	21.2	N/A	N/A	N/A	N/A	N/A	N/A	N/A	16.7	0.0	0.0	ENCOMPASS INDEMNITY CO
143.1	122.4	N/A	N/A	N/A	N/A	N/A	N/A	N/A	999 +	0.0	0.0	ENCOMPASS INDEPENDENT INS CO
155.5	80.1	N/A	N/A	N/A	N/A	N/A	N/A	N/A	N/A	0.0	0.0	ENCOMPASS INS CO
103.4	51.0	N/A	N/A	N/A	N/A	N/A	N/A	N/A	734.7	0.0	0.0	ENCOMPASS INS CO OF AM
129.3	116.4	N/A	N/A	N/A	N/A	N/A	N/A	N/A	195.2	0.0	0.0	ENCOMPASS INS CO OF MA
122.9	61.4	N/A	N/A	N/A	N/A	N/A	N/A	N/A	-62.3	0.0	0.0	ENCOMPASS INS CO OF NJ
105.9	52.1	N/A	N/A	N/A	N/A	N/A	N/A	N/A	999 +	0.0	0.0	ENCOMPASS PROP & CAS INS CO OF NJ
47.7	42.9	N/A	N/A	N/A	N/A	N/A	N/A	N/A	-20.1	0.0	0.0	ENCOMPASS PROPERTY & CASUALTY
88.2	43.2	N/A	N/A	N/A	N/A	N/A	N/A	N/A	N/A	0.0	0.0	ENDEAVOUR INS CO
1.6	1.1	89.7	93.7	5.9	3.2	79.3	14.9	94.2	119.2	8.9	20.0 ●	ENDURANCE AMERICAN INS CO
1.4	0.9	122.8	128.4	8.0	4.4	79.3	14.9	94.2	132.2	8.9	0.0	ENDURANCE AMERICAN SPECIALTY INS
2.1	1.8	38.0	67.0	-3.1	-8.3	55.9	35.7	91.6	133.9	13.9	26.3 ●	ENDURANCE ASR CORP
1.3	0.8	132.2	138.1	8.7	4.9	79.3	14.9	94.2	103.0	8.9	0.0	ENDURANCE RISK SOLUTIONS ASR CO
36.4	32.8	N/A	N/A	N/A	N/A	N/A	N/A	N/A	N/A	0.0	0.0	ENUMCLAW P&C INS CO
2.0	1.8	95.6	146.9	-5.5	-13.2	65.0	29.7	94.7	91.4	-4.0	0.0	EQUITABLE LIABILITY INS CO
1.4	1.2	178.1	77.3	0.5	-0.5	89.5	12.2	101.7	87.2	9.5	0.0	EQUITY INS CO
7.1	4.8	46.9	13.1	N/A	0.6	40.7	38.5	79.2	127.5	4.8	0.1	ERIE & NIAGARA INS ASSN
5.2	3.6	88.4	59.6	-1.6	-3.2	68.8	27.9	96.7	108.9	6.2	5.0 ●	ERIE INS CO
3.9	2.5	99.2	66.9	-1.8	-3.6	68.8	27.9	96.7	109.5	6.2	0.0	ERIE INS CO OF NEW YORK
4.0	2.6	76.6	51.7	-1.4	-2.7	68.8	27.9	96.7	109.6	6.2	5.0 ●	ERIE INS EXCHANGE
1.4	1.3	N/A	N/A	N/A	N/A	N/A	N/A	N/A	641.4	0.0	0.0	ERIE INS P&C CO
17.7	9.5	58.8	3.9	-1.0	-0.8	3.7	27.9	31.6	367.2	13.9	0.0 ●	ESSENT GUARANTY INC
7.0	6.3	31.2	3.6	-1.3	-1.1	3.0	28.7	31.7	318.5	-18.0	0.0	ESSENT GUARANTY OF PA INC
3.5	2.6	101.7	10.3	-0.4	N/A	45.3	51.4	96.7	415.2	0.0	0.0	ESSENTIA INS CO
3.2	3.1	N/A	N/A	N/A	N/A	N/A	N/A	N/A	81.4	0.0	38.3	ESURANCE INS CO
14.4	12.9	N/A	N/A	N/A	N/A	N/A	N/A	N/A	N/A	0.0	0.0	ESURANCE INS CO OF NJ
6.0	5.4	N/A	N/A	N/A	N/A	N/A	N/A	N/A	114.2	0.0	0.0	ESURANCE P&C INS CO
1.3	0.8	181.0	131.6	2.3	2.6	73.0	24.8	97.8	107.7	12.8	0.0	ETHIO-AMERICAN INS CO
6.6	4.1	55.3	29.8	-3.0	-4.5	48.4	28.8	77.2	116.0	-5.9	0.0	EULER HERMES NORTH AMERICA INS
1.7	1.1	106.7	175.0	-7.4	-21.6	54.0	36.8	90.8	115.7	63.4	0.0 ●	EVANSTON INS CO
74.6	38.8	6.7	0.8	-0.4	-0.4	23.4	22.9	46.3	228.3	0.0	0.0	EVER-GREENE MUTUAL INS CO
N/A	N/A	--	--	--	--	--	--	--	--	--	--	EVEREST DENALI INSURANCE CO
6.6	5.9	N/A	N/A	N/A	N/A	N/A	N/A	N/A	209.2	0.0	0.0	EVEREST INDEMNITY INS CO
8.6	4.4	N/A	N/A	N/A	N/A	N/A	N/A	N/A	151.2	0.0	0.0	EVEREST NATIONAL INS CO
N/A	N/A	--	--	--	--	--	--	--	--	--	--	EVEREST PREMIER INSURANCE CO

999 + Denotes number greater than 999.9%
999 - Denotes number less than -999.99%
● Bullets denote a more detailed analysis is available in Section II.

INSURANCE COMPANY NAME	DOM. STATE	RATING	TOTAL ASSETS ($MIL)	CAPITAL & SURPLUS ($MIL)	ANNUAL NET PREMIUM ($MIL)	NET INCOME ($MIL)	CAPITAL-IZATION INDEX (PTS)	RESERVE ADQ INDEX (PTS)	PROFIT-ABILITY INDEX (PTS)	LIQUIDITY INDEX (PTS)	STAB. INDEX (PTS)	STABILITY FACTORS
EVEREST REINS CO	DE	B-	10,186.8	3,789.8	2,050.6	85.5	8.0	5.8	8.8	7.0	4.7	RT
EVEREST SECURITY INS CO	GA	C	36.4	22.1	0.0	0.6	10.0	3.6	6.2	6.9	3.5	DGRT
EVERETT CASH MUTUAL INS CO	PA	B-	126.0	61.0	61.3	0.3	8.2	7.6	6.5	6.0	3.6	RT
EVERGREEN NATIONAL INDEMNITY CO	OH	C	47.7	33.8	12.0	0.8	8.8	8.8	6.5	7.5	3.6	RT
EVERGREEN USA RRG INC	VT	U (1)	--	--	--	--	N/A	--	--	--	--	Z
EVERSPAN FINANCIAL GUARANTEE CORP	WI	U	--	--	--	--	N/A	--	--	--	--	Z
EXACT PROPERTY & CASUALTY CO INC	CA	C+	285.7	116.5	147.6	-0.3	9.5	5.9	6.5	6.7	4.7	FRT
▲EXCALIBUR NATIONAL INS CO	LA	C-	11.7	8.0	2.3	-0.6	8.1	N/A	2.3	9.6	2.3	DFGT
EXCALIBUR REINS CORP	PA	U (5)	--	--	--	--	N/A	--	--	--	--	Z
EXCELA RECIPROCAL RRG	VT	E	13.2	2.1	3.3	0.1	0.3	0.3	2.2	9.4	0.0	CDGT
EXCELSIOR INS CO	NH	C	37.5	35.5	0.0	0.1	10.0	N/A	4.6	7.0	4.3	GR
EXCESS SHARE INS CORP	OH	C	52.1	21.1	1.7	0.1	10.0	9.0	5.5	9.8	3.1	D
EXECUTIVE INS CO	NY	U	--	--	--	--	N/A	--	--	--	--	Z
EXECUTIVE RISK INDEMNITY INC	DE	B-	2,961.8	1,279.0	506.9	29.2	9.2	8.6	6.8	6.9	3.7	T
EXECUTIVE RISK SPECIALTY INS CO	CT	B-	295.1	178.5	31.7	2.4	10.0	7.9	8.8	7.0	3.8	T
EXPLORER AMERICAN INS CO	CA	U	--	--	--	--	N/A	--	--	--	--	Z
EXPLORER INS CO	CA	C	371.6	129.7	146.0	3.5	6.8	5.0	8.9	6.4	3.7	RT
FACILITY INS CORP	TX	U	--	--	--	--	N/A	--	--	--	--	Z
FACTORY MUTUAL INS CO	RI	B-	17,343.3	11,852.3	2,795.2	100.4	8.5	6.1	8.5	6.9	3.8	RT
FAIR AMERICAN INS & REINS CO	NY	B-	205.5	189.0	3.9	1.6	10.0	5.1	3.2	10.0	4.6	T
FAIR AMERICAN SELECT INS CO	DE	B	108.0	103.4	2.3	0.2	10.0	3.6	4.8	10.0	4.2	DGT
FAIRMONT FARMERS MUTUAL INS CO	MN	C+	33.7	20.1	15.9	0.3	10.0	7.9	8.7	6.9	4.3	DGT
FAIRWAY PHYSICIANS INS CO RRG	DC	D	13.6	2.9	3.8	0.0	2.1	1.1	1.1	2.3	1.7	CDFG
FAITH AFFILIATED RRG INC	VT	E+ (2)	5.8	5.6	1.5	0.7	3.0	4.0	3.9	6.6	0.7	DGT
FALCON INS CO	IL	D+	37.3	9.1	15.7	-0.1	2.1	4.1	2.9	3.7	2.3	CDFG
FALLS LAKE FIRE & CASUALTY CO	CA	C	77.1	15.0	8.8	0.0	7.6	3.6	3.7	6.9	3.1	DT
FALLS LAKE GENERAL INS CO	OH	C	13.6	5.2	4.0	0.0	5.7	8.6	3.8	5.4	2.9	DFGT
FALLS LAKE NATIONAL INS CO	OH	B-	380.7	57.6	5.8	0.0	7.3	6.9	7.1	2.3	3.9	FLT
FAMILY SECURITY INS CO	HI	C+	40.5	20.5	19.1	2.9	5.6	4.9	4.1	6.9	3.2	DGT
FARM BU TOWN & COUNTRY INS CO OF MO	MO	B	413.9	185.4	201.5	-2.1	8.8	7.7	7.0	5.7	4.6	T
FARM BUREAU CNTY MUTUAL INS CO OF	TX	C	19.9	5.8	0.0	0.0	8.2	N/A	3.6	7.0	2.9	DGT
FARM BUREAU GENERAL INS CO OF MI	MI	B	681.2	306.9	336.4	4.2	9.7	6.5	6.9	5.8	4.9	RT
FARM BUREAU INS OF NC INC	NC	B	9.7	9.6	0.0	0.1	10.0	N/A	7.1	7.0	4.3	DG
FARM BUREAU MUTUAL INS CO OF AR	AR	B	404.2	241.6	197.3	-0.3	10.0	8.1	8.6	6.1	4.2	T
FARM BUREAU MUTUAL INS CO OF ID	ID	B	462.8	238.4	187.6	-10.2	9.1	5.9	3.9	6.4	4.1	T
FARM BUREAU MUTUAL INS CO OF MI	MI	B	746.2	373.7	357.5	6.2	9.5	8.6	8.4	5.9	4.6	T
FARM BUREAU NEW HORIZONS INS CO MO	MO	C	54.0	25.3	26.7	-0.6	7.2	6.1	3.2	6.8	3.8	T
FARM BUREAU P&C INS CO	IA	B+	2,529.1	1,241.9	1,214.8	38.0	9.9	8.1	8.9	6.1	5.3	T
FARM CREDIT SYS ASSOC CAPTIVE INS CO	CO	B-	122.9	89.1	16.2	3.0	10.0	9.3	8.9	7.3	3.9	DT
FARM FAMILY CASUALTY INS CO	NY	B+	1,188.8	428.8	428.8	4.3	9.4	9.2	6.8	6.6	5.3	T
FARMERS & MECH MU I ASN OF CECIL CTY	MD	D	1.0	0.6	0.4	0.0	7.7	7.5	2.4	7.0	1.0	DFGR
FARMERS & MECH MUTUAL INS CO	PA	B	5.9	4.9	0.2	0.1	8.1	5.0	8.4	9.1	4.5	ADFG
FARMERS & MECHANICS FIRE & CAS INS	WV	C	11.9	5.4	6.3	0.1	7.1	5.7	4.0	6.4	3.6	DGRT
FARMERS & MECHANICS MUTUAL IC OF WV	WV	B-	66.4	48.3	20.7	0.0	10.0	5.2	8.2	6.9	3.5	DRT
FARMERS & MERCHANTS MUTUAL FIRE I C	MI	C+	30.4	24.7	3.9	0.1	9.7	6.1	7.7	7.8	3.2	DGRT
FARMERS ALLIANCE MUTUAL INS CO	KS	B-	319.0	174.0	133.6	3.4	10.0	8.1	5.6	6.6	4.0	RT
FARMERS AUTOMOBILE INS ASN	IL	B+	1,277.1	504.1	491.2	-9.2	8.3	8.2	4.3	6.3	5.0	T
FARMERS FIRE INS CO	PA	C	28.9	14.5	15.0	0.2	7.6	5.7	4.8	6.9	3.6	DGRT
FARMERS INS CO	KS	C+	325.0	106.6	110.7	0.0	10.0	5.9	5.5	7.0	4.5	RT
FARMERS INS CO OF AZ	AZ	C+	48.4	4.5	0.0	0.2	4.4	N/A	4.4	0.7	3.2	CDFL
FARMERS INS CO OF FLEMINGTON	NJ	C+ (1)	66.6	27.7	22.8	2.3	7.2	9.2	8.1	7.2	3.4	T
FARMERS INS CO OF IDAHO	ID	C+	217.6	71.1	110.7	-0.3	8.9	5.9	4.2	6.6	4.2	FRT

See Page 27 for explanation of footnotes and
Page 28 for explanation of stability factors.
Arrows denote recent upgrades ▲ or downgrades ▼   (see Section VII for explanations)

62

www.weissratings.com

RISK ADJ. CAPITAL RATIO #1	CAPITAL RATIO #2	PREMIUM TO SURPLUS (%)	RESV. TO SURPLUS (%)	RESV. DEVELOP. 1 YEAR (%)	RESV. DEVELOP. 2 YEAR (%)	LOSS RATIO (%)	EXP. RATIO (%)	COMB RATIO (%)	CASH FROM UNDER-WRITING (%)	NET PREMIUM GROWTH (%)	INVEST. IN AFFIL (%)	INSURANCE COMPANY NAME
3.5	2.2	56.4	115.7	-2.6	-2.2	63.5	26.9	90.4	99.1	-1.4	3.4 ●	EVEREST REINS CO
7.5	6.8	N/A	N/A	N/A	N/A	N/A	N/A	N/A	67.3	0.0	0.0	EVEREST SECURITY INS CO
2.6	1.9	101.7	46.4	1.2	-0.3	77.7	28.7	106.4	105.3	3.1	7.2	EVERETT CASH MUTUAL INS CO
3.0	2.1	36.2	12.9	-8.0	-7.6	5.6	70.5	76.1	137.4	5.1	0.0	EVERGREEN NATIONAL INDEMNITY CO
N/A	N/A	--	--	--	--	--	--	--	--	--	--	EVERGREEN USA RRG INC
N/A	N/A	--	--	--	--	--	--	--	--	--	--	EVERSPAN FINANCIAL GUARANTEE
3.9	2.8	126.1	75.7	1.1	2.3	71.2	32.4	103.6	94.3	-1.1	0.0	EXACT PROPERTY & CASUALTY CO INC
1.9	1.4	28.5	0.6	N/A	N/A	12.9	80.3	93.2	88.6	0.0	0.0	EXCALIBUR NATIONAL INS CO
N/A	N/A	--	--	--	--	--	--	--	--	--	--	EXCALIBUR REINS CORP
0.1	0.1	161.3	365.8	65.9	73.8	101.0	9.4	110.4	378.6	12.2	0.0	EXCELA RECIPROCAL RRG
49.5	44.5	N/A	N/A	N/A	N/A	N/A	N/A	N/A	N/A	0.0	0.0	EXCELSIOR INS CO
4.7	4.2	8.0	10.5	-6.1	-9.2	3.5	101.3	104.8	97.2	9.7	0.0	EXCESS SHARE INS CORP
N/A	N/A	--	--	--	--	--	--	--	--	--	--	EXECUTIVE INS CO
4.0	2.8	40.5	99.0	-4.2	-7.3	53.6	34.2	87.8	93.9	-35.2	6.6 ●	EXECUTIVE RISK INDEMNITY INC
7.4	4.7	18.0	43.9	-2.0	-3.8	53.5	34.2	87.7	91.5	-35.2	0.0	EXECUTIVE RISK SPECIALTY INS CO
N/A	N/A	--	--	--	--	--	--	--	--	--	--	EXPLORER AMERICAN INS CO
1.5	1.1	116.7	161.8	-2.0	-4.1	64.9	22.5	87.4	157.8	9.2	0.0	EXPLORER INS CO
N/A	N/A	--	--	--	--	--	--	--	--	--	--	FACILITY INS CORP
2.6	2.0	24.3	16.5	-1.9	0.4	54.5	29.5	84.0	115.7	0.5	18.1 ●	FACTORY MUTUAL INS CO
54.2	37.1	2.1	2.9	-0.3	-0.4	52.3	65.4	117.7	106.1	10.0	0.0	FAIR AMERICAN INS & REINS CO
72.4	45.8	2.2	0.8	-0.2	-0.1	72.3	44.2	116.5	169.9	154.0	0.0	FAIR AMERICAN SELECT INS CO
6.4	3.6	80.9	10.0	-1.2	-0.7	56.8	32.2	89.0	122.7	8.0	0.0	FAIRMONT FARMERS MUTUAL INS CO
0.5	0.4	119.7	267.0	32.0	73.6	89.7	56.6	146.3	78.6	-63.8	0.0	FAIRWAY PHYSICIANS INS CO RRG
5.8	4.3	29.5	90.2	10.7	10.6	128.8	18.4	147.2	109.1	13.7	0.0	FAITH AFFILIATED RRG INC
0.6	0.4	172.8	91.8	13.3	10.7	98.5	14.8	113.3	84.6	16.8	0.0	FALCON INS CO
2.1	1.9	60.4	82.5	-2.9	N/A	85.1	12.8	97.9	-957.4	0.0	0.0	FALLS LAKE FIRE & CASUALTY CO
1.9	1.4	97.2	144.0	-5.2	-9.0	85.1	14.0	99.1	99.5	352.2	0.0	FALLS LAKE GENERAL INS CO
1.3	1.2	10.3	24.7	-0.9	-1.8	85.1	22.6	107.7	7.2	-49.9	65.4	FALLS LAKE NATIONAL INS CO
1.7	1.2	117.2	12.1	0.5	-18.0	46.4	49.0	95.4	103.6	11.8	0.0	FAMILY SECURITY INS CO
3.4	2.3	108.0	38.6	0.8	-0.9	68.8	20.7	89.5	115.5	7.3	4.7	FARM BU TOWN & COUNTRY INS CO OF
2.0	1.8	N/A	N/A	N/A	N/A	N/A	N/A	N/A	N/A	0.0	0.0	FARM BUREAU CNTY MUTUAL INS CO OF
4.6	3.2	112.0	55.7	1.6	-1.3	71.2	24.5	95.7	111.2	7.6	0.0 ●	FARM BUREAU GENERAL INS CO OF MI
101.9	50.9	N/A	N/A	N/A	N/A	N/A	N/A	N/A	N/A	0.0	0.0	FARM BUREAU INS OF NC INC
6.0	4.2	81.4	11.3	-1.2	-4.2	71.6	21.1	92.7	102.7	-2.2	0.5 ●	FARM BUREAU MUTUAL INS CO OF AR
2.6	2.2	73.8	30.1	-0.7	-0.1	70.9	26.2	97.1	102.7	11.1	19.3 ●	FARM BUREAU MUTUAL INS CO OF ID
4.5	2.9	98.4	55.1	-2.0	-6.2	66.8	28.6	95.4	106.5	3.5	0.0 ●	FARM BUREAU MUTUAL INS CO OF MI
2.1	1.5	103.5	44.0	9.7	8.9	54.1	32.7	86.8	111.3	-4.9	0.0	FARM BUREAU NEW HORIZONS INS CO
4.4	3.4	101.8	41.5	-3.8	-4.4	59.9	26.6	86.5	115.2	0.5	5.7 ●	FARM BUREAU P&C INS CO
15.8	9.1	18.9	29.1	-9.0	-8.6	48.7	9.0	57.7	156.4	-3.3	0.0	FARM CREDIT SYS ASSOC CAPTIVE INS
4.2	2.7	101.0	116.1	-6.0	-9.6	64.4	29.7	94.1	113.6	5.2	0.0 ●	FARM FAMILY CASUALTY INS CO
2.1	1.3	71.9	7.2	-2.4	-1.2	53.2	57.1	110.3	93.2	1.9	0.0	FARMERS & MECH MU I ASN OF CECIL
2.7	1.6	5.2	3.2	-0.8	-0.7	50.1	19.9	70.0	155.9	1.9	0.0	FARMERS & MECH MUTUAL INS CO
1.5	1.2	121.5	45.7	-7.0	-20.8	63.3	27.2	90.5	124.4	30.5	0.0	FARMERS & MECHANICS FIRE & CAS INS
4.2	3.2	43.3	8.4	N/A	-1.5	58.3	39.1	97.4	103.0	-1.3	8.8	FARMERS & MECHANICS MUTUAL IC OF
4.5	2.7	16.1	2.5	-0.2	-0.6	43.4	47.7	91.1	118.4	4.8	0.0	FARMERS & MERCHANTS MUTUAL FIRE I
4.8	3.8	79.0	28.3	-1.6	-5.1	70.8	30.6	101.4	98.2	1.0	6.9	FARMERS ALLIANCE MUTUAL INS CO
2.0	1.7	95.5	76.8	0.8	-0.7	77.7	28.9	106.6	99.6	2.2	21.7 ●	FARMERS AUTOMOBILE INS ASN
2.3	1.5	106.0	23.6	2.3	6.6	53.9	36.8	90.7	113.1	-3.0	0.0	FARMERS FIRE INS CO
4.6	3.2	103.7	65.2	1.8	3.1	72.0	32.3	104.3	98.0	-1.1	0.0	FARMERS INS CO
0.7	0.6	N/A	N/A	N/A	N/A	N/A	N/A	N/A	2.4	0.0	0.0	FARMERS INS CO OF AZ
2.0	1.2	82.3	78.3	-1.5	-0.5	54.0	37.4	91.4	112.1	0.4	0.0	FARMERS INS CO OF FLEMINGTON
3.2	2.2	154.6	92.7	1.4	2.8	71.2	32.4	103.6	94.6	-1.1	0.0	FARMERS INS CO OF IDAHO

999 + Denotes number greater than 999.9%
999 - Denotes number less than -999.99%
● Bullets denote a more detailed analysis is available in Section II.

INSURANCE COMPANY NAME	DOM. STATE	RATING	TOTAL ASSETS ($MIL)	CAPITAL & SURPLUS ($MIL)	ANNUAL NET PREMIUM ($MIL)	NET INCOME ($MIL)	CAPITAL-IZATION INDEX (PTS)	RESERVE ADQ INDEX (PTS)	PROFIT-ABILITY INDEX (PTS)	LIQUIDITY INDEX (PTS)	STAB. INDEX (PTS)	STABILITY FACTORS
FARMERS INS CO OF OREGON	OR	B	1,693.2	530.6	1,033.3	-0.7	8.2	5.7	6.0	5.9	4.7	FRT
FARMERS INS CO OF WA	WA	B-	554.9	205.4	295.2	-0.2	9.1	5.9	6.4	6.2	4.6	RT
FARMERS INS EXCHANGE	CA	C	16,534.7	4,207.3	7,639.3	-39.8	5.4	5.6	3.7	2.6	4.3	FLRT
FARMERS INS HAWAII INC	HI	B	101.6	94.4	0.0	0.1	10.0	4.6	3.3	10.0	4.4	T
FARMERS INS OF COLUMBUS INC	OH	C+	291.4	101.4	147.6	-0.2	9.1	5.9	5.8	6.7	4.5	FRT
FARMERS MUTUAL F I C OF MCCANDLESS	PA	C-	11.7	6.6	5.6	0.1	7.2	6.4	8.6	6.8	2.1	DGRT
FARMERS MUTUAL F I C OF OKARCHE OK	OK	C	19.9	14.4	8.4	1.0	8.7	6.2	5.8	6.4	2.6	DGT
FARMERS MUTUAL F I C OF SALEM CTY	NJ	B-	150.6	74.1	40.3	1.0	9.6	9.2	8.5	6.9	3.8	RT
FARMERS MUTUAL FIRE INS CO OF	PA	C	32.1	21.9	9.3	0.7	8.5	8.7	8.8	7.0	2.9	DGRT
FARMERS MUTUAL HAIL INS CO OF IA	IA	B-	681.3	429.6	334.2	3.5	7.5	7.7	5.2	5.1	4.3	RT
FARMERS MUTUAL INS CO	WV	C	15.3	11.1	5.6	0.3	10.0	5.2	8.7	7.2	2.4	DGRT
FARMERS MUTUAL INS CO OF ELLINWOOD	KS	D-	4.8	2.7	2.7	0.1	7.4	4.1	4.9	6.6	1.3	DGRT
FARMERS MUTUAL INS CO OF MI	MI	D-	1.7	1.1	0.9	0.1	6.1	5.6	1.3	4.5	1.0	DFGL
FARMERS MUTUAL INS CO OF NE	NE	B	673.1	354.3	327.4	22.0	10.0	7.7	6.5	6.6	4.8	RT
FARMERS MUTUAL OF TENNESSEE	TN	C	24.0	13.8	11.4	-0.3	7.9	6.2	5.3	6.8	2.7	DGRT
FARMERS NEW CENTURY INS CO	IL	C+	204.5	71.5	110.7	-0.3	8.9	5.9	4.5	6.7	4.7	FRT
FARMERS REINS CO	CA	U	--	--	--	--	N/A	--	--	--	--	Z
FARMERS SPECIALTY INS CO	MI	B-	61.0	17.1	0.0	0.1	9.4	N/A	6.7	9.6	3.8	DFT
FARMERS TEXAS COUNTY MUTUAL INS CO	TX	C+	183.4	51.8	0.0	1.5	10.0	N/A	8.8	6.5	4.0	RT
FARMERS UNION MUTUAL INS CO	MT	C+	62.7	38.1	23.1	0.8	9.7	7.0	6.2	6.9	3.4	RT
FARMERS UNION MUTUAL INS CO	ND	B-	113.1	66.9	62.5	2.5	10.0	8.0	8.8	6.7	3.6	FRT
FARMERS UNION MUTUAL INS CO	AR	D	4.5	1.9	1.9	-0.1	5.9	5.9	1.6	7.4	1.5	DGT
FARMINGTON CASUALTY CO	CT	B	1,032.4	296.4	322.2	6.9	7.9	8.7	6.5	6.7	4.6	T
FARMINGTON MUTUAL INS CO	WI	E	8.5	7.2	1.1	0.1	8.9	6.1	8.0	8.0	0.0	DGR
FARMLAND MUTUAL INS CO	IA	B	590.2	170.2	194.9	-0.3	9.9	6.0	4.1	6.2	4.6	AT
FB INS CO	KY	U	--	--	--	--	N/A	--	--	--	--	Z
FBALLIANCE INS CO	IL	B	47.2	46.5	0.1	-0.9	10.0	N/A	2.7	7.0	4.1	DFT
FBALLIANCE INS INC	VA	D	4.7	4.5	0.0	0.0	10.0	N/A	4.9	7.0	2.3	DFGT
FCCI ADVANTAGE INS CO	FL	U	--	--	--	--	N/A	--	--	--	--	Z
FCCI COMMERCIAL INS CO	FL	U	--	--	--	--	N/A	--	--	--	--	Z
FCCI INS CO	FL	C+	2,020.6	572.1	750.1	-4.9	7.9	7.0	4.2	6.4	4.2	RT
FD INS CO	FL	C+	29.3	20.7	-52.4	0.1	9.9	10.0	3.9	6.9	4.4	DFGT
FDM PREFERRED INS CO	NY	C-	14.3	2.9	2.1	0.0	4.4	9.3	8.5	8.0	2.4	CDGT
FEDERAL INS CO	IN	B-	28,149.3	11,889.4	4,708.0	429.4	7.2	8.3	3.3	6.8	3.8	T
FEDERATED MUTUAL INS CO	MN	B	5,543.6	3,165.9	1,460.6	52.4	10.0	9.0	8.6	6.9	5.1	T
FEDERATED NATIONAL INS CO	FL	C	548.5	140.8	326.3	-3.1	3.6	6.1	4.1	5.6	4.1	CRT
FEDERATED RESERVE INS CO	MN	U	--	--	--	--	N/A	--	--	--	--	Z
FEDERATED RURAL ELECTRIC INS EXCH	KS	B	542.2	183.7	123.5	5.5	8.7	9.4	8.9	6.8	6.3	T
FEDERATED SERVICE INS CO	MN	B-	433.6	233.6	162.3	4.4	10.0	9.3	8.6	6.9	4.5	T
▲FFVA MUTUAL INS CO	FL	B-	348.5	162.6	113.5	3.1	8.4	5.8	6.6	6.7	5.0	T
FHM INS CO	FL	C	78.2	39.0	27.6	-0.2	7.7	6.3	2.9	7.0	3.9	FRT
FIDELITY & DEPOSIT CO OF MARYLAND	MD	C+	211.2	168.5	0.0	0.5	10.0	N/A	5.2	7.0	4.6	RT
FIDELITY & GUARANTY INS	WI	C+	153.5	91.0	21.8	1.0	10.0	7.4	3.9	7.7	4.4	T
FIDELITY & GUARANTY INS CO	IA	C+	21.9	19.3	0.0	0.1	10.0	N/A	5.9	9.4	3.4	DFGT
FIDELITY MOHAWK INS CO	NJ	U (1)	--	--	--	--	N/A	--	--	--	--	Z
▼FIDUCIARY INS CO OF AMERICA	NY	F	38.5	-160.6	0.0	-2.1	0.0	0.2	0.2	0.0	0.0	CLRT
FINANCIAL AMERICAN PROP & CAS INS CO	TX	C-	12.8	8.7	1.1	-0.2	10.0	6.0	2.1	10.0	2.8	DFGR
FINANCIAL CASUALTY & SURETY INC	TX	C	28.4	16.7	14.8	0.0	7.2	7.0	8.5	7.2	2.8	DGT
FINANCIAL GUARANTY INS CO	NY	E	2,467.9	66.4	9.1	23.1	0.0	1.6	0.9	4.7	0.0	CLRT
FINANCIAL INDEMNITY CO	IL	B-	100.3	22.7	0.0	0.3	9.6	N/A	3.6	10.0	3.8	DRT
FINANCIAL PACIFIC INS CO	CA	B	237.6	96.8	77.2	1.5	9.5	8.2	7.4	6.8	4.5	RT
FINGER LAKES FIRE & CASUALTY CO	NY	C+	41.6	27.0	9.8	-0.2	9.2	6.2	5.5	7.1	3.2	DRT

See Page 27 for explanation of footnotes and Page 28 for explanation of stability factors.

Arrows denote recent upgrades ▲ or downgrades ▼ (see Section VII for explanations)

64

www.weissratings.com

RISK ADJ. CAPITAL RATIO #1	CAPITAL RATIO #2	PREMIUM TO SURPLUS (%)	RESV. TO SURPLUS (%)	RESV. DEVELOP. 1 YEAR (%)	RESV. DEVELOP. 2 YEAR (%)	LOSS RATIO (%)	EXP. RATIO (%)	COMB RATIO (%)	CASH FROM UNDER-WRITING (%)	NET PREMIUM GROWTH (%)	INVEST. IN AFFIL (%)	INSURANCE COMPANY NAME
2.5	1.8	193.9	120.4	2.9	5.2	71.8	32.4	104.2	94.4	-1.1	0.0 ●	FARMERS INS CO OF OREGON
3.4	2.4	143.3	86.0	1.3	2.6	71.2	32.4	103.6	95.7	-1.1	0.0 ●	FARMERS INS CO OF WA
0.8	0.7	181.1	117.0	4.1	6.7	72.5	33.1	105.6	93.9	-1.1	46.3 ●	FARMERS INS EXCHANGE
8.8	8.5	N/A	0.9	0.2	N/A	N/A	N/A	N/A	N/A	0.0	10.9	FARMERS INS HAWAII INC
3.4	2.4	145.0	87.0	1.3	2.6	71.2	32.4	103.6	94.4	-1.1	0.0	FARMERS INS OF COLUMBUS INC
1.7	1.1	87.9	15.9	0.8	1.3	42.6	35.1	77.7	128.7	4.0	0.0	FARMERS MUTUAL F I C OF
3.9	2.3	62.7	5.2	0.1	-1.7	61.3	42.6	103.9	96.8	0.7	0.0	FARMERS MUTUAL F I C OF OKARCHE
4.1	2.6	56.0	61.0	-4.1	-8.3	63.1	33.9	97.0	112.0	3.3	0.1	FARMERS MUTUAL F I C OF SALEM CTY
3.2	2.0	44.5	11.3	-3.0	-5.1	46.3	33.3	79.6	127.1	8.0	0.0	FARMERS MUTUAL FIRE INS CO OF
2.1	1.6	78.3	28.6	-5.9	-1.9	63.6	18.8	82.4	122.6	-7.3	35.4 ●	FARMERS MUTUAL HAIL INS CO OF IA
5.2	3.3	51.9	4.1	-0.3	-0.4	39.9	46.3	86.2	110.4	2.0	0.0	FARMERS MUTUAL INS CO
3.4	2.1	116.5	4.6	-0.6	-2.7	31.2	36.4	67.6	138.2	-6.2	6.7	FARMERS MUTUAL INS CO OF
1.4	1.0	92.4	1.7	-1.1	7.2	40.0	69.1	109.1	97.9	-23.3	0.0	FARMERS MUTUAL INS CO OF MI
4.4	3.2	98.1	28.4	0.5	-0.7	65.4	27.1	92.5	117.1	3.8	0.0 ●	FARMERS MUTUAL INS CO OF NE
2.5	1.7	80.7	18.9	1.1	-0.1	59.0	36.4	95.4	106.3	3.6	0.3	FARMERS MUTUAL OF TENNESSEE
3.2	2.3	153.8	92.2	1.4	2.8	71.2	32.4	103.6	94.1	-1.1	0.0	FARMERS NEW CENTURY INS CO
N/A	N/A	--	--	--	--	--	--	--	--	--	--	FARMERS REINS CO
2.8	2.5	N/A	N/A	N/A	N/A	N/A	N/A	N/A	-5.7	0.0	0.0	FARMERS SPECIALTY INS CO
5.5	5.0	N/A	N/A	N/A	N/A	N/A	N/A	N/A	-78.6	0.0	0.0	FARMERS TEXAS COUNTY MUTUAL INS
4.4	3.1	61.8	22.0	-3.4	-7.4	58.5	33.8	92.3	114.4	11.5	3.4	FARMERS UNION MUTUAL INS CO
4.5	3.9	98.2	14.8	-2.2	-3.6	70.0	30.3	100.3	98.2	0.3	0.0	FARMERS UNION MUTUAL INS CO
1.2	0.8	103.8	8.9	2.1	0.1	73.4	43.4	116.8	80.2	8.1	0.0	FARMERS UNION MUTUAL INS CO
2.4	1.6	111.3	184.7	-2.2	-5.7	63.4	30.0	93.4	109.1	4.8	0.1 ●	FARMINGTON CASUALTY CO
3.7	2.2	15.3	3.3	0.2	0.1	44.6	42.2	86.8	119.2	-2.9	0.0	FARMINGTON MUTUAL INS CO
3.9	2.7	113.7	83.8	2.1	2.8	74.7	31.1	105.8	97.4	4.3	0.0	FARMLAND MUTUAL INS CO
N/A	N/A	--	--	--	--	--	--	--	--	--	--	FB INS CO
10.2	9.2	0.2	0.1	N/A	N/A	-204.0	999 +	999 +	-1.9	0.0	9.5	FBALLIANCE INS CO
71.4	64.2	N/A	N/A	N/A	N/A	N/A	N/A	N/A	999 +	0.0	0.0	FBALLIANCE INS INC
N/A	N/A	--	--	--	--	--	--	--	--	--	--	FCCI ADVANTAGE INS CO
N/A	N/A	--	--	--	--	--	--	--	--	--	--	FCCI COMMERCIAL INS CO
2.1	1.5	131.1	147.4	4.6	0.1	80.6	28.7	109.3	108.1	5.5	7.6 ●	FCCI INS CO
11.4	10.3	-253.1	3.8	-197.0	-102.9	97.5	1.8	99.3	-534.8	-338.5	0.0	FD INS CO
1.1	0.4	72.5	178.9	-0.2	-7.8	73.5	16.9	90.4	143.7	5.8	0.0	FDM PREFERRED INS CO
1.3	1.2	41.2	99.7	-3.7	-6.5	52.0	35.0	87.0	95.4	-35.8	38.2 ●	FEDERAL INS CO
3.4	2.7	47.3	47.0	-3.9	-7.7	68.8	23.8	92.6	113.8	12.3	15.4 ●	FEDERATED MUTUAL INS CO
0.9	0.6	230.5	87.6	-2.1	1.4	79.5	33.9	113.4	108.2	35.2	0.0	FEDERATED NATIONAL INS CO
N/A	N/A	--	--	--	--	--	--	--	--	--	--	FEDERATED RESERVE INS CO
2.9	2.0	66.6	144.6	-8.1	-17.3	78.7	14.5	93.2	133.8	2.7	0.0	FEDERATED RURAL ELECTRIC INS EXCH
7.6	4.9	71.1	70.6	-5.9	-11.7	68.8	24.0	92.8	113.6	12.3	0.0 ●	FEDERATED SERVICE INS CO
2.7	2.1	72.7	79.5	-5.2	-8.0	61.8	26.6	88.4	110.7	0.3	0.0	FFVA MUTUAL INS CO
2.2	1.6	70.9	88.9	-7.3	-15.8	63.5	33.6	97.1	82.3	-1.5	0.0	FHM INS CO
7.7	7.3	N/A	N/A	N/A	N/A	N/A	N/A	N/A	-12.3	0.0	13.6	FIDELITY & DEPOSIT CO OF MARYLAND
10.8	6.9	24.2	40.1	-0.5	-1.1	63.4	30.9	94.3	94.4	4.8	0.0	FIDELITY & GUARANTY INS
21.9	19.7	N/A	N/A	N/A	N/A	N/A	N/A	N/A	16.3	0.0	0.0	FIDELITY & GUARANTY INS CO
N/A	N/A	--	--	--	--	--	--	--	--	--	--	FIDELITY MOHAWK INS CO
-16.2	-14.6	N/A	N/A	N/A	N/A	N/A	N/A	N/A	N/A	0.0	0.0	FIDUCIARY INS CO OF AMERICA
6.2	4.1	11.9	1.9	-0.7	0.8	14.8	114.2	129.0	-21.3	-11.7	0.0	FINANCIAL AMERICAN PROP & CAS INS
1.5	1.3	88.5	19.0	-10.8	-15.6	23.2	70.4	93.6	156.5	6.9	0.0	FINANCIAL CASUALTY & SURETY INC
0.1	0.0	13.7	999 +	484.1	-85.8	807.2	-270.9	536.3	7.6	-24.1	1.3	FINANCIAL GUARANTY INS CO
2.8	2.5	N/A	N/A	N/A	N/A	N/A	N/A	N/A	27.5	0.0	0.0	FINANCIAL INDEMNITY CO
4.5	2.9	81.2	89.2	-0.7	-2.6	69.8	30.1	99.9	117.5	8.7	0.0	FINANCIAL PACIFIC INS CO
3.6	2.3	36.6	19.3	2.1	-1.6	54.5	34.6	89.1	131.6	4.2	0.0	FINGER LAKES FIRE & CASUALTY CO

999 + Denotes number greater than 999.9%
999 - Denotes number less than -999.99%
● Bullets denote a more detailed analysis is available in Section II.

INSURANCE COMPANY NAME	DOM. STATE	RATING	TOTAL ASSETS ($MIL)	CAPITAL & SURPLUS ($MIL)	ANNUAL NET PREMIUM ($MIL)	NET INCOME ($MIL)	CAPITAL- IZATION INDEX (PTS)	RESERVE ADQ INDEX (PTS)	PROFIT- ABILITY INDEX (PTS)	LIQUIDITY INDEX (PTS)	STAB. INDEX (PTS)	STABILITY FACTORS
FINIAL REINS CO	CT	D+	1,530.0	1,007.7	72.4	1.5	9.7	4.6	8.6	10.0	2.5	RT
FIRE DISTRICTS INS CO	NY	C	17.2	4.5	3.2	0.0	4.6	9.3	8.5	7.5	2.5	CDGT
FIRE DISTRICTS OF NY MUT INS CO INC	NY	C+	95.2	30.1	15.8	0.1	7.1	6.2	8.0	7.5	3.3	DRT
FIRE INS EXCHANGE	CA	C+	2,573.2	770.5	1,107.1	-3.5	5.1	5.7	3.9	2.9	4.8	LRT
FIREMANS FUND INDEMNITY CORP	NJ	C+	15.4	14.8	0.0	-0.4	10.0	N/A	3.9	7.0	3.7	DFGT
FIREMANS FUND INS CO	CA	C	2,291.0	1,675.6	-503.1	12.6	8.1	5.0	3.0	5.9	4.2	RT
FIREMANS FUND INS CO OF HI INC	HI	C+	11.5	9.2	0.0	0.0	10.0	N/A	6.3	7.0	3.4	DFGR
FIREMENS INS CO OF WASHINGTON DC	DE	C	101.3	33.0	0.0	0.2	10.0	N/A	6.5	9.3	3.8	T
FIRST ACCEPTANCE INS CO	TX	D+	266.4	60.7	197.3	-0.2	4.4	5.8	1.3	0.6	2.5	FLRT
FIRST ACCEPTANCE INS CO OF GEORGIA	GA	D+	105.5	19.0	77.7	-0.2	2.1	4.6	1.4	0.9	2.4	CDFL
FIRST ACCEPTANCE INS CO OF TN INC	TN	D+	32.6	6.4	23.9	0.0	2.5	5.8	1.6	1.4	2.8	CDFG
FIRST AMERICAN PROP & CAS INS CO	CA	C	100.0	43.6	59.2	-0.2	7.2	6.0	3.9	4.4	3.4	LRT
FIRST AMERICAN SPECIALTY INS CO	CA	C	116.8	54.4	68.8	-1.5	7.0	4.8	6.5	4.7	3.6	LRT
FIRST BENEFITS INS MUTUAL INC	NC	D	47.2	8.8	18.4	-0.3	2.0	9.9	5.6	6.9	2.3	DT
FIRST CHICAGO INS CO	IL	D	85.2	14.6	46.9	-1.0	4.3	6.8	4.3	5.7	2.3	DRT
▲FIRST CHOICE CASUALTY INS CO	NV	C-	15.1	4.9	6.6	0.2	4.2	3.9	3.2	3.3	2.3	CDFG
FIRST COLONIAL INS CO	FL	B	338.9	147.4	38.4	-2.8	10.0	6.2	2.8	7.0	4.5	FRT
FIRST COMMUNITY INS CO	FL	C	101.2	41.6	40.4	0.8	8.8	6.3	8.2	6.8	3.7	RT
FIRST DAKOTA INDEMNITY CO	SD	C	48.0	15.1	16.5	0.5	6.1	6.2	8.9	6.5	4.3	DRT
FIRST F&C INS OF HI INC	HI	C	9.2	9.2	0.0	-0.2	10.0	N/A	2.9	7.0	2.9	DGRT
FIRST FINANCIAL INS CO	IL	C-	548.9	434.7	20.9	0.9	7.3	7.9	7.9	7.7	2.6	RT
FIRST FLORIDIAN AUTO & HOME INS CO	FL	B	263.1	190.5	55.6	-0.2	10.0	6.3	4.8	7.0	5.8	T
FIRST FOUNDERS ASR CO	NJ	D+	5.5	4.5	0.4	0.0	10.0	6.0	8.4	9.2	2.3	DG
FIRST GUARD INS CO	AZ	B-	28.7	26.2	22.4	0.6	10.0	7.3	9.0	7.4	5.0	DGT
FIRST INDEMNITY INS OF HI INC	HI	C	7.5	7.5	0.0	0.0	10.0	N/A	3.7	7.0	2.8	DGRT
FIRST INDEMNITY OF AMERICA INS CO	NJ	D+	10.6	6.0	7.2	0.1	6.3	2.8	6.6	6.2	2.1	DGRT
FIRST INS CO OF HI LTD	HI	C	667.4	278.0	205.2	4.7	10.0	9.0	4.5	6.8	4.2	RT
FIRST JERSEY CASUALTY INS CO INC	NJ	U (1)	--	--	--	--	N/A	--	--	--	--	Z
FIRST LIBERTY INS CORP	IL	C+	22.5	22.2	0.0	0.0	10.0	3.6	4.0	7.0	3.5	ADGT
FIRST MEDICAL INS CO RRG	VT	C+	98.1	51.9	10.5	1.7	8.3	9.3	3.3	6.9	4.6	DT
FIRST MERCURY INS CO	DE	C	105.0	52.3	0.0	0.3	10.0	3.6	3.5	7.0	4.0	AFRT
FIRST MUTUAL INS CO	NC	D+	6.7	5.0	1.5	0.0	10.0	7.3	8.1	9.1	2.1	DFGR
FIRST NATIONAL INS CO OF AMERICA	NH	B	57.3	56.7	0.0	0.2	10.0	3.9	7.2	7.0	4.1	ART
FIRST NET INS CO	GU	D+(1)	20.5	13.1	6.4	1.6	8.0	4.1	5.9	7.1	2.5	D
FIRST NONPROFIT INS CO	DE	C	71.9	30.0	26.8	0.9	8.0	5.1	2.9	7.1	3.6	GRT
FIRST PROFESSIONALS INS CO INC	FL	U	--	--	--	--	N/A	--	--	--	--	Z
FIRST PROTECTIVE INS CO	FL	U	--	--	--	--	N/A	--	--	--	--	Z
FIRST SECURITY INS OF HI INC	HI	C	5.6	5.6	0.0	-0.3	10.0	N/A	3.4	7.0	3.6	DGR
FIRST SPECIALTY INS CORP	MO	C	180.0	73.8	0.0	1.2	9.4	3.9	5.5	6.7	4.2	FGRT
FIRST STATE INS CO	CT	U	--	--	--	--	N/A	--	--	--	--	Z
FIRST SURETY CORP	WV	C-	40.0	13.4	2.0	0.5	8.1	4.9	3.8	10.0	2.3	DGRT
FIRST WASHINGTON INS CO	DC	U	--	--	--	--	N/A	--	--	--	--	Z
FIRSTCOMP INS CO	NE	B	289.9	128.6	44.5	3.4	8.2	9.3	6.9	7.8	4.6	RT
FIRSTLINE NATIONAL INS CO	MD	C+	96.1	52.6	39.0	0.7	8.7	6.5	8.5	6.7	3.7	T
FITCHBURG MUTUAL INS CO	MA	C+	127.3	61.5	43.9	1.0	8.9	5.9	6.8	6.9	3.8	RT
FLAGSHIP CITY INS CO	PA	C+	55.1	12.5	0.0	0.1	8.7	N/A	7.2	10.0	3.1	DT
FLORIDA FAMILY INS CO	FL	B	107.1	57.9	56.1	0.8	8.7	6.1	8.0	6.2	6.0	T
FLORIDA FARM BU CASUALTY INS CO	FL	B-	562.9	283.7	250.8	-0.3	10.0	7.8	5.5	6.5	4.5	FT
FLORIDA FARM BUREAU GENERAL INS CO	FL	B	10.3	10.3	0.0	0.1	10.0	N/A	6.9	7.0	4.5	DGT
FLORIDA LAWYERS MUTUAL INS CO	FL	C+	86.8	46.6	11.6	0.0	9.3	9.4	8.4	7.7	3.4	DRT
▲FLORIDA PENINSULA INS CO	FL	B-	293.4	120.5	109.9	-0.1	7.6	5.2	7.7	6.8	5.0	FT
FLORIDA SELECT INS CO	FL	F (5)	0.0	0.0	-0.3	0.0	0.0	5.0	1.9	7.0	0.0	CDFT

See Page 27 for explanation of footnotes and
Page 28 for explanation of stability factors.
Arrows denote recent upgrades ▲ or downgrades ▼   (see Section VII for explanations)

66

www.weissratings.com

RISK ADJ. RATIO #1	CAPITAL RATIO #2	PREMIUM TO SURPLUS (%)	RESV. TO SURPLUS (%)	RESV. DEVELOP. 1 YEAR (%)	RESV. DEVELOP. 2 YEAR (%)	LOSS RATIO (%)	EXP. RATIO (%)	COMB RATIO (%)	CASH FROM UNDER-WRITING (%)	NET PREMIUM GROWTH (%)	INVEST. IN AFFIL (%)	INSURANCE COMPANY NAME
5.4	2.9	7.4	45.4	5.2	12.3	78.6	-12.3	66.3	338.6	-27.2	0.0 ●	FINIAL REINS CO
1.3	0.5	70.5	174.0	-0.2	-7.3	73.5	15.3	88.8	149.2	5.8	0.0	FIRE DISTRICTS INS CO
1.7	1.2	53.2	164.0	-0.9	-3.8	69.2	14.8	84.0	151.7	5.8	9.0	FIRE DISTRICTS OF NY MUT INS CO INC
0.8	0.7	142.4	91.8	3.1	5.1	72.5	32.3	104.8	98.0	-1.1	57.4 ●	FIRE INS EXCHANGE
51.0	45.9	N/A	N/A	N/A	N/A	N/A	N/A	N/A	865.2	0.0	0.0	FIREMANS FUND INDEMNITY CORP
3.8	3.5	-30.1	N/A	N/A	N/A	N/A	-1.1	N/A	72.5	57.7	30.0 ●	FIREMANS FUND INS CO
11.3	10.2	N/A	N/A	N/A	N/A	N/A	N/A	N/A	-33.5	0.0	0.0	FIREMANS FUND INS CO OF HI INC
4.3	3.9	N/A	N/A	N/A	N/A	N/A	N/A	N/A	164.3	0.0	0.0	FIREMENS INS CO OF WASHINGTON DC
0.8	0.6	335.1	179.7	20.2	6.2	101.9	18.6	120.5	87.1	5.8	13.2	FIRST ACCEPTANCE INS CO
0.5	0.4	452.0	242.3	31.9	10.7	101.9	18.6	120.5	86.6	5.8	0.0	FIRST ACCEPTANCE INS CO OF
0.5	0.4	370.1	198.4	24.5	7.0	101.9	18.6	120.5	88.5	5.8	0.0	FIRST ACCEPTANCE INS CO OF TN INC
1.7	1.1	135.8	41.0	9.1	4.5	69.2	34.1	103.3	97.1	-0.6	0.0	FIRST AMERICAN PROP & CAS INS CO
1.8	1.1	123.6	33.9	-0.2	-1.0	58.2	33.8	92.0	109.1	2.5	0.0	FIRST AMERICAN SPECIALTY INS CO
0.6	0.4	208.3	289.2	-23.2	-50.0	70.1	26.8	96.9	134.4	2.0	0.0	FIRST BENEFITS INS MUTUAL INC
1.0	0.6	307.2	230.9	-9.1	-5.2	65.5	27.9	93.4	118.0	16.9	3.5	FIRST CHICAGO INS CO
0.8	0.4	140.2	123.7	-13.0	-12.0	67.0	38.7	105.7	93.8	-9.1	0.0	FIRST CHOICE CASUALTY INS CO
6.6	5.2	25.1	9.7	2.4	1.3	106.0	45.3	151.3	55.0	-50.0	0.0	FIRST COLONIAL INS CO
3.4	2.7	98.9	44.2	2.7	0.8	61.7	43.9	105.6	99.4	-12.2	0.0	FIRST COMMUNITY INS CO
1.1	0.9	112.7	147.6	-5.0	-2.8	67.5	20.7	88.2	116.3	6.4	0.0	FIRST DAKOTA INDEMNITY CO
113.5	56.7	N/A	N/A	N/A	N/A	N/A	N/A	N/A	N/A	0.0	0.0	FIRST F&C INS OF HI INC
1.2	1.2	4.8	14.0	-0.8	-2.1	47.6	55.3	102.9	85.6	-14.9	76.3 ●	FIRST FINANCIAL INS CO
12.1	9.0	29.1	23.2	2.6	-1.3	82.2	23.5	105.7	94.5	-7.0	0.0	FIRST FLORIDIAN AUTO & HOME INS CO
8.5	5.7	8.7	7.5	-0.8	0.3	10.7	67.1	77.8	112.1	3.3	0.0	FIRST FOUNDERS ASR CO
9.5	5.0	87.8	5.5	-2.0	-1.3	56.4	21.6	78.0	122.2	34.0	0.0	FIRST GUARD INS CO
120.3	60.1	N/A	N/A	N/A	N/A	N/A	N/A	N/A	N/A	0.0	0.0	FIRST INDEMNITY INS OF HI INC
1.0	0.8	123.0	27.4	-1.0	-1.0	31.8	66.9	98.7	136.1	-1.2	0.0	FIRST INDEMNITY OF AMERICA INS CO
4.7	3.2	75.1	88.6	1.2	-0.9	68.5	36.5	105.0	106.6	8.0	3.8 ●	FIRST INS CO OF HI LTD
N/A	N/A	--	--	--	--	--	--	--	--	--	--	FIRST JERSEY CASUALTY INS CO INC
67.2	33.6	N/A	N/A	N/A	N/A	N/A	N/A	N/A	N/A	0.0	0.0	FIRST LIBERTY INS CORP
2.2	1.8	20.9	81.9	0.8	-7.6	105.3	4.9	110.2	124.6	5.4	0.0	FIRST MEDICAL INS CO RRG
7.6	6.8	N/A	N/A	N/A	N/A	N/A	N/A	N/A	357.3	-100.0	0.0	FIRST MERCURY INS CO
7.8	6.8	29.5	2.3	-0.9	-0.7	54.2	36.2	90.4	102.4	-5.8	0.0	FIRST MUTUAL INS CO
150.5	75.1	N/A	N/A	N/A	N/A	N/A	N/A	N/A	N/A	0.0	0.0	FIRST NATIONAL INS CO OF AMERICA
2.3	1.7	49.1	15.4	-1.9	-3.5	36.4	44.4	80.8	119.2	0.2	0.0	FIRST NET INS CO
2.1	1.7	91.9	45.6	-6.2	N/A	32.1	60.0	92.1	135.3	16.9	15.1	FIRST NONPROFIT INS CO
N/A	N/A	--	--	--	--	--	--	--	--	--	--	FIRST PROFESSIONALS INS CO INC
N/A	N/A	--	--	--	--	--	--	--	--	--	--	FIRST PROTECTIVE INS CO
159.7	79.8	N/A	N/A	N/A	N/A	N/A	N/A	N/A	N/A	0.0	0.0	FIRST SECURITY INS OF HI INC
7.6	4.4	N/A	41.3	3.1	9.1	999 +	999 +	999 +	20.5	119.2	0.0	FIRST SPECIALTY INS CORP
N/A	N/A	--	--	--	--	--	--	--	--	--	--	FIRST STATE INS CO
3.0	2.2	20.1	21.7	3.6	1.8	31.8	62.4	94.2	150.5	54.0	0.0	FIRST SURETY CORP
N/A	N/A	--	--	--	--	--	--	--	--	--	--	FIRST WASHINGTON INS CO
2.8	1.8	36.2	93.0	-7.9	-15.8	39.1	32.7	71.8	107.0	-2.1	0.0	FIRSTCOMP INS CO
3.3	2.3	75.6	64.4	-0.8	2.5	61.2	33.8	95.0	126.2	8.5	0.0	FIRSTLINE NATIONAL INS CO
3.2	2.3	73.3	42.3	-3.8	-0.5	52.5	37.6	90.1	128.8	20.1	6.3	FITCHBURG MUTUAL INS CO
2.1	1.9	N/A	N/A	N/A	N/A	N/A	N/A	N/A	999 +	0.0	0.0	FLAGSHIP CITY INS CO
2.3	2.1	98.0	18.0	-0.3	-0.1	54.6	43.2	97.8	97.7	13.5	17.0	FLORIDA FAMILY INS CO
4.9	3.6	87.8	42.1	-2.5	-4.1	88.6	20.6	109.2	93.7	5.1	2.8 ●	FLORIDA FARM BU CASUALTY INS CO
96.2	48.1	N/A	N/A	N/A	N/A	N/A	N/A	N/A	N/A	0.0	0.0	FLORIDA FARM BUREAU GENERAL INS
3.9	2.4	25.4	54.1	-12.2	-20.6	68.6	23.0	91.6	146.1	-7.2	0.0	FLORIDA LAWYERS MUTUAL INS CO
2.1	1.7	84.2	66.4	1.7	-5.4	70.9	33.2	104.1	89.8	-4.8	1.8	FLORIDA PENINSULA INS CO
-1.9	-1.7	2.3	-16.5	8.4	0.3	537.6	-780.2	-242.6	28.4	0.0	0.0	FLORIDA SELECT INS CO

999 + Denotes number greater than 999.9%
999 - Denotes number less than -999.99%
● Bullets denote a more detailed analysis is available in Section II.

INSURANCE COMPANY NAME	DOM. STATE	RATING	TOTAL ASSETS ($MIL)	CAPITAL & SURPLUS ($MIL)	ANNUAL NET PREMIUM ($MIL)	NET INCOME ($MIL)	CAPITAL-IZATION INDEX (PTS)	RESERVE ADQ INDEX (PTS)	PROFIT-ABILITY INDEX (PTS)	LIQUIDITY INDEX (PTS)	STAB. INDEX (PTS)	STABILITY FACTORS
FLORIDA SPECIALTY INS CO	FL	C-	48.3	19.8	29.6	-0.5	4.5	7.3	1.6	6.8	2.9	DGRT
FLORISTS INS CO	IL	C	6.6	5.6	0.0	0.0	10.0	N/A	3.4	7.0	2.2	DGRT
FLORISTS MUTUAL INS CO	IL	C-	125.4	22.8	20.1	0.1	7.4	4.2	1.6	6.9	2.1	DT
FMH AG RISK INS CO	IA	B	125.9	113.2	0.0	0.7	10.0	6.8	2.9	7.0	4.2	FRT
FMI INS CO	NJ	B- (1)	49.4	37.1	0.0	5.2	7.3	N/A	6.9	7.0	3.8	T
FOREMOST COUNTY MUTUAL INS CO	TX	C+	83.9	5.2	0.0	0.1	3.7	N/A	8.9	9.9	3.2	CDT
FOREMOST INS CO	MI	B	2,309.5	1,141.8	0.0	7.5	10.0	7.3	7.8	8.3	5.5	FT
FOREMOST LLOYDS OF TEXAS	TX	C+	63.7	4.8	0.0	0.1	4.0	N/A	8.6	6.6	3.2	CDFT
FOREMOST P&C INS CO	MI	C+	63.3	18.2	0.0	0.1	9.4	N/A	6.3	6.9	4.6	DF
FOREMOST SIGNATURE INS CO	MI	C+	65.3	20.1	0.0	0.1	9.9	N/A	5.9	9.5	3.4	DT
▲FORESTRY MUTUAL INS CO	NC	B-	61.7	21.8	23.5	-1.1	7.2	9.8	4.4	6.5	4.7	DRT
FORT WAYNE MEDICAL ASR CO RRG	AZ	D+	4.1	2.7	0.9	0.1	8.2	7.0	6.8	7.7	2.0	DG
FORTRESS INS CO	IL	B-	135.7	63.7	23.2	0.6	5.4	4.6	4.7	7.9	4.7	CDT
FORTUITY INS CO	MI	B	43.0	18.4	18.0	0.4	9.3	9.3	8.8	6.7	5.5	DT
FOUNDERS INS CO (IL)	IL	C	161.3	71.8	44.4	0.1	9.3	4.3	3.3	6.7	4.2	RT
FOUNDERS INS CO (NJ)	NJ	C (1)	6.5	6.5	0.0	0.1	10.0	N/A	4.0	10.0	3.8	D
FOUNDERS INS CO OF MI	MI	U	--	--	--	--	N/A	--	--	--	--	Z
FRANDISCO P&C INS CO	GA	B-	111.6	85.4	32.1	3.6	10.0	6.1	8.7	7.0	3.9	T
FRANK WINSTON CRUM INS CO	FL	C-	86.6	20.1	20.4	0.4	4.3	3.7	6.7	8.0	3.3	DGRT
FRANKENMUTH MUTUAL INS CO	MI	B	1,272.5	570.7	467.8	11.2	9.2	9.3	8.8	6.7	4.9	T
FRANKLIN CASUALTY INS CO RRG	VT	D+	21.0	4.1	3.1	-0.1	4.5	7.0	6.0	8.2	2.2	DFGR
FRANKLIN INS CO	PA	C	30.8	13.2	9.6	0.2	8.3	8.2	8.3	6.9	3.7	DGRT
FRANKLIN MUTUAL INS CO	NJ	B (1)	934.5	626.8	119.2	32.9	8.1	8.0	8.1	8.7	4.6	T
FREDERICK MUTUAL INS CO	MD	C-	44.9	19.6	18.7	-0.5	7.1	4.3	1.7	6.6	2.9	DFT
FREDERICKSBURG PROFESSIONAL RISK	VT	D	20.2	12.4	1.9	0.3	8.3	9.6	5.1	7.0	1.6	DFGR
FREEDOM ADVANTAGE INS CO	PA	D+	11.0	4.1	3.4	0.0	5.2	7.1	4.7	7.9	2.2	DFGR
FREEDOM SPECIALTY INS CO	OH	B	69.7	21.6	0.0	0.2	10.0	N/A	7.6	10.0	4.3	DT
FREMONT INS CO	MI	D	150.7	45.0	60.5	-0.4	8.8	4.4	5.5	6.4	1.7	RT
FRIENDS COVE MUTUAL INS CO	PA	C-	5.7	3.1	2.9	-0.1	7.5	5.8	4.2	6.9	2.0	DGRT
FRONTIER - MT CARROLL MUTL INS	IL	D+	23.3	16.2	2.7	0.2	8.2	7.8	8.7	6.7	2.1	DGRT
FRONTLINE INS UNLIMITED CO	IL	U	--	--	--	--	N/A	--	--	--	--	Z
▼FULMONT MUTUAL INS CO	NY	E+	3.3	0.9	1.5	-0.3	5.2	3.7	1.6	7.2	0.4	DFGR
GABLES RRG INC	VT	E	11.6	5.6	3.3	0.2	7.2	5.1	3.0	6.8	0.0	DGT
▼GALEN INS CO	MO	F	9.3	-2.3	1.2	-0.1	0.0	4.8	0.0	7.0	0.0	CDFG
GARRISON P&C INS CO	TX	B	2,075.2	770.0	1,376.4	8.3	8.2	8.1	5.2	2.6	4.9	LRT
GATEWAY INS CO	MO	D	81.1	17.6	28.8	0.0	2.4	2.3	2.9	2.5	2.3	DFLR
GEICO ADVANTAGE INS CO	NE	B	1,962.4	957.1	788.3	-51.2	8.1	5.7	2.7	6.2	4.9	FGT
GEICO CASUALTY CO	MD	C	3,272.5	984.5	1,834.2	-13.0	7.1	9.5	2.8	2.3	4.0	LT
GEICO CHOICE INS CO	NE	B+	919.4	370.7	469.2	-11.3	7.6	5.8	2.8	2.8	5.0	FGLT
GEICO COUNTY MUTUAL INS CO	TX	C	132.0	5.0	0.0	0.0	3.0	N/A	3.9	0.0	2.8	CDGL
GEICO GENERAL INS CO	MD	B+	166.1	166.0	0.0	0.1	10.0	N/A	7.1	7.0	5.0	FT
GEICO INDEMNITY CO	MD	B	8,771.2	4,856.3	2,542.6	47.5	7.9	9.4	8.9	6.3	5.1	T
GEICO MARINE INS CO	MD	C+	134.5	50.9	41.7	0.1	7.7	8.3	2.6	5.8	3.1	GRT
GEICO SECURE INS CO	NE	A-	555.9	287.8	214.1	-1.7	8.1	5.6	3.5	5.9	5.7	GT
GEISINGER INS CORP RRG	VT	D	16.4	11.8	1.2	0.2	10.0	4.5	5.8	8.6	2.0	DGR
GEM STATE INS CO	ID	C-	12.1	8.9	3.8	-0.2	9.6	6.2	6.1	7.0	2.3	DGT
GEMINI INS CO	DE	C	110.0	57.1	0.0	0.3	10.0	N/A	6.2	10.0	4.3	RT
GENERAL AUTOMOBILE INS CO	OH	C+	132.3	35.6	97.2	-1.3	6.5	4.3	3.3	2.8	3.8	LT
GENERAL CASUALTY CO OF WI	WI	C+	970.0	294.1	369.5	7.9	7.5	5.7	3.5	6.5	4.5	GRT
GENERAL CASUALTY INS CO	WI	C	8.5	7.5	-8.4	0.0	10.0	3.8	1.9	2.2	2.8	DFGL
▲GENERAL INS CO OF AM	NH	B-	110.5	107.9	0.0	0.2	10.0	3.9	3.7	7.0	4.5	ART
GENERAL REINS CORP	DE	C+	15,274.7	11,011.2	550.2	174.2	7.5	7.8	3.9	9.3	3.9	RT

See Page 27 for explanation of footnotes and
Page 28 for explanation of stability factors.
Arrows denote recent upgrades ▲ or downgrades ▼   (see Section VII for explanations)

68   www.weissratings.com

RISK ADJ. CAPITAL RATIO #1	RISK ADJ. CAPITAL RATIO #2	PREMIUM TO SURPLUS (%)	RESV. TO SURPLUS (%)	RESV. DEVELOP. 1 YEAR (%)	RESV. DEVELOP. 2 YEAR (%)	LOSS RATIO (%)	EXP. RATIO (%)	COMB RATIO (%)	CASH FROM UNDER-WRITING (%)	NET PREMIUM GROWTH (%)	INVEST. IN AFFIL (%)	INSURANCE COMPANY NAME
0.8	0.7	146.1	14.4	-0.2	-0.5	58.4	57.6	116.0	132.8	275.7	0.0	FLORIDA SPECIALTY INS CO
13.0	11.7	N/A	4.7	N/A	N/A	N/A	N/A	N/A	452.8	0.0	0.0	FLORISTS INS CO
2.1	1.4	88.6	139.0	-1.0	-2.3	73.9	28.2	102.1	96.4	-4.4	5.5	FLORISTS MUTUAL INS CO
42.0	37.8	N/A	N/A	N/A	2.8	N/A	N/A	N/A	119.8	100.0	0.0	FMH AG RISK INS CO
2.0	1.2	N/A	N/A	N/A	N/A	N/A	N/A	N/A	N/A	0.0	0.0	FMI INS CO
0.6	0.5	N/A	N/A	N/A	N/A	N/A	N/A	N/A	93.6	0.0	0.0	FOREMOST COUNTY MUTUAL INS CO
9.5	6.8	N/A	0.4	N/A	-0.2	N/A	N/A	N/A	-19.8	0.0	6.5 ●	FOREMOST INS CO
0.6	0.6	N/A	N/A	N/A	N/A	N/A	N/A	N/A	136.1	0.0	0.0	FOREMOST LLOYDS OF TEXAS
2.9	2.6	N/A	N/A	N/A	N/A	N/A	N/A	N/A	-16.5	0.0	0.0	FOREMOST P&C INS CO
3.2	2.9	N/A	N/A	N/A	N/A	N/A	N/A	N/A	68.3	0.0	0.0	FOREMOST SIGNATURE INS CO
1.3	1.0	104.7	88.5	-1.2	-22.9	64.5	30.7	95.2	104.5	2.5	5.5	FORESTRY MUTUAL INS CO
2.4	1.8	34.0	37.3	8.3	2.0	48.0	44.8	92.8	122.0	-1.4	0.0	FORT WAYNE MEDICAL ASR CO RRG
1.1	0.8	37.0	88.8	-0.9	N/A	75.6	28.7	104.3	102.6	6.5	0.0	FORTRESS INS CO
3.7	2.7	99.9	72.0	-7.0	-10.9	63.3	29.4	92.7	116.9	3.8	0.0	FORTUITY INS CO
4.4	3.1	62.1	86.9	-0.9	-2.9	65.5	32.8	98.3	110.3	8.0	4.4	FOUNDERS INS CO (IL)
90.3	44.8	N/A	N/A	N/A	N/A	N/A	N/A	N/A	-62.3	0.0	0.0	FOUNDERS INS CO (NJ)
N/A	N/A	--	--	--	--	--	--	--	--	--	--	FOUNDERS INS CO OF MI
8.6	7.2	39.1	2.1	-0.4	0.1	11.9	56.2	68.1	146.0	-17.8	0.0	FRANDISCO P&C INS CO
1.0	0.5	103.8	106.6	10.1	19.8	52.5	42.1	94.6	118.1	18.6	0.0	FRANK WINSTON CRUM INS CO
3.0	2.4	84.1	60.6	-5.9	-9.2	63.3	29.4	92.7	113.9	3.8	14.5 ●	FRANKENMUTH MUTUAL INS CO
1.3	0.9	72.4	157.6	2.3	-25.9	58.5	40.1	98.6	86.9	-4.2	0.0	FRANKLIN CASUALTY INS CO RRG
3.2	2.1	74.6	82.0	-0.8	-2.5	69.8	30.1	99.9	117.3	8.7	0.0	FRANKLIN INS CO
2.7	1.7	19.0	17.8	-2.1	-2.9	52.6	28.0	80.6	123.5	6.3	6.1	FRANKLIN MUTUAL INS CO
1.8	1.0	94.3	63.5	6.6	3.9	66.6	51.1	117.7	86.6	-11.2	0.0	FREDERICK MUTUAL INS CO
2.9	1.9	15.8	51.4	-2.1	-20.4	106.2	14.0	120.2	103.4	-3.5	0.0	FREDERICKSBURG PROFESSIONAL RISK
1.4	0.9	82.5	120.3	-1.6	-46.8	50.8	32.2	83.0	93.6	-15.9	0.0	FREEDOM ADVANTAGE INS CO
3.3	2.9	N/A	N/A	N/A	N/A	N/A	N/A	N/A	-195.9	0.0	0.0	FREEDOM SPECIALTY INS CO
2.9	2.3	134.1	100.1	1.2	1.3	69.2	28.3	97.5	107.7	4.1	0.0	FREMONT INS CO
2.0	1.3	93.2	21.4	-1.0	3.0	39.5	46.6	86.1	124.9	-1.0	0.0	FRIENDS COVE MUTUAL INS CO
4.9	2.9	51.2	4.8	-4.7	-1.0	31.6	33.5	65.1	130.2	2.3	0.4	FRONTIER - MT CARROLL MUTL INS
N/A	N/A	--	--	--	--	--	--	--	--	--	--	FRONTLINE INS UNLIMITED CO
0.8	0.5	131.5	136.3	25.9	10.2	84.0	26.1	110.1	72.5	-34.0	7.1	FULMONT MUTUAL INS CO
2.0	1.5	61.9	65.2	8.0	-31.9	53.9	9.5	63.4	152.9	6.5	0.0	GABLES RRG INC
-0.0	-0.0	-59.6	-502.5	164.5	25.1	152.1	194.5	346.6	40.4	-79.3	0.0	GALEN INS CO
2.4	1.8	183.1	88.1	-1.1	-1.1	91.8	12.4	104.2	103.6	15.6	0.0 ●	GARRISON P&C INS CO
0.6	0.4	164.0	95.0	27.7	47.3	78.5	26.6	105.1	97.4	2.1	0.0	GATEWAY INS CO
2.3	1.6	80.7	32.4	-3.0	-3.1	105.9	30.3	136.2	80.1	65.4	0.0 ●	GEICO ADVANTAGE INS CO
1.4	1.0	198.4	90.7	-5.9	-3.7	87.3	18.5	105.8	99.5	13.2	0.0 ●	GEICO CASUALTY CO
1.9	1.3	129.8	46.1	-3.2	-3.0	93.2	21.4	114.6	92.8	48.9	0.0 ●	GEICO CHOICE INS CO
0.5	0.4	N/A	N/A	N/A	N/A	N/A	N/A	N/A	133.8	0.0	0.0	GEICO COUNTY MUTUAL INS CO
156.9	78.4	N/A	N/A	N/A	N/A	N/A	N/A	N/A	N/A	0.0	0.0 ●	GEICO GENERAL INS CO
2.1	1.5	55.3	30.6	-1.4	-1.6	80.7	13.5	94.2	110.0	6.0	14.1 ●	GEICO INDEMNITY CO
2.4	1.8	87.0	18.9	-2.3	-2.9	95.1	21.6	116.7	107.3	74.5	0.0	GEICO MARINE INS CO
2.5	1.6	79.6	28.3	-1.3	-1.2	85.6	22.4	108.0	99.4	45.4	0.0 ●	GEICO SECURE INS CO
8.2	6.3	10.5	4.3	N/A	4.4	41.1	40.7	81.8	112.6	2.2	0.0	GEISINGER INS CORP RRG
3.8	2.6	42.8	6.6	0.5	-0.4	51.3	30.9	82.2	124.3	9.4	0.0	GEM STATE INS CO
8.3	7.4	N/A	N/A	N/A	N/A	N/A	N/A	N/A	N/A	0.0	0.0	GEMINI INS CO
0.9	0.8	265.2	97.5	9.7	2.0	82.9	24.6	107.5	106.0	26.2	0.0	GENERAL AUTOMOBILE INS CO
1.8	1.3	131.7	106.1	-13.5	-10.0	58.8	32.1	90.9	151.8	105.1	23.8 ●	GENERAL CASUALTY CO OF WI
16.3	14.7	-113.9	N/A	N/A	N/A	N/A	N/A	N/A	-21.1	-138.0	0.0	GENERAL CASUALTY INS CO
10.0	9.7	N/A	N/A	N/A	N/A	N/A	N/A	N/A	N/A	0.0	13.7	GENERAL INS CO OF AM
1.4	1.3	5.2	27.0	-1.2	-2.2	54.4	37.9	92.3	103.0	0.3	47.2 ●	GENERAL REINS CORP

999 + Denotes number greater than 999.9%
999 - Denotes number less than -999.99%
● Bullets denote a more detailed analysis is available in Section II.

INSURANCE COMPANY NAME	DOM. STATE	RATING	TOTAL ASSETS ($MIL)	CAPITAL & SURPLUS ($MIL)	ANNUAL NET PREMIUM ($MIL)	NET INCOME ($MIL)	CAPITAL-IZATION INDEX (PTS)	RESERVE ADQ INDEX (PTS)	PROFIT-ABILITY INDEX (PTS)	LIQUIDITY INDEX (PTS)	STAB. INDEX (PTS)	STABILITY FACTORS
GENERAL SECURITY IND CO OF AZ	AZ	C-	373.9	49.3	18.1	-4.1	7.4	6.5	4.1	7.2	3.0	FRT
GENERAL SECURITY NATIONAL INS CO	NY	C-	390.0	133.5	82.5	-2.3	7.3	6.9	5.4	6.9	3.2	RT
GENERAL STAR INDEMNITY CO	DE	C	862.0	605.1	67.7	2.8	9.7	8.5	5.8	9.8	4.0	RT
GENERAL STAR NATIONAL INS CO	DE	B-	239.8	180.9	10.2	0.3	10.0	8.8	5.3	10.0	4.9	DFRT
GENERALI - US BRANCH	NY	C	66.4	26.5	0.7	-0.4	7.5	3.5	2.6	7.0	3.5	FRT
GENESEE PATRONS COOP INS	NY	D+	9.6	5.3	4.4	-0.2	7.9	6.4	4.9	6.8	2.4	DGRT
GENESIS INS CO	DE	C	182.4	127.0	8.6	1.3	10.0	8.9	4.3	10.0	2.9	DFRT
GENEVA INS CO	IN	D+	4.1	1.7	3.4	0.1	4.1	3.4	2.1	2.2	1.4	DFGL
GENWORTH FINANCIAL ASR CORP	NC	U	--	--	--	--	N/A	--	--	--	--	Z
GENWORTH MORTGAGE INS CORP	NC	C	3,038.7	1,259.7	675.6	107.0	7.3	4.3	5.3	6.6	4.0	RT
GENWORTH MORTGAGE REINS CORP	NC	B	15.1	11.3	1.0	0.2	10.0	4.9	3.5	9.7	4.6	ADG
▲GENWORTH MTG INS CORP OF NC	NC	B-	360.3	174.8	68.6	16.2	8.0	5.8	8.1	6.9	4.5	T
GEORGIA CASUALTY & SURETY CO	GA	C	43.3	19.7	15.2	0.2	9.1	6.3	6.2	6.7	3.9	DT
GEORGIA DEALERS INS CO	GA	D	9.4	3.4	1.1	0.0	2.6	3.8	1.2	1.2	1.5	CDFG
GEORGIA FARM BUREAU CASUALTY INS CO	GA	B	3.5	3.5	0.0	0.0	10.0	N/A	3.8	10.0	4.6	DGT
GEORGIA FARM BUREAU MUTUAL INS CO	GA	C	628.4	198.5	450.0	-14.1	7.2	4.4	2.2	4.5	4.1	FLT
GEORGIA MUNICIPAL CAPTIVE INS CO	GA	D+	11.2	3.5	2.8	0.0	5.9	6.0	7.3	7.2	2.0	DGT
GEORGIA TRANSPORTATION CAPTIVE INS	GA	D (1)	2.8	1.5	0.8	0.1	7.7	9.5	8.0	8.4	1.2	DT
GEOVERA INS CO	CA	D+	85.9	26.2	31.3	1.4	0.9	7.8	3.6	5.5	2.4	CRT
GEOVERA SPECIALTY INS CO	DE	C	126.2	20.3	14.6	0.6	2.9	7.5	3.9	6.2	3.4	CDRT
GERMAN AMERICAN FARM MUTUAL	TX	B-	4.4	3.3	0.9	0.0	10.0	5.5	4.6	9.1	3.5	DG
GERMAN MUTUAL INS CO	OH	D	41.5	17.9	20.6	0.5	7.3	5.9	3.4	6.8	2.0	DRT
GERMANIA FARM MUTUAL INS ASN	TX	C	396.1	188.6	190.3	-11.1	7.1	5.9	3.7	4.5	4.0	LRT
GERMANIA FIRE & CASUALTY CO	TX	C	31.8	11.5	19.9	-0.6	7.7	5.9	2.2	4.2	3.0	DFGL
GERMANIA INS CO	TX	C+	77.3	49.1	24.3	1.3	10.0	6.1	8.9	6.8	3.8	RT
GERMANIA SELECT INS CO	TX	B-	211.2	71.2	153.1	-1.5	8.4	6.4	2.5	2.6	5.1	FLT
GERMANTOWN INS CO	PA	C+	100.2	47.5	30.7	0.5	10.0	6.4	6.7	6.7	4.7	T
GERMANTOWN MUTUAL INS CO	WI	B-	107.2	58.6	46.8	1.6	10.0	8.6	8.4	6.1	3.6	RT
GLOBAL HAWK INS CO RRG	VT	E-	51.8	3.8	23.2	0.0	0.0	0.7	0.6	0.0	0.0	CDFL
GLOBAL HAWK PROPERTY CAS INS CO	DE	U	--	--	--	--	N/A	--	--	--	--	Z
GLOBAL INS CO	GA	U (5)	--	--	--	--	N/A	--	--	--	--	Z
GLOBAL LIBERTY INS CO OF NY	NY	D	69.7	21.9	36.1	0.8	7.2	1.8	5.2	6.3	2.3	DFRT
GLOBAL REINS CORP OF AM	NY	U	--	--	--	--	N/A	--	--	--	--	Z
GNY CUSTOM INS CO	AZ	B+	59.3	53.2	2.9	0.3	10.0	5.0	7.0	9.0	6.5	DT
GOAUTO INS CO	LA	D	60.9	10.4	22.1	-0.1	2.5	5.8	2.5	2.1	2.3	CDGL
GOLDEN BEAR INS CO	CA	C+	144.8	54.4	28.4	0.3	7.6	9.6	8.8	7.3	3.5	RT
GOLDEN EAGLE INS CORP	NH	C	59.5	56.2	0.0	0.2	10.0	3.8	3.9	7.0	4.3	R
GOLDEN INS CO A RRG	NV	E+ (1)	13.7	2.6	4.7	-0.9	0.9	1.3	2.3	7.6	0.8	CDT
GOLDSTREET INS CO	NY	U	--	--	--	--	N/A	--	--	--	--	Z
GOOD SHEPHERD RECIPROCAL RRG	SC	D	11.2	6.3	1.7	0.2	3.3	3.6	5.3	7.9	1.8	DG
GOODVILLE MUTUAL CAS CO	PA	B	255.2	150.0	117.0	2.5	10.0	6.0	8.9	6.8	4.1	RT
GOTHAM INS CO	NY	C	242.7	74.8	73.8	-0.5	6.8	4.2	3.7	6.9	2.9	T
GOVERNMENT EMPLOYEES INS CO	MD	B	28,989.0	16,833.4	6,988.3	208.3	8.4	9.4	8.8	6.7	5.1	T
GOVERNMENT ENTITIES MUTUAL INC	DC	U (5)	--	--	--	--	N/A	--	--	--	--	Z
GOVERNMENTAL INTERINS	IL	B	65.0	48.0	5.8	0.3	10.0	8.3	5.1	7.0	4.1	DFT
▼GOVT TECHNOLOGY INS CO RRG INC	NV	E	2.0	0.6	0.3	-0.2	6.2	N/A	3.9	2.9	0.0	DGLT
GRACO RRG INC	SC	U	--	--	--	--	N/A	--	--	--	--	Z
GRAIN DEALERS MUTUAL INS CO	IN	C-	11.3	9.1	0.0	0.3	10.0	N/A	7.5	10.0	1.9	DGRT
GRANADA INS CO	FL	E+	38.5	9.7	10.2	0.1	0.5	0.5	4.4	6.2	0.6	CDFG
GRANGE INDEMNITY INS CO	OH	C	99.4	56.3	46.8	2.2	10.0	6.0	8.7	6.7	3.9	T
GRANGE INS ASSN	WA	B-	287.8	140.0	154.2	-6.0	9.1	5.9	3.9	6.3	4.0	RT
GRANGE INS CO OF MI	OH	C	70.8	43.2	29.3	1.4	10.0	6.0	8.7	6.8	4.2	T

See Page 27 for explanation of footnotes and
Page 28 for explanation of stability factors.
Arrows denote recent upgrades ▲ or downgrades ▼   (see Section VII for explanations)

70

www.weissratings.com

RISK ADJ. RATIO #1	CAPITAL RATIO #2	PREMIUM TO SURPLUS (%)	RESV. TO SURPLUS (%)	RESV. DEVELOP. 1 YEAR (%)	RESV. DEVELOP. 2 YEAR (%)	LOSS RATIO (%)	EXP. RATIO (%)	COMB RATIO (%)	CASH FROM UNDER-WRITING (%)	NET PREMIUM GROWTH (%)	INVEST. IN AFFIL (%)	INSURANCE COMPANY NAME
1.9	1.2	33.8	58.7	4.2	-7.6	75.9	38.8	114.7	8.1	-37.8	0.0	GENERAL SECURITY IND CO OF AZ
2.4	1.1	59.6	92.1	-3.5	-3.5	48.0	41.7	89.7	116.7	-7.6	0.0	GENERAL SECURITY NATIONAL INS CO
4.5	2.7	11.4	23.1	-4.4	-4.6	46.6	46.8	93.4	93.6	1.3	0.0 ●	GENERAL STAR INDEMNITY CO
7.1	4.6	5.8	21.2	-4.3	-6.3	26.8	45.5	72.3	75.1	4.3	0.0	GENERAL STAR NATIONAL INS CO
3.9	2.1	2.8	55.7	2.5	-0.4	130.8	203.1	333.9	35.7	-96.8	0.3	GENERALI - US BRANCH
2.3	1.5	81.5	13.7	-1.3	-1.2	61.5	30.0	91.5	119.0	14.0	0.0	GENESEE PATRONS COOP INS
6.1	4.1	6.9	38.0	-5.5	-8.4	44.4	30.8	75.2	63.6	-17.3	0.0	GENESIS INS CO
0.8	0.7	223.4	87.3	24.2	14.4	68.3	36.5	104.8	88.4	-22.3	0.0	GENEVA INS CO
N/A	N/A	--	--	--	--	--	--	--	--	--	--	GENWORTH FINANCIAL ASR CORP
1.8	1.5	56.9	46.7	-3.6	-2.3	23.9	26.1	50.0	137.8	8.8	14.8 ●	GENWORTH MORTGAGE INS CORP
9.1	8.2	9.3	3.7	1.6	1.0	25.4	6.3	31.7	999 +	-18.3	0.0	GENWORTH MORTGAGE REINS CORP
3.3	2.5	42.5	50.2	-2.9	-0.3	29.0	0.3	29.3	110.0	11.3	14.7	GENWORTH MTG INS CORP OF NC
3.3	2.3	76.9	54.4	-0.5	-3.2	68.2	31.2	99.4	107.7	13.7	0.0	GEORGIA CASUALTY & SURETY CO
0.7	0.5	33.5	193.2	-43.5	11.9	121.6	44.2	165.8	71.1	-73.6	0.0	GEORGIA DEALERS INS CO
149.0	68.9	N/A	N/A	N/A	N/A	N/A	N/A	N/A	N/A	0.0	0.0	GEORGIA FARM BUREAU CASUALTY INS
1.6	1.1	215.8	78.5	9.2	11.0	78.3	29.1	107.4	93.5	2.8	1.6 ●	GEORGIA FARM BUREAU MUTUAL INS
1.7	0.7	80.1	173.1	-19.5	-22.6	64.9	14.2	79.1	161.6	2.6	0.0	GEORGIA MUNICIPAL CAPTIVE INS CO
2.6	1.6	52.0	72.9	-2.4	-10.0	69.7	22.4	92.1	112.7	10.5	0.0	GEORGIA TRANSPORTATION CAPTIVE
0.3	0.2	124.9	28.4	-0.1	-2.7	41.5	30.2	71.7	173.7	21.7	0.0	GEOVERA INS CO
0.6	0.4	70.7	16.0	-0.1	-1.7	41.5	30.2	71.7	210.4	21.7	0.0	GEOVERA SPECIALTY INS CO
6.8	6.2	26.1	8.6	1.1	-0.6	102.7	8.7	111.4	108.2	21.2	0.0	GERMAN AMERICAN FARM MUTUAL
2.3	1.6	123.1	38.5	-2.1	0.8	59.4	27.6	87.0	123.2	4.0	0.0	GERMAN MUTUAL INS CO
1.2	1.1	95.3	7.7	2.2	0.6	69.8	25.6	95.4	96.8	9.0	52.5 ●	GERMANIA FARM MUTUAL INS ASN
1.7	1.3	164.9	62.8	2.5	6.3	89.8	24.6	114.4	91.2	6.8	0.0	GERMANIA FIRE & CASUALTY CO
4.3	3.6	50.9	27.3	0.5	1.8	63.8	28.2	92.0	110.6	-8.5	0.0	GERMANIA INS CO
2.2	1.8	211.3	67.8	2.7	2.6	81.4	26.9	108.3	96.4	8.4	1.6	GERMANIA SELECT INS CO
4.5	3.6	65.5	41.2	-1.3	2.5	67.4	27.4	94.8	107.9	0.6	0.0	GERMANTOWN INS CO
5.8	4.1	82.5	40.1	-6.7	-7.6	58.2	30.4	88.6	111.8	2.4	0.0	GERMANTOWN MUTUAL INS CO
0.0	0.0	630.9	921.0	185.8	164.7	148.5	22.5	171.0	82.8	-4.5	0.0	GLOBAL HAWK INS CO RRG
N/A	N/A	--	--	--	--	--	--	--	--	--	--	GLOBAL HAWK PROPERTY CAS INS CO
N/A	N/A	--	--	--	--	--	--	--	--	--	--	GLOBAL INS CO
1.9	1.2	173.2	103.8	44.7	56.0	79.6	24.2	103.8	92.5	-2.1	0.0	GLOBAL LIBERTY INS CO OF NY
N/A	N/A	--	--	--	--	--	--	--	--	--	--	GLOBAL REINS CORP OF AM
23.4	18.7	5.4	7.8	0.3	0.2	66.5	29.3	95.8	107.4	5.2	0.0 ●	GNY CUSTOM INS CO
0.5	0.4	209.6	109.4	1.2	-8.5	126.4	20.1	146.5	107.5	42.6	0.0	GOAUTO INS CO
2.1	1.4	52.9	111.2	-31.0	-48.2	44.2	38.6	82.8	179.4	33.5	0.0	GOLDEN BEAR INS CO
64.5	58.0	N/A	N/A	N/A	N/A	N/A	N/A	N/A	N/A	0.0	0.0	GOLDEN EAGLE INS CORP
0.3	0.2	184.2	194.8	7.0	29.9	94.3	30.2	124.5	140.1	-5.7	0.0	GOLDEN INS CO A RRG
N/A	N/A	--	--	--	--	--	--	--	--	--	--	GOLDSTREET INS CO
0.7	0.6	28.5	38.3	3.6	-23.4	76.0	12.5	88.5	123.2	-22.4	0.0	GOOD SHEPHERD RECIPROCAL RRG
5.1	3.4	79.2	24.8	-1.3	0.4	59.4	27.4	86.8	115.1	4.0	0.0	GOODVILLE MUTUAL CAS CO
1.5	0.9	99.8	148.8	9.4	13.2	74.0	35.3	109.3	105.9	-2.6	0.0	GOTHAM INS CO
3.1	1.9	44.5	30.9	-1.2	-1.5	82.9	8.8	91.7	117.0	8.0	0.7 ●	GOVERNMENT EMPLOYEES INS CO
N/A	N/A	--	--	--	--	--	--	--	--	--	--	GOVERNMENT ENTITIES MUTUAL INC
6.8	5.1	12.1	26.4	-1.7	-2.9	77.9	53.0	130.9	69.8	-26.6	0.0	GOVERNMENTAL INTERINS
0.6	0.6	38.9	N/A	N/A	N/A	4.0	209.7	213.7	94.6	-54.1	0.0	GOVT TECHNOLOGY INS CO RRG INC
N/A	N/A	--	--	--	--	--	--	--	--	--	--	GRACO RRG INC
11.6	10.4	N/A	N/A	N/A	N/A	N/A	N/A	N/A	N/A	0.0	0.0	GRAIN DEALERS MUTUAL INS CO
0.2	0.1	105.7	127.4	19.5	43.8	86.7	5.4	92.1	53.4	38.5	0.0	GRANADA INS CO
9.3	7.7	84.1	50.1	-1.9	0.6	62.3	27.9	90.2	109.3	-4.3	0.0	GRANGE INDEMNITY INS CO
3.0	2.2	105.8	42.4	1.1	3.5	71.4	28.3	99.7	102.7	6.3	8.2	GRANGE INS ASSN
10.0	7.2	68.3	40.6	-1.5	0.4	62.3	29.8	92.1	115.9	-4.3	0.0	GRANGE INS CO OF MI

999 + Denotes number greater than 999.9%
999 - Denotes number less than -999.99%
● Bullets denote a more detailed analysis is available in Section II.

INSURANCE COMPANY NAME	DOM. STATE	RATING	TOTAL ASSETS ($MIL)	CAPITAL & SURPLUS ($MIL)	ANNUAL NET PREMIUM ($MIL)	NET INCOME ($MIL)	CAPITAL-IZATION INDEX (PTS)	RESERVE ADQ INDEX (PTS)	PROFIT-ABILITY INDEX (PTS)	LIQUIDITY INDEX (PTS)	STAB. INDEX (PTS)	STABILITY FACTORS
GRANGE MUTUAL CAS CO	OH	B	2,463.8	1,142.2	983.1	16.4	8.4	6.0	8.4	6.3	4.8	RT
GRANGE MUTUAL FIRE INS CO	PA	D+	4.7	3.7	1.1	0.1	9.2	7.4	8.1	7.0	2.0	DGRT
GRANGE P&C INS CO	OH	B-	67.0	43.0	23.4	1.2	10.0	6.0	8.8	6.9	5.2	T
GRANITE MUTUAL INS CO	VT	C+	4.5	4.5	0.0	0.0	10.0	N/A	6.3	7.0	3.4	DGRT
GRANITE RE INC	OK	C+	49.8	23.7	25.8	1.2	5.3	10.0	8.5	7.6	3.1	DRT
GRANITE STATE INS CO	IL	B-	40.3	33.1	0.0	1.4	10.0	N/A	4.1	7.0	3.8	GT
GRANWEST P&C	WA	C	22.6	20.5	0.0	0.1	10.0	6.5	6.8	9.5	3.5	DFGR
GRAPHIC ARTS MUTUAL INS CO	NY	C+	149.7	58.8	44.4	0.3	9.9	6.4	6.7	6.9	4.1	T
GRAY CASUALTY & SURETY CO	LA	C	17.9	14.7	2.2	0.0	10.0	3.6	3.9	10.0	3.1	DGR
GRAY INS CO	LA	C+	284.6	114.9	58.1	0.9	7.5	4.7	6.6	6.9	3.4	FRT
GRAY INS CO OF LOUISIANA	LA	U	--	--	--	--	N/A	--	--	--	--	Z
GREAT AMERICAN ALLIANCE INS CO	OH	C	30.5	30.5	0.0	0.1	10.0	N/A	5.8	7.0	3.7	AGRT
GREAT AMERICAN ASR CO	OH	C+	19.8	19.8	0.0	0.1	10.0	N/A	6.1	7.0	3.4	ADGR
GREAT AMERICAN CASUALTY INS CO	OH	U	--	--	--	--	N/A	--	--	--	--	Z
GREAT AMERICAN CONTEMPORARY INS CO	OH	U	--	--	--	--	N/A	--	--	--	--	Z
GREAT AMERICAN E & S INS CO	DE	C	47.3	47.2	0.0	0.2	10.0	N/A	5.8	7.0	3.9	ART
GREAT AMERICAN FIDELITY INS CO	DE	C	47.4	47.3	0.0	0.2	10.0	N/A	5.8	7.0	3.9	ADRT
GREAT AMERICAN INS CO	OH	B	6,930.2	2,064.0	2,471.4	79.1	7.5	8.0	8.7	6.9	4.0	ART
GREAT AMERICAN INS CO OF NEW YORK	NY	C	48.6	48.5	0.0	0.3	10.0	N/A	6.1	7.0	3.9	ART
GREAT AMERICAN LLOYDS INS CO	TX	U	--	--	--	--	N/A	--	--	--	--	Z
GREAT AMERICAN PROTECTION INS CO	OH	U	--	--	--	--	N/A	--	--	--	--	Z
GREAT AMERICAN SECURITY INS CO	OH	C	15.4	15.4	0.0	0.0	10.0	N/A	3.4	7.0	3.2	ADGR
GREAT AMERICAN SPIRIT INS CO	OH	C	16.9	16.9	0.0	0.1	10.0	N/A	3.4	7.0	3.3	ADGR
GREAT CENTRAL FIRE INS CO	LA	D+(1)	3.9	3.1	2.8	0.0	7.1	6.0	6.5	6.2	2.2	DT
GREAT DIVIDE INS CO	ND	C	258.9	69.9	0.0	0.4	10.0	3.6	6.2	10.0	4.1	RT
GREAT FALLS INS CO	ME	D+	13.3	3.7	3.0	-0.2	3.3	5.0	3.9	6.7	2.0	DGT
GREAT LAKES CASUALTY INS CO	MI	U	--	--	--	--	N/A	--	--	--	--	Z
GREAT LAKES MUTUAL INS CO	MI	C-	11.7	8.0	3.9	0.3	9.8	8.7	8.8	7.4	2.2	DGT
GREAT MIDWEST INS CO	TX	B	208.8	105.4	86.2	0.6	7.8	4.2	3.6	7.4	4.2	FT
GREAT NORTHERN INS CO	IN	B-	1,694.3	516.5	253.5	14.5	8.5	9.0	8.4	6.8	3.6	T
GREAT NORTHWEST INS CO	MN	C-	19.8	7.6	0.0	0.2	9.3	3.4	5.7	10.0	2.8	DGRT
GREAT PLAINS CASUALTY INC	IA	C+	21.0	18.4	5.2	0.4	10.0	8.5	8.9	7.0	4.0	DGT
GREAT WEST CASUALTY CO	NE	B	2,063.9	621.5	831.1	10.5	8.7	9.3	8.9	6.4	6.2	AT
GREATER NEW YORK MUTUAL INS CO	NY	B-	986.2	483.8	240.8	7.7	8.5	6.0	8.0	6.9	4.3	RT
GREEN HILLS INS CO A RRG	VT	E	12.8	5.8	3.9	0.5	7.2	10.0	3.6	6.6	0.0	DGT
GREEN MOUNTAIN INS CO	VT	B	12.4	11.8	0.0	0.1	10.0	N/A	7.5	7.0	4.0	DGT
GREEN TREE PERPETUAL ASR CO	PA	U	--	--	--	--	N/A	--	--	--	--	Z
GREENVILLE CASUALTY INS CO INC	SC	C-	11.9	7.5	5.2	0.0	7.7	4.6	2.9	6.9	2.9	DFGT
GREENWICH INS CO	DE	C	1,132.8	369.0	200.1	4.7	7.8	6.2	3.8	7.3	3.8	AFRT
GREYHAWK INSURANCE CO	CO	C	20.2	18.3	-6.2	-0.7	10.0	9.6	2.0	9.1	3.4	DFGR
GRINNELL MUTUAL REINS CO	IA	B-	1,140.1	605.7	556.5	12.5	9.1	8.1	8.2	6.2	4.4	RT
GRINNELL SELECT INS CO	IA	C	42.0	24.7	0.0	0.0	10.0	N/A	3.4	10.0	3.7	FGT
GROWERS AUTOMOBILE INS ASN	IN	D+	7.2	5.5	0.1	0.0	7.4	4.9	4.7	9.2	2.1	DFGT
GUARANTEE CO OF NORTH AMERICA USA	MI	B	223.8	182.1	46.1	3.6	10.0	6.2	7.9	8.7	4.1	RT
GUARANTEE INS CO	FL	E+	400.4	50.5	103.4	3.1	0.8	0.2	2.6	0.5	0.4	CFLR
GUARDIAN INDEMNITY INC	MT	E (5)	6.2	2.8	1.1	0.2	3.6	6.9	2.2	8.8	0.0	DT
GUARDIAN INS CO	VI	C	28.0	13.3	18.6	-0.4	7.6	5.9	2.4	4.7	2.8	DFGL
GUIDEONE AMERICA INS CO	IA	C+	12.9	10.9	0.0	0.0	10.0	N/A	6.6	10.0	3.3	DFGR
GUIDEONE ELITE INS CO	IA	C+	30.2	25.2	0.0	0.1	10.0	N/A	7.4	7.0	3.7	GRT
GUIDEONE MUTUAL INS CO	IA	B	1,199.6	398.8	353.8	-11.5	7.5	8.6	2.6	6.6	4.5	FRT
GUIDEONE NATIONAL INS CO	IA	C+	55.2	48.0	0.0	0.3	10.0	N/A	8.3	9.1	3.9	T
GUIDEONE P&C INS CO	IA	B	434.6	221.2	110.6	-2.9	8.6	8.0	2.8	6.8	4.4	RT

See Page 27 for explanation of footnotes and
Page 28 for explanation of stability factors.
Arrows denote recent upgrades ▲ or downgrades ▼   (see Section VII for explanations)

72

www.weissratings.com

RISK ADJ. RATIO #1	CAPITAL RATIO #2	PREMIUM TO SURPLUS (%)	RESV. TO SURPLUS (%)	RESV. 1 YEAR (%)	DEVELOP. 2 YEAR (%)	LOSS RATIO (%)	EXP. RATIO (%)	COMB RATIO (%)	CASH FROM UNDER-WRITING (%)	NET PREMIUM GROWTH (%)	INVEST. IN AFFIL (%)	INSURANCE COMPANY NAME
2.5	1.9	88.8	52.8	-1.9	0.5	62.3	32.1	94.4	108.4	-4.3	14.2 ●	GRANGE MUTUAL CAS CO
4.0	2.4	29.4	3.7	-0.9	-1.6	41.9	51.8	93.7	117.2	1.1	0.0	GRANGE MUTUAL FIRE INS CO
10.9	8.7	54.9	32.7	-1.3	0.4	62.3	14.3	76.6	107.8	-4.3	0.0	GRANGE P&C INS CO
90.1	46.4	N/A	N/A	N/A	N/A	N/A	N/A	N/A	N/A	0.0	0.0	GRANITE MUTUAL INS CO
1.0	0.8	114.6	73.6	-35.3	-63.1	4.9	71.4	76.3	118.6	4.8	0.0	GRANITE RE INC
17.2	14.8	N/A	N/A	N/A	N/A	N/A	N/A	N/A	N/A	0.0	4.0	GRANITE STATE INS CO
27.2	24.4	N/A	N/A	-4.1	-5.2	N/A	N/A	N/A	-0.2	-100.0	0.0	GRANWEST P&C
4.5	3.0	76.4	107.0	-1.1	-3.6	65.5	32.8	98.3	110.1	8.0	2.6	GRAPHIC ARTS MUTUAL INS CO
7.1	4.9	15.2	16.8	0.2	N/A	36.6	50.8	87.4	156.9	6.7	0.0	GRAY CASUALTY & SURETY CO
1.8	1.2	51.5	137.9	N/A	N/A	54.0	46.1	100.1	89.1	-13.3	10.9	GRAY INS CO
N/A	N/A	--	--	--	--	--	--	--	--	--	--	GRAY INS CO OF LOUISIANA
94.3	47.1	N/A	N/A	N/A	N/A	N/A	N/A	N/A	N/A	0.0	0.0	GREAT AMERICAN ALLIANCE INS CO
113.7	55.8	N/A	N/A	N/A	N/A	N/A	N/A	N/A	N/A	0.0	0.0	GREAT AMERICAN ASR CO
N/A	N/A	--	--	--	--	--	--	--	--	--	--	GREAT AMERICAN CASUALTY INS CO
N/A	N/A	--	--	--	--	--	--	--	--	--	--	GREAT AMERICAN CONTEMPORARY INS
89.4	45.9	N/A	N/A	N/A	N/A	N/A	N/A	N/A	N/A	0.0	0.0	GREAT AMERICAN E & S INS CO
85.6	43.8	N/A	N/A	N/A	N/A	N/A	N/A	N/A	N/A	0.0	0.0	GREAT AMERICAN FIDELITY INS CO
1.8	1.4	123.6	141.5	-5.7	-4.1	52.4	34.0	86.4	128.0	5.0	15.0 ●	GREAT AMERICAN INS CO
68.9	37.7	N/A	N/A	N/A	N/A	N/A	N/A	N/A	N/A	0.0	0.0	GREAT AMERICAN INS CO OF NEW
N/A	N/A	--	--	--	--	--	--	--	--	--	--	GREAT AMERICAN LLOYDS INS CO
N/A	N/A	--	--	--	--	--	--	--	--	--	--	GREAT AMERICAN PROTECTION INS CO
182.1	91.0	N/A	N/A	N/A	N/A	N/A	N/A	N/A	N/A	0.0	0.0	GREAT AMERICAN SECURITY INS CO
165.8	82.9	N/A	N/A	N/A	N/A	N/A	N/A	N/A	N/A	0.0	0.0	GREAT AMERICAN SPIRIT INS CO
1.3	1.1	88.7	6.6	-0.7	1.3	22.8	77.8	100.6	98.6	-6.8	0.0	GREAT CENTRAL FIRE INS CO
7.0	6.3	N/A	N/A	N/A	N/A	N/A	N/A	N/A	280.1	0.0	0.0	GREAT DIVIDE INS CO
1.2	0.6	79.4	60.0	-7.0	-2.7	67.1	6.2	73.3	143.7	32.1	0.0	GREAT FALLS INS CO
N/A	N/A	--	--	--	--	--	--	--	--	--	--	GREAT LAKES CASUALTY INS CO
5.4	3.3	49.3	14.3	-6.2	-9.3	23.8	34.8	58.6	173.7	8.2	0.0	GREAT LAKES MUTUAL INS CO
2.4	1.6	82.3	73.6	17.5	10.6	94.5	37.9	132.4	84.0	-7.7	0.4	GREAT MIDWEST INS CO
3.8	2.4	50.3	122.8	-5.7	-9.7	53.6	34.1	87.7	98.3	-35.2	0.0 ●	GREAT NORTHERN INS CO
2.8	2.5	N/A	4.8	-1.9	7.5	N/A	N/A	N/A	14.1	0.0	0.0	GREAT NORTHWEST INS CO
6.3	3.7	29.4	9.5	-1.9	-8.5	49.0	10.3	59.3	229.9	-12.2	0.0	GREAT PLAINS CASUALTY INC
3.3	2.0	133.5	126.8	0.1	-7.3	74.0	22.4	96.4	110.9	-2.1	0.0 ●	GREAT WEST CASUALTY CO
2.3	1.9	50.9	72.9	2.9	1.7	66.5	29.3	95.8	107.4	5.2	16.3 ●	GREATER NEW YORK MUTUAL INS CO
1.9	1.1	72.9	84.5	-43.2	-122.5	-2.4	24.1	21.7	304.1	8.3	0.0	GREEN HILLS INS CO A RRG
5.2	3.0	N/A	N/A	N/A	N/A	N/A	N/A	N/A	N/A	0.0	0.0	GREEN MOUNTAIN INS CO
N/A	N/A	--	--	--	--	--	--	--	--	--	--	GREEN TREE PERPETUAL ASR CO
2.5	2.3	70.1	27.6	-6.3	-9.3	41.1	33.1	74.2	68.9	0.8	45.4	GREENVILLE CASUALTY INS CO INC
1.8	1.5	54.9	110.8	0.1	0.4	69.3	23.5	92.8	105.0	25.6	24.2 ●	GREENWICH INS CO
29.1	26.1	-32.6	N/A	-28.5	-42.1	94.0	-33.3	60.7	-36.5	N/A	0.0	GREYHAWK INSURANCE CO
3.8	2.6	94.3	43.6	-2.2	-3.7	59.3	27.4	86.7	119.6	6.0	3.1 ●	GRINNELL MUTUAL REINS CO
7.6	6.9	N/A	N/A	N/A	N/A	N/A	N/A	N/A	-156.2	0.0	0.0	GRINNELL SELECT INS CO
2.1	1.3	2.1	-0.3	-1.3	1.0	80.7	99.8	180.5	25.7	-6.0	0.0	GROWERS AUTOMOBILE INS ASN
7.6	5.7	25.5	4.9	-1.0	-0.7	14.1	63.9	78.0	128.0	11.9	0.0	GUARANTEE CO OF NORTH AMERICA
0.2	0.1	203.6	129.9	71.9	122.0	82.0	31.6	113.6	65.4	59.5	8.2	GUARANTEE INS CO
0.7	0.5	39.9	106.7	-15.2	1.7	68.4	18.9	87.3	114.2	0.6	0.0	GUARDIAN INDEMNITY INC
1.6	1.3	131.2	25.7	3.3	3.4	67.0	41.8	108.8	90.4	-4.2	17.0	GUARDIAN INS CO
14.6	13.2	N/A	N/A	N/A	N/A	N/A	N/A	N/A	-160.3	0.0	0.0	GUIDEONE AMERICA INS CO
16.3	14.7	N/A	N/A	N/A	N/A	N/A	N/A	N/A	43.7	0.0	0.0	GUIDEONE ELITE INS CO
1.7	1.3	83.9	99.8	0.1	-4.4	78.6	48.1	126.7	93.8	-1.8	21.5 ●	GUIDEONE MUTUAL INS CO
24.9	22.4	N/A	N/A	N/A	N/A	N/A	N/A	N/A	36.7	0.0	0.0	GUIDEONE NATIONAL INS CO
2.5	2.1	49.4	58.8	0.1	-2.5	78.6	36.3	114.9	92.7	-1.8	23.1 ●	GUIDEONE P&C INS CO

999 + Denotes number greater than 999.9%
999 - Denotes number less than -999.99%
● Bullets denote a more detailed analysis is available in Section II.

INSURANCE COMPANY NAME	DOM. STATE	RATING	TOTAL ASSETS ($MIL)	CAPITAL & SURPLUS ($MIL)	ANNUAL NET PREMIUM ($MIL)	NET INCOME ($MIL)	CAPITAL-IZATION INDEX (PTS)	RESERVE ADQ INDEX (PTS)	PROFIT-ABILITY INDEX (PTS)	LIQUIDITY INDEX (PTS)	STAB. INDEX (PTS)	STABILITY FACTORS
GUIDEONE SPECIALTY MUTUAL INS CO	IA	B	270.7	92.1	88.4	-0.1	8.2	8.9	3.5	6.6	4.4	FRT
GUILDERLAND REINS CO	NY	U	--	--	--	--	N/A	--	--	--	--	Z
GUILFORD INS CO	IL	C-	379.3	277.1	27.9	0.3	7.9	8.0	6.0	7.8	2.6	FRT
GULF BUILDERS RRG INC	SC	F (5)	0.0	0.0	-0.1	0.0	3.0	4.6	0.8	10.0	0.0	FGT
GULF GUARANTY INS CO	MS	C	4.3	3.8	0.4	0.1	10.0	6.2	3.1	8.4	2.3	DFGT
GULF STATES INS CO (LA)	LA	U	--	--	--	--	N/A	--	--	--	--	Z
GULF UNDERWRITERS INS CO	CT	U	--	--	--	--	N/A	--	--	--	--	Z
GULFSTREAM P&C INS CO	FL	B-	112.6	32.9	61.4	0.6	7.3	9.3	4.2	7.0	5.2	FT
GUTHRIE RRG	SC	C	53.1	18.4	7.6	0.6	5.1	9.4	3.7	6.9	4.0	DT
HALIFAX MUTUAL INS CO	NC	D (1)	8.2	4.2	3.8	0.3	7.4	8.8	5.2	6.9	1.5	DFRT
HALLMARK COUNTY MUTUAL INS CO	TX	C	5.6	5.5	0.0	0.0	10.0	N/A	4.9	7.6	2.4	DFGR
HALLMARK INS CO	AZ	D+	305.8	105.6	115.8	2.2	8.1	4.9	6.9	7.0	2.2	RT
HALLMARK NATIONAL INS CO	AZ	C	85.0	26.2	36.2	0.5	7.9	4.8	5.5	7.2	2.7	FRT
HALLMARK SPECIALTY INS CO	OK	B-	233.5	60.7	86.8	1.6	8.0	4.8	5.5	6.7	3.7	FRT
HAMDEN ASR RRG INC	VT	U	--	--	--	--	N/A	--	--	--	--	Z
HAMILTON INS CO	DE	C+	30.7	21.7	2.6	-1.4	7.9	4.9	1.5	7.5	3.1	DFGR
HAMILTON MUTUAL INS CO	IA	C	76.6	38.6	31.4	3.2	9.3	8.0	8.6	6.9	3.8	T
HAMILTON SPECIALTY INS CO	DE	B-	101.9	55.2	18.4	-2.5	7.6	3.6	2.6	6.8	3.5	GT
HANNAHSTOWN MUTUAL INS CO	PA	D+(2)	4.3	2.6	1.5	0.1	8.1	6.5	6.3	7.3	1.9	DGRT
HANOVER AMERICAN INS CO	NH	C	31.1	30.8	0.0	0.2	10.0	N/A	7.3	7.0	3.7	GRT
HANOVER FIRE & CASUALTY INS CO	PA	D+	5.9	3.2	4.5	0.0	5.3	6.8	8.0	6.9	2.0	DGRT
HANOVER INS CO	NH	B	7,505.1	2,224.2	3,171.5	34.4	7.2	3.4	6.3	6.0	5.1	AT
HANOVER LLOYDS INS CO	TX	C+	6.1	6.1	0.0	0.0	10.0	N/A	7.2	7.0	3.0	DGRT
HANOVER NATIONAL INS CO	NH	U	--	--	--	--	N/A	--	--	--	--	Z
HANOVER NJ INS CO	NH	U	--	--	--	--	N/A	--	--	--	--	Z
HARBOR INS CO	OK	D+	12.2	3.3	4.9	0.1	7.5	6.9	4.3	7.5	2.0	DGT
HARCO NATIONAL INS CO	IL	B-	480.5	177.4	123.4	2.9	4.9	5.8	5.5	2.8	4.1	CGLR
HARFORD MUTUAL INS CO	MD	B-	434.7	212.5	123.6	2.3	8.5	6.4	8.3	6.9	4.1	RT
HARLEYSVILLE INS CO	PA	C	163.7	26.4	0.0	0.1	9.7	3.9	4.3	8.0	3.7	AT
HARLEYSVILLE INS CO OF NEW YORK	PA	C	60.6	24.0	0.0	0.1	10.0	3.8	5.0	10.0	3.8	DFRT
HARLEYSVILLE INS CO OF NJ	NJ	C	89.1	47.5	0.0	0.1	10.0	3.9	3.5	10.0	3.6	AT
HARLEYSVILLE LAKE STATES INS CO	MI	C	57.9	36.8	0.0	0.1	10.0	3.9	3.5	7.0	3.8	AT
HARLEYSVILLE PREFERRED INS CO	PA	C	138.4	48.5	0.0	0.2	10.0	3.9	3.5	7.0	3.6	AT
HARLEYSVILLE WORCESTER INS CO	PA	C	192.5	57.7	0.0	0.2	10.0	3.9	3.4	7.0	3.6	AT
HARTFORD ACCIDENT & INDEMNITY CO	CT	B	12,150.0	3,166.7	3,444.1	109.8	7.7	5.8	4.8	6.7	4.9	AT
HARTFORD CASUALTY INS CO	IN	B	2,325.1	912.3	579.5	19.4	10.0	5.9	5.4	6.8	4.9	AT
HARTFORD FIRE INS CO	CT	B	24,977.6	12,287.1	4,372.3	227.6	7.6	6.0	3.8	6.8	5.1	AT
HARTFORD INS CO OF IL	IL	B	3,906.5	1,300.1	1,064.1	34.8	9.1	5.8	4.5	6.7	5.0	AT
HARTFORD INS CO OF THE MIDWEST	IN	B	628.9	495.6	52.7	4.3	10.0	5.0	8.1	7.0	4.7	AT
HARTFORD INS CO OF THE SOUTHEAST	CT	B	191.5	58.4	52.7	1.9	8.5	5.8	5.9	6.8	4.1	AT
HARTFORD LLOYDS INS CO	TX	B	74.1	71.6	1.1	0.5	10.0	4.6	7.8	9.8	4.3	AGT
HARTFORD SM BOIL INSPECTION & INS	CT	B	1,316.7	616.8	451.7	27.2	9.2	8.7	3.9	6.9	6.1	T
HARTFORD SM BOIL INSPECTION IC OF CT	CT	B	31.0	27.3	17.7	3.1	10.0	7.9	3.5	9.2	4.2	DT
HARTFORD UNDERWRITERS INS CO	CT	B	1,654.8	606.4	421.4	14.3	9.7	5.9	4.6	6.8	4.8	AT
HARTLAND MUTUAL INS CO	ND	C	12.5	8.2	5.5	0.6	9.5	6.3	7.0	7.1	2.7	DFGT
HASTINGS MUTUAL INS CO	MI	B	902.9	428.3	401.8	2.6	10.0	5.8	8.3	6.7	4.7	T
HAULERS INS CO	TN	B-	78.0	39.6	37.8	0.4	9.6	6.9	6.0	6.3	3.9	T
▲HAWAII EMPLOYERS MUTUAL INS CO	HI	B-	387.5	231.2	71.8	2.3	10.0	6.0	6.9	7.0	5.0	T
HAWAIIAN INS & GUARANTY CO LTD	HI	B-	28.4	14.1	10.6	-0.2	8.5	6.0	5.6	7.2	5.0	DGT
HAWKEYE-SECURITY INS CO	WI	C	13.4	13.1	0.0	0.0	10.0	N/A	5.8	7.0	3.1	DGRT
HAY CREEK MUTUAL INS CO	MN	D+	5.8	3.2	2.6	0.1	8.7	6.1	5.6	6.6	2.1	DGT
HCC SPECIALTY INS CO	OK	B-	19.6	16.7	0.0	0.1	10.0	N/A	5.9	9.1	4.9	DGR

Arrows denote recent upgrades ▲ or downgrades ▼   (see Section VII for explanations)

RISK ADJ. CAPITAL RATIO #1	CAPITAL RATIO #2	PREMIUM TO SURPLUS (%)	RESV. TO SURPLUS (%)	RESV. DEVELOP. 1 YEAR (%)	2 YEAR (%)	LOSS RATIO (%)	EXP. RATIO (%)	COMB RATIO (%)	CASH FROM UNDER-WRITING (%)	NET PREMIUM GROWTH (%)	INVEST. IN AFFIL (%)	INSURANCE COMPANY NAME
2.7	1.9	93.9	111.6	0.1	-5.0	78.6	36.3	114.9	91.1	-1.8	7.3	GUIDEONE SPECIALTY MUTUAL INS CO
N/A	N/A	--	--	--	--	--	--	--	--	--	--	GUILDERLAND REINS CO
1.6	1.6	10.2	29.5	-1.8	-3.2	47.9	54.5	102.4	72.9	-14.9	49.0 ●	GUILFORD INS CO
0.5	0.5	-52.9	20.2	-3.2	-0.7	27.2	-79.2	-52.0	1.0	-167.1	0.0	GULF BUILDERS RRG INC
7.1	5.6	11.1	1.5	-0.9	-0.9	54.0	96.3	150.3	50.7	15.7	0.0	GULF GUARANTY INS CO
N/A	N/A	--	--	--	--	--	--	--	--	--	--	GULF STATES INS CO (LA)
N/A	N/A	--	--	--	--	--	--	--	--	--	--	GULF UNDERWRITERS INS CO
1.5	1.4	195.1	47.2	N/A	-9.7	79.1	34.1	113.2	85.4	9.8	0.0	GULFSTREAM P&C INS CO
1.0	0.7	42.9	176.3	5.7	-7.7	87.0	4.4	91.4	146.3	4.1	0.0	GUTHRIE RRG
2.2	1.5	92.2	8.6	-4.2	-8.1	66.6	22.7	89.3	84.7	12.2	0.0	HALIFAX MUTUAL INS CO
81.3	36.4	N/A	N/A	N/A	N/A	N/A	N/A	N/A	N/A	0.0	0.0	HALLMARK COUNTY MUTUAL INS CO
2.4	1.7	111.6	110.1	1.8	1.3	71.3	27.7	99.0	129.8	-4.3	10.6	HALLMARK INS CO
2.9	1.9	140.6	138.8	2.3	1.5	71.3	31.5	102.8	72.4	13.2	0.0	HALLMARK NATIONAL INS CO
3.0	1.8	146.9	144.9	2.4	1.5	71.3	29.3	100.6	70.7	13.3	0.0	HALLMARK SPECIALTY INS CO
N/A	N/A	--	--	--	--	--	--	--	--	--	--	HAMDEN ASR RRG INC
1.4	1.3	12.1	4.8	-0.5	N/A	63.1	404.0	467.1	40.1	151.5	0.0	HAMILTON INS CO
7.2	6.4	87.9	89.6	-4.7	-5.4	65.2	31.4	96.6	108.5	3.8	0.0	HAMILTON MUTUAL INS CO
1.6	1.3	36.7	17.3	0.2	N/A	89.0	129.3	218.3	143.4	385.5	22.9	HAMILTON SPECIALTY INS CO
2.9	1.8	63.0	7.7	-1.6	-2.8	46.6	39.6	86.2	114.6	16.8	0.0	HANNAHSTOWN MUTUAL INS CO
78.3	36.6	N/A	N/A	N/A	N/A	N/A	N/A	N/A	N/A	0.0	0.0	HANOVER AMERICAN INS CO
0.9	0.7	140.8	14.7	-7.1	-8.8	17.1	73.9	91.0	107.7	0.8	0.0	HANOVER FIRE & CASUALTY INS CO
1.4	1.1	146.3	137.8	12.5	17.2	69.4	34.3	103.7	110.5	4.1	20.2 ●	HANOVER INS CO
68.3	30.3	N/A	N/A	N/A	N/A	N/A	N/A	N/A	N/A	0.0	0.0	HANOVER LLOYDS INS CO
N/A	N/A	--	--	--	--	--	--	--	--	--	--	HANOVER NATIONAL INS CO
N/A	N/A	--	--	--	--	--	--	--	--	--	--	HANOVER NJ INS CO
1.5	1.3	148.1	58.7	-17.1	-6.4	62.2	22.6	84.8	102.8	3.1	0.0	HARBOR INS CO
1.1	0.8	73.0	60.3	10.9	4.1	77.7	22.4	100.1	101.1	43.5	14.2	HARCO NATIONAL INS CO
2.5	1.9	59.2	47.8	-0.6	1.8	61.2	32.3	93.5	114.6	8.3	14.5 ●	HARFORD MUTUAL INS CO
3.0	2.7	N/A	N/A	N/A	N/A	N/A	N/A	N/A	196.7	0.0	0.0	HARLEYSVILLE INS CO
4.7	4.2	N/A	N/A	N/A	N/A	N/A	N/A	N/A	-462.0	0.0	0.0	HARLEYSVILLE INS CO OF NEW YORK
10.4	9.4	N/A	N/A	N/A	N/A	N/A	N/A	N/A	-644.2	0.0	0.0	HARLEYSVILLE INS CO OF NJ
11.6	10.4	N/A	N/A	N/A	N/A	N/A	N/A	N/A	66.9	0.0	0.0	HARLEYSVILLE LAKE STATES INS CO
7.2	6.5	N/A	N/A	N/A	N/A	N/A	N/A	N/A	330.6	0.0	0.0	HARLEYSVILLE PREFERRED INS CO
7.8	7.0	N/A	N/A	N/A	N/A	N/A	N/A	N/A	13.8	0.0	0.0	HARLEYSVILLE WORCESTER INS CO
1.9	1.4	109.2	194.8	3.8	3.0	70.4	29.1	99.5	105.5	0.0	9.2 ●	HARTFORD ACCIDENT & INDEMNITY CO
4.6	3.0	64.8	115.6	2.3	1.9	70.4	27.9	98.3	105.5	0.0	0.0 ●	HARTFORD CASUALTY INS CO
2.0	1.5	34.9	62.3	1.2	0.9	70.4	47.8	118.2	104.9	0.0	26.4 ●	HARTFORD FIRE INS CO
3.7	2.4	84.6	150.9	3.0	2.3	70.4	29.1	99.5	105.5	0.0	0.0 ●	HARTFORD INS CO OF IL
26.8	16.9	10.7	19.1	0.4	0.3	70.4	15.4	85.8	105.5	0.0	0.0 ●	HARTFORD INS CO OF THE MIDWEST
3.1	2.0	93.3	166.5	3.4	2.6	70.4	27.4	97.8	105.5	0.0	0.0	HARTFORD INS CO OF THE SOUTHEAST
83.0	51.2	1.5	2.6	0.1	0.1	70.4	-11.3	59.1	105.5	0.0	0.0	HARTFORD LLOYDS INS CO
2.9	2.5	75.4	24.7	-3.8	-6.1	29.4	54.5	83.9	124.2	66.4	14.2 ●	HARTFORD SM BOIL INSPECTION & INS
4.6	4.6	43.7	13.5	-2.4	-3.3	28.1	8.3	36.4	232.0	58.8	0.0	HARTFORD SM BOIL INSPECTION IC OF
4.1	2.7	71.2	127.0	2.5	2.0	70.4	27.1	97.5	105.5	0.0	0.0 ●	HARTFORD UNDERWRITERS INS CO
4.8	3.0	71.2	12.9	-0.8	-0.7	76.9	33.9	110.8	95.0	-3.9	1.3	HARTLAND MUTUAL INS CO
5.1	3.4	95.0	58.0	-3.0	-5.4	60.8	31.0	91.8	113.3	3.4	0.0 ●	HASTINGS MUTUAL INS CO
3.5	2.6	96.8	54.8	-6.1	-7.2	75.3	25.5	100.8	90.5	5.5	0.0	HAULERS INS CO
4.6	3.2	31.4	48.8	-0.7	1.7	71.8	28.1	99.9	115.8	6.3	0.0 ●	HAWAII EMPLOYERS MUTUAL INS CO
3.4	2.6	74.4	25.6	-6.3	-3.7	37.5	48.0	85.5	107.7	-6.1	0.0	HAWAIIAN INS & GUARANTY CO LTD
101.4	91.2	N/A	N/A	N/A	N/A	N/A	N/A	N/A	N/A	0.0	0.0	HAWKEYE-SECURITY INS CO
3.0	2.3	85.6	8.3	-6.4	-2.9	53.3	38.3	91.6	106.6	2.6	0.0	HAY CREEK MUTUAL INS CO
17.5	15.7	N/A	N/A	N/A	N/A	N/A	N/A	N/A	-348.0	0.0	0.0	HCC SPECIALTY INS CO

999 + Denotes number greater than 999.9%
999 - Denotes number less than -999.99%
● Bullets denote a more detailed analysis is available in Section II.

INSURANCE COMPANY NAME	DOM. STATE	RATING	TOTAL ASSETS ($MIL)	CAPITAL & SURPLUS ($MIL)	ANNUAL NET PREMIUM ($MIL)	NET INCOME ($MIL)	CAPITAL-IZATION INDEX (PTS)	RESERVE ADQ INDEX (PTS)	PROFIT-ABILITY INDEX (PTS)	LIQUIDITY INDEX (PTS)	STAB. INDEX (PTS)	STABILITY FACTORS
HDI GLOBAL INS CO	IL	C	436.2	143.8	5.3	2.6	10.0	6.6	7.7	10.0	3.6	FRT
HDI SPECIALTY INSURANCE CO	IL	U	--	--	--	--	N/A	--	--	--	--	Z
HEALTH CARE CASUALTY RRG INC	DC	D	11.4	2.1	1.5	-0.1	5.1	10.0	5.2	9.4	1.8	DFGR
HEALTH CARE INDEMNITY INC	CO	C-	366.3	110.7	21.6	1.7	7.0	9.7	2.9	7.7	2.7	FRT
▲HEALTH CARE INDUSTRY LIAB RECIP INS	DC	C-	44.6	17.1	3.6	0.1	8.5	5.2	7.9	6.9	3.0	DRT
HEALTH CARE INS RECPL	MN	C-	30.2	8.5	7.1	0.3	5.4	9.7	4.5	7.0	2.9	DGRT
HEALTH CARE MUT CAPTIVE INS CO	GA	D	14.5	5.5	4.9	-0.3	5.7	9.4	2.9	6.9	2.0	DGRT
HEALTH PROVIDERS INS RECIPROCAL RRG	HI	B-	84.2	59.1	8.0	-0.6	10.0	9.3	5.4	7.3	4.8	DRT
HEALTHCARE PROFESSIONAL INS CO INC	NY	D+	231.0	66.5	21.1	-0.2	4.2	5.1	6.6	6.8	2.6	DFRT
HEALTHCARE PROVIDERS INS EXCH	PA	E-	37.4	6.4	-23.1	1.1	0.1	0.9	0.4	9.5	0.1	CFRT
▲HEALTHCARE UNDERWRITERS GRP MUT	OH	B-	86.7	48.2	16.0	-0.2	9.9	9.3	4.6	7.7	5.0	DFT
HEALTHCARE UNDERWRITING CO RRG	VT	D	130.9	24.5	45.4	1.0	1.9	3.7	3.0	8.0	2.3	DFT
HEARTLAND MUTUAL INS CO	MN	D	8.0	4.7	4.2	0.3	10.0	6.6	8.6	7.1	2.0	DGT
HEREFORD INS CO	NY	C	256.7	31.8	72.3	-0.3	5.9	3.1	5.7	6.6	3.2	RT
HERITAGE CASUALTY INS CO	KS	U	--	--	--	--	N/A	--	--	--	--	Z
HERITAGE INDEMNITY CO	CA	C+	115.6	38.5	-34.6	0.1	10.0	4.9	3.1	8.9	3.1	FRT
HERITAGE P&C INS CO	FL	C+	606.2	195.0	319.1	-5.4	5.1	5.5	4.9	6.0	4.1	CT
▼HERMITAGE INS CO	NY	F (5)	167.6	10.7	-32.3	0.0	5.2	0.9	0.1	2.3	0.0	DFLR
HIGH POINT P&C INS CO	NJ	B (1)	390.9	367.2	0.0	1.3	7.9	N/A	7.1	7.0	5.5	F
HIGH POINT PREFERRED INS CO	NJ	B (1)	276.7	152.0	117.0	31.7	8.4	7.0	7.2	6.6	4.3	T
HIGH POINT SAFETY & INS CO	NJ	B- (1)	65.2	52.0	0.0	1.0	10.0	N/A	7.4	7.0	5.0	
HIGHLANDS INS CO	TX	F (5)	0.0	0.0	40.8	0.0	0.0	0.7	0.0	1.9	0.0	CDFL
HIGHMARK CASUALTY INS CO	PA	C	272.8	181.3	218.0	1.9	8.3	6.9	8.0	0.9	4.2	FLRT
HILLSTAR INS CO	IN	U	--	--	--	--	N/A	--	--	--	--	Z
HINGHAM MUTUAL FIRE INS CO	MA	C+	63.4	42.0	20.7	0.5	8.6	8.0	5.1	6.9	3.7	RT
HISCOX INS CO	IL	C+	246.0	61.1	70.3	2.1	3.9	6.3	6.0	7.2	4.3	CGRT
HLTHCR PROVIDERS INS CO	SC	C	81.2	48.2	10.2	-0.3	9.2	9.4	6.8	9.1	4.0	DGRT
HM CASUALTY INS CO	PA	B-	63.3	17.7	0.0	0.0	10.0	N/A	9.3	10.0	4.9	DG
HOCHHEIM PRAIRIE CASUALTY INS CO	TX	C	78.4	34.4	43.1	0.2	7.9	7.0	5.7	5.7	3.5	FRT
HOCHHEIM PRAIRIE FARM MUT INS ASN	TX	D	132.7	65.1	78.0	-0.3	7.2	4.4	2.9	3.4	2.0	FLRT
HOME & FARM INS CO	OH	C	9.9	7.0	2.2	0.1	10.0	6.5	4.2	6.9	2.7	DGRT
HOME CONSTRUCTION INS CO	NV	U (5)	--	--	--	--	N/A	--	--	--	--	Z
HOME STATE COUNTY MUTUAL INS CO	TX	C-	104.3	7.1	4.9	0.1	3.8	8.5	8.9	9.9	2.7	DFRT
HOME VALUE INS CO	OH	F (5)	0.0	0.0	0.0	0.0	8.4	N/A	0.9	10.0	0.0	DFGT
HOME-OWNERS INS CO	MI	A-	2,197.5	1,097.9	831.4	19.4	10.0	6.0	8.9	6.8	5.9	T
HOMELAND INS CO OF DE	DE	B	52.3	52.0	0.0	0.1	10.0	N/A	6.3	7.0	4.3	T
HOMELAND INS CO OF NY	NY	C	116.9	114.8	0.0	0.6	8.8	N/A	5.9	7.0	4.2	RT
HOMEOWNERS CHOICE ASR CO INC	AL	U (4)	--	--	--	--	N/A	--	--	--	--	Z
HOMEOWNERS CHOICE PROP & CAS INS	FL	C	411.8	172.9	217.0	8.4	7.5	4.4	7.9	7.1	3.6	T
▲HOMEOWNERS OF AMERICA INS CO	TX	C-	47.4	18.7	3.5	-0.4	8.5	6.1	6.2	6.9	3.0	DFRT
HOMESHIELD FIRE & CASUALTY INS CO	OK	U	--	--	--	--	N/A	--	--	--	--	Z
HOMESITE INDEMNITY CO	WI	C	54.3	40.3	0.0	0.1	10.0	3.6	8.0	10.0	3.5	RT
HOMESITE INS CO	WI	C	156.8	87.3	0.0	0.3	10.0	3.6	8.0	7.0	3.6	FRT
HOMESITE INS CO OF CA	CA	C	58.8	37.1	0.0	0.1	10.0	3.6	8.1	8.7	3.5	FRT
HOMESITE INS CO OF FL	IL	C	14.2	11.1	0.0	0.0	10.0	3.6	5.9	10.0	3.4	DFGR
HOMESITE INS CO OF GA	GA	C	30.8	21.8	0.0	0.1	10.0	3.6	7.9	7.0	3.5	DFGR
HOMESITE INS CO OF IL	IL	C	12.8	9.5	0.0	0.0	10.0	3.6	7.3	10.0	3.5	DGR
HOMESITE INS CO OF NY	NY	C	37.4	17.6	11.6	-0.6	9.7	3.6	5.7	8.0	3.5	DGRT
HOMESITE INS CO OF THE MIDWEST	WI	C	416.2	102.7	0.0	0.1	10.0	5.1	6.4	6.8	3.8	RT
HOMESITE LLOYDS OF TEXAS	TX	C	32.1	15.9	0.0	0.0	10.0	3.6	7.7	6.9	3.2	DFGR
HOMESTEAD INS CO	PA	U	--	--	--	--	N/A	--	--	--	--	Z
HOMESTEAD MUTUAL INS CO	WI	C	9.6	7.2	2.1	0.0	7.9	6.2	5.1	6.9	2.5	DGT

See Page 27 for explanation of footnotes and
Page 28 for explanation of stability factors.

76

www.weissratings.com

Arrows denote recent upgrades ▲ or downgrades ▼   (see Section VII for explanations)

RISK ADJ. RATIO #1	CAPITAL RATIO #2	PREMIUM TO SURPLUS (%)	RESV. TO SURPLUS (%)	RESV. DEVELOP. 1 YEAR (%)	RESV. DEVELOP. 2 YEAR (%)	LOSS RATIO (%)	EXP. RATIO (%)	COMB RATIO (%)	CASH FROM UNDER-WRITING (%)	NET PREMIUM GROWTH (%)	INVEST. IN AFFIL (%)	INSURANCE COMPANY NAME
6.3	4.0	3.8	25.4	1.0	1.1	124.5	-253.8	-129.3	60.3	-36.9	2.8	HDI GLOBAL INS CO
N/A	N/A	--	--	--	--	--	--	--	--	--	--	HDI SPECIALTY INSURANCE CO
0.9	0.8	71.6	333.6	-30.7	-45.0	65.0	58.9	123.9	53.9	-51.6	0.0	HEALTH CARE CASUALTY RRG INC
1.2	0.9	19.8	226.9	-9.5	-15.9	90.3	29.2	119.5	22.2	-42.3	0.0	HEALTH CARE INDEMNITY INC
3.0	2.4	21.4	52.2	-0.9	-1.6	80.8	3.2	84.0	107.8	-8.7	0.0	HEALTH CARE INDUSTRY LIAB RECIP
1.2	0.9	77.9	169.2	-30.7	-51.7	35.4	29.8	65.2	115.3	1.5	0.0	HEALTH CARE INS RECPL
1.6	1.2	89.7	76.6	-40.0	-11.1	35.8	27.6	63.4	113.7	48.0	0.0	HEALTH CARE MUT CAPTIVE INS CO
6.7	4.3	13.5	30.5	-0.8	-9.7	73.7	29.4	103.1	138.6	9.4	0.0	HEALTH PROVIDERS INS RECIPROCAL
1.0	0.9	30.1	222.2	-102.9	-122.2	22.4	35.5	57.9	63.5	-30.4	0.0	HEALTHCARE PROFESSIONAL INS CO
0.2	0.1	-440.6	620.7	-56.1	4.5	40.8	6.3	47.1	-126.2	-192.1	0.0	HEALTHCARE PROVIDERS INS EXCH
4.6	3.5	33.3	57.9	-5.2	-12.1	61.3	41.1	102.4	76.2	-6.6	0.0	HEALTHCARE UNDERWRITERS GRP
0.6	0.4	193.6	412.5	27.5	8.8	110.2	5.7	115.9	94.2	3.9	0.0	HEALTHCARE UNDERWRITING CO RRG
4.5	4.0	93.9	18.1	-3.1	-2.2	48.1	31.7	79.8	157.0	5.1	0.0	HEARTLAND MUTUAL INS CO
1.4	0.9	233.0	325.3	-0.4	17.7	80.5	12.0	92.5	114.4	11.7	0.0	HEREFORD INS CO
N/A	N/A	--	--	--	--	--	--	--	--	--	--	HERITAGE CASUALTY INS CO
4.9	4.4	-68.6	1.7	-17.0	1.2	85.7	19.0	104.7	-376.2	-159.8	0.0	HERITAGE INDEMNITY CO
1.4	0.9	159.8	69.9	9.0	-2.7	70.9	46.8	117.7	99.0	-18.5	0.0 •	HERITAGE P&C INS CO
1.2	1.1	-431.0	N/A	-101.2	69.8	108.5	-15.2	93.3	-35.1	-119.2	0.0	HERMITAGE INS CO
1.6	1.6	N/A	N/A	N/A	N/A	N/A	N/A	N/A	N/A	0.0	60.6	HIGH POINT P&C INS CO
3.0	2.3	77.0	34.0	-4.7	-4.9	37.9	23.3	61.2	154.4	1.3	5.1	HIGH POINT PREFERRED INS CO
5.1	3.0	N/A	N/A	N/A	N/A	N/A	N/A	N/A	N/A	0.0	0.0	HIGH POINT SAFETY & INS CO
-0.0	-0.0	196.4	999 +	74.9	99.7	109.3	70.8	180.1	41.8	-86.8	0.0	HIGHLANDS INS CO
4.6	3.0	121.6	35.1	-10.5	-3.2	74.5	32.2	106.7	57.9	-23.0	0.0	HIGHMARK CASUALTY INS CO
N/A	N/A	--	--	--	--	--	--	--	--	--	--	HILLSTAR INS CO
3.2	2.4	50.3	17.8	-1.5	-1.8	48.0	45.7	93.7	110.9	0.1	14.6	HINGHAM MUTUAL FIRE INS CO
0.8	0.6	106.8	94.8	0.8	-2.4	63.9	21.7	85.6	215.5	39.3	9.0	HISCOX INS CO
4.0	2.5	21.6	49.6	-9.7	-21.1	43.8	33.5	77.3	148.1	29.9	0.0	HLTHCR PROVIDERS INS CO
2.8	2.5	N/A	N/A	N/A	N/A	N/A	N/A	N/A	91.8	0.0	0.0	HM CASUALTY INS CO
2.5	1.7	126.9	58.0	-5.0	-16.1	87.0	22.9	109.9	90.9	7.0	0.9	HOCHHEIM PRAIRIE CASUALTY INS CO
1.2	1.0	120.1	12.5	-4.8	N/A	79.2	25.8	105.0	91.5	-2.1	38.7	HOCHHEIM PRAIRIE FARM MUT INS ASN
7.3	6.5	31.1	7.2	-0.4	-1.3	70.3	35.3	105.6	96.6	12.3	0.0	HOME & FARM INS CO
N/A	N/A	--	--	--	--	--	--	--	--	--	--	HOME CONSTRUCTION INS CO
0.8	0.7	69.6	41.2	-1.2	-8.1	88.2	-2.4	85.8	80.4	3.2	0.0	HOME STATE COUNTY MUTUAL INS CO
0.4	0.4	0.3	N/A	N/A	N/A	999 +	999 +	999 +	0.2	0.0	0.0	HOME VALUE INS CO
6.1	4.5	77.6	55.3	-0.2	-1.4	67.6	24.9	92.5	108.0	2.7	0.0 •	HOME-OWNERS INS CO
80.8	37.0	N/A	N/A	N/A	N/A	N/A	N/A	N/A	N/A	0.0	0.0	HOMELAND INS CO OF DE
2.2	2.2	N/A	N/A	N/A	N/A	N/A	N/A	N/A	N/A	0.0	47.9	HOMELAND INS CO OF NY
N/A	N/A	--	--	--	--	--	--	--	--	--	--	HOMEOWNERS CHOICE ASR CO INC
2.3	2.0	118.5	35.9	9.5	9.0	61.1	37.6	98.7	125.8	0.6	0.0	HOMEOWNERS CHOICE PROP & CAS INS
2.5	1.7	18.5	10.5	-4.7	1.9	298.5	-121.4	177.1	121.7	-53.9	0.0	HOMEOWNERS OF AMERICA INS CO
N/A	N/A	--	--	--	--	--	--	--	--	--	--	HOMESHIELD FIRE & CASUALTY INS CO
14.1	12.7	N/A	N/A	N/A	N/A	N/A	N/A	N/A	64.1	0.0	0.0	HOMESITE INDEMNITY CO
11.5	10.3	N/A	N/A	N/A	N/A	N/A	N/A	N/A	-420.1	0.0	0.0	HOMESITE INS CO
10.1	9.1	N/A	N/A	N/A	N/A	N/A	N/A	N/A	-350.7	0.0	0.0	HOMESITE INS CO OF CA
10.9	9.8	N/A	N/A	N/A	N/A	N/A	N/A	N/A	-280.2	0.0	0.0	HOMESITE INS CO OF FL
9.7	8.7	N/A	N/A	N/A	N/A	N/A	N/A	N/A	230.4	0.0	0.0	HOMESITE INS CO OF GA
8.9	8.0	N/A	N/A	N/A	N/A	N/A	N/A	N/A	153.5	0.0	0.0	HOMESITE INS CO OF IL
2.0	1.8	63.7	3.3	N/A	N/A	28.5	12.7	41.2	513.5	0.0	0.0	HOMESITE INS CO OF NY
10.7	9.6	N/A	N/A	N/A	N/A	N/A	N/A	N/A	192.0	0.0	0.0	HOMESITE INS CO OF THE MIDWEST
5.1	4.6	N/A	N/A	N/A	N/A	N/A	N/A	N/A	208.1	0.0	0.0	HOMESITE LLOYDS OF TEXAS
N/A	N/A	--	--	--	--	--	--	--	--	--	--	HOMESTEAD INS CO
2.5	1.6	30.1	3.4	-0.2	-1.1	42.6	44.6	87.2	116.4	0.4	0.5	HOMESTEAD MUTUAL INS CO

999 + Denotes number greater than 999.9%
999 - Denotes number less than -999.99%
• Bullets denote a more detailed analysis is available in Section II.

INSURANCE COMPANY NAME	DOM. STATE	RATING	TOTAL ASSETS ($MIL)	CAPITAL & SURPLUS ($MIL)	ANNUAL NET PREMIUM ($MIL)	NET INCOME ($MIL)	CAPITAL- IZATION INDEX (PTS)	RESERVE ADQ INDEX (PTS)	PROFIT- ABILITY INDEX (PTS)	LIQUIDITY INDEX (PTS)	STAB. INDEX (PTS)	STABILITY FACTORS
HOOSIER INS CO	IN	C	8.3	7.4	-9.3	0.0	10.0	3.8	1.9	1.5	2.7	FGLR
HORACE MANN INS CO	IL	B	465.2	187.8	258.9	1.0	7.9	8.5	6.3	4.4	4.4	ALT
HORACE MANN LLOYDS	TX	B-	4.9	2.9	0.0	0.0	10.0	N/A	7.3	7.0	3.8	DG
HORACE MANN P&C INS CO	IL	B	293.0	122.7	166.7	0.7	7.7	8.5	6.8	4.4	4.4	ALRT
HORIZON MIDWEST CASUALTY CO	KS	U	--	--	--	--	N/A	--	--	--	--	Z
HOSPITALITY INS CO	MA	C+	13.7	10.7	0.0	0.0	10.0	N/A	7.0	7.0	3.1	DFGT
HOSPITALITY MUT CAPT INS CO	GA	F (5)	0.0	0.0	2.5	0.0	0.0	5.8	2.5	0.0	0.0	CDFG
HOSPITALITY MUTUAL INS CO	MA	C	65.3	26.8	16.8	0.0	4.0	6.4	2.8	7.1	4.0	CDT
▲HOSPITALITY RRG INC	VT	E+	3.9	2.5	0.8	0.0	10.0	N/A	3.5	10.0	0.5	DGT
HOSPITALS INS CO	NY	C-	1,672.5	546.1	191.9	1.8	5.7	10.0	7.9	6.9	3.2	RT
HOUSING & REDEVELOPMENT INS EXCH	PA	C	45.5	14.7	22.7	-1.0	5.6	7.0	4.0	6.3	2.7	DFRT
HOUSING AUTHORITY PROP A MUTUAL CO	VT	B	177.5	114.3	43.5	-2.2	10.0	8.6	4.6	6.9	6.3	T
HOUSING AUTHORITY RISK RET GROUP	VT	B-	303.1	173.4	31.2	-1.7	9.2	9.3	2.8	7.1	4.1	FRT
HOUSING ENTERPRISE INS CO	VT	C+	79.3	30.1	27.5	-2.2	5.2	6.6	3.9	6.5	4.6	CT
HOUSING SPECIALTY INS CO	VT	C+	17.0	15.6	1.2	0.0	10.0	3.6	4.7	8.9	3.3	DGT
HOUSTON CASUALTY CO	TX	B-	3,518.1	1,977.3	860.4	10.0	7.8	7.6	6.4	6.7	4.5	RT
HOUSTON GENERAL INS EXCH	TX	U	--	--	--	--	N/A	--	--	--	--	Z
HOUSTON SPECIALTY INS CO	TX	B	460.3	262.8	111.8	4.2	6.1	5.5	4.5	7.0	5.5	CFT
HOW INS CO A RRG	VA	U (5)	--	--	--	--	N/A	--	--	--	--	Z
HPIC RRG	SC	D	1.0	0.6	0.0	-0.1	7.8	3.6	0.7	9.0	0.9	DGT
HSB SPECIALTY INS CO	CT	B	54.2	49.9	0.0	0.3	10.0	N/A	5.5	10.0	4.3	DFT
HUDSON EXCESS INS CO	DE	B	69.7	56.7	0.0	0.6	10.0	N/A	7.9	10.0	4.2	T
HUDSON INS CO	DE	C-	1,035.1	458.9	158.6	-0.1	8.4	6.5	6.7	7.4	3.2	RT
HUDSON SPECIALTY INS CO	NY	D+	356.6	202.3	53.0	-1.8	9.5	8.1	6.9	8.2	2.6	FRT
HUTTERIAN BRETHREN MUTUAL INS CORP	IL	D	3.5	2.9	0.3	0.0	10.0	4.8	5.7	10.0	2.0	DGT
HYUNDAI MARINE & FIRE INS CO LTD	CA	B	111.0	53.4	25.5	0.3	10.0	8.2	5.2	8.3	5.3	T
ICI MUTUAL INS CO A RRG	VT	B	352.1	259.5	30.6	1.7	10.0	8.8	7.0	8.6	6.3	T
ID COUNTIES RISK MGMT PROGRAM UNDW	ID	C	70.5	28.7	24.4	-5.8	7.9	5.8	2.9	7.0	3.2	RT
IDS PROPERTY CASUALTY INS CO	WI	B-	1,787.4	806.0	1,065.3	7.5	8.5	3.3	3.7	5.1	4.9	RT
IFA INS CO	NJ	F (1)	3.0	-4.3	0.6	-7.0	0.0	0.3	0.0	7.0	0.0	CDFR
IL STATE BAR ASSOC MUTUAL INS CO	IL	C+	77.6	37.2	15.6	1.7	9.1	9.4	7.1	7.8	3.4	DRT
ILLINOIS CASUALTY CO	IL	C+	121.4	50.4	43.2	1.1	7.2	9.3	6.9	6.5	3.3	RT
ILLINOIS EMCASCO INS CO	IA	B-	360.0	109.7	154.6	1.3	8.0	8.6	8.5	6.6	4.5	T
ILLINOIS FARMERS INS CO	IL	C+	255.7	86.6	110.7	-0.4	7.3	5.8	3.9	6.5	4.4	RT
▲ILLINOIS INS CO	IA	B-	53.9	33.5	18.2	1.3	8.0	8.2	9.0	9.0	3.8	DT
ILLINOIS NATIONAL INS CO	IL	B-	52.9	39.9	0.0	1.4	10.0	N/A	3.6	7.0	3.9	T
ILLINOIS UNION INS CO	IL	C	354.5	126.4	0.0	0.6	10.0	N/A	3.3	10.0	4.0	RT
IMPERIAL F&C INS CO	LA	C-	117.4	25.5	0.0	0.1	10.0	4.6	2.6	9.3	2.9	FRT
IMPERIUM INS CO	TX	C-	375.7	175.6	89.9	1.2	5.8	1.7	3.7	7.0	2.9	FRT
IMT INS CO	IA	B	368.3	189.1	218.4	7.4	9.5	5.9	8.2	6.4	4.1	RT
INDEMNITY CO OF CA	CA	C	22.2	16.7	3.9	0.3	8.4	8.0	3.4	7.6	2.4	DGRT
INDEMNITY INS CO OF NORTH AMERICA	PA	C	469.6	133.6	99.9	4.0	8.4	6.3	8.3	6.9	3.8	RT
INDEMNITY NATIONAL INS CO	MS	C	25.0	14.4	1.3	1.0	8.7	9.3	8.4	9.8	2.7	DGRT
INDEPENDENCE AMERICAN INS CO	DE	B-	105.6	67.7	91.2	1.8	8.2	5.8	8.5	2.8	3.9	FLRT
▲INDEPENDENCE CASUALTY INS CO	MA	C-	4.7	4.6	0.0	0.0	10.0	N/A	7.7	7.0	3.0	DGR
INDEPENDENT MUTUAL FIRE INS CO	IL	C+	47.3	40.4	3.6	-0.1	7.6	3.6	6.7	7.0	3.4	DFT
INDEPENDENT SPECIALTY INS CO	DE	U	--	--	--	--	N/A	--	--	--	--	Z
INDIAN HARBOR INS CO	DE	C-	191.0	47.5	33.3	1.0	8.5	6.3	4.3	8.1	3.0	ART
INDIANA FARMERS MUTUAL INS CO	IN	B	422.8	199.7	198.5	3.0	8.2	7.0	5.3	6.0	4.6	RT
INDIANA INS CO	IN	C	69.6	65.8	0.0	-0.1	10.0	3.9	3.8	7.0	4.1	RT
INDIANA LUMBERMENS MUTUAL INS CO	IN	C	55.5	16.3	14.8	0.6	7.2	7.0	2.4	7.0	3.0	DRT
INDIANA OLD NATIONAL INS CO	VT	C (2)	2,179.7	2,166.2	1.3	37.9	10.0	N/A	7.5	10.0	3.3	RT

See Page 27 for explanation of footnotes and Page 28 for explanation of stability factors.

Arrows denote recent upgrades ▲ or downgrades ▼ (see Section VII for explanations)

78

www.weissratings.com

RISK ADJ. RATIO #1	CAPITAL RATIO #2	PREMIUM TO SURPLUS (%)	RESV. TO SURPLUS (%)	RESV. DEVELOP. 1 YEAR (%)	RESV. DEVELOP. 2 YEAR (%)	LOSS RATIO (%)	EXP. RATIO (%)	COMB RATIO (%)	CASH FROM UNDER-WRITING (%)	NET PREMIUM GROWTH (%)	INVEST. IN AFFIL (%)	INSURANCE COMPANY NAME
16.7	15.1	-126.3	N/A	N/A	N/A	N/A	N/A	N/A	-21.1	-136.3	0.0	HOOSIER INS CO
3.1	2.0	138.9	54.3	-1.0	-5.3	75.1	26.0	101.1	98.1	4.7	0.0	HORACE MANN INS CO
4.1	3.7	N/A	N/A	N/A	N/A	N/A	N/A	N/A	40.5	0.0	0.0	HORACE MANN LLOYDS
2.7	1.7	135.9	53.1	-0.9	-5.2	75.1	26.0	101.1	97.1	4.7	0.0	HORACE MANN P&C INS CO
N/A	N/A	--	--	--	--	--	--	--	--	--	--	HORIZON MIDWEST CASUALTY CO
10.9	6.7	N/A	N/A	N/A	N/A	N/A	N/A	N/A	365.1	0.0	0.0	HOSPITALITY INS CO
0.1	0.1	408.3	213.6	77.4	0.4	85.4	54.4	139.8	89.5	84.7	0.0	HOSPITALITY MUT CAPT INS CO
0.8	0.6	64.5	108.9	12.7	8.5	92.3	37.8	130.1	110.7	15.6	18.7	HOSPITALITY MUTUAL INS CO
2.9	1.8	31.5	0.8	N/A	N/A	67.7	7.2	74.9	-38.9	0.0	0.0	HOSPITALITY RRG INC
1.2	1.0	36.4	178.8	-18.1	-18.1	54.1	18.2	72.3	120.3	-11.2	0.0 ●	HOSPITALS INS CO
1.2	0.7	145.6	127.8	9.7	-3.3	76.6	28.5	105.1	90.2	-5.8	0.0	HOUSING & REDEVELOPMENT INS EXCH
3.6	3.2	37.1	23.0	-2.1	-4.9	68.4	32.8	101.2	113.7	5.3	16.0	HOUSING AUTHORITY PROP A MUTUAL
3.0	2.4	17.7	53.9	N/A	-4.4	120.3	32.5	152.8	89.1	0.9	12.4	HOUSING AUTHORITY RISK RET GROUP
1.1	0.6	85.0	85.4	-5.1	-8.9	67.7	31.3	99.0	113.0	26.9	0.0	HOUSING ENTERPRISE INS CO
14.7	9.2	7.4	3.8	-0.5	N/A	57.6	61.3	118.9	98.5	5.6	0.0	HOUSING SPECIALTY INS CO
1.7	1.5	45.0	41.5	-1.0	-1.4	64.4	28.1	92.5	108.6	6.5	42.2 ●	HOUSTON CASUALTY CO
N/A	N/A	--	--	--	--	--	--	--	--	--	--	HOUSTON GENERAL INS EXCH
0.9	0.8	42.9	28.0	4.7	6.3	69.1	40.4	109.5	88.2	-8.5	50.6 ●	HOUSTON SPECIALTY INS CO
N/A	N/A	--	--	--	--	--	--	--	--	--	--	HOW INS CO A RRG
2.4	2.0	7.1	21.5	6.1	N/A	376.9	285.0	661.9	361.0	0.0	0.0	HPIC RRG
37.2	33.5	N/A	N/A	N/A	N/A	N/A	N/A	N/A	12.9	0.0	0.0	HSB SPECIALTY INS CO
20.5	18.5	N/A	1.4	N/A	N/A	N/A	N/A	N/A	14.6	0.0	0.0	HUDSON EXCESS INS CO
2.1	1.9	35.0	38.2	-0.9	-2.3	71.9	20.5	92.4	136.2	6.2	31.9 ●	HUDSON INS CO
3.3	2.9	26.4	42.3	-4.1	-8.0	56.7	38.3	95.0	68.6	4.0	19.4 ●	HUDSON SPECIALTY INS CO
10.4	8.5	9.5	0.7	-1.1	-7.4	3.5	31.5	35.0	170.6	0.0	0.0	HUTTERIAN BRETHREN MUTUAL INS
4.9	3.1	48.6	38.2	4.5	-0.2	62.1	34.5	96.6	111.4	3.2	0.0	HYUNDAI MARINE & FIRE INS CO LTD
10.0	6.2	12.0	25.8	-3.1	-7.2	49.3	40.4	89.7	155.4	-1.1	-0.2 ●	ICI MUTUAL INS CO A RRG
1.4	1.2	71.3	72.6	6.2	16.6	57.0	25.3	82.3	125.1	2.9	0.0	ID COUNTIES RISK MGMT PROGRAM
2.9	2.3	133.1	76.7	-2.0	10.2	91.2	17.4	108.6	95.6	-0.3	2.8 ●	IDS PROPERTY CASUALTY INS CO
-0.6	-0.4	-15.0	-169.1	125.5	241.6	536.0	426.0	962.0	9.5	-95.6	0.0	IFA INS CO
3.9	2.6	44.6	79.5	-14.8	-17.5	55.5	28.3	83.8	122.6	5.7	0.0	IL STATE BAR ASSOC MUTUAL INS CO
3.3	2.3	144.3	135.9	-16.0	-9.8	57.1	37.3	94.4	99.4	3.8	0.1	ILLINOIS CASUALTY CO
2.6	1.7	144.5	147.5	-8.0	-9.0	64.6	31.9	96.5	106.9	2.0	0.0	ILLINOIS EMCASCO INS CO
1.2	1.1	126.2	79.2	2.1	3.7	72.0	32.4	104.4	98.0	-1.1	37.8	ILLINOIS FARMERS INS CO
2.1	1.7	56.6	53.9	3.6	-1.1	43.9	28.7	72.6	200.7	-4.6	0.0	ILLINOIS INS CO
14.5	13.0	N/A	N/A	N/A	N/A	N/A	N/A	N/A	N/A	0.0	3.9	ILLINOIS NATIONAL INS CO
12.4	7.7	N/A	25.4	N/A	N/A	N/A	N/A	N/A	117.1	0.0	0.0	ILLINOIS UNION INS CO
2.9	2.6	N/A	N/A	N/A	N/A	N/A	N/A	N/A	-65.5	0.0	0.0	IMPERIAL F&C INS CO
1.2	1.0	50.6	92.5	13.5	20.7	98.7	21.7	120.4	79.4	-23.0	33.5	IMPERIUM INS CO
4.7	2.9	122.0	35.5	4.3	4.9	60.4	32.0	92.4	112.3	9.3	0.3	IMT INS CO
2.0	1.8	23.9	1.4	-2.7	-0.9	0.7	80.9	81.6	100.0	41.6	3.2	INDEMNITY CO OF CA
3.0	2.0	77.1	140.7	1.0	0.8	76.5	17.3	93.8	122.9	5.0	0.0	INDEMNITY INS CO OF NORTH AMERICA
4.2	2.3	10.2	27.9	-3.9	-12.2	10.0	39.3	49.3	183.0	-24.9	0.0	INDEMNITY NATIONAL INS CO
4.5	2.6	136.6	45.6	3.7	6.2	62.4	33.7	96.1	92.9	-39.1	0.0	INDEPENDENCE AMERICAN INS CO
95.1	47.5	N/A	N/A	N/A	N/A	N/A	N/A	N/A	N/A	0.0	0.0	INDEPENDENCE CASUALTY INS CO
2.3	1.4	9.2	0.6	-0.2	N/A	27.0	105.7	132.7	77.4	1.8	0.0	INDEPENDENT MUTUAL FIRE INS CO
N/A	N/A	--	--	--	--	--	--	--	--	--	--	INDEPENDENT SPECIALTY INS CO
3.0	1.9	70.9	142.9	0.2	0.6	69.3	28.5	97.8	105.0	25.6	0.0	INDIAN HARBOR INS CO
3.3	1.9	101.6	50.3	-9.2	-15.2	69.0	29.7	98.7	109.3	4.7	0.0 ●	INDIANA FARMERS MUTUAL INS CO
7.0	6.8	N/A	N/A	N/A	N/A	N/A	N/A	N/A	N/A	0.0	19.0	INDIANA INS CO
1.6	1.2	94.4	106.6	1.5	-2.3	64.2	31.3	95.5	125.2	-5.2	24.4	INDIANA LUMBERMENS MUTUAL INS CO
56.9	21.2	0.1	N/A	N/A	N/A	4.6	41.6	46.2	221.4	-6.8	0.0	INDIANA OLD NATIONAL INS CO

999 + Denotes number greater than 999.9%
999 - Denotes number less than -999.99%
● Bullets denote a more detailed analysis is available in Section II.

INSURANCE COMPANY NAME	DOM. STATE	RATING	TOTAL ASSETS ($MIL)	CAPITAL & SURPLUS ($MIL)	ANNUAL NET PREMIUM ($MIL)	NET INCOME ($MIL)	CAPITAL-IZATION INDEX (PTS)	RESERVE ADQ INDEX (PTS)	PROFIT-ABILITY INDEX (PTS)	LIQUIDITY INDEX (PTS)	STAB. INDEX (PTS)	STABILITY FACTORS
INFINITY ASSURANCE INS CO	OH	B-	7.1	5.6	1.4	0.0	10.0	5.2	5.1	8.8	3.5	ADGT
INFINITY AUTO INS CO	OH	C	10.7	7.7	1.4	0.0	10.0	5.2	5.2	6.8	4.1	ADFG
INFINITY CASUALTY INS CO	OH	B-	7.6	6.2	1.4	0.0	10.0	5.2	5.4	9.2	3.5	ADGT
INFINITY COUNTY MUTUAL INS CO	TX	C	62.8	5.1	0.0	0.0	4.7	N/A	5.4	10.0	2.9	CDGT
INFINITY INDEMNITY INS CO	IN	C	6.3	4.5	1.4	0.0	10.0	5.2	3.4	7.7	3.5	ADFG
INFINITY INS CO	IN	B	2,050.3	663.5	1,379.9	10.9	7.9	6.7	5.4	3.2	4.5	ALRT
INFINITY PREFERRED INS CO	OH	C	4.8	3.3	1.4	0.0	10.0	6.2	3.7	7.8	3.2	ADG
INFINITY SAFEGUARD INS CO	OH	C+	5.1	3.6	1.4	0.0	10.0	6.1	3.7	7.6	3.2	ADGT
INFINITY SECURITY INS CO	IN	C	5.8	4.4	1.4	0.0	10.0	5.2	3.7	6.9	2.9	ADGT
INFINITY SELECT INS CO	IN	B-	7.1	5.4	1.4	0.0	10.0	5.2	5.4	6.9	3.5	ADFG
INFINITY STANDARD INS CO	IN	C	7.1	5.6	1.4	0.0	10.0	5.2	5.6	9.2	3.6	ADG
INLAND INS CO	NE	C	276.0	208.4	0.5	2.4	8.3	3.6	6.9	10.0	2.6	GRT
INLAND MUTUAL INS CO	WV	C-	6.8	6.2	0.4	0.0	10.0	7.9	6.0	8.5	2.1	DGRT
INNOVATIVE PHYSICIAN SOLUTIONS RRG	VT	E	4.7	1.1	1.3	0.0	0.0	1.8	1.1	8.4	0.0	CDGT
INS CO OF GREATER NY	NY	C+	120.4	62.9	28.7	1.0	10.0	6.0	8.0	6.9	4.0	T
INS CO OF ILLINOIS	IL	B	21.9	20.9	0.0	0.1	10.0	N/A	3.8	7.0	4.1	ADGT
INS CO OF NORTH AMERICA	PA	C	929.9	259.3	249.8	9.2	7.7	6.4	7.9	7.1	3.6	RT
INS CO OF THE AMERICAS	FL	U	--	--	--	--	N/A	--	--	--	--	Z
INS CO OF THE SOUTH	GA	D+	39.9	14.7	30.4	0.3	2.1	6.5	8.7	5.0	2.4	CDT
INS CO OF THE STATE OF PA	IL	C	274.5	116.1	0.0	2.1	10.0	3.6	1.9	7.0	4.2	AT
INS CO OF THE WEST	CA	C	2,306.1	909.3	812.7	21.3	7.3	5.0	8.9	6.5	3.7	RT
INS PLACEMENT FACILITY OF PA	PA	E- (1)	7.5	-4.9	7.4	-1.7	0.0	5.3	0.1	7.2	0.0	CDFT
▲INSPIRIEN INS CO	AL	C-	40.5	17.3	6.0	-0.4	8.5	9.6	4.0	8.1	3.0	DFGR
INSUREMAX INS CO	IN	E-	2.9	0.9	-0.2	-0.2	6.1	3.7	0.4	0.8	0.0	DFGL
INSURORS INDEMNITY CO	TX	C-	34.1	17.1	15.3	-0.2	7.7	9.3	6.1	7.0	2.7	DGT
INSURORS INDEMNITY LLOYDS	TX	C	5.2	2.7	0.0	0.0	9.9	N/A	4.1	7.1	3.0	DGRT
INTEGON CASUALTY INS CO	NC	C	39.4	6.3	0.0	0.0	7.2	3.9	3.0	7.0	2.7	DGRT
INTEGON GENERAL INS CORP	NC	C	51.9	6.4	0.0	0.1	7.2	3.9	2.5	6.7	2.7	DGRT
INTEGON INDEMNITY CORP	NC	C	140.2	23.1	0.0	0.2	8.1	3.9	3.0	1.9	3.6	DFGL
INTEGON NATIONAL INS CO	NC	C+	3,052.5	627.0	1,522.0	-22.9	6.4	4.2	2.9	1.5	4.7	GLRT
INTEGON PREFERRED INS CO	NC	C	81.5	6.5	0.0	0.1	5.4	3.9	3.5	5.6	2.7	DRT
INTEGRA INS INC	MN	D	1.8	1.8	2.7	0.0	4.0	N/A	4.3	3.1	1.6	DGLT
INTEGRAND ASR CO	PR	C	116.9	62.1	44.3	1.1	8.1	5.8	2.7	6.5	3.5	RT
INTEGRITY MUTUAL INS CO	WI	B-	106.0	51.4	38.6	0.8	8.4	6.0	8.5	6.8	3.8	T
INTEGRITY P&C INS CO	WI	D+	15.8	13.7	8.2	0.4	10.0	6.0	8.7	6.8	2.1	DGT
INTEGRITY SELECT INSURANCE CO	WI	U	--	--	--	--	N/A	--	--	--	--	Z
▲INTERBORO INS CO	NY	C-	80.9	43.9	33.6	2.1	8.0	8.5	7.4	6.5	3.0	FRT
INTERINS EXCHANGE	CA	B+	9,670.8	6,006.7	3,261.5	-26.2	9.9	7.3	4.9	6.5	5.1	T
INTERNATIONAL FIDELITY INS CO	NJ	B-	223.4	90.9	98.5	1.4	7.5	9.2	4.1	6.9	4.4	RT
INTERSTATE FIRE & CAS CO	IL	C-	110.2	68.3	0.0	0.1	10.0	3.6	2.0	6.9	3.2	RT
INTREPID INS CO	IA	C	30.4	30.1	0.0	0.1	10.0	3.6	1.9	7.0	4.3	DFGR
IOWA AMERICAN INS CO	IA	B	27.3	9.8	7.1	-0.1	9.4	7.7	5.0	6.7	4.7	DFGT
IOWA MUTUAL INS CO	IA	B	101.5	36.5	21.4	-0.2	7.9	7.6	5.1	6.6	4.1	FT
IQS INS RRG INC	VT	D	1.6	1.3	0.4	0.0	10.0	4.7	7.3	8.3	1.2	DGT
IRONSHORE INDEMNITY INC	MN	B-	431.9	165.7	44.7	-1.6	8.3	5.3	4.4	7.1	3.7	FRT
IRONSHORE RRG (DC) INC	DC	D	2.5	0.6	0.1	-0.1	5.6	5.0	1.3	9.7	1.0	DFGT
IRONSHORE SPECIALTY INS CO	AZ	C	999.7	352.8	109.7	-1.2	7.8	6.0	5.7	7.1	3.7	FRT
ISLAND HOME INS CO	GU	D	23.7	12.9	31.5	0.8	7.9	3.3	4.5	2.3	1.7	DGLT
ISLAND INS CO LTD	HI	B-	322.5	114.0	101.0	2.0	9.1	9.4	8.0	7.0	3.8	RT
ISLAND PREMIER INS CO LTD	HI	C	11.5	5.7	0.0	0.0	10.0	N/A	6.7	9.5	3.6	DG
ISMIE INDEMNITY CO	IL	U	--	--	--	--	N/A	--	--	--	--	Z
ISMIE MUTUAL INS CO	IL	B-	1,443.8	692.1	149.4	-2.7	10.0	9.5	6.1	7.7	4.5	FRT

See Page 27 for explanation of footnotes and
Page 28 for explanation of stability factors.
Arrows denote recent upgrades ▲ or downgrades ▼   (see Section VII for explanations)

80

www.weissratings.com

RISK ADJ. CAPITAL RATIO #1	RATIO #2	PREMIUM TO SURPLUS (%)	RESV. TO SURPLUS (%)	RESV. DEVELOP. 1 YEAR (%)	2 YEAR (%)	LOSS RATIO (%)	EXP. RATIO (%)	COMB RATIO (%)	CASH FROM UNDER-WRITING (%)	NET PREMIUM GROWTH (%)	INVEST. IN AFFIL (%)	INSURANCE COMPANY NAME
9.7	8.7	25.0	12.0	-0.4	-0.9	79.0	17.5	96.5	99.6	1.4	0.0	INFINITY ASSURANCE INS CO
7.6	6.8	18.2	8.8	-0.3	-0.7	79.0	17.5	96.5	64.4	1.4	0.0	INFINITY AUTO INS CO
10.9	9.8	22.7	10.9	-0.3	-0.9	79.0	17.5	96.5	100.1	1.4	0.0	INFINITY CASUALTY INS CO
0.7	0.6	N/A	N/A	N/A	N/A	N/A	N/A	N/A	N/A	0.0	0.0	INFINITY COUNTY MUTUAL INS CO
7.0	6.3	30.7	14.7	-0.5	-0.9	79.0	17.5	96.5	90.7	1.4	0.0	INFINITY INDEMNITY INS CO
1.8	1.6	208.9	100.2	-3.1	-7.6	79.0	17.5	96.5	99.3	1.4	3.4 ●	INFINITY INS CO
5.8	5.3	41.7	20.0	-0.6	-1.4	79.0	17.5	96.5	98.8	1.4	0.0	INFINITY PREFERRED INS CO
6.2	5.6	39.0	18.7	-0.6	-1.3	79.0	17.5	96.5	98.8	1.4	0.0	INFINITY SAFEGUARD INS CO
7.6	6.9	32.0	15.4	-0.5	-1.2	79.0	17.5	96.5	98.8	1.4	0.0	INFINITY SECURITY INS CO
8.2	7.3	26.0	12.5	-0.4	-1.0	79.0	17.5	96.5	83.6	1.4	0.0	INFINITY SELECT INS CO
8.8	7.9	24.8	11.9	-0.4	-0.9	79.0	17.5	96.5	107.2	1.4	6.8	INFINITY STANDARD INS CO
3.2	1.9	0.2	1.2	N/A	N/A	-0.7	110.9	110.2	54.7	-15.3	0.0 ●	INLAND INS CO
5.5	3.2	6.3	3.4	-1.9	-3.2	42.9	56.7	99.6	110.3	-7.4	0.0	INLAND MUTUAL INS CO
0.1	0.0	120.3	294.2	17.9	23.9	82.1	56.8	138.9	109.4	-11.9	0.0	INNOVATIVE PHYSICIAN SOLUTIONS
4.0	3.3	46.2	66.1	2.6	1.5	66.5	29.3	95.8	107.4	5.2	0.0	INS CO OF GREATER NY
44.6	40.1	N/A	N/A	N/A	N/A	N/A	N/A	N/A	N/A	0.0	0.0	INS CO OF ILLINOIS
2.3	1.5	99.9	182.3	1.3	0.9	76.5	20.1	96.6	118.3	5.0	0.0 ●	INS CO OF NORTH AMERICA
N/A	N/A	--	--	--	--	--	--	--	--	--	--	INS CO OF THE AMERICAS
0.5	0.4	208.9	29.2	2.0	-1.4	48.1	35.7	83.8	120.9	6.9	0.0	INS CO OF THE SOUTH
8.8	7.9	N/A	N/A	N/A	N/A	N/A	N/A	N/A	N/A	0.0	0.0	INS CO OF THE STATE OF PA
1.6	1.2	90.1	124.9	-1.5	-2.8	64.9	22.5	87.4	163.1	9.2	9.2 ●	INS CO OF THE WEST
-0.7	-0.6	-150.0	-32.7	10.8	16.3	67.7	57.1	124.8	81.5	-7.8	0.0	INS PLACEMENT FACILITY OF PA
2.0	1.7	30.8	79.7	-6.1	-17.3	39.1	72.5	111.6	67.8	21.8	0.2	INSPIRIEN INS CO
1.1	1.0	-16.6	176.7	1.8	13.3	112.7	-346.3	-233.6	24.8	-102.7	0.0	INSUREMAX INS CO
1.8	1.3	89.2	36.7	-4.2	-13.8	46.0	49.1	95.1	119.6	24.8	8.9	INSURORS INDEMNITY CO
3.0	2.7	N/A	N/A	N/A	N/A	N/A	N/A	N/A	999 +	0.0	0.0	INSURORS INDEMNITY LLOYDS
1.2	1.1	N/A	N/A	N/A	N/A	N/A	N/A	N/A	65.7	0.0	0.0	INTEGON CASUALTY INS CO
1.0	0.9	N/A	N/A	N/A	N/A	N/A	N/A	N/A	157.7	0.0	0.0	INTEGON GENERAL INS CORP
1.7	1.5	N/A	N/A	N/A	N/A	N/A	N/A	N/A	93.3	0.0	47.7	INTEGON INDEMNITY CORP
1.3	1.0	256.0	74.6	2.3	4.3	74.3	22.4	96.7	92.4	31.7	9.8 ●	INTEGON NATIONAL INS CO
0.8	0.7	N/A	N/A	N/A	N/A	N/A	N/A	N/A	152.9	0.0	0.0	INTEGON PREFERRED INS CO
0.6	0.6	140.3	N/A	N/A	N/A	N/A	98.5	98.5	101.3	-2.7	0.0	INTEGRA INS INC
2.4	1.7	71.6	32.8	-0.8	3.7	63.9	35.4	99.3	101.7	13.9	0.2	INTEGRAND ASR CO
2.8	2.2	76.7	45.6	-1.7	0.5	62.3	31.4	93.7	110.2	-4.3	15.7	INTEGRITY MUTUAL INS CO
10.7	7.7	60.4	35.9	-1.4	0.4	62.3	19.2	81.5	103.9	-4.3	0.0	INTEGRITY P&C INS CO
N/A	N/A	--	--	--	--	--	--	--	--	--	--	INTEGRITY SELECT INSURANCE CO
3.0	2.6	83.1	27.4	0.2	-1.6	41.4	46.8	88.2	81.1	-35.9	0.0	INTERBORO INS CO
4.6	2.8	55.2	19.7	0.9	-0.3	79.4	21.2	100.6	102.6	8.1	0.8 ●	INTERINS EXCHANGE
1.5	1.3	110.6	7.0	-8.2	-14.1	14.3	76.4	90.7	118.7	-2.8	13.2	INTERNATIONAL FIDELITY INS CO
12.8	11.5	N/A	N/A	N/A	N/A	N/A	N/A	N/A	999 +	0.0	0.0	INTERSTATE FIRE & CAS CO
226.7	113.4	N/A	N/A	N/A	N/A	N/A	N/A	N/A	1.5	0.0	0.0	INTREPID INS CO
3.0	2.6	72.9	53.8	-0.6	-1.5	64.1	37.9	102.0	90.2	-0.4	0.0	IOWA AMERICAN INS CO
2.1	1.6	59.1	43.7	-0.5	-1.2	64.1	38.0	102.1	89.1	-0.4	17.1	IOWA MUTUAL INS CO
6.1	4.0	34.0	18.5	-13.1	-10.7	-1.6	45.4	43.8	322.3	-1.8	0.0	IQS INS RRG INC
3.2	1.9	27.0	51.2	-2.4	2.1	78.2	26.0	104.2	51.9	-13.4	0.0	IRONSHORE INDEMNITY INC
0.8	0.8	16.5	48.5	10.5	3.5	105.0	176.6	281.6	-24.8	-33.5	0.0	IRONSHORE RRG (DC) INC
2.4	1.5	31.4	80.6	1.7	0.6	82.7	40.9	123.6	80.7	-2.1	0.0 ●	IRONSHORE SPECIALTY INS CO
2.6	1.4	232.4	37.2	N/A	N/A	71.9	17.6	89.5	106.7	12.9	0.0	ISLAND HOME INS CO
3.5	2.3	77.1	100.9	-8.6	-16.6	58.3	34.0	92.3	108.2	4.0	4.9	ISLAND INS CO LTD
3.4	3.1	N/A	N/A	N/A	N/A	N/A	N/A	N/A	N/A	0.0	0.0	ISLAND PREMIER INS CO LTD
N/A	N/A	--	--	--	--	--	--	--	--	--	--	ISMIE INDEMNITY CO
4.4	3.7	21.6	86.8	-5.3	-11.8	61.9	34.6	96.5	86.2	-11.2	4.2 ●	ISMIE MUTUAL INS CO

999 + Denotes number greater than 999.9%
999 - Denotes number less than -999.99%
● Bullets denote a more detailed analysis is available in Section II.

INSURANCE COMPANY NAME	DOM. STATE	RATING	TOTAL ASSETS ($MIL)	CAPITAL & SURPLUS ($MIL)	ANNUAL NET PREMIUM ($MIL)	NET INCOME ($MIL)	CAPITAL-IZATION INDEX (PTS)	RESERVE ADQ INDEX (PTS)	PROFIT-ABILITY INDEX (PTS)	LIQUIDITY INDEX (PTS)	STAB. INDEX (PTS)	STABILITY FACTORS
IU HEALTH RRG INC	SC	D+	3.8	2.8	0.0	0.0	9.7	N/A	1.9	7.0	2.0	DGR
JAMES RIVER CASUALTY CO	VA	C+	47.0	16.7	11.5	0.0	6.5	6.8	4.4	6.5	3.4	DGT
JAMES RIVER INS CO	OH	C	600.9	134.6	63.8	3.1	7.6	9.0	3.4	7.1	4.0	FRT
JEFFERSON INS CO	NY	C	96.4	56.8	96.2	-3.8	7.4	7.4	4.7	6.4	3.5	RT
JEWELERS MUTUAL INS CO	WI	B	401.1	249.4	180.6	8.4	10.0	6.4	8.8	6.7	4.4	T
JM SPECIALTY INSURANCE CO	WI	U	--	--	--	--	N/A	--	--	--	--	Z
JM WOODWORTH RRG INC	NV	U	--	--	--	--	N/A	--	--	--	--	Z
JUNIATA MUTUAL INS CO	PA	D+	8.7	5.3	5.0	-0.3	8.2	6.1	4.8	7.1	2.1	DGRT
KAMMCO CASUALTY CO	KS	U	--	--	--	--	N/A	--	--	--	--	Z
KANSAS MEDICAL MUTUAL INS CO	KS	B	152.0	103.0	19.6	-0.9	10.0	8.4	2.9	7.0	4.1	DFRT
KANSAS MUTUAL INS CO	KS	C- (1)	14.9	8.8	6.9	1.4	9.9	8.1	8.2	7.0	2.2	DT
KEMPER FINANCIAL INDEMNITY CO	IL	U	--	--	--	--	N/A	--	--	--	--	Z
KEMPER INDEPENDENCE INS CO	IL	B	93.4	9.6	0.0	0.1	7.0	3.6	7.0	7.0	4.3	DFRT
KENSINGTON INS CO	NY	D	15.5	3.9	6.5	-0.2	1.9	3.1	2.8	7.1	2.2	CDGT
▲KENTUCKIANA MEDICAL RRG & INS CO INC	KY	D-	53.8	36.0	4.3	-0.2	8.0	7.0	5.9	8.3	1.0	DRT
KENTUCKY EMPLOYERS MUTUAL INS	KY	B	921.1	188.3	146.1	0.1	6.8	6.9	3.8	6.9	5.7	T
KENTUCKY FARM BUREAU MUTUAL INS CO	KY	B	2,426.2	1,306.1	937.9	15.1	10.0	6.6	6.8	6.1	4.8	T
▲KENTUCKY HOSPITAL INS CO RRG	KY	C-	20.9	8.1	2.1	0.7	7.3	9.6	3.1	6.8	2.6	DFGR
KENTUCKY NATIONAL INS CO	KY	D+	31.9	10.6	27.1	0.1	2.6	4.8	3.5	0.7	2.5	DGLR
KESWICK GUARANTY INC	VI	B- (1)	5.3	5.2	0.4	0.3	9.2	N/A	8.7	6.9	3.5	DT
KEY INS CO	KS	D	36.1	8.0	52.7	0.1	0.8	2.6	3.8	0.0	1.7	CDGL
KEY RISK INS CO	IA	C	47.1	31.0	0.0	0.1	10.0	N/A	7.3	9.0	4.2	R
KEYSTONE MUTUAL INS CO	MO	E	3.0	0.4	1.8	0.0	0.0	0.5	2.4	7.6	0.0	CDGT
KEYSTONE NATIONAL INS CO	PA	B-	17.8	9.6	2.2	0.1	10.0	7.5	7.9	8.8	4.3	DGR
KINGSTONE INS CO	NY	C	149.9	74.0	65.9	1.6	7.5	3.7	8.8	6.6	3.4	RT
KINSALE INS CO	AR	B	523.4	200.4	167.3	5.4	7.1	8.9	7.0	7.5	4.1	GT
KNIGHT SPECIALTY INS CO	DE	B	73.9	48.7	0.0	0.2	8.9	N/A	4.9	10.0	4.1	T
KNIGHTBROOK INS CO	DE	D	206.6	61.3	7.7	0.3	3.9	0.7	2.7	6.9	2.2	CFRT
KOOKMIN BEST INS CO LTD US BR	NY	E+	296.6	121.4	25.4	-3.2	1.5	0.1	1.2	6.4	0.5	CFRT
LACKAWANNA AMERICAN INS CO	PA	B	88.5	42.3	23.1	0.3	8.9	8.2	8.7	6.8	6.0	DT
LACKAWANNA CASUALTY CO	PA	B-	234.0	92.1	80.9	1.3	7.2	8.3	7.0	5.9	4.5	RT
LACKAWANNA NATIONAL INS CO	PA	B-	36.8	15.4	11.5	0.1	7.5	8.2	8.9	6.8	5.1	DGT
LAFAYETTE INS CO	LA	B-	207.9	89.7	67.5	1.4	9.4	8.3	8.4	6.8	4.3	T
LAKE STREET RRG INC	VT	D	2.3	1.5	0.4	0.0	9.8	7.1	4.1	9.5	1.3	DFGT
LAKEVIEW INS CO	FL	C+	35.9	17.6	18.7	0.3	8.3	6.1	8.3	6.7	3.3	DGT
LAMMICO	LA	B	416.2	229.2	49.8	1.5	10.0	8.9	8.4	8.6	4.2	RT
▲LAMMICO RRG INC	DC	C-	5.9	5.5	0.0	0.1	10.0	5.5	3.7	10.0	1.7	DGT
LAMORAK INS CO	PA	U	--	--	--	--	N/A	--	--	--	--	Z
LANCER INDEMNITY CO	NY	C+	29.0	11.4	9.4	0.1	5.4	3.5	5.3	6.9	3.1	DGRT
LANCER INS CO	IL	B	677.9	202.8	260.6	3.0	8.1	3.5	6.1	6.8	4.1	RT
LANCET IND RRG INC	NV	E+	21.7	4.9	17.2	0.1	0.3	1.2	2.3	1.3	0.5	CFGL
LANDCAR CASUALTY CO	UT	C+	41.5	16.3	10.6	-0.2	7.2	6.0	5.0	7.0	3.1	DT
LANDMARK AMERICAN INS CO	NH	C	385.2	232.9	38.3	4.2	10.0	7.8	7.8	7.7	3.1	ART
LAUNDRY OWNERS MUTUAL LIAB INS ASN	PA	C-	16.7	8.2	4.6	0.1	7.5	6.0	8.6	6.9	2.3	DGRT
LAWYERS MUTUAL INS CO	CA	B	329.2	229.6	35.2	3.4	10.0	9.4	8.9	8.2	4.2	RT
LAWYERS MUTUAL INS CO OF KENTUCKY	KY	C	23.5	10.7	4.5	0.1	8.0	9.8	7.4	7.4	2.4	DGRT
LAWYERS MUTUAL LIAB INS CO OF NC	NC	B-	103.9	76.7	14.6	1.6	10.0	9.3	8.9	7.8	3.8	DRT
LCTA CASUALTY INS CO	LA	B-	79.1	32.9	22.5	-1.8	6.1	N/A	3.7	6.8	3.9	DT
LE MARS INS CO	IA	C+	64.8	26.5	32.6	0.9	7.9	5.8	3.2	6.6	3.7	RT
▼LEAGUE OF WI MUNICIPALITIES MUT INS	WI	C+	79.8	29.6	24.1	-4.5	8.2	9.7	2.9	7.1	4.4	RT
LEATHERSTOCKING COOP INS CO	NY	C+	38.1	20.3	16.5	0.6	8.3	9.2	8.9	6.8	4.3	DGRT
LEBANON VALLEY INS CO	PA	C	25.2	12.1	8.5	0.3	8.6	9.3	5.1	7.0	3.0	DGRT

See Page 27 for explanation of footnotes and
Page 28 for explanation of stability factors.

82

www.weissratings.com

Arrows denote recent upgrades ▲ or downgrades ▼   (see Section VII for explanations)

RISK ADJ. RATIO #1	CAPITAL RATIO #2	PREMIUM TO SURPLUS (%)	RESV. TO SURPLUS (%)	RESV. DEVELOP. 1 YEAR (%)	RESV. DEVELOP. 2 YEAR (%)	LOSS RATIO (%)	EXP. RATIO (%)	COMB RATIO (%)	CASH FROM UNDER- WRITING (%)	NET PREMIUM GROWTH (%)	INVEST. IN AFFIL (%)	INSURANCE COMPANY NAME
5.8	5.2	N/A	N/A	N/A	N/A	N/A	N/A	N/A	N/A	0.0	0.0	IU HEALTH RRG INC
1.6	1.2	69.4	108.8	-4.0	-7.1	85.1	14.0	99.1	109.8	156.2	0.0	JAMES RIVER CASUALTY CO
3.0	1.8	49.8	95.1	-3.7	-4.8	85.1	11.4	96.5	73.4	-5.0	5.9	JAMES RIVER INS CO
1.6	1.4	167.7	10.7	-1.4	-1.5	30.4	56.7	87.1	119.4	11.4	0.0	JEFFERSON INS CO
5.3	3.3	73.0	10.5	-2.2	-1.2	48.4	42.3	90.7	115.2	8.9	0.2 ●	JEWELERS MUTUAL INS CO
N/A	N/A	--	--	--	--	--	--	--	--	--	--	JM SPECIALTY INSURANCE CO
N/A	N/A	--	--	--	--	--	--	--	--	--	--	JM WOODWORTH RRG INC
2.5	1.8	93.4	8.4	4.1	3.3	47.1	41.5	88.6	123.8	4.8	0.0	JUNIATA MUTUAL INS CO
N/A	N/A	--	--	--	--	--	--	--	--	--	--	KAMMCO CASUALTY CO
6.2	4.5	19.0	27.6	-1.1	-1.2	71.3	46.0	117.3	67.5	-1.6	1.9	KANSAS MEDICAL MUTUAL INS CO
3.5	2.9	79.0	10.6	-3.5	-3.7	50.8	22.9	73.7	113.5	1.9	0.0	KANSAS MUTUAL INS CO
N/A	N/A	--	--	--	--	--	--	--	--	--	--	KEMPER FINANCIAL INDEMNITY CO
1.1	1.0	N/A	N/A	N/A	N/A	N/A	N/A	N/A	-30.2	0.0	0.0	KEMPER INDEPENDENCE INS CO
0.6	0.4	159.4	139.1	8.6	19.1	65.2	41.4	106.6	99.0	7.3	0.0	KENSINGTON INS CO
2.5	1.9	11.9	37.4	-9.1	-33.6	28.1	27.1	55.2	177.4	-22.1	0.0	KENTUCKIANA MEDICAL RRG & INS CO
1.3	0.9	78.3	314.8	-3.3	-3.6	88.5	22.1	110.6	90.5	3.6	0.0	KENTUCKY EMPLOYERS MUTUAL INS
5.6	3.7	73.3	31.9	-1.6	-2.3	80.6	20.8	101.4	100.7	6.8	0.7 ●	KENTUCKY FARM BUREAU MUTUAL INS
1.4	1.1	28.6	123.9	-19.9	-39.2	77.3	34.4	111.7	53.4	-11.5	0.0	KENTUCKY HOSPITAL INS CO RRG
0.7	0.5	257.5	91.6	-8.2	5.8	72.5	30.8	103.3	94.7	3.7	14.9	KENTUCKY NATIONAL INS CO
4.6	2.6	7.8	1.7	N/A	N/A	19.0	13.9	32.9	81.1	4.7	0.0	KESWICK GUARANTY INC
0.2	0.2	661.3	280.6	45.7	43.1	81.7	22.9	104.6	108.0	22.8	0.0	KEY INS CO
10.0	9.0	N/A	N/A	N/A	N/A	N/A	N/A	N/A	87.6	0.0	0.0	KEY RISK INS CO
0.2	0.2	547.0	288.8	-122.7	259.7	18.8	63.3	82.1	111.6	0.4	0.0	KEYSTONE MUTUAL INS CO
4.5	3.6	23.7	5.0	-3.0	-2.3	42.8	36.2	79.0	143.2	16.1	0.0	KEYSTONE NATIONAL INS CO
3.5	2.3	132.0	52.0	-1.0	-2.0	45.3	34.4	79.7	134.1	9.2	1.7	KINGSTONE INS CO
1.9	1.0	86.5	100.7	-10.0	-15.8	53.0	20.2	73.2	223.5	99.1	0.0	KINSALE INS CO
3.5	2.0	N/A	N/A	N/A	N/A	N/A	N/A	N/A	23.7	0.0	0.0	KNIGHT SPECIALTY INS CO
0.8	0.6	12.6	91.6	49.6	46.3	398.4	46.0	444.4	43.2	-35.1	1.9	KNIGHTBROOK INS CO
0.6	0.4	20.6	133.3	2.9	349.3	122.6	80.6	203.2	18.2	-7.0	0.0	KOOKMIN BEST INS CO LTD US BR
2.9	2.3	55.4	62.9	0.2	-1.8	77.2	16.1	93.3	112.9	2.7	0.0	LACKAWANNA AMERICAN INS CO
1.2	1.1	91.3	107.4	0.6	-2.3	77.1	16.1	93.2	112.2	2.8	30.3	LACKAWANNA CASUALTY CO
1.7	1.4	75.9	83.3	0.2	-2.6	77.2	16.1	93.3	113.2	2.7	0.0	LACKAWANNA NATIONAL INS CO
4.5	2.9	77.3	84.9	-0.8	-2.6	69.8	30.0	99.8	117.7	8.7	0.0	LAFAYETTE INS CO
4.5	4.1	23.7	30.3	-47.0	-46.8	-73.2	49.5	-23.7	80.5	52.9	0.0	LAKE STREET RRG INC
2.1	1.9	107.3	19.7	-0.3	-0.2	54.6	43.2	97.8	97.7	13.5	0.0	LAKEVIEW INS CO
5.4	4.1	22.0	68.8	-4.1	-6.5	67.2	27.5	94.7	102.8	1.8	0.1 ●	LAMMICO
26.9	24.2	0.3	1.1	-0.1	-0.1	80.3	187.3	267.6	49.8	-19.4	0.0	LAMMICO RRG INC
N/A	N/A	--	--	--	--	--	--	--	--	--	--	LAMORAK INS CO
1.2	0.7	83.5	94.1	-2.6	13.8	57.1	30.4	87.5	124.8	4.8	0.0	LANCER INDEMNITY CO
2.5	1.7	130.5	170.6	3.7	18.9	70.2	29.4	99.6	110.3	-0.9	0.0 ●	LANCER INS CO
0.1	0.1	381.3	259.5	258.7	286.1	120.0	19.3	139.3	95.4	104.6	10.7	LANCET IND RRG INC
1.5	1.0	62.8	11.5	0.7	1.6	83.2	7.9	91.1	148.5	-3.6	0.0	LANDCAR CASUALTY CO
14.8	9.1	16.7	28.3	-2.8	-4.4	50.6	28.6	79.2	140.3	-10.6	0.0 ●	LANDMARK AMERICAN INS CO
2.4	1.9	55.8	70.0	-12.7	-24.2	42.5	38.5	81.0	115.7	10.7	0.0	LAUNDRY OWNERS MUTUAL LIAB INS
9.6	6.0	15.7	32.8	-6.1	-11.6	50.4	17.8	68.2	126.1	-3.1	0.1 ●	LAWYERS MUTUAL INS CO
2.9	2.0	42.8	86.0	-10.3	-39.2	84.0	21.4	105.4	96.5	5.6	0.0	LAWYERS MUTUAL INS CO OF
6.3	4.1	19.6	21.3	-5.4	-6.8	42.7	28.7	71.4	117.6	1.4	3.3	LAWYERS MUTUAL LIAB INS CO OF NC
1.4	1.0	64.8	70.2	N/A	N/A	52.6	44.1	96.7	107.1	0.0	0.0	LCTA CASUALTY INS CO
2.6	1.6	127.5	66.9	0.2	2.7	68.3	31.5	99.8	95.3	11.3	0.0	LE MARS INS CO
2.3	1.7	70.9	80.2	-12.5	-14.0	61.3	16.3	77.6	132.3	1.4	5.0	LEAGUE OF WI MUNICIPALITIES MUT INS
2.5	1.8	84.5	32.6	-6.8	-7.4	44.5	28.7	73.2	165.7	23.9	0.0	LEATHERSTOCKING COOP INS CO
2.9	2.1	71.8	60.3	-13.3	-13.3	46.7	43.4	90.1	105.0	5.0	0.0	LEBANON VALLEY INS CO

999 + Denotes number greater than 999.9%
999 - Denotes number less than -999.99%
● Bullets denote a more detailed analysis is available in Section II.

INSURANCE COMPANY NAME	DOM. STATE	RATING		TOTAL ASSETS ($MIL)	CAPITAL & SURPLUS ($MIL)	ANNUAL NET PREMIUM ($MIL)	NET INCOME ($MIL)	CAPITAL-IZATION INDEX (PTS)	RESERVE ADQ INDEX (PTS)	PROFIT-ABILITY INDEX (PTS)	LIQUIDITY INDEX (PTS)	STAB. INDEX (PTS)	STABILITY FACTORS
LEGAL MUTUAL LIAB INS SOCIETY OF MD	MD	U	(5)	--	--	--	--	N/A	--	--	--	--	Z
LEMIC INS CO	LA	F	(5)	0.0	0.0	15.4	0.0	0.0	1.6	0.1	7.0	0.0	CDFR
LEMONADE INS CO	NY	D+		11.3	10.6	0.2	-2.5	10.0	N/A	1.3	10.0	2.1	DFGT
LEON HIX INS CO	SC	U		--	--	--	--	N/A	--	--	--	--	Z
LEXINGTON INS CO	DE	C		21,929.5	5,943.6	4,837.1	146.2	7.4	3.1	3.5	6.4	2.8	FRT
LEXINGTON NATIONAL INS CORP	FL	D-		58.8	17.5	13.3	0.5	7.5	6.1	6.5	7.1	1.3	DRT
LEXON INS CO	TX	C-		225.9	64.6	74.4	1.0	7.3	2.5	5.8	7.9	3.3	RT
LIBERTY AMERICAN INS CO	FL	U	(3)	--	--	--	--	N/A	--	--	--	--	Z
LIBERTY AMERICAN SELECT INS CO	FL	U	(2)	--	--	--	--	N/A	--	--	--	--	Z
LIBERTY COUNTY MUTUAL INS CO	TX	C-		7.2	5.2	0.0	0.0	10.0	N/A	3.4	9.9	2.6	DGT
LIBERTY FIRST RRG INS CO	UT	F	(5)	0.0	0.0	2.5	0.0	0.2	0.5	1.9	8.5	0.0	CDGR
LIBERTY INS CORP	IL	C		252.7	241.1	0.0	2.1	10.0	3.0	4.5	7.0	3.8	AT
LIBERTY INS UNDERWRITERS INC	IL	C		175.7	128.0	0.0	0.9	10.0	3.6	6.2	10.0	4.3	AFRT
LIBERTY LLOYDS OF TX INS CO	TX	B		6.5	6.5	0.0	0.0	10.0	N/A	6.4	7.0	4.3	DG
LIBERTY MUTUAL FIRE INS CO	WI	B-		5,597.8	1,479.1	2,119.9	-10.2	7.6	4.7	5.4	6.1	3.6	AT
LIBERTY MUTUAL INS CO	MA	B		44,306.8	16,551.8	13,249.4	-193.4	7.6	5.9	5.2	6.4	4.3	ART
LIBERTY MUTUAL MID ATLANTIC INS CO	MA	C		20.6	19.8	0.0	0.1	10.0	N/A	7.5	7.0	3.4	DGT
LIBERTY MUTUAL PERSONAL INS CO	MA	B		6.9	6.9	0.0	0.0	10.0	N/A	6.3	7.0	4.0	DG
LIBERTY NORTHWEST INS CORP	OR	C		56.2	55.9	0.0	0.1	10.0	N/A	3.6	7.0	4.0	RT
LIBERTY PERSONAL INS CO	NH	C		16.7	16.1	0.0	0.1	10.0	N/A	3.6	7.0	3.2	DGT
LIBERTY SURPLUS INS CORP	NH	C		178.9	97.9	0.0	0.3	10.0	N/A	3.9	8.5	4.3	AT
LIGHTHOUSE CASUALTY CO	IL	D-		27.4	4.4	18.7	-0.1	0.5	1.0	3.1	4.3	1.2	CDGL
LIGHTHOUSE PROPERTY INS CORP	LA	B-		73.2	23.4	39.8	0.0	5.8	6.2	6.1	7.2	4.7	DT
LIGHTNING ROD MUTUAL INS CO	OH	B-		282.8	168.2	112.5	2.9	10.0	7.8	6.1	6.9	4.1	T
LION INS CO (FL)	FL	B		266.5	91.4	28.3	1.4	7.8	8.6	8.7	9.4	4.9	RT
LITITZ MUTUAL INS CO	PA	B-		280.1	179.4	76.4	0.7	7.6	6.4	6.1	6.2	4.0	ART
LITTLE BLACK MUTUAL INS CO	WI	D+		6.1	2.7	2.6	-1.0	6.4	6.0	3.9	6.7	2.1	DGRT
LIVINGSTON MUTUAL INS CO	PA	C		2.8	1.6	0.5	0.0	8.2	6.5	2.8	6.8	2.3	DFGT
LM GENERAL INS CO	IL	B-		10.9	10.7	0.0	0.1	10.0	4.7	4.9	8.7	3.8	DGT
LM INS CORP	IL	C		119.7	117.3	0.0	0.5	10.0	3.8	6.4	10.0	4.3	AT
LM P&C INS CO	IN	U		--	--	--	--	N/A	--	--	--	--	Z
LOCUST MUTUAL FIRE INS CO	PA	D	(1)	1.2	1.2	0.0	0.0	7.6	3.7	3.1	7.4	1.0	DT
LONE STAR ALLIANCE INC A RRG	DC	D		11.3	3.2	0.7	0.3	7.9	3.7	3.5	8.9	2.0	DGT
LONE STAR NATIONAL INS CO	IN	D		4.3	4.3	-0.1	0.0	10.0	4.7	4.8	6.8	1.9	DFGR
LOUISIANA FARM BUREAU CAS INS CO	LA	B		11.1	11.0	0.0	0.1	10.0	N/A	7.4	10.0	4.3	DGT
LOUISIANA FARM BUREAU MUTUAL INS CO	LA	B		223.0	139.3	84.0	3.0	10.0	6.9	8.9	6.8	4.3	T
LOYA CASUALTY INS CO	CA	D		106.9	26.5	151.1	-3.2	4.0	8.5	1.4	0.0	2.0	FLT
LOYA INS CO	TX	D		272.8	118.4	347.8	1.0	6.0	3.7	1.9	0.0	2.0	FLT
LR INS INC	DE	U		--	--	--	--	N/A	--	--	--	--	Z
LUBA CASUALTY INS CO	LA	B		240.1	90.0	74.3	-0.5	8.1	9.3	6.8	6.9	6.3	T
LUBA INDEMNITY INS CO	LA	D		5.3	5.0	0.0	0.0	10.0	N/A	4.9	10.0	2.3	DGT
LUMBER MUTUAL INS CO	MA	F	(5)	0.0	0.0	0.0	0.0	0.3	2.4	1.8	9.1	0.0	CFGR
LUMBERMENS UNDERWRITING ALLIANCE	MO	F	(5)	354.2	-41.9	63.8	0.0	0.0	4.1	0.1	7.0	0.0	CDFR
LUTHERAN MUTUAL FIRE INS CO	IL	C		10.7	10.4	0.3	0.0	10.0	5.0	5.7	7.0	2.3	DGT
LVHN RRG	SC	U		--	--	--	--	N/A	--	--	--	--	Z
LYNDON SOUTHERN INS CO	DE	B		181.7	53.0	89.2	0.9	7.4	5.1	8.6	6.4	4.2	RT
MA EMPLOYERS INS CO	MA	C		4.3	3.6	0.0	0.0	10.0	N/A	6.2	7.0	3.3	DFGR
MACHINERY INS INC	FL	D-		2.8	2.5	0.4	0.0	10.0	N/A	5.2	9.1	0.0	DGT
MADA INS EXCHANGE	MN	U		--	--	--	--	N/A	--	--	--	--	Z
MADISON MUTUAL INS CO	IL	B-		63.5	39.6	31.2	-0.2	8.5	5.3	3.3	6.2	3.5	FRT
MADISON MUTUAL INS CO	NY	C+		14.0	9.8	4.0	0.3	9.9	7.6	7.2	6.9	3.0	DGRT
MAG MUTUAL INS CO	GA	B-		1,840.1	927.8	243.9	2.4	9.3	9.4	8.0	7.4	4.7	RT

See Page 27 for explanation of footnotes and
Page 28 for explanation of stability factors.
Arrows denote recent upgrades ▲ or downgrades ▼   (see Section VII for explanations)

84

www.weissratings.com

RISK ADJ. RATIO #1	CAPITAL RATIO #2	PREMIUM TO SURPLUS (%)	RESV. TO SURPLUS (%)	RESV. 1 YEAR (%)	DEVELOP. 2 YEAR (%)	LOSS RATIO (%)	EXP. RATIO (%)	COMB RATIO (%)	CASH FROM UNDER- WRITING (%)	NET PREMIUM GROWTH (%)	INVEST. IN AFFIL (%)	INSURANCE COMPANY NAME
N/A	N/A	--	--	--	--	--	--	--	--	--	--	LEGAL MUTUAL LIAB INS SOCIETY OF
-0.0	-0.0	-739.3	999 +	53.8	50.0	121.0	52.5	173.5	71.1	-29.6	0.0	LEMIC INS CO
9.9	9.6	2.9	0.1	N/A	N/A	397.5	999 +	999 +	1.2	0.0	0.0	LEMONADE INS CO
N/A	N/A	--	--	--	--	--	--	--	--	--	--	LEON HIX INS CO
2.2	1.5	82.6	232.0	22.0	30.9	99.8	26.1	125.9	85.9	-13.1	0.3 ●	LEXINGTON INS CO
1.4	1.2	76.3	1.5	2.1	0.3	10.8	83.5	94.3	105.9	15.8	19.2	LEXINGTON NATIONAL INS CORP
1.6	1.3	117.8	37.8	-4.8	2.7	29.9	62.8	92.7	97.8	6.9	1.3	LEXON INS CO
N/A	N/A	--	--	--	--	--	--	--	--	--	--	LIBERTY AMERICAN INS CO
N/A	N/A	--	--	--	--	--	--	--	--	--	--	LIBERTY AMERICAN SELECT INS CO
7.1	6.4	N/A	N/A	N/A	N/A	N/A	N/A	N/A	N/A	0.0	0.0	LIBERTY COUNTY MUTUAL INS CO
-0.3	-0.2	149.9	267.7	21.4	98.2	41.3	11.6	52.9	222.4	-50.3	0.0	LIBERTY FIRST RRG INS CO
83.2	59.6	N/A	N/A	N/A	N/A	N/A	N/A	N/A	N/A	0.0	0.0 ●	LIBERTY INS CORP
19.6	17.6	N/A	N/A	N/A	N/A	N/A	N/A	N/A	999 +	0.0	0.0	LIBERTY INS UNDERWRITERS INC
247.4	123.7	N/A	N/A	N/A	N/A	N/A	N/A	N/A	N/A	0.0	0.0	LIBERTY LLOYDS OF TX INS CO
2.1	1.5	143.8	187.0	1.2	-0.5	69.8	32.0	101.8	100.8	3.4	4.9 ●	LIBERTY MUTUAL FIRE INS CO
1.5	1.4	80.2	104.3	0.7	-0.3	69.8	32.5	102.3	99.6	3.4	27.6 ●	LIBERTY MUTUAL INS CO
53.3	25.1	N/A	N/A	N/A	N/A	N/A	N/A	N/A	N/A	0.0	0.0	LIBERTY MUTUAL MID ATLANTIC INS CO
222.6	111.3	N/A	N/A	N/A	N/A	N/A	N/A	N/A	N/A	0.0	0.0	LIBERTY MUTUAL PERSONAL INS CO
3.9	3.8	N/A	N/A	N/A	N/A	N/A	N/A	N/A	N/A	0.0	28.7	LIBERTY NORTHWEST INS CORP
57.3	51.5	N/A	N/A	N/A	N/A	N/A	N/A	N/A	N/A	0.0	0.0	LIBERTY PERSONAL INS CO
12.0	10.8	N/A	N/A	N/A	N/A	N/A	N/A	N/A	999 +	0.0	0.0	LIBERTY SURPLUS INS CORP
0.2	0.1	435.5	224.6	40.6	71.1	69.2	29.9	99.1	119.0	65.1	0.0	LIGHTHOUSE CASUALTY CO
1.4	0.9	173.6	31.3	-2.2	-4.4	41.9	42.7	84.6	134.6	29.4	0.0	LIGHTHOUSE PROPERTY INS CORP
5.1	3.2	68.7	29.4	-1.4	-2.6	65.1	31.0	96.1	109.1	4.6	0.1	LIGHTNING ROD MUTUAL INS CO
2.5	1.5	31.5	56.3	-1.7	-5.7	41.0	35.7	76.7	142.9	0.5	0.0	LION INS CO (FL)
2.4	1.4	44.1	11.3	-1.4	-2.2	58.7	37.6	96.3	102.6	2.3	0.0	LITITZ MUTUAL INS CO
1.2	0.8	71.5	5.1	-1.6	1.6	32.0	39.7	71.7	121.7	5.0	0.0	LITTLE BLACK MUTUAL INS CO
2.7	1.7	32.4	10.2	-1.6	-6.2	59.7	70.6	130.3	85.2	-0.1	0.0	LIVINGSTON MUTUAL INS CO
126.9	71.3	N/A	0.5	N/A	N/A	N/A	N/A	N/A	999 +	0.0	0.0	LM GENERAL INS CO
145.4	70.4	N/A	N/A	N/A	N/A	N/A	N/A	N/A	N/A	0.0	0.0	LM INS CORP
N/A	N/A	--	--	--	--	--	--	--	--	--	--	LM P&C INS CO
2.2	1.3	3.3	N/A	-0.7	-3.1	-12.3	172.1	159.8	69.1	29.4	0.0	LOCUST MUTUAL FIRE INS CO
1.5	1.3	22.2	31.5	2.0	-2.2	153.3	-24.8	128.5	-603.8	244.4	0.0	LONE STAR ALLIANCE INC A RRG
22.0	12.4	-1.6	N/A	0.6	-0.3	66.7	-344.7	-278.0	41.6	-108.0	0.0	LONE STAR NATIONAL INS CO
31.3	17.6	N/A	N/A	N/A	N/A	N/A	N/A	N/A	N/A	0.0	0.0	LOUISIANA FARM BUREAU CAS INS CO
5.6	5.0	61.1	10.8	-1.4	-3.5	64.8	21.8	86.6	112.7	-3.0	4.6	LOUISIANA FARM BUREAU MUTUAL INS
0.6	0.5	510.2	199.2	21.4	-2.3	87.0	34.0	121.0	83.2	4.0	0.0	LOYA CASUALTY INS CO
1.0	0.9	314.3	121.7	19.8	8.9	87.9	29.2	117.1	80.8	5.2	24.4	LOYA INS CO
N/A	N/A	--	--	--	--	--	--	--	--	--	--	LR INS INC
2.3	1.8	81.8	98.3	-9.0	-18.1	52.1	32.7	84.8	116.8	-0.6	2.6	LUBA CASUALTY INS CO
43.5	39.1	N/A	N/A	N/A	N/A	N/A	N/A	N/A	N/A	0.0	0.0	LUBA INDEMNITY INS CO
0.1	0.1	0.7	407.0	33.1	32.6	999 +	999 +	999 +	0.4	146.2	54.4	LUMBER MUTUAL INS CO
-0.3	-0.2	-283.3	-645.8	3.0	15.1	97.4	177.7	275.1	71.0	-23.8	0.0	LUMBERMENS UNDERWRITING
13.9	9.5	2.9	0.2	N/A	1.0	84.4	108.8	193.2	51.4	16.7	0.0	LUTHERAN MUTUAL FIRE INS CO
N/A	N/A	--	--	--	--	--	--	--	--	--	--	LVHN RRG
3.2	1.8	171.1	23.9	1.6	-1.1	48.1	35.9	84.0	121.2	17.9	0.0	LYNDON SOUTHERN INS CO
11.5	10.3	N/A	N/A	N/A	N/A	N/A	N/A	N/A	999 +	0.0	0.0	MA EMPLOYERS INS CO
7.1	5.1	17.1	1.2	N/A	N/A	-0.8	59.8	59.0	165.6	-13.7	0.0	MACHINERY INS INC
N/A	N/A	--	--	--	--	--	--	--	--	--	--	MADA INS EXCHANGE
3.2	2.1	78.6	27.9	-1.1	-1.7	82.3	26.7	109.0	91.2	-4.1	0.0	MADISON MUTUAL INS CO
4.8	2.9	42.3	10.4	-1.7	-2.1	49.0	37.5	86.5	102.5	11.5	0.0	MADISON MUTUAL INS CO
3.0	2.3	26.7	57.0	-2.2	-9.4	71.8	25.2	97.0	112.9	21.8	12.5 ●	MAG MUTUAL INS CO

999 + Denotes number greater than 999.9%
999 - Denotes number less than -999.99%
● Bullets denote a more detailed analysis is available in Section II.

INSURANCE COMPANY NAME	DOM. STATE	RATING	TOTAL ASSETS ($MIL)	CAPITAL & SURPLUS ($MIL)	ANNUAL NET PREMIUM ($MIL)	NET INCOME ($MIL)	CAPITAL-IZATION INDEX (PTS)	RESERVE ADQ INDEX (PTS)	PROFIT-ABILITY INDEX (PTS)	LIQUIDITY INDEX (PTS)	STAB. INDEX (PTS)	STABILITY FACTORS
MAIDEN RE NORTH AMERICA INC	MO	B-	1,411.2	288.8	433.2	-7.9	5.3	4.3	3.9	5.6	5.3	CFT
MAIDSTONE INS CO	NY	E+	54.6	5.7	38.8	-0.2	0.3	7.0	0.6	4.8	0.5	CDGL
MAIN STREET AMER PROTECTION INS CO	FL	C	15.9	15.8	0.0	0.1	10.0	N/A	7.7	7.0	2.9	DGT
MAIN STREET AMERICA ASR CO	FL	C	68.4	43.2	0.0	0.2	10.0	N/A	5.8	7.0	3.7	T
MAISON INS CO	LA	C+	69.7	35.9	30.8	0.4	5.6	4.9	3.7	6.7	3.3	DT
MAKE TRANSPORTATION INS INC RRG	DE	D	3.9	2.0	1.3	-0.2	9.1	6.8	4.2	7.9	1.8	DGRT
MANHATTAN RE-INS CO	DE	F (5)	0.0	0.0	0.0	0.0	5.6	9.8	0.8	9.2	2.0	FRT
MANUFACTURERS ALLIANCE INS CO	PA	C-	207.0	65.0	53.0	-0.1	7.4	2.5	4.3	6.6	3.3	ART
▼MANUFACTURING TECHNOLOGY MUT INS	MI	C+	57.7	25.2	20.0	-3.1	6.0	9.8	3.0	6.9	4.4	DRT
MAPFRE INS CO	NJ	C	82.4	22.5	47.4	0.0	6.9	3.8	3.8	2.7	3.4	DLRT
MAPFRE INS CO OF FLORIDA	FL	C	108.3	31.3	67.1	-0.1	7.6	4.3	2.5	4.6	2.9	FLT
MAPFRE INS CO OF NY	NY	C+	157.9	46.5	98.7	0.1	8.1	4.2	2.5	4.4	3.3	LT
MAPFRE PAN AMERICAN INS CO	PR	C	34.5	12.7	7.7	1.0	5.6	7.3	6.8	6.3	2.4	DGT
MAPFRE PRAICO INS CO	PR	C	402.8	164.0	183.3	2.9	7.0	8.3	6.6	5.6	2.9	FT
MAPLE VALLEY MUTUAL INS CO	WI	C	14.0	9.3	5.3	0.1	9.3	7.6	6.9	7.4	2.3	DGRT
MARATHON FINANCIAL INS INC RRG	DE	D+	4.4	2.1	0.2	0.0	7.6	7.6	3.7	10.0	1.7	DFGR
MARKEL AMERICAN INS CO	VA	C	470.1	163.2	212.2	4.3	7.7	9.4	8.0	6.8	2.8	AGRT
MARKEL GLOBAL REINS CO	DE	B+	1,943.5	826.2	254.7	-15.5	7.7	7.5	4.0	7.0	6.5	T
MARKEL INS CO	IL	C	1,643.1	396.8	537.3	10.2	6.6	9.3	5.1	6.7	3.7	ART
MARYSVILLE MUTUAL INS CO	KS	C+	48.1	30.0	23.1	0.8	8.9	6.2	8.8	6.7	3.3	RT
MASSACHUSETTS BAY INS CO	NH	C+	66.3	66.1	0.0	0.4	10.0	N/A	7.4	7.0	4.1	RT
▼MASSACHUSETTS HOMELAND INS CO	MA	F (5)	8.9	8.3	0.0	0.0	10.0	N/A	4.5	7.0	0.0	DFGR
MAXUM CASUALTY INS CO	CT	C+	23.5	17.4	14.5	1.3	6.7	4.1	4.1	6.9	4.7	DRT
MAXUM INDEMNITY CO	CT	C	120.7	108.4	76.2	7.7	7.6	4.3	3.2	7.0	4.0	FRT
MAYA ASR CO	NY	E+	18.0	3.2	6.1	0.0	0.5	0.1	4.7	5.7	0.8	CDFG
MBIA INS CORP	NY	E+	228.8	286.1	52.0	177.9	1.5	1.0	0.6	0.6	0.4	CFLT
MCIC VERMONT INC RRG	VT	C	2,024.1	581.3	289.3	0.0	0.7	0.5	4.9	6.4	3.4	CRT
MCMILLAN WARNER MUTUAL INS CO	WI	C	16.7	10.0	7.0	0.2	8.0	7.6	5.4	7.0	3.0	DGRT
▲MD RRG INC	MT	C-	25.6	16.5	3.9	0.6	9.7	9.8	8.5	9.2	3.0	DGRT
MDADVANTAGE INS CO OF NJ	NJ	C	345.1	146.5	34.5	1.7	8.3	9.3	8.3	8.3	3.5	T
MDOW INS CO	TX	B-	22.9	13.9	0.0	0.3	10.0	N/A	9.0	7.0	4.4	DG
MED MAL RRG INC	TN	D	4.0	1.4	0.1	0.0	8.0	4.9	2.3	10.0	1.3	DFGT
MEDCHOICE RRG INC	VT	D	2.3	2.0	0.1	0.0	10.0	3.6	3.2	10.0	2.2	DFGT
MEDICAL ALLIANCE INS CO	IL	D+	12.1	5.2	2.7	0.0	9.5	N/A	5.4	8.7	2.4	DFGR
MEDICAL INS EXCHANGE OF CALIFORNIA	CA	B	425.7	180.7	50.0	-0.5	9.9	9.0	4.0	7.7	4.1	FRT
MEDICAL LIABILITY ALLIANCE	MO	B	77.6	55.6	10.9	0.5	10.0	9.0	8.4	7.3	5.8	DT
MEDICAL LIABILITY MUTUAL INS CO	NY	D+	5,590.6	2,095.0	393.7	32.4	7.6	9.5	8.2	7.5	2.4	FRT
MEDICAL MUTUAL INS CO OF MAINE	ME	B	292.7	168.2	36.3	1.6	10.0	9.4	8.6	9.0	4.1	RT
MEDICAL MUTUAL INS CO OF NC	NC	B-	559.8	264.3	114.3	5.4	9.6	9.3	7.0	8.8	4.1	GRT
MEDICAL MUTUAL LIAB INS SOC OF MD	MD	B-	851.5	399.1	104.2	-3.4	10.0	9.4	4.9	8.0	4.3	RT
MEDICAL PROFESSIONAL MUTUAL INS CO	MA	B-	3,165.3	1,585.5	250.4	-5.6	8.0	9.4	5.8	7.1	4.5	RT
MEDICAL PROTECTIVE CO	IN	B	3,184.7	1,781.8	255.8	27.2	9.7	9.7	8.7	9.9	5.5	FT
MEDICAL PROVIDERS MUTUAL INS CO RRG	DC	D+	7.6	3.2	1.2	0.1	7.8	9.7	4.0	7.7	2.1	DGR
MEDICAL SECURITY INS CO	NC	C+	22.3	17.6	0.0	0.0	10.0	6.9	7.9	8.8	3.3	DGRT
MEDICUS INS CO	TX	B-	54.5	36.0	0.0	0.3	10.0	4.1	7.7	7.0	3.9	DRT
MEDMAL DIRECT INS CO	FL	B-	44.5	21.6	12.5	0.0	7.1	6.4	4.8	7.4	3.5	DT
MEDMARC CASUALTY INS CO	VT	C	304.0	188.2	33.9	1.4	8.6	6.9	7.0	8.1	4.1	GRT
MEDPRO RRG	DC	C-	93.8	6.8	2.7	-0.1	5.3	9.4	3.7	10.0	2.0	DFT
MEDSTAR LIABILITY LTD INS CO INC RRG	DC	U (5)	--	--	--	--	N/A	--	--	--	--	Z
MEEMIC INS CO	MI	C	268.1	80.6	100.8	-0.3	9.0	4.4	5.6	6.1	4.2	T
▲MEMBERS INS CO	NC	C-	31.9	13.6	19.6	0.3	7.0	8.2	4.2	5.4	3.0	DGT
MEMBERSELECT INS CO	MI	B-	527.1	154.3	181.5	-0.7	9.2	4.6	5.2	6.7	4.5	T

See Page 27 for explanation of footnotes and
Page 28 for explanation of stability factors.
Arrows denote recent upgrades ▲ or downgrades ▼   (see Section VII for explanations)

86

www.weissratings.com

RISK ADJ. RATIO #1	CAPITAL RATIO #2	PREMIUM TO SURPLUS (%)	RESV. TO SURPLUS (%)	RESV. DEVELOP. 1 YEAR (%)	RESV. DEVELOP. 2 YEAR (%)	LOSS RATIO (%)	EXP. RATIO (%)	COMB RATIO (%)	CASH FROM UNDER-WRITING (%)	NET PREMIUM GROWTH (%)	INVEST. IN AFFIL (%)	INSURANCE COMPANY NAME
1.1	0.6	148.8	173.1	17.5	14.3	79.6	30.5	110.1	96.3	4.0	0.0 ●	MAIDEN RE NORTH AMERICA INC
0.2	0.2	678.8	574.4	-26.2	-22.1	91.1	28.1	119.2	101.1	36.6	0.0	MAIDSTONE INS CO
104.1	52.0	N/A	N/A	N/A	N/A	N/A	N/A	N/A	N/A	0.0	0.0	MAIN STREET AMER PROTECTION INS
10.6	9.5	N/A	N/A	N/A	N/A	N/A	N/A	N/A	N/A	0.0	0.0	MAIN STREET AMERICA ASR CO
2.7	1.8	155.2	16.8	-1.5	4.8	54.4	50.9	105.3	106.2	1.2	0.0	MAISON INS CO
2.9	2.6	57.6	56.2	-12.6	10.0	39.8	25.0	64.8	146.0	-2.8	0.0	MAKE TRANSPORTATION INS INC RRG
2.4	0.9	-0.2	102.5	-76.7	-71.0	999 +	999 +	999 +	0.9	-120.0	0.0	MANHATTAN RE-INS CO
1.6	1.1	81.7	145.8	7.0	14.6	78.6	24.8	103.4	98.3	18.1	6.5	MANUFACTURERS ALLIANCE INS CO
1.6	1.2	72.2	87.5	-17.4	-37.8	48.8	18.8	67.6	144.4	4.2	0.0	MANUFACTURING TECHNOLOGY MUT
1.4	1.1	212.5	100.6	3.8	4.6	78.1	23.4	101.5	100.5	-8.1	0.0	MAPFRE INS CO
1.7	1.3	216.5	102.5	4.0	4.5	78.1	25.1	103.2	93.6	-11.6	0.0	MAPFRE INS CO OF FLORIDA
2.0	1.7	215.3	101.9	3.8	4.7	78.1	24.3	102.4	99.3	-5.0	0.0	MAPFRE INS CO OF NY
1.0	0.6	64.8	1.8	-0.5	-0.6	20.1	1.1	21.2	424.7	190.9	0.0	MAPFRE PAN AMERICAN INS CO
1.5	1.0	113.2	44.5	-4.6	-4.7	48.9	46.0	94.9	96.6	11.8	0.0	MAPFRE PRAICO INS CO
3.7	2.6	58.4	7.5	-0.3	-2.0	39.9	38.3	78.2	113.2	2.6	0.0	MAPLE VALLEY MUTUAL INS CO
2.6	2.3	8.0	1.7	-1.1	-1.1	N/A	-44.0	-44.0	280.9	117.9	0.0	MARATHON FINANCIAL INS INC RRG
2.1	1.4	146.5	88.4	-13.8	-15.9	52.7	39.6	92.3	142.6	63.4	0.0	MARKEL AMERICAN INS CO
2.0	1.3	31.7	56.8	-0.9	-1.0	68.9	33.2	102.1	113.9	20.3	14.9 ●	MARKEL GLOBAL REINS CO
1.8	0.9	141.8	223.5	-10.1	-6.7	61.7	34.9	96.6	112.2	0.6	0.0 ●	MARKEL INS CO
3.0	2.3	79.7	7.3	-0.7	-1.2	48.7	27.3	76.0	137.3	7.9	0.0	MARYSVILLE MUTUAL INS CO
83.7	38.8	N/A	N/A	N/A	N/A	N/A	N/A	N/A	N/A	0.0	0.0	MASSACHUSETTS BAY INS CO
30.8	27.1	N/A	N/A	N/A	N/A	N/A	N/A	N/A	N/A	0.0	0.0	MASSACHUSETTS HOMELAND INS CO
3.1	2.0	85.6	129.6	8.0	10.6	86.7	37.5	124.2	92.2	10.3	0.0	MAXUM CASUALTY INS CO
2.9	2.0	74.0	112.0	6.7	8.6	86.7	37.9	124.6	91.0	10.3	7.2	MAXUM INDEMNITY CO
0.1	0.1	191.5	219.2	66.2	159.2	98.4	4.5	102.9	84.8	-15.3	0.0	MAYA ASR CO
0.4	0.1	21.8	-87.0	-17.1	47.2	357.1	42.0	399.1	51.6	-40.2	39.0 ●	MBIA INS CORP
0.2	0.2	52.3	183.2	-4.5	-9.9	97.4	14.1	111.5	93.4	25.7	0.0 ●	MCIC VERMONT INC RRG
2.4	1.8	72.0	13.0	-3.7	-2.7	53.0	34.6	87.6	107.7	2.4	0.0	MCMILLAN WARNER MUTUAL INS CO
4.3	3.0	24.6	47.3	-17.9	-30.3	24.3	14.3	38.6	159.3	-0.3	0.0	MD RRG INC
2.3	2.0	23.8	110.0	-8.1	-14.6	56.4	35.3	91.7	109.1	-4.5	0.0	MDADVANTAGE INS CO OF NJ
6.1	5.5	N/A	N/A	N/A	N/A	N/A	N/A	N/A	16.5	0.0	0.0	MDOW INS CO
1.7	1.5	9.4	46.5	-9.5	-14.6	-4.7	151.8	147.1	-273.9	-63.3	0.0	MED MAL RRG INC
14.7	13.2	2.6	1.0	0.1	N/A	60.0	19.9	79.9	-27.3	594.4	0.0	MEDCHOICE RRG INC
2.7	2.5	52.2	N/A	N/A	N/A	18.4	70.8	89.2	80.5	6.9	0.0	MEDICAL ALLIANCE INS CO
3.9	2.8	28.2	76.6	-5.4	-9.5	83.0	17.8	100.8	108.6	-2.4	2.4	MEDICAL INS EXCHANGE OF
8.9	5.9	19.9	31.3	-1.5	-8.2	67.8	17.6	85.4	119.4	5.0	0.0	MEDICAL LIABILITY ALLIANCE
2.0	1.6	19.1	145.7	-14.8	-23.5	47.3	16.4	63.7	57.7	-4.2	0.2 ●	MEDICAL LIABILITY MUTUAL INS CO
6.3	4.5	21.9	55.1	-2.5	-7.5	70.2	25.2	95.4	134.1	-2.6	0.0	MEDICAL MUTUAL INS CO OF MAINE
3.8	2.7	44.9	68.7	-9.5	-16.0	59.2	13.8	73.0	256.6	78.7	3.5 ●	MEDICAL MUTUAL INS CO OF NC
3.5	3.2	25.9	48.4	-7.3	-15.9	55.2	16.3	71.5	128.9	-3.6	14.0 ●	MEDICAL MUTUAL LIAB INS SOC OF MD
1.9	1.6	15.7	73.4	-3.8	-11.4	88.7	36.6	125.3	79.9	3.8	23.6 ●	MEDICAL PROFESSIONAL MUTUAL INS
3.5	2.2	15.0	48.5	-3.6	-7.4	65.0	12.0	77.0	35.1	13.0	0.0 ●	MEDICAL PROTECTIVE CO
1.7	1.5	39.2	120.9	-0.1	-22.9	107.8	35.3	143.1	161.9	-18.1	0.0	MEDICAL PROVIDERS MUTUAL INS CO
12.2	11.0	N/A	1.3	-0.1	-2.0	999 +	999 +	999 +	185.7	0.0	0.0	MEDICAL SECURITY INS CO
10.7	9.6	N/A	23.7	N/A	N/A	N/A	N/A	N/A	121.2	0.0	0.0	MEDICUS INS CO
1.6	1.2	58.9	66.6	2.6	5.5	64.9	40.0	104.9	130.9	9.2	0.0	MEDMAL DIRECT INS CO
2.3	2.0	16.8	30.6	-5.9	-10.3	49.1	34.3	83.4	158.3	31.5	25.7 ●	MEDMARC CASUALTY INS CO
0.8	0.7	39.0	86.2	-0.2	-23.1	92.8	44.6	137.4	38.8	465.9	0.0	MEDPRO RRG
N/A	N/A	--	--	--	--	--	--	--	--	--	--	MEDSTAR LIABILITY LTD INS CO INC
3.1	2.4	124.5	92.9	1.1	1.2	69.2	28.3	97.5	115.0	4.1	0.0	MEEMIC INS CO
1.4	1.0	149.9	40.1	-1.1	-4.3	81.0	24.1	105.1	95.9	24.7	0.0	MEMBERS INS CO
3.2	2.4	117.1	97.1	0.4	-0.2	69.4	28.3	97.7	116.1	4.1	0.0	MEMBERSELECT INS CO

999 + Denotes number greater than 999.9%
999 - Denotes number less than -999.99%
● Bullets denote a more detailed analysis is available in Section II.

INSURANCE COMPANY NAME	DOM. STATE	RATING	TOTAL ASSETS ($MIL)	CAPITAL & SURPLUS ($MIL)	ANNUAL NET PREMIUM ($MIL)	NET INCOME ($MIL)	CAPITAL-IZATION INDEX (PTS)	RESERVE ADQ INDEX (PTS)	PROFIT-ABILITY INDEX (PTS)	LIQUIDITY INDEX (PTS)	STAB. INDEX (PTS)	STABILITY FACTORS
MEMIC CASUALTY CO	NH	B-	52.5	19.8	13.8	-0.6	5.7	5.7	3.9	7.3	3.5	CDT
MEMIC INDEMNITY CO	NH	C	472.7	132.5	167.6	-2.7	6.2	8.1	4.3	6.6	3.2	RT
MENDAKOTA INS CO	MN	B	12.4	9.4	0.0	0.0	10.0	3.3	6.0	7.0	4.4	DGRT
MENDOTA INS CO	MN	D+	125.4	40.6	114.9	-0.2	0.3	3.0	2.9	0.0	2.5	CFLR
MENNONITE MUTUAL INS CO	OH	C	27.8	15.1	13.5	0.1	8.7	6.5	8.7	7.0	2.7	DGT
MENTAL HEALTH RISK RETENTION GROUP	VT	C	30.0	17.1	4.0	0.4	9.1	9.7	8.9	9.1	2.8	DGT
MERASTAR INS CO	IL	B-	36.3	10.6	0.0	0.1	9.3	N/A	5.7	10.0	3.8	DGRT
MERCED PROPERTY & CASUALTY CO	CA	C+	23.5	17.3	4.9	-0.3	10.0	7.7	4.9	7.0	3.4	DGRT
MERCER INS CO	PA	C+	265.7	112.3	86.8	1.6	7.9	8.2	7.8	6.8	4.4	RT
MERCER INS CO OF NJ INC	NJ	C	88.5	34.4	28.9	0.5	8.2	8.4	8.3	6.7	3.8	RT
MERCHANTS BONDING CO (MUTUAL)	IA	B	183.7	112.3	80.1	3.0	8.7	8.5	8.7	6.9	4.1	RT
MERCHANTS MUTUAL INS CO	NY	B-	516.3	192.5	146.4	2.9	8.9	5.7	6.9	6.7	4.1	RT
MERCHANTS NATIONAL BONDING INC	IA	C+	31.2	14.3	10.9	0.4	7.6	6.6	8.7	7.6	3.2	DGRT
MERCHANTS NATIONAL INS CO	NH	B	130.2	53.1	41.8	0.4	7.3	5.3	5.7	6.7	5.9	T
MERCHANTS PREFERRED INS CO	NY	B	72.1	29.3	20.9	0.6	8.5	5.8	6.9	6.8	6.0	DT
MERCHANTS PROPERTY INS CO OF IN	IN	U	--	--	--	--	N/A	--	--	--	--	Z
MERCURY CASUALTY CO	CA	B	1,917.0	1,089.1	753.1	4.3	7.5	5.7	3.7	6.9	6.2	T
MERCURY COUNTY MUTUAL INS CO	TX	B	12.0	4.6	0.0	0.0	8.6	N/A	3.5	10.0	4.9	DFGT
▲MERCURY INDEMNITY CO OF AMERICA	FL	C-	60.7	38.4	0.0	0.0	10.0	N/A	6.1	7.0	3.0	T
MERCURY INDEMNITY CO OF GEORGIA	GA	B	17.5	10.8	0.0	0.0	10.0	N/A	6.6	7.0	4.9	DG
MERCURY INS CO	CA	B+	1,654.2	647.0	1,560.1	13.9	7.7	5.8	4.9	3.5	5.2	LT
MERCURY INS CO OF FL	FL	C+	42.6	41.9	0.0	0.2	10.0	N/A	6.5	7.0	4.8	T
MERCURY INS CO OF GA	GA	B	22.4	18.5	0.0	0.1	10.0	N/A	7.7	7.0	4.9	DGT
MERCURY INS CO OF IL	IL	B	36.5	34.0	0.0	0.1	8.3	N/A	6.9	10.0	4.6	DGT
MERCURY NATIONAL INS CO	IL	B	16.0	15.8	0.0	0.0	10.0	3.6	6.5	10.0	4.9	DGT
MERIDIAN SECURITY INS CO	IN	C	123.6	72.5	0.0	0.3	10.0	N/A	7.3	7.3	3.5	RT
MERITPLAN INS CO	CA	U	--	--	--	--	N/A	--	--	--	--	Z
MERRIMACK MUTUAL FIRE INS CO	MA	B-	1,487.7	968.9	269.6	7.0	7.9	6.5	7.9	7.2	4.8	T
MESA UNDERWRITERS SPECIALTY INS CO	NJ	C	329.1	87.2	111.9	3.3	7.7	9.3	8.3	6.8	3.6	RT
MET LLOYDS INS CO OF TX	TX	B	102.8	18.1	0.0	0.1	8.3	N/A	7.8	8.5	4.8	DT
METROMILE INS CO	DE	C	23.2	13.4	4.5	0.1	7.9	N/A	1.7	9.6	2.5	DFGR
METROPOLITAN CASUALTY INS CO	RI	B	199.2	57.2	0.0	0.5	10.0	N/A	7.9	10.0	4.2	T
METROPOLITAN DIRECT PROP & CAS INS	RI	B	140.1	32.9	0.0	0.3	10.0	N/A	7.7	7.0	4.5	T
METROPOLITAN GENERAL INS CO	RI	B	43.9	38.9	0.0	0.3	10.0	N/A	7.8	7.0	4.4	DT
METROPOLITAN GROUP PROP & CAS INS	RI	B	693.9	417.1	0.0	4.3	10.0	4.5	6.9	7.0	4.9	FT
METROPOLITAN P&C INS CO	RI	B-	5,686.1	2,307.5	3,558.3	30.4	7.9	8.3	6.2	2.4	5.1	LT
MFS MUTUAL INS CO	IA	C- (1)	3.9	2.8	1.2	-0.1	6.7	6.1	3.4	5.8	1.9	DFRT
MGA INS CO	TX	C	278.5	99.0	240.3	2.7	7.5	3.5	6.0	2.8	3.9	LRT
MGIC ASSURANCE CORP	WI	C-	18.5	14.0	1.8	-0.1	10.0	6.1	3.5	10.0	3.0	DFGT
MGIC CREDIT ASR CORP	WI	U	--	--	--	--	N/A	--	--	--	--	Z
MGIC INDEMNITY CORP	WI	D+	142.1	90.9	10.0	1.0	10.0	4.6	1.9	9.0	2.4	ADT
MGIC REINS CORP OF WI	WI	D	586.8	180.3	114.3	6.4	2.5	6.1	2.6	6.8	2.2	T
MHA INS CO	MI	C	600.1	310.9	65.9	-0.7	9.2	8.4	6.6	7.1	4.3	RT
MIAMI MUTUAL INS CO	OH	B	59.1	28.0	33.0	0.4	7.9	8.2	8.3	6.0	4.0	RT
MIC GENERAL INS CORP	MI	C	44.3	17.3	0.0	0.1	10.0	3.9	3.6	9.6	3.3	DFGR
MIC P&C INS CORP	MI	C	96.8	54.9	0.0	0.0	10.0	N/A	6.1	10.0	3.8	FRT
MICA RRG INC	DC	U	--	--	--	--	N/A	--	--	--	--	Z
MICHIGAN COMMERCIAL INS MUTUAL	MI	C-	74.7	16.8	36.7	-0.4	3.4	3.8	1.6	5.8	2.9	CDFR
MICHIGAN INS CO	MI	C+	147.9	51.2	74.9	1.2	9.0	8.0	8.0	6.6	4.6	T
MICHIGAN MILLERS MUTUAL INS CO	MI	C	177.1	54.3	57.8	1.1	8.1	3.1	2.9	6.6	3.9	RT
MICHIGAN PROFESSIONAL INS EXCHANGE	MI	C+	107.2	53.3	14.7	4.8	9.2	9.4	4.7	7.4	3.4	DRT
MICO INS CO	OH	U	--	--	--	--	N/A	--	--	--	--	Z

See Page 27 for explanation of footnotes and
Page 28 for explanation of stability factors.

Arrows denote recent upgrades ▲ or downgrades ▼ (see Section VII for explanations)

88

www.weissratings.com

RISK ADJ. RATIO #1	CAPITAL RATIO #2	PREMIUM TO SURPLUS (%)	RESV. TO SURPLUS (%)	RESV. DEVELOP. 1 YEAR (%)	RESV. DEVELOP. 2 YEAR (%)	LOSS RATIO (%)	EXP. RATIO (%)	COMB RATIO (%)	CASH FROM UNDER-WRITING (%)	NET PREMIUM GROWTH (%)	INVEST. IN AFFIL (%)	INSURANCE COMPANY NAME
1.4	0.6	68.6	89.0	-3.6	-6.0	76.0	22.2	98.2	179.1	-2.2	0.0	MEMIC CASUALTY CO
1.1	0.8	125.4	162.0	-0.3	-0.2	78.2	23.4	101.6	137.7	17.8	0.0	MEMIC INDEMNITY CO
9.4	8.4	N/A	N/A	N/A	N/A	N/A	N/A	N/A	5.1	0.0	0.0	MENDAKOTA INS CO
0.1	0.1	278.0	106.9	23.8	20.9	85.3	22.3	107.6	87.5	10.4	37.9	MENDOTA INS CO
3.0	2.1	91.4	15.5	-1.8	-2.8	43.4	41.1	84.5	126.7	6.9	0.0	MENNONITE MUTUAL INS CO
3.9	2.5	24.6	57.6	-16.4	-35.6	19.6	15.7	35.3	294.5	2.0	0.0	MENTAL HEALTH RISK RETENTION
2.5	2.3	N/A	N/A	N/A	N/A	N/A	N/A	N/A	0.4	0.0	0.0	MERASTAR INS CO
6.9	4.1	28.0	8.8	-3.7	-3.4	46.5	58.0	104.5	98.9	11.7	0.0	MERCED PROPERTY & CASUALTY CO
2.0	1.7	79.6	87.5	-0.8	-2.6	69.8	29.8	99.6	118.4	8.7	19.1	MERCER INS CO
3.5	2.2	85.8	94.3	-0.9	-3.0	69.8	30.1	99.9	120.3	8.7	0.0	MERCER INS CO OF NJ INC
2.6	2.1	73.9	17.0	-6.8	-8.0	7.6	70.1	77.7	131.1	9.4	5.1	MERCHANTS BONDING CO (MUTUAL)
2.7	2.2	76.9	108.2	-1.1	-2.0	59.7	34.8	94.5	106.8	-0.5	12.6	MERCHANTS MUTUAL INS CO
1.7	1.4	79.4	18.3	-7.3	-8.7	7.6	70.2	77.8	119.0	9.4	0.0	MERCHANTS NATIONAL BONDING INC
1.7	1.5	79.7	99.2	-1.1	-2.3	59.7	34.8	94.5	104.8	-0.5	26.4	MERCHANTS NATIONAL INS CO
3.5	2.6	71.8	89.4	-0.8	-1.6	59.7	34.8	94.5	114.3	-0.5	0.0	MERCHANTS PREFERRED INS CO
N/A	N/A	--	--	--	--	--	--	--	--	--	--	MERCHANTS PROPERTY INS CO OF IN
1.6	1.5	81.3	49.0	4.0	4.8	83.2	25.4	108.6	101.7	13.6	36.8 ●	MERCURY CASUALTY CO
2.3	2.1	N/A	N/A	N/A	N/A	N/A	N/A	N/A	16.0	0.0	0.0	MERCURY COUNTY MUTUAL INS CO
10.2	9.1	N/A	N/A	N/A	N/A	N/A	N/A	N/A	-32.9	0.0	0.0	MERCURY INDEMNITY CO OF AMERICA
5.9	5.3	N/A	N/A	N/A	N/A	N/A	N/A	N/A	365.1	0.0	0.0	MERCURY INDEMNITY CO OF GEORGIA
1.6	1.5	247.0	85.9	5.6	1.8	73.0	24.8	97.8	104.9	5.9	0.0 ●	MERCURY INS CO
71.5	45.3	N/A	N/A	N/A	N/A	N/A	N/A	N/A	21.7	0.0	0.0	MERCURY INS CO OF FL
15.0	13.5	N/A	N/A	N/A	N/A	N/A	N/A	N/A	-46.0	0.0	0.0	MERCURY INS CO OF GA
2.0	1.8	N/A	N/A	N/A	N/A	N/A	N/A	N/A	240.5	0.0	47.2	MERCURY INS CO OF IL
37.2	21.1	N/A	N/A	N/A	N/A	N/A	N/A	N/A	-182.0	0.0	0.0	MERCURY NATIONAL INS CO
10.6	9.6	N/A	N/A	N/A	N/A	N/A	N/A	N/A	130.4	0.0	0.0	MERIDIAN SECURITY INS CO
N/A	N/A	--	--	--	--	--	--	--	--	--	--	MERITPLAN INS CO
2.0	1.6	28.9	15.6	-0.4	-2.1	50.8	38.3	89.1	121.0	4.0	23.1 ●	MERRIMACK MUTUAL FIRE INS CO
2.5	1.7	131.3	179.7	-4.1	-10.7	57.4	34.2	91.6	113.5	8.1	0.0	MESA UNDERWRITERS SPECIALTY INS
2.1	1.9	N/A	N/A	N/A	N/A	N/A	N/A	N/A	117.0	0.0	0.0	MET LLOYDS INS CO OF TX
1.6	1.2	34.4	11.3	N/A	N/A	162.9	31.8	194.7	34.6	0.0	0.0	METROMILE INS CO
6.1	5.4	N/A	N/A	N/A	N/A	N/A	N/A	N/A	999 +	0.0	0.0	METROPOLITAN CASUALTY INS CO
3.6	3.2	N/A	N/A	N/A	N/A	N/A	N/A	N/A	999 +	0.0	0.0	METROPOLITAN DIRECT PROP & CAS
25.4	22.9	N/A	N/A	N/A	N/A	N/A	N/A	N/A	999 +	0.0	0.0	METROPOLITAN GENERAL INS CO
38.8	31.2	N/A	N/A	N/A	N/A	N/A	N/A	N/A	-1.5	0.0	0.0 ●	METROPOLITAN GROUP PROP & CAS
2.0	1.6	156.7	68.2	0.3	-3.1	74.0	26.4	100.4	100.1	1.0	23.6 ●	METROPOLITAN P&C INS CO
1.4	0.9	43.3	6.0	1.6	0.2	71.1	43.8	114.9	83.5	11.6	0.0	MFS MUTUAL INS CO
1.3	1.2	232.6	80.9	-2.3	-5.0	69.9	26.8	96.7	102.1	6.1	0.0	MGA INS CO
6.2	5.5	15.5	0.6	-1.7	-0.9	-55.9	8.6	-47.3	42.4	N/A	0.0	MGIC ASSURANCE CORP
N/A	N/A	--	--	--	--	--	--	--	--	--	--	MGIC CREDIT ASR CORP
8.6	7.7	11.1	2.4	-0.4	-0.1	3.6	126.3	129.9	376.6	-39.0	0.0	MGIC INDEMNITY CORP
0.9	0.7	74.6	147.9	-26.9	-239.8	23.8	67.2	91.0	432.6	18.4	0.0	MGIC REINS CORP OF WI
2.7	2.3	21.0	63.7	-5.5	-8.9	68.5	38.4	106.9	87.8	-9.9	0.0 ●	MHA INS CO
2.7	1.7	119.9	37.2	-6.4	-5.9	59.4	32.4	91.8	111.1	4.3	0.0	MIAMI MUTUAL INS CO
4.0	3.6	N/A	N/A	N/A	N/A	N/A	N/A	N/A	-620.1	0.0	0.0	MIC GENERAL INS CORP
9.3	8.4	N/A	N/A	N/A	N/A	N/A	N/A	N/A	-159.2	0.0	0.0	MIC P&C INS CORP
N/A	N/A	--	--	--	--	--	--	--	--	--	--	MICA RRG INC
0.6	0.5	208.3	242.8	1.2	13.1	75.1	33.1	108.2	85.6	0.7	0.0	MICHIGAN COMMERCIAL INS MUTUAL
3.6	2.4	150.1	97.4	-3.2	-6.6	59.6	27.6	87.2	124.6	2.9	0.0	MICHIGAN INS CO
2.7	1.8	107.9	119.2	-0.9	26.5	62.6	37.7	100.3	103.4	11.1	0.0	MICHIGAN MILLERS MUTUAL INS CO
3.1	2.5	28.9	78.4	-5.9	-10.5	74.9	10.9	85.8	141.2	22.4	0.0	MICHIGAN PROFESSIONAL INS
N/A	N/A	--	--	--	--	--	--	--	--	--	--	MICO INS CO

999 + Denotes number greater than 999.9%
999 - Denotes number less than -999.99%
● Bullets denote a more detailed analysis is available in Section II.

INSURANCE COMPANY NAME	DOM. STATE	RATING	TOTAL ASSETS ($MIL)	CAPITAL & SURPLUS ($MIL)	ANNUAL NET PREMIUM ($MIL)	NET INCOME ($MIL)	CAPITAL-IZATION INDEX (PTS)	RESERVE ADQ INDEX (PTS)	PROFIT-ABILITY INDEX (PTS)	LIQUIDITY INDEX (PTS)	STAB. INDEX (PTS)	STABILITY FACTORS
MID AMERICAN FIRE & CAS CO	NH	U	--	--	--	--	N/A	--	--	--	--	Z
MID-CENTURY INS CO	CA	B	4,011.1	1,057.9	2,361.9	1.2	7.6	6.0	6.2	4.5	4.9	FLRT
MID-CENTURY INS CO OF TX	TX	U	--	--	--	--	N/A	--	--	--	--	Z
MID-CONTINENT CAS CO	OH	C+	515.6	159.0	121.3	5.0	3.9	3.8	6.8	7.6	4.4	CRT
MID-CONTINENT EXCESS & SURPLUS INS	DE	C+	17.9	17.9	0.0	0.1	10.0	N/A	7.1	7.0	3.4	DGT
MID-CONTINENT INS CO	OH	C	20.4	20.2	-1.8	0.1	10.0	4.6	4.5	9.8	3.4	DFGR
MID-HUDSON CO-OPERTIVE INS CO	NY	C	26.1	11.1	13.6	-0.4	7.0	6.3	4.3	6.9	2.6	DGRT
MIDDLE STATES INS CO	OK	C-	5.7	5.3	1.2	0.0	10.0	5.0	3.8	7.3	2.1	DFGT
MIDDLESEX INS CO	WI	B	725.1	249.7	201.2	2.1	9.0	8.1	5.7	6.8	4.8	T
MIDROX INS CO	NY	D+	8.1	3.5	3.4	-0.1	7.4	8.3	5.4	6.5	2.0	DGRT
MIDSOUTH MUTUAL INS CO	TN	C	27.6	11.9	9.4	-0.1	5.0	7.0	4.0	7.3	2.5	DGT
MIDSTATE MUTUAL INS CO	NY	C+	40.6	27.1	11.3	0.2	9.6	7.7	8.1	6.8	3.3	DRT
MIDSTATES REINS CORP	IL	U	--	--	--	--	N/A	--	--	--	--	Z
MIDVALE INDEMNITY CO	IL	D-	12.1	13.4	0.0	0.3	10.0	6.3	7.4	6.6	1.0	DGRT
MIDWEST BUILDERS CASUALTY MUTUAL	KS	B	86.0	46.9	27.3	2.3	7.7	7.0	6.8	6.7	5.6	T
MIDWEST EMPLOYERS CAS CO	DE	C+	178.7	106.8	0.0	0.8	10.0	3.7	6.3	10.0	4.3	RT
MIDWEST FAMILY MUTUAL INS CO	IA	B-	227.1	66.8	117.3	2.7	7.9	6.1	6.8	6.4	3.6	RT
MIDWEST INS CO	IL	C	93.7	36.0	22.6	0.6	7.1	3.5	8.2	7.3	4.3	RT
MIDWEST INS GROUP INC RRG	VT	D	6.8	1.8	1.9	0.1	1.7	10.0	2.7	7.6	1.4	CDGR
MIDWESTERN EQUITY TITLE INS CO	IN	D+	4.0	3.3	0.1	0.0	7.8	3.6	7.6	10.0	2.1	DGR
MIDWESTERN INDEMNITY CO	NH	C	28.2	27.6	0.0	0.0	10.0	N/A	6.0	7.0	3.7	DGRT
MILBANK INS CO	IA	C+	624.1	148.2	278.6	-0.5	6.9	4.8	5.2	5.9	4.3	ART
MILLERS CAPITAL INS CO	PA	B-	134.2	66.6	49.4	-0.9	9.4	9.4	5.1	6.8	3.8	RT
MILLERS CLASSIFIED INS CO	IL	F (5)	2.7	0.0	-0.4	0.0	2.4	7.0	0.1	5.1	0.0	CFRT
MILLERS FIRST INS CO	IL	F (5)	7.8	-4.0	0.0	0.0	0.0	4.8	0.1	7.0	0.0	CDRT
MILLVILLE INS CO OF NY	NY	C-	2.9	2.7	0.0	0.0	10.0	3.6	5.9	7.0	2.3	DGT
MILLVILLE MUTUAL INS CO	PA	C+	85.5	55.4	30.2	1.5	9.8	6.2	8.8	6.9	3.5	T
MILWAUKEE CASUALTY INS CO	WI	B	102.8	25.9	43.6	-0.7	5.2	5.9	5.8	6.7	4.1	CGRT
MINNESOTA LAWYERS MUTUAL INS CO	MN	B	178.1	90.9	33.0	1.2	9.5	8.3	7.6	6.9	4.3	RT
MISSISSIPPI FARM BUREAU CAS INS CO	MS	B-	435.6	279.8	171.4	4.2	10.0	7.7	8.9	6.8	4.5	T
MISSOURI DOCTORS MUTUAL INS CO	MO	E-	4.5	0.0	3.8	-0.1	0.0	0.5	0.0	2.1	0.0	CDFG
MISSOURI HOSPITAL PLAN	MO	C+	197.4	156.6	19.0	2.7	8.8	6.7	4.2	7.1	3.4	FRT
MISSOURI PHYSICIANS ASSOCIATES	MO	U (1)	--	--	--	--	N/A	--	--	--	--	Z
MISSOURI PROFESSIONALS MUTUAL INS	MO	E-	15.5	0.1	8.2	-0.1	0.0	0.4	0.0	0.0	0.0	CDFG
MISSOURI VALLEY MUTUAL INS CO	SD	D+	6.3	3.8	3.4	0.2	9.0	6.4	8.6	6.5	2.0	DGRT
MITSUI SUMITOMO INS CO OF AMER	NY	B+	958.1	340.0	199.1	0.6	9.2	9.3	6.9	6.9	5.1	T
MITSUI SUMITOMO INS USA INC	NY	C+	137.4	63.8	24.9	-0.2	10.0	8.8	5.2	8.4	3.2	T
MLM RRG INC	DC	U	--	--	--	--	N/A	--	--	--	--	Z
MMG INS CO	ME	B	260.9	99.2	164.5	3.6	9.0	4.7	6.8	6.2	4.0	RT
MMIC INS INC	MN	B	723.2	320.9	105.4	5.2	7.9	9.4	8.3	7.1	4.7	RT
MMIC RRG INC	DC	U	--	--	--	--	N/A	--	--	--	--	Z
MO EMPLOYERS MUTUAL INS CO	MO	B	683.3	258.3	219.9	4.7	8.0	9.2	6.4	6.7	6.0	T
MODERN USA INS CO	FL	B-	53.5	19.2	27.6	-1.2	5.7	4.3	4.0	6.9	4.8	DT
MONARCH NATIONAL INS CO	FL	B-	40.1	30.8	10.8	0.3	9.9	3.6	3.8	8.6	3.7	DGT
MONROE GUARANTY INS CO	IN	C	53.0	53.3	0.0	0.3	10.0	N/A	6.3	9.1	3.5	RT
MONTEREY INS CO	CA	C+	85.8	32.7	40.4	-0.5	7.3	4.4	4.0	5.8	3.7	T
MONTGOMERY MUTUAL INS CO	MA	C	53.5	51.9	0.0	0.2	10.0	N/A	6.8	7.0	4.0	DRT
MONTOUR MUTUAL INS CO	PA	D	1.0	0.6	0.2	0.0	7.4	6.2	1.9	7.8	1.0	DGT
MORTGAGE GUARANTY INS CORP	WI	D+	4,529.7	1,520.5	844.0	16.2	6.0	3.5	2.9	6.2	2.4	ART
MOTOR CLUB INS CO	RI	B	50.1	48.1	1.5	0.0	9.4	4.6	6.0	9.2	4.1	DGT
▲MOTORISTS COMMERCIAL MUTUAL INS CO	OH	A-	358.9	155.6	132.2	-1.4	9.2	7.8	5.2	6.5	6.9	T
MOTORISTS MUTUAL INS CO	OH	B+	1,368.4	537.2	489.3	-1.6	8.9	7.8	4.3	6.4	5.1	T

See Page 27 for explanation of footnotes and
Page 28 for explanation of stability factors.
Arrows denote recent upgrades ▲ or downgrades ▼   (see Section VII for explanations)

90

www.weissratings.com

RISK ADJ. RATIO #1	CAPITAL RATIO #2	PREMIUM TO SURPLUS (%)	RESV. TO SURPLUS (%)	RESV. DEVELOP. 1 YEAR (%)	RESV. DEVELOP. 2 YEAR (%)	LOSS RATIO (%)	EXP. RATIO (%)	COMB RATIO (%)	CASH FROM UNDER-WRITING (%)	NET PREMIUM GROWTH (%)	INVEST. IN AFFIL (%)	INSURANCE COMPANY NAME
N/A	N/A	--	--	--	--	--	--	--	--	--	--	MID AMERICAN FIRE & CAS CO
1.9	1.4	224.4	142.4	1.6	3.4	70.9	32.3	103.2	93.7	-1.1	8.1 ●	MID-CENTURY INS CO
N/A	N/A	--	--	--	--	--	--	--	--	--	--	MID-CENTURY INS CO OF TX
0.9	0.6	80.3	188.2	1.1	20.2	58.8	39.0	97.8	101.6	-1.7	11.6	MID-CONTINENT CAS CO
106.2	52.3	N/A	N/A	N/A	N/A	N/A	N/A	N/A	N/A	0.0	0.0	MID-CONTINENT EXCESS & SURPLUS
88.7	44.1	-8.8	N/A	N/A	N/A	N/A	-0.2	N/A	N/A	-145.0	0.0	MID-CONTINENT INS CO
1.3	0.9	120.1	38.3	3.2	4.6	55.1	37.1	92.2	131.9	51.8	0.0	MID-HUDSON CO-OPERTIVE INS CO
5.1	3.3	21.9	8.2	1.9	1.4	83.6	45.4	129.0	83.6	40.9	0.0	MIDDLE STATES INS CO
3.5	2.3	81.5	127.9	-1.0	-3.1	73.9	28.2	102.1	103.0	7.2	4.1 ●	MIDDLESEX INS CO
1.8	1.2	97.5	37.2	-0.7	-1.6	68.0	34.6	102.6	103.4	4.8	0.0	MIDROX INS CO
1.1	0.7	78.5	48.1	-10.5	-7.6	45.8	33.5	79.3	145.4	48.9	0.0	MIDSOUTH MUTUAL INS CO
4.6	3.1	42.4	20.8	-0.9	-1.9	53.8	34.5	88.3	98.9	-0.9	0.0	MIDSTATE MUTUAL INS CO
N/A	N/A	--	--	--	--	--	--	--	--	--	--	MIDSTATES REINS CORP
92.0	46.0	N/A	N/A	N/A	-0.1	N/A	N/A	N/A	999 +	0.0	0.0	MIDVALE INDEMNITY CO
2.1	1.6	61.1	77.6	-3.0	-9.1	72.7	27.9	100.6	111.9	11.2	10.5	MIDWEST BUILDERS CASUALTY MUTUAL
14.1	12.7	N/A	N/A	N/A	N/A	N/A	N/A	N/A	64.9	0.0	0.0	MIDWEST EMPLOYERS CAS CO
2.4	1.7	185.9	125.2	-15.6	-4.7	68.6	23.8	92.4	117.9	10.5	0.0	MIDWEST FAMILY MUTUAL INS CO
2.1	1.3	64.1	103.9	-5.8	-0.7	55.5	34.0	89.5	103.9	-4.9	0.0	MIDWEST INS CO
0.4	0.3	119.2	194.2	-27.8	-53.4	80.5	37.9	118.4	132.3	34.1	0.0	MIDWEST INS GROUP INC RRG
2.4	1.4	2.6	N/A	N/A	N/A	N/A	32.0	32.0	322.0	-0.8	0.0	MIDWESTERN EQUITY TITLE INS CO
3.6	3.5	N/A	N/A	N/A	N/A	N/A	N/A	N/A	N/A	0.0	30.0	MIDWESTERN INDEMNITY CO
1.6	0.9	192.5	177.2	2.6	2.3	73.1	33.4	106.5	102.5	1.6	0.0	MILBANK INS CO
2.9	2.4	74.3	48.6	-5.1	-12.5	52.3	42.4	94.7	114.3	4.8	0.1	MILLERS CAPITAL INS CO
0.1	0.1	-78.8	746.7	-6.6	-14.0	357.3	-361.7	-4.4	-3.5	-106.7	0.0	MILLERS CLASSIFIED INS CO
-1.5	-1.3	N/A	N/A	N/A	N/A	N/A	N/A	N/A	N/A	-100.0	0.0	MILLERS FIRST INS CO
25.3	22.8	N/A	N/A	N/A	N/A	N/A	N/A	N/A	264.8	0.0	0.0	MILLVILLE INS CO OF NY
4.5	3.1	56.4	18.1	-1.7	-0.6	58.9	29.4	88.3	117.5	6.2	3.7	MILLVILLE MUTUAL INS CO
0.9	0.6	162.8	87.4	2.5	1.4	60.6	16.7	77.3	182.4	88.4	3.4	MILWAUKEE CASUALTY INS CO
4.4	2.8	37.1	62.4	-8.9	-6.6	54.0	25.1	79.1	114.3	2.4	0.0	MINNESOTA LAWYERS MUTUAL INS CO
6.2	5.6	62.1	10.3	-2.5	-2.5	60.5	22.7	83.2	109.7	-2.3	0.0 ●	MISSISSIPPI FARM BUREAU CAS INS CO
0.0	0.0	999 +	999 +	383.8	7.3	41.7	63.1	104.8	82.3	-1.5	0.0	MISSOURI DOCTORS MUTUAL INS CO
2.6	2.2	12.6	23.1	-0.2	-7.6	50.6	1.8	52.4	184.1	-10.1	27.0	MISSOURI HOSPITAL PLAN
N/A	N/A	--	--	--	--	--	--	--	--	--	--	MISSOURI PHYSICIANS ASSOCIATES
0.0	0.0	999 +	999 +	109.5	205.5	59.8	49.1	108.9	75.4	-8.3	43.7	MISSOURI PROFESSIONALS MUTUAL INS
4.1	2.9	95.7	8.1	-0.9	-0.5	49.2	37.8	87.0	116.0	0.8	0.0	MISSOURI VALLEY MUTUAL INS CO
3.7	2.3	57.2	119.3	-5.6	-11.3	66.5	27.9	94.4	106.5	14.1	0.0 ●	MITSUI SUMITOMO INS CO OF AMER
6.1	3.9	38.9	81.2	-3.8	-7.8	66.5	28.1	94.6	106.5	8.1	0.0	MITSUI SUMITOMO INS USA INC
N/A	N/A	--	--	--	--	--	--	--	--	--	--	MLM RRG INC
3.4	2.3	168.9	64.6	9.6	9.1	69.2	31.8	101.0	105.1	5.5	0.0	MMG INS CO
1.7	1.5	31.1	68.3	-9.4	-11.1	75.2	23.4	98.6	96.3	-3.0	22.2 ●	MMIC INS INC
N/A	N/A	--	--	--	--	--	--	--	--	--	--	MMIC RRG INC
2.1	1.6	86.2	105.3	-4.7	-9.0	68.9	28.0	96.9	113.3	8.5	0.1 ●	MO EMPLOYERS MUTUAL INS CO
1.3	1.2	137.4	43.1	-2.5	4.2	75.1	36.0	111.1	98.6	7.9	0.0	MODERN USA INS CO
3.6	3.1	35.3	5.4	0.1	N/A	59.2	27.2	86.4	252.4	419.7	0.0	MONARCH NATIONAL INS CO
82.2	37.9	N/A	N/A	N/A	N/A	N/A	N/A	N/A	127.6	0.0	0.0	MONROE GUARANTY INS CO
1.8	1.1	121.6	90.8	11.7	12.7	76.1	34.2	110.3	96.7	2.6	0.0	MONTEREY INS CO
85.5	48.0	N/A	N/A	N/A	N/A	N/A	N/A	N/A	N/A	0.0	0.0	MONTGOMERY MUTUAL INS CO
1.9	1.2	27.1	5.7	-0.2	0.3	31.3	109.8	141.1	102.8	-2.6	0.0	MONTOUR MUTUAL INS CO
1.1	1.0	56.1	77.0	-7.7	-10.7	25.9	74.1	100.0	112.7	-6.8	6.5 ●	MORTGAGE GUARANTY INS CORP
4.2	2.5	3.3	0.4	N/A	N/A	56.6	51.3	107.9	99.3	1.0	0.0	MOTOR CLUB INS CO
3.3	2.4	84.3	62.3	-0.7	-1.7	64.1	37.9	102.0	99.0	-0.4	6.6 ●	MOTORISTS COMMERCIAL MUTUAL INS
2.9	2.1	89.9	66.4	-0.7	-1.7	64.1	37.5	101.6	98.8	-0.4	10.4 ●	MOTORISTS MUTUAL INS CO

999 + Denotes number greater than 999.9%
999 - Denotes number less than -999.99%
● Bullets denote a more detailed analysis is available in Section II.

INSURANCE COMPANY NAME	DOM. STATE	RATING	TOTAL ASSETS ($MIL)	CAPITAL & SURPLUS ($MIL)	ANNUAL NET PREMIUM ($MIL)	NET INCOME ($MIL)	CAPITAL-IZATION INDEX (PTS)	RESERVE ADQ INDEX (PTS)	PROFIT-ABILITY INDEX (PTS)	LIQUIDITY INDEX (PTS)	STAB. INDEX (PTS)	STABILITY FACTORS
MOTORS INS CORP	MI	D	2,053.7	759.5	388.3	12.6	10.0	7.7	3.0	7.1	0.9	FRT
MOUND PRAIRIE MUTUAL INS CO	MN	D+	7.5	4.3	3.5	0.0	8.3	5.9	4.7	7.1	2.2	DGT
MOUNT BEACON INS CO	FL	D+	20.5	13.3	-9.6	-0.4	8.6	3.6	1.2	6.8	2.3	DFGT
MOUNT VERNON FIRE INS CO	PA	C	668.0	465.5	68.1	3.4	7.9	8.6	8.2	9.1	4.3	RT
MOUNT VERNON SPECIALTY INS CO	NE	B-	58.3	57.4	0.1	-0.7	7.3	N/A	3.5	10.0	4.1	DFGT
MOUNTAIN LAKE RRG INC	VT	D	1.6	1.1	0.1	0.0	10.0	9.4	2.6	7.9	1.1	DFGT
MOUNTAIN LAUREL ASR CO	OH	C	175.6	62.7	177.0	0.7	7.4	8.6	9.0	2.2	3.6	LRT
MOUNTAIN LAUREL RRG INC	VT	E	18.4	6.5	4.6	0.2	2.7	9.8	2.8	7.2	0.1	DGT
MOUNTAIN STATES COMM INS CO	NM	D	1.1	1.0	0.0	0.0	10.0	3.6	3.9	9.2	1.8	DGT
MOUNTAIN STATES HEALTHCARE RECIP	MT	D+	119.3	33.0	23.2	0.0	5.7	4.9	1.7	6.5	2.5	FT
MOUNTAIN STATES INDEMNITY CO	NM	C	50.2	28.5	4.9	-0.3	7.8	6.1	2.4	7.6	3.8	DFRT
MOUNTAIN VALLEY INDEMNITY CO	NY	D	68.2	23.0	12.0	-0.1	9.2	6.0	5.8	7.7	1.7	DRT
MOUNTAIN WEST FARM BU MUTUAL INS CO	WY	B	362.1	146.1	163.1	-0.8	7.5	9.3	3.0	3.3	4.1	FLT
MOUNTAINPOINT INS CO	AZ	U	--	--	--	--	N/A	--	--	--	--	Z
MOWER COUNTY FARMERS MUT INS CO	MN	D+	5.8	3.7	2.2	0.1	10.0	7.5	8.7	7.1	2.1	DG
MSA INS CO	SC	B-	18.7	18.5	0.0	0.1	10.0	N/A	6.9	7.0	4.1	DGT
MT HAWLEY INS CO	IL	C	906.2	471.7	217.0	9.1	8.3	9.3	3.9	6.9	4.0	ART
MT MORRIS MUTUAL INS CO	WI	C	37.7	18.1	20.1	0.3	7.3	6.2	8.2	6.0	4.0	DGRT
MT WASHINGTON ASR CORP	NH	C	7.0	3.6	0.0	0.0	10.0	N/A	4.4	6.0	2.4	DFGR
MULTINATIONAL INS CO	PR	C-	33.3	9.7	15.5	0.0	3.8	3.5	2.6	5.8	2.6	CDGT
MUNICH REINS AMERICA INC	DE	C+	18,335.4	4,650.8	3,117.7	-17.5	8.2	8.9	4.3	6.9	4.4	RT
MUNICIPAL ASR CORP	NY	E	1,091.2	486.2	1.2	18.7	10.0	N/A	4.6	7.0	0.0	T
MUNICIPAL MUTUAL INS CO	WV	C+	35.4	23.7	12.9	-0.7	8.7	8.1	4.2	6.7	3.2	DGT
▲MUNICIPAL PROPERTY INS CO	WI	C-	17.9	8.8	7.1	0.2	5.6	3.6	3.9	7.6	2.3	DGT
MUTUAL BENEFIT INS CO	PA	B-	226.4	94.9	92.4	0.5	9.0	9.3	8.2	6.5	3.9	RT
MUTUAL FIRE INS CO OF S BEND TOWNSHP	PA	D+(1)	3.6	3.5	0.1	0.1	10.0	5.0	6.6	10.0	2.0	DT
MUTUAL INS CO OF AZ	AZ	B	1,056.2	634.6	101.7	7.2	10.0	9.4	8.2	8.1	4.9	RT
MUTUAL INS CO OF LEHIGH CTY	PA	D	2.8	1.4	1.6	0.1	7.2	5.9	3.4	6.9	1.2	DGRT
MUTUAL OF ENUMCLAW INS CO	OR	B	737.9	319.8	385.1	-10.0	9.7	6.7	4.0	6.5	4.7	RT
MUTUAL OF WAUSAU INS CORP	WI	C+	24.4	15.9	9.2	0.1	8.0	6.4	5.8	6.8	4.1	DGT
MUTUAL RRG INC	HI	C+	133.2	49.8	24.4	1.4	10.0	9.6	9.0	7.7	3.4	RT
MUTUAL SAVINGS FIRE INS CO	AL	D	5.0	4.0	0.0	0.0	10.0	N/A	3.7	10.0	2.2	DGRT
MUTUALAID EXCHANGE	KS	C+	30.7	18.8	13.0	-0.4	7.7	7.9	5.9	6.9	4.2	DGRT
MYCOMPASS INC	IA	U	--	--	--	--	N/A	--	--	--	--	Z
NAMIC INS CO	IN	C+	53.6	28.4	5.1	0.5	9.1	9.2	5.9	7.2	3.2	DFT
▲NARRAGANSETT BAY INS CO	RI	C-	226.3	94.2	51.6	6.5	8.3	4.5	3.9	7.0	3.0	RT
▲NASW RRG INC	DC	C-	15.4	10.3	4.0	0.2	8.6	5.2	4.1	9.1	2.3	DGT
NATIONAL AMERICAN INS CO	OK	C+	201.0	67.9	67.5	0.7	8.9	6.5	8.7	6.6	3.6	RT
NATIONAL AMERICAN INS CO OF CA	CA	U	--	--	--	--	N/A	--	--	--	--	Z
NATIONAL ASSISTED LIVING RRG INC	DC	D+	8.3	4.4	2.0	0.0	6.6	9.8	6.1	6.9	2.2	DG
NATIONAL BAIL & SURETY CO	FL	U	--	--	--	--	N/A	--	--	--	--	Z
NATIONAL BUILDERS & CONTRACTORS INS	NV	U	--	--	--	--	N/A	--	--	--	--	Z
NATIONAL BUILDERS INS CO	DE	B	88.3	29.1	20.3	-0.1	7.7	9.3	6.6	7.0	4.1	RT
NATIONAL BUILDING MATERIAL ASR CO	IN	D-	6.4	4.4	0.8	0.0	10.0	4.8	5.0	6.9	1.3	GR
NATIONAL CASUALTY CO	OH	B+	404.6	140.1	0.0	0.8	10.0	N/A	7.7	9.7	6.4	GT
NATIONAL CATHOLIC RRG	VT	D	65.0	16.2	10.2	0.0	1.7	2.7	2.3	6.3	1.9	CDRT
NATIONAL CONTINENTAL INS CO	NY	C	144.6	67.0	13.3	3.0	10.0	9.3	4.8	8.8	3.6	FT
NATIONAL DIRECT INS CO	NV	D	6.3	2.3	5.4	0.1	3.9	4.7	3.7	0.6	1.7	DGLT
NATIONAL FARMERS UNION PROP & CAS	WI	C	170.4	47.5	54.4	1.2	7.6	4.9	4.0	7.0	3.9	RT
NATIONAL FIRE & CASUALTY CO	IL	C	10.2	6.4	2.6	0.2	8.1	9.3	6.4	6.9	2.8	DGRT
NATIONAL FIRE & INDEMNITY EXCHANGE	MO	C-	10.8	5.8	3.0	0.0	8.9	6.8	3.6	6.9	2.1	DFGR
NATIONAL FIRE & MARINE INS CO	NE	C	9,388.5	5,852.5	929.0	67.9	8.1	6.2	8.0	9.1	4.1	RT

See Page 27 for explanation of footnotes and
Page 28 for explanation of stability factors.
Arrows denote recent upgrades ▲ or downgrades ▼   (see Section VII for explanations)

92

www.weissratings.com

RISK ADJ. RATIO #1	CAPITAL RATIO #2	PREMIUM TO SURPLUS (%)	RESV. TO SURPLUS (%)	RESV. DEVELOP. 1 YEAR (%)	RESV. DEVELOP. 2 YEAR (%)	LOSS RATIO (%)	EXP. RATIO (%)	COMB RATIO (%)	CASH FROM UNDER- WRITING (%)	NET PREMIUM GROWTH (%)	INVEST. IN AFFIL (%)	INSURANCE COMPANY NAME
5.5	3.7	52.1	13.1	-1.3	-2.1	71.5	32.4	103.9	82.6	-7.6	3.8 ●	MOTORS INS CORP
2.5	2.0	80.5	7.7	0.3	2.2	33.3	39.4	72.7	145.0	-5.6	0.0	MOUND PRAIRIE MUTUAL INS CO
6.5	3.7	-70.5	46.7	9.8	0.2	183.1	-96.2	86.9	-47.8	-134.9	0.0	MOUNT BEACON INS CO
2.1	1.6	15.3	22.1	-2.4	-3.6	43.2	40.8	84.0	130.7	0.7	20.6 ●	MOUNT VERNON FIRE INS CO
1.2	1.2	0.2	0.1	N/A	N/A	753.8	999 +	999 +	5.7	831.4	90.0	MOUNT VERNON SPECIALTY INS CO
5.1	3.5	12.6	26.7	-0.8	-5.6	84.6	70.1	154.7	36.6	19.2	0.0	MOUNTAIN LAKE RRG INC
1.4	1.3	287.6	72.2	-5.7	-6.4	68.8	19.8	88.6	114.9	14.1	0.0	MOUNTAIN LAUREL ASR CO
0.7	0.4	76.5	152.9	-2.4	-15.8	52.8	43.2	96.0	173.1	-1.0	0.0	MOUNTAIN LAUREL RRG INC
22.7	20.4	1.0	1.4	0.4	N/A	218.9	17.7	236.6	470.9	0.0	0.0	MOUNTAIN STATES COMM INS CO
1.0	0.8	71.9	212.8	32.8	24.6	162.1	11.9	174.0	85.1	-3.5	0.0	MOUNTAIN STATES HEALTHCARE RECIP
2.6	1.5	16.9	64.7	11.8	4.8	171.4	49.1	220.5	79.9	-33.5	2.1	MOUNTAIN STATES INDEMNITY CO
3.7	2.9	52.3	28.7	-4.8	3.9	58.5	25.4	83.9	999 +	20.2	0.0	MOUNTAIN VALLEY INDEMNITY CO
1.8	1.2	111.8	70.3	-5.7	-8.4	88.8	28.8	117.6	84.8	-3.4	7.8	MOUNTAIN WEST FARM BU MUTUAL INS
N/A	N/A	--	--	--	--	--	--	--	--	--	--	MOUNTAINPOINT INS CO
4.9	3.4	62.9	12.6	-2.1	-0.3	48.6	39.9	88.5	126.6	15.4	0.0	MOWER COUNTY FARMERS MUT INS CO
83.9	40.3	N/A	N/A	N/A	N/A	N/A	N/A	N/A	N/A	0.0	0.0	MSA INS CO
2.4	1.9	47.9	69.3	-5.9	-8.4	44.8	38.4	83.2	132.9	4.2	12.3 ●	MT HAWLEY INS CO
1.9	1.3	113.0	25.7	2.1	1.1	49.6	31.5	81.1	126.5	11.6	0.0	MT MORRIS MUTUAL INS CO
3.2	2.9	N/A	N/A	N/A	N/A	N/A	N/A	N/A	451.8	0.0	0.0	MT WASHINGTON ASR CORP
0.8	0.4	152.4	66.3	1.9	20.4	43.6	48.0	91.6	117.5	5.3	0.0	MULTINATIONAL INS CO
3.0	1.8	64.7	128.1	-1.9	-5.0	65.4	36.5	101.9	105.7	-0.1	0.0 ●	MUNICH REINS AMERICA INC
21.2	15.4	0.2	N/A	N/A	N/A	N/A	999 +	999 +	-11.0	124.5	0.0 ●	MUNICIPAL ASR CORP
3.1	2.1	54.0	11.1	-4.9	-4.6	73.3	30.3	103.6	97.6	4.9	0.0	MUNICIPAL MUTUAL INS CO
1.3	1.0	82.4	32.7	-1.1	N/A	66.5	26.6	93.1	181.8	274.6	0.0	MUNICIPAL PROPERTY INS CO
3.1	2.3	99.8	66.6	-3.2	-11.0	65.6	32.0	97.6	108.1	5.6	9.1	MUTUAL BENEFIT INS CO
100.7	81.3	2.9	0.1	-0.1	-0.1	5.9	48.8	54.7	196.2	9.0	0.0	MUTUAL FIRE INS CO OF S BEND
7.4	4.9	16.3	45.1	-6.8	-14.0	56.9	17.2	74.1	129.3	-3.3	0.0 ●	MUTUAL INS CO OF AZ
1.8	1.1	123.0	14.5	-2.8	4.7	48.6	41.7	90.3	99.6	-3.2	1.9	MUTUAL INS CO OF LEHIGH CTY
4.1	2.9	118.0	62.0	-2.2	0.7	70.0	30.5	100.5	101.7	2.4	1.4 ●	MUTUAL OF ENUMCLAW INS CO
3.1	2.0	58.2	7.5	-1.5	-2.9	39.6	46.7	86.3	119.6	1.3	0.0	MUTUAL OF WAUSAU INS CORP
3.9	2.9	50.7	97.1	-10.4	-27.6	75.3	8.1	83.4	170.4	26.0	0.1	MUTUAL RRG INC
9.3	8.3	N/A	N/A	N/A	N/A	N/A	N/A	N/A	100.5	0.0	0.0	MUTUAL SAVINGS FIRE INS CO
1.9	1.6	68.2	10.8	-3.7	-3.7	61.4	30.6	92.0	100.6	16.7	26.0	MUTUALAID EXCHANGE
N/A	N/A	--	--	--	--	--	--	--	--	--	--	MYCOMPASS INC
3.8	2.3	18.6	22.6	-4.2	-9.2	75.6	45.0	120.6	78.0	1.7	0.0	NAMIC INS CO
4.9	4.0	57.8	25.8	-3.9	-6.0	52.4	-0.3	52.1	145.2	-34.1	1.1	NARRAGANSETT BAY INS CO
2.2	1.8	40.1	9.3	0.9	-0.4	46.6	22.7	69.3	255.5	826.9	0.0	NASW RRG INC
3.5	2.3	99.1	116.4	-1.2	-4.9	58.1	38.2	96.3	109.8	-1.3	0.0	NATIONAL AMERICAN INS CO
N/A	N/A	--	--	--	--	--	--	--	--	--	--	NATIONAL AMERICAN INS CO OF CA
1.6	1.0	45.9	59.6	-20.8	-28.9	42.0	46.5	88.5	104.2	22.2	0.0	NATIONAL ASSISTED LIVING RRG INC
N/A	N/A	--	--	--	--	--	--	--	--	--	--	NATIONAL BAIL & SURETY CO
N/A	N/A	--	--	--	--	--	--	--	--	--	--	NATIONAL BUILDERS & CONTRACTORS
2.5	1.7	70.0	104.4	-6.3	-16.0	60.0	28.4	88.4	139.2	2.3	0.0	NATIONAL BUILDERS INS CO
5.2	4.0	17.6	19.9	0.3	-0.6	63.3	33.3	96.6	105.2	-10.6	0.0	NATIONAL BUILDING MATERIAL ASR CO
13.3	12.0	N/A	N/A	N/A	N/A	N/A	N/A	N/A	-109.5	0.0	0.0 ●	NATIONAL CASUALTY CO
0.5	0.4	66.0	279.1	-15.7	14.9	67.3	27.6	94.9	98.3	-5.8	0.0	NATIONAL CATHOLIC RRG
8.6	7.7	20.8	47.0	-2.4	-18.9	89.4	-113.7	-24.3	11.6	-9.0	0.0	NATIONAL CONTINENTAL INS CO
0.6	0.6	262.5	118.7	17.7	10.3	82.9	23.8	106.7	89.8	34.1	0.0	NATIONAL DIRECT INS CO
2.6	1.6	120.3	109.7	-16.5	-12.8	58.8	36.4	95.2	108.3	10.7	0.0	NATIONAL FARMERS UNION PROP &
3.4	2.0	41.3	23.6	-7.3	-12.1	67.2	37.2	104.4	104.8	-8.6	0.0	NATIONAL FIRE & CASUALTY CO
2.8	2.2	51.0	35.3	-2.4	-2.9	34.5	63.2	97.7	90.3	-6.0	0.0	NATIONAL FIRE & INDEMNITY
2.4	1.5	16.8	23.8	-0.3	-1.6	58.3	28.5	86.8	183.6	13.0	5.6 ●	NATIONAL FIRE & MARINE INS CO

999 + Denotes number greater than 999.9%
999 - Denotes number less than -999.99%
● Bullets denote a more detailed analysis is available in Section II.

INSURANCE COMPANY NAME	DOM. STATE	RATING	TOTAL ASSETS ($MIL)	CAPITAL & SURPLUS ($MIL)	ANNUAL NET PREMIUM ($MIL)	NET INCOME ($MIL)	CAPITAL-IZATION INDEX (PTS)	RESERVE ADQ INDEX (PTS)	PROFIT-ABILITY INDEX (PTS)	LIQUIDITY INDEX (PTS)	STAB. INDEX (PTS)	STABILITY FACTORS
NATIONAL FIRE INS CO OF HARTFORD	IL	C	116.5	116.4	0.0	1.0	10.0	N/A	5.0	9.3	3.8	ART
NATIONAL GENERAL ASR CO	MO	C	39.8	17.0	0.0	0.1	10.0	3.8	5.4	7.0	3.3	DGRT
NATIONAL GENERAL INS CO	MO	C	59.8	25.3	0.0	0.2	10.0	3.8	3.7	7.0	3.7	RT
NATIONAL GENERAL INS ONLINE INC	MO	C	51.3	11.3	0.0	0.0	8.5	3.9	6.9	7.8	3.7	DR
NATIONAL GENL PREMIER INS CO	CA	B-	25.2	16.5	0.0	0.1	10.0	4.8	8.3	7.0	5.2	DG
NATIONAL GUARDIAN RRG INC	HI	C-	12.2	6.3	1.1	-0.1	7.6	10.0	3.8	8.5	2.1	DGRT
NATIONAL HERITAGE INS CO	IL	D+	3.7	1.7	2.9	-0.2	8.0	4.6	1.8	7.5	1.5	DFGT
NATIONAL HOME INS CO RRG	CO	U	--	--	--	--	N/A	--	--	--	--	Z
NATIONAL INDEMNITY CO	NE	B	194,845.0	100,280.0	20,030.1	2,960.7	7.8	6.0	5.8	6.6	4.3	T
NATIONAL INDEMNITY CO OF MID-AMERICA	IA	C	276.9	196.9	6.7	2.6	7.9	7.4	8.3	9.6	4.3	RT
NATIONAL INDEMNITY CO OF THE SOUTH	IA	C+	398.5	204.9	67.9	-2.0	8.0	6.0	6.1	9.0	4.3	RT
NATIONAL INDEPENDENT TRUCKERS IC	SC	C-	14.6	7.9	4.0	-0.1	7.9	5.9	5.0	6.9	2.7	DGRT
NATIONAL INS ASSN	IN	U	--	--	--	--	N/A	--	--	--	--	Z
NATIONAL INS CO OF WI	WI	C	13.6	12.0	0.0	-0.1	10.0	9.7	2.6	7.0	2.5	DFGT
NATIONAL INTERSTATE INS CO	OH	C+	1,308.6	343.4	309.0	6.9	7.3	3.9	6.8	6.9	4.7	RT
NATIONAL INTERSTATE INS CO OF HAWAII	OH	C	54.5	13.3	8.8	0.1	8.2	4.4	6.9	7.9	4.0	DRT
NATIONAL LIABILITY & FIRE INS CO	CT	C+	2,685.3	1,176.0	562.1	12.7	8.1	8.3	5.4	8.9	3.9	RT
NATIONAL LLOYDS INS CO	TX	B-	229.6	132.0	122.7	0.6	10.0	5.0	6.5	6.6	4.0	RT
NATIONAL MEDICAL PROFESSIONAL RRG	SC	U	--	--	--	--	N/A	--	--	--	--	Z
NATIONAL MORTGAGE INS CORP	WI	A-	645.5	377.5	129.8	-10.2	9.4	N/A	3.8	7.2	5.7	GT
NATIONAL MORTGAGE RE INC ONE	WI	C+	35.1	26.9	-2.4	0.1	10.0	3.6	3.8	10.0	3.7	DFGT
NATIONAL MUTUAL INS CO	OH	C	78.7	33.1	37.4	0.4	7.9	8.2	8.3	6.1	3.5	RT
NATIONAL PUBLIC FINANCE GUAR CORP	NY	B	4,389.8	2,787.9	19.0	31.7	10.0	5.8	8.6	9.8	5.1	AFT
NATIONAL SECURITY FIRE & CAS CO	AL	B-	75.8	34.4	54.7	-0.7	8.0	6.3	6.4	5.3	4.6	FRT
NATIONAL SERVICE CONTRACT INS CO	DC	C	12.5	10.6	0.6	0.1	10.0	3.6	3.4	9.9	4.3	DGR
NATIONAL SPECIALTY INS CO	TX	C+	86.2	49.8	27.8	0.7	10.0	6.0	8.2	7.1	3.8	RT
NATIONAL SURETY CORP	IL	C	136.9	71.8	0.0	0.2	10.0	3.6	2.5	7.0	3.7	RT
NATIONAL TRUST INS CO	IN	C	36.8	37.5	0.0	0.2	10.0	N/A	5.9	7.9	3.4	GRT
NATIONAL UNION FIRE INS CO	PA	C	26,559.6	6,825.9	4,837.1	183.3	7.5	2.8	3.5	6.3	2.8	ART
NATIONAL UNITY INS CO	TX	D	40.7	10.6	38.7	-0.4	2.5	2.5	1.1	0.4	1.9	CDFL
NATIONS INS CO	CA	D+	48.3	10.5	35.0	0.5	2.3	4.1	2.4	3.2	2.6	CDGL
NATIONWIDE AFFINITY INS CO OF AMER	OH	B	423.7	12.8	0.0	0.1	6.8	N/A	3.9	7.0	4.4	FT
NATIONWIDE AGRIBUSINESS INS CO	IA	B-	633.4	68.6	0.0	0.4	10.0	N/A	6.8	7.0	4.2	AT
NATIONWIDE ASR CO	OH	B-	140.6	62.5	0.0	0.2	10.0	N/A	6.5	7.0	5.2	AT
NATIONWIDE GENERAL INS CO	OH	B-	506.3	23.2	0.0	0.1	8.1	N/A	6.4	2.7	3.9	AFLT
NATIONWIDE INDEMNITY CO	OH	C+	2,976.0	1,014.6	1.2	37.4	5.9	2.1	2.9	10.0	4.5	FGT
NATIONWIDE INS CO OF AM	OH	B-	445.6	154.3	0.0	0.5	10.0	N/A	6.0	7.0	4.5	FT
NATIONWIDE INS CO OF FL	OH	B-	51.5	33.7	-20.7	0.0	10.0	5.1	1.9	7.1	5.0	FT
NATIONWIDE LLOYDS	TX	B	42.2	28.8	0.0	0.1	10.0	N/A	6.1	7.0	4.3	T
NATIONWIDE MUTUAL FIRE INS CO	OH	B+	8,809.3	2,565.8	2,338.5	-182.2	10.0	6.0	3.7	6.4	5.1	AT
NATIONWIDE MUTUAL INS CO	OH	B	35,852.6	13,003.2	16,174.4	116.6	7.4	6.0	4.5	4.7	5.1	ALT
NATIONWIDE P&C INS CO	OH	B-	691.9	46.2	0.0	0.2	9.4	N/A	3.2	7.2	3.9	AFT
NATL TRANSPORTATION INS CO RRG	NC	D	3.0	1.2	0.4	0.0	9.8	N/A	4.3	9.6	0.9	DGT
NAU COUNTRY INS CO	MN	C+	1,191.2	348.2	436.2	7.6	7.6	5.6	4.7	7.0	4.3	RT
NAUTILUS INS CO	AZ	C	265.8	164.1	0.0	1.0	10.0	3.9	3.8	7.0	4.0	RT
NAVIGATORS INS CO	NY	B	2,916.6	1,066.3	845.0	21.2	8.2	6.7	8.4	6.9	4.6	RT
NAVIGATORS SPECIALTY INS CO	NY	B-	179.9	139.7	0.0	0.7	10.0	N/A	6.9	7.0	4.4	T
NAZARETH MUTUAL INS CO	PA	C-	14.5	7.4	7.0	0.1	7.7	5.9	8.2	6.7	2.2	DGRT
NCMIC INS CO	IA	B	732.6	295.0	143.4	2.3	8.1	9.6	8.9	7.4	4.2	RT
NCMIC RRG INC	VT	C	7.0	4.3	0.8	0.0	9.7	4.8	5.2	9.9	2.5	DGT
NEIGHBORHOOD SPIRIT PROP & CAS CO	CA	C+	289.5	119.2	147.6	-0.2	9.6	5.9	6.5	6.7	4.7	FRT
NETHERLANDS INS CO	NH	C	98.3	88.6	0.0	0.4	10.0	3.8	5.5	7.0	4.3	RT

See Page 27 for explanation of footnotes and Page 28 for explanation of stability factors.

Arrows denote recent upgrades ▲ or downgrades ▼ (see Section VII for explanations)

94

www.weissratings.com

RISK ADJ. RATIO #1	CAPITAL RATIO #2	PREMIUM TO SURPLUS (%)	RESV. TO SURPLUS (%)	RESV. DEVELOP. 1 YEAR (%)	RESV. DEVELOP. 2 YEAR (%)	LOSS RATIO (%)	EXP. RATIO (%)	COMB RATIO (%)	CASH FROM UNDER-WRITING (%)	NET PREMIUM GROWTH (%)	INVEST. IN AFFIL (%)	INSURANCE COMPANY NAME
70.7	29.3	N/A	N/A	N/A	N/A	N/A	N/A	N/A	N/A	0.0	0.0	NATIONAL FIRE INS CO OF HARTFORD
4.4	4.0	N/A	N/A	N/A	N/A	N/A	N/A	N/A	19.6	0.0	0.0	NATIONAL GENERAL ASR CO
4.9	4.4	N/A	N/A	N/A	N/A	N/A	N/A	N/A	20.6	0.0	0.0	NATIONAL GENERAL INS CO
1.9	1.7	N/A	N/A	N/A	N/A	N/A	N/A	N/A	316.7	0.0	0.0	NATIONAL GENERAL INS ONLINE INC
7.6	6.8	N/A	N/A	N/A	N/A	N/A	N/A	N/A	999 +	0.0	0.0	NATIONAL GENL PREMIER INS CO
2.0	1.6	17.2	58.3	-2.9	-77.1	81.4	72.9	154.3	544.4	137.3	0.0	NATIONAL GUARDIAN RRG INC
2.2	1.8	164.0	13.0	4.6	N/A	65.2	38.5	103.7	96.7	-4.5	0.0	NATIONAL HERITAGE INS CO
N/A	N/A	--	--	--	--	--	--	--	--	--	--	NATIONAL HOME INS CO RRG
1.7	1.4	19.8	24.4	-1.2	-2.0	77.3	22.5	99.8	114.9	8.5	23.0 ●	NATIONAL INDEMNITY CO
2.8	1.7	3.6	7.8	N/A	-0.2	58.6	23.7	82.3	157.2	2.2	0.0	NATIONAL INDEMNITY CO OF
2.8	1.7	34.3	46.7	3.1	-0.3	74.3	23.4	97.7	105.4	-33.9	0.0 ●	NATIONAL INDEMNITY CO OF THE
1.9	1.5	50.9	38.3	2.9	1.3	46.8	50.1	96.9	106.4	21.4	0.0	NATIONAL INDEPENDENT TRUCKERS IC
N/A	N/A	--	--	--	--	--	--	--	--	--	--	NATIONAL INS ASSN
7.5	6.2	0.1	12.3	-10.4	-35.0	999 +	999 +	999 +	2.0	-99.7	0.0	NATIONAL INS CO OF WI
1.5	1.2	91.7	126.2	4.5	10.0	70.2	29.2	99.4	114.6	4.6	17.0 ●	NATIONAL INTERSTATE INS CO
2.2	1.7	66.7	91.8	3.0	6.6	70.2	32.0	102.2	103.6	4.6	0.0	NATIONAL INTERSTATE INS CO OF
2.7	1.7	49.9	80.4	1.0	-3.8	72.7	26.8	99.5	112.8	-26.2	2.5 ●	NATIONAL LIABILITY & FIRE INS CO
4.6	3.8	93.5	17.2	-1.3	2.7	57.0	31.8	88.8	102.9	-8.6	0.0	NATIONAL LLOYDS INS CO
N/A	N/A	--	--	--	--	--	--	--	--	--	--	NATIONAL MEDICAL PROFESSIONAL
2.8	2.5	33.5	0.6	N/A	N/A	2.3	104.0	106.3	96.7	24.9	0.0 ●	NATIONAL MORTGAGE INS CORP
12.7	11.4	-9.0	0.8	-0.1	-0.1	3.1	-120.6	-117.5	-42.8	-123.4	0.0	NATIONAL MORTGAGE RE INC ONE
2.9	1.8	114.8	35.6	-6.1	-5.7	59.4	32.4	91.8	110.4	4.3	0.0	NATIONAL MUTUAL INS CO
32.9	15.8	0.7	-3.6	-8.4	2.5	41.9	322.8	364.7	7.7	12.0	0.0 ●	NATIONAL PUBLIC FINANCE GUAR CORP
2.4	1.7	155.1	17.8	-4.9	-5.4	62.0	34.9	96.9	97.1	2.3	12.9	NATIONAL SECURITY FIRE & CAS CO
13.1	8.5	6.1	N/A	N/A	N/A	N/A	106.4	106.4	84.3	-6.7	0.0	NATIONAL SERVICE CONTRACT INS CO
5.7	4.0	56.9	5.2	0.2	1.0	47.6	39.2	86.8	130.7	11.4	0.0	NATIONAL SPECIALTY INS CO
10.7	9.6	N/A	N/A	N/A	N/A	N/A	N/A	N/A	22.7	0.0	0.0	NATIONAL SURETY CORP
148.9	74.4	N/A	N/A	N/A	N/A	N/A	N/A	N/A	111.1	0.0	0.0	NATIONAL TRUST INS CO
2.4	1.6	81.1	227.6	21.7	30.2	99.8	26.7	126.5	85.5	-13.1	0.9 ●	NATIONAL UNION FIRE INS CO
0.5	0.4	357.1	160.7	29.5	54.4	70.8	40.1	110.9	84.1	-10.0	3.4	NATIONAL UNITY INS CO
0.7	0.5	344.8	102.1	2.9	8.2	76.1	20.0	96.1	105.2	37.8	0.0	NATIONS INS CO
1.0	0.9	N/A	N/A	N/A	N/A	N/A	N/A	N/A	999 +	0.0	0.0	NATIONWIDE AFFINITY INS CO OF AMER
5.2	3.7	N/A	N/A	N/A	N/A	N/A	N/A	N/A	-7.3	0.0	0.0	NATIONWIDE AGRIBUSINESS INS CO
7.8	7.0	N/A	N/A	N/A	N/A	N/A	N/A	N/A	-48.2	0.0	0.0	NATIONWIDE ASR CO
1.8	1.6	N/A	N/A	N/A	N/A	N/A	N/A	N/A	53.6	0.0	0.0	NATIONWIDE GENERAL INS CO
1.6	0.7	0.1	194.9	14.9	23.0	999 +	366.0	999 +	1.3	219.5	0.0 ●	NATIONWIDE INDEMNITY CO
14.3	12.9	N/A	N/A	N/A	N/A	N/A	N/A	N/A	999 +	0.0	0.0	NATIONWIDE INS CO OF AM
10.3	9.3	-61.8	N/A	N/A	0.3	N/A	N/A	N/A	-69.3	-159.4	0.0	NATIONWIDE INS CO OF FL
10.3	9.2	N/A	N/A	N/A	N/A	N/A	N/A	N/A	165.0	0.0	0.0	NATIONWIDE LLOYDS
3.3	2.3	87.5	64.5	1.7	2.2	74.7	31.0	105.7	97.8	4.3	5.2 ●	NATIONWIDE MUTUAL FIRE INS CO
1.5	1.3	127.5	93.9	2.5	3.2	74.7	31.0	105.7	98.8	4.3	28.6 ●	NATIONWIDE MUTUAL INS CO
3.3	2.3	N/A	N/A	N/A	N/A	N/A	N/A	N/A	-72.8	0.0	0.0	NATIONWIDE P&C INS CO
1.8	1.6	36.4	1.0	N/A	N/A	32.7	12.3	45.0	999 +	0.0	0.0	NATL TRANSPORTATION INS CO RRG
2.5	1.6	129.3	113.3	-17.8	-15.6	58.8	35.0	93.8	119.3	26.8	0.0 ●	NAU COUNTRY INS CO
5.6	4.9	N/A	N/A	N/A	N/A	N/A	N/A	N/A	N/A	0.0	0.0	NAUTILUS INS CO
2.3	1.8	82.3	112.8	-2.2	-2.5	60.5	32.9	93.4	123.6	11.6	5.5 ●	NAVIGATORS INS CO
24.5	22.0	N/A	N/A	N/A	N/A	N/A	N/A	N/A	N/A	0.0	0.0	NAVIGATORS SPECIALTY INS CO
2.2	1.6	97.8	23.5	7.7	6.5	45.7	44.1	89.8	124.7	16.7	0.0	NAZARETH MUTUAL INS CO
2.6	1.8	49.1	96.0	-10.0	-19.6	52.8	28.1	80.9	124.1	-1.5	1.3 ●	NCMIC INS CO
3.5	2.6	18.3	34.7	-4.3	-5.9	43.2	-69.3	-26.1	-165.2	0.5	0.0	NCMIC RRG INC
4.0	2.8	123.3	74.0	1.1	2.2	71.2	32.4	103.6	94.8	-1.1	0.0	NEIGHBORHOOD SPIRIT PROP & CAS CO
40.2	36.2	N/A	N/A	N/A	N/A	N/A	N/A	N/A	N/A	0.0	0.0	NETHERLANDS INS CO

999 + Denotes number greater than 999.9%
999 - Denotes number less than -999.99%
● Bullets denote a more detailed analysis is available in Section II.

INSURANCE COMPANY NAME	DOM. STATE	RATING	TOTAL ASSETS ($MIL)	CAPITAL & SURPLUS ($MIL)	ANNUAL NET PREMIUM ($MIL)	NET INCOME ($MIL)	CAPITAL-IZATION INDEX (PTS)	RESERVE ADQ INDEX (PTS)	PROFIT-ABILITY INDEX (PTS)	LIQUIDITY INDEX (PTS)	STAB. INDEX (PTS)	STABILITY FACTORS
NEVADA CAPITAL INS CO	NV	B	107.8	51.1	44.0	-0.4	8.4	4.9	4.1	6.0	5.7	T
NEVADA DOCS MEDICAL RRG INC	NV	U (5)	--	--	--	--	N/A	--	--	--	--	Z
NEVADA GENERAL INS CO	NV	D	15.7	6.1	13.9	0.2	4.7	4.4	0.9	2.3	2.1	DFGL
NEVADA MUTUAL INS CO	NV	D+	20.7	9.9	1.3	0.7	5.8	5.1	5.7	7.0	2.7	DGRT
NEW CENTURY INS CO	TX	C	10.7	5.9	4.0	0.0	9.4	6.1	4.8	6.9	3.5	DGRT
NEW ENGLAND GUARANTY INS CO INC	VT	U	--	--	--	--	N/A	--	--	--	--	Z
NEW ENGLAND INS CO	CT	U	--	--	--	--	N/A	--	--	--	--	Z
NEW ENGLAND MUTUAL INS CO	MA	B	44.7	41.9	0.0	0.2	10.0	5.6	4.8	10.0	4.1	DT
NEW ENGLAND REINS CORP	CT	U	--	--	--	--	N/A	--	--	--	--	Z
NEW HAMPSHIRE EMPLOYERS INS CO	NH	B-	3.9	3.5	0.0	0.0	10.0	N/A	6.2	10.0	3.5	DG
NEW HAMPSHIRE INS CO	IL	C	205.0	176.7	0.0	-1.8	10.0	3.5	1.9	7.0	4.2	AT
NEW HOME WARRANTY INS CO RRG	DC	C+	21.7	6.6	3.6	-0.1	8.0	6.0	3.9	8.5	3.2	DGT
NEW HORIZON INS CO	TX	U	--	--	--	--	N/A	--	--	--	--	Z
NEW JERSEY CASUALTY INS CO	NJ	B- (1)	577.4	269.7	69.9	24.2	9.0	5.8	8.8	7.2	5.0	T
NEW JERSEY INDEMNITY INS CO	NJ	C+(1)	78.7	68.6	7.2	1.8	10.0	7.0	7.8	8.5	4.8	D
NEW JERSEY PHYS UNITED RECIP EXCH	NJ	D+	31.0	11.7	5.8	-0.6	4.0	3.2	1.8	7.0	2.6	DGT
NEW JERSEY RE-INS CO	NJ	B	546.9	415.3	16.0	2.4	8.8	6.6	7.8	9.2	4.7	FT
NEW JERSEY SKYLANDS INS ASSN	NJ	D+(1)	56.9	14.7	22.6	-1.0	3.0	2.0	1.7	6.8	2.5	CDT
NEW JERSEY SKYLANDS INS CO	NJ	C- (1)	35.1	11.4	12.2	-0.3	5.2	2.6	2.1	6.3	3.2	DFT
NEW LONDON COUNTY MUTUAL INS CO	CT	B-	117.5	66.7	35.7	1.4	8.7	8.1	6.1	6.8	3.8	RT
NEW MEXICO ASR CO	NM	C-	6.6	1.8	0.0	0.1	6.0	N/A	4.8	9.0	2.1	DGT
NEW MEXICO EMPLOYERS ASR CO	NM	B-	6.3	1.9	0.0	0.1	6.0	N/A	3.9	6.9	3.5	DFGT
NEW MEXICO FOUNDATION INS CO	NM	C	23.4	18.0	0.0	0.1	10.0	3.6	8.3	10.0	3.3	DGRT
NEW MEXICO MUTUAL CASUALTY CO	NM	C+	386.5	166.1	91.9	3.3	7.4	6.9	8.5	6.9	4.0	T
▼NEW MEXICO PREMIER INS CO	NM	C	3.9	1.3	0.0	0.1	7.2	N/A	4.3	7.3	2.8	DFGT
NEW MEXICO PROPERTY & CASUALTY CO	NM	U	--	--	--	--	N/A	--	--	--	--	Z
▲NEW MEXICO SAFETY CASUALTY CO	NM	C-	5.1	2.4	0.0	0.0	8.9	N/A	7.1	7.2	2.3	DGT
NEW MEXICO SECURITY INS CO	NM	D+	4.0	1.6	0.0	0.0	8.1	N/A	4.8	9.6	1.9	DGT
NEW MEXICO SOUTHWEST CASUALTY CO	NM	C-	18.1	11.3	0.0	0.1	9.4	N/A	4.2	10.0	3.3	DFGR
NEW SOUTH INS CO	NC	C	49.3	7.9	0.0	0.1	7.3	3.9	3.9	7.0	3.7	DFRT
NEW YORK CENTRAL MUTUAL FIRE INS CO	NY	B-	1,119.2	531.7	448.9	-1.1	9.9	6.1	6.8	6.6	4.3	RT
NEW YORK HEALTHCARE INS CO INC RRG	DC	E+	23.0	4.9	6.2	0.1	0.3	0.8	4.0	7.1	0.4	CDFG
NEW YORK MARINE & GENERAL INS CO	NY	B-	1,351.8	359.7	393.4	-3.0	6.5	5.4	3.7	6.7	4.3	RT
NEW YORK MUNICIPAL INS RECIPROCAL	NY	B-	167.7	58.4	52.3	-1.7	8.0	6.9	5.2	6.9	3.6	RT
NEW YORK SCHOOLS INS RECIPROCAL	NY	B	288.6	177.1	61.5	2.4	10.0	8.3	8.8	7.1	4.5	RT
NEW YORK TRANSPORTATION INS CORP	NY	U (5)	--	--	--	--	N/A	--	--	--	--	Z
NEWPORT BONDING & SURETY CO	PR	D (1)	4.3	2.5	1.4	0.2	5.0	0.1	3.0	6.1	0.6	DT
NEWPORT INS CO	AZ	U	--	--	--	--	N/A	--	--	--	--	Z
NGM INS CO	FL	B-	2,520.0	1,055.5	1,066.2	3.0	8.9	4.4	6.6	6.4	4.6	RT
NHRMA MUTUAL INS CO	IL	C	37.9	14.3	14.0	1.0	5.1	9.9	4.6	6.6	3.4	DGRT
NJ MANUFACTURERS INS CO	NJ	B	7,070.7	2,733.4	1,689.5	45.4	8.2	6.7	5.0	6.8	5.7	T
NLC MUTUAL INS CO	VT	B (3)	326.2	129.1	14.0	4.4	7.0	4.2	6.6	8.6	4.1	RT
NODAK INS CO	ND	B-	247.2	144.2	136.2	4.1	9.4	8.9	8.5	6.2	4.0	T
NOETIC SPECIALTY INS CO	VT	C	124.9	75.8	11.2	1.2	9.5	9.4	8.6	8.5	3.5	DRT
NORCAL MUTUAL INS CO	CA	B-	1,668.7	686.1	337.5	3.4	8.1	9.0	6.8	7.0	4.6	RT
NORCAL SPECIALTY INS CO	PA	C-	63.0	47.3	-2.5	-0.1	10.0	4.9	1.9	9.5	3.1	DT
NORFOLK & DEDHAM MUTUAL FIRE INS CO	MA	C+	413.7	197.9	140.6	3.1	9.4	5.9	6.8	6.8	4.1	RT
NORGUARD INS CO	PA	D	859.5	209.8	229.7	4.4	1.3	9.3	8.7	1.5	2.0	CLRT
NORMANDY INS CO	FL	D	46.9	10.6	30.1	-0.5	1.3	5.8	5.2	6.2	1.6	CDT
NORTH AMERICAN CAPACITY INS CO	NH	C	199.7	45.9	0.0	-0.5	10.0	4.6	3.9	9.1	3.5	FRT
NORTH AMERICAN ELITE INS CO	NH	C	131.3	40.1	0.0	1.3	10.0	N/A	8.4	10.0	3.7	RT
NORTH AMERICAN SPECIALTY INS CO	NH	C	477.7	316.4	0.2	2.4	10.0	6.3	3.5	7.6	3.6	FGRT

See Page 27 for explanation of footnotes and
Page 28 for explanation of stability factors.
Arrows denote recent upgrades ▲ or downgrades ▼   (see Section VII for explanations)

96

www.weissratings.com

RISK ADJ. RATIO #1	CAPITAL RATIO #2	PREMIUM TO SURPLUS (%)	RESV. TO SURPLUS (%)	RESV. DEVELOP. 1 YEAR (%)	RESV. DEVELOP. 2 YEAR (%)	LOSS RATIO (%)	EXP. RATIO (%)	COMB RATIO (%)	CASH FROM UNDER-WRITING (%)	NET PREMIUM GROWTH (%)	INVEST. IN AFFIL (%)	INSURANCE COMPANY NAME
3.1	1.9	85.6	63.9	8.3	8.8	76.1	34.2	110.3	96.7	2.6	0.0	NEVADA CAPITAL INS CO
N/A	N/A	--	--	--	--	--	--	--	--	--	--	NEVADA DOCS MEDICAL RRG INC
1.0	0.9	237.4	121.3	16.0	11.8	89.0	38.7	127.7	78.6	0.2	0.0	NEVADA GENERAL INS CO
1.9	1.5	14.4	81.1	-19.8	-51.0	59.0	75.6	134.6	95.9	-68.8	30.3	NEVADA MUTUAL INS CO
2.7	2.5	67.4	11.3	-0.4	0.8	64.0	29.0	93.0	133.2	31.2	0.0	NEW CENTURY INS CO
N/A	N/A	--	--	--	--	--	--	--	--	--	--	NEW ENGLAND GUARANTY INS CO INC
N/A	N/A	--	--	--	--	--	--	--	--	--	--	NEW ENGLAND INS CO
44.2	32.2	N/A	N/A	N/A	-2.9	N/A	N/A	N/A	-44.9	100.0	0.0	NEW ENGLAND MUTUAL INS CO
N/A	N/A	--	--	--	--	--	--	--	--	--	--	NEW ENGLAND REINS CORP
17.5	15.8	N/A	N/A	N/A	N/A	N/A	N/A	N/A	N/A	0.0	0.0	NEW HAMPSHIRE EMPLOYERS INS CO
32.7	25.7	N/A	N/A	N/A	N/A	N/A	N/A	N/A	N/A	0.0	0.0	NEW HAMPSHIRE INS CO
2.1	1.9	55.1	10.9	-0.7	-0.2	54.3	13.5	67.8	263.3	12.7	0.0	NEW HOME WARRANTY INS CO RRG
N/A	N/A	--	--	--	--	--	--	--	--	--	--	NEW HORIZON INS CO
4.3	3.0	25.9	102.7	-4.9	-4.4	49.3	23.7	73.0	135.6	-12.1	0.0	NEW JERSEY CASUALTY INS CO
19.5	17.5	10.5	7.6	-1.7	-6.6	59.1	22.3	81.4	89.3	18.5	0.0	NEW JERSEY INDEMNITY INS CO
0.9	0.8	47.7	107.6	9.4	9.3	87.6	44.7	132.3	110.8	11.0	0.0	NEW JERSEY PHYS UNITED RECIP EXCH
4.1	2.4	3.9	30.4	-0.4	0.7	67.8	39.1	106.9	54.0	-25.6	0.0 ●	NEW JERSEY RE-INS CO
0.6	0.5	153.9	128.9	13.1	43.4	84.5	22.0	106.5	102.5	32.3	27.2	NEW JERSEY SKYLANDS INS ASSN
0.9	0.7	106.9	89.6	8.0	32.6	84.0	22.4	106.4	85.2	32.3	0.0	NEW JERSEY SKYLANDS INS CO
2.8	2.2	54.2	19.2	-1.6	-1.9	48.0	44.4	92.4	105.9	0.1	19.5	NEW LONDON COUNTY MUTUAL INS CO
1.2	0.8	N/A	124.7	N/A	N/A	N/A	N/A	N/A	67.0	0.0	0.0	NEW MEXICO ASR CO
1.4	0.8	N/A	124.6	N/A	N/A	N/A	N/A	N/A	67.3	0.0	0.0	NEW MEXICO EMPLOYERS ASR CO
11.2	5.2	N/A	20.2	N/A	N/A	N/A	N/A	N/A	72.3	0.0	0.0	NEW MEXICO FOUNDATION INS CO
2.0	1.5	56.8	120.8	-4.9	-15.0	48.6	35.4	84.0	117.6	-8.8	11.6	NEW MEXICO MUTUAL CASUALTY CO
1.4	1.2	N/A	96.2	N/A	N/A	N/A	N/A	N/A	85.4	0.0	0.0	NEW MEXICO PREMIER INS CO
N/A	N/A	--	--	--	--	--	--	--	--	--	--	NEW MEXICO PROPERTY & CASUALTY
2.5	2.3	N/A	35.9	N/A	N/A	N/A	N/A	N/A	-159.6	0.0	0.0	NEW MEXICO SAFETY CASUALTY CO
1.9	1.7	N/A	49.4	N/A	N/A	N/A	N/A	N/A	20.6	0.0	0.0	NEW MEXICO SECURITY INS CO
6.0	2.5	N/A	41.5	N/A	N/A	N/A	N/A	N/A	20.1	0.0	0.0	NEW MEXICO SOUTHWEST CASUALTY
1.3	1.2	N/A	N/A	N/A	N/A	N/A	N/A	N/A	288.8	0.0	0.0	NEW SOUTH INS CO
3.9	2.9	84.0	55.8	1.6	-0.6	67.1	29.6	96.7	106.5	6.3	4.5 ●	NEW YORK CENTRAL MUTUAL FIRE INS
0.2	0.1	131.1	291.0	-63.0	-17.0	14.2	91.2	105.4	81.8	-2.3	0.0	NEW YORK HEALTHCARE INS CO INC
1.3	0.9	110.7	172.0	7.9	8.8	74.5	39.4	113.9	105.5	-1.9	14.0 ●	NEW YORK MARINE & GENERAL INS CO
2.0	1.5	88.3	125.4	0.2	-7.3	70.2	27.6	97.8	128.4	6.3	0.0	NEW YORK MUNICIPAL INS RECIPROCAL
5.0	3.5	35.9	53.2	-1.8	-4.6	72.9	19.5	92.4	118.1	-0.7	0.0	NEW YORK SCHOOLS INS RECIPROCAL
N/A	N/A	--	--	--	--	--	--	--	--	--	--	NEW YORK TRANSPORTATION INS
1.0	0.9	55.6	33.1	-3.0	N/A	17.3	86.5	103.8	93.7	0.0	0.0	NEWPORT BONDING & SURETY CO
N/A	N/A	--	--	--	--	--	--	--	--	--	--	NEWPORT INS CO
2.7	2.1	102.6	80.2	6.5	9.8	71.8	32.3	104.1	105.8	10.2	12.4 ●	NGM INS CO
1.5	1.1	104.8	132.3	-29.2	-38.5	62.7	9.0	71.7	121.8	2.3	11.1	NHRMA MUTUAL INS CO
2.3	1.7	63.6	118.2	-1.5	-2.7	82.0	13.9	95.9	110.0	3.7	12.2 ●	NJ MANUFACTURERS INS CO
1.6	1.1	11.2	147.0	-2.0	-0.9	81.2	18.7	99.9	98.7	4.4	0.0	NLC MUTUAL INS CO
4.0	2.9	97.9	32.3	-2.7	-8.4	77.3	25.2	102.5	105.8	9.1	10.2	NODAK INS CO
3.6	2.7	15.0	50.7	-8.9	-17.1	16.8	38.5	55.3	160.9	-2.9	0.0	NOETIC SPECIALTY INS CO
2.4	1.8	47.9	88.7	N/A	-5.6	77.7	21.6	99.3	103.4	7.4	10.1 ●	NORCAL MUTUAL INS CO
17.8	16.0	-5.7	11.4	N/A	N/A	N/A	20.0	N/A	-8.8	93.0	0.0	NORCAL SPECIALTY INS CO
3.9	2.7	72.6	43.4	-3.7	0.2	52.3	38.4	90.7	114.6	9.1	3.5 ●	NORFOLK & DEDHAM MUTUAL FIRE INS
0.3	0.2	115.8	126.8	-4.0	-2.2	59.0	23.7	82.7	168.1	22.0	0.0 ●	NORGUARD INS CO
0.4	0.2	274.5	141.0	N/A	12.1	64.9	30.5	95.4	118.7	29.4	0.0	NORMANDY INS CO
4.8	4.3	N/A	2.0	0.1	N/A	N/A	N/A	N/A	-23.4	0.0	0.0	NORTH AMERICAN CAPACITY INS CO
4.6	4.2	N/A	1.4	N/A	N/A	N/A	N/A	N/A	-5.3	-100.0	0.0	NORTH AMERICAN ELITE INS CO
4.1	3.8	0.1	8.9	-0.6	-0.3	999 +	999 +	999 +	21.4	-91.8	22.1 ●	NORTH AMERICAN SPECIALTY INS CO

999 + Denotes number greater than 999.9%
999 - Denotes number less than -999.99%
● Bullets denote a more detailed analysis is available in Section II.

INSURANCE COMPANY NAME	DOM. STATE	RATING	TOTAL ASSETS ($MIL)	CAPITAL & SURPLUS ($MIL)	ANNUAL NET PREMIUM ($MIL)	NET INCOME ($MIL)	CAPITAL-IZATION INDEX (PTS)	RESERVE ADQ INDEX (PTS)	PROFIT-ABILITY INDEX (PTS)	LIQUIDITY INDEX (PTS)	STAB. INDEX (PTS)	STABILITY FACTORS
NORTH CAROLINA FARM BU MUTUAL INS	NC	B	1,935.5	1,138.4	771.2	22.3	10.0	8.6	8.2	6.4	4.8	T
▲NORTH CAROLINA GRANGE MUTUAL INS	NC	C-	33.5	17.2	17.5	1.9	7.1	7.0	8.8	5.7	2.6	DGT
NORTH COUNTRY INS CO	NY	C	27.8	19.1	7.5	0.3	10.0	7.9	8.8	7.1	2.9	DGT
▼NORTH EAST INS CO	ME	F (5)	35.9	15.7	-6.2	0.0	7.4	1.6	1.3	7.7	0.0	DFRT
NORTH LIGHT SPECIALTY INS CO	IL	B-	89.8	54.6	47.5	1.5	8.7	3.6	8.3	7.3	5.0	GT
NORTH PACIFIC INS CO	OR	C	8.0	7.9	0.0	0.0	10.0	N/A	6.4	7.0	2.8	DGRT
NORTH POINTE INS CO	PA	C-	19.6	14.1	-11.8	0.1	10.0	4.0	2.3	6.3	3.1	DFGR
NORTH RIVER INS CO	NJ	C-	1,065.2	295.5	396.8	-2.6	6.0	5.9	5.1	7.4	3.3	ART
NORTH STAR GENERAL INS CO	MN	U	--	--	--	--	N/A	--	--	--	--	Z
NORTH STAR MUTUAL INS CO	MN	B-	712.4	429.1	349.1	18.1	10.0	7.6	8.8	6.7	4.2	RT
NORTHERN MUTUAL INS CO	MI	C+	35.4	23.2	14.9	0.3	8.9	7.0	8.5	6.8	3.1	DGRT
NORTHERN SECURITY INS CO	VT	C	8.5	8.4	0.0	0.0	10.0	N/A	6.3	7.0	2.8	DGRT
NORTHFIELD INS CO	IA	C+	390.3	128.0	113.2	2.5	7.9	8.3	6.0	6.7	4.5	T
NORTHLAND CASUALTY CO	CT	B	111.1	39.0	30.5	0.7	8.3	8.3	8.8	7.0	4.4	T
NORTHLAND INS CO	CT	B	1,191.7	546.3	265.6	7.2	9.1	7.8	5.9	6.9	4.7	T
NORTHSTONE INS CO	PA	C+	64.7	11.4	7.2	0.0	5.6	9.7	4.4	8.0	3.1	DT
NORTHWEST DENTISTS INS CO	WI	C	24.0	10.6	6.1	0.1	7.7	9.4	4.1	7.2	2.7	DFGT
NORTHWEST GF MUTUAL INS CO	SD	D	18.4	8.9	11.5	0.6	7.9	8.6	7.1	6.7	2.0	DGT
NORTHWESTERN NATL INS CO SEG ACCNT	WI	E-	22.3	1.6	0.4	0.2	0.1	N/A	0.2	6.8	0.1	CDFG
NORTHWESTERN NTL INS CO MILWAUKEE	WI	F	22.5	1.6	0.0	0.0	2.6	N/A	1.5	7.0	0.0	DFGR
NOVA CASUALTY CO	NY	C+	95.5	95.3	0.0	0.1	8.8	N/A	6.4	10.0	4.5	FRT
NOVANT HEALTH RRG INC	SC	E (3)	9.8	6.2	2.6	0.1	6.3	4.7	7.0	9.4	0.0	DFGR
NUCLEAR ELECTRIC INS LTD	DE	A+(1)	5,050.9	4,049.0	245.3	271.9	9.2	3.9	5.1	7.0	8.6	
▲NUTMEG INS CO	CT	C+	766.5	523.0	73.7	1.9	10.0	4.9	5.5	8.1	4.4	AT
NW FARMERS MUTUAL INSURANCE CO	NC	U	--	--	--	--	N/A	--	--	--	--	Z
OAK RIVER INS CO	NE	C	693.6	248.1	127.2	7.3	6.7	9.3	6.6	9.2	4.3	RT
OAKWOOD INS CO	TN	U	--	--	--	--	N/A	--	--	--	--	Z
OASIS RECIPROCAL RRG	VT	B-	16.6	6.0	3.6	0.2	6.7	10.0	9.5	6.9	3.5	DFGT
OBI AMERICA INS CO	PA	U	--	--	--	--	N/A	--	--	--	--	Z
OBI NATIONAL INS CO	PA	C+	13.2	13.2	0.0	0.0	10.0	N/A	4.0	7.0	3.2	DGT
OBSTETRICIANS & GYNECOLOGISTS RRG	MT	U (5)	--	--	--	--	N/A	--	--	--	--	Z
OCCIDENTAL FIRE & CAS CO OF NC	NC	C-	624.6	182.8	51.3	2.1	5.9	4.0	5.9	6.0	2.7	RT
OCEAN HARBOR CASUALTY INS CO	FL	B	277.9	58.2	198.6	-1.5	6.2	9.9	5.6	3.1	6.0	LT
OCEAN MARINE INDEMNITY INS CO	LA	C-	11.5	7.2	0.5	-0.2	9.9	4.3	3.1	7.5	2.2	DFGR
OCEANUS INS CO A RRG	SC	D-	52.9	6.9	10.8	-0.9	0.9	0.5	0.6	6.0	1.2	CDFR
ODYSSEY REINS CO	CT	C	7,252.6	3,283.8	1,575.2	93.9	7.3	9.4	5.8	7.0	2.7	ART
OGLESBY REINS CO	IL	A+	4,364.9	3,309.8	907.1	39.3	10.0	3.6	8.0	7.0	8.4	T
OHIC INS CO	OH	U	--	--	--	--	N/A	--	--	--	--	Z
OHIO BAR LIABILITY INS CO	OH	B-	40.0	29.4	6.3	0.2	10.0	7.9	8.3	9.0	3.9	DGT
OHIO CASUALTY INS CO	NH	C	5,711.1	1,738.2	2,119.9	-1.7	8.2	5.9	6.6	6.4	3.1	ART
OHIO FARMERS INS CO	OH	B-	2,975.6	2,266.4	343.8	2.6	7.3	7.5	7.4	7.0	4.6	T
OHIO INDEMNITY CO	OH	C	150.2	47.8	83.3	1.9	8.1	9.3	6.1	6.5	2.9	T
OHIO MUTUAL INS CO	OH	B-	282.0	222.8	56.4	0.8	7.5	7.6	7.7	6.9	4.7	T
OHIO SECURITY INS CO	NH	C-	16.2	15.8	0.0	0.1	10.0	N/A	6.5	7.0	3.1	ADGR
OKLAHOMA ATTORNEYS MUTUAL INS CO	OK	B	55.8	36.6	6.2	-0.4	10.0	6.9	4.3	8.2	4.1	DRT
OKLAHOMA FARM BUREAU MUTUAL INS CO	OK	B-	303.0	119.5	121.4	3.2	8.0	9.3	7.2	6.8	4.0	FT
OKLAHOMA P&C INS CO	OK	U	--	--	--	--	N/A	--	--	--	--	Z
OKLAHOMA SPECIALTY INS CO	OK	C+	24.5	18.9	0.0	0.1	10.0	N/A	8.0	10.0	3.4	DGT
OKLAHOMA SURETY CO	OH	C	16.4	16.3	-1.8	0.1	10.0	4.6	4.5	9.3	3.2	DFGR
OLD AMERICAN CTY MUTUAL FIRE INS CO	TX	E+	131.6	5.0	40.0	0.0	0.0	7.3	5.1	7.3	0.7	CDGR
OLD AMERICAN INDEMNITY CO	KY	B-	14.1	9.5	0.5	0.0	10.0	4.9	3.5	9.5	3.5	DFGR
OLD DOMINION INS CO	FL	B-	37.6	35.6	0.0	0.2	10.0	N/A	7.6	7.0	3.5	GT

See Page 27 for explanation of footnotes and
Page 28 for explanation of stability factors.
Arrows denote recent upgrades ▲ or downgrades ▼   (see Section VII for explanations)

98

www.weissratings.com

RISK ADJ. RATIO #1	CAPITAL RATIO #2	PREMIUM TO SURPLUS (%)	RESV. TO SURPLUS (%)	RESV. DEVELOP. 1 YEAR (%)	RESV. DEVELOP. 2 YEAR (%)	LOSS RATIO (%)	EXP. RATIO (%)	COMB RATIO (%)	CASH FROM UNDER-WRITING (%)	NET PREMIUM GROWTH (%)	INVEST. IN AFFIL (%)	INSURANCE COMPANY NAME
6.7	4.4	69.6	29.2	-2.5	-5.6	80.5	23.4	103.9	96.9	7.6	0.6 ●	NORTH CAROLINA FARM BU MUTUAL INS
1.8	1.3	116.4	33.2	-7.3	-6.7	69.4	30.0	99.4	110.2	1.6	0.0	NORTH CAROLINA GRANGE MUTUAL INS
5.4	3.9	40.1	20.8	-0.4	-2.5	30.0	40.3	70.3	138.3	4.1	3.6	NORTH COUNTRY INS CO
3.8	3.4	-42.0	N/A	10.6	46.4	108.5	-15.2	93.3	-35.1	-125.3	0.0	NORTH EAST INS CO
2.8	2.3	89.4	9.0	0.3	N/A	32.2	22.6	54.8	191.4	0.0	0.0	NORTH LIGHT SPECIALTY INS CO
164.5	109.8	N/A	N/A	N/A	N/A	N/A	N/A	N/A	N/A	0.0	0.0	NORTH PACIFIC INS CO
8.3	7.5	-84.4	N/A	N/A	N/A	N/A	N/A	N/A	-21.2	-132.1	0.0	NORTH POINTE INS CO
1.2	0.8	139.2	195.5	-1.5	-2.5	63.7	34.5	98.2	110.2	8.5	21.1 ●	NORTH RIVER INS CO
N/A	N/A	--	--	--	--	--	--	--	--	--	--	NORTH STAR GENERAL INS CO
6.5	4.4	85.4	25.9	-1.4	-3.4	56.1	27.9	84.0	120.4	3.1	0.7 ●	NORTH STAR MUTUAL INS CO
3.5	2.2	65.3	13.3	-9.1	-13.2	47.6	36.2	83.8	119.4	-1.4	0.0	NORTHERN MUTUAL INS CO
104.0	49.0	N/A	N/A	N/A	N/A	N/A	N/A	N/A	N/A	0.0	0.0	NORTHERN SECURITY INS CO
2.4	1.6	90.3	149.9	-1.8	-4.6	63.4	29.9	93.3	107.4	4.8	0.0	NORTHFIELD INS CO
3.0	1.9	79.9	132.5	-1.7	-4.4	63.4	29.9	93.3	118.5	4.8	0.0	NORTHLAND CASUALTY CO
2.9	2.4	49.6	82.4	-1.0	-2.5	63.4	30.0	93.4	110.2	4.8	15.5 ●	NORTHLAND INS CO
1.3	0.9	63.4	199.4	-12.4	-27.0	69.6	26.2	95.8	106.1	37.9	0.0	NORTHSTONE INS CO
1.9	1.4	59.3	74.3	3.5	-11.4	105.3	37.0	142.3	97.8	-2.6	0.0	NORTHWEST DENTISTS INS CO
2.4	2.1	140.7	25.6	-3.9	-8.3	54.5	35.9	90.4	113.0	3.6	0.2	NORTHWEST GF MUTUAL INS CO
0.1	0.1	20.0	728.9	N/A	N/A	510.8	621.3	999 +	11.8	-13.6	51.2	NORTHWESTERN NATL INS CO SEG
0.4	0.4	N/A	N/A	N/A	N/A	N/A	N/A	N/A	N/A	0.0	0.0	NORTHWESTERN NTL INS CO
2.2	2.1	N/A	N/A	N/A	N/A	N/A	N/A	N/A	-845.0	0.0	52.1	NOVA CASUALTY CO
1.3	1.0	42.1	45.6	-2.7	-12.4	49.3	30.2	79.5	64.2	4.3	0.0	NOVANT HEALTH RRG INC
3.6	2.5	6.1	7.3	-1.8	3.1	18.8	14.8	33.6	224.6	20.1	2.7	NUCLEAR ELECTRIC INS LTD
50.7	45.6	12.7	22.6	0.5	0.8	70.4	29.2	99.6	105.5	0.0	34.7 ●	NUTMEG INS CO
N/A	N/A	--	--	--	--	--	--	--	--	--	--	NW FARMERS MUTUAL INSURANCE CO
1.9	1.2	55.3	147.3	-9.7	-15.3	61.3	22.9	84.2	160.5	14.7	0.0 ●	OAK RIVER INS CO
N/A	N/A	--	--	--	--	--	--	--	--	--	--	OAKWOOD INS CO
1.7	1.0	64.0	97.0	-31.1	-44.0	19.8	25.1	44.9	83.5	5.3	0.0	OASIS RECIPROCAL RRG
N/A	N/A	--	--	--	--	--	--	--	--	--	--	OBI AMERICA INS CO
148.5	71.8	N/A	N/A	N/A	N/A	N/A	N/A	N/A	N/A	0.0	0.0	OBI NATIONAL INS CO
N/A	N/A	--	--	--	--	--	--	--	--	--	--	OBSTETRICIANS & GYNECOLOGISTS
1.1	0.9	29.7	52.3	5.4	12.2	76.6	23.5	100.1	97.4	-58.4	34.0	OCCIDENTAL FIRE & CAS CO OF NC
1.0	0.9	340.7	131.1	-16.9	-59.3	62.0	33.6	95.6	108.1	20.3	13.1	OCEAN HARBOR CASUALTY INS CO
4.4	2.8	7.4	53.9	0.1	0.6	117.8	72.9	190.7	39.1	-12.6	0.0	OCEAN MARINE INDEMNITY INS CO
0.2	0.2	141.0	517.3	32.5	81.9	88.8	67.9	156.7	59.6	-53.8	0.0	OCEANUS INS CO A RRG
1.5	1.2	49.3	89.9	-6.2	-11.3	55.3	33.9	89.2	106.3	0.0	29.7 ●	ODYSSEY REINS CO
16.4	10.6	27.8	21.6	-1.4	N/A	67.5	20.4	87.9	191.9	-24.8	0.0 ●	OGLESBY REINS CO
N/A	N/A	--	--	--	--	--	--	--	--	--	--	OHIC INS CO
5.0	3.4	21.8	21.9	N/A	-4.5	53.0	33.6	86.6	122.4	6.7	5.1	OHIO BAR LIABILITY INS CO
2.9	1.9	123.1	160.1	1.0	-0.5	69.8	32.0	101.8	100.7	3.4	2.2 ●	OHIO CASUALTY INS CO
1.2	1.2	15.5	14.0	-0.6	-0.9	62.3	35.7	98.0	109.0	2.3	69.7 ●	OHIO FARMERS INS CO
2.6	1.7	182.8	35.9	-7.6	-11.9	49.7	37.5	87.2	111.1	23.2	0.0	OHIO INDEMNITY CO
1.3	1.3	25.9	12.9	-0.8	-1.1	61.7	31.9	93.6	106.1	5.3	66.8 ●	OHIO MUTUAL INS CO
95.3	79.9	N/A	N/A	N/A	N/A	N/A	N/A	N/A	N/A	0.0	0.0	OHIO SECURITY INS CO
6.2	3.7	17.0	28.0	-1.9	-2.8	75.5	27.5	103.0	118.4	-4.2	0.0	OKLAHOMA ATTORNEYS MUTUAL INS
2.3	1.7	103.3	41.8	-6.5	-14.9	76.6	18.8	95.4	100.8	-2.0	13.0	OKLAHOMA FARM BUREAU MUTUAL INS
N/A	N/A	--	--	--	--	--	--	--	--	--	--	OKLAHOMA P&C INS CO
11.6	10.4	N/A	N/A	N/A	N/A	N/A	N/A	N/A	-131.4	0.0	0.0	OKLAHOMA SPECIALTY INS CO
89.7	44.8	-10.9	N/A	N/A	N/A	N/A	-0.2	N/A	N/A	-145.0	0.0	OKLAHOMA SURETY CO
0.1	0.1	800.2	N/A	N/A	-0.6	N/A	99.1	99.1	102.6	8.7	0.0	OLD AMERICAN CTY MUTUAL FIRE INS
6.6	5.9	5.3	4.1	-1.0	0.2	55.3	75.0	130.3	41.2	-49.2	0.0	OLD AMERICAN INDEMNITY CO
49.8	24.4	N/A	N/A	N/A	N/A	N/A	N/A	N/A	N/A	0.0	0.0	OLD DOMINION INS CO

999 + Denotes number greater than 999.9%
999 - Denotes number less than -999.99%
● Bullets denote a more detailed analysis is available in Section II.

INSURANCE COMPANY NAME	DOM. STATE	RATING	TOTAL ASSETS ($MIL)	CAPITAL & SURPLUS ($MIL)	ANNUAL NET PREMIUM ($MIL)	NET INCOME ($MIL)	CAPITAL-IZATION INDEX (PTS)	RESERVE ADQ INDEX (PTS)	PROFIT-ABILITY INDEX (PTS)	LIQUIDITY INDEX (PTS)	STAB. INDEX (PTS)	STABILITY FACTORS
OLD ELIZABETH MUTUAL FIRE INS CO	PA	U (1)	--	--	--	--	N/A	--	--	--	--	Z
OLD GLORY INS CO	TX	C	23.6	10.0	7.3	-0.2	7.2	7.0	4.2	6.6	3.0	DGRT
OLD GUARD INS CO	OH	C+	455.6	210.1	162.9	1.7	9.0	8.7	8.6	6.7	4.4	T
OLD RELIABLE CAS CO	MO	C-	5.8	4.8	0.0	0.0	10.0	3.6	2.4	7.0	2.5	DFGR
OLD REPUB INS CO	PA	B	2,863.9	1,113.7	470.7	20.9	9.2	6.2	8.8	7.0	4.8	ART
OLD REPUB UNION INS CO	IL	B	62.1	52.1	0.1	0.2	8.6	6.2	6.9	7.3	4.3	DGRT
OLD REPUBLIC GENERAL INS CORP	IL	B	2,060.4	561.0	184.4	9.7	7.4	8.6	8.9	7.0	4.8	CT
OLD REPUBLIC LLOYDS OF TX	TX	B (1)	2.2	0.8	0.6	0.0	7.5	9.3	3.9	8.2	4.9	DT
OLD REPUBLIC SECURITY ASR CO	IL	B	1,045.4	198.4	224.4	0.6	4.1	0.2	2.7	6.0	4.8	CFRT
OLD REPUBLIC SURETY CO	WI	B	122.7	65.3	47.9	2.3	8.1	9.5	8.6	6.9	4.3	RT
OLD UNITED CAS CO	KS	C	625.0	220.0	150.9	6.6	10.0	7.3	3.5	9.1	3.7	RT
OLYMPUS INS CO	FL	C	70.5	30.7	-16.8	0.2	7.9	3.2	2.9	7.0	3.7	FR
OMAHA INDEMNITY CO	WI	U	--	--	--	--	N/A	--	--	--	--	Z
OMEGA INS CO	FL	C	48.1	15.5	10.8	-0.8	7.6	3.7	3.4	7.0	3.2	DFRT
OMEGA ONE INS CO	AL	C	12.0	10.9	0.6	0.1	10.0	6.9	8.3	7.3	2.9	DFGR
OMNI INDEMNITY CO	IL	C	97.6	6.8	34.7	-1.2	0.8	1.4	0.5	2.7	2.7	CDFG
OMNI INS CO	IL	B-	126.8	20.3	45.8	-1.8	2.6	1.9	0.8	0.0	3.8	CDFL
OMS NATIONAL INS CO RRG	IL	B-	422.8	242.5	67.2	0.9	8.6	8.8	8.5	8.1	4.1	RT
ONE ALLIANCE INS CORP	PR	D+	14.0	6.9	2.9	-0.2	5.6	3.6	1.3	6.7	2.2	DFGT
ONECIS INS CO	IL	U	--	--	--	--	N/A	--	--	--	--	Z
ONTARIO INS CO	NY	C	17.3	12.2	4.3	0.3	10.0	7.9	8.0	7.3	2.5	DGRT
ONTARIO REINS CO LTD	GA	C	28.4	21.8	0.5	0.0	8.0	5.1	6.7	9.3	4.0	DFG
ONYX INS CO INC A RRG	TN	E+	29.1	5.9	13.9	-0.5	0.4	1.8	2.5	7.8	0.6	CDGT
OOIDA RISK RETENTION GROUP INC	VT	C	96.5	22.9	17.7	0.0	6.7	9.5	4.4	6.8	4.3	DRT
OPHTHALMIC MUTUAL INS CO RRG	VT	B	281.1	208.7	36.5	1.0	10.0	9.0	8.7	8.1	4.2	RT
ORANGE COUNTY MEDICAL RECIP INS RRG	AZ	D+	6.3	5.1	0.7	0.1	10.0	9.5	4.0	9.5	2.3	DG
ORDINARY MUTUAL A RRG CORP	VT	U (2)	--	--	--	--	N/A	--	--	--	--	Z
OREGON AUTOMOBILE INS CO	OR	C	8.3	7.9	0.0	0.0	10.0	N/A	6.0	7.0	2.8	DGRT
OREGON MUTUAL INS CO	OR	C-	211.9	65.9	123.6	-13.9	7.9	4.8	1.7	5.3	3.3	FRT
ORISKA INS CO	NY	E	38.8	11.9	16.5	0.6	0.0	0.9	3.7	0.0	0.2	CDGL
ORTHOFORUM INS CO	SC	E	22.7	2.8	6.8	0.0	0.0	0.5	1.7	7.7	0.1	CDGT
OSWEGO COUNTY MUTUAL INS CO	NY	C	27.9	16.2	7.4	0.6	8.5	8.9	8.7	6.9	2.7	DGT
OTSEGO COUNTY PATRONS CO-OP F R	NY	D	2.1	0.6	0.6	0.0	6.5	7.9	3.6	6.8	1.0	DGRT
OTSEGO MUTUAL FIRE INS CO	NY	B	122.5	106.5	4.6	0.6	10.0	7.4	8.4	7.9	4.4	DT
OWNERS INS CO	OH	A-	3,948.4	1,736.5	1,519.1	28.3	10.0	8.3	8.8	6.7	5.6	FT
P&C INS CO OF HARTFORD	IN	B	226.4	98.3	52.7	3.1	10.0	5.9	7.7	7.1	4.5	AT
P&S INS RRG INC	SC	U	--	--	--	--	N/A	--	--	--	--	Z
PACE RRG INC	VT	D+	4.9	3.1	0.1	0.0	7.0	5.0	3.5	7.0	2.0	DFGR
PACIFIC COMPENSATION INS CO	CA	C	376.9	111.9	138.2	-0.1	3.3	4.7	3.9	5.9	3.6	CRT
PACIFIC EMPLOYERS INS CO	PA	B-	3,736.2	1,358.0	889.3	37.8	8.9	6.3	8.4	6.9	3.9	RT
PACIFIC INDEMNITY CO	WI	B-	6,782.9	2,988.7	1,074.5	66.9	10.0	8.6	7.3	6.9	3.7	T
PACIFIC INDEMNITY INS CO	GU	C+	34.1	22.4	8.9	0.4	9.5	8.4	8.7	8.2	3.1	DGRT
PACIFIC INS CO LTD	CT	B	653.3	224.8	179.1	5.9	9.1	5.8	5.3	6.8	5.8	AT
▲PACIFIC PIONEER INS CO	CA	C-	22.8	8.4	4.7	0.1	5.1	5.4	2.4	4.9	2.3	DGLR
PACIFIC PROPERTY & CASUALTY CO	CA	B	85.4	42.6	44.0	-0.7	7.6	8.0	5.3	5.9	6.0	T
PACIFIC SPECIALTY INS CO	CA	B-	309.2	131.4	186.5	-0.3	7.4	6.0	3.6	6.5	4.0	RT
▲PACIFIC SPECIALTY PROPERTY & CAS CO	TX	D-	5.4	4.7	0.6	0.0	10.0	6.0	4.3	9.4	1.0	DGR
PACIFIC STAR INS CO	WI	C	14.7	10.4	1.5	0.0	10.0	5.9	4.0	9.2	2.8	DGRT
PACO ASR CO INC	IL	C	68.4	33.5	9.8	0.2	7.4	9.3	5.6	7.5	3.7	DRT
PAFCO GENERAL INS CO	IN	F (5)	0.0	0.0	6.3	0.0	1.5	4.9	0.3	2.9	0.0	CDFL
PALADIN REINS CORP	NY	U	--	--	--	--	N/A	--	--	--	--	Z
PALISADES INS CO	NJ	D+ (1)	35.1	12.3	0.0	0.1	9.9	N/A	5.1	7.0	2.5	DT

See Page 27 for explanation of footnotes and
Page 28 for explanation of stability factors.

Arrows denote recent upgrades ▲ or downgrades ▼   (see Section VII for explanations)

100

www.weissratings.com

RISK ADJ. RATIO #1	CAPITAL RATIO #2	PREMIUM TO SURPLUS (%)	RESV. TO SURPLUS (%)	RESV. DEVELOP. 1 YEAR (%)	RESV. DEVELOP. 2 YEAR (%)	LOSS RATIO (%)	EXP. RATIO (%)	COMB RATIO (%)	CASH FROM UNDER-WRITING (%)	NET PREMIUM GROWTH (%)	INVEST. IN AFFIL (%)	INSURANCE COMPANY NAME
N/A	N/A	--	--	--	--	--	--	--	--	--	--	OLD ELIZABETH MUTUAL FIRE INS CO
1.6	1.0	71.0	95.7	-9.0	-16.3	69.5	53.5	123.0	95.2	-14.5	0.0	OLD GLORY INS CO
3.7	2.4	79.0	71.0	-3.0	-4.4	62.3	35.8	98.1	106.4	2.3	0.0 ●	OLD GUARD INS CO
11.3	10.1	N/A	N/A	0.2	N/A	N/A	N/A	N/A	-15.0	0.0	0.0	OLD RELIABLE CAS CO
4.0	2.4	42.5	93.3	-0.6	-1.9	54.7	28.1	82.8	130.1	11.8	0.5 ●	OLD REPUB INS CO
3.5	2.0	0.2	7.4	N/A	-1.5	241.5	297.3	538.8	125.3	743.9	0.0	OLD REPUB UNION INS CO
2.7	1.2	33.1	195.9	-2.1	-6.0	85.0	4.7	89.7	118.4	-40.8	0.0 ●	OLD REPUBLIC GENERAL INS CORP
1.5	1.3	79.2	125.1	-3.0	-5.7	64.6	41.7	106.3	105.0	-1.7	0.0	OLD REPUBLIC LLOYDS OF TX
0.9	0.4	114.0	357.1	19.7	129.2	97.9	27.3	125.2	65.1	-32.0	0.0 ●	OLD REPUBLIC SECURITY ASR CO
2.2	1.7	74.5	34.3	-12.0	-19.1	15.4	71.0	86.4	119.7	1.8	0.2	OLD REPUBLIC SURETY CO
5.8	3.2	71.9	3.2	-0.2	-0.4	46.7	26.7	73.4	153.3	6.5	0.0 ●	OLD UNITED CAS CO
2.2	1.8	-55.3	34.0	-2.0	-0.8	-60.0	163.8	103.8	180.6	28.8	0.0	OLYMPUS INS CO
N/A	N/A	--	--	--	--	--	--	--	--	--	--	OMAHA INDEMNITY CO
2.1	1.4	68.1	48.6	0.6	16.3	89.2	49.4	138.6	93.7	-30.1	0.0	OMEGA INS CO
9.9	6.0	5.7	0.6	N/A	-2.5	164.8	10.5	175.3	57.0	0.0	0.0	OMEGA ONE INS CO
0.1	0.1	424.0	313.2	33.1	49.3	109.7	28.2	137.9	82.7	54.2	0.0	OMNI INDEMNITY CO
0.5	0.4	207.6	175.8	18.1	26.5	104.4	29.6	134.0	78.8	-30.9	23.1	OMNI INS CO
2.5	2.0	28.2	53.2	-3.3	-4.7	61.4	30.0	91.4	125.3	5.2	16.2 ●	OMS NATIONAL INS CO RRG
0.9	0.5	40.8	6.2	0.2	N/A	64.2	141.4	205.6	51.1	390.5	0.0	ONE ALLIANCE INS CORP
N/A	N/A	--	--	--	--	--	--	--	--	--	--	ONECIS INS CO
5.1	3.3	35.9	17.7	-1.7	-4.4	58.1	33.7	91.8	119.3	13.6	0.0	ONTARIO INS CO
2.8	1.6	2.1	3.8	0.8	-0.3	99.3	46.3	145.6	89.6	-1.7	0.0	ONTARIO REINS CO LTD
0.2	0.1	236.9	235.6	56.0	44.4	90.9	34.3	125.2	121.1	20.8	0.0	ONYX INS CO INC A RRG
1.4	1.2	78.0	145.3	-31.7	-30.2	45.9	29.5	75.4	124.7	-5.7	0.0	OOIDA RISK RETENTION GROUP INC
12.2	7.6	17.7	18.9	-3.3	-4.3	39.4	29.2	68.6	140.1	-8.4	0.0 ●	OPHTHALMIC MUTUAL INS CO RRG
9.0	5.6	14.5	14.3	0.1	-15.0	66.3	22.2	88.5	122.7	-0.1	0.0	ORANGE COUNTY MEDICAL RECIP INS
N/A	N/A	--	--	--	--	--	--	--	--	--	--	ORDINARY MUTUAL A RRG CORP
41.2	37.1	N/A	N/A	N/A	N/A	N/A	N/A	N/A	N/A	0.0	0.0	OREGON AUTOMOBILE INS CO
2.1	1.5	180.1	106.6	-8.0	10.7	68.3	35.9	104.2	84.5	-2.4	5.4	OREGON MUTUAL INS CO
0.1	0.1	150.0	166.2	1.9	7.9	54.8	41.0	95.8	135.5	61.9	0.0	ORISKA INS CO
0.1	0.0	238.0	542.1	56.5	79.6	110.8	17.8	128.6	134.5	5.4	0.0	ORTHOFORUM INS CO
3.0	2.0	48.3	41.7	-2.6	-5.7	58.9	33.2	92.1	136.0	11.9	0.0	OSWEGO COUNTY MUTUAL INS CO
1.1	0.8	100.4	24.2	-1.9	-0.8	81.9	14.8	96.7	134.7	42.2	0.0	OTSEGO COUNTY PATRONS CO-OP F R
7.2	4.2	4.4	2.3	-0.2	-0.5	51.6	5.2	56.8	164.1	4.6	0.0	OTSEGO MUTUAL FIRE INS CO
5.7	3.8	89.5	71.3	-0.2	-5.0	68.6	30.2	98.8	95.9	-10.9	0.0 ●	OWNERS INS CO
5.3	3.4	44.6	79.5	1.8	1.4	70.4	16.2	86.6	105.5	0.0	0.0	P&C INS CO OF HARTFORD
N/A	N/A	--	--	--	--	--	--	--	--	--	--	P&S INS RRG INC
2.1	1.8	3.2	26.7	1.8	-15.9	488.4	26.2	514.6	999 +	-11.5	0.0	PACE RRG INC
0.7	0.4	123.7	198.1	0.3	0.1	75.2	29.5	104.7	148.2	35.8	0.0	PACIFIC COMPENSATION INS CO
3.5	2.4	67.4	123.0	0.9	0.6	76.5	20.4	96.9	115.8	5.0	4.3 ●	PACIFIC EMPLOYERS INS CO
5.7	3.6	36.7	92.0	-4.1	-6.7	53.2	34.3	87.5	94.3	-36.5	0.1 ●	PACIFIC INDEMNITY CO
4.8	2.9	40.7	14.2	-3.2	-4.3	27.6	40.2	67.8	116.0	0.5	0.5	PACIFIC INDEMNITY INS CO
3.5	2.3	81.7	145.8	2.9	2.3	70.4	29.1	99.5	105.5	0.0	0.0 ●	PACIFIC INS CO LTD
1.6	1.0	58.2	75.3	-12.3	-27.1	72.7	27.1	99.8	94.4	-28.5	0.0	PACIFIC PIONEER INS CO
2.1	1.3	101.6	54.2	3.3	-0.2	81.7	24.2	105.9	105.4	11.9	0.0	PACIFIC PROPERTY & CASUALTY CO
1.9	1.5	141.3	51.4	-3.8	-3.3	57.2	41.6	98.8	99.4	3.4	1.6	PACIFIC SPECIALTY INS CO
13.0	11.8	13.0	3.8	1.2	1.2	80.0	46.5	126.5	88.5	45.1	0.0	PACIFIC SPECIALTY PROPERTY & CAS
7.6	6.0	14.7	11.5	-1.6	-5.4	57.0	38.5	95.5	103.8	-4.3	0.0	PACIFIC STAR INS CO
2.7	2.3	29.3	75.9	-17.3	-19.1	49.5	23.3	72.8	90.1	-1.9	0.0	PACO ASR CO INC
0.4	0.3	196.2	297.0	7.1	-17.7	95.7	39.4	135.1	51.3	-17.6	0.0	PAFCO GENERAL INS CO
N/A	N/A	--	--	--	--	--	--	--	--	--	--	PALADIN REINS CORP
3.2	2.9	N/A	N/A	N/A	N/A	N/A	N/A	N/A	N/A	0.0	0.0	PALISADES INS CO

999 + Denotes number greater than 999.9%
999 - Denotes number less than -999.99%
● Bullets denote a more detailed analysis is available in Section II.

INSURANCE COMPANY NAME	DOM. STATE	RATING	TOTAL ASSETS ($MIL)	CAPITAL & SURPLUS ($MIL)	ANNUAL NET PREMIUM ($MIL)	NET INCOME ($MIL)	CAPITAL-IZATION INDEX (PTS)	RESERVE ADQ INDEX (PTS)	PROFIT-ABILITY INDEX (PTS)	LIQUIDITY INDEX (PTS)	STAB. INDEX (PTS)	STABILITY FACTORS
PALISADES P&C INS CO	NJ	D (1)	15.1	12.3	0.0	0.0	10.0	N/A	6.9	7.0	1.5	D
PALISADES SAFETY & INS ASSOC	NJ	C (1)	1,244.1	412.9	587.5	-11.6	4.1	7.0	3.6	3.4	3.5	CLT
PALLADIUM RRG INC	VT	D+	99.9	12.1	27.7	0.2	1.2	3.6	3.6	7.8	1.3	CDGT
PALMETTO CASUALTY INS CO	SC	C+	7.1	7.0	0.0	0.0	10.0	N/A	6.9	7.0	3.0	DGT
PALMETTO SURETY CORP	SC	D+	13.2	3.7	9.4	-0.4	1.8	9.3	2.9	6.7	2.1	CDFG
PALOMAR SPECIALTY INS CO	OR	C-	123.9	69.0	40.3	0.5	3.4	3.6	4.4	6.1	2.3	CGT
PANHANDLE FARMERS MULT INS CO	WV	C-	4.8	2.6	2.7	0.0	7.8	5.7	4.2	6.5	2.0	DGRT
PARAMOUNT INS CO	MD	D	11.7	1.5	8.3	-0.3	1.3	3.7	0.9	6.7	1.3	CDGR
PARATRANSIT INS CO A MUTUAL RRG	TN	C	26.9	13.5	4.9	0.1	8.4	9.3	7.6	8.2	2.5	DGRT
▼PARK INS CO	NY	E-	34.5	2.1	9.1	-1.0	0.0	0.1	1.5	0.0	0.1	CDFG
PARTNER REINSURANCE CO OF THE US	NY	C+	4,720.1	1,372.1	1,188.2	0.8	7.6	9.6	7.6	6.7	4.4	RT
PARTNERRE AMERICA INS CO	DE	C+	366.5	115.6	32.1	-0.6	10.0	5.9	3.7	7.9	4.4	FRT
PARTNERRE INS CO OF NY	NY	C	122.0	107.8	0.0	-1.0	8.9	6.4	3.6	9.4	3.8	DFGR
PARTNERS MUTUAL INS CO	WI	C	44.2	11.9	13.7	0.1	7.5	5.6	7.8	6.5	3.3	DRT
PASSPORT INS CO	ND	U (5)	--	--	--	--	N/A	--	--	--	--	Z
PATRIOT GENERAL INS CO	WI	B	26.0	25.3	0.0	0.2	10.0	N/A	5.4	10.0	4.9	DGT
PATRIOT INS CO	ME	C	125.6	50.3	48.0	1.1	9.6	9.4	8.8	6.8	3.1	T
PATRONS MUTUAL FIRE INS CO OF IN PA	PA	D+(1)	2.8	2.6	0.3	0.1	10.0	8.1	6.9	10.0	1.9	DFT
PATRONS MUTUAL INS CO OF CT	CT	C	50.5	21.7	9.9	0.0	9.8	6.0	6.0	6.7	3.5	DFRT
PATRONS OXFORD INS CO	ME	C	21.2	12.9	0.0	0.0	10.0	3.6	6.9	9.3	3.0	DFGT
PAWTUCKET INS CO	RI	U	--	--	--	--	N/A	--	--	--	--	Z
PCH MUTUAL INS CO INC RRG	VT	D+	6.8	3.1	2.8	0.1	3.3	7.0	3.9	7.6	2.1	DFGR
▲PEACE CHURCH RRG INC	VT	C-	23.6	15.7	3.2	0.1	10.0	9.4	7.7	9.1	3.0	DGRT
PEACHTREE CASUALTY INS CO	FL	D	20.3	4.5	8.3	-0.6	2.3	4.1	0.5	5.0	1.5	CDFG
PEAK P&C INS CORP	WI	B	48.0	39.2	0.0	0.2	10.0	N/A	5.8	7.0	4.0	RT
PEERLESS INDEMNITY INS CO	IL	C+	198.3	188.6	0.0	1.0	10.0	3.8	7.0	7.0	4.3	RT
PEERLESS INS CO	NH	B-	13,521.2	3,569.9	5,299.8	-23.5	7.6	4.8	6.3	6.1	3.9	RT
PEKIN INS CO	IL	B+	306.7	127.1	122.8	-1.8	10.0	8.3	5.0	6.6	5.0	T
PELEUS INS CO	VA	D+	94.3	51.0	0.0	0.1	10.0	N/A	6.8	10.0	2.6	FRT
▲PELICAN INS RRG	VT	C-	20.2	13.6	2.8	-0.2	7.9	6.0	3.8	8.3	3.0	FGRT
PEMCO MUTUAL INS CO	WA	B-	735.5	282.9	421.5	0.9	8.8	6.0	5.9	6.1	4.1	RT
PENINSULA INDEMNITY CO	MD	C	11.0	10.0	0.0	0.0	10.0	N/A	6.6	8.2	2.9	DGRT
PENINSULA INS CO	MD	C+	91.8	41.5	50.7	-0.5	9.0	5.8	4.1	6.3	3.9	T
PENN CHARTER MUTL INS CO	PA	C	15.5	12.3	0.0	0.1	7.3	6.1	6.9	10.0	3.0	DGT
PENN MILLERS INS CO	PA	C	98.5	41.9	0.0	0.9	10.0	6.8	2.2	6.8	3.7	FRT
PENN NATIONAL SECURITY INS CO	PA	B-	982.6	324.4	336.1	1.7	9.2	6.3	6.9	6.5	4.4	T
PENN RESERVE INS CO LTD	PA	D	2.0	1.8	0.6	0.1	10.0	N/A	5.1	9.1	1.5	DGT
PENN-AMERICA INS CO	PA	C+	133.1	79.5	26.9	-0.3	7.2	6.3	3.6	6.9	4.0	RT
PENN-PATRIOT INS CO	VA	C	50.1	18.4	17.6	-0.2	6.3	5.8	2.8	9.1	3.2	DGRT
PENN-STAR INS CO	PA	C+	125.2	46.5	43.1	-0.3	8.1	6.7	4.2	6.4	4.5	RT
PENNSYLVANIA INS CO	IA	C	66.0	46.0	18.2	1.3	9.3	7.8	8.7	9.2	3.9	DRT
PENNSYLVANIA LUMBERMENS MUTUAL INS	PA	B	472.2	123.3	139.2	4.6	7.4	4.7	5.4	6.1	4.2	RT
PENNSYLVANIA MANUFACTURERS ASN INS	PA	C	945.8	284.3	159.1	0.7	8.2	2.8	6.5	6.7	3.7	ART
PENNSYLVANIA MANUFACTURERS IND CO	PA	C	218.6	74.9	53.0	-0.1	7.8	2.8	4.2	6.7	3.8	ART
PENNSYLVANIA NTL MUTUAL CAS INS CO	PA	B-	1,298.3	620.5	336.1	5.2	7.8	6.2	6.9	6.7	4.5	RT
PENNSYLVANIA PHYSICIANS RECIP INS	PA	U	--	--	--	--	N/A	--	--	--	--	Z
PEOPLES TRUST INS CO	FL	D	226.9	48.5	112.3	-3.5	3.1	4.4	1.6	0.1	2.1	FLT
PERMANENT GEN ASR CORP OF OHIO	OH	C-	249.0	90.3	142.9	-2.4	7.8	5.4	3.7	4.5	3.2	FLRT
PERMANENT GENERAL ASR CORP	OH	C-	455.8	129.0	331.5	-4.3	7.3	4.8	3.5	4.6	3.0	GLRT
PERSONAL SERVICE INS CO	PA	D+(1)	57.9	4.1	13.9	-4.3	1.2	1.3	0.7	0.9	2.4	CDFG
▲PETROLEUM CAS CO	TX	B-	34.7	25.0	4.9	1.1	5.4	5.8	6.9	10.0	4.9	CDGT
PETROLEUM MARKETERS MGMT INS CO	IA	C	34.5	24.1	4.4	0.1	7.5	6.4	4.3	7.5	4.0	DGT

See Page 27 for explanation of footnotes and
Page 28 for explanation of stability factors.
Arrows denote recent upgrades ▲ or downgrades ▼   (see Section VII for explanations)

102

www.weissratings.com

RISK ADJ. RATIO #1	CAPITAL RATIO #2	PREMIUM TO SURPLUS (%)	RESV. TO SURPLUS (%)	RESV. DEVELOP. 1 YEAR (%)	RESV. DEVELOP. 2 YEAR (%)	LOSS RATIO (%)	EXP. RATIO (%)	COMB RATIO (%)	CASH FROM UNDER-WRITING (%)	NET PREMIUM GROWTH (%)	INVEST. IN AFFIL (%)	INSURANCE COMPANY NAME
13.3	7.6	N/A	N/A	N/A	N/A	N/A	N/A	N/A	N/A	0.0	0.0	PALISADES P&C INS CO
0.8	0.7	142.3	135.0	-6.1	-8.5	76.9	30.0	106.9	95.9	2.1	33.7	PALISADES SAFETY & INS ASSOC
0.5	0.3	241.0	412.1	-48.1	N/A	90.2	6.8	97.0	727.0	5.7	0.0	PALLADIUM RRG INC
90.8	45.4	N/A	N/A	N/A	N/A	N/A	N/A	N/A	N/A	0.0	0.0	PALMETTO CASUALTY INS CO
0.3	0.3	208.1	27.3	-9.8	-12.6	15.7	84.2	99.9	90.2	51.7	0.0	PALMETTO SURETY CORP
0.8	0.5	60.0	5.0	-0.4	N/A	22.5	69.2	91.7	123.5	-1.2	0.0	PALOMAR SPECIALTY INS CO
2.4	1.9	107.0	12.6	3.2	-15.1	60.2	39.3	99.5	97.8	0.8	0.0	PANHANDLE FARMERS MULT INS CO
0.2	0.2	551.0	210.3	-3.8	4.2	76.1	36.9	113.0	134.7	85.0	0.0	PARAMOUNT INS CO
3.0	1.9	37.9	59.8	-2.8	-5.0	47.7	25.6	73.3	155.2	30.8	0.0	PARATRANSIT INS CO A MUTUAL RRG
0.0	0.0	343.8	590.5	245.1	663.0	148.6	-33.4	115.2	52.3	5.8	0.0	PARK INS CO
2.5	1.6	81.2	161.8	-12.4	-22.1	67.2	31.7	98.9	105.1	-1.1	3.0 ●	PARTNER REINSURANCE CO OF THE US
10.1	6.1	27.7	22.1	-0.9	-2.5	85.8	22.5	108.3	92.0	-0.5	0.0	PARTNERRE AMERICA INS CO
6.3	2.5	N/A	51.7	-1.2	-3.3	-221.7	999 +	999 +	-83.7	-84.5	0.0	PARTNERRE INS CO OF NY
2.3	1.5	115.1	117.5	-0.4	-5.2	64.2	32.8	97.0	97.3	1.6	0.0	PARTNERS MUTUAL INS CO
N/A	N/A	--	--	--	--	--	--	--	--	--	--	PASSPORT INS CO
86.1	49.7	N/A	N/A	N/A	N/A	N/A	N/A	N/A	88.9	0.0	0.0	PATRIOT GENERAL INS CO
5.4	3.8	97.1	70.0	-9.2	-14.4	63.3	29.4	92.7	121.3	3.8	0.0	PATRIOT INS CO
11.3	8.1	12.0	3.5	-4.4	-6.5	3.9	74.7	78.6	93.2	-14.3	0.0	PATRONS MUTUAL FIRE INS CO OF IN
4.6	2.7	45.8	42.2	0.6	0.5	73.1	33.4	106.5	75.6	1.6	0.0	PATRONS MUTUAL INS CO OF CT
6.0	5.4	N/A	N/A	N/A	N/A	N/A	N/A	N/A	318.4	0.0	0.0	PATRONS OXFORD INS CO
N/A	N/A	--	--	--	--	--	--	--	--	--	--	PAWTUCKET INS CO
1.1	0.8	91.7	84.2	-5.9	5.9	46.7	37.0	83.7	61.2	23.5	0.0	PCH MUTUAL INS CO INC RRG
6.4	4.3	20.4	31.1	-3.4	-3.9	39.5	16.2	55.7	188.4	8.7	0.0	PEACE CHURCH RRG INC
0.4	0.3	162.7	80.3	22.3	10.4	87.6	61.4	149.0	55.5	-38.9	0.0	PEACHTREE CASUALTY INS CO
17.7	15.9	N/A	N/A	N/A	N/A	N/A	N/A	N/A	79.9	0.0	0.0	PEAK P&C INS CORP
84.1	52.7	N/A	N/A	N/A	N/A	N/A	N/A	N/A	N/A	0.0	0.0	PEERLESS INDEMNITY INS CO
2.1	1.5	149.8	194.8	1.3	-0.6	69.8	32.0	101.8	100.7	3.4	5.9 ●	PEERLESS INS CO
4.4	3.1	95.8	77.0	0.8	-0.8	77.7	28.9	106.6	101.5	2.2	3.3 ●	PEKIN INS CO
8.4	5.9	N/A	N/A	N/A	N/A	N/A	N/A	N/A	-7.1	0.0	0.0	PELEUS INS CO
2.1	1.5	20.1	15.3	1.8	3.4	10.3	46.2	56.5	35.7	214.8	0.0	PELICAN INS RRG
2.7	2.2	149.5	74.3	7.0	3.6	80.7	21.6	102.3	93.7	6.3	0.4 ●	PEMCO MUTUAL INS CO
21.7	19.5	N/A	N/A	N/A	N/A	N/A	N/A	N/A	999 +	0.0	0.0	PENINSULA INDEMNITY CO
3.0	2.3	120.7	51.0	1.9	1.8	73.1	28.0	101.1	96.3	9.5	14.3	PENINSULA INS CO
2.0	1.2	0.4	0.3	-0.1	0.3	39.1	50.1	89.2	98.3	-0.1	0.0	PENN CHARTER MUTL INS CO
6.1	5.5	N/A	50.1	-2.7	-4.0	N/A	N/A	N/A	-12.0	0.0	0.0	PENN MILLERS INS CO
3.7	2.6	105.0	107.1	-0.3	-3.8	64.2	34.0	98.2	103.8	1.6	0.0 ●	PENN NATIONAL SECURITY INS CO
6.2	4.0	37.7	8.1	N/A	N/A	84.9	16.0	100.9	105.3	363.7	0.0	PENN RESERVE INS CO LTD
1.2	1.1	33.7	33.7	-2.0	-4.0	67.1	39.6	106.7	98.8	27.2	60.8	PENN-AMERICA INS CO
1.2	0.7	94.6	101.5	-5.6	-11.3	68.1	39.2	107.3	-148.9	821.3	0.0	PENN-PATRIOT INS CO
2.7	1.7	92.5	92.5	-5.7	-10.8	67.1	39.6	106.7	107.9	-11.1	0.0	PENN-STAR INS CO
3.1	2.5	40.8	38.9	2.5	-0.7	43.9	28.7	72.6	200.4	-4.6	0.0	PENNSYLVANIA INS CO
2.4	1.3	116.9	132.6	4.2	-1.2	64.3	33.2	97.5	100.8	-10.6	0.0	PENNSYLVANIA LUMBERMENS MUTUAL
2.4	1.6	56.1	100.0	4.9	10.1	78.6	25.0	103.6	111.1	18.1	0.0 ●	PENNSYLVANIA MANUFACTURERS ASN
2.0	1.4	70.8	126.3	5.9	12.5	78.6	24.8	103.4	96.4	18.1	0.0	PENNSYLVANIA MANUFACTURERS IND
1.7	1.5	54.9	56.1	-0.1	-2.0	64.2	33.1	97.3	101.7	1.6	34.5 ●	PENNSYLVANIA NTL MUTUAL CAS INS
N/A	N/A	--	--	--	--	--	--	--	--	--	--	PENNSYLVANIA PHYSICIANS RECIP INS
0.6	0.4	216.3	149.2	2.7	-16.2	112.8	29.1	141.9	82.7	-14.5	0.0	PEOPLES TRUST INS CO
1.5	1.4	153.9	56.5	5.6	1.2	82.9	24.6	107.5	82.9	26.2	27.6	PERMANENT GEN ASR CORP OF OHIO
1.2	1.1	251.2	92.3	9.2	1.9	82.9	24.6	107.5	100.8	26.2	0.8	PERMANENT GENERAL ASR CORP
0.3	0.2	341.2	257.4	33.2	48.9	108.7	26.7	135.4	78.9	30.9	0.0	PERSONAL SERVICE INS CO
1.2	0.8	20.4	40.1	0.2	3.0	24.1	27.4	51.5	175.1	-12.8	0.0	PETROLEUM CAS CO
2.1	1.3	18.9	21.1	-0.7	-0.7	27.3	43.2	70.5	167.0	20.2	4.0	PETROLEUM MARKETERS MGMT INS CO

999 + Denotes number greater than 999.9%
999 - Denotes number less than -999.99%
● Bullets denote a more detailed analysis is available in Section II.

INSURANCE COMPANY NAME	DOM. STATE	RATING	TOTAL ASSETS ($MIL)	CAPITAL & SURPLUS ($MIL)	ANNUAL NET PREMIUM ($MIL)	NET INCOME ($MIL)	CAPITAL-IZATION INDEX (PTS)	RESERVE ADQ INDEX (PTS)	PROFIT-ABILITY INDEX (PTS)	LIQUIDITY INDEX (PTS)	STAB. INDEX (PTS)	STABILITY FACTORS
PFD PHYSICIANS MED RRG A MUTL	MO	B	35.4	5.5	26.8	2.7	10.0	9.3	5.1	10.0	4.1	RT
PHARMACISTS MUTUAL INS CO	IA	B	292.9	120.0	107.0	4.2	9.0	7.0	8.8	6.6	4.2	RT
PHENIX MUTUAL FIRE INS CO	NH	B-	67.4	24.9	21.4	0.0	8.2	7.9	6.6	6.4	3.9	FT
PHILADELPHIA CBSP FOR INS OF HOUSES	PA	B-	340.6	261.2	36.8	2.6	7.2	7.3	6.6	6.7	4.1	FRT
PHILADELPHIA CONTRIBUTIONSHIP INS CO	PA	B-	225.1	126.2	55.3	3.3	8.6	6.3	6.9	6.7	4.1	RT
PHILADELPHIA INDEMNITY INS CO	PA	B-	8,309.9	2,354.2	2,872.8	82.4	8.3	7.7	7.4	6.7	4.6	RT
PHILADELPHIA REINS CORP	PA	U	--	--	--	--	N/A	--	--	--	--	Z
▼PHOEBE RECIPROCAL RRG	SC	E	4.6	3.0	0.4	0.0	9.0	9.3	7.0	10.0	0.0	DG
PHOENIX FUND INC	NC	F (5)	0.0	0.0	25.2	0.0	0.0	0.3	5.2	5.9	0.0	CDT
PHOENIX INS CO	CT	B	4,264.0	1,762.3	1,088.9	23.0	7.7	8.1	7.4	6.8	5.0	T
PHYSICIANS CASUALTY RRG INC	AL	E	13.9	3.5	7.7	0.3	2.3	7.1	6.9	8.6	0.1	DGT
PHYSICIANS IND RRG INC	NV	D	6.1	1.8	2.5	0.1	3.8	9.9	1.7	8.1	1.5	DFGT
PHYSICIANS INS A MUTL CO	WA	B-	541.3	240.5	78.2	4.2	10.0	9.4	6.8	7.5	4.1	RT
PHYSICIANS INS CO	FL	D+	13.7	6.1	4.9	-0.2	3.3	4.0	1.6	7.0	2.7	DGRT
PHYSICIANS INS EXCHANGE RESOURCE	VT	D- (1)	3.9	1.5	1.2	-0.6	1.9	5.1	1.8	7.6	1.0	DFT
▼PHYSICIANS INS MUTUAL	MO	E-	3.9	0.6	0.9	-0.4	4.6	10.0	1.5	6.4	0.1	DFGT
PHYSICIANS INS PROGRAM	PA	C	26.6	11.8	3.5	-0.1	5.6	6.8	5.0	9.6	4.0	DFGR
PHYSICIANS PROACTIVE PROTECTION INC	SC	D+	91.1	26.5	8.0	1.3	3.2	5.9	6.0	7.1	2.0	CDFR
PHYSICIANS PROFESSIONAL LIABILTY RRG	VT	C+	37.8	18.9	3.8	0.2	9.7	9.5	4.5	7.8	4.2	DFGR
PHYSICIANS RECIPROCAL INSURERS	NY	E-	1,189.6	-348.3	279.5	2.3	0.0	10.0	0.9	7.0	0.0	CFRT
PHYSICIANS REIMBURSEMENT FUND RRG	VT	C	31.3	11.1	2.2	-0.2	4.0	10.0	3.8	6.9	3.2	CDFG
PHYSICIANS SPECIALTY LTD RRG	SC	D+	11.5	5.7	0.4	0.0	6.1	9.6	4.4	6.9	2.4	DFGR
PHYSICIANS STANDARD INS CO	KS	D+	4.1	3.4	0.2	-0.1	10.0	4.9	1.7	10.0	2.0	DFGT
PIA PROFESSIONAL LIABILITY INS RRG	MT	D (3)	2.1	1.0	0.6	-0.3	4.4	5.7	1.7	8.4	1.2	DGT
PIEDMONT MUTUAL INS CO	NC	D+	4.8	3.2	1.8	0.0	7.6	8.0	4.3	7.0	2.0	DGRT
PIH INS CO A RECIP RRG	HI	B-	21.9	12.7	4.5	0.1	8.0	9.4	8.8	7.2	3.5	DGT
PILGRIM INS CO	MA	C	90.4	18.4	31.7	0.1	7.0	6.0	6.6	6.3	3.3	DT
PINNACLEPOINT INS CO	WV	C+	80.8	11.6	7.2	0.2	5.6	5.0	5.6	7.9	3.1	DT
PIONEER SPECIALTY INS CO	MN	C	67.7	27.7	27.9	0.3	9.0	8.3	8.7	6.4	3.4	RT
PIONEER STATE MUTUAL INS CO	MI	B	561.4	331.1	196.7	3.4	10.0	8.7	8.8	6.9	4.7	T
PLANS LIABILITY INS CO	OH	C	73.3	32.6	3.0	-0.3	2.0	4.6	1.6	7.2	2.4	CDFT
PLATEAU CASUALTY INS CO	TN	C+	43.6	21.0	21.7	0.6	7.4	7.4	6.5	6.7	4.4	DRT
▼PLATINUM TRANSPORT INS RRG INC	HI	D-	5.5	1.1	3.8	-0.1	3.5	3.6	2.2	8.5	0.7	DGT
PLATTE RIVER INS CO	NE	C	142.2	44.7	37.5	0.5	8.0	4.2	5.1	7.3	3.6	RT
PLAZA INS CO	IA	C+	78.3	27.4	0.0	0.1	10.0	N/A	6.6	6.9	3.7	RT
PLICO INC	OK	C	111.8	76.2	5.4	0.6	10.0	10.0	7.9	9.0	3.8	FRT
PLYMOUTH ROCK ASR CORP	MA	B-	605.4	188.0	365.1	1.6	7.5	6.1	6.1	4.2	4.0	LRT
PMI INS CO	AZ	F	115.2	59.9	22.9	3.0	8.7	4.8	5.7	6.1	0.0	DFGR
PMI MORTGAGE INS CO	AZ	F	926.7	-1,394.6	165.4	60.0	0.0	4.6	0.9	7.0	0.0	CDFR
PODIATRY INS CO OF AM	IL	C+	297.8	121.7	44.9	1.8	8.4	9.3	6.4	7.8	4.4	AT
POINT GUARD INS CO	PR	C-	53.1	15.2	49.7	-0.3	3.9	3.9	4.4	2.9	3.0	CDGL
POLICYHOLDERS MUTUAL INS CO	WI	U	--	--	--	--	N/A	--	--	--	--	Z
PONCE DE LEON LTC RRG INC	FL	D+	5.7	4.5	0.2	0.0	8.7	6.6	1.7	6.7	2.3	DFGR
POSITIVE PHYSICIANS INS	PA	C	58.7	17.1	9.5	0.1	4.8	9.8	8.1	7.3	3.7	DRT
POTOMAC INS CO	PA	U	--	--	--	--	N/A	--	--	--	--	Z
PRAETORIAN INS CO	PA	C	515.4	223.4	61.1	1.4	8.4	4.4	2.5	6.5	4.1	FRT
PRE-PAID LEGAL CAS INC	OK	C	18.6	15.8	46.4	1.5	5.7	7.2	6.1	1.9	2.8	DGLT
PREFERRED AUTO INS CO	TN	D+	9.9	3.3	2.9	0.1	8.3	9.4	5.9	9.0	2.1	DGRT
PREFERRED CONTRACTORS INS CO RRG	MT	E	96.7	11.3	9.1	0.1	0.0	0.5	2.4	3.7	0.1	CDLR
PREFERRED EMPLOYERS INS CO	CA	C	103.5	46.2	0.0	0.2	10.0	3.8	7.3	10.0	4.2	RT
PREFERRED MUTUAL INS CO	NY	B	531.3	234.0	213.2	-2.5	9.8	8.7	6.2	6.7	4.3	RT
PREFERRED PROFESSIONAL INS CO	NE	B	323.4	173.1	49.6	1.0	10.0	9.4	7.1	8.1	4.7	RT

See Page 27 for explanation of footnotes and Page 28 for explanation of stability factors.

Arrows denote recent upgrades ▲ or downgrades ▼ (see Section VII for explanations)

www.weissratings.com

RISK ADJ. CAPITAL RATIO #1	CAPITAL RATIO #2	PREMIUM TO SURPLUS (%)	RESV. TO SURPLUS (%)	RESV. DEVELOP. 1 YEAR (%)	RESV. DEVELOP. 2 YEAR (%)	LOSS RATIO (%)	EXP. RATIO (%)	COMB RATIO (%)	CASH FROM UNDER-WRITING (%)	NET PREMIUM GROWTH (%)	INVEST. IN AFFIL (%)	INSURANCE COMPANY NAME
1.9	1.0	20.5	50.0	-6.0	-8.1	43.4	35.0	78.4	135.1	-3.7	0.0	PFD PHYSICIANS MED RRG A MUTL
3.4	2.3	92.8	86.8	-4.6	-8.6	60.6	32.4	93.0	110.2	16.2	4.4	PHARMACISTS MUTUAL INS CO
2.8	1.9	85.6	63.2	-0.7	-1.7	64.1	37.8	101.9	93.6	-0.4	0.0	PHENIX MUTUAL FIRE INS CO
1.3	1.1	14.6	9.9	-0.4	-0.3	71.6	36.1	107.7	91.5	0.6	51.8 •	PHILADELPHIA CBSP FOR INS OF
3.3	2.0	45.5	28.7	-1.0	1.7	67.4	27.1	94.5	106.0	0.6	0.0	PHILADELPHIA CONTRIBUTIONSHIP INS
2.5	1.8	126.5	169.8	-2.2	-1.5	60.8	30.2	91.0	129.2	6.6	0.0 •	PHILADELPHIA INDEMNITY INS CO
N/A	N/A	--	--	--	--	--	--	--	--	--	--	PHILADELPHIA REINS CORP
3.1	1.9	7.2	26.9	-3.5	-11.1	18.7	39.5	58.2	158.5	-6.9	0.0	PHOEBE RECIPROCAL RRG
0.1	0.1	378.0	273.0	49.1	32.3	71.3	27.2	98.5	133.5	0.0	0.0	PHOENIX FUND INC
1.7	1.5	63.4	105.1	-1.3	-3.2	63.4	30.0	93.4	110.6	4.7	26.1 •	PHOENIX INS CO
0.8	0.6	245.0	169.8	17.0	-2.0	25.9	48.2	74.1	187.2	41.6	0.0	PHYSICIANS CASUALTY RRG INC
1.0	0.8	141.6	127.3	-14.9	-21.0	37.7	47.3	85.0	21.8	62.7	0.0	PHYSICIANS IND RRG INC
4.0	3.0	33.7	87.7	-9.4	-17.8	82.2	20.4	102.6	103.0	2.5	2.9 •	PHYSICIANS INS A MUTL CO
0.7	0.6	77.1	66.6	3.7	-1.3	79.7	44.6	124.3	190.7	12.9	0.0	PHYSICIANS INS CO
0.7	0.5	81.1	93.6	36.3	6.0	68.2	80.3	148.5	73.0	12.7	0.0	PHYSICIANS INS EXCHANGE RESOURCE
0.5	0.4	88.4	295.5	-35.4	-31.3	116.2	19.1	135.3	70.2	-3.6	0.0	PHYSICIANS INS MUTUAL
1.3	0.8	28.8	101.9	-20.9	-14.7	5.4	48.9	54.3	127.3	-26.9	0.0	PHYSICIANS INS PROGRAM
0.6	0.5	30.3	137.5	5.1	-9.3	104.7	23.5	128.2	50.3	-11.3	0.0	PHYSICIANS PROACTIVE PROTECTION
3.6	3.0	20.3	47.6	-10.7	-16.9	44.4	68.0	112.4	57.3	-7.5	0.0	PHYSICIANS PROFESSIONAL LIABILTY
-0.4	-0.3	-79.0	-433.5	-146.8	-243.1	148.1	31.5	179.6	80.0	-2.0	0.0	PHYSICIANS RECIPROCAL INSURERS
0.7	0.6	20.1	159.3	-46.1	-73.0	56.2	74.7	130.9	66.3	-12.3	0.0	PHYSICIANS REIMBURSEMENT FUND
1.4	1.0	6.9	81.0	-1.7	-24.4	83.4	190.4	273.8	32.9	86.5	0.0	PHYSICIANS SPECIALTY LTD RRG
11.4	10.2	4.4	15.8	-0.3	-1.6	98.5	50.5	149.0	51.3	-68.3	0.0	PHYSICIANS STANDARD INS CO
0.7	0.4	43.4	52.1	-15.8	-12.7	84.5	69.2	153.7	118.4	24.0	0.0	PIA PROFESSIONAL LIABILITY INS RRG
2.4	1.7	56.9	7.6	-2.7	-2.9	39.8	46.8	86.6	111.8	-1.6	0.2	PIEDMONT MUTUAL INS CO
2.8	1.7	37.1	37.6	0.9	-26.3	69.7	13.2	82.9	142.4	7.9	0.0	PIH INS CO A RECIP RRG
1.3	1.0	171.5	87.8	-5.2	-4.3	76.3	23.2	99.5	110.8	7.7	0.0	PILGRIM INS CO
1.3	0.9	62.7	197.2	-12.6	-29.1	69.6	26.3	95.9	113.1	37.9	0.0	PINNACLEPOINT INS CO
3.4	2.5	102.7	78.9	-3.3	-7.2	65.5	27.1	92.6	112.4	2.5	0.0	PIONEER SPECIALTY INS CO
5.0	3.1	60.8	29.3	-5.1	-7.1	60.1	25.3	85.4	124.8	7.3	0.0 •	PIONEER STATE MUTUAL INS CO
0.4	0.3	9.4	104.7	-0.2	-0.1	156.8	87.3	244.1	32.1	-23.2	0.0	PLANS LIABILITY INS CO
1.5	1.3	107.8	9.5	1.8	-0.5	50.7	41.0	91.7	127.1	29.7	29.6	PLATEAU CASUALTY INS CO
0.5	0.3	235.3	60.0	-2.2	N/A	64.4	25.1	89.5	239.5	996.0	0.0	PLATINUM TRANSPORT INS RRG INC
3.1	1.8	86.5	79.0	N/A	0.7	54.5	44.8	99.3	108.5	13.5	0.0	PLATTE RIVER INS CO
4.0	3.6	N/A	N/A	N/A	N/A	N/A	N/A	N/A	999 +	0.0	0.0	PLAZA INS CO
6.4	4.0	7.4	20.8	-0.7	-70.7	82.7	29.4	112.1	4.2	113.3	0.7	PLICO INC
1.7	1.3	195.7	100.2	-5.8	-5.0	76.3	22.9	99.2	110.0	7.7	0.0	PLYMOUTH ROCK ASR CORP
2.8	2.1	38.4	39.3	7.1	11.3	33.7	34.3	68.0	51.5	41.4	0.0	PMI INS CO
-1.1	-0.8	-11.5	-148.2	6.1	2.1	54.7	-0.4	54.3	47.7	-18.3	7.0	PMI MORTGAGE INS CO
3.1	2.2	37.4	112.0	-3.8	-9.7	84.3	13.0	97.3	96.9	-3.6	0.0	PODIATRY INS CO OF AM
0.5	0.5	287.9	30.8	0.5	16.7	89.7	9.6	99.3	109.3	7.4	0.0	POINT GUARD INS CO
N/A	N/A	--	--	--	--	--	--	--	--	--	--	POLICYHOLDERS MUTUAL INS CO
4.7	3.5	4.8	33.6	-10.7	1.9	47.9	173.4	221.3	9.6	-81.2	0.0	PONCE DE LEON LTC RRG INC
1.0	0.8	54.2	170.2	-29.0	-44.3	44.8	48.2	93.0	106.2	-22.5	0.0	POSITIVE PHYSICIANS INS
N/A	N/A	--	--	--	--	--	--	--	--	--	--	POTOMAC INS CO
4.2	2.9	27.0	52.5	-7.0	-4.7	58.8	89.2	148.0	43.3	-79.7	0.0 •	PRAETORIAN INS CO
1.0	0.8	285.2	0.5	0.1	-0.1	38.0	47.9	85.9	116.4	4.2	0.0	PRE-PAID LEGAL CAS INC
1.8	1.7	90.5	65.9	-5.5	-18.3	89.1	7.6	96.7	108.9	12.9	0.0	PREFERRED AUTO INS CO
0.1	0.0	90.2	584.5	-0.5	27.4	82.1	80.4	162.5	186.6	-69.4	0.0	PREFERRED CONTRACTORS INS CO
6.5	5.9	N/A	N/A	N/A	N/A	N/A	N/A	N/A	69.9	0.0	0.0	PREFERRED EMPLOYERS INS CO
4.8	3.0	90.9	60.9	-2.4	-4.3	60.4	33.0	93.4	105.9	4.3	0.0 •	PREFERRED MUTUAL INS CO
5.3	4.0	29.1	61.1	-12.5	-17.5	59.4	19.3	78.7	170.2	36.3	0.3	PREFERRED PROFESSIONAL INS CO

999 + Denotes number greater than 999.9%
999 - Denotes number less than -999.99%
• Bullets denote a more detailed analysis is available in Section II.

INSURANCE COMPANY NAME	DOM. STATE	RATING	TOTAL ASSETS ($MIL)	CAPITAL & SURPLUS ($MIL)	ANNUAL NET PREMIUM ($MIL)	NET INCOME ($MIL)	CAPITAL-IZATION INDEX (PTS)	RESERVE ADQ INDEX (PTS)	PROFIT-ABILITY INDEX (PTS)	LIQUIDITY INDEX (PTS)	STAB. INDEX (PTS)	STABILITY FACTORS
PREFERRED PROFESSIONAL RRG	DC	U	--	--	--	--	N/A	--	--	--	--	Z
▲PREMIER GROUP INS CO	TN	B-	68.1	35.4	15.6	0.9	9.4	8.6	8.9	7.0	5.0	DT
PREMIER INS CO OF MA	CT	B	255.2	236.2	-0.5	2.2	10.0	6.0	6.7	7.0	4.6	FT
PREMIER INS EXCHANGE RRG	VT	U (5)	--	--	--	--	N/A	--	--	--	--	Z
PREMIER PHYSICIANS INS CO	NV	E (2)	12.4	1.1	4.0	-1.5	1.2	4.2	0.3	4.7	0.1	CDFG
PREPARED INS CO	FL	C-	52.1	19.5	26.1	0.3	4.4	4.3	2.9	2.9	2.9	CDFL
▲PREVISOR INS CO	CO	C-	9.7	8.5	0.2	-0.1	10.0	3.6	3.5	10.0	2.2	DFGT
▲PRIME INS CO	IL	B-	91.1	43.3	30.3	1.2	7.4	5.9	8.9	7.0	5.0	T
PRIME P&C INS INC	IL	C+	33.0	12.4	8.5	-0.3	8.2	3.8	4.7	9.0	3.1	DGT
PRIMEONE INS CO	UT	D+	16.1	7.9	2.2	-0.1	6.6	7.0	1.6	6.2	2.2	DFGT
PRIMERO INS CO	NV	C	16.5	8.4	10.8	-0.3	7.6	8.4	3.6	5.7	4.0	DFGR
PRINCETON EXCESS & SURPLUS LINES INS	DE	C	150.7	60.4	0.0	2.2	10.0	N/A	8.6	7.0	3.6	RT
PRINCETON INS CO	NJ	C	695.0	483.8	29.1	3.3	10.0	9.3	7.4	10.0	3.8	RT
PRIORITY ONE INS CO	TX	C	18.6	10.8	6.2	0.5	8.1	4.5	2.0	6.3	2.9	DFGR
PRIVILEGE UNDERWRITERS RECIP EXCH	FL	B-	443.8	168.0	163.6	-0.3	7.3	5.7	2.8	6.9	4.3	FT
PROAIR RRG INC	NV	F (5)	0.5	0.0	0.2	0.0	7.1	6.5	0.1	2.6	0.0	LT
PROASSURANCE AMER MUTL A RRG	DC	C-	10.8	10.3	0.1	0.0	10.0	N/A	5.3	10.0	2.9	DGT
PROASSURANCE CASUALTY CO	MI	B-	1,100.5	417.9	157.3	14.4	9.1	9.6	3.2	7.3	4.5	ART
PROASSURANCE INDEMNTIY CO INC	AL	C	1,268.8	485.2	197.8	23.0	8.8	9.6	2.7	7.0	3.9	ART
PROASSURANCE SPECIALTY INS CO INC	AL	C	47.2	31.3	0.0	0.9	10.0	N/A	5.1	9.1	3.7	T
PROBUILDERS SPECIALTY INS CO RRG	DC	U	--	--	--	--	N/A	--	--	--	--	Z
PROCENTURY INS CO	MI	C-	89.3	79.9	0.0	0.4	10.0	1.9	4.9	6.1	3.3	FRT
PRODUCERS AGRICULTURE INS CO	TX	C	515.8	71.8	0.0	9.7	10.0	4.5	6.4	7.0	3.9	RT
PRODUCERS LLOYDS INS CO	TX	C	6.1	6.0	0.0	0.0	10.0	N/A	5.6	10.0	2.7	DFGR
PROFESSIONAL CASUALTY ASSN	PA	C-	41.3	13.4	9.8	-0.2	6.2	7.0	5.7	7.8	3.1	DFRT
PROFESSIONAL EXCHANGE ASR CO (A	HI	D	17.0	4.6	4.6	0.0	1.0	5.0	5.9	8.5	1.4	CDGT
PROFESSIONAL INS EXCHANGE MUTUAL	UT	D+	8.1	5.4	1.2	0.0	7.4	5.6	4.9	7.6	2.1	DFGT
PROFESSIONAL QUALITY LIABILITY INS	VT	U	--	--	--	--	N/A	--	--	--	--	Z
PROFESSIONAL SECURITY INS CO	AZ	C+	78.8	68.5	0.0	0.5	10.0	3.6	5.0	7.2	4.1	T
PROFESSIONAL SOLUTIONS INS CO	IA	C	22.8	7.9	3.2	-0.2	4.9	8.6	2.4	7.2	3.4	DGRT
PROFESSIONALS ADVOCATE INS CO	MD	B-	139.6	110.3	5.2	1.1	10.0	8.3	8.2	9.7	4.1	DT
PROFESSIONALS RRG INC	MT	D	4.7	1.2	0.4	0.0	7.8	6.7	2.0	7.0	1.1	DFGT
PROGRESSIVE ADVANCED INS CO	OH	C	476.8	203.8	328.2	4.2	8.5	7.5	8.7	2.0	3.7	FLRT
PROGRESSIVE AMERICAN INS CO	OH	C	511.0	213.0	229.2	3.3	10.0	6.1	8.4	6.1	3.8	FRT
PROGRESSIVE BAYSIDE INS CO	OH	C	132.6	38.8	114.6	1.6	7.4	6.3	8.9	5.5	3.5	RT
PROGRESSIVE CASUALTY INS CO	OH	B-	8,195.0	2,020.5	5,614.2	83.5	5.6	6.3	9.5	1.7	4.5	LRT
PROGRESSIVE CHOICE INS CO	OH	U	--	--	--	--	N/A	--	--	--	--	Z
PROGRESSIVE CLASSIC INS CO	WI	C	413.3	116.2	343.7	4.6	7.4	6.3	8.9	3.4	3.8	LRT
PROGRESSIVE COMMERCIAL CASUALTY	OH	U	--	--	--	--	N/A	--	--	--	--	Z
PROGRESSIVE COUNTY MUTUAL INS CO	TX	D+	578.4	5.0	0.0	0.0	1.9	N/A	3.9	2.4	2.4	CFLR
PROGRESSIVE DIRECT INS CO	OH	C+	7,217.2	2,204.7	6,358.9	101.4	7.3	7.7	8.9	1.7	4.1	LRT
PROGRESSIVE EXPRESS INS CO	OH	C	237.6	70.9	44.8	1.0	10.0	4.7	8.2	4.0	3.6	FLRT
PROGRESSIVE FREEDOM INS CO	NJ	C	6.6	5.2	0.2	0.0	10.0	6.4	7.8	9.3	3.2	DFGR
PROGRESSIVE GARDEN STATE INS CO	NJ	B	382.6	66.5	57.4	1.8	9.8	6.1	8.5	6.7	4.2	RT
PROGRESSIVE GULF INS CO	OH	C	283.1	77.8	229.2	3.9	7.4	6.3	3.5	4.3	3.6	LRT
PROGRESSIVE HAWAII INS CORP	OH	C	208.8	67.2	185.1	2.3	7.7	9.4	9.6	5.1	3.6	RT
PROGRESSIVE MARATHON INS CO	MI	C	552.3	175.2	492.3	6.9	7.3	7.7	8.9	1.9	3.8	LRT
PROGRESSIVE MAX INS CO	OH	C	528.9	170.2	492.3	6.9	7.2	7.7	8.9	2.6	3.8	LRT
PROGRESSIVE MICHIGAN INS CO	MI	C	562.3	162.2	458.3	6.7	7.4	6.3	8.9	2.9	3.8	LRT
PROGRESSIVE MOUNTAIN INS CO	OH	C	291.9	81.1	114.6	2.8	9.2	6.2	8.7	6.2	3.6	FRT
PROGRESSIVE NORTHERN INS CO	WI	C+	1,676.6	475.9	1,374.9	22.1	7.2	6.3	9.2	4.5	4.3	LRT
PROGRESSIVE NORTHWESTERN INS CO	OH	C+	1,622.9	473.5	1,374.9	21.5	7.2	6.3	9.1	4.6	4.3	LRT

See Page 27 for explanation of footnotes and Page 28 for explanation of stability factors.

Arrows denote recent upgrades ▲ or downgrades ▼   (see Section VII for explanations)

106   www.weissratings.com

RISK ADJ. RATIO #1	CAPITAL RATIO #2	PREMIUM TO SURPLUS (%)	RESV. TO SURPLUS (%)	RESV. DEVELOP. 1 YEAR (%)	RESV. DEVELOP. 2 YEAR (%)	LOSS RATIO (%)	EXP. RATIO (%)	COMB RATIO (%)	CASH FROM UNDER-WRITING (%)	NET PREMIUM GROWTH (%)	INVEST. IN AFFIL (%)	INSURANCE COMPANY NAME
N/A	N/A	--	--	--	--	--	--	--	--	--	--	PREFERRED PROFESSIONAL RRG
3.1	2.5	44.5	47.1	-5.9	-6.5	52.0	26.7	78.7	136.0	6.1	0.0	PREMIER GROUP INS CO
69.5	45.5	-0.2	9.5	-0.8	-2.9	46.3	999 +	999 +	24.8	-100.7	0.0 ●	PREMIER INS CO OF MA
N/A	N/A	--	--	--	--	--	--	--	--	--	--	PREMIER INS EXCHANGE RRG
0.2	0.1	223.5	218.6	28.8	27.4	90.1	60.0	150.1	61.4	-8.0	0.0	PREMIER PHYSICIANS INS CO
1.1	0.7	129.9	76.1	2.7	7.9	83.9	50.0	133.9	71.7	-38.4	0.0	PREPARED INS CO
5.2	4.6	3.0	1.8	-0.2	N/A	135.5	238.2	373.7	-18.2	982.3	0.0	PREVISOR INS CO
2.1	1.5	72.9	47.8	3.5	2.4	52.0	24.4	76.4	127.4	8.8	17.9	PRIME INS CO
2.1	1.5	68.8	44.4	9.0	15.9	82.4	15.7	98.1	210.1	117.9	0.0	PRIME P&C INS INC
2.2	1.3	27.5	37.7	-14.5	-18.5	17.6	85.7	103.3	100.5	-45.4	0.0	PRIMEONE INS CO
1.5	1.3	125.4	68.9	-1.7	-4.4	93.4	13.5	106.9	86.3	-4.2	0.0	PRIMERO INS CO
7.0	6.3	N/A	N/A	N/A	N/A	N/A	N/A	N/A	23.7	0.0	0.0	PRINCETON EXCESS & SURPLUS LINES
6.6	4.8	6.1	29.7	-1.9	-2.8	65.8	15.2	81.0	999 +	-6.2	0.0 ●	PRINCETON INS CO
2.9	1.9	60.5	39.7	7.3	11.1	80.0	42.2	122.2	73.5	-18.7	10.8	PRIORITY ONE INS CO
3.1	2.0	104.2	23.6	2.0	4.0	60.9	39.1	100.0	97.1	18.6	1.2	PRIVILEGE UNDERWRITERS RECIP
0.0	0.0	44.4	12.2	-1.6	-3.5	64.5	81.9	146.4	101.6	70.3	0.0	PROAIR RRG INC
43.9	39.5	0.6	0.3	N/A	N/A	103.4	-204.2	-100.8	-2.0	653.0	0.0	PROASSURANCE AMER MUTL A RRG
3.3	2.4	38.7	134.8	-11.2	-18.0	63.0	27.9	90.9	94.2	4.1	0.0 ●	PROASSURANCE CASUALTY CO
3.1	2.2	42.6	133.4	-10.1	-18.2	52.5	17.7	70.2	103.7	0.2	0.8 ●	PROASSURANCE INDEMNTIY CO INC
10.1	9.1	N/A	16.6	N/A	N/A	N/A	N/A	N/A	41.2	0.0	0.0	PROASSURANCE SPECIALTY INS CO INC
N/A	N/A	--	--	--	--	--	--	--	--	--	--	PROBUILDERS SPECIALTY INS CO RRG
33.3	30.0	N/A	N/A	N/A	N/A	N/A	N/A	N/A	-4.8	-100.0	0.0	PROCENTURY INS CO
5.1	2.7	N/A	N/A	N/A	N/A	N/A	N/A	N/A	86.2	-100.0	38.7	PRODUCERS AGRICULTURE INS CO
192.8	152.2	N/A	N/A	N/A	N/A	N/A	N/A	N/A	N/A	0.0	0.0	PRODUCERS LLOYDS INS CO
1.3	1.0	72.3	156.2	-9.3	-10.2	51.4	47.0	98.4	58.5	-21.2	0.0	PROFESSIONAL CASUALTY ASSN
0.4	0.2	105.9	144.3	9.4	-16.0	62.8	18.8	81.6	334.7	174.1	0.0	PROFESSIONAL EXCHANGE ASR CO (A
2.0	1.3	23.5	41.6	-0.6	-5.9	56.4	50.6	107.0	82.7	-4.1	0.0	PROFESSIONAL INS EXCHANGE MUTUAL
N/A	N/A	--	--	--	--	--	--	--	--	--	--	PROFESSIONAL QUALITY LIABILITY INS
15.4	7.6	N/A	N/A	N/A	N/A	N/A	N/A	N/A	265.7	-100.0	0.0	PROFESSIONAL SECURITY INS CO
0.9	0.6	40.3	101.9	-9.2	-4.8	85.5	23.2	108.7	109.3	-5.0	0.0	PROFESSIONAL SOLUTIONS INS CO
8.8	5.3	4.8	10.7	-1.6	-2.3	51.3	51.7	103.0	91.1	-4.6	0.0	PROFESSIONALS ADVOCATE INS CO
1.0	0.9	31.6	53.4	-4.3	-2.2	66.7	59.1	125.8	-68.1	60.5	0.0	PROFESSIONALS RRG INC
2.2	2.0	164.9	62.7	-0.4	-2.4	76.5	18.4	94.9	97.5	15.2	0.0 ●	PROGRESSIVE ADVANCED INS CO
3.9	3.4	109.5	44.9	0.1	-1.6	75.3	19.3	94.6	95.4	11.2	0.0 ●	PROGRESSIVE AMERICAN INS CO
1.4	1.2	310.5	127.3	0.1	-4.4	75.3	19.9	95.2	115.1	11.2	0.0	PROGRESSIVE BAYSIDE INS CO
1.1	0.9	308.7	126.5	0.1	-4.4	75.3	20.2	95.5	109.8	11.2	16.8 ●	PROGRESSIVE CASUALTY INS CO
N/A	N/A	--	--	--	--	--	--	--	--	--	--	PROGRESSIVE CHOICE INS CO
1.4	1.2	310.0	127.1	0.1	-4.4	75.3	19.6	94.9	112.5	11.2	0.0	PROGRESSIVE CLASSIC INS CO
N/A	N/A	--	--	--	--	--	--	--	--	--	--	PROGRESSIVE COMMERCIAL CASUALTY
0.4	0.2	N/A	N/A	N/A	N/A	N/A	N/A	N/A	-43.6	0.0	0.0	PROGRESSIVE COUNTY MUTUAL INS CO
1.4	1.2	307.9	117.0	-0.8	-4.3	76.5	18.6	95.1	113.3	15.2	0.0 ●	PROGRESSIVE DIRECT INS CO
6.9	4.5	64.0	44.2	1.6	N/A	76.4	18.3	94.7	69.3	12.0	0.0	PROGRESSIVE EXPRESS INS CO
9.3	8.3	3.2	4.9	-2.5	-0.6	33.0	14.5	47.5	58.4	-53.2	0.0	PROGRESSIVE FREEDOM INS CO
3.3	2.8	88.9	56.7	-2.8	-0.9	79.1	15.4	94.5	109.2	12.5	0.0	PROGRESSIVE GARDEN STATE INS CO
1.4	1.2	311.8	127.8	0.1	-3.8	75.3	18.9	94.2	110.6	11.2	0.0	PROGRESSIVE GULF INS CO
1.8	1.5	286.9	102.1	-0.5	-14.5	70.4	18.3	88.7	117.3	12.5	0.0	PROGRESSIVE HAWAII INS CORP
1.3	1.2	294.6	111.9	-0.7	-4.0	76.5	18.2	94.7	109.3	15.2	0.0	PROGRESSIVE MARATHON INS CO
1.2	1.1	303.6	115.3	-0.8	-4.3	76.5	18.6	95.1	111.2	15.2	0.0	PROGRESSIVE MAX INS CO
1.4	1.3	296.5	121.6	0.1	-4.1	75.3	19.6	94.9	111.6	11.2	0.0	PROGRESSIVE MICHIGAN INS CO
2.9	2.5	146.1	59.9	0.1	-2.3	75.3	17.2	92.5	80.6	11.2	0.0	PROGRESSIVE MOUNTAIN INS CO
1.4	1.2	310.8	127.4	0.1	-4.5	75.3	19.1	94.4	113.2	11.2	0.0 ●	PROGRESSIVE NORTHERN INS CO
1.4	1.2	311.3	127.6	0.1	-4.4	75.3	19.6	94.9	115.0	11.2	0.0 ●	PROGRESSIVE NORTHWESTERN INS CO

999 + Denotes number greater than 999.9%
999 - Denotes number less than -999.99%
● Bullets denote a more detailed analysis is available in Section II.

INSURANCE COMPANY NAME	DOM. STATE	RATING	TOTAL ASSETS ($MIL)	CAPITAL & SURPLUS ($MIL)	ANNUAL NET PREMIUM ($MIL)	NET INCOME ($MIL)	CAPITAL-IZATION INDEX (PTS)	RESERVE ADQ INDEX (PTS)	PROFIT-ABILITY INDEX (PTS)	LIQUIDITY INDEX (PTS)	STAB. INDEX (PTS)	STABILITY FACTORS
PROGRESSIVE PALOVERDE INS CO	IN	C	160.2	53.3	41.0	0.8	9.9	7.3	8.5	6.5	3.6	FRT
PROGRESSIVE PREFERRED INS CO	OH	C	839.7	233.9	687.5	10.9	7.3	6.3	9.1	3.0	3.9	LRT
PROGRESSIVE PREMIER INS CO OF IL	OH	C	251.8	74.3	164.1	2.2	7.6	7.6	8.9	5.1	4.0	RT
▲PROGRESSIVE PROPERTY INS CO	FL	B-	91.8	43.1	60.6	2.1	7.3	8.9	7.0	6.5	5.0	T
PROGRESSIVE SECURITY INS CO	LA	C	241.5	52.8	41.9	0.7	10.0	6.2	5.4	7.1	3.6	RT
PROGRESSIVE SELECT INS CO	OH	C	732.6	200.5	155.9	1.6	10.0	6.2	7.9	2.9	3.9	FLRT
PROGRESSIVE SOUTHEASTERN INS CO	IN	C	191.2	68.9	114.6	2.1	8.1	6.2	8.9	2.7	4.0	LRT
PROGRESSIVE SPECIALTY INS CO	OH	C	997.9	291.2	802.0	25.3	7.3	6.3	3.1	2.2	4.0	LRT
PROGRESSIVE UNIVERSAL INS CO	WI	C	405.9	136.6	328.2	5.3	7.6	7.6	8.9	1.6	3.8	LRT
PROGRESSIVE WEST INS CO	OH	C	127.7	32.5	27.7	0.5	9.7	5.9	4.1	7.0	3.5	RT
PROPERTY-OWNERS INS CO	IN	B+	289.0	129.5	119.5	5.0	7.4	5.6	8.7	6.3	5.1	T
PROSELECT INS CO	NE	C	158.2	24.0	0.0	0.2	10.0	N/A	5.2	5.6	4.2	DRT
PROSELECT NATIONAL INS CO INC	AZ	U	--	--	--	--	N/A	--	--	--	--	Z
PROTECTION MUTUAL INS CO	PA	U	--	--	--	--	N/A	--	--	--	--	Z
▲PROTECTIVE INS CO	IN	A-	799.3	403.3	255.7	16.3	7.2	8.2	7.3	6.8	6.9	T
PROTECTIVE P&C INS CO	MO	B-	383.6	173.4	61.8	5.6	10.0	6.3	7.9	7.0	4.4	RT
PROTECTIVE SPECIALTY INS CO	IN	B	67.1	60.2	1.4	0.2	10.0	4.2	5.8	9.5	5.1	DFT
PROTUCKET INSURANCE CO	RI	U	--	--	--	--	N/A	--	--	--	--	Z
PROVIDENCE MUTUAL FIRE INS CO	RI	B-	195.2	95.9	78.8	2.5	8.6	7.7	2.9	6.5	3.9	RT
PROVIDENCE PLANTATIONS INS CO	RI	U (2)	--	--	--	--	N/A	--	--	--	--	Z
PROVIDENCE WASHINGTON INS CO	RI	U	--	--	--	--	N/A	--	--	--	--	Z
PUBLIC SERVICE INS CO	IL	F (1)	295.1	28.3	46.6	-51.3	0.0	1.1	0.2	0.4	0.0	CDFL
PUBLIC UTILITY MUTUAL INS CO RRG	VT	E	7.8	6.1	0.9	0.0	10.0	9.3	8.6	8.8	0.0	DGR
PUERTO RICO MED DEFENSE MUT INS CO	PR	D	18.4	3.9	3.2	0.2	2.2	3.5	7.7	7.4	2.2	CDGT
PURE INS CO	FL	B	298.4	158.2	163.6	0.8	7.8	5.7	3.6	6.5	5.4	T
PYMATUNING MUTUAL FIRE INS CO	PA	D+(1)	3.3	3.2	0.0	0.0	10.0	N/A	3.3	10.0	2.0	DFT
QBE INS CORP	PA	B	2,405.5	786.7	846.9	15.5	8.0	4.9	4.6	6.6	4.8	RT
QBE REINS CORP	PA	B	1,232.9	904.2	147.5	-0.6	7.5	6.0	5.5	6.5	5.4	FT
QBE SEGUROS	PR	D	56.0	12.2	16.8	-0.4	2.3	4.6	2.9	7.0	2.0	CDFR
QBE SPECIALTY INS CO	ND	C-	412.8	127.7	75.5	-0.1	7.8	4.5	2.5	5.5	3.3	FRT
QUALITAS INS CO	CA	D	66.9	15.3	41.3	-0.8	1.9	3.6	2.8	6.9	2.2	CDGR
QUALITY CASUALTY INS CO	AL	U	--	--	--	--	N/A	--	--	--	--	Z
QUEEN CITY ASR INC	VT	U (2)	--	--	--	--	N/A	--	--	--	--	Z
QUINCY MUTUAL FIRE INS CO	MA	B	1,647.4	1,103.4	307.7	14.1	9.3	7.9	7.7	6.9	4.7	RT
R&Q REINS CO	PA	U	--	--	--	--	N/A	--	--	--	--	Z
RADIAN GUARANTY INC	PA	D+	3,818.7	1,167.7	628.7	94.2	7.5	4.6	5.1	6.8	2.4	ART
RADIAN GUARANTY REINS INC	PA	U	--	--	--	--	N/A	--	--	--	--	Z
RADIAN INS INC	PA	D+	22.6	19.3	0.7	0.2	10.0	9.0	1.9	10.0	2.4	DFGT
RADIAN INVESTOR SURETY INC	PA	U	--	--	--	--	N/A	--	--	--	--	Z
RADIAN MORTGAGE ASR INC	PA	U	--	--	--	--	N/A	--	--	--	--	Z
RADIAN MORTGAGE GUARANTY INC	PA	U	--	--	--	--	N/A	--	--	--	--	Z
RADIAN MORTGAGE INS INC	PA	U	--	--	--	--	N/A	--	--	--	--	Z
RADIAN REINS INC	PA	A-	684.6	321.0	104.3	14.3	8.1	3.6	8.6	7.2	5.7	GT
RADNOR SPECIALTY INS CO	NE	B	53.1	52.3	0.0	0.1	10.0	N/A	4.9	10.0	4.3	DGT
RAINIER INS CO	AZ	C+	25.6	21.1	2.5	-0.1	10.0	6.3	4.5	10.0	3.3	DGT
RAM MUTUAL INS CO	MN	B-	110.3	66.6	48.6	0.9	9.3	8.9	8.7	7.1	3.7	RT
RAMPART INS CO	NY	U	--	--	--	--	N/A	--	--	--	--	Z
RANCHERS & FARMERS MUTUAL INS CO	TX	D+	41.8	4.3	-0.5	0.1	5.0	5.8	9.0	7.5	2.2	DGRT
REAL LEGACY ASR CO INC	PR	D+	131.2	34.1	51.1	-2.2	5.6	6.8	1.6	6.6	2.5	RT
REAMSTOWN MUTUAL INS CO	PA	D+	8.3	3.4	5.9	-0.1	6.7	6.4	5.4	6.5	2.0	DGRT
RECREATION RRG INC	VT	D	4.1	3.1	0.8	0.1	9.1	N/A	5.9	10.0	2.0	DGT
RED CLAY RRG INC	SC	B-	9.6	4.5	0.8	-0.1	8.5	9.9	5.7	9.1	3.5	DGT

See Page 27 for explanation of footnotes and
Page 28 for explanation of stability factors.
Arrows denote recent upgrades ▲ or downgrades ▼   (see Section VII for explanations)

108

www.weissratings.com

RISK ADJ. RATIO #1	CAPITAL RATIO #2	PREMIUM TO SURPLUS (%)	RESV. TO SURPLUS (%)	RESV. 1 YEAR (%)	DEVELOP. 2 YEAR (%)	LOSS RATIO (%)	EXP. RATIO (%)	COMB RATIO (%)	CASH FROM UNDER-WRITING (%)	NET PREMIUM GROWTH (%)	INVEST. IN AFFIL (%)	INSURANCE COMPANY NAME
3.4	3.0	78.6	29.9	-0.2	-1.1	76.5	17.4	93.9	86.0	15.2	0.0	PROGRESSIVE PALOVERDE INS CO
1.4	1.2	310.1	127.1	0.1	-4.4	75.3	19.1	94.4	111.3	11.2	0.0 •	PROGRESSIVE PREFERRED INS CO
1.6	1.5	229.5	87.2	-0.6	-3.4	76.5	19.4	95.9	100.4	15.2	0.0	PROGRESSIVE PREMIER INS CO OF IL
2.2	1.6	144.8	41.8	-1.7	-8.0	67.0	35.9	102.9	103.2	23.3	0.0	PROGRESSIVE PROPERTY INS CO
4.6	3.8	80.5	28.8	1.2	-1.2	96.0	19.5	115.5	876.2	10.2	0.0	PROGRESSIVE SECURITY INS CO
4.2	3.7	78.5	29.2	0.3	-0.8	78.7	16.9	95.6	86.1	14.7	0.0 •	PROGRESSIVE SELECT INS CO
1.8	1.5	172.2	70.6	0.1	-2.5	75.3	16.5	91.8	102.6	11.2	0.0	PROGRESSIVE SOUTHEASTERN INS CO
1.4	1.2	304.5	124.8	0.1	-3.2	75.3	18.8	94.1	110.9	11.2	0.0 •	PROGRESSIVE SPECIALTY INS CO
1.5	1.4	251.3	95.5	-0.6	-3.3	76.5	16.7	93.2	106.8	15.2	0.0	PROGRESSIVE UNIVERSAL INS CO
3.2	2.7	87.0	36.6	1.5	0.9	77.2	20.3	97.5	97.1	-7.9	0.0	PROGRESSIVE WEST INS CO
2.0	1.2	96.3	45.2	-1.6	0.9	56.5	31.7	88.2	139.6	51.6	0.0 •	PROPERTY-OWNERS INS CO
2.5	2.3	N/A	N/A	N/A	N/A	N/A	N/A	N/A	148.5	0.0	0.0	PROSELECT INS CO
N/A	N/A	--	--	--	--	--	--	--	--	--	--	PROSELECT NATIONAL INS CO INC
N/A	N/A	--	--	--	--	--	--	--	--	--	--	PROTECTION MUTUAL INS CO
1.5	1.2	64.3	75.8	2.5	-0.4	65.7	31.0	96.7	111.1	9.6	26.1 •	PROTECTIVE INS CO
7.7	4.8	36.6	7.6	-2.0	-3.6	65.5	19.9	85.4	118.0	-5.0	0.0	PROTECTIVE P&C INS CO
5.7	4.0	2.3	10.3	3.2	4.1	65.4	39.6	105.0	39.0	36.4	0.0	PROTECTIVE SPECIALTY INS CO
N/A	N/A	--	--	--	--	--	--	--	--	--	--	PROTUCKET INSURANCE CO
3.3	2.1	85.0	51.7	-3.0	-4.3	64.5	38.5	103.0	98.4	7.4	0.7	PROVIDENCE MUTUAL FIRE INS CO
N/A	N/A	--	--	--	--	--	--	--	--	--	--	PROVIDENCE PLANTATIONS INS CO
N/A	N/A	--	--	--	--	--	--	--	--	--	--	PROVIDENCE WASHINGTON INS CO
0.1	0.0	164.9	999 +	32.2	53.8	95.5	133.2	228.7	50.6	-53.4	6.2	PUBLIC SERVICE INS CO
7.9	5.1	15.6	12.9	-5.3	-8.9	16.4	50.6	67.0	185.7	6.3	0.0	PUBLIC UTILITY MUTUAL INS CO RRG
0.8	0.5	85.9	250.0	N/A	-0.1	68.5	39.0	107.5	149.3	-49.6	0.0	PUERTO RICO MED DEFENSE MUT INS
2.9	1.8	105.5	23.9	1.3	2.0	60.6	38.9	99.5	113.4	18.6	1.6	PURE INS CO
42.9	40.4	0.4	N/A	N/A	N/A	163.8	374.4	538.2	15.4	-12.6	0.0	PYMATUNING MUTUAL FIRE INS CO
2.5	1.7	113.1	96.7	-14.2	-11.1	58.8	34.3	93.1	127.8	41.9	9.6 •	QBE INS CORP
1.4	1.3	17.1	16.7	-2.6	-1.8	58.8	38.5	97.3	91.9	-21.0	71.4 •	QBE REINS CORP
0.5	0.3	119.6	66.3	-39.6	-9.0	37.7	82.2	119.9	70.4	-49.7	0.0	QBE SEGUROS
2.9	1.9	60.2	95.0	-9.3	-6.3	58.8	63.0	121.8	50.8	-73.8	0.0	QBE SPECIALTY INS CO
0.6	0.4	264.8	103.8	6.9	0.6	65.5	30.7	96.2	214.5	146.1	0.0	QUALITAS INS CO
N/A	N/A	--	--	--	--	--	--	--	--	--	--	QUALITY CASUALTY INS CO
N/A	N/A	--	--	--	--	--	--	--	--	--	--	QUEEN CITY ASR INC
4.4	2.8	28.5	18.1	-2.3	-3.3	52.4	37.1	89.5	107.0	-1.8	3.5 •	QUINCY MUTUAL FIRE INS CO
N/A	N/A	--	--	--	--	--	--	--	--	--	--	R&Q REINS CO
1.9	1.5	46.6	48.5	0.8	-5.5	22.7	37.7	60.4	129.7	-25.7	0.0 •	RADIAN GUARANTY INC
N/A	N/A	--	--	--	--	--	--	--	--	--	--	RADIAN GUARANTY REINS INC
20.9	17.6	3.7	3.8	-6.2	-6.1	-73.7	107.1	33.4	84.3	-95.4	0.0	RADIAN INS INC
N/A	N/A	--	--	--	--	--	--	--	--	--	--	RADIAN INVESTOR SURETY INC
N/A	N/A	--	--	--	--	--	--	--	--	--	--	RADIAN MORTGAGE ASR INC
N/A	N/A	--	--	--	--	--	--	--	--	--	--	RADIAN MORTGAGE GUARANTY INC
N/A	N/A	--	--	--	--	--	--	--	--	--	--	RADIAN MORTGAGE INS INC
7.6	4.9	70.7	66.3	-4.1	N/A	21.7	4.6	26.3	178.6	63.3	0.0 •	RADIAN REINS INC
13.8	8.1	N/A	N/A	N/A	N/A	54.3	999 +	999 +	4.3	0.0	0.0	RADNOR SPECIALTY INS CO
5.3	3.2	11.8	16.0	-2.8	-0.4	31.0	54.8	85.8	104.8	2.7	0.0	RAINIER INS CO
4.8	3.1	74.1	30.9	-5.9	-9.3	47.6	29.9	77.5	132.8	3.2	0.0	RAM MUTUAL INS CO
N/A	N/A	--	--	--	--	--	--	--	--	--	--	RAMPART INS CO
0.7	0.7	-10.7	1.6	-2.6	2.8	-23.5	431.6	408.1	36.5	-144.5	0.0	RANCHERS & FARMERS MUTUAL INS CO
1.2	0.7	140.4	70.1	11.2	4.8	69.8	46.6	116.4	113.3	-8.4	-7.6	REAL LEGACY ASR CO INC
1.4	0.9	174.9	29.3	-3.7	-5.6	49.3	44.9	94.2	113.3	-6.6	0.0	REAMSTOWN MUTUAL INS CO
3.1	2.0	27.6	4.6	N/A	N/A	30.9	26.2	57.1	351.5	0.0	0.0	RECREATION RRG INC
2.7	1.7	17.3	50.5	-17.4	-42.7	7.7	81.6	89.3	320.4	-44.3	0.0	RED CLAY RRG INC

999 + Denotes number greater than 999.9%
999 - Denotes number less than -999.99%
• Bullets denote a more detailed analysis is available in Section II.

INSURANCE COMPANY NAME	DOM. STATE	RATING	TOTAL ASSETS ($MIL)	CAPITAL & SURPLUS ($MIL)	ANNUAL NET PREMIUM ($MIL)	NET INCOME ($MIL)	CAPITAL-IZATION INDEX (PTS)	RESERVE ADQ INDEX (PTS)	PROFIT-ABILITY INDEX (PTS)	LIQUIDITY INDEX (PTS)	STAB. INDEX (PTS)	STABILITY FACTORS
RED ROCK RISK RETENTION GROUP INC	AZ	D+	7.4	4.8	2.1	0.1	6.9	1.9	2.4	8.7	2.1	DGT
RED SHIELD INS CO	WA	B	39.9	22.1	13.1	0.1	8.3	6.4	6.8	8.8	4.0	DGRT
REDPOINT COUNTY MUTUAL INS CO	TX	C-	32.4	5.0	0.0	0.0	7.5	N/A	7.8	4.3	2.1	DGLR
REDWOOD FIRE & CAS INS CO	NE	C	1,728.1	655.7	386.1	3.7	4.1	8.1	8.1	8.6	4.3	CT
REGENT INS CO	WI	C	38.9	31.9	-13.5	0.0	10.0	3.8	3.9	6.8	3.5	FGRT
RELIABLE LLOYDS INS CO	TX	C+	16.9	13.0	0.0	0.3	10.0	N/A	8.8	10.0	3.2	DGRT
▲RELIAMAX INS CO	SD	C-	17.0	6.7	5.6	0.3	4.2	6.0	5.1	6.5	3.0	DGRT
RELIAMAX SURETY CO	SD	C+	61.3	20.2	28.8	0.1	9.3	8.2	4.1	7.3	4.5	DT
RENAISSANCE RE US INC	MD	B	1,742.0	529.1	248.6	3.5	8.1	9.5	5.0	7.1	4.8	FRT
REPUB MORTGAGE INS CO	NC	F	638.1	54.9	124.8	16.0	0.7	4.1	2.0	2.9	0.0	CFLR
REPUBLIC CREDIT INDEMNITY CO	IL	D+	64.8	7.0	14.9	-0.2	1.0	5.1	1.7	9.1	2.7	CDT
REPUBLIC FIRE & CASUALTY INS CO	OK	C	8.2	8.2	0.0	0.0	10.0	N/A	6.3	7.1	2.1	DFGR
REPUBLIC INDEMNITY CO OF AMERICA	CA	B-	2,366.6	529.7	791.2	16.5	5.6	9.3	7.9	6.7	4.7	ART
REPUBLIC INDEMNITY OF CA	CA	C	33.0	32.1	0.0	0.1	10.0	3.6	6.6	7.0	3.8	GRT
REPUBLIC LLOYDS	TX	C	12.3	12.3	0.0	0.0	10.0	N/A	3.9	10.0	2.1	DFGR
▲REPUBLIC MORTGAGE INS CO OF FLORIDA	FL	B	22.9	9.0	2.2	0.3	6.8	5.0	3.5	8.0	4.2	DFGT
▲REPUBLIC MORTGAGE INS CO OF NC	NC	C	152.1	20.2	22.1	2.7	1.6	5.1	2.9	6.3	3.4	CDFR
REPUBLIC RRG	SC	U (1)	--	--	--	--	N/A	--	--	--	--	Z
REPUBLIC UNDERWRITERS INS CO	TX	C	774.6	219.9	-11.7	-1.7	8.3	4.6	2.3	6.7	4.1	FRT
REPUBLIC-FRANKLIN INS CO	OH	C+	109.5	53.3	26.6	0.2	10.0	6.3	6.8	7.0	4.3	T
REPUBLIC-VANGUARD INS CO	AZ	B-	25.1	24.8	0.0	0.1	10.0	N/A	6.4	10.0	3.7	DGRT
REPWEST INS CO	AZ	D+	325.7	179.9	41.9	3.3	2.0	4.4	8.5	7.3	2.6	CRT
RESIDENCE MUTUAL INS CO	CA	C-	128.3	86.4	42.2	0.9	7.8	8.1	8.1	6.5	2.7	RT
RESPONSE INDEMNITY CO OF CA	CA	C-	7.9	5.2	2.9	0.1	10.0	5.0	8.3	6.7	1.5	DGRT
RESPONSE INS CO	IL	C-	38.6	36.1	0.0	0.0	7.4	N/A	7.0	7.0	2.9	DGRT
RESPONSE WORLDWIDE DIRECT AUTO INS	IL	U	--	--	--	--	N/A	--	--	--	--	Z
RESPONSE WORLDWIDE INS CO	IL	U	--	--	--	--	N/A	--	--	--	--	Z
RESPONSIVE AUTO INS CO	FL	C	23.5	8.3	18.7	-0.6	3.9	4.3	3.0	3.2	2.9	CDFG
▲RESTORATION RRG INC	VT	B-	82.4	32.6	13.9	0.6	6.9	9.5	8.7	7.4	5.0	DT
▲RETAILERS CASUALTY INS CO	LA	B-	81.9	42.8	24.3	0.6	8.2	7.0	8.7	6.7	5.0	T
▲RETAILERS INS CO	MI	C-	21.8	10.0	8.6	-0.1	7.2	9.3	4.9	6.9	3.0	DFGR
▲RETAILFIRST INS CO	FL	A-	305.0	147.1	110.5	1.5	8.4	6.6	7.9	6.6	7.0	T
RIDER INS CO	NJ	D+	36.7	9.6	12.7	0.1	4.5	3.8	1.1	5.4	2.3	DFGR
RIVERPORT INS CO	IA	B	70.8	42.3	0.0	0.3	10.0	3.8	7.6	7.0	4.1	FRT
RLI INS CO	IL	B	1,782.6	897.3	456.3	12.1	7.2	8.0	7.5	6.9	5.7	AT
ROCHDALE INS CO	NY	C-	308.5	86.9	135.8	-15.5	6.4	2.9	2.9	5.1	2.9	RT
ROCHE SURETY & CASUALTY INC	FL	C	23.8	9.4	3.1	0.0	9.5	N/A	8.4	9.1	2.3	DGT
ROCKFORD MUTUAL INS CO	IL	C+	79.3	37.7	47.5	0.3	6.6	6.8	7.6	6.0	3.4	RT
ROCKHILL INS CO	AZ	C	153.4	88.0	0.0	0.2	10.0	N/A	3.4	6.9	4.0	RT
ROCKINGHAM CASUALTY CO	VA	C	32.4	29.2	0.0	0.1	10.0	N/A	6.6	8.3	3.5	FGRT
ROCKINGHAM INS CO	VA	B	133.7	71.5	47.7	1.4	6.7	8.7	5.3	6.2	6.0	T
ROCKWOOD CASUALTY INS CO	PA	C-	259.8	93.8	40.1	6.4	7.7	9.4	8.0	7.6	3.2	RT
ROMULUS INS RRG INC	SC	D	2.3	1.7	0.6	0.0	7.5	3.6	2.7	7.3	1.4	DGT
ROOT INS CO	OH	U	--	--	--	--	N/A	--	--	--	--	Z
RPX RRG INC	HI	U	--	--	--	--	N/A	--	--	--	--	Z
RSUI INDEMNITY CO	NH	C+	3,458.4	1,574.4	681.0	57.7	8.1	8.0	7.8	6.9	2.9	ART
RURAL COMMUNITY INS CO	MN	C+	1,821.5	267.9	-35.3	0.9	9.7	7.6	1.9	0.0	4.4	GLRT
RURAL MUTUAL INS CO	WI	B-	472.0	247.4	171.4	3.3	10.0	8.3	8.9	6.7	4.1	RT
RURAL TRUST INS CO	TX	C	24.8	12.9	5.4	0.3	7.2	6.1	4.8	8.2	2.5	DGRT
RUTGERS CASUALTY INS CO	NJ	C-	20.9	7.7	4.0	-0.3	8.1	6.3	2.0	7.4	2.8	DFGR
RUTGERS ENHANCED INS CO	NJ	C- (1)	11.2	4.4	2.7	0.0	7.9	6.4	3.2	7.3	3.0	FT
RVI AMERICA INS CO	CT	C	105.2	72.4	6.0	0.7	10.0	5.6	7.4	9.7	3.3	RT

See Page 27 for explanation of footnotes and
Page 28 for explanation of stability factors.
Arrows denote recent upgrades ▲ or downgrades ▼ (see Section VII for explanations)

www.weissratings.com

RISK RATIO #1	ADJ. CAPITAL RATIO #2	PREMIUM TO SURPLUS (%)	RESV. TO SURPLUS (%)	RESV. DEVELOP. 1 YEAR (%)	RESV. DEVELOP. 2 YEAR (%)	LOSS RATIO (%)	EXP. RATIO (%)	COMB. RATIO (%)	CASH FROM UNDER-WRITING (%)	NET PREMIUM GROWTH (%)	INVEST. IN AFFIL (%)	INSURANCE COMPANY NAME
1.4	1.1	44.0	31.1	1.0	24.9	40.8	15.3	56.1	130.5	71.0	0.0	RED ROCK RISK RETENTION GROUP INC
2.9	1.8	60.0	36.3	-1.9	-1.7	42.7	53.2	95.9	106.5	1.6	0.0	RED SHIELD INS CO
1.1	1.0	N/A	N/A	N/A	N/A	N/A	N/A	N/A	108.8	0.0	0.0	REDPOINT COUNTY MUTUAL INS CO
0.9	0.5	60.6	116.0	-7.4	-7.2	63.8	20.0	83.8	169.8	-3.8	0.0 ●	REDWOOD FIRE & CAS INS CO
16.4	14.8	-42.4	N/A	N/A	N/A	N/A	N/A	N/A	-21.2	-137.3	0.0	REGENT INS CO
10.4	9.4	N/A	N/A	N/A	N/A	N/A	N/A	N/A	-8.1	0.0	0.0	RELIABLE LLOYDS INS CO
1.4	0.9	86.9	104.6	-31.3	-60.4	36.1	22.0	58.1	178.4	-10.1	0.0	RELIAMAX INS CO
3.5	2.5	143.2	10.7	-2.0	-8.8	75.2	27.1	102.3	126.9	72.0	0.0	RELIAMAX SURETY CO
3.0	1.9	47.5	145.9	-4.8	-16.5	55.8	37.7	93.5	78.6	-23.2	0.0 ●	RENAISSANCE RE US INC
0.4	0.3	243.8	584.6	-141.1	-328.3	34.5	10.5	45.0	57.3	-20.6	0.1	REPUB MORTGAGE INS CO
0.3	0.2	205.5	688.2	-215.6	-363.0	102.2	14.7	116.9	143.1	-16.6	0.0	REPUBLIC CREDIT INDEMNITY CO
95.5	47.8	N/A	N/A	N/A	N/A	N/A	N/A	N/A	-29.6	0.0	0.0	REPUBLIC FIRE & CASUALTY INS CO
1.0	0.7	148.6	309.6	-10.6	-12.8	64.1	24.9	89.0	115.5	-0.3	1.5 ●	REPUBLIC INDEMNITY CO OF AMERICA
83.1	47.8	N/A	N/A	N/A	N/A	N/A	N/A	N/A	N/A	0.0	0.0	REPUBLIC INDEMNITY OF CA
110.5	55.2	N/A	N/A	N/A	N/A	N/A	N/A	N/A	-282.0	0.0	0.0	REPUBLIC LLOYDS
2.0	1.5	24.1	57.6	-7.3	-22.9	34.6	19.9	54.5	55.0	-20.7	0.0	REPUBLIC MORTGAGE INS CO OF
0.7	0.5	113.3	375.8	-65.9	-180.2	40.6	16.2	56.8	47.8	-22.6	0.0	REPUBLIC MORTGAGE INS CO OF NC
N/A	N/A	--	--	--	--	--	--	--	--	--	--	REPUBLIC RRG
2.3	1.9	-5.3	54.8	-18.2	-9.6	112.5	-458.8	-346.3	-9.6	-104.1	13.2 ●	REPUBLIC UNDERWRITERS INS CO
7.0	4.5	50.8	71.1	-0.7	-2.4	65.5	32.8	98.3	110.4	8.0	0.0	REPUBLIC-FRANKLIN INS CO
77.1	36.1	N/A	N/A	N/A	N/A	N/A	N/A	N/A	N/A	0.0	0.0	REPUBLIC-VANGUARD INS CO
0.5	0.4	23.8	75.2	0.2	-0.3	22.8	57.3	80.1	107.8	5.3	0.0	REPWEST INS CO
2.7	1.7	49.7	14.4	-2.8	-4.2	71.2	20.8	92.0	110.5	1.9	1.5	RESIDENCE MUTUAL INS CO
5.6	4.5	56.1	7.8	0.5	1.1	48.1	35.7	83.8	133.1	5.0	0.0	RESPONSE INDEMNITY CO OF CA
1.2	1.2	N/A	N/A	N/A	N/A	N/A	N/A	N/A	192.2	0.0	88.9	RESPONSE INS CO
N/A	N/A	--	--	--	--	--	--	--	--	--	--	RESPONSE WORLDWIDE DIRECT AUTO
N/A	N/A	--	--	--	--	--	--	--	--	--	--	RESPONSE WORLDWIDE INS CO
0.8	0.6	206.5	69.8	2.1	-10.7	73.9	36.2	110.1	88.0	-11.1	0.0	RESPONSIVE AUTO INS CO
1.8	1.4	44.5	115.9	-3.5	-22.4	46.7	15.2	61.9	175.1	2.8	0.0	RESTORATION RRG INC
2.8	2.1	57.6	64.4	-17.9	-33.0	40.6	32.0	72.6	116.0	6.2	0.0	RETAILERS CASUALTY INS CO
1.5	1.2	84.6	71.9	-6.4	-7.3	53.0	37.7	90.7	98.9	4.7	0.0	RETAILERS INS CO
2.4	1.9	76.2	94.1	-3.9	-4.7	69.9	27.4	97.3	115.3	10.4	0.0 ●	RETAILFIRST INS CO
0.9	0.7	140.6	79.7	12.8	10.3	77.9	49.0	126.9	81.8	20.9	0.0	RIDER INS CO
10.3	9.2	N/A	N/A	N/A	N/A	N/A	N/A	N/A	123.7	0.0	0.0	RIVERPORT INS CO
1.3	1.1	53.1	56.9	-0.9	-2.9	52.1	41.0	93.1	111.1	1.2	35.5 ●	RLI INS CO
1.1	0.7	133.4	158.1	10.8	21.2	63.4	33.3	96.7	168.9	-6.2	0.0	ROCHDALE INS CO
3.2	2.5	32.7	N/A	N/A	N/A	N/A	78.7	78.7	128.1	7.8	0.0	ROCHE SURETY & CASUALTY INC
1.6	1.0	127.1	53.5	-8.4	-9.6	58.9	38.8	97.7	103.8	4.3	0.0	ROCKFORD MUTUAL INS CO
3.4	3.3	N/A	N/A	N/A	N/A	N/A	N/A	N/A	85.1	0.0	29.1	ROCKHILL INS CO
28.0	25.2	N/A	N/A	N/A	N/A	N/A	N/A	N/A	-42.5	0.0	0.0	ROCKINGHAM CASUALTY CO
1.2	1.1	69.3	26.9	-5.1	-6.6	61.2	35.7	96.9	119.4	8.5	23.2	ROCKINGHAM INS CO
1.8	1.5	46.1	110.9	-8.7	-11.4	41.3	36.2	77.5	125.0	-8.3	19.4	ROCKWOOD CASUALTY INS CO
1.3	1.1	33.1	24.0	10.8	N/A	97.1	28.7	125.8	135.1	0.0	0.0	ROMULUS INS RRG INC
N/A	N/A	--	--	--	--	--	--	--	--	--	--	ROOT INS CO
N/A	N/A	--	--	--	--	--	--	--	--	--	--	RPX RRG INC
2.7	2.0	44.5	88.6	-4.0	-4.2	53.3	28.7	82.0	125.5	-5.5	8.7 ●	RSUI INDEMNITY CO
5.9	2.9	-13.2	N/A	-3.1	-0.2	999 +	-17.3	999 +	116.3	-109.7	0.0 ●	RURAL COMMUNITY INS CO
6.1	4.1	70.9	44.5	-1.4	-2.0	57.7	24.0	81.7	129.3	5.4	0.0 ●	RURAL MUTUAL INS CO
2.0	1.2	42.8	25.3	0.1	-1.1	81.1	26.2	107.3	121.5	22.0	0.0	RURAL TRUST INS CO
2.7	1.8	49.9	91.0	0.3	-0.4	66.6	40.4	107.0	69.0	-7.7	0.0	RUTGERS CASUALTY INS CO
2.4	1.7	60.4	110.2	0.4	-0.8	66.6	40.4	107.0	75.9	-7.7	0.0	RUTGERS ENHANCED INS CO
14.8	13.3	8.3	2.9	-0.1	-2.9	2.9	47.3	50.2	519.3	37.8	0.0	RVI AMERICA INS CO

999 + Denotes number greater than 999.9%
999 - Denotes number less than -999.99%
● Bullets denote a more detailed analysis is available in Section II.

INSURANCE COMPANY NAME	DOM. STATE	RATING	TOTAL ASSETS ($MIL)	CAPITAL & SURPLUS ($MIL)	ANNUAL NET PREMIUM ($MIL)	NET INCOME ($MIL)	CAPITAL-IZATION INDEX (PTS)	RESERVE ADQ INDEX (PTS)	PROFIT-ABILITY INDEX (PTS)	LIQUIDITY INDEX (PTS)	STAB. INDEX (PTS)	STABILITY FACTORS
▲RVOS FARM MUTUAL INS CO	TX	C-	87.3	38.2	57.2	-0.9	6.8	5.4	3.9	3.2	3.0	LRT
SAFE AUTO INS CO	OH	B	440.2	163.7	312.1	-2.3	7.7	8.8	4.6	2.4	4.1	LT
▲SAFE HARBOR INS CO	FL	B-	82.7	26.7	49.5	-0.2	5.9	4.0	7.7	6.6	5.0	T
▲SAFE INS CO	WV	C-	11.2	9.1	2.7	0.1	10.0	8.0	8.7	7.6	2.3	DGRT
SAFECARD SERVICES INS CO	ND	D (1)	2.0	1.9	0.2	0.1	10.0	3.6	7.2	10.0	1.5	DT
SAFECO INS CO OF AMERICA	NH	B-	4,520.7	1,523.2	1,589.9	1.5	8.1	5.9	6.6	6.4	3.9	ART
SAFECO INS CO OF IL	IL	B	193.9	184.5	0.0	0.6	10.0	3.8	6.7	10.0	4.6	ART
SAFECO INS CO OF INDIANA	IN	B	15.3	15.3	0.0	0.0	10.0	N/A	6.3	10.0	5.1	DG
SAFECO INS CO OF OREGON	OR	B	14.1	13.8	0.0	0.1	10.0	N/A	7.4	10.0	4.9	DGR
SAFECO LLOYDS INS CO	TX	B-	13.2	13.1	0.0	0.0	10.0	N/A	6.4	7.0	4.8	DGR
SAFECO NATIONAL INS CO	NH	B-	15.0	14.7	0.0	0.1	10.0	N/A	3.6	7.0	3.9	ADGR
SAFECO SURPLUS LINES INS CO	NH	U	--	--	--	--	N/A	--	--	--	--	Z
SAFEPOINT INS CO	FL	C+	146.2	50.4	51.1	0.8	8.0	3.0	5.2	6.8	3.4	FT
SAFETY FIRST INS CO	IL	C	72.8	68.1	1.1	0.4	10.0	7.7	6.9	10.0	4.0	DRT
SAFETY INDEMNITY INS CO	MA	C+	123.2	58.0	53.7	0.6	10.0	8.7	5.3	6.6	4.0	T
SAFETY INS CO	MA	B-	1,470.8	603.5	689.8	11.8	8.9	8.9	4.4	6.2	4.4	RT
SAFETY NATIONAL CASUALTY CORP	MO	C	6,646.8	1,860.3	778.4	42.2	7.2	2.5	6.4	7.4	3.4	RT
SAFETY P&C INS CO	MA	C	45.8	18.8	23.0	0.2	8.1	9.2	5.2	6.6	4.3	DT
SAFETY SPECIALTY INS CO	MO	C	71.4	68.1	0.2	0.5	10.0	2.5	3.9	10.0	3.5	DGT
SAFEWAY INS CO	IL	B-	555.5	285.4	210.5	-1.6	7.6	4.9	3.8	5.4	4.5	FRT
SAFEWAY INS CO OF AL	IL	C	89.7	30.0	41.3	-0.3	7.9	4.7	3.2	6.4	4.2	FRT
SAFEWAY INS CO OF GA	GA	C	81.2	30.7	41.3	-0.4	8.0	5.9	2.8	6.0	3.7	FRT
SAFEWAY INS CO OF LA	LA	C+	159.8	60.4	82.7	-0.8	9.1	5.8	3.1	5.6	4.5	RT
SAGAMORE INS CO	IN	B-	160.7	129.4	14.4	0.1	10.0	6.0	6.0	9.1	4.2	DT
SAGE RRG INC	NV	D	3.7	1.1	1.9	0.0	6.8	3.6	8.9	8.6	1.1	DGT
SAINT LUKES HEALTH SYSTEM RRG	SC	C-	13.9	9.6	2.3	0.1	6.6	4.9	2.9	6.6	2.9	DFGR
SALEM COUNTY MUTUAL FIRE INS CO	NJ	U (5)	--	--	--	--	N/A	--	--	--	--	Z
SAMARITAN RRG INC	SC	C	36.8	20.2	9.4	1.3	8.0	6.3	8.0	8.4	4.0	DGT
SAMSUNG FIRE & MARINE INS CO LTD US	NY	D	249.7	65.2	61.0	-6.3	5.3	1.9	2.3	8.1	1.9	RT
SAN ANTONIO INDEMNITY CO	TX	F (5)	0.0	0.0	4.2	0.0	0.3	5.5	1.1	0.0	0.0	CDGL
SAN DIEGO INS CO	CA	U	--	--	--	--	N/A	--	--	--	--	Z
SAN FRANCISCO REINS CO	CA	C	3,469.2	625.6	-443.3	10.9	7.5	0.4	3.8	9.0	3.6	FRT
SAUCON MUTUAL INS CO	PA	U (1)	--	--	--	--	N/A	--	--	--	--	Z
SAUQUOIT VALLEY INS CO	NY	C-	4.7	4.0	0.6	0.0	7.5	7.4	4.0	7.3	2.2	DGR
SAVERS P&C INS CO	MO	C-	75.8	58.4	0.0	0.2	10.0	1.8	3.6	0.3	2.9	FLRT
SAWGRASS MUTUAL INS CO	FL	D+	32.3	20.3	8.2	5.0	3.0	2.2	3.5	6.8	2.7	DGT
SCOR REINS CO	NY	C	3,212.4	1,103.1	1,123.7	-7.7	7.1	6.9	5.4	6.9	3.4	RT
SCOTTSDALE INDEMNITY CO	OH	B	85.0	39.0	0.0	0.1	10.0	N/A	6.8	9.5	4.2	RT
SCOTTSDALE INS CO	OH	B-	2,531.5	772.0	779.5	-3.6	8.3	6.0	4.4	6.0	4.9	AT
SCOTTSDALE SURPLUS LINES INS CO	AZ	B	50.8	48.0	0.0	0.2	10.0	N/A	8.2	9.2	6.1	D
SCRUBS MUTUAL ASR CO RRG	NV	D	17.8	4.2	6.0	0.0	3.6	1.3	3.7	6.1	2.1	DFGR
SEABRIGHT INS CO	TX	D-	58.9	55.7	0.0	-1.3	10.0	6.1	1.5	7.3	1.0	DFGR
▼SEAVIEW INS CO	CA	D+	22.6	11.2	8.5	0.5	8.6	7.1	7.9	7.2	1.6	DGT
SEAWAY MUTUAL INS CO	PA	U (1)	--	--	--	--	N/A	--	--	--	--	Z
SECURA INS A MUTUAL CO	WI	B-	1,124.9	412.7	491.3	4.8	8.3	9.1	8.8	6.6	4.2	RT
SECURA SUPREME INS CO	WI	C+	139.5	61.8	54.6	0.6	10.0	8.6	8.8	6.7	4.7	T
▲SECURIAN CASUALTY CO	MN	A-	288.6	122.2	231.6	1.3	7.9	6.3	8.7	5.8	6.9	T
SECURITY AMERICA RRG INC	VT	E	4.8	1.4	1.6	0.0	0.0	2.6	0.9	2.1	0.1	CDFG
SECURITY FIRST INS CO	FL	B-	273.9	84.0	169.1	6.0	6.6	3.9	2.9	4.0	5.1	FGLT
SECURITY MUTUAL INS CO	NY	C+	106.0	56.8	35.9	0.8	10.0	6.8	8.7	6.7	3.5	RT
SECURITY NATIONAL INS CO	DE	B	1,280.4	218.6	228.4	3.1	7.5	5.6	9.4	6.8	4.7	GRT
SECURITY NATIONAL INS CO	FL	D+	118.2	35.6	0.0	0.2	10.0	4.0	3.9	10.0	2.5	FRT

See Page 27 for explanation of footnotes and
Page 28 for explanation of stability factors.

112

www.weissratings.com

Arrows denote recent upgrades ▲ or downgrades ▼   (see Section VII for explanations)

RISK ADJ. RATIO #1	CAPITAL RATIO #2	PREMIUM TO SURPLUS (%)	RESV. TO SURPLUS (%)	RESV. DEVELOP. 1 YEAR (%)	RESV. DEVELOP. 2 YEAR (%)	LOSS RATIO (%)	EXP. RATIO (%)	COMB RATIO (%)	CASH FROM UNDER-WRITING (%)	NET PREMIUM GROWTH (%)	INVEST. IN AFFIL (%)	INSURANCE COMPANY NAME
1.5	1.2	151.6	19.5	-0.4	3.6	60.2	28.1	88.3	104.9	-5.5	24.3	RVOS FARM MUTUAL INS CO
1.7	1.5	189.5	75.7	2.6	-1.8	73.4	22.9	96.3	92.8	-1.2	0.0	SAFE AUTO INS CO
1.4	1.2	185.8	56.8	-12.5	-3.8	57.5	37.1	94.6	110.9	-1.0	0.0	SAFE HARBOR INS CO
5.2	3.2	30.7	8.2	-2.8	-3.9	36.3	43.7	80.0	115.8	-4.2	0.0	SAFE INS CO
20.3	18.3	8.4	0.5	-0.6	N/A	N/A	24.8	24.8	403.8	0.0	0.0	SAFECARD SERVICES INS CO
2.7	1.9	106.1	138.1	0.9	-0.4	69.8	32.0	101.8	100.7	3.4	6.8 ●	SAFECO INS CO OF AMERICA
3.7	3.6	N/A	N/A	N/A	N/A	N/A	N/A	N/A	N/A	0.0	29.8	SAFECO INS CO OF IL
143.8	71.9	N/A	N/A	N/A	N/A	N/A	N/A	N/A	N/A	0.0	0.0	SAFECO INS CO OF INDIANA
89.2	51.7	N/A	N/A	N/A	N/A	N/A	N/A	N/A	N/A	0.0	0.0	SAFECO INS CO OF OREGON
193.5	96.7	N/A	N/A	N/A	N/A	N/A	N/A	N/A	N/A	0.0	0.0	SAFECO LLOYDS INS CO
152.6	88.2	N/A	N/A	N/A	N/A	N/A	N/A	N/A	N/A	0.0	0.0	SAFECO NATIONAL INS CO
N/A	N/A	--	--	--	--	--	--	--	--	--	--	SAFECO SURPLUS LINES INS CO
2.2	1.5	102.8	67.4	14.1	13.9	107.4	17.2	124.6	88.7	22.4	0.0	SAFEPOINT INS CO
41.2	19.9	1.7	4.6	-0.8	-3.5	38.2	38.0	76.2	123.5	-19.8	0.0	SAFETY FIRST INS CO
5.0	3.4	91.7	57.0	-5.2	-7.8	65.3	28.4	93.7	103.7	2.7	0.0	SAFETY INDEMNITY INS CO
3.2	2.2	114.1	70.9	-6.4	-9.1	65.3	28.1	93.4	107.1	2.7	6.4 ●	SAFETY INS CO
1.7	1.2	42.9	206.2	3.0	11.0	84.6	20.2	104.8	187.1	6.8	4.3 ●	SAFETY NATIONAL CASUALTY CORP
2.5	1.7	122.2	76.0	-7.0	-10.2	65.3	30.1	95.4	105.2	2.7	0.0	SAFETY P&C INS CO
59.3	28.9	0.3	0.1	N/A	N/A	70.0	-145.1	-75.1	-188.8	-78.2	0.0	SAFETY SPECIALTY INS CO
1.5	1.3	73.1	30.6	3.6	2.9	86.1	21.0	107.1	94.2	3.0	43.2 ●	SAFEWAY INS CO
1.7	1.5	137.3	57.4	6.9	5.4	86.1	20.4	106.5	91.8	7.9	0.0	SAFEWAY INS CO OF AL
1.7	1.5	133.8	56.0	6.6	5.2	86.1	21.9	108.0	92.8	10.3	0.0	SAFEWAY INS CO OF GA
2.6	2.3	136.0	56.9	6.8	5.4	86.1	21.9	108.0	93.4	9.1	0.0	SAFEWAY INS CO OF LA
27.3	19.1	11.2	9.5	0.9	1.5	65.4	29.0	94.4	108.0	-24.0	0.0	SAGAMORE INS CO
1.4	0.9	169.1	109.2	-9.8	N/A	64.7	24.6	89.3	261.3	24.7	0.0	SAGE RRG INC
1.6	1.1	23.8	40.6	-14.1	-3.2	15.8	26.8	42.6	19.5	21.2	0.0	SAINT LUKES HEALTH SYSTEM RRG
N/A	N/A	--	--	--	--	--	--	--	--	--	--	SALEM COUNTY MUTUAL FIRE INS CO
2.5	1.5	49.6	49.9	-4.4	3.6	64.2	13.1	77.3	193.3	6.1	0.0	SAMARITAN RRG INC
1.0	0.5	85.2	185.8	80.5	67.3	168.9	42.7	211.6	108.2	4.8	0.0	SAMSUNG FIRE & MARINE INS CO LTD
0.2	0.1	394.1	58.1	-14.1	1.3	76.0	26.0	102.0	99.2	75.3	0.0	SAN ANTONIO INDEMNITY CO
N/A	N/A	--	--	--	--	--	--	--	--	--	--	SAN DIEGO INS CO
2.0	1.3	-72.2	282.5	-54.2	999 +	76.5	-12.2	64.3	-401.9	-119.4	0.0 ●	SAN FRANCISCO REINS CO
N/A	N/A	--	--	--	--	--	--	--	--	--	--	SAUCON MUTUAL INS CO
2.2	1.3	16.1	5.4	0.3	-1.8	74.9	33.2	108.1	99.0	-0.4	0.0	SAUQUOIT VALLEY INS CO
17.1	15.3	N/A	N/A	N/A	N/A	N/A	N/A	N/A	-14.3	-100.0	0.0	SAVERS P&C INS CO
1.0	0.7	40.6	42.4	-8.6	4.2	187.7	-22.2	165.5	75.1	188.7	0.0	SAWGRASS MUTUAL INS CO
1.7	1.0	101.9	114.0	-4.0	-10.4	53.2	40.5	93.7	122.9	32.7	0.0 ●	SCOR REINS CO
6.1	5.5	N/A	N/A	N/A	N/A	N/A	N/A	N/A	-122.1	0.0	0.0	SCOTTSDALE INDEMNITY CO
2.1	1.8	100.5	74.1	1.9	2.4	74.7	31.1	105.8	95.2	4.3	19.3 ●	SCOTTSDALE INS CO
52.1	45.9	N/A	N/A	N/A	N/A	N/A	N/A	N/A	226.0	0.0	0.0	SCOTTSDALE SURPLUS LINES INS CO
0.8	0.5	145.9	177.4	-8.5	89.8	61.8	41.7	103.5	38.5	-9.9	0.0	SCRUBS MUTUAL ASR CO RRG
55.5	39.1	N/A	N/A	N/A	-230.3	N/A	N/A	N/A	N/A	100.0	0.0	SEABRIGHT INS CO
3.1	2.5	64.3	4.2	-2.8	-4.8	-0.3	59.8	59.5	150.3	-12.2	0.0	SEAVIEW INS CO
N/A	N/A	--	--	--	--	--	--	--	--	--	--	SEAWAY MUTUAL INS CO
2.5	1.8	121.5	94.7	-6.6	-7.6	59.9	31.1	91.0	118.3	6.2	7.0 ●	SECURA INS A MUTUAL CO
5.1	3.8	89.2	69.5	-4.6	-5.5	59.9	30.0	89.9	114.3	6.2	0.0	SECURA SUPREME INS CO
2.0	1.5	192.8	24.1	-1.0	-2.2	55.5	36.2	91.7	123.5	28.1	0.0 ●	SECURIAN CASUALTY CO
0.1	0.1	114.4	167.6	59.3	46.6	140.2	76.7	216.9	48.9	-20.9	0.0	SECURITY AMERICA RRG INC
1.3	1.1	236.8	82.0	13.3	9.2	94.9	31.7	126.6	96.9	19.4	0.0	SECURITY FIRST INS CO
4.6	3.5	64.4	44.5	-1.8	-5.9	53.4	37.6	91.0	108.9	0.3	0.0	SECURITY MUTUAL INS CO
1.8	1.1	105.2	66.2	-3.8	1.7	48.6	23.8	72.4	177.4	59.3	3.0 ●	SECURITY NATIONAL INS CO
4.2	3.8	N/A	0.3	0.7	3.1	N/A	N/A	N/A	999 +	0.0	0.0	SECURITY NATIONAL INS CO

999 + Denotes number greater than 999.9%
999 - Denotes number less than -999.99%
● Bullets denote a more detailed analysis is available in Section II.

INSURANCE COMPANY NAME	DOM. STATE	RATING		TOTAL ASSETS ($MIL)	CAPITAL & SURPLUS ($MIL)	ANNUAL NET PREMIUM ($MIL)	NET INCOME ($MIL)	CAPITAL-IZATION INDEX (PTS)	RESERVE ADQ INDEX (PTS)	PROFIT-ABILITY INDEX (PTS)	LIQUIDITY INDEX (PTS)	STAB. INDEX (PTS)	STABILITY FACTORS
SECURITY PLAN FIRE INS CO	LA	D		8.0	6.8	5.1	0.0	8.4	7.9	6.2	6.9	1.8	DGRT
SELECT INS CO	TX	U		--	--	--	--	N/A	--	--	--	--	Z
SELECT MARKETS INS CO	IL	U		--	--	--	--	N/A	--	--	--	--	Z
SELECT MD RRG INC	MT	D+		3.0	0.7	0.2	0.0	7.9	6.0	1.7	10.0	1.2	DFGT
SELECT RISK INS CO	PA	C		43.8	16.7	16.3	0.1	8.4	9.3	8.3	6.5	3.2	DT
SELECTIVE AUTO INS CO OF NJ	NJ	B		368.1	89.0	134.2	3.1	7.7	9.3	8.4	6.7	6.3	AT
SELECTIVE CASUALTY INS CO	NJ	B	(1)	431.5	101.0	156.6	12.6	7.8	6.0	8.6	6.7	4.9	T
SELECTIVE F&C INS CO	NJ	B	(1)	187.6	43.2	67.1	5.5	7.8	6.0	8.6	6.7	4.1	T
SELECTIVE INS CO OF AM	NJ	B		2,389.7	584.2	715.9	22.1	8.1	9.2	8.3	6.9	5.6	AT
SELECTIVE INS CO OF NEW ENGLAND	NJ	C		188.7	44.9	67.1	1.8	7.8	9.3	8.6	6.7	4.0	AT
SELECTIVE INS CO OF NY	NY	B		427.4	104.2	156.6	3.7	7.8	9.3	8.4	6.7	4.4	AT
SELECTIVE INS CO OF SC	IN	B		636.7	144.0	201.4	4.9	7.9	9.3	8.4	6.8	4.5	AT
SELECTIVE INS CO OF THE SOUTHEAST	IN	B		497.6	110.9	156.6	3.8	7.8	9.3	8.4	6.8	4.4	AT
SELECTIVE WAY INS CO	NJ	B		1,310.0	316.1	469.8	10.9	7.7	9.3	8.4	6.6	4.6	AT
SENECA INS CO	NY	D+		190.2	142.4	0.0	0.3	9.9	3.9	5.1	8.5	2.8	FRT
SENECA SPECIALTY INS CO	DE	C+		50.7	50.7	0.0	0.2	10.0	N/A	6.7	10.0	4.8	R
SENIOR AMERICAN INS CO	PA	E-	(2)	13.3	-1.8	2.4	-1.8	0.0	0.5	0.5	0.0	0.0	CDFG
SENIORSFIRST RRG INC	NC	U		--	--	--	--	N/A	--	--	--	--	Z
SENTINEL ASR RRG INC	HI	E	(2)	17.2	7.3	4.0	-2.9	7.2	5.9	2.2	7.7	0.0	DGRT
SENTINEL INS CO LTD	CT	B		263.7	186.3	31.6	3.8	10.0	4.9	8.9	7.5	5.8	AT
SENTRUITY CASUALTY CO	TX	B		196.6	48.9	12.0	0.0	10.0	5.0	8.3	9.1	5.6	FT
SENTRY CASUALTY CO	WI	B		311.4	73.6	50.3	1.7	9.7	7.9	5.6	7.0	4.5	T
SENTRY INS A MUTUAL CO	WI	A		7,779.6	4,846.9	1,086.7	52.4	8.6	7.5	6.8	6.9	6.1	T
SENTRY LLOYDS OF TX	TX	B		7.1	7.0	0.0	0.0	10.0	N/A	7.4	10.0	4.9	DGT
SENTRY SELECT INS CO	WI	B+		715.6	233.9	201.2	2.6	9.0	8.1	5.7	6.7	5.1	T
SEQUOIA INDEMNITY CO	NV	B-		11.1	10.1	0.8	-0.1	10.0	6.9	4.4	8.1	3.6	DGRT
SEQUOIA INS CO	CA	C		241.4	97.4	-5.1	0.4	10.0	6.0	2.9	9.3	3.0	FRT
SERVICE INS CO (FL)	FL	B		53.3	42.6	5.4	0.4	9.3	6.0	6.5	6.9	4.1	RT
▲SERVICE INS CO (NJ)	NJ	C-		14.9	7.9	2.4	0.2	10.0	8.9	8.7	9.0	2.2	DGRT
SERVICE LLOYDS INS CO	TX	B-		304.6	124.8	82.1	-0.7	9.6	8.9	6.9	7.0	4.0	FRT
SEVEN SEAS INS CO	FL	C		24.9	21.6	18.1	2.3	9.2	6.1	8.3	7.7	2.9	DGRT
SFM MUTUAL INS CO	MN	B		585.5	140.0	163.2	3.2	6.6	6.2	8.9	6.6	6.2	T
SFM SAFE INS CO	MN	D		5.3	5.0	0.0	0.0	10.0	N/A	4.9	7.0	2.3	DGT
▲SFM SELECT INS CO	MN	C-		5.0	3.5	0.0	0.0	10.0	5.1	5.6	7.0	2.4	DGRT
SHEBOYGAN FALLS INS CO	WI	C+		36.6	14.1	20.9	0.0	7.3	4.5	5.9	6.6	3.2	DGRT
SHELBY INS CO	TX	F	(5)	0.0	0.0	0.0	0.0	10.0	N/A	2.6	7.0	0.0	
SHELTER GENERAL INS CO	MO	C+		132.7	70.6	38.9	1.2	8.6	8.4	2.8	6.3	3.7	FRT
SHELTER MUTUAL INS CO	MO	B		3,367.5	1,924.8	1,449.1	16.8	8.1	7.6	6.8	5.8	5.0	T
SHELTER REINS CO	MO	B-		457.1	335.7	113.0	8.3	9.5	7.0	8.9	6.8	3.8	RT
SIGMA RRG INC	DC	B-		17.9	7.0	2.4	0.2	7.4	9.3	8.6	9.7	3.5	DGT
SILVER OAK CASUALTY INC	NE	B-		239.0	93.9	53.2	2.4	8.6	9.3	8.3	7.0	4.1	RT
▲SIMED	PR	B-		161.0	97.8	18.5	2.2	10.0	8.8	8.1	7.9	5.0	DT
SIRIUS AMERICA INS CO	NY	B-		1,381.3	557.7	217.3	13.4	4.7	6.6	5.2	7.4	3.5	CFRT
SLAVONIC INS CO OF TEXAS	TX	U		--	--	--	--	N/A	--	--	--	--	Z
SLAVONIC MUTUAL FIRE INS ASN	TX	C+		30.1	29.6	0.8	0.2	10.0	3.6	6.9	9.3	3.3	DGRT
SOCIETY INS A MUTUAL CO	WI	B		412.1	143.7	159.0	1.4	8.5	6.4	8.8	6.6	4.1	T
SOMERSET CASUALTY INS CO	PA	D+		42.9	24.9	7.1	0.6	10.0	8.7	8.9	7.3	2.4	DRT
▲SOMPO AM FIRE & MARINE INS CO	NY	B-		78.6	74.4	0.1	0.4	10.0	4.6	4.9	10.0	4.1	DGT
▲SOMPO AMERICA INSURANCE CO	NY	A-		1,235.5	568.1	182.3	4.8	9.4	8.8	5.8	7.1	7.0	T
SOMPO JAPAN CANOPIUS RE AG	DE	U		--	--	--	--	N/A	--	--	--	--	Z
SOMPO JAPAN NIPPONKOA INS INC	GU	D	(1)	8.6	1.1	6.1	0.7	0.3	6.8	3.7	7.5	0.6	CDGT
SONNENBERG MUTUAL INS CO	OH	C		26.0	15.7	10.2	0.3	8.6	7.8	6.2	6.9	2.7	DGT

See Page 27 for explanation of footnotes and
Page 28 for explanation of stability factors.
Arrows denote recent upgrades ▲ or downgrades ▼   (see Section VII for explanations)

114

www.weissratings.com

RISK ADJ. RATIO #1	CAPITAL RATIO #2	PREMIUM TO SURPLUS (%)	RESV. TO SURPLUS (%)	RESV. DEVELOP. 1 YEAR (%)	RESV. DEVELOP. 2 YEAR (%)	LOSS RATIO (%)	EXP. RATIO (%)	COMB RATIO (%)	CASH FROM UNDER-WRITING (%)	NET PREMIUM GROWTH (%)	INVEST. IN AFFIL (%)	INSURANCE COMPANY NAME
2.7	2.2	73.9	7.3	-2.0	-2.7	38.2	57.8	96.0	105.4	-2.4	0.0	SECURITY PLAN FIRE INS CO
N/A	N/A	--	--	--	--	--	--	--	--	--	--	SELECT INS CO
N/A	N/A	--	--	--	--	--	--	--	--	--	--	SELECT MARKETS INS CO
1.0	0.9	27.6	66.5	-7.6	-43.2	189.8	48.5	238.3	3.3	44.9	0.0	SELECT MD RRG INC
3.0	1.9	100.0	66.8	-3.2	-10.9	65.6	32.0	97.6	107.5	5.6	0.0	SELECT RISK INS CO
2.3	1.5	154.9	212.1	-4.8	-12.1	57.4	34.2	91.6	110.9	8.1	0.0	SELECTIVE AUTO INS CO OF NJ
2.3	1.6	155.0	212.3	-4.7	-12.1	57.4	34.2	91.6	109.1	8.1	0.0	SELECTIVE CASUALTY INS CO
2.3	1.6	155.2	212.5	-4.7	-12.0	57.4	34.2	91.6	107.7	8.1	0.0	SELECTIVE F&C INS CO
2.8	1.8	125.9	172.4	-3.8	-9.3	57.4	34.2	91.6	116.6	8.1	0.0 ●	SELECTIVE INS CO OF AM
2.3	1.6	153.5	210.2	-4.7	-12.1	57.4	34.2	91.6	110.9	8.1	0.0	SELECTIVE INS CO OF NEW ENGLAND
2.3	1.6	153.8	210.6	-4.6	-12.1	57.4	34.2	91.6	112.6	8.1	0.0	SELECTIVE INS CO OF NY
2.5	1.7	141.9	194.3	-4.3	-11.1	57.4	34.1	91.5	110.7	8.1	0.0	SELECTIVE INS CO OF SC
2.5	1.6	143.6	196.6	-4.5	-11.7	57.4	34.1	91.5	112.5	8.1	0.0	SELECTIVE INS CO OF THE SOUTHEAST
2.3	1.5	151.8	207.8	-4.7	-12.0	57.4	34.2	91.6	111.8	8.1	0.0 ●	SELECTIVE WAY INS CO
3.1	2.9	N/A	N/A	N/A	N/A	N/A	N/A	N/A	-11.0	0.0	45.8	SENECA INS CO
68.8	28.2	N/A	N/A	N/A	N/A	N/A	N/A	N/A	N/A	0.0	0.0	SENECA SPECIALTY INS CO
-0.3	-0.2	999 +	999 +	999 +	999 +	155.6	-3.8	151.8	41.7	-6.2	0.0	SENIOR AMERICAN INS CO
N/A	N/A	--	--	--	--	--	--	--	--	--	--	SENIORSFIRST RRG INC
1.0	0.8	38.9	43.6	-36.3	-25.7	-15.8	23.1	7.3	166.6	8.1	0.0	SENTINEL ASR RRG INC
16.8	10.7	17.3	30.9	0.7	0.6	70.4	-15.1	55.3	105.5	0.0	0.0	SENTINEL INS CO LTD
5.1	4.1	25.1	1.0	0.6	0.2	54.7	51.9	106.6	93.5	54.6	0.0	SENTRUITY CASUALTY CO
4.3	2.6	70.1	110.0	-0.8	-2.7	73.9	28.2	102.1	107.7	7.2	0.0	SENTRY CASUALTY CO
2.6	2.2	23.0	36.1	-0.3	-1.0	73.9	28.2	102.1	111.7	7.1	21.8 ●	SENTRY INS A MUTUAL CO
218.2	109.1	N/A	N/A	N/A	N/A	N/A	N/A	N/A	-21.4	0.0	0.0	SENTRY LLOYDS OF TX
3.5	2.2	87.0	136.5	-1.0	-3.3	73.9	28.2	102.1	104.4	7.2	0.0 ●	SENTRY SELECT INS CO
7.0	4.9	7.5	4.2	0.5	0.2	64.8	66.3	131.1	194.5	18.5	8.3	SEQUOIA INDEMNITY CO
4.3	3.4	-5.3	48.2	-28.2	-20.2	720.8	-259.9	460.9	18.0	-122.4	8.8	SEQUOIA INS CO
5.3	2.9	12.9	7.2	1.3	-0.3	50.6	28.9	79.5	97.1	-61.4	0.0	SERVICE INS CO (FL)
4.1	2.9	30.3	9.8	-1.9	-5.0	14.8	57.2	72.0	239.4	26.9	0.0	SERVICE INS CO (NJ)
3.8	2.8	65.8	56.9	-3.8	-12.3	52.3	47.6	99.9	88.4	1.2	0.0	SERVICE LLOYDS INS CO
2.9	2.8	92.9	5.2	-0.7	0.8	17.9	12.9	30.8	348.8	1.1	1.4	SEVEN SEAS INS CO
1.3	0.9	119.9	236.6	0.7	3.3	73.0	20.9	93.9	123.2	9.6	2.4	SFM MUTUAL INS CO
53.4	46.1	N/A	N/A	N/A	N/A	N/A	N/A	N/A	N/A	0.0	0.0	SFM SAFE INS CO
6.0	5.4	N/A	N/A	N/A	-0.6	N/A	N/A	N/A	N/A	0.0	0.0	SFM SELECT INS CO
1.8	1.2	159.1	71.1	-0.1	0.6	65.8	28.6	94.4	115.0	10.9	0.0	SHEBOYGAN FALLS INS CO
19.5	17.2	N/A	N/A	N/A	N/A	N/A	N/A	N/A	1.9	0.0	0.0	SHELBY INS CO
2.4	2.1	58.2	67.4	-9.5	-9.1	80.2	38.9	119.1	81.5	8.8	11.1	SHELTER GENERAL INS CO
2.2	1.8	77.2	27.8	-2.4	-2.6	73.9	28.0	101.9	101.8	5.0	23.9 ●	SHELTER MUTUAL INS CO
5.4	3.5	34.6	28.9	-8.0	-8.1	44.3	27.9	72.2	128.5	9.2	0.0 ●	SHELTER REINS CO
1.8	1.2	34.4	126.4	2.3	-11.8	92.1	10.7	102.8	143.4	-1.7	0.0	SIGMA RRG INC
2.9	2.2	58.0	107.8	-8.1	-16.2	53.8	22.8	76.6	134.4	-3.6	0.0	SILVER OAK CASUALTY INC
5.8	4.1	19.5	57.4	-5.2	-7.7	60.8	26.6	87.4	94.7	-4.1	0.0	SIMED
1.0	0.7	39.9	117.8	-0.2	-4.4	73.8	36.6	110.4	63.7	-23.5	0.0 ●	SIRIUS AMERICA INS CO
N/A	N/A	--	--	--	--	--	--	--	--	--	--	SLAVONIC INS CO OF TEXAS
6.2	5.9	2.8	0.1	N/A	N/A	36.3	58.8	95.1	109.4	0.1	16.5	SLAVONIC MUTUAL FIRE INS ASN
2.7	1.9	112.4	114.0	-3.3	-4.3	65.2	28.8	94.0	113.0	3.9	0.0	SOCIETY INS A MUTUAL CO
4.2	3.3	29.3	36.8	-5.6	-2.8	41.8	23.2	65.0	177.0	-9.5	0.0	SOMERSET CASUALTY INS CO
56.1	50.5	0.2	0.4	0.1	0.1	260.2	731.9	992.1	42.6	112.8	0.0	SOMPO AM FIRE & MARINE INS CO
4.6	2.9	32.6	77.3	-4.9	-5.6	61.2	33.2	94.4	101.1	-0.4	1.3 ●	SOMPO AMERICA INSURANCE CO
N/A	N/A	--	--	--	--	--	--	--	--	--	--	SOMPO JAPAN CANOPIUS RE AG
0.2	0.1	556.4	38.3	-18.3	-5.5	34.1	34.0	68.1	182.7	70.0	0.0	SOMPO JAPAN NIPPONKOA INS INC
3.3	2.1	66.8	28.6	-1.3	-2.5	65.1	31.0	96.1	109.1	4.6	0.0	SONNENBERG MUTUAL INS CO

999 + Denotes number greater than 999.9%
999 - Denotes number less than -999.99%
● Bullets denote a more detailed analysis is available in Section II.

INSURANCE COMPANY NAME	DOM. STATE	RATING	TOTAL ASSETS ($MIL)	CAPITAL & SURPLUS ($MIL)	ANNUAL NET PREMIUM ($MIL)	NET INCOME ($MIL)	CAPITAL-IZATION INDEX (PTS)	RESERVE ADQ INDEX (PTS)	PROFIT-ABILITY INDEX (PTS)	LIQUIDITY INDEX (PTS)	STAB. INDEX (PTS)	STABILITY FACTORS
SOUTH CAROLINA FARM BU MUTUAL INS	SC	C+	106.5	51.3	54.8	0.3	8.5	7.8	3.2	5.9	3.5	FT
▲SOUTH CAROLINA FARM BUREAU INS	SC	C-	3.6	3.1	0.0	0.0	10.0	N/A	5.8	7.0	2.4	DGT
SOUTHERN COUNTY MUTUAL INS CO	TX	C	34.0	30.0	0.0	0.0	10.0	N/A	4.2	10.0	3.7	FGRT
SOUTHERN FARM BUREAU CAS INS CO	MS	B-	2,172.7	1,293.5	870.0	9.8	8.3	7.8	4.2	6.2	4.8	FT
SOUTHERN FARM BUREAU PROPERTY	MS	U	--	--	--	--	N/A	--	--	--	--	Z
SOUTHERN FIDELITY INS CO	FL	B	199.1	85.9	100.0	0.3	8.9	6.3	8.2	5.9	6.3	T
SOUTHERN FIDELITY P&C INC	FL	C+	111.0	33.3	65.9	0.0	5.6	5.3	7.8	6.7	3.3	T
SOUTHERN FIRE & CASUALTY CO	WI	C	6.8	6.7	-2.5	0.0	10.0	4.0	4.3	6.9	2.7	FGRT
▲SOUTHERN GENERAL INS CO	GA	C-	54.1	18.3	40.0	-0.3	6.1	5.6	2.9	0.8	2.8	DFLR
SOUTHERN GUARANTY INS CO	WI	C (1)	13.2	4.5	-11.0	2.2	7.2	3.9	1.9	1.7	3.5	FLRT
SOUTHERN INS CO	TX	C	40.6	29.3	0.2	0.2	7.2	4.1	3.1	7.6	3.5	FGRT
SOUTHERN INS CO OF VA	VA	C+	150.3	62.3	76.7	-1.3	9.9	6.0	4.6	6.5	4.0	RT
SOUTHERN MUTUAL CHURCH INS CO	SC	C+	65.1	34.6	25.9	1.7	8.0	8.2	8.7	6.9	3.4	RT
SOUTHERN MUTUAL INS CO	GA	C+	19.1	14.4	0.1	0.0	10.0	4.6	8.3	7.6	3.2	DFGR
▲SOUTHERN OAK INS CO	FL	B-	120.0	55.2	59.8	0.3	8.2	5.6	8.7	6.6	5.0	T
SOUTHERN PILOT INS CO	WI	C	7.2	6.9	-4.2	0.0	10.0	3.9	2.8	6.4	2.7	DFGR
SOUTHERN PIONEER PROP & CAS INS CO	AR	C+	46.9	20.5	26.1	-0.3	7.2	6.2	5.1	6.9	3.1	DFRT
SOUTHERN STATES INS EXCHANGE	VA	C+	38.6	19.2	15.9	1.1	7.8	9.3	7.0	6.6	3.0	DRT
SOUTHERN TRUST INS CO	GA	B (1)	48.3	22.6	31.4	0.3	7.9	6.1	5.6	6.2	4.7	DR
SOUTHERN UNDERWRITERS INS CO	OK	C	5.3	5.2	0.0	0.0	10.0	N/A	5.6	9.2	2.1	DFGR
SOUTHERN VANGUARD INS CO	TX	C	19.9	10.2	6.0	-0.3	7.5	4.6	3.9	6.6	2.5	DFGR
SOUTHERN-OWNERS INS CO	MI	A-	774.5	241.4	293.2	7.0	8.4	8.5	7.8	6.7	7.3	T
SOUTHLAND LLOYDS INS CO	TX	U (5)	--	--	--	--	N/A	--	--	--	--	Z
SOUTHWEST GENERAL INS CO	NM	D	2.2	1.3	0.6	0.0	8.6	9.3	1.9	7.4	1.5	DFGT
SOUTHWEST MARINE & GEN INS CO	AZ	C+	128.4	61.7	24.5	-0.1	7.8	3.0	3.9	7.2	3.6	T
SOUTHWEST PHYSICIANS RRG INC	SC	U	--	--	--	--	N/A	--	--	--	--	Z
SPARTA INS CO	CT	D+	283.6	74.9	6.3	2.2	2.3	1.0	0.6	6.4	2.5	CFRT
SPARTAN INS CO	TX	C-	7.4	6.3	3.4	0.2	9.6	6.1	8.6	8.1	2.1	DGRT
SPARTAN PROPERTY INS CO	SC	C+	29.3	23.0	10.7	1.0	7.6	5.2	6.3	7.6	3.2	DGT
SPECIALTY RISK OF AMERICA	IL	C-	16.3	5.7	7.3	0.0	4.0	6.5	4.4	7.1	2.1	DGT
SPECIALTY SURPLUS INS CO	IL	U	--	--	--	--	N/A	--	--	--	--	Z
SPINNAKER INS CO	IL	B-	38.6	28.6	8.4	-0.4	9.2	4.6	3.3	7.7	3.7	DFGR
SPIRIT COMMERCIAL AUTO RRG INC	NV	E	103.2	15.7	53.9	1.0	0.0	0.1	2.3	7.0	0.2	CDGT
SPIRIT MOUNTAIN INS CO RRG INC	DC	D+	6.9	3.8	2.1	0.0	8.6	10.0	8.7	9.4	2.2	DGR
SPRING VALLEY MUTUAL INS CO	MN	E	4.6	4.5	0.0	0.1	10.0	4.9	6.2	10.0	0.0	DGR
▲ST CHARLES INS CO RRG	SC	D-	16.1	13.7	1.8	0.3	10.0	10.0	8.8	8.7	1.0	DG
ST CLAIR INS CO	NY	U	--	--	--	--	N/A	--	--	--	--	Z
ST JOHNS INS CO	FL	C-	142.6	50.9	33.1	-0.3	2.9	5.5	3.9	4.5	3.0	CFLT
ST LUKES HEALTH NETWORK INS CO RRG	VT	E	65.0	19.3	11.0	0.5	2.0	3.6	6.1	6.9	0.1	DT
ST PAUL FIRE & MARINE INS CO	CT	B	18,495.1	5,497.0	5,490.5	137.7	7.6	8.5	4.0	6.8	5.1	T
ST PAUL GUARDIAN INS CO	CT	C+	75.1	24.8	21.8	0.5	7.7	8.2	3.9	7.3	3.7	DT
ST PAUL MERCURY INS CO	CT	B-	334.5	123.8	87.1	2.6	9.2	8.0	3.9	7.2	4.5	T
ST PAUL PROTECTIVE INS CO	CT	B-	521.8	226.4	126.4	3.6	10.0	7.9	5.4	6.9	4.6	T
ST PAUL SURPLUS LINES INS CO	DE	C	636.3	197.3	191.6	4.5	5.0	8.5	6.0	6.6	4.0	CT
STANDARD CASUALTY CO	TX	C+	38.8	18.1	28.7	0.2	7.5	4.7	3.9	6.4	4.1	DFGT
STANDARD FIRE INS CO	CT	B	3,717.4	1,195.4	1,053.7	24.0	7.8	8.3	6.6	6.8	5.0	T
STANDARD GUARANTY INS CO	DE	B-	345.2	148.3	199.8	5.7	8.2	6.2	6.9	6.2	4.5	RT
STANDARD P&C INS CO	IL	C	33.7	23.0	14.5	0.3	8.0	9.4	2.3	5.1	3.4	DFRT
STAR & SHIELD INS EXCHANGE	FL	D (1)	9.9	4.2	6.5	-0.8	2.4	3.2	0.6	3.8	1.4	CDFL
STAR CASUALTY INS CO	FL	D	15.4	4.6	6.2	-0.7	2.1	1.4	0.8	0.5	1.8	CDFG
STAR INS CO	MI	C	1,819.3	520.8	587.1	56.1	7.1	2.4	6.0	9.1	3.6	GRT
STARNET INS CO	DE	C	238.4	117.3	0.0	0.5	10.0	N/A	4.5	7.9	3.9	RT

See Page 27 for explanation of footnotes and
Page 28 for explanation of stability factors.
Arrows denote recent upgrades ▲ or downgrades ▼   (see Section VII for explanations)

116

www.weissratings.com

RISK ADJ. RATIO #1	CAPITAL RATIO #2	PREMIUM TO SURPLUS (%)	RESV. TO SURPLUS (%)	RESV. DEVELOP. 1 YEAR (%)	2 YEAR (%)	LOSS RATIO (%)	EXP. RATIO (%)	COMB RATIO (%)	CASH FROM UNDER-WRITING (%)	NET PREMIUM GROWTH (%)	INVEST. IN AFFIL (%)	INSURANCE COMPANY NAME
2.5	2.2	108.4	22.5	-4.1	-4.3	77.1	28.9	106.0	91.9	4.9	8.5	SOUTH CAROLINA FARM BU MUTUAL INS
14.2	12.8	N/A	N/A	N/A	N/A	N/A	N/A	N/A	N/A	0.0	0.0	SOUTH CAROLINA FARM BUREAU INS
23.5	21.2	N/A	N/A	N/A	N/A	N/A	N/A	N/A	-11.9	0.0	0.0	SOUTHERN COUNTY MUTUAL INS CO
1.9	1.8	67.6	31.7	-1.5	-2.9	92.2	20.1	112.3	91.8	3.8	33.0 ●	SOUTHERN FARM BUREAU CAS INS CO
N/A	N/A	--	--	--	--	--	--	--	--	--	--	SOUTHERN FARM BUREAU PROPERTY
3.4	2.7	115.9	31.3	-2.5	1.5	55.1	46.0	101.1	99.5	-6.5	2.4	SOUTHERN FIDELITY INS CO
1.7	1.1	198.1	74.9	5.5	2.9	67.3	34.0	101.3	106.3	4.0	1.7	SOUTHERN FIDELITY P&C INC
133.7	66.8	-38.0	N/A	N/A	N/A	N/A	N/A	N/A	-21.1	-131.5	0.0	SOUTHERN FIRE & CASUALTY CO
1.2	1.0	215.6	63.3	19.4	6.1	78.1	28.0	106.1	81.4	6.4	0.0	SOUTHERN GENERAL INS CO
1.7	1.5	-245.2	N/A	N/A	N/A	N/A	N/A	N/A	-21.1	-136.3	0.0	SOUTHERN GUARANTY INS CO
1.9	1.1	0.6	35.2	9.0	8.8	999 +	263.1	999 +	-112.7	-62.5	0.0	SOUTHERN INS CO
3.8	2.7	121.1	57.9	-1.9	-1.4	65.8	33.0	98.8	100.5	11.8	0.0	SOUTHERN INS CO OF VA
2.8	2.0	78.7	24.9	-5.6	-6.5	43.8	37.6	81.4	125.8	3.9	0.0	SOUTHERN MUTUAL CHURCH INS CO
9.8	8.8	0.6	0.3	0.1	N/A	24.4	-831.6	-807.2	31.3	-13.5	0.0	SOUTHERN MUTUAL INS CO
3.1	2.5	110.1	38.4	-2.9	-5.2	62.2	33.0	95.2	104.2	-12.2	0.0	SOUTHERN OAK INS CO
46.6	42.0	-61.2	N/A	N/A	N/A	N/A	N/A	N/A	-21.1	-133.2	0.0	SOUTHERN PILOT INS CO
1.7	1.1	127.4	42.6	-3.3	-4.2	66.7	31.5	98.2	99.0	5.2	0.0	SOUTHERN PIONEER PROP & CAS INS
2.5	1.6	89.7	76.2	-0.1	-1.3	67.5	26.5	94.0	117.6	10.4	0.0	SOUTHERN STATES INS EXCHANGE
2.3	1.6	139.0	21.7	3.1	-1.9	56.7	42.5	99.2	97.3	8.4	0.0	SOUTHERN TRUST INS CO
76.2	35.9	N/A	N/A	N/A	N/A	N/A	N/A	N/A	-199.1	0.0	0.0	SOUTHERN UNDERWRITERS INS CO
1.8	1.3	57.4	8.4	-2.7	-1.4	104.2	17.4	121.6	82.3	-11.7	0.0	SOUTHERN VANGUARD INS CO
2.7	1.9	126.3	137.7	0.6	-1.6	75.5	25.8	101.3	119.4	10.2	0.0 ●	SOUTHERN-OWNERS INS CO
N/A	N/A	--	--	--	--	--	--	--	--	--	--	SOUTHLAND LLOYDS INS CO
2.7	2.2	43.2	19.4	-5.4	-9.4	55.2	97.2	152.4	55.7	-28.9	0.0	SOUTHWEST GENERAL INS CO
3.3	1.8	39.9	59.9	4.0	15.5	74.8	36.8	111.6	227.8	-15.1	0.0	SOUTHWEST MARINE & GEN INS CO
N/A	N/A	--	--	--	--	--	--	--	--	--	--	SOUTHWEST PHYSICIANS RRG INC
0.7	0.4	8.6	286.9	53.5	64.0	999 +	149.7	999 +	3.4	46.6	0.0	SPARTA INS CO
2.9	2.6	55.5	1.6	-0.8	-0.9	2.8	72.0	74.8	119.6	9.3	0.0	SPARTAN INS CO
2.4	1.5	49.6	1.0	-0.8	-1.5	8.4	61.4	69.8	138.9	7.0	0.0	SPARTAN PROPERTY INS CO
0.8	0.5	129.0	94.6	-0.3	-3.7	57.6	42.5	100.1	113.9	19.6	0.0	SPECIALTY RISK OF AMERICA
N/A	N/A	--	--	--	--	--	--	--	--	--	--	SPECIALTY SURPLUS INS CO
2.7	1.9	28.8	4.2	N/A	N/A	70.2	66.9	137.1	80.6	N/A	0.0	SPINNAKER INS CO
0.0	0.0	404.4	379.3	96.0	284.4	88.6	16.0	104.6	122.4	58.9	0.0	SPIRIT COMMERCIAL AUTO RRG INC
3.8	2.2	55.0	37.5	-24.6	-44.6	4.2	49.5	53.7	170.4	0.9	0.0	SPIRIT MOUNTAIN INS CO RRG INC
73.4	35.0	N/A	N/A	N/A	N/A	N/A	N/A	N/A	N/A	0.0	0.0	SPRING VALLEY MUTUAL INS CO
6.2	3.6	13.7	11.9	-10.7	-16.6	15.3	27.7	43.0	354.6	19.4	0.0	ST CHARLES INS CO RRG
N/A	N/A	--	--	--	--	--	--	--	--	--	--	ST CLAIR INS CO
0.5	0.5	64.3	29.7	0.1	3.6	116.5	9.2	125.7	84.6	-2.8	0.0	ST JOHNS INS CO
0.7	0.5	59.0	239.6	-23.2	-34.7	75.2	9.7	84.9	140.5	-24.1	0.0	ST LUKES HEALTH NETWORK INS CO
2.0	1.4	98.8	167.1	-1.9	-4.5	63.8	30.1	93.9	109.8	4.5	12.1 ●	ST PAUL FIRE & MARINE INS CO
2.2	1.4	89.6	148.7	-1.7	-4.3	63.4	29.9	93.3	140.6	4.8	0.0	ST PAUL GUARDIAN INS CO
3.7	2.4	71.8	119.1	-1.4	-3.4	63.4	30.0	93.4	140.0	4.8	0.0	ST PAUL MERCURY INS CO
4.7	3.0	56.7	94.1	-1.1	-2.9	63.3	30.0	93.3	106.5	4.8	0.0 ●	ST PAUL PROTECTIVE INS CO
1.0	0.6	99.3	164.8	-2.0	-5.0	63.4	29.9	93.3	99.2	4.8	0.0	ST PAUL SURPLUS LINES INS CO
2.1	1.4	159.0	14.0	0.4	6.6	66.9	40.6	107.5	91.9	11.5	0.0	STANDARD CASUALTY CO
1.9	1.5	87.7	145.5	-1.8	-4.4	63.4	30.1	93.5	108.8	4.8	16.6 ●	STANDARD FIRE INS CO
2.4	1.9	139.4	30.5	-12.7	-9.0	35.6	50.1	85.7	102.3	-8.9	0.0	STANDARD GUARANTY INS CO
3.2	2.5	63.8	N/A	-28.7	-19.9	74.3	77.7	152.0	52.6	-66.7	0.0	STANDARD P&C INS CO
0.7	0.6	155.5	113.3	-10.5	-39.3	103.0	11.1	114.1	60.6	-35.5	0.0	STAR & SHIELD INS EXCHANGE
0.5	0.4	150.5	59.6	35.3	36.9	124.3	46.2	170.5	62.4	-28.3	0.0	STAR CASUALTY INS CO
1.2	1.0	115.5	203.8	5.7	32.6	64.6	32.7	97.3	-532.7	175.6	18.8 ●	STAR INS CO
12.7	11.4	N/A	N/A	N/A	N/A	N/A	N/A	N/A	804.1	0.0	0.0	STARNET INS CO

999 + Denotes number greater than 999.9%
999 - Denotes number less than -999.99%
● Bullets denote a more detailed analysis is available in Section II.

INSURANCE COMPANY NAME	DOM. STATE	RATING	TOTAL ASSETS ($MIL)	CAPITAL & SURPLUS ($MIL)	ANNUAL NET PREMIUM ($MIL)	NET INCOME ($MIL)	CAPITAL-IZATION INDEX (PTS)	RESERVE ADQ INDEX (PTS)	PROFIT-ABILITY INDEX (PTS)	LIQUIDITY INDEX (PTS)	STAB. INDEX (PTS)	STABILITY FACTORS
STARR INDEMNITY & LIABILITY CO	TX	B	4,442.6	1,874.5	1,003.2	8.0	7.2	4.5	6.2	6.8	4.7	RT
STARR SPECIALTY INSURANCE CO	TX	U	--	--	--	--	N/A	--	--	--	--	Z
STARR SURPLUS LINES INS CO	IL	B-	347.2	125.4	65.6	9.3	7.3	3.6	8.9	6.5	3.6	FT
STARSTONE NATIONAL INS CO	DE	C	390.8	94.0	93.1	-1.8	7.3	7.0	4.6	5.3	3.6	FGT
STARSTONE SPECIALTY INS CO	DE	C-	198.0	114.7	34.7	-1.4	7.0	2.8	3.6	7.0	3.3	GRT
STATE AUTO INS CO OF OH	OH	C-	29.0	17.1	0.0	0.1	10.0	N/A	7.2	9.2	3.3	ADFG
STATE AUTO INS CO OF WI	WI	B-	15.9	12.1	0.0	0.0	10.0	N/A	5.6	7.0	3.6	ADFG
STATE AUTO P&C INS CO	IA	C+	2,496.9	685.3	1,014.7	1.0	7.4	5.7	5.3	6.3	4.3	ART
STATE AUTOMOBILE MUTUAL INS CO	OH	C+	2,488.5	826.4	686.4	-1.5	7.0	5.9	3.8	6.2	4.3	AT
STATE FARM CTY MUTUAL INS CO OF TX	TX	B-	184.3	19.3	32.6	0.7	7.1	6.0	1.0	5.7	3.5	DFT
STATE FARM FIRE & CAS CO	IL	B+	38,866.0	16,715.8	16,167.1	244.2	7.7	6.5	8.3	5.5	5.1	T
STATE FARM FLORIDA INS CO	FL	B	2,095.9	1,114.1	570.7	27.7	9.6	6.4	8.9	6.7	5.4	T
STATE FARM GENERAL INS CO	IL	B	7,137.5	3,999.3	1,930.7	-70.9	10.0	6.4	5.9	6.7	4.9	T
STATE FARM GUARANTY INS CO	IL	C+	36.9	13.5	0.0	0.0	10.0	N/A	6.2	10.0	4.8	DFGR
STATE FARM INDEMNITY CO	IL	B	2,255.2	1,230.4	631.2	10.0	10.0	8.9	6.6	6.8	5.0	T
STATE FARM LLOYDS	TX	B	3,502.3	1,360.9	1,671.2	18.3	8.5	6.6	7.1	6.0	5.0	T
STATE FARM MUTUAL AUTOMOBILE INS CO	IL	B+	150,198.0	89,522.3	40,455.0	534.4	8.1	7.6	4.2	6.5	5.3	FT
STATE MUTUAL INS CO (ME)	ME	C	2.5	2.3	0.0	0.0	9.1	N/A	7.7	7.0	2.3	DGT
STATE NATIONAL FIRE INS CO	LA	C	3.9	2.7	1.6	0.0	7.9	7.5	3.2	8.0	2.5	DGT
STATE NATIONAL INS CO	TX	B-	357.8	274.3	62.6	3.1	7.8	5.0	7.6	7.0	4.8	RT
STATE VOLUNTEER MUTUAL INS CO	TN	B	1,215.1	567.5	111.8	-5.4	10.0	9.4	5.4	8.4	4.9	RT
STATES SELF-INSURERS RISK RET GROUP	VT	D-	26.0	9.0	4.3	0.3	0.5	4.0	2.8	7.4	1.2	CDGR
STEADFAST INS CO	DE	C+	577.2	500.2	0.0	0.9	9.0	N/A	7.3	7.0	4.7	RT
STEADPOINT INS CO	TN	C-	26.4	9.9	9.2	0.2	6.5	7.0	8.8	6.9	3.0	DGRT
STERLING CASUALTY INS CO	CA	D	16.6	3.8	7.4	-0.1	4.5	1.7	2.3	7.1	1.9	DGT
STERLING INS CO	NY	B	181.5	114.0	60.1	2.7	10.0	9.1	8.8	6.9	4.1	RT
STERLING INS COOP INC	NY	U	--	--	--	--	N/A	--	--	--	--	Z
STICO MUTUAL INS CO RRG	VT	D	23.1	12.2	2.8	0.0	7.5	9.3	6.5	7.0	1.9	DFGR
STILLWATER INS CO	CA	B-	377.0	190.2	221.7	0.5	6.2	7.9	5.7	2.0	4.1	LRT
STILLWATER P&C INS CO	NY	C+	135.0	123.0	2.5	2.4	10.0	N/A	8.2	10.0	4.1	T
STONE VALLEY MUTUAL FIRE INS CO	PA	U (1)	--	--	--	--	N/A	--	--	--	--	Z
STONEGATE INS CO	IL	D	22.9	5.0	15.2	-0.7	1.7	0.8	2.9	6.2	1.5	CDGT
▲STONETRUST COMMERCIAL INS CO	NE	B-	161.2	60.6	53.1	0.4	7.1	3.7	4.5	6.7	4.9	RT
STONEWOOD INS CO	NC	C+	114.1	25.7	18.4	0.1	7.0	8.2	3.1	7.0	3.6	GRT
STONINGTON INS CO	PA	E+	15.1	13.5	-21.1	-0.7	10.0	4.1	1.9	0.8	0.6	DFGL
STRATFORD INS CO	NH	B-	144.3	84.7	15.2	-0.3	10.0	9.4	5.4	7.5	4.1	FRT
STRATHMORE INS CO	NY	C	55.0	26.3	14.3	0.5	8.2	6.0	8.1	6.8	4.0	T
SU INS CO	WI	C	19.8	12.5	15.4	-0.3	9.7	6.1	4.6	7.2	3.2	DGT
SUBLIMITY INS CO	OR	C+	40.4	16.4	26.6	-0.6	7.9	5.6	5.6	5.4	3.4	DGRT
SUBURBAN HEALTH ORG RRG LLC	SC	U	--	--	--	--	N/A	--	--	--	--	Z
SUECIA INS CO	NY	U	--	--	--	--	N/A	--	--	--	--	Z
SUMMITPOINT INS CO	WV	C+	55.6	11.6	7.2	0.1	5.6	5.0	5.5	8.8	3.1	DT
SUN SURETY INS CO	SD	C-	20.7	10.2	3.7	0.2	8.4	N/A	8.6	7.6	3.0	DGT
SUNAPEE MUTL FIRE INS CO	NH	B	4.5	4.1	0.0	0.0	8.9	N/A	7.6	7.0	4.0	DGT
SUNDERLAND MARINE INS CO LTD	AK	D+	10.3	5.8	0.3	0.1	8.8	5.8	2.0	10.0	2.4	DFGR
SUNLAND RRG INC	TN	B-	6.3	1.5	0.6	0.2	7.4	6.8	6.2	5.2	3.5	DFGT
SUNZ INS CO	FL	E	140.2	28.2	41.1	0.0	0.3	1.2	2.9	0.5	0.3	CDGL
SURETEC INDEMNITY CO	CA	C+	23.0	12.7	7.2	0.3	8.2	4.8	5.8	7.6	3.1	DGT
SURETEC INS CO	TX	B	228.9	97.5	61.7	2.9	9.3	8.5	8.6	7.9	6.0	T
SURETY BONDING CO OF AMERICA	SD	C+	7.6	7.6	0.0	0.0	10.0	N/A	3.9	10.0	3.0	DGRT
SUSSEX INS CO	IL	C+	634.7	134.2	1.5	1.9	2.5	4.9	1.0	7.0	4.3	CFT
SUTTER INS CO	CA	C	35.8	20.8	13.1	-0.1	9.3	5.9	3.4	6.6	2.9	DFGR

See Page 27 for explanation of footnotes and
Page 28 for explanation of stability factors.

Arrows denote recent upgrades ▲ or downgrades ▼   (see Section VII for explanations)

118

www.weissratings.com

RISK RATIO #1	ADJ. CAPITAL RATIO #2	PREMIUM TO SURPLUS (%)	RESV. TO SURPLUS (%)	RESV. 1 YEAR (%)	DEVELOP. 2 YEAR (%)	LOSS RATIO (%)	EXP. RATIO (%)	COMB RATIO (%)	CASH FROM UNDER-WRITING (%)	NET PREMIUM GROWTH (%)	INVEST. IN AFFIL (%)	INSURANCE COMPANY NAME
1.3	1.1	52.2	89.2	6.7	8.6	85.9	19.0	104.9	127.9	-6.9	34.1 •	STARR INDEMNITY & LIABILITY CO
N/A	N/A	--	--	--	--	--	--	--	--	--	--	STARR SPECIALTY INSURANCE CO
2.2	1.3	57.4	80.0	-0.8	8.4	64.4	10.2	74.6	62.0	41.6	0.0	STARR SURPLUS LINES INS CO
2.6	1.1	98.9	113.2	1.4	-3.1	68.1	31.3	99.4	67.1	18.7	0.0	STARSTONE NATIONAL INS CO
1.1	1.0	29.5	62.4	1.2	14.0	83.0	19.0	102.0	101.2	43.7	63.1	STARSTONE SPECIALTY INS CO
6.5	5.8	N/A	N/A	N/A	N/A	N/A	N/A	N/A	-204.3	0.0	0.0	STATE AUTO INS CO OF OH
9.8	8.9	N/A	N/A	N/A	N/A	N/A	N/A	N/A	782.9	0.0	0.0	STATE AUTO INS CO OF WI
2.0	1.2	148.7	136.8	2.0	1.8	73.1	33.4	106.5	104.1	1.6	0.0 •	STATE AUTO P&C INS CO
1.1	1.0	83.5	76.8	1.1	0.9	73.1	34.2	107.3	97.4	1.6	46.1 •	STATE AUTOMOBILE MUTUAL INS CO
1.7	1.3	176.8	96.2	4.8	4.6	116.5	25.7	142.2	58.4	-5.8	0.0	STATE FARM CTY MUTUAL INS CO OF TX
2.7	1.7	98.9	45.0	2.4	0.5	65.2	26.7	91.9	110.7	1.6	0.0 •	STATE FARM FIRE & CAS CO
5.1	3.6	52.7	28.2	-0.2	0.1	48.4	25.7	74.1	133.7	-2.3	0.0 •	STATE FARM FLORIDA INS CO
6.4	4.3	47.4	33.2	2.7	0.2	75.3	27.6	102.9	102.6	1.4	0.0 •	STATE FARM GENERAL INS CO
3.4	3.1	N/A	N/A	N/A	N/A	N/A	N/A	N/A	999 +	0.0	0.0	STATE FARM GUARANTY INS CO
5.9	5.0	51.8	58.1	-3.2	-5.1	83.3	23.0	106.3	91.9	1.6	0.6 •	STATE FARM INDEMNITY CO
2.7	2.4	124.6	35.9	0.8	1.5	60.4	29.1	89.5	113.1	6.3	0.0 •	STATE FARM LLOYDS
2.0	1.7	46.2	32.5	0.4	-0.6	91.9	25.3	117.2	92.8	7.8	28.0 •	STATE FARM MUTUAL AUTOMOBILE INS
3.9	2.3	N/A	N/A	N/A	N/A	N/A	N/A	N/A	N/A	0.0	0.0	STATE MUTUAL INS CO (ME)
2.1	1.6	60.1	1.1	-1.4	-2.3	23.4	59.7	83.1	134.4	95.5	0.0	STATE NATIONAL FIRE INS CO
1.6	1.5	23.2	2.1	0.1	0.5	47.6	39.2	86.8	114.8	11.4	55.9 •	STATE NATIONAL INS CO
4.5	3.4	19.7	86.7	-7.1	-11.6	79.3	19.6	98.9	91.4	-1.4	0.0 •	STATE VOLUNTEER MUTUAL INS CO
0.2	0.1	49.7	159.1	-1.5	-1.4	95.6	30.1	125.7	181.0	66.6	0.0	STATES SELF-INSURERS RISK RET
2.3	2.3	N/A	N/A	N/A	N/A	N/A	N/A	N/A	8.3	0.0	46.1 •	STEADFAST INS CO
1.4	1.1	94.7	106.5	-2.0	-8.3	48.2	27.9	76.1	134.8	1.3	0.0	STEADPOINT INS CO
0.9	0.7	190.3	111.6	29.6	44.3	92.4	21.6	114.0	245.5	22.6	0.0	STERLING CASUALTY INS CO
6.5	4.8	54.1	22.9	-2.8	-6.0	47.1	33.7	80.8	130.5	4.0	0.2	STERLING INS CO
N/A	N/A	--	--	--	--	--	--	--	--	--	--	STERLING INS COOP INC
3.4	2.1	23.8	35.4	-12.6	-22.2	37.4	63.8	101.2	69.5	-16.8	0.0	STICO MUTUAL INS CO RRG
1.1	0.8	119.2	31.8	3.0	-0.7	66.9	33.4	100.3	108.2	18.6	38.2	STILLWATER INS CO
10.4	5.6	2.1	N/A	N/A	N/A	N/A	15.7	15.7	295.2	10.9	0.0	STILLWATER P&C INS CO
N/A	N/A	--	--	--	--	--	--	--	--	--	--	STONE VALLEY MUTUAL FIRE INS CO
0.4	0.3	282.9	117.7	37.7	51.1	59.2	34.7	93.9	114.5	7.3	0.0	STONEGATE INS CO
1.6	1.1	94.5	116.9	-0.4	10.0	63.8	37.0	100.8	104.6	-7.6	0.0	STONETRUST COMMERCIAL INS CO
1.9	1.3	72.8	110.5	-4.1	-4.9	85.1	14.6	99.7	130.2	243.3	0.0	STONEWOOD INS CO
21.2	19.1	-148.6	N/A	N/A	N/A	N/A	N/A	N/A	-21.2	-134.4	0.0	STONINGTON INS CO
8.0	5.5	17.9	47.4	-1.6	-3.2	68.3	39.3	107.6	57.9	25.4	0.0	STRATFORD INS CO
2.2	1.8	55.4	79.3	3.1	1.8	66.5	29.3	95.8	107.4	5.2	0.0	STRATHMORE INS CO
3.8	2.4	119.8	10.3	-0.8	-1.6	60.5	35.5	96.0	106.8	12.5	0.0	SU INS CO
2.0	1.6	157.6	50.5	1.0	6.4	71.6	31.7	103.3	106.4	3.4	0.0	SUBLIMITY INS CO
N/A	N/A	--	--	--	--	--	--	--	--	--	--	SUBURBAN HEALTH ORG RRG LLC
N/A	N/A	--	--	--	--	--	--	--	--	--	--	SUECIA INS CO
1.3	0.9	62.6	197.0	-12.6	-29.0	69.6	26.3	95.9	143.1	37.9	0.0	SUMMITPOINT INS CO
2.4	1.9	37.3	N/A	N/A	N/A	1.8	72.9	74.7	137.3	19.1	20.6	SUN SURETY INS CO
3.6	2.1	N/A	N/A	N/A	N/A	N/A	N/A	N/A	N/A	0.0	0.0	SUNAPEE MUTL FIRE INS CO
4.2	3.8	4.8	N/A	1.9	12.0	-16.9	99.8	82.9	-48.0	-87.4	0.0	SUNDERLAND MARINE INS CO LTD
1.0	0.9	42.7	34.6	0.3	-8.9	62.6	42.6	105.2	53.1	-1.3	0.0	SUNLAND RRG INC
0.3	0.2	202.8	112.3	29.3	22.4	48.0	52.1	100.1	110.9	64.7	0.0	SUNZ INS CO
2.5	2.1	58.2	22.8	-6.9	-6.8	22.2	63.7	85.9	117.4	-7.1	0.0	SURETEC INDEMNITY CO
3.3	2.7	65.3	11.5	-4.6	-5.5	12.6	60.5	73.1	134.2	4.0	5.8	SURETEC INS CO
86.9	41.2	N/A	N/A	N/A	N/A	N/A	N/A	N/A	N/A	0.0	0.0	SURETY BONDING CO OF AMERICA
0.7	0.4	1.1	222.7	3.4	-62.4	247.8	999 +	999 +	6.2	100.8	0.0	SUSSEX INS CO
3.3	2.6	62.8	37.1	-5.6	4.3	60.4	41.9	102.3	81.9	-6.2	0.0	SUTTER INS CO

999 + Denotes number greater than 999.9%
999 - Denotes number less than -999.99%
• Bullets denote a more detailed analysis is available in Section II.

INSURANCE COMPANY NAME	DOM. STATE	RATING	TOTAL ASSETS ($MIL)	CAPITAL & SURPLUS ($MIL)	ANNUAL NET PREMIUM ($MIL)	NET INCOME ($MIL)	CAPITAL-IZATION INDEX (PTS)	RESERVE ADQ INDEX (PTS)	PROFIT-ABILITY INDEX (PTS)	LIQUIDITY INDEX (PTS)	STAB. INDEX (PTS)	STABILITY FACTORS
SWISS REINS AMERICA CORP	NY	C-	13,505.3	3,418.9	1,882.9	79.7	5.0	8.9	3.2	7.0	2.0	RT
SYNCORA CAPITAL ASR INC	NY	E	424.2	226.2	9.9	2.0	8.9	0.5	2.8	9.8	0.0	DFT
SYNCORA GUARANTEE INC	NY	E-	1,267.9	1,185.1	8.2	-8.8	10.0	1.9	6.1	10.0	0.0	FT
▲SYNERGY COMP INS CO	PA	C-	37.2	14.0	14.8	0.2	5.1	9.9	8.8	6.8	3.0	DGRT
SYNERGY INS CO	NC	C-	68.5	23.2	17.5	-0.3	5.2	7.0	5.5	7.2	3.3	DRT
TANK OWNER MEMBERS INS CO	TX	C	28.3	14.0	5.7	0.4	7.8	8.9	9.4	7.5	3.4	DGRT
TDC NATIONAL ASR CO	OR	C+	318.3	93.4	18.7	4.2	7.4	6.4	6.2	7.4	4.4	T
TDC SPECIALTY INS CO	DC	C	76.8	50.2	3.9	-2.9	10.0	6.2	3.7	8.3	3.8	DGT
TEACHERS AUTO INS CO	NJ	B- (1)	25.5	13.6	0.0	0.4	10.0	6.1	7.9	10.0	4.6	D
TEACHERS INS CO	IL	B	350.8	150.3	205.8	1.2	7.9	8.5	6.8	5.0	4.4	AT
TECHNOLOGY INS CO	DE	C	2,471.3	557.5	1,140.4	-16.7	5.6	3.0	3.7	5.6	3.6	RT
TECUMSEH HEALTH RECIPROCAL RRG	VT	C	55.8	28.2	6.2	0.1	7.7	7.0	6.5	7.6	4.0	DGT
TENNESSEE FARMERS ASR CO	TN	B+	1,442.2	994.9	600.4	4.6	10.0	8.1	8.6	6.3	5.1	T
TENNESSEE FARMERS MUTUAL INS CO	TN	B+	2,919.9	2,301.8	603.3	6.8	8.1	7.6	8.5	6.7	5.1	T
TERRA INS CO (A RRG)	VT	B-	36.0	18.1	7.7	0.5	9.2	5.9	6.9	8.0	4.1	DGRT
TERRAFIRMA RRG LLC	VT	D+	7.7	4.8	1.3	0.1	9.8	4.0	4.6	8.1	2.1	DGT
TEXAS BUILDERS INS CO	TX	U	--	--	--	--	N/A	--	--	--	--	Z
TEXAS FAIR PLAN ASSN	TX	E-	70.7	-14.6	80.4	1.5	0.0	3.8	0.2	7.0	0.0	CDFT
TEXAS FARM BUREAU CASUALTY INS CO	TX	B+	1,206.1	668.2	687.1	11.2	10.0	6.1	4.2	5.5	6.6	LT
TEXAS FARM BUREAU MUTUAL INS CO	TX	C	746.2	340.0	423.3	-8.1	9.3	6.2	4.6	5.8	4.0	T
TEXAS FARM BUREAU UNDERWRITERS	TX	C	68.6	19.8	0.0	0.0	9.9	N/A	5.2	7.0	3.4	DT
TEXAS FARMERS INS CO	TX	C+	333.0	87.0	147.6	-0.3	8.5	5.7	4.4	6.4	4.4	FRT
TEXAS HERITAGE INS CO	TX	C	19.9	17.1	4.7	0.4	9.5	6.0	2.5	6.8	4.0	DFGR
TEXAS HOSPITAL INS EXCHANGE	TX	C-	36.2	23.6	7.5	0.3	9.6	10.0	8.8	7.0	2.5	DGRT
TEXAS INS CO	TX	C	34.8	15.6	18.2	1.2	5.0	7.0	9.3	7.7	3.1	CDGT
TEXAS LAWYERS INS EXCHANGE	TX	C+	90.8	64.1	16.9	1.8	10.0	9.4	8.9	7.6	3.5	DRT
▲TEXAS MEDICAL INS CO	TX	C-	58.2	32.2	19.0	0.0	7.8	9.3	8.7	7.5	3.0	DGRT
TEXAS PACIFIC INDEMNITY CO	TX	B	7.7	7.5	0.0	0.0	10.0	N/A	6.7	10.0	4.5	DGT
THAMES INS CO	CT	C	29.1	17.1	10.7	0.3	8.5	8.3	7.4	6.8	3.3	DGT
THE INS CO	LA	C	206.4	48.9	69.1	0.4	5.9	7.0	2.2	6.8	4.2	RT
THIRD COAST INS CO	WI	U	--	--	--	--	N/A	--	--	--	--	Z
TIG INS CO	CA	C	2,718.7	726.4	63.5	-43.8	2.7	3.7	2.4	8.7	3.7	CFGR
TITAN INDEMNITY CO	TX	B-	211.1	145.7	0.0	0.2	7.8	N/A	3.6	7.0	5.0	T
TITAN INS CO	MI	B-	132.3	101.2	0.0	-0.7	10.0	N/A	3.8	7.0	4.5	DT
TITAN INS CO INC A RRG	SC	C	65.9	47.3	7.6	1.4	8.8	N/A	8.9	8.4	4.0	RT
TITLE INDUSTRY ASR CO RRG	VT	D+	7.3	4.9	0.9	0.0	10.0	9.3	8.9	9.7	2.3	DGR
TM SPECIALTY INS CO	AZ	U	--	--	--	--	N/A	--	--	--	--	Z
TNUS INS CO	NY	B	68.1	57.2	0.0	0.3	10.0	3.6	7.3	10.0	4.1	DT
TOA REINS CO OF AMERICA	DE	B+	1,749.0	640.1	397.0	12.0	8.0	6.4	5.7	6.9	5.1	T
TOKIO MARINE AMERICA INS CO	NY	A	1,401.2	547.5	302.7	5.2	8.4	6.9	4.7	6.8	7.4	T
TOKIO MARINE PACIFIC INS LTD	GU	C	112.7	70.4	143.9	2.7	8.6	7.9	6.4	1.0	3.4	FLT
TOKIO MARINE SPECIALTY INS CO	DE	C	583.4	201.3	151.2	4.3	9.5	7.6	8.9	6.9	3.9	T
TOKIO MILLENNIUM RE AG (US BRANCH)	NY	C	1,036.3	207.7	538.6	12.8	6.0	3.6	2.3	6.3	3.2	GT
TOPA INS CO	CA	B-	189.4	78.6	72.5	0.0	8.5	6.3	4.1	6.7	3.8	RT
TOWER BONDING & SURETY CO	PR	D+	3.7	2.7	1.5	0.0	7.2	5.0	4.9	6.3	2.0	DFG
TOWER HILL PREFERRED INS CO	FL	D	102.8	48.5	38.3	0.4	9.2	4.5	7.5	7.0	2.1	RT
TOWER HILL PRIME INS CO	FL	D	204.3	93.6	37.5	1.2	10.0	3.3	4.5	7.0	1.6	RT
TOWER HILL SELECT INS CO	FL	C	77.5	29.9	18.9	-0.7	5.7	3.1	2.9	6.6	4.1	FRT
TOWER HILL SIGNATURE INS CO	FL	C	121.7	45.8	49.7	1.7	3.7	3.8	3.8	5.5	3.8	CT
TOYOTA MOTOR INS CO	IA	C+	534.8	252.3	89.2	5.3	10.0	5.0	8.9	7.5	4.0	RT
▲TRADERS INS CO	MO	C-	78.4	23.5	63.8	0.2	2.8	6.4	9.1	5.1	3.0	CDRT
TRADEWIND INS CO LTD	HI	C	13.8	8.3	0.0	0.0	10.0	N/A	6.5	9.0	2.8	DGT

See Page 27 for explanation of footnotes and Page 28 for explanation of stability factors.
Arrows denote recent upgrades ▲ or downgrades ▼ (see Section VII for explanations)

120

www.weissratings.com

RISK ADJ. RATIO #1	CAPITAL RATIO #2	PREMIUM TO SURPLUS (%)	RESV. TO SURPLUS (%)	RESV. DEVELOP. 1 YEAR (%)	RESV. DEVELOP. 2 YEAR (%)	LOSS RATIO (%)	EXP. RATIO (%)	COMB RATIO (%)	CASH FROM UNDER-WRITING (%)	NET PREMIUM GROWTH (%)	INVEST. IN AFFIL (%)	INSURANCE COMPANY NAME
1.0	0.7	56.2	127.8	1.4	-3.4	57.2	36.7	93.9	154.0	-5.3	0.0 ●	SWISS REINS AMERICA CORP
3.5	2.2	4.4	25.5	24.4	53.4	69.7	248.0	317.7	22.9	-15.2	0.0 ●	SYNCORA CAPITAL ASR INC
16.0	9.1	0.7	-10.4	-17.6	-42.1	-296.4	277.8	-18.6	19.3	-36.1	2.1 ●	SYNCORA GUARANTEE INC
1.2	1.0	108.5	96.4	-31.7	-42.3	41.9	25.9	67.8	152.1	22.2	0.0	SYNERGY COMP INS CO
1.9	1.5	75.7	68.8	-28.6	-21.8	26.3	21.6	47.9	137.3	-2.6	0.0	SYNERGY INS CO
2.7	1.7	43.3	66.6	-4.7	-7.1	36.1	12.9	49.0	221.1	-3.3	3.2	TANK OWNER MEMBERS INS CO
1.9	1.2	21.0	35.9	-7.2	-6.0	10.9	11.0	21.9	196.9	-1.2	0.0	TDC NATIONAL ASR CO
5.5	4.5	7.3	13.0	1.5	1.3	346.0	67.7	413.7	75.1	640.1	6.7	TDC SPECIALTY INS CO
5.1	4.6	N/A	N/A	N/A	-0.5	N/A	N/A	N/A	N/A	0.0	0.0	TEACHERS AUTO INS CO
3.1	2.0	136.2	53.2	-1.0	-5.2	75.1	25.9	101.0	97.8	4.7	0.0	TEACHERS INS CO
1.0	0.7	197.6	181.6	-0.7	11.8	64.8	29.5	94.3	137.3	15.8	4.4 ●	TECHNOLOGY INS CO
3.0	1.9	31.9	78.8	-6.0	-8.4	72.7	10.7	83.4	146.8	-1.3	0.0	TECUMSEH HEALTH RECIPROCAL RRG
5.8	4.0	61.0	18.5	-2.8	-4.5	72.2	14.7	86.9	117.9	2.4	1.7 ●	TENNESSEE FARMERS ASR CO
1.8	1.7	26.4	10.9	-1.2	-2.0	72.0	14.5	86.5	120.3	2.4	49.4 ●	TENNESSEE FARMERS MUTUAL INS CO
3.7	2.5	42.2	13.4	2.9	3.1	17.7	54.1	71.8	145.8	6.6	0.0	TERRA INS CO (A RRG)
4.3	2.7	28.0	33.2	6.9	7.9	67.8	34.7	102.5	142.4	8.1	0.0	TERRAFIRMA RRG LLC
N/A	N/A	--	--	--	--	--	--	--	--	--	--	TEXAS BUILDERS INS CO
-0.2	-0.1	-528.8	-155.4	-21.9	-93.6	92.4	33.4	125.8	75.1	-8.9	0.0	TEXAS FAIR PLAN ASSN
4.3	3.4	105.1	36.6	0.2	0.2	86.9	17.9	104.8	94.4	6.6	0.0 ●	TEXAS FARM BUREAU CASUALTY INS
2.7	2.5	122.2	17.8	-3.6	-3.1	74.8	20.9	95.7	97.7	3.9	1.3 ●	TEXAS FARM BUREAU MUTUAL INS CO
2.9	2.6	N/A	N/A	N/A	N/A	N/A	N/A	N/A	N/A	0.0	0.0	TEXAS FARM BUREAU UNDERWRITERS
2.8	2.0	168.6	106.9	3.2	5.4	72.2	30.8	103.0	92.2	-1.1	0.0	TEXAS FARMERS INS CO
2.9	2.6	27.9	4.0	-0.6	-0.8	85.6	38.6	124.2	83.7	8.7	0.0	TEXAS HERITAGE INS CO
6.2	4.0	32.2	35.9	-15.9	-72.0	7.4	46.2	53.6	121.3	-0.9	0.0	TEXAS HOSPITAL INS EXCHANGE
0.9	0.7	127.4	121.4	9.4	-4.5	43.9	28.7	72.6	161.4	-41.7	0.0	TEXAS INS CO
12.9	8.3	27.3	25.3	-3.9	-10.0	36.6	10.7	47.3	214.0	5.5	0.1	TEXAS LAWYERS INS EXCHANGE
2.4	1.8	59.1	41.9	-1.8	-15.2	54.7	33.2	87.9	244.6	136.2	0.0	TEXAS MEDICAL INS CO
81.6	38.2	N/A	N/A	N/A	N/A	N/A	N/A	N/A	N/A	0.0	0.0	TEXAS PACIFIC INDEMNITY CO
3.3	2.2	64.1	22.7	-1.9	-2.4	48.0	45.6	93.6	110.1	0.1	0.0	THAMES INS CO
1.0	0.7	132.1	231.3	18.9	0.3	107.5	31.8	139.3	99.4	7.6	0.0	THE INS CO
N/A	N/A	--	--	--	--	--	--	--	--	--	--	THIRD COAST INS CO
0.8	0.6	8.6	256.5	8.7	18.3	235.1	94.4	329.5	13.2	N/A	11.6 ●	TIG INS CO
1.5	1.5	N/A	N/A	N/A	N/A	N/A	N/A	N/A	28.3	0.0	69.5	TITAN INDEMNITY CO
21.4	15.5	N/A	N/A	N/A	N/A	N/A	N/A	N/A	36.7	0.0	0.0	TITAN INS CO
2.3	2.2	16.7	N/A	N/A	N/A	N/A	-35.6	-35.6	999 +	16.9	34.0	TITAN INS CO INC A RRG
5.9	4.1	18.8	24.0	-3.6	-5.4	50.8	-13.0	37.8	511.3	56.1	0.0	TITLE INDUSTRY ASR CO RRG
N/A	N/A	--	--	--	--	--	--	--	--	--	--	TM SPECIALTY INS CO
22.5	20.3	N/A	1.5	N/A	N/A	N/A	N/A	N/A	-94.1	0.0	0.0	TNUS INS CO
2.4	1.5	59.3	124.9	3.8	1.1	76.3	28.0	104.3	99.0	9.1	0.0 ●	TOA REINS CO OF AMERICA
2.5	1.9	56.1	141.8	-1.7	-1.4	75.4	38.2	113.6	97.8	-1.9	13.4 ●	TOKIO MARINE AMERICA INS CO
4.2	2.2	229.2	35.3	-14.7	-7.7	82.5	13.1	95.6	96.6	6.4	0.0	TOKIO MARINE PACIFIC INS LTD
3.6	2.7	76.5	102.7	-1.2	-1.1	60.8	30.1	90.9	108.2	6.6	0.0 ●	TOKIO MARINE SPECIALTY INS CO
1.5	0.9	276.6	143.2	1.2	0.3	65.2	36.7	101.9	134.6	-16.8	0.0 ●	TOKIO MILLENNIUM RE AG (US BRANCH)
2.8	1.9	92.2	80.6	0.2	1.3	66.6	34.5	101.1	112.1	11.1	7.1	TOPA INS CO
1.5	1.4	53.3	9.0	N/A	N/A	2.0	108.4	110.4	80.3	-15.9	0.0	TOWER BONDING & SURETY CO
3.1	2.7	80.7	34.2	-0.7	8.4	57.8	38.1	95.9	125.2	28.5	0.0	TOWER HILL PREFERRED INS CO
6.9	4.3	41.2	32.5	5.5	10.5	98.7	21.8	120.5	112.8	-8.2	0.0	TOWER HILL PRIME INS CO
1.2	0.9	62.7	56.3	10.3	19.6	93.4	44.6	138.0	80.7	-19.9	0.0	TOWER HILL SELECT INS CO
0.8	0.6	112.5	61.5	5.9	10.1	72.9	39.6	112.5	118.3	15.6	0.0	TOWER HILL SIGNATURE INS CO
7.0	6.0	36.2	6.5	0.5	0.6	66.1	19.5	85.6	152.3	-2.8	0.0 ●	TOYOTA MOTOR INS CO
0.6	0.5	278.2	124.0	1.5	7.2	75.4	15.5	90.9	117.1	23.3	0.0	TRADERS INS CO
5.0	4.5	N/A	N/A	N/A	N/A	N/A	N/A	N/A	N/A	0.0	4.7	TRADEWIND INS CO LTD

999 + Denotes number greater than 999.9%
999 - Denotes number less than -999.99%
● Bullets denote a more detailed analysis is available in Section II.

INSURANCE COMPANY NAME	DOM. STATE	RATING	TOTAL ASSETS ($MIL)	CAPITAL & SURPLUS ($MIL)	ANNUAL NET PREMIUM ($MIL)	NET INCOME ($MIL)	CAPITAL- IZATION INDEX (PTS)	RESERVE ADQ INDEX (PTS)	PROFIT- ABILITY INDEX (PTS)	LIQUIDITY INDEX (PTS)	STAB. INDEX (PTS)	STABILITY FACTORS
TRANS CITY CASUALTY INS CO	AZ	C	18.3	12.8	3.1	0.5	10.0	9.4	8.4	9.6	2.8	DGRT
TRANS PACIFIC INS CO	NY	B	71.5	53.5	0.0	0.4	10.0	6.0	4.8	9.7	4.5	FT
TRANSAMERICA CASUALTY INS CO	OH	B-	360.8	183.3	358.5	3.5	8.3	5.2	8.5	2.9	5.3	LT
TRANSATLANTIC REINS CO	NY	B	14,157.0	5,035.1	3,574.2	111.9	7.7	8.9	7.3	6.8	4.8	ART
TRANSGUARD INS CO OF AMERICA INC	IL	B	321.4	142.8	119.5	2.0	7.5	9.3	7.8	6.8	4.6	GRT
▲TRANSIT GENERAL INS CO	IL	C-	32.1	7.5	10.9	0.3	4.5	7.0	8.9	6.4	2.2	DGT
TRANSIT MUTUAL INS CORP OF WI	WI	D-	16.0	10.9	2.7	0.3	10.0	9.6	8.9	7.6	0.8	DGT
TRANSPORT INS CO	OH	U	--	--	--	--	N/A	--	--	--	--	Z
TRANSPORT RISK SOLUTIONS RRG	SC	U	--	--	--	--	N/A	--	--	--	--	Z
TRANSPORTATION INS CO	IL	C	77.9	77.7	0.0	0.3	10.0	N/A	3.9	9.4	3.8	ART
TRANSPORTATION INS SVCS RRG	SC	D	1.4	0.6	0.5	0.0	6.6	3.6	5.6	7.9	0.6	DGT
TRAVCO INS CO	CT	B	217.8	70.7	58.8	1.3	8.6	8.3	5.9	6.8	4.4	T
TRAVEL AIR INS CO (KS)	KS	U (2)	--	--	--	--	N/A	--	--	--	--	Z
TRAVELERS CASUALTY & SURETY CO	CT	A-	16,679.3	6,493.2	4,432.6	105.0	7.7	8.1	7.5	6.9	5.5	T
TRAVELERS CASUALTY & SURETY CO OF	CT	C+	4,334.2	2,205.5	1,419.8	92.0	10.0	9.6	8.0	7.0	3.0	RT
TRAVELERS CASUALTY CO	CT	C+	207.1	63.7	63.1	1.4	8.1	8.5	6.0	6.7	4.1	T
TRAVELERS CASUALTY CO OF	CT	B	324.9	92.2	102.3	2.3	7.9	8.6	5.1	6.6	4.5	T
TRAVELERS CASUALTY INS CO OF	CT	B	1,971.9	574.0	594.4	16.0	8.0	8.6	6.3	6.6	4.7	T
TRAVELERS COMMERCIAL CASUALTY CO	CT	B	333.3	97.7	102.3	2.5	8.0	8.6	6.1	6.8	4.5	T
TRAVELERS COMMERCIAL INS CO	CT	B	371.1	95.8	102.3	1.9	8.0	8.6	6.1	7.0	4.5	T
TRAVELERS CONSTITUTION STATE INS CO	CT	C+	209.2	63.7	63.1	1.4	8.1	8.5	5.8	6.9	4.1	T
TRAVELERS EXCESS & SURPLUS LINES CO	CT	B	207.7	65.9	58.8	1.4	8.4	8.3	5.9	6.8	4.4	T
TRAVELERS HOME & MARINE INS CO	CT	B	379.1	111.8	58.8	1.7	10.0	7.8	3.7	7.0	4.5	T
TRAVELERS INDEMNITY CO	CT	B+	21,493.8	6,957.5	5,070.5	217.9	7.8	8.1	6.9	6.9	5.4	T
TRAVELERS INDEMNITY CO OF AMERICA	CT	B	647.6	190.6	167.6	4.0	8.5	8.3	4.7	6.8	4.6	T
TRAVELERS INDEMNITY CO OF CT	CT	B	1,108.2	354.2	298.3	9.1	8.6	8.2	4.0	6.8	4.7	T
TRAVELERS LLOYDS INS CO	TX	B	20.2	12.4	0.0	0.3	10.0	N/A	2.9	8.9	4.3	DGT
TRAVELERS LLOYDS OF TEXAS INS CO	TX	B	20.8	14.0	0.0	0.2	10.0	N/A	4.9	9.5	4.2	DFGT
TRAVELERS PERSONAL INS CO	CT	B	212.8	65.5	58.8	1.3	8.4	8.4	6.0	6.7	4.4	T
TRAVELERS PERSONAL SECURITY INS CO	CT	B	212.0	68.1	58.8	1.4	8.5	8.3	6.1	6.7	4.4	T
TRAVELERS PROPERTY CAS OF AMERICA	CT	B	863.1	440.6	78.4	3.5	10.0	7.4	3.8	7.6	4.7	T
TRAVELERS PROPERTY CASUALTY INS CO	CT	B	265.7	72.8	65.3	1.7	8.4	8.4	6.3	6.9	4.4	T
TRENWICK AMERICA REINSURANCE CORP	CT	U	--	--	--	--	N/A	--	--	--	--	Z
TRI-CENTURY INS CO	PA	C+	41.4	10.0	2.2	-0.1	7.3	7.9	5.5	8.6	3.1	DRT
TRI-STATE CONSUMER INS CO	NY	B	102.2	43.6	26.7	1.7	8.2	9.4	5.9	6.9	4.1	RT
TRI-STATE INS CO OF MN	IA	C	51.6	33.1	0.0	0.2	10.0	N/A	6.8	7.0	3.8	T
TRIAD GUARANTY ASR CORP	IL	F (5)	0.0	0.0	2.5	0.0	6.1	7.1	2.5	6.9	0.0	DFGT
TRIAD GUARANTY INS CORP	IL	F (5)	0.0	0.0	156.7	0.0	3.0	3.5	0.9	6.5	0.0	FT
TRIANGLE INS CO	OK	C+	88.3	29.4	40.4	-0.8	6.8	9.4	5.8	6.5	3.3	RT
TRIDENT INSURANCE GROUP INC	MD	U	--	--	--	--	N/A	--	--	--	--	Z
TRINITY RISK SOLUTIONS RECIP INS RRG	DC	E	9.1	4.3	1.5	0.3	4.0	4.7	2.0	7.0	0.1	DFGR
TRINITY UNIVERSAL INS CO	TX	B	1,927.8	737.7	1,194.5	-20.5	7.9	8.9	3.4	1.5	4.7	ALRT
TRIPLE S PROPIEDAD INC	PR	B	281.7	135.4	87.2	3.2	8.2	6.1	7.0	6.5	4.1	RT
TRITON INS CO	TX	C+	412.2	150.5	101.5	12.6	10.0	7.5	2.9	7.2	4.2	RT
TRIUMPHE CASUALTY CO	OH	C	62.2	20.3	8.8	0.2	9.8	5.7	8.3	8.5	3.4	DRT
TRUCK INS EXCHANGE	CA	C+	2,234.1	612.6	1,144.0	7.8	5.2	5.6	3.8	2.8	4.8	FLRT
TRUMBULL INS CO	CT	B	226.4	99.3	52.7	3.9	10.0	5.9	6.2	7.1	4.5	AT
TRUSTGARD INS CO	OH	B-	109.4	70.8	41.0	2.0	10.0	6.0	8.7	6.8	3.7	T
TRUSTSTAR INS CO	MD	U (5)	--	--	--	--	N/A	--	--	--	--	Z
TUDOR INS CO	NH	C	186.6	122.1	15.2	1.3	10.0	9.3	6.7	8.4	4.0	FRT
TUSCARORA WAYNE INS CO	PA	B-	106.4	68.0	40.2	0.9	9.8	8.1	8.7	6.9	3.7	RT
TWIN CITY FIRE INS CO	IN	B	680.6	287.2	158.0	6.1	10.0	5.9	5.0	6.8	4.6	AT

See Page 27 for explanation of footnotes and
Page 28 for explanation of stability factors.
Arrows denote recent upgrades ▲ or downgrades ▼   (see Section VII for explanations)

122

www.weissratings.com

RISK ADJ. RATIO #1	CAPITAL RATIO #2	PREMIUM TO SURPLUS (%)	RESV. TO SURPLUS (%)	RESV. DEVELOP. 1 YEAR (%)	RESV. DEVELOP. 2 YEAR (%)	LOSS RATIO (%)	EXP. RATIO (%)	COMB RATIO (%)	CASH FROM UNDER-WRITING (%)	NET PREMIUM GROWTH (%)	INVEST. IN AFFIL (%)	INSURANCE COMPANY NAME
6.1	4.6	25.2	33.8	-10.2	-16.8	16.4	38.8	55.2	141.0	1.0	1.9	TRANS CITY CASUALTY INS CO
16.2	12.1	N/A	15.5	1.7	1.2	999 +	999 +	999 +	-4.2	100.3	0.0	TRANS PACIFIC INS CO
2.7	1.9	199.7	44.9	-0.6	0.7	59.3	39.9	99.2	100.4	12.7	0.0	TRANSAMERICA CASUALTY INS CO
2.2	1.5	72.8	151.3	-6.0	-9.7	58.2	36.1	94.3	112.4	20.4	9.0 ●	TRANSATLANTIC REINS CO
2.9	1.7	87.2	66.4	-4.0	-8.9	58.2	41.1	99.3	124.6	82.8	0.0	TRANSGUARD INS CO OF AMERICA INC
1.7	0.9	149.4	184.6	-2.4	3.9	71.6	13.0	84.6	126.9	-0.6	0.0	TRANSIT GENERAL INS CO
7.4	6.7	24.7	24.2	-10.5	-17.8	12.6	18.5	31.1	152.0	11.4	0.0	TRANSIT MUTUAL INS CORP OF WI
N/A	N/A	--	--	--	--	--	--	--	--	--	--	TRANSPORT INS CO
N/A	N/A	--	--	--	--	--	--	--	--	--	--	TRANSPORT RISK SOLUTIONS RRG
60.0	24.3	N/A	N/A	N/A	N/A	N/A	N/A	N/A	N/A	0.0	0.0	TRANSPORTATION INS CO
1.6	1.1	83.0	38.4	-11.3	N/A	19.1	30.2	49.3	206.5	51.0	0.0	TRANSPORTATION INS SVCS RRG
3.1	2.0	84.7	140.6	-1.7	-4.3	63.4	30.4	93.8	104.7	4.8	0.0	TRAVCO INS CO
N/A	N/A	--	--	--	--	--	--	--	--	--	--	TRAVEL AIR INS CO (KS)
1.6	1.4	68.3	113.4	-1.4	-3.5	63.4	29.9	93.3	110.4	4.8	26.3 ●	TRAVELERS CASUALTY & SURETY CO
4.7	3.5	68.0	47.0	-10.1	-18.3	20.3	40.1	60.4	159.7	3.4	8.4 ●	TRAVELERS CASUALTY & SURETY CO
2.6	1.7	101.4	168.2	-2.0	-5.1	63.4	29.9	93.3	109.7	4.8	0.0	TRAVELERS CASUALTY CO
2.4	1.5	113.9	189.0	-2.2	-5.6	63.4	30.0	93.4	108.3	4.8	0.0	TRAVELERS CASUALTY CO OF
2.6	1.6	106.1	176.1	-2.1	-5.4	63.4	30.1	93.5	111.9	4.8	0.0 ●	TRAVELERS CASUALTY INS CO OF
2.5	1.6	107.4	178.2	-2.1	-5.4	63.4	29.9	93.3	109.4	4.8	0.0	TRAVELERS COMMERCIAL CASUALTY
2.4	1.6	108.9	180.7	-2.1	-5.6	63.4	30.3	93.7	116.7	4.8	0.0	TRAVELERS COMMERCIAL INS CO
2.6	1.7	101.4	168.2	-2.0	-5.1	63.4	29.9	93.3	109.5	4.8	0.0	TRAVELERS CONSTITUTION STATE INS
2.9	1.9	91.1	151.2	-1.8	-4.6	63.4	30.3	93.7	114.8	4.8	0.0	TRAVELERS EXCESS & SURPLUS LINES
4.8	3.1	53.4	88.6	-1.0	-2.2	63.4	32.1	95.5	135.8	4.8	0.0	TRAVELERS HOME & MARINE INS CO
1.8	1.5	72.4	120.3	-1.5	-3.9	63.4	26.4	89.8	113.5	4.8	20.5 ●	TRAVELERS INDEMNITY CO
3.0	1.9	89.8	149.0	-1.8	-4.2	63.4	30.4	93.8	111.5	4.8	0.0	TRAVELERS INDEMNITY CO OF AMERICA
3.1	2.0	86.4	143.4	-1.7	-4.0	63.4	30.3	93.7	112.6	4.8	0.0 ●	TRAVELERS INDEMNITY CO OF CT
6.0	5.4	N/A	N/A	N/A	N/A	N/A	N/A	N/A	-54.7	0.0	0.0	TRAVELERS LLOYDS INS CO
7.5	6.7	N/A	N/A	N/A	N/A	N/A	N/A	N/A	224.2	0.0	0.0	TRAVELERS LLOYDS OF TEXAS INS CO
2.9	1.9	91.6	151.9	-1.8	-4.6	63.4	30.1	93.5	106.9	4.8	0.0	TRAVELERS PERSONAL INS CO
3.0	2.0	88.1	146.2	-1.7	-4.5	63.4	29.8	93.2	99.2	4.8	0.0	TRAVELERS PERSONAL SECURITY INS
13.9	8.9	17.9	29.8	-0.4	-0.8	63.4	34.6	98.0	109.3	4.8	0.0 ●	TRAVELERS PROPERTY CAS OF
2.9	1.9	91.9	152.5	-1.8	-4.7	63.4	30.4	93.8	106.9	4.8	0.0	TRAVELERS PROPERTY CASUALTY INS
N/A	N/A	--	--	--	--	--	--	--	--	--	--	TRENWICK AMERICA REINSURANCE
1.4	1.2	21.9	90.4	1.7	-2.6	108.4	16.9	125.3	120.5	0.7	0.0	TRI-CENTURY INS CO
3.0	1.8	60.8	93.7	-6.3	-16.9	66.9	36.9	103.8	93.0	-6.4	0.0	TRI-STATE CONSUMER INS CO
9.8	8.8	N/A	N/A	N/A	N/A	N/A	N/A	N/A	107.6	0.0	0.0	TRI-STATE INS CO OF MN
1.6	1.3	29.6	92.6	-5.4	-76.8	122.9	39.9	162.8	47.9	-19.1	0.0	TRIAD GUARANTY ASR CORP
0.9	0.7	66.9	208.6	72.1	117.6	223.0	11.0	234.0	51.4	-20.7	1.1	TRIAD GUARANTY INS CORP
1.3	0.9	133.7	99.8	-10.9	-19.2	67.5	27.9	95.4	112.4	10.3	0.0	TRIANGLE INS CO
N/A	N/A	--	--	--	--	--	--	--	--	--	--	TRIDENT INSURANCE GROUP INC
0.7	0.5	39.0	83.7	-3.7	2.5	73.6	33.1	106.7	64.8	166.8	0.0	TRINITY RISK SOLUTIONS RECIP INS
2.0	1.5	154.8	76.6	-3.2	-4.6	71.5	30.4	101.9	95.5	-1.4	15.3 ●	TRINITY UNIVERSAL INS CO
2.7	1.8	62.4	50.9	-4.7	-3.0	51.2	43.2	94.4	103.9	1.7	0.0	TRIPLE S PROPIEDAD INC
5.2	3.6	72.8	18.5	-2.3	-2.0	41.3	45.9	87.2	115.3	-13.8	0.0	TRITON INS CO
3.4	2.7	44.2	60.9	2.0	4.4	70.2	27.9	98.1	167.7	4.6	0.0	TRIUMPHE CASUALTY CO
0.8	0.7	185.8	119.8	4.1	6.6	72.5	32.4	104.9	94.4	-1.1	44.2 ●	TRUCK INS EXCHANGE
5.4	3.4	55.2	98.4	2.0	1.6	70.4	7.6	78.0	105.5	0.0	0.0	TRUMBULL INS CO
12.8	11.0	58.4	34.8	-1.3	0.4	62.3	24.2	86.5	107.4	-4.3	0.0	TRUSTGARD INS CO
N/A	N/A	--	--	--	--	--	--	--	--	--	--	TRUSTSTAR INS CO
9.9	6.6	8.2	22.9	-0.7	-1.5	68.3	39.3	107.6	49.7	25.9	0.0	TUDOR INS CO
3.8	2.7	61.2	19.0	-5.1	-5.3	37.6	41.6	79.2	124.8	4.9	9.3	TUSCARORA WAYNE INS CO
5.2	3.4	56.2	100.2	2.0	1.6	70.4	24.9	95.3	105.5	0.0	0.0 ●	TWIN CITY FIRE INS CO

999 + Denotes number greater than 999.9%
999 - Denotes number less than -999.99%
● Bullets denote a more detailed analysis is available in Section II.

INSURANCE COMPANY NAME	DOM. STATE	RATING	TOTAL ASSETS ($MIL)	CAPITAL & SURPLUS ($MIL)	ANNUAL NET PREMIUM ($MIL)	NET INCOME ($MIL)	CAPITAL- IZATION INDEX (PTS)	RESERVE ADQ INDEX (PTS)	PROFIT- ABILITY INDEX (PTS)	LIQUIDITY INDEX (PTS)	STAB. INDEX (PTS)	STABILITY FACTORS
TWIN LIGHTS INS CO	NJ	D+(1)	8.5	8.3	0.0	0.1	10.0	N/A	6.4	7.0	2.5	DT
TYPTAP INS CO	FL	B-	26.9	24.9	2.0	0.1	10.0	N/A	3.8	10.0	3.6	DGT
UFB CASUALTY INS CO	IN	B	8.8	8.8	0.0	0.0	10.0	N/A	6.5	10.0	4.8	DGT
UFG SPECIALTY INS CO	IA	C	42.9	20.6	9.6	0.2	9.7	8.3	5.1	6.6	3.3	DFGR
UMIA INS INC	OR	B	255.4	112.0	39.2	1.8	8.9	9.5	5.8	7.0	4.2	FRT
UMIALIK INS CO	AK	B-	61.4	26.0	23.3	0.4	9.3	8.3	8.9	6.6	3.8	RT
UNDERWRITERS AT LLOYDS (IL)	IL	D	352.1	193.7	69.9	12.3	8.4	6.7	3.9	9.1	2.3	RT
UNDERWRITERS AT LLOYDS (KY)	KY	D	171.1	33.4	37.4	0.9	1.9	6.0	5.9	8.8	2.3	CFT
UNDERWRITERS AT LLOYDS (VI)	VI	C	66.4	25.0	62.7	10.1	0.3	0.3	5.9	0.2	3.1	CLT
UNIGARD INDEMNITY CO	WI	C	7.5	7.5	-5.9	0.0	7.6	3.8	2.0	5.2	2.8	FGRT
UNIGARD INS CO	WI	C	452.8	110.1	174.2	-0.3	7.5	5.0	3.1	6.5	4.2	RT
UNION INS CO	IA	C	142.3	45.2	0.0	0.2	10.0	N/A	6.9	10.0	3.9	T
UNION INS CO OF PROVIDENCE	IA	C	65.4	63.5	-17.1	0.4	10.0	4.7	8.5	8.8	4.0	T
UNION MUTUAL FIRE INS CO	VT	B-	221.7	93.0	102.2	1.1	7.6	8.5	8.4	6.7	3.9	T
UNION MUTUAL INS CO	OK	F	5.1	0.8	3.7	0.1	1.2	3.9	0.7	7.4	0.0	CDGR
UNION NATIONAL FIRE INS CO	LA	B	9.5	6.3	0.0	0.1	10.0	N/A	5.5	7.0	4.1	DGR
UNION STANDARD LLOYDS	TX	C	2.5	0.9	0.0	0.0	7.4	N/A	6.3	10.0	2.8	DGT
UNIQUE INS CO	IL	D	89.1	16.0	60.9	0.0	1.4	1.3	5.0	3.2	1.5	CDGL
UNITED AMERICAS INS CO	NY	U	--	--	--	--	N/A	--	--	--	--	Z
UNITED AUTOMOBILE INS CO	FL	E	290.3	41.7	150.7	-5.1	2.5	0.4	1.3	0.0	0.1	FLRT
UNITED BUS INS CO	GA	D	11.7	3.3	6.6	-0.1	2.3	3.5	2.9	6.7	2.0	CDGR
▲UNITED CASUALTY & SURETY CO INC	MA	C-	10.4	7.9	2.1	0.0	9.2	7.7	8.6	9.4	2.1	DGRT
UNITED CASUALTY INS CO OF AMERICA	IL	B	13.5	10.3	0.0	0.0	10.0	N/A	7.7	7.0	4.4	DGR
UNITED CENTRAL PA RRG	VT	E	21.8	9.5	4.2	0.3	3.9	4.6	5.1	6.9	0.0	DGT
UNITED EDUCATORS INS A RECIP RRG	VT	B	878.3	292.5	140.9	6.0	7.4	8.9	8.0	7.3	6.0	T
UNITED EQUITABLE INS CO	IL	D+	25.5	5.1	12.5	-0.5	4.3	9.6	2.9	6.7	2.2	DGT
UNITED FARM FAMILY INS CO	NY	B	39.6	13.4	8.8	0.0	9.6	8.5	6.9	2.8	4.6	DFLT
UNITED FARM FAMILY MUTUAL INS CO	IN	B	1,055.2	450.5	544.4	1.9	8.8	8.2	4.9	5.5	4.5	T
UNITED FINANCIAL CASUALTY CO	OH	B-	2,973.9	711.6	1,981.2	45.4	7.7	6.5	9.4	6.0	4.5	T
UNITED FIRE & CAS CO	IA	B	1,950.1	793.5	617.6	8.3	7.2	8.3	8.4	6.7	5.5	T
UNITED FIRE & INDEMNITY CO	TX	C+	55.7	20.2	19.3	0.3	7.6	8.6	8.2	6.7	3.4	DT
UNITED FIRE LLOYDS	TX	C+	32.1	9.0	9.6	0.1	7.3	9.3	7.5	6.9	3.1	DGT
UNITED FRONTIER MUTUAL INS CO	NY	C	16.5	10.7	4.1	-0.2	8.9	7.9	5.4	7.0	2.4	DGRT
UNITED GROUP CAPTIVE INS CO	GA	D	1.3	0.6	0.6	0.0	7.6	4.7	2.1	9.0	1.0	DFGT
UNITED GUAR RESIDENTIAL INS CO OF NC	NC	C+	331.6	312.8	27.1	6.4	7.5	5.8	3.5	9.8	4.6	T
UNITED GUARANTY COML INS CO OF NC	NC	U	--	--	--	--	N/A	--	--	--	--	Z
UNITED GUARANTY CREDIT INS CO	NC	B-	25.9	24.2	0.2	0.1	10.0	6.7	4.9	10.0	3.8	DGT
UNITED GUARANTY INS CO	NC	B-	92.4	19.0	14.2	3.3	4.5	4.6	1.9	7.2	5.2	CDT
UNITED GUARANTY MORTGAGE INDEM CO	NC	C+	438.7	290.7	18.5	4.0	10.0	5.0	4.7	7.0	4.6	FRT
UNITED GUARANTY MORTGAGE INS CO	NC	B-	93.1	19.9	14.2	3.6	4.7	4.6	1.9	7.1	5.2	CDT
UNITED GUARANTY MTG INS CO OF NC	NC	B-	92.9	19.7	14.2	3.6	4.7	4.6	1.9	6.9	5.2	CDT
UNITED GUARANTY RESIDENTIAL INS CO	NC	C+	3,389.7	1,192.3	548.8	104.1	8.6	4.4	3.5	6.7	4.8	RT
▼UNITED HERITAGE PROP & CAS CO	ID	E+	42.3	15.7	23.6	-1.6	7.5	6.1	3.4	5.5	0.6	DT
▲UNITED HOME INS CO	AR	C-	38.8	12.9	29.9	-1.0	3.4	5.7	4.4	3.1	2.5	DGLR
UNITED HOME INS CO A RRG	VT	U	--	--	--	--	N/A	--	--	--	--	Z
UNITED INS CO	UT	C-	46.2	11.3	42.4	0.3	2.8	7.0	8.8	0.7	3.0	CDGL
UNITED INTERNATIONAL INS CO	NY	U	--	--	--	--	N/A	--	--	--	--	Z
UNITED NATIONAL INS CO	PA	C	356.1	180.6	80.8	0.3	7.4	6.4	3.6	6.9	4.1	FRT
UNITED OHIO INS CO	OH	B-	327.8	164.1	135.8	2.8	10.0	8.6	8.6	6.7	4.7	T
UNITED P&C INS CO	FL	B-	603.9	157.2	398.7	-6.0	5.4	4.6	5.0	5.8	5.1	T
UNITED SECURITY HEALTH & CASUALTY	IL	D	2.9	1.7	0.5	-0.1	7.2	3.6	1.2	7.3	2.0	DFGT
UNITED SERVICES AUTOMOBILE ASN	TX	B+	33,965.5	25,653.7	7,038.1	278.7	7.6	7.3	7.7	6.7	5.2	T

See Page 27 for explanation of footnotes and
Page 28 for explanation of stability factors.
Arrows denote recent upgrades ▲ or downgrades ▼   (see Section VII for explanations)

124

www.weissratings.com

RISK ADJ. CAPITAL RATIO #1	CAPITAL RATIO #2	PREMIUM TO SURPLUS (%)	RESV. TO SURPLUS (%)	RESV. DEVELOP. 1 YEAR (%)	RESV. DEVELOP. 2 YEAR (%)	LOSS RATIO (%)	EXP. RATIO (%)	COMB RATIO (%)	CASH FROM UNDER-WRITING (%)	NET PREMIUM GROWTH (%)	INVEST. IN AFFIL (%)	INSURANCE COMPANY NAME
12.3	7.1	N/A	N/A	N/A	N/A	N/A	N/A	N/A	N/A	0.0	0.0	TWIN LIGHTS INS CO
21.0	12.9	8.0	0.1	N/A	N/A	60.4	39.6	100.0	198.5	0.0	0.0	TYPTAP INS CO
99.8	49.9	N/A	N/A	N/A	N/A	N/A	N/A	N/A	N/A	0.0	0.0	UFB CASUALTY INS CO
5.0	3.3	55.4	60.9	-0.6	-1.9	69.8	30.0	99.8	81.0	-23.6	0.0	UFG SPECIALTY INS CO
3.6	2.5	36.3	96.3	-5.1	-24.0	76.7	15.8	92.5	85.0	-5.8	0.0	UMIA INS INC
3.6	2.6	91.0	69.9	-3.1	-6.8	65.5	26.5	92.0	103.9	2.5	0.0	UMIALIK INS CO
3.2	2.2	40.5	85.9	18.9	1.3	83.3	17.8	101.1	117.1	3.4	0.0	UNDERWRITERS AT LLOYDS (IL)
0.6	0.4	112.1	356.7	-50.1	-83.4	10.0	28.1	38.1	89.7	-11.4	0.0	UNDERWRITERS AT LLOYDS (KY)
0.1	0.1	251.0	141.4	70.3	97.3	29.4	30.4	59.8	190.6	10.0	0.0	UNDERWRITERS AT LLOYDS (VI)
174.6	87.2	-79.5	N/A	N/A	N/A	N/A	N/A	N/A	-21.1	-136.3	0.0	UNIGARD INDEMNITY CO
2.0	1.3	162.2	138.6	-18.7	-13.9	58.8	34.1	92.9	127.3	37.6	3.2	UNIGARD INS CO
5.1	4.5	N/A	N/A	N/A	N/A	N/A	N/A	N/A	73.9	0.0	0.0	UNION INS CO
73.4	38.9	-27.2	N/A	N/A	N/A	N/A	17.1	N/A	77.6	-145.2	0.0	UNION INS CO OF PROVIDENCE
1.8	1.5	112.6	44.7	-0.1	-6.5	50.8	35.0	85.8	126.6	6.7	23.5	UNION MUTUAL FIRE INS CO
0.5	0.4	597.3	89.9	16.3	6.3	57.4	29.7	87.1	108.3	24.2	0.0	UNION MUTUAL INS CO
6.1	5.4	N/A	N/A	N/A	N/A	N/A	N/A	N/A	362.0	0.0	0.0	UNION NATIONAL FIRE INS CO
1.4	1.2	N/A	N/A	N/A	N/A	N/A	N/A	N/A	86.1	0.0	0.0	UNION STANDARD LLOYDS
0.3	0.3	379.2	227.7	22.8	49.7	68.0	31.4	99.4	97.4	43.1	9.1	UNIQUE INS CO
N/A	N/A	--	--	--	--	--	--	--	--	--	--	UNITED AMERICAS INS CO
0.4	0.3	312.4	248.8	39.6	56.8	98.4	8.5	106.9	82.3	-17.6	2.0	UNITED AUTOMOBILE INS CO
0.6	0.5	204.2	85.5	5.4	-42.1	53.9	26.5	80.4	138.4	24.6	0.0	UNITED BUS INS CO
4.3	3.9	33.6	1.5	-2.2	-2.1	0.8	84.0	84.8	116.9	-19.7	0.0	UNITED CASUALTY & SURETY CO INC
9.9	8.9	N/A	N/A	N/A	N/A	N/A	N/A	N/A	81.4	0.0	0.0	UNITED CASUALTY INS CO OF AMERICA
0.8	0.6	47.0	91.9	0.3	-4.7	110.2	8.5	118.7	93.1	3.0	0.0	UNITED CENTRAL PA RRG
1.5	1.2	48.4	160.2	-3.2	-3.2	78.3	23.0	101.3	103.3	-2.6	0.0 ●	UNITED EDUCATORS INS A RECIP RRG
0.8	0.6	234.8	223.4	-29.2	-50.1	49.4	46.2	95.6	106.0	-16.1	0.0	UNITED EQUITABLE INS CO
3.2	2.9	65.7	75.5	-3.8	-5.9	64.4	29.7	94.1	64.4	5.2	0.0	UNITED FARM FAMILY INS CO
3.5	2.3	121.5	55.1	-3.4	-5.7	69.7	27.5	97.2	102.9	1.5	3.3 ●	UNITED FARM FAMILY MUTUAL INS CO
2.2	1.5	298.2	179.0	-0.5	-5.2	74.1	18.6	92.7	119.6	13.7	0.0 ●	UNITED FINANCIAL CASUALTY CO
1.4	1.2	80.1	88.0	-0.8	-2.7	69.8	29.2	99.0	113.1	9.4	34.4 ●	UNITED FIRE & CAS CO
2.5	1.6	96.9	106.5	-1.0	-3.3	69.8	30.0	99.8	110.3	8.7	0.0	UNITED FIRE & INDEMNITY CO
2.2	1.4	108.8	119.6	-1.1	-3.7	69.8	30.0	99.8	111.0	8.7	0.0	UNITED FIRE LLOYDS
3.3	2.0	38.1	25.8	-0.7	-2.9	55.3	36.4	91.7	122.3	0.8	0.0	UNITED FRONTIER MUTUAL INS CO
1.9	1.4	92.0	105.9	-3.0	10.4	72.9	17.0	89.9	91.0	-11.4	0.0	UNITED GROUP CAPTIVE INS CO
1.2	1.2	8.4	4.8	-4.4	-9.6	-48.9	13.6	-35.3	-427.1	-29.3	85.2 ●	UNITED GUAR RESIDENTIAL INS CO OF
N/A	N/A	--	--	--	--	--	--	--	--	--	--	UNITED GUARANTY COML INS CO OF NC
27.1	18.6	0.7	5.7	-2.4	-4.0	-118.2	40.8	-77.4	301.4	-24.7	0.0	UNITED GUARANTY CREDIT INS CO
1.0	0.8	82.5	140.0	-4.7	-7.1	27.9	20.0	47.9	99.0	46.5	0.0	UNITED GUARANTY INS CO
7.2	5.5	6.1	25.6	-5.5	-21.9	41.8	27.1	68.9	48.3	-37.0	0.0 ●	UNITED GUARANTY MORTGAGE INDEM
1.0	0.8	80.5	136.6	-4.8	-7.3	27.9	20.0	47.9	99.0	46.5	0.0	UNITED GUARANTY MORTGAGE INS CO
1.0	0.8	81.1	137.6	-4.6	-7.0	27.9	20.0	47.9	99.0	46.5	0.0	UNITED GUARANTY MTG INS CO OF NC
2.5	2.1	46.3	31.7	-0.8	-0.6	17.8	30.6	48.4	152.9	-2.8	9.2 ●	UNITED GUARANTY RESIDENTIAL INS
1.7	1.3	138.9	42.5	1.7	5.9	72.6	29.0	101.6	98.6	-11.9	0.0	UNITED HERITAGE PROP & CAS CO
0.8	0.7	221.4	47.2	-9.8	3.3	55.9	29.1	85.0	114.3	5.0	0.0	UNITED HOME INS CO
N/A	N/A	--	--	--	--	--	--	--	--	--	--	UNITED HOME INS CO A RRG
0.5	0.4	388.9	171.5	-9.4	-14.3	75.3	20.9	96.2	116.7	50.1	0.0	UNITED INS CO
N/A	N/A	--	--	--	--	--	--	--	--	--	--	UNITED INTERNATIONAL INS CO
1.6	1.3	45.3	45.3	-2.9	-5.1	67.1	36.2	103.3	73.0	0.3	26.9	UNITED NATIONAL INS CO
7.1	5.0	84.7	42.1	-2.6	-3.5	61.7	31.0	92.7	107.8	5.3	0.0	UNITED OHIO INS CO
1.1	0.8	256.2	69.1	12.2	2.0	63.9	41.8	105.7	109.4	7.8	0.0	UNITED P&C INS CO
1.5	1.2	29.9	51.4	-44.3	N/A	29.8	123.9	153.7	60.7	48.2	0.0	UNITED SECURITY HEALTH & CASUALTY
1.4	1.4	27.8	13.8	-0.2	-0.4	90.1	12.1	102.2	100.4	3.3	58.6 ●	UNITED SERVICES AUTOMOBILE ASN

999 + Denotes number greater than 999.9%
999 - Denotes number less than -999.99%
● Bullets denote a more detailed analysis is available in Section II.

INSURANCE COMPANY NAME	DOM. STATE	RATING	TOTAL ASSETS ($MIL)	CAPITAL & SURPLUS ($MIL)	ANNUAL NET PREMIUM ($MIL)	NET INCOME ($MIL)	CAPITAL-IZATION INDEX (PTS)	RESERVE ADQ INDEX (PTS)	PROFIT-ABILITY INDEX (PTS)	LIQUIDITY INDEX (PTS)	STAB. INDEX (PTS)	STABILITY FACTORS
UNITED SPECIALTY INS CO	DE	B	230.3	130.7	48.7	2.7	10.0	6.0	8.4	8.1	4.5	GT
UNITED STATES FIDELITY & GUARANTY CO	CT	C-	3,291.3	1,068.3	960.1	23.7	8.5	7.7	1.9	6.6	3.3	T
UNITED STATES SURETY CO	MD	B-	70.5	47.9	23.1	0.8	9.4	9.3	8.7	7.1	5.3	DT
UNITED SURETY & INDEMNITY CO	PR	B	102.7	62.6	26.3	2.6	7.3	8.9	6.1	6.7	4.2	RT
UNITED WISCONSIN INS CO	WI	C+	202.4	123.8	114.9	10.3	7.7	4.2	8.9	6.7	4.4	RT
▲UNITRIN ADVANTAGE INS CO	NY	C-	3.3	2.6	0.0	0.0	10.0	N/A	7.6	7.0	3.0	DGRT
UNITRIN AUTO & HOME INS CO	NY	D+	74.8	33.9	0.0	0.4	10.0	3.6	6.3	10.0	2.5	FRT
UNITRIN COUNTY MUTUAL INS CO	TX	B	32.7	4.6	0.0	0.0	7.0	N/A	5.7	10.0	4.1	DFGR
UNITRIN DIRECT INS CO	IL	B	12.2	8.3	0.0	0.1	10.0	N/A	5.4	7.0	4.2	DGR
UNITRIN DIRECT PROPERTY & CAS CO	IL	B	14.6	10.1	0.0	0.1	10.0	N/A	7.3	7.0	4.4	DGR
UNITRIN PREFERRED INS CO	NY	D+	22.0	9.7	0.0	0.1	10.0	N/A	6.1	7.0	2.4	DFGR
UNITRIN SAFEGUARD INS CO	WI	B	27.6	7.6	0.0	0.0	8.4	N/A	7.8	7.0	4.1	DGRT
UNIVERSAL FIRE & CASUALTY INS CO	IN	C-	15.5	7.4	3.1	0.2	8.7	N/A	8.2	7.4	2.1	DGT
▲UNIVERSAL INS CO	NC	C-	41.8	12.0	23.3	0.1	7.0	3.9	3.5	1.7	2.7	DFGL
UNIVERSAL INS CO (PR)	PR	B-	858.1	267.4	203.7	2.4	7.5	6.1	6.0	6.6	4.2	RT
UNIVERSAL INS CO OF NORTH AMERICA	FL	C-	112.5	29.2	64.1	-3.8	5.6	5.0	1.7	4.0	3.3	FLOT
UNIVERSAL NORTH AMERICA INS CO	TX	C	186.6	75.2	112.7	-0.2	4.0	6.3	7.3	2.5	4.2	CLRT
UNIVERSAL P&C INS CO	FL	D	957.5	332.6	652.3	11.7	7.1	6.7	5.2	6.3	2.0	RT
UNIVERSAL SURETY CO	NE	C	214.6	157.0	2.8	3.1	8.2	7.4	8.4	10.0	2.6	DRT
UNIVERSAL SURETY OF AMERICA	SD	C	14.7	14.7	0.0	0.0	10.0	N/A	3.9	10.0	3.8	DGR
UNIVERSAL UNDERWRITERS INS CO	IL	C+	396.7	323.9	0.0	1.2	10.0	N/A	4.3	7.0	4.7	FRT
UNIVERSAL UNDERWRITERS OF TX	IL	C+	11.4	9.6	0.0	0.0	10.0	N/A	5.2	7.0	3.2	DGRT
UPLAND MUTUAL INS INC	KS	C	30.3	14.5	15.9	-0.3	8.1	6.5	6.6	5.9	2.6	DGRT
▼UPMC HEALTH BENEFITS INC	PA	D	174.4	56.4	101.0	-1.1	1.8	4.9	3.7	5.5	2.3	CT
▲UPMC WORK ALLIANCE INC	PA	C-	6.3	2.3	0.6	0.3	5.3	4.7	2.7	7.3	2.2	CDFG
UPPER HUDSON NATIONAL INS CO	NE	U	--	--	--	--	N/A	--	--	--	--	Z
URGENT CARE ASR CO RRG INC	NV	D	5.7	1.8	1.5	0.0	2.9	2.7	4.3	9.5	1.5	DGRT
URGENT MD RRG INC	VT	D	5.9	2.7	3.9	0.1	1.0	N/A	5.9	5.5	1.9	CDGT
▲US COASTAL INS CO	NY	C-	22.3	8.8	3.7	-0.5	7.1	3.6	2.9	6.8	2.7	DGT
US COASTAL P&C INS CO	FL	C+	32.8	23.0	7.2	-0.5	9.1	N/A	2.9	8.5	3.4	DGT
US FIRE INS CO	DE	C	3,994.4	1,233.0	1,370.7	-19.5	7.1	5.8	5.0	6.9	3.7	ART
US INS CO OF AMERICA	IL	D+	6.1	2.8	1.0	0.1	4.9	7.0	6.4	6.7	2.0	DGR
US LEGAL SERVICES INC	TN	D	3.6	2.9	3.5	0.2	4.8	5.2	8.7	7.7	1.9	DGT
US LIABILITY INS CO	PA	C	1,058.6	684.3	204.3	2.8	7.1	8.7	7.8	7.3	4.3	RT
US LLOYDS INS CO	TX	C	29.7	9.6	20.4	0.0	7.3	4.5	6.6	6.4	2.3	DFGR
US SPECIALTY INS CO	TX	B-	1,826.5	547.2	464.1	28.8	7.8	6.9	3.8	6.7	3.5	RT
US UNDERWRITERS INS CO	ND	C	170.8	127.2	12.5	0.2	10.0	4.9	8.0	10.0	4.0	FRT
USA INS CO	MS	D+	15.9	6.4	11.5	0.0	7.6	6.4	2.3	6.6	2.5	DGRT
USA UNDERWRITERS	MI	C-	10.0	6.6	6.2	0.3	2.7	5.9	5.3	4.4	2.1	CDGL
USAA CASUALTY INS CO	TX	A-	10,235.4	4,644.9	6,471.9	61.8	8.5	7.7	7.1	5.0	5.7	LT
USAA COUNTY MUTUAL INS CO	TX	U	--	--	--	--	N/A	--	--	--	--	Z
USAA GENERAL INDEMNITY CO	TX	B+	4,214.9	1,520.5	2,752.8	16.1	8.2	8.6	6.0	2.7	5.0	LT
USPLATE GLASS INS CO	IL	C+	29.8	23.3	9.9	0.6	7.4	5.1	8.2	7.1	3.1	DGRT
UTAH BUSINESS INS CO	UT	D	21.7	5.1	14.4	0.1	1.7	5.9	4.4	5.4	1.9	CDFG
UTICA FIRST INS CO	NY	B	277.3	133.3	83.2	0.5	9.6	8.4	8.5	6.7	4.1	RT
UTICA LLOYDS OF TX	TX	B	7.8	7.4	0.0	0.1	10.0	N/A	8.2	10.0	4.0	DG
UTICA MUTUAL INS CO	NY	B-	2,393.6	882.9	745.1	5.2	8.1	6.4	6.7	6.8	4.6	RT
UTICA NATIONAL ASR CO	NY	C	66.6	30.1	17.7	0.1	9.9	6.3	6.8	6.9	4.1	T
UTICA NATIONAL INS CO OF OHIO	OH	C+	18.8	14.1	0.0	0.2	10.0	N/A	6.6	7.0	3.2	DGT
UTICA NATIONAL INS CO OF TX	TX	C	36.2	16.2	8.9	0.1	10.0	6.3	6.8	6.9	3.2	DGT
UTICA SPECIALTY RISK INS CO	TX	U	--	--	--	--	N/A	--	--	--	--	Z
UV INS RRG INC	HI	D+	1.3	0.8	0.3	-0.1	8.8	7.0	3.0	8.9	1.3	DGT

See Page 27 for explanation of footnotes and
Page 28 for explanation of stability factors.
Arrows denote recent upgrades ▲ or downgrades ▼   (see Section VII for explanations)

www.weissratings.com

RISK ADJ. RATIO #1	CAPITAL RATIO #2	PREMIUM TO SURPLUS (%)	RESV. TO SURPLUS (%)	RESV. DEVELOP. 1 YEAR (%)	2 YEAR (%)	LOSS RATIO (%)	EXP. RATIO (%)	COMB RATIO (%)	CASH FROM UNDER-WRITING (%)	NET PREMIUM GROWTH (%)	INVEST. IN AFFIL (%)	INSURANCE COMPANY NAME
3.6	2.6	37.8	3.5	0.2	1.0	47.6	39.2	86.8	133.4	11.4	11.0	UNITED SPECIALTY INS CO
3.0	2.0	92.0	152.7	-1.4	-2.0	63.4	29.9	93.3	107.4	4.8	3.8 •	UNITED STATES FIDELITY & GUARANTY
3.8	3.0	49.1	19.2	-4.6	-8.1	18.0	54.2	72.2	163.2	1.7	0.0	UNITED STATES SURETY CO
2.1	1.3	44.0	14.2	-4.4	-11.2	-2.8	58.8	56.0	154.5	1.8	0.0	UNITED SURETY & INDEMNITY CO
3.5	3.2	97.8	112.3	-2.1	-0.9	60.1	22.3	82.4	146.4	13.9	0.0	UNITED WISCONSIN INS CO
8.1	7.3	N/A	N/A	N/A	N/A	N/A	N/A	N/A	N/A	0.0	0.0	UNITRIN ADVANTAGE INS CO
5.8	5.2	N/A	N/A	N/A	N/A	N/A	N/A	N/A	-37.2	0.0	0.0	UNITRIN AUTO & HOME INS CO
1.0	0.9	N/A	N/A	N/A	N/A	N/A	N/A	N/A	-10.0	0.0	0.0	UNITRIN COUNTY MUTUAL INS CO
6.8	6.1	N/A	N/A	N/A	N/A	N/A	N/A	N/A	-94.7	0.0	0.0	UNITRIN DIRECT INS CO
7.3	6.6	N/A	N/A	N/A	N/A	N/A	N/A	N/A	-15.9	0.0	0.0	UNITRIN DIRECT PROPERTY & CAS CO
3.6	3.2	N/A	N/A	N/A	N/A	N/A	N/A	N/A	-18.0	0.0	0.0	UNITRIN PREFERRED INS CO
2.1	1.9	N/A	N/A	N/A	N/A	N/A	N/A	N/A	7.7	0.0	0.0	UNITRIN SAFEGUARD INS CO
2.7	2.2	42.0	N/A	N/A	N/A	N/A	82.6	82.6	122.6	19.3	0.0	UNIVERSAL FIRE & CASUALTY INS CO
1.5	0.9	197.2	69.6	-2.2	5.0	86.2	19.7	105.9	87.1	13.3	0.0	UNIVERSAL INS CO
1.7	1.3	78.5	24.4	-1.2	-0.3	66.2	34.5	100.7	102.7	4.8	17.6 •	UNIVERSAL INS CO (PR)
0.9	0.6	195.9	78.5	-9.7	-22.5	94.8	30.9	125.7	75.1	21.4	0.0	UNIVERSAL INS CO OF NORTH AMERICA
0.9	0.5	149.6	39.5	-4.7	-4.4	66.3	30.6	96.9	108.8	-1.2	0.0	UNIVERSAL NORTH AMERICA INS CO
1.7	1.6	207.9	18.4	-0.7	-9.4	49.9	36.2	86.1	114.0	4.7	0.0 •	UNIVERSAL P&C INS CO
3.1	1.9	1.8	4.2	-0.4	-1.3	1.4	56.7	58.1	141.9	-7.4	0.0	UNIVERSAL SURETY CO
73.2	33.1	N/A	N/A	N/A	N/A	N/A	N/A	N/A	N/A	0.0	0.0	UNIVERSAL SURETY OF AMERICA
29.6	24.1	N/A	N/A	N/A	N/A	N/A	N/A	N/A	999 +	0.0	3.6 •	UNIVERSAL UNDERWRITERS INS CO
14.6	13.2	N/A	N/A	N/A	N/A	N/A	N/A	N/A	36.8	0.0	0.0	UNIVERSAL UNDERWRITERS OF TX
2.5	2.1	108.4	15.8	-0.5	-4.9	55.3	27.9	83.2	116.3	-2.5	0.0	UPLAND MUTUAL INS INC
0.5	0.3	195.6	109.5	8.0	17.2	74.5	20.2	94.7	115.3	10.7	0.0	UPMC HEALTH BENEFITS INC
1.8	0.8	30.2	122.5	-23.1	-0.3	126.1	56.0	182.1	66.6	-73.5	0.0	UPMC WORK ALLIANCE INC
N/A	N/A	--	--	--	--	--	--	--	--	--	--	UPPER HUDSON NATIONAL INS CO
0.6	0.5	89.6	121.7	-1.8	0.5	37.5	34.9	72.4	143.2	-8.6	0.0	URGENT CARE ASR CO RRG INC
0.4	0.2	146.1	75.4	N/A	N/A	68.3	17.8	86.1	502.8	0.0	0.0	URGENT MD RRG INC
2.3	1.3	40.1	34.6	-23.6	2.2	49.6	50.8	100.4	131.3	-69.2	0.0	US COASTAL INS CO
3.4	2.3	30.8	4.7	N/A	N/A	59.4	38.7	98.1	234.6	0.0	0.0	US COASTAL P&C INS CO
1.3	1.0	112.5	157.9	-1.4	-2.6	63.7	35.0	98.7	110.2	8.5	22.0 •	US FIRE INS CO
1.7	0.9	38.7	92.1	-45.7	-42.6	16.8	67.9	84.7	91.9	0.3	0.0	US INS CO OF AMERICA
1.1	0.8	127.3	9.0	N/A	-0.8	13.4	59.7	73.1	133.8	39.4	0.0	US LEGAL SERVICES INC
1.2	1.0	31.6	30.0	-3.5	-7.2	38.8	42.9	81.7	129.6	9.2	53.6 •	US LIABILITY INS CO
1.5	1.2	214.0	45.5	7.6	15.6	67.4	33.2	100.6	90.5	4.6	0.0	US LLOYDS INS CO
2.4	1.5	89.6	167.3	1.7	1.3	59.7	32.5	92.2	105.0	6.4	0.0 •	US SPECIALTY INS CO
6.7	4.8	9.9	27.2	N/A	N/A	54.4	39.1	93.5	91.9	-3.9	0.0	US UNDERWRITERS INS CO
1.6	1.3	180.1	82.0	-0.7	4.7	75.1	23.1	98.2	92.8	6.8	0.9	USA INS CO
0.5	0.5	98.0	19.1	N/A	-3.0	40.7	54.5	95.2	105.8	44.4	0.0	USA UNDERWRITERS
2.7	2.0	144.1	69.2	-0.8	-0.7	91.8	11.9	103.7	104.7	14.0	8.5 •	USAA CASUALTY INS CO
N/A	N/A	--	--	--	--	--	--	--	--	--	--	USAA COUNTY MUTUAL INS CO
2.5	1.9	185.7	89.4	-1.1	-1.2	91.7	11.8	103.5	107.2	20.2	0.0 •	USAA GENERAL INDEMNITY CO
1.9	1.3	44.7	0.5	-0.1	-0.3	5.5	80.4	85.9	118.3	2.8	0.0	USPLATE GLASS INS CO
0.5	0.4	291.3	254.2	-13.2	1.8	61.3	39.8	101.1	95.4	1.0	0.0	UTAH BUSINESS INS CO
3.4	2.7	63.1	65.2	-0.2	-2.5	69.5	25.6	95.1	96.7	4.6	0.0	UTICA FIRST INS CO
35.6	32.0	N/A	N/A	N/A	N/A	N/A	N/A	N/A	N/A	0.0	0.0	UTICA LLOYDS OF TX
2.4	1.8	86.0	120.5	-1.3	-4.1	65.5	32.9	98.4	110.1	8.0	11.0 •	UTICA MUTUAL INS CO
4.6	3.0	59.4	83.1	-0.9	-2.8	65.5	32.8	98.3	110.2	8.0	0.0	UTICA NATIONAL ASR CO
9.8	8.8	N/A	N/A	N/A	N/A	N/A	N/A	N/A	N/A	0.0	0.0	UTICA NATIONAL INS CO OF OHIO
4.6	3.0	55.0	77.1	-0.8	-2.6	65.5	32.8	98.3	110.2	8.0	0.0	UTICA NATIONAL INS CO OF TX
N/A	N/A	--	--	--	--	--	--	--	--	--	--	UTICA SPECIALTY RISK INS CO
3.1	2.5	35.3	21.7	-4.3	-34.0	33.2	70.7	103.9	115.1	-18.8	0.0	UV INS RRG INC

999 + Denotes number greater than 999.9%
999 - Denotes number less than -999.99%
• Bullets denote a more detailed analysis is available in Section II.

INSURANCE COMPANY NAME	DOM. STATE	RATING	TOTAL ASSETS ($MIL)	CAPITAL & SURPLUS ($MIL)	ANNUAL NET PREMIUM ($MIL)	NET INCOME ($MIL)	CAPITAL- IZATION INDEX (PTS)	RESERVE ADQ INDEX (PTS)	PROFIT- ABILITY INDEX (PTS)	LIQUIDITY INDEX (PTS)	STAB. INDEX (PTS)	STABILITY FACTORS
VA FARM BUREAU TOWN & COUNTRY INS	VA	C+	66.9	24.9	26.7	0.8	8.7	9.3	7.4	6.7	4.4	DRT
VALLEY FORGE INS CO	PA	C	71.2	70.9	0.0	0.6	10.0	N/A	4.4	7.4	3.8	ART
VALLEY P&C INS CO	OR	B	12.7	7.8	0.0	0.1	10.0	N/A	6.9	7.0	4.1	DGR
VANLINER INS CO	MO	B	427.3	143.0	114.8	2.1	8.9	4.1	6.9	6.9	4.8	RT
VANTAGE CASUALTY INS CO	IN	U	--	--	--	--	N/A	--	--	--	--	Z
VANTAPRO SPECIALTY INS CO	AR	U	--	--	--	--	N/A	--	--	--	--	Z
VASA SPRING GARDEN MUTUAL INS CO	MN	D+	5.4	3.1	2.4	0.3	9.1	6.2	4.4	6.5	2.0	DG
VEHICULAR SERVICE INS CO RRG	OK	U	--	--	--	--	N/A	--	--	--	--	Z
VELOCITY INS CO A RRG	SC	D	2.4	1.5	1.1	0.0	7.6	N/A	5.2	8.5	1.2	DGT
VERLAN FIRE INS CO	NH	B-	26.9	26.7	0.0	0.1	10.0	N/A	6.8	7.0	5.0	G
VERMONT ACCIDENT INS CO	VT	B	9.1	8.3	0.0	0.1	9.1	N/A	7.6	7.0	4.3	DG
VERMONT MUTUAL INS CO	VT	B-	840.2	427.0	384.0	7.1	9.9	8.8	8.7	6.7	4.2	RT
VERSANT CASUALTY INS CO	MS	C	45.5	15.2	7.9	0.2	9.3	6.1	8.9	7.1	3.9	DT
VERTERRA INS CO	TX	C-	75.9	51.6	14.6	0.3	9.1	6.1	8.3	8.6	3.0	DRT
VERTI INSURANCE CO	OH	D+	23.9	7.7	15.8	-0.1	5.2	3.6	2.0	5.2	1.0	DGT
VESTA INS CORP	TX	F (5)	0.0	0.0	0.0	0.0	10.0	N/A	3.9	8.1	0.0	DGT
VETERINARY PET INS CO	OH	B	238.1	99.1	-142.7	-0.2	10.0	5.8	4.7	6.8	4.5	FT
VFH CAPTIVE INS CO	GA	E	5.9	0.9	3.6	0.1	0.1	3.6	0.5	0.9	0.0	CDFG
VICTORIA AUTOMOBILE INS CO	OH	B-	27.8	11.0	0.0	0.0	9.8	N/A	6.6	7.0	4.5	DG
VICTORIA FIRE & CASUALTY CO	OH	C+	116.6	42.9	0.0	0.2	8.0	N/A	3.3	7.0	3.9	T
VICTORIA NATIONAL INS CO	OH	U	--	--	--	--	N/A	--	--	--	--	Z
VICTORIA SELECT INS CO	OH	B-	21.5	8.6	0.0	0.0	9.4	N/A	6.7	7.0	4.2	DG
VICTORIA SPECIALTY INSURANCE CO	OH	C	18.0	3.5	0.0	0.0	7.1	N/A	3.9	7.0	3.2	DG
VICTORY INS CO	MT	E+	12.1	5.0	2.5	0.0	3.2	0.5	2.1	7.2	0.8	DFGR
VIGILANT INS CO	NY	B	529.7	320.3	31.7	3.1	10.0	7.6	8.6	7.4	4.6	T
VIKING INS CO OF WI	WI	C	418.5	179.9	100.6	1.3	10.0	7.8	5.5	6.9	3.5	T
VIRGINIA FARM BUREAU FIRE & CAS INS	VA	C	63.6	21.9	30.9	0.7	8.1	9.4	6.0	6.4	3.5	DRT
VIRGINIA FARM BUREAU MUTUAL INS CO	VA	B-	399.7	192.4	196.5	6.7	7.9	9.2	5.0	6.4	3.5	RT
▼VIRGINIA PHYSICIANS RRG INC	MT	D	2.7	1.0	0.4	0.0	8.0	7.0	3.0	8.4	1.0	DGT
VIRGINIA SURETY CO INC	IL	B	1,198.0	418.9	45.9	4.2	10.0	6.3	8.2	6.9	4.3	FRT
VISION INS CO	TX	D	29.8	14.4	45.0	0.3	2.5	4.0	2.1	0.0	1.5	CDFG
VOYAGER INDEMNITY INS CO	GA	C	115.3	63.0	106.9	8.1	8.3	6.3	7.4	6.6	2.3	DRT
WADENA INS CO	IA	C	5.5	5.5	0.0	0.0	10.0	N/A	2.7	7.0	3.3	DG
WALL ROSE MUTUAL INS CO	PA	U	--	--	--	--	N/A	--	--	--	--	Z
WARNER INS CO	IL	U	--	--	--	--	N/A	--	--	--	--	Z
WARRANTY UNDERWRITERS INS CO	TX	C-	31.5	15.9	1.9	0.2	7.6	10.0	3.8	7.0	3.0	DFGR
▲WASHINGTON CASUALTY CO	WA	D-	24.9	21.5	0.0	0.1	10.0	N/A	6.9	7.0	1.0	DFGR
WASHINGTON COUNTY CO-OPERATIVE INS	NY	D+	8.2	5.8	1.6	0.1	10.0	7.4	8.2	7.6	2.4	DG
WASHINGTON INTL INS CO	NH	C	103.6	80.7	0.0	0.5	10.0	7.6	7.8	7.0	3.5	DGRT
WATFORD INS CO	NJ	U	--	--	--	--	N/A	--	--	--	--	Z
WATFORD SPECIALTY INS CO	NJ	B	70.5	66.0	0.9	0.1	8.2	N/A	3.8	9.4	4.7	DGT
WAUSAU BUSINESS INS CO	WI	C	36.8	28.9	0.0	0.2	10.0	3.5	4.0	7.0	3.7	ADGR
WAUSAU GENERAL INS CO	WI	C	16.1	12.4	0.0	0.1	10.0	N/A	3.8	7.0	3.0	ADGR
WAUSAU UNDERWRITERS INS CO	WI	C	123.7	68.0	0.0	0.5	10.0	3.6	4.2	6.8	4.1	AGRT
WAWANESA GENERAL INS CO	CA	B-	567.6	240.4	360.8	3.9	8.2	4.4	3.5	5.1	5.3	FT
WAYNE COOPERATIVE INS CO	NY	C	31.4	16.3	14.6	0.2	8.9	9.1	8.0	6.7	2.8	DGRT
WAYNE MUTUAL INS CO	OH	C+	75.9	39.2	47.9	1.0	8.8	8.2	8.8	6.4	3.4	T
WEA P&C INS CO	WI	C	18.4	5.8	12.1	0.2	7.4	9.4	5.1	6.1	2.1	DGT
WELLINGTON INS CO	TX	C	33.9	19.4	9.6	0.6	10.0	6.5	8.7	7.0	2.9	DGRT
▼WELLSPAN RRG	VT	E+	34.0	6.4	10.0	0.1	7.3	10.0	7.2	6.9	0.5	DGT
WESCAP INS CO	CO	U	--	--	--	--	N/A	--	--	--	--	Z
WESCO INS CO	DE	B-	2,042.3	441.0	607.0	-5.0	5.7	4.9	5.7	6.1	4.7	GRT

See Page 27 for explanation of footnotes and
Page 28 for explanation of stability factors.
Arrows denote recent upgrades ▲ or downgrades ▼ (see Section VII for explanations)

128

www.weissratings.com

RISK ADJ. CAPITAL RATIO #1	CAPITAL RATIO #2	PREMIUM TO SURPLUS (%)	RESV. TO SURPLUS (%)	RESV. DEVELOP. 1 YEAR (%)	RESV. DEVELOP. 2 YEAR (%)	LOSS RATIO (%)	EXP. RATIO (%)	COMB RATIO (%)	CASH FROM UNDER-WRITING (%)	NET PREMIUM GROWTH (%)	INVEST. IN AFFIL (%)	INSURANCE COMPANY NAME
2.8	2.3	111.0	58.8	-3.1	-10.9	72.3	29.5	101.8	97.1	0.6	0.0	VA FARM BUREAU TOWN & COUNTRY
62.4	26.5	N/A	N/A	N/A	N/A	N/A	N/A	N/A	N/A	0.0	0.0	VALLEY FORGE INS CO
5.2	4.6	N/A	N/A	N/A	N/A	N/A	N/A	N/A	-38.8	0.0	0.0	VALLEY P&C INS CO
3.1	2.2	81.8	112.5	3.8	8.4	70.2	27.6	97.8	91.4	4.6	0.0	VANLINER INS CO
N/A	N/A	--	--	--	--	--	--	--	--	--	--	VANTAGE CASUALTY INS CO
N/A	N/A	--	--	--	--	--	--	--	--	--	--	VANTAPRO SPECIALTY INS CO
3.9	2.7	88.6	14.5	-1.3	-2.8	61.9	32.9	94.8	117.4	9.1	0.0	VASA SPRING GARDEN MUTUAL INS CO
N/A	N/A	--	--	--	--	--	--	--	--	--	--	VEHICULAR SERVICE INS CO RRG
2.6	1.5	73.0	21.7	N/A	N/A	70.9	11.5	82.4	646.0	0.0	0.0	VELOCITY INS CO A RRG
66.8	29.7	N/A	N/A	N/A	N/A	N/A	N/A	N/A	-41.5	0.0	0.0	VERLAN FIRE INS CO
4.0	2.4	N/A	N/A	N/A	N/A	N/A	N/A	N/A	N/A	0.0	0.0	VERMONT ACCIDENT INS CO
4.5	3.0	92.3	35.1	-2.4	-5.4	51.1	37.2	88.3	126.9	7.1	1.2 ●	VERMONT MUTUAL INS CO
3.2	2.5	52.6	6.0	-1.4	0.1	52.9	25.9	78.8	246.7	-6.7	8.5	VERSANT CASUALTY INS CO
3.8	2.5	28.6	39.7	-0.4	-1.1	64.9	22.5	87.4	156.7	9.2	0.0	VERTERRA INS CO
1.4	1.1	295.3	139.8	4.6	N/A	78.1	25.2	103.3	120.2	-30.1	0.0	VERTI INSURANCE CO
4.8	4.3	N/A	N/A	N/A	N/A	N/A	N/A	N/A	159.8	0.0	0.0	VESTA INS CORP
10.4	9.4	-141.1	N/A	N/A	3.5	N/A	-2.4	N/A	-91.0	-151.5	1.3	VETERINARY PET INS CO
0.2	0.1	537.3	651.1	24.1	33.5	83.9	30.6	114.5	97.3	-8.9	35.6	VFH CAPTIVE INS CO
3.4	3.1	N/A	N/A	N/A	N/A	N/A	N/A	N/A	68.7	0.0	0.0	VICTORIA AUTOMOBILE INS CO
1.7	1.6	N/A	N/A	N/A	N/A	N/A	N/A	N/A	121.0	0.0	42.6	VICTORIA FIRE & CASUALTY CO
N/A	N/A	--	--	--	--	--	--	--	--	--	--	VICTORIA NATIONAL INS CO
3.1	2.8	N/A	N/A	N/A	N/A	N/A	N/A	N/A	97.6	0.0	0.0	VICTORIA SELECT INS CO
1.2	1.0	N/A	N/A	N/A	N/A	N/A	N/A	N/A	41.0	0.0	0.0	VICTORIA SPECIALTY INSURANCE CO
1.5	1.0	47.2	57.7	-7.7	64.4	73.1	26.1	99.2	39.3	-61.7	0.0	VICTORY INS CO
9.1	7.1	9.9	24.2	-1.1	-2.0	53.5	33.8	87.3	118.9	-35.2	7.2 ●	VIGILANT INS CO
4.1	2.9	56.5	88.6	-0.7	-2.2	73.9	28.2	102.1	105.3	7.2	8.0	VIKING INS CO OF WI
2.1	1.7	146.4	67.1	-3.5	-11.9	72.3	25.9	98.2	100.6	6.1	0.0	VIRGINIA FARM BUREAU FIRE & CAS INS
2.1	1.7	108.0	46.7	-2.9	-6.1	60.5	33.1	93.6	108.6	0.2	21.1	VIRGINIA FARM BUREAU MUTUAL INS CO
1.6	1.4	37.7	41.3	-5.5	-14.0	51.6	35.8	87.4	87.2	59.2	0.0	VIRGINIA PHYSICIANS RRG INC
9.3	6.4	11.2	13.8	4.6	2.2	62.8	133.9	196.7	9.5	-84.7	2.4 ●	VIRGINIA SURETY CO INC
0.7	0.5	319.3	106.8	26.8	15.4	100.1	29.5	129.6	75.9	0.4	0.0	VISION INS CO
3.9	2.2	170.2	26.9	-13.9	-0.9	20.6	24.1	44.7	195.0	-23.4	0.0	VOYAGER INDEMNITY INS CO
99.1	46.4	N/A	N/A	N/A	N/A	N/A	N/A	N/A	46.4	0.0	0.0	WADENA INS CO
N/A	N/A	--	--	--	--	--	--	--	--	--	--	WALL ROSE MUTUAL INS CO
N/A	N/A	--	--	--	--	--	--	--	--	--	--	WARNER INS CO
2.6	1.9	12.4	49.2	-16.9	-33.6	70.2	74.9	145.1	33.2	0.2	4.2	WARRANTY UNDERWRITERS INS CO
19.5	17.6	N/A	N/A	N/A	N/A	N/A	N/A	N/A	194.4	0.0	0.0	WASHINGTON CASUALTY CO
7.2	5.2	27.9	7.2	-2.4	-2.1	36.5	34.2	70.7	153.2	4.1	0.0	WASHINGTON COUNTY CO-OPERATIVE
21.2	19.0	N/A	3.1	-1.8	-3.1	999 +	999 +	999 +	15.1	-99.1	0.0	WASHINGTON INTL INS CO
N/A	N/A	--	--	--	--	--	--	--	--	--	--	WATFORD INS CO
2.2	1.7	1.3	0.2	N/A	N/A	58.4	193.8	252.2	105.3	0.0	42.5	WATFORD SPECIALTY INS CO
12.8	11.6	N/A	N/A	N/A	N/A	N/A	N/A	N/A	-15.3	0.0	0.0	WAUSAU BUSINESS INS CO
10.6	9.5	N/A	N/A	N/A	N/A	N/A	N/A	N/A	270.2	0.0	0.0	WAUSAU GENERAL INS CO
9.3	8.4	N/A	N/A	N/A	N/A	N/A	N/A	N/A	999 +	0.0	0.0	WAUSAU UNDERWRITERS INS CO
2.4	1.8	152.0	73.3	-4.9	4.9	94.7	12.0	106.7	89.6	-1.4	0.0 ●	WAWANESA GENERAL INS CO
3.1	2.3	91.4	35.5	-2.0	-9.7	62.2	30.5	92.7	116.1	4.9	0.0	WAYNE COOPERATIVE INS CO
3.8	2.6	125.0	25.4	-1.7	-3.0	47.4	35.1	82.5	124.3	11.5	0.0	WAYNE MUTUAL INS CO
1.7	1.3	201.9	71.3	-15.2	-24.9	65.1	33.6	98.7	102.1	6.5	0.0	WEA P&C INS CO
4.8	4.0	51.1	19.8	-6.8	-5.8	48.2	25.4	73.6	107.6	32.9	0.0	WELLINGTON INS CO
1.0	0.8	107.7	200.4	-48.5	-56.2	64.6	5.0	69.6	187.6	14.1	0.0	WELLSPAN RRG
N/A	N/A	--	--	--	--	--	--	--	--	--	--	WESCAP INS CO
1.4	0.9	167.0	89.0	4.9	5.4	67.5	29.5	97.0	159.1	45.6	6.6 ●	WESCO INS CO

999 + Denotes number greater than 999.9%
999 - Denotes number less than -999.99%
● Bullets denote a more detailed analysis is available in Section II.

INSURANCE COMPANY NAME	DOM. STATE	RATING	TOTAL ASSETS ($MIL)	CAPITAL & SURPLUS ($MIL)	ANNUAL NET PREMIUM ($MIL)	NET INCOME ($MIL)	CAPITAL-IZATION INDEX (PTS)	RESERVE ADQ INDEX (PTS)	PROFIT-ABILITY INDEX (PTS)	LIQUIDITY INDEX (PTS)	STAB. INDEX (PTS)	STABILITY FACTORS
WEST AMERICAN INS CO	IN	C-	51.7	50.5	0.0	0.2	10.0	N/A	3.1	7.0	3.1	ART
WEST BEND MUTUAL INS CO	WI	B+	2,580.8	977.6	1,016.1	16.9	8.7	8.9	8.6	6.4	5.1	T
WEST BRANCH MUTL INS CO	PA	C+	1.1	0.9	0.3	0.0	7.5	7.3	3.9	7.0	3.0	DFGT
WEST VIRGINIA FARMERS MUT INS ASSOC	WV	C-	7.5	5.6	1.9	0.1	9.4	5.2	7.9	6.8	2.6	DGRT
WEST VIRGINIA INS CO	WV	C	52.1	43.3	11.4	0.4	10.0	7.5	8.0	6.8	4.0	DT
▲WEST VIRGINIA MUTUAL INS CO	WV	C-	165.8	98.3	17.1	0.7	10.0	9.4	3.1	7.4	3.0	DFRT
WEST VIRGINIA NATIONAL AUTO INS CO	WV	D+	6.5	2.7	3.7	0.0	7.2	4.9	1.3	5.4	2.0	DFGR
WESTCHESTER FIRE INS CO	PA	C	1,849.8	703.3	361.8	4.1	9.2	6.6	3.4	6.9	2.9	RT
WESTCHESTER SURPLUS LINES INS CO	GA	C	329.9	119.9	43.2	1.3	10.0	6.4	3.1	7.4	4.0	RT
WESTERN AGRICULTURAL INS CO	IA	B+	217.1	106.3	105.6	3.3	10.0	8.1	8.9	6.3	5.1	T
WESTERN CATHOLIC INS CO RRG	VT	E+	4.0	1.3	1.3	-0.1	0.3	0.3	2.9	8.0	0.5	CDFG
WESTERN COMMUNITY INS CO	ID	B-	41.0	32.4	0.0	0.4	10.0	N/A	8.2	10.0	3.8	T
WESTERN GENERAL INS CO	CA	D+	90.0	21.5	59.0	0.2	2.0	3.6	3.0	1.9	2.7	CDGL
WESTERN HERITAGE INS CO	AZ	B	134.0	113.6	0.0	0.4	10.0	N/A	7.0	7.0	4.5	RT
WESTERN HOME INS CO	MN	C	70.3	31.5	27.9	0.5	9.5	8.3	8.9	6.7	3.4	RT
WESTERN MUTL INS CO (CA)	CA	C-	85.2	58.1	27.9	0.6	7.2	8.1	8.1	6.6	2.7	RT
WESTERN MUTUAL FIRE INS CO	MN	B-	7.3	5.2	2.6	0.2	10.0	4.8	8.5	7.2	3.5	DGT
WESTERN NATIONAL ASR CO	MN	C	72.1	28.1	27.9	0.3	9.0	8.3	8.9	6.3	3.7	FRT
WESTERN NATIONAL MUTUAL INS CO	MN	B-	996.7	447.3	349.2	5.7	8.6	8.2	8.6	6.6	4.3	RT
WESTERN PACIFIC MUT INS CO RISK RET	CO	B-	140.3	113.2	3.3	-0.1	10.0	8.9	6.6	9.9	3.6	DFRT
WESTERN PROFESSIONAL INS CO	WA	U	--	--	--	--	N/A	--	--	--	--	Z
WESTERN PROTECTORS INS CO	OR	C	9.1	9.0	-1.1	0.0	10.0	3.6	5.6	7.0	2.9	DFGR
WESTERN RESERVE MUTUAL CAS CO	OH	B-	193.5	114.2	81.8	2.1	9.9	7.8	6.1	6.2	4.0	T
WESTERN SELECT INS CO	IL	C	16.7	15.2	0.2	0.2	10.0	5.0	5.4	10.0	3.6	DG
WESTERN SURETY CO	SD	C	2,015.0	1,439.5	370.2	17.7	10.0	9.3	8.1	8.0	3.9	RT
WESTERN WORLD INS CO	NH	C	836.8	387.5	121.4	63.6	7.6	9.5	6.0	6.8	4.1	FRT
WESTFIELD INS CO	OH	B-	2,777.2	1,209.8	977.1	16.6	9.7	8.7	8.6	6.7	4.6	T
WESTFIELD NATIONAL INS CO	OH	B-	664.5	305.5	235.2	4.7	9.5	8.7	8.6	6.7	4.6	T
WESTGUARD INS CO	PA	B-	1,130.2	537.1	23.0	4.1	7.1	9.2	7.5	10.0	4.4	FRT
WESTMINSTER AMERICAN INS CO	MD	C	32.7	18.3	16.0	0.2	8.0	7.7	8.9	7.6	2.9	DGRT
WESTON INS CO	FL	C	78.7	46.0	0.7	0.5	10.0	4.6	3.9	9.5	2.2	DGT
WESTPORT INS CORP	MO	B	4,649.0	1,562.8	287.1	21.6	7.1	8.3	4.2	7.5	4.3	FRT
WHITE PINE INS CO	MI	C	77.2	31.6	42.5	-1.0	3.2	7.0	3.7	6.6	3.4	CGRT
WHITECAP SURETY CO	MN	D-	1.6	1.4	3.4	0.0	1.6	N/A	8.3	2.6	1.2	CDGL
WI LAWYERS MUTUAL INS CO	WI	C+	33.5	23.3	3.9	0.0	10.0	8.0	6.8	7.7	3.1	DGRT
WILLIAMSBURG NATIONAL INS CO	MI	C-	53.2	46.9	0.0	0.2	10.0	1.8	4.1	7.7	2.9	FRT
WILMINGTON INS CO	DE	D+	5.1	3.4	1.0	0.0	10.0	6.3	7.3	9.2	2.1	DG
WILSHIRE INS CO	NC	C-	301.1	116.4	88.5	4.8	5.6	3.4	4.7	5.9	2.7	RT
WILSON MUTUAL INS CO	WI	B	92.7	25.9	21.4	0.0	8.0	7.8	4.9	6.5	4.1	FT
▲WINDHAVEN INS CO	FL	D-	227.6	50.3	117.7	0.7	0.8	1.0	5.5	0.3	0.9	CLRT
WINDHAVEN NATIONAL INS CO	TX	C	5.9	5.5	0.0	-0.1	8.4	2.8	3.0	9.2	2.7	DFGT
WINDSOR MOUNT JOY MUTUAL INS CO	PA	C+	79.1	50.6	32.5	1.3	10.0	8.1	8.7	7.0	3.4	RT
WINTHROP PHYSICIANS RECIP RRG	VT	B- (2)	2.9	2.4	0.2	-0.1	10.0	4.6	3.8	10.0	3.5	DFGT
WISCONSIN COUNTY MUTUAL INS CORP	WI	C	93.8	28.5	24.3	-3.1	7.3	6.9	2.5	6.7	3.3	RT
WISCONSIN MUNICIPAL MUTUAL INS CO	WI	C	52.0	33.3	3.2	0.6	7.4	6.5	2.4	8.5	3.2	DFRT
WISCONSIN MUTUAL INS CO	WI	B-	154.9	88.5	73.2	2.4	10.0	6.9	8.9	6.6	3.9	RT
WISCONSIN REINS CORP	WI	C+	96.6	58.9	39.9	0.1	7.4	7.0	8.6	6.8	3.5	RT
WOLVERINE MUTUAL INS CO	MI	C+	56.4	22.6	34.5	0.6	7.8	8.2	7.9	6.3	3.1	DT
WOODLANDS INS CO	TX	C	28.5	11.5	1.7	0.4	10.0	3.6	5.1	9.0	2.4	DGT
▲WORK FIRST CASUALTY CO	DE	C-	43.1	13.2	16.2	0.3	3.1	5.0	3.1	6.2	2.5	DRT
WORKERS COMPENSATION EXCHANGE	ID	E	7.8	0.5	2.4	0.0	0.1	3.6	3.3	7.5	0.3	CDGR
WORKMENS AUTO INS CO	CA	D	44.7	19.0	26.4	0.2	5.1	0.6	3.6	5.7	1.9	DFRT

See Page 27 for explanation of footnotes and Page 28 for explanation of stability factors.

Arrows denote recent upgrades ▲ or downgrades ▼ (see Section VII for explanations)

130

www.weissratings.com

RISK ADJ. CAPITAL RATIO #1	CAPITAL RATIO #2	PREMIUM TO SURPLUS (%)	RESV. TO SURPLUS (%)	RESV. DEVELOP. 1 YEAR (%)	RESV. DEVELOP. 2 YEAR (%)	LOSS RATIO (%)	EXP. RATIO (%)	COMB RATIO (%)	CASH FROM UNDER-WRITING (%)	NET PREMIUM GROWTH (%)	INVEST. IN AFFIL (%)	INSURANCE COMPANY NAME
98.5	52.0	N/A	N/A	N/A	N/A	N/A	N/A	N/A	N/A	0.0	0.0	WEST AMERICAN INS CO
3.2	2.2	107.3	97.2	-3.2	-9.7	65.5	30.6	96.1	116.0	5.8	0.0 ●	WEST BEND MUTUAL INS CO
2.1	1.3	40.1	1.1	-0.6	-0.5	37.9	80.7	118.6	86.9	-1.9	0.0	WEST BRANCH MUTL INS CO
3.6	2.5	34.3	3.1	-0.4	-1.0	42.5	49.4	91.9	108.2	3.4	0.0	WEST VIRGINIA FARMERS MUT INS
11.0	9.6	26.5	4.9	-1.4	-1.7	72.0	19.6	91.6	109.4	-0.1	0.0	WEST VIRGINIA INS CO
5.2	4.1	17.6	45.2	-6.4	-12.4	94.6	40.1	134.7	75.0	-6.9	0.0	WEST VIRGINIA MUTUAL INS CO
1.2	1.1	139.5	91.4	3.2	10.4	93.5	29.7	123.2	80.8	-17.1	0.0	WEST VIRGINIA NATIONAL AUTO INS CO
3.8	2.5	51.5	121.1	6.1	2.7	76.5	26.9	103.4	88.2	-3.3	0.0 ●	WESTCHESTER FIRE INS CO
5.3	3.3	36.4	51.9	-0.9	1.1	58.2	23.2	81.4	236.3	1.9	0.0	WESTCHESTER SURPLUS LINES INS CO
5.0	3.9	102.5	41.6	-3.7	-4.2	59.9	26.6	86.5	115.8	0.5	2.2 ●	WESTERN AGRICULTURAL INS CO
0.1	0.1	84.8	127.6	30.9	71.6	58.2	32.8	91.0	27.1	-2.4	0.0	WESTERN CATHOLIC INS CO RRG
14.9	13.4	N/A	N/A	N/A	N/A	N/A	N/A	N/A	7.0	0.0	0.0	WESTERN COMMUNITY INS CO
0.7	0.4	283.4	79.4	11.7	18.2	58.9	41.6	100.5	109.2	8.1	0.0	WESTERN GENERAL INS CO
32.0	28.8	N/A	N/A	N/A	N/A	N/A	N/A	N/A	84.8	0.0	0.0	WESTERN HERITAGE INS CO
4.3	3.1	90.4	69.5	-3.0	-6.5	65.5	27.4	92.9	135.4	2.5	0.0	WESTERN HOME INS CO
1.8	1.2	48.9	14.2	-2.9	-4.2	71.2	21.1	92.3	110.7	1.9	24.3	WESTERN MUTL INS CO (CA)
7.0	6.3	51.5	16.3	-2.3	-0.5	77.1	21.8	98.9	118.5	1.9	0.0	WESTERN MUTUAL FIRE INS CO
3.5	2.5	100.8	77.5	-3.4	-7.1	65.5	26.9	92.4	94.2	2.5	0.0	WESTERN NATIONAL ASR CO
2.5	2.1	80.6	61.9	-2.7	-6.1	65.5	26.0	91.5	118.6	2.5	18.8 ●	WESTERN NATIONAL MUTUAL INS CO
7.7	4.7	2.9	7.8	-2.7	-3.5	62.2	115.6	177.8	41.2	2.2	0.0	WESTERN PACIFIC MUT INS CO RISK
N/A	N/A	--	--	--	--	--	--	--	--	--	--	WESTERN PROFESSIONAL INS CO
96.4	46.4	-12.4	N/A	N/A	N/A	N/A	12.1	N/A	169.7	N/A	0.0	WESTERN PROTECTORS INS CO
4.8	2.9	73.5	31.4	-1.4	-2.7	65.1	31.0	96.1	104.5	4.6	0.2	WESTERN RESERVE MUTUAL CAS CO
25.6	23.0	1.4	1.9	0.2	0.2	104.0	-122.0	-18.0	-47.9	-3.6	0.0	WESTERN SELECT INS CO
7.6	5.7	25.5	20.6	-3.9	-6.0	14.7	53.6	68.3	171.1	25.1	1.2 ●	WESTERN SURETY CO
1.4	1.3	29.1	77.6	-2.5	-5.0	68.3	38.5	106.8	71.9	25.6	34.6 ●	WESTERN WORLD INS CO
4.4	2.9	83.0	74.6	-3.0	-4.5	62.3	34.3	96.6	106.4	2.3	0.0 ●	WESTFIELD INS CO
4.2	2.8	78.3	70.3	-2.9	-4.3	62.3	35.5	97.8	106.4	2.3	0.0 ●	WESTFIELD NATIONAL INS CO
1.3	1.2	4.5	4.8	-0.2	-0.1	58.9	13.7	72.6	999 +	21.0	65.2 ●	WESTGUARD INS CO
2.0	1.8	88.0	12.2	N/A	-1.4	32.6	33.2	65.8	143.3	8.2	0.0	WESTMINSTER AMERICAN INS CO
9.3	8.4	1.6	2.5	0.2	0.3	999 +	-709.3	388.3	324.1	-1.3	0.0	WESTON INS CO
1.7	1.2	18.4	73.6	0.9	-3.3	80.1	37.6	117.7	56.0	2.0	12.2 ●	WESTPORT INS CORP
0.7	0.5	131.3	52.3	12.9	3.1	63.9	44.0	107.9	121.6	94.0	0.0	WHITE PINE INS CO
0.4	0.3	246.8	N/A	N/A	N/A	N/A	96.3	96.3	104.2	-2.7	0.0	WHITECAP SURETY CO
4.5	3.0	16.8	26.8	-4.4	-6.7	58.7	34.5	93.2	107.1	2.9	0.0	WI LAWYERS MUTUAL INS CO
25.5	22.9	N/A	N/A	N/A	N/A	N/A	N/A	N/A	-134.8	-100.0	0.0	WILLIAMSBURG NATIONAL INS CO
5.4	4.0	30.0	11.4	-5.8	-2.5	15.5	20.6	36.1	206.7	-2.3	0.0	WILMINGTON INS CO
1.7	1.0	81.2	83.6	21.1	27.6	85.3	15.1	100.4	100.0	-3.9	0.0	WILSHIRE INS CO
2.7	1.7	82.8	61.2	-0.6	-1.7	64.1	37.6	101.7	90.0	-0.4	0.0	WILSON MUTUAL INS CO
0.3	0.3	255.0	94.4	-7.1	-4.9	67.7	35.1	102.8	100.1	21.6	0.0	WINDHAVEN INS CO
3.2	2.3	N/A	26.0	-0.9	26.7	N/A	N/A	N/A	5.4	-100.0	0.0	WINDHAVEN NATIONAL INS CO
5.2	4.4	65.9	13.8	-2.6	-2.8	42.8	39.5	82.3	134.6	13.2	0.0	WINDSOR MOUNT JOY MUTUAL INS CO
5.9	4.9	8.7	5.4	-1.7	-1.7	0.2	108.8	109.0	89.1	-32.6	0.0	WINTHROP PHYSICIANS RECIP RRG
1.7	1.1	78.3	119.8	4.4	0.5	80.6	28.6	109.2	103.2	5.5	7.6	WISCONSIN COUNTY MUTUAL INS CORP
2.6	1.6	10.1	33.5	9.6	6.9	184.4	27.1	211.5	152.2	1.7	6.4	WISCONSIN MUNICIPAL MUTUAL INS CO
6.2	4.5	85.7	37.5	-3.6	-7.6	62.1	23.2	85.3	116.4	3.8	0.0	WISCONSIN MUTUAL INS CO
2.0	1.6	67.5	49.0	-7.8	-16.2	47.0	21.9	68.9	152.1	-3.3	12.5	WISCONSIN REINS CORP
2.4	1.8	156.3	67.5	-3.6	-3.2	66.8	29.9	96.7	111.3	-4.9	0.0	WOLVERINE MUTUAL INS CO
3.6	3.2	15.4	2.7	-0.1	N/A	61.8	14.2	76.0	171.0	569.8	0.0	WOODLANDS INS CO
0.9	0.6	127.8	217.0	-7.3	-37.7	68.3	29.8	98.1	108.0	26.9	0.0	WORK FIRST CASUALTY CO
0.1	0.1	465.7	999 +	76.5	40.0	98.0	13.2	111.2	122.4	12.8	0.0	WORKERS COMPENSATION EXCHANGE
1.1	0.8	141.6	73.2	-10.4	-1.8	81.6	25.4	107.0	81.5	33.6	0.0	WORKMENS AUTO INS CO

999 + Denotes number greater than 999.9%
999 - Denotes number less than -999.99%
● Bullets denote a more detailed analysis is available in Section II.

INSURANCE COMPANY NAME	DOM. STATE	RATING	TOTAL ASSETS ($MIL)	CAPITAL & SURPLUS ($MIL)	ANNUAL NET PREMIUM ($MIL)	NET INCOME ($MIL)	CAPITAL-IZATION INDEX (PTS)	RESERVE ADQ INDEX (PTS)	PROFIT-ABILITY INDEX (PTS)	LIQUIDITY INDEX (PTS)	STAB. INDEX (PTS)	STABILITY FACTORS
WORTH CASUALTY CO	TX	C (1)	14.8	8.4	0.0	0.1	10.0	4.6	4.2	9.3	2.8	DFRT
▲WRIGHT NATIONAL FLOOD INS CO	TX	B-	31.2	24.3	0.0	0.7	10.0	5.0	7.5	6.9	4.8	DG
WRM AMERICA INDEMNITY CO	NY	U	--	--	--	--	N/A	--	--	--	--	Z
XL INS AMERICA INC	DE	C	724.0	196.2	166.7	3.7	7.2	6.3	3.4	8.3	3.7	RT
XL INS CO OF NY INC	NY	C-	227.5	77.0	50.0	3.2	8.7	6.3	4.0	7.6	3.1	ART
XL REINS AMERICA INC	NY	C	6,087.9	2,122.4	1,083.7	38.0	8.4	6.2	4.2	6.8	3.8	ART
XL SELECT INS CO	DE	D	141.0	47.6	33.3	0.9	8.0	6.3	3.7	6.9	2.3	FRT
XL SPECIALTY INS CO	DE	C	956.4	289.3	100.0	6.5	8.8	6.3	5.0	9.8	3.8	AGRT
YEL CO INS	FL	C	16.8	11.2	1.2	0.3	10.0	9.1	8.2	10.0	2.4	DGT
▲YELLOWSTONE INS EXCHANGE	VT	C-	22.5	9.3	5.1	0.0	8.1	10.0	5.5	8.0	2.9	DGRT
▼YORK INS CO OF MAINE	ME	F (5)	47.0	46.3	0.0	0.0	10.0	N/A	7.5	7.0	0.0	RT
YOSEMITE INS CO	IN	C+	166.7	65.6	31.4	2.5	10.0	6.4	1.9	8.9	3.9	T
YOUNG AMERICA INS CO	TX	D	56.2	17.3	67.1	-0.3	1.2	2.9	0.9	0.0	1.5	CDFL
ZALE INDEMNITY CO	TX	C+	52.7	17.7	15.2	0.0	7.3	8.3	7.4	6.7	3.0	DRT
ZENITH INS CO	CA	C+	1,864.4	605.5	792.7	30.1	7.0	7.0	4.3	7.3	4.4	ART
ZEPHYR INS CO	HI	C	104.0	72.3	29.8	3.1	10.0	N/A	9.1	8.7	3.7	RT
ZNAT INS CO	CA	C	70.6	27.3	16.2	0.9	8.3	7.0	5.1	9.3	3.4	ART
ZURICH AMERICAN INS CO	NY	B-	30,708.0	7,592.2	4,215.2	202.4	8.1	6.0	5.9	7.2	3.5	RT
ZURICH AMERICAN INS CO OF IL	IL	C+	53.9	34.3	0.0	0.1	10.0	N/A	5.3	10.0	3.8	RT

See Page 27 for explanation of footnotes and
Page 28 for explanation of stability factors.
Arrows denote recent upgrades ▲ or downgrades ▼   (see Section VII for explanations)

132

www.weissratings.com

RISK ADJ. RATIO #1	CAPITAL RATIO #2	PREMIUM TO SURPLUS (%)	RESV. TO SURPLUS (%)	RESV. DEVELOP. 1 YEAR (%)	RESV. DEVELOP. 2 YEAR (%)	LOSS RATIO (%)	EXP. RATIO (%)	COMB RATIO (%)	CASH FROM UNDER-WRITING	NET PREMIUM GROWTH (%)	INVEST. IN AFFIL (%)	INSURANCE COMPANY NAME
4.7	4.2	N/A	N/A	N/A	N/A	N/A	N/A	N/A	-824.0	0.0	0.0	WORTH CASUALTY CO
13.0	11.7	0.1	N/A	N/A	0.1	999 +	999 +	999 +	1.8	-15.6	0.0	WRIGHT NATIONAL FLOOD INS CO
N/A	N/A	--	--	--	--	--	--	--	--	--	--	WRM AMERICA INDEMNITY CO
1.4	1.1	86.2	173.9	0.2	0.6	69.3	29.3	98.6	105.1	25.6	18.4 ●	XL INS AMERICA INC
3.3	2.1	66.8	134.7	0.1	0.5	69.3	27.3	96.6	105.0	25.6	0.0	XL INS CO OF NY INC
2.3	1.9	52.2	105.2	0.1	0.4	69.3	27.1	96.4	122.8	25.6	16.6 ●	XL REINS AMERICA INC
5.4	4.9	70.7	142.5	0.2	0.5	69.3	27.3	96.6	105.0	25.6	0.0	XL SELECT INS CO
4.2	3.1	35.3	71.2	0.2	0.6	69.3	28.0	97.3	105.2	25.6	5.8 ●	XL SPECIALTY INS CO
6.9	6.2	11.0	42.8	-4.1	-7.7	17.9	3.4	21.3	602.3	0.0	0.0	YEL CO INS
2.4	1.9	56.4	63.7	-10.1	-46.6	29.8	50.6	80.4	126.5	36.8	0.0	YELLOWSTONE INS EXCHANGE
60.4	34.5	N/A	N/A	N/A	N/A	N/A	N/A	N/A	N/A	-100.0	0.0	YORK INS CO OF MAINE
7.4	3.8	50.0	31.9	-0.6	-3.6	27.8	37.9	65.7	145.6	-13.6	0.0	YOSEMITE INS CO
0.5	0.4	532.8	302.5	49.5	36.5	99.3	28.8	128.1	75.8	-0.1	0.0	YOUNG AMERICA INS CO
1.2	1.1	88.0	5.3	1.5	-3.1	14.1	69.7	83.8	107.6	-23.5	37.3	ZALE INDEMNITY CO
1.3	1.0	140.7	199.0	-16.0	-29.4	44.6	31.7	76.3	123.7	5.0	9.5 ●	ZENITH INS CO
7.0	6.5	39.0	N/A	-0.1	N/A	-0.1	37.7	37.6	199.3	-27.2	0.0	ZEPHYR INS CO
2.5	1.9	61.4	86.9	-7.7	-12.6	44.6	31.9	76.5	212.9	5.0	0.0	ZNAT INS CO
2.3	1.6	53.7	181.7	-1.6	1.2	78.5	20.5	99.0	95.0	-7.2	8.0 ●	ZURICH AMERICAN INS CO
9.8	8.9	N/A	N/A	N/A	N/A	N/A	N/A	N/A	-83.4	0.0	0.0	ZURICH AMERICAN INS CO OF IL

999 + Denotes number greater than 999.9%
999 - Denotes number less than -999.99%
● Bullets denote a more detailed analysis is available in Section II.

Section II

Analysis of Largest Companies

A summary analysis of Weiss Recommended

U.S. Property and Casualty Insurers,

along with the largest companies based on capital and surplus.

Companies are listed in alphabetical order.

Section II Contents

This section contains rating factors, historical data and general information on each of the largest property and casualty insurers in the U.S. that have the most recent quarterly financial information available.

1. **Safety Rating**   The current rating appears to the right of the company name. Our ratings are designed to distinguish levels of insolvency risk and are measured on a scale from A (Excellent) to F (Failed). Highly-rated companies are, in our opinion, less likely to experience financial difficulties than lower-rated firms. See *About Weiss Safety Ratings* for more information.

2. **Major Rating Factors**   A synopsis of the key indexes and sub-factors that have most influenced the rating of a particular insurer. Items are presented in the approximate order of their importance to the rating. There may be additional factors which have influenced the rating but do not appear due to space limitations or confidentiality agreements with insurers.

3. **Other Rating Factors**   A summary of those Weiss Ratings indexes that were not included as Major Rating Factors, but nevertheless, may have had some impact on the final grade.

4. **Principal Business**   The major types of policies written by an insurer along with the percentages for each line in relation to the entire book of business. Lines of business written by property and casualty insurers include personal and commercial insurance lines such as homeowners', auto, workers' compensation, commercial multiple peril, medical malpractice and product liability, among others.

5. **Principal Investments**   The major investments in an insurer's portfolio. These include cash, investment grade bonds, non investment grade bonds, common and preferred stock, and real estate.

6. **Investments in Affiliates**   The percentage of bonds, common and preferred stocks and other financial instruments an insurer has invested with affiliated companies.

7. **Group Affiliation**   The name of the group of companies to which a particular insurer belongs.

8. **Licensed in**   List of the states in which an insurer is licensed to conduct business.

9. **Commenced Business**   The month and year the company started its operations.

10. **Address**   The address of an insurer's corporate headquarters. This location may differ from the company's state of domicile.

11. **Phone**   The telephone number of an insurer's corporate headquarters.

12. Domicile State	The state that has primary regulatory responsibility for this company. You do not have to live in the domicile state to do business with this firm, provided it is registered to do business in your state.
13. NAIC Code	The identification number assigned to an insurer by the National Association of Insurance Commissioners (NAIC).
14. Historical Data	Five years of background data for Weiss Safety Rating, risk-adjusted capital ratios (moderate and severe loss scenarios), total assets, capital, net premium, and net income. See the following page for more details on how to read the historical data table.
15. Customized Graph (or Table)	A graph or table depicting one of the company's major strengths or weaknesses.

How to Read the Historical Data Table

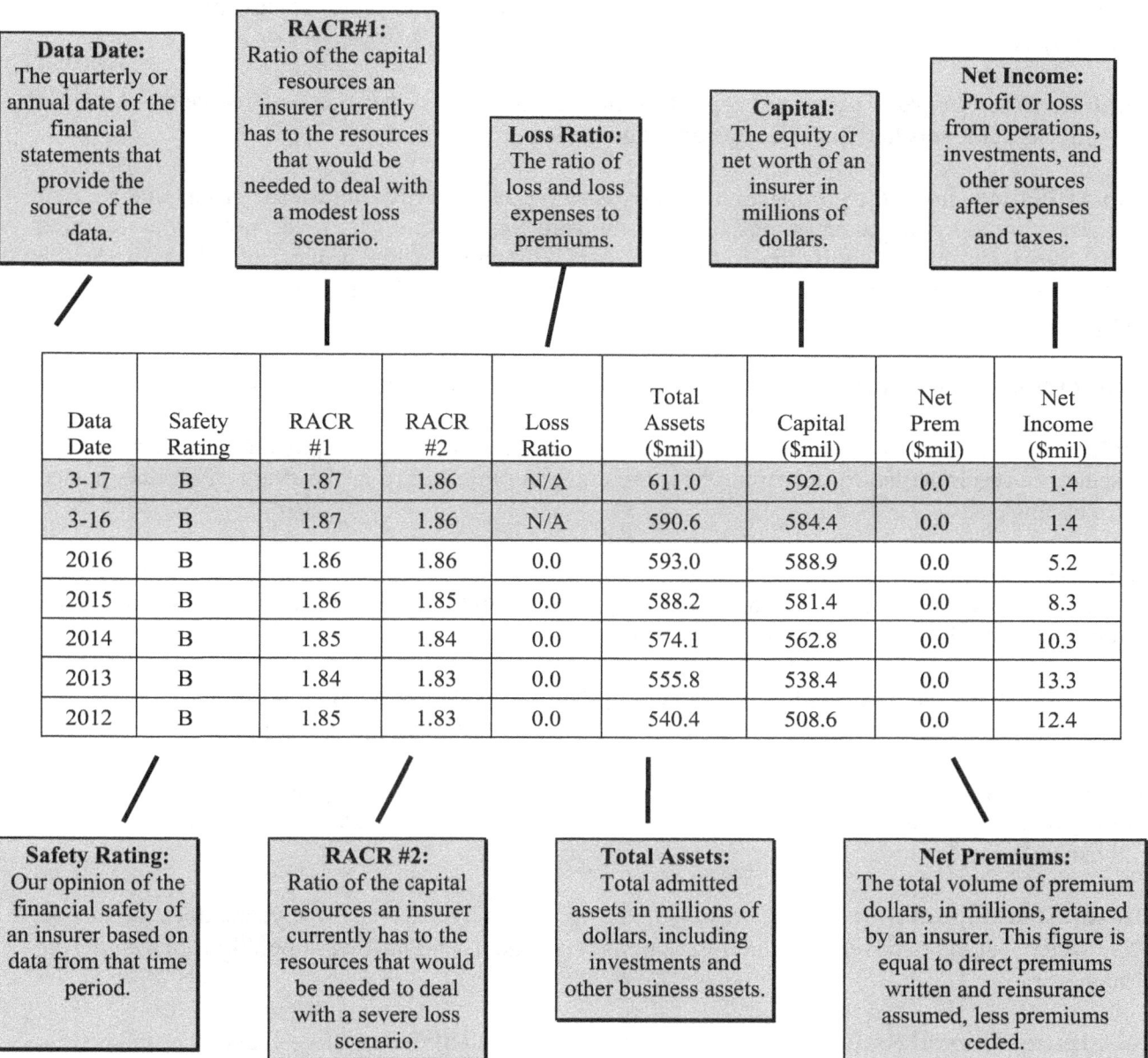

Data Date:
The quarterly or annual date of the financial statements that provide the source of the data.

RACR#1:
Ratio of the capital resources an insurer currently has to the resources that would be needed to deal with a modest loss scenario.

Loss Ratio:
The ratio of loss and loss expenses to premiums.

Capital:
The equity or net worth of an insurer in millions of dollars.

Net Income:
Profit or loss from operations, investments, and other sources after expenses and taxes.

Data Date	Safety Rating	RACR #1	RACR #2	Loss Ratio	Total Assets ($mil)	Capital ($mil)	Net Prem ($mil)	Net Income ($mil)
3-17	B	1.87	1.86	N/A	611.0	592.0	0.0	1.4
3-16	B	1.87	1.86	N/A	590.6	584.4	0.0	1.4
2016	B	1.86	1.86	0.0	593.0	588.9	0.0	5.2
2015	B	1.86	1.85	0.0	588.2	581.4	0.0	8.3
2014	B	1.85	1.84	0.0	574.1	562.8	0.0	10.3
2013	B	1.84	1.83	0.0	555.8	538.4	0.0	13.3
2012	B	1.85	1.83	0.0	540.4	508.6	0.0	12.4

Safety Rating:
Our opinion of the financial safety of an insurer based on data from that time period.

RACR #2:
Ratio of the capital resources an insurer currently has to the resources that would be needed to deal with a severe loss scenario.

Total Assets:
Total admitted assets in millions of dollars, including investments and other business assets.

Net Premiums:
The total volume of premium dollars, in millions, retained by an insurer. This figure is equal to direct premiums written and reinsurance assumed, less premiums ceded.

Row Descriptions:

Row 1 contains the most recent quarterly data as filed with state regulators and is presented on a year-to-date basis. For example, the figure for year-end premiums includes premiums received through the year-end. **Row 2** consists of data from the same quarter of the prior year so that you can compare current quarterly results to those of a year ago.

Row 3 contains data from the most recent annual statutory filing. **Rows 4-7** include data from year-end statements going back four years from the most recent annual filing so that you can compare current year-end results to those of the previous four years. With the exception of Total Assets and Capital, quarterly data are not comparable with annual data.

Customized Graphs

In the lower right-hand corner of each company section, a customized graph or text block highlights a key factor affecting that company's financial strength. One of nine types of information is found, identified by one of the following headings:

Capital plots the company's reported capital in millions of dollars over the last five years. Volatile changes in capital levels may indicate unstable operations.

Group Affiliation shows the group name, a composite Weiss Safety Rating for the group, and a list of the largest members with their ratings. The composite Safety Rating is made up of the weighted average, by assets, of the individual ratings of each company in the group (including life/health companies, property/casualty companies or HMOs) plus a factor for the financial strength of the holding company, where applicable.

Income Trends shows underwriting and net income results over the last five years.

Liquidity Index evaluates a company's ability to raise the cash necessary to pay claims. Various cash flow scenarios are modeled to determine how the company might fare in the event of an unexpected spike in claims costs.

Rating Indexes illustrate the score and range -- strong, good, fair or weak -- on the five Weiss indexes: Risk-Adjusted Capital Index #2 (Cap2), Stability Index (Stab.), Reserve Adequacy Index (Res.), Profitability Index (Prof.), and Liquidity Index (Liq.).

Reserve Deficiency shows whether the company has set aside sufficient funds to pay claims. A positive number indicates insufficient reserving and a negative number adequate reserving.

Reserves to Capital analyzes the relationship between loss and loss expense reserves to capital. Operating results and capital levels for companies with a high ratio are more susceptible to fluctuations than those with lower ratios.

Risk-Adjusted Capital Ratio #1 answers the question: In each of the past five years, does the insurer have sufficient capital to cover potential losses in its investments and business operations in a *moderate* loss scenario?

Risk-Adjusted Capital Ratio #2 answers the question: In each of the past five years, does the insurer have sufficient capital to cover potential losses in its investments and business operations in a *severe* loss scenario?

21ST CENTURY CENTENNIAL INS CO   B   Good

Major Rating Factors: Good overall profitability index (6.9 on a scale of 0 to 10). Fair expense controls. Return on equity has been low, averaging 1.8% over the past five years. Fair reserve development (4.6) as reserves have generally been sufficient to cover claims.

Other Rating Factors: Fair overall results on stability tests (4.8) including weak results on operational trends. Affiliation with Farmers Insurance Group of Companies is a strength. Strong long-term capitalization index (8.3) based on excellent current risk adjusted capital (severe and moderate loss scenarios), despite some fluctuation in capital levels. Superior liquidity (10.0) with ample operational cash flow and liquid investments.

Principal Business: Auto liability (69%) and auto physical damage (31%).

Principal Investments: Misc. investments (58%), investment grade bonds (39%), and cash (3%).

Investments in Affiliates: 59%

Group Affiliation: Farmers Insurance Group of Companies

Licensed in: All states except PR

Commenced Business: November 1977

Address: 2595 INTERSTATE DRIVE STE 103, Harrisburg, PA 17110

Phone: (302) 252-2000   **Domicile State:** PA   **NAIC Code:** 34789

Data Date	Rating	RACR #1	RACR #2	Loss Ratio %	Total Assets ($mil)	Capital ($mil)	Net Premium ($mil)	Net Income ($mil)
3-17	B	1.87	1.86	N/A	611.0	592.0	0.0	1.4
3-16	B	1.87	1.86	N/A	590.6	584.4	0.0	1.4
2016	B	1.86	1.86	0.0	593.0	588.9	0.0	5.2
2015	B	1.86	1.85	0.0	588.2	581.4	0.0	8.3
2014	B	1.85	1.84	0.0	574.1	562.8	0.0	10.3
2013	B	1.84	1.83	0.0	555.8	538.4	0.0	13.3
2012	B	1.85	1.83	0.0	540.4	508.6	0.0	12.4

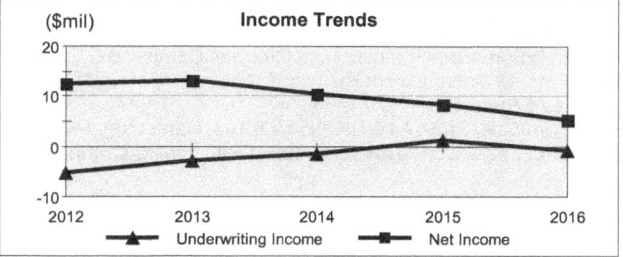

21ST CENTURY INS CO   B   Good

Major Rating Factors: Good overall profitability index (6.6 on a scale of 0 to 10). Fair expense controls. Return on equity has been low, averaging 2.3% over the past five years. Good overall results on stability tests (6.0). Stability strengths include good operational trends and excellent risk diversification.

Other Rating Factors: Fair reserve development (4.6) as reserves have generally been sufficient to cover claims. Strong long-term capitalization index (10.0) based on excellent current risk adjusted capital (severe and moderate loss scenarios), despite some fluctuation in capital levels. Superior liquidity (10.0) with ample operational cash flow and liquid investments.

Principal Business: Auto liability (57%) and auto physical damage (43%).

Principal Investments: Investment grade bonds (95%), misc. investments (3%), and cash (2%).

Investments in Affiliates: None

Group Affiliation: Farmers Insurance Group of Companies

Licensed in: All states except HI, LA, MA, NH, NM, RI, WY, PR

Commenced Business: December 1968

Address: 2710 GATEWAY OAKS DR STE 150N, Sacramento, CA 95833-3505

Phone: (302) 252-2000   **Domicile State:** CA   **NAIC Code:** 12963

Data Date	Rating	RACR #1	RACR #2	Loss Ratio %	Total Assets ($mil)	Capital ($mil)	Net Premium ($mil)	Net Income ($mil)
3-17	B	106.70	48.17	N/A	956.7	939.7	0.0	4.5
3-16	B	101.10	45.88	N/A	922.1	909.1	0.0	6.6
2016	B	102.28	46.19	0.0	945.0	934.9	0.0	31.3
2015	B	100.94	45.85	0.0	912.6	902.6	0.0	24.3
2014	B	101.87	48.43	0.0	895.4	880.6	0.0	21.1
2013	B	55.30	36.29	0.0	880.8	861.7	0.0	15.0
2012	B	33.35	26.04	0.0	931.9	897.4	0.0	13.1

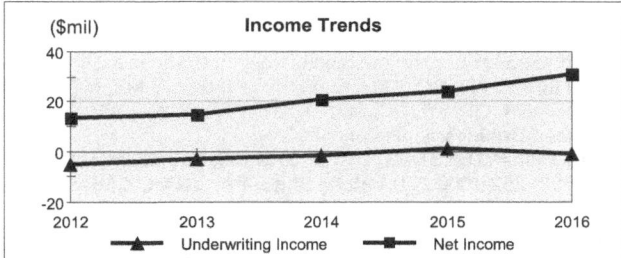

21ST CENTURY NORTH AMERICA INS   B   Good

Major Rating Factors: Good overall profitability index (6.1 on a scale of 0 to 10). Fair expense controls. Return on equity has been low, averaging 1.9% over the past five years. Fair reserve development (4.6) as reserves have generally been sufficient to cover claims.

Other Rating Factors: Fair overall results on stability tests (4.7) including weak results on operational trends. Affiliation with Farmers Insurance Group of Companies is a strength. Strong long-term capitalization index (10.0) based on excellent current risk adjusted capital (severe and moderate loss scenarios), despite some fluctuation in capital levels. Superior liquidity (10.0) with ample operational cash flow and liquid investments.

Principal Business: Auto liability (64%) and auto physical damage (36%).

Principal Investments: Investment grade bonds (79%), misc. investments (18%), and cash (3%).

Investments in Affiliates: 18%

Group Affiliation: Farmers Insurance Group of Companies

Licensed in: All states except PR

Commenced Business: May 1975

Address: 100 DUFFY AVENUE SUITE 501, Hicksville, NY 11801

Phone: (302) 252-2000   **Domicile State:** NY   **NAIC Code:** 32220

Data Date	Rating	RACR #1	RACR #2	Loss Ratio %	Total Assets ($mil)	Capital ($mil)	Net Premium ($mil)	Net Income ($mil)
3-17	B	5.88	5.61	N/A	600.1	565.6	0.0	1.4
3-16	B	5.90	5.67	N/A	577.8	558.6	0.0	1.8
2016	B	5.87	5.61	0.0	584.9	563.6	0.0	4.9
2015	B	5.89	5.67	0.0	583.0	556.5	0.0	7.5
2014	B	5.90	5.73	0.0	577.6	545.0	0.0	6.0
2013	B	5.76	5.47	0.0	572.0	532.6	0.0	15.2
2012	B	5.74	5.45	0.0	569.0	517.3	0.0	17.1

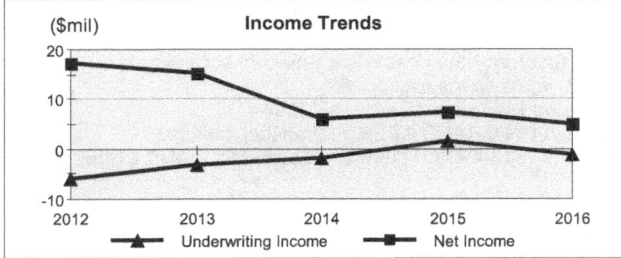

21ST CENTURY PREMIER INS CO   B-   Good

Major Rating Factors: Fair reserve development (4.6 on a scale of 0 to 10) as reserves have generally been sufficient to cover claims. Fair overall results on stability tests (4.6) including weak results on operational trends.

Other Rating Factors: Good overall profitability index (6.9). Weak expense controls. Return on equity has been low, averaging 3.1% over the past five years. Strong long-term capitalization index (10.0) based on excellent current risk adjusted capital (severe and moderate loss scenarios), despite some fluctuation in capital levels. Superior liquidity (10.0) with ample operational cash flow and liquid investments.

Principal Business: Auto liability (62%), auto physical damage (33%), homeowners multiple peril (3%), and group accident & health (1%).

Principal Investments: Investment grade bonds (71%), misc. investments (23%), and cash (6%).

Investments in Affiliates: 24%

Group Affiliation: Farmers Insurance Group of Companies

Licensed in: All states except PR

Commenced Business: April 1866

Address: 2595 INTERSTATE DRIVE STE 103, Harrisburg, PA 17110

Phone: (302) 252-2000 **Domicile State:** PA **NAIC Code:** 20796

Data Date	Rating	RACR #1	RACR #2	Loss Ratio %	Total Assets ($mil)	Capital ($mil)	Net Premium ($mil)	Net Income ($mil)
3-17	B-	4.60	4.52	N/A	302.2	284.6	0.0	1.2
3-16	B-	4.57	4.49	N/A	283.7	281.1	0.0	1.2
2016	B-	4.59	4.52	0.0	285.2	283.0	0.0	4.5
2015	B-	4.55	4.49	0.0	282.2	279.5	0.0	6.1
2014	B-	4.53	4.43	0.0	275.7	270.6	0.0	8.9
2013	B-	4.58	4.46	0.0	264.5	257.9	0.0	11.3
2012	B-	4.74	4.60	0.0	256.4	240.6	0.0	10.9

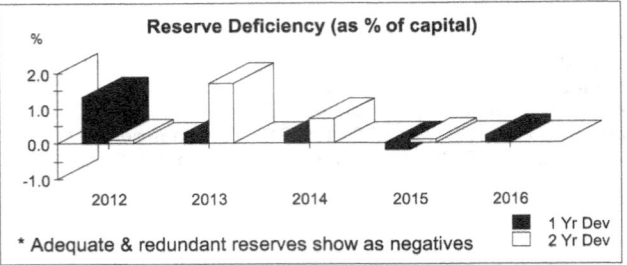

Reserve Deficiency (as % of capital)

* Adequate & redundant reserves show as negatives

■ 1 Yr Dev □ 2 Yr Dev

21ST CENTURY SECURITY INS CO   B   Good

Major Rating Factors: Good overall profitability index (5.9 on a scale of 0 to 10). Fair expense controls. Return on equity has been low, averaging 1.8% over the past five years. Fair reserve development (4.6) as reserves have generally been sufficient to cover claims.

Other Rating Factors: Fair overall results on stability tests (4.6) including weak results on operational trends. Affiliation with Farmers Insurance Group of Companies is a strength. Strong long-term capitalization index (10.0) based on excellent current risk adjusted capital (severe and moderate loss scenarios), despite some fluctuation in capital levels. Superior liquidity (10.0) with ample operational cash flow and liquid investments.

Principal Business: Auto liability (74%) and auto physical damage (26%).

Principal Investments: Investment grade bonds (78%), misc. investments (11%), and cash (11%).

Investments in Affiliates: 12%

Group Affiliation: Farmers Insurance Group of Companies

Licensed in: AK, AR, CO, DC, DE, FL, ID, IN, IA, LA, ME, MD, MI, MN, MS, NE, NH, NY, ND, OK, OR, PA, SC, SD, TX, UT, VT, VA, WA, WV, WI

Commenced Business: January 1952

Address: 2595 INTERSTATE DRIVE STE 103, Harrisburg, PA 17110

Phone: (302) 252-2000 **Domicile State:** PA **NAIC Code:** 23833

Data Date	Rating	RACR #1	RACR #2	Loss Ratio %	Total Assets ($mil)	Capital ($mil)	Net Premium ($mil)	Net Income ($mil)
3-17	B	8.74	8.47	N/A	222.0	198.1	0.0	0.5
3-16	B	8.77	8.52	N/A	198.4	196.1	0.0	0.5
2016	B	8.77	8.54	0.0	199.7	197.6	0.0	1.7
2015	B	8.75	8.51	0.0	198.3	195.7	0.0	3.6
2014	B	8.54	8.13	0.0	196.4	191.9	0.0	3.2
2013	B	8.39	7.89	0.0	195.3	188.5	0.0	4.0
2012	B	8.25	7.73	0.0	196.9	184.2	0.0	4.6

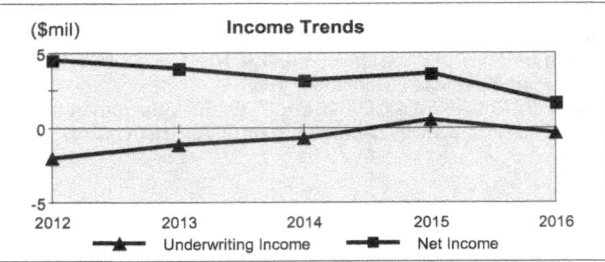

Income Trends

▲ Underwriting Income ■ Net Income

ACCIDENT FUND INS CO OF AMERICA   B-   Good

Major Rating Factors: Fair overall results on stability tests (4.6 on a scale of 0 to 10) including potential drain of affiliation with Blue Cross Blue Shield of Michigan and excessive premium growth. Fair reserve development (4.2) as reserves have generally been sufficient to cover claims.

Other Rating Factors: Good liquidity (6.8) with sufficient resources (cash flows and marketable investments) to handle a spike in claims. Strong long-term capitalization index (7.0) based on good current risk adjusted capital (severe and moderate loss scenarios), although results have slipped from the excellent range during the last year. Excellent profitability (8.7) with operating gains in each of the last five years.

Principal Business: Workers compensation (100%).

Principal Investments: Investment grade bonds (58%), misc. investments (38%), and non investment grade bonds (4%).

Investments in Affiliates: 17%

Group Affiliation: Blue Cross Blue Shield of Michigan

Licensed in: All states except PR

Commenced Business: December 1994

Address: 200 N GRAND AVENUE, Lansing, MI 48933

Phone: (517) 342-4200 **Domicile State:** MI **NAIC Code:** 10166

Data Date	Rating	RACR #1	RACR #2	Loss Ratio %	Total Assets ($mil)	Capital ($mil)	Net Premium ($mil)	Net Income ($mil)
3-17	B-	1.19	0.94	N/A	3,785.0	926.6	299.3	5.6
3-16	B-	1.25	0.99	N/A	2,962.8	832.3	209.4	3.6
2016	B-	1.27	1.03	63.0	3,114.1	897.4	925.0	93.5
2015	B-	1.26	1.01	64.5	2,780.5	813.8	812.6	107.0
2014	B-	1.31	1.07	72.5	2,387.0	750.9	717.4	62.6
2013	C+	1.46	1.18	65.9	2,257.7	684.1	546.7	30.5
2012	C+	1.40	1.12	73.2	2,300.3	633.6	489.0	37.5

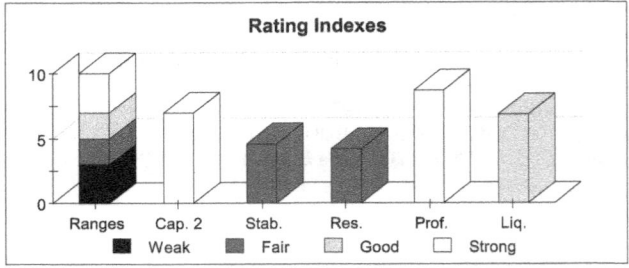

Rating Indexes

Ranges Cap. 2 Stab. Res. Prof. Liq.

■ Weak ▨ Fair ▨ Good □ Strong

ACE AMERICAN INS CO
B-   **Good**

Major Rating Factors: Fair overall results on stability tests (3.9 on a scale of 0 to 10) including potential drain of affiliation with Chubb Limited and weak results on operational trends. The largest net exposure for one risk is acceptable at 2.1% of capital. History of adequate reserve strength (6.3) as reserves have been consistently at an acceptable level.

Other Rating Factors: Good liquidity (6.6) with sufficient resources (cash flows and marketable investments) to handle a spike in claims. Strong long-term capitalization index (7.2) based on excellent current risk adjusted capital (severe and moderate loss scenarios), despite some fluctuation in capital levels. Excellent profitability (7.0) with operating gains in each of the last five years.

Principal Business: Other liability (31%), workers compensation (18%), commercial multiple peril (12%), group accident & health (11%), auto liability (7%), fire (4%), and other lines (16%).

Principal Investments: Investment grade bonds (52%), non investment grade bonds (26%), misc. investments (18%), cash (3%), and real estate (1%).

Investments in Affiliates: 19%

Group Affiliation: Chubb Limited

Licensed in: All states, the District of Columbia and Puerto Rico

Commenced Business: January 1946

Address: 436 Walnut Street, Philadelphia, PA 19106

Phone: (215) 640-1000   **Domicile State:** PA   **NAIC Code:** 22667

Data Date	Rating	RACR #1	RACR #2	Loss Ratio %	Total Assets ($mil)	Capital ($mil)	Net Premium ($mil)	Net Income ($mil)
3-17	B-	1.47	1.14	N/A	13,190.9	2,916.9	345.3	95.1
3-16	B-	1.37	1.10	N/A	11,864.2	2,630.9	342.2	44.6
2016	B-	1.42	1.10	76.5	13,035.8	2,812.4	1,848.6	180.9
2015	B-	1.36	1.09	72.8	12,074.0	2,578.8	1,760.5	214.0
2014	B-	1.57	1.29	77.6	12,150.7	2,992.9	1,656.5	251.2
2013	B-	1.39	1.16	72.2	11,697.3	2,677.0	1,610.8	412.3
2012	B-	1.20	1.05	89.9	11,040.6	2,425.8	1,658.0	58.9

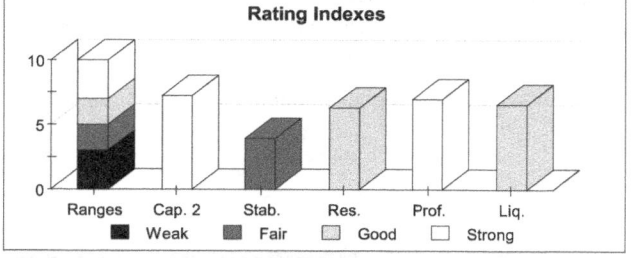

Rating Indexes

ACE P&C INS CO
B-   **Good**

Major Rating Factors: Fair overall results on stability tests (3.9 on a scale of 0 to 10) including weak results on operational trends. The largest net exposure for one risk is acceptable at 2.6% of capital. History of adequate reserve strength (6.3) as reserves have been consistently at an acceptable level.

Other Rating Factors: Good liquidity (6.9) with sufficient resources (cash flows and marketable investments) to handle a spike in claims. Strong long-term capitalization index (8.4) based on excellent current risk adjusted capital (severe and moderate loss scenarios), despite some fluctuation in capital levels. Excellent profitability (7.9) with operating gains in each of the last five years.

Principal Business: Allied lines (75%), other liability (20%), auto liability (3%), and auto physical damage (1%).

Principal Investments: Investment grade bonds (76%), misc. investments (18%), and non investment grade bonds (6%).

Investments in Affiliates: 3%

Group Affiliation: Chubb Limited

Licensed in: All states, the District of Columbia and Puerto Rico

Commenced Business: August 1819

Address: 436 WALNUT STREET, Philadelphia, PA 19106

Phone: (215) 640-1000   **Domicile State:** PA   **NAIC Code:** 20699

Data Date	Rating	RACR #1	RACR #2	Loss Ratio %	Total Assets ($mil)	Capital ($mil)	Net Premium ($mil)	Net Income ($mil)
3-17	B-	2.93	1.97	N/A	9,120.3	2,222.5	326.4	77.4
3-16	B-	2.66	1.79	N/A	8,638.1	2,031.5	323.7	49.3
2016	B-	2.90	1.96	76.5	8,192.2	2,157.6	1,748.7	181.2
2015	C+	2.67	1.81	72.8	7,748.8	1,995.9	1,665.3	136.2
2014	C	3.02	2.05	77.6	7,360.7	2,064.4	1,567.0	115.6
2013	C	2.95	2.01	72.2	7,214.1	1,920.5	1,523.8	165.6
2012	C	2.93	1.96	89.9	7,925.9	1,802.5	1,568.4	68.6

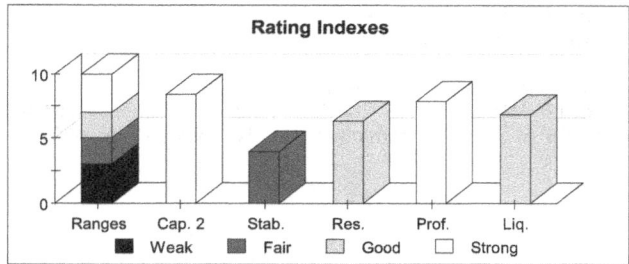

Rating Indexes

ACUITY A MUTUAL INS CO *
B+   **Good**

Major Rating Factors: Good liquidity (6.7 on a scale of 0 to 10) with sufficient resources (cash flows and marketable investments) to handle a spike in claims. Good overall results on stability tests (5.1) despite weak results on operational trends.

Other Rating Factors: Strong long-term capitalization index (9.3) based on excellent current risk adjusted capital (severe and moderate loss scenarios). Moreover, capital levels have been consistent in recent years. Ample reserve history (9.1) that helps to protect the company against sharp claims increases. Excellent profitability (8.9) with operating gains in each of the last five years.

Principal Business: Workers compensation (23%), auto liability (22%), auto physical damage (15%), commercial multiple peril (11%), homeowners multiple peril (10%), other liability (9%), and other lines (9%).

Principal Investments: Investment grade bonds (60%), misc. investments (31%), real estate (7%), and non investment grade bonds (3%).

Investments in Affiliates: None

Group Affiliation: None

Licensed in: AL, AZ, AR, CO, DE, GA, ID, IL, IN, IA, KS, KY, ME, MI, MN, MS, MO, MT, NE, NV, NH, NM, ND, OH, OK, OR, PA, SD, TN, TX, UT, VT, VA, WA, WV, WI, WY

Commenced Business: September 1925

Address: 2800 South Taylor Drive, Sheboygan, WI 53081-8470

Phone: (920) 458-9131   **Domicile State:** WI   **NAIC Code:** 14184

Data Date	Rating	RACR #1	RACR #2	Loss Ratio %	Total Assets ($mil)	Capital ($mil)	Net Premium ($mil)	Net Income ($mil)
3-17	B+	4.51	2.66	N/A	3,686.4	1,668.5	321.9	33.8
3-16	B+	4.39	2.66	N/A	3,386.7	1,479.9	314.8	49.3
2016	B+	4.53	2.69	61.3	3,621.3	1,606.6	1,316.3	145.8
2015	B+	4.33	2.64	61.9	3,349.5	1,429.9	1,269.9	142.0
2014	B	3.83	2.36	65.1	3,101.0	1,323.4	1,189.2	113.2
2013	B	3.77	2.33	62.0	2,826.4	1,202.3	1,074.0	111.1
2012	B	3.85	2.40	63.2	2,475.2	994.3	937.8	95.4

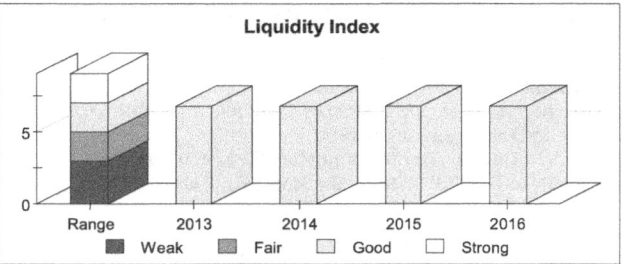

Liquidity Index

ADMIRAL INS CO — C — Fair

Major Rating Factors: Fair profitability index (3.9). Fair expense controls. Return on equity has been fair, averaging 29.0% over the past five years.
Other Rating Factors: Fair overall results on stability tests (4.1) including weak results on operational trends. Strong long-term capitalization index (8.1) based on excellent current risk adjusted capital (severe and moderate loss scenarios), despite some fluctuation in capital levels. Superior liquidity (10.0) with ample operational cash flow and liquid investments.
Principal Business: Other liability (72%), medical malpractice (12%), products liability (9%), fire (5%), and allied lines (1%).
Principal Investments: Misc. investments (50%) and investment grade bonds (50%).
Investments in Affiliates: 50%
Group Affiliation: W R Berkley Corp
Licensed in: All states, the District of Columbia and Puerto Rico
Commenced Business: November 1952
Address: 1209 ORANGE STREET, Wilmington, DE 19801-1000
Phone: (480) 951-0905 **Domicile State:** DE **NAIC Code:** 24856

Data Date	Rating	RACR #1	RACR #2	Loss Ratio %	Total Assets ($mil)	Capital ($mil)	Net Premium ($mil)	Net Income ($mil)
3-17	C	1.57	1.56	N/A	744.4	655.8	0.0	2.0
3-16	C	1.65	1.64	N/A	719.0	637.6	0.0	1.9
2016	C	1.74	1.88	0.0	737.3	652.1	0.0	10.4
2015	C	1.81	1.92	0.0	710.2	634.0	0.0	8.4
2014	C-	1.82	1.94	0.0	688.5	615.6	0.0	11.2
2013	C-	1.91	2.07	0.0	667.4	597.6	-255.7	826.2
2012	C	1.50	1.39	62.2	3,142.1	1,688.4	520.3	150.7

Rating Indexes

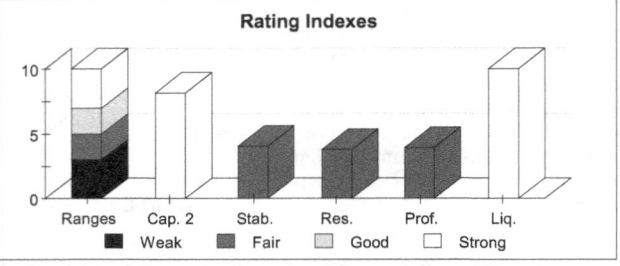

Ranges | Cap. 2 | Stab. | Res. | Prof. | Liq.
■ Weak ■ Fair ▨ Good ☐ Strong

ADVANTAGE WORKERS COMP INS CO — B- — Good

Major Rating Factors: Fair reserve development (4.6 on a scale of 0 to 10) as reserves have generally been sufficient to cover claims. Fair profitability index (4.0) with operating losses during 2012, 2013, 2014 and the first three months of 2017. Average return on equity over the last five years has been poor at -1.2%.
Other Rating Factors: Fair overall results on stability tests (4.0) including weak results on operational trends. Strong long-term capitalization index (7.1) based on excellent current risk adjusted capital (severe and moderate loss scenarios), despite some fluctuation in capital levels. Excellent liquidity (7.0) with ample operational cash flow and liquid investments.
Principal Business: Workers compensation (100%).
Principal Investments: Investment grade bonds (95%), non investment grade bonds (3%), cash (1%), and misc. investments (1%).
Investments in Affiliates: None
Group Affiliation: Workers Compensation Fund
Licensed in: All states except PR
Commenced Business: November 1981
Address: 111 MONUMENT CIRCLE SUITE 2700, Indianapolis, IN 46204
Phone: (888) 595-8750 **Domicile State:** IN **NAIC Code:** 40517

Data Date	Rating	RACR #1	RACR #2	Loss Ratio %	Total Assets ($mil)	Capital ($mil)	Net Premium ($mil)	Net Income ($mil)
3-17	B-	1.89	1.30	N/A	497.8	209.5	16.3	-1.1
3-16	C+	4.11	2.29	N/A	476.2	194.5	15.3	-8.2
2016	B-	1.52	1.03	71.5	491.5	210.6	70.6	3.5
2015	C+	4.20	2.49	77.8	110.5	52.8	14.1	1.9
2014	C	4.33	2.68	119.3	107.9	50.8	9.3	-1.2
2013	C	3.98	2.50	107.7	118.6	50.2	8.9	-0.2
2012	C	3.35	1.67	125.4	125.7	50.3	12.1	-4.1

Reserve Deficiency (as % of capital)

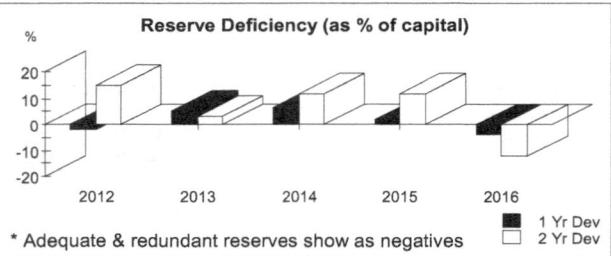

2012 | 2013 | 2014 | 2015 | 2016
■ 1 Yr Dev ☐ 2 Yr Dev
* Adequate & redundant reserves show as negatives

AFFILIATED FM INS CO — C — Fair

Major Rating Factors: Fair overall results on stability tests (3.5 on a scale of 0 to 10). The largest net exposure for one risk is excessive at 8.8% of capital. History of adequate reserve strength (6.2) as reserves have been consistently at an acceptable level.
Other Rating Factors: Strong long-term capitalization index (9.1) based on excellent current risk adjusted capital (severe and moderate loss scenarios). Moreover, capital levels have been consistent in recent years. Excellent profitability (8.8) with operating gains in each of the last five years. Excellent liquidity (7.1) with ample operational cash flow and liquid investments.
Principal Business: Fire (34%), allied lines (24%), inland marine (23%), commercial multiple peril (10%), boiler & machinery (7%), and ocean marine (2%).
Principal Investments: Investment grade bonds (50%), misc. investments (48%), and cash (2%).
Investments in Affiliates: None
Group Affiliation: Factory Mutual Ins
Licensed in: All states, the District of Columbia and Puerto Rico
Commenced Business: June 1950
Address: 270 Central Avenue, Johnston, RI 02919-4949
Phone: (401) 275-3000 **Domicile State:** RI **NAIC Code:** 10014

Data Date	Rating	RACR #1	RACR #2	Loss Ratio %	Total Assets ($mil)	Capital ($mil)	Net Premium ($mil)	Net Income ($mil)
3-17	C	4.38	2.65	N/A	2,969.7	1,676.6	116.9	38.8
3-16	C	4.37	2.69	N/A	2,581.1	1,508.6	104.5	31.2
2016	C	4.29	2.60	56.9	2,992.9	1,618.7	423.6	83.4
2015	C	4.39	2.71	58.8	2,589.3	1,479.6	420.5	121.6
2014	C	4.35	2.70	52.5	2,528.7	1,397.6	386.6	119.1
2013	C	3.60	2.27	50.6	2,327.1	1,262.1	387.6	124.4
2012	C	2.70	1.77	59.7	2,302.2	1,034.1	444.2	86.0

Rating Indexes

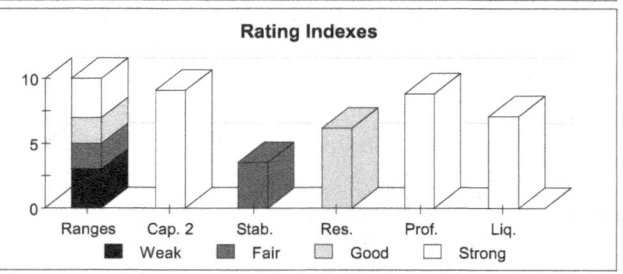

Ranges | Cap. 2 | Stab. | Res. | Prof. | Liq.
■ Weak ■ Fair ▨ Good ☐ Strong

AIG PROPERTY CASUALTY CO

C   **Fair**

Major Rating Factors: Fair reserve development (3.3 on a scale of 0 to 10) as reserves have generally been sufficient to cover claims. In 2016, the two year reserve development was 21% deficient. Weak overall results on stability tests (2.8) including weak results on operational trends and negative cash flow from operations for 2016. The largest net exposure for one risk is excessive at 36.0% of capital. Strengths include potentially strong support from affiliation with AIG.

Other Rating Factors: Weak profitability index (1.9). Fair expense controls. Return on equity has been fair, averaging 35.6% over the past five years. Good liquidity (6.3) with sufficient resources (cash flows and marketable investments) to handle a spike in claims. Strong long-term capitalization index (7.4) based on excellent current risk adjusted capital (severe and moderate loss scenarios), despite some fluctuation in capital levels.

Principal Business: Homeowners multiple peril (51%), inland marine (12%), other liability (9%), auto physical damage (8%), auto liability (8%), earthquake (5%), and other lines (8%).

Principal Investments: Investment grade bonds (166%) and non investment grade bonds (5%).

Investments in Affiliates: 0%

Group Affiliation: American International Group

Licensed in: All states except HI, PR

Commenced Business: August 1871

Address: 2595 INTERSTATE DRIVE STE 102, Harrisburg, PA 17110

Phone: (212) 770-7000   **Domicile State:** PA   **NAIC Code:** 19402

Data Date	Rating	RACR #1	RACR #2	Loss Ratio %	Total Assets ($mil)	Capital ($mil)	Net Premium ($mil)	Net Income ($mil)
3-17	C	2.11	1.37	N/A	2,027.7	344.1	0.0	136.2
3-16	C	2.13	1.34	N/A	4,614.1	1,275.0	221.8	29.9
2016	C	1.82	1.22	99.8	4,180.0	951.7	806.2	440.2
2015	C	2.16	1.36	88.8	4,730.2	1,312.8	927.5	246.8
2014	C+	2.27	1.45	76.5	5,025.9	1,587.1	1,034.9	158.0
2013	C+	2.30	1.46	76.6	3,656.5	1,166.3	713.5	124.6
2012	C+	2.27	1.47	87.1	3,475.7	1,080.2	615.3	668.0

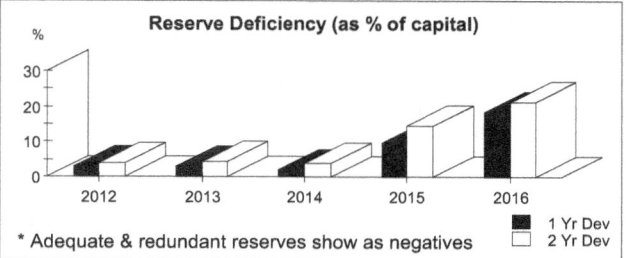

Reserve Deficiency (as % of capital)

* Adequate & redundant reserves show as negatives
■ 1 Yr Dev □ 2 Yr Dev

ALAMANCE INS CO

C-   **Fair**

Major Rating Factors: Weak overall results on stability tests (2.6 on a scale of 0 to 10) including potential drain of affiliation with IFG Companies. Good overall profitability index (6.1). Weak expense controls. Return on equity has been low, averaging 3.0% over the past five years.

Other Rating Factors: Strong long-term capitalization index (7.7) based on excellent current risk adjusted capital (severe and moderate loss scenarios), despite some fluctuation in capital levels. Ample reserve history (7.8) that can protect against increases in claims costs. Excellent liquidity (8.0) with ample operational cash flow and liquid investments.

Principal Business: (This company is a reinsurer.)

Principal Investments: Misc. investments (62%) and investment grade bonds (38%).

Investments in Affiliates: 59%

Group Affiliation: IFG Companies

Licensed in: All states except CA, PR

Commenced Business: December 1998

Address: 400 South Ninth Street, Springfield, IL 62701-1822

Phone: (336) 586-2500   **Domicile State:** IL   **NAIC Code:** 10957

Data Date	Rating	RACR #1	RACR #2	Loss Ratio %	Total Assets ($mil)	Capital ($mil)	Net Premium ($mil)	Net Income ($mil)
3-17	C-	1.48	1.45	N/A	476.9	375.2	6.8	0.6
3-16	C-	1.48	1.45	N/A	486.6	376.8	8.0	2.4
2016	C-	1.47	1.45	47.9	475.0	371.6	27.9	11.7
2015	C-	1.48	1.45	44.4	485.3	373.8	32.8	11.0
2014	C-	1.46	1.43	56.5	488.1	369.5	36.6	8.4
2013	C-	1.45	1.42	50.6	480.6	358.1	40.7	14.7
2012	C-	1.46	1.43	60.2	460.9	334.1	43.1	9.6

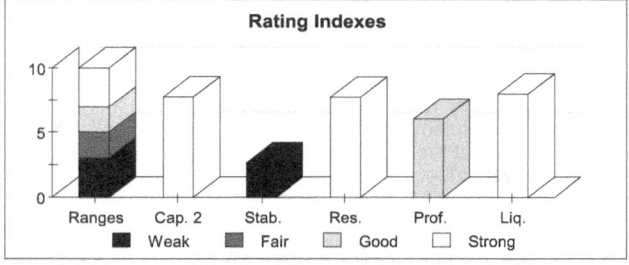

Rating Indexes

Ranges Cap. 2 Stab. Res. Prof. Liq.
■ Weak ■ Fair □ Good □ Strong

ALASKA NATIONAL INS CO

B   **Good**

Major Rating Factors: Fair overall results on stability tests (4.7 on a scale of 0 to 10) including weak results on operational trends. Strong long-term capitalization index (9.2) based on excellent current risk adjusted capital (severe and moderate loss scenarios). Moreover, capital levels have been consistent in recent years.

Other Rating Factors: Ample reserve history (9.4) that helps to protect the company against sharp claims increases. Excellent profitability (8.8) with operating gains in each of the last five years. Return on equity has been good over the last five years, averaging 11.4%. Excellent liquidity (7.1) with ample operational cash flow and liquid investments.

Principal Business: Workers compensation (77%), commercial multiple peril (6%), auto liability (6%), other liability (5%), inland marine (2%), auto physical damage (1%), and other lines (2%).

Principal Investments: Investment grade bonds (74%), misc. investments (24%), and cash (2%).

Investments in Affiliates: None

Group Affiliation: Alaska National Corp

Licensed in: AL, AK, AZ, CA, CO, FL, HI, ID, IL, IA, KS, LA, MN, MS, MO, MT, NV, NM, ND, OK, OR, SD, TX, UT, WA, WY

Commenced Business: October 1980

Address: 7001 Jewel Lake Road, Anchorage, AK 99502-2800

Phone: (907) 248-2642   **Domicile State:** AK   **NAIC Code:** 38733

Data Date	Rating	RACR #1	RACR #2	Loss Ratio %	Total Assets ($mil)	Capital ($mil)	Net Premium ($mil)	Net Income ($mil)
3-17	B	3.82	2.66	N/A	976.4	447.5	53.3	15.5
3-16	B	3.37	2.38	N/A	903.4	395.3	53.1	8.6
2016	B	3.83	2.67	56.7	951.4	438.0	221.5	53.4
2015	B	3.48	2.47	56.3	889.0	387.8	228.5	36.4
2014	B	3.10	2.13	55.7	879.8	380.5	212.3	50.5
2013	B	3.18	2.20	51.3	830.4	352.2	200.6	50.3
2012	B	3.45	2.42	69.2	753.4	293.6	183.9	20.9

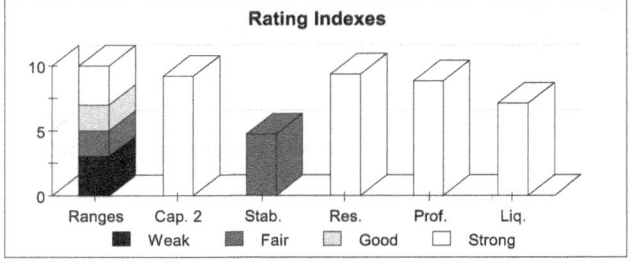

Rating Indexes

Ranges Cap. 2 Stab. Res. Prof. Liq.
■ Weak ■ Fair □ Good □ Strong

ALFA MUTUAL FIRE INS CO

B **Good**

Major Rating Factors: Good profitability index (5.0 on a scale of 0 to 10) despite operating losses during the first three months of 2017. Good liquidity (6.2) with sufficient resources (cash flows and marketable investments) to handle a spike in claims.

Other Rating Factors: Fair overall results on stability tests (4.9) including weak results on operational trends. Strong long-term capitalization index (8.5) based on excellent current risk adjusted capital (severe and moderate loss scenarios), despite some fluctuation in capital levels. Ample reserve history (7.7) that can protect against increases in claims costs.

Principal Business: Fire (48%), allied lines (43%), and inland marine (9%).

Principal Investments: Misc. investments (49%), investment grade bonds (47%), non investment grade bonds (2%), cash (1%), and real estate (1%).

Investments in Affiliates: 26%

Group Affiliation: Alfa Ins Group

Licensed in: AL, VA

Commenced Business: August 1946

Address: 2108 East South Boulevard, Montgomery, AL 36116-2015

Phone: (334) 288-3900   **Domicile State:** AL   **NAIC Code:** 19143

Data Date	Rating	RACR #1	RACR #2	Loss Ratio %	Total Assets ($mil)	Capital ($mil)	Net Premium ($mil)	Net Income ($mil)
3-17	B	2.48	1.99	N/A	768.8	425.4	93.1	-3.3
3-16	B	2.40	1.89	N/A	720.2	406.0	86.4	-1.2
2016	B	2.47	2.01	72.1	728.0	420.1	368.8	11.4
2015	B	2.43	1.93	70.6	699.0	409.8	341.5	16.2
2014	B	2.23	1.71	70.2	697.1	419.8	336.0	8.0
2013	B	1.96	1.48	68.6	659.5	399.3	327.1	25.7
2012	B	1.65	1.23	68.5	608.2	362.6	311.3	12.3

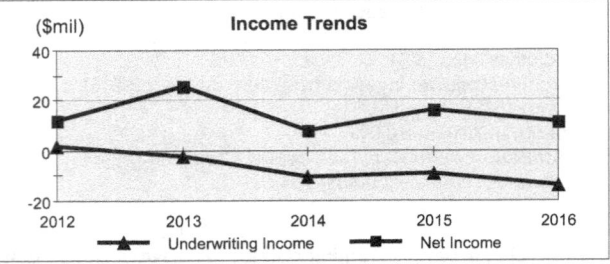

ALFA MUTUAL GENERAL INS CO *

B+ **Good**

Major Rating Factors: Good overall profitability index (5.9 on a scale of 0 to 10) despite modest operating losses during the first three months of 2017. Good liquidity (6.7) with sufficient resources (cash flows and marketable investments) to handle a spike in claims.

Other Rating Factors: Good overall results on stability tests (5.0) despite weak results on operational trends. The largest net exposure for one risk is conservative at 1.3% of capital. Strong long-term capitalization index (9.1) based on excellent current risk adjusted capital (severe and moderate loss scenarios), despite some fluctuation in capital levels. Ample reserve history (7.6) that can protect against increases in claims costs.

Principal Business: Homeowners multiple peril (47%), auto liability (29%), auto physical damage (23%), and other liability (1%).

Principal Investments: Investment grade bonds (49%), misc. investments (45%), cash (5%), and non investment grade bonds (1%).

Investments in Affiliates: 1%

Group Affiliation: Alfa Ins Group

Licensed in: AL, GA, MS

Commenced Business: October 1955

Address: 2108 East South Boulevard, Montgomery, AL 36116-2015

Phone: (334) 288-3900   **Domicile State:** AL   **NAIC Code:** 19151

Data Date	Rating	RACR #1	RACR #2	Loss Ratio %	Total Assets ($mil)	Capital ($mil)	Net Premium ($mil)	Net Income ($mil)
3-17	B+	3.89	2.56	N/A	111.8	58.3	12.4	-0.1
3-16	B+	3.14	2.02	N/A	104.5	56.4	11.5	-0.2
2016	B+	3.57	2.38	72.1	103.3	57.1	49.2	1.8
2015	B+	3.12	2.04	70.7	100.9	56.9	45.5	5.8
2014	B+	2.40	1.57	70.3	99.0	57.9	44.8	3.4
2013	B+	2.35	1.58	68.8	94.8	54.3	43.6	4.1
2012	B	1.89	1.28	69.0	86.8	48.3	41.5	3.2

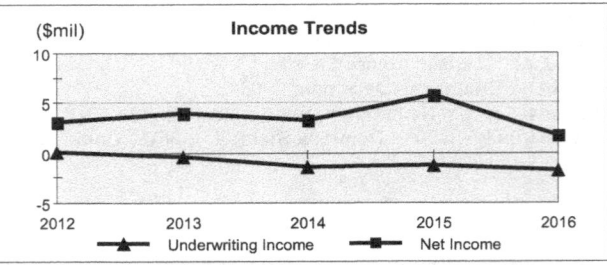

ALFA MUTUAL INS CO

B **Good**

Major Rating Factors: Fair overall results on stability tests (4.5 on a scale of 0 to 10) including weak results on operational trends. Strengths include potentially strong support from affiliation with Alfa Ins Group. Fair profitability index (3.0) with operating losses during the first three months of 2017.

Other Rating Factors: Fair liquidity (4.1) as cash resources may not be adequate to cover a spike in claims. Strong long-term capitalization index (7.1) based on excellent current risk adjusted capital (severe and moderate loss scenarios), despite some fluctuation in capital levels. Ample reserve history (7.7) that can protect against increases in claims costs.

Principal Business: Auto physical damage (30%), auto liability (29%), homeowners multiple peril (29%), farmowners multiple peril (7%), commercial multiple peril (3%), and inland marine (1%).

Principal Investments: Misc. investments (58%), investment grade bonds (35%), real estate (4%), non investment grade bonds (2%), and cash (1%).

Investments in Affiliates: 37%

Group Affiliation: Alfa Ins Group

Licensed in: AL, FL, GA, IL, IN, KY, NC, OH, PA, VA

Commenced Business: October 1947

Address: 2108 East South Boulevard, Montgomery, AL 36116-2015

Phone: (334) 288-3900   **Domicile State:** AL   **NAIC Code:** 19135

Data Date	Rating	RACR #1	RACR #2	Loss Ratio %	Total Assets ($mil)	Capital ($mil)	Net Premium ($mil)	Net Income ($mil)
3-17	B	1.21	1.04	N/A	1,307.1	446.3	161.3	-9.3
3-16	B	1.32	1.09	N/A	1,302.7	490.7	149.7	-4.8
2016	B	1.24	1.07	72.3	1,251.2	451.8	639.3	5.6
2015	B	1.35	1.13	70.5	1,239.6	497.9	592.0	24.9
2014	B	1.38	1.11	70.2	1,275.0	537.8	582.4	12.4
2013	B	1.59	1.25	68.7	1,231.2	580.4	566.7	48.5
2012	B	1.40	1.09	69.5	1,150.4	525.1	539.4	11.8

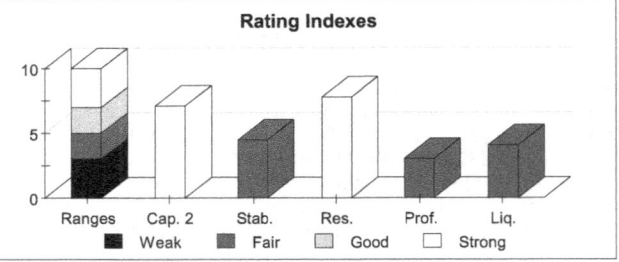

ALFA SPECIALTY INS CORP *   B+   Good

Major Rating Factors: Good overall profitability index (5.3 on a scale of 0 to 10) despite operating losses during the first three months of 2017. Return on equity has been low, averaging 4.6% over the past five years. Good overall results on stability tests (6.5). Stability strengths include good operational trends and excellent risk diversification. The largest net exposure for one risk is conservative at 1.8% of capital.

Other Rating Factors: Strong long-term capitalization index (8.7) based on excellent current risk adjusted capital (severe and moderate loss scenarios), despite some fluctuation in capital levels. Ample reserve history (7.8) that can protect against increases in claims costs. Excellent liquidity (7.0) with ample operational cash flow and liquid investments.

Principal Business: Auto liability (73%) and auto physical damage (27%).

Principal Investments: Investment grade bonds (70%) and misc. investments (33%).

Investments in Affiliates: None

Group Affiliation: Alfa Ins Group

Licensed in: AL, AR, GA, IN, KY, MS, MO, OH, TN, TX, VA

Commenced Business: December 1999

Address: 2108 East South Boulevard, Montgomery, AL 36116-2015

Phone: (334) 288-3900   **Domicile State:** VA   **NAIC Code:** 11004

Data Date	Rating	RACR #1	RACR #2	Loss Ratio %	Total Assets ($mil)	Capital ($mil)	Net Premium ($mil)	Net Income ($mil)
3-17	B+	3.17	2.17	N/A	57.1	28.1	6.2	-0.4
3-16	B	2.93	1.96	N/A	51.6	26.0	5.8	0.1
2016	B+	3.17	2.24	72.2	53.8	27.9	24.6	0.8
2015	B	2.81	1.90	70.7	50.8	26.2	22.8	1.0
2014	C+	2.35	1.61	70.4	52.8	26.8	22.4	0.6
2013	C+	1.45	1.00	68.8	43.4	18.6	21.8	1.8
2012	C	1.11	0.78	69.1	40.0	17.2	20.7	1.3

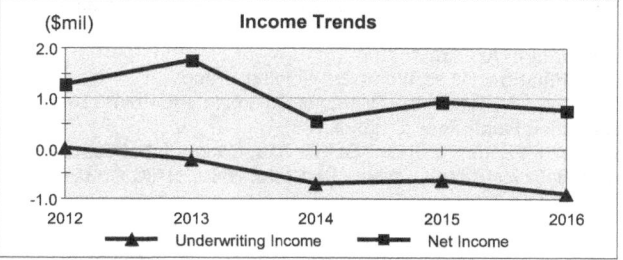

Income Trends

ALL AMERICA INS CO *   B+   Good

Major Rating Factors: Good liquidity (6.8 on a scale of 0 to 10) with sufficient resources (cash flows and marketable investments) to handle a spike in claims. Good overall results on stability tests (5.0) despite weak results on operational trends.

Other Rating Factors: Strong long-term capitalization index (10.0) based on excellent current risk adjusted capital (severe and moderate loss scenarios). Moreover, capital levels have been consistent in recent years. Ample reserve history (9.1) that helps to protect the company against sharp claims increases. Excellent profitability (8.4) with operating gains in each of the last five years.

Principal Business: Commercial multiple peril (57%), auto liability (21%), auto physical damage (9%), workers compensation (8%), and products liability (4%).

Principal Investments: Investment grade bonds (94%) and cash (6%).

Investments in Affiliates: 0%

Group Affiliation: Central Mutual Ins Group

Licensed in: AZ, AR, CA, CO, CT, GA, ID, IL, IN, IA, KY, ME, MD, MA, MI, MN, MS, MT, NV, NH, NJ, NM, NY, NC, OH, OK, OR, PA, SC, TN, TX, UT, VT, VA, WA, WI

Commenced Business: August 1961

Address: 800 SOUTH WASHINGTON STREET, Van Wert, OH 45891-2357

Phone: (419) 238-1010   **Domicile State:** OH   **NAIC Code:** 20222

Data Date	Rating	RACR #1	RACR #2	Loss Ratio %	Total Assets ($mil)	Capital ($mil)	Net Premium ($mil)	Net Income ($mil)
3-17	B+	6.41	4.34	N/A	285.9	153.8	24.8	1.1
3-16	B+	6.12	4.18	N/A	275.6	147.0	23.5	1.0
2016	B+	6.52	4.46	64.0	283.9	152.6	98.8	6.5
2015	B+	6.26	4.32	57.9	275.8	146.0	93.0	11.2
2014	B+	5.95	4.08	59.8	258.8	134.7	85.3	10.3
2013	B+	5.49	3.68	58.4	247.7	124.7	76.6	11.5
2012	B	5.05	3.35	70.7	240.3	113.5	70.4	5.0

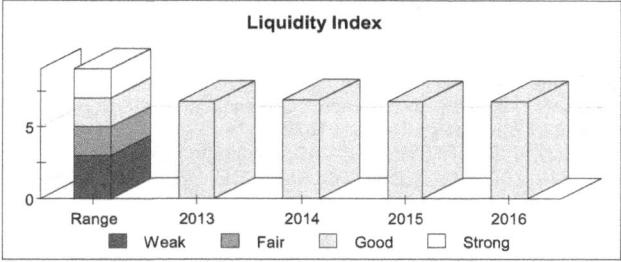

Liquidity Index

ALLIANZ GLOBAL RISKS US INS CO   C   Fair

Major Rating Factors: Fair profitability index (3.7 on a scale of 0 to 10) with operating losses during 2012 and 2016. Average return on equity over the last five years has been poor at -2.4%. Fair overall results on stability tests (3.8) including excessive premium growth, weak results on operational trends and negative cash flow from operations for 2016. The largest net exposure for one risk is acceptable at 2.6% of capital.

Other Rating Factors: Good long-term capitalization index (5.1) based on good current risk adjusted capital (severe and moderate loss scenarios), although results have slipped from the excellent range over the last two years. Good liquidity (6.8) with sufficient resources (cash flows and marketable investments) to handle a spike in claims. Ample reserve history (9.7) that helps to protect the company against sharp claims increases.

Principal Business: Fire (28%), aircraft (16%), other liability (16%), products liability (11%), allied lines (11%), inland marine (7%), and other lines (10%).

Principal Investments: Investment grade bonds (56%), misc. investments (43%), and non investment grade bonds (1%).

Investments in Affiliates: 32%

Group Affiliation: Allianz Ins Group

Licensed in: All states, the District of Columbia and Puerto Rico

Commenced Business: December 1977

Address: 225 W WASHINGTON ST STE 1800, Chicago, IL 60606-3484

Phone: (888) 466-7883   **Domicile State:** IL   **NAIC Code:** 35300

Data Date	Rating	RACR #1	RACR #2	Loss Ratio %	Total Assets ($mil)	Capital ($mil)	Net Premium ($mil)	Net Income ($mil)
3-17	C	0.95	0.76	N/A	7,630.3	1,989.9	483.3	52.0
3-16	C	0.92	0.69	N/A	8,158.7	1,894.8	246.3	-90.8
2016	C	0.95	0.77	73.3	8,002.5	1,931.8	2,124.9	-268.6
2015	C	1.22	1.06	72.0	4,345.4	1,862.2	1,093.4	32.8
2014	C	0.80	0.51	73.1	3,322.7	759.1	1,236.6	44.4
2013	C-	0.74	0.52	79.5	3,176.9	867.3	868.2	10.0
2012	C-	0.75	0.54	82.8	3,099.8	866.9	916.0	-86.7

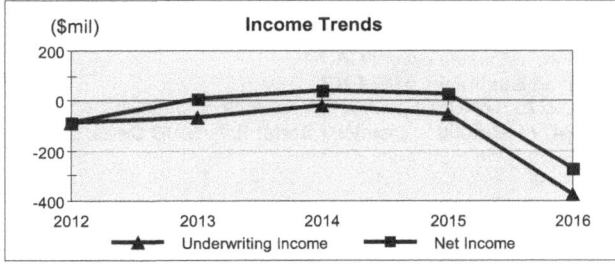

Income Trends

ALLIED WORLD INS CO | C | Fair

Major Rating Factors: Fair overall results on stability tests (3.4 on a scale of 0 to 10) including potential drain of affiliation with Allied World Asr Holding Group and weak results on operational trends. History of adequate reserve strength (6.1) as reserves have been consistently at an acceptable level.

Other Rating Factors: Good overall profitability index (5.3) with small operating losses during 2012. Return on equity has been low, averaging 1.1% over the past five years. Strong long-term capitalization index (8.1) based on excellent current risk adjusted capital (severe and moderate loss scenarios), despite some fluctuation in capital levels. Excellent liquidity (7.2) with ample operational cash flow and liquid investments.

Principal Business: Other liability (60%), surety (16%), medical malpractice (11%), commercial multiple peril (11%), inland marine (1%), and credit (1%).

Principal Investments: Misc. investments (52%), investment grade bonds (45%), non investment grade bonds (2%), and cash (1%).

Investments in Affiliates: 46%

Group Affiliation: Allied World Asr Holding Group

Licensed in: All states, the District of Columbia and Puerto Rico

Commenced Business: October 1986

Address: 10 FERRY STREET SUITE 313, Concord, NH 03301

Phone: (646) 794-0500   **Domicile State:** NH   **NAIC Code:** 22730

Data Date	Rating	RACR #1	RACR #2	Loss Ratio %	Total Assets ($mil)	Capital ($mil)	Net Premium ($mil)	Net Income ($mil)
3-17	C	1.78	1.70	N/A	1,787.4	1,026.7	48.8	1.0
3-16	C	1.75	1.62	N/A	1,867.8	1,059.4	49.9	9.0
2016	C	1.79	1.71	74.7	1,713.4	1,030.7	199.4	11.3
2015	C	1.68	1.52	69.1	1,749.6	1,082.3	214.6	15.3
2014	C	1.56	1.40	69.9	1,727.2	1,092.9	198.3	24.7
2013	C	1.57	1.44	67.8	1,687.3	1,044.5	177.2	13.6
2012	C	1.72	1.68	74.2	1,435.6	868.5	168.2	-4.2

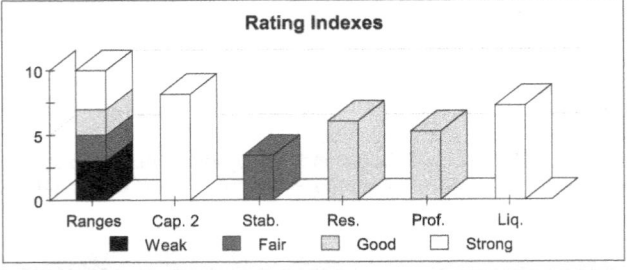

Rating Indexes

ALLIED WORLD SPECIALTY INS CO | B | Good

Major Rating Factors: History of adequate reserve strength (6.2 on a scale of 0 to 10) as reserves have been consistently at an acceptable level. Good overall profitability index (6.9). Fair expense controls. Return on equity has been low, averaging 3.0% over the past five years.

Other Rating Factors: Fair overall results on stability tests (4.7) including weak results on operational trends. Strong long-term capitalization index (9.5) based on excellent current risk adjusted capital (severe and moderate loss scenarios), despite some fluctuation in capital levels. Excellent liquidity (7.0) with ample operational cash flow and liquid investments.

Principal Business: Other liability (48%), inland marine (16%), auto liability (8%), commercial multiple peril (8%), medical malpractice (6%), fire (6%), and other lines (8%).

Principal Investments: Investment grade bonds (76%), misc. investments (20%), and cash (4%).

Investments in Affiliates: 21%

Group Affiliation: Allied World Asr Holding Group

Licensed in: All states, the District of Columbia and Puerto Rico

Commenced Business: January 1972

Address: 2711 CENTERVILLE ROAD, Wilmington, DE 19808

Phone: (646) 794-0500   **Domicile State:** DE   **NAIC Code:** 16624

Data Date	Rating	RACR #1	RACR #2	Loss Ratio %	Total Assets ($mil)	Capital ($mil)	Net Premium ($mil)	Net Income ($mil)
3-17	B	3.21	2.75	N/A	808.2	416.2	27.1	0.1
3-16	B	3.19	2.72	N/A	832.1	413.1	27.7	6.8
2016	B	3.21	2.76	74.7	795.2	413.1	110.8	7.8
2015	B	3.18	2.74	69.1	786.7	405.7	119.2	12.2
2014	B-	2.49	2.00	69.9	752.0	397.4	110.2	13.3
2013	B-	2.98	2.36	67.8	689.3	364.0	98.5	11.0
2012	B-	3.74	2.86	74.2	737.0	368.4	98.7	15.7

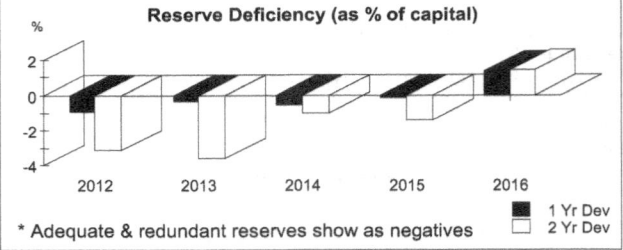

Reserve Deficiency (as % of capital)

* Adequate & redundant reserves show as negatives

ALLSTATE F&C INS CO | C+ | Fair

Major Rating Factors: Fair overall results on stability tests (4.6 on a scale of 0 to 10) including weak results on operational trends.

Other Rating Factors: Strong long-term capitalization index (10.0) based on excellent current risk adjusted capital (severe and moderate loss scenarios). Moreover, capital levels have been consistent in recent years. Excellent profitability (7.2) with operating gains in each of the last five years. Excellent expense controls. Superior liquidity (10.0) with ample operational cash flow and liquid investments.

Principal Business: Auto liability (57%), auto physical damage (40%), and homeowners multiple peril (3%).

Principal Investments: Investment grade bonds (99%) and misc. investments (1%).

Investments in Affiliates: None

Group Affiliation: Allstate Group

Licensed in: All states except CA, PR

Commenced Business: May 1973

Address: 2775 SANDERS ROAD, Northbrook, IL 60062-6127

Phone: (847) 402-5000   **Domicile State:** IL   **NAIC Code:** 29688

Data Date	Rating	RACR #1	RACR #2	Loss Ratio %	Total Assets ($mil)	Capital ($mil)	Net Premium ($mil)	Net Income ($mil)
3-17	C+	125.80	58.77	N/A	267.7	259.7	0.0	0.9
3-16	C+	121.32	58.27	N/A	217.8	211.6	0.0	0.6
2016	C+	135.61	60.57	0.0	262.0	258.7	0.0	2.6
2015	C+	129.99	57.65	0.0	215.7	211.2	0.0	2.1
2014	C	136.54	60.77	0.0	175.3	173.9	0.0	1.6
2013	C	130.27	57.28	0.0	148.7	147.5	0.0	2.3
2012	C	171.45	77.79	0.0	141.7	140.1	0.0	2.1

Allstate Group Composite Group Rating: B Largest Group Members	Assets ($mil)	Rating
ALLSTATE INS CO	45624	B
ALLSTATE LIFE INS CO	32127	B
ALLSTATE LIFE INS CO OF NEW YORK	6279	C+
ALLSTATE NJ INS CO	2495	B+
AMERICAN HERITAGE LIFE INS CO	1886	B

ALLSTATE INS CO
B   Good

Major Rating Factors: History of adequate reserve strength (6.1 on a scale of 0 to 10) as reserves have been consistently at an acceptable level. Good overall results on stability tests (5.1) despite weak results on operational trends.
Other Rating Factors: Fair profitability index (4.5). Fair expense controls. Return on equity has been fair, averaging 12.6% over the past five years. Fair liquidity (4.2) as cash resources may not be adequate to cover a spike in claims. Strong long-term capitalization index (7.7) based on excellent current risk adjusted capital (severe and moderate loss scenarios), despite some fluctuation in capital levels.
Principal Business: Homeowners multiple peril (33%), auto liability (31%), auto physical damage (25%), allied lines (4%), commercial multiple peril (4%), other liability (1%), and inland marine (1%).
Principal Investments: Investment grade bonds (53%), misc. investments (33%), non investment grade bonds (15%), and real estate (1%).
Investments in Affiliates: 13%
Group Affiliation: Allstate Group
Licensed in: All states except NJ
Commenced Business: April 1931
Address: 2775 SANDERS ROAD, Northbrook, IL 60062-6127
Phone: (847) 402-5000   **Domicile State:** IL   **NAIC Code:** 19232

Data Date	Rating	RACR #1	RACR #2	Loss Ratio %	Total Assets ($mil)	Capital ($mil)	Net Premium ($mil)	Net Income ($mil)
3-17	B	1.97	1.52	N/A	46,626.9	16,259.2	7,166.7	874.9
3-16	B	1.89	1.45	N/A	42,990.7	14,767.4	7,010.7	148.0
2016	B	1.89	1.47	71.9	45,624.2	15,559.9	28,491.4	1,379.8
2015	B	1.97	1.52	70.1	43,271.2	15,318.3	27,774.3	1,705.4
2014	B+	2.15	1.68	68.0	43,246.3	16,265.6	26,453.4	2,313.8
2013	A-	2.21	1.72	66.4	43,733.3	17,254.7	25,108.5	2,465.5
2012	B+	2.07	1.62	69.4	42,133.1	16,260.9	24,193.4	1,950.4

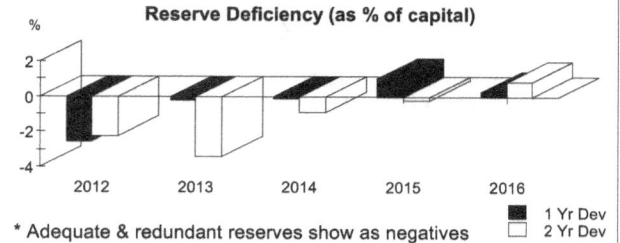

Reserve Deficiency (as % of capital)

* Adequate & redundant reserves show as negatives   ■ 1 Yr Dev   □ 2 Yr Dev

ALLSTATE NJ INS CO *
B+   Good

Major Rating Factors: History of adequate reserve strength (6.8 on a scale of 0 to 10) as reserves have been consistently at an acceptable level. Good overall profitability index (5.2) despite operating losses during 2012. Return on equity has been good over the last five years, averaging 11.2%.
Other Rating Factors: Good liquidity (6.3) with sufficient resources (cash flows and marketable investments) to handle a spike in claims. Good overall results on stability tests (6.7). Stability strengths include good operational trends and excellent risk diversification. Strong long-term capitalization index (8.2) based on excellent current risk adjusted capital (severe and moderate loss scenarios), despite some fluctuation in capital levels.
Principal Business: Auto liability (42%), homeowners multiple peril (32%), auto physical damage (20%), allied lines (2%), other liability (2%), commercial multiple peril (1%), and inland marine (1%).
Principal Investments: Investment grade bonds (92%), misc. investments (7%), and non investment grade bonds (2%).
Investments in Affiliates: 5%
Group Affiliation: Allstate Group
Licensed in: IL, NJ, PA
Commenced Business: November 1997
Address: 2775 SANDERS ROAD, Northbrook, IL 60062-6127
Phone: (908) 252-5000   **Domicile State:** IL   **NAIC Code:** 10852

Data Date	Rating	RACR #1	RACR #2	Loss Ratio %	Total Assets ($mil)	Capital ($mil)	Net Premium ($mil)	Net Income ($mil)
3-17	B+	2.47	1.90	N/A	2,557.8	849.5	287.9	41.2
3-16	B	2.35	1.81	N/A	2,477.8	798.8	289.9	23.2
2016	B+	2.22	1.81	65.6	2,495.4	807.5	1,164.9	123.7
2015	B	2.18	1.78	70.2	2,444.8	774.9	1,157.5	87.6
2014	B	2.22	1.75	63.4	2,478.3	802.8	1,163.9	134.9
2013	B	2.45	1.93	62.4	2,680.7	930.9	1,190.1	162.7
2012	B	1.97	1.53	91.5	2,647.6	767.5	1,199.4	-52.0

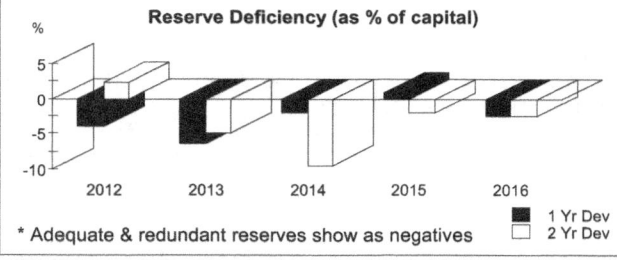

Reserve Deficiency (as % of capital)

* Adequate & redundant reserves show as negatives   ■ 1 Yr Dev   □ 2 Yr Dev

ALLSTATE P&C INS CO
B   Good

Major Rating Factors: Fair overall results on stability tests (4.7 on a scale of 0 to 10) including weak results on operational trends. Strengths include potentially strong support from affiliation with Allstate Group. Strong long-term capitalization index (10.0) based on excellent current risk adjusted capital (severe and moderate loss scenarios). Moreover, capital levels have been consistent in recent years.
Other Rating Factors: Excellent profitability (7.3) with operating gains in each of the last five years. Excellent expense controls. Superior liquidity (10.0) with ample operational cash flow and liquid investments.
Principal Business: Auto liability (43%), auto physical damage (32%), homeowners multiple peril (23%), and inland marine (1%).
Principal Investments: Investment grade bonds (100%).
Investments in Affiliates: None
Group Affiliation: Allstate Group
Licensed in: All states except HI, MA, NJ, PR
Commenced Business: April 1985
Address: 2775 SANDERS ROAD, Northbrook, IL 60062-6127
Phone: (847) 402-5000   **Domicile State:** IL   **NAIC Code:** 17230

Data Date	Rating	RACR #1	RACR #2	Loss Ratio %	Total Assets ($mil)	Capital ($mil)	Net Premium ($mil)	Net Income ($mil)
3-17	B	67.13	55.76	N/A	257.5	237.3	0.0	0.8
3-16	B	83.34	57.83	N/A	242.4	229.4	0.0	0.7
2016	B	82.10	58.37	0.0	250.6	236.5	0.0	2.5
2015	B	73.27	57.90	0.0	245.3	228.8	0.0	2.5
2014	B	87.44	62.79	0.0	215.5	206.0	0.0	2.2
2013	B	87.25	59.92	0.0	213.7	204.2	0.0	5.5
2012	B	109.24	64.02	0.0	204.4	197.8	0.0	4.6

Allstate Group Composite Group Rating: B Largest Group Members	Assets ($mil)	Rating
ALLSTATE INS CO	45624	B
ALLSTATE LIFE INS CO	32127	B
ALLSTATE LIFE INS CO OF NEW YORK	6279	C+
ALLSTATE NJ INS CO	2495	B+
AMERICAN HERITAGE LIFE INS CO	1886	B

AMBAC ASSURANCE CORP   E   Very Weak

Major Rating Factors: Poor long-term capitalization index (1.8 on a scale of 0 to 10) based on weak current risk adjusted capital (severe and moderate loss scenarios). A history of deficient reserves (2.7). Underreserving can have an adverse impact on capital and profits.

Other Rating Factors: overall results on stability tests (-0.5) including weak results on operational trends and weak risk adjusted capital in prior years. The largest net exposure for one risk is excessive at 454.0% of capital. Fair profitability index (4.2) with operating losses during 2013. Return on equity has been fair, averaging 284.2% over the past five years. Good liquidity (6.8) with sufficient resources (cash flows and marketable investments) to handle a spike in claims.

Principal Business: Financial guaranty (100%).

Principal Investments: Misc. investments (49%), investment grade bonds (47%), non investment grade bonds (3%), and cash (1%).

Investments in Affiliates: 8%

Group Affiliation: AMBAC Financial Group Inc

Licensed in: All states except TN

Commenced Business: March 1970

Address: 2 East Mifflin St, Madison, WI 53703

Phone: (212) 658-7470   **Domicile State:** WI   **NAIC Code:** 18708

Data Date	Rating	RACR #1	RACR #2	Loss Ratio %	Total Assets ($mil)	Capital ($mil)	Net Premium ($mil)	Net Income ($mil)
3-17	E	0.98	0.46	N/A	5,496.2	944.8	46.4	176.5
3-16	E	0.71	0.34	N/A	5,485.4	646.5	47.8	21.6
2016	E	0.98	0.45	1.2	5,442.1	976.5	45.2	359.1
2015	E	0.77	0.34	N/A	4,813.4	624.8	53.2	772.3
2014	E	0.36	0.16	N/A	4,451.6	100.0	63.6	724.8
2013	E	0.60	0.30	145.2	5,793.6	840.3	90.3	-235.6
2012	E	0.30	0.14	157.6	5,216.2	100.0	104.0	616.1

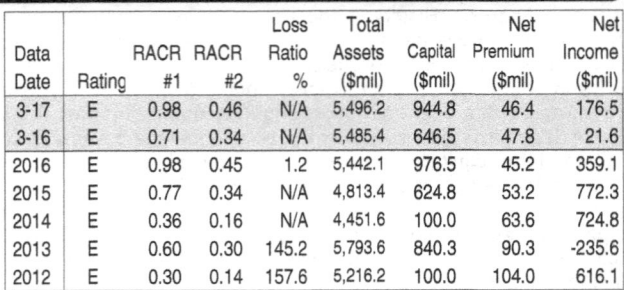

AMCO INS CO   C+   Fair

Major Rating Factors: Fair profitability index (3.2 on a scale of 0 to 10). Good expense controls. Return on equity has been low, averaging 4.9% over the past five years. Fair overall results on stability tests (4.5) including weak results on operational trends.

Other Rating Factors: Strong long-term capitalization index (10.0) based on excellent current risk adjusted capital (severe and moderate loss scenarios), despite some fluctuation in capital levels. Excellent liquidity (8.1) with ample operational cash flow and liquid investments.

Principal Business: Auto liability (25%), commercial multiple peril (22%), auto physical damage (18%), homeowners multiple peril (18%), other liability (7%), fire (3%), and other lines (8%).

Principal Investments: Investment grade bonds (105%) and misc. investments (12%).

Investments in Affiliates: 16%

Group Affiliation: Nationwide Corp

Licensed in: All states except AK, HI, LA, MA, NH, NJ, OK, PR

Commenced Business: April 1959

Address: 1100 LOCUST STREET, Des Moines, IA 50391-1100

Phone: (515) 508-4211   **Domicile State:** IA   **NAIC Code:** 19100

Data Date	Rating	RACR #1	RACR #2	Loss Ratio %	Total Assets ($mil)	Capital ($mil)	Net Premium ($mil)	Net Income ($mil)
3-17	C+	5.42	4.57	N/A	989.3	203.3	0.0	1.0
3-16	C+	5.30	4.56	N/A	930.2	203.2	0.0	1.1
2016	C+	6.05	5.46	0.0	951.7	201.3	0.0	2.7
2015	C+	5.63	5.01	0.0	947.9	206.3	0.0	4.1
2014	C+	4.59	4.17	0.0	1,001.0	208.0	0.0	33.6
2013	B	8.61	7.54	0.0	1,067.8	363.8	0.0	7.8
2012	B	8.97	7.99	0.0	1,057.5	429.2	0.0	15.6

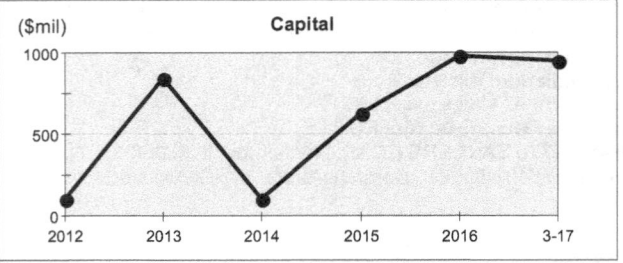

AMERICAN AGRICULTURAL INS CO   B   Good

Major Rating Factors: Good overall results on stability tests (6.3 on a scale of 0 to 10). Stability strengths include good operational trends and excellent risk diversification. Strong long-term capitalization index (8.1) based on excellent current risk adjusted capital (severe and moderate loss scenarios). Moreover, capital levels have been consistent in recent years.

Other Rating Factors: Ample reserve history (7.0) that can protect against increases in claims costs. Excellent profitability (8.8) with operating gains in each of the last five years. Excellent liquidity (7.0) with ample operational cash flow and liquid investments.

Principal Business: Allied lines (100%).

Principal Investments: Investment grade bonds (75%), misc. investments (22%), and cash (3%).

Investments in Affiliates: 0%

Group Affiliation: None

Licensed in: All states except AK, CA, HI, NV

Commenced Business: May 1948

Address: 225 South East Street, Indianapolis, IN 46202

Phone: (847) 969-2900   **Domicile State:** IN   **NAIC Code:** 10103

Data Date	Rating	RACR #1	RACR #2	Loss Ratio %	Total Assets ($mil)	Capital ($mil)	Net Premium ($mil)	Net Income ($mil)
3-17	B	2.44	1.77	N/A	1,309.2	584.2	76.3	6.0
3-16	B	2.23	1.61	N/A	1,212.0	554.4	74.6	10.3
2016	B	2.43	1.77	73.8	1,249.2	575.9	340.6	29.3
2015	B	2.22	1.61	71.4	1,152.6	541.2	304.9	38.5
2014	C+	2.16	1.59	65.8	1,105.1	525.7	295.4	56.1
2013	C+	1.86	1.38	73.3	1,093.1	489.3	342.2	55.3
2012	C	1.74	1.35	86.3	1,041.0	440.1	283.6	10.0

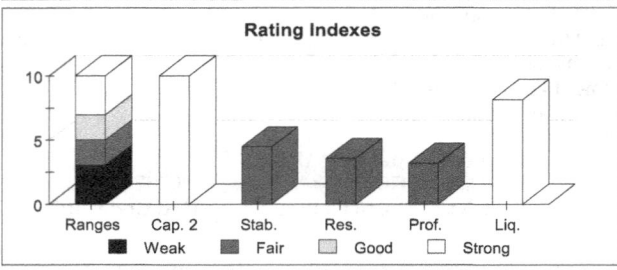

AMERICAN ALTERNATIVE INS CORP   C   Fair

Major Rating Factors: Fair overall results on stability tests (3.7 on a scale of 0 to 10) including potential drain of affiliation with Münchener Rückversicherungs-Gesellsc and weak results on operational trends.

Other Rating Factors: Strong long-term capitalization index (10.0) based on excellent current risk adjusted capital (severe and moderate loss scenarios), despite some fluctuation in capital levels. Excellent profitability (8.7) with operating gains in each of the last five years. Excellent expense controls. Return on equity has been excellent over the last five years averaging 16.2%. Superior liquidity (10.0) with ample operational cash flow and liquid investments.

Principal Business: Commercial multiple peril (26%), other accident & health (18%), other liability (17%), auto liability (15%), auto physical damage (8%), aircraft (8%), and other lines (8%).

Principal Investments: Investment grade bonds (107%) and non investment grade bonds (3%).

Investments in Affiliates: None
Group Affiliation: Münchener Rückversicherungs-Gesellsc
Licensed in: All states, the District of Columbia and Puerto Rico
Commenced Business: May 1923
Address: 2711 CENTERVILLE ROAD SUITE 40, Wilmington, DE 19808
Phone: (609) 243-4200   **Domicile State:** DE   **NAIC Code:** 19720

Data Date	Rating	RACR #1	RACR #2	Loss Ratio %	Total Assets ($mil)	Capital ($mil)	Net Premium ($mil)	Net Income ($mil)
3-17	C	16.00	12.08	N/A	521.1	178.9	0.0	8.5
3-16	C	15.42	9.04	N/A	570.3	179.1	0.0	9.2
2016	C	17.82	14.89	0.0	535.3	198.4	0.0	27.9
2015	C	17.71	13.80	0.0	550.8	199.5	0.0	30.7
2014	C	14.93	13.43	0.0	526.4	168.9	0.0	30.8
2013	C	15.10	13.59	0.0	452.2	161.7	0.0	28.6
2012	C	14.37	12.94	0.0	464.7	156.2	0.0	23.1

Münchener Rückversicherungs-Gesellsc
Composite Group Rating: C+

Largest Group Members	Assets ($mil)	Rating
MUNICH REINS AMERICA INC	17710	C+
MUNICH AMERICAN REASSURANCE CO	7664	C
HARTFORD SM BOIL INSPECTION INS	1256	B
AMERICAN MODERN HOME INS CO	1115	C+
AMERICAN ALTERNATIVE INS CORP	535	C

AMERICAN BANKERS INS CO OF FL   B   Good

Major Rating Factors: Good overall results on stability tests (5.8 on a scale of 0 to 10) despite potential drain of affiliation with Assurant Inc. Stability strengths include good operational trends and excellent risk diversification. History of adequate reserve strength (6.7) as reserves have been consistently at an acceptable level.

Other Rating Factors: Good overall profitability index (6.2). Weak expense controls. Return on equity has been excellent over the last five years averaging 22.2%. Good liquidity (6.1) with sufficient resources (cash flows and marketable investments) to handle a spike in claims. Strong long-term capitalization index (8.0) based on excellent current risk adjusted capital (severe and moderate loss scenarios), despite some fluctuation in capital levels.

Principal Business: Other liability (50%), homeowners multiple peril (14%), allied lines (12%), inland marine (11%), credit (4%), credit accident & health (4%), and other lines (5%).

Principal Investments: Investment grade bonds (75%), misc. investments (17%), non investment grade bonds (7%), and cash (1%).

Investments in Affiliates: 1%
Group Affiliation: Assurant Inc
Licensed in: All states, the District of Columbia and Puerto Rico
Commenced Business: October 1947
Address: 11222 QUAIL ROOST DRIVE, Miami, FL 33157-6596
Phone: (305) 253-2244   **Domicile State:** FL   **NAIC Code:** 10111

Data Date	Rating	RACR #1	RACR #2	Loss Ratio %	Total Assets ($mil)	Capital ($mil)	Net Premium ($mil)	Net Income ($mil)
3-17	B	2.89	1.79	N/A	2,070.3	588.0	217.4	55.0
3-16	B	2.10	1.24	N/A	1,954.3	503.9	213.9	48.5
2016	B	2.65	1.60	45.2	1,986.3	528.5	915.1	143.6
2015	B	2.06	1.20	39.9	1,877.6	483.2	867.5	142.3
2014	B	2.68	1.55	40.8	1,967.5	563.9	870.1	146.5
2013	B	2.62	1.49	40.1	1,844.9	542.1	884.0	96.5
2012	B	2.76	1.56	44.7	1,707.5	506.5	817.8	33.4

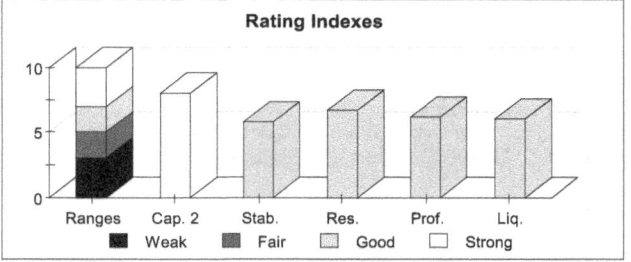

Rating Indexes

Ranges   Cap. 2   Stab.   Res.   Prof.   Liq.
■ Weak   ■ Fair   □ Good   □ Strong

AMERICAN FAMILY MUTL INS CO SI *   B+   Good

Major Rating Factors: Good liquidity (6.3 on a scale of 0 to 10) with sufficient resources (cash flows and marketable investments) to handle a spike in claims. Good overall results on stability tests (5.2) despite weak results on operational trends.

Other Rating Factors: Strong long-term capitalization index (8.1) based on excellent current risk adjusted capital (severe and moderate loss scenarios). Moreover, capital levels have been consistent in recent years. Ample reserve history (8.3) that helps to protect the company against sharp claims increases. Excellent profitability (7.7) with operating gains in each of the last five years.

Principal Business: Homeowners multiple peril (33%), auto liability (29%), auto physical damage (23%), commercial multiple peril (8%), other liability (3%), farmowners multiple peril (2%), and other lines (3%).

Principal Investments: Investment grade bonds (56%), misc. investments (40%), non investment grade bonds (3%), and real estate (2%).

Investments in Affiliates: 16%
Group Affiliation: American Family Ins Group
Licensed in: AZ, CO, FL, GA, ID, IL, IN, IA, KS, MN, MO, MT, NE, NV, NM, NC, ND, OH, OR, SC, SD, TN, TX, UT, VA, WA, WI, WY
Commenced Business: October 1927
Address: 6000 AMERICAN PARKWAY, Madison, WI 53783-0001
Phone: (608) 249-2111   **Domicile State:** WI   **NAIC Code:** 19275

Data Date	Rating	RACR #1	RACR #2	Loss Ratio %	Total Assets ($mil)	Capital ($mil)	Net Premium ($mil)	Net Income ($mil)
3-17	B+	2.16	1.70	N/A	16,206.4	6,884.7	1,830.5	177.2
3-16	B+	2.22	1.71	N/A	15,643.6	6,608.4	1,713.6	170.9
2016	B+	2.17	1.71	68.2	16,193.7	6,867.0	7,291.3	211.7
2015	B+	2.20	1.71	63.5	15,299.1	6,503.1	6,854.8	570.5
2014	B+	2.10	1.66	70.8	14,500.5	6,030.1	6,656.3	659.2
2013	B+	2.17	1.73	72.6	13,229.6	5,791.7	5,595.6	281.2
2012	B	2.56	1.94	73.0	12,038.9	5,165.0	5,435.1	323.7

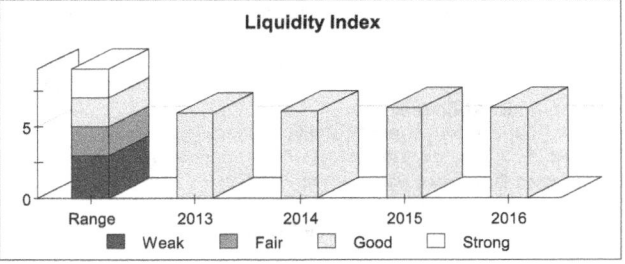

Liquidity Index

Range   2013   2014   2015   2016
■ Weak   ■ Fair   □ Good   □ Strong

AMERICAN HOME ASR CO

C　　**Fair**

Major Rating Factors: Fair reserve development (3.0 on a scale of 0 to 10) as the level of reserves has at times been insufficient to cover claims. In 2015 and 2016 the two year reserve development was 18% and 22% deficient respectively. Fair profitability index (4.9) with operating losses during 2015 and 2016. Return on equity has been fair, averaging 5.9% over the past five years.

Other Rating Factors: Weak overall results on stability tests (2.8) including weak results on operational trends. The largest net exposure for one risk is excessive at 10.5% of capital. Good liquidity (5.7) with sufficient resources (cash flows and marketable investments) to handle a spike in claims. Strong long-term capitalization index (7.8) based on excellent current risk adjusted capital (severe and moderate loss scenarios), despite some fluctuation in capital levels.

Principal Business: Fire (52%), workers compensation (9%), allied lines (8%), boiler & machinery (6%), inland marine (5%), auto liability (5%), and other lines (15%).

Principal Investments: Investment grade bonds (81%), misc. investments (14%), non investment grade bonds (4%), and cash (1%).

Investments in Affiliates: 1%

Group Affiliation: American International Group

Licensed in: All states except PR

Commenced Business: February 1899

Address: 175 WATER STREET 18TH FLOOR, New York, NY 10038

Phone: (212) 770-7000　**Domicile State:** NY　**NAIC Code:** 19380

Data Date	Rating	RACR #1	RACR #2	Loss Ratio %	Total Assets ($mil)	Capital ($mil)	Net Premium ($mil)	Net Income ($mil)
3-17	C	2.51	1.65	N/A	26,144.8	6,979.5	1,320.0	418.4
3-16	C	2.38	1.62	N/A	30,005.9	7,393.5	1,579.2	357.6
2016	C	2.28	1.50	90.5	29,684.9	6,447.6	6,267.6	-243.8
2015	C	2.39	1.63	90.5	26,103.9	6,640.8	5,708.9	-75.2
2014	C+	2.48	1.69	74.2	26,376.9	7,247.9	5,499.4	808.2
2013	C	1.77	1.17	70.0	23,671.1	5,091.7	5,852.4	703.0
2012	C	2.16	1.46	79.5	24,302.3	6,004.3	5,204.4	285.5

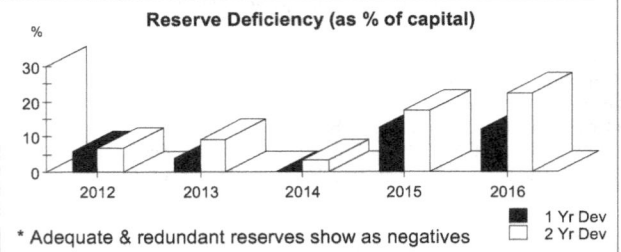

Reserve Deficiency (as % of capital)

2012　2013　2014　2015　2016

■ 1 Yr Dev　□ 2 Yr Dev

* Adequate & redundant reserves show as negatives

AMERICAN INTERSTATE INS CO

B-　　**Good**

Major Rating Factors: Fair overall results on stability tests (4.3 on a scale of 0 to 10) including potential drain of affiliation with Amerisafe Inc and weak results on operational trends. Strong long-term capitalization index (7.7) based on excellent current risk adjusted capital (severe and moderate loss scenarios), despite some fluctuation in capital levels.

Other Rating Factors: Ample reserve history (9.4) that helps to protect the company against sharp claims increases. Excellent profitability (8.6) with operating gains in each of the last five years. Return on equity has been good over the last five years, averaging 13.2%. Excellent liquidity (7.2) with ample operational cash flow and liquid investments.

Principal Business: Workers compensation (100%).

Principal Investments: Investment grade bonds (85%), misc. investments (13%), cash (1%), and non investment grade bonds (1%).

Investments in Affiliates: 12%

Group Affiliation: Amerisafe Inc

Licensed in: All states except CT, NJ, OH, PR

Commenced Business: April 1974

Address: 13321 California St Ste 310, Omaha, NE 68154

Phone: (800) 256-9052　**Domicile State:** NE　**NAIC Code:** 31895

Data Date	Rating	RACR #1	RACR #2	Loss Ratio %	Total Assets ($mil)	Capital ($mil)	Net Premium ($mil)	Net Income ($mil)
3-17	B-	1.98	1.57	N/A	1,247.4	408.3	73.2	11.1
3-16	B-	1.88	1.50	N/A	1,281.1	397.2	77.3	20.1
2016	B-	1.95	1.57	54.1	1,225.5	394.0	291.9	79.0
2015	B-	1.81	1.46	57.1	1,207.7	371.4	301.8	66.9
2014	B-	1.73	1.38	65.2	1,185.6	377.7	305.3	40.3
2013	B-	1.74	1.35	69.4	1,093.7	354.3	284.8	35.3
2012	B-	2.02	1.60	75.7	1,001.8	323.9	251.2	25.4

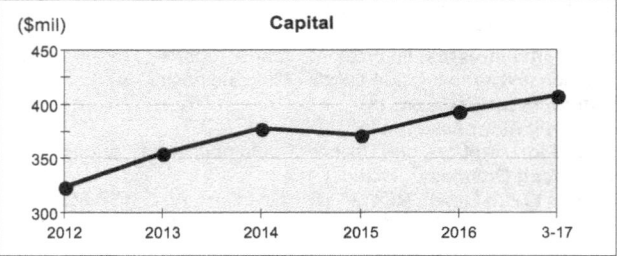

($mil)　Capital

2012　2013　2014　2015　2016　3-17

AMERICAN MODERN HOME INS CO

C+　　**Fair**

Major Rating Factors: Fair overall results on stability tests (4.3 on a scale of 0 to 10) including fair financial strength of affiliated Münchener Rückversicherungs-Gesellsc and weak results on operational trends. Good overall profitability index (5.4) despite operating losses during the first three months of 2017. Return on equity has been low, averaging 3.8% over the past five years.

Other Rating Factors: Good liquidity (6.4) with sufficient resources (cash flows and marketable investments) to handle a spike in claims. Strong long-term capitalization index (7.4) based on excellent current risk adjusted capital (severe and moderate loss scenarios), despite some fluctuation in capital levels. Ample reserve history (7.8) that can protect against increases in claims costs.

Principal Business: Homeowners multiple peril (38%), fire (20%), allied lines (13%), inland marine (11%), auto physical damage (6%), commercial multiple peril (3%), and other lines (9%).

Principal Investments: Investment grade bonds (49%), misc. investments (39%), real estate (11%), and non investment grade bonds (3%).

Investments in Affiliates: 39%

Group Affiliation: Münchener Rückversicherungs-Gesellsc

Licensed in: All states, the District of Columbia and Puerto Rico

Commenced Business: September 1965

Address: 7000 MIDLAND BLVD, Amelia, OH 45102-2607

Phone: (800) 543-2644　**Domicile State:** OH　**NAIC Code:** 23469

Data Date	Rating	RACR #1	RACR #2	Loss Ratio %	Total Assets ($mil)	Capital ($mil)	Net Premium ($mil)	Net Income ($mil)
3-17	C+	1.98	1.56	N/A	1,044.3	419.6	77.3	-5.9
3-16	C+	2.01	1.57	N/A	1,247.9	417.6	91.9	7.8
2016	C+	1.91	1.50	54.8	1,115.1	406.9	329.0	15.8
2015	C+	2.09	1.62	48.2	1,277.2	436.1	370.2	54.2
2014	C+	1.99	1.51	48.3	1,286.2	380.5	496.5	8.0
2013	C+	2.17	1.66	43.8	1,256.4	373.6	431.7	5.8
2012	C+	2.52	1.95	50.3	1,156.6	389.8	361.7	5.6

Münchener Rückversicherungs-Gesellsc
Composite Group Rating: C+
Largest Group Members

	Assets ($mil)	Rating
MUNICH REINS AMERICA INC	17710	C+
MUNICH AMERICAN REASSURANCE CO	7664	C
HARTFORD SM BOIL INSPECTION INS	1256	B
AMERICAN MODERN HOME INS CO	1115	C+
AMERICAN ALTERNATIVE INS CORP	535	C

AMERICAN MUTUAL SHARE INS CORP   C-   Fair

Major Rating Factors: Weak overall results on stability tests (1.5 on a scale of 0 to 10) including negative cash flow from operations for 2016. The largest net exposure for one risk is excessive at 447.9% of capital. Strengths include potentially strong support from affiliation with American Mutual Share Group. Fair profitability index (4.6) with operating losses during the first three months of 2017.

Other Rating Factors: Strong long-term capitalization index (10.0) based on excellent current risk adjusted capital (severe and moderate loss scenarios). Moreover, capital levels have been consistent in recent years. Ample reserve history (7.0) that can protect against increases in claims costs. Superior liquidity (10.0) with ample operational cash flow and liquid investments.

Principal Business: Aggregate write-ins for other lines of business (100%).

Principal Investments: Investment grade bonds (75%), misc. investments (15%), and cash (10%).

Investments in Affiliates: 9%

Group Affiliation: American Mutual Share Group

Licensed in: AL, AZ, CA, ID, IL, IN, ME, NV, NH, OH, TX

Commenced Business: June 1974

Address: 5656 Frantz Rd, Dublin, OH 43017

Phone: (614) 764-1900   **Domicile State:** OH   **NAIC Code:** 12700

Data Date	Rating	RACR #1	RACR #2	Loss Ratio %	Total Assets ($mil)	Capital ($mil)	Net Premium ($mil)	Net Income ($mil)
3-17	C-	9.99	8.86	N/A	267.3	239.7	0.1	-0.8
3-16	C-	8.97	7.90	N/A	245.2	218.7	0.0	-1.2
2016	C-	10.01	8.92	N/A	262.8	238.2	0.2	0.1
2015	C-	8.87	7.79	N/A	249.2	219.4	0.2	5.4
2014	C-	8.36	7.32	N/A	230.4	202.3	0.2	11.0
2013	C-	7.89	6.66	N/A	230.2	188.1	0.2	1.6
2012	C-	7.73	6.53	N/A	223.0	183.3	0.2	1.4

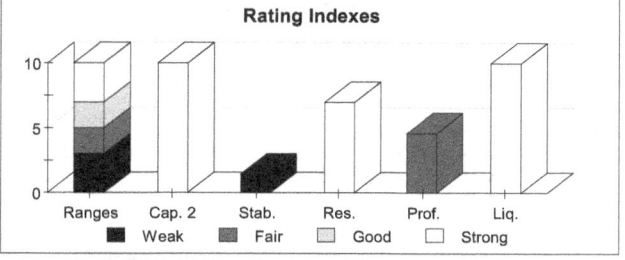

Rating Indexes

AMERICAN NATIONAL PROPERTY & CAS CO   B   Good

Major Rating Factors: Good overall profitability index (6.8 on a scale of 0 to 10). Fair expense controls. Return on equity has been low, averaging 4.2% over the past five years. Good liquidity (6.0) with sufficient resources (cash flows and marketable investments) to handle a spike in claims.

Other Rating Factors: Fair overall results on stability tests (4.9) including weak results on operational trends. Strong long-term capitalization index (8.1) based on excellent current risk adjusted capital (severe and moderate loss scenarios), despite some fluctuation in capital levels. Ample reserve history (8.4) that helps to protect the company against sharp claims increases.

Principal Business: Homeowners multiple peril (26%), auto liability (25%), credit (16%), auto physical damage (15%), allied lines (6%), other liability (4%), and other lines (7%).

Principal Investments: Investment grade bonds (61%), misc. investments (38%), and real estate (1%).

Investments in Affiliates: 21%

Group Affiliation: American National Group Inc

Licensed in: All states except CT, MA, NY

Commenced Business: January 1974

Address: 1949 EAST SUNSHINE, Springfield, MO 65899-0001

Phone: (417) 887-4990   **Domicile State:** MO   **NAIC Code:** 28401

Data Date	Rating	RACR #1	RACR #2	Loss Ratio %	Total Assets ($mil)	Capital ($mil)	Net Premium ($mil)	Net Income ($mil)
3-17	B	2.12	1.73	N/A	1,339.7	632.8	136.9	5.9
3-16	B	2.15	1.78	N/A	1,280.6	634.9	124.6	7.4
2016	B	2.11	1.73	77.2	1,320.1	627.0	542.6	7.1
2015	B	2.15	1.79	70.4	1,275.6	635.9	496.5	33.1
2014	B	2.12	1.75	71.1	1,218.5	596.9	481.3	40.0
2013	B	2.02	1.65	75.2	1,155.6	537.5	468.0	25.4
2012	B	1.95	1.57	79.7	1,105.8	495.5	467.6	17.6

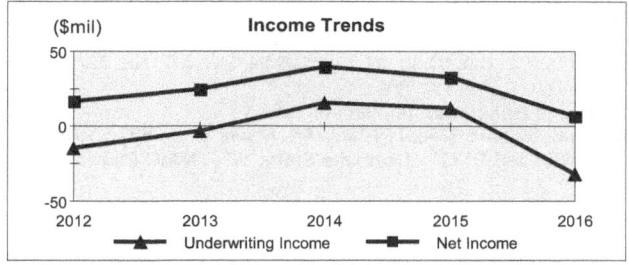

Income Trends

AMERICAN ROAD INS CO   C+   Fair

Major Rating Factors: Fair overall results on stability tests (3.0 on a scale of 0 to 10) including weak results on operational trends and negative cash flow from operations for 2016. The largest net exposure for one risk is excessive at 8.0% of capital. History of adequate reserve strength (6.1) as reserves have been consistently at an acceptable level.

Other Rating Factors: Good overall profitability index (6.4). Excellent expense controls. Return on equity has been fair, averaging 8.1% over the past five years. Strong long-term capitalization index (10.0) based on excellent current risk adjusted capital (severe and moderate loss scenarios), despite some fluctuation in capital levels. Excellent liquidity (7.4) with ample operational cash flow and liquid investments.

Principal Business: (Not applicable due to unusual reinsurance transactions.)

Principal Investments: Investment grade bonds (90%), misc. investments (9%), and cash (1%).

Investments in Affiliates: None

Group Affiliation: Ford Motor Co

Licensed in: All states except PR

Commenced Business: December 1959

Address: One American Road MD 7600, Dearborn, MI 48126-2701

Phone: (313) 337-1102   **Domicile State:** MI   **NAIC Code:** 19631

Data Date	Rating	RACR #1	RACR #2	Loss Ratio %	Total Assets ($mil)	Capital ($mil)	Net Premium ($mil)	Net Income ($mil)
3-17	C+	7.78	5.15	N/A	711.3	248.7	40.7	1.2
3-16	C+	19.81	10.04	N/A	677.2	266.0	39.7	14.3
2016	C+	19.38	10.50	99.0	658.8	247.9	157.6	3.7
2015	C+	21.55	11.34	65.0	642.2	251.1	134.6	30.3
2014	C+	22.71	12.29	97.5	556.9	246.6	125.8	3.3
2013	C+	21.22	11.60	64.2	564.2	276.0	118.1	48.6
2012	C	4.82	4.11	77.5	482.8	214.0	99.5	19.9

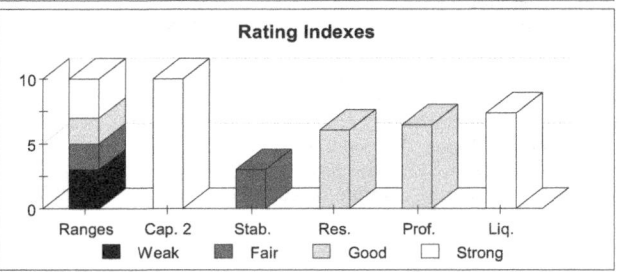

Rating Indexes

AMERICAN SECURITY INS CO | B- | Good

Major Rating Factors: Fair profitability index (3.5 on a scale of 0 to 10). Weak expense controls. Return on equity has been fair, averaging 36.6% over the past five years. Fair overall results on stability tests (4.7) including weak results on operational trends.

Other Rating Factors: History of adequate reserve strength (6.3) as reserves have been consistently at an acceptable level. Good liquidity (6.0) with sufficient resources (cash flows and marketable investments) to handle a spike in claims. Strong long-term capitalization index (7.5) based on excellent current risk adjusted capital (severe and moderate loss scenarios), despite some fluctuation in capital levels.

Principal Business: Allied lines (51%), fire (31%), inland marine (8%), other liability (6%), homeowners multiple peril (3%), and credit (1%).

Principal Investments: Investment grade bonds (71%), misc. investments (25%), non investment grade bonds (6%), and real estate (2%).

Investments in Affiliates: 12%

Group Affiliation: Assurant Inc

Licensed in: All states except NH

Commenced Business: September 1938

Address: 2711 CENTERVILLE ROAD STE 400, Wilmington, DE 19808

Phone: (770) 763-1000 **Domicile State:** DE **NAIC Code:** 42978

Data Date	Rating	RACR #1	RACR #2	Loss Ratio %	Total Assets ($mil)	Capital ($mil)	Net Premium ($mil)	Net Income ($mil)
3-17	B-	2.09	1.61	N/A	1,531.8	594.3	222.4	35.2
3-16	B-	2.07	1.54	N/A	1,533.5	560.7	256.6	63.2
2016	B-	1.91	1.48	49.0	1,552.5	555.2	945.8	84.2
2015	B-	2.02	1.51	36.6	1,584.9	558.8	1,047.3	298.5
2014	B	1.53	1.20	38.0	1,915.8	661.5	1,369.2	251.2
2013	B	2.55	1.82	33.6	2,078.0	740.8	1,601.9	294.2
2012	B	3.84	2.39	43.1	1,949.3	703.1	1,496.0	279.8

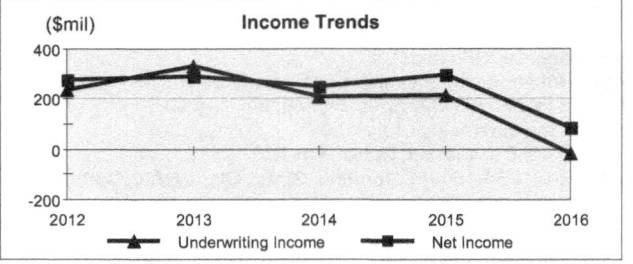

Income Trends

AMERICAN STANDARD INS CO OF WI * | B+ | Good

Major Rating Factors: Good overall results on stability tests (5.0 on a scale of 0 to 10) despite weak results on operational trends and negative cash flow from operations for 2016. Strengths include potential support from affiliation with American Family Ins Group. Strong long-term capitalization index (10.0) based on excellent current risk adjusted capital (severe and moderate loss scenarios), despite some fluctuation in capital levels.

Other Rating Factors: Excellent profitability (7.2) with operating gains in each of the last five years. Excellent expense controls. Superior liquidity (10.0) with ample operational cash flow and liquid investments.

Principal Business: Auto liability (65%) and auto physical damage (35%).

Principal Investments: Investment grade bonds (93%), cash (4%), misc. investments (2%), and non investment grade bonds (1%).

Investments in Affiliates: None

Group Affiliation: American Family Ins Group

Licensed in: AZ, CO, ID, IL, IN, IA, KS, MN, MO, MT, NE, NV, NM, NC, ND, OH, OR, SC, SD, UT, WA, WI, WY

Commenced Business: September 1961

Address: 6000 AMERICAN PARKWAY, Madison, WI 53783-0001

Phone: (608) 249-2111 **Domicile State:** WI **NAIC Code:** 19283

Data Date	Rating	RACR #1	RACR #2	Loss Ratio %	Total Assets ($mil)	Capital ($mil)	Net Premium ($mil)	Net Income ($mil)
3-17	B+	48.55	43.69	N/A	401.3	343.9	0.0	0.7
3-16	B+	43.29	38.96	N/A	414.2	339.8	0.0	1.4
2016	B+	48.08	43.27	0.0	401.7	343.1	0.0	5.7
2015	B+	37.42	33.68	0.0	433.0	338.3	0.0	9.1
2014	B+	39.45	35.50	0.0	414.8	329.3	0.0	10.3
2013	B+	40.40	36.36	0.0	393.9	318.6	0.0	8.0
2012	B+	39.71	35.74	0.0	384.6	310.7	0.0	11.7

American Family Ins Group Composite Group Rating: B+ Largest Group Members	Assets ($mil)	Rating
AMERICAN FAMILY MUTL INS CO SI	16194	B+
AMERICAN FAMILY LIFE INS CO	5497	A+
PERMANENT GENERAL ASR CORP	418	C-
HOMESITE INS CO OF THE MIDWEST	403	C
AMERICAN STANDARD INS CO OF WI	402	B+

AMERICAN STRATEGIC INS CO | C | Fair

Major Rating Factors: Fair overall results on stability tests (3.9 on a scale of 0 to 10) including potential drain of affiliation with Progressive Corp. Good overall profitability index (6.2) despite operating losses during 2012. Return on equity has been low, averaging 4.6% over the past five years.

Other Rating Factors: Good liquidity (6.5) with sufficient resources (cash flows and marketable investments) to handle a spike in claims. Strong long-term capitalization index (8.8) based on excellent current risk adjusted capital (severe and moderate loss scenarios). Moreover, capital levels have been consistent in recent years. Ample reserve history (9.4) that helps to protect the company against sharp claims increases.

Principal Business: Homeowners multiple peril (71%), allied lines (22%), fire (5%), and other liability (2%).

Principal Investments: Investment grade bonds (87%), misc. investments (10%), and real estate (4%).

Investments in Affiliates: 2%

Group Affiliation: Progressive Corp

Licensed in: All states except AK, AR, CA, HI, ID, IN, LA, NY, SD, WY, PR

Commenced Business: December 1997

Address: 1 ASI Way, St Petersburg, FL 33702-2514

Phone: (727) 821-8765 **Domicile State:** FL **NAIC Code:** 10872

Data Date	Rating	RACR #1	RACR #2	Loss Ratio %	Total Assets ($mil)	Capital ($mil)	Net Premium ($mil)	Net Income ($mil)
3-17	C	2.77	2.43	N/A	1,100.4	505.1	153.5	14.2
3-16	C	2.54	2.24	N/A	1,009.7	441.7	135.8	0.6
2016	C	2.81	2.31	64.5	1,080.0	489.4	618.3	19.8
2015	C	2.68	2.22	57.9	980.9	441.8	576.1	51.5
2014	C	2.34	1.89	63.7	885.3	375.4	500.6	11.3
2013	B-	2.34	1.88	54.1	736.4	307.4	409.5	30.1
2012	B-	1.95	1.56	69.3	603.9	227.7	343.9	-15.9

Progressive Corp Composite Group Rating: C+ Largest Group Members	Assets ($mil)	Rating
PROGRESSIVE CASUALTY INS CO	6967	B-
PROGRESSIVE DIRECT INS CO	6727	C+
UNITED FINANCIAL CASUALTY CO	2897	B-
PROGRESSIVE NORTHERN INS CO	1576	C+
PROGRESSIVE NORTHWESTERN INS CO	1538	C+

AMERICAN ZURICH INS CO   C+   Fair

Major Rating Factors: Fair overall results on stability tests (4.6 on a scale of 0 to 10) including fair financial strength of affiliated Zurich Financial Services Group and weak results on operational trends.

Other Rating Factors: Strong long-term capitalization index (10.0) based on excellent current risk adjusted capital (severe and moderate loss scenarios). Moreover, capital levels have been consistent in recent years. Excellent profitability (7.5) with operating gains in each of the last five years. Superior liquidity (10.0) with ample operational cash flow and liquid investments.

Principal Business: Workers compensation (73%), inland marine (19%), commercial multiple peril (4%), other liability (2%), and auto liability (1%).

Principal Investments: Investment grade bonds (80%) and misc. investments (20%).

Investments in Affiliates: 15%
Group Affiliation: Zurich Financial Services Group
Licensed in: All states except PR
Commenced Business: September 1981
Address: 1299 ZURICH WAY, Schaumburg, IL 60196-1056
Phone: (847) 605-6000   **Domicile State:** IL   **NAIC Code:** 40142

Data Date	Rating	RACR #1	RACR #2	Loss Ratio %	Total Assets ($mil)	Capital ($mil)	Net Premium ($mil)	Net Income ($mil)
3-17	C+	7.13	6.78	N/A	319.1	231.4	0.0	0.5
3-16	C+	6.97	6.65	N/A	299.1	227.1	0.0	0.7
2016	C+	7.18	6.88	0.0	315.9	230.7	0.0	4.7
2015	C+	7.00	6.72	0.0	314.3	226.3	0.0	4.7
2014	C	4.79	4.61	0.0	264.5	157.5	0.0	2.9
2013	C	4.86	4.71	0.0	234.2	153.3	0.0	3.3
2012	C	4.68	4.53	0.0	212.7	151.0	0.0	8.3

Zurich Financial Services Group
Composite Group Rating: C+

Largest Group Members	Assets ($mil)	Rating
ZURICH AMERICAN INS CO	31003	B-
ZURICH AMERICAN LIFE INS CO	12330	C
FARMERS NEW WORLD LIFE INS CO	7155	B-
CENTRE LIFE INS CO	1810	B-
RURAL COMMUNITY INS CO	1754	C+

AMERISURE INS CO   B-   Good

Major Rating Factors: Fair overall results on stability tests (4.4 on a scale of 0 to 10) including potential drain of affiliation with Amerisure Companies and weak results on operational trends. History of adequate reserve strength (5.9) as reserves have been consistently at an acceptable level.

Other Rating Factors: Good liquidity (6.8) with sufficient resources (cash flows and marketable investments) to handle a spike in claims. Strong long-term capitalization index (8.2) based on excellent current risk adjusted capital (severe and moderate loss scenarios). Moreover, capital levels have been consistent in recent years. Excellent profitability (7.5) with operating gains in each of the last five years.

Principal Business: Workers compensation (54%), commercial multiple peril (18%), auto liability (15%), other liability (7%), auto physical damage (4%), and products liability (2%).

Principal Investments: Investment grade bonds (99%) and cash (1%).

Investments in Affiliates: None
Group Affiliation: Amerisure Companies
Licensed in: All states except CA
Commenced Business: September 1968
Address: 26777 Halsted Road, Farmington Hills, MI 48331-3586
Phone: (248) 615-9000   **Domicile State:** MI   **NAIC Code:** 19488

Data Date	Rating	RACR #1	RACR #2	Loss Ratio %	Total Assets ($mil)	Capital ($mil)	Net Premium ($mil)	Net Income ($mil)
3-17	B-	2.48	1.75	N/A	968.8	245.8	61.4	1.3
3-16	B-	2.63	1.86	N/A	926.9	239.8	58.3	2.5
2016	B-	2.57	1.83	69.5	836.4	245.8	244.0	7.5
2015	B-	2.70	1.93	64.5	785.9	238.7	232.8	14.2
2014	B-	2.65	1.87	67.2	752.2	224.5	215.4	8.1
2013	B-	2.57	1.75	73.1	721.6	215.7	199.3	3.4
2012	B-	2.83	1.93	71.1	690.5	212.3	173.2	4.5

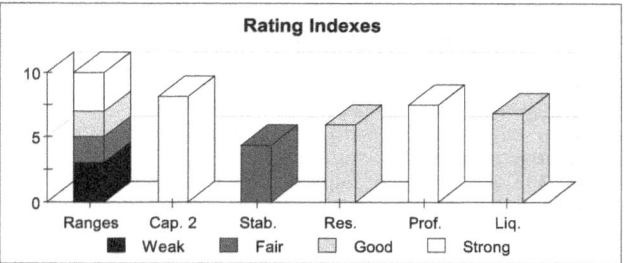

AMERISURE MUTUAL INS CO   B-   Good

Major Rating Factors: Fair overall results on stability tests (4.7 on a scale of 0 to 10) including potential drain of affiliation with Amerisure Companies and weak results on operational trends. History of adequate reserve strength (6.0) as reserves have been consistently at an acceptable level.

Other Rating Factors: Good liquidity (6.8) with sufficient resources (cash flows and marketable investments) to handle a spike in claims. Strong long-term capitalization index (8.3) based on excellent current risk adjusted capital (severe and moderate loss scenarios). Moreover, capital levels have been consistent in recent years. Excellent profitability (8.3) with operating gains in each of the last five years.

Principal Business: Workers compensation (55%), commercial multiple peril (17%), other liability (13%), auto liability (9%), auto physical damage (2%), products liability (2%), and other lines (2%).

Principal Investments: Investment grade bonds (59%), misc. investments (39%), non investment grade bonds (1%), and real estate (1%).

Investments in Affiliates: 14%
Group Affiliation: Amerisure Companies
Licensed in: All states, the District of Columbia and Puerto Rico
Commenced Business: September 1912
Address: 26777 Halsted Road, Farmington Hills, MI 48331-3586
Phone: (248) 615-9000   **Domicile State:** MI   **NAIC Code:** 23396

Data Date	Rating	RACR #1	RACR #2	Loss Ratio %	Total Assets ($mil)	Capital ($mil)	Net Premium ($mil)	Net Income ($mil)
3-17	B-	2.36	1.87	N/A	2,397.2	945.7	137.2	9.0
3-16	B-	2.23	1.76	N/A	2,243.2	876.7	130.3	10.3
2016	B-	2.34	1.86	69.5	2,231.8	937.9	545.0	40.4
2015	B-	2.26	1.80	64.5	2,124.5	875.2	519.9	71.2
2014	B-	2.25	1.77	67.2	2,069.7	843.0	481.1	48.1
2013	B-	2.16	1.69	73.1	1,981.8	803.8	445.2	41.0
2012	B-	2.15	1.69	71.1	1,843.4	732.9	386.7	36.1

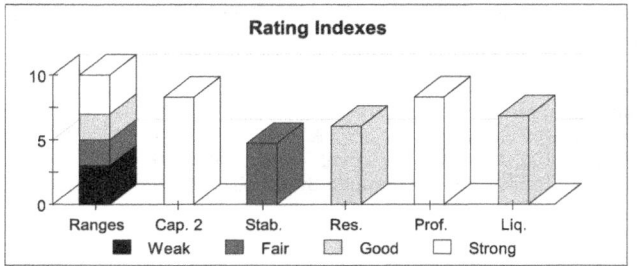

AMICA MUTUAL INS CO *

B+   Good

Major Rating Factors: Good overall profitability index (5.2 on a scale of 0 to 10). Good expense controls. Good liquidity (5.6) with sufficient resources (cash flows and marketable investments) to handle a spike in claims.

Other Rating Factors: Good overall results on stability tests (5.4) despite weak results on operational trends. Strong long-term capitalization index (8.2) based on excellent current risk adjusted capital (severe and moderate loss scenarios), despite some fluctuation in capital levels. Ample reserve history (8.2) that helps to protect the company against sharp claims increases.

Principal Business: Homeowners multiple peril (37%), auto liability (34%), auto physical damage (23%), other liability (3%), earthquake (1%), allied lines (1%), and inland marine (1%).

Principal Investments: Investment grade bonds (51%), misc. investments (49%), and real estate (1%).

Investments in Affiliates: 8%

Group Affiliation: Amica Mutual Group

Licensed in: All states except PR

Commenced Business: April 1907

Address: 100 AMICA WAY, Lincoln, RI 02865-1156

Phone: (800) 652-6422   **Domicile State:** RI   **NAIC Code:** 19976

Data Date	Rating	RACR #1	RACR #2	Loss Ratio %	Total Assets ($mil)	Capital ($mil)	Net Premium ($mil)	Net Income ($mil)
3-17	B+	2.64	1.76	N/A	5,140.7	2,600.1	517.7	7.5
3-16	B+	2.70	1.82	N/A	4,975.2	2,576.9	483.5	9.1
2016	B+	2.65	1.78	77.9	5,120.6	2,583.7	2,086.5	146.2
2015	B+	2.72	1.84	80.9	4,961.9	2,611.3	1,942.8	56.2
2014	B+	2.97	1.97	66.3	5,061.7	2,759.8	1,841.5	185.5
2013	B+	2.97	1.95	69.9	4,855.2	2,649.7	1,746.7	145.2
2012	B+	2.94	1.92	76.5	4,391.2	2,377.5	1,633.4	69.9

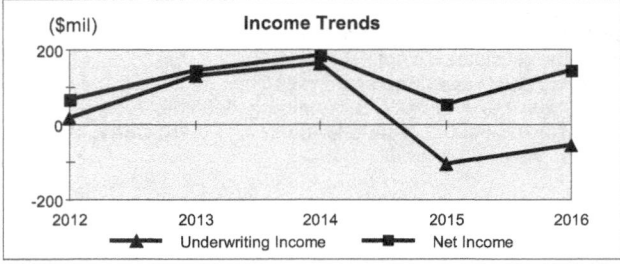
Income Trends

APPALACHIAN INS CO

C   Fair

Major Rating Factors: Fair reserve development (3.1 on a scale of 0 to 10) as the level of reserves has at times been insufficient to cover claims. In 2013 and 2014 the two year reserve development was 20% and 25% deficient respectively. Fair overall results on stability tests (3.1). The largest net exposure for one risk is excessive at 9.6% of capital.

Other Rating Factors: Strong long-term capitalization index (9.6) based on excellent current risk adjusted capital (severe and moderate loss scenarios). Moreover, capital levels have been consistent in recent years. Excellent profitability (8.4) despite modest operating losses during the first three months of 2017. Excellent liquidity (8.4) with ample operational cash flow and liquid investments.

Principal Business: Inland marine (47%), allied lines (22%), ocean marine (17%), and fire (14%).

Principal Investments: Investment grade bonds (56%), misc. investments (27%), and cash (17%).

Investments in Affiliates: None

Group Affiliation: Factory Mutual Ins

Licensed in: All states, the District of Columbia and Puerto Rico

Commenced Business: January 1942

Address: 270 Central Avenue, Johnston, RI 02919-4949

Phone: (401) 275-3000   **Domicile State:** RI   **NAIC Code:** 10316

Data Date	Rating	RACR #1	RACR #2	Loss Ratio %	Total Assets ($mil)	Capital ($mil)	Net Premium ($mil)	Net Income ($mil)
3-17	C	4.69	2.88	N/A	330.5	217.2	17.6	-0.2
3-16	C	4.25	2.55	N/A	316.1	210.2	16.2	4.3
2016	C	4.76	2.92	54.8	322.5	217.4	66.1	11.0
2015	C	4.19	2.50	58.1	324.1	205.9	65.2	9.2
2014	C	4.37	2.67	50.5	287.6	197.0	63.6	14.0
2013	C	4.26	2.68	50.6	290.5	182.9	64.5	13.0
2012	C	5.38	4.46	59.8	233.6	169.7	66.1	14.4

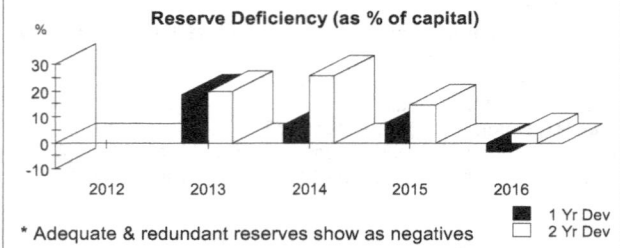
Reserve Deficiency (as % of capital)

* Adequate & redundant reserves show as negatives

ARBELLA MUTUAL INS CO

C+   Fair

Major Rating Factors: Fair overall results on stability tests (4.3 on a scale of 0 to 10) including potential drain of affiliation with Arbella Ins Group and weak results on operational trends. Good profitability index (5.0) despite operating losses during 2015.

Other Rating Factors: Good liquidity (6.2) with sufficient resources (cash flows and marketable investments) to handle a spike in claims. Strong long-term capitalization index (8.4) based on excellent current risk adjusted capital (severe and moderate loss scenarios), despite some fluctuation in capital levels. Ample reserve history (7.7) that can protect against increases in claims costs.

Principal Business: Auto liability (40%), auto physical damage (32%), homeowners multiple peril (25%), fire (1%), other liability (1%), allied lines (1%), and inland marine (1%).

Principal Investments: Investment grade bonds (74%) and misc. investments (26%).

Investments in Affiliates: 14%

Group Affiliation: Arbella Ins Group

Licensed in: MA

Commenced Business: October 1988

Address: 1100 Crown Colony Drive, Quincy, MA 02269-9103

Phone: (617) 328-2800   **Domicile State:** MA   **NAIC Code:** 17000

Data Date	Rating	RACR #1	RACR #2	Loss Ratio %	Total Assets ($mil)	Capital ($mil)	Net Premium ($mil)	Net Income ($mil)
3-17	C+	2.57	1.96	N/A	1,376.4	576.7	151.1	14.7
3-16	C+	2.35	1.78	N/A	1,341.8	510.7	154.6	0.1
2016	C+	2.51	1.94	64.1	1,404.4	557.6	619.2	41.6
2015	C+	2.38	1.83	82.2	1,334.2	510.5	609.1	-45.0
2014	C+	2.65	2.13	62.9	1,285.7	561.2	577.0	28.6
2013	C+	2.69	2.06	64.5	1,177.8	523.9	496.4	22.8
2012	C+	2.71	2.09	64.1	1,139.1	480.9	464.9	35.2

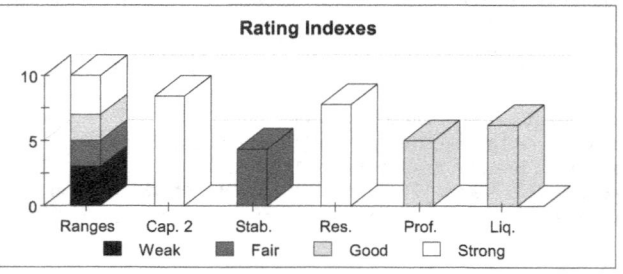
Rating Indexes

ARCH INS CO   C   Fair

Major Rating Factors: Fair overall results on stability tests (3.4 on a scale of 0 to 10) including potential drain of affiliation with Arch Capital Group Ltd. Good overall profitability index (5.8) despite operating losses during 2012. Return on equity has been low, averaging 3.2% over the past five years.

Other Rating Factors: Good liquidity (6.9) with sufficient resources (cash flows and marketable investments) to handle a spike in claims. Strong long-term capitalization index (7.4) based on excellent current risk adjusted capital (severe and moderate loss scenarios). Moreover, capital levels have been consistent in recent years. Ample reserve history (7.5) that can protect against increases in claims costs.

Principal Business: Other liability (30%), workers compensation (25%), auto liability (10%), inland marine (6%), surety (5%), commercial multiple peril (5%), and other lines (19%).

Principal Investments: Investment grade bonds (76%), misc. investments (23%), and cash (1%).

Investments in Affiliates: 15%

Group Affiliation: Arch Capital Group Ltd

Licensed in: All states, the District of Columbia and Puerto Rico

Commenced Business: June 1980

Address: 2345 GRAND BLVD SUITE 900, Kansas City, MO 64108

Phone: (201) 743-4000   **Domicile State:** MO   **NAIC Code:** 11150

Data Date	Rating	RACR #1	RACR #2	Loss Ratio %	Total Assets ($mil)	Capital ($mil)	Net Premium ($mil)	Net Income ($mil)
3-17	C	1.63	1.32	N/A	3,951.7	890.3	194.3	3.6
3-16	C	1.58	1.25	N/A	3,665.3	855.8	194.5	12.5
2016	C	1.66	1.36	71.5	3,729.3	888.6	793.2	49.7
2015	C	1.56	1.25	68.5	3,545.4	826.5	772.9	52.8
2014	C	1.39	1.07	67.3	3,200.9	778.4	785.5	37.6
2013	C	1.38	1.06	68.2	2,840.9	736.6	659.6	28.7
2012	C	1.21	0.88	75.6	2,696.9	563.5	750.0	-23.0

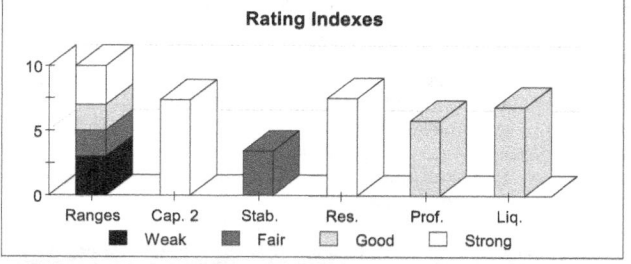

Rating Indexes

ARCH REINS CO   C-   Fair

Major Rating Factors: Weak overall results on stability tests (2.7 on a scale of 0 to 10) including potential drain of affiliation with Arch Capital Group Ltd. The largest net exposure for one risk is conservative at 1.1% of capital. Strong long-term capitalization index (7.6) based on excellent current risk adjusted capital (severe and moderate loss scenarios), despite some fluctuation in capital levels.

Other Rating Factors: Ample reserve history (8.2) that helps to protect the company against sharp claims increases. Excellent profitability (7.7) with operating gains in each of the last five years. Excellent liquidity (7.3) with ample operational cash flow and liquid investments.

Principal Business: (This company is a reinsurer.)

Principal Investments: Misc. investments (52%), investment grade bonds (44%), and cash (4%).

Investments in Affiliates: 50%

Group Affiliation: Arch Capital Group Ltd

Licensed in: All states except PR

Commenced Business: July 1995

Address: 1209 ORANGE STREET, Wilmington, DE 19801

Phone: (973) 898-9575   **Domicile State:** DE   **NAIC Code:** 10348

Data Date	Rating	RACR #1	RACR #2	Loss Ratio %	Total Assets ($mil)	Capital ($mil)	Net Premium ($mil)	Net Income ($mil)
3-17	C-	1.55	1.52	N/A	2,016.7	1,245.4	51.6	9.4
3-16	C-	1.63	1.58	N/A	2,011.1	1,244.8	57.4	7.9
2016	C-	1.60	1.57	46.9	2,040.4	1,284.1	215.7	36.9
2015	C-	1.59	1.56	49.2	1,904.9	1,201.4	219.0	32.7
2014	C-	1.61	1.57	52.1	1,736.9	1,104.0	245.5	33.3
2013	C-	1.61	1.58	46.8	1,547.9	1,013.2	204.0	33.0
2012	C-	1.71	1.67	65.1	1,315.9	822.6	190.0	7.2

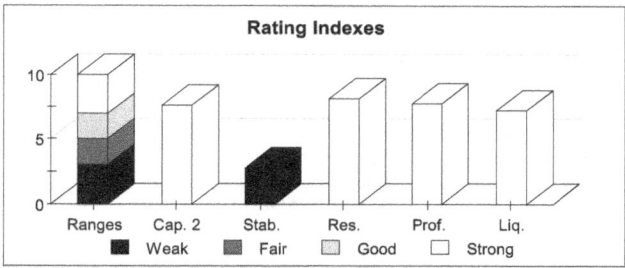

Rating Indexes

ARCH SPECIALTY INS CO   B   Good

Major Rating Factors: History of adequate reserve strength (6.0 on a scale of 0 to 10) as reserves have been consistently at an acceptable level. Fair profitability index (4.8) with operating losses during 2012 and the first three months of 2017. Return on equity has been low, averaging 1.7% over the past five years.

Other Rating Factors: Fair overall results on stability tests (4.7) including weak results on operational trends and negative cash flow from operations for 2016. Strong long-term capitalization index (10.0) based on excellent current risk adjusted capital (severe and moderate loss scenarios), despite some fluctuation in capital levels. Superior liquidity (9.1) with ample operational cash flow and liquid investments.

Principal Business: Other liability (47%), fire (21%), medical malpractice (11%), commercial multiple peril (6%), products liability (6%), earthquake (5%), and allied lines (3%).

Principal Investments: Investment grade bonds (87%), misc. investments (9%), and cash (4%).

Investments in Affiliates: None

Group Affiliation: Arch Capital Group Ltd

Licensed in: All states, the District of Columbia and Puerto Rico

Commenced Business: January 1965

Address: 2345 GRAND BLVD SUITE 900, Kansas City, MO 64108

Phone: (201) 743-4000   **Domicile State:** MO   **NAIC Code:** 21199

Data Date	Rating	RACR #1	RACR #2	Loss Ratio %	Total Assets ($mil)	Capital ($mil)	Net Premium ($mil)	Net Income ($mil)
3-17	B	5.89	4.68	N/A	496.9	297.4	0.0	-4.4
3-16	B	5.65	4.50	N/A	486.6	301.1	0.0	-7.9
2016	B	6.01	4.82	N/A	481.0	301.9	0.1	2.1
2015	B	5.76	4.62	N/A	503.0	305.9	0.3	23.3
2014	B	5.61	4.47	N/A	470.6	292.4	0.9	7.7
2013	B	21.66	13.74	N/A	473.5	283.5	0.0	5.6
2012	B	18.93	12.13	N/A	437.8	271.8	0.0	-6.8

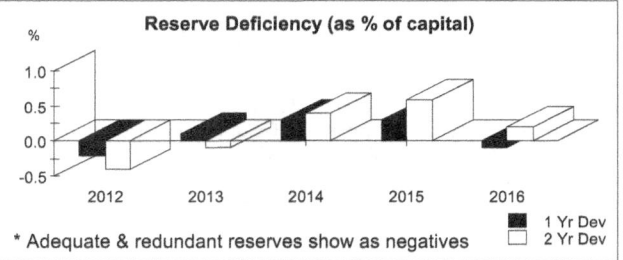

Reserve Deficiency (as % of capital)

* Adequate & redundant reserves show as negatives

ARGONAUT INS CO
C · Fair

Major Rating Factors: Fair overall results on stability tests (3.3 on a scale of 0 to 10) including potential drain of affiliation with Argo Group Intl Holdings Ltd and weak results on operational trends. The largest net exposure for one risk is conservative at 1.0% of capital. Fair reserve development (3.3) as the level of reserves has at times been insufficient to cover claims. In four of the last five years reserves (two year development) were between 16% and 20% deficient.

Other Rating Factors: Good long-term capitalization index (6.1) based on good current risk adjusted capital (moderate loss scenario), despite some fluctuation in capital levels. Good overall profitability index (6.2) despite operating losses during 2012. Return on equity has been fair, averaging 5.4% over the past five years. Excellent liquidity (7.2) with ample operational cash flow and liquid investments.

Principal Business: Other liability (33%), workers compensation (22%), surety (19%), commercial multiple peril (12%), auto liability (6%), inland marine (2%), and other lines (6%).

Principal Investments: Misc. investments (54%), investment grade bonds (39%), non investment grade bonds (6%), and cash (1%).

Investments in Affiliates: 33%

Group Affiliation: Argo Group Intl Holdings Ltd

Licensed in: All states, the District of Columbia and Puerto Rico

Commenced Business: May 1957

Address: 225 W WASHINGTON ST 24TH FL, Chicago, IL 60606

Phone: (800) 470-7958   **Domicile State:** IL   **NAIC Code:** 19801

Data Date	Rating	RACR #1	RACR #2	Loss Ratio %	Total Assets ($mil)	Capital ($mil)	Net Premium ($mil)	Net Income ($mil)
3-17	C	1.46	1.23	N/A	1,695.6	817.0	55.1	3.7
3-16	C	2.32	1.53	N/A	1,598.6	752.9	47.2	20.3
2016	C	1.44	1.22	61.8	1,675.0	799.7	223.7	52.0
2015	C	1.72	1.14	70.4	1,271.0	416.1	192.2	38.5
2014	C	1.43	0.94	88.6	1,280.4	390.8	185.2	13.4
2013	C	1.86	1.21	82.8	1,308.9	409.4	196.9	49.8
2012	C	1.66	1.05	93.0	1,337.3	380.5	217.8	-13.8

Rating Indexes

(Bar chart: Ranges, Cap. 2, Stab., Res., Prof., Liq. — legend: ■ Weak, ▨ Fair, ▢ Good, □ Strong)

ARROWOOD INDEMNITY CO
D · Weak

Major Rating Factors: Weak overall results on stability tests (2.0 on a scale of 0 to 10) including weak risk adjusted capital in prior years, weak results on operational trends and negative cash flow from operations for 2016. Strengths include potentially strong support from affiliation with Arrowpoint Capital Group. The largest net exposure for one risk is acceptable at 2.3% of capital. Poor long-term capitalization index (0.4) based on weak current risk adjusted capital (severe and moderate loss scenarios).

Other Rating Factors: Weak profitability index (1.6) with operating losses during each of the last five years and the first three months of 2017. Average return on equity over the last five years has been poor at -9.4%. Fair reserve development (4.4) as reserves have generally been sufficient to cover claims. Excellent liquidity (7.0) with ample operational cash flow and liquid investments.

Principal Business: (Not applicable due to unusual reinsurance transactions.)

Principal Investments: Investment grade bonds (69%), misc. investments (18%), non investment grade bonds (12%), and cash (1%).

Investments in Affiliates: 7%

Group Affiliation: Arrowpoint Capital Group

Licensed in: All states except PR

Commenced Business: February 1911

Address: 2711 Centerville Road Ste 400, Wilmington, DE 19808

Phone: (704) 522-2000   **Domicile State:** DE   **NAIC Code:** 24678

Data Date	Rating	RACR #1	RACR #2	Loss Ratio %	Total Assets ($mil)	Capital ($mil)	Net Premium ($mil)	Net Income ($mil)
3-17	D	0.31	0.18	N/A	1,284.4	220.7	0.0	-4.8
3-16	D+	0.36	0.21	N/A	1,319.2	224.4	0.1	-12.7
2016	D	0.27	0.16	N/A	1,322.4	219.3	0.0	-37.5
2015	D+	0.37	0.21	N/A	1,354.0	230.8	-1.8	-16.2
2014	U	0.28	0.17	N/A	1,473.7	249.0	-1.9	-38.1
2013	U	0.31	0.19	673.6	1,540.0	260.5	1.5	-3.2
2012	D	0.33	0.20	N/A	1,554.9	273.4	-2.6	-18.3

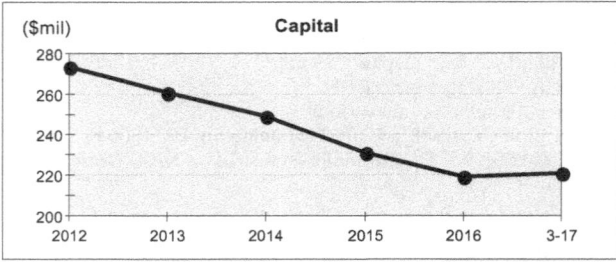

($mil) **Capital**

ASPEN AMERICAN INS CO
B · Good

Major Rating Factors: Fair reserve development (4.8 on a scale of 0 to 10) as reserves have generally been sufficient to cover claims. In 2016, the one year reserve development was 18% deficient. Fair profitability index (4.2) with operating losses during 2012, 2013, 2014 and 2015. Average return on equity over the last five years has been poor at -7.7%.

Other Rating Factors: Fair overall results on stability tests (4.3) including weak results on operational trends. Strong long-term capitalization index (7.6) based on excellent current risk adjusted capital (severe and moderate loss scenarios). Moreover, capital levels have been consistent in recent years. Excellent liquidity (7.1) with ample operational cash flow and liquid investments.

Principal Business: Other liability (32%), commercial multiple peril (30%), surety (13%), inland marine (8%), allied lines (7%), ocean marine (4%), and other lines (6%).

Principal Investments: Investment grade bonds (45%), misc. investments (30%), and cash (25%).

Investments in Affiliates: 27%

Group Affiliation: Aspen Insurance Holdings Ltd

Licensed in: All states, the District of Columbia and Puerto Rico

Commenced Business: December 1990

Address: 1999 BRYAN STREET SUITE 900, Dallas, TX 75201

Phone: (860) 258-3500   **Domicile State:** TX   **NAIC Code:** 43460

Data Date	Rating	RACR #1	RACR #2	Loss Ratio %	Total Assets ($mil)	Capital ($mil)	Net Premium ($mil)	Net Income ($mil)
3-17	B	2.26	1.71	N/A	791.5	464.8	18.1	8.7
3-16	B-	3.64	2.37	N/A	572.6	273.6	43.3	4.0
2016	B	2.13	1.59	69.2	881.1	454.5	89.7	14.4
2015	C+	4.99	3.26	83.5	504.9	268.5	69.4	-14.8
2014	C	3.85	2.55	66.9	502.3	262.8	64.0	-24.1
2013	C	6.46	4.35	102.9	443.7	257.5	26.8	-27.4
2012	C	4.93	3.35	98.3	277.9	172.0	21.0	-34.6

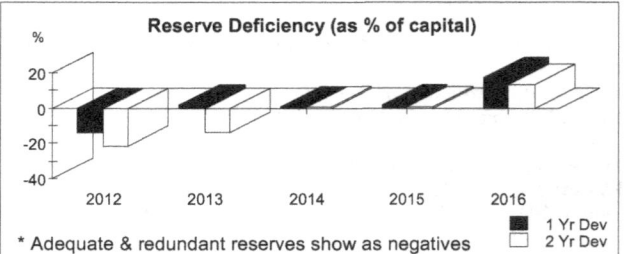

Reserve Deficiency (as % of capital)

* Adequate & redundant reserves show as negatives   ■ 1 Yr Dev   □ 2 Yr Dev

ASSOCIATED INDUSTRIES OF MA MUT INS   **B-**   **Good**

Major Rating Factors: Fair overall results on stability tests (4.1 on a scale of 0 to 10) including potential drain of affiliation with AIM Mutual Group and weak results on operational trends. Good liquidity (6.8) with sufficient resources (cash flows and marketable investments) to handle a spike in claims.

Other Rating Factors: Strong long-term capitalization index (8.2) based on excellent current risk adjusted capital (severe and moderate loss scenarios). Moreover, capital levels have been consistent in recent years. Ample reserve history (9.4) that helps to protect the company against sharp claims increases. Excellent profitability (8.7) with operating gains in each of the last five years.

Principal Business: Workers compensation (100%).

Principal Investments: Investment grade bonds (87%), misc. investments (12%), and cash (1%).

Investments in Affiliates: 2%

Group Affiliation: AIM Mutual Group

Licensed in: CT, MA, NH

Commenced Business: January 1989

Address: 54 Third Avenue, Burlington, MA 01803

Phone: (781) 221-1600   **Domicile State:** MA   **NAIC Code:** 33758

Data Date	Rating	RACR #1	RACR #2	Loss Ratio %	Total Assets ($mil)	Capital ($mil)	Net Premium ($mil)	Net Income ($mil)
3-17	B-	2.44	1.82	N/A	615.2	218.0	37.2	2.3
3-16	C+	2.33	1.73	N/A	578.8	195.9	32.2	2.0
2016	B-	2.55	1.90	71.6	593.7	215.0	137.3	19.6
2015	C+	2.39	1.79	71.7	560.3	193.8	132.8	14.7
2014	C	2.31	1.73	74.6	530.9	180.6	129.2	11.6
2013	C	1.99	1.47	76.7	492.9	178.2	126.1	8.0
2012	C	2.12	1.57	75.7	448.4	164.4	113.0	10.0

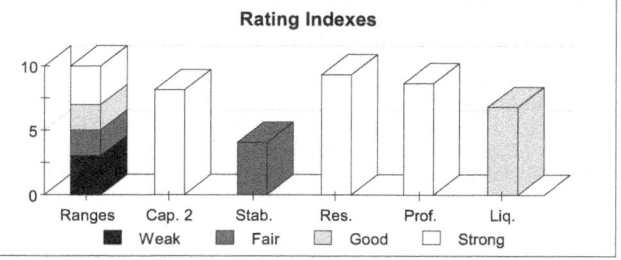

Rating Indexes

ASSURED GUARANTY CORP   **C-**   **Fair**

Major Rating Factors: Weak overall results on stability tests (2.4 on a scale of 0 to 10) including weak results on operational trends and negative cash flow from operations for 2016. The largest net exposure for one risk is excessive at 9.6% of capital. Strengths include potentially strong support from affiliation with Assured Guaranty/Financial Sec Asr. A history of deficient reserves (1.0). Underreserving can have an adverse impact on capital and profits. In 2015 and 2016 the two year reserve development was 57% and 134% deficient respectively.

Other Rating Factors: Good overall profitability index (5.5) despite operating losses during 2015 and the first three months of 2017. Return on equity has been fair, averaging 8.3% over the past five years. Strong long-term capitalization index (10.0) based on excellent current risk adjusted capital (severe and moderate loss scenarios), despite some fluctuation in capital levels. Superior liquidity (10.0) with ample operational cash flow and liquid investments.

Principal Business: Financial guaranty (100%).

Principal Investments: Investment grade bonds (77%), misc. investments (15%), non investment grade bonds (6%), cash (1%), and real estate (1%).

Investments in Affiliates: 11%

Group Affiliation: Assured Guaranty/Financial Sec Asr

Licensed in: All states, the District of Columbia and Puerto Rico

Commenced Business: January 1988

Address: 1633 Broadway, New York, NY 10019

Phone: (212) 974-0100   **Domicile State:** MD   **NAIC Code:** 30180

Data Date	Rating	RACR #1	RACR #2	Loss Ratio %	Total Assets ($mil)	Capital ($mil)	Net Premium ($mil)	Net Income ($mil)
3-17	C-	3.94	2.99	N/A	3,281.8	1,872.8	25.0	-31.9
3-16	C-	2.93	2.45	N/A	2,997.5	1,416.3	27.2	36.2
2016	C-	5.00	4.01	38.1	3,272.0	1,895.6	58.1	107.6
2015	C-	2.81	2.35	74.5	3,791.1	1,454.1	57.2	-52.7
2014	D+	2.98	2.46	N/A	3,888.9	1,421.9	58.6	129.3
2013	D+	2.15	1.82	N/A	2,504.4	692.6	-186.7	211.2
2012	D+	3.61	2.97	46.2	2,963.0	905.4	88.1	31.3

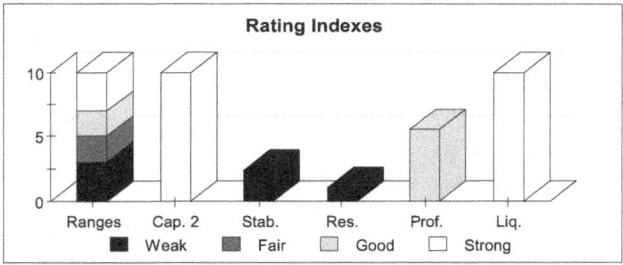

Rating Indexes

ASSURED GUARANTY MUNICIPAL CORP   **D+**   **Weak**

Major Rating Factors: Weak overall results on stability tests (1.9 on a scale of 0 to 10) including weak results on operational trends and negative cash flow from operations for 2016. The largest net exposure for one risk is excessive at 17.5% of capital. Strengths include potentially strong support from affiliation with Assured Guaranty/Financial Sec Asr. Strong long-term capitalization index (8.4) based on excellent current risk adjusted capital (severe and moderate loss scenarios), despite some fluctuation in capital levels.

Other Rating Factors: Fair reserve development (3.9) as reserves have generally been sufficient to cover claims. Excellent profitability (7.2) with operating gains in each of the last five years. Return on equity has been good over the last five years, averaging 12.0%. Excellent liquidity (8.5) with ample operational cash flow and liquid investments.

Principal Business: Financial guaranty (100%).

Principal Investments: Investment grade bonds (79%), misc. investments (19%), and non investment grade bonds (2%).

Investments in Affiliates: 11%

Group Affiliation: Assured Guaranty/Financial Sec Asr

Licensed in: All states, the District of Columbia and Puerto Rico

Commenced Business: September 1985

Address: 1633 Broadway, New York, NY 10019

Phone: (212) 974-0100   **Domicile State:** NY   **NAIC Code:** 18287

Data Date	Rating	RACR #1	RACR #2	Loss Ratio %	Total Assets ($mil)	Capital ($mil)	Net Premium ($mil)	Net Income ($mil)
3-17	D+	3.12	1.90	N/A	5,395.9	2,203.8	37.9	32.4
3-16	D+	2.70	1.68	N/A	5,684.9	2,361.7	70.6	22.3
2016	D+	3.24	1.91	34.8	5,333.5	2,321.0	143.5	190.7
2015	D+	2.85	1.80	59.6	5,788.5	2,440.8	141.8	216.7
2014	D+	2.75	1.69	N/A	5,961.2	2,266.9	173.9	303.9
2013	D+	2.49	1.48	N/A	5,712.1	1,733.1	-191.3	339.6
2012	D+	2.07	1.42	65.6	4,498.5	1,780.1	196.1	203.3

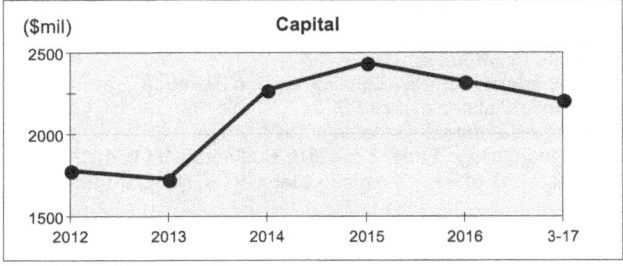

Capital

ATLANTIC SPECIALTY INS CO

B-　　**Good**

Major Rating Factors: Fair reserve development (4.4 on a scale of 0 to 10) as reserves have generally been sufficient to cover claims. Fair profitability index (3.2) with operating losses during 2012 and 2014. Return on equity has been low, averaging 3.5% over the past five years.

Other Rating Factors: Fair overall results on stability tests (4.5) including weak results on operational trends and negative cash flow from operations for 2016. Good liquidity (6.9) with sufficient resources (cash flows and marketable investments) to handle a spike in claims. Strong long-term capitalization index (7.3) based on excellent current risk adjusted capital (severe and moderate loss scenarios), despite some fluctuation in capital levels.

Principal Business: Other liability (25%), ocean marine (12%), commercial multiple peril (11%), group accident & health (10%), inland marine (7%), auto liability (7%), and other lines (28%).

Principal Investments: Investment grade bonds (71%), misc. investments (23%), non investment grade bonds (5%), and cash (1%).

Investments in Affiliates: 13%

Group Affiliation: White Mountains Group

Licensed in: All states, the District of Columbia and Puerto Rico

Commenced Business: December 1986

Address: 77 Water Street 17th Floor, New York, NY 10005-4488

Phone: (952) 852-2431　**Domicile State:** NY　**NAIC Code:** 27154

Data Date	Rating	RACR #1	RACR #2	Loss Ratio %	Total Assets ($mil)	Capital ($mil)	Net Premium ($mil)	Net Income ($mil)
3-17	B-	1.93	1.48	N/A	2,210.6	637.9	131.5	0.0
3-16	C+	1.81	1.38	N/A	2,296.1	631.9	139.9	4.8
2016	B-	1.92	1.48	68.9	2,232.7	624.8	552.8	34.9
2015	C+	1.79	1.37	65.9	2,340.3	622.3	590.1	45.0
2014	C	1.03	0.72	72.2	2,550.9	721.5	1,109.0	-14.1
2013	C	1.33	0.96	54.6	2,258.8	665.8	969.2	116.3
2012	C	1.87	1.31	68.7	2,248.4	716.7	850.5	-72.8

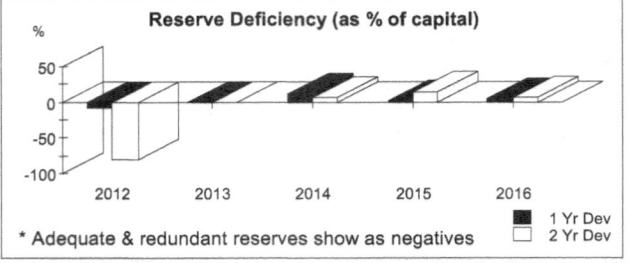

Reserve Deficiency (as % of capital)

* Adequate & redundant reserves show as negatives
■ 1 Yr Dev　□ 2 Yr Dev

ATLANTIC STATES INS CO

B-　　**Good**

Major Rating Factors: Fair overall results on stability tests (4.3 on a scale of 0 to 10) including potential drain of affiliation with Donegal Mutual Insurance Company and weak results on operational trends. History of adequate reserve strength (5.8) as reserves have been consistently at an acceptable level.

Other Rating Factors: Good liquidity (6.2) with sufficient resources (cash flows and marketable investments) to handle a spike in claims. Strong long-term capitalization index (8.7) based on excellent current risk adjusted capital (severe and moderate loss scenarios). Moreover, capital levels have been consistent in recent years. Excellent profitability (8.2) with operating gains in each of the last five years.

Principal Business: Auto liability (33%), auto physical damage (21%), commercial multiple peril (18%), homeowners multiple peril (13%), and workers compensation (13%).

Principal Investments: Investment grade bonds (84%), misc. investments (15%), and cash (1%).

Investments in Affiliates: None

Group Affiliation: Donegal Mutual Insurance Company

Licensed in: CT, DC, DE, GA, IL, IN, IA, ME, MD, MI, NE, NH, NY, NC, OH, PA, SC, SD, TN, VT, VA, WV

Commenced Business: October 1986

Address: 1195 River Road, Marietta, PA 17547-0302

Phone: (717) 426-1931　**Domicile State:** PA　**NAIC Code:** 22586

Data Date	Rating	RACR #1	RACR #2	Loss Ratio %	Total Assets ($mil)	Capital ($mil)	Net Premium ($mil)	Net Income ($mil)
3-17	B-	2.92	2.09	N/A	780.1	228.9	105.2	1.5
3-16	B-	2.86	2.08	N/A	728.0	214.0	99.8	5.8
2016	B-	2.98	2.13	64.1	758.1	227.9	426.3	15.8
2015	B-	2.85	2.08	66.0	705.5	207.6	393.1	13.4
2014	B-	2.82	2.06	68.4	636.4	191.2	371.3	6.1
2013	B-	2.83	2.01	64.7	595.4	186.6	346.9	12.6
2012	B-	3.35	2.47	67.6	538.8	180.5	303.3	12.5

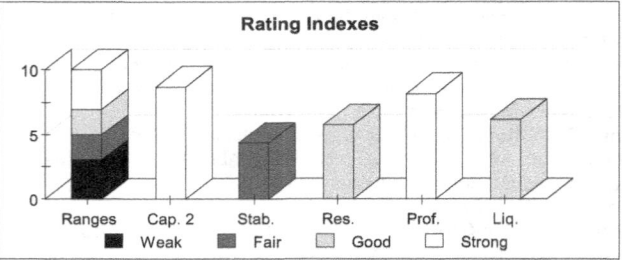

Rating Indexes

Ranges　Cap. 2　Stab.　Res.　Prof.　Liq.
■ Weak　■ Fair　□ Good　□ Strong

ATTORNEYS LIAB ASR SOCIETY INC RRG

D　　**Weak**

Major Rating Factors: Poor long-term capitalization index (1.7 on a scale of 0 to 10) based on weak current risk adjusted capital (severe and moderate loss scenarios). A history of deficient reserves (1.7). Underreserving can have an adverse impact on capital and profits. In 2014 and 2015 the two year reserve development was 53% and 70% deficient respectively.

Other Rating Factors: Weak overall results on stability tests (1.9) including weak risk adjusted capital in prior years and weak results on operational trends. The largest net exposure for one risk is high at 3.6% of capital. Good overall profitability index (5.4) despite operating losses during 2013 and 2014. Return on equity has been low, averaging 2.2% over the past five years. Excellent liquidity (7.0) with ample operational cash flow and liquid investments.

Principal Business: Other liability (100%).

Principal Investments: Misc. investments (55%), investment grade bonds (44%), and cash (1%).

Investments in Affiliates: 32%

Group Affiliation: Attorneys Liability Asr Soc Bermuda

Licensed in: All states except PR

Commenced Business: December 1987

Address: 148 College Street Suite 204, Burlington, VT 05401

Phone: (312) 697-6900　**Domicile State:** VT　**NAIC Code:** 10639

Data Date	Rating	RACR #1	RACR #2	Loss Ratio %	Total Assets ($mil)	Capital ($mil)	Net Premium ($mil)	Net Income ($mil)
3-17	D	0.49	0.39	N/A	2,203.2	629.0	48.8	12.7
3-16	D	0.31	0.24	N/A	2,133.4	548.3	50.9	-5.6
2016	D	0.46	0.37	79.0	1,933.5	604.5	206.2	37.7
2015	D	0.32	0.26	115.2	1,944.7	557.2	222.9	20.4
2014	D	0.45	0.36	111.6	2,036.0	594.1	243.3	-33.4
2013	C-	4.53	3.11	102.4	239.1	80.3	25.9	-3.2
2012	C-	3.66	2.62	85.9	153.7	59.2	23.2	5.3

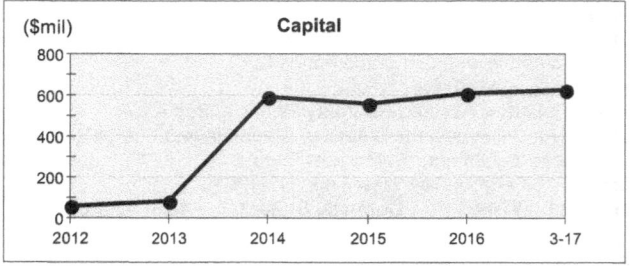

Capital

AUTO CLUB INDEMNITY CO *   B+   Good

Major Rating Factors: Good overall profitability index (6.5 on a scale of 0 to 10). Excellent expense controls. Return on equity has been low, averaging 0.9% over the past five years. Good overall results on stability tests (5.0) despite negative cash flow from operations for 2016. Stability strengths include good operational trends and excellent risk diversification.

Other Rating Factors: Strong long-term capitalization index (7.7) based on excellent current risk adjusted capital (severe and moderate loss scenarios), despite some fluctuation in capital levels. Superior liquidity (9.5) with ample operational cash flow and liquid investments.

Principal Business: Homeowners multiple peril (99%) and other liability (1%).

Principal Investments: Investment grade bonds (89%) and cash (11%).

Investments in Affiliates: None

Group Affiliation: Auto Club Enterprises Ins Group

Licensed in: TX

Commenced Business: December 1999

Address: 1225 FREEPORT PARKWAY, Coppell, TX 75019-4413

Phone: (714) 850-5111   **Domicile State:** TX   **NAIC Code:** 11008

Data Date	Rating	RACR #1	RACR #2	Loss Ratio %	Total Assets ($mil)	Capital ($mil)	Net Premium ($mil)	Net Income ($mil)
3-17	B+	1.53	1.38	N/A	25.9	5.4	0.0	0.0
3-16	B+	1.57	1.41	N/A	24.6	5.4	0.0	0.0
2016	B+	1.70	1.53	0.0	22.4	5.4	0.0	0.1
2015	B+	1.73	1.55	0.0	21.6	5.4	0.0	0.0
2014	B+	1.80	1.62	0.0	20.0	5.3	0.0	0.0
2013	B+	1.92	1.72	0.0	18.0	5.2	0.0	0.0
2012	B+	2.00	1.80	0.0	16.7	5.2	0.0	0.0

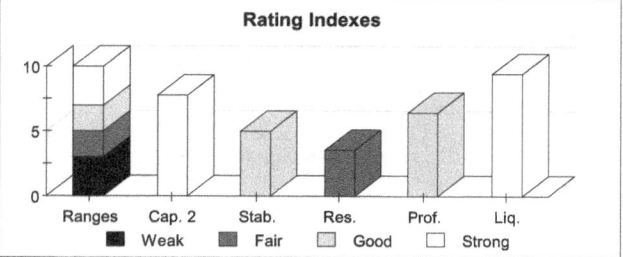

Rating Indexes

Ranges · Cap. 2 · Stab. · Res. · Prof. · Liq.
■ Weak ■ Fair ▨ Good □ Strong

AUTO CLUB INS ASSN   B   Good

Major Rating Factors: Good overall profitability index (5.8 on a scale of 0 to 10) despite operating losses during the first three months of 2017. Good liquidity (6.6) with sufficient resources (cash flows and marketable investments) to handle a spike in claims.

Other Rating Factors: Fair overall results on stability tests (4.9) including potential drain of affiliation with Automobile Club of Michigan Group and weak results on operational trends. Fair reserve development (4.7) as reserves have generally been sufficient to cover claims. Strong long-term capitalization index (7.9) based on excellent current risk adjusted capital (severe and moderate loss scenarios), despite some fluctuation in capital levels.

Principal Business: Auto liability (38%), homeowners multiple peril (35%), auto physical damage (26%), and other liability (1%).

Principal Investments: Investment grade bonds (49%), misc. investments (44%), non investment grade bonds (7%), and real estate (1%).

Investments in Affiliates: 18%

Group Affiliation: Automobile Club of Michigan Group

Licensed in: IL, MI, MN, NE, NY, ND, PA, WI

Commenced Business: March 1922

Address: 1 Auto Club Drive, Dearborn, MI 48126

Phone: (313) 336-1234   **Domicile State:** MI   **NAIC Code:** 21202

Data Date	Rating	RACR #1	RACR #2	Loss Ratio %	Total Assets ($mil)	Capital ($mil)	Net Premium ($mil)	Net Income ($mil)
3-17	B	2.07	1.61	N/A	4,174.1	1,817.5	378.0	-5.1
3-16	B	1.87	1.50	N/A	3,854.9	1,626.9	355.8	15.7
2016	B	2.10	1.66	69.4	4,074.6	1,809.4	1,492.1	97.0
2015	B	1.84	1.49	70.5	3,783.3	1,592.8	1,432.8	127.5
2014	B	1.82	1.46	77.5	3,673.6	1,524.8	1,355.0	51.3
2013	B	1.89	1.53	74.0	3,650.4	1,575.8	1,351.3	48.5
2012	B	1.89	1.57	86.3	3,350.4	1,526.3	1,229.1	18.2

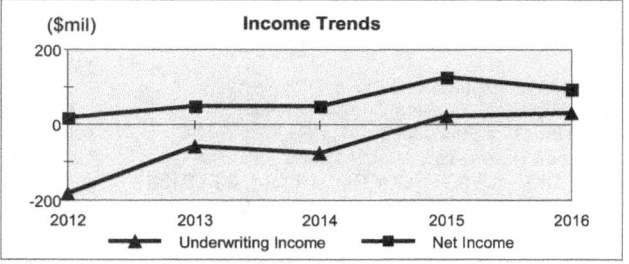

($mil)   Income Trends

2012 · 2013 · 2014 · 2015 · 2016
▲ Underwriting Income   ■ Net Income

AUTO-OWNERS INS CO *   A-   Excellent

Major Rating Factors: Strong long-term capitalization index (8.6 on a scale of 0 to 10) based on excellent current risk adjusted capital (severe and moderate loss scenarios). Furthermore, this high level of risk adjusted capital has been consistently maintained in previous years. Excellent profitability (8.2) with operating gains in each of the last five years.

Other Rating Factors: History of adequate reserve strength (6.1) as reserves have been consistently at an acceptable level. Good liquidity (6.9) with sufficient resources (cash flows and marketable investments) to handle a spike in claims. Good overall results on stability tests (5.7) despite weak results on operational trends.

Principal Business: Homeowners multiple peril (34%), auto liability (18%), auto physical damage (10%), commercial multiple peril (9%), fire (9%), workers compensation (6%), and other lines (13%).

Principal Investments: Misc. investments (50%), investment grade bonds (50%), and real estate (1%).

Investments in Affiliates: 29%

Group Affiliation: Auto-Owners Group

Licensed in: AL, AZ, AR, CO, FL, GA, ID, IL, IN, IA, KS, KY, MI, MN, MS, MO, NE, NV, NM, NC, ND, OH, OR, PA, SC, SD, TN, UT, VA, WA, WI

Commenced Business: July 1916

Address: 6101 ANACAPRI BOULEVARD, Lansing, MI 48917-3968

Phone: (517) 323-1200   **Domicile State:** MI   **NAIC Code:** 18988

Data Date	Rating	RACR #1	RACR #2	Loss Ratio %	Total Assets ($mil)	Capital ($mil)	Net Premium ($mil)	Net Income ($mil)
3-17	A-	2.38	2.06	N/A	14,502.3	9,939.5	799.7	106.5
3-16	A-	2.44	2.09	N/A	13,351.7	9,023.9	719.3	118.0
2016	A-	2.35	2.05	52.4	14,313.5	9,690.1	3,219.4	454.9
2015	A-	2.44	2.12	51.7	13,117.6	8,777.0	2,873.1	476.6
2014	A-	2.42	2.10	63.1	12,207.7	7,969.1	2,541.0	344.2
2013	A	2.42	2.08	60.9	11,392.8	7,510.8	2,325.4	340.3
2012	A	2.43	2.08	67.0	10,308.1	6,591.0	2,230.3	260.7

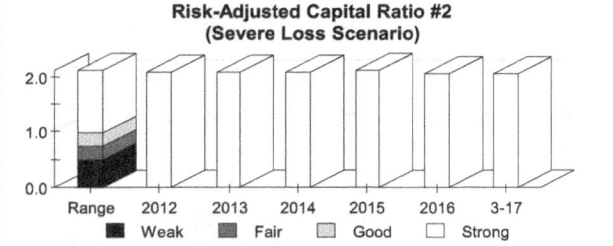

Risk-Adjusted Capital Ratio #2
(Severe Loss Scenario)

Range · 2012 · 2013 · 2014 · 2015 · 2016 · 3-17
■ Weak ■ Fair ▨ Good □ Strong

AUTOMOBILE CLUB INTERINSURANCE EXCH

C   **Fair**

Major Rating Factors: Fair profitability index (4.2 on a scale of 0 to 10) with operating losses during 2013 and the first three months of 2017. Fair overall results on stability tests (4.2) including fair financial strength of affiliated Auto Club Enterprises Ins Group and weak results on operational trends.

Other Rating Factors: Good liquidity (6.3) with sufficient resources (cash flows and marketable investments) to handle a spike in claims. Strong long-term capitalization index (8.6) based on excellent current risk adjusted capital (severe and moderate loss scenarios). Moreover, capital levels have been consistent in recent years. Ample reserve history (7.3) that can protect against increases in claims costs.

Principal Business: Auto liability (53%) and auto physical damage (46%).

Principal Investments: Misc. investments (51%), investment grade bonds (51%), non investment grade bonds (4%), and real estate (1%).

Investments in Affiliates: 14%

Group Affiliation: Auto Club Enterprises Ins Group

Licensed in: AL, AR, CA, IL, IN, KS, LA, MS, MO, OH

Commenced Business: April 1927

Address: 12901 NORTH FORTY DRIVE, St Louis, MO 63141-8634

Phone: (714) 850-5111   **Domicile State:** MO   **NAIC Code:** 15512

Data Date	Rating	RACR #1	RACR #2	Loss Ratio %	Total Assets ($mil)	Capital ($mil)	Net Premium ($mil)	Net Income ($mil)
3-17	C	2.74	2.05	N/A	445.8	228.7	34.4	-2.2
3-16	C	2.74	2.06	N/A	414.1	208.1	31.8	-2.4
2016	C	2.77	2.08	79.4	434.5	226.3	137.3	-2.1
2015	C	2.79	2.12	71.9	406.3	209.9	127.0	5.1
2014	C	2.78	2.10	71.6	402.1	205.7	120.6	9.4
2013	C	2.71	2.03	71.1	415.9	198.0	115.9	-5.3
2012	C	3.10	2.37	72.4	414.6	188.0	110.0	7.6

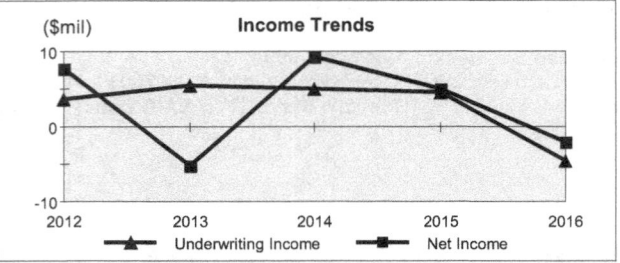

AUTOMOBILE INS CO OF HARTFORD CT

B   **Good**

Major Rating Factors: Good overall profitability index (6.1 on a scale of 0 to 10). Fair expense controls. Return on equity has been good over the last five years, averaging 12.8%. Good liquidity (6.7) with sufficient resources (cash flows and marketable investments) to handle a spike in claims.

Other Rating Factors: Fair overall results on stability tests (4.7) including weak results on operational trends. Affiliation with Travelers Companies Inc is a strength. Strong long-term capitalization index (8.3) based on excellent current risk adjusted capital (severe and moderate loss scenarios), despite some fluctuation in capital levels. Ample reserve history (8.4) that helps to protect the company against sharp claims increases.

Principal Business: Homeowners multiple peril (46%), fire (13%), auto liability (11%), other liability (11%), allied lines (10%), auto physical damage (9%), and inland marine (1%).

Principal Investments: Investment grade bonds (98%) and misc. investments (2%).

Investments in Affiliates: None

Group Affiliation: Travelers Companies Inc

Licensed in: All states except CA, PR

Commenced Business: August 1968

Address: ONE TOWER SQUARE, Hartford, CT 06183

Phone: (860) 277-0111   **Domicile State:** CT   **NAIC Code:** 19062

Data Date	Rating	RACR #1	RACR #2	Loss Ratio %	Total Assets ($mil)	Capital ($mil)	Net Premium ($mil)	Net Income ($mil)
3-17	B	2.89	1.88	N/A	1,021.0	323.7	73.9	7.2
3-16	B	2.96	1.87	N/A	1,016.7	329.8	71.2	7.4
2016	B	2.90	1.89	63.4	1,006.6	316.4	298.3	35.6
2015	B	2.97	1.89	58.7	1,008.5	322.4	284.7	43.1
2014	B	2.97	1.87	60.5	1,013.2	320.8	276.6	43.1
2013	B	2.99	1.90	60.9	1,002.2	317.3	275.9	47.3
2012	B	2.83	1.82	68.4	983.1	295.1	268.0	36.1

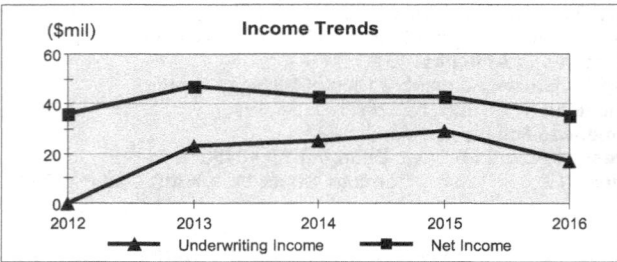

AXIS INS CO

B   **Good**

Major Rating Factors: History of adequate reserve strength (6.9 on a scale of 0 to 10) as reserves have been consistently at an acceptable level. Good liquidity (6.9) with sufficient resources (cash flows and marketable investments) to handle a spike in claims.

Other Rating Factors: Fair overall results on stability tests (4.2) including potential drain of affiliation with AXIS Specialty Ltd and weak results on operational trends. The largest net exposure for one risk is conservative at 1.6% of capital. Fair profitability index (4.1) with operating losses during 2012, 2013, 2014 and the first three months of 2017. Return on equity has been low, averaging 0.2% over the past five years. Strong long-term capitalization index (7.9) based on excellent current risk adjusted capital (severe and moderate loss scenarios), despite some fluctuation in capital levels.

Principal Business: Other liability (63%), group accident & health (8%), fire (7%), allied lines (7%), inland marine (3%), commercial multiple peril (2%), and other lines (10%).

Principal Investments: Investment grade bonds (82%), misc. investments (17%), and cash (1%).

Investments in Affiliates: 19%

Group Affiliation: AXIS Specialty Ltd

Licensed in: All states except PR

Commenced Business: November 1979

Address: 111 South Wacker Dr Ste 3500, Chicago, IL 60606

Phone: (678) 746-9400   **Domicile State:** IL   **NAIC Code:** 37273

Data Date	Rating	RACR #1	RACR #2	Loss Ratio %	Total Assets ($mil)	Capital ($mil)	Net Premium ($mil)	Net Income ($mil)
3-17	B	2.00	1.53	N/A	1,508.9	567.4	80.8	-7.9
3-16	B	1.93	1.27	N/A	1,545.9	563.7	75.9	-5.5
2016	B	2.05	1.58	68.0	1,505.4	574.5	313.7	13.9
2015	B	1.96	1.29	62.2	1,488.0	565.1	307.5	32.1
2014	C+	1.91	1.28	78.0	1,483.8	578.1	282.3	-2.1
2013	C+	1.79	1.25	80.0	1,366.0	526.2	306.8	-10.1
2012	C+	1.94	1.52	80.0	1,196.5	538.9	227.4	-17.5

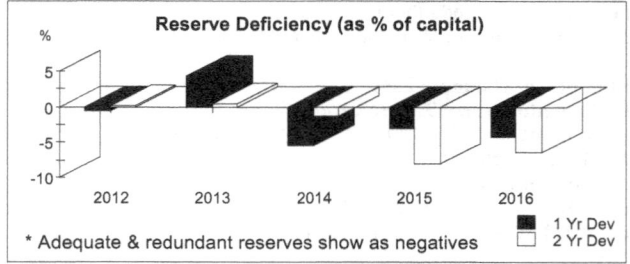

AXIS REINS CO   C+   Fair

Major Rating Factors: Fair overall results on stability tests (4.2 on a scale of 0 to 10) including potential drain of affiliation with AXIS Specialty Ltd and weak results on operational trends. Good overall profitability index (5.2) despite operating losses during the first three months of 2017. Return on equity has been low, averaging 4.0% over the past five years.

Other Rating Factors: Strong long-term capitalization index (7.9) based on excellent current risk adjusted capital (severe and moderate loss scenarios), despite some fluctuation in capital levels. Ample reserve history (9.3) that helps to protect the company against sharp claims increases. Excellent liquidity (7.0) with ample operational cash flow and liquid investments.

Principal Business: Other liability (86%), allied lines (5%), fidelity (4%), medical malpractice (3%), and fire (2%).

Principal Investments: Investment grade bonds (67%), misc. investments (25%), non investment grade bonds (6%), and cash (2%).

Investments in Affiliates: None

Group Affiliation: AXIS Specialty Ltd

Licensed in: All states, the District of Columbia and Puerto Rico

Commenced Business: January 1992

Address: 1211 Ave of Americas 24th Fl, New York, NY 10036

Phone: (678) 746-9400   **Domicile State:** NY   **NAIC Code:** 20370

Data Date	Rating	RACR #1	RACR #2	Loss Ratio %	Total Assets ($mil)	Capital ($mil)	Net Premium ($mil)	Net Income ($mil)
3-17	C+	2.63	1.60	N/A	3,236.5	900.1	141.3	-3.0
3-16	C+	2.61	1.59	N/A	2,991.8	865.0	122.8	-16.6
2016	C+	2.68	1.63	71.3	3,003.2	896.2	531.8	17.2
2015	C+	2.69	1.64	68.1	2,863.3	860.9	513.4	24.6
2014	C+	2.63	1.62	73.7	2,872.8	864.9	528.4	40.5
2013	C+	2.74	1.71	57.8	2,675.9	822.7	494.2	58.0
2012	C+	2.27	1.35	69.4	2,501.2	756.8	407.5	35.0

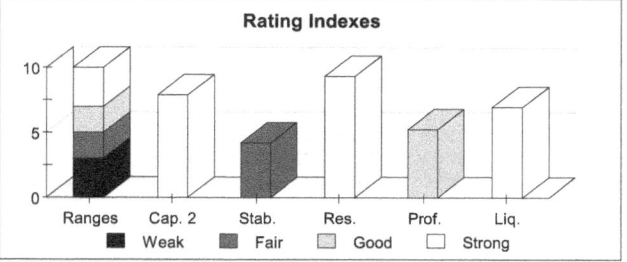

Rating Indexes

BAY STATE INS CO   B-   Good

Major Rating Factors: Fair overall results on stability tests (4.5 on a scale of 0 to 10) including potential drain of affiliation with Andover Group and weak results on operational trends. History of adequate reserve strength (6.4) as reserves have been consistently at an acceptable level.

Other Rating Factors: Strong long-term capitalization index (8.3) based on excellent current risk adjusted capital (severe and moderate loss scenarios), despite some fluctuation in capital levels. Excellent profitability (8.1) with operating gains in each of the last five years. Excellent liquidity (7.3) with ample operational cash flow and liquid investments.

Principal Business: Homeowners multiple peril (86%), other liability (5%), commercial multiple peril (4%), and inland marine (4%).

Principal Investments: Misc. investments (73%), investment grade bonds (14%), and cash (13%).

Investments in Affiliates: None

Group Affiliation: Andover Group

Licensed in: CT, IL, ME, MA, NH, NJ, NY, RI

Commenced Business: July 1955

Address: 95 Old River Road, Andover, MA 01810-1078

Phone: (978) 475-3300   **Domicile State:** MA   **NAIC Code:** 19763

Data Date	Rating	RACR #1	RACR #2	Loss Ratio %	Total Assets ($mil)	Capital ($mil)	Net Premium ($mil)	Net Income ($mil)
3-17	B-	3.19	1.93	N/A	493.9	317.6	19.1	11.6
3-16	B-	3.26	1.97	N/A	439.2	280.4	18.6	2.2
2016	B-	3.13	1.89	50.9	476.0	300.0	80.9	15.3
2015	B-	3.23	1.95	68.5	450.4	284.5	77.8	4.8
2014	B-	3.17	1.93	43.4	456.7	287.3	78.5	15.9
2013	B-	3.33	2.06	43.3	412.6	260.3	73.9	16.6
2012	B-	3.36	2.13	64.9	361.4	217.4	71.9	5.9

Andover Group
Composite Group Rating: B-

Largest Group Members	Assets ($mil)	Rating
MERRIMACK MUTUAL FIRE INS CO	1467	B-
CAMBRIDGE MUTUAL FIRE INS CO	877	B-
BAY STATE INS CO	476	B-

BERKLEY INS CO   B   Good

Major Rating Factors: Good overall results on stability tests (5.1 on a scale of 0 to 10) despite potential drain of affiliation with W R Berkley Corp and weak results on operational trends. Good liquidity (6.9) with sufficient resources (cash flows and marketable investments) to handle a spike in claims.

Other Rating Factors: Strong long-term capitalization index (7.3) based on excellent current risk adjusted capital (severe and moderate loss scenarios), despite some fluctuation in capital levels. Ample reserve history (8.0) that helps to protect the company against sharp claims increases. Excellent profitability (7.7) with operating gains in each of the last five years. Return on equity has been excellent over the last five years averaging 15.1%.

Principal Business: Other liability (74%), surety (16%), other accident & health (5%), auto liability (3%), and medical malpractice (1%).

Principal Investments: Investment grade bonds (56%), misc. investments (39%), non investment grade bonds (2%), real estate (2%), and cash (1%).

Investments in Affiliates: 20%

Group Affiliation: W R Berkley Corp

Licensed in: All states, the District of Columbia and Puerto Rico

Commenced Business: December 1975

Address: 1209 Orange Street, Wilmington, DE 19801

Phone: (203) 542-3800   **Domicile State:** DE   **NAIC Code:** 32603

Data Date	Rating	RACR #1	RACR #2	Loss Ratio %	Total Assets ($mil)	Capital ($mil)	Net Premium ($mil)	Net Income ($mil)
3-17	B	1.33	1.11	N/A	17,896.8	5,028.8	1,396.9	121.8
3-16	B-	1.31	1.06	N/A	17,171.2	4,856.9	1,324.5	91.6
2016	B	1.47	1.24	60.6	17,940.5	5,493.0	5,711.5	702.8
2015	C+	1.44	1.17	56.5	17,109.3	5,295.6	5,338.8	765.4
2014	C	1.40	1.15	59.3	16,934.1	5,437.2	5,070.0	710.5
2013	C	1.38	1.09	61.6	16,122.7	4,907.2	5,744.1	1,493.8
2012	C	1.44	1.31	67.3	10,223.8	4,656.3	1,719.3	294.5

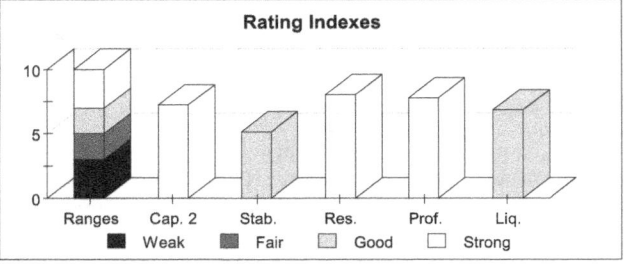

Rating Indexes

BERKLEY REGIONAL INS CO — C+ — Fair

Major Rating Factors: Fair overall results on stability tests (4.5) including fair financial strength of affiliated W R Berkley Corp and weak results on operational trends.

Other Rating Factors: Good overall profitability index (6.9). Fair expense controls. Return on equity has been fair, averaging 8.4% over the past five years. Strong long-term capitalization index (7.9) based on excellent current risk adjusted capital (severe and moderate loss scenarios), despite some fluctuation in capital levels. Excellent liquidity (7.0) with ample operational cash flow and liquid investments.

Principal Business: Fidelity (26%), workers compensation (24%), auto liability (17%), commercial multiple peril (15%), auto physical damage (6%), burglary & theft (4%), and other lines (7%).

Principal Investments: Misc. investments (53%) and investment grade bonds (47%).

Investments in Affiliates: 48%

Group Affiliation: W R Berkley Corp

Licensed in: All states except PR

Commenced Business: January 1987

Address: 1209 Orange Street, Wilmington, DE 19801

Phone: (515) 473-3000 **Domicile State:** DE **NAIC Code:** 29580

Data Date	Rating	RACR #1	RACR #2	Loss Ratio %	Total Assets ($mil)	Capital ($mil)	Net Premium ($mil)	Net Income ($mil)
3-17	C+	1.41	1.40	N/A	755.9	714.3	0.0	2.8
3-16	C+	1.53	1.52	N/A	717.5	686.4	0.0	2.6
2016	C+	1.61	1.77	0.0	748.2	706.9	0.0	13.0
2015	C+	1.73	1.88	0.0	711.6	679.9	0.0	11.6
2014	C+	1.75	1.90	0.0	700.4	666.6	0.0	11.0
2013	C+	1.89	2.08	0.0	681.2	643.2	-547.4	134.5
2012	B	1.39	1.17	58.7	2,700.8	717.3	1,185.6	127.2

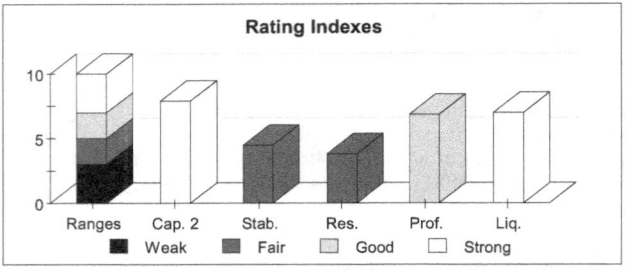

Rating Indexes

BERKSHIRE HATHAWAY ASR CORP * — A+ — Excellent

Major Rating Factors: Strong long-term capitalization index (9.6 on a scale of 0 to 10) based on excellent current risk adjusted capital (severe and moderate loss scenarios). Furthermore, this high level of risk adjusted capital has been consistently maintained in previous years. Excellent profitability (8.6) with operating gains in each of the last five years.

Other Rating Factors: Superior liquidity (10.0) with ample operational cash flow and liquid investments. Excellent overall results on stability tests (7.6). Stability strengths include excellent risk diversification. Fair reserve development (4.6) as reserves have generally been sufficient to cover claims.

Principal Business: Financial guaranty (90%) and surety (10%).

Principal Investments: Misc. investments (64%), investment grade bonds (34%), and cash (2%).

Investments in Affiliates: None

Group Affiliation: Berkshire-Hathaway

Licensed in: All states, the District of Columbia and Puerto Rico

Commenced Business: December 2007

Address: Marine Air Terminal LaGuardia, Flushing, NY 11371

Phone: (402) 916-3000 **Domicile State:** NY **NAIC Code:** 13070

Data Date	Rating	RACR #1	RACR #2	Loss Ratio %	Total Assets ($mil)	Capital ($mil)	Net Premium ($mil)	Net Income ($mil)
3-17	A+	4.96	2.97	N/A	2,454.3	1,869.2	14.3	4.7
3-16	A+	4.08	2.44	N/A	2,181.7	1,447.3	12.1	3.7
2016	A+	4.56	2.73	9.7	2,351.4	1,793.8	2.9	254.1
2015	A+	4.18	2.50	N/A	2,176.5	1,449.3	12.9	78.1
2014	A+	4.11	2.46	1.7	2,275.7	1,459.6	2.3	95.2
2013	A+	4.45	2.64	31.1	2,255.6	1,426.8	12.4	195.5
2012	A+	6.70	3.41	0.0	1,841.2	1,149.3	10.2	78.1

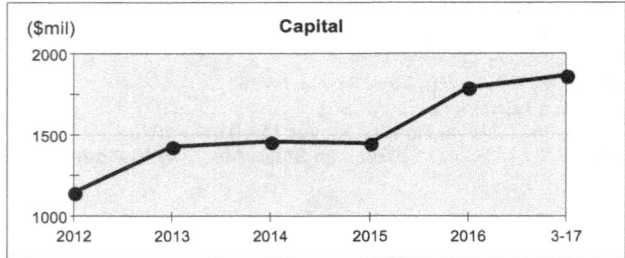

Capital

BERKSHIRE HATHAWAY HOMESTATE INS — C+ — Fair

Major Rating Factors: Fair overall results on stability tests (4.1 on a scale of 0 to 10) including potential drain of affiliation with Berkshire-Hathaway and weak results on operational trends. The largest net exposure for one risk is conservative at 1.8% of capital. History of adequate reserve strength (6.1) as reserves have been consistently at an acceptable level.

Other Rating Factors: Strong long-term capitalization index (7.6) based on excellent current risk adjusted capital (severe and moderate loss scenarios). Moreover, capital levels have been consistent in recent years. Excellent profitability (8.0) with operating gains in each of the last five years. Excellent liquidity (7.7) with ample operational cash flow and liquid investments.

Principal Business: Workers compensation (70%), auto liability (15%), commercial multiple peril (7%), auto physical damage (4%), allied lines (2%), fire (2%), and inland marine (1%).

Principal Investments: Misc. investments (68%), investment grade bonds (24%), and cash (8%).

Investments in Affiliates: None

Group Affiliation: Berkshire-Hathaway

Licensed in: All states except PR

Commenced Business: February 1970

Address: 1314 Douglas Street, Omaha, NE 68102

Phone: (402) 393-7255 **Domicile State:** NE **NAIC Code:** 20044

Data Date	Rating	RACR #1	RACR #2	Loss Ratio %	Total Assets ($mil)	Capital ($mil)	Net Premium ($mil)	Net Income ($mil)
3-17	C+	2.46	1.46	N/A	2,541.9	1,310.1	108.4	21.4
3-16	C+	2.60	1.57	N/A	2,087.6	1,105.4	108.4	14.8
2016	C+	2.38	1.41	87.4	2,467.2	1,257.5	441.4	4.0
2015	C+	2.69	1.62	70.4	2,175.0	1,167.7	461.5	55.7
2014	C+	1.63	1.04	64.5	2,008.1	1,159.5	376.5	152.7
2013	C+	1.23	0.80	77.8	1,587.5	963.8	280.1	22.4
2012	C+	1.94	1.25	77.0	1,254.2	884.8	179.5	3.6

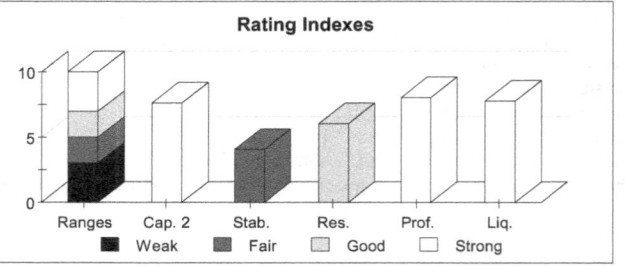

Rating Indexes

BERKSHIRE HATHAWAY SPECIALTY INS CO   C+   Fair

Major Rating Factors: Fair reserve development (4.9 on a scale of 0 to 10) as reserves have generally been sufficient to cover claims. Fair profitability index (3.9) with operating losses during 2012 and 2016. Average return on equity over the last five years has been poor at -0.1%.

Other Rating Factors: Fair overall results on stability tests (3.5) including fair financial strength of affiliated Berkshire-Hathaway, excessive premium growth and weak results on operational trends. The largest net exposure for one risk is high at 3.7% of capital. Strong long-term capitalization index (9.6) based on excellent current risk adjusted capital (severe and moderate loss scenarios), despite some fluctuation in capital levels. Superior liquidity (9.3) with ample operational cash flow and liquid investments.

Principal Business: Other liability (56%), workers compensation (9%), fire (7%), auto liability (7%), commercial multiple peril (6%), surety (4%), and other lines (11%).

Principal Investments: Misc. investments (54%), cash (24%), and investment grade bonds (22%).

Investments in Affiliates: None

Group Affiliation: Berkshire-Hathaway

Licensed in: All states, the District of Columbia and Puerto Rico

Commenced Business: February 1866

Address: 1314 Douglas Street Suite 1400, Omaha, NE 68102-1944

Phone: (402) 916-3000   **Domicile State:** NE   **NAIC Code:** 22276

Data Date	Rating	RACR #1	RACR #2	Loss Ratio %	Total Assets ($mil)	Capital ($mil)	Net Premium ($mil)	Net Income ($mil)
3-17	C+	5.10	3.07	N/A	4,330.5	3,399.6	65.5	10.6
3-16	C+	4.13	2.48	N/A	3,372.8	3,003.3	23.8	2.7
2016	C+	4.47	2.69	70.5	4,086.5	3,337.1	267.4	-58.0
2015	C+	4.32	2.60	75.7	3,371.4	3,044.1	95.5	37.7
2014	C+	4.11	2.46	N/A	3,521.6	3,234.1	0.7	7.6
2013	C+	3.20	1.92	156.6	3,357.7	3,106.7	1.6	0.2
2012	C+	1.81	0.86	339.9	90.2	71.3	2.3	-0.5

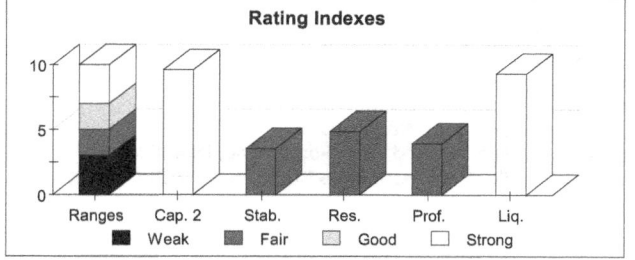

Rating Indexes

BITCO GENERAL INS CORP   B   Good

Major Rating Factors: Good overall profitability index (6.8 on a scale of 0 to 10) despite modest operating losses during the first three months of 2017. Return on equity has been good over the last five years, averaging 10.5%. Good liquidity (6.8) with sufficient resources (cash flows and marketable investments) to handle a spike in claims.

Other Rating Factors: Fair overall results on stability tests (4.8) including weak results on operational trends and excessive premium growth. Strong long-term capitalization index (8.3) based on excellent current risk adjusted capital (severe and moderate loss scenarios), despite some fluctuation in capital levels. Ample reserve history (8.7) that helps to protect the company against sharp claims increases.

Principal Business: Workers compensation (35%), auto liability (20%), commercial multiple peril (19%), other liability (11%), auto physical damage (8%), and inland marine (7%).

Principal Investments: Investment grade bonds (70%), misc. investments (24%), and non investment grade bonds (6%).

Investments in Affiliates: None

Group Affiliation: Old Republic Group

Licensed in: All states except HI, NH, PR

Commenced Business: August 1928

Address: PO BOX 7146, Rock Island, IL 61201

Phone: (800) 475-4477   **Domicile State:** IL   **NAIC Code:** 20095

Data Date	Rating	RACR #1	RACR #2	Loss Ratio %	Total Assets ($mil)	Capital ($mil)	Net Premium ($mil)	Net Income ($mil)
3-17	B	2.88	1.77	N/A	886.0	291.8	79.6	-0.5
3-16	B	3.04	1.90	N/A	839.6	286.0	57.2	5.6
2016	B	3.13	1.92	72.5	851.8	295.6	231.5	24.1
2015	B	3.08	1.95	71.9	820.8	275.1	237.6	27.2
2014	B	3.45	2.20	71.2	810.9	288.5	230.2	42.5
2013	A-	3.87	2.49	67.2	788.4	290.2	204.3	39.5
2012	A-	4.18	2.58	65.0	719.8	274.2	178.1	24.3

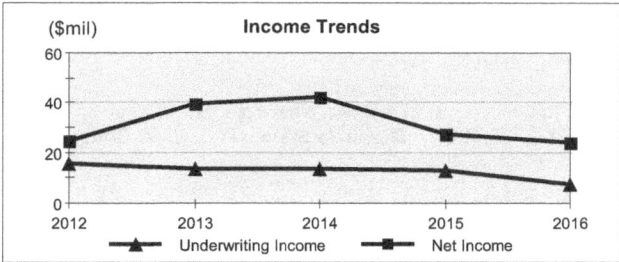

($mil) Income Trends

BRICKSTREET MUTUAL INS CO   B-   Good

Major Rating Factors: Good overall results on stability tests (5.0 on a scale of 0 to 10) despite excessive premium growth. Strong long-term capitalization index (8.5) based on excellent current risk adjusted capital (severe and moderate loss scenarios). Moreover, capital levels have been consistent in recent years.

Other Rating Factors: Ample reserve history (9.5) that helps to protect the company against sharp claims increases. Excellent profitability (8.6) with operating gains in each of the last five years. Excellent liquidity (7.1) with ample operational cash flow and liquid investments.

Principal Business: Workers compensation (100%).

Principal Investments: Investment grade bonds (87%), misc. investments (11%), cash (1%), and real estate (1%).

Investments in Affiliates: 2%

Group Affiliation: BrickStreet Mutual Ins

Licensed in: AL, DC, DE, GA, IL, IN, IA, KS, KY, MD, MO, NJ, NC, PA, SC, TN, VA, WV

Commenced Business: January 2006

Address: 400 Quarrier St, Charleston, WV 25301

Phone: (304) 941-1000   **Domicile State:** WV   **NAIC Code:** 12372

Data Date	Rating	RACR #1	RACR #2	Loss Ratio %	Total Assets ($mil)	Capital ($mil)	Net Premium ($mil)	Net Income ($mil)
3-17	B-	2.73	1.90	N/A	2,228.6	769.5	88.5	8.1
3-16	C	3.10	2.03	N/A	1,921.0	714.7	62.9	10.4
2016	C+	2.89	2.00	69.6	2,182.6	756.1	337.9	42.1
2015	C	3.15	2.06	69.2	1,918.4	705.8	245.0	49.2
2014	C-	2.35	0.88	76.1	1,886.9	658.9	290.2	50.9
2013	C-	2.38	0.88	75.1	1,791.0	603.7	301.3	49.6
2012	C-	2.52	0.86	64.8	1,703.1	552.6	287.6	36.8

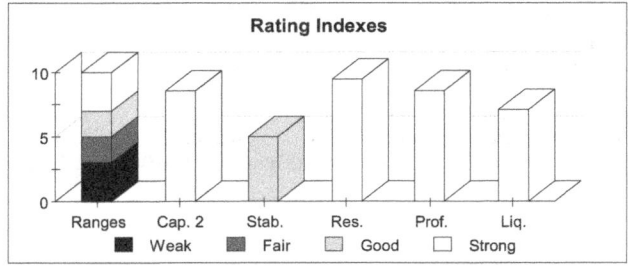

Rating Indexes

BROTHERHOOD MUTUAL INS CO *

B+   **Good**

Major Rating Factors: History of adequate reserve strength (5.0 on a scale of 0 to 10) as reserves have been consistently at an acceptable level. Good overall profitability index (5.7) despite operating losses during the first three months of 2017.

Other Rating Factors: Good liquidity (5.6) with sufficient resources (cash flows and marketable investments) to handle a spike in claims. Good overall results on stability tests (6.5). Strong long-term capitalization index (8.0) based on excellent current risk adjusted capital (severe and moderate loss scenarios), despite some fluctuation in capital levels.

Principal Business: Commercial multiple peril (73%), workers compensation (13%), auto liability (5%), other liability (4%), boiler & machinery (3%), and auto physical damage (2%).

Principal Investments: Misc. investments (48%), investment grade bonds (45%), real estate (6%), and cash (1%).

Investments in Affiliates: None

Group Affiliation: None

Licensed in: All states except PR

Commenced Business: November 1935

Address: 6400 Brotherhood Way, Fort Wayne, IN 46825

Phone: (260) 482-8668   **Domicile State:** IN   **NAIC Code:** 13528

Data Date	Rating	RACR #1	RACR #2	Loss Ratio %	Total Assets ($mil)	Capital ($mil)	Net Premium ($mil)	Net Income ($mil)
3-17	B+	2.04	1.56	N/A	591.8	242.2	84.6	-7.1
3-16	B	2.30	1.79	N/A	533.9	231.0	79.3	3.2
2016	B+	2.17	1.67	62.2	600.7	244.7	341.1	12.2
2015	B	2.35	1.83	61.0	542.0	229.1	304.9	19.1
2014	B	2.02	1.54	66.2	469.7	189.4	277.3	10.0
2013	A-	2.01	1.53	64.5	443.3	178.2	252.5	9.5
2012	A-	2.31	1.80	62.5	384.9	159.7	217.3	7.3

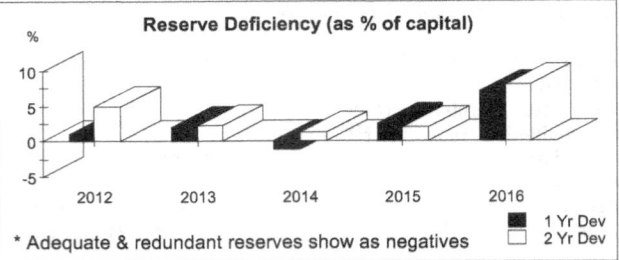

Reserve Deficiency (as % of capital)

* Adequate & redundant reserves show as negatives   ■ 1 Yr Dev   □ 2 Yr Dev

BUILD AMERICA MUTUAL ASR CO

D+   **Weak**

Major Rating Factors: Weak profitability index (2.3) with operating losses during each of the last five years and the first three months of 2017.

Other Rating Factors: Weak overall results on stability tests (1.1) including excessive premium growth, weak results on operational trends and negative cash flow from operations for 2016. The largest net exposure for one risk is excessive at 78.9% of capital. Strong long-term capitalization index (10.0) based on excellent current risk adjusted capital (severe and moderate loss scenarios), despite some fluctuation in capital levels. Superior liquidity (10.0) with ample operational cash flow and liquid investments.

Principal Business: Financial guaranty (100%).

Principal Investments: Investment grade bonds (93%), misc. investments (5%), and cash (2%).

Investments in Affiliates: None

Group Affiliation: None

Licensed in: All states except PR

Commenced Business: July 2012

Address: 200 Liberty St 27th Floor, New York, NY 10281

Phone: (212) 235-2500   **Domicile State:** NY   **NAIC Code:** 14380

Data Date	Rating	RACR #1	RACR #2	Loss Ratio %	Total Assets ($mil)	Capital ($mil)	Net Premium ($mil)	Net Income ($mil)
3-17	D+	9.59	9.20	N/A	504.2	432.7	0.2	-5.6
3-16	D+	10.02	9.71	N/A	475.0	433.4	0.1	-8.2
2016	D+	10.89	10.36	0.0	496.7	431.5	11.4	-32.7
2015	D+	11.84	11.38	0.0	479.6	437.3	6.3	-32.0
2014	D+	12.00	11.69	0.0	475.7	448.8	3.6	-31.8
2013	D+	14.08	13.68	0.0	486.5	469.0	3.0	-29.3
2012	A+	24.08	23.22	0.0	491.2	483.7	0.0	-18.2

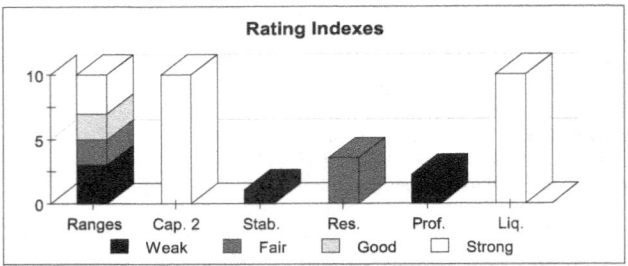

Rating Indexes

■ Weak   ▨ Fair   ▤ Good   □ Strong

BUILDERS INS (A MUTUAL CAPTIVE CO)

C   **Fair**

Major Rating Factors: Fair overall results on stability tests (3.5 on a scale of 0 to 10) including potential drain of affiliation with Builders Financial Group Inc. Good liquidity (6.9) with sufficient resources (cash flows and marketable investments) to handle a spike in claims.

Other Rating Factors: Strong long-term capitalization index (8.1) based on excellent current risk adjusted capital (severe and moderate loss scenarios). Moreover, capital levels have been consistent in recent years. Ample reserve history (9.3) that helps to protect the company against sharp claims increases. Excellent profitability (8.5) with operating gains in each of the last five years.

Principal Business: Workers compensation (82%), other liability (12%), and commercial multiple peril (6%).

Principal Investments: Investment grade bonds (63%), misc. investments (34%), real estate (2%), and cash (1%).

Investments in Affiliates: 13%

Group Affiliation: Builders Financial Group Inc

Licensed in: DE, FL, GA, NC, TX

Commenced Business: July 1996

Address: 2410 Paces Ferry Road Ste 300, Atlanta, GA 30339-1802

Phone: (678) 309-4000   **Domicile State:** GA   **NAIC Code:** 10704

Data Date	Rating	RACR #1	RACR #2	Loss Ratio %	Total Assets ($mil)	Capital ($mil)	Net Premium ($mil)	Net Income ($mil)
3-17	C	2.38	1.81	N/A	592.6	260.8	38.6	1.7
3-16	C	2.30	1.75	N/A	536.4	233.1	37.2	2.9
2016	C	2.40	1.84	59.5	579.3	254.9	154.8	17.6
2015	C	2.30	1.77	54.6	518.1	227.3	144.7	19.9
2014	C	1.96	1.47	62.9	482.6	201.8	141.3	13.9
2013	C	1.78	1.34	69.8	441.6	185.9	125.9	7.2
2012	C	1.60	1.20	67.2	406.7	170.0	106.3	4.8

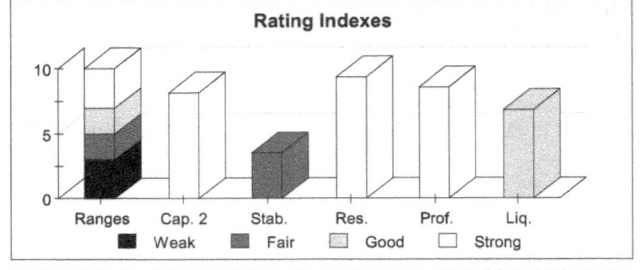

Rating Indexes

■ Weak   ▨ Fair   ▤ Good   □ Strong

BUILDERS MUTUAL INS CO *   A-   Excellent

Major Rating Factors: Strong long-term capitalization index (7.9 on a scale of 0 to 10) based on excellent current risk adjusted capital (severe and moderate loss scenarios). Furthermore, this high level of risk adjusted capital has been consistently maintained in previous years. Ample reserve history (8.5) that helps to protect the company against sharp claims increases.

Other Rating Factors: Excellent profitability (8.7) with operating gains in each of the last five years. Excellent overall results on stability tests (7.3). Stability strengths include excellent operational trends and excellent risk diversification. Good liquidity (6.7) with sufficient resources (cash flows and marketable investments) to handle a spike in claims.

Principal Business: Workers compensation (75%), commercial multiple peril (12%), products liability (5%), other liability (3%), inland marine (3%), and auto liability (2%).

Principal Investments: Investment grade bonds (71%), misc. investments (27%), and cash (2%).

Investments in Affiliates: 2%

Group Affiliation: Builders Group

Licensed in: DC, FL, GA, MD, MS, NC, SC, TN, VA, WI

Commenced Business: September 1997

Address: 5580 Centerview Drive, Raleigh, NC 27606

Phone: (919) 845-1976   **Domicile State:** NC   **NAIC Code:** 10844

Data Date	Rating	RACR #1	RACR #2	Loss Ratio %	Total Assets ($mil)	Capital ($mil)	Net Premium ($mil)	Net Income ($mil)
3-17	A-	2.24	1.61	N/A	803.9	319.8	71.4	5.4
3-16	B+	2.32	1.69	N/A	715.7	288.2	64.4	4.7
2016	A-	2.25	1.62	63.9	779.8	310.0	284.3	19.6
2015	B+	2.37	1.72	63.1	701.7	281.6	246.8	19.9
2014	B+	2.29	1.63	62.3	638.7	262.6	215.5	18.3
2013	B+	2.24	1.56	61.5	576.4	242.0	181.7	13.4
2012	B+	2.30	1.60	64.8	536.2	218.7	148.4	10.2

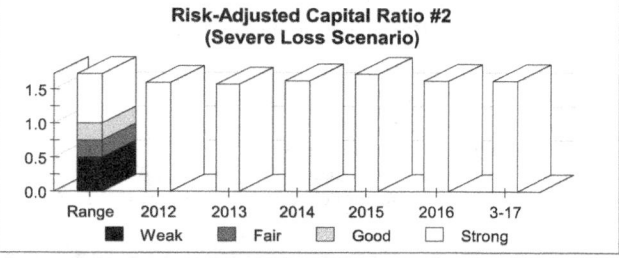

Risk-Adjusted Capital Ratio #2
(Severe Loss Scenario)

Range / 2012 / 2013 / 2014 / 2015 / 2016 / 3-17
■ Weak   ▨ Fair   ▢ Good   ☐ Strong

CALIFORNIA AUTOMOBILE INS CO   B   Good

Major Rating Factors: Good long-term capitalization index (6.9 on a scale of 0 to 10) based on good current risk adjusted capital (moderate loss scenario), despite some fluctuation in capital levels. Fair reserve development (4.2) as reserves have generally been sufficient to cover claims.

Other Rating Factors: Fair overall results on stability tests (4.0) including weak results on operational trends. The largest net exposure for one risk is high at 3.7% of capital. Weak profitability index (2.9) with operating losses during 2012, 2013, 2014, 2015 and the first three months of 2017. Average return on equity over the last five years has been poor at -6.4%. Vulnerable liquidity (2.6) as a spike in claims may stretch capacity.

Principal Business: Homeowners multiple peril (41%), auto liability (36%), and auto physical damage (24%).

Principal Investments: Investment grade bonds (96%), misc. investments (9%), and non investment grade bonds (1%).

Investments in Affiliates: 3%

Group Affiliation: Mercury General Group

Licensed in: CA

Commenced Business: August 1992

Address: 555 West Imperial Highway, Brea, CA 92821

Phone: (714) 671-6600   **Domicile State:** CA   **NAIC Code:** 38342

Data Date	Rating	RACR #1	RACR #2	Loss Ratio %	Total Assets ($mil)	Capital ($mil)	Net Premium ($mil)	Net Income ($mil)
3-17	B	1.28	0.96	N/A	745.8	190.7	158.5	-16.8
3-16	B	1.50	1.21	N/A	589.7	174.0	131.1	8.1
2016	B	1.50	1.10	76.0	739.3	206.6	600.2	7.8
2015	B	1.35	1.08	77.5	637.3	165.3	634.4	-15.3
2014	B	1.11	0.97	77.4	436.4	114.5	477.3	-5.9
2013	B	1.29	1.16	80.3	372.9	119.9	410.8	-6.2
2012	B+	2.42	2.19	79.5	301.5	133.4	234.4	-11.6

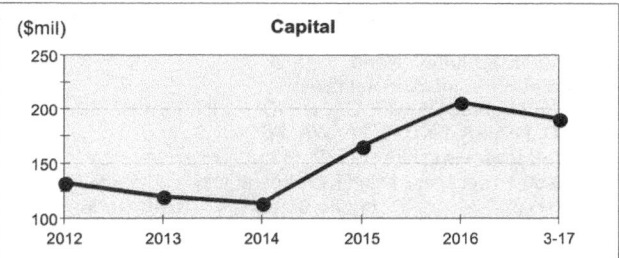

($mil)   Capital

2012 / 2013 / 2014 / 2015 / 2016 / 3-17

CALIFORNIA CAPITAL INS CO   B-   Good

Major Rating Factors: Fair overall results on stability tests (4.7 on a scale of 0 to 10) including potential drain of affiliation with CIG Holding Company Inc. Fair profitability index (3.5) with operating losses during the first three months of 2017. Return on equity has been low, averaging 2.0% over the past five years.

Other Rating Factors: History of adequate reserve strength (5.6) as reserves have been consistently at an acceptable level. Good liquidity (6.5) with sufficient resources (cash flows and marketable investments) to handle a spike in claims. Strong long-term capitalization index (7.8) based on excellent current risk adjusted capital (severe and moderate loss scenarios), despite some fluctuation in capital levels.

Principal Business: Commercial multiple peril (37%), homeowners multiple peril (21%), auto liability (14%), auto physical damage (10%), fire (5%), other liability (4%), and other lines (10%).

Principal Investments: Investment grade bonds (71%), misc. investments (25%), non investment grade bonds (4%), and real estate (3%).

Investments in Affiliates: 26%

Group Affiliation: CIG Holding Company Inc

Licensed in: AZ, CA, ID, MT, NV, OR, TX

Commenced Business: August 1898

Address: 2300 GARDEN ROAD, Monterey, CA 93940

Phone: (831) 233-5500   **Domicile State:** CA   **NAIC Code:** 13544

Data Date	Rating	RACR #1	RACR #2	Loss Ratio %	Total Assets ($mil)	Capital ($mil)	Net Premium ($mil)	Net Income ($mil)
3-17	B-	1.92	1.55	N/A	567.4	293.4	54.6	-2.4
3-16	B-	2.10	1.73	N/A	584.8	315.7	55.4	1.6
2016	B-	1.96	1.57	76.2	578.9	297.6	223.8	-4.4
2015	B-	2.10	1.73	69.9	580.3	314.1	218.1	13.4
2014	B-	2.16	1.77	65.1	593.5	315.6	245.0	10.8
2013	B-	2.15	1.76	65.1	569.5	303.3	234.0	9.2
2012	B-	2.18	1.79	67.2	536.6	289.7	210.8	6.6

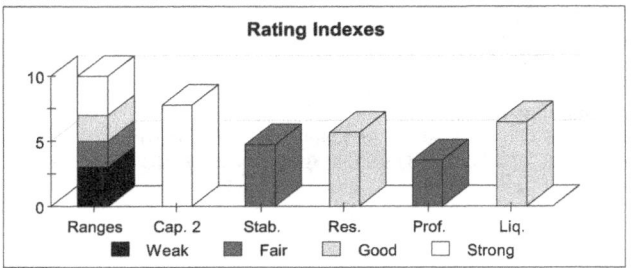

Rating Indexes

Ranges / Cap. 2 / Stab. / Res. / Prof. / Liq.
■ Weak   ▨ Fair   ▢ Good   ☐ Strong

CALIFORNIA CASUALTY INDEMNITY EXCH

C+   **Fair**

Major Rating Factors: Fair overall results on stability tests (3.9 on a scale of 0 to 10) including weak results on operational trends and negative cash flow from operations for 2016. The largest net exposure for one risk is acceptable at 2.2% of capital. History of adequate reserve strength (6.2) as reserves have been consistently at an acceptable level.

Other Rating Factors: Good liquidity (6.1) with sufficient resources (cash flows and marketable investments) to handle a spike in claims. Weak profitability index (2.4) with operating losses during 2012, 2014, 2015 and the first three months of 2017. Strong long-term capitalization index (7.9) based on excellent current risk adjusted capital (severe and moderate loss scenarios), despite some fluctuation in capital levels.

Principal Business: Auto physical damage (37%), auto liability (36%), and homeowners multiple peril (26%).

Principal Investments: Investment grade bonds (53%) and misc. investments (47%).

Investments in Affiliates: 33%

Group Affiliation: California Casualty Ins Group

Licensed in: All states except MI, NJ, PR

Commenced Business: January 1914

Address: 1900 Alameda de las Pulgas, San Mateo, CA 94403-1298

Phone: (650) 574-4000   **Domicile State:** CA   **NAIC Code:** 20117

Data Date	Rating	RACR #1	RACR #2	Loss Ratio %	Total Assets ($mil)	Capital ($mil)	Net Premium ($mil)	Net Income ($mil)
3-17	C+	1.82	1.58	N/A	581.9	271.4	60.0	-3.0
3-16	C+	1.82	1.58	N/A	577.7	279.5	59.0	-1.6
2016	C+	1.83	1.60	81.6	582.8	273.0	242.1	-7.0
2015	C+	1.87	1.63	84.1	582.3	284.3	238.6	-26.7
2014	C+	2.10	1.89	82.5	557.6	319.1	163.8	-6.2
2013	C+	2.08	1.88	79.4	571.8	336.5	158.7	2.6
2012	C+	2.10	1.89	79.9	557.6	320.0	152.7	-1.8

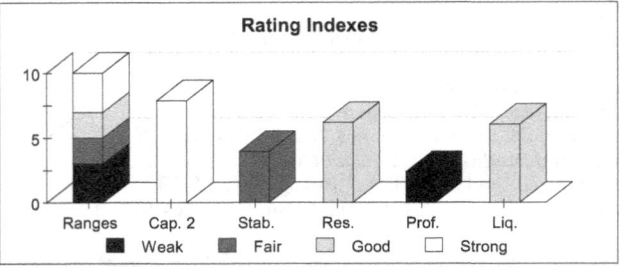

Rating Indexes — Ranges, Cap. 2, Stab., Res., Prof., Liq. — Weak, Fair, Good, Strong

CALIFORNIA INS CO

B   **Good**

Major Rating Factors: Fair overall results on stability tests (4.7 on a scale of 0 to 10) including weak results on operational trends. Affiliation with Berkshire-Hathaway is a strength. Strong long-term capitalization index (9.2) based on excellent current risk adjusted capital (severe and moderate loss scenarios). Moreover, capital levels have been consistent in recent years.

Other Rating Factors: Ample reserve history (7.9) that can protect against increases in claims costs. Excellent profitability (8.9) with operating gains in each of the last five years. Return on equity has been excellent over the last five years averaging 16.1%. Excellent liquidity (7.9) with ample operational cash flow and liquid investments.

Principal Business: Workers compensation (97%), surety (2%), other liability (1%), and aggregate write-ins for other lines of business (1%).

Principal Investments: Investment grade bonds (73%), misc. investments (21%), and cash (6%).

Investments in Affiliates: None

Group Affiliation: Berkshire-Hathaway

Licensed in: AK, AZ, CA, CT, GA, HI, ID, IL, IN, IA, KS, MD, MO, MT, NV, NJ, NY, NC, ND, OR, PA, TX, UT, VA, WA, WI

Commenced Business: June 1980

Address: 950 Tower Lane 14th Floor, Foster City, CA 94404

Phone: (402) 827-3424   **Domicile State:** CA   **NAIC Code:** 38865

Data Date	Rating	RACR #1	RACR #2	Loss Ratio %	Total Assets ($mil)	Capital ($mil)	Net Premium ($mil)	Net Income ($mil)
3-17	B	3.64	2.80	N/A	889.6	558.4	69.4	18.5
3-16	B-	3.61	2.92	N/A	767.8	479.9	57.2	14.4
2016	B	3.63	2.80	43.7	851.1	528.7	255.0	55.0
2015	B-	3.67	2.96	21.1	751.2	468.8	255.3	88.5
2014	B-	2.95	2.30	30.1	631.7	379.8	241.6	65.5
2013	B-	3.98	2.18	32.2	521.1	317.4	186.9	48.9
2012	B-	3.99	1.97	12.6	443.9	244.7	136.2	47.6

Berkshire-Hathaway
Composite Group Rating: B

Largest Group Members	Assets ($mil)	Rating
NATIONAL INDEMNITY CO	178623	B
GOVERNMENT EMPLOYEES INS CO	27198	B
COLUMBIA INS CO	20707	U
BERKSHIRE HATHAWAY LIFE INS CO OF NE	17970	C+
GENERAL REINS CORP	14780	C+

CAMBRIDGE MUTUAL FIRE INS CO

B-   **Good**

Major Rating Factors: Fair overall results on stability tests (4.6 on a scale of 0 to 10) including potential drain of affiliation with Andover Group and weak results on operational trends. History of adequate reserve strength (6.6) as reserves have been consistently at an acceptable level.

Other Rating Factors: Good overall profitability index (6.0) despite operating losses during 2015. Strong long-term capitalization index (8.4) based on excellent current risk adjusted capital (severe and moderate loss scenarios), despite some fluctuation in capital levels. Excellent liquidity (7.6) with ample operational cash flow and liquid investments.

Principal Business: Homeowners multiple peril (61%), commercial multiple peril (16%), fire (8%), allied lines (7%), other liability (6%), and inland marine (2%).

Principal Investments: Misc. investments (70%), investment grade bonds (18%), and cash (12%).

Investments in Affiliates: None

Group Affiliation: Andover Group

Licensed in: CT, IL, ME, MA, NH, NJ, NY, RI

Commenced Business: January 1834

Address: 95 Old River Road, Andover, MA 01810-1078

Phone: (978) 475-3300   **Domicile State:** MA   **NAIC Code:** 19771

Data Date	Rating	RACR #1	RACR #2	Loss Ratio %	Total Assets ($mil)	Capital ($mil)	Net Premium ($mil)	Net Income ($mil)
3-17	B-	3.14	1.92	N/A	896.4	536.1	44.6	5.3
3-16	B-	3.37	2.06	N/A	815.6	485.2	43.4	4.3
2016	B-	3.32	2.04	50.9	877.5	512.7	188.8	39.4
2015	B-	3.40	2.08	68.5	805.2	474.1	181.5	-9.3
2014	B-	3.23	1.99	43.4	830.2	479.0	183.3	30.1
2013	B-	3.15	2.01	43.3	738.7	421.9	172.5	51.3
2012	B-	3.02	2.01	64.9	679.7	352.6	167.8	11.9

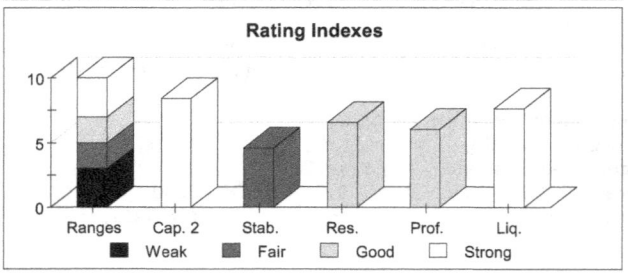

Rating Indexes — Ranges, Cap. 2, Stab., Res., Prof., Liq. — Weak, Fair, Good, Strong

CANAL INS CO   B   Good

Major Rating Factors: Good overall results on stability tests (5.8 on a scale of 0 to 10) despite potential drain of affiliation with Canal Group. History of adequate reserve strength (5.3) as reserves have been consistently at an acceptable level.
Other Rating Factors: Good profitability index (5.0). Fair expense controls. Return on equity has been low, averaging 2.8% over the past five years. Strong long-term capitalization index (8.5) based on excellent current risk adjusted capital (severe and moderate loss scenarios), despite some fluctuation in capital levels. Excellent liquidity (7.3) with ample operational cash flow and liquid investments.
Principal Business: Auto liability (72%), auto physical damage (21%), and inland marine (6%).
Principal Investments: Misc. investments (48%), investment grade bonds (48%), non investment grade bonds (2%), and real estate (2%).
Investments in Affiliates: 6%
Group Affiliation: Canal Group
Licensed in: All states except AK, HI, PR
Commenced Business: March 1939
Address: 400 East Stone Ave, Greenville, SC 29601
Phone: (864) 242-5365   **Domicile State:** SC   **NAIC Code:** 10464

Data Date	Rating	RACR #1	RACR #2	Loss Ratio %	Total Assets ($mil)	Capital ($mil)	Net Premium ($mil)	Net Income ($mil)
3-17	B	2.91	1.97	N/A	823.5	444.5	53.7	6.5
3-16	B	2.85	1.98	N/A	777.2	433.8	46.7	4.9
2016	B	2.95	2.01	82.9	819.0	439.7	210.0	10.3
2015	B	2.88	2.01	71.6	787.0	428.0	185.5	20.0
2014	B	2.69	1.92	76.9	818.8	447.2	177.4	20.3
2013	B	2.63	1.89	86.6	849.0	444.8	191.9	1.7
2012	B	2.60	1.89	79.1	831.0	421.3	200.1	6.2

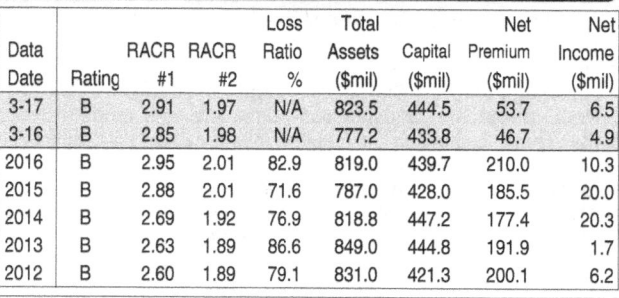

Rating Indexes

CAPITOL INDEMNITY CORP   C   Fair

Major Rating Factors: Fair reserve development (4.3 on a scale of 0 to 10) as reserves have generally been sufficient to cover claims. Fair overall results on stability tests (4.0) including fair financial strength of affiliated Alleghany Corp Group.
Other Rating Factors: Good overall profitability index (5.6) despite operating losses during 2013 and 2014. Return on equity has been low, averaging 1.0% over the past five years. Good liquidity (6.8) with sufficient resources (cash flows and marketable investments) to handle a spike in claims. Strong long-term capitalization index (7.3) based on excellent current risk adjusted capital (severe and moderate loss scenarios). Moreover, capital levels have been consistent in recent years.
Principal Business: Commercial multiple peril (54%), other liability (26%), surety (8%), auto liability (4%), medical malpractice (2%), products liability (1%), and other lines (4%).
Principal Investments: Misc. investments (56%), investment grade bonds (43%), and cash (1%).
Investments in Affiliates: 21%
Group Affiliation: Alleghany Corp Group
Licensed in: All states except VT, PR
Commenced Business: June 1960
Address: 1600 Aspen Commons, Middleton, WI 53562-4718
Phone: (608) 829-4200   **Domicile State:** WI   **NAIC Code:** 10472

Data Date	Rating	RACR #1	RACR #2	Loss Ratio %	Total Assets ($mil)	Capital ($mil)	Net Premium ($mil)	Net Income ($mil)
3-17	C	1.76	1.34	N/A	535.5	243.8	43.4	4.3
3-16	C	1.56	1.19	N/A	484.0	227.2	38.8	1.7
2016	C	1.56	1.18	53.1	520.0	234.2	175.0	8.5
2015	C	1.55	1.18	54.8	478.8	225.5	154.2	5.1
2014	C	1.58	1.21	55.8	462.4	221.9	134.7	-0.9
2013	C	1.69	1.18	65.6	411.2	172.9	120.0	-11.3
2012	C	1.81	1.28	59.7	386.0	162.5	104.4	7.3

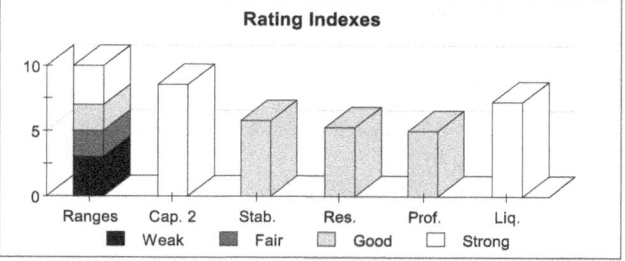

Reserve Deficiency (as % of capital)

* Adequate & redundant reserves show as negatives   ■ 1 Yr Dev   □ 2 Yr Dev

CASTLE KEY INS CO   B   Good

Major Rating Factors: History of adequate reserve strength (6.4 on a scale of 0 to 10) as reserves have been consistently at an acceptable level. Good liquidity (6.8) with sufficient resources (cash flows and marketable investments) to handle a spike in claims.
Other Rating Factors: Fair overall results on stability tests (4.3) including weak results on operational trends. The largest net exposure for one risk is conservative at 1.5% of capital. Strong long-term capitalization index (10.0) based on excellent current risk adjusted capital (severe and moderate loss scenarios). Moreover, capital levels have been consistent in recent years. Excellent profitability (8.8) with operating gains in each of the last five years. Return on equity has been good over the last five years, averaging 10.7%.
Principal Business: Homeowners multiple peril (96%) and inland marine (3%).
Principal Investments: Investment grade bonds (90%), misc. investments (9%), and non investment grade bonds (1%).
Investments in Affiliates: 6%
Group Affiliation: Allstate Group
Licensed in: FL, IL, PA
Commenced Business: November 1988
Address: 2775 SANDERS ROAD, Northbrook, IL 60062-6127
Phone: (727) 573-6800   **Domicile State:** IL   **NAIC Code:** 30511

Data Date	Rating	RACR #1	RACR #2	Loss Ratio %	Total Assets ($mil)	Capital ($mil)	Net Premium ($mil)	Net Income ($mil)
3-17	B	4.45	3.91	N/A	372.8	218.9	31.6	4.3
3-16	B-	4.59	3.34	N/A	361.2	209.4	31.5	3.0
2016	B	4.41	3.66	71.0	370.5	214.4	122.7	7.5
2015	B-	4.49	3.29	60.5	360.4	206.3	123.0	16.6
2014	B-	2.11	1.53	53.5	360.6	190.0	142.5	26.3
2013	B-	0.77	0.56	50.6	354.0	165.7	153.5	24.4
2012	B-	0.69	0.50	53.5	345.8	141.6	130.7	20.2

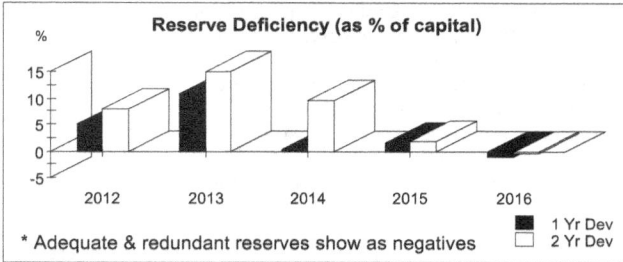

Reserve Deficiency (as % of capital)

* Adequate & redundant reserves show as negatives   ■ 1 Yr Dev   □ 2 Yr Dev

CATASTROPHE REINS CO
C-   Fair

Major Rating Factors: Fair overall results on stability tests (3.0 on a scale of 0 to 10). History of adequate reserve strength (5.3) as reserves have been consistently at an acceptable level.

Other Rating Factors: Strong long-term capitalization index (10.0) based on excellent current risk adjusted capital (severe and moderate loss scenarios), despite some fluctuation in capital levels. Excellent profitability (8.6) with operating gains in each of the last five years. Excellent expense controls. Return on equity has been good over the last five years, averaging 11.6%. Superior liquidity (9.1) with ample operational cash flow and liquid investments.

Principal Business: (This company is a reinsurer.)

Principal Investments: Investment grade bonds (73%), misc. investments (23%), and non investment grade bonds (4%).

Investments in Affiliates: None

Group Affiliation: USAA Group

Licensed in: TX

Commenced Business: June 2006

Address: 9800 Fredericksburg Road, San Antonio, TX 78288

Phone: (210) 498-1411   **Domicile State:** TX   **NAIC Code:** 12578

Data Date	Rating	RACR #1	RACR #2	Loss Ratio %	Total Assets ($mil)	Capital ($mil)	Net Premium ($mil)	Net Income ($mil)
3-17	C-	15.24	8.73	N/A	1,886.3	1,800.4	37.0	37.3
3-16	D	14.14	8.82	N/A	1,800.2	1,703.1	41.4	32.5
2016	D+	15.67	9.00	N/A	1,831.9	1,743.1	148.2	158.1
2015	D	13.80	8.54	N/A	1,775.4	1,659.6	165.5	153.2
2014	D-	9.87	5.93	N/A	1,715.5	1,577.2	178.0	250.6
2013	D-	4.93	3.10	67.6	1,930.5	1,589.2	356.9	136.1
2012	D-	4.94	3.04	24.1	1,976.7	1,680.2	446.7	271.6

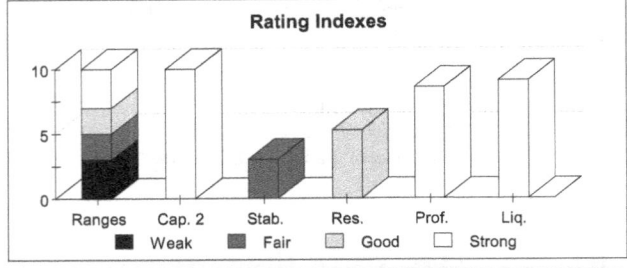

Rating Indexes

CATERPILLAR INS CO
B   Good

Major Rating Factors: History of adequate reserve strength (6.6 on a scale of 0 to 10) as reserves have been consistently at an acceptable level. Good overall results on stability tests (6.3). Stability strengths include good operational trends and excellent risk diversification.

Other Rating Factors: Strong long-term capitalization index (9.2) based on excellent current risk adjusted capital (severe and moderate loss scenarios). Moreover, capital levels have been consistent in recent years. Excellent profitability (8.9) with operating gains in each of the last five years. Return on equity has been good over the last five years, averaging 13.2%. Excellent liquidity (7.1) with ample operational cash flow and liquid investments.

Principal Business: Other liability (91%), aggregate write-ins for other lines of business (5%), and inland marine (3%).

Principal Investments: Investment grade bonds (64%), misc. investments (28%), cash (7%), and non investment grade bonds (1%).

Investments in Affiliates: None

Group Affiliation: Caterpillar Ins Holdings Inc

Licensed in: All states except PR

Commenced Business: February 1963

Address: 237 East High Street, Jefferson City, MO 65101

Phone: (615) 341-8147   **Domicile State:** MO   **NAIC Code:** 11255

Data Date	Rating	RACR #1	RACR #2	Loss Ratio %	Total Assets ($mil)	Capital ($mil)	Net Premium ($mil)	Net Income ($mil)
3-17	B	3.71	2.62	N/A	701.1	326.7	41.2	1.6
3-16	B	4.52	3.21	N/A	654.6	299.7	42.3	3.7
2016	B	3.70	2.66	72.4	687.2	316.2	180.7	18.9
2015	B	4.38	3.17	63.5	650.3	286.6	142.5	49.0
2014	B-	3.23	2.60	72.9	660.7	271.9	204.7	31.5
2013	B-	2.62	2.16	55.2	639.6	243.4	214.6	33.2
2012	B-	2.26	1.87	51.0	575.6	203.9	199.2	41.5

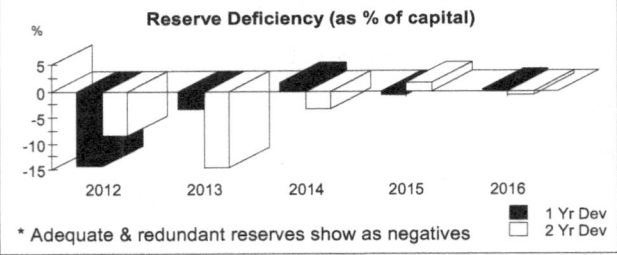

Reserve Deficiency (as % of capital)

* Adequate & redundant reserves show as negatives

1 Yr Dev   2 Yr Dev

CATLIN SPECIALTY INS CO
C+   Fair

Major Rating Factors: Fair overall results on stability tests (4.1 on a scale of 0 to 10) including potential drain of affiliation with XL Group Ltd and weak results on operational trends. The largest net exposure for one risk is conservative at 1.8% of capital. Fair reserve development (4.0) as reserves have generally been sufficient to cover claims.

Other Rating Factors: Fair profitability index (4.2) with operating losses during 2015. Return on equity has been low, averaging 1.2% over the past five years. Strong long-term capitalization index (7.4) based on excellent current risk adjusted capital (severe and moderate loss scenarios). Moreover, capital levels have been consistent in recent years. Excellent liquidity (7.2) with ample operational cash flow and liquid investments.

Principal Business: Other liability (64%), commercial multiple peril (10%), auto liability (8%), products liability (7%), medical malpractice (5%), auto physical damage (4%), and other lines (2%).

Principal Investments: Investment grade bonds (80%), misc. investments (17%), and cash (3%).

Investments in Affiliates: 15%

Group Affiliation: XL Group Ltd

Licensed in: All states except PR

Commenced Business: January 1942

Address: 1209 Orange St, Wilmington, DE 19801

Phone: (404) 443-4910   **Domicile State:** DE   **NAIC Code:** 15989

Data Date	Rating	RACR #1	RACR #2	Loss Ratio %	Total Assets ($mil)	Capital ($mil)	Net Premium ($mil)	Net Income ($mil)
3-17	C+	2.47	1.83	N/A	728.2	235.2	11.7	1.9
3-16	C+	2.35	1.74	N/A	672.5	222.6	19.7	2.6
2016	C+	2.46	1.81	86.8	744.0	234.2	50.3	3.5
2015	C+	2.33	1.74	90.9	668.4	213.1	76.8	-6.8
2014	C+	2.01	1.64	76.3	591.4	204.3	86.8	3.0
2013	C+	2.12	1.68	62.0	483.8	201.5	78.0	7.4
2012	C+	1.70	1.08	71.3	355.2	112.8	63.7	2.5

XL Group Ltd Composite Group Rating: C Largest Group Members	Assets ($mil)	Rating
XL REINS AMERICA INC	6274	C
GREENWICH INS CO	1203	C
XL SPECIALTY INS CO	920	C
XL INS AMERICA INC	825	C
CATLIN SPECIALTY INS CO	744	C+

CENTRAL MUTUAL INS CO   B   Good

Major Rating Factors: Good liquidity (6.6 on a scale of 0 to 10) with sufficient resources (cash flows and marketable investments) to handle a spike in claims. Fair overall results on stability tests (4.7) including weak results on operational trends.

Other Rating Factors: Strong long-term capitalization index (8.8) based on excellent current risk adjusted capital (severe and moderate loss scenarios). Moreover, capital levels have been consistent in recent years. Ample reserve history (9.3) that helps to protect the company against sharp claims increases. Excellent profitability (8.4) with operating gains in each of the last five years.

Principal Business: Homeowners multiple peril (26%), auto liability (23%), commercial multiple peril (20%), auto physical damage (16%), other liability (6%), inland marine (3%), and other lines (7%).

Principal Investments: Investment grade bonds (58%), misc. investments (38%), real estate (3%), and cash (1%).

Investments in Affiliates: 12%

Group Affiliation: Central Mutual Ins Group

Licensed in: AZ, AR, CA, CO, CT, DE, GA, ID, IL, IN, IA, KY, ME, MD, MA, MI, MN, MS, MT, NV, NH, NJ, NM, NY, NC, OH, OK, OR, PA, SC, TN, TX, UT, VT, VA, WA, WI

Commenced Business: October 1876

Address: 800 SOUTH WASHINGTON STREET, Van Wert, OH 45891-2357

Phone: (419) 238-1010   **Domicile State:** OH   **NAIC Code:** 20230

Data Date	Rating	RACR #1	RACR #2	Loss Ratio %	Total Assets ($mil)	Capital ($mil)	Net Premium ($mil)	Net Income ($mil)
3-17	B	2.92	2.17	N/A	1,538.9	765.7	130.2	5.0
3-16	B	2.90	2.16	N/A	1,446.5	708.1	123.5	7.3
2016	B	2.91	2.18	64.0	1,514.5	743.0	518.8	32.5
2015	B	2.93	2.20	57.9	1,451.2	705.8	488.0	57.0
2014	B	2.79	2.08	59.8	1,359.6	640.1	447.6	50.4
2013	B	2.91	2.14	58.4	1,266.0	619.4	402.3	62.9
2012	B	2.63	1.92	70.7	1,184.2	510.5	369.9	23.0

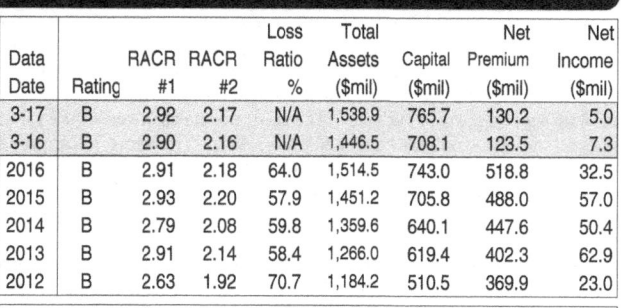

Liquidity Index

Range · 2013 · 2014 · 2015 · 2016
■ Weak   ▨ Fair   ☐ Good   ☐ Strong

CENTRAL STATES INDEMNITY CO OF OMAHA   C+   Fair

Major Rating Factors: Fair overall results on stability tests (4.5 on a scale of 0 to 10) including potential drain of affiliation with Berkshire-Hathaway and weak results on operational trends. Good profitability index (5.0) despite operating losses during the first three months of 2017. Return on equity has been low, averaging 3.3% over the past five years.

Other Rating Factors: Strong long-term capitalization index (9.1) based on excellent current risk adjusted capital (severe and moderate loss scenarios), despite some fluctuation in capital levels. Ample reserve history (7.4) that can protect against increases in claims costs. Excellent liquidity (8.1) with ample operational cash flow and liquid investments.

Principal Business: Other accident & health (59%), inland marine (26%), aggregate write-ins for other lines of business (9%), credit accident & health (4%), and aircraft (2%).

Principal Investments: Misc. investments (70%), investment grade bonds (29%), and cash (1%).

Investments in Affiliates: 3%

Group Affiliation: Berkshire-Hathaway

Licensed in: All states, the District of Columbia and Puerto Rico

Commenced Business: June 1977

Address: 1212 North 96th Street, Omaha, NE 68114

Phone: (402) 997-8000   **Domicile State:** NE   **NAIC Code:** 34274

Data Date	Rating	RACR #1	RACR #2	Loss Ratio %	Total Assets ($mil)	Capital ($mil)	Net Premium ($mil)	Net Income ($mil)
3-17	C+	3.88	2.46	N/A	468.7	388.8	15.8	-1.0
3-16	C+	4.16	2.62	N/A	394.9	339.7	14.5	0.4
2016	C+	3.82	2.42	60.2	447.9	378.0	59.6	8.0
2015	C+	4.00	2.50	55.4	417.3	354.9	55.0	9.5
2014	C+	4.12	2.63	44.6	435.0	363.7	50.2	11.4
2013	B+	4.34	2.79	36.2	412.3	346.0	43.0	17.7
2012	B+	4.34	2.69	18.3	335.1	285.5	32.2	13.1

Berkshire-Hathaway
Composite Group Rating: B

Largest Group Members	Assets ($mil)	Rating
NATIONAL INDEMNITY CO	178623	B
GOVERNMENT EMPLOYEES INS CO	27198	B
COLUMBIA INS CO	20707	U
BERKSHIRE HATHAWAY LIFE INS CO OF NE	17970	C+
GENERAL REINS CORP	14780	C+

CENTURY-NATIONAL INS CO   C   Fair

Major Rating Factors: Fair overall results on stability tests (4.0 on a scale of 0 to 10) including weak results on operational trends. Weak profitability index (2.8). Fair expense controls. Return on equity has been low, averaging 3.8% over the past five years.

Other Rating Factors: History of adequate reserve strength (6.5) as reserves have been consistently at an acceptable level. Good liquidity (6.0) with sufficient resources (cash flows and marketable investments) to handle a spike in claims. Strong long-term capitalization index (7.8) based on excellent current risk adjusted capital (severe and moderate loss scenarios), despite some fluctuation in capital levels.

Principal Business: Auto liability (32%), homeowners multiple peril (29%), auto physical damage (16%), commercial multiple peril (11%), fire (5%), allied lines (4%), and earthquake (2%).

Principal Investments: Investment grade bonds (94%), misc. investments (6%), and non investment grade bonds (1%).

Investments in Affiliates: None

Group Affiliation: National General Holdings Corporatio

Licensed in: All states except DC, HI, MA, NH, NY, RI, PR

Commenced Business: December 1956

Address: 16650 Sherman Way, Van Nuys, CA 91406

Phone: (336) 435-2000   **Domicile State:** CA   **NAIC Code:** 26905

Data Date	Rating	RACR #1	RACR #2	Loss Ratio %	Total Assets ($mil)	Capital ($mil)	Net Premium ($mil)	Net Income ($mil)
3-17	C	2.18	1.54	N/A	544.4	251.4	51.9	4.5
3-16	B	3.87	2.58	N/A	632.1	390.6	43.9	18.2
2016	C	2.23	1.57	70.8	513.7	248.0	210.5	10.4
2015	B	3.65	2.38	70.3	594.1	367.5	165.1	7.5
2014	B	3.64	2.29	72.2	593.1	385.0	141.0	19.4
2013	B	3.54	2.20	78.4	587.7	386.5	124.8	15.5
2012	B	3.52	2.21	66.6	531.6	336.9	117.4	9.7

National General Holdings Corporatio
Composite Group Rating: C+

Largest Group Members	Assets ($mil)	Rating
INTEGON NATIONAL INS CO	2489	C+
TECHNOLOGY INS CO	2350	C
WESCO INS CO	1904	B-
SECURITY NATIONAL INS CO	1205	B
REPUBLIC UNDERWRITERS INS CO	701	C

CHARTER OAK FIRE INS CO   B   Good

Major Rating Factors: Good overall profitability index (5.3 on a scale of 0 to 10). Fair expense controls. Return on equity has been excellent over the last five years averaging 15.1%. Good liquidity (6.7) with sufficient resources (cash flows and marketable investments) to handle a spike in claims.

Other Rating Factors: Fair overall results on stability tests (4.6) including weak results on operational trends. Affiliation with Travelers Companies Inc is a strength. Strong long-term capitalization index (7.9) based on excellent current risk adjusted capital (severe and moderate loss scenarios), despite some fluctuation in capital levels. Ample reserve history (8.7) that helps to protect the company against sharp claims increases.

Principal Business: Commercial multiple peril (33%), workers compensation (32%), auto liability (12%), other liability (7%), homeowners multiple peril (7%), auto physical damage (4%), and other lines (6%).

Principal Investments: Investment grade bonds (98%) and misc. investments (2%).

Investments in Affiliates: None
Group Affiliation: Travelers Companies Inc
Licensed in: All states except CA
Commenced Business: October 1935
Address: ONE TOWER SQUARE, Hartford, CT 06183
Phone: (860) 277-0111   **Domicile State:** CT   **NAIC Code:** 25615

Data Date	Rating	RACR #1	RACR #2	Loss Ratio %	Total Assets ($mil)	Capital ($mil)	Net Premium ($mil)	Net Income ($mil)
3-17	B	2.41	1.56	N/A	950.9	249.5	68.5	6.1
3-16	B	2.54	1.61	N/A	937.4	263.2	66.0	7.9
2016	B	2.41	1.57	63.4	918.0	242.9	276.5	30.9
2015	B	2.54	1.62	58.7	922.9	255.7	263.9	42.1
2014	B	2.53	1.60	60.5	926.1	253.6	256.4	41.7
2013	B	2.50	1.59	60.9	916.9	245.9	255.8	42.6
2012	B	2.40	1.54	68.4	918.5	232.2	248.4	32.0

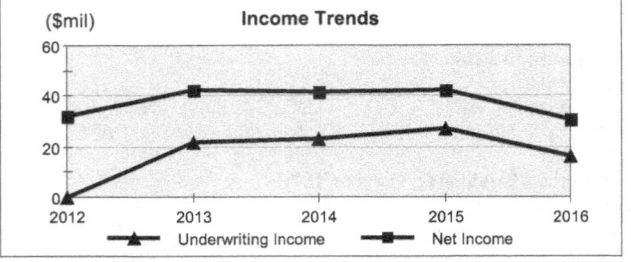

Income Trends

CHESAPEAKE EMPLOYERS INS CO   B   Good

Major Rating Factors: Good overall profitability index (6.5 on a scale of 0 to 10). Fair expense controls. Return on equity has been good over the last five years, averaging 11.1%. Good liquidity (6.9) with sufficient resources (cash flows and marketable investments) to handle a spike in claims.

Other Rating Factors: Fair overall results on stability tests (4.4) including weak results on operational trends. Strong long-term capitalization index (7.1) based on excellent current risk adjusted capital (severe and moderate loss scenarios). Moreover, capital levels have been consistent in recent years. Ample reserve history (9.4) that helps to protect the company against sharp claims increases.

Principal Business: Workers compensation (100%).

Principal Investments: Investment grade bonds (78%), misc. investments (19%), and non investment grade bonds (3%).

Investments in Affiliates: None
Group Affiliation: None
Licensed in: MD
Commenced Business: July 1914
Address: 8722 Loch Raven Boulevard, Towson, MD 21286-2235
Phone: (410) 494-2000   **Domicile State:** MD   **NAIC Code:** 11039

Data Date	Rating	RACR #1	RACR #2	Loss Ratio %	Total Assets ($mil)	Capital ($mil)	Net Premium ($mil)	Net Income ($mil)
3-17	B	2.03	1.25	N/A	2,252.8	579.2	58.3	21.5
3-16	B	1.70	1.05	N/A	2,133.3	475.5	57.5	16.4
2016	B	1.99	1.22	81.4	2,212.5	543.4	237.4	81.5
2015	B	1.72	1.05	73.1	2,067.8	463.1	231.1	85.4
2014	U	1.41	0.88	83.8	2,005.8	399.7	227.9	50.8
2013	N/A	N/A	N/A	89.3	1,865.6	337.4	225.6	19.3
2012	N/A	N/A	N/A	98.1	1,843.2	287.2	199.9	7.7

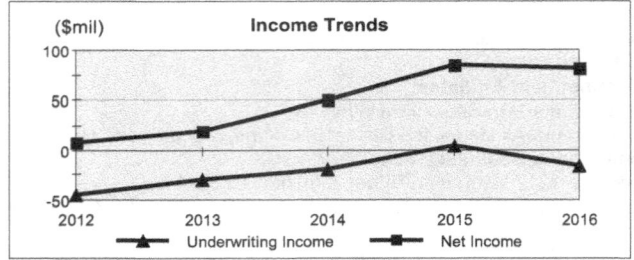

Income Trends

CHUBB CUSTOM INS CO   B-   Good

Major Rating Factors: Fair overall results on stability tests (3.9 on a scale of 0 to 10) including weak results on operational trends. The largest net exposure for one risk is acceptable at 2.1% of capital. Strong long-term capitalization index (10.0) based on excellent current risk adjusted capital (severe and moderate loss scenarios). Moreover, capital levels have been consistent in recent years.

Other Rating Factors: Ample reserve history (7.9) that can protect against increases in claims costs. Excellent profitability (8.7) with operating gains in each of the last five years. Excellent liquidity (7.2) with ample operational cash flow and liquid investments.

Principal Business: Fire (30%), commercial multiple peril (20%), allied lines (19%), other liability (16%), products liability (5%), homeowners multiple peril (3%), and other lines (6%).

Principal Investments: Investment grade bonds (98%), misc. investments (1%), and non investment grade bonds (1%).

Investments in Affiliates: None
Group Affiliation: Chubb Limited
Licensed in: All states, the District of Columbia and Puerto Rico
Commenced Business: December 1980
Address: 15 Mountain View Road, Warren, NJ 07059
Phone: (908) 903-2000   **Domicile State:** NJ   **NAIC Code:** 38989

Data Date	Rating	RACR #1	RACR #2	Loss Ratio %	Total Assets ($mil)	Capital ($mil)	Net Premium ($mil)	Net Income ($mil)
3-17	B-	11.59	7.27	N/A	370.4	217.5	7.4	2.7
3-16	B-	8.90	5.57	N/A	430.5	201.1	9.8	3.7
2016	B-	11.41	7.18	53.5	372.9	215.0	31.7	12.4
2015	B-	8.99	5.66	55.1	405.5	200.8	48.9	13.5
2014	B-	8.42	5.36	56.7	398.7	187.4	47.0	13.5
2013	B-	7.78	4.98	51.1	346.3	173.9	45.1	14.1
2012	B-	6.99	4.44	66.4	337.3	160.0	43.3	11.1

Chubb Limited
Composite Group Rating: B-

Largest Group Members	Assets ($mil)	Rating
FEDERAL INS CO	27371	B-
ACE AMERICAN INS CO	13036	B-
ACE PC INS CO	8192	B-
PACIFIC INDEMNITY CO	6555	B-
PACIFIC EMPLOYERS INS CO	3774	B-

CHURCH MUTUAL INS CO   **B**   **Good**

Major Rating Factors: Good overall profitability index (6.8 on a scale of 0 to 10) despite operating losses during 2013. Good liquidity (6.5) with sufficient resources (cash flows and marketable investments) to handle a spike in claims.
Other Rating Factors: Fair overall results on stability tests (4.9) including weak results on operational trends. Strong long-term capitalization index (8.2) based on excellent current risk adjusted capital (severe and moderate loss scenarios). Moreover, capital levels have been consistent in recent years. Ample reserve history (8.3) that helps to protect the company against sharp claims increases.
Principal Business: Commercial multiple peril (66%), workers compensation (23%), auto liability (5%), other liability (3%), auto physical damage (1%), medical malpractice (1%), and allied lines (1%).
Principal Investments: Investment grade bonds (68%), misc. investments (30%), cash (1%), and real estate (1%).
Investments in Affiliates: 7%
Group Affiliation: None
Licensed in: All states except PR
Commenced Business: June 1897
Address: 3000 SCHUSTER LANE, Merrill, WI 54452
Phone: (715) 536-5577   **Domicile State:** WI   **NAIC Code:** 18767

Data Date	Rating	RACR #1	RACR #2	Loss Ratio %	Total Assets ($mil)	Capital ($mil)	Net Premium ($mil)	Net Income ($mil)
3-17	B	2.83	1.95	N/A	1,701.0	688.3	161.6	12.2
3-16	B	3.00	2.13	N/A	1,564.6	602.8	149.1	11.8
2016	B	2.77	1.92	55.9	1,625.6	663.8	645.8	49.4
2015	B	2.97	2.12	57.7	1,643.9	585.1	615.7	58.1
2014	B	3.18	2.34	58.2	1,453.6	536.7	589.0	76.0
2013	A	2.71	1.83	63.6	1,357.7	473.2	557.3	-4.9
2012	A	2.76	2.22	66.4	1,229.7	415.3	492.5	78.1

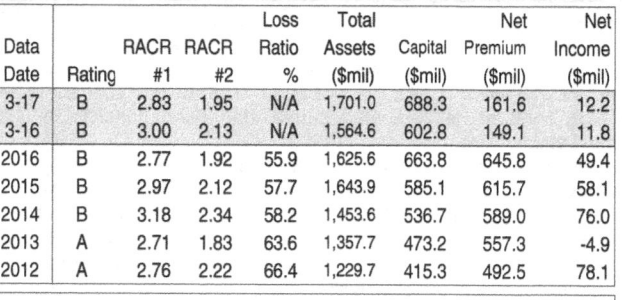

Income Trends

CINCINNATI CASUALTY CO   **B**   **Good**

Major Rating Factors: Fair overall results on stability tests (4.7 on a scale of 0 to 10) including weak results on operational trends. Strong long-term capitalization index (10.0) based on excellent current risk adjusted capital (severe and moderate loss scenarios). Moreover, capital levels have been consistent in recent years.
Other Rating Factors: Excellent profitability (8.1) with operating gains in each of the last five years. Superior liquidity (10.0) with ample operational cash flow and liquid investments.
Principal Business: Workers compensation (42%), commercial multiple peril (30%), other liability (10%), auto liability (8%), auto physical damage (3%), products liability (3%), and other lines (4%).
Principal Investments: Investment grade bonds (68%), misc. investments (27%), cash (4%), and non investment grade bonds (1%).
Investments in Affiliates: None
Group Affiliation: Cincinnati Financial Corp
Licensed in: All states except PR
Commenced Business: March 1973
Address: 6200 SOUTH GILMORE ROAD, Fairfield, OH 45014-5141
Phone: (513) 870-2000   **Domicile State:** OH   **NAIC Code:** 28665

Data Date	Rating	RACR #1	RACR #2	Loss Ratio %	Total Assets ($mil)	Capital ($mil)	Net Premium ($mil)	Net Income ($mil)
3-17	B	9.99	5.79	N/A	424.0	365.5	0.0	11.6
3-16	B	11.54	6.64	N/A	386.2	342.9	0.0	2.7
2016	B	10.29	5.96	0.0	408.3	359.9	0.0	11.1
2015	B	12.12	6.96	0.0	377.7	336.5	0.0	12.2
2014	B	10.94	6.34	0.0	371.8	330.2	0.0	12.0
2013	B	10.60	6.13	0.0	361.1	316.5	0.0	9.9
2012	B	12.67	7.29	0.0	329.3	292.6	0.0	9.8

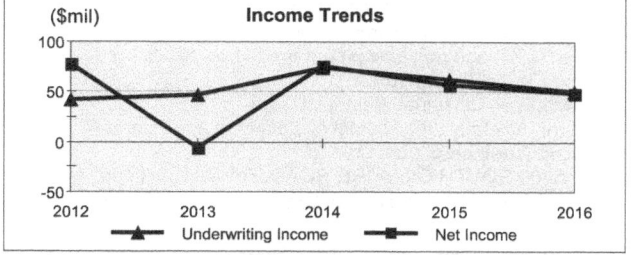

Cincinnati Financial Corp Composite Group Rating: A Largest Group Members	Assets ($mil)	Rating
CINCINNATI INS CO	12093	A
CINCINNATI LIFE INS CO	4266	B
CINCINNATI SPECIALTY UNDERWRITER	719	A-
CINCINNATI CASUALTY CO	408	B
CINCINNATI INDEMNITY CO	130	A-

CINCINNATI INDEMNITY CO *   **A-**   **Excellent**

Major Rating Factors: Strong long-term capitalization index (10.0 on a scale of 0 to 10) based on excellent current risk adjusted capital (severe and moderate loss scenarios). Moreover, capital levels have been consistent in recent years. Excellent profitability (8.0) with operating gains in each of the last five years.
Other Rating Factors: Superior liquidity (9.1) with ample operational cash flow and liquid investments. Good overall results on stability tests (5.5) despite weak results on operational trends and negative cash flow from operations for 2016. Strengths include potential support from affiliation with Cincinnati Financial Corp.
Principal Business: Workers compensation (29%), commercial multiple peril (24%), other liability (15%), auto liability (13%), auto physical damage (6%), allied lines (4%), and other lines (8%).
Principal Investments: Investment grade bonds (72%), misc. investments (25%), and cash (3%).
Investments in Affiliates: None
Group Affiliation: Cincinnati Financial Corp
Licensed in: All states except PR
Commenced Business: January 1989
Address: 6200 SOUTH GILMORE ROAD, Fairfield, OH 45014-5141
Phone: (513) 870-2000   **Domicile State:** OH   **NAIC Code:** 23280

Data Date	Rating	RACR #1	RACR #2	Loss Ratio %	Total Assets ($mil)	Capital ($mil)	Net Premium ($mil)	Net Income ($mil)
3-17	A-	11.17	6.43	N/A	132.7	94.4	0.0	1.5
3-16	A-	11.27	6.48	N/A	128.9	89.6	0.0	1.7
2016	A-	11.23	6.48	0.0	130.3	93.2	0.0	4.1
2015	A-	11.16	6.44	0.0	124.4	87.8	0.0	2.7
2014	A-	10.55	6.12	0.0	123.0	85.6	0.0	3.1
2013	A-	9.53	5.44	0.0	110.7	82.0	0.0	2.4
2012	A-	10.66	6.00	0.0	101.4	76.2	0.0	2.4

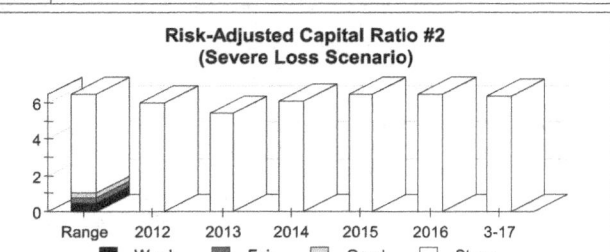

Risk-Adjusted Capital Ratio #2
(Severe Loss Scenario)

CINCINNATI INS CO *

A   **Excellent**

Major Rating Factors: Excellent overall results on stability tests (7.5 on a scale of 0 to 10). Stability strengths include excellent operational trends and excellent risk diversification. Strong long-term capitalization index (8.0) based on excellent current risk adjusted capital (severe and moderate loss scenarios). Furthermore, this high level of risk adjusted capital has been consistently maintained in previous years.

Other Rating Factors: Ample reserve history (8.4) that helps to protect the company against sharp claims increases. Excellent profitability (8.5) with operating gains in each of the last five years. Good liquidity (6.4) with sufficient resources (cash flows and marketable investments) to handle a spike in claims.

Principal Business: Commercial multiple peril (26%), auto liability (18%), other liability (16%), homeowners multiple peril (14%), auto physical damage (11%), inland marine (3%), and other lines (12%).

Principal Investments: Investment grade bonds (51%), misc. investments (44%), cash (3%), and non investment grade bonds (2%).

Investments in Affiliates: 10%

Group Affiliation: Cincinnati Financial Corp

Licensed in: All states, the District of Columbia and Puerto Rico

Commenced Business: January 1951

Address: 6200 SOUTH GILMORE ROAD, Fairfield, OH 45014-5141

Phone: (513) 870-2000   **Domicile State:** OH   **NAIC Code:** 10677

Data Date	Rating	RACR #1	RACR #2	Loss Ratio %	Total Assets ($mil)	Capital ($mil)	Net Premium ($mil)	Net Income ($mil)
3-17	A	2.28	1.67	N/A	12,253.3	4,763.3	1,106.6	147.5
3-16	A-	2.36	1.73	N/A	11,416.1	4,533.7	1,056.7	146.2
2016	A	2.30	1.70	64.9	12,092.7	4,686.0	4,393.9	434.1
2015	A-	2.36	1.75	60.9	11,194.2	4,412.4	4,189.4	534.1
2014	A-	2.40	1.75	65.5	11,017.2	4,472.2	3,993.2	435.8
2013	A	2.41	1.76	62.1	10,559.8	4,325.7	3,769.2	417.7
2012	A	2.50	1.86	63.7	9,767.3	3,913.6	3,380.3	334.7

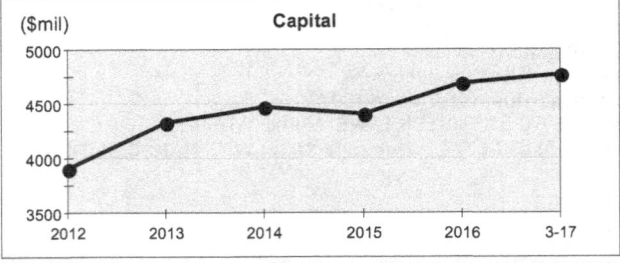

CINCINNATI SPECIALTY UNDERWRITER *

A-   **Excellent**

Major Rating Factors: Strong long-term capitalization index (7.8 on a scale of 0 to 10) based on excellent current risk adjusted capital (severe and moderate loss scenarios). Furthermore, this high level of risk adjusted capital has been consistently maintained in previous years. Ample reserve history (9.4) that helps to protect the company against sharp claims increases.

Other Rating Factors: Excellent profitability (8.7) with operating gains in each of the last five years. Return on equity has been good over the last five years, averaging 11.3%. Excellent overall results on stability tests (7.0). Stability strengths include excellent operational trends and excellent risk diversification. Good liquidity (6.9) with sufficient resources (cash flows and marketable investments) to handle a spike in claims.

Principal Business: Other liability (71%), products liability (15%), fire (8%), and allied lines (6%).

Principal Investments: Investment grade bonds (78%), misc. investments (15%), cash (6%), and non investment grade bonds (1%).

Investments in Affiliates: None

Group Affiliation: Cincinnati Financial Corp

Licensed in: All states except PR

Commenced Business: November 2007

Address: 1807 NORTH MARKET ST, Wilmington, DE 19802-4810

Phone: (513) 870-2000   **Domicile State:** DE   **NAIC Code:** 13037

Data Date	Rating	RACR #1	RACR #2	Loss Ratio %	Total Assets ($mil)	Capital ($mil)	Net Premium ($mil)	Net Income ($mil)
3-17	A-	3.22	1.67	N/A	744.7	381.1	47.9	18.3
3-16	B	3.01	1.55	N/A	650.7	324.1	43.2	15.5
2016	B+	3.24	1.67	37.6	719.2	372.1	189.8	56.8
2015	B	2.93	1.50	41.9	630.0	306.5	174.7	49.0
2014	B	2.77	1.41	50.5	545.8	265.6	153.3	32.3
2013	B	2.96	1.50	56.7	453.5	228.4	127.7	18.2
2012	B-	3.33	1.65	69.3	377.7	199.1	105.0	5.7

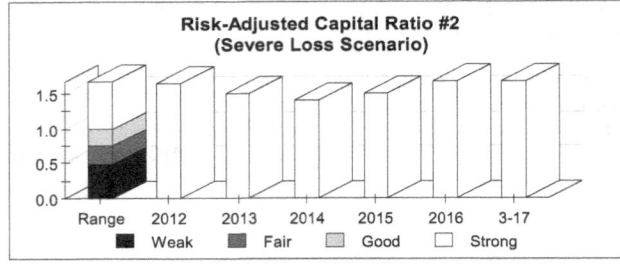

CITIZENS INS CO OF AM

B   **Good**

Major Rating Factors: Good liquidity (6.2 on a scale of 0 to 10) with sufficient resources (cash flows and marketable investments) to handle a spike in claims. Fair overall results on stability tests (4.8) including potential drain of affiliation with Hanover Ins Group Inc and weak results on operational trends.

Other Rating Factors: Strong long-term capitalization index (10.0) based on excellent current risk adjusted capital (severe and moderate loss scenarios), despite some fluctuation in capital levels. Ample reserve history (8.0) that helps to protect the company against sharp claims increases. Excellent profitability (8.1) with operating gains in each of the last five years. Return on equity has been good over the last five years, averaging 10.6%.

Principal Business: Homeowners multiple peril (32%), commercial multiple peril (32%), auto liability (14%), auto physical damage (11%), workers compensation (6%), other liability (2%), and other lines (3%).

Principal Investments: Investment grade bonds (80%), misc. investments (13%), non investment grade bonds (7%), and real estate (1%).

Investments in Affiliates: None

Group Affiliation: Hanover Ins Group Inc

Licensed in: All states except FL, KY, LA, WY, PR

Commenced Business: August 1974

Address: 808 NORTH HIGHLANDER WAY, Howell, MI 48843-1070

Phone: (508) 853-7200   **Domicile State:** MI   **NAIC Code:** 31534

Data Date	Rating	RACR #1	RACR #2	Loss Ratio %	Total Assets ($mil)	Capital ($mil)	Net Premium ($mil)	Net Income ($mil)
3-17	B	4.60	3.06	N/A	1,541.6	717.8	180.7	9.1
3-16	B	4.84	3.29	N/A	1,469.6	699.8	167.1	45.9
2016	B	4.49	3.03	57.7	1,596.2	705.5	714.0	105.5
2015	B	4.36	2.98	58.3	1,526.4	660.4	680.7	100.8
2014	B	4.03	2.69	76.7	1,501.0	633.6	675.3	35.6
2013	B	4.35	3.04	67.1	1,476.6	662.2	679.8	67.9
2012	B	4.49	3.19	74.0	1,525.1	682.6	716.9	55.8

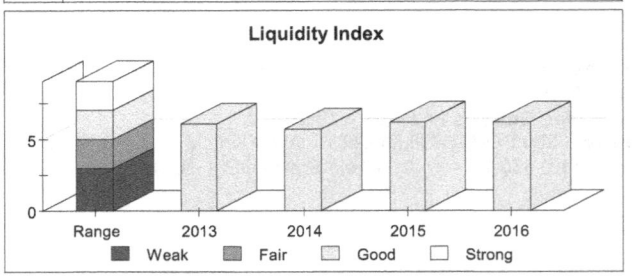

CLEARWATER SELECT INS CO D Weak

Major Rating Factors: Weak overall results on stability tests (1.7 on a scale of 0 to 10) including potential drain of affiliation with Fairfax Financial. The largest net exposure for one risk is excessive at 7.3% of capital. A history of deficient reserves (1.9). Underreserving can have an adverse impact on capital and profits. In 2013 and 2014 the two year reserve development was 401% and 466% deficient respectively.

Other Rating Factors: Good long-term capitalization index (6.9) based on good current risk adjusted capital (moderate loss scenario), despite some fluctuation in capital levels. Excellent profitability (8.6) with operating gains in each of the last five years. Excellent liquidity (8.7) with ample operational cash flow and liquid investments.

Principal Business: (This company is a reinsurer.)

Principal Investments: Investment grade bonds (66%), misc. investments (29%), non investment grade bonds (4%), and cash (1%).

Investments in Affiliates: 11%

Group Affiliation: Fairfax Financial

Licensed in: All states except CA, FL

Commenced Business: March 1994

Address: 300 FIRST STAMFORD PLACE, Stamford, CT 06902

Phone: (203) 977-8000 **Domicile State:** CT **NAIC Code:** 10019

Data Date	Rating	RACR #1	RACR #2	Loss Ratio %	Total Assets ($mil)	Capital ($mil)	Net Premium ($mil)	Net Income ($mil)
3-17	D	1.50	1.11	N/A	1,239.0	494.2	50.3	11.7
3-16	D	0.87	0.69	N/A	1,219.8	483.7	44.6	11.5
2016	D	1.49	1.11	57.6	1,193.5	473.4	196.7	54.5
2015	D	0.84	0.68	58.4	1,192.2	476.9	200.4	62.1
2014	D	0.69	0.56	58.4	1,177.7	431.6	222.5	48.3
2013	D	0.11	0.09	93.1	1,111.8	372.6	808.4	2.0
2012	U	43.36	27.71	N/A	118.6	111.3	0.0	6.0

Fairfax Financial
Composite Group Rating: C
Largest Group Members

	Assets ($mil)	Rating
ODYSSEY REINS CO	7163	C
US FIRE INS CO	3950	C
TIG INS CO	2818	C
ZENITH INS CO	1825	C+
CLEARWATER SELECT INS CO	1193	D

COAST NATIONAL INS CO D+ Weak

Major Rating Factors: Weak overall results on stability tests (2.7 on a scale of 0 to 10) including potential drain of affiliation with Farmers Insurance Group of Companies and weak results on operational trends. History of adequate reserve strength (6.0) as reserves have been consistently at an acceptable level.

Other Rating Factors: Good overall profitability index (6.7). Excellent expense controls. Return on equity has been low, averaging 1.7% over the past five years. Strong long-term capitalization index (10.0) based on excellent current risk adjusted capital (severe and moderate loss scenarios), despite some fluctuation in capital levels. Superior liquidity (10.0) with ample operational cash flow and liquid investments.

Principal Business: Auto liability (64%) and auto physical damage (36%).

Principal Investments: Investment grade bonds (82%), misc. investments (13%), cash (4%), and non investment grade bonds (1%).

Investments in Affiliates: 12%

Group Affiliation: Farmers Insurance Group of Companies

Licensed in: AZ, CA, FL, GA, MS, NV, OR, PA, TN, WA

Commenced Business: March 1987

Address: 333 S ANITA DR SUITE 150, Orange, CA 92868

Phone: (888) 888-0080 **Domicile State:** CA **NAIC Code:** 25089

Data Date	Rating	RACR #1	RACR #2	Loss Ratio %	Total Assets ($mil)	Capital ($mil)	Net Premium ($mil)	Net Income ($mil)
3-17	D+	7.94	7.28	N/A	598.4	429.0	0.0	2.0
3-16	D+	7.78	7.13	N/A	604.5	421.5	0.0	2.6
2016	D+	7.97	7.37	0.0	583.3	427.0	0.0	8.9
2015	D+	7.81	7.22	0.0	597.5	418.6	0.0	7.4
2014	D+	7.87	7.35	0.0	609.5	411.3	0.0	6.7
2013	D+	7.94	7.38	N/A	587.0	403.1	0.0	7.1
2012	D+	7.47	6.72	0.0	621.8	395.7	0.0	5.7

Farmers Insurance Group of Companies
Composite Group Rating: C
Largest Group Members

	Assets ($mil)	Rating
FARMERS INS EXCHANGE	16057	C
MID-CENTURY INS CO	3981	B
FIRE INS EXCHANGE	2429	C+
FOREMOST INS CO	2269	B
TRUCK INS EXCHANGE	2144	C+

COLONY INS CO C Fair

Major Rating Factors: Fair overall results on stability tests (3.3 on a scale of 0 to 10) including potential drain of affiliation with Argo Group Intl Holdings Ltd and weak results on operational trends. The largest net exposure for one risk is conservative at 1.3% of capital. Strong long-term capitalization index (7.3) based on excellent current risk adjusted capital (severe and moderate loss scenarios), despite some fluctuation in capital levels.

Other Rating Factors: Ample reserve history (9.3) that helps to protect the company against sharp claims increases. Excellent profitability (8.5) with operating gains in each of the last five years. Return on equity has been good over the last five years, averaging 13.5%. Excellent liquidity (7.3) with ample operational cash flow and liquid investments.

Principal Business: Other liability (55%), products liability (20%), commercial multiple peril (10%), allied lines (7%), auto liability (3%), earthquake (2%), and other lines (4%).

Principal Investments: Investment grade bonds (56%), misc. investments (34%), non investment grade bonds (9%), and cash (1%).

Investments in Affiliates: 5%

Group Affiliation: Argo Group Intl Holdings Ltd

Licensed in: All states except PR

Commenced Business: July 1981

Address: 8720 Stony Point Pkwy Ste 400, Richmond, VA 23235

Phone: (804) 560-2000 **Domicile State:** VA **NAIC Code:** 39993

Data Date	Rating	RACR #1	RACR #2	Loss Ratio %	Total Assets ($mil)	Capital ($mil)	Net Premium ($mil)	Net Income ($mil)
3-17	C	1.80	1.24	N/A	1,554.7	386.9	61.5	6.0
3-16	C	1.54	1.07	N/A	1,412.6	327.1	61.8	7.5
2016	C	1.77	1.22	59.6	1,494.7	368.9	261.8	30.3
2015	C	1.63	1.14	56.1	1,409.4	349.6	278.8	32.4
2014	C	1.88	1.30	43.3	1,318.8	319.8	234.6	81.1
2013	C	1.97	1.40	42.5	1,309.8	324.4	199.8	46.9
2012	C	1.87	1.31	46.1	1,277.1	328.0	175.7	39.6

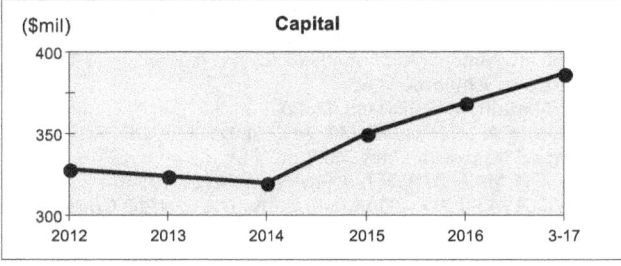

Capital ($mil)

COLUMBIA CASUALTY CO

C   **Fair**

Major Rating Factors: Fair overall results on stability tests (3.9 on a scale of 0 to 10) including fair financial strength of affiliated CNA Financial Corp and weak results on operational trends.

Other Rating Factors: Good overall profitability index (5.7). Fair expense controls. Return on equity has been low, averaging 2.8% over the past five years. Strong long-term capitalization index (10.0) based on excellent current risk adjusted capital (severe and moderate loss scenarios), despite some fluctuation in capital levels. Superior liquidity (10.0) with ample operational cash flow and liquid investments.

Principal Business: Other liability (70%), medical malpractice (20%), products liability (4%), fire, (3%), allied lines (1%), and burglary & theft (1%).

Principal Investments: Investment grade bonds (97%), misc. investments (2%), and non investment grade bonds (1%).

Investments in Affiliates: None

Group Affiliation: CNA Financial Corp

Licensed in: All states, the District of Columbia and Puerto Rico

Commenced Business: March 1974

Address: 333 S WABASH AVE, Chicago, IL 60604

Phone: (312) 822-5000   **Domicile State:** IL   **NAIC Code:** 31127

Data Date	Rating	RACR #1	RACR #2	Loss Ratio %	Total Assets ($mil)	Capital ($mil)	Net Premium ($mil)	Net Income ($mil)
3-17	C	67.76	28.06	N/A	240.6	240.1	0.0	1.6
3-16	C	70.58	29.31	N/A	250.3	247.3	0.0	1.9
2016	C	68.01	28.17	0.0	238.8	238.5	0.0	7.2
2015	C	68.89	28.58	0.0	247.4	247.3	0.0	5.3
2014	C	68.00	28.39	0.0	242.0	241.6	0.0	6.9
2013	C	67.97	28.36	0.0	235.2	234.9	0.0	6.8
2012	C	65.96	27.41	0.0	234.7	234.3	0.0	7.6

CNA Financial Corp
Composite Group Rating: C+

Largest Group Members	Assets ($mil)	Rating
CONTINENTAL CASUALTY CO	43520	C+
WESTERN SURETY CO	1999	C
CONTINENTAL INS CO	1667	C
COLUMBIA CASUALTY CO	239	C
AMERICAN CASUALTY CO OF READING	140	C

COMMERCE & INDUSTRY INS CO

C   **Fair**

Major Rating Factors: Fair overall results on stability tests (4.2 on a scale of 0 to 10) including weak results on operational trends and negative cash flow from operations for 2016. Strengths include potentially strong support from affiliation with American International Group.

Other Rating Factors: Weak profitability index (1.9). Fair expense controls. Return on equity has been fair, averaging 28.2% over the past five years. Vulnerable liquidity (0.0) as a spike in claims may stretch capacity. Strong long-term capitalization index (10.0) based on excellent current risk adjusted capital (severe and moderate loss scenarios), despite some fluctuation in capital levels.

Principal Business: (Not applicable due to unusual reinsurance transactions.)

Principal Investments: Investment grade bonds (91%), misc. investments (8%), and cash (1%).

Investments in Affiliates: 10%

Group Affiliation: American International Group

Licensed in: All states except PR

Commenced Business: December 1957

Address: 175 WATER STREET 18TH FLOOR, New York, NY 10038

Phone: (212) 770-7000   **Domicile State:** NY   **NAIC Code:** 19410

Data Date	Rating	RACR #1	RACR #2	Loss Ratio %	Total Assets ($mil)	Capital ($mil)	Net Premium ($mil)	Net Income ($mil)
3-17	C	8.94	8.17	N/A	403.2	394.2	0.0	9.1
3-16	C	1.85	1.22	N/A	3,216.4	367.8	0.0	71.0
2016	C	11.10	12.02	0.0	387.3	381.9	-521.1	152.8
2015	C	1.92	1.33	91.2	4,142.7	974.0	927.4	650.2
2014	C	2.79	1.87	85.6	4,770.8	1,624.9	590.4	263.8
2013	C	2.05	1.37	73.0	7,339.2	1,905.6	1,569.7	309.1
2012	C	2.28	1.56	85.3	7,350.7	2,041.5	1,353.6	131.7

American International Group
Composite Group Rating: B

Largest Group Members	Assets ($mil)	Rating
AMERICAN GENERAL LIFE INS CO	170850	B
VARIABLE ANNUITY LIFE INS CO	76675	B
AMERICAN HOME ASR CO	29685	C
UNITED STATES LIFE INS CO IN NYC	28610	B
NATIONAL UNION FIRE INS CO	26517	C

COMMERCE INS CO

C+   **Fair**

Major Rating Factors: Fair overall results on stability tests (4.6 on a scale of 0 to 10) including potential drain of affiliation with MAPFRE Ins Group, weak results on operational trends and negative cash flow from operations for 2016. Fair reserve development (4.2) as reserves have generally been sufficient to cover claims.

Other Rating Factors: Fair profitability index (3.4) with small operating losses during 2015. Return on equity has been fair, averaging 7.4% over the past five years. Fair liquidity (3.0) as cash resources may not be adequate to cover a spike in claims. Strong long-term capitalization index (8.1) based on excellent current risk adjusted capital (severe and moderate loss scenarios), despite some fluctuation in capital levels.

Principal Business: Auto liability (50%), auto physical damage (38%), homeowners multiple peril (8%), commercial multiple peril (2%), and fire (1%).

Principal Investments: Investment grade bonds (81%), misc. investments (16%), non investment grade bonds (3%), and real estate (3%).

Investments in Affiliates: 4%

Group Affiliation: MAPFRE Ins Group

Licensed in: CA, CT, FL, ME, MA, NH, NJ, NY, OH, OR, RI, TX, VT

Commenced Business: May 1972

Address: 211 MAIN STREET, Webster, MA 01570-0758

Phone: (508) 943-9000   **Domicile State:** MA   **NAIC Code:** 34754

Data Date	Rating	RACR #1	RACR #2	Loss Ratio %	Total Assets ($mil)	Capital ($mil)	Net Premium ($mil)	Net Income ($mil)
3-17	C+	2.20	1.74	N/A	2,144.7	630.5	318.6	5.7
3-16	C	2.43	1.88	N/A	2,196.6	658.4	306.8	4.6
2016	C+	2.13	1.75	78.2	2,183.7	621.3	1,285.1	48.0
2015	C	2.37	1.90	84.1	2,235.2	660.6	1,157.6	-1.7
2014	C	2.32	1.91	76.6	2,217.4	682.8	1,370.1	63.7
2013	B-	3.04	2.42	73.5	2,272.1	834.8	1,320.3	88.0
2012	B+	3.74	2.94	75.0	2,372.6	987.8	1,209.8	106.1

Rating Indexes

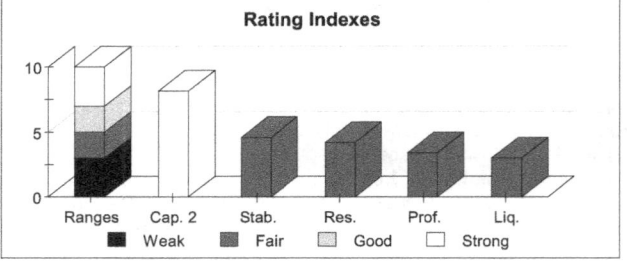

CONCORD GENERAL MUTUAL INS CO   B-   Good

Major Rating Factors: Fair overall results on stability tests (4.1 on a scale of 0 to 10) including potential drain of affiliation with Concord Group and weak results on operational trends. Good overall profitability index (6.8). Fair expense controls.

Other Rating Factors: Good liquidity (6.8) with sufficient resources (cash flows and marketable investments) to handle a spike in claims. Strong long-term capitalization index (7.9) based on excellent current risk adjusted capital (severe and moderate loss scenarios), despite some fluctuation in capital levels. Ample reserve history (8.5) that helps to protect the company against sharp claims increases.

Principal Business: Homeowners multiple peril (35%), auto liability (27%), auto physical damage (25%), commercial multiple peril (8%), other liability (3%), and inland marine (1%).

Principal Investments: Misc. investments (55%), investment grade bonds (40%), cash (2%), non investment grade bonds (2%), and real estate (1%).

Investments in Affiliates: 6%

Group Affiliation: Concord Group

Licensed in: ME, NH, SC, VT

Commenced Business: June 1928

Address: 4 BOUTON STREET, Concord, NH 03301-5023

Phone: (603) 224-4086   **Domicile State:** NH   **NAIC Code:** 20672

Data Date	Rating	RACR #1	RACR #2	Loss Ratio %	Total Assets ($mil)	Capital ($mil)	Net Premium ($mil)	Net Income ($mil)
3-17	B-	2.68	1.75	N/A	473.5	251.5	39.5	3.2
3-16	B-	2.56	1.71	N/A	434.5	222.8	40.2	1.0
2016	B-	2.68	1.76	60.5	469.6	245.8	162.5	13.6
2015	B-	2.55	1.71	74.6	438.2	221.6	164.1	0.4
2014	B-	2.60	1.74	72.2	449.5	226.2	167.7	4.4
2013	B-	2.60	1.72	67.4	426.1	211.9	164.6	10.1
2012	B-	2.88	1.90	68.8	373.6	187.2	155.0	7.9

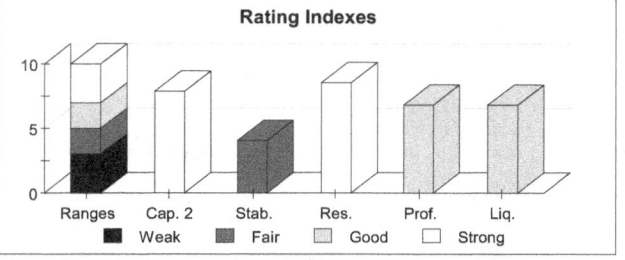

Rating Indexes

CONNECTICUT MEDICAL INS CO   B   Good

Major Rating Factors: Good profitability index (5.0 on a scale of 0 to 10) despite operating losses during the first three months of 2017. Fair overall results on stability tests (4.2) including weak results on operational trends.

Other Rating Factors: Strong long-term capitalization index (7.3) based on excellent current risk adjusted capital (severe and moderate loss scenarios). Moreover, capital levels have been consistent in recent years. Ample reserve history (9.3) that helps to protect the company against sharp claims increases. Excellent liquidity (7.8) with ample operational cash flow and liquid investments.

Principal Business: Medical malpractice (100%).

Principal Investments: Investment grade bonds (81%), misc. investments (18%), and cash (1%).

Investments in Affiliates: None

Group Affiliation: Connecticut Medical

Licensed in: CT, MA

Commenced Business: October 1984

Address: 80 Glastonbury Boulevard, Glastonbury, CT 06033

Phone: (860) 633-7788   **Domicile State:** CT   **NAIC Code:** 15890

Data Date	Rating	RACR #1	RACR #2	Loss Ratio %	Total Assets ($mil)	Capital ($mil)	Net Premium ($mil)	Net Income ($mil)
3-17	B	1.37	1.18	N/A	509.6	298.0	7.4	-1.1
3-16	B	1.52	1.30	N/A	492.9	288.3	9.0	0.8
2016	B	1.42	1.22	93.7	492.8	296.7	34.1	3.1
2015	B	1.57	1.35	67.5	476.7	286.8	31.8	8.9
2014	C+	1.65	1.41	63.2	480.2	279.1	31.1	10.7
2013	C+	1.73	1.48	58.6	468.6	264.4	35.9	11.2
2012	C+	7.50	5.50	24.7	440.8	243.7	34.1	21.0

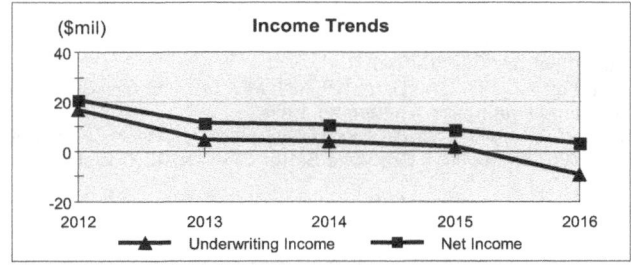

Income Trends

CONTINENTAL CASUALTY CO   C+   Fair

Major Rating Factors: Fair overall results on stability tests (3.3 on a scale of 0 to 10) including weak results on operational trends. The largest net exposure for one risk is high at 5.0% of capital. History of adequate reserve strength (6.3) as reserves have been consistently at an acceptable level.

Other Rating Factors: Good overall profitability index (5.3). Fair expense controls. Return on equity has been fair, averaging 7.6% over the past five years. Strong long-term capitalization index (7.8) based on excellent current risk adjusted capital (severe and moderate loss scenarios), despite some fluctuation in capital levels. Excellent liquidity (7.0) with ample operational cash flow and liquid investments.

Principal Business: Inland marine (51%), other liability (27%), other accident & health (5%), commercial multiple peril (4%), group accident & health (3%), workers compensation (2%), and other lines (9%).

Principal Investments: Investment grade bonds (75%), misc. investments (19%), and non investment grade bonds (6%).

Investments in Affiliates: 11%

Group Affiliation: CNA Financial Corp

Licensed in: All states, the District of Columbia and Puerto Rico

Commenced Business: December 1897

Address: 333 S WABASH AVE, Chicago, IL 60604

Phone: (312) 822-5000   **Domicile State:** IL   **NAIC Code:** 20443

Data Date	Rating	RACR #1	RACR #2	Loss Ratio %	Total Assets ($mil)	Capital ($mil)	Net Premium ($mil)	Net Income ($mil)
3-17	C+	1.92	1.45	N/A	43,255.0	10,414.8	1,328.9	262.5
3-16	C+	1.90	1.44	N/A	43,059.4	10,260.0	1,283.9	187.5
2016	C+	2.02	1.53	82.5	43,519.5	10,748.3	5,997.0	1,009.9
2015	C+	2.01	1.54	83.1	43,531.4	10,723.3	6,036.8	1,078.8
2014	C	2.09	1.60	85.1	43,309.7	11,155.2	6,007.1	839.3
2013	C+	2.04	1.59	87.8	42,642.3	11,136.7	6,246.7	788.0
2012	C+	1.94	1.48	94.8	41,292.2	9,998.4	6,162.5	348.2

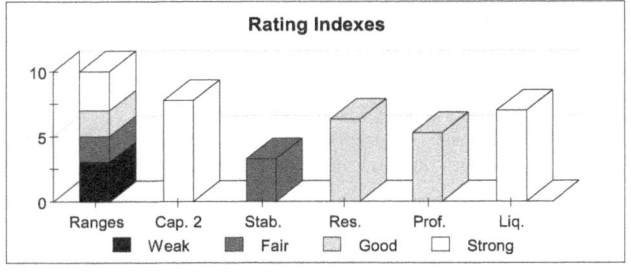

Rating Indexes

CONTINENTAL INS CO   C   Fair

Major Rating Factors: Fair reserve development (3.7 on a scale of 0 to 10) as reserves have generally been sufficient to cover claims. In 2013, the two year reserve development was 16% deficient. Fair overall results on stability tests (4.2) including fair financial strength of affiliated CNA Financial Corp and weak results on operational trends.

Other Rating Factors: Good overall profitability index (6.2). Weak expense controls. Return on equity has been low, averaging 4.6% over the past five years. Strong long-term capitalization index (10.0) based on excellent current risk adjusted capital (severe and moderate loss scenarios), despite some fluctuation in capital levels. Excellent liquidity (7.0) with ample operational cash flow and liquid investments.

Principal Business: Other liability (27%), commercial multiple peril (18%), workers compensation (14%), ocean marine (11%), auto liability (8%), surety (4%), and other lines (17%).

Principal Investments: Investment grade bonds (88%), misc. investments (11%), and non investment grade bonds (1%).

Investments in Affiliates: 10%

Group Affiliation: CNA Financial Corp

Licensed in: All states, the District of Columbia and Puerto Rico

Commenced Business: December 1977

Address: 100 MATSONFORD RD - STE 200, Radnor, PA 19087

Phone: (312) 822-5000   **Domicile State:** PA   **NAIC Code:** 35289

Data Date	Rating	RACR #1	RACR #2	Loss Ratio %	Total Assets ($mil)	Capital ($mil)	Net Premium ($mil)	Net Income ($mil)
3-17	C	6.35	3.44	N/A	1,694.4	1,519.1	0.0	14.1
3-16	C	5.93	3.19	N/A	1,650.2	1,469.1	0.0	11.5
2016	C	6.35	3.44	0.0	1,667.5	1,500.3	0.0	55.4
2015	C	6.41	3.56	0.0	1,666.9	1,469.3	0.0	53.1
2014	C	5.27	2.92	0.0	1,995.3	1,437.3	0.0	55.8
2013	C	4.78	2.58	0.0	2,345.5	1,366.9	0.0	121.8
2012	C	5.14	2.85	0.0	2,708.5	1,323.0	0.0	41.4

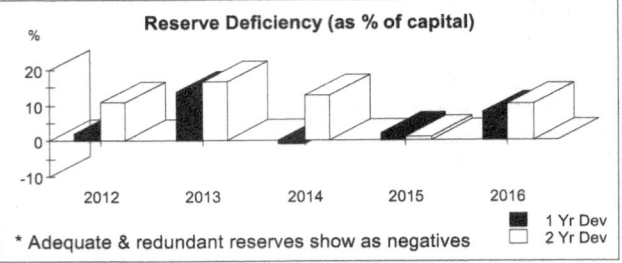

Reserve Deficiency (as % of capital)

* Adequate & redundant reserves show as negatives   ■ 1 Yr Dev   □ 2 Yr Dev

COPIC INS CO *   A-   Excellent

Major Rating Factors: Strong long-term capitalization index (10.0 on a scale of 0 to 10) based on excellent current risk adjusted capital (severe and moderate loss scenarios). Furthermore, this high level of risk adjusted capital has been consistently maintained in previous years. Ample reserve history (9.4) that helps to protect the company against sharp claims increases.

Other Rating Factors: Excellent profitability (7.7) with operating gains in each of the last five years. Excellent liquidity (8.1) with ample operational cash flow and liquid investments. Excellent overall results on stability tests (7.0). Stability strengths include excellent operational trends and excellent risk diversification.

Principal Business: Medical malpractice (95%), other liability (4%), and group accident & health (1%).

Principal Investments: Investment grade bonds (53%), misc. investments (45%), cash (1%), and non investment grade bonds (1%).

Investments in Affiliates: None

Group Affiliation: COPIC Trust

Licensed in: AZ, CO, GA, ID, IA, KS, MN, MO, MT, NE, OK, SD, UT, WY

Commenced Business: September 1984

Address: 7351 LOWRY BOULEVARD SUITE 400, Denver, CO 80230

Phone: (720) 858-6000   **Domicile State:** CO   **NAIC Code:** 11860

Data Date	Rating	RACR #1	RACR #2	Loss Ratio %	Total Assets ($mil)	Capital ($mil)	Net Premium ($mil)	Net Income ($mil)
3-17	A-	5.87	3.84	N/A	716.3	417.7	24.0	1.2
3-16	B	6.27	4.12	N/A	667.2	397.9	25.5	1.0
2016	B+	6.06	3.99	63.6	696.8	410.5	100.4	7.0
2015	B	6.43	4.21	56.3	657.3	396.1	82.1	1.9
2014	B	4.75	3.19	49.3	526.5	268.1	81.1	12.8
2013	A-	4.57	3.08	59.4	525.0	260.6	82.0	11.9
2012	A-	4.44	3.08	56.5	525.0	238.9	88.2	27.8

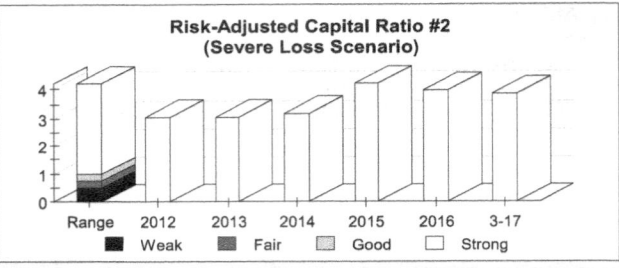

Risk-Adjusted Capital Ratio #2
(Severe Loss Scenario)

Range   2012   2013   2014   2015   2016   3-17
■ Weak   ■ Fair   ▨ Good   □ Strong

COPPERPOINT MUTUAL INS CO *   A+   Excellent

Major Rating Factors: Strong long-term capitalization index (8.5 on a scale of 0 to 10) based on excellent current risk adjusted capital (severe and moderate loss scenarios). Furthermore, this high level of risk adjusted capital has been consistently maintained in previous years. Excellent liquidity (7.6) with ample operational cash flow and liquid investments.

Other Rating Factors: Excellent overall results on stability tests (7.7). Stability strengths include excellent risk diversification. History of adequate reserve strength (6.9) as reserves have been consistently at an acceptable level. Good overall profitability index (6.7). Fair expense controls.

Principal Business: Workers compensation (100%).

Principal Investments: Investment grade bonds (74%), misc. investments (24%), non investment grade bonds (1%), and real estate (1%).

Investments in Affiliates: 2%

Group Affiliation: CopperPoint Group

Licensed in: AZ

Commenced Business: January 2013

Address: 3030 N 3RD STREET, Phoenix, AZ 85012

Phone: (602) 631-2240   **Domicile State:** AZ   **NAIC Code:** 14216

Data Date	Rating	RACR #1	RACR #2	Loss Ratio %	Total Assets ($mil)	Capital ($mil)	Net Premium ($mil)	Net Income ($mil)
3-17	A+	3.27	2.02	N/A	3,655.7	1,385.9	61.1	12.2
3-16	A+	3.08	1.92	N/A	3,576.8	1,266.4	60.3	7.8
2016	A+	3.31	2.03	76.2	3,606.3	1,351.8	247.6	57.5
2015	A+	3.16	1.96	78.5	3,562.5	1,258.8	242.1	61.9
2014	A+	2.59	1.61	78.2	3,560.4	1,229.7	239.6	51.2
2013	A+	2.22	1.38	89.2	3,536.2	1,186.2	222.5	44.7
2012	U	266.05	133.00	101.8	3,729.6	1,066.6	183.5	287.6

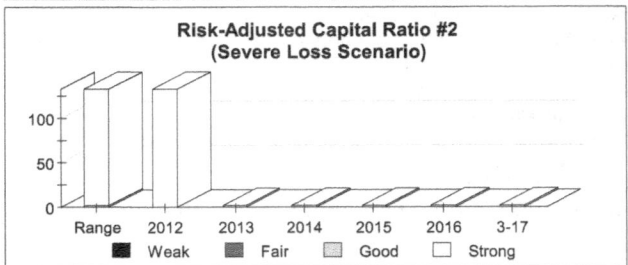

Risk-Adjusted Capital Ratio #2
(Severe Loss Scenario)

Range   2012   2013   2014   2015   2016   3-17
■ Weak   ■ Fair   ▨ Good   □ Strong

COUNTRY CASUALTY INS CO *　　　　　　　　B+　　　Good

Major Rating Factors: Good overall profitability index (6.5 on a scale of 0 to 10). Excellent expense controls. Return on equity has been low, averaging 1.4% over the past five years. Good overall results on stability tests (5.0) despite weak results on operational trends. Strengths include potential support from affiliation with COUNTRY Financial.

Other Rating Factors: Strong long-term capitalization index (10.0) based on excellent current risk adjusted capital (severe and moderate loss scenarios), despite some fluctuation in capital levels. Superior liquidity (10.0) with ample operational cash flow and liquid investments.

Principal Business: Auto liability (43%), homeowners multiple peril (34%), and auto physical damage (23%).

Principal Investments: Investment grade bonds (85%), misc. investments (14%), and cash (1%).

Investments in Affiliates: None

Group Affiliation: COUNTRY Financial

Licensed in: AL, AK, AZ, AR, CO, CT, DE, GA, ID, IL, IN, IA, KS, KY, ME, MD, MA, MI, MN, MO, MT, NE, NV, NM, ND, OH, OK, OR, PA, RI, SD, TN, TX, WA, WI, WY

Commenced Business: March 1964

Address: 1701 N TOWANDA AVENUE, Bloomington, IL 61701-2090

Phone: (309) 821-3000　　**Domicile State:** IL　　**NAIC Code:** 20982

Data Date	Rating	RACR #1	RACR #2	Loss Ratio %	Total Assets ($mil)	Capital ($mil)	Net Premium ($mil)	Net Income ($mil)
3-17	B+	22.73	20.46	N/A	85.4	69.6	0.0	0.1
3-16	B+	22.24	20.02	N/A	85.5	69.2	0.0	0.3
2016	B+	24.12	21.71	0.0	83.8	69.6	0.0	0.6
2015	B+	25.60	23.04	0.0	81.3	68.9	0.0	0.8
2014	B+	27.50	24.75	0.0	78.2	67.9	0.0	1.0
2013	B+	26.67	24.00	0.0	77.7	67.0	0.0	1.2
2012	B+	26.57	23.91	0.0	77.0	66.4	0.0	1.1

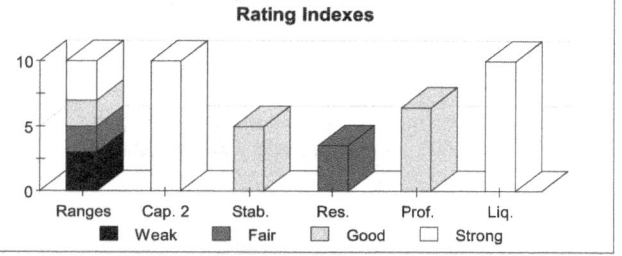

Rating Indexes

COUNTRY MUTUAL INS CO *　　　　　　　　A-　　　Excellent

Major Rating Factors: Strong long-term capitalization index (9.9 on a scale of 0 to 10) based on excellent current risk adjusted capital (severe and moderate loss scenarios). Furthermore, this high level of risk adjusted capital has been consistently maintained in previous years. History of adequate reserve strength (5.5) as reserves have been consistently at an acceptable level.

Other Rating Factors: Good overall profitability index (6.8). Fair expense controls. Good liquidity (6.2) with sufficient resources (cash flows and marketable investments) to handle a spike in claims. Good overall results on stability tests (5.9) despite weak results on operational trends.

Principal Business: Homeowners multiple peril (42%), auto liability (16%), auto physical damage (12%), farmowners multiple peril (10%), commercial multiple peril (7%), allied lines (6%), and other lines (8%).

Principal Investments: Investment grade bonds (63%), misc. investments (34%), and non investment grade bonds (3%).

Investments in Affiliates: 4%

Group Affiliation: COUNTRY Financial

Licensed in: All states except DC, FL, HI, LA, MS, PR

Commenced Business: November 1925

Address: 1701 N TOWANDA AVENUE, Bloomington, IL 61701-2090

Phone: (309) 821-3000　　**Domicile State:** IL　　**NAIC Code:** 20990

Data Date	Rating	RACR #1	RACR #2	Loss Ratio %	Total Assets ($mil)	Capital ($mil)	Net Premium ($mil)	Net Income ($mil)
3-17	A-	4.58	3.26	N/A	4,756.8	2,425.9	544.3	2.5
3-16	A-	4.38	3.13	N/A	4,337.5	2,118.5	480.9	51.8
2016	A-	4.45	3.19	71.6	4,390.6	2,207.7	2,023.8	109.2
2015	A-	4.26	3.05	70.7	4,295.7	2,072.0	2,023.5	120.0
2014	A-	3.74	2.70	70.3	4,255.7	1,964.2	2,055.1	178.0
2013	A-	3.56	2.56	69.3	4,150.3	1,825.5	2,051.7	151.3
2012	B+	3.41	2.46	75.5	3,930.7	1,635.9	1,979.7	47.1

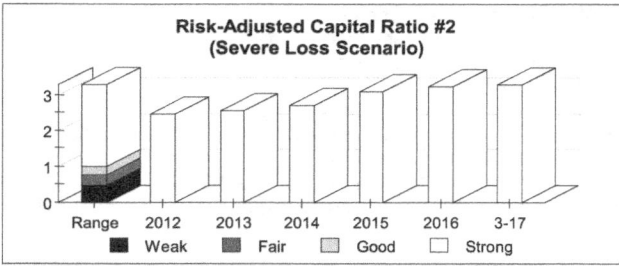

Risk-Adjusted Capital Ratio #2
(Severe Loss Scenario)

COURTESY INS CO　　　　　　　　　　　　　B　　　Good

Major Rating Factors: History of adequate reserve strength (6.0 on a scale of 0 to 10) as reserves have been consistently at an acceptable level. Fair overall results on stability tests (4.2) including potential drain of affiliation with J M Family Enterprise Group and weak results on operational trends.

Other Rating Factors: Strong long-term capitalization index (10.0) based on excellent current risk adjusted capital (severe and moderate loss scenarios). Moreover, capital levels have been consistent in recent years. Excellent profitability (8.7) with operating gains in each of the last five years. Excellent liquidity (7.1) with ample operational cash flow and liquid investments.

Principal Business: Aggregate write-ins for other lines of business (26%).

Principal Investments: Investment grade bonds (84%) and misc. investments (16%).

Investments in Affiliates: None

Group Affiliation: J M Family Enterprise Group

Licensed in: All states except MI

Commenced Business: May 1988

Address: 100 Jim Moran Boulevard, Deerfield Beach, FL 33442

Phone: (954) 429-2150　　**Domicile State:** FL　　**NAIC Code:** 26492

Data Date	Rating	RACR #1	RACR #2	Loss Ratio %	Total Assets ($mil)	Capital ($mil)	Net Premium ($mil)	Net Income ($mil)
3-17	B	9.54	5.44	N/A	810.4	384.1	33.9	1.1
3-16	B	10.01	5.65	N/A	781.3	363.5	30.9	2.5
2016	B	10.02	5.73	85.7	789.6	377.8	128.8	10.7
2015	B	10.51	5.95	67.6	764.8	360.1	135.6	23.2
2014	B	9.84	5.60	57.9	735.4	341.6	121.7	33.2
2013	B	9.23	5.31	52.7	686.5	308.4	124.9	38.3
2012	B	8.81	5.04	45.1	627.2	265.0	138.6	29.8

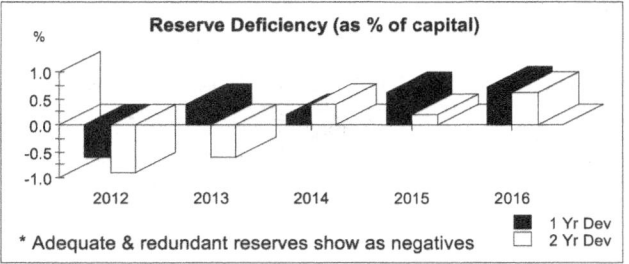

Reserve Deficiency (as % of capital)

* Adequate & redundant reserves show as negatives

CSAA INS EXCHANGE

B-   **Good**

Major Rating Factors: Fair overall results on stability tests (4.8 on a scale of 0 to 10) including weak results on operational trends. History of adequate reserve strength (6.1) as reserves have been consistently at an acceptable level.

Other Rating Factors: Good liquidity (6.1) with sufficient resources (cash flows and marketable investments) to handle a spike in claims. Strong long-term capitalization index (9.0) based on excellent current risk adjusted capital (severe and moderate loss scenarios), despite some fluctuation in capital levels. Weak profitability index (2.9) with operating losses during 2015 and the first three months of 2017.

Principal Business: Auto liability (38%), auto physical damage (36%), homeowners multiple peril (23%), and other liability (1%).

Principal Investments: Investment grade bonds (52%), misc. investments (39%), non investment grade bonds (8%), and real estate (2%).

Investments in Affiliates: 5%

Group Affiliation: CSAA Insurance Group

Licensed in: AZ, CA, IN, MO, NV, NJ, NY, UT, WY

Commenced Business: August 1914

Address: 3055 OAK ROAD, Walnut Creek, CA 94597-2098

Phone: (925) 279-2300   **Domicile State:** CA   **NAIC Code:** 15539

Data Date	Rating	RACR #1	RACR #2	Loss Ratio %	Total Assets ($mil)	Capital ($mil)	Net Premium ($mil)	Net Income ($mil)
3-17	B-	3.44	2.33	N/A	7,009.7	3,443.4	816.9	-20.3
3-16	B-	3.12	2.14	N/A	6,614.2	3,352.0	777.6	-23.0
2016	B-	3.42	2.35	75.0	6,812.9	3,387.8	3,290.5	68.3
2015	B-	3.17	2.19	81.6	6,572.3	3,378.1	3,116.8	-120.8
2014	B	3.51	2.45	73.4	6,983.9	3,749.3	2,899.6	122.6
2013	A-	3.82	2.68	74.1	6,672.1	3,830.2	2,714.9	114.9
2012	A-	3.79	2.69	69.5	6,430.9	3,624.9	2,637.5	131.2

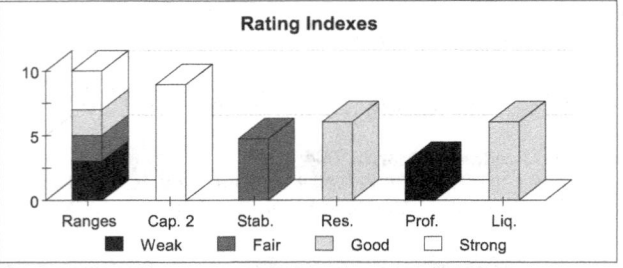

Rating Indexes

CUMIS INS SOCIETY INC *

A-   **Excellent**

Major Rating Factors: Strong long-term capitalization index (10.0 on a scale of 0 to 10) based on excellent current risk adjusted capital (severe and moderate loss scenarios). Moreover, capital levels have been consistent in recent years. Ample reserve history (9.2) that helps to protect the company against sharp claims increases.

Other Rating Factors: Excellent profitability (8.8) with operating gains in each of the last five years. Good overall results on stability tests (6.9). Stability strengths include good operational trends and excellent risk diversification. The largest net exposure for one risk is conservative at 1.1% of capital. Good liquidity (6.3) with sufficient resources (cash flows and marketable investments) to handle a spike in claims.

Principal Business: Other liability (67%), fidelity (15%), commercial multiple peril (13%), auto physical damage (2%), auto liability (1%), and credit (1%).

Principal Investments: Investment grade bonds (83%), misc. investments (14%), non investment grade bonds (2%), and cash (1%).

Investments in Affiliates: 4%

Group Affiliation: CUNA Mutual Ins Group

Licensed in: All states, the District of Columbia and Puerto Rico

Commenced Business: June 1960

Address: 2000 HERITAGE WAY, Waverly, IA 50677

Phone: (608) 238-5851   **Domicile State:** IA   **NAIC Code:** 10847

Data Date	Rating	RACR #1	RACR #2	Loss Ratio %	Total Assets ($mil)	Capital ($mil)	Net Premium ($mil)	Net Income ($mil)
3-17	A-	5.21	3.78	N/A	1,894.2	885.4	207.7	13.6
3-16	B	5.24	3.74	N/A	1,736.7	820.6	190.4	21.7
2016	B+	5.22	3.81	64.8	1,832.6	869.2	820.9	69.8
2015	B	4.99	3.58	64.4	1,711.8	800.5	826.3	110.9
2014	B	4.48	3.25	63.4	2,062.8	714.9	652.2	80.9
2013	B	4.63	3.27	63.8	1,637.6	621.7	621.0	58.5
2012	B	4.67	3.28	63.5	1,636.9	562.0	553.1	29.1

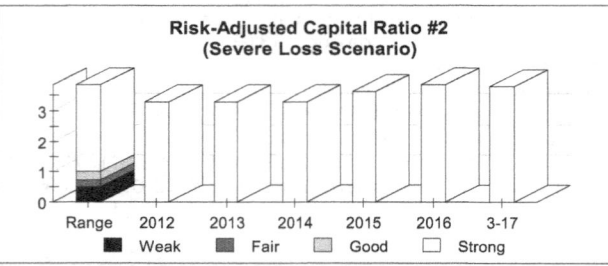

Risk-Adjusted Capital Ratio #2
(Severe Loss Scenario)

CYPRESS INS CO

C+   **Fair**

Major Rating Factors: Good long-term capitalization (5.0 on a scale of 0 to 10) based on good current risk adjusted capital (severe loss scenario) reflecting some improvement over results in 2016. Fair overall results on stability tests (4.4) including fair financial strength of affiliated Berkshire-Hathaway and fair risk adjusted capital in prior years.

Other Rating Factors: Ample reserve history (9.3) that helps to protect the company against sharp claims increases. Excellent profitability (8.5) with operating gains in each of the last five years. Superior liquidity (9.0) with ample operational cash flow and liquid investments.

Principal Business: Workers compensation (91%), auto liability (6%), auto physical damage (2%), and commercial multiple peril (1%).

Principal Investments: Investment grade bonds (61%), misc. investments (38%), and cash (1%).

Investments in Affiliates: 10%

Group Affiliation: Berkshire-Hathaway

Licensed in: AL, AR, CA, CO, DE, GA, HI, ID, IA, MS, NE, NM, OK, SC, TN, TX, VA

Commenced Business: March 1963

Address: 1 California Street Suite 600, San Francisco, CA 94111

Phone: (888) 495-8949   **Domicile State:** CA   **NAIC Code:** 10855

Data Date	Rating	RACR #1	RACR #2	Loss Ratio %	Total Assets ($mil)	Capital ($mil)	Net Premium ($mil)	Net Income ($mil)
3-17	C+	1.04	0.76	N/A	1,573.5	397.3	106.6	14.1
3-16	C+	1.10	0.77	N/A	1,319.8	306.8	104.6	35.7
2016	C+	1.00	0.73	68.0	1,499.7	366.0	428.9	76.8
2015	C+	1.21	0.84	77.3	1,284.2	305.7	327.0	6.8
2014	C	1.26	0.85	77.4	1,203.2	311.5	254.3	26.6
2013	C	1.45	1.01	78.9	1,140.2	264.4	271.9	25.3
2012	C	1.22	0.87	85.7	1,065.2	207.2	265.5	12.7

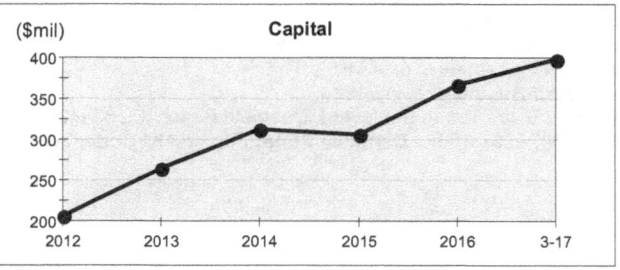

Capital

DAIRYLAND INS CO *   B+   Good

Major Rating Factors: Good overall profitability index (5.6 on a scale of 0 to 10). Fair expense controls. Return on equity has been fair, averaging 5.6% over the past five years. Good liquidity (6.8) with sufficient resources (cash flows and marketable investments) to handle a spike in claims.

Other Rating Factors: Good overall results on stability tests (5.3) despite weak results on operational trends. Strong long-term capitalization index (9.6) based on excellent current risk adjusted capital (severe and moderate loss scenarios), despite some fluctuation in capital levels. Ample reserve history (8.0) that helps to protect the company against sharp claims increases.

Principal Business: Auto liability (68%) and auto physical damage (32%).

Principal Investments: Investment grade bonds (89%), misc. investments (10%), and non investment grade bonds (1%).

Investments in Affiliates: None

Group Affiliation: Sentry Ins Group

Licensed in: All states except CA, DC, HI, LA, NJ, OK, PR

Commenced Business: February 1953

Address: 1800 NORTH POINT DRIVE, Stevens Point, WI 54481

Phone: (715) 346-6000   **Domicile State:** WI   **NAIC Code:** 21164

Data Date	Rating	RACR #1	RACR #2	Loss Ratio %	Total Assets ($mil)	Capital ($mil)	Net Premium ($mil)	Net Income ($mil)
3-17	B+	4.23	2.68	N/A	1,297.4	484.6	87.5	4.8
3-16	B+	4.48	2.82	N/A	1,266.0	485.5	83.2	4.6
2016	B+	4.26	2.73	73.9	1,272.8	475.4	352.2	24.1
2015	B+	4.57	2.92	72.7	1,239.6	482.0	328.5	29.3
2014	B+	5.05	3.38	74.9	1,194.9	485.3	317.4	34.8
2013	A+	4.86	3.30	76.3	1,163.2	471.7	318.1	25.6
2012	A+	4.95	3.35	77.3	1,129.0	460.8	302.3	21.7

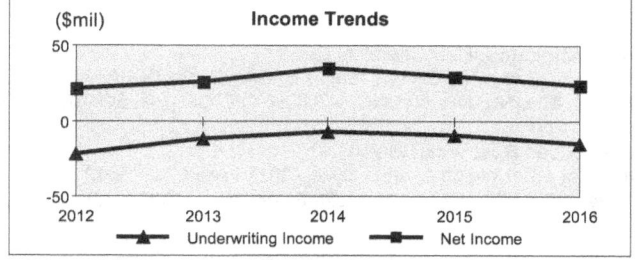

Income Trends

DOCTORS CO AN INTERINS   B-   Good

Major Rating Factors: Fair overall results on stability tests (4.7 on a scale of 0 to 10) including potential drain of affiliation with Doctors Co Group and weak results on operational trends. Fair profitability index (3.7) with operating losses during 2015 and the first three months of 2017.

Other Rating Factors: Strong long-term capitalization index (7.7) based on excellent current risk adjusted capital (severe and moderate loss scenarios), despite some fluctuation in capital levels. Ample reserve history (8.8) that helps to protect the company against sharp claims increases. Excellent liquidity (7.1) with ample operational cash flow and liquid investments.

Principal Business: Medical malpractice (99%) and other liability (1%).

Principal Investments: Misc. investments (53%), investment grade bonds (42%), cash (3%), and non investment grade bonds (2%).

Investments in Affiliates: 18%

Group Affiliation: Doctors Co Group

Licensed in: All states except PR

Commenced Business: April 1976

Address: 185 GREENWOOD ROAD, Napa, CA 94558

Phone: (707) 226-0100   **Domicile State:** CA   **NAIC Code:** 34495

Data Date	Rating	RACR #1	RACR #2	Loss Ratio %	Total Assets ($mil)	Capital ($mil)	Net Premium ($mil)	Net Income ($mil)
3-17	B-	1.97	1.59	N/A	4,272.9	1,929.6	144.8	-23.1
3-16	B-	1.89	1.49	N/A	4,182.1	1,779.1	153.9	-20.7
2016	B-	2.01	1.63	77.7	4,132.2	1,925.9	602.4	-70.2
2015	B-	1.95	1.54	74.5	3,585.4	1,808.9	622.9	-72.8
2014	B-	1.93	1.53	78.3	3,559.8	1,821.9	644.0	31.3
2013	B-	1.88	1.54	75.1	3,313.2	1,731.7	675.7	27.7
2012	B-	1.61	1.40	69.1	2,769.5	1,358.3	596.5	120.9

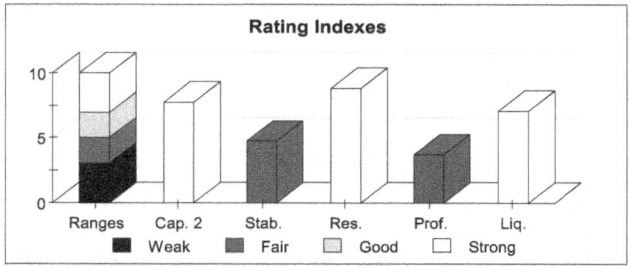

Rating Indexes

DONEGAL MUTUAL INS CO   B-   Good

Major Rating Factors: Fair overall results on stability tests (4.3 on a scale of 0 to 10) including potential drain of affiliation with Donegal Mutual Insurance Company and weak results on operational trends. Good long-term capitalization index (6.7) based on good current risk adjusted capital (moderate loss scenario). Moreover, capital levels have been consistent over the last several years.

Other Rating Factors: History of adequate reserve strength (5.9) as reserves have been consistently at an acceptable level. Excellent profitability (8.3) with operating gains in each of the last five years. Excellent liquidity (7.0) with ample operational cash flow and liquid investments.

Principal Business: Homeowners multiple peril (24%), auto liability (22%), commercial multiple peril (17%), auto physical damage (16%), workers compensation (11%), other liability (5%), and other lines (5%).

Principal Investments: Misc. investments (76%), real estate (12%), investment grade bonds (7%), and cash (5%).

Investments in Affiliates: 65%

Group Affiliation: Donegal Mutual Insurance Company

Licensed in: AL, DC, DE, GA, IL, IN, IA, ME, MD, MI, NE, NH, NC, OH, OK, PA, SC, SD, TN, TX, VT, VA, WV, WI

Commenced Business: May 1889

Address: 1195 River Road, Marietta, PA 17547-0302

Phone: (717) 426-1931   **Domicile State:** PA   **NAIC Code:** 13692

Data Date	Rating	RACR #1	RACR #2	Loss Ratio %	Total Assets ($mil)	Capital ($mil)	Net Premium ($mil)	Net Income ($mil)
3-17	B-	1.01	0.96	N/A	462.3	237.4	31.8	0.3
3-16	B-	0.97	0.92	N/A	437.6	218.1	27.6	2.8
2016	B-	1.01	0.96	59.1	469.0	235.2	118.0	16.8
2015	B-	0.94	0.90	65.7	431.2	209.4	109.8	14.0
2014	B-	1.08	1.02	75.7	393.7	204.4	102.7	3.5
2013	B-	1.09	1.02	59.2	383.8	204.4	97.8	15.4
2012	B-	1.03	0.96	73.0	350.7	187.7	84.7	5.9

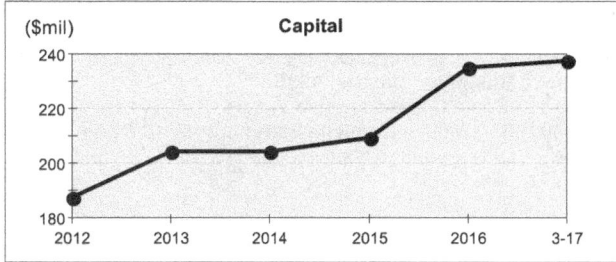

Capital

DORINCO REINS CO

C- **Fair**

Major Rating Factors: Weak overall results on stability tests (2.6 on a scale of 0 to 10) including potential drain of affiliation with Dow Chemical Co and weak results on operational trends. The largest net exposure for one risk is high at 4.4% of capital. Good overall profitability index (6.3). Good expense controls. Return on equity has been good over the last five years, averaging 13.9%.

Other Rating Factors: Good liquidity (6.7) with sufficient resources (cash flows and marketable investments) to handle a spike in claims. Strong long-term capitalization index (7.2) based on excellent current risk adjusted capital (severe and moderate loss scenarios), despite some fluctuation in capital levels. Ample reserve history (7.0) that can protect against increases in claims costs.

Principal Business: Fire (52%), other liability (48%), and products liability (1%).

Principal Investments: Investment grade bonds (71%) and misc. investments (29%).

Investments in Affiliates: None

Group Affiliation: Dow Chemical Co

Licensed in: AL, AZ, CA, CT, DE, FL, GA, ID, IL, IN, IA, KS, KY, LA, MD, MI, MN, MS, MO, NE, NH, NY, NC, ND, OH, OK, OR, PA, SC, SD, TX, UT, VT, VA, WV, WI, WY

Commenced Business: March 1977

Address: 1320 Waldo Avenue Suite 200, Midland, MI 48642

Phone: (989) 636-0047   **Domicile State:** MI   **NAIC Code:** 33499

Data Date	Rating	RACR #1	RACR #2	Loss Ratio %	Total Assets ($mil)	Capital ($mil)	Net Premium ($mil)	Net Income ($mil)
3-17	C-	1.48	1.10	N/A	1,538.0	549.5	43.5	11.4
3-16	C-	1.50	1.09	N/A	1,536.2	544.0	40.2	37.0
2016	C-	1.49	1.11	50.9	1,522.9	532.0	172.7	85.5
2015	C-	1.42	1.02	60.2	1,536.2	514.0	153.7	85.8
2014	D+	1.37	1.10	70.8	1,565.9	531.8	171.7	75.0
2013	D+	1.32	1.04	72.9	1,571.4	529.5	196.8	73.2
2012	D+	1.25	1.00	77.5	1,553.3	524.0	208.4	54.4

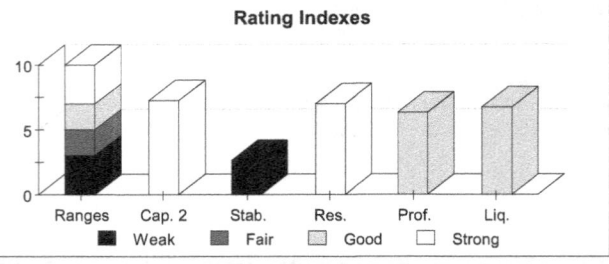

Rating Indexes

Ranges   Cap. 2   Stab.   Res.   Prof.   Liq.
■ Weak   ■ Fair   ▨ Good   ☐ Strong

EAGLESTONE REINS CO

C **Fair**

Major Rating Factors: Fair overall results on stability tests (3.1 on a scale of 0 to 10) including weak risk adjusted capital in prior years and weak results on operational trends. The largest net exposure for one risk is excessive at 5.3% of capital. Strengths include potentially strong support from affiliation with American International Group. Fair profitability index (3.6) with operating losses during 2014, 2015 and 2016. Return on equity has been low, averaging 0.2% over the past five years.

Other Rating Factors: Poor long-term capitalization index (0.6) based on weak current risk adjusted capital (severe and moderate loss scenarios), although results have slipped from the excellent range over the last two years. A history of deficient reserves (1.6) that places pressure on both capital and profits. In four of the last five years reserves (two year development) were between 21% and 45% deficient. Superior liquidity (9.6) with ample operational cash flow and liquid investments.

Principal Business: (This company is a reinsurer.)

Principal Investments: Investment grade bonds (89%), misc. investments (8%), and non investment grade bonds (3%).

Investments in Affiliates: None

Group Affiliation: American International Group

Licensed in: DE, IL, NY, PA

Commenced Business: April 1996

Address: 2595 INTERSTATE DRIVE STE 103, Harrisburg, PA 17110

Phone: (212) 770-7000   **Domicile State:** PA   **NAIC Code:** 10651

Data Date	Rating	RACR #1	RACR #2	Loss Ratio %	Total Assets ($mil)	Capital ($mil)	Net Premium ($mil)	Net Income ($mil)
3-17	C	0.27	0.22	N/A	6,355.1	1,881.2	28.0	52.0
3-16	B	1.68	1.12	N/A	6,600.1	1,878.5	24.5	26.6
2016	C	0.26	0.21	766.6	6,461.9	1,828.4	4.5	-228.8
2015	B	1.63	1.10	N/A	6,792.3	1,858.7	40.4	-3.4
2014	U	2.14	1.37	N/A	5,593.6	1,727.9	0.0	-209.4
2013	B	2.32	1.46	N/A	5,805.7	1,937.4	0.5	377.9
2012	B	1.41	0.91	223.5	6,199.7	1,358.8	539.9	49.8

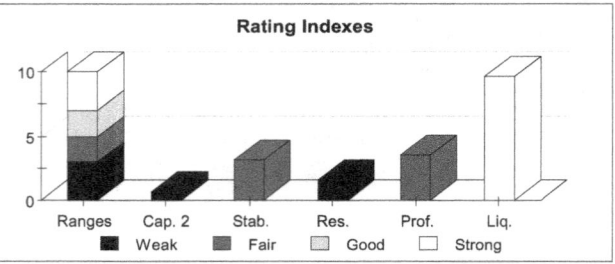

Rating Indexes

Ranges   Cap. 2   Stab.   Res.   Prof.   Liq.
■ Weak   ■ Fair   ▨ Good   ☐ Strong

ECONOMY FIRE & CAS CO

B- **Good**

Major Rating Factors: Fair overall results on stability tests (4.7 on a scale of 0 to 10) including weak results on operational trends. Good overall profitability index (6.6). Fair expense controls. Return on equity has been low, averaging 4.2% over the past five years.

Other Rating Factors: Strong long-term capitalization index (10.0) based on excellent current risk adjusted capital (severe and moderate loss scenarios), despite some fluctuation in capital levels. Excellent liquidity (7.0) with ample operational cash flow and liquid investments.

Principal Business: Auto liability (47%), auto physical damage (41%), and homeowners multiple peril (12%).

Principal Investments: Investment grade bonds (84%), misc. investments (15%), and real estate (1%).

Investments in Affiliates: 15%

Group Affiliation: MetLife Inc

Licensed in: All states except DC, DE, ME, MA, NH, NJ, RI, SC, PR

Commenced Business: January 1935

Address: 177 South Commons Drive, Aurora, IL 60504

Phone: (401) 827-2400   **Domicile State:** IL   **NAIC Code:** 22926

Data Date	Rating	RACR #1	RACR #2	Loss Ratio %	Total Assets ($mil)	Capital ($mil)	Net Premium ($mil)	Net Income ($mil)
3-17	B-	6.58	6.04	N/A	503.8	384.8	0.0	2.7
3-16	B-	6.69	6.11	N/A	487.0	379.5	0.0	3.5
2016	B-	6.59	6.08	0.0	502.0	381.7	0.0	15.0
2015	B-	6.68	6.13	0.0	477.8	375.5	0.0	12.7
2014	B-	6.75	6.16	0.0	467.9	369.3	0.0	15.1
2013	B-	6.85	6.23	0.0	456.3	362.8	0.0	17.4
2012	B-	7.15	6.50	0.0	450.6	364.1	0.0	18.2

MetLife Inc Composite Group Rating: B- Largest Group Members	Assets ($mil)	Rating
METROPOLITAN LIFE INS CO	396367	B-
BRIGHTHOUSE LIFE INSURANCE CO	170910	B
GENERAL AMERICAN LIFE INS CO	12412	B
AMERICAN LIFE INS CO	10378	C
NEW ENGLAND LIFE INS CO	9802	B

ELECTRIC INS CO | C+ | Fair

Major Rating Factors: Fair overall results on stability tests (3.4 on a scale of 0 to 10) including potential drain of affiliation with Wilmington Trust and weak results on operational trends. The largest net exposure for one risk is conservative at 1.3% of capital. Good overall profitability index (6.0). Good expense controls. Return on equity has been fair, averaging 5.3% over the past five years.

Other Rating Factors: Good liquidity (6.7) with sufficient resources (cash flows and marketable investments) to handle a spike in claims. Strong long-term capitalization index (8.7) based on excellent current risk adjusted capital (severe and moderate loss scenarios), despite some fluctuation in capital levels. Ample reserve history (9.3) that helps to protect the company against sharp claims increases.

Principal Business: Workers compensation (30%), homeowners multiple peril (21%), auto liability (20%), auto physical damage (14%), products liability (11%), other liability (2%), and inland marine (1%).

Principal Investments: Investment grade bonds (88%), misc. investments (12%), and real estate (1%).

Investments in Affiliates: 2%

Group Affiliation: Wilmington Trust

Licensed in: All states, the District of Columbia and Puerto Rico

Commenced Business: September 1966

Address: 75 Sam Fonzo Drive, Beverly, MA 01915-1000

Phone: (978) 921-2080 **Domicile State:** MA **NAIC Code:** 21261

Data Date	Rating	RACR #1	RACR #2	Loss Ratio %	Total Assets ($mil)	Capital ($mil)	Net Premium ($mil)	Net Income ($mil)
3-17	C+	3.60	2.17	N/A	1,577.7	539.7	79.3	7.1
3-16	C+	3.48	2.14	N/A	1,703.4	555.5	102.4	5.2
2016	C+	3.57	2.16	76.0	1,488.6	534.1	329.3	30.2
2015	C+	3.62	2.24	81.6	1,507.8	545.5	346.5	23.6
2014	C+	3.68	2.30	82.4	1,467.2	537.6	302.0	25.4
2013	C+	3.16	1.92	79.8	1,448.7	522.6	353.3	33.6
2012	C+	2.64	1.63	85.5	1,442.4	481.7	367.0	25.6

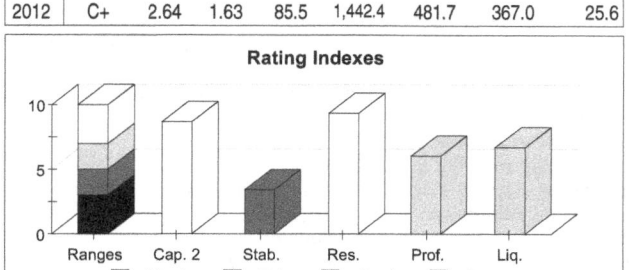

Rating Indexes

Ranges Cap. 2 Stab. Res. Prof. Liq.

■ Weak ■ Fair ☐ Good ☐ Strong

EMC REINS CO | B- | Good

Major Rating Factors: Fair overall results on stability tests (3.8 on a scale of 0 to 10) including weak results on operational trends. The largest net exposure for one risk is acceptable at 2.7% of capital. Good liquidity (6.8) with sufficient resources (cash flows and marketable investments) to handle a spike in claims.

Other Rating Factors: Strong long-term capitalization index (8.1) based on excellent current risk adjusted capital (severe and moderate loss scenarios). Moreover, capital levels have been consistent in recent years. Ample reserve history (9.4) that helps to protect the company against sharp claims increases. Excellent profitability (8.8) with operating gains in each of the last five years. Return on equity has been good over the last five years, averaging 10.5%.

Principal Business: (This company is a reinsurer.)

Principal Investments: Investment grade bonds (80%) and misc. investments (20%).

Investments in Affiliates: None

Group Affiliation: Employers Mutual Group

Licensed in: CO, CT, FL, GA, IA, KS, MD, NY, NC, PA, SC, TX

Commenced Business: February 1981

Address: 717 MULBERRY STREET, Des Moines, IA 50309-3872

Phone: (515) 280-2511 **Domicile State:** IA **NAIC Code:** 40509

Data Date	Rating	RACR #1	RACR #2	Loss Ratio %	Total Assets ($mil)	Capital ($mil)	Net Premium ($mil)	Net Income ($mil)
3-17	B-	2.70	1.85	N/A	472.2	214.5	30.8	4.3
3-16	C+	2.46	1.66	N/A	450.2	194.8	32.3	4.0
2016	B-	2.65	1.82	68.1	467.2	208.6	131.0	18.8
2015	C+	2.50	1.70	64.1	443.9	191.2	124.5	20.4
2014	C+	2.24	1.50	73.9	409.2	177.0	118.9	12.4
2013	C+	2.02	1.38	59.0	378.9	160.4	129.0	22.3
2012	C+	2.00	1.40	68.4	327.7	132.7	107.2	16.4

Employers Mutual Group Composite Group Rating: B- Largest Group Members	Assets ($mil)	Rating
EMPLOYERS MUTUAL CAS CO	3198	B-
EMCASCO INS CO	486	B-
EMC REINS CO	467	B-
ILLINOIS EMCASCO INS CO	361	B-
DAKOTA FIRE INS CO	231	C

EMPLOYERS COMPENSATION INS CO * | A- | Excellent

Major Rating Factors: Strong long-term capitalization index (7.7 on a scale of 0 to 10) based on excellent current risk adjusted capital (severe and moderate loss scenarios). Furthermore, this high level of risk adjusted capital has been consistently maintained in previous years. Ample reserve history (8.0) that helps to protect the company against sharp claims increases.

Other Rating Factors: Excellent profitability (8.6) with operating gains in each of the last five years. Good liquidity (6.8) with sufficient resources (cash flows and marketable investments) to handle a spike in claims. Good overall results on stability tests (6.5). Stability strengths include good operational trends and excellent risk diversification.

Principal Business: Workers compensation (100%).

Principal Investments: Investment grade bonds (94%), misc. investments (5%), and non investment grade bonds (1%).

Investments in Affiliates: None

Group Affiliation: Employers Group Inc

Licensed in: AL, AZ, AR, CA, CO, CT, DC, FL, GA, ID, IL, IN, IA, KS, KY, LA, MD, MA, MI, MN, MS, MO, MT, NE, NV, NJ, NM, NY, OK, OR, PA, SC, TN, TX, UT, VT, VA, WI

Commenced Business: September 2002

Address: 500 North Brand Boulevard, Glendale, CA 91203-4707

Phone: (775) 327-2700 **Domicile State:** CA **NAIC Code:** 11512

Data Date	Rating	RACR #1	RACR #2	Loss Ratio %	Total Assets ($mil)	Capital ($mil)	Net Premium ($mil)	Net Income ($mil)
3-17	A-	2.13	1.46	N/A	1,095.5	367.1	61.4	8.9
3-16	B	1.90	1.27	N/A	1,063.9	340.7	60.4	3.6
2016	B+	2.15	1.45	62.5	1,083.8	358.3	243.1	38.1
2015	B	1.93	1.27	65.1	1,094.1	335.1	265.0	19.6
2014	B	2.04	1.46	67.4	1,802.2	318.5	185.7	15.7
2013	B	1.69	1.20	73.8	1,712.3	299.0	183.2	8.3
2012	B	2.32	1.59	57.4	1,477.8	292.9	153.8	5.8

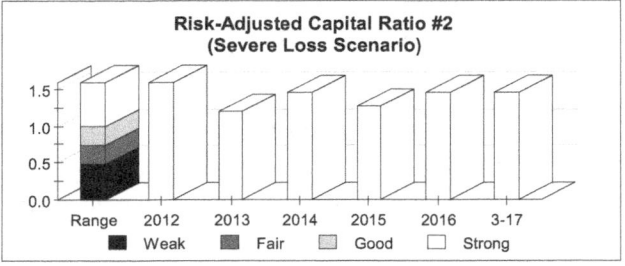

Risk-Adjusted Capital Ratio #2 (Severe Loss Scenario)

Range 2012 2013 2014 2015 2016 3-17

■ Weak ■ Fair ☐ Good ☐ Strong

EMPLOYERS INS OF WAUSAU

B-   **Good**

Major Rating Factors: Fair overall results on stability tests (3.6 on a scale of 0 to 10) including weak results on operational trends. The largest net exposure for one risk is excessive at 5.6% of capital. History of adequate reserve strength (5.8) as reserves have been consistently at an acceptable level.

Other Rating Factors: Good overall profitability index (6.0) despite operating losses during 2012 and the first three months of 2017. Return on equity has been low, averaging 4.1% over the past five years. Good liquidity (6.2) with sufficient resources (cash flows and marketable investments) to handle a spike in claims. Strong long-term capitalization index (8.1) based on excellent current risk adjusted capital (severe and moderate loss scenarios). Moreover, capital levels have been consistent in recent years.

Principal Business: Workers compensation (79%), auto liability (9%), other liability (6%), commercial multiple peril (2%), auto physical damage (2%), and products liability (1%).

Principal Investments: Investment grade bonds (80%), misc. investments (15%), and non investment grade bonds (6%).

Investments in Affiliates: 3%

Group Affiliation: Liberty Mutual Group

Licensed in: All states, the District of Columbia and Puerto Rico

Commenced Business: September 1911

Address: 2000 Westwood Drive, Wausau, WI 54401

Phone: (617) 357-9500   **Domicile State:** WI   **NAIC Code:** 21458

Data Date	Rating	RACR #1	RACR #2	Loss Ratio %	Total Assets ($mil)	Capital ($mil)	Net Premium ($mil)	Net Income ($mil)
3-17	B-	2.50	1.74	N/A	5,648.8	1,592.5	523.5	-10.6
3-16	B-	2.48	1.71	N/A	5,465.6	1,547.3	505.4	37.1
2016	B-	2.54	1.78	69.9	5,614.3	1,585.8	2,119.9	57.9
2015	B-	2.44	1.69	68.4	5,477.2	1,514.4	2,050.6	155.1
2014	B-	2.19	1.51	70.0	5,277.7	1,393.2	2,030.1	119.7
2013	B-	1.83	1.26	73.5	5,599.8	1,283.7	2,427.2	48.9
2012	B-	2.77	1.89	90.3	3,940.7	1,229.7	1,044.5	-47.7

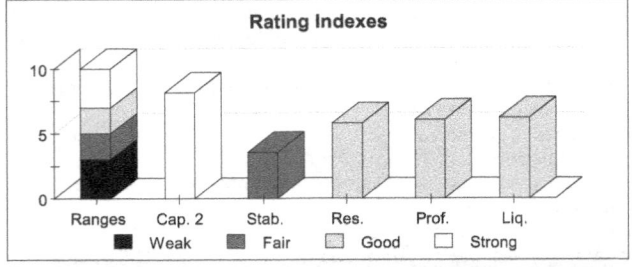

Rating Indexes

EMPLOYERS MUTUAL CAS CO

B-   **Good**

Major Rating Factors: Fair overall results on stability tests (4.8 on a scale of 0 to 10) including potential drain of affiliation with Employers Mutual Group and weak results on operational trends. Good liquidity (6.5) with sufficient resources (cash flows and marketable investments) to handle a spike in claims.

Other Rating Factors: Strong long-term capitalization index (8.0) based on excellent current risk adjusted capital (severe and moderate loss scenarios). Moreover, capital levels have been consistent in recent years. Ample reserve history (7.8) that can protect against increases in claims costs. Excellent profitability (8.1) with operating gains in each of the last five years.

Principal Business: Other liability (22%), auto liability (20%), workers compensation (14%), auto physical damage (10%), allied lines (9%), inland marine (6%), and other lines (18%).

Principal Investments: Misc. investments (48%), investment grade bonds (48%), and real estate (5%).

Investments in Affiliates: 20%

Group Affiliation: Employers Mutual Group

Licensed in: All states except PR

Commenced Business: July 1913

Address: 717 MULBERRY STREET, Des Moines, IA 50309-3872

Phone: (515) 280-2511   **Domicile State:** IA   **NAIC Code:** 21415

Data Date	Rating	RACR #1	RACR #2	Loss Ratio %	Total Assets ($mil)	Capital ($mil)	Net Premium ($mil)	Net Income ($mil)
3-17	B-	2.08	1.63	N/A	3,269.9	1,413.0	276.3	11.5
3-16	B-	2.08	1.63	N/A	3,052.6	1,323.0	260.9	26.7
2016	B-	2.09	1.66	65.2	3,198.0	1,378.6	1,123.0	65.9
2015	B-	2.08	1.66	65.7	2,890.6	1,276.3	946.0	61.4
2014	B-	2.06	1.65	70.0	2,721.4	1,215.0	902.2	45.4
2013	B-	2.06	1.65	66.7	2,538.0	1,121.9	845.0	56.1
2012	B-	1.99	1.57	66.4	2,308.9	963.0	772.9	36.1

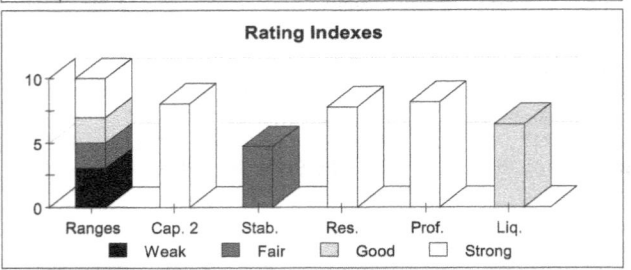

Rating Indexes

ENDURANCE AMERICAN INS CO

B-   **Good**

Major Rating Factors: Fair profitability index (3.6 on a scale of 0 to 10) with operating losses during 2012, 2013, 2014 and the first three months of 2017. Average return on equity over the last five years has been poor at -7.3%. Good long-term capitalization index (6.7) based on good current risk adjusted capital (moderate loss scenario), despite some fluctuation in capital levels.

Other Rating Factors: History of adequate reserve strength (6.1) as reserves have been consistently at an acceptable level. Good liquidity (6.2) with sufficient resources (cash flows and marketable investments) to handle a spike in claims. Good overall results on stability tests (5.3). Stability strengths include good operational trends and excellent risk diversification. The largest net exposure for one risk is acceptable at 2.0% of capital.

Principal Business: Other liability (67%), aircraft (15%), inland marine (8%), ocean marine (6%), commercial multiple peril (2%), and surety (1%).

Principal Investments: Investment grade bonds (76%), misc. investments (21%), and cash (3%).

Investments in Affiliates: 20%

Group Affiliation: Endurance Specialty Holdings

Licensed in: All states except CA, MN, PR

Commenced Business: April 1996

Address: 1209 ORANGE STREET, Wilmington, DE 19801

Phone: (914) 468-8000   **Domicile State:** DE   **NAIC Code:** 10641

Data Date	Rating	RACR #1	RACR #2	Loss Ratio %	Total Assets ($mil)	Capital ($mil)	Net Premium ($mil)	Net Income ($mil)
3-17	B-	1.61	1.13	N/A	1,717.5	283.1	49.2	-3.7
3-16	C+	1.35	0.99	N/A	1,556.1	261.3	43.6	-1.2
2016	B-	1.60	1.12	79.3	1,293.3	283.1	253.8	20.3
2015	C+	1.29	0.94	78.4	1,227.4	262.7	233.1	16.5
2014	C	1.31	0.94	87.3	1,243.9	241.2	312.0	-4.9
2013	D+	1.27	0.87	94.4	1,313.8	247.5	362.2	-42.9
2012	D	0.73	0.56	103.1	1,305.2	231.0	358.0	-71.4

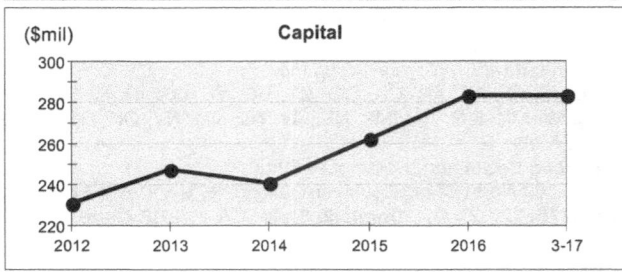

Capital

ENDURANCE ASR CORP *   A-   Excellent

Major Rating Factors: Strong long-term capitalization index (8.4 on a scale of 0 to 10) based on excellent current risk adjusted capital (severe and moderate loss scenarios). Furthermore, this high level of risk adjusted capital has been consistently maintained in previous years. Ample reserve history (8.6) that helps to protect the company against sharp claims increases.

Other Rating Factors: Excellent liquidity (7.3) with ample operational cash flow and liquid investments. Excellent overall results on stability tests (7.0). Stability strengths include excellent operational trends and excellent risk diversification. Good overall profitability index (5.5) despite operating losses during 2012. Return on equity has been low, averaging 2.9% over the past five years.

Principal Business: Other liability (41%), aircraft (33%), surety (9%), ocean marine (8%), inland marine (7%), and commercial multiple peril (1%).

Principal Investments: Investment grade bonds (65%), misc. investments (29%), and cash (6%).

Investments in Affiliates: 26%

Group Affiliation: Endurance Specialty Holdings

Licensed in: All states, the District of Columbia and Puerto Rico

Commenced Business: December 2002

Address: 1209 ORANGE STREET, Wilmington, DE 19801

Phone: (914) 468-8000   **Domicile State:** DE   **NAIC Code:** 11551

Data Date	Rating	RACR #1	RACR #2	Loss Ratio %	Total Assets ($mil)	Capital ($mil)	Net Premium ($mil)	Net Income ($mil)
3-17	A-	2.18	1.88	N/A	1,824.1	792.9	70.9	10.0
3-16	B	2.23	1.92	N/A	1,689.3	743.7	66.8	7.2
2016	B+	2.19	1.91	55.9	1,786.4	786.8	299.0	24.2
2015	B	2.24	1.94	47.7	1,642.9	739.3	262.4	35.7
2014	B	2.18	1.89	49.5	1,562.1	674.1	250.9	33.5
2013	B	1.92	1.61	51.2	1,489.7	629.0	263.2	28.4
2012	B-	1.84	1.50	81.6	1,466.6	587.4	239.8	-19.9

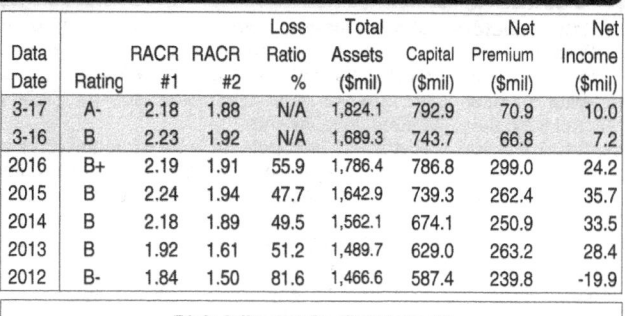

Risk-Adjusted Capital Ratio #2
(Severe Loss Scenario)

Range 2012 2013 2014 2015 2016 3-17
■ Weak   ■ Fair   ▨ Good   □ Strong

ERIE INS CO   B-   Good

Major Rating Factors: Fair overall results on stability tests (4.7 on a scale of 0 to 10) including potential drain of affiliation with Erie Ins Group and weak results on operational trends. Good liquidity (6.6) with sufficient resources (cash flows and marketable investments) to handle a spike in claims.

Other Rating Factors: Strong long-term capitalization index (10.0) based on excellent current risk adjusted capital (severe and moderate loss scenarios). Moreover, capital levels have been consistent in recent years. Ample reserve history (7.9) that can protect against increases in claims costs. Excellent profitability (8.3) with operating gains in each of the last five years.

Principal Business: Homeowners multiple peril (53%), auto liability (20%), auto physical damage (14%), commercial multiple peril (7%), workers compensation (3%), and other liability (1%).

Principal Investments: Investment grade bonds (89%), misc. investments (8%), and non investment grade bonds (3%).

Investments in Affiliates: 5%

Group Affiliation: Erie Ins Group

Licensed in: DC, IL, IN, KY, MD, MN, NY, NC, OH, PA, TN, VA, WV, WI

Commenced Business: January 1973

Address: 100 Erie Insurance Place, Erie, PA 16530

Phone: (814) 870-2000   **Domicile State:** PA   **NAIC Code:** 26263

Data Date	Rating	RACR #1	RACR #2	Loss Ratio %	Total Assets ($mil)	Capital ($mil)	Net Premium ($mil)	Net Income ($mil)
3-17	B-	5.22	3.61	N/A	987.1	358.3	78.2	3.7
3-16	B-	5.09	3.54	N/A	916.0	339.5	73.7	4.3
2016	B-	5.29	3.73	68.8	967.7	353.7	312.7	19.5
2015	B-	5.15	3.65	69.4	899.7	334.6	294.6	19.2
2014	B-	5.13	3.66	73.0	839.3	311.9	274.4	12.0
2013	B-	5.04	3.48	69.4	771.8	294.4	252.3	17.1
2012	B-	5.16	3.57	76.0	713.3	276.4	230.1	13.8

Erie Ins Group
Composite Group Rating: B

Largest Group Members	Assets ($mil)	Rating
ERIE INS EXCHANGE	15017	B
ERIE FAMILY LIFE INS CO	2247	A-
ERIE INS CO	968	B-
ERIE INS CO OF NEW YORK	109	B
ERIE INS PC CO	103	B-

ERIE INS EXCHANGE   B   Good

Major Rating Factors: Good overall results on stability tests (5.1 on a scale of 0 to 10) despite potential drain of affiliation with Erie Ins Group and weak results on operational trends. Good liquidity (6.6) with sufficient resources (cash flows and marketable investments) to handle a spike in claims.

Other Rating Factors: Strong long-term capitalization index (9.4) based on excellent current risk adjusted capital (severe and moderate loss scenarios). Moreover, capital levels have been consistent in recent years. Ample reserve history (7.8) that can protect against increases in claims costs. Excellent profitability (8.4) with operating gains in each of the last five years.

Principal Business: Auto liability (32%), auto physical damage (24%), homeowners multiple peril (19%), commercial multiple peril (16%), workers compensation (4%), other liability (3%), and inland marine (1%).

Principal Investments: Investment grade bonds (49%), misc. investments (40%), non investment grade bonds (11%), and real estate (1%).

Investments in Affiliates: 5%

Group Affiliation: Erie Ins Group

Licensed in: AL, CT, DC, DE, GA, IL, IN, IA, KY, ME, MD, MN, MO, MT, NE, NV, NH, NJ, NM, NY, NC, ND, OH, PA, RI, SC, SD, TN, TX, VT, VA, WV, WI, WY

Commenced Business: April 1925

Address: 100 Erie Insurance Place, Erie, PA 16530

Phone: (814) 870-2000   **Domicile State:** PA   **NAIC Code:** 26271

Data Date	Rating	RACR #1	RACR #2	Loss Ratio %	Total Assets ($mil)	Capital ($mil)	Net Premium ($mil)	Net Income ($mil)
3-17	B	4.08	2.64	N/A	15,885.8	7,924.5	1,478.7	138.8
3-16	B	3.96	2.62	N/A	14,011.1	7,228.9	1,392.7	100.4
2016	B	4.03	2.63	68.8	15,016.9	7,710.6	5,910.0	509.8
2015	B	3.97	2.65	69.4	13,930.7	7,141.5	5,567.1	465.6
2014	B	3.74	2.51	73.0	13,344.7	6,816.6	5,185.5	353.0
2013	B	3.68	2.51	69.4	12,591.7	6,467.0	4,767.7	478.8
2012	B	3.70	2.57	76.0	11,229.2	5,633.4	4,349.3	311.0

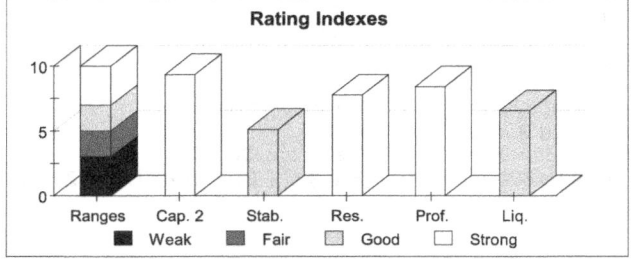

Rating Indexes

Ranges   Cap. 2   Stab.   Res.   Prof.   Liq.
■ Weak   ■ Fair   ▨ Good   □ Strong

ESSENT GUARANTY INC *

A- Excellent

Major Rating Factors: Strong long-term capitalization index (10.0 on a scale of 0 to 10) based on excellent current risk adjusted capital (severe and moderate loss scenarios). Furthermore, this high level of risk adjusted capital has been consistently maintained in previous years. Excellent liquidity (7.7) with ample operational cash flow and liquid investments.

Other Rating Factors: History of adequate reserve strength (5.2) as reserves have been consistently at an acceptable level. Good overall profitability index (6.5) despite operating losses during 2012. Return on equity has been good over the last five years, averaging 21.0%. Good overall results on stability tests (5.7) despite weak results on operational trends.

Principal Business: Mortgage guaranty (100%).

Principal Investments: Investment grade bonds (94%), misc. investments (5%), and cash (1%).

Investments in Affiliates: None

Group Affiliation: Essent Group Ltd

Licensed in: All states except PR

Commenced Business: July 2009

Address: 2 Radnor Corp 100 Matsonford, Radnor, PA 19087

Phone: (877) 673-8190   **Domicile State:** PA   **NAIC Code:** 13634

Data Date	Rating	RACR #1	RACR #2	Loss Ratio %	Total Assets ($mil)	Capital ($mil)	Net Premium ($mil)	Net Income ($mil)
3-17	A-	17.70	9.51	N/A	1,384.2	595.1	88.9	60.8
3-16	A-	7.61	4.62	N/A	1,131.2	532.2	76.0	48.5
2016	A-	10.85	6.38	3.7	1,323.6	578.9	340.6	216.0
2015	A-	6.05	3.77	3.6	1,072.6	522.2	299.0	172.7
2014	A-	6.33	4.08	2.8	817.3	465.2	239.6	118.2
2013	A-	6.30	4.22	1.9	546.8	346.4	169.8	49.8
2012	A-	3.11	2.58	3.4	246.2	163.8	66.8	-16.3

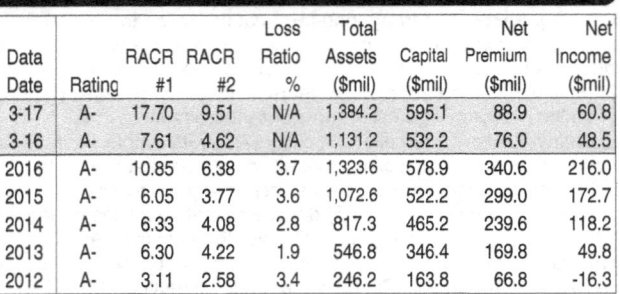

Risk-Adjusted Capital Ratio #2
(Severe Loss Scenario)

EVANSTON INS CO

C Fair

Major Rating Factors: Fair overall results on stability tests (3.8 on a scale of 0 to 10) including weak results on operational trends. The largest net exposure for one risk is conservative at 1.1% of capital. Good liquidity (6.8) with sufficient resources (cash flows and marketable investments) to handle a spike in claims.

Other Rating Factors: Strong long-term capitalization index (7.2) based on excellent current risk adjusted capital (severe and moderate loss scenarios). Moreover, capital levels have been consistent in recent years. Ample reserve history (9.5) that helps to protect the company against sharp claims increases. Excellent profitability (8.7) with operating gains in each of the last five years. Return on equity has been good over the last five years, averaging 14.0%.

Principal Business: Other liability (52%), commercial multiple peril (10%), medical malpractice (8%), allied lines (8%), products liability (6%), fire (5%), and other lines (11%).

Principal Investments: Investment grade bonds (65%) and misc. investments (35%).

Investments in Affiliates: None

Group Affiliation: Markel Corp

Licensed in: All states, the District of Columbia and Puerto Rico

Commenced Business: December 1977

Address: Ten Parkway North, Deerfield, IL 60015

Phone: (847) 572-6000   **Domicile State:** IL   **NAIC Code:** 35378

Data Date	Rating	RACR #1	RACR #2	Loss Ratio %	Total Assets ($mil)	Capital ($mil)	Net Premium ($mil)	Net Income ($mil)
3-17	C	1.72	1.17	N/A	4,551.2	1,346.5	255.7	31.2
3-16	C	1.56	1.06	N/A	2,760.1	753.4	219.9	29.4
2016	C	1.58	1.08	54.0	4,413.7	1,284.4	1,370.0	172.6
2015	C	1.52	1.03	46.2	4,399.9	1,204.3	1,281.2	257.2
2014	C	1.45	0.97	52.7	2,792.9	1,160.9	758.8	86.7
2013	C	1.34	0.90	48.7	2,152.3	574.2	642.2	82.0
2012	C	1.42	0.99	53.5	2,010.2	568.4	451.1	84.1

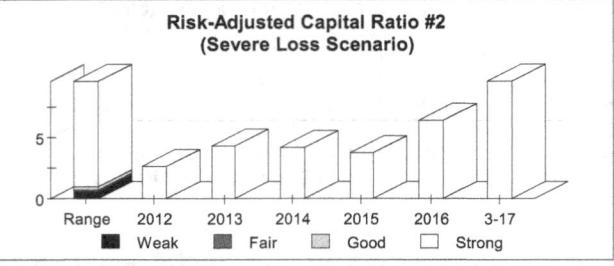

Rating Indexes

EVEREST REINS CO

B- Good

Major Rating Factors: Fair overall results on stability tests (4.7 on a scale of 0 to 10) including potential drain of affiliation with Everest Reinsurance Group and weak results on operational trends. History of adequate reserve strength (5.8) as reserves have been consistently at an acceptable level.

Other Rating Factors: Strong long-term capitalization index (8.4) based on excellent current risk adjusted capital (severe and moderate loss scenarios). Moreover, capital levels have been consistent in recent years. Excellent profitability (8.8) with operating gains in each of the last five years. Return on equity has been good over the last five years, averaging 14.8%. Excellent liquidity (7.0) with ample operational cash flow and liquid investments.

Principal Business: Other liability (82%), group accident & health (11%), fidelity (4%), surety (1%), and other accident & health (1%).

Principal Investments: Investment grade bonds (61%), misc. investments (35%), cash (2%), and non investment grade bonds (2%).

Investments in Affiliates: 3%

Group Affiliation: Everest Reinsurance Group

Licensed in: All states, the District of Columbia and Puerto Rico

Commenced Business: June 1973

Address: 1209 Orange Street, Wilmington, DE 19801

Phone: (908) 604-3000   **Domicile State:** DE   **NAIC Code:** 26921

Data Date	Rating	RACR #1	RACR #2	Loss Ratio %	Total Assets ($mil)	Capital ($mil)	Net Premium ($mil)	Net Income ($mil)
3-17	B-	3.51	2.24	N/A	10,186.8	3,789.8	475.6	85.5
3-16	B-	2.68	1.75	N/A	9,964.2	3,308.0	487.4	119.1
2016	B-	3.40	2.18	63.5	10,224.8	3,635.1	2,050.6	523.5
2015	B-	2.61	1.71	58.8	9,979.6	3,210.9	2,079.5	498.5
2014	C+	2.27	1.47	61.7	9,616.2	2,893.0	2,121.8	357.3
2013	C+	1.13	0.93	59.5	9,288.4	2,814.3	2,024.4	540.0
2012	C+	1.11	0.92	64.9	9,046.7	2,613.0	1,581.0	359.8

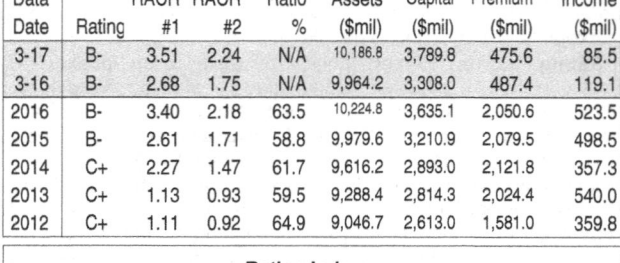

Rating Indexes

EXECUTIVE RISK INDEMNITY INC

B-   **Good**

Major Rating Factors: Fair overall results on stability tests (3.7 on a scale of 0 to 10) including weak results on operational trends. The largest net exposure for one risk is excessive at 5.5% of capital. Good overall profitability index (6.8). Fair expense controls. Return on equity has been good over the last five years, averaging 13.0%.

Other Rating Factors: Good liquidity (6.9) with sufficient resources (cash flows and marketable investments) to handle a spike in claims. Strong long-term capitalization index (8.7) based on excellent current risk adjusted capital (severe and moderate loss scenarios), despite some fluctuation in capital levels. Ample reserve history (8.6) that helps to protect the company against sharp claims increases.

Principal Business: Other liability (73%), homeowners multiple peril (12%), commercial multiple peril (6%), products liability (5%), inland marine (1%), fidelity (1%), and burglary & theft (1%).

Principal Investments: Investment grade bonds (91%), misc. investments (7%), non investment grade bonds (1%), and real estate (1%).

Investments in Affiliates: 7%

Group Affiliation: Chubb Limited

Licensed in: All states except PR

Commenced Business: January 1978

Address: 1209 Orange Street, Wilmington, DE 19801-1120

Phone: (908) 903-2000   **Domicile State:** DE   **NAIC Code:** 35181

Data Date	Rating	RACR #1	RACR #2	Loss Ratio %	Total Assets ($mil)	Capital ($mil)	Net Premium ($mil)	Net Income ($mil)
3-17	B-	4.07	2.84	N/A	2,961.8	1,279.0	118.6	29.2
3-16	B	3.46	2.35	N/A	3,025.9	1,239.5	156.5	78.4
2016	B-	3.97	2.77	53.6	2,901.4	1,251.0	506.9	189.0
2015	B	3.41	2.32	56.5	3,068.2	1,267.1	782.7	168.4
2014	B	3.42	2.33	56.7	3,024.8	1,258.0	751.6	164.2
2013	B+	3.43	2.34	52.7	2,977.3	1,218.6	721.2	174.1
2012	B+	3.17	2.12	67.3	2,899.9	1,100.6	694.2	115.4

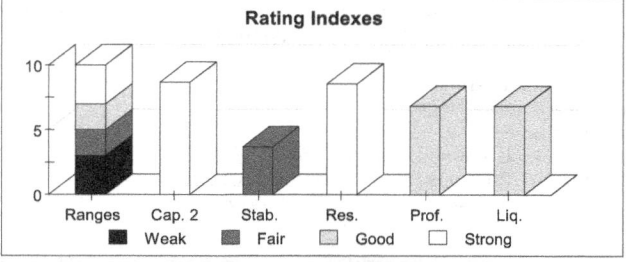

Rating Indexes

FACTORY MUTUAL INS CO

B-   **Good**

Major Rating Factors: Fair overall results on stability tests (3.8 on a scale of 0 to 10) including potential drain of affiliation with Factory Mutual Ins and weak results on operational trends. The largest net exposure for one risk is acceptable at 2.6% of capital. History of adequate reserve strength (6.1) as reserves have been consistently at an acceptable level.

Other Rating Factors: Good liquidity (6.9) with sufficient resources (cash flows and marketable investments) to handle a spike in claims. Strong long-term capitalization index (8.3) based on excellent current risk adjusted capital (severe and moderate loss scenarios). Moreover, capital levels have been consistent in recent years. Excellent profitability (8.5) with operating gains in each of the last five years.

Principal Business: Allied lines (34%), inland marine (30%), boiler & machinery (20%), and fire (15%).

Principal Investments: Misc. investments (73%), investment grade bonds (24%), non investment grade bonds (2%), and cash (1%).

Investments in Affiliates: 18%

Group Affiliation: Factory Mutual Ins

Licensed in: All states, the District of Columbia and Puerto Rico

Commenced Business: December 1835

Address: 270 Central Avenue, Johnston, RI 02919-4949

Phone: (401) 275-3000   **Domicile State:** RI   **NAIC Code:** 21482

Data Date	Rating	RACR #1	RACR #2	Loss Ratio %	Total Assets ($mil)	Capital ($mil)	Net Premium ($mil)	Net Income ($mil)
3-17	B-	2.69	2.07	N/A	17,343.3	11,852.3	746.2	100.4
3-16	B-	2.60	1.99	N/A	15,872.4	10,773.0	690.8	212.1
2016	B-	2.64	2.04	54.5	16,764.3	11,519.4	2,795.2	601.6
2015	C+	2.57	1.98	58.0	15,682.9	10,546.7	2,782.1	550.1
2014	C	2.50	1.91	50.2	15,070.1	10,141.8	2,838.5	670.8
2013	C	2.48	1.90	50.6	13,795.7	9,153.5	2,824.5	662.5
2012	C	2.47	1.89	59.8	12,239.9	7,525.1	2,855.3	612.1

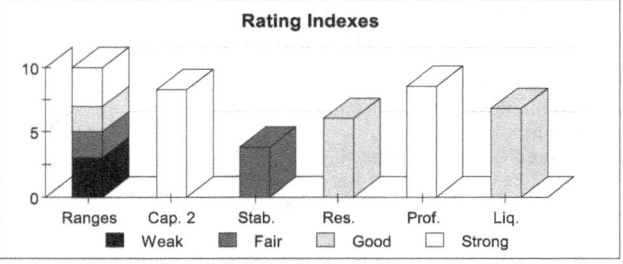

Rating Indexes

FARM BUREAU GENERAL INS CO OF MI

B   **Good**

Major Rating Factors: History of adequate reserve strength (6.5 on a scale of 0 to 10) as reserves have been consistently at an acceptable level. Good overall profitability index (6.9). Good expense controls. Return on equity has been fair, averaging 5.6% over the past five years.

Other Rating Factors: Good liquidity (5.8) with sufficient resources (cash flows and marketable investments) to handle a spike in claims. Fair overall results on stability tests (4.9) including weak results on operational trends. Strong long-term capitalization index (9.7) based on excellent current risk adjusted capital (severe and moderate loss scenarios). Moreover, capital levels have been consistent in recent years.

Principal Business: Auto liability (33%), auto physical damage (27%), homeowners multiple peril (26%), commercial multiple peril (6%), workers compensation (3%), inland marine (1%), and other lines (4%).

Principal Investments: Investment grade bonds (87%) and misc. investments (16%).

Investments in Affiliates: None

Group Affiliation: Michigan Farm Bureau

Licensed in: MI

Commenced Business: July 1962

Address: 7373 W SAGINAW, Lansing, MI 48917

Phone: (517) 323-7000   **Domicile State:** MI   **NAIC Code:** 21547

Data Date	Rating	RACR #1	RACR #2	Loss Ratio %	Total Assets ($mil)	Capital ($mil)	Net Premium ($mil)	Net Income ($mil)
3-17	B	4.60	3.21	N/A	681.2	306.9	83.7	4.2
3-16	B	4.45	3.07	N/A	638.6	277.3	79.0	4.0
2016	B	4.54	3.17	71.2	677.8	300.2	336.4	23.9
2015	B	4.41	3.06	72.1	651.5	273.2	312.7	20.9
2014	B	3.26	2.31	79.7	528.8	178.5	287.3	7.3
2013	B	3.12	2.20	74.8	503.8	170.3	286.4	5.3
2012	B	3.86	2.64	77.9	413.2	147.7	182.6	7.8

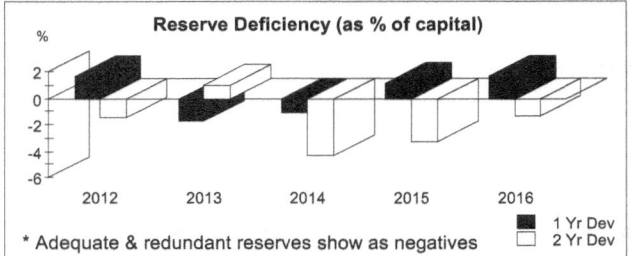

Reserve Deficiency (as % of capital)

* Adequate & redundant reserves show as negatives

FARM BUREAU MUTUAL INS CO OF AR | B | Good

Major Rating Factors: Good liquidity (6.1 on a scale of 0 to 10) with sufficient resources (cash flows and marketable investments) to handle a spike in claims. Fair overall results on stability tests (4.2) including weak results on operational trends.

Other Rating Factors: Strong long-term capitalization index (10.0) based on excellent current risk adjusted capital (severe and moderate loss scenarios). Moreover, capital levels have been consistent in recent years. Ample reserve history (8.1) that helps to protect the company against sharp claims increases. Excellent profitability (8.6) despite modest operating losses during the first three months of 2017. Return on equity has been good over the last five years, averaging 13.5%.

Principal Business: Homeowners multiple peril (56%), fire (16%), inland marine (16%), allied lines (9%), other liability (2%), and commercial multiple peril (1%).

Principal Investments: Investment grade bonds (91%), misc. investments (13%), and real estate (1%).

Investments in Affiliates: 1%

Group Affiliation: None

Licensed in: AR

Commenced Business: March 1950

Address: 10720 Kanis Road, Little Rock, AR 72211

Phone: (501) 224-4400   **Domicile State:** AR   **NAIC Code:** 13757

Data Date	Rating	RACR #1	RACR #2	Loss Ratio %	Total Assets ($mil)	Capital ($mil)	Net Premium ($mil)	Net Income ($mil)
3-17	B	6.03	4.21	N/A	404.2	241.6	48.9	-0.3
3-16	B	5.08	3.46	N/A	403.3	229.7	49.9	4.7
2016	B	6.11	4.29	71.6	402.0	242.4	197.3	17.2
2015	B	5.06	3.47	60.6	387.2	224.9	201.9	32.0
2014	C+	4.58	3.14	71.0	355.5	192.5	195.2	18.9
2013	C+	4.04	2.77	55.3	336.4	172.8	194.5	37.0
2012	C	2.75	1.86	70.2	294.1	126.5	186.8	23.3

Liquidity Index

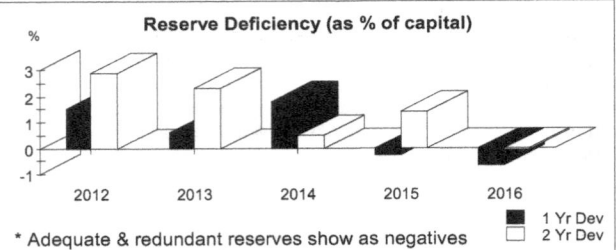

Range / 2013 / 2014 / 2015 / 2016

■ Weak ■ Fair □ Good □ Strong

FARM BUREAU MUTUAL INS CO OF ID | B | Good

Major Rating Factors: History of adequate reserve strength (5.9 on a scale of 0 to 10) as reserves have been consistently at an acceptable level. Good liquidity (6.4) with sufficient resources (cash flows and marketable investments) to handle a spike in claims.

Other Rating Factors: Fair overall results on stability tests (4.1) including potential drain of affiliation with Farm Bureau Group of Idaho and weak results on operational trends. Fair profitability index (3.9) with operating losses during 2012, 2015 and the first three months of 2017. Strong long-term capitalization index (9.0) based on excellent current risk adjusted capital (severe and moderate loss scenarios), despite some fluctuation in capital levels.

Principal Business: Auto liability (31%), auto physical damage (25%), homeowners multiple peril (19%), farmowners multiple peril (18%), inland marine (3%), allied lines (2%), and other liability (2%).

Principal Investments: Investment grade bonds (65%), misc. investments (32%), and real estate (3%).

Investments in Affiliates: 19%

Group Affiliation: Farm Bureau Group of Idaho

Licensed in: ID

Commenced Business: May 1947

Address: 275 Tierra Vista Drive, Pocatello, ID 83201

Phone: (208) 232-7914   **Domicile State:** ID   **NAIC Code:** 13765

Data Date	Rating	RACR #1	RACR #2	Loss Ratio %	Total Assets ($mil)	Capital ($mil)	Net Premium ($mil)	Net Income ($mil)
3-17	B	2.66	2.22	N/A	462.8	238.4	45.9	-10.2
3-16	B	2.89	2.37	N/A	453.6	240.1	42.6	1.0
2016	B	2.83	2.37	70.9	470.4	254.1	187.6	13.0
2015	B	2.90	2.40	82.1	447.8	238.5	169.0	-2.9
2014	B	3.08	2.55	77.9	440.3	241.5	162.4	4.8
2013	B+	3.30	2.70	78.2	418.0	233.1	151.7	5.4
2012	B+	3.46	2.76	86.9	396.6	220.7	137.4	-8.9

Reserve Deficiency (as % of capital)

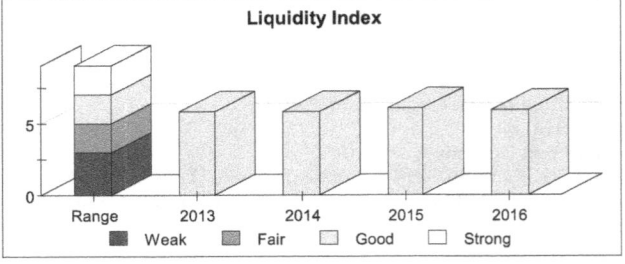

2012 / 2013 / 2014 / 2015 / 2016

■ 1 Yr Dev   □ 2 Yr Dev

* Adequate & redundant reserves show as negatives

FARM BUREAU MUTUAL INS CO OF MI | B | Good

Major Rating Factors: Good liquidity (5.9 on a scale of 0 to 10) with sufficient resources (cash flows and marketable investments) to handle a spike in claims. Fair overall results on stability tests (4.6) including weak results on operational trends.

Other Rating Factors: Strong long-term capitalization index (9.5) based on excellent current risk adjusted capital (severe and moderate loss scenarios). Moreover, capital levels have been consistent in recent years. Ample reserve history (8.6) that helps to protect the company against sharp claims increases. Excellent profitability (8.4) with operating gains in each of the last five years.

Principal Business: Farmowners multiple peril (46%), auto liability (25%), auto physical damage (19%), workers compensation (6%), inland marine (2%), other liability (2%), and boiler & machinery (1%).

Principal Investments: Investment grade bonds (79%), misc. investments (22%), and non investment grade bonds (1%).

Investments in Affiliates: None

Group Affiliation: Michigan Farm Bureau

Licensed in: AL, CA, CT, DE, GA, IL, IN, IA, KS, KY, LA, ME, MD, MA, MI, MN, MO, MT, NE, NH, NJ, NC, ND, OH, OK, OR, PA, RI, SC, SD, TN, TX, UT, VT, VA, WV, WI

Commenced Business: March 1949

Address: 7373 W SAGINAW, Lansing, MI 48917

Phone: (517) 323-7000   **Domicile State:** MI   **NAIC Code:** 21555

Data Date	Rating	RACR #1	RACR #2	Loss Ratio %	Total Assets ($mil)	Capital ($mil)	Net Premium ($mil)	Net Income ($mil)
3-17	B	4.52	2.98	N/A	746.2	373.7	86.9	6.2
3-16	B	4.20	2.75	N/A	721.2	338.8	86.1	7.3
2016	B	4.41	2.89	66.8	740.3	363.2	357.5	28.7
2015	B	4.22	2.75	65.5	706.3	331.1	345.3	36.7
2014	B-	4.08	2.65	70.8	651.9	290.3	324.9	23.7
2013	B-	3.82	2.49	69.8	630.6	262.8	286.9	21.4
2012	C+	2.76	1.84	74.4	597.8	203.9	337.8	12.4

Liquidity Index

Range / 2013 / 2014 / 2015 / 2016

■ Weak ■ Fair □ Good □ Strong

FARM BUREAU P&C INS CO *   B+   Good

Major Rating Factors: Good liquidity (6.1 on a scale of 0 to 10) with sufficient resources (cash flows and marketable investments) to handle a spike in claims. Good overall results on stability tests (5.3) despite weak results on operational trends.

Other Rating Factors: Strong long-term capitalization index (9.8) based on excellent current risk adjusted capital (severe and moderate loss scenarios). Moreover, capital levels have been consistent in recent years. Ample reserve history (8.1) that helps to protect the company against sharp claims increases. Excellent profitability (8.9) with operating gains in each of the last five years. Return on equity has been good over the last five years, averaging 10.5%.

Principal Business: Farmowners multiple peril (26%), homeowners multiple peril (24%), auto liability (20%), auto physical damage (20%), commercial multiple peril (4%), workers compensation (3%), and other liability (3%).

Principal Investments: Investment grade bonds (77%), misc. investments (23%), non investment grade bonds (1%), and real estate (1%).

Investments in Affiliates: 6%

Group Affiliation: Iowa Farm Bureau

Licensed in: AZ, ID, IA, KS, MN, MO, NE, NM, SD, UT, WI

Commenced Business: May 1939

Address: 5400 University Avenue, West Des Moines, IA 50266-5997

Phone: (515) 225-5400   **Domicile State:** IA   **NAIC Code:** 13773

Data Date	Rating	RACR #1	RACR #2	Loss Ratio %	Total Assets ($mil)	Capital ($mil)	Net Premium ($mil)	Net Income ($mil)
3-17	B+	4.47	3.45	N/A	2,529.1	1,241.9	287.2	38.0
3-16	B+	4.17	3.23	N/A	2,331.6	1,092.4	283.3	66.0
2016	B+	4.35	3.29	59.9	2,443.5	1,193.5	1,214.8	157.3
2015	B+	3.85	2.91	62.2	2,243.1	1,020.4	1,209.0	129.0
2014	B+	3.57	2.69	70.3	2,036.2	880.6	1,166.7	65.4
2013	A-	3.45	2.57	70.2	1,931.3	802.3	1,127.9	68.6
2012	A-	3.38	2.49	71.4	1,768.5	714.8	1,052.9	74.0

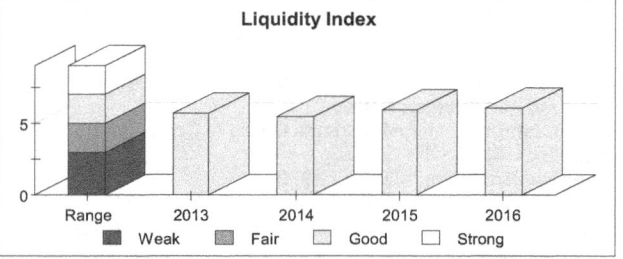

Liquidity Index

FARM FAMILY CASUALTY INS CO *   B+   Good

Major Rating Factors: Good overall profitability index (6.8 on a scale of 0 to 10). Fair expense controls. Return on equity has been fair, averaging 6.6% over the past five years. Good liquidity (6.6) with sufficient resources (cash flows and marketable investments) to handle a spike in claims.

Other Rating Factors: Good overall results on stability tests (5.3) despite weak results on operational trends. Strong long-term capitalization index (9.6) based on excellent current risk adjusted capital (severe and moderate loss scenarios). Moreover, capital levels have been consistent in recent years. Ample reserve history (9.2) that helps to protect the company against sharp claims increases.

Principal Business: Auto liability (19%), workers compensation (15%), other liability (12%), commercial multiple peril (12%), allied lines (11%), fire (10%), and other lines (20%).

Principal Investments: Investment grade bonds (87%), misc. investments (11%), cash (1%), and non investment grade bonds (1%).

Investments in Affiliates: None

Group Affiliation: American National Group Inc

Licensed in: CT, DE, ME, MD, MA, MO, NH, NJ, NY, PA, RI, VT, VA, WV

Commenced Business: November 1956

Address: 344 ROUTE 9W, Glenmont, NY 12077

Phone: (518) 431-5000   **Domicile State:** NY   **NAIC Code:** 13803

Data Date	Rating	RACR #1	RACR #2	Loss Ratio %	Total Assets ($mil)	Capital ($mil)	Net Premium ($mil)	Net Income ($mil)
3-17	B+	4.20	2.73	N/A	1,188.8	428.8	106.3	4.3
3-16	B+	3.79	2.48	N/A	1,113.3	380.2	101.0	0.8
2016	B+	4.30	2.84	64.4	1,164.4	424.4	428.8	41.4
2015	B+	3.85	2.55	71.0	1,096.5	376.5	407.6	24.9
2014	B+	3.64	2.43	72.8	1,080.0	365.7	392.7	17.5
2013	B+	3.57	2.39	72.1	1,036.7	347.1	371.1	27.6
2012	B+	3.40	2.29	78.9	984.6	308.3	352.7	13.5

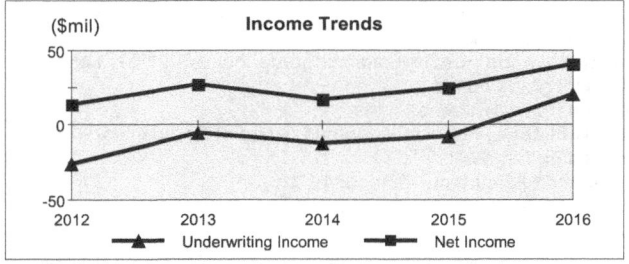

($mil) Income Trends

FARMERS AUTOMOBILE INS ASN *   B+   Good

Major Rating Factors: Good liquidity (6.3 on a scale of 0 to 10) with sufficient resources (cash flows and marketable investments) to handle a spike in claims. Good overall results on stability tests (5.0) despite weak results on operational trends.

Other Rating Factors: Strong long-term capitalization index (8.3) based on excellent current risk adjusted capital (severe and moderate loss scenarios), despite some fluctuation in capital levels. Ample reserve history (8.2) that helps to protect the company against sharp claims increases. Fair profitability index (4.3) with operating losses during the first three months of 2017.

Principal Business: Homeowners multiple peril (33%), auto liability (31%), auto physical damage (30%), allied lines (3%), fire (2%), and inland marine (1%).

Principal Investments: Investment grade bonds (68%), misc. investments (28%), cash (2%), and real estate (2%).

Investments in Affiliates: 22%

Group Affiliation: Farmers Automobile Ins Assn

Licensed in: AZ, IL, IN, IA, MI, OH, WI

Commenced Business: April 1921

Address: 2505 COURT STREET, Pekin, IL 61558

Phone: (309) 346-1161   **Domicile State:** IL   **NAIC Code:** 24201

Data Date	Rating	RACR #1	RACR #2	Loss Ratio %	Total Assets ($mil)	Capital ($mil)	Net Premium ($mil)	Net Income ($mil)
3-17	B+	2.08	1.78	N/A	1,277.1	504.1	119.3	-9.2
3-16	B+	2.22	1.90	N/A	1,250.2	517.5	117.7	1.6
2016	B+	2.15	1.86	77.7	1,266.9	514.6	491.2	-1.8
2015	B+	2.25	1.95	71.5	1,228.6	519.1	480.8	15.4
2014	B+	2.24	1.95	74.3	1,171.2	491.2	455.1	10.5
2013	B+	2.36	2.06	75.4	1,153.5	497.8	428.5	10.2
2012	B+	2.35	2.07	75.1	1,079.7	471.3	402.0	22.8

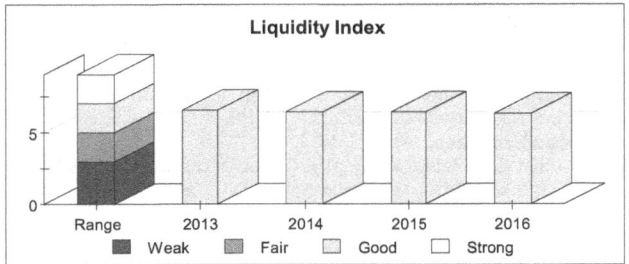

Liquidity Index

FARMERS INS CO OF OREGON   B   Good

Major Rating Factors: History of adequate reserve strength (5.7 on a scale of 0 to 10) as reserves have been consistently at an acceptable level. Good overall profitability index (6.0) despite modest operating losses during the first three months of 2017. Return on equity has been low, averaging 2.8% over the past five years.

Other Rating Factors: Good liquidity (5.9) with sufficient resources (cash flows and marketable investments) to handle a spike in claims. Fair overall results on stability tests (4.7) including potential drain of affiliation with Farmers Insurance Group of Companies, weak results on operational trends and negative cash flow from operations for 2016. Strong long-term capitalization index (8.2) based on excellent current risk adjusted capital (severe and moderate loss scenarios), despite some fluctuation in capital levels.

Principal Business: Auto liability (59%), auto physical damage (22%), homeowners multiple peril (13%), commercial multiple peril (4%), earthquake (1%), and allied lines (1%).

Principal Investments: Investment grade bonds (100%) and cash (2%).

Investments in Affiliates: None

Group Affiliation: Farmers Insurance Group of Companies

Licensed in: CA, MI, OR

Commenced Business: October 1970

Address: 23175 NW BENNETT ST, Hillsboro, OR 97124

Phone: (503) 372-2000   **Domicile State:** OR   **NAIC Code:** 21636

Data Date	Rating	RACR #1	RACR #2	Loss Ratio %	Total Assets ($mil)	Capital ($mil)	Net Premium ($mil)	Net Income ($mil)
3-17	B	2.55	1.82	N/A	1,693.2	530.6	251.7	-0.7
3-16	B	2.48	1.77	N/A	1,687.2	526.5	261.6	-0.2
2016	B	2.53	1.79	71.8	1,691.3	533.1	1,033.3	7.7
2015	B	2.48	1.77	68.7	1,681.5	529.8	1,045.1	18.0
2014	B	2.56	1.85	65.7	1,627.9	514.6	984.4	21.3
2013	B	2.48	1.81	66.8	1,614.9	490.3	954.6	21.9
2012	B-	2.36	1.73	72.3	1,600.3	470.2	969.9	6.4

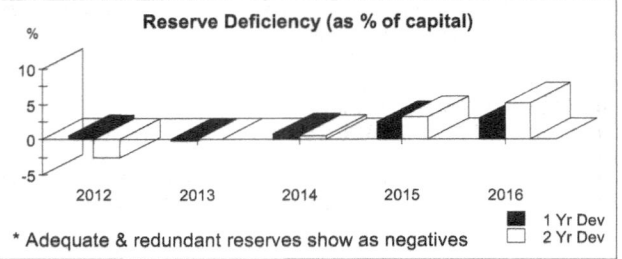

Reserve Deficiency (as % of capital)

* Adequate & redundant reserves show as negatives

■ 1 Yr Dev   □ 2 Yr Dev

FARMERS INS CO OF WA   B-   Good

Major Rating Factors: Fair overall results on stability tests (4.6 on a scale of 0 to 10) including fair financial strength of affiliated Farmers Insurance Group of Companies and weak results on operational trends. History of adequate reserve strength (5.9) as reserves have been consistently at an acceptable level.

Other Rating Factors: Good overall profitability index (6.4) despite modest operating losses during the first three months of 2017. Return on equity has been low, averaging 2.7% over the past five years. Good liquidity (6.2) with sufficient resources (cash flows and marketable investments) to handle a spike in claims. Strong long-term capitalization index (9.1) based on excellent current risk adjusted capital (severe and moderate loss scenarios), despite some fluctuation in capital levels.

Principal Business: Auto liability (50%), auto physical damage (22%), homeowners multiple peril (20%), commercial multiple peril (6%), allied lines (1%), and earthquake (1%).

Principal Investments: Investment grade bonds (97%), cash (2%), and non investment grade bonds (1%).

Investments in Affiliates: None

Group Affiliation: Farmers Insurance Group of Companies

Licensed in: CA, WA

Commenced Business: October 1970

Address: 3003 77TH AVE SE, Mercer Island, WA 98040-2890

Phone: (503) 372-2000   **Domicile State:** WA   **NAIC Code:** 21644

Data Date	Rating	RACR #1	RACR #2	Loss Ratio %	Total Assets ($mil)	Capital ($mil)	Net Premium ($mil)	Net Income ($mil)
3-17	B-	3.48	2.46	N/A	554.9	205.4	71.9	-0.2
3-16	B-	3.36	2.39	N/A	555.4	203.5	74.7	1.3
2016	B-	3.45	2.43	71.2	548.3	206.1	295.2	1.9
2015	B-	3.36	2.37	68.5	548.9	203.4	298.6	6.6
2014	B-	3.46	2.49	65.5	531.4	197.1	281.2	6.9
2013	B-	3.39	2.46	66.9	513.8	189.4	272.7	7.5
2012	C+	3.23	2.36	71.3	511.4	181.7	277.1	4.5

Farmers Insurance Group of Companies
Composite Group Rating: C
Largest Group Members

	Assets ($mil)	Rating
FARMERS INS EXCHANGE	16057	C
MID-CENTURY INS CO	3981	B
FIRE INS EXCHANGE	2429	C+
FOREMOST INS CO	2269	B
TRUCK INS EXCHANGE	2144	C+

FARMERS INS EXCHANGE   C   Fair

Major Rating Factors: Fair profitability index (3.7 on a scale of 0 to 10) with operating losses during 2012, 2015 and the first three months of 2017. Fair overall results on stability tests (4.3) including weak results on operational trends and negative cash flow from operations for 2016.

Other Rating Factors: Vulnerable liquidity (2.6) as a spike in claims may stretch capacity. Good overall long-term capitalization (5.4) based on good current risk adjusted capital (severe and moderate loss scenarios). However, capital levels have fluctuated somewhat during past years. History of adequate reserve strength (5.6) as reserves have been consistently at an acceptable level.

Principal Business: Homeowners multiple peril (33%), auto liability (30%), auto physical damage (20%), commercial multiple peril (11%), other liability (2%), and workers compensation (2%).

Principal Investments: Misc. investments (53%), investment grade bonds (43%), real estate (3%), and non investment grade bonds (1%).

Investments in Affiliates: 46%

Group Affiliation: Farmers Insurance Group of Companies

Licensed in: All states except AK, CT, HI, PR

Commenced Business: April 1928

Address: 6301 OWENSMOUTH AVE, Woodland Hills, CA 91367

Phone: (323) 932-3200   **Domicile State:** CA   **NAIC Code:** 21652

Data Date	Rating	RACR #1	RACR #2	Loss Ratio %	Total Assets ($mil)	Capital ($mil)	Net Premium ($mil)	Net Income ($mil)
3-17	C	0.86	0.79	N/A	16,534.7	4,207.3	1,860.8	-39.8
3-16	C	0.88	0.81	N/A	16,090.8	4,184.1	1,933.8	-19.4
2016	C	0.87	0.80	72.5	16,057.2	4,218.8	7,639.3	-147.9
2015	C	0.89	0.82	69.0	15,566.6	4,206.8	7,726.6	-113.7
2014	C	0.92	0.85	65.8	15,591.3	4,181.5	7,277.2	2.5
2013	C	0.90	0.84	66.8	15,557.1	3,879.7	7,057.1	55.0
2012	C	0.91	0.85	73.4	15,530.2	3,750.8	7,170.1	-162.0

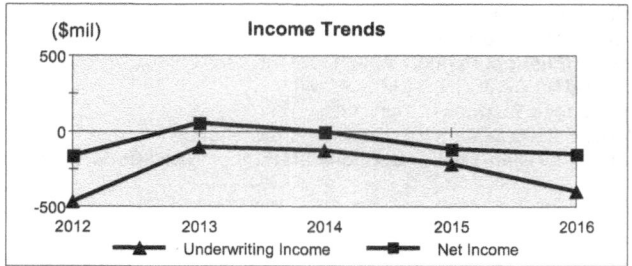

($mil)   **Income Trends**

▲ Underwriting Income   ■ Net Income

FARMERS MUTUAL HAIL INS CO OF IA   B-   Good

Major Rating Factors: Fair overall results on stability tests (4.3 on a scale of 0 to 10) including potential drain of affiliation with Farmers Mutual Hail Ins Co and weak results on operational trends. The largest net exposure for one risk is conservative at 1.0% of capital. Good overall profitability index (5.2) despite operating losses during 2012 and 2014.

Other Rating Factors: Good liquidity (5.1) with sufficient resources (cash flows and marketable investments) to handle a spike in claims. Strong long-term capitalization index (7.3) based on excellent current risk adjusted capital (severe and moderate loss scenarios), despite some fluctuation in capital levels. Ample reserve history (7.7) that can protect against increases in claims costs.

Principal Business: Allied lines (94%), fire (3%), auto liability (1%), auto physical damage (1%), and other liability (1%).

Principal Investments: Misc. investments (53%), investment grade bonds (37%), non investment grade bonds (4%), cash (3%), and real estate (3%).

Investments in Affiliates: 35%

Group Affiliation: Farmers Mutual Hail Ins Co

Licensed in: All states except AK, DC, HI, ME, NV, PR

Commenced Business: March 1893

Address: 6785 WESTOWN PARKWAY, West Des Moines, IA 50266

Phone: (515) 724-5007   **Domicile State:** IA   **NAIC Code:** 13897

Data Date	Rating	RACR #1	RACR #2	Loss Ratio %	Total Assets ($mil)	Capital ($mil)	Net Premium ($mil)	Net Income ($mil)
3-17	B-	2.10	1.64	N/A	681.3	429.6	43.8	3.5
3-16	B-	1.83	1.43	N/A	718.9	377.3	43.3	2.7
2016	B-	2.00	1.54	63.6	702.8	427.0	334.2	48.2
2015	B-	1.67	1.27	77.9	744.5	366.6	360.4	9.4
2014	B-	1.77	1.14	91.0	676.3	309.5	390.2	-31.2
2013	B-	1.98	1.24	85.9	832.8	358.3	431.1	3.9
2012	B-	1.91	1.18	92.6	879.9	317.5	470.4	-15.1

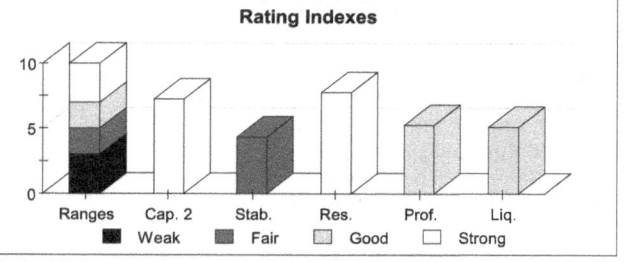

Rating Indexes

FARMERS MUTUAL INS CO OF NE   B   Good

Major Rating Factors: Good overall profitability index (6.5 on a scale of 0 to 10) despite operating losses during 2014. Good liquidity (6.6) with sufficient resources (cash flows and marketable investments) to handle a spike in claims.

Other Rating Factors: Fair overall results on stability tests (4.8) including weak results on operational trends. Strong long-term capitalization index (10.0) based on excellent current risk adjusted capital (severe and moderate loss scenarios), despite some fluctuation in capital levels. Ample reserve history (7.7) that can protect against increases in claims costs.

Principal Business: Farmowners multiple peril (30%), homeowners multiple peril (28%), auto physical damage (20%), auto liability (16%), allied lines (2%), fire (2%), and other liability (2%).

Principal Investments: Investment grade bonds (71%), misc. investments (22%), real estate (5%), and cash (2%).

Investments in Affiliates: None

Group Affiliation: None

Licensed in: IL, IN, IA, KS, NE, ND, SD

Commenced Business: November 1891

Address: 501 S 13th Street, Lincoln, NE 68508

Phone: (402) 434-8300   **Domicile State:** NE   **NAIC Code:** 13889

Data Date	Rating	RACR #1	RACR #2	Loss Ratio %	Total Assets ($mil)	Capital ($mil)	Net Premium ($mil)	Net Income ($mil)
3-17	B	4.48	3.28	N/A	673.1	354.3	83.6	22.0
3-16	B	4.28	3.16	N/A	618.2	326.8	79.9	24.3
2016	B	4.25	3.03	65.4	653.5	333.6	327.4	26.4
2015	B	4.08	2.92	65.8	591.0	304.3	315.3	27.3
2014	B	4.31	3.01	83.8	536.2	282.4	267.3	-7.7
2013	B	4.70	3.34	67.1	512.4	293.2	264.9	20.0
2012	B	5.08	3.60	70.0	461.8	269.7	224.5	18.2

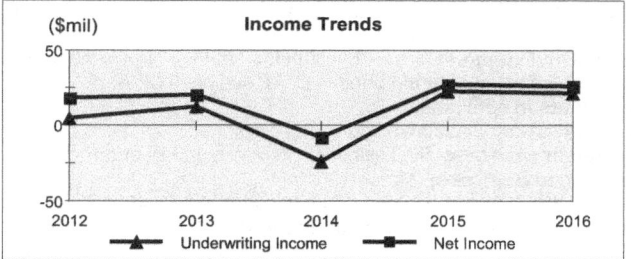

Income Trends

FARMINGTON CASUALTY CO   B   Good

Major Rating Factors: Good overall profitability index (6.5 on a scale of 0 to 10). Fair expense controls. Return on equity has been good over the last five years, averaging 13.9%. Good liquidity (6.7) with sufficient resources (cash flows and marketable investments) to handle a spike in claims.

Other Rating Factors: Fair overall results on stability tests (4.6) including weak results on operational trends. Affiliation with Travelers Companies Inc is a strength. Strong long-term capitalization index (7.9) based on excellent current risk adjusted capital (severe and moderate loss scenarios), despite some fluctuation in capital levels. Ample reserve history (8.7) that helps to protect the company against sharp claims increases.

Principal Business: Workers compensation (62%), homeowners multiple peril (36%), and auto liability (1%).

Principal Investments: Investment grade bonds (97%) and misc. investments (3%).

Investments in Affiliates: 0%

Group Affiliation: Travelers Companies Inc

Licensed in: All states except PR

Commenced Business: October 1982

Address: ONE TOWER SQUARE, Hartford, CT 06183

Phone: (860) 277-0111   **Domicile State:** CT   **NAIC Code:** 41483

Data Date	Rating	RACR #1	RACR #2	Loss Ratio %	Total Assets ($mil)	Capital ($mil)	Net Premium ($mil)	Net Income ($mil)
3-17	B	2.46	1.60	N/A	1,032.4	296.4	79.8	6.9
3-16	B	2.51	1.59	N/A	1,019.7	301.4	76.9	8.4
2016	B	2.46	1.61	63.4	1,017.7	289.5	322.2	37.0
2015	B	2.49	1.59	58.7	1,005.4	291.3	307.5	42.0
2014	B	2.48	1.56	60.5	1,009.6	287.7	298.8	46.4
2013	B	2.52	1.60	60.9	1,000.6	287.4	298.1	45.9
2012	B	2.39	1.54	68.4	1,003.0	269.2	289.5	29.7

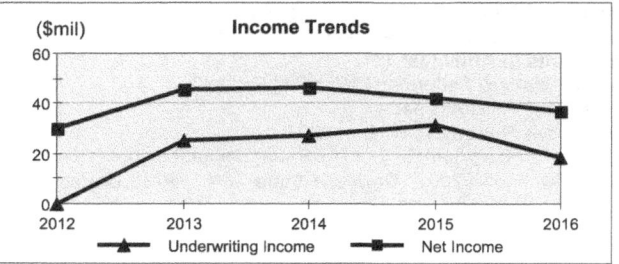

Income Trends

FCCI INS CO   C+   Fair

Major Rating Factors: Fair overall results on stability tests (4.2 on a scale of 0 to 10) including potential drain of affiliation with FCCI Ins Group. Fair profitability index (4.2) with operating losses during the first three months of 2017. Return on equity has been low, averaging 3.5% over the past five years.

Other Rating Factors: Good liquidity (6.4) with sufficient resources (cash flows and marketable investments) to handle a spike in claims. Strong long-term capitalization index (7.9) based on excellent current risk adjusted capital (severe and moderate loss scenarios), despite some fluctuation in capital levels. Ample reserve history (7.0) that can protect against increases in claims costs.

Principal Business: Workers compensation (47%), auto liability (15%), commercial multiple peril (13%), other liability (8%), auto physical damage (4%), surety (3%), and other lines (9%).

Principal Investments: Investment grade bonds (75%), misc. investments (22%), real estate (2%), and non investment grade bonds (1%).

Investments in Affiliates: 8%

Group Affiliation: FCCI Ins Group

Licensed in: AL, AZ, AR, CO, DC, FL, GA, IL, IN, IA, KS, KY, LA, MD, MI, MS, MO, NE, NC, OH, OK, PA, SC, TN, TX, VA

Commenced Business: April 1959

Address: 6300 University Parkway, Sarasota, FL 34240-8424

Phone: (941) 907-3224   **Domicile State:** FL   **NAIC Code:** 10178

Data Date	Rating	RACR #1	RACR #2	Loss Ratio %	Total Assets ($mil)	Capital ($mil)	Net Premium ($mil)	Net Income ($mil)
3-17	C+	2.10	1.51	N/A	2,020.6	572.1	187.2	-4.9
3-16	C+	2.40	1.73	N/A	1,875.2	585.2	182.1	1.8
2016	C+	2.22	1.61	80.6	1,920.9	572.0	750.1	-17.6
2015	C+	2.51	1.83	65.8	1,802.2	581.1	711.1	35.5
2014	C+	2.54	1.85	63.4	1,709.1	578.7	639.2	39.4
2013	C+	2.63	1.90	66.0	1,628.9	552.1	559.1	26.7
2012	C+	2.63	1.91	67.1	1,529.4	520.8	492.2	24.7

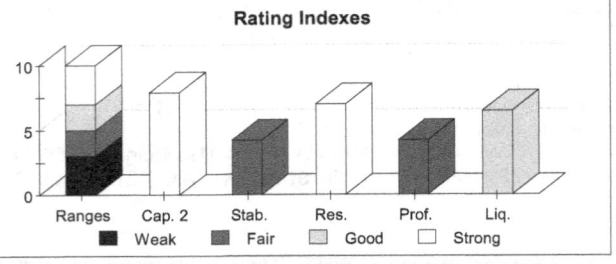
Rating Indexes

FEDERAL INS CO   B-   Good

Major Rating Factors: Fair profitability index (3.3 on a scale of 0 to 10). Fair expense controls. Return on equity has been fair, averaging 16.3% over the past five years. Fair overall results on stability tests (3.8) including weak results on operational trends. The largest net exposure for one risk is excessive at 5.1% of capital.

Other Rating Factors: Good liquidity (6.8) with sufficient resources (cash flows and marketable investments) to handle a spike in claims. Strong long-term capitalization index (7.0) based on excellent current risk adjusted capital (severe and moderate loss scenarios), despite some fluctuation in capital levels. Ample reserve history (8.3) that helps to protect the company against sharp claims increases.

Principal Business: Other liability (34%), commercial multiple peril (17%), workers compensation (12%), homeowners multiple peril (9%), fidelity (4%), inland marine (4%), and other lines (21%).

Principal Investments: Misc. investments (44%), investment grade bonds (43%), non investment grade bonds (11%), and cash (2%).

Investments in Affiliates: 38%

Group Affiliation: Chubb Limited

Licensed in: All states, the District of Columbia and Puerto Rico

Commenced Business: March 1901

Address: 202 N Illinois St Suite 2600, Indianapolis, IN 46282

Phone: (908) 903-2000   **Domicile State:** IN   **NAIC Code:** 20281

Data Date	Rating	RACR #1	RACR #2	Loss Ratio %	Total Assets ($mil)	Capital ($mil)	Net Premium ($mil)	Net Income ($mil)
3-17	B-	1.33	1.20	N/A	28,149.3	11,889.4	1,085.8	429.4
3-16	B	1.25	1.16	N/A	31,030.9	13,224.1	1,504.3	682.5
2016	B-	1.28	1.16	52.0	27,371.2	11,423.8	4,708.0	3,239.2
2015	B	1.24	1.15	54.3	32,240.6	13,278.7	7,338.2	2,154.1
2014	B	1.36	1.26	56.8	32,484.3	14,828.4	7,113.5	1,855.3
2013	B+	1.42	1.31	51.7	31,761.3	14,741.3	6,844.9	2,021.9
2012	B+	1.36	1.25	64.8	31,246.7	13,841.0	6,586.4	1,564.7

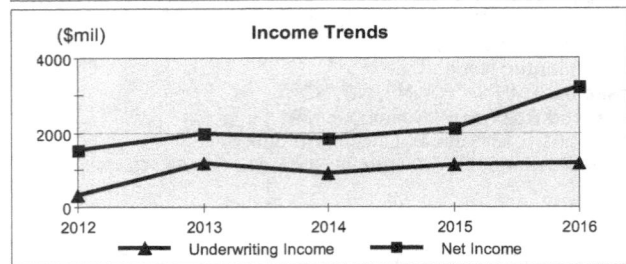
Income Trends

FEDERATED MUTUAL INS CO   B   Good

Major Rating Factors: Good overall results on stability tests (5.1 on a scale of 0 to 10) despite potential drain of affiliation with Federated Mutual Ins Group and weak results on operational trends. Good liquidity (6.9) with sufficient resources (cash flows and marketable investments) to handle a spike in claims.

Other Rating Factors: Strong long-term capitalization index (9.9) based on excellent current risk adjusted capital (severe and moderate loss scenarios). Moreover, capital levels have been consistent in recent years. Ample reserve history (9.0) that helps to protect the company against sharp claims increases. Excellent profitability (8.6) with operating gains in each of the last five years.

Principal Business: Group accident & health (33%), workers compensation (17%), other liability (14%), auto liability (12%), commercial multiple peril (5%), auto physical damage (5%), and other lines (13%).

Principal Investments: Investment grade bonds (70%), misc. investments (28%), non investment grade bonds (1%), and real estate (1%).

Investments in Affiliates: 15%

Group Affiliation: Federated Mutual Ins Group

Licensed in: All states except HI, PR

Commenced Business: August 1904

Address: 121 EAST PARK SQUARE, Owatonna, MN 55060

Phone: (507) 455-5200   **Domicile State:** MN   **NAIC Code:** 13935

Data Date	Rating	RACR #1	RACR #2	Loss Ratio %	Total Assets ($mil)	Capital ($mil)	Net Premium ($mil)	Net Income ($mil)
3-17	B	3.47	2.79	N/A	5,543.6	3,165.9	365.4	52.4
3-16	B	3.85	3.13	N/A	5,138.6	2,918.5	343.2	49.5
2016	B	3.61	2.97	68.8	5,456.8	3,091.1	1,460.6	185.4
2015	B	3.82	3.13	66.9	5,076.2	2,862.4	1,301.0	189.1
2014	B	3.79	3.11	63.2	4,783.7	2,657.1	1,183.9	187.6
2013	A-	3.67	3.00	69.6	4,523.5	2,518.3	1,083.5	127.9
2012	A-	3.86	3.19	74.6	4,233.8	2,365.4	942.3	106.1

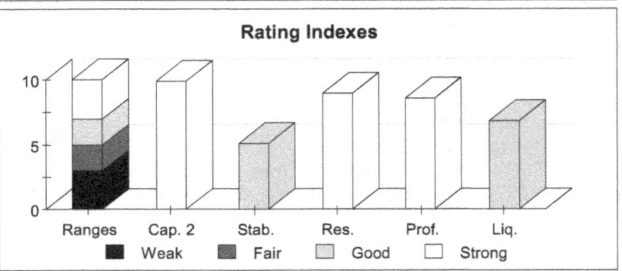
Rating Indexes

FEDERATED SERVICE INS CO   B-   Good

Major Rating Factors: Fair overall results on stability tests (4.5 on a scale of 0 to 10) including potential drain of affiliation with Federated Mutual Ins Group and weak results on operational trends. The largest net exposure for one risk is conservative at 1.2% of capital. Good liquidity (6.9) with sufficient resources (cash flows and marketable investments) to handle a spike in claims.

Other Rating Factors: Strong long-term capitalization index (10.0) based on excellent current risk adjusted capital (severe and moderate loss scenarios). Moreover, capital levels have been consistent in recent years. Ample reserve history (9.3) that helps to protect the company against sharp claims increases. Excellent profitability (8.6) with operating gains in each of the last five years.

Principal Business: Auto liability (27%), other liability (24%), workers compensation (17%), auto physical damage (13%), allied lines (7%), fire (5%), and other lines (7%).

Principal Investments: Investment grade bonds (107%) and non investment grade bonds (2%).

Investments in Affiliates: None

Group Affiliation: Federated Mutual Ins Group

Licensed in: All states except HI, NH, NJ, VT, PR

Commenced Business: January 1975

Address: 121 EAST PARK SQUARE, Owatonna, MN 55060

Phone: (507) 455-5200   **Domicile State:** MN   **NAIC Code:** 28304

Data Date	Rating	RACR #1	RACR #2	Loss Ratio %	Total Assets ($mil)	Capital ($mil)	Net Premium ($mil)	Net Income ($mil)
3-17	B-	7.69	4.92	N/A	433.6	233.6	30.4	4.4
3-16	B-	6.29	4.00	N/A	460.9	216.2	38.1	5.6
2016	B-	6.64	4.24	68.8	488.8	228.3	162.3	19.1
2015	B-	6.40	4.08	66.9	455.8	211.2	144.6	20.2
2014	B-	5.82	3.81	63.2	428.3	193.3	131.5	19.6
2013	B	5.31	3.50	69.6	406.0	184.1	120.4	11.6
2012	B	5.97	3.82	74.6	377.3	171.1	104.7	8.4

Federated Mutual Ins Group
Composite Group Rating: B

Largest Group Members	Assets ($mil)	Rating
FEDERATED MUTUAL INS CO	5457	B
FEDERATED LIFE INS CO	1777	A
FEDERATED SERVICE INS CO	489	B-
FEDERATED RESERVE INS CO	53	U
GRANITE RE INC	47	C+

FINIAL REINS CO   D+   Weak

Major Rating Factors: Weak overall results on stability tests (2.5 on a scale of 0 to 10) including potential drain of affiliation with Berkshire-Hathaway and weak results on operational trends. The largest net exposure for one risk is conservative at 1.3% of capital. Fair reserve development (4.6) as reserves have generally been sufficient to cover claims.

Other Rating Factors: Strong long-term capitalization index (9.7) based on excellent current risk adjusted capital (severe and moderate loss scenarios). Moreover, capital levels have been consistent in recent years. Excellent profitability (8.6) with operating gains in each of the last five years. Excellent expense controls. Superior liquidity (10.0) with ample operational cash flow and liquid investments.

Principal Business: (This company is a reinsurer.)

Principal Investments: Investment grade bonds (61%), misc. investments (33%), and cash (6%).

Investments in Affiliates: None

Group Affiliation: Berkshire-Hathaway

Licensed in: All states except MS, PR

Commenced Business: February 1993

Address: 100 First Stamford Place, Stamford, CT 06902-6745

Phone: (402) 916-3000   **Domicile State:** CT   **NAIC Code:** 39136

Data Date	Rating	RACR #1	RACR #2	Loss Ratio %	Total Assets ($mil)	Capital ($mil)	Net Premium ($mil)	Net Income ($mil)
3-17	D+	5.42	2.94	N/A	1,530.0	1,007.7	0.0	1.5
3-16	D+	5.30	3.37	N/A	1,239.7	835.8	0.1	9.3
2016	D+	5.21	2.80	78.6	1,487.0	975.5	72.4	43.5
2015	D+	5.21	3.30	73.2	1,336.8	881.3	99.4	32.3
2014	D+	6.13	3.75	N/A	1,230.2	880.1	-0.5	29.6
2013	D+	7.17	4.28	N/A	1,257.7	812.1	-2.2	59.1
2012	U	6.71	3.93	N/A	1,203.0	716.3	-0.1	47.1

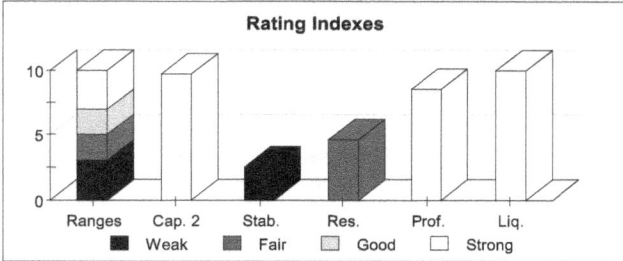

Rating Indexes

FIRE INS EXCHANGE   C+   Fair

Major Rating Factors: Fair profitability index (3.9 on a scale of 0 to 10) with operating losses during 2012 and the first three months of 2017. Fair overall results on stability tests (4.8) including weak results on operational trends.

Other Rating Factors: Good overall long-term capitalization (5.1) based on good current risk adjusted capital (severe and moderate loss scenarios). However, capital levels have fluctuated somewhat during past years. History of adequate reserve strength (5.7) as reserves have been consistently at an acceptable level. Vulnerable liquidity (2.9) as a spike in claims may stretch capacity.

Principal Business: Homeowners multiple peril (67%), commercial multiple peril (15%), allied lines (10%), fire (5%), other liability (1%), and inland marine (1%).

Principal Investments: Misc. investments (63%), investment grade bonds (44%), and real estate (3%).

Investments in Affiliates: 57%

Group Affiliation: Farmers Insurance Group of Companies

Licensed in: AL, AZ, AR, CA, CO, FL, GA, ID, IL, IN, IA, KS, MI, MN, MO, MT, NE, NV, NH, NJ, NM, NY, ND, OH, OK, OR, SD, TX, UT, WA, WI, WY

Commenced Business: November 1942

Address: 6301 OWENSMOUTH AVE, Woodland Hills, CA 91367

Phone: (323) 932-3200   **Domicile State:** CA   **NAIC Code:** 21660

Data Date	Rating	RACR #1	RACR #2	Loss Ratio %	Total Assets ($mil)	Capital ($mil)	Net Premium ($mil)	Net Income ($mil)
3-17	C+	0.81	0.76	N/A	2,573.2	770.5	269.7	-3.5
3-16	C+	0.83	0.78	N/A	2,503.0	778.2	280.3	-6.2
2016	C+	0.81	0.76	72.5	2,429.4	777.2	1,107.1	-14.3
2015	C+	0.84	0.79	69.0	2,335.3	786.9	1,119.8	12.5
2014	C+	0.84	0.80	65.8	2,281.7	771.1	1,054.7	6.8
2013	C+	0.83	0.78	66.9	2,254.8	721.3	1,022.8	12.7
2012	C+	0.83	0.78	73.3	2,204.0	662.2	1,039.1	-10.7

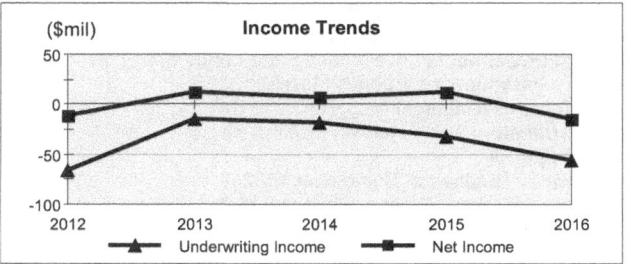

Income Trends

FIREMANS FUND INS CO
C   Fair

Major Rating Factors: Fair profitability index (3.0 on a scale of 0 to 10) with operating losses during 2012. Return on equity has been fair, averaging 5.1% over the past five years. Fair overall results on stability tests (4.2) including weak results on operational trends.

Other Rating Factors: Good liquidity (5.9) with sufficient resources (cash flows and marketable investments) to handle a spike in claims. Strong long-term capitalization index (9.4) based on excellent current risk adjusted capital (severe and moderate loss scenarios), despite some fluctuation in capital levels.

Principal Business: Commercial multiple peril (38%), other liability (27%), inland marine (12%), fire (5%), workers compensation (4%), auto liability (4%), and other lines (10%).

Principal Investments: Investment grade bonds (51%), misc. investments (46%), non investment grade bonds (2%), and cash (1%).

Investments in Affiliates: 30%

Group Affiliation: Allianz Ins Group

Licensed in: All states, the District of Columbia and Puerto Rico

Commenced Business: September 1864

Address: 777 SAN MARIN DRIVE, Novato, CA 94998

Phone: (888) 466-7883   **Domicile State:** CA   **NAIC Code:** 21873

Data Date	Rating	RACR #1	RACR #2	Loss Ratio %	Total Assets ($mil)	Capital ($mil)	Net Premium ($mil)	Net Income ($mil)
3-17	C	3.85	3.55	N/A	2,291.0	1,675.6	0.0	12.6
3-16	C	1.90	1.80	N/A	2,654.6	1,536.6	0.0	349.9
2016	C	3.83	3.53	0.0	2,811.3	1,670.6	-503.1	389.3
2015	C	1.25	0.97	132.5	5,500.4	1,296.3	-1,189.5	292.2
2014	C	1.12	0.75	90.0	9,434.6	2,134.2	2,460.5	62.9
2013	C	1.39	0.92	68.6	9,843.7	2,478.7	2,577.7	237.4
2012	C	1.15	0.75	103.2	11,835.8	2,522.1	3,638.2	-814.8

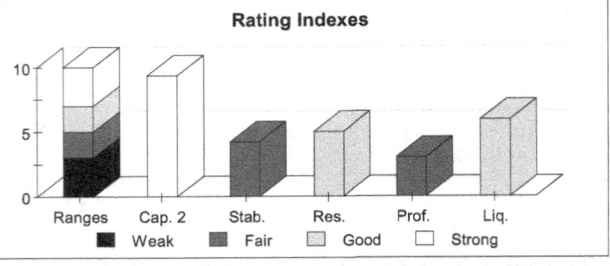

Rating Indexes

FIRST FINANCIAL INS CO
C-   Fair

Major Rating Factors: Weak overall results on stability tests (2.6 on a scale of 0 to 10) including potential drain of affiliation with IFG Companies. Strong long-term capitalization index (7.3) based on excellent current risk adjusted capital (severe and moderate loss scenarios). Moreover, capital levels have been consistent in recent years.

Other Rating Factors: Ample reserve history (7.9) that can protect against increases in claims costs. Excellent profitability (7.9) with operating gains in each of the last five years. Excellent liquidity (7.7) with ample operational cash flow and liquid investments.

Principal Business: Inland marine (76%), auto liability (21%), and auto physical damage (3%).

Principal Investments: Misc. investments (77%) and investment grade bonds (23%).

Investments in Affiliates: 76%

Group Affiliation: IFG Companies

Licensed in: All states except PR

Commenced Business: May 1970

Address: 400 South Ninth Street, Springfield, IL 62701-1822

Phone: (336) 586-2500   **Domicile State:** IL   **NAIC Code:** 11177

Data Date	Rating	RACR #1	RACR #2	Loss Ratio %	Total Assets ($mil)	Capital ($mil)	Net Premium ($mil)	Net Income ($mil)
3-17	C-	1.23	1.20	N/A	548.9	434.7	5.1	0.9
3-16	C-	1.22	1.20	N/A	551.2	428.7	6.0	2.2
2016	C-	1.23	1.20	47.6	551.1	432.6	20.9	12.7
2015	C-	1.21	1.19	35.1	544.2	423.7	24.6	5.6
2014	C-	1.18	1.17	56.3	540.2	406.4	27.4	5.0
2013	C-	1.18	1.17	36.2	533.6	393.5	30.5	16.3
2012	C-	1.13	1.13	26.2	507.2	354.7	32.3	18.8

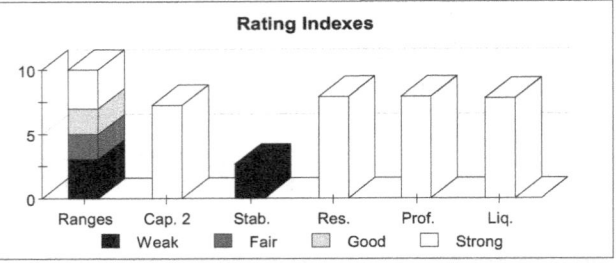

Rating Indexes

FIRST INS CO OF HI LTD
C   Fair

Major Rating Factors: Fair profitability index (4.5 on a scale of 0 to 10). Fair expense controls. Return on equity has been fair, averaging 7.9% over the past five years. Fair overall results on stability tests (4.2) including fair financial strength of affiliated Tokio Marine Holdings Inc and weak results on operational trends. The largest net exposure for one risk is conservative at 1.4% of capital.

Other Rating Factors: Good liquidity (6.8) with sufficient resources (cash flows and marketable investments) to handle a spike in claims. Strong long-term capitalization index (10.0) based on excellent current risk adjusted capital (severe and moderate loss scenarios), despite some fluctuation in capital levels. Ample reserve history (9.0) that helps to protect the company against sharp claims increases.

Principal Business: Workers compensation (25%), allied lines (20%), other liability (13%), commercial multiple peril (13%), auto liability (10%), homeowners multiple peril (10%), and other lines (10%).

Principal Investments: Investment grade bonds (93%), misc. investments (7%), and non investment grade bonds (1%).

Investments in Affiliates: 4%

Group Affiliation: Tokio Marine Holdings Inc

Licensed in: HI

Commenced Business: September 1982

Address: 1100 Ward Avenue, Honolulu, HI 96814

Phone: (808) 527-7777   **Domicile State:** HI   **NAIC Code:** 41742

Data Date	Rating	RACR #1	RACR #2	Loss Ratio %	Total Assets ($mil)	Capital ($mil)	Net Premium ($mil)	Net Income ($mil)
3-17	C	4.73	3.28	N/A	667.4	278.0	51.3	4.7
3-16	C	5.20	3.68	N/A	641.5	279.6	47.9	5.0
2016	C	4.76	3.33	68.5	664.7	273.1	205.2	6.5
2015	C	5.24	3.75	67.2	640.2	274.9	190.1	15.8
2014	C	5.03	3.55	62.9	631.0	288.8	181.0	20.0
2013	C	5.23	3.66	59.2	640.8	286.4	171.8	19.6
2012	C	6.38	4.14	41.1	646.9	286.9	148.7	50.8

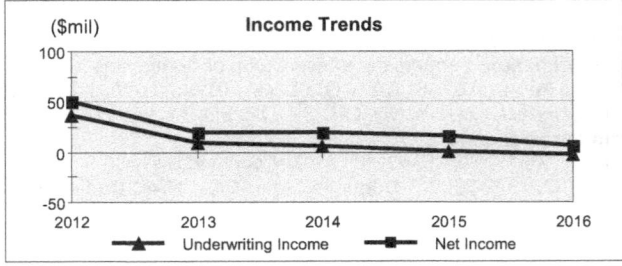

Income Trends

FLORIDA FARM BU CASUALTY INS CO

B-   **Good**

Major Rating Factors: Fair overall results on stability tests (4.5 on a scale of 0 to 10) including potential drain of affiliation with Southern Farm Bureau Casualty, weak results on operational trends and negative cash flow from operations for 2016. Good overall profitability index (5.5) despite operating losses during the first three months of 2017. Return on equity has been fair, averaging 5.3% over the past five years.

Other Rating Factors: Good liquidity (6.5) with sufficient resources (cash flows and marketable investments) to handle a spike in claims. Strong long-term capitalization index (10.0) based on excellent current risk adjusted capital (severe and moderate loss scenarios), despite some fluctuation in capital levels. Ample reserve history (7.8) that can protect against increases in claims costs.

Principal Business: Homeowners multiple peril (68%), auto liability (24%), and auto physical damage (8%).

Principal Investments: Investment grade bonds (91%), misc. investments (6%), real estate (2%), and cash (1%).

Investments in Affiliates: 3%

Group Affiliation: Southern Farm Bureau Casualty

Licensed in: FL

Commenced Business: July 1974

Address: 5700 SW 34th Street, Gainesville, FL 32608-5330

Phone: (352) 378-8100   **Domicile State:** FL   **NAIC Code:** 31216

Data Date	Rating	RACR #1	RACR #2	Loss Ratio %	Total Assets ($mil)	Capital ($mil)	Net Premium ($mil)	Net Income ($mil)
3-17	B-	4.98	3.63	N/A	562.9	283.7	64.0	-0.3
3-16	B-	5.01	3.58	N/A	557.1	288.1	62.3	-2.9
2016	B-	4.93	3.71	88.7	557.4	285.8	250.8	-8.2
2015	B-	5.05	3.71	73.4	554.4	292.3	238.6	21.4
2014	B-	4.43	3.19	71.3	532.2	269.0	237.3	24.6
2013	B-	3.02	2.11	73.4	502.8	246.3	235.5	19.9
2012	B-	3.00	2.08	74.6	474.0	227.5	226.3	14.8

Southern Farm Bureau Casualty
Composite Group Rating: B-
Largest Group Members

	Assets ($mil)	Rating
SOUTHERN FARM BUREAU CAS INS CO	2162	B-
FLORIDA FARM BU CASUALTY INS CO	557	B-
MISSISSIPPI FARM BUREAU CAS INS CO	426	B-
SOUTHERN FARM BUREAU PROPERTY	56	U
LOUISIANA FARM BUREAU CAS INS CO	12	B

FOREMOST INS CO

B   **Good**

Major Rating Factors: Good overall results on stability tests (5.5 on a scale of 0 to 10) despite potential drain of affiliation with Farmers Insurance Group of Companies and negative cash flow from operations for 2016. Stability strengths include good operational trends and excellent risk diversification. Strong long-term capitalization index (10.0) based on excellent current risk adjusted capital (severe and moderate loss scenarios), despite some fluctuation in capital levels.

Other Rating Factors: Ample reserve history (7.3) that can protect against increases in claims costs. Excellent profitability (7.8) with operating gains in each of the last five years. Excellent liquidity (8.3) with ample operational cash flow and liquid investments.

Principal Business: Homeowners multiple peril (43%), fire (19%), allied lines (11%), auto physical damage (9%), auto liability (7%), other liability (4%), and other lines (6%).

Principal Investments: Investment grade bonds (80%), misc. investments (14%), and real estate (6%).

Investments in Affiliates: 7%

Group Affiliation: Farmers Insurance Group of Companies

Licensed in: All states except PR

Commenced Business: June 1952

Address: 5600 BEECH TREE LANE, Caledonia, MI 49316-0050

Phone: (616) 942-3000   **Domicile State:** MI   **NAIC Code:** 11185

Data Date	Rating	RACR #1	RACR #2	Loss Ratio %	Total Assets ($mil)	Capital ($mil)	Net Premium ($mil)	Net Income ($mil)
3-17	B	9.53	6.83	N/A	2,309.5	1,141.8	0.0	7.5
3-16	B	9.54	6.82	N/A	2,252.1	1,103.1	0.0	9.7
2016	B	9.77	7.10	0.0	2,269.5	1,131.6	0.0	33.8
2015	B	9.74	7.04	0.0	2,172.2	1,093.2	0.0	33.9
2014	B	8.71	6.20	0.0	2,093.3	1,060.1	0.0	27.1
2013	B	10.90	7.99	0.0	1,938.6	1,029.9	0.0	38.5
2012	B	10.73	7.90	0.0	1,774.4	993.5	0.0	40.4

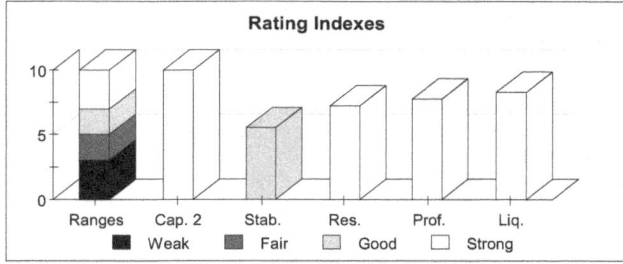

Rating Indexes

Ranges   Cap. 2   Stab.   Res.   Prof.   Liq.

■ Weak   ▨ Fair   ▢ Good   ☐ Strong

FRANKENMUTH MUTUAL INS CO

B   **Good**

Major Rating Factors: Good liquidity (6.7 on a scale of 0 to 10) with sufficient resources (cash flows and marketable investments) to handle a spike in claims. Fair overall results on stability tests (4.9) including weak results on operational trends.

Other Rating Factors: Strong long-term capitalization index (9.2) based on excellent current risk adjusted capital (severe and moderate loss scenarios). Moreover, capital levels have been consistent in recent years. Ample reserve history (9.3) that helps to protect the company against sharp claims increases. Excellent profitability (8.8) with operating gains in each of the last five years.

Principal Business: Auto liability (23%), commercial multiple peril (22%), auto physical damage (17%), homeowners multiple peril (15%), workers compensation (13%), other liability (5%), and other lines (6%).

Principal Investments: Investment grade bonds (77%), misc. investments (22%), and real estate (2%).

Investments in Affiliates: 15%

Group Affiliation: Frankenmuth Mutual Group

Licensed in: All states except AK, CA, DC, HI, PR

Commenced Business: March 1922

Address: One Mutual Avenue, Frankenmuth, MI 48787-0001

Phone: (989) 652-6121   **Domicile State:** MI   **NAIC Code:** 13986

Data Date	Rating	RACR #1	RACR #2	Loss Ratio %	Total Assets ($mil)	Capital ($mil)	Net Premium ($mil)	Net Income ($mil)
3-17	B	3.09	2.48	N/A	1,272.5	570.7	116.7	11.2
3-16	B	3.25	2.60	N/A	1,183.1	524.3	112.5	13.2
2016	B	3.17	2.61	63.3	1,259.5	556.0	467.8	37.0
2015	B	3.02	2.40	62.1	1,174.2	508.3	450.8	33.2
2014	B	3.06	2.45	68.9	1,107.4	463.8	427.9	22.1
2013	A	3.13	2.51	63.2	1,069.3	445.0	410.9	40.1
2012	A-	2.81	2.16	70.2	1,015.6	389.8	396.8	29.2

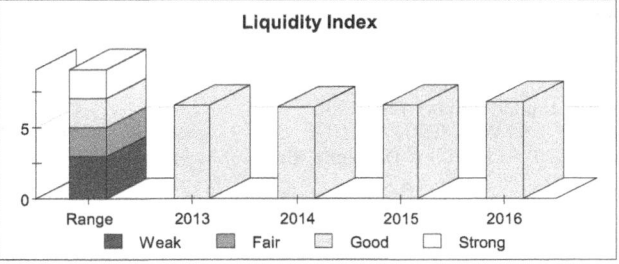

Liquidity Index

Range   2013   2014   2015   2016

■ Weak   ▨ Fair   ▢ Good   ☐ Strong

GARRISON P&C INS CO | B | Good

Major Rating Factors: Good overall profitability index (5.2 on a scale of 0 to 10) despite operating losses during 2016. Return on equity has been low, averaging 4.6% over the past five years. Fair overall results on stability tests (4.9) including weak results on operational trends. The largest net exposure for one risk is conservative at 1.2% of capital.

Other Rating Factors: Strong long-term capitalization index (8.2) based on excellent current risk adjusted capital (severe and moderate loss scenarios). Moreover, capital levels have been consistent in recent years. Ample reserve history (8.1) that helps to protect the company against sharp claims increases. Vulnerable liquidity (2.6) as a spike in claims may stretch capacity.

Principal Business: Auto liability (43%), auto physical damage (33%), homeowners multiple peril (21%), inland marine (1%), allied lines (1%), and fire (1%).

Principal Investments: Investment grade bonds (75%), misc. investments (21%), and non investment grade bonds (4%).

Investments in Affiliates: None

Group Affiliation: USAA Group

Licensed in: All states except PR

Commenced Business: December 1997

Address: 9800 Fredericksburg Road, San Antonio, TX 78288

Phone: (210) 498-1411 **Domicile State:** TX **NAIC Code:** 21253

Data Date	Rating	RACR #1	RACR #2	Loss Ratio %	Total Assets ($mil)	Capital ($mil)	Net Premium ($mil)	Net Income ($mil)
3-17	B	2.47	1.82	N/A	2,075.2	770.0	369.4	8.3
3-16	B	2.54	1.88	N/A	1,739.1	660.3	305.0	1.3
2016	B	2.43	1.83	91.8	1,981.5	751.6	1,376.4	-17.9
2015	B	2.49	1.89	86.0	1,707.7	655.3	1,190.8	19.0
2014	B	2.10	1.56	81.3	1,492.6	600.1	1,048.0	43.4
2013	B	2.70	2.06	77.4	1,255.5	506.4	710.0	49.2
2012	B	2.69	2.10	83.6	1,107.9	417.8	617.7	22.9

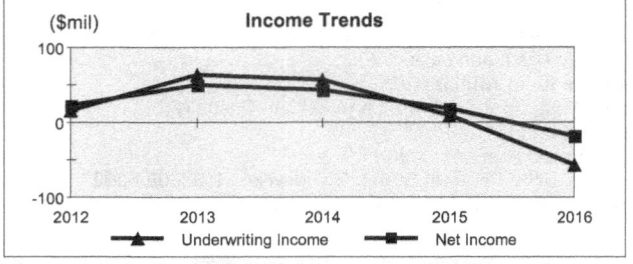

Income Trends

GEICO ADVANTAGE INS CO | B | Good

Major Rating Factors: History of adequate reserve strength (5.7 on a scale of 0 to 10) as reserves have been consistently at an acceptable level. Good liquidity (6.2) with sufficient resources (cash flows and marketable investments) to handle a spike in claims.

Other Rating Factors: Fair overall results on stability tests (4.9) including excessive premium growth, weak results on operational trends and negative cash flow from operations for 2016. Strong long-term capitalization index (8.1) based on excellent current risk adjusted capital (severe and moderate loss scenarios), despite some fluctuation in capital levels. Weak profitability index (2.7) with operating losses during each of the last five years and the first three months of 2017. Average return on equity over the last five years has been poor at -16.2%.

Principal Business: Auto liability (59%) and auto physical damage (41%).

Principal Investments: Misc. investments (52%) and investment grade bonds (48%).

Investments in Affiliates: None

Group Affiliation: Berkshire-Hathaway

Licensed in: All states except CA, FL, HI, ME, MA, MI, MN, NY, ND, SD, VT, PR

Commenced Business: November 2011

Address: 1440 KIEWIT PLAZA, Omaha, NE 68131

Phone: (800) 841-3000 **Domicile State:** NE **NAIC Code:** 14138

Data Date	Rating	RACR #1	RACR #2	Loss Ratio %	Total Assets ($mil)	Capital ($mil)	Net Premium ($mil)	Net Income ($mil)
3-17	B	2.39	1.66	N/A	1,962.4	957.1	233.9	-51.2
3-16	B-	1.98	1.47	N/A	1,186.0	594.5	144.1	-36.8
2016	B	2.47	1.76	105.9	1,805.2	977.4	788.3	-195.7
2015	B-	1.89	1.39	100.5	1,011.4	532.8	476.5	-115.2
2014	C+	2.49	1.65	103.0	779.7	446.6	192.6	-54.7
2013	C+	4.75	3.61	107.4	629.6	484.6	215.6	-85.3
2012	A-	10.23	7.53	102.7	249.1	208.2	44.3	-17.1

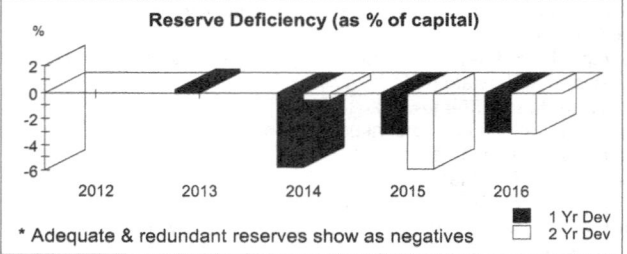

Reserve Deficiency (as % of capital)

* Adequate & redundant reserves show as negatives   ■ 1 Yr Dev   □ 2 Yr Dev

GEICO CASUALTY CO | C | Fair

Major Rating Factors: Fair overall results on stability tests (4.0 on a scale of 0 to 10) including weak results on operational trends. Weak profitability index (2.8) with operating losses during each of the last five years and the first three months of 2017. Average return on equity over the last five years has been poor at -18.8%.

Other Rating Factors: Vulnerable liquidity (2.3) as a spike in claims may stretch capacity. Strong long-term capitalization index (7.1) based on excellent current risk adjusted capital (severe and moderate loss scenarios), despite some fluctuation in capital levels. Ample reserve history (9.5) that helps to protect the company against sharp claims increases.

Principal Business: (Not applicable due to unusual reinsurance transactions.)

Principal Investments: Misc. investments (62%) and investment grade bonds (38%).

Investments in Affiliates: None

Group Affiliation: Berkshire-Hathaway

Licensed in: All states except MI, PR

Commenced Business: May 1983

Address: 5260 WESTERN AVENUE, Chevy Chase, MD 20815-3799

Phone: (800) 841-3000 **Domicile State:** MD **NAIC Code:** 41491

Data Date	Rating	RACR #1	RACR #2	Loss Ratio %	Total Assets ($mil)	Capital ($mil)	Net Premium ($mil)	Net Income ($mil)
3-17	C	1.48	1.05	N/A	3,272.5	984.5	479.1	-13.0
3-16	C-	1.68	1.23	N/A	2,811.8	929.9	422.2	-9.1
2016	C	1.46	1.09	87.3	2,920.5	924.5	1,834.2	-67.0
2015	D+	1.74	1.28	90.8	2,605.9	929.8	1,619.8	-125.3
2014	D	2.45	1.63	83.2	2,347.3	979.9	657.8	-44.1
2013	D-	1.64	1.37	90.9	2,707.2	1,001.0	2,209.4	-342.5
2012	D-	1.73	1.48	87.7	1,712.6	661.8	1,381.8	-252.0

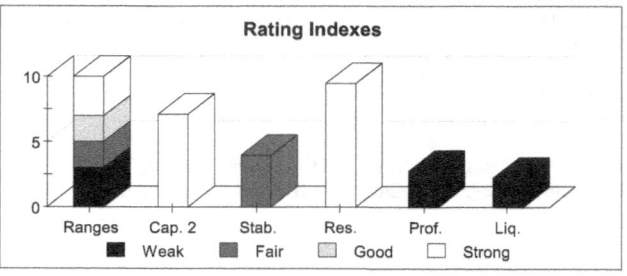

Rating Indexes

Ranges   Cap. 2   Stab.   Res.   Prof.   Liq.

■ Weak   ▨ Fair   ▧ Good   □ Strong

GEICO CHOICE INS CO *   B+   Good

Major Rating Factors: History of adequate reserve strength (5.8 on a scale of 0 to 10) as reserves have been consistently at an acceptable level. Good overall results on stability tests (5.0) despite weak results on operational trends, excessive premium growth and negative cash flow from operations for 2016.

Other Rating Factors: Strong long-term capitalization index (7.5) based on excellent current risk adjusted capital (severe and moderate loss scenarios), despite some fluctuation in capital levels. Weak profitability index (2.8) with operating losses during each of the last five years and the first three months of 2017. Average return on equity over the last five years has been poor at -11.1%. Vulnerable liquidity (2.8) as a spike in claims may stretch capacity.

Principal Business: Auto liability (61%) and auto physical damage (39%).

Principal Investments: Misc. investments (64%) and investment grade bonds (36%).

Investments in Affiliates: None

Group Affiliation: Berkshire-Hathaway

Licensed in: All states except CA, FL, HI, ME, MA, MI, MN, NY, ND, SD, VT, PR

Commenced Business: November 2011

Address: 1440 KIEWIT PLAZA, Omaha, NE 68131

Phone: (800) 841-3000   **Domicile State:** NE   **NAIC Code:** 14139

Data Date	Rating	RACR #1	RACR #2	Loss Ratio %	Total Assets ($mil)	Capital ($mil)	Net Premium ($mil)	Net Income ($mil)
3-17	B+	1.91	1.31	N/A	919.4	370.7	134.2	-11.3
3-16	A-	2.21	1.53	N/A	649.2	283.6	91.2	-11.9
2016	B+	1.96	1.38	93.2	826.9	361.6	469.2	-48.1
2015	A-	2.37	1.65	93.2	600.9	295.7	315.1	-41.5
2014	A-	2.58	1.65	90.7	411.4	229.4	134.5	-13.9
2013	A-	3.88	2.79	99.4	339.5	236.8	163.6	-37.4
2012	A-	13.29	9.34	104.2	248.5	212.9	40.1	-12.5

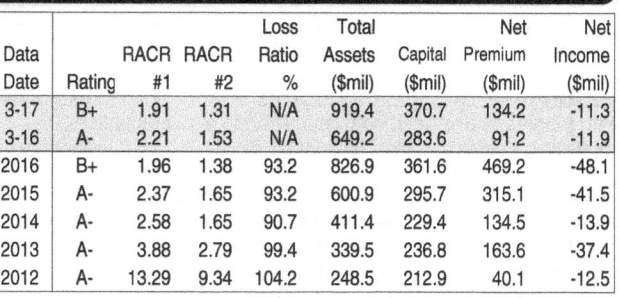

Reserve Deficiency (as % of capital)

* Adequate & redundant reserves show as negatives   ■ 1 Yr Dev   □ 2 Yr Dev

GEICO GENERAL INS CO *   B+   Good

Major Rating Factors: Good overall results on stability tests (5.0 on a scale of 0 to 10) despite weak results on operational trends and negative cash flow from operations for 2016. Strong long-term capitalization index (10.0) based on excellent current risk adjusted capital (severe and moderate loss scenarios). Moreover, capital levels have been consistent in recent years.

Other Rating Factors: Excellent profitability (7.1) with operating gains in each of the last five years. Excellent expense controls. Excellent liquidity (7.0) with ample operational cash flow and liquid investments.

Principal Business: Auto liability (60%) and auto physical damage (40%).

Principal Investments: Investment grade bonds (79%) and misc. investments (21%).

Investments in Affiliates: None

Group Affiliation: Berkshire-Hathaway

Licensed in: All states except PR

Commenced Business: May 1934

Address: 5260 WESTERN AVENUE, Chevy Chase, MD 20815-3799

Phone: (800) 841-3000   **Domicile State:** MD   **NAIC Code:** 35882

Data Date	Rating	RACR #1	RACR #2	Loss Ratio %	Total Assets ($mil)	Capital ($mil)	Net Premium ($mil)	Net Income ($mil)
3-17	B+	156.90	78.44	N/A	166.1	166.0	0.0	0.1
3-16	B+	19.23	17.31	N/A	230.8	153.5	0.0	0.1
2016	B+	181.11	90.56	0.0	154.1	153.9	0.0	0.5
2015	B+	18.69	16.82	0.0	209.5	141.4	0.0	0.2
2014	B+	15.86	14.27	0.0	214.8	131.1	0.0	0.3
2013	B+	14.30	12.87	0.0	215.7	123.6	0.0	2.8
2012	B+	14.96	13.47	0.0	184.2	114.4	0.0	1.7

Berkshire-Hathaway
Composite Group Rating: B
Largest Group Members

Largest Group Members	Assets ($mil)	Rating
NATIONAL INDEMNITY CO	178623	B
GOVERNMENT EMPLOYEES INS CO	27198	B
COLUMBIA INS CO	20707	U
BERKSHIRE HATHAWAY LIFE INS CO OF NE	17970	C+
GENERAL REINS CORP	14780	C+

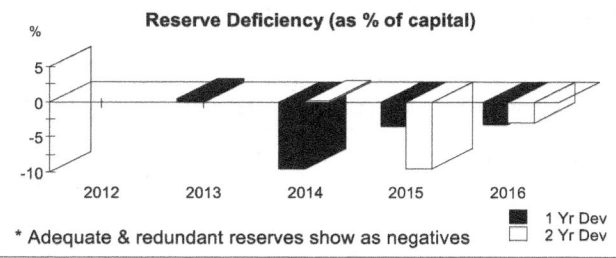

GEICO INDEMNITY CO   B   Good

Major Rating Factors: Good overall results on stability tests (5.1 on a scale of 0 to 10) despite potential drain of affiliation with Berkshire-Hathaway and weak results on operational trends. Good liquidity (6.3) with sufficient resources (cash flows and marketable investments) to handle a spike in claims.

Other Rating Factors: Strong long-term capitalization index (7.5) based on excellent current risk adjusted capital (severe and moderate loss scenarios). Moreover, capital levels have been consistent in recent years. Ample reserve history (9.4) that helps to protect the company against sharp claims increases. Excellent profitability (8.9) with operating gains in each of the last five years. Return on equity has been good over the last five years, averaging 11.1%.

Principal Business: (Not applicable due to unusual reinsurance transactions.)

Principal Investments: Misc. investments (84%) and investment grade bonds (16%).

Investments in Affiliates: 14%

Group Affiliation: Berkshire-Hathaway

Licensed in: All states except PR

Commenced Business: September 1961

Address: 5260 WESTERN AVENUE, Chevy Chase, MD 20815-3799

Phone: (800) 841-3000   **Domicile State:** MD   **NAIC Code:** 22055

Data Date	Rating	RACR #1	RACR #2	Loss Ratio %	Total Assets ($mil)	Capital ($mil)	Net Premium ($mil)	Net Income ($mil)
3-17	B	2.18	1.58	N/A	8,771.2	4,856.3	649.1	47.5
3-16	B	2.20	1.68	N/A	7,101.5	3,919.5	602.2	46.3
2016	B	2.13	1.57	80.7	8,166.9	4,598.2	2,542.6	160.0
2015	B	2.19	1.66	80.3	7,138.7	4,075.9	2,397.8	133.0
2014	B	2.25	1.67	47.4	6,962.8	4,018.3	530.9	409.2
2013	B+	1.75	1.38	73.2	7,811.2	3,636.3	4,411.5	663.6
2012	B+	1.71	1.38	69.0	6,443.7	2,748.9	4,206.7	607.7

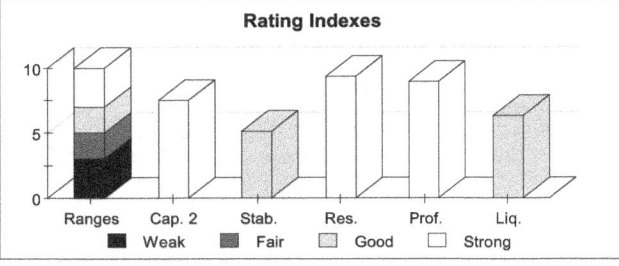

Rating Indexes

Ranges   Cap. 2   Stab.   Res.   Prof.   Liq.
■ Weak   ▨ Fair   ▧ Good   □ Strong

GEICO SECURE INS CO *

A-   Excellent

Major Rating Factors: Strong long-term capitalization index (8.0 on a scale of 0 to 10) based on excellent current risk adjusted capital (severe and moderate loss scenarios). Furthermore, this high level of risk adjusted capital has been consistently maintained in previous years. History of adequate reserve strength (5.6) as reserves have been consistently at an acceptable level.

Other Rating Factors: Good liquidity (5.9) with sufficient resources (cash flows and marketable investments) to handle a spike in claims. Good overall results on stability tests (5.7) despite weak results on operational trends and excessive premium growth. Fair profitability index (3.5) with operating losses during each of the last five years and the first three months of 2017. Average return on equity over the last five years has been poor at -3.5%.

Principal Business: Auto liability (67%) and auto physical damage (33%).

Principal Investments: Misc. investments (75%) and investment grade bonds (25%).

Investments in Affiliates: None

Group Affiliation: Berkshire-Hathaway

Licensed in: All states except CA, FL, HI, ME, MA, MI, MN, NY, ND, SD, VT, PR

Commenced Business: November 2011

Address: 1440 KIEWIT PLAZA, Omaha, NE 68131

Phone: (800) 841-3000   **Domicile State:** NE   **NAIC Code:** 14137

Data Date	Rating	RACR #1	RACR #2	Loss Ratio %	Total Assets ($mil)	Capital ($mil)	Net Premium ($mil)	Net Income ($mil)
3-17	A-	2.54	1.68	N/A	555.9	287.8	60.8	-1.7
3-16	A-	3.45	2.27	N/A	444.3	266.6	42.1	-1.7
2016	A-	2.53	1.70	85.6	489.5	269.1	214.1	-11.6
2015	A-	3.26	2.12	86.7	417.5	269.1	147.3	-13.3
2014	A-	3.65	2.24	80.4	413.6	273.1	66.3	-1.9
2013	A-	7.75	5.16	91.7	322.2	266.6	82.7	-14.3
2012	A-	20.77	13.14	92.2	238.9	220.3	21.1	-5.1

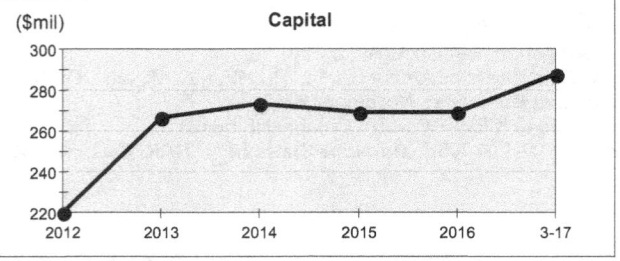

Capital ($mil)

GENERAL CASUALTY CO OF WI

C+   Fair

Major Rating Factors: Fair overall results on stability tests (4.5 on a scale of 0 to 10) including potential drain of affiliation with QBE Ins Group Ltd and weak results on operational trends. Fair profitability index (3.5) with small operating losses during 2012 and 2013. Return on equity has been low, averaging 2.9% over the past five years.

Other Rating Factors: History of adequate reserve strength (5.7) as reserves have been consistently at an acceptable level. Good liquidity (6.5) with sufficient resources (cash flows and marketable investments) to handle a spike in claims. Strong long-term capitalization index (7.5) based on excellent current risk adjusted capital (severe and moderate loss scenarios), despite some fluctuation in capital levels.

Principal Business: Commercial multiple peril (33%), auto liability (20%), workers compensation (13%), homeowners multiple peril (10%), auto physical damage (9%), other liability (9%), and other lines (6%).

Principal Investments: Investment grade bonds (73%), misc. investments (23%), and real estate (9%).

Investments in Affiliates: 24%

Group Affiliation: QBE Ins Group Ltd

Licensed in: All states, the District of Columbia and Puerto Rico

Commenced Business: May 1925

Address: One General Drive, Sun Prairie, WI 53596

Phone: (608) 825-5160   **Domicile State:** WI   **NAIC Code:** 24414

Data Date	Rating	RACR #1	RACR #2	Loss Ratio %	Total Assets ($mil)	Capital ($mil)	Net Premium ($mil)	Net Income ($mil)
3-17	C+	1.81	1.36	N/A	970.0	294.1	79.8	7.9
3-16	C	1.77	1.46	N/A	1,150.4	330.4	78.9	12.4
2016	C+	1.73	1.30	58.8	873.5	280.7	369.5	21.9
2015	C	1.75	1.51	63.9	695.4	317.9	180.2	13.0
2014	C	1.62	1.41	69.2	762.3	309.6	228.3	1.7
2013	C	1.41	1.20	75.2	866.6	312.7	312.2	0.0
2012	B-	1.57	1.36	73.5	1,025.0	448.1	280.2	-0.1

QBE Ins Group Ltd Composite Group Rating: B Largest Group Members	Assets ($mil)	Rating
QBE INS CORP	2325	B
NAU COUNTRY INS CO	1342	C+
QBE REINS CORP	1171	B
GENERAL CASUALTY CO OF WI	874	C+
PRAETORIAN INS CO	492	C

GENERAL REINS CORP

C+   Fair

Major Rating Factors: Fair overall results on stability tests (3.9 on a scale of 0 to 10) including potential drain of affiliation with Berkshire-Hathaway and weak results on operational trends. The largest net exposure for one risk is acceptable at 2.0% of capital. Fair profitability index (3.9). Weak expense controls. Return on equity has been fair, averaging 5.8% over the past five years.

Other Rating Factors: Strong long-term capitalization index (7.5) based on excellent current risk adjusted capital (severe and moderate loss scenarios), despite some fluctuation in capital levels. Ample reserve history (7.8) that can protect against increases in claims costs. Superior liquidity (9.3) with ample operational cash flow and liquid investments.

Principal Business: Aircraft (100%).

Principal Investments: Misc. investments (83%) and investment grade bonds (17%).

Investments in Affiliates: 47%

Group Affiliation: Berkshire-Hathaway

Licensed in: All states, the District of Columbia and Puerto Rico

Commenced Business: January 1973

Address: 1209 ORANGE STREET, Wilmington, DE 19801

Phone: (203) 328-5000   **Domicile State:** DE   **NAIC Code:** 22039

Data Date	Rating	RACR #1	RACR #2	Loss Ratio %	Total Assets ($mil)	Capital ($mil)	Net Premium ($mil)	Net Income ($mil)
3-17	C+	1.49	1.33	N/A	15,274.7	11,011.2	166.9	174.2
3-16	C+	1.54	1.38	N/A	15,138.1	10,947.9	141.6	322.9
2016	C+	1.46	1.31	54.5	14,780.1	10,660.5	550.2	742.0
2015	C+	1.51	1.34	56.8	15,320.5	11,050.5	548.5	570.7
2014	C+	1.56	1.36	41.8	16,157.5	11,706.6	593.4	538.2
2013	B-	1.51	1.33	30.7	16,219.7	11,561.7	543.0	930.9
2012	B-	1.51	1.31	54.8	15,532.9	10,693.2	567.5	432.9

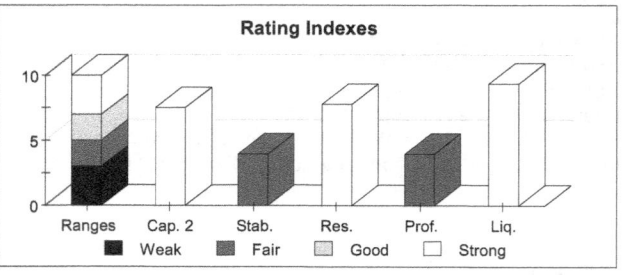

Rating Indexes

Ranges   Cap. 2   Stab.   Res.   Prof.   Liq.

■ Weak   ▨ Fair   ▧ Good   □ Strong

GENERAL STAR INDEMNITY CO   C   Fair

Major Rating Factors: Fair overall results on stability tests (4.0 on a scale of 0 to 10) including weak results on operational trends. The largest net exposure for one risk is conservative at 1.5% of capital. Good overall profitability index (5.8). Weak expense controls. Return on equity has been low, averaging 3.1% over the past five years.

Other Rating Factors: Strong long-term capitalization index (9.7) based on excellent current risk adjusted capital (severe and moderate loss scenarios), despite some fluctuation in capital levels. Ample reserve history (8.5) that helps to protect the company against sharp claims increases. Superior liquidity (9.8) with ample operational cash flow and liquid investments.

Principal Business: Other liability (45%), allied lines (26%), fire (9%), medical malpractice (8%), products liability (7%), homeowners multiple peril (2%), and inland marine (2%).

Principal Investments: Investment grade bonds (57%) and misc. investments (43%).

Investments in Affiliates: None
Group Affiliation: Berkshire-Hathaway
Licensed in: All states, the District of Columbia and Puerto Rico
Commenced Business: May 1979
Address: 1209 ORANGE STREET, Wilmington, DE 19801
Phone: (203) 328-5700   **Domicile State:** DE   **NAIC Code:** 37362

Data Date	Rating	RACR #1	RACR #2	Loss Ratio %	Total Assets ($mil)	Capital ($mil)	Net Premium ($mil)	Net Income ($mil)
3-17	C	4.54	2.79	N/A	862.0	605.1	17.3	2.8
3-16	C	4.70	2.92	N/A	747.6	527.0	16.1	1.9
2016	C	4.56	2.82	46.6	841.0	595.2	67.7	15.8
2015	C	4.60	2.85	60.3	774.7	543.3	66.8	7.9
2014	C	4.82	3.00	54.6	848.9	616.0	72.3	10.4
2013	B-	6.24	3.84	39.8	859.4	645.8	70.3	47.6
2012	B-	7.17	4.49	27.6	748.4	566.4	58.6	14.0

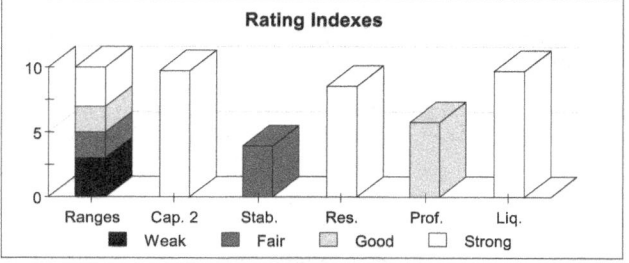

Rating Indexes

GENWORTH MORTGAGE INS CORP   C   Fair

Major Rating Factors: Fair overall results on stability tests (4.0 on a scale of 0 to 10) including weak results on operational trends. Strengths include potentially strong support from affiliation with Genworth Financial. Fair reserve development (4.3) as reserves have generally been sufficient to cover claims. In 2012, the two year reserve development was 43% deficient.

Other Rating Factors: Good overall profitability index (5.3) despite operating losses during 2012. Return on equity has been good over the last five years, averaging 10.5%. Good liquidity (6.6) with sufficient resources (cash flows and marketable investments) to handle a spike in claims. Strong long-term capitalization index (7.7) based on excellent current risk adjusted capital (severe and moderate loss scenarios), despite some fluctuation in capital levels.

Principal Business: Mortgage guaranty (100%).

Principal Investments: Investment grade bonds (81%), misc. investments (16%), and non investment grade bonds (3%).

Investments in Affiliates: 15%
Group Affiliation: Genworth Financial
Licensed in: All states except PR
Commenced Business: May 1980
Address: 8325 Six Forks Road, Raleigh, NC 27615
Phone: (919) 846-4100   **Domicile State:** NC   **NAIC Code:** 38458

Data Date	Rating	RACR #1	RACR #2	Loss Ratio %	Total Assets ($mil)	Capital ($mil)	Net Premium ($mil)	Net Income ($mil)
3-17	C	1.81	1.55	N/A	3,038.7	1,259.7	151.2	107.0
3-16	C	1.49	1.27	N/A	2,676.2	1,121.9	144.7	81.3
2016	C	1.70	1.46	23.9	2,944.7	1,187.0	675.6	390.4
2015	C	1.42	1.21	35.9	2,627.1	1,073.1	621.1	261.7
2014	C	1.50	1.30	61.0	2,866.0	1,395.8	572.6	179.1
2013	C-	0.88	0.77	77.1	2,390.3	960.3	477.9	77.3
2012	D+	0.41	0.32	139.4	2,247.3	485.6	455.3	-152.3

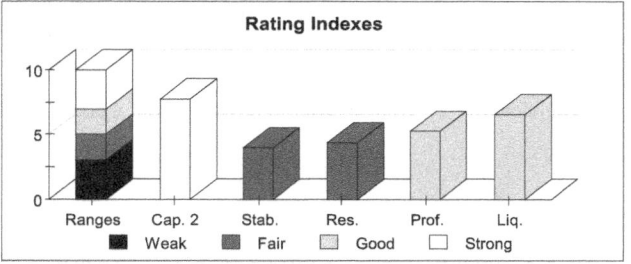

Rating Indexes

GEORGIA FARM BUREAU MUTUAL INS CO   C   Fair

Major Rating Factors: Fair reserve development (4.4 on a scale of 0 to 10) as reserves have generally been sufficient to cover claims. Fair liquidity (4.5) as cash resources may not be adequate to cover a spike in claims.

Other Rating Factors: Fair overall results on stability tests (4.1) including weak results on operational trends and negative cash flow from operations for 2016. Weak profitability index (2.2) with operating losses during 2015 and the first three months of 2017. Strong long-term capitalization index (7.2) based on excellent current risk adjusted capital (severe and moderate loss scenarios), despite some fluctuation in capital levels.

Principal Business: Auto liability (35%), homeowners multiple peril (24%), auto physical damage (22%), farmowners multiple peril (15%), commercial multiple peril (2%), allied lines (1%), and fire (1%).

Principal Investments: Investment grade bonds (80%), misc. investments (14%), and cash (6%).

Investments in Affiliates: 2%
Group Affiliation: Georgia Farm Bureau Ins
Licensed in: GA
Commenced Business: January 1959
Address: 1620 Bass Road, Macon, GA 31210
Phone: (478) 474-8411   **Domicile State:** GA   **NAIC Code:** 14001

Data Date	Rating	RACR #1	RACR #2	Loss Ratio %	Total Assets ($mil)	Capital ($mil)	Net Premium ($mil)	Net Income ($mil)
3-17	C	1.64	1.13	N/A	628.4	198.5	98.5	-14.1
3-16	C+	1.87	1.27	N/A	666.0	239.0	112.9	1.8
2016	C	1.66	1.16	78.3	645.4	208.6	450.0	-19.6
2015	C+	1.85	1.28	73.5	665.6	237.2	437.9	-4.1
2014	C	2.13	1.47	67.7	651.1	260.4	414.2	19.7
2013	C	2.07	1.41	74.3	620.6	258.1	401.4	2.6
2012	C	2.06	1.40	69.7	609.5	243.5	380.7	19.3

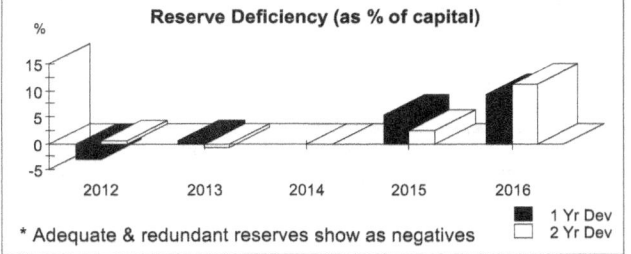

Reserve Deficiency (as % of capital)

* Adequate & redundant reserves show as negatives

GERMANIA FARM MUTUAL INS ASN

C   **Fair**

Major Rating Factors: Fair profitability index (3.7 on a scale of 0 to 10) with operating losses during 2012, 2013 and the first three months of 2017. Fair liquidity (4.5) as cash resources may not be adequate to cover a spike in claims.
Other Rating Factors: Fair overall results on stability tests (4.0) including fair financial strength of affiliated Germania Ins Group and weak results on operational trends. History of adequate reserve strength (5.9) as reserves have been consistently at an acceptable level. Strong long-term capitalization index (7.2) based on excellent current risk adjusted capital (severe and moderate loss scenarios), despite some fluctuation in capital levels.
Principal Business: Fire (99%) and inland marine (1%).
Principal Investments: Misc. investments (63%), investment grade bonds (34%), non investment grade bonds (5%), and real estate (1%).
Investments in Affiliates: 53%
Group Affiliation: Germania Ins Group
Licensed in: TX
Commenced Business: November 1897
Address: 507 Highway 290 East, Brenham, TX 77833
Phone: (979) 836-5224   **Domicile State:** TX   **NAIC Code:** 29610

Data Date	Rating	RACR #1	RACR #2	Loss Ratio %	Total Assets ($mil)	Capital ($mil)	Net Premium ($mil)	Net Income ($mil)
3-17	C	1.22	1.12	N/A	396.1	188.6	47.7	-11.1
3-16	C-	1.05	0.96	N/A	393.3	172.2	46.6	-3.1
2016	C	1.31	1.22	69.8	375.6	199.6	190.3	11.3
2015	D+	1.06	0.98	80.1	393.2	172.7	174.6	0.8
2014	D	1.19	1.12	74.3	401.4	184.2	178.3	18.0
2013	D	1.03	0.97	82.5	376.1	176.6	202.7	-17.2
2012	B-	1.08	1.00	80.8	364.7	172.1	199.4	-10.9

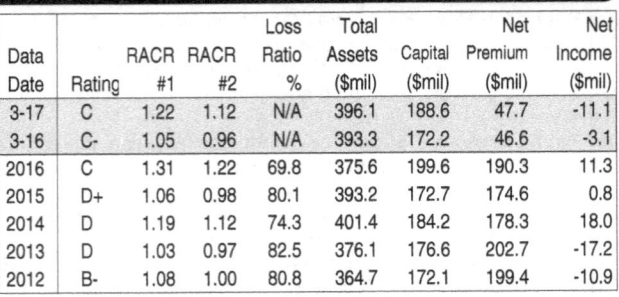

GNY CUSTOM INS CO *

B+   **Good**

Major Rating Factors: History of adequate reserve strength (5.0 on a scale of 0 to 10) as reserves have been consistently at an acceptable level. Good overall results on stability tests (6.5).
Other Rating Factors: Strong long-term capitalization index (10.0) based on excellent current risk adjusted capital (severe and moderate loss scenarios), despite some fluctuation in capital levels. Excellent profitability (7.0) with operating gains in each of the last five years. Superior liquidity (9.0) with ample operational cash flow and liquid investments.
Principal Business: Commercial multiple peril (100%).
Principal Investments: Investment grade bonds (99%) and misc. investments (1%).
Investments in Affiliates: None
Group Affiliation: Greater New York Group
Licensed in: AZ, CT, DC, DE, IL, IN, MD, MA, MI, NJ, NY, NC, OH, PA, VT, VA
Commenced Business: June 2006
Address: 200 Madison Avenue, New York, NY 10016-3904
Phone: (212) 683-9700   **Domicile State:** AZ   **NAIC Code:** 10814

Data Date	Rating	RACR #1	RACR #2	Loss Ratio %	Total Assets ($mil)	Capital ($mil)	Net Premium ($mil)	Net Income ($mil)
3-17	B+	23.44	18.75	N/A	59.3	53.2	0.7	0.3
3-16	B	23.40	18.43	N/A	58.2	52.2	0.7	0.3
2016	B+	23.60	18.98	66.5	59.0	52.9	2.9	1.1
2015	B	23.49	18.60	68.7	57.6	51.8	2.7	1.2
2014	B	24.16	18.76	67.6	56.2	50.7	2.5	1.3
2013	B+	24.88	17.89	61.1	54.8	49.5	2.3	1.4
2012	B+	25.44	20.16	75.1	54.2	47.9	2.1	1.1

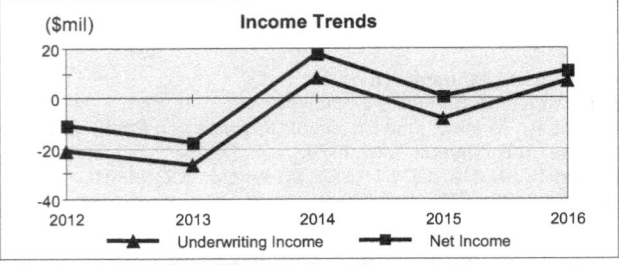

GOVERNMENT EMPLOYEES INS CO

B   **Good**

Major Rating Factors: Good overall results on stability tests (5.1 on a scale of 0 to 10) despite potential drain of affiliation with Berkshire-Hathaway and weak results on operational trends. Good liquidity (6.7) with sufficient resources (cash flows and marketable investments) to handle a spike in claims.
Other Rating Factors: Strong long-term capitalization index (8.0) based on excellent current risk adjusted capital (severe and moderate loss scenarios). Moreover, capital levels have been consistent in recent years. Ample reserve history (9.4) that helps to protect the company against sharp claims increases. Excellent profitability (8.8) with operating gains in each of the last five years. Return on equity has been good over the last five years, averaging 10.7%.
Principal Business: Auto liability (59%), auto physical damage (39%), and other liability (3%).
Principal Investments: Misc. investments (80%), investment grade bonds (21%), non investment grade bonds (1%), and real estate (1%).
Investments in Affiliates: 1%
Group Affiliation: Berkshire-Hathaway
Licensed in: All states except PR
Commenced Business: December 1937
Address: 5260 WESTERN AVENUE, Chevy Chase, MD 20815-3799
Phone: (800) 841-3000   **Domicile State:** MD   **NAIC Code:** 22063

Data Date	Rating	RACR #1	RACR #2	Loss Ratio %	Total Assets ($mil)	Capital ($mil)	Net Premium ($mil)	Net Income ($mil)
3-17	B	3.10	1.93	N/A	28,989.0	16,833.4	1,781.3	208.3
3-16	B	3.33	2.11	N/A	23,788.5	13,717.8	1,655.4	247.9
2016	B	3.09	1.95	82.9	27,197.9	15,702.6	6,988.3	728.6
2015	B	3.21	2.04	82.3	24,036.2	13,930.5	6,468.3	1,152.6
2014	B	3.43	2.13	36.2	23,472.6	13,443.0	649.5	1,725.3
2013	B+	2.67	1.81	77.3	25,778.8	12,089.8	11,644.8	2,010.1
2012	B+	2.14	1.52	80.2	19,089.6	8,017.6	11,118.7	1,026.0

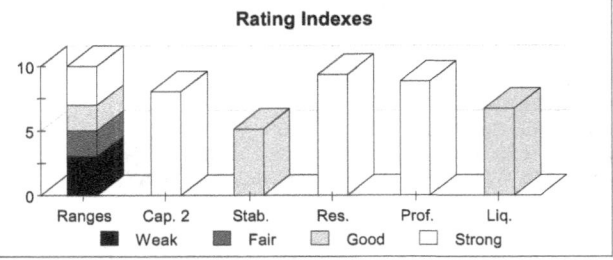

GRANGE MUTUAL CAS CO   B   Good

Major Rating Factors: History of adequate reserve strength (6.0 on a scale of 0 to 10) as reserves have been consistently at an acceptable level. Good liquidity (6.3) with sufficient resources (cash flows and marketable investments) to handle a spike in claims.

Other Rating Factors: Fair overall results on stability tests (4.8) including potential drain of affiliation with Grange Mutual Casualty Group and weak results on operational trends. Strong long-term capitalization index (8.2) based on excellent current risk adjusted capital (severe and moderate loss scenarios), despite some fluctuation in capital levels. Excellent profitability (8.4) with operating gains in each of the last five years.

Principal Business: Auto liability (27%), auto physical damage (22%), commercial multiple peril (19%), homeowners multiple peril (19%), farmowners multiple peril (4%), fire (3%), and other lines (6%).

Principal Investments: Investment grade bonds (43%), misc. investments (40%), non investment grade bonds (9%), real estate (5%), and cash (3%).

Investments in Affiliates: 14%

Group Affiliation: Grange Mutual Casualty Group

Licensed in: AL, GA, IL, IN, IA, KS, KY, MN, MO, OH, PA, SC, TN, VA, WI

Commenced Business: April 1935

Address: 671 South High Street, Columbus, OH 43206-1014

Phone: (614) 445-2900   **Domicile State:** OH   **NAIC Code:** 14060

Data Date	Rating	RACR #1	RACR #2	Loss Ratio %	Total Assets ($mil)	Capital ($mil)	Net Premium ($mil)	Net Income ($mil)
3-17	B	2.58	1.92	N/A	2,463.8	1,142.2	275.6	16.4
3-16	B	2.85	2.07	N/A	2,185.0	1,097.7	250.2	27.3
2016	B	2.55	1.91	62.3	2,311.7	1,106.8	983.1	82.5
2015	B	2.83	2.06	69.1	2,192.2	1,068.1	1,026.8	57.2
2014	B	3.01	2.22	68.9	2,120.6	1,047.3	1,021.2	33.1
2013	B+	3.02	2.18	67.0	2,011.8	1,010.2	957.4	47.4
2012	B+	2.97	2.14	69.0	1,858.6	915.3	888.7	37.7

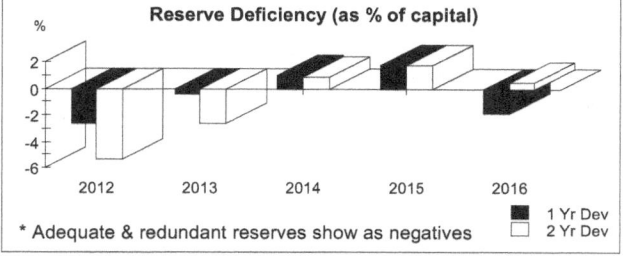

Reserve Deficiency (as % of capital)

* Adequate & redundant reserves show as negatives

■ 1 Yr Dev   □ 2 Yr Dev

GREAT AMERICAN INS CO   B   Good

Major Rating Factors: Good liquidity (6.9 on a scale of 0 to 10) with sufficient resources (cash flows and marketable investments) to handle a spike in claims. Fair overall results on stability tests (4.0) including weak results on operational trends. The largest net exposure for one risk is acceptable at 2.7% of capital.

Other Rating Factors: Strong long-term capitalization index (7.4) based on excellent current risk adjusted capital (severe and moderate loss scenarios), despite some fluctuation in capital levels. Ample reserve history (8.0) that helps to protect the company against sharp claims increases. Excellent profitability (8.7) with operating gains in each of the last five years. Return on equity has been excellent over the last five years averaging 16.2%.

Principal Business: Allied lines (47%), other liability (20%), credit (6%), surety (5%), ocean marine (5%), fidelity (4%), and other lines (12%).

Principal Investments: Investment grade bonds (55%), misc. investments (42%), non investment grade bonds (2%), and real estate (1%).

Investments in Affiliates: 15%

Group Affiliation: American Financial Group Inc

Licensed in: All states, the District of Columbia and Puerto Rico

Commenced Business: March 1872

Address: 301 E Fourth Street, Cincinnati, OH 45202

Phone: (513) 369-5000   **Domicile State:** OH   **NAIC Code:** 16691

Data Date	Rating	RACR #1	RACR #2	Loss Ratio %	Total Assets ($mil)	Capital ($mil)	Net Premium ($mil)	Net Income ($mil)
3-17	B	1.83	1.40	N/A	6,930.2	2,064.0	565.2	79.1
3-16	B-	1.80	1.31	N/A	6,023.9	1,608.7	524.3	78.6
2016	B	1.82	1.40	52.4	6,851.2	1,998.9	2,471.4	349.1
2015	B-	1.76	1.28	55.6	6,110.9	1,550.9	2,354.2	294.2
2014	B-	1.62	1.19	59.0	5,811.7	1,413.6	2,256.9	221.5
2013	B-	1.79	1.31	59.1	5,376.9	1,403.3	2,100.1	273.7
2012	C+	1.86	1.40	65.4	5,132.6	1,469.6	1,862.4	141.1

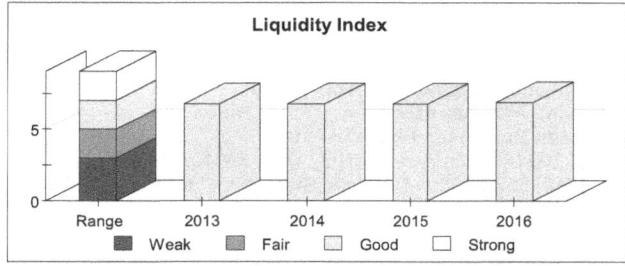

Liquidity Index

■ Weak   ▨ Fair   ▢ Good   □ Strong

GREAT NORTHERN INS CO   B-   Good

Major Rating Factors: Fair overall results on stability tests (3.6 on a scale of 0 to 10) including weak results on operational trends. The largest net exposure for one risk is excessive at 6.8% of capital. Good liquidity (6.8) with sufficient resources (cash flows and marketable investments) to handle a spike in claims.

Other Rating Factors: Strong long-term capitalization index (8.2) based on excellent current risk adjusted capital (severe and moderate loss scenarios), despite some fluctuation in capital levels. Ample reserve history (9.0) that helps to protect the company against sharp claims increases. Excellent profitability (8.4) with operating gains in each of the last five years. Return on equity has been excellent over the last five years averaging 16.0%.

Principal Business: Homeowners multiple peril (41%), commercial multiple peril (23%), inland marine (9%), auto liability (8%), auto physical damage (5%), other liability (5%), and other lines (9%).

Principal Investments: Investment grade bonds (99%) and non investment grade bonds (1%).

Investments in Affiliates: None

Group Affiliation: Chubb Limited

Licensed in: All states except PR

Commenced Business: August 1952

Address: 202 N Illinois St Suite 2600, Indianapolis, IN 46282

Phone: (908) 903-2000   **Domicile State:** IN   **NAIC Code:** 20303

Data Date	Rating	RACR #1	RACR #2	Loss Ratio %	Total Assets ($mil)	Capital ($mil)	Net Premium ($mil)	Net Income ($mil)
3-17	B-	3.86	2.45	N/A	1,694.3	516.5	59.3	14.5
3-16	B	2.81	1.79	N/A	1,612.5	455.0	78.2	33.4
2016	B-	3.75	2.39	53.6	1,607.6	504.2	253.5	88.0
2015	B	2.87	1.83	56.5	1,647.5	469.2	391.3	81.2
2014	B	2.94	1.88	56.7	1,641.7	477.0	375.8	80.3
2013	B	2.97	1.92	52.7	1,653.1	478.8	360.6	83.4
2012	B	2.68	1.71	67.3	1,625.6	438.6	347.1	54.2

Chubb Limited
Composite Group Rating: B-

Largest Group Members	Assets ($mil)	Rating
FEDERAL INS CO	27371	B-
ACE AMERICAN INS CO	13036	B-
ACE PC INS CO	8192	B-
PACIFIC INDEMNITY CO	6555	B-
PACIFIC EMPLOYERS INS CO	3774	B-

GREAT WEST CASUALTY CO | B | Good

Major Rating Factors: Good liquidity (6.4 on a scale of 0 to 10) with sufficient resources (cash flows and marketable investments) to handle a spike in claims. Good overall results on stability tests (6.2).

Other Rating Factors: Strong long-term capitalization index (8.6) based on excellent current risk adjusted capital (severe and moderate loss scenarios). Moreover, capital levels have been consistent in recent years. Ample reserve history (9.3) that helps to protect the company against sharp claims increases. Excellent profitability (8.9) with operating gains in each of the last five years. Return on equity has been good over the last five years, averaging 11.4%.

Principal Business: Auto liability (46%), auto physical damage (28%), workers compensation (13%), inland marine (8%), and other liability (4%).

Principal Investments: Investment grade bonds (69%), misc. investments (25%), non investment grade bonds (5%), and cash (1%).

Investments in Affiliates: None

Group Affiliation: Old Republic Group

Licensed in: All states except HI, PR

Commenced Business: April 1956

Address: 1100 WEST 29TH STREET, South Sioux City, NE 68776-3130

Phone: (402) 494-2411   **Domicile State:** NE   **NAIC Code:** 11371

Data Date	Rating	RACR #1	RACR #2	Loss Ratio %	Total Assets ($mil)	Capital ($mil)	Net Premium ($mil)	Net Income ($mil)
3-17	B	3.36	2.01	N/A	2,063.9	621.5	204.6	10.5
3-16	B	3.41	2.08	N/A	2,000.4	599.6	205.4	18.8
2016	B	3.51	2.10	74.0	2,015.9	622.3	831.1	63.4
2015	B	3.58	2.20	71.4	1,953.1	586.2	849.2	70.5
2014	B	3.89	2.38	71.4	1,848.4	573.1	787.9	88.9
2013	A-	4.30	2.67	71.3	1,736.6	546.9	712.5	65.1
2012	A-	4.47	2.79	74.0	1,635.6	514.9	668.8	44.1

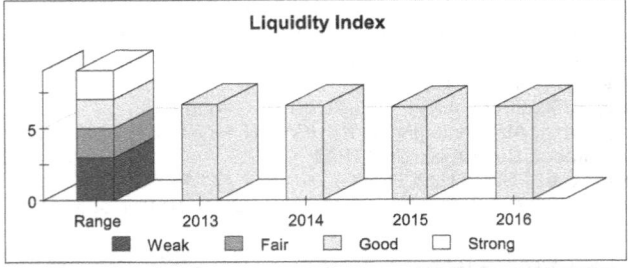

Liquidity Index

GREATER NEW YORK MUTUAL INS CO | B- | Good

Major Rating Factors: Fair overall results on stability tests (4.3 on a scale of 0 to 10) including potential drain of affiliation with Greater New York Group and weak results on operational trends. History of adequate reserve strength (6.0) as reserves have been consistently at an acceptable level.

Other Rating Factors: Good liquidity (6.9) with sufficient resources (cash flows and marketable investments) to handle a spike in claims. Strong long-term capitalization index (8.5) based on excellent current risk adjusted capital (severe and moderate loss scenarios). Moreover, capital levels have been consistent in recent years. Excellent profitability (8.0) with operating gains in each of the last five years.

Principal Business: Commercial multiple peril (95%), workers compensation (2%), and other liability (1%).

Principal Investments: Investment grade bonds (69%), misc. investments (28%), cash (2%), and non investment grade bonds (1%).

Investments in Affiliates: 16%

Group Affiliation: Greater New York Group

Licensed in: All states except AK, CA, FL, HI, TX, PR

Commenced Business: November 1927

Address: 200 Madison Avenue, New York, NY 10016-3904

Phone: (212) 683-9700   **Domicile State:** NY   **NAIC Code:** 22187

Data Date	Rating	RACR #1	RACR #2	Loss Ratio %	Total Assets ($mil)	Capital ($mil)	Net Premium ($mil)	Net Income ($mil)
3-17	B-	2.32	1.97	N/A	986.2	483.8	60.7	7.7
3-16	B-	2.30	1.96	N/A	943.6	454.1	58.0	7.2
2016	B-	2.31	1.98	66.5	987.0	472.6	240.8	20.1
2015	B-	2.29	1.97	68.7	942.0	443.9	228.8	13.4
2014	B-	2.37	2.02	67.6	905.4	430.8	213.1	15.6
2013	B-	2.41	2.00	61.1	863.7	414.5	196.7	18.0
2012	B-	2.53	2.26	75.1	859.6	388.6	179.2	2.9

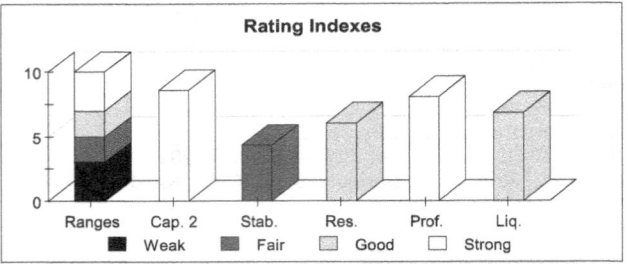

Rating Indexes

GREENWICH INS CO | C | Fair

Major Rating Factors: Fair overall results on stability tests (3.8 on a scale of 0 to 10) including potential drain of affiliation with XL Group Ltd, weak results on operational trends and negative cash flow from operations for 2016. The largest net exposure for one risk is conservative at 1.8% of capital. Fair profitability index (3.8). Fair expense controls. Return on equity has been fair, averaging 6.5% over the past five years.

Other Rating Factors: History of adequate reserve strength (6.2) as reserves have been consistently at an acceptable level. Strong long-term capitalization index (7.8) based on excellent current risk adjusted capital (severe and moderate loss scenarios), despite some fluctuation in capital levels. Excellent liquidity (7.3) with ample operational cash flow and liquid investments.

Principal Business: Other liability (56%), allied lines (17%), auto liability (15%), commercial multiple peril (3%), workers compensation (2%), aggregate write-ins for other lines of business (2%), and other lines (5%).

Principal Investments: Investment grade bonds (65%), misc. investments (26%), and cash (9%).

Investments in Affiliates: 24%

Group Affiliation: XL Group Ltd

Licensed in: All states, the District of Columbia and Puerto Rico

Commenced Business: May 1946

Address: 1200 Orange Street, Wilmington, DE 19801

Phone: (203) 964-5200   **Domicile State:** DE   **NAIC Code:** 22322

Data Date	Rating	RACR #1	RACR #2	Loss Ratio %	Total Assets ($mil)	Capital ($mil)	Net Premium ($mil)	Net Income ($mil)
3-17	C	1.81	1.55	N/A	1,132.8	369.0	37.2	4.7
3-16	C	1.59	1.38	N/A	1,095.1	347.8	40.6	-2.4
2016	C	1.81	1.56	69.3	1,202.5	364.2	200.1	31.1
2015	C	1.63	1.42	71.2	1,088.3	350.4	159.3	21.0
2014	C	1.71	1.51	61.5	1,073.1	397.3	152.0	35.3
2013	C	1.69	1.51	65.3	1,053.3	416.6	159.7	30.8
2012	C	1.75	1.55	73.4	1,102.6	440.8	155.3	9.4

XL Group Ltd Composite Group Rating: C Largest Group Members	Assets ($mil)	Rating
XL REINS AMERICA INC	6274	C
GREENWICH INS CO	1203	C
XL SPECIALTY INS CO	920	C
XL INS AMERICA INC	825	C
CATLIN SPECIALTY INS CO	744	C+

GRINNELL MUTUAL REINS CO   B-   Good

Major Rating Factors: Fair overall results on stability tests (4.4 on a scale of 0 to 10) including potential drain of affiliation with Grinnell Mutual Group and weak results on operational trends. Good liquidity (6.2) with sufficient resources (cash flows and marketable investments) to handle a spike in claims.

Other Rating Factors: Strong long-term capitalization index (9.2) based on excellent current risk adjusted capital (severe and moderate loss scenarios). Moreover, capital levels have been consistent in recent years. Ample reserve history (8.1) that helps to protect the company against sharp claims increases. Excellent profitability (8.2) despite modest operating losses during 2012. Return on equity has been good over the last five years, averaging 10.1%.

Principal Business: Commercial multiple peril (19%), other liability (16%), workers compensation (16%), allied lines (14%), auto liability (14%), auto physical damage (12%), and other lines (8%).

Principal Investments: Investment grade bonds (78%), misc. investments (16%), cash (3%), real estate (2%), and non investment grade bonds (1%).

Investments in Affiliates: 3%

Group Affiliation: Grinnell Mutual Group

Licensed in: IL, IN, IA, MN, MO, MT, NE, NY, ND, OH, OK, PA, SD, WI

Commenced Business: April 1909

Address: 4215 HIGHWAY 146 PO BOX 790, Grinnell, IA 50112-0790

Phone: (641) 269-8000   **Domicile State:** IA   **NAIC Code:** 14117

Data Date	Rating	RACR #1	RACR #2	Loss Ratio %	Total Assets ($mil)	Capital ($mil)	Net Premium ($mil)	Net Income ($mil)
3-17	B-	3.86	2.66	N/A	1,140.1	605.7	138.0	12.5
3-16	B-	3.58	2.44	N/A	1,036.3	543.1	132.6	26.7
2016	B-	3.82	2.65	59.3	1,104.3	589.9	556.5	68.7
2015	B-	3.47	2.38	53.2	1,008.1	517.0	525.1	89.4
2014	B-	3.20	2.25	63.8	913.7	440.1	483.5	58.7
2013	B-	2.90	2.07	65.9	858.6	399.9	451.7	36.8
2012	B-	2.64	1.95	76.0	796.0	351.0	410.5	-2.1

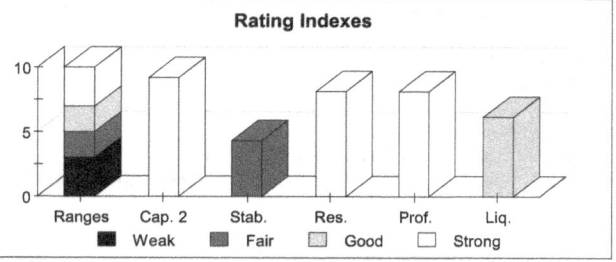

Rating Indexes

GUIDEONE MUTUAL INS CO   B   Good

Major Rating Factors: Good liquidity (6.6 on a scale of 0 to 10) with sufficient resources (cash flows and marketable investments) to handle a spike in claims. Fair overall results on stability tests (4.5) including weak results on operational trends and negative cash flow from operations for 2016.

Other Rating Factors: Strong long-term capitalization index (7.5) based on excellent current risk adjusted capital (severe and moderate loss scenarios), despite some fluctuation in capital levels. Ample reserve history (8.6) that helps to protect the company against sharp claims increases. Weak profitability index (2.6) with operating losses during 2013 and the first three months of 2017.

Principal Business: Commercial multiple peril (52%), workers compensation (17%), auto liability (11%), other liability (7%), homeowners multiple peril (6%), auto physical damage (5%), and allied lines (2%).

Principal Investments: Investment grade bonds (64%), misc. investments (37%), and real estate (1%).

Investments in Affiliates: 22%

Group Affiliation: GuideOne Group

Licensed in: All states except PR

Commenced Business: April 1947

Address: 1111 Ashworth Road, West Des Moines, IA 50265-3538

Phone: (515) 267-5000   **Domicile State:** IA   **NAIC Code:** 15032

Data Date	Rating	RACR #1	RACR #2	Loss Ratio %	Total Assets ($mil)	Capital ($mil)	Net Premium ($mil)	Net Income ($mil)
3-17	B	1.70	1.36	N/A	1,199.6	398.8	77.4	-11.5
3-16	B	1.61	1.34	N/A	1,220.7	456.3	84.6	-0.4
2016	B	1.69	1.35	78.6	1,214.7	421.8	353.8	-55.5
2015	B	1.66	1.39	67.1	1,232.0	464.1	360.2	19.6
2014	B-	1.44	1.17	68.0	1,695.2	442.1	355.0	22.3
2013	B-	1.51	1.23	70.5	1,814.5	460.0	334.8	-9.4
2012	B-	1.90	1.66	59.8	1,134.8	423.4	295.7	24.4

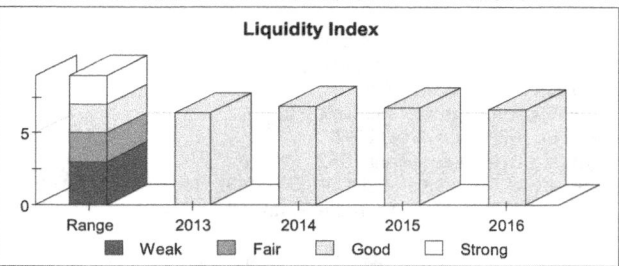

Liquidity Index

GUIDEONE P&C INS CO   B   Good

Major Rating Factors: Good liquidity (6.8 on a scale of 0 to 10) with sufficient resources (cash flows and marketable investments) to handle a spike in claims. Fair overall results on stability tests (4.4) including weak results on operational trends.

Other Rating Factors: Strong long-term capitalization index (8.6) based on excellent current risk adjusted capital (severe and moderate loss scenarios), despite some fluctuation in capital levels. Ample reserve history (8.0) that helps to protect the company against sharp claims increases. Weak profitability index (2.8) with operating losses during the first three months of 2017. Return on equity has been low, averaging 1.1% over the past five years.

Principal Business: (This company is a reinsurer.)

Principal Investments: Investment grade bonds (63%), misc. investments (36%), and non investment grade bonds (1%).

Investments in Affiliates: 23%

Group Affiliation: GuideOne Group

Licensed in: IA

Commenced Business: December 1993

Address: 1111 Ashworth Road, West Des Moines, IA 50265-3538

Phone: (515) 267-5000   **Domicile State:** IA   **NAIC Code:** 13984

Data Date	Rating	RACR #1	RACR #2	Loss Ratio %	Total Assets ($mil)	Capital ($mil)	Net Premium ($mil)	Net Income ($mil)
3-17	B	2.51	2.18	N/A	434.6	221.2	24.2	-2.9
3-16	B	2.55	2.14	N/A	451.1	249.9	26.4	0.2
2016	B	2.38	2.04	78.6	429.3	223.7	110.6	-5.5
2015	B	2.57	2.17	67.1	450.3	248.6	112.6	5.3
2014	B	2.31	1.90	68.0	547.5	245.6	110.9	6.3
2013	B	2.77	2.18	70.5	526.5	241.4	104.6	1.8
2012	B	4.07	3.34	59.8	417.1	234.9	92.4	9.2

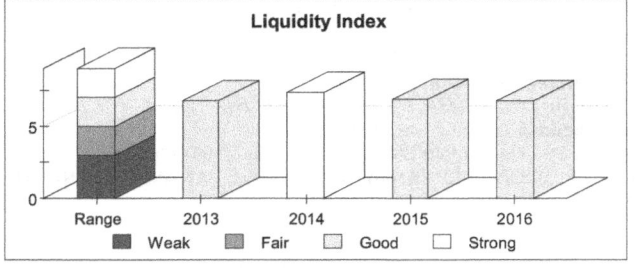

Liquidity Index

GUILFORD INS CO | C- | Fair

Major Rating Factors: Weak overall results on stability tests (2.6 on a scale of 0 to 10) including potential drain of affiliation with IFG Companies and negative cash flow from operations for 2016. Good overall profitability index (6.0). Weak expense controls. Return on equity has been low, averaging 3.0% over the past five years.

Other Rating Factors: Strong long-term capitalization index (7.9) based on excellent current risk adjusted capital (severe and moderate loss scenarios), despite some fluctuation in capital levels. Ample reserve history (8.0) that helps to protect the company against sharp claims increases. Excellent liquidity (7.8) with ample operational cash flow and liquid investments.

Principal Business: Other liability (55%), inland marine (40%), fire (3%), auto liability (1%), and allied lines (1%).

Principal Investments: Misc. investments (50%) and investment grade bonds (50%).

Investments in Affiliates: 49%
Group Affiliation: IFG Companies
Licensed in: All states except CA, PR
Commenced Business: December 1998
Address: 400 South Ninth Street, Springfield, IL 62701-1822
Phone: (336) 586-2500 **Domicile State:** IL **NAIC Code:** 10956

Data Date	Rating	RACR #1	RACR #2	Loss Ratio %	Total Assets ($mil)	Capital ($mil)	Net Premium ($mil)	Net Income ($mil)
3-17	C-	1.66	1.62	N/A	379.3	277.1	6.8	0.3
3-16	C-	1.67	1.63	N/A	387.7	277.4	8.0	1.7
2016	C-	1.65	1.61	47.9	377.9	274.3	27.9	5.9
2015	C-	1.66	1.62	44.4	386.9	275.2	32.8	9.5
2014	C-	1.63	1.59	56.5	393.3	274.3	36.6	6.9
2013	C-	1.61	1.57	50.6	390.3	267.5	40.7	12.3
2012	C-	1.61	1.57	60.2	377.8	250.7	43.1	7.6

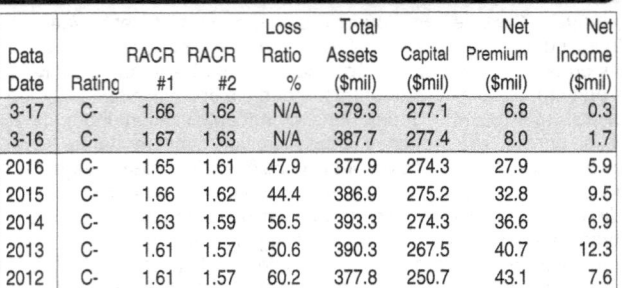

Rating Indexes

HANOVER INS CO | B | Good

Major Rating Factors: Good overall profitability index (6.3 on a scale of 0 to 10) despite operating losses during 2012. Return on equity has been fair, averaging 5.9% over the past five years. Good liquidity (6.0) with sufficient resources (cash flows and marketable investments) to handle a spike in claims.

Other Rating Factors: Good overall results on stability tests (5.1) despite weak results on operational trends. Fair reserve development (3.4) as reserves have generally been sufficient to cover claims. In 2016, the two year reserve development was 17% deficient. Strong long-term capitalization index (7.2) based on excellent current risk adjusted capital (severe and moderate loss scenarios), despite some fluctuation in capital levels.

Principal Business: Other liability (26%), commercial multiple peril (20%), inland marine (15%), homeowners multiple peril (8%), surety (7%), auto liability (6%), and other lines (19%).

Principal Investments: Investment grade bonds (59%), misc. investments (35%), non investment grade bonds (5%), and real estate (1%).

Investments in Affiliates: 20%
Group Affiliation: Hanover Ins Group Inc
Licensed in: All states except PR
Commenced Business: April 1852
Address: 1 EXEC PARK DR 2ND FL STE 200, Bedford, NH 03110-5905
Phone: (508) 853-7200 **Domicile State:** NH **NAIC Code:** 22292

Data Date	Rating	RACR #1	RACR #2	Loss Ratio %	Total Assets ($mil)	Capital ($mil)	Net Premium ($mil)	Net Income ($mil)
3-17	B	1.41	1.14	N/A	7,505.1	2,224.2	788.5	34.4
3-16	B	1.60	1.30	N/A	6,984.1	2,272.0	763.9	43.0
2016	B	1.40	1.14	69.5	7,409.3	2,168.2	3,171.5	117.1
2015	B	1.56	1.28	66.4	6,926.3	2,188.0	3,046.3	128.8
2014	B	1.53	1.27	63.3	6,482.1	2,052.4	2,905.8	225.0
2013	B	1.42	1.21	64.8	6,047.1	1,829.7	2,759.4	184.3
2012	B-	1.21	1.03	76.1	5,696.5	1,518.9	2,661.5	-42.6

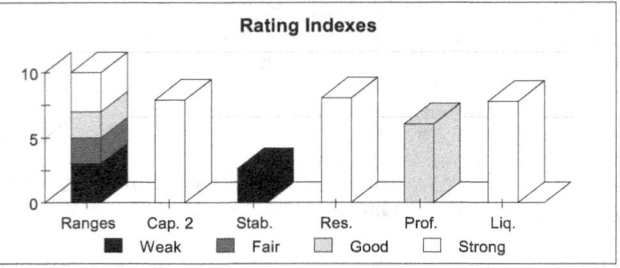

Income Trends

HARFORD MUTUAL INS CO | B- | Good

Major Rating Factors: Fair overall results on stability tests (4.1 on a scale of 0 to 10) including potential drain of affiliation with Harford Group Inc and weak results on operational trends. History of adequate reserve strength (6.4) as reserves have been consistently at an acceptable level.

Other Rating Factors: Good liquidity (6.9) with sufficient resources (cash flows and marketable investments) to handle a spike in claims. Strong long-term capitalization index (8.5) based on excellent current risk adjusted capital (severe and moderate loss scenarios), despite some fluctuation in capital levels. Excellent profitability (8.3) with operating gains in each of the last five years.

Principal Business: Commercial multiple peril (47%), workers compensation (26%), auto liability (12%), other liability (8%), auto physical damage (4%), homeowners multiple peril (1%), and inland marine (1%).

Principal Investments: Investment grade bonds (54%), misc. investments (41%), cash (4%), and real estate (1%).

Investments in Affiliates: 15%
Group Affiliation: Harford Group Inc
Licensed in: DC, DE, GA, MD, NJ, NC, PA, SC, TN, VA, WV
Commenced Business: January 1843
Address: 200 North Main Street, Bel Air, MD 21014-3544
Phone: (410) 838-4000 **Domicile State:** MD **NAIC Code:** 14141

Data Date	Rating	RACR #1	RACR #2	Loss Ratio %	Total Assets ($mil)	Capital ($mil)	Net Premium ($mil)	Net Income ($mil)
3-17	B-	2.51	1.97	N/A	434.7	212.5	30.0	2.3
3-16	B-	2.35	1.82	N/A	390.2	191.4	28.2	-2.6
2016	B-	2.52	1.99	61.2	420.3	208.6	123.6	8.9
2015	B-	2.42	1.89	60.9	384.5	193.4	114.1	10.9
2014	B-	2.52	1.96	62.3	370.6	194.6	104.0	8.8
2013	B-	2.66	2.06	55.6	352.8	187.5	95.3	11.5
2012	B-	2.76	2.13	55.8	317.8	162.6	81.8	11.6

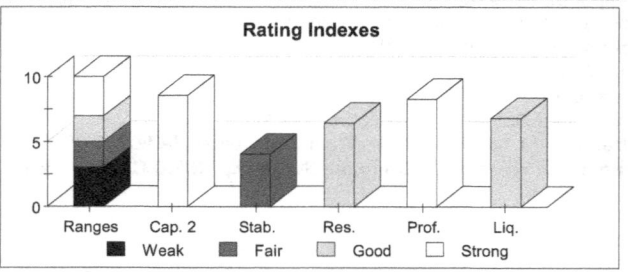

Rating Indexes

HARTFORD ACCIDENT & INDEMNITY CO   B   Good

Major Rating Factors: History of adequate reserve strength (5.8 on a scale of 0 to 10) as reserves have been consistently at an acceptable level. Good liquidity (6.7) with sufficient resources (cash flows and marketable investments) to handle a spike in claims.

Other Rating Factors: Fair profitability index (4.8). Fair expense controls. Return on equity has been fair, averaging 14.4% over the past five years. Fair overall results on stability tests (4.9) including weak results on operational trends. Strong long-term capitalization index (7.7) based on excellent current risk adjusted capital (severe and moderate loss scenarios), despite some fluctuation in capital levels.

Principal Business: Workers compensation (46%), auto liability (26%), auto physical damage (11%), commercial multiple peril (5%), homeowners multiple peril (5%), other liability (5%), and surety (2%).

Principal Investments: Investment grade bonds (63%), misc. investments (33%), and non investment grade bonds (4%).

Investments in Affiliates: 9%

Group Affiliation: Hartford Financial Services Inc

Licensed in: All states, the District of Columbia and Puerto Rico

Commenced Business: August 1913

Address: One Hartford Plaza, Hartford, CT 06155-0001

Phone: (860) 547-5000   **Domicile State:** CT   **NAIC Code:** 22357

Data Date	Rating	RACR #1	RACR #2	Loss Ratio %	Total Assets ($mil)	Capital ($mil)	Net Premium ($mil)	Net Income ($mil)
3-17	B	1.94	1.41	N/A	12,150.0	3,166.7	903.3	109.8
3-16	B	2.10	1.53	N/A	11,697.4	3,361.3	849.7	104.2
2016	B	1.99	1.46	70.4	11,604.5	3,154.5	3,444.1	409.9
2015	B	2.09	1.53	66.1	11,521.7	3,276.6	3,444.7	582.3
2014	B	2.18	1.60	67.0	11,348.4	3,324.9	3,349.1	509.1
2013	B	2.18	1.60	68.8	11,122.4	3,271.5	3,252.5	468.7
2012	B	2.17	1.60	72.7	11,063.3	3,107.6	3,218.3	362.2

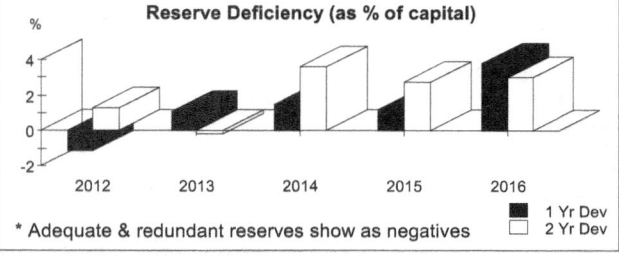

Reserve Deficiency (as % of capital)
* Adequate & redundant reserves show as negatives   ■ 1 Yr Dev   □ 2 Yr Dev

HARTFORD CASUALTY INS CO   B   Good

Major Rating Factors: History of adequate reserve strength (5.9 on a scale of 0 to 10) as reserves have been consistently at an acceptable level. Good overall profitability index (5.4). Fair expense controls. Return on equity has been fair, averaging 9.6% over the past five years.

Other Rating Factors: Good liquidity (6.8) with sufficient resources (cash flows and marketable investments) to handle a spike in claims. Fair overall results on stability tests (4.9) including weak results on operational trends. Strong long-term capitalization index (10.0) based on excellent current risk adjusted capital (severe and moderate loss scenarios), despite some fluctuation in capital levels.

Principal Business: Workers compensation (38%), commercial multiple peril (23%), auto liability (14%), other liability (13%), auto physical damage (7%), homeowners multiple peril (2%), and other lines (3%).

Principal Investments: Investment grade bonds (85%), misc. investments (14%), and non investment grade bonds (1%).

Investments in Affiliates: None

Group Affiliation: Hartford Financial Services Inc

Licensed in: All states except PR

Commenced Business: July 1987

Address: 501 Pennsylvania Pkwy Ste 400, Indianapolis, IN 46280-0014

Phone: (860) 547-5000   **Domicile State:** IN   **NAIC Code:** 29424

Data Date	Rating	RACR #1	RACR #2	Loss Ratio %	Total Assets ($mil)	Capital ($mil)	Net Premium ($mil)	Net Income ($mil)
3-17	B	4.67	3.00	N/A	2,325.1	912.3	152.0	19.4
3-16	B	4.91	3.17	N/A	2,312.1	945.0	143.0	24.6
2016	B	4.74	3.08	70.4	2,267.2	894.0	579.5	77.9
2015	B	4.80	3.13	66.1	2,249.9	904.4	579.6	95.0
2014	B	4.97	3.23	67.0	2,233.8	913.3	563.5	95.9
2013	B	5.01	3.28	68.8	2,207.0	905.8	547.2	83.6
2012	B	5.13	3.36	72.7	2,196.5	907.3	541.5	82.2

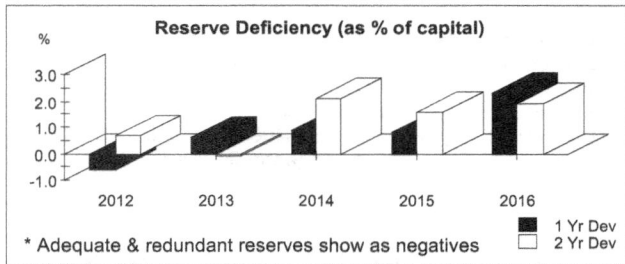

Reserve Deficiency (as % of capital)
* Adequate & redundant reserves show as negatives   ■ 1 Yr Dev   □ 2 Yr Dev

HARTFORD FIRE INS CO   B   Good

Major Rating Factors: History of adequate reserve strength (6.0 on a scale of 0 to 10) as reserves have been consistently at an acceptable level. Good liquidity (6.8) with sufficient resources (cash flows and marketable investments) to handle a spike in claims.

Other Rating Factors: Good overall results on stability tests (5.1) despite weak results on operational trends. Fair profitability index (3.8). Weak expense controls. Return on equity has been fair, averaging 6.8% over the past five years. Strong long-term capitalization index (7.7) based on excellent current risk adjusted capital (severe and moderate loss scenarios), despite some fluctuation in capital levels.

Principal Business: Commercial multiple peril (29%), workers compensation (19%), inland marine (13%), other liability (10%), auto liability (9%), surety (8%), and other lines (11%).

Principal Investments: Misc. investments (34%), investment grade bonds (32%), non investment grade bonds (32%), and real estate (2%).

Investments in Affiliates: 26%

Group Affiliation: Hartford Financial Services Inc

Licensed in: All states, the District of Columbia and Puerto Rico

Commenced Business: August 1810

Address: One Hartford Plaza, Hartford, CT 06155-0001

Phone: (860) 547-5000   **Domicile State:** CT   **NAIC Code:** 19682

Data Date	Rating	RACR #1	RACR #2	Loss Ratio %	Total Assets ($mil)	Capital ($mil)	Net Premium ($mil)	Net Income ($mil)
3-17	B	2.00	1.56	N/A	24,977.6	12,287.1	1,146.8	227.6
3-16	B	2.03	1.44	N/A	25,141.1	13,098.5	1,078.7	179.9
2016	B	1.96	1.41	70.4	25,540.6	12,514.6	4,372.3	526.5
2015	B	2.09	1.48	66.1	25,426.3	13,440.5	4,373.1	1,188.3
2014	B	2.11	1.48	67.0	25,520.2	13,797.4	4,251.7	1,068.2
2013	B	2.16	1.50	68.8	25,684.8	14,081.4	4,129.1	1,006.6
2012	B	2.09	1.47	72.7	24,620.3	13,012.5	4,085.7	735.6

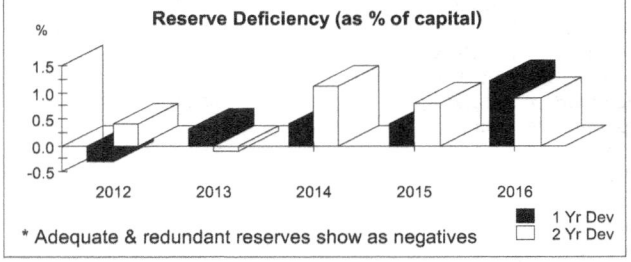

Reserve Deficiency (as % of capital)
* Adequate & redundant reserves show as negatives   ■ 1 Yr Dev   □ 2 Yr Dev

HARTFORD INS CO OF IL

B **Good**

Major Rating Factors: History of adequate reserve strength (5.8 on a scale of 0 to 10) as reserves have been consistently at an acceptable level. Good liquidity (6.7) with sufficient resources (cash flows and marketable investments) to handle a spike in claims.

Other Rating Factors: Good overall results on stability tests (5.0) despite weak results on operational trends. Fair profitability index (4.5). Fair expense controls. Return on equity has been fair, averaging 10.7% over the past five years. Strong long-term capitalization index (9.1) based on excellent current risk adjusted capital (severe and moderate loss scenarios), despite some fluctuation in capital levels.

Principal Business: Workers compensation (43%), auto liability (28%), auto physical damage (15%), homeowners multiple peril (11%), and other liability (2%).

Principal Investments: Investment grade bonds (88%), misc. investments (10%), and non investment grade bonds (2%).

Investments in Affiliates: None

Group Affiliation: Hartford Financial Services Inc

Licensed in: CT, HI, IL, MI, NY, PA

Commenced Business: January 1980

Address: 4245 Meridian Parkway, Aurora, IL 60504-7901

Phone: (860) 547-5000　**Domicile State:** IL　**NAIC Code:** 38288

Data Date	Rating	RACR #1	RACR #2	Loss Ratio %	Total Assets ($mil)	Capital ($mil)	Net Premium ($mil)	Net Income ($mil)
3-17	B	3.71	2.41	N/A	3,906.5	1,300.1	279.1	34.8
3-16	B	3.81	2.48	N/A	3,859.1	1,329.6	262.5	40.5
2016	B	3.70	2.43	70.4	3,832.8	1,258.0	1,064.1	119.6
2015	B	3.78	2.47	66.1	3,787.8	1,289.3	1,064.3	151.8
2014	B	4.00	2.59	67.0	3,781.9	1,334.8	1,034.8	164.6
2013	B	3.99	2.60	68.8	3,725.2	1,309.1	1,004.9	136.4
2012	B	4.06	2.67	72.7	3,698.8	1,301.0	994.3	123.1

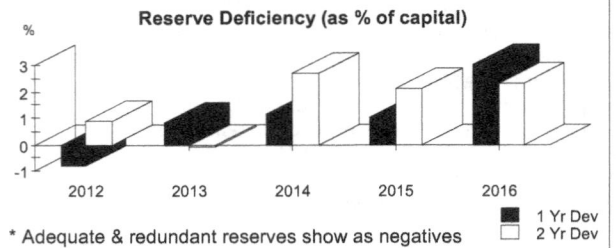

Reserve Deficiency (as % of capital)

* Adequate & redundant reserves show as negatives

■ 1 Yr Dev　□ 2 Yr Dev

HARTFORD INS CO OF THE MIDWEST

B **Good**

Major Rating Factors: History of adequate reserve strength (5.0 on a scale of 0 to 10) as reserves have been consistently at an acceptable level. Fair overall results on stability tests (4.7) including weak results on operational trends.

Other Rating Factors: Strong long-term capitalization index (10.0) based on excellent current risk adjusted capital (severe and moderate loss scenarios). Moreover, capital levels have been consistent in recent years. Excellent profitability (8.1) with operating gains in each of the last five years. Excellent liquidity (7.0) with ample operational cash flow and liquid investments.

Principal Business: Workers compensation (35%), allied lines (23%), auto liability (15%), homeowners multiple peril (13%), auto physical damage (8%), commercial multiple peril (4%), and other liability (1%).

Principal Investments: Investment grade bonds (97%) and misc. investments (3%).

Investments in Affiliates: None

Group Affiliation: Hartford Financial Services Inc

Licensed in: All states except PR

Commenced Business: January 1980

Address: 501 Pennsylvania Pkwy Ste 400, Indianapolis, IN 46280-0014

Phone: (860) 547-5000　**Domicile State:** IN　**NAIC Code:** 37478

Data Date	Rating	RACR #1	RACR #2	Loss Ratio %	Total Assets ($mil)	Capital ($mil)	Net Premium ($mil)	Net Income ($mil)
3-17	B	26.80	16.98	N/A	628.9	495.6	13.8	4.3
3-16	B	26.33	17.14	N/A	601.5	478.5	13.0	5.5
2016	B	27.53	17.58	70.4	617.2	491.4	52.7	18.2
2015	B	26.66	17.49	66.1	595.6	473.3	52.7	20.4
2014	B	25.97	17.00	67.0	581.5	452.9	51.2	21.2
2013	B	25.12	16.51	68.8	550.1	432.1	49.7	19.2
2012	B+	20.83	13.70	72.7	470.1	352.7	49.2	21.0

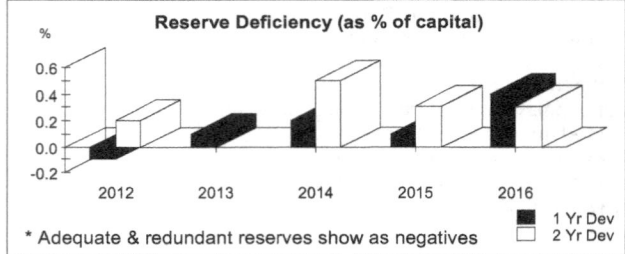

Reserve Deficiency (as % of capital)

* Adequate & redundant reserves show as negatives

■ 1 Yr Dev　□ 2 Yr Dev

HARTFORD SM BOIL INSPECTION & INS

B **Good**

Major Rating Factors: Good liquidity (6.9 on a scale of 0 to 10) with sufficient resources (cash flows and marketable investments) to handle a spike in claims. Good overall results on stability tests (6.1). The largest net exposure for one risk is conservative at 1.5% of capital.

Other Rating Factors: Fair profitability index (3.9). Weak expense controls. Return on equity has been fair, averaging 19.2% over the past five years. Strong long-term capitalization index (9.3) based on excellent current risk adjusted capital (severe and moderate loss scenarios), despite some fluctuation in capital levels. Ample reserve history (8.7) that helps to protect the company against sharp claims increases.

Principal Business: Boiler & machinery (93%), inland marine (3%), commercial multiple peril (3%), and other liability (1%).

Principal Investments: Investment grade bonds (70%), misc. investments (23%), real estate (4%), non investment grade bonds (2%), and cash (1%).

Investments in Affiliates: 14%

Group Affiliation: Münchener Rückversicherungs-Gesellsc

Licensed in: All states, the District of Columbia and Puerto Rico

Commenced Business: October 1866

Address: ONE STATE STREET, Hartford, CT 06102-5024

Phone: (860) 722-1866　**Domicile State:** CT　**NAIC Code:** 11452

Data Date	Rating	RACR #1	RACR #2	Loss Ratio %	Total Assets ($mil)	Capital ($mil)	Net Premium ($mil)	Net Income ($mil)
3-17	B	2.99	2.56	N/A	1,316.7	616.8	116.8	27.2
3-16	B	3.51	2.94	N/A	1,334.5	672.1	110.9	21.0
2016	B	2.97	2.55	29.4	1,256.1	598.9	451.7	97.4
2015	B	3.40	2.89	27.3	1,293.0	635.8	271.5	151.5
2014	B	2.24	1.98	29.4	1,406.6	641.1	771.8	127.8
2013	B	2.30	2.08	26.8	1,372.0	640.9	727.6	105.2
2012	B	2.40	2.19	26.8	1,353.9	649.2	668.4	128.0

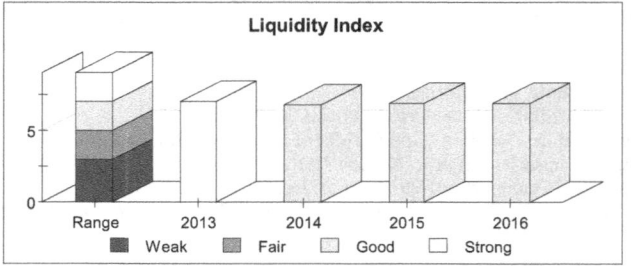

Liquidity Index

■ Weak　▨ Fair　▨ Good　□ Strong

HARTFORD UNDERWRITERS INS CO

B **Good**

Major Rating Factors: History of adequate reserve strength (5.9 on a scale of 0 to 10) as reserves have been consistently at an acceptable level. Good liquidity (6.8) with sufficient resources (cash flows and marketable investments) to handle a spike in claims.

Other Rating Factors: Fair profitability index (4.6). Fair expense controls. Return on equity has been fair, averaging 9.5% over the past five years. Fair overall results on stability tests (4.8) including weak results on operational trends. Strong long-term capitalization index (9.6) based on excellent current risk adjusted capital (severe and moderate loss scenarios), despite some fluctuation in capital levels.

Principal Business: Workers compensation (36%), auto liability (32%), auto physical damage (16%), homeowners multiple peril (8%), other liability (3%), commercial multiple peril (2%), and allied lines (1%).

Principal Investments: Investment grade bonds (86%), misc. investments (13%), and non investment grade bonds (1%).

Investments in Affiliates: None

Group Affiliation: Hartford Financial Services Inc

Licensed in: All states except PR

Commenced Business: December 1987

Address: One Hartford Plaza, Hartford, CT 06155-0001

Phone: (860) 547-5000 **Domicile State:** CT **NAIC Code:** 30104

Data Date	Rating	RACR #1	RACR #2	Loss Ratio %	Total Assets ($mil)	Capital ($mil)	Net Premium ($mil)	Net Income ($mil)
3-17	B	4.16	2.72	N/A	1,654.8	606.4	110.5	14.3
3-16	B	4.36	2.84	N/A	1,626.6	625.7	104.0	19.0
2016	B	4.21	2.78	70.4	1,594.1	591.9	421.4	49.7
2015	B	4.36	2.86	66.1	1,590.0	608.8	421.5	66.1
2014	B	4.53	2.97	67.0	1,581.8	620.3	409.8	69.3
2013	B+	4.53	2.99	68.8	1,561.3	611.4	398.0	52.8
2012	B+	4.65	3.07	72.7	1,558.0	614.3	393.8	53.2

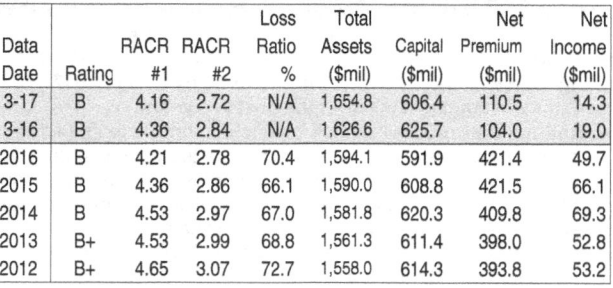

Reserve Deficiency (as % of capital)

* Adequate & redundant reserves show as negatives
■ 1 Yr Dev □ 2 Yr Dev

HASTINGS MUTUAL INS CO

B **Good**

Major Rating Factors: History of adequate reserve strength (5.8 on a scale of 0 to 10) as reserves have been consistently at an acceptable level. Good liquidity (6.7) with sufficient resources (cash flows and marketable investments) to handle a spike in claims.

Other Rating Factors: Fair overall results on stability tests (4.7) including weak results on operational trends. Strong long-term capitalization index (10.0) based on excellent current risk adjusted capital (severe and moderate loss scenarios). Moreover, capital levels have been consistent in recent years. Excellent profitability (8.3) with operating gains in each of the last five years.

Principal Business: Auto liability (18%), workers compensation (18%), commercial multiple peril (17%), farmowners multiple peril (16%), homeowners multiple peril (13%), auto physical damage (12%), and other lines (6%).

Principal Investments: Investment grade bonds (81%), misc. investments (14%), non investment grade bonds (4%), and cash (1%).

Investments in Affiliates: None

Group Affiliation: None

Licensed in: IL, IN, IA, KY, MI, OH, PA, TN, WI

Commenced Business: April 1885

Address: 404 E Woodlawn Ave, Hastings, MI 49058-1091

Phone: (269) 945-3405 **Domicile State:** MI **NAIC Code:** 14176

Data Date	Rating	RACR #1	RACR #2	Loss Ratio %	Total Assets ($mil)	Capital ($mil)	Net Premium ($mil)	Net Income ($mil)
3-17	B	5.14	3.44	N/A	902.9	428.3	101.1	2.6
3-16	B	5.13	3.53	N/A	835.2	396.8	97.7	10.8
2016	B	5.23	3.47	60.8	888.9	422.8	401.8	31.7
2015	B	5.10	3.47	58.2	830.1	386.4	388.6	38.3
2014	B	4.74	3.26	67.9	783.1	354.0	374.2	18.7
2013	A-	4.73	3.30	76.8	759.0	335.5	354.9	3.3
2012	A-	5.18	3.65	71.0	697.4	327.3	328.7	6.6

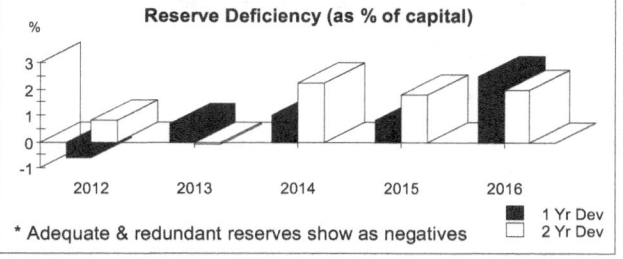

Reserve Deficiency (as % of capital)

* Adequate & redundant reserves show as negatives
■ 1 Yr Dev □ 2 Yr Dev

HAWAII EMPLOYERS MUTUAL INS CO

B- **Good**

Major Rating Factors: History of adequate reserve strength (6.0 on a scale of 0 to 10) as reserves have been consistently at an acceptable level. Good overall profitability index (6.9). Fair expense controls.

Other Rating Factors: Good overall results on stability tests (5.0). Strong long-term capitalization index (10.0) based on excellent current risk adjusted capital (severe and moderate loss scenarios), despite some fluctuation in capital levels. Excellent liquidity (7.0) with ample operational cash flow and liquid investments.

Principal Business: Workers compensation (100%).

Principal Investments: Investment grade bonds (78%), misc. investments (14%), non investment grade bonds (6%), and real estate (2%).

Investments in Affiliates: None

Group Affiliation: None

Licensed in: HI

Commenced Business: October 1996

Address: 1100 Alakea Street Suite 1400, Honolulu, HI 96813-3407

Phone: (808) 524-3642 **Domicile State:** HI **NAIC Code:** 10781

Data Date	Rating	RACR #1	RACR #2	Loss Ratio %	Total Assets ($mil)	Capital ($mil)	Net Premium ($mil)	Net Income ($mil)
3-17	B-	4.62	3.24	N/A	387.5	231.2	17.5	2.3
3-16	C	4.20	2.95	N/A	370.0	223.5	17.2	2.3
2016	C+	4.73	3.33	71.8	380.9	228.9	71.8	7.2
2015	C	4.28	3.00	72.9	360.6	221.0	67.6	7.5
2014	C-	4.68	3.26	75.8	341.2	217.5	61.3	11.5
2013	C-	5.90	3.93	72.0	313.6	209.4	45.5	9.3
2012	C-	7.08	4.60	67.7	285.0	190.1	33.6	10.6

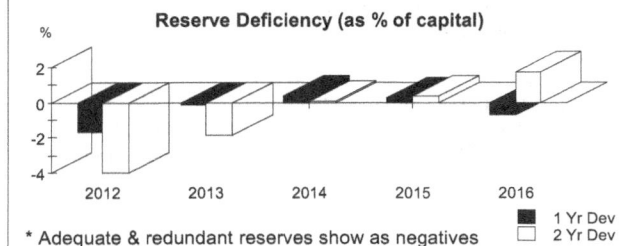

Reserve Deficiency (as % of capital)

* Adequate & redundant reserves show as negatives
■ 1 Yr Dev □ 2 Yr Dev

HERITAGE P&C INS CO

C+ | **Fair**

Major Rating Factors: Good long-term capitalization (5.1 on a scale of 0 to 10) based on good current risk adjusted capital (severe loss scenario) reflecting some improvement over results in 2016. Fair profitability index (4.9) with operating losses during 2012 and the first three months of 2017. Return on equity has been fair, averaging 8.3% over the past five years.

Other Rating Factors: Fair overall results on stability tests (4.1) including weak results on operational trends and fair risk adjusted capital in prior years. History of adequate reserve strength (5.5) as reserves have been consistently at an acceptable level. Good liquidity (6.0) with sufficient resources (cash flows and marketable investments) to handle a spike in claims.

Principal Business: Homeowners multiple peril (70%), commercial multiple peril (21%), allied lines (7%), and fire (1%).

Principal Investments: Investment grade bonds (76%), misc. investments (18%), and cash (6%).

Investments in Affiliates: None

Group Affiliation: Heritage Ins Holdings LLC

Licensed in: AL, FL, GA, MS, NC, SC

Commenced Business: August 2012

Address: 2600 MCCORMICK DRIVE SUITE 300, Clearwater, FL 33759

Phone: (727) 362-7200   **Domicile State:** FL   **NAIC Code:** 14407

Data Date	Rating	RACR #1	RACR #2	Loss Ratio %	Total Assets ($mil)	Capital ($mil)	Net Premium ($mil)	Net Income ($mil)
3-17	C+	1.48	0.91	N/A	606.2	195.0	75.2	-5.4
3-16	C+	1.19	0.80	N/A	637.6	211.2	102.9	-5.3
2016	C+	1.15	0.64	70.9	626.1	199.7	319.1	-16.5
2015	C+	1.06	0.65	44.7	601.9	216.4	391.7	43.4
2014	C	1.01	0.69	46.5	496.7	172.7	331.7	9.8
2013	C	0.81	0.60	44.4	207.8	63.1	139.6	21.0
2012	B-	0.90	0.70	27.2	78.0	26.5	45.2	-1.1

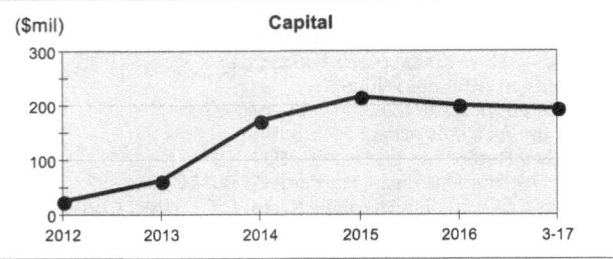

HOME-OWNERS INS CO *

A- | **Excellent**

Major Rating Factors: Strong long-term capitalization index (10.0 on a scale of 0 to 10) based on excellent current risk adjusted capital (severe and moderate loss scenarios). Furthermore, this high level of risk adjusted capital has been consistently maintained in previous years. Excellent profitability (8.9) with operating gains in each of the last five years.

Other Rating Factors: History of adequate reserve strength (6.0) as reserves have been consistently at an acceptable level. Good liquidity (6.8) with sufficient resources (cash flows and marketable investments) to handle a spike in claims. Good overall results on stability tests (5.9) despite weak results on operational trends.

Principal Business: Auto liability (49%), auto physical damage (35%), commercial multiple peril (9%), workers compensation (3%), other liability (2%), and inland marine (1%).

Principal Investments: Investment grade bonds (83%), misc. investments (16%), and cash (1%).

Investments in Affiliates: None

Group Affiliation: Auto-Owners Group

Licensed in: AL, AR, CO, GA, IL, IN, IA, KY, MI, MO, NE, NV, ND, OH, PA, SC, SD, UT, VA, WI

Commenced Business: May 1863

Address: 6101 ANACAPRI BOULEVARD, Lansing, MI 48917-3968

Phone: (517) 323-1200   **Domicile State:** MI   **NAIC Code:** 26638

Data Date	Rating	RACR #1	RACR #2	Loss Ratio %	Total Assets ($mil)	Capital ($mil)	Net Premium ($mil)	Net Income ($mil)
3-17	A-	6.19	4.53	N/A	2,197.5	1,097.9	204.4	19.4
3-16	A-	6.19	4.42	N/A	2,105.7	1,017.3	204.4	39.1
2016	A-	5.82	4.52	67.6	2,168.8	1,071.3	831.4	80.7
2015	A-	5.27	3.99	66.8	2,063.8	976.4	809.4	102.6
2014	A-	4.42	3.16	72.3	2,104.5	886.7	993.4	89.4
2013	A-	3.77	2.62	69.3	2,069.7	799.4	1,045.3	73.7
2012	A-	3.32	2.29	73.3	1,854.4	684.9	980.9	46.6

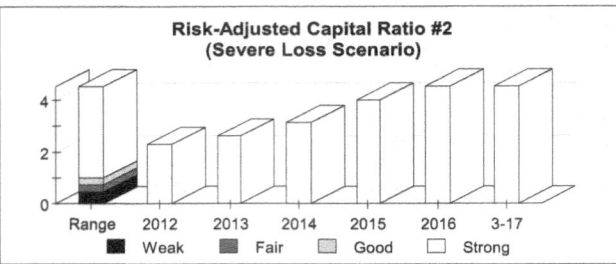

HOSPITALS INS CO

C- | **Fair**

Major Rating Factors: Fair overall results on stability tests (3.2 on a scale of 0 to 10) including weak results on operational trends. The largest net exposure for one risk is conservative at 1.7% of capital. Good long-term capitalization index (5.3) based on excellent current risk adjusted capital (severe and moderate loss scenarios), despite some fluctuation in capital levels.

Other Rating Factors: Good liquidity (6.9) with sufficient resources (cash flows and marketable investments) to handle a spike in claims. Ample reserve history (10.0) that helps to protect the company against sharp claims increases. Excellent profitability (7.9) with operating gains in each of the last five years. Return on equity has been good over the last five years, averaging 14.4%.

Principal Business: Medical malpractice (96%) and other liability (4%).

Principal Investments: Misc. investments (50%), investment grade bonds (46%), and non investment grade bonds (4%).

Investments in Affiliates: None

Group Affiliation: None

Licensed in: NY

Commenced Business: August 1987

Address: 50 Main Street Suite 1220, White Plains, NY 10606

Phone: (914) 220-1800   **Domicile State:** NY   **NAIC Code:** 30317

Data Date	Rating	RACR #1	RACR #2	Loss Ratio %	Total Assets ($mil)	Capital ($mil)	Net Premium ($mil)	Net Income ($mil)
3-17	C-	1.21	1.01	N/A	1,672.5	546.1	48.5	1.8
3-16	C-	0.96	0.81	N/A	1,571.1	441.7	46.5	-8.9
2016	C-	1.20	1.01	54.1	1,568.5	526.6	191.9	61.6
2015	D+	0.99	0.84	88.7	1,472.8	448.2	216.1	11.5
2014	D	1.08	0.92	9.5	1,414.4	460.2	229.2	134.6
2013	D	0.65	0.56	55.3	1,397.5	318.7	234.1	76.5
2012	D-	0.40	0.34	100.0	1,282.6	214.6	221.5	17.1

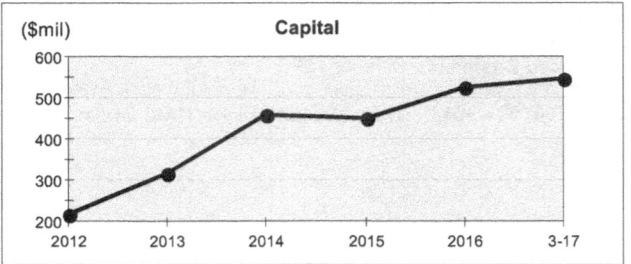

HOUSTON CASUALTY CO   B-   Good

Major Rating Factors: Fair overall results on stability tests (4.5 on a scale of 0 to 10) including weak results on operational trends. The largest net exposure for one risk is conservative at 1.4% of capital. Good overall profitability index (6.4). Fair expense controls. Return on equity has been good over the last five years, averaging 13.8%.

Other Rating Factors: Good liquidity (6.7) with sufficient resources (cash flows and marketable investments) to handle a spike in claims. Strong long-term capitalization index (7.8) based on excellent current risk adjusted capital (severe and moderate loss scenarios), despite some fluctuation in capital levels. Ample reserve history (7.6) that can protect against increases in claims costs.

Principal Business: Other liability (49%), ocean marine (14%), other accident & health (6%), commercial multiple peril (5%), products liability (5%), inland marine (5%), and other lines (15%).

Principal Investments: Misc. investments (50%), investment grade bonds (43%), non investment grade bonds (5%), and cash (2%).

Investments in Affiliates: 42%

Group Affiliation: HCC Ins Holdings Inc

Licensed in: All states, the District of Columbia and Puerto Rico

Commenced Business: June 1981

Address: 13403 Northwest Freeway, Houston, TX 77040

Phone: (713) 462-1000   **Domicile State:** TX   **NAIC Code:** 42374

Data Date	Rating	RACR #1	RACR #2	Loss Ratio %	Total Assets ($mil)	Capital ($mil)	Net Premium ($mil)	Net Income ($mil)
3-17	B-	1.75	1.55	N/A	3,518.1	1,977.3	116.7	10.0
3-16	B-	1.89	1.73	N/A	3,549.1	1,991.5	125.4	3.9
2016	B-	1.72	1.54	64.4	3,329.6	1,913.0	860.4	239.2
2015	B-	1.87	1.73	66.4	3,404.1	1,936.9	808.3	313.8
2014	B-	1.72	1.60	51.2	2,960.2	1,891.9	336.7	215.3
2013	B-	1.88	1.71	40.6	2,967.1	1,909.7	301.7	323.6
2012	B-	1.87	1.70	50.1	2,930.4	1,795.1	332.1	264.2

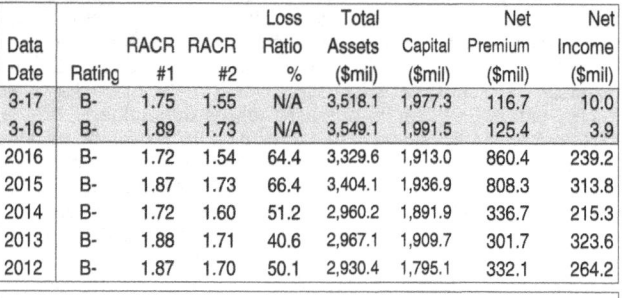

Rating Indexes

HOUSTON SPECIALTY INS CO   B   Good

Major Rating Factors: Good long-term capitalization index (6.1 on a scale of 0 to 10) based on good current risk adjusted capital (severe and moderate loss scenarios). Over the last several years, capital levels have remained relatively consistent. History of adequate reserve strength (5.5) as reserves have been consistently at an acceptable level.

Other Rating Factors: Good overall results on stability tests (5.5) despite negative cash flow from operations for 2016. Stability strengths include good operational trends and excellent risk diversification. Fair profitability index (4.5) with operating losses during 2012, 2015 and 2016. Return on equity has been low, averaging 1.7% over the past five years. Excellent liquidity (7.0) with ample operational cash flow and liquid investments.

Principal Business: Other liability (41%), inland marine (29%), auto liability (15%), allied lines (6%), auto physical damage (4%), commercial multiple peril (3%), and other lines (4%).

Principal Investments: Misc. investments (57%), investment grade bonds (37%), and cash (6%).

Investments in Affiliates: 51%

Group Affiliation: Houston International Ins Group Ltd

Licensed in: All states except PR

Commenced Business: April 2007

Address: 800 Gessner Suite 600, Houston, TX 77024

Phone: (713) 935-4820   **Domicile State:** TX   **NAIC Code:** 12936

Data Date	Rating	RACR #1	RACR #2	Loss Ratio %	Total Assets ($mil)	Capital ($mil)	Net Premium ($mil)	Net Income ($mil)
3-17	B	0.96	0.86	N/A	460.3	262.8	29.8	4.2
3-16	B-	1.07	0.96	N/A	489.3	275.1	32.4	2.7
2016	B	0.99	0.89	69.1	458.0	260.8	111.8	-0.1
2015	B-	1.03	0.91	63.5	497.3	268.9	122.1	-5.8
2014	B	1.01	0.90	61.0	471.1	263.6	74.3	14.0
2013	B	0.78	0.70	51.1	361.7	187.7	109.1	8.2
2012	A-	1.18	1.08	58.6	281.8	187.6	67.5	-0.2

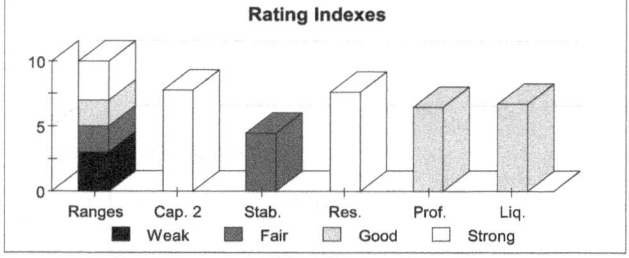

($mil)   Capital

HUDSON INS CO   C-   Fair

Major Rating Factors: Fair overall results on stability tests (3.2 on a scale of 0 to 10) including weak financial strength of affiliated Fairfax Financial and weak results on operational trends. History of adequate reserve strength (6.5) as reserves have been consistently at an acceptable level.

Other Rating Factors: Good overall profitability index (6.7). Fair expense controls. Return on equity has been low, averaging 4.6% over the past five years. Strong long-term capitalization index (8.4) based on excellent current risk adjusted capital (severe and moderate loss scenarios), despite some fluctuation in capital levels. Excellent liquidity (7.4) with ample operational cash flow and liquid investments.

Principal Business: Allied lines (42%), other liability (36%), surety (8%), auto liability (7%), auto physical damage (6%), medical malpractice (1%), and commercial multiple peril (1%).

Principal Investments: Investment grade bonds (52%), misc. investments (39%), non investment grade bonds (5%), and cash (4%).

Investments in Affiliates: 32%

Group Affiliation: Fairfax Financial

Licensed in: All states, the District of Columbia and Puerto Rico

Commenced Business: December 1918

Address: 1209 ORANGE STREET, Wilmington, DE 19801

Phone: (212) 978-2800   **Domicile State:** DE   **NAIC Code:** 25054

Data Date	Rating	RACR #1	RACR #2	Loss Ratio %	Total Assets ($mil)	Capital ($mil)	Net Premium ($mil)	Net Income ($mil)
3-17	C-	2.19	1.95	N/A	1,035.1	458.9	32.0	-0.1
3-16	C-	2.04	1.85	N/A	973.7	452.1	27.0	-2.1
2016	C-	2.17	1.91	71.9	1,159.9	453.2	158.6	36.8
2015	C-	2.06	1.87	76.0	1,082.8	457.9	149.4	40.0
2014	C-	2.11	1.91	81.4	1,042.7	440.2	166.6	9.6
2013	C-	2.48	2.22	86.0	819.0	413.9	129.6	6.0
2012	C-	2.76	2.54	82.8	821.1	398.9	108.4	14.0

Fairfax Financial Composite Group Rating: C Largest Group Members	Assets ($mil)	Rating
ODYSSEY REINS CO	7163	C
US FIRE INS CO	3950	C
TIG INS CO	2818	C
ZENITH INS CO	1825	C+
CLEARWATER SELECT INS CO	1193	D

HUDSON SPECIALTY INS CO   D+   Weak

Major Rating Factors: Weak overall results on stability tests (2.6 on a scale of 0 to 10) including potential drain of affiliation with Fairfax Financial, weak results on operational trends and negative cash flow from operations for 2016. The largest net exposure for one risk is conservative at 1.1% of capital. Good overall profitability index (6.9) despite operating losses during the first three months of 2017. Return on equity has been fair, averaging 9.7% over the past five years.

Other Rating Factors: Strong long-term capitalization index (9.6) based on excellent current risk adjusted capital (severe and moderate loss scenarios), despite some fluctuation in capital levels. Ample reserve history (8.1) that helps to protect the company against sharp claims increases. Excellent liquidity (8.2) with ample operational cash flow and liquid investments.

Principal Business: Other liability (52%), medical malpractice (16%), ocean marine (13%), commercial multiple peril (10%), fire (7%), auto liability (1%), and inland marine (1%).

Principal Investments: Investment grade bonds (76%), misc. investments (21%), and non investment grade bonds (3%).

Investments in Affiliates: 19%

Group Affiliation: Fairfax Financial

Licensed in: All states, the District of Columbia and Puerto Rico

Commenced Business: December 1985

Address: 100 WILLIAM STREET 5TH FLOOR, New York, NY 10038

Phone: (212) 978-2800   **Domicile State:** NY   **NAIC Code:** 37079

Data Date	Rating	RACR #1	RACR #2	Loss Ratio %	Total Assets ($mil)	Capital ($mil)	Net Premium ($mil)	Net Income ($mil)
3-17	D+	3.35	2.90	N/A	356.6	202.3	13.4	-1.8
3-16	D+	3.22	2.79	N/A	376.6	202.7	12.7	2.2
2016	D+	3.34	2.89	56.7	365.7	200.9	53.0	3.4
2015	D+	3.20	2.78	46.8	373.2	201.2	51.0	50.6
2014	D+	2.79	2.39	60.9	366.9	186.8	63.2	22.2
2013	D+	2.70	2.27	68.7	311.7	157.7	50.5	12.5
2012	D+	2.86	2.58	87.9	263.5	143.8	35.1	7.7

Fairfax Financial
Composite Group Rating: C

Largest Group Members	Assets ($mil)	Rating
ODYSSEY REINS CO	7163	C
US FIRE INS CO	3950	C
TIG INS CO	2818	C
ZENITH INS CO	1825	C+
CLEARWATER SELECT INS CO	1193	D

ICI MUTUAL INS CO A RRG   B   Good

Major Rating Factors: Good overall results on stability tests (6.3 on a scale of 0 to 10). The largest net exposure for one risk is high at 3.0% of capital. Stability strengths include good operational trends and excellent risk diversification. Strong long-term capitalization index (10.0) based on excellent current risk adjusted capital (severe and moderate loss scenarios), despite some fluctuation in capital levels.

Other Rating Factors: Ample reserve history (8.8) that helps to protect the company against sharp claims increases. Excellent profitability (7.0) with operating gains in each of the last five years. Excellent liquidity (8.6) with ample operational cash flow and liquid investments.

Principal Business: Other liability (89%) and fidelity (11%).

Principal Investments: Investment grade bonds (82%), misc. investments (16%), cash (1%), and non investment grade bonds (1%).

Investments in Affiliates: 0%

Group Affiliation: None

Licensed in: AZ, CA, CO, CT, DC, FL, GA, IL, IA, KS, MD, MA, MI, MN, MO, NE, NJ, NM, NY, ND, OH, PA, SC, TN, TX, UT, VT, VA, WA, WI

Commenced Business: March 1988

Address: 126 COLLEGE STREET SUITE 400, Burlington, VT 05401

Phone: (800) 643-4246   **Domicile State:** VT   **NAIC Code:** 11268

Data Date	Rating	RACR #1	RACR #2	Loss Ratio %	Total Assets ($mil)	Capital ($mil)	Net Premium ($mil)	Net Income ($mil)
3-17	B	10.09	6.27	N/A	352.1	259.5	6.3	1.7
3-16	B	11.49	7.11	N/A	343.8	256.8	6.9	4.2
2016	B	10.21	6.41	49.3	355.6	255.0	30.6	6.3
2015	B	11.20	6.98	59.5	340.8	249.1	31.0	3.8
2014	B	12.56	7.50	18.6	333.9	249.6	30.1	12.0
2013	A-	10.76	6.82	17.7	322.1	235.8	29.2	12.5
2012	A-	11.83	7.43	45.3	314.0	224.6	28.3	9.4

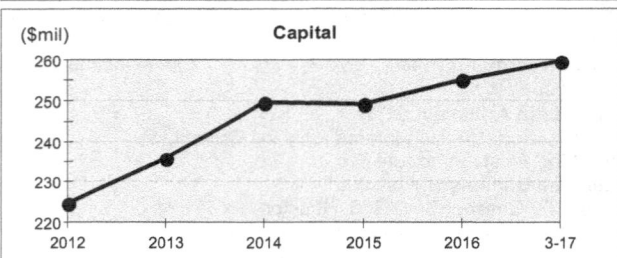

Capital ($mil)

IDS PROPERTY CASUALTY INS CO   B-   Good

Major Rating Factors: Fair reserve development (3.3 on a scale of 0 to 10) as reserves have generally been sufficient to cover claims. In 2015, the two year reserve development was 18% deficient. Fair profitability index (3.7) with operating losses during 2014, 2015 and 2016. Average return on equity over the last five years has been poor at -0.6%.

Other Rating Factors: Fair overall results on stability tests (4.9) including weak results on operational trends. Good liquidity (5.1) with sufficient resources (cash flows and marketable investments) to handle a spike in claims. Strong long-term capitalization index (8.4) based on excellent current risk adjusted capital (severe and moderate loss scenarios). Moreover, capital levels have been consistent in recent years.

Principal Business: Auto liability (38%), homeowners multiple peril (33%), auto physical damage (29%), and other liability (1%).

Principal Investments: Investment grade bonds (101%) and misc. investments (2%).

Investments in Affiliates: 3%

Group Affiliation: Ameriprise Financial Group

Licensed in: All states except PR

Commenced Business: January 1973

Address: 3500 Packerland Drive, De Pere, WI 54115-9070

Phone: (920) 330-5100   **Domicile State:** WI   **NAIC Code:** 29068

Data Date	Rating	RACR #1	RACR #2	Loss Ratio %	Total Assets ($mil)	Capital ($mil)	Net Premium ($mil)	Net Income ($mil)
3-17	B-	2.94	2.30	N/A	1,787.4	806.0	241.9	7.5
3-16	B-	2.69	2.10	N/A	1,754.6	753.2	265.2	-3.4
2016	B-	2.87	2.21	91.2	1,826.3	800.3	1,065.3	-8.4
2015	B-	2.49	1.91	97.7	1,661.8	683.6	1,068.2	-44.4
2014	B	2.25	1.74	95.6	1,414.3	559.9	1,000.9	-25.3
2013	B	2.57	2.13	88.2	1,268.3	530.7	883.7	11.3
2012	B	2.45	2.02	87.0	1,109.4	462.2	801.0	27.4

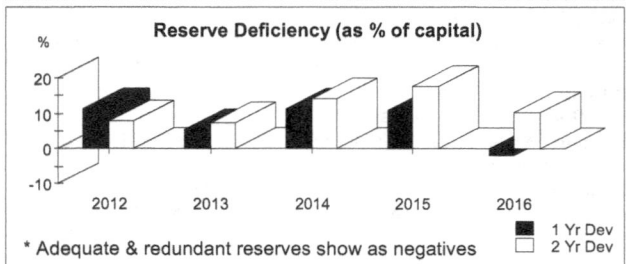

Reserve Deficiency (as % of capital)

* Adequate & redundant reserves show as negatives

■ 1 Yr Dev   □ 2 Yr Dev

INDIANA FARMERS MUTUAL INS CO   B   Good

Major Rating Factors: Good overall profitability index (5.3 on a scale of 0 to 10) despite operating losses during 2012. Good liquidity (6.0) with sufficient resources (cash flows and marketable investments) to handle a spike in claims.
Other Rating Factors: Fair overall results on stability tests (4.6) including weak results on operational trends. Strong long-term capitalization index (8.3) based on excellent current risk adjusted capital (severe and moderate loss scenarios). Moreover, capital levels have been consistent in recent years. Ample reserve history (7.0) that can protect against increases in claims costs.
Principal Business: Homeowners multiple peril (23%), auto liability (23%), auto physical damage (18%), farmowners multiple peril (13%), commercial multiple peril (11%), workers compensation (4%), and other lines (8%).
Principal Investments: Investment grade bonds (86%), misc. investments (13%), and cash (1%).
Investments in Affiliates: None
Group Affiliation: None
Licensed in: IN
Commenced Business: August 1877
Address: 10 West 106th Street, Indianapolis, IN 46290-1002
Phone: (317) 846-4211   **Domicile State:** IN   **NAIC Code:** 22624

Data Date	Rating	RACR #1	RACR #2	Loss Ratio %	Total Assets ($mil)	Capital ($mil)	Net Premium ($mil)	Net Income ($mil)
3-17	B	3.33	1.98	N/A	422.8	199.7	48.7	3.0
3-16	B	3.16	1.89	N/A	400.7	188.7	47.4	7.8
2016	B	3.26	1.95	69.0	428.4	195.3	198.5	13.5
2015	B	3.01	1.81	59.1	391.0	180.1	189.5	20.8
2014	B	2.91	1.75	62.5	359.6	161.7	180.0	24.4
2013	B+	2.56	1.54	67.3	331.7	139.4	169.5	14.2
2012	B+	2.33	1.42	100.4	305.0	125.0	153.1	-22.0

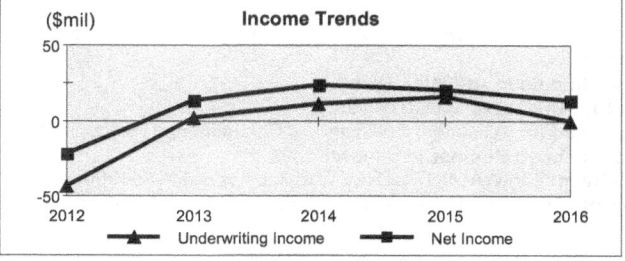

INFINITY INS CO   B   Good

Major Rating Factors: History of adequate reserve strength (6.7 on a scale of 0 to 10) as reserves have been consistently at an acceptable level. Good overall profitability index (5.4). Good expense controls. Return on equity has been fair, averaging 8.2% over the past five years.
Other Rating Factors: Fair overall results on stability tests (4.5) including potential drain of affiliation with Infinity Property & Casualty Group and weak results on operational trends. Fair liquidity (3.2) as cash resources may not be adequate to cover a spike in claims. Strong long-term capitalization index (7.9) based on excellent current risk adjusted capital (severe and moderate loss scenarios), despite some fluctuation in capital levels.
Principal Business: Auto liability (62%) and auto physical damage (38%).
Principal Investments: Investment grade bonds (79%), misc. investments (11%), non investment grade bonds (8%), and real estate (4%).
Investments in Affiliates: 3%
Group Affiliation: Infinity Property & Casualty Group
Licensed in: All states except KS, LA, NH, NJ, VT, WY, PR
Commenced Business: October 1978
Address: 500 East 96th Street Suite 100, Indianapolis, IN 46240
Phone: (205) 870-4000   **Domicile State:** IN   **NAIC Code:** 22268

Data Date	Rating	RACR #1	RACR #2	Loss Ratio %	Total Assets ($mil)	Capital ($mil)	Net Premium ($mil)	Net Income ($mil)
3-17	B	1.88	1.60	N/A	2,050.3	663.5	338.3	10.9
3-16	B	1.81	1.55	N/A	2,026.8	645.0	333.2	5.3
2016	B	1.83	1.61	79.0	2,012.7	660.6	1,379.9	62.0
2015	B	1.79	1.59	77.1	1,992.7	652.8	1,360.9	61.4
2014	B	1.84	1.63	75.7	1,991.5	674.6	1,334.7	68.0
2013	B	1.73	1.53	78.2	1,966.4	666.6	1,316.0	47.8
2012	B	1.60	1.39	79.7	1,860.6	605.7	1,233.1	33.8

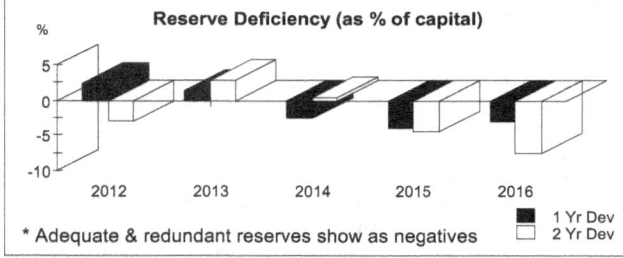

INLAND INS CO   C   Fair

Major Rating Factors: Fair reserve development (3.6 on a scale of 0 to 10) as reserves have generally been sufficient to cover claims. Weak overall results on stability tests (2.6) including weak results on operational trends. The largest net exposure for one risk is excessive at 8.8% of capital.
Other Rating Factors: Good overall profitability index (6.9). Weak expense controls. Return on equity has been low, averaging 4.5% over the past five years. Strong long-term capitalization index (8.4) based on excellent current risk adjusted capital (severe and moderate loss scenarios), despite some fluctuation in capital levels. Superior liquidity (10.0) with ample operational cash flow and liquid investments.
Principal Business: Surety (100%).
Principal Investments: Misc. investments (86%), investment grade bonds (9%), and cash (5%).
Investments in Affiliates: None
Group Affiliation: Universal Surety
Licensed in: AZ, CO, IA, KS, MN, MO, MT, NE, ND, OK, SD, WY
Commenced Business: November 1958
Address: 601 S 12th Street, Lincoln, NE 68508
Phone: (402) 435-4302   **Domicile State:** NE   **NAIC Code:** 23264

Data Date	Rating	RACR #1	RACR #2	Loss Ratio %	Total Assets ($mil)	Capital ($mil)	Net Premium ($mil)	Net Income ($mil)
3-17	C	3.27	1.95	N/A	276.0	208.4	0.1	2.4
3-16	C	3.17	1.89	N/A	241.5	184.0	0.1	1.3
2016	C	3.22	1.92	N/A	273.2	206.9	0.5	11.3
2015	C	3.16	1.89	N/A	240.4	182.8	0.5	8.5
2014	C	3.00	1.79	4.1	262.5	195.7	0.7	8.7
2013	C	2.93	1.75	14.8	254.7	190.0	0.4	9.7
2012	C	2.96	1.77	1.7	209.6	158.5	0.4	4.4

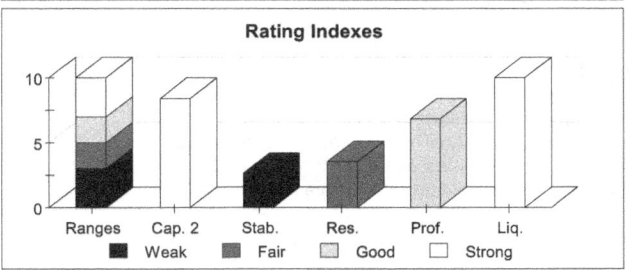

INS CO OF NORTH AMERICA · C · Fair

Major Rating Factors: Fair overall results on stability tests (3.6 on a scale of 0 to 10) including fair financial strength of affiliated Chubb Limited and weak results on operational trends. The largest net exposure for one risk is high at 3.1% of capital. History of adequate reserve strength (6.4) as reserves have been consistently at an acceptable level.

Other Rating Factors: Strong long-term capitalization index (7.7) based on excellent current risk adjusted capital (severe and moderate loss scenarios), despite some fluctuation in capital levels. Excellent profitability (7.9) with operating gains in each of the last five years. Excellent liquidity (7.1) with ample operational cash flow and liquid investments.

Principal Business: Other accident & health (24%), other liability (20%), fire (18%), international (14%), group accident & health (10%), ocean marine (5%), and other lines (9%).

Principal Investments: Investment grade bonds (80%), cash (19%), and real estate (3%).

Investments in Affiliates: None

Group Affiliation: Chubb Limited

Licensed in: All states, the District of Columbia and Puerto Rico

Commenced Business: January 1792

Address: 436 WALNUT STREET, Philadelphia, PA 19106

Phone: (215) 640-1000   **Domicile State:** PA   **NAIC Code:** 22713

Data Date	Rating	RACR #1	RACR #2	Loss Ratio %	Total Assets ($mil)	Capital ($mil)	Net Premium ($mil)	Net Income ($mil)
3-17	C	2.37	1.58	N/A	929.9	259.3	46.7	9.2
3-16	C	2.10	1.40	N/A	862.6	238.7	46.2	5.4
2016	C	2.29	1.53	76.5	944.2	250.2	249.8	16.5
2015	C	2.08	1.40	72.8	883.8	233.6	237.9	8.6
2014	C	2.29	1.53	77.6	869.9	225.2	223.9	12.7
2013	C	1.88	1.26	72.2	787.1	182.8	217.7	15.3
2012	C	2.22	1.46	89.9	831.8	195.6	224.1	3.2

Chubb Limited Composite Group Rating: B- Largest Group Members	Assets ($mil)	Rating
FEDERAL INS CO	27371	B-
ACE AMERICAN INS CO	13036	B-
ACE PC INS CO	8192	B-
PACIFIC INDEMNITY CO	6555	B-
PACIFIC EMPLOYERS INS CO	3774	B-

INS CO OF THE WEST · C · Fair

Major Rating Factors: Fair overall results on stability tests (3.7 on a scale of 0 to 10) including potential drain of affiliation with American Assets Inc and weak results on operational trends. The largest net exposure for one risk is conservative at 1.3% of capital. History of adequate reserve strength (5.0) as reserves have been consistently at an acceptable level.

Other Rating Factors: Good liquidity (6.5) with sufficient resources (cash flows and marketable investments) to handle a spike in claims. Strong long-term capitalization index (7.3) based on excellent current risk adjusted capital (severe and moderate loss scenarios). Moreover, capital levels have been consistent in recent years. Excellent profitability (8.9) with operating gains in each of the last five years. Return on equity has been good over the last five years, averaging 10.0%.

Principal Business: Workers compensation (95%), earthquake (4%), and inland marine (1%).

Principal Investments: Investment grade bonds (56%), misc. investments (35%), non investment grade bonds (6%), and cash (3%).

Investments in Affiliates: 9%

Group Affiliation: American Assets Inc

Licensed in: All states except PR

Commenced Business: May 1972

Address: 15025 INNOVATION DRIVE, San Diego, CA 92128

Phone: (858) 350-2400   **Domicile State:** CA   **NAIC Code:** 27847

Data Date	Rating	RACR #1	RACR #2	Loss Ratio %	Total Assets ($mil)	Capital ($mil)	Net Premium ($mil)	Net Income ($mil)
3-17	C	1.68	1.24	N/A	2,306.1	909.3	197.6	21.3
3-16	C	1.45	1.07	N/A	1,986.3	781.5	193.0	27.1
2016	C	1.71	1.27	64.9	2,252.8	902.0	812.7	104.0
2015	C	1.47	1.08	63.0	1,917.0	753.3	744.1	90.4
2014	C	1.50	1.07	64.0	1,613.2	658.2	621.4	68.1
2013	C	1.72	1.21	61.1	1,314.5	533.5	514.8	68.8
2012	C	1.78	1.20	71.3	1,032.3	417.5	367.5	14.4

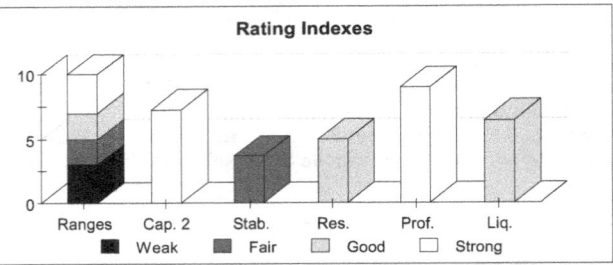

Rating Indexes — Ranges, Cap. 2, Stab., Res., Prof., Liq. · Weak, Fair, Good, Strong

INTEGON NATIONAL INS CO · C+ · Fair

Major Rating Factors: Fair overall results on stability tests (4.7 on a scale of 0 to 10) including potential drain of affiliation with AmTrust Financial Services Inc, weak results on operational trends and excessive premium growth. Fair reserve development (4.2) as reserves have generally been sufficient to cover claims. In 2012, the two year reserve development was 40% deficient.

Other Rating Factors: Weak profitability index (2.9) with operating losses during 2012, 2013, 2015 and the first three months of 2017. Average return on equity over the last five years has been poor at -7.5%. Vulnerable liquidity (1.5) as a spike in claims may stretch capacity. Strong long-term capitalization index (7.0) based on excellent current risk adjusted capital (severe and moderate loss scenarios). Moreover, capital levels have been consistent in recent years.

Principal Business: Auto liability (46%), auto physical damage (27%), homeowners multiple peril (20%), commercial multiple peril (3%), group accident & health (2%), allied lines (2%), and fire (1%).

Principal Investments: Investment grade bonds (70%), misc. investments (28%), non investment grade bonds (4%), and real estate (1%).

Investments in Affiliates: 10%

Group Affiliation: AmTrust Financial Services Inc

Licensed in: All states except PR

Commenced Business: December 1988

Address: 5630 University Parkway, Winston-salem, NC 27105

Phone: (336) 435-2000   **Domicile State:** NC   **NAIC Code:** 29742

Data Date	Rating	RACR #1	RACR #2	Loss Ratio %	Total Assets ($mil)	Capital ($mil)	Net Premium ($mil)	Net Income ($mil)
3-17	C+	1.36	1.00	N/A	3,052.5	627.0	412.3	-22.9
3-16	C	1.13	0.81	N/A	2,321.5	444.5	291.3	-5.7
2016	C+	1.45	1.06	74.3	2,489.2	594.4	1,522.0	50.4
2015	C	1.18	0.85	75.2	2,339.5	448.3	1,155.3	-10.0
2014	C-	1.22	0.97	74.3	1,741.0	332.4	928.7	11.4
2013	D+	1.27	0.96	87.6	1,149.5	159.8	349.1	-33.2
2012	D	0.31	0.26	79.1	1,145.1	139.7	869.0	-34.3

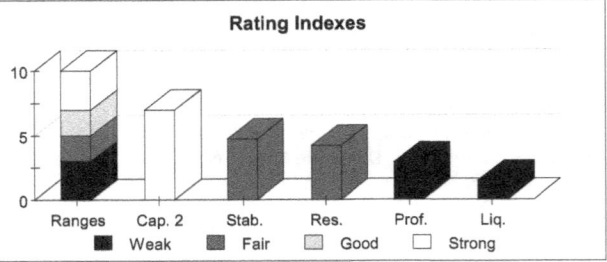

Rating Indexes — Ranges, Cap. 2, Stab., Res., Prof., Liq. · Weak, Fair, Good, Strong

INTERINS EXCHANGE *   B+   Good

Major Rating Factors: Good overall results on stability tests (5.1 on a scale of 0 to 10) despite potential drain of affiliation with Auto Club Enterprises Ins Group and weak results on operational trends. Good liquidity (6.5) with sufficient resources (cash flows and marketable investments) to handle a spike in claims.
Other Rating Factors: Strong long-term capitalization index (9.8) based on excellent current risk adjusted capital (severe and moderate loss scenarios). Moreover, capital levels have been consistent in recent years. Ample reserve history (7.3) that can protect against increases in claims costs. Fair profitability index (4.9) with operating losses during the first three months of 2017.
Principal Business: Auto liability (44%), auto physical damage (35%), homeowners multiple peril (19%), fire (1%), and other liability (1%).
Principal Investments: Investment grade bonds (46%), misc. investments (45%), non investment grade bonds (8%), and real estate (2%).
Investments in Affiliates: 1%
Group Affiliation: Auto Club Enterprises Ins Group
Licensed in: CA, FL, HI, ME, MI, MO, NH, NM, OH, PA, TX, VT, VA
Commenced Business: October 1912
Address: 3333 FAIRVIEW ROAD, Costa Mesa, CA 92626-1698
Phone: (714) 850-5111   **Domicile State:** CA   **NAIC Code:** 15598

Data Date	Rating	RACR #1	RACR #2	Loss Ratio %	Total Assets ($mil)	Capital ($mil)	Net Premium ($mil)	Net Income ($mil)
3-17	B+	4.63	2.83	N/A	9,670.8	6,006.7	815.9	-26.2
3-16	B+	4.94	3.04	N/A	8,852.7	5,564.0	755.9	-56.5
2016	B+	4.72	2.91	79.4	9,326.9	5,911.1	3,261.5	35.6
2015	B+	5.05	3.13	71.9	8,707.0	5,633.7	3,017.0	183.2
2014	B+	5.11	3.16	71.6	8,547.9	5,496.7	2,864.6	200.7
2013	A+	5.26	3.26	71.1	8,106.5	5,214.6	2,752.1	269.8
2012	A+	5.69	3.60	72.4	7,254.0	4,609.7	2,612.8	220.0

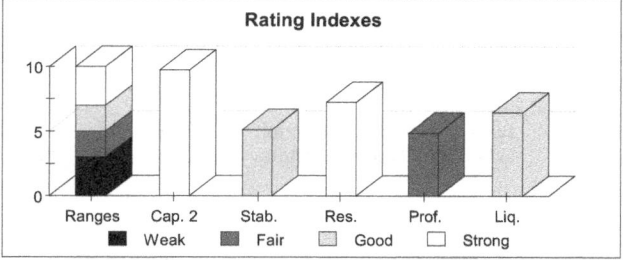

IRONSHORE SPECIALTY INS CO   C   Fair

Major Rating Factors: Fair overall results on stability tests (3.7 on a scale of 0 to 10) including potential drain of affiliation with Ironshore Holdings Inc, weak results on operational trends and negative cash flow from operations for 2016. The largest net exposure for one risk is conservative at 1.8% of capital. History of adequate reserve strength (6.0) as reserves have been consistently at an acceptable level.
Other Rating Factors: Good overall profitability index (5.7) despite operating losses during the first three months of 2017. Return on equity has been fair, averaging 5.4% over the past five years. Strong long-term capitalization index (7.6) based on excellent current risk adjusted capital (severe and moderate loss scenarios). Moreover, capital levels have been consistent in recent years. Excellent liquidity (7.1) with ample operational cash flow and liquid investments.
Principal Business: Other liability (67%), medical malpractice (10%), fire (8%), homeowners multiple peril (8%), products liability (4%), aircraft (1%), and other lines (2%).
Principal Investments: Investment grade bonds (95%), non investment grade bonds (3%), and cash (2%).
Investments in Affiliates: None
Group Affiliation: Ironshore Holdings Inc
Licensed in: All states, the District of Columbia and Puerto Rico
Commenced Business: February 1953
Address: 8601 N SCOTTSDALE ROAD STE 300, Scottsdale, AZ 85253
Phone: (646) 826-6600   **Domicile State:** AZ   **NAIC Code:** 25445

Data Date	Rating	RACR #1	RACR #2	Loss Ratio %	Total Assets ($mil)	Capital ($mil)	Net Premium ($mil)	Net Income ($mil)
3-17	C	2.46	1.59	N/A	999.7	352.8	26.9	-1.2
3-16	C	2.39	1.44	N/A	1,068.5	340.0	30.3	0.2
2016	C	2.42	1.56	82.7	1,082.9	349.3	109.7	-0.4
2015	C	2.41	1.46	76.6	987.1	334.0	112.0	20.9
2014	C	2.28	1.40	85.1	974.0	325.8	127.1	31.3
2013	C	2.59	1.58	68.3	832.9	300.3	119.2	21.4
2012	C	3.02	1.76	84.5	804.3	291.3	101.4	17.1

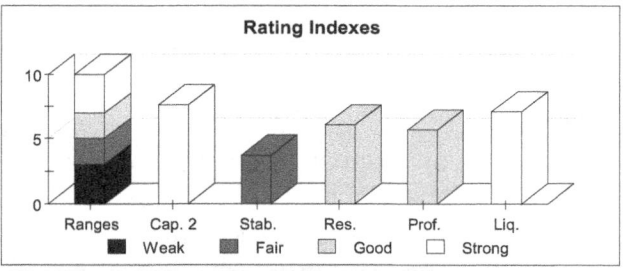

ISMIE MUTUAL INS CO   B-   Good

Major Rating Factors: Fair overall results on stability tests (4.5 on a scale of 0 to 10) including potential drain of affiliation with ISMIE Group, weak results on operational trends and negative cash flow from operations for 2016. Good overall profitability index (6.1) despite operating losses during the first three months of 2017.
Other Rating Factors: Strong long-term capitalization index (10.0) based on excellent current risk adjusted capital (severe and moderate loss scenarios). Moreover, capital levels have been consistent in recent years. Ample reserve history (9.5) that helps to protect the company against sharp claims increases. Excellent liquidity (7.7) with ample operational cash flow and liquid investments.
Principal Business: Medical malpractice (99%) and aggregate write-ins for other lines of business (1%).
Principal Investments: Investment grade bonds (91%), misc. investments (6%), cash (2%), and non investment grade bonds (1%).
Investments in Affiliates: 4%
Group Affiliation: ISMIE Group
Licensed in: GA, IL, IN, IA, KS, KY, LA, MI, MO, NE, NM, PA, SC, WI
Commenced Business: June 1976
Address: 20 North Michigan Avenue, Chicago, IL 60602-4811
Phone: (312) 782-2749   **Domicile State:** IL   **NAIC Code:** 32921

Data Date	Rating	RACR #1	RACR #2	Loss Ratio %	Total Assets ($mil)	Capital ($mil)	Net Premium ($mil)	Net Income ($mil)
3-17	B-	4.43	3.70	N/A	1,443.8	692.1	36.9	-2.7
3-16	B-	4.12	3.43	N/A	1,500.6	670.5	39.2	-0.9
2016	B-	4.51	3.79	61.9	1,468.4	693.3	149.4	24.4
2015	B-	4.15	3.48	57.9	1,525.9	670.1	168.4	37.4
2014	B-	3.73	3.10	53.4	1,625.1	647.4	189.2	34.8
2013	B-	3.66	2.98	37.6	1,616.4	609.9	229.6	80.1
2012	B-	2.99	2.47	52.9	1,544.7	522.9	242.2	57.0

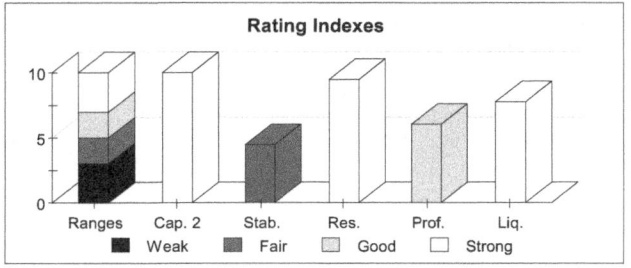

JEWELERS MUTUAL INS CO

B **Good**

Major Rating Factors: History of adequate reserve strength (6.4 on a scale of 0 to 10) as reserves have been consistently at an acceptable level. Good liquidity (6.7) with sufficient resources (cash flows and marketable investments) to handle a spike in claims.

Other Rating Factors: Fair overall results on stability tests (4.4) including weak results on operational trends. The largest net exposure for one risk is conservative at 2.0% of capital. Strong long-term capitalization index (10.0) based on excellent current risk adjusted capital (severe and moderate loss scenarios). Moreover, capital levels have been consistent in recent years. Excellent profitability (8.8) with operating gains in each of the last five years.

Principal Business: Inland marine (86%) and commercial multiple peril (13%).

Principal Investments: Investment grade bonds (58%), misc. investments (36%), cash (3%), and real estate (3%).

Investments in Affiliates: 0%

Group Affiliation: None

Licensed in: All states except PR

Commenced Business: June 1914

Address: 24 Jewelers Park Drive, Neenah, WI 54956-3703

Phone: (920) 725-4326   **Domicile State:** WI   **NAIC Code:** 14354

Data Date	Rating	RACR #1	RACR #2	Loss Ratio %	Total Assets ($mil)	Capital ($mil)	Net Premium ($mil)	Net Income ($mil)
3-17	B	5.37	3.39	N/A	401.1	249.4	44.9	8.4
3-16	B	5.52	3.44	N/A	368.4	228.7	41.7	0.7
2016	B	5.34	3.36	48.4	397.8	247.3	180.6	11.7
2015	B	5.77	3.60	45.0	365.3	226.5	165.9	15.5
2014	B	5.50	3.45	44.2	338.7	207.7	154.0	16.3
2013	A-	5.07	3.14	43.5	304.9	182.6	143.8	17.4
2012	A-	5.10	3.12	54.2	261.7	153.2	133.4	14.5

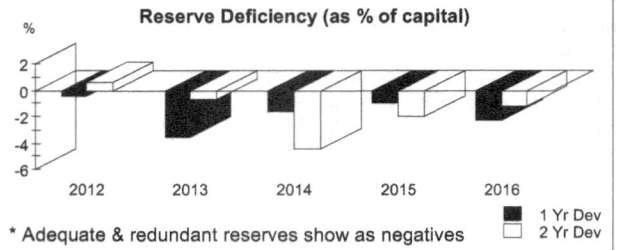

Reserve Deficiency (as % of capital)

* Adequate & redundant reserves show as negatives   ■ 1 Yr Dev   □ 2 Yr Dev

KENTUCKY FARM BUREAU MUTUAL INS CO

B **Good**

Major Rating Factors: History of adequate reserve strength (6.6 on a scale of 0 to 10) as reserves have been consistently at an acceptable level. Good overall profitability index (6.8). Good expense controls.

Other Rating Factors: Good liquidity (6.1) with sufficient resources (cash flows and marketable investments) to handle a spike in claims. Fair overall results on stability tests (4.8) including potential drain of affiliation with Kentucky Farm Bureau Group and weak results on operational trends. Strong long-term capitalization index (10.0) based on excellent current risk adjusted capital (severe and moderate loss scenarios). Moreover, capital levels have been consistent in recent years.

Principal Business: Auto liability (34%), homeowners multiple peril (26%), auto physical damage (20%), farmowners multiple peril (11%), commercial multiple peril (7%), other liability (1%), and allied lines (1%).

Principal Investments: Investment grade bonds (75%), misc. investments (25%), and non investment grade bonds (1%).

Investments in Affiliates: 1%

Group Affiliation: Kentucky Farm Bureau Group

Licensed in: CA, CT, DE, GA, ID, IL, IN, IA, KY, LA, MD, MA, MI, MO, MT, NH, NJ, NC, ND, OH, OK, OR, PA, RI, SD, TX, UT, VT, VA, WA, WV, WI

Commenced Business: December 1943

Address: 9201 Bunsen Parkway, Louisville, KY 40220-3793

Phone: (502) 495-5000   **Domicile State:** KY   **NAIC Code:** 22993

Data Date	Rating	RACR #1	RACR #2	Loss Ratio %	Total Assets ($mil)	Capital ($mil)	Net Premium ($mil)	Net Income ($mil)
3-17	B	5.69	3.72	N/A	2,426.2	1,306.1	239.1	15.1
3-16	B	5.66	3.68	N/A	2,333.2	1,251.3	222.8	27.6
2016	B	5.65	3.76	80.6	2,391.6	1,279.0	937.9	52.6
2015	B	5.58	3.68	79.6	2,286.1	1,226.1	877.8	39.9
2014	B	5.53	3.62	71.1	2,222.2	1,155.1	851.1	120.4
2013	A-	5.04	3.32	67.2	2,119.7	1,066.3	845.5	147.6
2012	A-	4.27	2.84	85.9	1,915.4	938.4	850.8	19.6

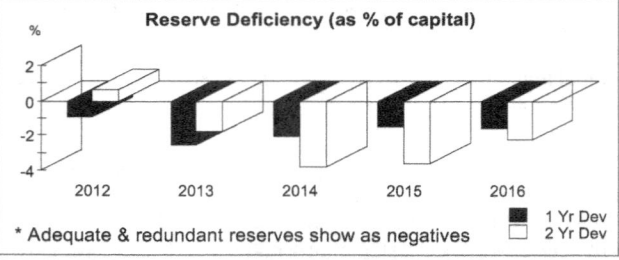

Reserve Deficiency (as % of capital)

* Adequate & redundant reserves show as negatives   ■ 1 Yr Dev   □ 2 Yr Dev

LAMMICO

B **Good**

Major Rating Factors: Fair overall results on stability tests (4.2 on a scale of 0 to 10) including weak results on operational trends. Strong long-term capitalization index (10.0) based on excellent current risk adjusted capital (severe and moderate loss scenarios). Moreover, capital levels have been consistent in recent years.

Other Rating Factors: Ample reserve history (8.9) that helps to protect the company against sharp claims increases. Excellent profitability (8.4) with operating gains in each of the last five years. Excellent liquidity (8.6) with ample operational cash flow and liquid investments.

Principal Business: Medical malpractice (99%) and other liability (1%).

Principal Investments: Investment grade bonds (84%), misc. investments (15%), and cash (1%).

Investments in Affiliates: 0%

Group Affiliation: None

Licensed in: AR, LA, MS, TN, TX

Commenced Business: January 1982

Address: One Galleria Boulevard Ste 700, Metairie, LA 70001

Phone: (504) 831-3756   **Domicile State:** LA   **NAIC Code:** 43656

Data Date	Rating	RACR #1	RACR #2	Loss Ratio %	Total Assets ($mil)	Capital ($mil)	Net Premium ($mil)	Net Income ($mil)
3-17	B	5.49	4.17	N/A	416.2	229.2	12.0	1.5
3-16	B	5.33	4.11	N/A	408.1	215.8	11.5	1.2
2016	B	5.57	4.28	67.2	431.3	226.6	49.8	9.4
2015	B	5.38	4.17	64.3	427.1	214.9	49.0	11.6
2014	C+	5.12	3.95	63.8	421.5	206.0	49.3	12.3
2013	C+	4.81	3.76	57.6	411.9	194.0	49.4	13.9
2012	C+	4.35	3.38	57.2	412.5	177.7	54.9	17.1

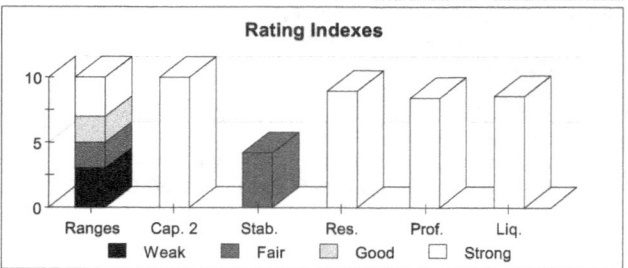

Rating Indexes

■ Weak   ▨ Fair   ▥ Good   □ Strong

LANCER INS CO　　　　　　　　　　　　　　　　　　　　　B　　Good

Major Rating Factors: Good overall profitability index (6.1 on a scale of 0 to 10) despite operating losses during 2015. Return on equity has been fair, averaging 7.0% over the past five years. Good liquidity (6.8) with sufficient resources (cash flows and marketable investments) to handle a spike in claims.

Other Rating Factors: Fair reserve development (3.5) as reserves have generally been sufficient to cover claims. In 2016, the two year reserve development was 19% deficient. Fair overall results on stability tests (4.1) including weak results on operational trends. The largest net exposure for one risk is acceptable at 2.5% of capital. Strong long-term capitalization index (8.1) based on excellent current risk adjusted capital (severe and moderate loss scenarios), despite some fluctuation in capital levels.

Principal Business: Auto liability (74%), auto physical damage (18%), other liability (4%), inland marine (3%), and ocean marine (1%).

Principal Investments: Investment grade bonds (94%), misc. investments (2%), cash (2%), non investment grade bonds (1%), and real estate (1%).

Investments in Affiliates: None

Group Affiliation: Lancer Financial Group Inc

Licensed in: All states, the District of Columbia and Puerto Rico

Commenced Business: May 1945

Address: 77 West Washington Street, Chicago, IL 60602

Phone: (516) 431-4441　**Domicile State:** IL　**NAIC Code:** 26077

Data Date	Rating	RACR #1	RACR #2	Loss Ratio %	Total Assets ($mil)	Capital ($mil)	Net Premium ($mil)	Net Income ($mil)
3-17	B	2.52	1.71	N/A	677.9	202.8	63.2	3.0
3-16	B	2.13	1.46	N/A	639.5	191.2	64.3	8.0
2016	B	2.51	1.72	70.2	674.4	199.7	260.6	15.2
2015	B	2.08	1.43	81.8	632.7	183.0	263.0	-4.9
2014	C+	2.73	1.85	67.9	575.0	189.5	242.5	16.1
2013	C+	3.59	2.35	73.7	517.5	171.7	218.3	19.7
2012	C+	4.27	2.94	67.3	444.0	149.9	168.6	15.3

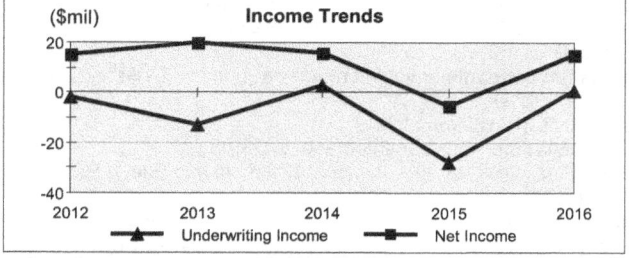

Income Trends

LANDMARK AMERICAN INS CO　　　　　　　　　　　　　　　C　　Fair

Major Rating Factors: Fair overall results on stability tests (3.1 on a scale of 0 to 10) including potential drain of affiliation with Alleghany Corp Group and weak results on operational trends. The largest net exposure for one risk is excessive at 5.3% of capital. Strong long-term capitalization index (10.0) based on excellent current risk adjusted capital (severe and moderate loss scenarios), despite some fluctuation in capital levels.

Other Rating Factors: Ample reserve history (7.8) that can protect against increases in claims costs. Excellent profitability (7.8) with operating gains in each of the last five years. Excellent liquidity (7.7) with ample operational cash flow and liquid investments.

Principal Business: Other liability (33%), allied lines (27%), fire (17%), medical malpractice (10%), inland marine (8%), products liability (3%), and earthquake (2%).

Principal Investments: Investment grade bonds (97%), misc. investments (5%), and non investment grade bonds (1%).

Investments in Affiliates: None

Group Affiliation: Alleghany Corp Group

Licensed in: All states, the District of Columbia and Puerto Rico

Commenced Business: April 1976

Address: 201 Robert S Kerr Ave Ste 600, Oklahoma City, OK 73102-4267

Phone: (404) 231-2366　**Domicile State:** NH　**NAIC Code:** 33138

Data Date	Rating	RACR #1	RACR #2	Loss Ratio %	Total Assets ($mil)	Capital ($mil)	Net Premium ($mil)	Net Income ($mil)
3-17	C	14.86	9.12	N/A	385.2	232.9	9.7	4.2
3-16	C	15.68	9.69	N/A	381.8	235.3	9.5	5.9
2016	C	14.76	9.12	50.7	380.0	228.8	38.3	14.4
2015	C	14.75	9.18	33.6	387.8	228.7	42.9	19.7
2014	C	13.79	8.66	44.4	388.9	224.4	45.2	17.0
2013	C	12.07	7.60	43.7	397.2	208.1	48.9	16.5
2012	C	8.35	4.56	58.0	370.4	191.6	51.4	11.3

Alleghany Corp Group
Composite Group Rating: B

Largest Group Members	Assets ($mil)	Rating
TRANSATLANTIC REINS CO	14019	B
RSUI INDEMNITY CO	3402	C+
CAPITOL INDEMNITY CORP	520	C
LANDMARK AMERICAN INS CO	380	C
PACIFIC COMPENSATION INS CO	361	C

LAWYERS MUTUAL INS CO　　　　　　　　　　　　　　　　　B　　Good

Major Rating Factors: Fair overall results on stability tests (4.2 on a scale of 0 to 10) including weak results on operational trends. Strong long-term capitalization index (10.0) based on excellent current risk adjusted capital (severe and moderate loss scenarios). Moreover, capital levels have been consistent in recent years.

Other Rating Factors: Ample reserve history (9.4) that helps to protect the company against sharp claims increases. Excellent profitability (8.9) with operating gains in each of the last five years. Excellent liquidity (8.2) with ample operational cash flow and liquid investments.

Principal Business: Other liability (100%).

Principal Investments: Investment grade bonds (82%), misc. investments (15%), cash (2%), and real estate (1%).

Investments in Affiliates: 0%

Group Affiliation: None

Licensed in: CA

Commenced Business: September 1978

Address: 3110 W Empire Ave, Burbank, CA 91504

Phone: (818) 565-5512　**Domicile State:** CA　**NAIC Code:** 36706

Data Date	Rating	RACR #1	RACR #2	Loss Ratio %	Total Assets ($mil)	Capital ($mil)	Net Premium ($mil)	Net Income ($mil)
3-17	B	9.66	6.05	N/A	329.2	229.6	8.7	3.4
3-16	B-	9.25	5.86	N/A	314.8	212.5	9.0	3.1
2016	B	9.73	6.12	50.4	319.6	224.0	35.2	13.4
2015	C+	9.16	5.82	44.8	308.5	208.7	36.4	15.2
2014	C	8.41	5.40	42.9	303.2	196.0	35.9	16.3
2013	C	6.95	4.43	53.6	296.0	183.2	35.7	14.4
2012	C	6.16	3.99	63.7	288.2	164.0	36.1	15.0

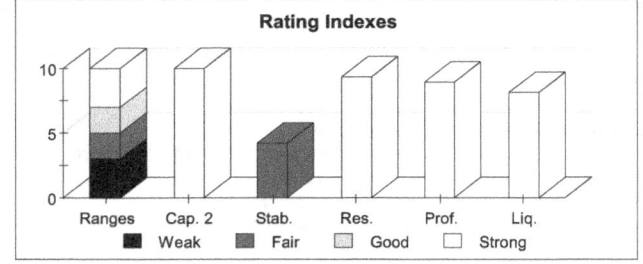

Rating Indexes

LEXINGTON INS CO   C   Fair

Major Rating Factors: Fair reserve development (3.1 on a scale of 0 to 10) as reserves have generally been sufficient to cover claims. In 2016, the two year reserve development was 31% deficient. Fair profitability index (3.5). Fair expense controls. Return on equity has been fair, averaging 9.2% over the past five years.

Other Rating Factors: Weak overall results on stability tests (2.8) including weak results on operational trends and negative cash flow from operations for 2016. The largest net exposure for one risk is excessive at 10.7% of capital. Good liquidity (6.4) with sufficient resources (cash flows and marketable investments) to handle a spike in claims. Strong long-term capitalization index (7.5) based on excellent current risk adjusted capital (severe and moderate loss scenarios), despite some fluctuation in capital levels.

Principal Business: Other liability (27%), fire (25%), allied lines (18%), homeowners multiple peril (8%), inland marine (7%), medical malpractice (5%), and other lines (10%).

Principal Investments: Investment grade bonds (94%) and non investment grade bonds (6%).

Investments in Affiliates: 0%

Group Affiliation: American International Group

Licensed in: All states, the District of Columbia and Puerto Rico

Commenced Business: April 1965

Address: 2711 CENTERVILLE ROAD STE 400, Wilmington, DE 19808

Phone: (617) 330-1100   **Domicile State:** DE   **NAIC Code:** 19437

Data Date	Rating	RACR #1	RACR #2	Loss Ratio %	Total Assets ($mil)	Capital ($mil)	Net Premium ($mil)	Net Income ($mil)
3-17	C	2.29	1.52	N/A	21,929.5	5,943.6	1,107.8	146.2
3-16	C+	2.23	1.51	N/A	25,334.3	6,649.6	1,330.9	245.4
2016	C	1.92	1.29	99.8	25,180.0	5,857.0	4,837.1	246.4
2015	C+	2.22	1.51	88.8	25,504.7	6,593.0	5,564.4	6.0
2014	C+	2.11	1.45	62.3	25,328.9	6,534.1	6,098.6	862.0
2013	C+	2.85	1.92	69.4	22,120.5	7,224.1	3,755.8	1,660.2
2012	C+	2.87	1.94	100.0	24,567.8	7,925.6	3,621.9	409.0

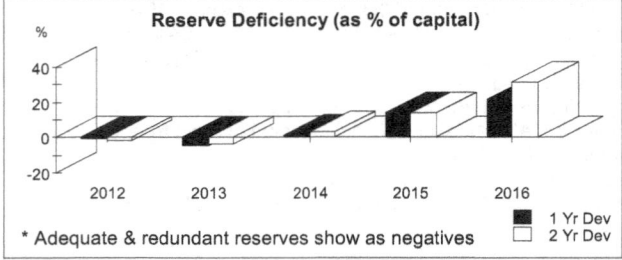

Reserve Deficiency (as % of capital)

* Adequate & redundant reserves show as negatives

■ 1 Yr Dev   □ 2 Yr Dev

LIBERTY INS CORP   C   Fair

Major Rating Factors: Fair profitability index (4.5) with operating losses during 2012. Return on equity has been low, averaging 1.1% over the past five years.

Other Rating Factors: Fair overall results on stability tests (3.8) including weak results on operational trends. Strong long-term capitalization index (10.0) based on excellent current risk adjusted capital (severe and moderate loss scenarios). Moreover, capital levels have been consistent in recent years. Excellent liquidity (7.0) with ample operational cash flow and liquid investments.

Principal Business: Homeowners multiple peril (65%), workers compensation (20%), other liability (9%), auto liability (3%), auto physical damage (1%), inland marine (1%), and products liability (1%).

Principal Investments: Investment grade bonds (92%) and misc. investments (8%).

Investments in Affiliates: None

Group Affiliation: Liberty Mutual Group

Licensed in: All states, the District of Columbia and Puerto Rico

Commenced Business: November 1988

Address: 2815 Forbs Avenue Suite 200, Hoffman Estates, IL 60192

Phone: (617) 357-9500   **Domicile State:** IL   **NAIC Code:** 42404

Data Date	Rating	RACR #1	RACR #2	Loss Ratio %	Total Assets ($mil)	Capital ($mil)	Net Premium ($mil)	Net Income ($mil)
3-17	C	83.28	59.62	N/A	252.7	241.1	0.0	2.1
3-16	C-	128.63	63.54	N/A	246.5	240.6	0.0	2.5
2016	C	132.31	64.30	0.0	242.0	240.8	0.0	1.1
2015	C-	135.45	65.78	0.0	244.8	239.7	0.0	16.6
2014	D	96.71	51.72	0.0	232.0	223.2	0.0	8.3
2013	D	135.89	66.60	0.0	218.6	215.4	-215.2	48.2
2012	D	0.80	0.53	90.3	1,449.7	168.7	522.2	-48.5

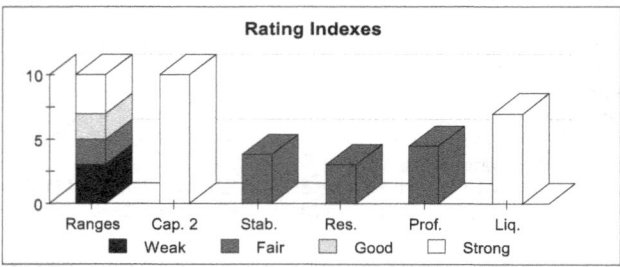

Rating Indexes

Ranges Cap. 2 Stab. Res. Prof. Liq.

■ Weak   ▨ Fair   ▥ Good   □ Strong

LIBERTY MUTUAL FIRE INS CO   B-   Good

Major Rating Factors: Fair reserve development (4.7 on a scale of 0 to 10) as reserves have generally been sufficient to cover claims. Fair overall results on stability tests (3.6) including weak results on operational trends. The largest net exposure for one risk is excessive at 6.0% of capital.

Other Rating Factors: Good overall profitability index (5.4) despite operating losses during 2012 and the first three months of 2017. Return on equity has been low, averaging 4.4% over the past five years. Good liquidity (6.1) with sufficient resources (cash flows and marketable investments) to handle a spike in claims. Strong long-term capitalization index (7.7) based on excellent current risk adjusted capital (severe and moderate loss scenarios). Moreover, capital levels have been consistent in recent years.

Principal Business: Auto liability (28%), homeowners multiple peril (22%), auto physical damage (15%), workers compensation (11%), other liability (9%), fire (6%), and other lines (8%).

Principal Investments: Investment grade bonds (73%), misc. investments (23%), and non investment grade bonds (5%).

Investments in Affiliates: 5%

Group Affiliation: Liberty Mutual Group

Licensed in: All states, the District of Columbia and Puerto Rico

Commenced Business: November 1908

Address: 2000 Westwood Drive, Wausau, WI 54401

Phone: (617) 357-9500   **Domicile State:** WI   **NAIC Code:** 23035

Data Date	Rating	RACR #1	RACR #2	Loss Ratio %	Total Assets ($mil)	Capital ($mil)	Net Premium ($mil)	Net Income ($mil)
3-17	B-	2.16	1.52	N/A	5,597.8	1,479.1	523.5	-10.2
3-16	B-	2.15	1.49	N/A	5,453.9	1,426.3	505.4	22.3
2016	B-	2.19	1.55	69.9	5,650.7	1,474.6	2,119.9	36.2
2015	B-	2.12	1.48	68.4	5,477.8	1,399.0	2,050.6	252.1
2014	C+	1.93	1.34	70.0	5,297.9	1,302.1	2,030.1	132.2
2013	C+	1.75	1.20	73.5	5,561.6	1,216.3	2,163.5	87.5
2012	C	1.37	0.92	90.3	5,235.7	939.1	1,684.2	-130.8

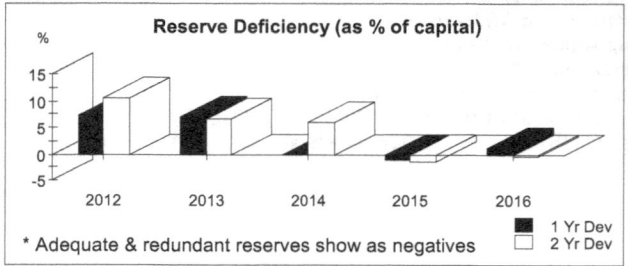

Reserve Deficiency (as % of capital)

* Adequate & redundant reserves show as negatives

■ 1 Yr Dev   □ 2 Yr Dev

LIBERTY MUTUAL INS CO
B | **Good**

Major Rating Factors: History of adequate reserve strength (5.9 on a scale of 0 to 10) as reserves have been consistently at an acceptable level. Good overall profitability index (5.2) despite operating losses during the first three months of 2017. Return on equity has been low, averaging 3.3% over the past five years.
Other Rating Factors: Good liquidity (6.4) with sufficient resources (cash flows and marketable investments) to handle a spike in claims. Fair overall results on stability tests (4.3) including weak results on operational trends. The largest net exposure for one risk is high at 3.3% of capital. Strong long-term capitalization index (7.6) based on excellent current risk adjusted capital (severe and moderate loss scenarios), despite some fluctuation in capital levels.
Principal Business: Surety (29%), other liability (20%), inland marine (14%), auto liability (12%), auto physical damage (11%), homeowners multiple peril (3%), and other lines (12%).
Principal Investments: Misc. investments (62%), investment grade bonds (35%), non investment grade bonds (3%), and real estate (1%).
Investments in Affiliates: 28%
Group Affiliation: Liberty Mutual Group
Licensed in: All states, the District of Columbia and Puerto Rico
Commenced Business: July 1912
Address: 175 Berkeley Street, Boston, MA 02116
Phone: (617) 357-9500 **Domicile State:** MA **NAIC Code:** 23043

Data Date	Rating	RACR #1	RACR #2	Loss Ratio %	Total Assets ($mil)	Capital ($mil)	Net Premium ($mil)	Net Income ($mil)
3-17	B	1.59	1.40	N/A	44,306.8	16,551.8	3,271.8	-193.4
3-16	B	1.60	1.39	N/A	41,882.1	15,884.5	3,158.5	121.7
2016	B	1.60	1.41	69.9	44,001.9	16,528.2	13,249.4	404.3
2015	B	1.60	1.40	68.4	42,343.2	15,815.3	12,816.1	973.0
2014	B	1.73	1.49	70.0	42,655.2	16,569.3	12,688.4	888.4
2013	B	1.63	1.39	73.5	44,475.8	15,126.4	13,889.2	507.4
2012	B	1.73	1.46	90.3	40,205.4	14,510.5	9,635.4	163.6

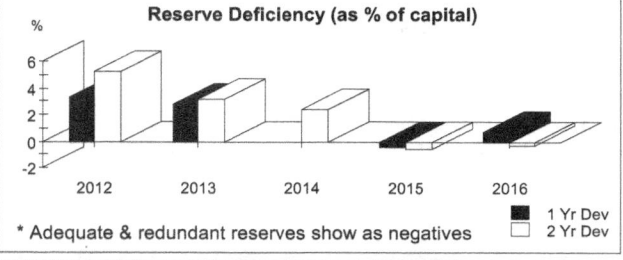

Reserve Deficiency (as % of capital)

* Adequate & redundant reserves show as negatives
■ 1 Yr Dev □ 2 Yr Dev

MAG MUTUAL INS CO
B- | **Good**

Major Rating Factors: Fair overall results on stability tests (4.7 on a scale of 0 to 10) including potential drain of affiliation with MAG Mutual Group and weak results on operational trends. Strong long-term capitalization index (9.2) based on excellent current risk adjusted capital (severe and moderate loss scenarios). Moreover, capital levels have been consistent in recent years.
Other Rating Factors: Ample reserve history (9.4) that helps to protect the company against sharp claims increases. Excellent profitability (8.0) with operating gains in each of the last five years. Excellent liquidity (7.4) with ample operational cash flow and liquid investments.
Principal Business: Medical malpractice (94%), workers compensation (4%), and commercial multiple peril (1%).
Principal Investments: Investment grade bonds (57%), misc. investments (34%), and non investment grade bonds (9%).
Investments in Affiliates: 13%
Group Affiliation: MAG Mutual Group
Licensed in: AL, AZ, AR, CO, FL, GA, IN, KY, LA, MD, MI, MS, MO, NM, NC, OH, SC, TN, VA, WA, WV
Commenced Business: June 1982
Address: 3535 Piedmont Rd NE Bldg 1, Atlanta, GA 30305-1518
Phone: (404) 842-5600 **Domicile State:** GA **NAIC Code:** 42617

Data Date	Rating	RACR #1	RACR #2	Loss Ratio %	Total Assets ($mil)	Capital ($mil)	Net Premium ($mil)	Net Income ($mil)
3-17	B-	3.09	2.38	N/A	1,840.1	927.8	62.5	2.4
3-16	B-	3.20	2.50	N/A	1,719.7	872.8	58.2	-10.2
2016	B-	3.20	2.51	71.9	1,773.9	914.9	243.9	15.9
2015	B-	3.25	2.55	71.3	1,719.2	880.7	200.2	40.8
2014	B-	5.19	3.44	74.4	1,635.6	773.3	194.1	45.2
2013	B-	4.96	3.43	64.5	1,609.9	740.3	197.5	52.0
2012	B-	4.86	3.53	71.6	1,543.7	667.5	197.3	43.7

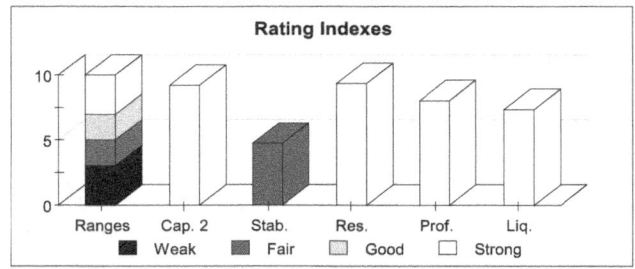

Rating Indexes

Ranges | Cap. 2 | Stab. | Res. | Prof. | Liq.
■ Weak ■ Fair □ Good □ Strong

MAIDEN RE NORTH AMERICA INC
B- | **Good**

Major Rating Factors: Good long-term capitalization index (5.3 on a scale of 0 to 10) based on fair current risk adjusted capital (severe loss scenario), although results have slipped from the good range over the last two years. Fair reserve development (4.3) as reserves have generally been sufficient to cover claims. In 2016, the one year reserve development was 18% deficient.
Other Rating Factors: Fair profitability index (3.9) with operating losses during 2012, 2013 and the first three months of 2017. Average return on equity over the last five years has been poor at -0.5%. Good liquidity (5.6) with sufficient resources (cash flows and marketable investments) to handle a spike in claims. Good overall results on stability tests (5.3) despite negative cash flow from operations for 2016 and fair risk adjusted capital in prior years. The largest net exposure for one risk is acceptable at 2.0% of capital.
Principal Business: (This company is a reinsurer.)
Principal Investments: Investment grade bonds (94%), non investment grade bonds (6%), and cash (3%).
Investments in Affiliates: None
Group Affiliation: Maiden Holdings Ltd
Licensed in: All states except PR
Commenced Business: August 2000
Address: PO Box 275 127 A East High St, Jefferson City, MO 65102-0275
Phone: (856) 359-2400 **Domicile State:** MO **NAIC Code:** 11054

Data Date	Rating	RACR #1	RACR #2	Loss Ratio %	Total Assets ($mil)	Capital ($mil)	Net Premium ($mil)	Net Income ($mil)
3-17	B-	1.14	0.66	N/A	1,411.2	288.8	117.1	-7.9
3-16	B-	1.22	0.70	N/A	1,339.6	281.2	97.3	-17.6
2016	B-	1.19	0.69	79.6	1,302.6	291.1	433.2	-11.8
2015	B-	1.31	0.75	69.9	1,240.0	294.3	416.4	17.4
2014	B-	1.46	0.80	68.9	1,216.1	289.2	438.7	16.6
2013	B-	1.55	0.87	75.6	1,159.6	269.6	391.8	-1.3
2012	B-	1.13	0.68	78.4	1,189.0	267.9	346.2	-19.2

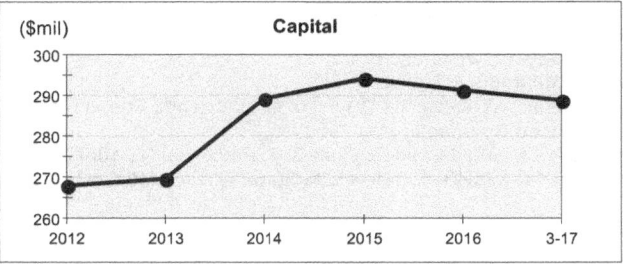

Capital

MARKEL GLOBAL REINS CO *   B+   Good

Major Rating Factors: Good overall results on stability tests (6.5 on a scale of 0 to 10) despite excessive premium growth. The largest net exposure for one risk is conservative at 1.7% of capital. Strong long-term capitalization index (7.6) based on excellent current risk adjusted capital (severe and moderate loss scenarios), despite some fluctuation in capital levels.

Other Rating Factors: Ample reserve history (7.5) that can protect against increases in claims costs. Excellent liquidity (7.0) with ample operational cash flow and liquid investments. Fair profitability index (4.0) with operating losses during the first three months of 2017. Return on equity has been low, averaging 0.9% over the past five years.

Principal Business: (This company is a reinsurer.)

Principal Investments: Misc. investments (54%), investment grade bonds (45%), and cash (1%).

Investments in Affiliates: 15%

Group Affiliation: Markel Corp

Licensed in: All states except PR

Commenced Business: September 1997

Address: 1209 Orange Street, Wilmington, DE 19801

Phone: (908) 630-2700   **Domicile State:** DE   **NAIC Code:** 10829

Data Date	Rating	RACR #1	RACR #2	Loss Ratio %	Total Assets ($mil)	Capital ($mil)	Net Premium ($mil)	Net Income ($mil)
3-17	B+	2.04	1.34	N/A	1,943.5	826.2	147.3	-15.5
3-16	B	2.57	1.71	N/A	1,674.7	734.6	55.4	-16.3
2016	B+	2.16	1.45	68.9	1,692.9	804.1	254.7	4.9
2015	B	2.58	1.72	71.7	1,546.4	727.1	211.7	1.7
2014	B+	3.21	2.22	71.4	1,491.6	749.4	220.7	11.6
2013	B+	3.62	2.60	68.0	1,364.7	715.0	186.9	19.6
2012	B+	5.26	3.44	73.5	1,299.2	671.6	201.7	9.7

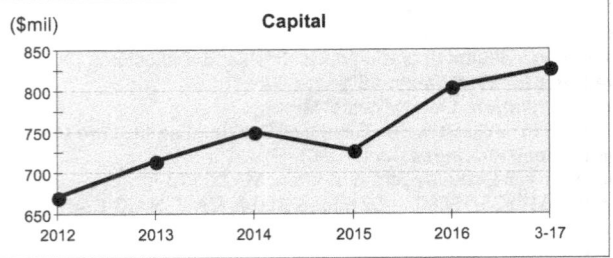

MARKEL INS CO   C   Fair

Major Rating Factors: Fair overall results on stability tests (3.7 on a scale of 0 to 10) including potential drain of affiliation with Markel Corp and weak results on operational trends. The largest net exposure for one risk is high at 3.1% of capital. Good overall long-term capitalization (6.6) based on good current risk adjusted capital (moderate loss scenario). However, capital levels have fluctuated somewhat during past years.

Other Rating Factors: Good overall profitability index (5.1) despite operating losses during 2012. Return on equity has been low, averaging 3.2% over the past five years. Good liquidity (6.7) with sufficient resources (cash flows and marketable investments) to handle a spike in claims. Ample reserve history (9.3) that helps to protect the company against sharp claims increases.

Principal Business: Workers compensation (40%), commercial multiple peril (21%), other liability (17%), inland marine (7%), auto liability (7%), other accident & health (4%), and other lines (5%).

Principal Investments: Investment grade bonds (66%) and misc. investments (34%).

Investments in Affiliates: None

Group Affiliation: Markel Corp

Licensed in: All states except PR

Commenced Business: December 1980

Address: Ten Parkway North, Deerfield, IL 60015

Phone: (800) 431-1270   **Domicile State:** IL   **NAIC Code:** 38970

Data Date	Rating	RACR #1	RACR #2	Loss Ratio %	Total Assets ($mil)	Capital ($mil)	Net Premium ($mil)	Net Income ($mil)
3-17	C	1.82	0.96	N/A	1,643.1	396.8	130.9	10.2
3-16	C	1.80	0.92	N/A	1,507.9	368.2	131.5	8.7
2016	C	1.79	0.95	61.7	1,564.0	378.8	537.3	37.6
2015	C	1.77	0.91	68.2	1,459.2	352.9	534.2	8.8
2014	C	1.85	1.11	65.0	1,506.5	407.2	517.9	5.6
2013	C	1.74	1.07	61.3	1,225.7	347.4	493.9	7.3
2012	C	1.80	1.10	64.6	1,019.5	272.8	416.6	-5.3

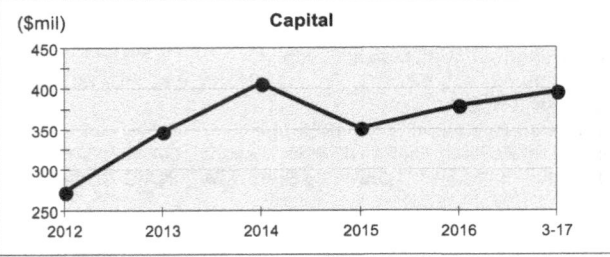

MBIA INS CORP   E+   Very Weak

Major Rating Factors: Poor long-term capitalization index (0.5 on a scale of 0 to 10) based on weak current risk adjusted capital (severe and moderate loss scenarios). A history of deficient reserves (1.0). Underreserving can have an adverse impact on capital and profits. In 2015 and 2014 the one year reserve development was 26% and 38% deficient respectively.

Other Rating Factors: Weak profitability index (0.6) with operating losses during 2012, 2013, 2014 and 2016. Average return on equity over the last five years has been poor at -54.4%. Vulnerable liquidity (0.6) as a spike in claims may stretch capacity. Weak overall results on stability tests (0.4) including weak risk adjusted capital in prior years and negative cash flow from operations for 2016.

Principal Business: Financial guaranty (100%).

Principal Investments: Investment grade bonds (111%), cash (17%), and non investment grade bonds (1%).

Investments in Affiliates: 39%

Group Affiliation: MBIA Inc

Licensed in: All states, the District of Columbia and Puerto Rico

Commenced Business: May 1968

Address: 1 Manhattanville Rd Suite 301, Purchase, NY 10577-2100

Phone: (914) 273-4545   **Domicile State:** NY   **NAIC Code:** 12041

Data Date	Rating	RACR #1	RACR #2	Loss Ratio %	Total Assets ($mil)	Capital ($mil)	Net Premium ($mil)	Net Income ($mil)
3-17	E+	0.43	0.14	N/A	228.8	286.1	14.9	177.9
3-16	D	0.77	0.26	N/A	795.5	571.3	18.9	-55.3
2016	E+	0.56	0.19	357.1	514.9	238.2	52.0	-322.6
2015	D	0.77	0.26	81.8	796.8	609.1	87.0	24.6
2014	D	0.75	0.25	131.4	960.2	541.5	104.6	-35.2
2013	D	0.78	0.26	378.6	1,280.1	403.0	133.5	-494.0
2012	D+	1.20	0.41	338.8	1,012.7	965.1	204.2	-843.4

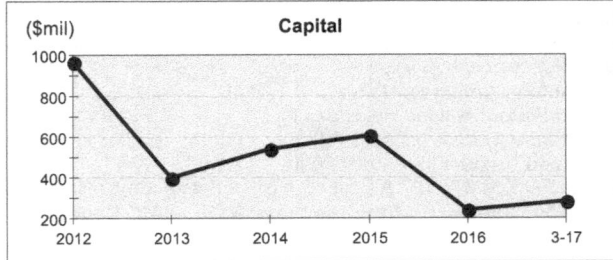

MCIC VERMONT INC RRG   C   Fair

Major Rating Factors: Fair profitability index (4.9 on a scale of 0 to 10) with operating losses during 2012. Fair overall results on stability tests (3.4) including weak results on operational trends and weak risk adjusted capital in prior years.
Other Rating Factors: Poor long-term capitalization index (0.7) based on weak current risk adjusted capital (severe and moderate loss scenarios). A history of deficient reserves (0.5). Underreserving can have an adverse impact on capital and profits. In 2014 and 2015 the two year reserve development was 6273% and 8875% deficient respectively. Good liquidity (6.4) with sufficient resources (cash flows and marketable investments) to handle a spike in claims.
Principal Business: Medical malpractice (96%) and other liability (4%).
Principal Investments: Misc. investments (71%), investment grade bonds (26%), and cash (3%).
Investments in Affiliates: None
Group Affiliation: MCIC Vermont Holdings Inc
Licensed in: CT, DC, FL, MD, MA, NJ, NY, VT
Commenced Business: January 1997
Address: 76 St Paul Street Suite 500, Burlington, VT 05401-4477
Phone: (802) 652-1571   **Domicile State:** VT   **NAIC Code:** 10697

Data Date	Rating	RACR #1	RACR #2	Loss Ratio %	Total Assets ($mil)	Capital ($mil)	Net Premium ($mil)	Net Income ($mil)
3-17	C	0.25	0.22	N/A	2,024.1	581.3	70.8	0.0
3-16	N/A	N/A	N/A	N/A	1,858.0	500.8	58.7	0.0
2016	C	0.23	0.20	97.4	1,650.0	553.5	289.3	19.1
2015	N/A	N/A	N/A	107.2	1,604.3	499.6	230.2	38.3
2014	N/A	N/A	N/A	534.3	1,674.1	576.3	218.5	21.8
2013	E	0.43	0.33	42.7	204.4	10.3	42.2	0.1
2012	E	0.44	0.35	43.9	136.9	11.2	41.1	-0.1

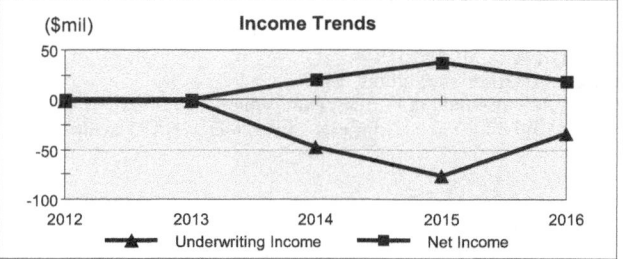
Income Trends

MEDICAL LIABILITY MUTUAL INS CO   D+   Weak

Major Rating Factors: Weak overall results on stability tests (2.4 on a scale of 0 to 10) including weak results on operational trends and negative cash flow from operations for 2016. Strong long-term capitalization index (7.5) based on excellent current risk adjusted capital (severe and moderate loss scenarios). Moreover, capital levels have been consistent in recent years.
Other Rating Factors: Ample reserve history (9.5) that helps to protect the company against sharp claims increases. Excellent profitability (8.2) with operating gains in each of the last five years. Excellent liquidity (7.5) with ample operational cash flow and liquid investments.
Principal Business: Medical malpractice (99%) and other liability (1%).
Principal Investments: Investment grade bonds (79%), misc. investments (11%), and non investment grade bonds (10%).
Investments in Affiliates: 0%
Group Affiliation: None
Licensed in: CT, DE, ME, MA, NJ, NY, PA, RI, VT
Commenced Business: May 1977
Address: Two Park Avenue Room 2500, New York, NY 10016
Phone: (212) 576-9801   **Domicile State:** NY   **NAIC Code:** 34231

Data Date	Rating	RACR #1	RACR #2	Loss Ratio %	Total Assets ($mil)	Capital ($mil)	Net Premium ($mil)	Net Income ($mil)
3-17	D+	2.03	1.69	N/A	5,590.6	2,095.0	96.5	32.4
3-16	D+	1.65	1.38	N/A	5,642.1	1,836.7	100.0	-5.3
2016	D+	2.01	1.69	47.3	5,499.8	2,064.7	393.7	162.7
2015	D+	1.64	1.38	77.6	5,452.2	1,826.9	410.9	114.5
2014	D+	1.52	1.28	78.4	5,881.1	1,783.9	490.3	263.8
2013	D+	1.27	1.08	93.4	5,777.6	1,538.8	533.9	172.2
2012	D+	1.04	0.89	106.5	5,567.8	1,271.0	550.1	94.5

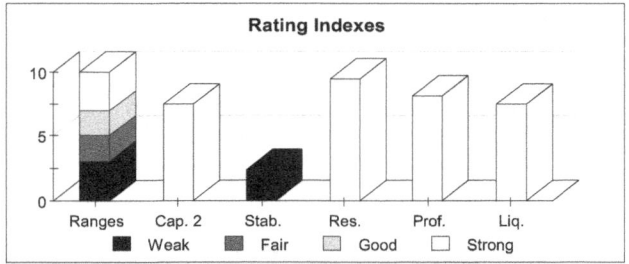
Rating Indexes

MEDICAL MUTUAL INS CO OF NC   B-   Good

Major Rating Factors: Fair overall results on stability tests (4.1 on a scale of 0 to 10) including potential drain of affiliation with Medical Ins Group and weak results on operational trends. Strong long-term capitalization index (9.6) based on excellent current risk adjusted capital (severe and moderate loss scenarios), despite some fluctuation in capital levels.
Other Rating Factors: Ample reserve history (9.3) that helps to protect the company against sharp claims increases. Excellent profitability (7.0) with operating gains in each of the last five years. Excellent liquidity (8.8) with ample operational cash flow and liquid investments.
Principal Business: Medical malpractice (100%).
Principal Investments: Investment grade bonds (60%), misc. investments (32%), cash (7%), and non investment grade bonds (1%).
Investments in Affiliates: 4%
Group Affiliation: Medical Ins Group
Licensed in: AL, AR, DE, FL, GA, KY, LA, MD, MS, NJ, NC, OH, PA, SC, TN, TX, VA, WV
Commenced Business: October 1975
Address: 700 Spring Forest Road Ste 400, Raleigh, NC 27609
Phone: (919) 872-7117   **Domicile State:** NC   **NAIC Code:** 32522

Data Date	Rating	RACR #1	RACR #2	Loss Ratio %	Total Assets ($mil)	Capital ($mil)	Net Premium ($mil)	Net Income ($mil)
3-17	B-	3.80	2.71	N/A	559.8	264.3	21.1	5.4
3-16	B-	4.12	2.95	N/A	525.1	240.6	23.2	4.7
2016	B-	3.77	2.71	59.2	555.0	254.8	114.3	24.1
2015	B-	4.50	3.35	57.2	485.7	229.0	64.0	21.8
2014	B-	4.83	3.72	55.0	475.5	221.3	68.7	30.3
2013	B-	6.28	4.56	54.7	598.0	334.2	75.4	26.1
2012	B-	6.22	4.43	54.4	558.2	295.1	72.2	23.4

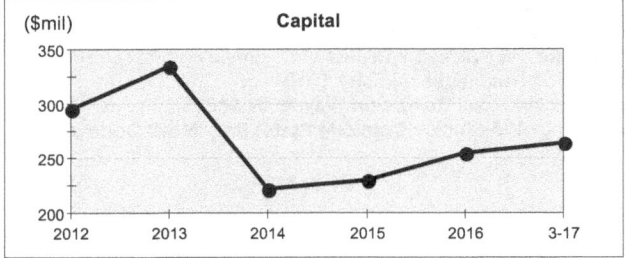
Capital

MEDICAL MUTUAL LIAB INS SOC OF MD — B- — Good

Major Rating Factors: Fair overall results on stability tests (4.3 on a scale of 0 to 10) including potential drain of affiliation with Medical Ins Group Of MD and weak results on operational trends. Fair profitability index (4.9) with operating losses during the first three months of 2017.

Other Rating Factors: Strong long-term capitalization index (10.0) based on excellent current risk adjusted capital (severe and moderate loss scenarios), despite some fluctuation in capital levels. Ample reserve history (9.4) that helps to protect the company against sharp claims increases. Excellent liquidity (8.0) with ample operational cash flow and liquid investments.

Principal Business: Medical malpractice (100%).

Principal Investments: Investment grade bonds (85%) and misc. investments (15%).

Investments in Affiliates: 14%

Group Affiliation: Medical Ins Group Of MD

Licensed in: MD, MI, NC, PA

Commenced Business: June 1975

Address: 225 International Circle, Hunt Valley, MD 21030

Phone: (410) 785-0050 **Domicile State:** MD **NAIC Code:** 32328

Data Date	Rating	RACR #1	RACR #2	Loss Ratio %	Total Assets ($mil)	Capital ($mil)	Net Premium ($mil)	Net Income ($mil)
3-17	B-	3.57	3.22	N/A	851.5	399.1	26.3	-3.4
3-16	B-	3.58	3.20	N/A	846.8	385.1	26.9	-3.1
2016	B-	3.69	3.36	55.2	806.1	401.5	104.2	10.3
2015	B-	3.68	3.33	53.9	800.7	385.8	108.1	15.1
2014	B-	3.50	3.15	52.2	812.1	369.3	114.5	15.8
2013	B-	3.35	2.99	50.3	804.9	339.9	120.7	3.4
2012	B-	3.41	3.02	65.3	785.6	331.8	128.9	3.2

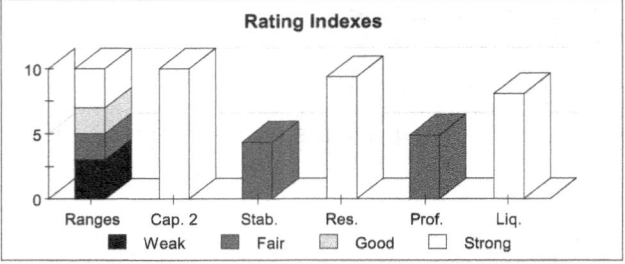

Rating Indexes

MEDICAL PROFESSIONAL MUTUAL INS CO — B- — Good

Major Rating Factors: Fair overall results on stability tests (4.5 on a scale of 0 to 10) including potential drain of affiliation with Medical Professional Mutual. Good overall profitability index (5.8) despite operating losses during the first three months of 2017.

Other Rating Factors: Strong long-term capitalization index (7.9) based on excellent current risk adjusted capital (severe and moderate loss scenarios), despite some fluctuation in capital levels. Ample reserve history (9.4) that helps to protect the company against sharp claims increases. Excellent liquidity (7.1) with ample operational cash flow and liquid investments.

Principal Business: Medical malpractice (99%) and other liability (1%).

Principal Investments: Misc. investments (47%), investment grade bonds (45%), and non investment grade bonds (8%).

Investments in Affiliates: 24%

Group Affiliation: Medical Professional Mutual

Licensed in: CO, FL, MA, NY, NC, TN, VA

Commenced Business: July 1975

Address: One Financial Center, Boston, MA 02111-2621

Phone: (617) 330-1755 **Domicile State:** MA **NAIC Code:** 10206

Data Date	Rating	RACR #1	RACR #2	Loss Ratio %	Total Assets ($mil)	Capital ($mil)	Net Premium ($mil)	Net Income ($mil)
3-17	B-	1.91	1.64	N/A	3,165.3	1,585.5	64.3	-5.6
3-16	B-	2.01	1.77	N/A	2,987.3	1,527.1	63.7	1.1
2016	B-	1.93	1.66	88.7	3,176.7	1,594.4	250.4	29.4
2015	B-	2.03	1.80	60.0	2,997.3	1,538.2	241.3	72.9
2014	B-	1.93	1.72	65.3	3,012.9	1,474.0	263.6	107.8
2013	B-	2.36	2.01	60.1	3,151.4	1,423.4	277.0	135.3
2012	B-	2.23	1.92	72.0	3,103.7	1,282.8	280.3	87.5

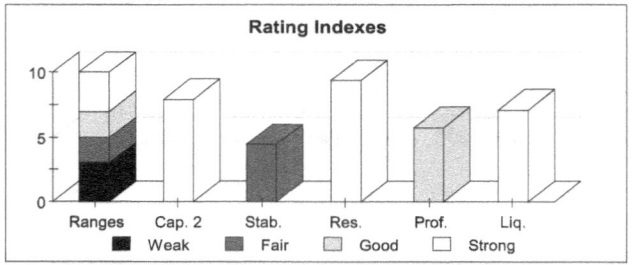

Rating Indexes

MEDICAL PROTECTIVE CO — B — Good

Major Rating Factors: Good overall results on stability tests (5.5 on a scale of 0 to 10) despite negative cash flow from operations for 2016. Affiliation with Berkshire-Hathaway is a strength. Strong long-term capitalization index (9.0) based on excellent current risk adjusted capital (severe and moderate loss scenarios), despite some fluctuation in capital levels.

Other Rating Factors: Ample reserve history (9.7) that helps to protect the company against sharp claims increases. Excellent profitability (8.7) with operating gains in each of the last five years. Superior liquidity (9.9) with ample operational cash flow and liquid investments.

Principal Business: Medical malpractice (99%) and other liability (1%).

Principal Investments: Investment grade bonds (54%), misc. investments (44%), and cash (2%).

Investments in Affiliates: None

Group Affiliation: Berkshire-Hathaway

Licensed in: All states, the District of Columbia and Puerto Rico

Commenced Business: January 1910

Address: 5814 Reed Road, Fort Wayne, IN 46835

Phone: (260) 485-9622 **Domicile State:** IN **NAIC Code:** 11843

Data Date	Rating	RACR #1	RACR #2	Loss Ratio %	Total Assets ($mil)	Capital ($mil)	Net Premium ($mil)	Net Income ($mil)
3-17	B	3.51	2.29	N/A	3,184.7	1,781.8	62.3	27.2
3-16	B	4.35	3.05	N/A	2,762.1	1,553.4	51.8	25.5
2016	B	4.13	2.83	65.0	2,996.1	1,709.5	255.8	109.2
2015	B	4.32	3.00	59.5	2,790.4	1,570.8	226.5	130.1
2014	B	4.98	3.33	114.5	2,699.6	1,589.1	-680.0	140.1
2013	B	2.74	2.15	51.3	3,286.3	1,405.7	366.9	205.3
2012	B	1.79	1.45	71.7	3,013.5	1,075.4	643.8	133.3

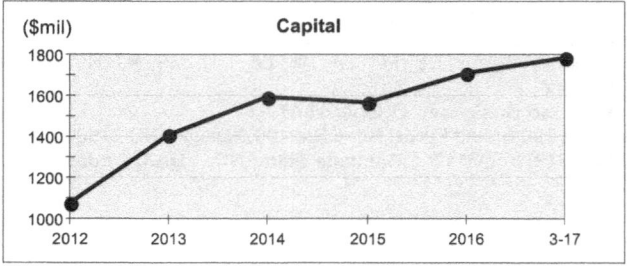

Capital

MEDMARC CASUALTY INS CO   C   Fair

Major Rating Factors: Fair overall results on stability tests (4.1 on a scale of 0 to 10) including potential drain of affiliation with ProAssurance Corp and weak results on operational trends. The largest net exposure for one risk is conservative at 1.5% of capital. History of adequate reserve strength (6.9) as reserves have been consistently at an acceptable level.

Other Rating Factors: Strong long-term capitalization index (8.7) based on excellent current risk adjusted capital (severe and moderate loss scenarios), despite some fluctuation in capital levels. Excellent profitability (7.0) with operating gains in each of the last five years. Excellent liquidity (8.1) with ample operational cash flow and liquid investments.

Principal Business: Other liability (60%) and products liability (40%).

Principal Investments: Misc. investments (58%), investment grade bonds (37%), and cash (5%).

Investments in Affiliates: 26%

Group Affiliation: ProAssurance Corp

Licensed in: All states except PR

Commenced Business: July 1950

Address: 100 East State Street, Montpelier, VT 05602

Phone: (703) 652-1300   **Domicile State:** VT   **NAIC Code:** 22241

Data Date	Rating	RACR #1	RACR #2	Loss Ratio %	Total Assets ($mil)	Capital ($mil)	Net Premium ($mil)	Net Income ($mil)
3-17	C	2.32	2.00	N/A	304.0	188.2	8.4	1.4
3-16	C	2.33	1.96	N/A	268.3	186.6	7.3	0.7
2016	C	2.48	2.14	49.1	290.2	202.0	33.9	10.6
2015	C	2.35	2.00	47.5	260.4	184.1	25.7	8.0
2014	C	2.24	1.89	51.7	251.0	172.6	20.4	14.1
2013	C	2.64	2.18	60.4	275.3	187.2	18.6	11.1
2012	C	2.66	1.94	57.2	289.7	166.2	22.7	6.5

ProAssurance Corp
Composite Group Rating: C

Largest Group Members	Assets ($mil)	Rating
PROASSURANCE INDEMNTIY CO INC	1247	C
PROASSURANCE CASUALTY CO	1093	B-
PODIATRY INS CO OF AM	301	C+
MEDMARC CASUALTY INS CO	290	C
EASTERN ALLIANCE INS CO	279	D

MERCURY CASUALTY CO   B   Good

Major Rating Factors: History of adequate reserve strength (5.7 on a scale of 0 to 10) as reserves have been consistently at an acceptable level. Good liquidity (6.9) with sufficient resources (cash flows and marketable investments) to handle a spike in claims.

Other Rating Factors: Good overall results on stability tests (6.2). Fair profitability index (3.7). Fair expense controls. Return on equity has been fair, averaging 12.7% over the past five years. Strong long-term capitalization index (7.6) based on excellent current risk adjusted capital (severe and moderate loss scenarios), despite some fluctuation in capital levels.

Principal Business: Commercial multiple peril (35%), auto liability (26%), auto physical damage (12%), homeowners multiple peril (12%), fire (7%), other liability (5%), and other lines (3%).

Principal Investments: Investment grade bonds (50%), misc. investments (42%), real estate (5%), and cash (3%).

Investments in Affiliates: 37%

Group Affiliation: Mercury General Group

Licensed in: AZ, CA, FL, GA, IL, MI, NV, NJ, NY, OK, PA, TX, VA, WA

Commenced Business: April 1962

Address: 555 West Imperial Highway, Brea, CA 92821

Phone: (714) 671-6600   **Domicile State:** CA   **NAIC Code:** 11908

Data Date	Rating	RACR #1	RACR #2	Loss Ratio %	Total Assets ($mil)	Capital ($mil)	Net Premium ($mil)	Net Income ($mil)
3-17	B	1.68	1.54	N/A	1,917.0	1,089.1	174.7	4.3
3-16	B	1.44	1.33	N/A	1,965.2	943.4	196.8	-10.1
2016	B	1.44	1.34	83.2	1,889.0	925.8	753.1	93.9
2015	B	1.50	1.40	77.5	1,849.4	977.7	662.7	119.9
2014	B	1.58	1.46	74.7	1,952.2	1,024.6	735.8	133.9
2013	B+	1.73	1.57	69.4	2,041.5	1,151.3	738.1	226.2
2012	B+	1.49	1.32	77.9	2,040.1	1,065.5	889.0	120.6

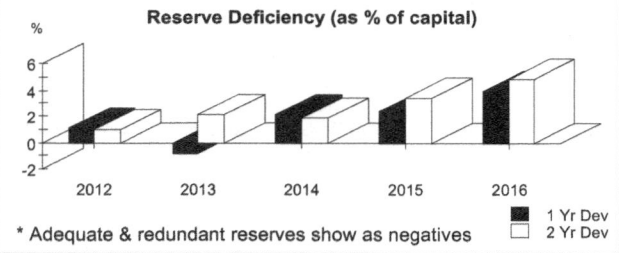

Reserve Deficiency (as % of capital)

* Adequate & redundant reserves show as negatives   ■ 1 Yr Dev □ 2 Yr Dev

MERCURY INS CO *   B+   Good

Major Rating Factors: History of adequate reserve strength (5.8 on a scale of 0 to 10) as reserves have been consistently at an acceptable level. Good overall results on stability tests (5.2) despite weak results on operational trends.

Other Rating Factors: Strong long-term capitalization index (7.7) based on excellent current risk adjusted capital (severe and moderate loss scenarios), despite some fluctuation in capital levels. Fair profitability index (4.9). Fair expense controls. Return on equity has been fair, averaging 9.4% over the past five years. Fair liquidity (3.5) as cash resources may not be adequate to cover a spike in claims.

Principal Business: Auto liability (58%) and auto physical damage (42%).

Principal Investments: Investment grade bonds (96%), misc. investments (4%), and non investment grade bonds (3%).

Investments in Affiliates: None

Group Affiliation: Mercury General Group

Licensed in: CA

Commenced Business: July 1978

Address: 555 West Imperial Highway, Brea, CA 92821

Phone: (714) 671-6600   **Domicile State:** CA   **NAIC Code:** 27553

Data Date	Rating	RACR #1	RACR #2	Loss Ratio %	Total Assets ($mil)	Capital ($mil)	Net Premium ($mil)	Net Income ($mil)
3-17	B+	1.69	1.51	N/A	1,654.2	647.0	395.6	13.9
3-16	B+	1.87	1.67	N/A	1,593.3	662.1	377.2	9.1
2016	B+	1.61	1.49	73.0	1,651.6	631.5	1,560.1	57.7
2015	B+	1.82	1.68	69.6	1,559.3	657.0	1,472.7	90.3
2014	B+	1.84	1.69	70.3	1,561.2	648.7	1,415.9	66.6
2013	A-	1.99	1.81	75.2	1,532.9	652.6	1,350.1	66.5
2012	A-	2.05	1.84	77.1	1,476.2	645.4	1,287.8	24.2

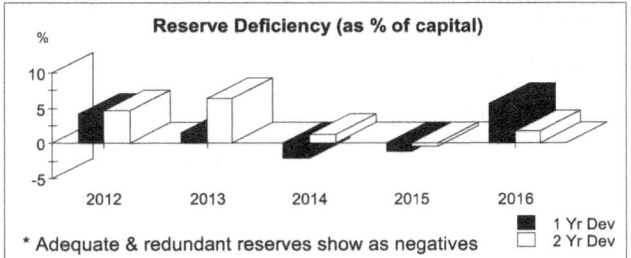

Reserve Deficiency (as % of capital)

* Adequate & redundant reserves show as negatives   ■ 1 Yr Dev □ 2 Yr Dev

MERRIMACK MUTUAL FIRE INS CO

B- **Good**

Major Rating Factors: Fair overall results on stability tests (4.8 on a scale of 0 to 10) including potential drain of affiliation with Andover Group and weak results on operational trends. History of adequate reserve strength (6.5) as reserves have been consistently at an acceptable level.

Other Rating Factors: Strong long-term capitalization index (7.7) based on excellent current risk adjusted capital (severe and moderate loss scenarios), despite some fluctuation in capital levels. Excellent profitability (7.9) with operating gains in each of the last five years. Excellent liquidity (7.2) with ample operational cash flow and liquid investments.

Principal Business: Homeowners multiple peril (54%), commercial multiple peril (14%), fire (13%), allied lines (9%), other liability (8%), and inland marine (2%).

Principal Investments: Misc. investments (75%), investment grade bonds (15%), cash (8%), and real estate (2%).

Investments in Affiliates: 23%

Group Affiliation: Andover Group

Licensed in: CT, IL, ME, MA, NH, NJ, NY, RI

Commenced Business: April 1828

Address: 95 Old River Road, Andover, MA 01810-1078

Phone: (978) 475-3300 **Domicile State:** MA **NAIC Code:** 19798

Data Date	Rating	RACR #1	RACR #2	Loss Ratio %	Total Assets ($mil)	Capital ($mil)	Net Premium ($mil)	Net Income ($mil)
3-17	B-	2.09	1.61	N/A	1,487.7	968.9	63.7	7.0
3-16	B-	2.02	1.57	N/A	1,339.6	858.7	62.0	6.1
2016	B-	2.03	1.57	50.9	1,467.0	933.1	269.6	43.7
2015	B-	2.01	1.58	68.5	1,341.1	844.1	259.3	8.7
2014	B	2.02	1.58	43.4	1,363.6	857.8	261.8	49.7
2013	B	2.02	1.58	43.3	1,251.0	785.2	246.4	60.1
2012	B	1.92	1.49	64.9	1,117.6	643.9	239.8	19.4

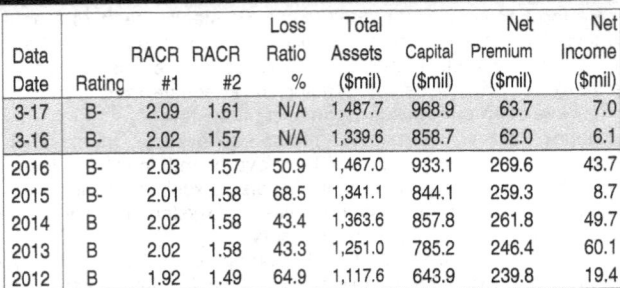

Rating Indexes

METROPOLITAN GROUP PROP & CAS INS CO

B **Good**

Major Rating Factors: Good overall profitability index (6.9 on a scale of 0 to 10). Good expense controls. Return on equity has been low, averaging 4.6% over the past five years.

Other Rating Factors: Fair overall results on stability tests (4.9) including weak results on operational trends and negative cash flow from operations for 2016. Strong long-term capitalization index (10.0) based on excellent current risk adjusted capital (severe and moderate loss scenarios). Moreover, capital levels have been consistent in recent years. Excellent liquidity (7.0) with ample operational cash flow and liquid investments.

Principal Business: (Not applicable due to unusual reinsurance transactions.)

Principal Investments: Investment grade bonds (97%), non investment grade bonds (2%), and cash (1%).

Investments in Affiliates: None

Group Affiliation: MetLife Inc

Licensed in: All states except HI, KY, ME, MN, NM, NC, OR, VA, WY, PR

Commenced Business: December 1977

Address: 700 Quaker Lane, Warwick, RI 02886-6669

Phone: (401) 827-2400 **Domicile State:** RI **NAIC Code:** 34339

Data Date	Rating	RACR #1	RACR #2	Loss Ratio %	Total Assets ($mil)	Capital ($mil)	Net Premium ($mil)	Net Income ($mil)
3-17	B	38.86	31.21	N/A	693.9	417.1	0.0	4.3
3-16	B	31.01	14.27	N/A	683.9	396.3	0.0	17.7
2016	B	38.37	34.53	0.0	695.7	413.7	0.0	28.0
2015	B	27.20	12.43	0.0	651.1	379.2	0.0	3.4
2014	B	22.37	10.27	0.0	611.7	378.3	0.0	25.7
2013	B	16.98	8.60	0.0	582.5	344.9	0.0	13.0
2012	B	14.32	7.10	0.0	555.8	305.5	0.0	14.4

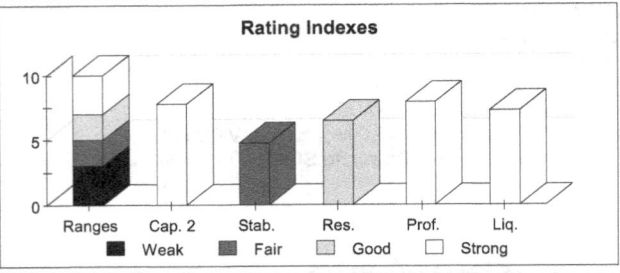

Income Trends

METROPOLITAN P&C INS CO

B- **Good**

Major Rating Factors: Good overall profitability index (6.2 on a scale of 0 to 10). Fair expense controls. Return on equity has been fair, averaging 9.5% over the past five years. Good overall results on stability tests (5.1) despite weak results on operational trends.

Other Rating Factors: Strong long-term capitalization index (7.9) based on excellent current risk adjusted capital (severe and moderate loss scenarios), despite some fluctuation in capital levels. Ample reserve history (8.3) that helps to protect the company against sharp claims increases. Vulnerable liquidity (2.4) as a spike in claims may stretch capacity.

Principal Business: Homeowners multiple peril (46%), auto liability (26%), auto physical damage (21%), other liability (3%), other accident & health (1%), inland marine (1%), and other lines (2%).

Principal Investments: Investment grade bonds (68%), misc. investments (31%), and non investment grade bonds (4%).

Investments in Affiliates: 24%

Group Affiliation: MetLife Inc

Licensed in: All states except AK, CA, PR

Commenced Business: December 1972

Address: 700 Quaker Lane, Warwick, RI 02886-6669

Phone: (401) 827-2400 **Domicile State:** RI **NAIC Code:** 26298

Data Date	Rating	RACR #1	RACR #2	Loss Ratio %	Total Assets ($mil)	Capital ($mil)	Net Premium ($mil)	Net Income ($mil)
3-17	B-	2.01	1.63	N/A	5,686.1	2,307.5	876.0	30.4
3-16	B-	2.13	1.70	N/A	5,673.9	2,372.7	871.6	30.0
2016	B-	1.97	1.60	74.0	5,630.7	2,271.1	3,558.3	131.3
2015	B-	2.10	1.69	70.2	5,599.1	2,335.5	3,524.3	191.6
2014	B	2.16	1.73	67.3	5,645.6	2,388.0	3,465.7	253.5
2013	B	2.07	1.65	68.8	5,499.7	2,224.9	3,372.1	265.8
2012	B	1.95	1.54	71.7	5,146.4	1,987.3	3,173.9	235.2

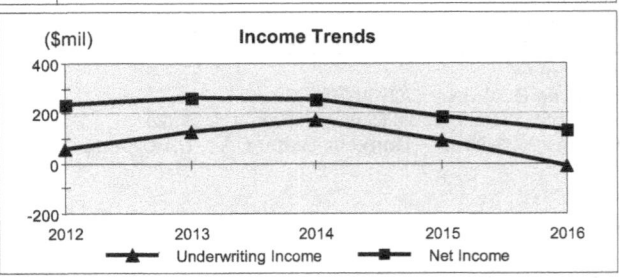

Income Trends

MHA INS CO   C   Fair

Major Rating Factors: Fair overall results on stability tests (4.3 on a scale of 0 to 10) including weak results on operational trends. Good overall profitability index (6.6) despite modest operating losses during the first three months of 2017. Return on equity has been low, averaging 2.8% over the past five years.

Other Rating Factors: Strong long-term capitalization index (8.8) based on excellent current risk adjusted capital (severe and moderate loss scenarios), despite some fluctuation in capital levels. Ample reserve history (8.4) that helps to protect the company against sharp claims increases. Excellent liquidity (7.1) with ample operational cash flow and liquid investments.

Principal Business: Medical malpractice (84%), workers compensation (11%), and other liability (5%).

Principal Investments: Investment grade bonds (93%), cash (4%), misc. investments (2%), and non investment grade bonds (1%).

Investments in Affiliates: None

Group Affiliation: Medical Professional Mutual

Licensed in: IL, IN, IA, KS, KY, MI, MN, MO, NE, ND, OH, OK, SD, WA, WI

Commenced Business: May 1976

Address: 3100 West Rd Bldg 1 Suite 200, East Lansing, MI 48823

Phone: (517) 703-8500   **Domicile State:** MI   **NAIC Code:** 33111

Data Date	Rating	RACR #1	RACR #2	Loss Ratio %	Total Assets ($mil)	Capital ($mil)	Net Premium ($mil)	Net Income ($mil)
3-17	C	2.74	2.34	N/A	600.1	310.9	16.9	-0.7
3-16	C	4.89	3.68	N/A	547.9	271.0	16.9	1.1
2016	C	2.86	2.44	68.5	582.7	313.5	65.9	13.9
2015	C	5.03	3.80	79.2	583.8	299.6	72.7	7.8
2014	C	5.01	3.61	79.1	539.6	289.0	72.7	8.9
2013	B	6.36	4.80	84.5	528.8	277.8	68.2	8.3
2012	B	6.63	5.19	91.4	482.7	269.1	61.9	5.2

Medical Professional Mutual
Composite Group Rating: C+

Largest Group Members	Assets ($mil)	Rating
MEDICAL PROFESSIONAL MUTUAL INS CO	3177	B-
MHA INS CO	583	C
PREFERRED PROFESSIONAL INS CO	326	B
PROSELECT INS CO	83	C
COVERYS SPECIALTY INS CO	59	B

MID-CENTURY INS CO   B   Good

Major Rating Factors: History of adequate reserve strength (6.0 on a scale of 0 to 10) as reserves have been consistently at an acceptable level. Good overall profitability index (6.2). Fair expense controls. Return on equity has been low, averaging 4.5% over the past five years.

Other Rating Factors: Fair overall results on stability tests (4.9) including potential drain of affiliation with Farmers Insurance Group of Companies, weak results on operational trends and negative cash flow from operations for 2016. Fair liquidity (4.5) as cash resources may not be adequate to cover a spike in claims. Strong long-term capitalization index (7.6) based on excellent current risk adjusted capital (severe and moderate loss scenarios). Moreover, capital levels have been consistent in recent years.

Principal Business: Auto liability (40%), auto physical damage (24%), homeowners multiple peril (18%), commercial multiple peril (11%), and workers compensation (7%).

Principal Investments: Investment grade bonds (85%), misc. investments (10%), real estate (3%), and non investment grade bonds (2%).

Investments in Affiliates: 8%

Group Affiliation: Farmers Insurance Group of Companies

Licensed in: All states except AK, ME, PR

Commenced Business: February 1953

Address: 6301 OWENSMOUTH AVE, Woodland Hills, CA 91367

Phone: (323) 932-3200   **Domicile State:** CA   **NAIC Code:** 21687

Data Date	Rating	RACR #1	RACR #2	Loss Ratio %	Total Assets ($mil)	Capital ($mil)	Net Premium ($mil)	Net Income ($mil)
3-17	B	1.95	1.44	N/A	4,011.1	1,057.9	575.3	1.2
3-16	B-	1.87	1.38	N/A	3,944.6	1,023.0	597.9	0.6
2016	B	1.93	1.42	71.0	3,980.6	1,052.8	2,361.9	28.4
2015	C+	1.88	1.38	68.3	3,904.9	1,023.6	2,388.9	45.1
2014	C	1.86	1.40	65.0	3,765.9	986.4	2,250.0	58.9
2013	C	1.82	1.38	67.2	3,714.7	921.3	2,181.9	56.0
2012	C	1.70	1.28	70.9	3,657.5	854.4	2,216.8	37.2

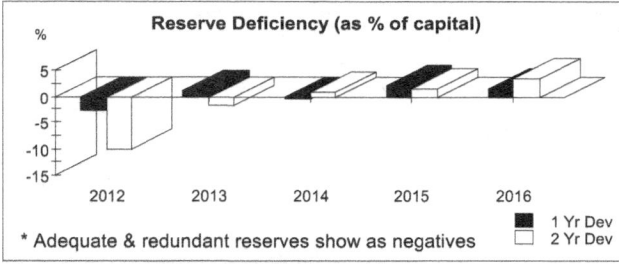

Reserve Deficiency (as % of capital)

* Adequate & redundant reserves show as negatives
   ■ 1 Yr Dev   □ 2 Yr Dev

MIDDLESEX INS CO   B   Good

Major Rating Factors: Good overall profitability index (5.7 on a scale of 0 to 10). Fair expense controls. Return on equity has been fair, averaging 5.3% over the past five years. Good liquidity (6.8) with sufficient resources (cash flows and marketable investments) to handle a spike in claims.

Other Rating Factors: Fair overall results on stability tests (4.8) including weak results on operational trends. The largest net exposure for one risk is conservative at 1.2% of capital. Strong long-term capitalization index (9.0) based on excellent current risk adjusted capital (severe and moderate loss scenarios), despite some fluctuation in capital levels. Ample reserve history (8.1) that helps to protect the company against sharp claims increases.

Principal Business: Workers compensation (54%), auto liability (33%), allied lines (4%), auto physical damage (3%), other liability (2%), fire (2%), and products liability (1%).

Principal Investments: Investment grade bonds (90%), misc. investments (9%), and non investment grade bonds (1%).

Investments in Affiliates: 4%

Group Affiliation: Sentry Ins Group

Licensed in: All states except PR

Commenced Business: March 1826

Address: 1800 NORTH POINT DRIVE, Stevens Point, WI 54481

Phone: (715) 346-6000   **Domicile State:** WI   **NAIC Code:** 23434

Data Date	Rating	RACR #1	RACR #2	Loss Ratio %	Total Assets ($mil)	Capital ($mil)	Net Premium ($mil)	Net Income ($mil)
3-17	B	3.50	2.30	N/A	725.1	249.7	50.0	2.1
3-16	B	3.71	2.44	N/A	707.9	251.4	47.6	2.0
2016	B	3.54	2.36	73.9	717.7	246.8	201.2	12.2
2015	B	3.79	2.52	72.7	695.2	249.9	187.7	15.8
2014	B	4.08	2.86	74.9	673.1	251.1	181.4	16.5
2013	B	3.92	2.77	76.3	653.2	242.8	181.8	11.8
2012	B	4.00	2.81	77.3	628.2	237.4	172.7	10.3

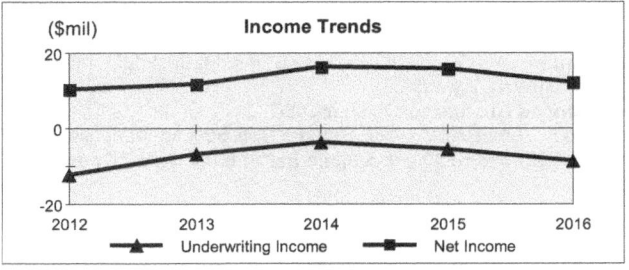

Income Trends

—▲— Underwriting Income   —■— Net Income

MISSISSIPPI FARM BUREAU CAS INS CO

B-   **Good**

Major Rating Factors: Fair overall results on stability tests (4.5 on a scale of 0 to 10) including potential drain of affiliation with Southern Farm Bureau Casualty and weak results on operational trends. Good liquidity (6.8) with sufficient resources (cash flows and marketable investments) to handle a spike in claims.

Other Rating Factors: Strong long-term capitalization index (10.0) based on excellent current risk adjusted capital (severe and moderate loss scenarios). Moreover, capital levels have been consistent in recent years. Ample reserve history (7.7) that can protect against increases in claims costs. Excellent profitability (8.9) with operating gains in each of the last five years.

Principal Business: Homeowners multiple peril (38%), auto liability (27%), auto physical damage (22%), allied lines (4%), fire (3%), inland marine (2%), and other lines (4%).

Principal Investments: Investment grade bonds (94%), cash (4%), and misc. investments (2%).

Investments in Affiliates: None
Group Affiliation: Southern Farm Bureau Casualty
Licensed in: FL, LA, MS, SC, TX
Commenced Business: September 1986
Address: 6311 Ridgewood Road, Jackson, MS 39211
Phone: (601) 957-3200   **Domicile State:** MS   **NAIC Code:** 27669

Data Date	Rating	RACR #1	RACR #2	Loss Ratio %	Total Assets ($mil)	Capital ($mil)	Net Premium ($mil)	Net Income ($mil)
3-17	B-	6.20	5.65	N/A	435.6	279.8	42.4	4.2
3-16	B-	5.22	4.69	N/A	424.0	248.0	43.5	2.8
2016	B-	6.15	5.18	60.5	426.2	275.8	171.4	30.6
2015	B-	5.45	4.52	59.4	417.6	255.4	175.3	31.6
2014	B-	4.93	4.16	72.9	375.4	228.5	170.2	15.3
2013	B	4.81	3.70	70.4	351.8	212.0	159.2	15.7
2012	B	4.69	3.56	69.8	331.3	197.8	151.3	14.6

Southern Farm Bureau Casualty
Composite Group Rating: B-
Largest Group Members

	Assets ($mil)	Rating
SOUTHERN FARM BUREAU CAS INS CO	2162	B-
FLORIDA FARM BU CASUALTY INS CO	557	B-
MISSISSIPPI FARM BUREAU CAS INS CO	426	B-
SOUTHERN FARM BUREAU PROPERTY	56	U
LOUISIANA FARM BUREAU CAS INS CO	12	B

MITSUI SUMITOMO INS CO OF AMER *

B+   **Good**

Major Rating Factors: Good overall profitability index (6.9 on a scale of 0 to 10). Fair expense controls. Return on equity has been fair, averaging 5.8% over the past five years. Good liquidity (6.9) with sufficient resources (cash flows and marketable investments) to handle a spike in claims.

Other Rating Factors: Good overall results on stability tests (5.1) despite weak results on operational trends. Strong long-term capitalization index (9.1) based on excellent current risk adjusted capital (severe and moderate loss scenarios), despite some fluctuation in capital levels. Ample reserve history (9.3) that helps to protect the company against sharp claims increases.

Principal Business: Workers compensation (29%), commercial multiple peril (24%), other liability (10%), allied lines (10%), ocean marine (7%), auto liability (6%), and other lines (14%).

Principal Investments: Investment grade bonds (76%), misc. investments (16%), cash (5%), and real estate (3%).

Investments in Affiliates: None
Group Affiliation: MS & AD Ins Group Holdings Inc
Licensed in: All states, the District of Columbia and Puerto Rico
Commenced Business: January 1971
Address: 560 Lexington Avenue 20th Floo, New York, NY 10022-6828
Phone: (908) 604-2900   **Domicile State:** NY   **NAIC Code:** 20362

Data Date	Rating	RACR #1	RACR #2	Loss Ratio %	Total Assets ($mil)	Capital ($mil)	Net Premium ($mil)	Net Income ($mil)
3-17	B+	3.71	2.31	N/A	958.1	340.0	48.6	0.6
3-16	B+	3.91	2.46	N/A	903.6	323.3	47.0	0.0
2016	B+	3.94	2.47	66.5	929.6	348.2	199.1	25.5
2015	B+	4.18	2.65	71.2	904.3	335.3	174.4	21.3
2014	B+	3.99	2.58	71.3	900.6	332.3	191.9	20.3
2013	B+	4.02	2.65	73.5	845.2	319.6	182.7	18.5
2012	B+	4.28	2.60	77.9	789.8	298.2	156.6	13.4

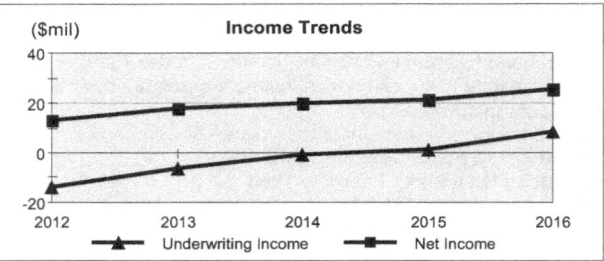

MMIC INS INC

B   **Good**

Major Rating Factors: Fair overall results on stability tests (4.7 on a scale of 0 to 10) including weak results on operational trends. The largest net exposure for one risk is conservative at 1.2% of capital. Strong long-term capitalization index (7.7) based on excellent current risk adjusted capital (severe and moderate loss scenarios), despite some fluctuation in capital levels.

Other Rating Factors: Ample reserve history (9.4) that helps to protect the company against sharp claims increases. Excellent profitability (8.3) with operating gains in each of the last five years. Excellent liquidity (7.1) with ample operational cash flow and liquid investments.

Principal Business: Medical malpractice (95%) and other liability (5%).

Principal Investments: Investment grade bonds (57%), misc. investments (42%), and non investment grade bonds (1%).

Investments in Affiliates: 22%
Group Affiliation: Constellation Inc
Licensed in: AR, CO, ID, IL, IN, IA, KS, KY, MI, MN, MO, MT, NE, ND, OH, OR, SD, TN, UT, WA, WI, WY
Commenced Business: October 1980
Address: 7701 FRANCE AVE SOUTH STE 500, Minneapolis, MN 55435-5288
Phone: (952) 838-6700   **Domicile State:** MN   **NAIC Code:** 16942

Data Date	Rating	RACR #1	RACR #2	Loss Ratio %	Total Assets ($mil)	Capital ($mil)	Net Premium ($mil)	Net Income ($mil)
3-17	B	1.79	1.51	N/A	723.2	320.9	25.2	5.2
3-16	B	1.70	1.46	N/A	742.6	320.5	25.5	1.0
2016	B	1.91	1.62	75.2	709.2	339.5	105.4	27.3
2015	B	1.76	1.52	77.4	718.1	327.1	108.7	36.9
2014	B	1.79	1.53	68.8	706.5	310.2	106.5	33.1
2013	A-	1.66	1.40	72.9	708.2	273.6	110.4	14.4
2012	A-	3.78	2.64	72.0	554.2	257.0	115.9	27.0

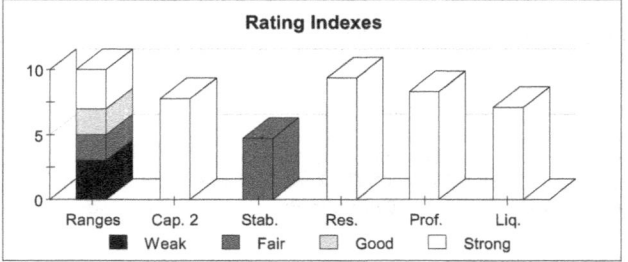

MO EMPLOYERS MUTUAL INS CO   B   Good

Major Rating Factors: Good overall profitability index (6.4 on a scale of 0 to 10) despite operating losses during 2012. Good liquidity (6.7) with sufficient resources (cash flows and marketable investments) to handle a spike in claims.
Other Rating Factors: Good overall results on stability tests (6.0). Strong long-term capitalization index (8.1) based on excellent current risk adjusted capital (severe and moderate loss scenarios). Moreover, capital levels have been consistent in recent years. Ample reserve history (9.2) that helps to protect the company against sharp claims increases.
Principal Business: Workers compensation (100%).
Principal Investments: Investment grade bonds (79%), misc. investments (16%), non investment grade bonds (2%), real estate (2%), and cash (1%).
Investments in Affiliates: 0%
Group Affiliation: Missouri Employers Mutual
Licensed in: MO
Commenced Business: March 1995
Address: 101 North Keene St, Columbia, MO 65201
Phone: (573) 499-9714   **Domicile State:** MO   **NAIC Code:** 10191

Data Date	Rating	RACR #1	RACR #2	Loss Ratio %	Total Assets ($mil)	Capital ($mil)	Net Premium ($mil)	Net Income ($mil)
3-17	B	2.17	1.68	N/A	683.3	258.3	54.2	4.7
3-16	B-	2.15	1.64	N/A	627.4	247.7	48.7	8.3
2016	B	2.25	1.74	68.9	667.1	255.2	219.9	15.4
2015	C+	2.12	1.62	62.1	614.5	237.8	202.6	30.6
2014	C	2.10	1.61	72.3	563.2	211.0	189.5	14.9
2013	C	2.01	1.51	72.3	508.8	194.4	166.1	5.9
2012	C	2.32	1.76	83.7	446.1	172.6	137.2	-1.9

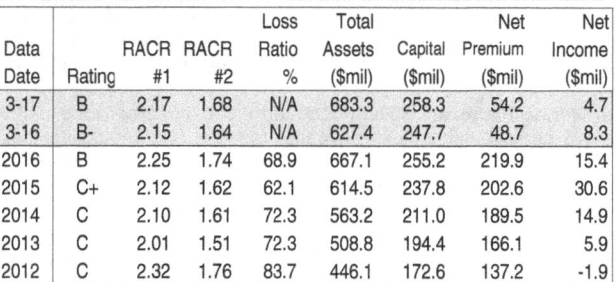

MORTGAGE GUARANTY INS CORP   D+   Weak

Major Rating Factors: Weak profitability index (2.9 on a scale of 0 to 10) with operating losses during 2012, 2013, 2014 and 2015. Average return on equity over the last five years has been poor at -22.4%. Weak overall results on stability tests (2.4) including weak results on operational trends.
Other Rating Factors: Fair reserve development (3.5) as the level of reserves has at times been insufficient to cover claims. In 2012 and 2013 the two year reserve development was 29% and 53% deficient respectively. Good long-term capitalization (6.9) based on good current risk adjusted capital (moderate loss scenario) reflecting improvement over results in 2016. Good liquidity (6.2) with sufficient resources (cash flows and marketable investments) to handle a spike in claims.
Principal Business: Mortgage guaranty (100%).
Principal Investments: Investment grade bonds (90%), misc. investments (6%), and non investment grade bonds (4%).
Investments in Affiliates: 7%
Group Affiliation: MGIC Investment Corp
Licensed in: All states, the District of Columbia and Puerto Rico
Commenced Business: March 1979
Address: 250 EAST KILBOURN AVENUE, Milwaukee, WI 53202
Phone: (800) 558-9900   **Domicile State:** WI   **NAIC Code:** 29858

Data Date	Rating	RACR #1	RACR #2	Loss Ratio %	Total Assets ($mil)	Capital ($mil)	Net Premium ($mil)	Net Income ($mil)
3-17	D+	1.16	1.01	N/A	4,529.7	1,520.5	199.8	16.2
3-16	D+	1.00	0.86	N/A	4,321.3	1,431.9	192.4	-8.5
2016	D+	1.14	0.99	26.0	4,475.7	1,504.7	844.0	68.3
2015	D+	1.08	0.92	36.8	4,274.8	1,573.9	905.5	-77.9
2014	D+	1.04	0.87	59.2	4,162.5	1,517.7	758.1	-7.8
2013	D+	0.99	0.79	91.1	4,406.2	1,520.6	793.5	-7.0
2012	D+	0.34	0.27	202.5	4,355.0	689.1	904.2	-808.5

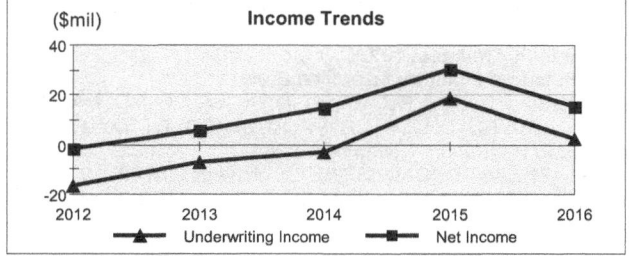

MOTORISTS COMMERCIAL MUTUAL INS CO *   A-   Excellent

Major Rating Factors: Strong long-term capitalization index (9.2 on a scale of 0 to 10) based on excellent current risk adjusted capital (severe and moderate loss scenarios), despite some fluctuation in capital levels. Ample reserve history (7.8) that can protect against increases in claims costs.
Other Rating Factors: Good overall results on stability tests (6.9). Affiliation with Motorists Insurance Group is a strength. Good overall profitability index (5.2) despite operating losses during the first three months of 2017. Good liquidity (6.5) with sufficient resources (cash flows and marketable investments) to handle a spike in claims.
Principal Business: Auto liability (33%), commercial multiple peril (19%), other liability (16%), auto physical damage (15%), inland marine (8%), workers compensation (3%), and other lines (6%).
Principal Investments: Investment grade bonds (65%), misc. investments (33%), and real estate (2%).
Investments in Affiliates: 7%
Group Affiliation: Motorists Insurance Group
Licensed in: All states except AL, AK, AR, FL, HI, LA, MS, MT, PR
Commenced Business: January 1900
Address: 471 EAST BROAD STREET, Columbus, OH 43215
Phone: (614) 225-8211   **Domicile State:** OH   **NAIC Code:** 13331

Data Date	Rating	RACR #1	RACR #2	Loss Ratio %	Total Assets ($mil)	Capital ($mil)	Net Premium ($mil)	Net Income ($mil)
3-17	A-	3.35	2.41	N/A	358.9	155.6	32.2	-1.4
3-16	B	3.29	2.40	N/A	352.0	151.8	32.4	1.9
2016	B+	3.48	2.57	64.1	354.7	156.7	132.2	4.6
2015	B	3.33	2.46	64.5	347.6	150.1	132.7	3.3
2014	B	3.27	2.38	64.0	342.9	146.2	136.9	8.3
2013	B	3.15	2.27	66.8	336.9	140.9	126.0	9.0
2012	B	2.93	2.13	70.9	322.8	128.6	120.2	3.6

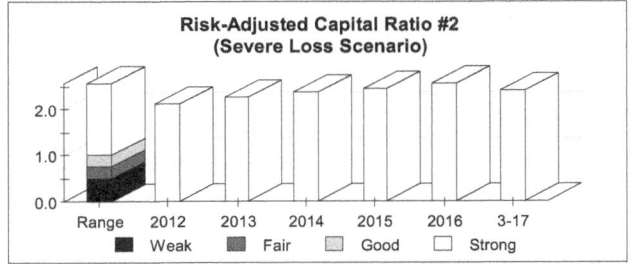

MOTORISTS MUTUAL INS CO * B+ Good

Major Rating Factors: Good liquidity (6.4 on a scale of 0 to 10) with sufficient resources (cash flows and marketable investments) to handle a spike in claims. Good overall results on stability tests (5.1) despite weak results on operational trends.

Other Rating Factors: Strong long-term capitalization index (8.8) based on excellent current risk adjusted capital (severe and moderate loss scenarios), despite some fluctuation in capital levels. Ample reserve history (7.8) that can protect against increases in claims costs. Fair profitability index (4.3) with operating losses during the first three months of 2017.

Principal Business: Auto liability (28%), auto physical damage (17%), other liability (16%), homeowners multiple peril (15%), commercial multiple peril (12%), workers compensation (5%), and other lines (7%).

Principal Investments: Investment grade bonds (64%), misc. investments (34%), and real estate (3%).

Investments in Affiliates: 10%

Group Affiliation: Motorists Insurance Group

Licensed in: AL, CA, CT, DE, GA, IL, IN, IA, KY, ME, MD, MA, MI, MO, MT, NE, NH, NJ, NY, NC, ND, OH, OK, OR, PA, RI, SC, SD, TN, TX, UT, VT, VA, WV, WI

Commenced Business: November 1928

Address: 471 EAST BROAD STREET, Columbus, OH 43215

Phone: (614) 225-8211 **Domicile State:** OH **NAIC Code:** 14621

Data Date	Rating	RACR #1	RACR #2	Loss Ratio %	Total Assets ($mil)	Capital ($mil)	Net Premium ($mil)	Net Income ($mil)
3-17	B+	2.90	2.18	N/A	1,368.4	537.2	119.2	-1.6
3-16	B+	2.95	2.21	N/A	1,360.7	556.7	119.9	6.1
2016	B+	2.96	2.24	64.1	1,359.7	544.3	489.3	19.7
2015	B+	2.96	2.24	64.5	1,387.4	553.9	491.5	7.8
2014	B+	3.24	2.37	64.0	1,373.9	557.4	500.9	40.4
2013	A-	3.53	2.48	66.8	1,335.8	568.8	480.0	37.9
2012	B+	3.06	2.17	70.9	1,272.1	480.6	458.1	7.3

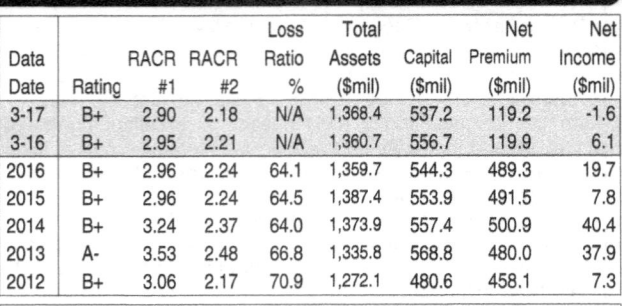

Liquidity Index

MOTORS INS CORP D Weak

Major Rating Factors: Weak overall results on stability tests (0.9 on a scale of 0 to 10) including weak results on operational trends and negative cash flow from operations for 2016. The largest net exposure for one risk is excessive at 22.6% of capital. Strengths include potentially strong support from affiliation with Ally Financial Inc. Fair profitability index (3.0). Weak expense controls. Return on equity has been fair, averaging 9.6% over the past five years.

Other Rating Factors: Strong long-term capitalization index (10.0) based on excellent current risk adjusted capital (severe and moderate loss scenarios), despite some fluctuation in capital levels. Ample reserve history (7.7) that can protect against increases in claims costs. Excellent liquidity (7.1) with ample operational cash flow and liquid investments.

Principal Business: Auto physical damage (63%).

Principal Investments: Investment grade bonds (76%), misc. investments (17%), and cash (7%).

Investments in Affiliates: 4%

Group Affiliation: Ally Financial Inc

Licensed in: All states except PR

Commenced Business: November 1939

Address: 500 WOODWARD AVE 14TH FLOOR, Detroit, MI 48226

Phone: (313) 656-5437 **Domicile State:** MI **NAIC Code:** 22012

Data Date	Rating	RACR #1	RACR #2	Loss Ratio %	Total Assets ($mil)	Capital ($mil)	Net Premium ($mil)	Net Income ($mil)
3-17	D	5.54	3.79	N/A	2,053.7	759.5	115.7	12.6
3-16	D	4.42	2.98	N/A	2,104.3	775.5	105.6	23.3
2016	D	5.04	3.45	71.5	2,038.0	745.5	388.3	50.4
2015	D	4.49	3.07	54.7	2,077.4	746.8	420.5	115.1
2014	C	5.19	3.53	72.1	2,458.7	1,059.9	475.5	84.4
2013	C	4.35	2.71	66.9	2,605.0	1,095.6	462.9	117.7
2012	C	2.49	1.63	73.2	2,770.1	1,183.2	479.8	93.0

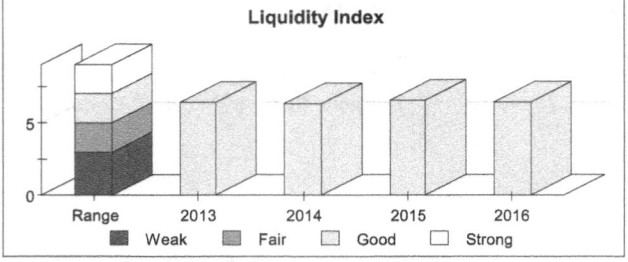

Rating Indexes

MOUNT VERNON FIRE INS CO C Fair

Major Rating Factors: Fair overall results on stability tests (4.3 on a scale of 0 to 10) including weak results on operational trends. Strong long-term capitalization index (7.8) based on excellent current risk adjusted capital (severe and moderate loss scenarios). Moreover, capital levels have been consistent in recent years.

Other Rating Factors: Ample reserve history (8.6) that helps to protect the company against sharp claims increases. Excellent profitability (8.2) with operating gains in each of the last five years. Superior liquidity (9.1) with ample operational cash flow and liquid investments.

Principal Business: Other liability (80%), fire (17%), products liability (1%), inland marine (1%), and homeowners multiple peril (1%).

Principal Investments: Misc. investments (74%), investment grade bonds (25%), and cash (1%).

Investments in Affiliates: 21%

Group Affiliation: Berkshire-Hathaway

Licensed in: All states except PR

Commenced Business: December 1958

Address: 1190 Devon Park Drive, Wayne, PA 19087

Phone: (800) 523-5545 **Domicile State:** PA **NAIC Code:** 26522

Data Date	Rating	RACR #1	RACR #2	Loss Ratio %	Total Assets ($mil)	Capital ($mil)	Net Premium ($mil)	Net Income ($mil)
3-17	C	2.11	1.61	N/A	668.0	465.5	16.8	3.4
3-16	C	2.09	1.67	N/A	548.7	382.5	16.6	2.7
2016	C	2.09	1.61	43.2	643.0	445.4	68.1	18.7
2015	C	2.09	1.64	37.8	580.2	399.7	67.7	17.0
2014	C	1.97	1.53	33.8	586.9	395.2	67.3	18.0
2013	B-	1.84	1.48	33.5	526.4	348.2	63.0	24.1
2012	B-	1.80	1.41	43.7	433.8	273.7	59.4	15.6

Berkshire-Hathaway Composite Group Rating: B Largest Group Members	Assets ($mil)	Rating
NATIONAL INDEMNITY CO	178623	B
GOVERNMENT EMPLOYEES INS CO	27198	B
COLUMBIA INS CO	20707	U
BERKSHIRE HATHAWAY LIFE INS CO OF NE	17970	C+
GENERAL REINS CORP	14780	C+

MT HAWLEY INS CO   C   Fair

Major Rating Factors: Fair profitability index (3.9 on a scale of 0 to 10). Weak expense controls. Return on equity has been fair, averaging 16.3% over the past five years. Fair overall results on stability tests (4.0) including weak results on operational trends. The largest net exposure for one risk is conservative at 1.8% of capital.

Other Rating Factors: Good liquidity (6.9) with sufficient resources (cash flows and marketable investments) to handle a spike in claims. Strong long-term capitalization index (8.3) based on excellent current risk adjusted capital (severe and moderate loss scenarios), despite some fluctuation in capital levels. Ample reserve history (9.3) that helps to protect the company against sharp claims increases.

Principal Business: Other liability (56%), allied lines (15%), fire (8%), earthquake (7%), medical malpractice (7%), inland marine (6%), and products liability (1%).

Principal Investments: Investment grade bonds (75%), misc. investments (23%), and non investment grade bonds (2%).

Investments in Affiliates: 12%

Group Affiliation: RLI Corp

Licensed in: All states, the District of Columbia and Puerto Rico

Commenced Business: December 1979

Address: 9025 N Lindbergh Drive, Peoria, IL 61615

Phone: (309) 692-1000   **Domicile State:** IL   **NAIC Code:** 37974

Data Date	Rating	RACR #1	RACR #2	Loss Ratio %	Total Assets ($mil)	Capital ($mil)	Net Premium ($mil)	Net Income ($mil)
3-17	C	2.43	1.90	N/A	906.2	471.7	52.4	9.1
3-16	C	2.37	1.87	N/A	885.1	470.5	51.9	14.1
2016	C	2.40	1.88	44.8	884.6	452.5	217.0	58.2
2015	C	2.31	1.82	37.4	861.2	447.8	208.2	85.5
2014	C	2.27	1.79	32.3	874.2	461.1	209.5	111.8
2013	C	2.63	2.01	26.0	925.3	523.0	202.9	76.0
2012	C	3.13	2.30	42.4	978.0	546.2	166.9	71.5

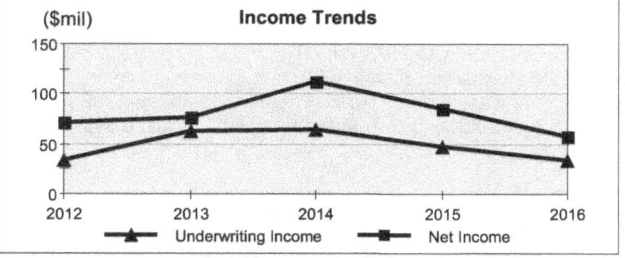

MUNICH REINS AMERICA INC   C+   Fair

Major Rating Factors: Fair overall results on stability tests (4.4 on a scale of 0 to 10) including potential drain of affiliation with Münchener Rückversicherungs-Gesellsc. The largest net exposure for one risk is high at 4.6% of capital. Fair profitability index (4.3) with operating losses during the first three months of 2017. Return on equity has been fair, averaging 10.1% over the past five years.

Other Rating Factors: Good liquidity (6.9) with sufficient resources (cash flows and marketable investments) to handle a spike in claims. Strong long-term capitalization index (8.5) based on excellent current risk adjusted capital (severe and moderate loss scenarios), despite some fluctuation in capital levels. Ample reserve history (8.9) that helps to protect the company against sharp claims increases.

Principal Business: (This company is a reinsurer.)

Principal Investments: Investment grade bonds (89%), misc. investments (6%), non investment grade bonds (4%), and real estate (1%).

Investments in Affiliates: None

Group Affiliation: Münchener Rückversicherungs-Gesellsc

Licensed in: All states, the District of Columbia and Puerto Rico

Commenced Business: April 1917

Address: 2711 CENTERVILLE ROAD STE 400, Wilmington, DE 19808

Phone: (609) 243-4200   **Domicile State:** DE   **NAIC Code:** 10227

Data Date	Rating	RACR #1	RACR #2	Loss Ratio %	Total Assets ($mil)	Capital ($mil)	Net Premium ($mil)	Net Income ($mil)
3-17	C+	3.00	1.89	N/A	18,335.4	4,650.8	814.5	-17.5
3-16	C+	2.84	1.78	N/A	18,138.7	4,656.6	751.9	-4.6
2016	C+	3.21	2.03	65.4	17,710.3	4,819.5	3,117.7	301.0
2015	C+	3.08	1.95	62.4	17,497.9	4,957.4	3,120.4	436.6
2014	C+	2.83	1.72	57.2	16,484.8	5,254.8	3,247.7	781.7
2013	C+	2.31	1.40	57.1	16,840.8	5,288.0	3,195.8	806.1
2012	C+	1.80	1.12	66.4	17,362.6	4,624.8	3,113.0	378.2

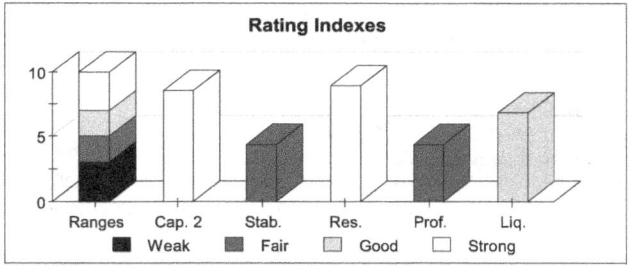

MUNICIPAL ASR CORP   E   Very Weak

Major Rating Factors: Weak overall results on stability tests (0.0) including weak results on operational trends. The largest net exposure for one risk is excessive at 31.1% of capital.

Other Rating Factors: Fair profitability index (4.6). Weak expense controls. Return on equity has been fair, averaging 12.4% over the past five years. Strong long-term capitalization index (10.0) based on excellent current risk adjusted capital (severe and moderate loss scenarios), despite some fluctuation in capital levels. Excellent liquidity (7.0) with ample operational cash flow and liquid investments.

Principal Business: Financial guaranty (100%).

Principal Investments: Investment grade bonds (99%) and misc. investments (1%).

Investments in Affiliates: None

Group Affiliation: Assured Guaranty Ltd

Licensed in: All states, the District of Columbia and Puerto Rico

Commenced Business: October 2008

Address: 1633 Broadway, New York, NY 10019

Phone: (212) 974-0100   **Domicile State:** NY   **NAIC Code:** 13559

Data Date	Rating	RACR #1	RACR #2	Loss Ratio %	Total Assets ($mil)	Capital ($mil)	Net Premium ($mil)	Net Income ($mil)
3-17	E	21.26	15.46	N/A	1,091.2	486.2	21.0	18.7
3-16	A+	49.42	24.88	N/A	1,507.3	741.1	26.2	24.1
2016	E	22.54	17.09	0.0	1,104.8	486.9	1.2	141.6
2015	A+	48.25	27.40	0.0	1,509.3	729.5	-4.8	101.9
2014	A+	37.58	22.45	0.0	1,519.8	611.5	-5.0	74.8
2013	A+	3.74	2.27	0.0	1,516.2	514.4	709.9	25.7
2012	U	111.74	55.87	0.0	77.0	76.9	0.0	0.6

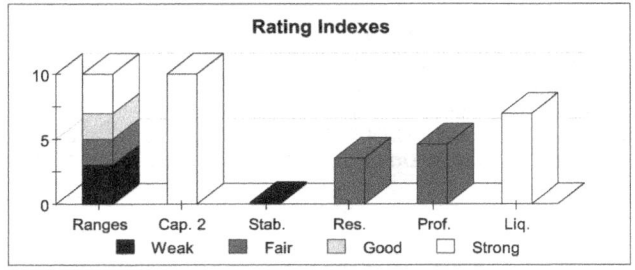

MUTUAL INS CO OF AZ

B   **Good**

Major Rating Factors: Fair overall results on stability tests (4.9 on a scale of 0 to 10) including weak results on operational trends. Strong long-term capitalization index (10.0) based on excellent current risk adjusted capital (severe and moderate loss scenarios). Moreover, capital levels have been consistent in recent years.

Other Rating Factors: Ample reserve history (9.4) that helps to protect the company against sharp claims increases. Excellent profitability (8.2) with operating gains in each of the last five years. Excellent liquidity (8.1) with ample operational cash flow and liquid investments.

Principal Business: (Not applicable due to unusual reinsurance transactions.)

Principal Investments: Investment grade bonds (84%), misc. investments (15%), and cash (1%).

Investments in Affiliates: None

Group Affiliation: None

Licensed in: AZ, CA, CO, NV, NM, UT

Commenced Business: March 1976

Address: 2602 East Thomas Road, Phoenix, AZ 85016-8202

Phone: (602) 956-5276   **Domicile State:** AZ   **NAIC Code:** 32832

Data Date	Rating	RACR #1	RACR #2	Loss Ratio %	Total Assets ($mil)	Capital ($mil)	Net Premium ($mil)	Net Income ($mil)
3-17	B	7.41	4.98	N/A	1,056.2	634.6	25.3	7.2
3-16	B	7.16	5.04	N/A	1,020.2	595.5	26.3	7.3
2016	B	7.51	5.09	56.9	1,067.7	623.6	101.7	25.3
2015	B	7.31	5.15	53.7	1,038.1	588.8	105.2	28.0
2014	B	7.02	4.95	57.9	1,017.4	565.6	105.4	27.4
2013	A	6.77	4.81	63.3	1,008.0	536.5	109.5	20.9
2012	A	7.08	5.44	41.3	989.4	504.2	113.3	33.2

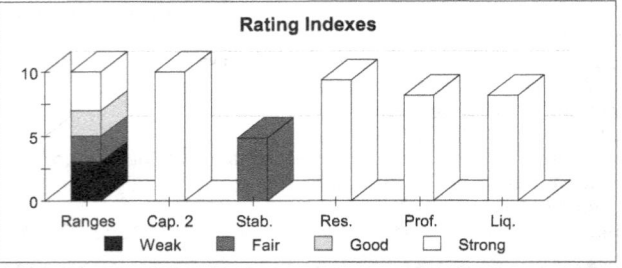

Rating Indexes

MUTUAL OF ENUMCLAW INS CO

B   **Good**

Major Rating Factors: History of adequate reserve strength (6.7 on a scale of 0 to 10) as reserves have been consistently at an acceptable level. Good liquidity (6.5) with sufficient resources (cash flows and marketable investments) to handle a spike in claims.

Other Rating Factors: Fair profitability index (4.0) with operating losses during 2015 and the first three months of 2017. Return on equity has been low, averaging 1.8% over the past five years. Fair overall results on stability tests (4.7) including weak results on operational trends. Strong long-term capitalization index (9.9) based on excellent current risk adjusted capital (severe and moderate loss scenarios), despite some fluctuation in capital levels.

Principal Business: Auto liability (30%), commercial multiple peril (20%), homeowners multiple peril (19%), auto physical damage (13%), farmowners multiple peril (12%), other liability (3%), and other lines (3%).

Principal Investments: Investment grade bonds (85%), misc. investments (14%), and real estate (1%).

Investments in Affiliates: 1%

Group Affiliation: Enumclaw Ins Group

Licensed in: AK, AZ, CO, ID, MT, NV, NM, OR, UT, WA

Commenced Business: March 1898

Address: 4000 KRUSE WAY PLACE BLDG 3, Lake Oswego, OR 97035

Phone: (360) 825-2591   **Domicile State:** OR   **NAIC Code:** 14761

Data Date	Rating	RACR #1	RACR #2	Loss Ratio %	Total Assets ($mil)	Capital ($mil)	Net Premium ($mil)	Net Income ($mil)
3-17	B	4.10	2.93	N/A	737.9	319.8	95.5	-10.0
3-16	B	3.48	2.51	N/A	693.7	292.8	93.1	0.1
2016	B	4.23	3.00	70.0	745.3	326.3	385.1	9.9
2015	B	3.45	2.48	77.5	697.0	290.0	376.1	-11.6
2014	B	3.86	2.80	68.1	666.7	302.9	350.2	11.3
2013	B	4.05	2.99	68.4	634.8	286.9	331.0	8.0
2012	B	3.90	2.89	68.0	598.9	266.3	309.1	18.2

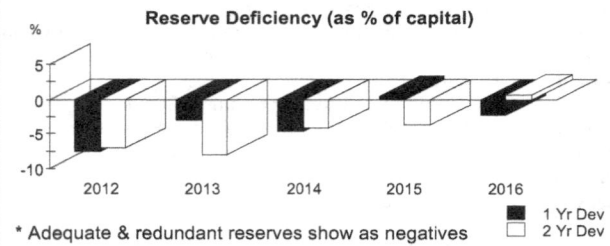

Reserve Deficiency (as % of capital)

* Adequate & redundant reserves show as negatives

NATIONAL CASUALTY CO *

B+   **Good**

Major Rating Factors: Good overall results on stability tests (6.4 on a scale of 0 to 10). Strengths include potential support from affiliation with Nationwide Corp, good operational trends and excellent risk diversification. Strong long-term capitalization index (10.0) based on excellent current risk adjusted capital (severe and moderate loss scenarios), despite some fluctuation in capital levels.

Other Rating Factors: Excellent profitability (7.7) with operating gains in each of the last five years. Superior liquidity (9.7) with ample operational cash flow and liquid investments.

Principal Business: Inland marine (32%), auto liability (24%), other liability (16%), commercial multiple peril (10%), auto physical damage (8%), workers compensation (5%), and other lines (6%).

Principal Investments: Investment grade bonds (94%) and misc. investments (6%).

Investments in Affiliates: None

Group Affiliation: Nationwide Corp

Licensed in: All states except PR

Commenced Business: December 1904

Address: 8877 N GAINEY CENTER DRIVE, Scottsdale, AZ 85258-2108

Phone: (480) 365-4000   **Domicile State:** OH   **NAIC Code:** 11991

Data Date	Rating	RACR #1	RACR #2	Loss Ratio %	Total Assets ($mil)	Capital ($mil)	Net Premium ($mil)	Net Income ($mil)
3-17	B+	13.36	12.03	N/A	404.6	140.1	0.0	0.8
3-16	B+	13.06	11.76	N/A	381.4	134.8	0.0	0.8
2016	B+	12.28	11.06	0.0	487.1	138.1	0.0	3.2
2015	B+	14.13	12.72	0.0	288.5	134.1	0.0	5.5
2014	B+	13.70	12.33	0.0	285.4	130.1	0.0	3.0
2013	B+	13.26	11.93	0.0	280.9	125.9	0.0	2.7
2012	B+	12.92	11.63	0.0	277.2	122.6	0.0	2.6

Nationwide Corp Composite Group Rating: B- Largest Group Members	Assets ($mil)	Rating
NATIONWIDE LIFE INS CO	133345	B-
NATIONWIDE MUTUAL INS CO	37185	B
NATIONWIDE LIFE ANNUITY INS CO	14466	C
NATIONWIDE MUTUAL FIRE INS CO	6122	B+
JEFFERSON NATIONAL LIFE INS CO	4611	C

NATIONAL FIRE & MARINE INS CO   C   Fair

Major Rating Factors: Fair overall results on stability tests (4.1 on a scale of 0 to 10) including weak results on operational trends. The largest net exposure for one risk is conservative at 1.7% of capital. History of adequate reserve strength (6.2) as reserves have been consistently at an acceptable level.

Other Rating Factors: Strong long-term capitalization index (8.1) based on excellent current risk adjusted capital (severe and moderate loss scenarios), despite some fluctuation in capital levels. Excellent profitability (8.0) with operating gains in each of the last five years. Superior liquidity (9.1) with ample operational cash flow and liquid investments.

Principal Business: Other liability (40%), medical malpractice (18%), allied lines (13%), fire (10%), earthquake (6%), auto liability (5%), and other lines (8%).

Principal Investments: Misc. investments (72%), investment grade bonds (26%), and cash (2%).

Investments in Affiliates: 6%

Group Affiliation: Berkshire-Hathaway

Licensed in: All states, the District of Columbia and Puerto Rico

Commenced Business: January 1950

Address: 1314 Douglas Street Suite 1400, Omaha, NE 68102-1944

Phone: (402) 916-3000   **Domicile State:** NE   **NAIC Code:** 20079

Data Date	Rating	RACR #1	RACR #2	Loss Ratio %	Total Assets ($mil)	Capital ($mil)	Net Premium ($mil)	Net Income ($mil)
3-17	C	2.44	1.58	N/A	9,388.5	5,852.5	242.3	67.9
3-16	C	2.66	1.77	N/A	8,502.0	5,559.4	201.4	215.5
2016	C	2.70	1.78	58.3	8,875.2	5,515.7	929.0	919.0
2015	C	2.53	1.67	44.7	8,664.8	5,695.9	822.2	327.2
2014	C	2.40	1.58	49.2	8,437.0	5,604.7	710.9	657.8
2013	C	2.57	1.70	69.8	7,335.1	5,010.4	316.5	233.2
2012	C	2.80	1.86	54.6	5,597.0	3,857.6	131.4	279.5

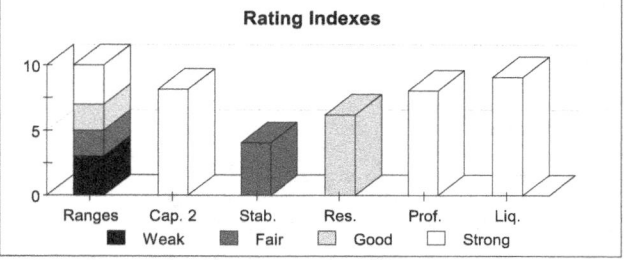

NATIONAL INDEMNITY CO   B   Good

Major Rating Factors: History of adequate reserve strength (6.0 on a scale of 0 to 10) as reserves have been consistently at an acceptable level. Good overall profitability index (5.8) despite operating losses during the first three months of 2017. Return on equity has been fair, averaging 7.8% over the past five years.

Other Rating Factors: Good liquidity (6.6) with sufficient resources (cash flows and marketable investments) to handle a spike in claims. Fair overall results on stability tests (4.3) including weak results on operational trends. The largest net exposure for one risk is conservative at 1.8% of capital. Strong long-term capitalization index (7.6) based on excellent current risk adjusted capital (severe and moderate loss scenarios), despite some fluctuation in capital levels.

Principal Business: Auto liability (65%), auto physical damage (15%), aircraft (11%), surety (4%), and inland marine (4%).

Principal Investments: Misc. investments (92%), investment grade bonds (6%), and cash (2%).

Investments in Affiliates: 23%

Group Affiliation: Berkshire-Hathaway

Licensed in: All states except PR

Commenced Business: May 1940

Address: 1314 Douglas Street Suite 1400, Omaha, NE 68102-1944

Phone: (402) 916-3000   **Domicile State:** NE   **NAIC Code:** 20087

Data Date	Rating	RACR #1	RACR #2	Loss Ratio %	Total Assets ($mil)	Capital ($mil)	Net Premium ($mil)	Net Income ($mil)
3-17	B	1.78	1.49	N/A	194,845.0	100,280.0	5,112.5	-2,960.7
3-16	B	1.81	1.51	N/A	163,907.2	90,209.6	4,676.1	1,589.9
2016	B	1.80	1.51	77.3	178,623.0	101,286.0	20,030.1	7,577.1
2015	B	1.81	1.52	75.1	161,777.0	89,828.6	18,456.6	7,270.9
2014	B-	1.66	1.43	79.3	166,985.0	93,997.7	26,655.0	12,007.5
2013	B-	2.24	1.87	49.2	151,912.0	97,226.1	5,650.4	8,390.8
2012	B-	2.48	2.01	62.8	128,203.0	79,408.9	7,469.8	5,489.3

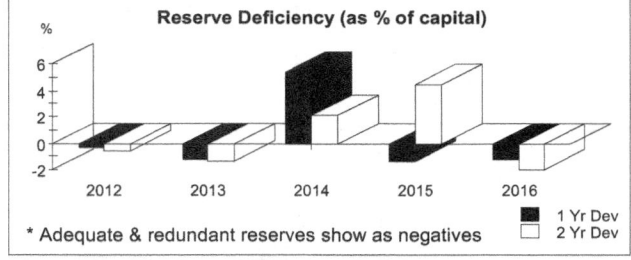

NATIONAL INDEMNITY CO OF THE SOUTH   C+   Fair

Major Rating Factors: Fair overall results on stability tests (4.3 on a scale of 0 to 10) including weak results on operational trends. History of adequate reserve strength (6.0) as reserves have been consistently at an acceptable level.

Other Rating Factors: Good overall profitability index (6.1) despite operating losses during the first three months of 2017. Return on equity has been low, averaging 2.9% over the past five years. Strong long-term capitalization index (7.5) based on excellent current risk adjusted capital (severe and moderate loss scenarios). Moreover, capital levels have been consistent in recent years. Superior liquidity (9.0) with ample operational cash flow and liquid investments.

Principal Business: Auto liability (81%), auto physical damage (11%), aircraft (4%), inland marine (3%), and other liability (1%).

Principal Investments: Misc. investments (51%), investment grade bonds (33%), and cash (16%).

Investments in Affiliates: None

Group Affiliation: Berkshire-Hathaway

Licensed in: AL, FL, GA, IA, NE, NJ, TN, PR

Commenced Business: October 1983

Address: 208 North Laura Street Ste 600, Jacksonville, FL 32202-2935

Phone: (402) 916-3000   **Domicile State:** IA   **NAIC Code:** 42137

Data Date	Rating	RACR #1	RACR #2	Loss Ratio %	Total Assets ($mil)	Capital ($mil)	Net Premium ($mil)	Net Income ($mil)
3-17	C+	2.82	1.75	N/A	398.5	204.9	17.9	-2.0
3-16	C+	2.52	1.58	N/A	356.7	180.5	22.8	3.2
2016	C+	2.65	1.64	74.3	378.5	198.3	67.9	10.3
2015	C+	2.52	1.58	72.8	355.8	179.1	102.8	6.8
2014	C+	2.69	1.64	71.7	319.2	177.4	84.2	0.7
2013	C+	3.17	1.91	55.2	256.9	167.3	33.0	6.1
2012	C+	3.48	2.10	51.9	211.8	141.8	19.1	4.9

Berkshire-Hathaway Composite Group Rating: B Largest Group Members	Assets ($mil)	Rating
NATIONAL INDEMNITY CO	178623	B
GOVERNMENT EMPLOYEES INS CO	27198	B
COLUMBIA INS CO	20707	U
BERKSHIRE HATHAWAY LIFE INS CO OF NE	17970	C+
GENERAL REINS CORP	14780	C+

NATIONAL INTERSTATE INS CO   C+   Fair

Major Rating Factors: Fair overall results on stability tests (4.7 on a scale of 0 to 10) including potential drain of affiliation with American Financial Group Inc and weak results on operational trends. The largest net exposure for one risk is conservative at 1.0% of capital. Fair reserve development (3.9) as reserves have generally been sufficient to cover claims.

Other Rating Factors: Good overall profitability index (6.8). Fair expense controls. Return on equity has been fair, averaging 7.7% over the past five years. Good liquidity (6.9) with sufficient resources (cash flows and marketable investments) to handle a spike in claims. Strong long-term capitalization index (7.3) based on excellent current risk adjusted capital (severe and moderate loss scenarios). Moreover, capital levels have been consistent in recent years.

Principal Business: Auto liability (51%), workers compensation (22%), auto physical damage (14%), other liability (10%), inland marine (1%), and allied lines (1%).

Principal Investments: Investment grade bonds (69%), misc. investments (27%), real estate (2%), cash (1%), and non investment grade bonds (1%).

Investments in Affiliates: 17%

Group Affiliation: American Financial Group Inc

Licensed in: All states except PR

Commenced Business: March 1989

Address: 3250 Interstate Drive, Richfield, OH 44286

Phone: (330) 659-8900   **Domicile State:** OH   **NAIC Code:** 32620

Data Date	Rating	RACR #1	RACR #2	Loss Ratio %	Total Assets ($mil)	Capital ($mil)	Net Premium ($mil)	Net Income ($mil)
3-17	C+	1.51	1.23	N/A	1,308.6	343.4	75.2	6.9
3-16	C+	1.44	1.17	N/A	1,214.8	301.4	72.3	3.7
2016	C+	1.51	1.25	70.2	1,286.5	337.0	309.0	16.1
2015	C+	1.43	1.18	75.1	1,200.1	295.6	295.3	12.5
2014	C+	1.45	1.20	78.7	1,117.6	284.7	291.2	5.4
2013	C+	1.52	1.26	70.8	1,054.1	283.4	277.6	21.9
2012	C+	1.61	1.36	62.3	1,017.5	269.7	260.7	52.9

American Financial Group Inc Composite Group Rating: B- Largest Group Members	Assets ($mil)	Rating
GREAT AMERICAN LIFE INS CO	29302	B-
GREAT AMERICAN INS CO	6851	B
ANNUITY INVESTORS LIFE INS CO	3063	A-
REPUBLIC INDEMNITY CO OF AMERICA	2300	B-
NATIONAL INTERSTATE INS CO	1287	C+

NATIONAL LIABILITY & FIRE INS CO   C+   Fair

Major Rating Factors: Fair overall results on stability tests (3.9 on a scale of 0 to 10) including fair financial strength of affiliated Berkshire-Hathaway and weak results on operational trends. The largest net exposure for one risk is acceptable at 2.1% of capital. Good overall profitability index (5.4) despite operating losses during 2014 and 2015. Return on equity has been low, averaging 3.4% over the past five years.

Other Rating Factors: Strong long-term capitalization index (7.8) based on excellent current risk adjusted capital (severe and moderate loss scenarios), despite some fluctuation in capital levels. Ample reserve history (8.3) that helps to protect the company against sharp claims increases. Excellent liquidity (8.9) with ample operational cash flow and liquid investments.

Principal Business: Auto liability (42%), workers compensation (19%), other liability (10%), auto physical damage (10%), ocean marine (7%), aircraft (5%), and other lines (8%).

Principal Investments: Misc. investments (47%), investment grade bonds (40%), and cash (13%).

Investments in Affiliates: 3%

Group Affiliation: Berkshire-Hathaway

Licensed in: All states except PR

Commenced Business: December 1958

Address: 100 First Stamford Place, Stamford, CT 06902-6745

Phone: (402) 916-3000   **Domicile State:** CT   **NAIC Code:** 20052

Data Date	Rating	RACR #1	RACR #2	Loss Ratio %	Total Assets ($mil)	Capital ($mil)	Net Premium ($mil)	Net Income ($mil)
3-17	C+	2.71	1.75	N/A	2,685.3	1,176.0	146.0	12.7
3-16	B-	2.68	1.68	N/A	2,345.0	930.4	182.6	25.8
2016	C+	2.65	1.71	72.7	2,605.4	1,126.6	562.1	89.4
2015	B-	2.86	1.81	68.9	2,377.3	957.1	762.1	-12.5
2014	B-	2.89	1.83	74.2	2,229.9	967.4	631.8	-0.9
2013	B+	4.12	2.55	64.8	1,836.1	899.0	388.3	70.5
2012	B+	3.88	2.35	77.5	1,419.0	714.5	343.0	18.1

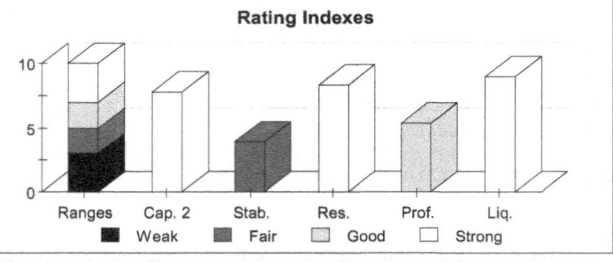

Rating Indexes

Ranges   Cap. 2   Stab.   Res.   Prof.   Liq.
■ Weak   ▨ Fair   ▢ Good   □ Strong

NATIONAL MORTGAGE INS CORP *   A-   Excellent

Major Rating Factors: Strong long-term capitalization index (9.4 on a scale of 0 to 10) based on excellent current risk adjusted capital (severe and moderate loss scenarios). Furthermore, this high level of risk adjusted capital has been consistently maintained in previous years. Excellent liquidity (7.2) with ample operational cash flow and liquid investments.

Other Rating Factors: Good overall results on stability tests (5.7) despite excessive premium growth and weak results on operational trends. Fair profitability index (3.8) with operating losses during each of the last five years and the first three months of 2017. Average return on equity over the last five years has been poor at -12.0%. Fair reserve development (3.6) as reserves have generally been sufficient to cover claims.

Principal Business: Mortgage guaranty (100%).

Principal Investments: Investment grade bonds (95%), misc. investments (3%), cash (1%), and non investment grade bonds (1%).

Investments in Affiliates: None

Group Affiliation: NMI Holdings Inc

Licensed in: All states except PR

Commenced Business: N/A

Address: 8040 Excelsior Drive Suite 200, Madison, WI 53717

Phone: (855) 873-2584   **Domicile State:** WI   **NAIC Code:** 13695

Data Date	Rating	RACR #1	RACR #2	Loss Ratio %	Total Assets ($mil)	Capital ($mil)	Net Premium ($mil)	Net Income ($mil)
3-17	A-	2.88	2.52	N/A	645.5	377.5	27.5	-10.2
3-16	A-	3.44	3.00	N/A	510.8	356.8	18.1	-10.1
2016	A-	3.01	2.59	2.3	634.8	387.0	129.8	-28.5
2015	A-	4.06	3.43	1.4	487.7	366.9	103.9	-50.3
2014	A-	3.69	3.41	0.6	261.9	223.1	31.3	-47.2
2013	A-	4.93	4.85	0.0	194.2	180.3	3.3	-32.7
2012	U	23.24	23.15	0.0	210.0	210.0	0.0	0.0

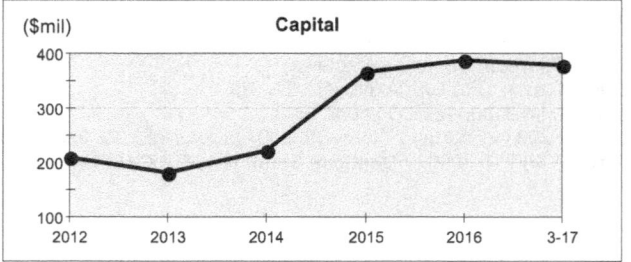

($mil)   **Capital**

NATIONAL PUBLIC FINANCE GUAR CORP — B — Good

Major Rating Factors: History of adequate reserve strength (5.8 on a scale of 0 to 10) as reserves have been consistently at an acceptable level. Good overall results on stability tests (5.1) despite weak results on operational trends and negative cash flow from operations for 2016.

Other Rating Factors: Strong long-term capitalization index (10.0) based on excellent current risk adjusted capital (severe and moderate loss scenarios). Moreover, capital levels have been consistent in recent years. Excellent profitability (8.6) with operating gains in each of the last five years. Return on equity has been good over the last five years, averaging 12.1%. Superior liquidity (9.8) with ample operational cash flow and liquid investments.

Principal Business: Financial guaranty (100%).

Principal Investments: Investment grade bonds (90%), non investment grade bonds (6%), misc. investments (3%), and cash (1%).

Investments in Affiliates: None

Group Affiliation: MBIA Inc

Licensed in: All states, the District of Columbia and Puerto Rico

Commenced Business: March 1960

Address: 1 Manhattanville Road Ste 301, Purchase Ny, NY 10577-2100

Phone: (914) 765-3333   **Domicile State:** NY   **NAIC Code:** 23825

Data Date	Rating	RACR #1	RACR #2	Loss Ratio %	Total Assets ($mil)	Capital ($mil)	Net Premium ($mil)	Net Income ($mil)
3-17	B	32.91	15.80	N/A	4,389.8	2,787.9	47.2	31.7
3-16	B	21.42	13.55	N/A	4,615.4	2,549.5	63.3	36.0
2016	B	33.03	16.16	41.9	4,355.2	2,730.8	19.0	191.8
2015	B	21.59	13.94	N/A	4,676.6	2,477.5	17.3	283.8
2014	B	25.38	13.47	27.9	5,142.4	2,190.4	13.5	238.1
2013	B	11.85	5.09	18.3	5,339.7	2,086.1	12.1	255.9
2012	B	12.49	6.44	5.5	5,726.2	1,998.5	-4.8	415.5

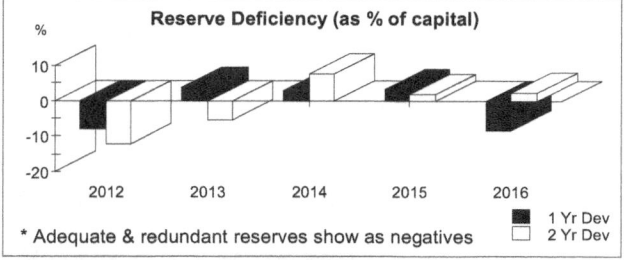

Reserve Deficiency (as % of capital)

* Adequate & redundant reserves show as negatives

■ 1 Yr Dev   □ 2 Yr Dev

NATIONAL UNION FIRE INS CO — C — Fair

Major Rating Factors: Fair profitability index (3.5 on a scale of 0 to 10) with operating losses during 2016. Return on equity has been fair, averaging 30.0% over the past five years. A history of deficient reserves (2.8) that places pressure on both capital and profits. In 2015 and 2016 the two year reserve development was 17% and 30% deficient respectively.

Other Rating Factors: Weak overall results on stability tests (2.8) including weak results on operational trends. The largest net exposure for one risk is excessive at 9.3% of capital. Good liquidity (6.3) with sufficient resources (cash flows and marketable investments) to handle a spike in claims. Strong long-term capitalization index (7.6) based on excellent current risk adjusted capital (severe and moderate loss scenarios), despite some fluctuation in capital levels.

Principal Business: Other liability (38%), group accident & health (15%), ocean marine (10%), auto liability (9%), commercial multiple peril (6%), workers compensation (6%), and other lines (17%).

Principal Investments: Investment grade bonds (64%), misc. investments (32%), and non investment grade bonds (4%).

Investments in Affiliates: 1%

Group Affiliation: American International Group

Licensed in: All states, the District of Columbia and Puerto Rico

Commenced Business: March 1901

Address: 2595 INTERSTATE DRIVE STE 102, Harrisburg, PA 17110

Phone: (212) 770-7000   **Domicile State:** PA   **NAIC Code:** 19445

Data Date	Rating	RACR #1	RACR #2	Loss Ratio %	Total Assets ($mil)	Capital ($mil)	Net Premium ($mil)	Net Income ($mil)
3-17	C	2.46	1.62	N/A	26,559.6	6,825.9	1,292.4	183.3
3-16	C	2.44	1.64	N/A	28,974.7	6,792.5	1,330.9	379.5
2016	C	1.99	1.33	99.8	26,517.3	5,967.4	4,837.1	-72.6
2015	C	2.43	1.64	88.8	26,764.2	6,682.8	5,564.4	110.6
2014	C	2.20	1.50	80.2	26,135.8	6,680.8	5,616.6	572.0
2013	C	2.03	1.38	76.7	24,709.6	5,836.5	5,422.5	8,102.0
2012	B-	1.60	1.46	87.1	32,520.8	14,398.9	4,676.2	1,039.0

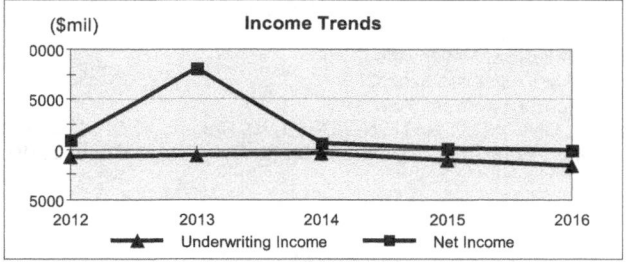

Income Trends

▲ Underwriting Income   ■ Net Income

NATIONWIDE INDEMNITY CO — C+ — Fair

Major Rating Factors: Fair overall results on stability tests (4.5 on a scale of 0 to 10) including excessive premium growth, weak results on operational trends and negative cash flow from operations for 2016. Strengths include potentially strong support from affiliation with Nationwide Corp. Good overall long-term capitalization (5.9) based on good current risk adjusted capital (severe loss scenario). However, capital levels have fluctuated during prior years.

Other Rating Factors: A history of deficient reserves (2.1) that places pressure on both capital and profits. In four of the last five years reserves (two year development) were between 21% and 26% deficient. Weak profitability index (2.9) with operating losses during 2013 and 2016. Return on equity has been low, averaging 2.5% over the past five years. Superior liquidity (10.0) with ample operational cash flow and liquid investments.

Principal Business: (This company is a reinsurer.)

Principal Investments: Investment grade bonds (92%), misc. investments (6%), and non investment grade bonds (2%).

Investments in Affiliates: None

Group Affiliation: Nationwide Corp

Licensed in: IL, IA, NY, OH, WI

Commenced Business: April 1994

Address: ONE WEST NATIONWIDE BLVD, Columbus, OH 43215-2220

Phone: (614) 249-7111   **Domicile State:** OH   **NAIC Code:** 10070

Data Date	Rating	RACR #1	RACR #2	Loss Ratio %	Total Assets ($mil)	Capital ($mil)	Net Premium ($mil)	Net Income ($mil)
3-17	C+	1.67	0.77	N/A	2,976.0	1,014.6	0.1	37.4
3-16	C+	1.76	0.81	N/A	2,982.2	1,030.0	0.0	25.0
2016	C+	1.63	0.75	N/A	2,981.4	997.6	1.2	-15.6
2015	C+	1.71	0.79	N/A	2,995.0	1,010.1	0.4	54.7
2014	C+	1.84	0.83	N/A	3,165.3	1,044.9	-0.4	4.0
2013	B-	2.21	0.89	N/A	3,251.9	1,069.4	0.2	-8.5
2012	B-	2.66	1.02	N/A	3,357.2	1,120.6	1.4	65.6

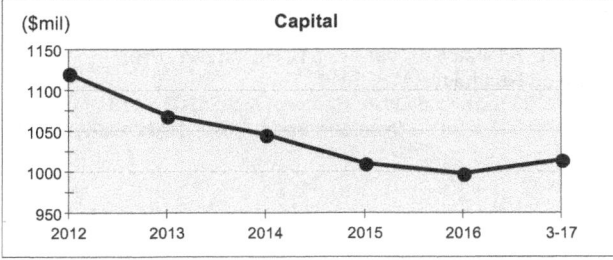

Capital

NATIONWIDE MUTUAL FIRE INS CO *   B+   Good

Major Rating Factors: History of adequate reserve strength (6.0 on a scale of 0 to 10) as reserves have been consistently at an acceptable level. Good liquidity (6.4) with sufficient resources (cash flows and marketable investments) to handle a spike in claims.

Other Rating Factors: Good overall results on stability tests (5.1) despite excessive premium growth and weak results on operational trends. Strong long-term capitalization index (10.0) based on excellent current risk adjusted capital (severe and moderate loss scenarios), despite some fluctuation in capital levels. Fair profitability index (3.7) with operating losses during 2015 and the first three months of 2017.

Principal Business: Homeowners multiple peril (48%), auto liability (16%), auto physical damage (10%), commercial multiple peril (7%), allied lines (6%), other liability (5%), and other lines (7%).

Principal Investments: Investment grade bonds (55%), misc. investments (40%), and non investment grade bonds (5%).

Investments in Affiliates: 5%

Group Affiliation: Nationwide Corp

Licensed in: All states except PR

Commenced Business: April 1934

Address: ONE WEST NATIONWIDE BLVD, Columbus, OH 43215-2220

Phone: (614) 249-7111   **Domicile State:** OH   **NAIC Code:** 23779

Data Date	Rating	RACR #1	RACR #2	Loss Ratio %	Total Assets ($mil)	Capital ($mil)	Net Premium ($mil)	Net Income ($mil)
3-17	B+	3.34	2.36	N/A	8,809.3	2,565.8	1,104.9	-182.2
3-16	B+	4.82	3.50	N/A	6,009.3	2,609.6	569.1	-3.2
2016	B+	4.83	3.54	74.7	6,121.6	2,671.6	2,338.5	12.4
2015	B+	4.90	3.59	71.1	5,938.4	2,604.3	2,242.5	-10.6
2014	B+	5.00	3.67	71.1	5,733.3	2,559.1	2,163.3	64.1
2013	B+	4.96	3.51	66.2	5,410.1	2,445.1	2,162.4	73.7
2012	B+	5.59	4.02	71.9	4,729.7	2,317.4	1,691.9	33.9

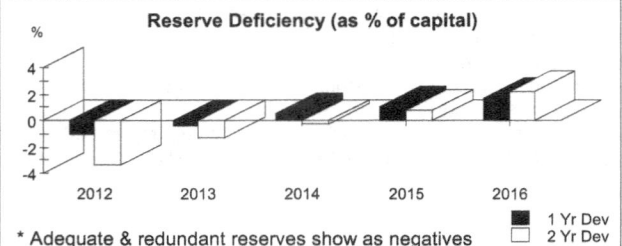

Reserve Deficiency (as % of capital)

* Adequate & redundant reserves show as negatives   ■ 1 Yr Dev   □ 2 Yr Dev

NATIONWIDE MUTUAL INS CO   B   Good

Major Rating Factors: History of adequate reserve strength (6.0 on a scale of 0 to 10) as reserves have been consistently at an acceptable level. Good overall results on stability tests (5.1) despite weak results on operational trends.

Other Rating Factors: Fair profitability index (4.5) with operating losses during 2016. Fair liquidity (4.7) as cash resources may not be adequate to cover a spike in claims. Strong long-term capitalization index (7.5) based on excellent current risk adjusted capital (severe and moderate loss scenarios), despite some fluctuation in capital levels.

Principal Business: Auto liability (40%), auto physical damage (26%), commercial multiple peril (12%), other liability (7%), homeowners multiple peril (5%), inland marine (3%), and other lines (7%).

Principal Investments: Misc. investments (48%), investment grade bonds (46%), non investment grade bonds (5%), and real estate (2%).

Investments in Affiliates: 29%

Group Affiliation: Nationwide Corp

Licensed in: All states except PR

Commenced Business: April 1926

Address: ONE WEST NATIONWIDE BLVD, Columbus, OH 43215-2220

Phone: (614) 249-7111   **Domicile State:** OH   **NAIC Code:** 23787

Data Date	Rating	RACR #1	RACR #2	Loss Ratio %	Total Assets ($mil)	Capital ($mil)	Net Premium ($mil)	Net Income ($mil)
3-17	B	1.53	1.35	N/A	35,852.6	13,003.2	3,458.8	116.6
3-16	B	1.42	1.24	N/A	35,947.3	12,183.0	3,936.0	-85.6
2016	B	1.49	1.31	74.7	37,185.2	12,690.3	16,174.4	-314.6
2015	B	1.45	1.27	71.1	35,923.7	12,315.9	15,510.8	184.1
2014	B	1.46	1.29	71.1	34,711.2	12,138.0	14,962.7	718.4
2013	B	1.49	1.31	66.2	32,675.8	11,792.5	14,630.9	499.8
2012	B	1.44	1.28	71.9	29,551.8	11,344.0	12,492.6	21.7

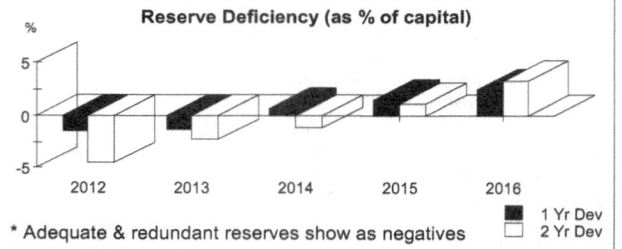

Reserve Deficiency (as % of capital)

* Adequate & redundant reserves show as negatives   ■ 1 Yr Dev   □ 2 Yr Dev

NAU COUNTRY INS CO   C+   Fair

Major Rating Factors: Fair overall results on stability tests (4.3 on a scale of 0 to 10) including potential drain of affiliation with QBE Ins Group Ltd and weak results on operational trends. Fair profitability index (4.7) with operating losses during 2012 and 2013. Average return on equity over the last five years has been poor at -0.8%.

Other Rating Factors: History of adequate reserve strength (5.6) as reserves have been consistently at an acceptable level. Strong long-term capitalization index (7.8) based on excellent current risk adjusted capital (severe and moderate loss scenarios), despite some fluctuation in capital levels. Excellent liquidity (7.0) with ample operational cash flow and liquid investments.

Principal Business: Allied lines (100%).

Principal Investments: Investment grade bonds (117%) and real estate (1%).

Investments in Affiliates: None

Group Affiliation: QBE Ins Group Ltd

Licensed in: All states except AK, DC, HI, ME, NY, PR

Commenced Business: May 1919

Address: 7333 Sunwood Drive, Ramsey, MN 55303-5119

Phone: (608) 825-5160   **Domicile State:** MN   **NAIC Code:** 25240

Data Date	Rating	RACR #1	RACR #2	Loss Ratio %	Total Assets ($mil)	Capital ($mil)	Net Premium ($mil)	Net Income ($mil)
3-17	C+	2.59	1.66	N/A	1,191.2	348.2	102.3	7.6
3-16	C	2.40	1.58	N/A	1,304.6	356.2	101.3	1.6
2016	C+	2.50	1.60	58.8	1,342.3	337.2	436.2	14.0
2015	C	2.32	1.54	63.9	1,305.1	309.3	343.9	19.7
2014	C	1.72	1.19	69.2	1,330.5	254.3	415.4	2.0
2013	C	1.53	1.04	75.2	1,300.1	274.8	444.3	-29.0
2012	C	1.28	0.90	73.5	1,458.6	335.4	693.9	-23.7

QBE Ins Group Ltd Composite Group Rating: B Largest Group Members	Assets ($mil)	Rating
QBE INS CORP	2325	B
NAU COUNTRY INS CO	1342	C+
QBE REINS CORP	1171	B
GENERAL CASUALTY CO OF WI	874	C+
PRAETORIAN INS CO	492	C

NAVIGATORS INS CO　　　　　　　　　　　　B　　　Good

Major Rating Factors: History of adequate reserve strength (6.7 on a scale of 0 to 10) as reserves have been consistently at an acceptable level. Good liquidity (6.9) with sufficient resources (cash flows and marketable investments) to handle a spike in claims.

Other Rating Factors: Fair overall results on stability tests (4.6) including weak results on operational trends. The largest net exposure for one risk is conservative at 1.4% of capital. Strong long-term capitalization index (8.2) based on excellent current risk adjusted capital (severe and moderate loss scenarios). Moreover, capital levels have been consistent in recent years. Excellent profitability (8.4) with operating gains in each of the last five years.

Principal Business: Other liability (58%), ocean marine (30%), auto liability (6%), inland marine (3%), surety (1%), and auto physical damage (1%).

Principal Investments: Investment grade bonds (75%), misc. investments (20%), non investment grade bonds (3%), and cash (2%).

Investments in Affiliates: 6%

Group Affiliation: Navigators Group Inc

Licensed in: All states, the District of Columbia and Puerto Rico

Commenced Business: March 1983

Address: One Penn Plaza - 32nd Floor, New York, NY 10119-0002

Phone: (203) 905-6090　**Domicile State:** NY　**NAIC Code:** 42307

Data Date	Rating	RACR #1	RACR #2	Loss Ratio %	Total Assets ($mil)	Capital ($mil)	Net Premium ($mil)	Net Income ($mil)
3-17	B	2.37	1.84	N/A	2,916.6	1,066.3	205.8	21.2
3-16	B	2.37	1.87	N/A	2,626.6	969.3	187.2	17.4
2016	B	2.34	1.83	60.5	2,808.1	1,026.8	845.0	80.7
2015	B	2.31	1.83	62.4	2,568.5	950.3	757.1	58.7
2014	B	2.33	1.81	61.7	2,454.0	893.9	752.8	72.4
2013	B	2.26	1.70	65.0	2,215.0	804.1	680.0	56.6
2012	B	2.48	1.88	73.0	2,102.4	682.9	623.0	25.2

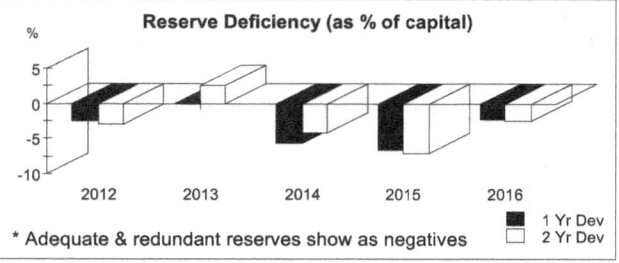

Reserve Deficiency (as % of capital)

* Adequate & redundant reserves show as negatives　　■ 1 Yr Dev　□ 2 Yr Dev

NCMIC INS CO　　　　　　　　　　　　　　B　　　Good

Major Rating Factors: Fair overall results on stability tests (4.2 on a scale of 0 to 10) including weak results on operational trends. Strong long-term capitalization index (8.2) based on excellent current risk adjusted capital (severe and moderate loss scenarios). Moreover, capital levels have been consistent in recent years.

Other Rating Factors: Ample reserve history (9.6) that helps to protect the company against sharp claims increases. Excellent profitability (8.9) with operating gains in each of the last five years. Excellent liquidity (7.4) with ample operational cash flow and liquid investments.

Principal Business: Medical malpractice (100%).

Principal Investments: Investment grade bonds (81%), misc. investments (18%), and cash (1%).

Investments in Affiliates: 1%

Group Affiliation: NCMIC Group

Licensed in: All states, the District of Columbia and Puerto Rico

Commenced Business: January 1946

Address: 14001 UNIVERSITY AVENUE, Clive, IA 50325-8258

Phone: (515) 313-4500　**Domicile State:** IA　**NAIC Code:** 15865

Data Date	Rating	RACR #1	RACR #2	Loss Ratio %	Total Assets ($mil)	Capital ($mil)	Net Premium ($mil)	Net Income ($mil)
3-17	B	2.66	1.83	N/A	732.6	295.0	23.6	2.3
3-16	B	2.19	1.50	N/A	713.1	266.8	23.7	4.5
2016	B	2.68	1.85	52.8	732.7	292.4	143.4	29.2
2015	B	2.20	1.51	58.1	683.9	261.7	145.6	17.7
2014	B	2.23	1.57	50.2	654.9	252.1	147.1	21.1
2013	B	2.68	2.02	50.2	593.9	241.5	102.2	27.2
2012	B	2.40	1.80	43.4	583.1	218.2	100.7	29.5

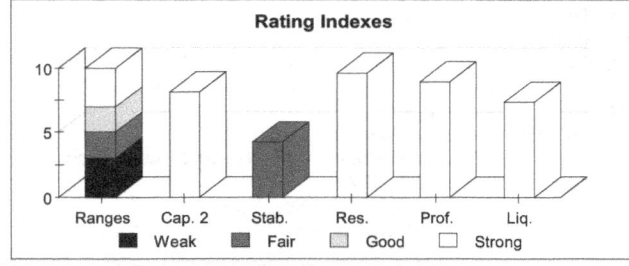

Rating Indexes

Ranges　Cap. 2　Stab.　Res.　Prof.　Liq.

■ Weak　▨ Fair　▧ Good　□ Strong

NEW JERSEY RE-INS CO　　　　　　　　　B　　　Good

Major Rating Factors: History of adequate reserve strength (6.6 on a scale of 0 to 10) as reserves have been consistently at an acceptable level. Fair overall results on stability tests (4.7) including potential drain of affiliation with NJ Manufacturers, weak results on operational trends and negative cash flow from operations for 2016.

Other Rating Factors: Strong long-term capitalization index (9.1) based on excellent current risk adjusted capital (severe and moderate loss scenarios). Moreover, capital levels have been consistent in recent years. Excellent profitability (7.8) with operating gains in each of the last five years. Superior liquidity (9.2) with ample operational cash flow and liquid investments.

Principal Business: Other liability (41%), allied lines (38%), workers compensation (16%), fire (2%), homeowners multiple peril (2%), and auto liability (1%).

Principal Investments: Investment grade bonds (99%) and cash (1%).

Investments in Affiliates: None

Group Affiliation: NJ Manufacturers

Licensed in: All states except AR, CA, CO, DC, ID, KS, LA, NM, UT, WY, PR

Commenced Business: January 1978

Address: 301 SULLIVAN WAY, West Trenton, NJ 08628-3496

Phone: (609) 883-1300　**Domicile State:** NJ　**NAIC Code:** 35432

Data Date	Rating	RACR #1	RACR #2	Loss Ratio %	Total Assets ($mil)	Capital ($mil)	Net Premium ($mil)	Net Income ($mil)
3-17	B	4.10	2.46	N/A	546.9	415.3	4.2	2.4
3-16	B	4.09	2.41	N/A	548.9	404.0	5.0	2.8
2016	B	4.11	2.43	67.8	548.6	412.8	16.0	9.0
2015	B	4.06	2.36	95.1	549.8	400.6	21.5	6.2
2014	B	3.86	2.28	33.1	556.8	393.1	33.6	19.8
2013	B	2.99	1.77	47.4	553.6	362.3	37.1	21.1
2012	B	2.52	1.49	92.5	546.8	330.4	41.2	12.0

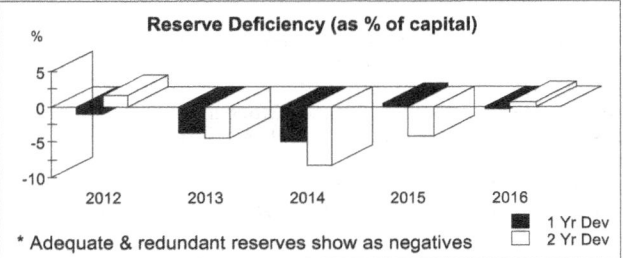

Reserve Deficiency (as % of capital)

* Adequate & redundant reserves show as negatives　　■ 1 Yr Dev　□ 2 Yr Dev

NEW YORK CENTRAL MUTUAL FIRE INS CO   B-   Good

Major Rating Factors: Fair overall results on stability tests (4.3 on a scale of 0 to 10) including potential drain of affiliation with Central Services Group and weak results on operational trends. History of adequate reserve strength (6.1) as reserves have been consistently at an acceptable level.

Other Rating Factors: Good overall profitability index (6.8) despite modest operating losses during the first three months of 2017. Good liquidity (6.6) with sufficient resources (cash flows and marketable investments) to handle a spike in claims. Strong long-term capitalization index (9.8) based on excellent current risk adjusted capital (severe and moderate loss scenarios), despite some fluctuation in capital levels.

Principal Business: Homeowners multiple peril (37%), auto liability (34%), auto physical damage (22%), commercial multiple peril (2%), fire (2%), other liability (1%), and inland marine (1%).

Principal Investments: Investment grade bonds (80%), misc. investments (20%), and real estate (1%).

Investments in Affiliates: 5%

Group Affiliation: Central Services Group

Licensed in: NY

Commenced Business: April 1899

Address: 1899 CENTRAL PLAZA EAST, Edmeston, NY 13335-1899

Phone: (607) 965-8321   **Domicile State:** NY   **NAIC Code:** 14834

Data Date	Rating	RACR #1	RACR #2	Loss Ratio %	Total Assets ($mil)	Capital ($mil)	Net Premium ($mil)	Net Income ($mil)
3-17	B-	3.94	2.90	N/A	1,119.2	531.7	111.0	-1.1
3-16	B-	4.02	2.98	N/A	1,054.2	494.5	106.9	1.7
2016	B-	3.92	2.93	67.1	1,117.7	534.3	448.9	23.3
2015	B-	3.94	2.97	66.9	1,051.1	491.7	422.4	20.0
2014	B-	3.93	2.98	73.7	1,016.7	480.1	420.6	9.7
2013	B-	3.82	2.93	67.9	1,010.8	466.4	421.8	30.7
2012	B-	3.60	2.83	70.7	980.7	423.9	414.7	18.6

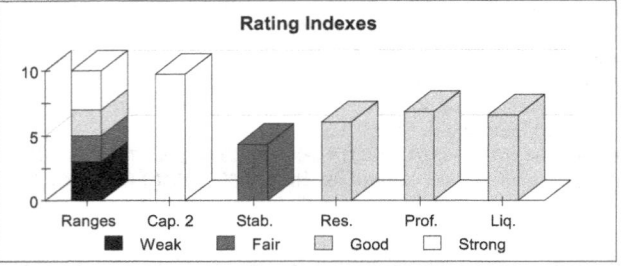

Rating Indexes

NEW YORK MARINE & GENERAL INS CO   B-   Good

Major Rating Factors: Fair profitability index (3.7 on a scale of 0 to 10) with operating losses during 2015 and the first three months of 2017. Average return on equity over the last five years has been poor at -0.6%. Fair overall results on stability tests (4.3) including weak results on operational trends. The largest net exposure for one risk is conservative at 1.4% of capital.

Other Rating Factors: Good long-term capitalization index (6.8) based on good current risk adjusted capital (moderate loss scenario). Over the last several years, capital levels have remained relatively consistent. History of adequate reserve strength (5.4) as reserves have been consistently at an acceptable level. Good liquidity (6.7) with sufficient resources (cash flows and marketable investments) to handle a spike in claims.

Principal Business: Workers compensation (21%), other liability (21%), auto liability (19%), commercial multiple peril (9%), ocean marine (5%), inland marine (4%), and other lines (20%).

Principal Investments: Investment grade bonds (72%), misc. investments (18%), cash (8%), and non investment grade bonds (2%).

Investments in Affiliates: 14%

Group Affiliation: ProSight Specialty Ins Group Inc

Licensed in: All states, the District of Columbia and Puerto Rico

Commenced Business: July 1972

Address: 59 Maiden Lane 27th Floor, New York, NY 10038

Phone: (973) 532-1900   **Domicile State:** NY   **NAIC Code:** 16608

Data Date	Rating	RACR #1	RACR #2	Loss Ratio %	Total Assets ($mil)	Capital ($mil)	Net Premium ($mil)	Net Income ($mil)
3-17	B-	1.38	0.97	N/A	1,351.8	359.7	97.6	-3.0
3-16	B-	1.36	0.97	N/A	1,247.3	382.2	102.5	1.8
2016	B-	1.38	0.98	74.5	1,277.9	355.4	393.4	-28.6
2015	B-	1.37	0.98	70.3	1,191.9	379.2	401.2	-8.3
2014	B-	1.10	0.79	57.7	1,062.9	352.6	347.1	12.6
2013	B-	1.21	0.88	60.6	891.7	240.1	270.9	1.8
2012	B	1.55	1.16	60.0	738.9	230.6	197.9	8.0

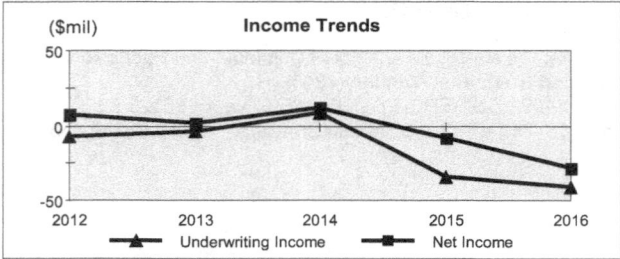

Income Trends

NGM INS CO   B-   Good

Major Rating Factors: Fair overall results on stability tests (4.6 on a scale of 0 to 10) including potential drain of affiliation with Main Street America Group Inc and weak results on operational trends. Fair reserve development (4.4) as reserves have generally been sufficient to cover claims.

Other Rating Factors: Good overall profitability index (6.6). Fair expense controls. Return on equity has been low, averaging 4.4% over the past five years. Good liquidity (6.4) with sufficient resources (cash flows and marketable investments) to handle a spike in claims. Strong long-term capitalization index (8.8) based on excellent current risk adjusted capital (severe and moderate loss scenarios). Moreover, capital levels have been consistent in recent years.

Principal Business: Auto liability (31%), homeowners multiple peril (21%), auto physical damage (16%), workers compensation (13%), surety (7%), other liability (5%), and other lines (7%).

Principal Investments: Investment grade bonds (70%), misc. investments (25%), and non investment grade bonds (5%).

Investments in Affiliates: 12%

Group Affiliation: Main Street America Group Inc

Licensed in: All states except AK, CA, HI, MN, PR

Commenced Business: July 1923

Address: 4601 TOUCHTON RD E STE 3400, Jacksonville, FL 32246

Phone: (904) 380-7282   **Domicile State:** FL   **NAIC Code:** 14788

Data Date	Rating	RACR #1	RACR #2	Loss Ratio %	Total Assets ($mil)	Capital ($mil)	Net Premium ($mil)	Net Income ($mil)
3-17	B-	2.76	2.14	N/A	2,520.0	1,055.5	270.7	3.0
3-16	B-	2.96	2.27	N/A	2,336.9	1,026.6	244.4	4.4
2016	B-	2.85	2.25	71.9	2,468.0	1,039.4	1,066.2	0.1
2015	B-	2.99	2.31	68.0	2,344.8	1,020.6	967.6	66.2
2014	B-	3.07	2.34	70.6	2,314.4	968.2	968.6	30.3
2013	B-	2.98	2.26	68.2	2,265.3	936.9	1,018.2	53.7
2012	B-	2.56	1.87	69.2	2,120.1	838.4	981.6	62.1

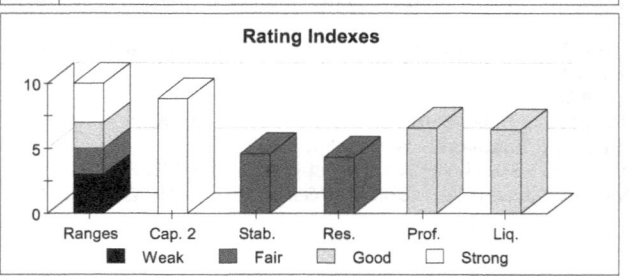

Rating Indexes

NJ MANUFACTURERS INS CO   B   Good

Major Rating Factors: Good overall results on stability tests (5.7 on a scale of 0 to 10) despite potential drain of affiliation with NJ Manufacturers. History of adequate reserve strength (6.7) as reserves have been consistently at an acceptable level.

Other Rating Factors: Good profitability index (5.0) despite operating losses during 2012. Return on equity has been low, averaging 0.8% over the past five years. Good liquidity (6.8) with sufficient resources (cash flows and marketable investments) to handle a spike in claims. Strong long-term capitalization index (8.1) based on excellent current risk adjusted capital (severe and moderate loss scenarios). Moreover, capital levels have been consistent in recent years.

Principal Business: Auto liability (39%), workers compensation (26%), auto physical damage (20%), and homeowners multiple peril (14%).

Principal Investments: Investment grade bonds (68%), misc. investments (31%), and real estate (1%).

Investments in Affiliates: 12%

Group Affiliation: NJ Manufacturers

Licensed in: CT, DE, ME, NJ, NY, PA, RI

Commenced Business: July 1913

Address: 301 SULLIVAN WAY, West Trenton, NJ 08628-3496

Phone: (609) 883-1300   **Domicile State:** NJ   **NAIC Code:** 12122

Data Date	Rating	RACR #1	RACR #2	Loss Ratio %	Total Assets ($mil)	Capital ($mil)	Net Premium ($mil)	Net Income ($mil)
3-17	B	2.39	1.79	N/A	7,070.7	2,733.4	418.6	45.4
3-16	B	2.41	1.81	N/A	6,747.1	2,517.4	407.9	7.3
2016	B	2.36	1.79	82.0	6,957.2	2,655.6	1,689.5	24.8
2015	B	2.39	1.82	78.6	6,687.0	2,445.0	1,629.6	79.7
2014	B-	2.48	1.87	79.7	6,568.2	2,379.9	1,660.1	162.5
2013	B-	2.38	1.80	83.1	6,282.4	2,273.9	1,597.6	123.6
2012	C+	2.25	1.69	107.5	5,945.3	2,057.3	1,459.1	-289.4

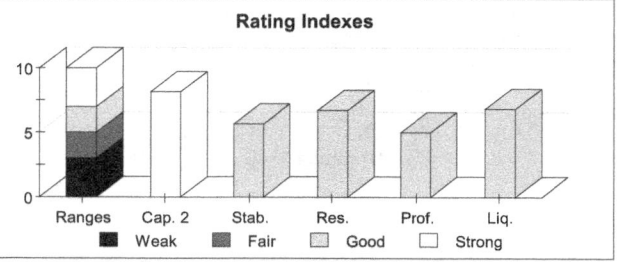

Rating Indexes

NORCAL MUTUAL INS CO   B-   Good

Major Rating Factors: Fair overall results on stability tests (4.6 on a scale of 0 to 10) including potential drain of affiliation with NORCAL Mutual, weak results on operational trends and excessive premium growth. Good overall profitability index (6.8). Good expense controls.

Other Rating Factors: Strong long-term capitalization index (8.5) based on excellent current risk adjusted capital (severe and moderate loss scenarios), despite some fluctuation in capital levels. Ample reserve history (9.0) that helps to protect the company against sharp claims increases. Excellent liquidity (7.0) with ample operational cash flow and liquid investments.

Principal Business: Medical malpractice (100%).

Principal Investments: Investment grade bonds (63%), misc. investments (34%), and non investment grade bonds (3%).

Investments in Affiliates: 10%

Group Affiliation: NORCAL Mutual

Licensed in: All states except NY, PR

Commenced Business: November 1975

Address: 560 Davis Street Suite 200, San Francisco, CA 94111-1966

Phone: (415) 397-9700   **Domicile State:** CA   **NAIC Code:** 33200

Data Date	Rating	RACR #1	RACR #2	Loss Ratio %	Total Assets ($mil)	Capital ($mil)	Net Premium ($mil)	Net Income ($mil)
3-17	B-	2.41	1.86	N/A	1,668.7	686.1	144.7	3.4
3-16	B-	1.64	1.40	N/A	1,628.4	662.2	109.1	-10.1
2016	B-	2.66	2.07	77.7	1,562.1	705.1	337.5	136.1
2015	B-	1.69	1.46	80.3	1,610.5	670.1	314.1	25.8
2014	B-	1.87	1.58	74.9	1,359.3	642.1	207.8	16.8
2013	B-	1.86	1.56	79.3	1,323.3	634.2	212.3	31.6
2012	B-	1.75	1.46	71.9	1,323.6	607.6	209.6	29.8

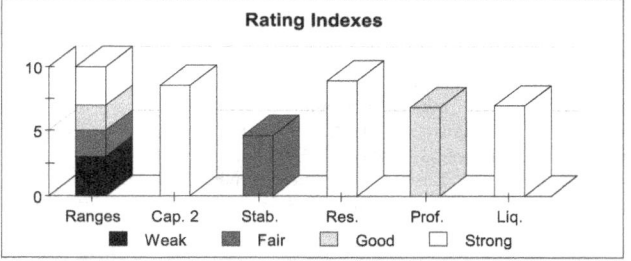

Rating Indexes

NORFOLK & DEDHAM MUTUAL FIRE INS CO   C+   Fair

Major Rating Factors: Fair overall results on stability tests (4.1 on a scale of 0 to 10) including potential drain of affiliation with Norfolk & Dedham Group and weak results on operational trends. History of adequate reserve strength (5.9) as reserves have been consistently at an acceptable level.

Other Rating Factors: Good overall profitability index (6.8). Weak expense controls. Good liquidity (6.8) with sufficient resources (cash flows and marketable investments) to handle a spike in claims. Strong long-term capitalization index (9.7) based on excellent current risk adjusted capital (severe and moderate loss scenarios), despite some fluctuation in capital levels.

Principal Business: Commercial multiple peril (29%), auto liability (24%), homeowners multiple peril (19%), auto physical damage (15%), workers compensation (5%), farmowners multiple peril (4%), and other lines (5%).

Principal Investments: Investment grade bonds (74%) and misc. investments (26%).

Investments in Affiliates: 4%

Group Affiliation: Norfolk & Dedham Group

Licensed in: AR, CT, MA, MO, NH, NJ, NY, PA, RI

Commenced Business: July 1825

Address: 222 AMES STREET, Dedham, MA 02026-1850

Phone: (781) 326-4010   **Domicile State:** MA   **NAIC Code:** 23965

Data Date	Rating	RACR #1	RACR #2	Loss Ratio %	Total Assets ($mil)	Capital ($mil)	Net Premium ($mil)	Net Income ($mil)
3-17	C+	3.93	2.73	N/A	413.7	197.9	34.5	3.1
3-16	C+	3.58	2.44	N/A	378.7	177.1	33.8	-0.2
2016	C+	3.98	2.80	52.3	411.9	193.7	140.6	11.8
2015	C+	3.75	2.57	75.3	381.2	177.3	128.9	3.4
2014	C+	3.51	2.36	66.4	359.9	182.0	123.9	5.3
2013	C+	3.83	2.60	59.5	331.3	178.6	112.5	15.0
2012	C+	3.63	2.46	59.6	305.5	161.0	106.0	9.4

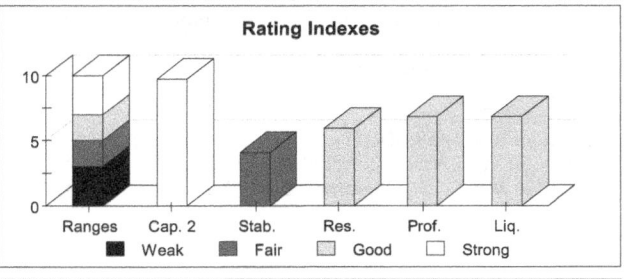

Rating Indexes

NORGUARD INS CO   D   Weak

Major Rating Factors: Poor long-term capitalization index (1.3 on a scale of 0 to 10) based on weak current risk adjusted capital (severe and moderate loss scenarios). Vulnerable liquidity (1.5) as a spike in claims may stretch capacity.

Other Rating Factors: Weak overall results on stability tests (2.0) including weak risk adjusted capital in prior years and weak results on operational trends. The largest net exposure for one risk is acceptable at 2.7% of capital. Ample reserve history (9.3) that helps to protect the company against sharp claims increases. Excellent profitability (8.7) with operating gains in each of the last five years. Return on equity has been good over the last five years, averaging 10.1%.

Principal Business: Workers compensation (95%) and commercial multiple peril (4%).

Principal Investments: Investment grade bonds (66%), misc. investments (31%), cash (2%), and non investment grade bonds (1%).

Investments in Affiliates: None

Group Affiliation: Berkshire-Hathaway

Licensed in: All states except WY, PR

Commenced Business: April 1988

Address: 16 SOUTH RIVER STREET, Wilkes-barre, PA 18702

Phone: (570) 825-9900   **Domicile State:** PA   **NAIC Code:** 31470

Data Date	Rating	RACR #1	RACR #2	Loss Ratio %	Total Assets ($mil)	Capital ($mil)	Net Premium ($mil)	Net Income ($mil)
3-17	D	0.38	0.29	N/A	859.5	209.8	58.5	4.4
3-16	D	0.39	0.29	N/A	687.6	171.5	44.0	2.4
2016	D	0.39	0.29	59.0	760.7	198.4	229.7	18.4
2015	D	0.41	0.31	59.9	615.7	166.2	188.3	19.8
2014	D+	0.52	0.40	62.7	482.7	162.4	121.3	12.1
2013	C	0.94	0.74	66.9	426.9	151.0	62.6	17.8
2012	B-	2.30	1.95	N/A	511.8	148.5	17.9	15.8

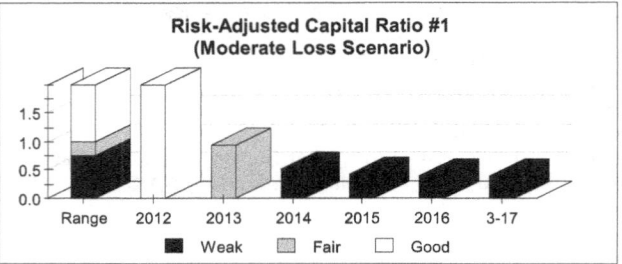

Risk-Adjusted Capital Ratio #1 (Moderate Loss Scenario)

Range 2012 2013 2014 2015 2016 3-17
■ Weak ▨ Fair □ Good

NORTH AMERICAN SPECIALTY INS CO   C   Fair

Major Rating Factors: Fair overall results on stability tests (3.6 on a scale of 0 to 10) including potential drain of affiliation with Swiss Reinsurance, weak results on operational trends and negative cash flow from operations for 2016. The largest net exposure for one risk is high at 3.2% of capital. Fair profitability index (3.5). Excellent expense controls. Return on equity has been low, averaging 2.2% over the past five years.

Other Rating Factors: History of adequate reserve strength (6.3) as reserves have been consistently at an acceptable level. Strong long-term capitalization index (10.0) based on excellent current risk adjusted capital (severe and moderate loss scenarios), despite some fluctuation in capital levels. Excellent liquidity (7.6) with ample operational cash flow and liquid investments.

Principal Business: Surety (36%), other liability (35%), inland marine (21%), ocean marine (5%), fire (1%), allied lines (1%), and other lines (2%).

Principal Investments: Investment grade bonds (71%) and misc. investments (29%).

Investments in Affiliates: 22%

Group Affiliation: Swiss Reinsurance

Licensed in: All states, the District of Columbia and Puerto Rico

Commenced Business: October 1974

Address: 650 ELM STREET, Manchester, NH 03101

Phone: (913) 676-5200   **Domicile State:** NH   **NAIC Code:** 29874

Data Date	Rating	RACR #1	RACR #2	Loss Ratio %	Total Assets ($mil)	Capital ($mil)	Net Premium ($mil)	Net Income ($mil)
3-17	C	4.14	3.87	N/A	477.7	316.4	0.0	2.4
3-16	C	5.35	4.91	N/A	568.2	398.0	-0.2	3.5
2016	C	4.15	3.91	N/A	488.1	313.6	0.2	7.2
2015	C	5.34	4.93	16.6	576.7	395.3	2.8	9.5
2014	C	5.35	4.92	34.3	547.3	384.2	14.2	6.4
2013	C	5.38	4.98	8.4	514.2	373.0	11.4	4.6
2012	C	5.50	5.09	N/A	503.5	363.7	10.4	12.5

Swiss Reinsurance
Composite Group Rating: C

Largest Group Members	Assets ($mil)	Rating
SWISS RE LIFE HEALTH AMER INC	14227	C
SWISS REINS AMERICA CORP	12927	C-
WESTPORT INS CORP	4730	B
NORTH AMERICAN SPECIALTY INS CO	488	C
FIRST SPECIALTY INS CORP	179	C

NORTH CAROLINA FARM BU MUTUAL INS CO   B   Good

Major Rating Factors: Good liquidity (6.4 on a scale of 0 to 10) with sufficient resources (cash flows and marketable investments) to handle a spike in claims. Fair overall results on stability tests (4.8) including potential drain of affiliation with NC Farm Bureau Ins and weak results on operational trends.

Other Rating Factors: Strong long-term capitalization index (10.0) based on excellent current risk adjusted capital (severe and moderate loss scenarios). Moreover, capital levels have been consistent in recent years. Ample reserve history (8.6) that helps to protect the company against sharp claims increases. Excellent profitability (8.2) with operating gains in each of the last five years.

Principal Business: Homeowners multiple peril (30%), auto liability (30%), auto physical damage (24%), allied lines (3%), farmowners multiple peril (3%), workers compensation (2%), and other lines (8%).

Principal Investments: Investment grade bonds (81%) and misc. investments (20%).

Investments in Affiliates: 1%

Group Affiliation: NC Farm Bureau Ins

Licensed in: NC

Commenced Business: October 1953

Address: 5301 GLENWOOD AVENUE, Raleigh, NC 27612

Phone: (919) 782-1705   **Domicile State:** NC   **NAIC Code:** 14842

Data Date	Rating	RACR #1	RACR #2	Loss Ratio %	Total Assets ($mil)	Capital ($mil)	Net Premium ($mil)	Net Income ($mil)
3-17	B	6.74	4.43	N/A	1,935.5	1,138.4	194.5	22.3
3-16	B	5.99	4.00	N/A	1,829.2	1,089.6	182.2	6.8
2016	B	6.69	4.45	80.5	1,895.4	1,107.2	771.2	8.6
2015	B	6.02	4.06	68.5	1,815.1	1,077.2	716.6	78.8
2014	B-	5.77	3.90	68.0	1,740.3	1,008.9	675.7	94.7
2013	B-	3.87	2.60	68.5	1,664.7	933.1	737.3	86.8
2012	C+	3.82	2.56	76.0	1,568.5	836.0	701.8	33.1

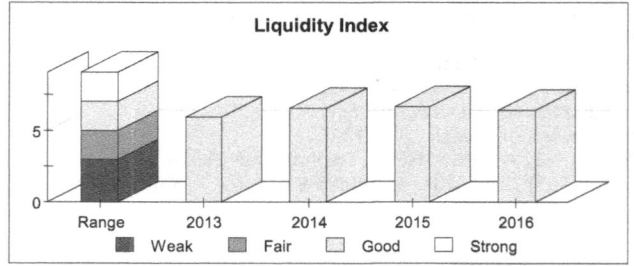

Liquidity Index

Range 2013 2014 2015 2016
■ Weak ▨ Fair □ Good □ Strong

NORTH RIVER INS CO   C-   Fair

Major Rating Factors: Fair overall results on stability tests (3.3 on a scale of 0 to 10) including weak financial strength of affiliated Fairfax Financial and weak results on operational trends. Good overall long-term capitalization (6.0) based on good current risk adjusted capital (moderate loss scenario). However, capital levels have fluctuated somewhat during past years.

Other Rating Factors: History of adequate reserve strength (5.9) as reserves have been consistently at an acceptable level. Good overall profitability index (5.1) despite operating losses during 2012 and the first three months of 2017. Return on equity has been fair, averaging 8.3% over the past five years. Excellent liquidity (7.4) with ample operational cash flow and liquid investments.

Principal Business: Other liability (44%), workers compensation (30%), products liability (8%), commercial multiple peril (7%), auto liability (6%), auto physical damage (2%), and other lines (3%).

Principal Investments: Investment grade bonds (67%), misc. investments (26%), and non investment grade bonds (7%).

Investments in Affiliates: 21%

Group Affiliation: Fairfax Financial

Licensed in: All states except PR

Commenced Business: October 1972

Address: 305 MADISON AVENUE, Township Of Morris, NJ 07960

Phone: (973) 490-6600   **Domicile State:** NJ   **NAIC Code:** 21105

Data Date	Rating	RACR #1	RACR #2	Loss Ratio %	Total Assets ($mil)	Capital ($mil)	Net Premium ($mil)	Net Income ($mil)
3-17	C-	1.21	0.88	N/A	1,065.2	295.5	98.0	-2.6
3-16	C-	1.26	0.97	N/A	1,049.5	303.8	92.9	6.7
2016	C-	1.19	0.87	63.7	1,051.4	285.0	396.8	-6.6
2015	C-	1.31	1.02	64.1	1,030.5	306.2	365.6	55.3
2014	C-	1.16	0.92	67.5	945.8	264.8	296.7	4.4
2013	C-	1.13	0.89	71.4	938.2	263.1	281.3	87.7
2012	C-	1.19	0.94	81.2	869.7	277.0	234.5	-17.2

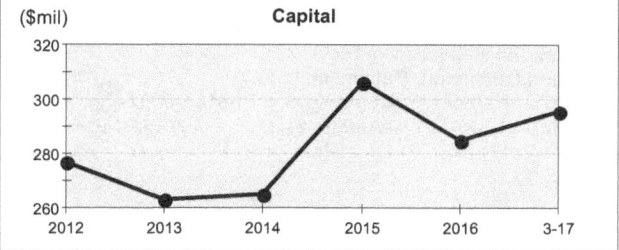

NORTH STAR MUTUAL INS CO   B-   Good

Major Rating Factors: Fair overall results on stability tests (4.2 on a scale of 0 to 10) including potential drain of affiliation with North Star Companies and weak results on operational trends. Good liquidity (6.7) with sufficient resources (cash flows and marketable investments) to handle a spike in claims.

Other Rating Factors: Strong long-term capitalization index (10.0) based on excellent current risk adjusted capital (severe and moderate loss scenarios). Moreover, capital levels have been consistent in recent years. Ample reserve history (7.6) that can protect against increases in claims costs. Excellent profitability (8.8) with operating gains in each of the last five years. Return on equity has been good over the last five years, averaging 10.1%.

Principal Business: Allied lines (24%), homeowners multiple peril (23%), auto physical damage (14%), auto liability (12%), farmowners multiple peril (12%), other liability (6%), and other lines (10%).

Principal Investments: Investment grade bonds (80%), misc. investments (18%), and real estate (2%).

Investments in Affiliates: 1%

Group Affiliation: North Star Companies

Licensed in: IA, KS, MN, NE, ND, OK, SD, WI

Commenced Business: February 1920

Address: 269 Barstad Road South, Cottonwood, MN 56229-0000

Phone: (507) 423-6262   **Domicile State:** MN   **NAIC Code:** 14850

Data Date	Rating	RACR #1	RACR #2	Loss Ratio %	Total Assets ($mil)	Capital ($mil)	Net Premium ($mil)	Net Income ($mil)
3-17	B-	6.56	4.49	N/A	712.4	429.1	87.7	18.1
3-16	B-	6.35	4.41	N/A	658.2	391.0	84.6	29.5
2016	B-	6.40	4.32	56.1	694.3	409.0	349.1	47.0
2015	B-	5.90	4.01	49.2	637.4	361.9	338.6	57.4
2014	B-	4.93	3.40	63.0	566.7	306.5	317.4	29.0
2013	B-	4.61	3.18	64.3	520.2	280.0	288.7	20.9
2012	B-	5.17	3.63	70.9	460.3	253.3	251.5	11.5

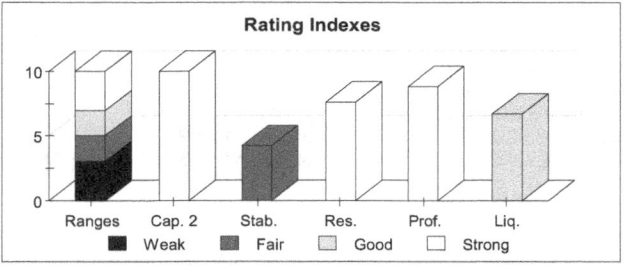

NORTHLAND INS CO   B   Good

Major Rating Factors: Good overall profitability index (5.9 on a scale of 0 to 10). Fair expense controls. Return on equity has been fair, averaging 10.0% over the past five years. Good liquidity (6.9) with sufficient resources (cash flows and marketable investments) to handle a spike in claims.

Other Rating Factors: Fair overall results on stability tests (4.7) including weak results on operational trends. Affiliation with Travelers Companies Inc is a strength. Strong long-term capitalization index (9.1) based on excellent current risk adjusted capital (severe and moderate loss scenarios), despite some fluctuation in capital levels. Ample reserve history (7.8) that can protect against increases in claims costs.

Principal Business: Auto liability (60%), auto physical damage (27%), inland marine (10%), other liability (2%), and allied lines (1%).

Principal Investments: Investment grade bonds (84%) and misc. investments (17%).

Investments in Affiliates: 16%

Group Affiliation: Travelers Companies Inc

Licensed in: All states except AK, PR

Commenced Business: March 1948

Address: ONE TOWER SQUARE, Hartford, CT 06183

Phone: (860) 277-0111   **Domicile State:** CT   **NAIC Code:** 24015

Data Date	Rating	RACR #1	RACR #2	Loss Ratio %	Total Assets ($mil)	Capital ($mil)	Net Premium ($mil)	Net Income ($mil)
3-17	B	2.94	2.40	N/A	1,191.7	546.3	65.8	7.2
3-16	B	2.98	2.41	N/A	1,194.9	557.1	63.4	8.3
2016	B	2.92	2.41	63.4	1,176.9	535.1	265.6	52.7
2015	B	2.96	2.42	58.7	1,171.6	544.0	253.5	62.1
2014	B	2.97	2.41	60.5	1,166.2	538.9	246.3	60.6
2013	B	2.97	2.43	60.9	1,157.6	533.3	245.7	56.8
2012	B	3.05	2.48	68.4	1,150.6	524.6	238.6	41.9

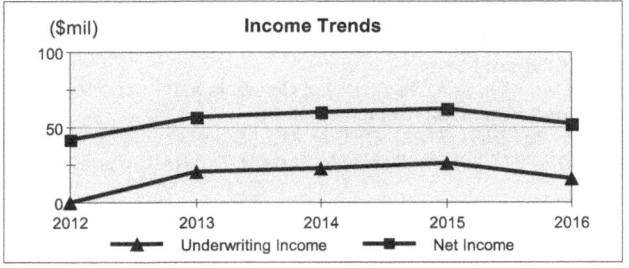

NUTMEG INS CO · C+ · Fair

Major Rating Factors: Fair reserve development (4.9 on a scale of 0 to 10) as reserves have generally been sufficient to cover claims. Fair overall results on stability tests (4.4) including weak results on operational trends.

Other Rating Factors: Good overall profitability index (5.5) despite operating losses during 2016. Return on equity has been fair, averaging 5.4% over the past five years. Strong long-term capitalization index (10.0) based on excellent current risk adjusted capital (severe and moderate loss scenarios), despite some fluctuation in capital levels. Excellent liquidity (8.1) with ample operational cash flow and liquid investments.

Principal Business: N/A

Principal Investments: Investment grade bonds (53%) and misc. investments (47%).

Investments in Affiliates: 35%

Group Affiliation: Hartford Financial Services Inc

Licensed in: All states except PR

Commenced Business: December 1980

Address: One Hartford Plaza, Hartford, CT 06155-0001

Phone: (860) 547-5000 **Domicile State:** CT **NAIC Code:** 39608

Data Date	Rating	RACR #1	RACR #2	Loss Ratio %	Total Assets ($mil)	Capital ($mil)	Net Premium ($mil)	Net Income ($mil)
3-17	C+	50.76	45.68	N/A	766.5	523.0	19.3	1.9
3-16	D+	57.76	51.98	N/A	739.7	561.1	18.2	10.5
2016	C	56.41	50.77	70.4	825.4	581.5	73.7	-62.8
2015	D	54.75	49.28	66.1	706.6	530.6	73.8	102.6
2014	D	0.06	0.04	67.0	448.1	280.2	71.7	11.8
2013	C-	26.77	24.09	68.8	421.7	256.6	69.6	28.3
2012	C-	23.82	21.44	72.7	392.0	227.9	68.9	8.9

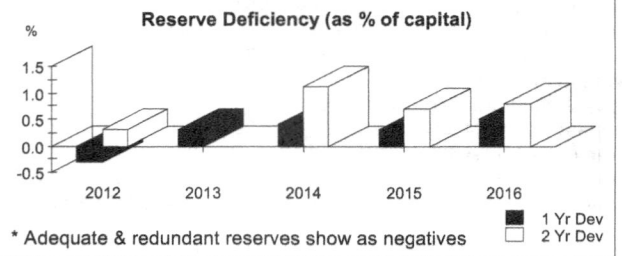

Reserve Deficiency (as % of capital)

* Adequate & redundant reserves show as negatives
■ 1 Yr Dev □ 2 Yr Dev

OAK RIVER INS CO · C · Fair

Major Rating Factors: Fair overall results on stability tests (4.3 on a scale of 0 to 10) including weak results on operational trends. Good overall profitability index (6.6) despite operating losses during 2012. Return on equity has been fair, averaging 6.1% over the past five years.

Other Rating Factors: Strong long-term capitalization index (7.2) based on excellent current risk adjusted capital (severe and moderate loss scenarios). Moreover, capital levels have been consistent in recent years. Ample reserve history (9.3) that helps to protect the company against sharp claims increases. Superior liquidity (9.2) with ample operational cash flow and liquid investments.

Principal Business: Workers compensation (90%), auto liability (5%), commercial multiple peril (3%), auto physical damage (1%), and allied lines (1%).

Principal Investments: Investment grade bonds (55%), misc. investments (30%), and cash (15%).

Investments in Affiliates: None

Group Affiliation: Berkshire-Hathaway

Licensed in: All states except ME, OR, PR

Commenced Business: December 1993

Address: 1314 Douglas Street, Omaha, NE 68102

Phone: (402) 393-7255 **Domicile State:** NE **NAIC Code:** 34630

Data Date	Rating	RACR #1	RACR #2	Loss Ratio %	Total Assets ($mil)	Capital ($mil)	Net Premium ($mil)	Net Income ($mil)
3-17	C	1.91	1.22	N/A	693.6	248.1	32.2	7.3
3-16	C	1.77	1.16	N/A	601.4	197.9	27.0	1.3
2016	C	1.85	1.18	61.3	665.6	230.0	127.2	18.6
2015	C	1.83	1.20	60.5	594.7	200.4	110.9	18.2
2014	C-	0.60	0.37	67.1	571.1	191.9	108.0	16.0
2013	C	1.64	1.07	66.3	527.4	170.9	111.9	14.0
2012	C	0.85	0.50	81.2	459.0	137.7	100.2	-6.1

Berkshire-Hathaway Composite Group Rating: B Largest Group Members	Assets ($mil)	Rating
NATIONAL INDEMNITY CO	178623	B
GOVERNMENT EMPLOYEES INS CO	27198	B
COLUMBIA INS CO	20707	U
BERKSHIRE HATHAWAY LIFE INS CO OF NE	17970	C+
GENERAL REINS CORP	14780	C+

ODYSSEY REINS CO · C · Fair

Major Rating Factors: Weak overall results on stability tests (2.7 on a scale of 0 to 10) including weak results on operational trends. The largest net exposure for one risk is excessive at 8.6% of capital. Good overall profitability index (5.8). Fair expense controls. Return on equity has been fair, averaging 7.0% over the past five years.

Other Rating Factors: Strong long-term capitalization index (7.4) based on excellent current risk adjusted capital (severe and moderate loss scenarios), despite some fluctuation in capital levels. Ample reserve history (9.4) that helps to protect the company against sharp claims increases. Excellent liquidity (7.0) with ample operational cash flow and liquid investments.

Principal Business: (This company is a reinsurer.)

Principal Investments: Misc. investments (54%), investment grade bonds (40%), cash (3%), and non investment grade bonds (3%).

Investments in Affiliates: 30%

Group Affiliation: Fairfax Financial

Licensed in: All states, the District of Columbia and Puerto Rico

Commenced Business: September 1986

Address: 300 FIRST STAMFORD PLACE, Stamford, CT 06902

Phone: (203) 977-8000 **Domicile State:** CT **NAIC Code:** 23680

Data Date	Rating	RACR #1	RACR #2	Loss Ratio %	Total Assets ($mil)	Capital ($mil)	Net Premium ($mil)	Net Income ($mil)
3-17	C	1.50	1.25	N/A	7,252.6	3,283.8	377.1	93.9
3-16	C	1.44	1.20	N/A	7,468.6	3,136.8	350.1	242.1
2016	C	1.50	1.26	55.3	7,162.6	3,193.9	1,575.2	158.4
2015	C	1.48	1.24	52.2	7,308.2	3,288.5	1,575.5	449.6
2014	C	1.41	1.13	51.8	7,577.4	3,248.7	1,799.8	191.7
2013	C	1.63	1.23	29.2	7,448.0	3,102.5	1,267.5	112.5
2012	C	1.65	1.21	57.5	8,171.6	3,154.8	2,129.9	174.7

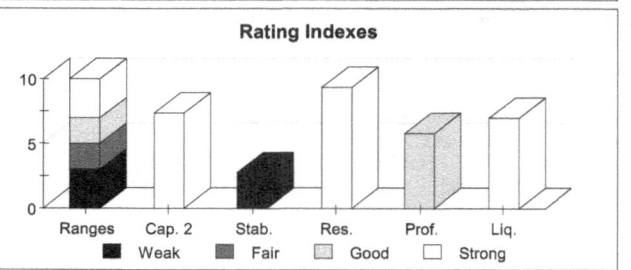

Rating Indexes

Ranges Cap. 2 Stab. Res. Prof. Liq.
■ Weak ■ Fair □ Good □ Strong

OGLESBY REINS CO *   A+   Excellent

Major Rating Factors: Strong long-term capitalization index (10.0 on a scale of 0 to 10) based on excellent current risk adjusted capital (severe and moderate loss scenarios). Furthermore, this high level of risk adjusted capital has been consistently maintained in previous years. Excellent profitability (8.0) with operating gains in each of the last five years.

Other Rating Factors: Excellent liquidity (7.0) with ample operational cash flow and liquid investments. Excellent overall results on stability tests (8.4). Stability strengths include excellent risk diversification.

Principal Business: (This company is a reinsurer.)

Principal Investments: Investment grade bonds (94%) and misc. investments (6%).

Investments in Affiliates: None

Group Affiliation: State Farm Group

Licensed in: IL, TX

Commenced Business: July 2011

Address: One State Farm Plaza, Bloomington, IL 61710

Phone: (309) 766-2311   **Domicile State:** IL   **NAIC Code:** 14103

Data Date	Rating	RACR #1	RACR #2	Loss Ratio %	Total Assets ($mil)	Capital ($mil)	Net Premium ($mil)	Net Income ($mil)
3-17	A+	16.43	10.68	N/A	4,364.9	3,309.8	105.7	39.3
3-16	A+	11.41	8.48	N/A	4,167.0	3,156.2	168.3	17.6
2016	A+	13.96	9.98	67.5	4,410.3	3,267.6	907.1	145.0
2015	A+	12.04	9.41	72.0	3,998.0	3,119.4	1,206.2	34.4
2014	A+	48.48	43.38	0.0	3,171.6	3,071.8	177.2	146.4
2013	A+	52.33	46.32	0.0	3,022.7	2,923.9	155.3	161.7
2012	A+	39.07	35.40	0.0	2,930.5	2,775.3	199.3	165.2

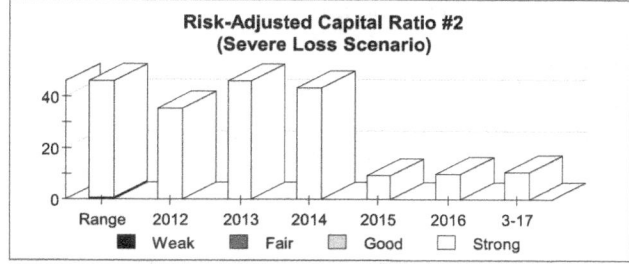

Risk-Adjusted Capital Ratio #2
(Severe Loss Scenario)

OHIO CASUALTY INS CO   C   Fair

Major Rating Factors: Fair overall results on stability tests (3.1 on a scale of 0 to 10) including potential drain of affiliation with Liberty Mutual Group and weak results on operational trends. The largest net exposure for one risk is excessive at 5.1% of capital. History of adequate reserve strength (5.9) as reserves have been consistently at an acceptable level.

Other Rating Factors: Good overall profitability index (6.6) despite modest operating losses during the first three months of 2017. Return on equity has been good over the last five years, averaging 10.3%. Good liquidity (6.4) with sufficient resources (cash flows and marketable investments) to handle a spike in claims. Strong long-term capitalization index (8.4) based on excellent current risk adjusted capital (severe and moderate loss scenarios). Moreover, capital levels have been consistent in recent years.

Principal Business: Other liability (36%), commercial multiple peril (22%), surety (15%), inland marine (9%), auto liability (7%), workers compensation (5%), and other lines (5%).

Principal Investments: Investment grade bonds (77%), misc. investments (18%), non investment grade bonds (5%), and real estate (1%).

Investments in Affiliates: 2%

Group Affiliation: Liberty Mutual Group

Licensed in: All states except PR

Commenced Business: March 1920

Address: 62 Maple Avenue, Keene, NH 03431

Phone: (617) 357-9500   **Domicile State:** NH   **NAIC Code:** 24074

Data Date	Rating	RACR #1	RACR #2	Loss Ratio %	Total Assets ($mil)	Capital ($mil)	Net Premium ($mil)	Net Income ($mil)
3-17	C	2.94	1.97	N/A	5,711.1	1,738.2	523.5	-1.7
3-16	C	2.89	1.92	N/A	5,585.4	1,666.5	505.4	36.2
2016	C	2.98	2.01	69.9	5,641.6	1,721.9	2,119.9	73.2
2015	C	2.82	1.87	68.4	5,578.6	1,637.4	2,050.6	157.4
2014	C	2.56	1.68	70.0	5,408.2	1,529.8	2,030.1	133.7
2013	C	2.34	1.52	73.5	5,639.6	1,384.1	1,791.9	313.5
2012	C	1.97	1.41	66.7	5,100.5	1,274.6	2,227.3	112.0

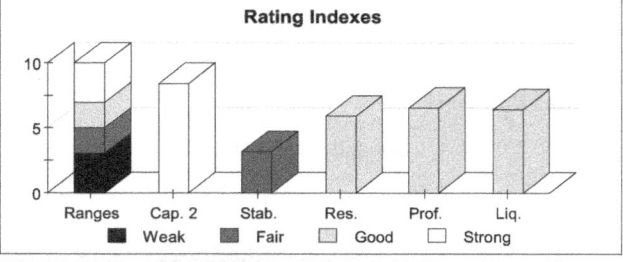

Rating Indexes

OHIO FARMERS INS CO   B-   Good

Major Rating Factors: Fair overall results on stability tests (4.6 on a scale of 0 to 10) including potential drain of affiliation with Westfield Companies and weak results on operational trends. Strong long-term capitalization index (7.2) based on excellent current risk adjusted capital (severe and moderate loss scenarios). Moreover, capital levels have been consistent in recent years.

Other Rating Factors: Ample reserve history (7.5) that can protect against increases in claims costs. Excellent profitability (7.4) with operating gains in each of the last five years. Excellent liquidity (7.0) with ample operational cash flow and liquid investments.

Principal Business: Surety (100%).

Principal Investments: Misc. investments (80%), investment grade bonds (17%), real estate (2%), and cash (1%).

Investments in Affiliates: 70%

Group Affiliation: Westfield Companies

Licensed in: All states except AK, CA, CT, HI, ID, ME, NH, OR, PR

Commenced Business: July 1848

Address: One Park Circle, Westfield Center, OH 44251-5001

Phone: (330) 887-0101   **Domicile State:** OH   **NAIC Code:** 24104

Data Date	Rating	RACR #1	RACR #2	Loss Ratio %	Total Assets ($mil)	Capital ($mil)	Net Premium ($mil)	Net Income ($mil)
3-17	B-	1.25	1.21	N/A	2,975.6	2,266.4	84.6	2.6
3-16	B-	1.26	1.21	N/A	2,743.0	2,056.1	83.8	6.7
2016	B-	1.23	1.20	62.3	2,964.7	2,211.9	343.8	63.0
2015	B-	1.23	1.20	62.7	2,701.1	1,997.1	336.1	22.0
2014	B-	1.22	1.19	63.5	2,595.1	1,902.4	329.3	39.3
2013	B-	1.25	1.21	59.8	2,404.6	1,808.7	318.3	21.1
2012	B-	1.22	1.18	64.9	2,131.9	1,525.6	305.3	36.9

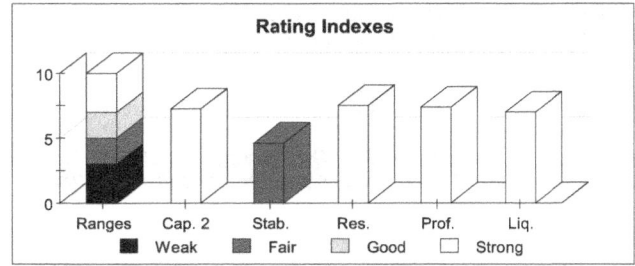

Rating Indexes

OHIO MUTUAL INS CO

B-   **Good**

Major Rating Factors: Fair overall results on stability tests (4.7 on a scale of 0 to 10) including potential drain of affiliation with Ohio Mutual Group. Good liquidity (6.9) with sufficient resources (cash flows and marketable investments) to handle a spike in claims.

Other Rating Factors: Strong long-term capitalization index (7.4) based on excellent current risk adjusted capital (severe and moderate loss scenarios). Moreover, capital levels have been consistent in recent years. Ample reserve history (7.6) that can protect against increases in claims costs. Excellent profitability (7.7) with operating gains in each of the last five years.

Principal Business: Auto liability (37%), auto physical damage (32%), homeowners multiple peril (22%), fire (5%), and farmowners multiple peril (3%).

Principal Investments: Misc. investments (71%), investment grade bonds (25%), cash (2%), and real estate (2%).

Investments in Affiliates: 67%

Group Affiliation: Ohio Mutual Group

Licensed in: CT, IN, IA, KS, ME, MN, NE, NH, OH, OR, RI, TN, VT, VA, WI

Commenced Business: March 1901

Address: 1725 HOPLEY AVENUE, Bucyrus, OH 44820-0111

Phone: (419) 562-3011   **Domicile State:** OH   **NAIC Code:** 10202

Data Date	Rating	RACR #1	RACR #2	Loss Ratio %	Total Assets ($mil)	Capital ($mil)	Net Premium ($mil)	Net Income ($mil)
3-17	B-	1.37	1.33	N/A	282.0	222.8	13.9	0.8
3-16	B-	1.37	1.32	N/A	261.4	204.7	13.3	0.7
2016	B-	1.35	1.31	61.7	276.6	217.6	56.4	3.3
2015	B-	1.36	1.32	61.6	256.8	201.3	53.5	2.9
2014	B-	1.37	1.32	64.0	239.7	187.5	51.9	2.4
2013	B-	1.35	1.31	65.8	227.4	177.8	49.4	1.8
2012	B-	1.38	1.33	67.7	222.7	165.2	45.3	2.1

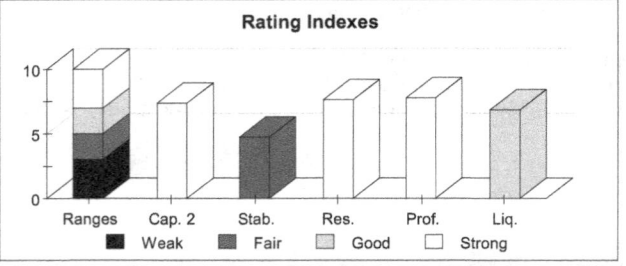

Rating Indexes

Ranges — Cap. 2 — Stab. — Res. — Prof. — Liq.

■ Weak   ■ Fair   □ Good   □ Strong

OLD GUARD INS CO

C+   **Fair**

Major Rating Factors: Fair overall results on stability tests (4.4 on a scale of 0 to 10) including potential drain of affiliation with Westfield Companies and weak results on operational trends. The largest net exposure for one risk is conservative at 1.4% of capital. Good liquidity (6.7) with sufficient resources (cash flows and marketable investments) to handle a spike in claims.

Other Rating Factors: Strong long-term capitalization index (8.9) based on excellent current risk adjusted capital (severe and moderate loss scenarios). Moreover, capital levels have been consistent in recent years. Ample reserve history (8.7) that helps to protect the company against sharp claims increases. Excellent profitability (8.6) with operating gains in each of the last five years.

Principal Business: (This company is a reinsurer.)

Principal Investments: Investment grade bonds (66%) and misc. investments (34%).

Investments in Affiliates: None

Group Affiliation: Westfield Companies

Licensed in: DE, IL, IN, IA, KY, MD, ND, OH, OR, PA, SD, VA, WV

Commenced Business: December 1896

Address: One Park Circle, Westfield Center, OH 44251

Phone: (330) 887-0101   **Domicile State:** OH   **NAIC Code:** 17558

Data Date	Rating	RACR #1	RACR #2	Loss Ratio %	Total Assets ($mil)	Capital ($mil)	Net Premium ($mil)	Net Income ($mil)
3-17	C+	3.76	2.44	N/A	455.6	210.1	40.1	1.7
3-16	C+	3.69	2.44	N/A	423.5	191.0	39.7	2.2
2016	C+	3.78	2.46	62.3	453.5	206.2	162.9	11.4
2015	C+	3.74	2.49	62.7	421.4	185.6	159.2	12.6
2014	C+	3.53	2.32	63.5	410.2	179.8	156.0	13.3
2013	C+	3.31	2.17	59.8	392.0	164.4	150.8	19.5
2012	C+	2.92	1.92	64.9	356.2	136.8	144.6	16.1

Westfield Companies
Composite Group Rating: B-
Largest Group Members

	Assets ($mil)	Rating
OHIO FARMERS INS CO	2965	B-
WESTFIELD INS CO	2740	B-
WESTFIELD NATIONAL INS CO	659	B-
OLD GUARD INS CO	453	C+
AMERICAN SELECT INS CO	255	C

OLD REPUB INS CO

B   **Good**

Major Rating Factors: History of adequate reserve strength (6.2 on a scale of 0 to 10) as reserves have been consistently at an acceptable level. Fair overall results on stability tests (4.8) including weak results on operational trends. The largest net exposure for one risk is conservative at 1.1% of capital.

Other Rating Factors: Strong long-term capitalization index (9.3) based on excellent current risk adjusted capital (severe and moderate loss scenarios), despite some fluctuation in capital levels. Excellent profitability (8.8) with operating gains in each of the last five years. Excellent liquidity (7.0) with ample operational cash flow and liquid investments.

Principal Business: Workers compensation (40%), other liability (17%), auto liability (11%), inland marine (9%), credit (8%), aircraft (7%), and other lines (9%).

Principal Investments: Investment grade bonds (70%), misc. investments (24%), non investment grade bonds (5%), and cash (1%).

Investments in Affiliates: 1%

Group Affiliation: Old Republic Group

Licensed in: All states, the District of Columbia and Puerto Rico

Commenced Business: April 1935

Address: 133 OAKLAND AVENUE, Greensburg, PA 15601-0789

Phone: (724) 834-5000   **Domicile State:** PA   **NAIC Code:** 24147

Data Date	Rating	RACR #1	RACR #2	Loss Ratio %	Total Assets ($mil)	Capital ($mil)	Net Premium ($mil)	Net Income ($mil)
3-17	B	4.02	2.47	N/A	2,863.9	1,113.7	105.7	20.9
3-16	B	4.06	2.52	N/A	2,718.1	1,053.5	102.4	28.5
2016	B	4.13	2.54	54.7	2,813.8	1,106.9	470.7	106.5
2015	B	4.16	2.58	53.5	2,668.8	1,034.0	420.9	98.9
2014	B+	3.85	2.35	61.7	2,609.4	1,035.8	400.4	105.6
2013	A-	4.02	2.48	52.2	2,472.7	937.8	365.4	107.4
2012	A-	3.96	2.36	57.2	2,439.8	874.9	359.3	84.4

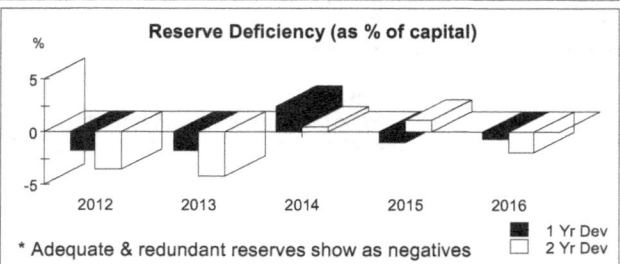

Reserve Deficiency (as % of capital)

2012 — 2013 — 2014 — 2015 — 2016

■ 1 Yr Dev   □ 2 Yr Dev

* Adequate & redundant reserves show as negatives

OLD REPUBLIC GENERAL INS CORP   B   Good

Major Rating Factors: Good long-term capitalization index (6.5 on a scale of 0 to 10) based on excellent current risk adjusted capital (severe loss scenario). Moreover, capital levels have been consistent in recent years. Fair overall results on stability tests (4.8) including weak results on operational trends.

Other Rating Factors: Ample reserve history (8.6) that helps to protect the company against sharp claims increases. Excellent profitability (8.9) with operating gains in each of the last five years. Excellent expense controls. Return on equity has been good over the last five years, averaging 11.2%. Excellent liquidity (7.0) with ample operational cash flow and liquid investments.

Principal Business: Workers compensation (66%), other liability (25%), auto liability (8%), and auto physical damage (2%).

Principal Investments: Investment grade bonds (76%), misc. investments (18%), non investment grade bonds (5%), and cash (1%).

Investments in Affiliates: None

Group Affiliation: Old Republic Group

Licensed in: All states, the District of Columbia and Puerto Rico

Commenced Business: January 1961

Address: 307 NORTH MICHIGAN AVENUE, Chicago, IL 60601

Phone: (312) 346-8100   **Domicile State:** IL   **NAIC Code:** 24139

Data Date	Rating	RACR #1	RACR #2	Loss Ratio %	Total Assets ($mil)	Capital ($mil)	Net Premium ($mil)	Net Income ($mil)
3-17	B	2.79	1.26	N/A	2,060.4	561.0	53.7	9.7
3-16	B	2.55	1.17	N/A	1,996.7	517.8	47.9	13.2
2016	B	2.86	1.28	85.0	2,021.2	556.8	184.4	53.0
2015	B	2.48	1.14	81.7	2,004.0	500.2	311.4	60.6
2014	B	2.50	1.18	88.8	1,925.7	494.1	303.1	62.8
2013	A-	2.74	1.63	83.2	1,730.6	431.7	286.3	54.2
2012	A-	2.22	1.06	88.0	1,507.9	332.6	278.6	33.4

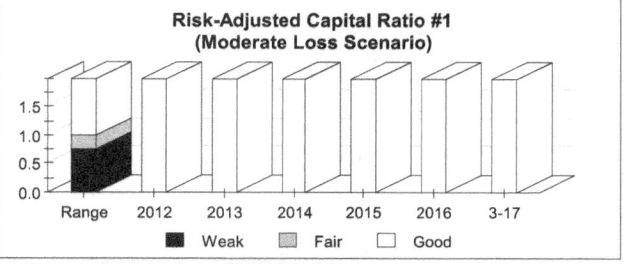

Risk-Adjusted Capital Ratio #1 (Moderate Loss Scenario)

OLD REPUBLIC SECURITY ASR CO   B   Good

Major Rating Factors: Good liquidity (6.0 on a scale of 0 to 10) with sufficient resources (cash flows and marketable investments) to handle a spike in claims. Fair overall results on stability tests (4.8) including weak results on operational trends, weak risk adjusted capital in prior years and negative cash flow from operations for 2016. Strengths include potentially strong support from affiliation with Old Republic Group.

Other Rating Factors: Poor long-term capitalization index (2.2) based on weak current risk adjusted capital (severe loss scenario). A history of deficient reserves (0.2) that places pressure on both capital and profits. In four of the last five years reserves (two year development) were between 44% and 129% deficient. Weak profitability index (2.7) with operating losses during each of the last five years. However, profits have turned positive in the first three months of 2017. Average return on equity over the last five years has been poor at -27.5%.

Principal Business: (This company is a reinsurer.)

Principal Investments: Investment grade bonds (92%), non investment grade bonds (5%), and misc. investments (3%).

Investments in Affiliates: None

Group Affiliation: Old Republic Group

Licensed in: All states except HI, MI, WA, PR

Commenced Business: August 1977

Address: 307 NORTH MICHIGAN AVENUE, Chicago, IL 60601

Phone: (312) 346-8100   **Domicile State:** IL   **NAIC Code:** 35424

Data Date	Rating	RACR #1	RACR #2	Loss Ratio %	Total Assets ($mil)	Capital ($mil)	Net Premium ($mil)	Net Income ($mil)
3-17	B	0.91	0.46	N/A	1,045.4	198.4	56.6	0.6
3-16	U	0.76	0.41	N/A	1,070.8	189.9	66.7	2.9
2016	B	0.89	0.45	97.9	1,056.6	196.8	224.4	-10.9
2015	U	0.72	0.39	106.4	1,092.5	184.3	329.9	-47.3
2014	U	10.40	6.20	117.0	1,022.9	86.5	362.5	-73.6
2013	U	346.80	173.40	104.2	908.3	154.2	345.2	-38.4
2012	D	1.59	1.48	91.0	793.4	184.9	279.9	-6.8

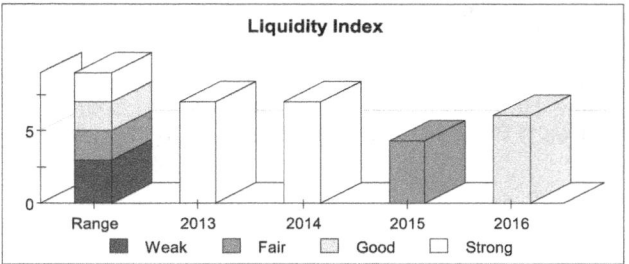

Liquidity Index

OLD UNITED CAS CO   C   Fair

Major Rating Factors: Fair profitability index (3.5 on a scale of 0 to 10). Fair expense controls. Return on equity has been fair, averaging 11.6% over the past five years. Fair overall results on stability tests (3.7) including fair financial strength of affiliated Berkshire-Hathaway and weak results on operational trends.

Other Rating Factors: Strong long-term capitalization index (10.0) based on excellent current risk adjusted capital (severe and moderate loss scenarios), despite some fluctuation in capital levels. Ample reserve history (7.3) that can protect against increases in claims costs. Superior liquidity (9.1) with ample operational cash flow and liquid investments.

Principal Business: Credit (14%).

Principal Investments: Investment grade bonds (83%), misc. investments (14%), and non investment grade bonds (3%).

Investments in Affiliates: None

Group Affiliation: Berkshire-Hathaway

Licensed in: All states except PR

Commenced Business: April 1989

Address: 8500 Shawnee Mission Pkwy #200, Merriam, KS 66202

Phone: (913) 895-0200   **Domicile State:** KS   **NAIC Code:** 37060

Data Date	Rating	RACR #1	RACR #2	Loss Ratio %	Total Assets ($mil)	Capital ($mil)	Net Premium ($mil)	Net Income ($mil)
3-17	C	5.81	3.26	N/A	625.0	220.0	29.1	6.6
3-16	C	7.08	3.87	N/A	552.2	187.2	26.7	7.6
2016	C	6.45	3.58	46.7	605.3	209.7	150.9	20.9
2015	C	6.61	3.57	43.4	540.1	184.1	141.7	33.2
2014	B-	8.20	4.44	43.3	656.6	335.4	126.5	39.0
2013	B-	8.22	4.39	44.7	603.8	302.6	119.9	27.3
2012	B-	8.02	4.18	45.7	522.5	262.0	108.8	24.6

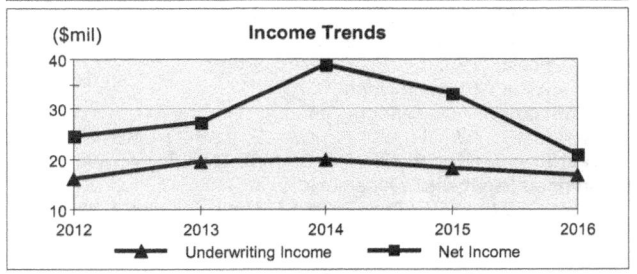

Income Trends

OMS NATIONAL INS CO RRG　　　　　　　　　　　　B-　　　Good

Major Rating Factors: Fair overall results on stability tests (4.1 on a scale of 0 to 10) including potential drain of affiliation with OMS National Ins and weak results on operational trends. The largest net exposure for one risk is conservative at 1.2% of capital. Strong long-term capitalization index (8.4) based on excellent current risk adjusted capital (severe and moderate loss scenarios). Moreover, capital levels have been consistent in recent years.

Other Rating Factors: Ample reserve history (8.8) that helps to protect the company against sharp claims increases. Excellent profitability (8.5) with operating gains in each of the last five years. Excellent liquidity (8.1) with ample operational cash flow and liquid investments.

Principal Business: Medical malpractice (100%).

Principal Investments: Investment grade bonds (55%), misc. investments (43%), and cash (2%).

Investments in Affiliates: 16%

Group Affiliation: OMS National Ins

Licensed in: All states except PR

Commenced Business: April 1988

Address: 6133 N RIVER ROAD SUITE 650, Rosemont, IL 60018-5173

Phone: (847) 384-0041　　**Domicile State:** IL　　**NAIC Code:** 44121

Data Date	Rating	RACR #1	RACR #2	Loss Ratio %	Total Assets ($mil)	Capital ($mil)	Net Premium ($mil)	Net Income ($mil)
3-17	B-	2.57	2.05	N/A	422.8	242.5	15.7	0.9
3-16	B-	2.48	2.00	N/A	384.6	220.1	16.1	1.1
2016	B-	2.59	2.08	61.4	419.0	238.3	67.2	13.8
2015	B-	2.50	2.03	68.0	384.3	216.8	63.8	8.9
2014	B-	2.46	1.98	67.9	374.8	215.1	65.7	12.9
2013	B-	2.43	1.98	51.3	342.9	191.5	69.9	21.4
2012	B-	2.88	2.19	55.1	383.0	166.6	77.3	15.6

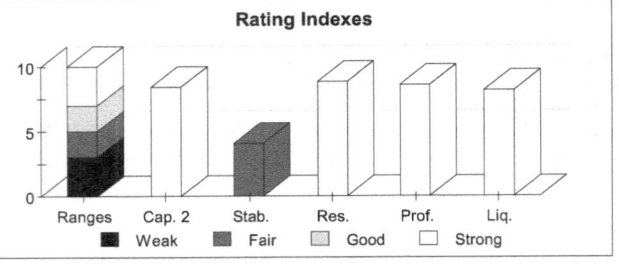

Rating Indexes

OPHTHALMIC MUTUAL INS CO RRG　　　　　　　　B　　　Good

Major Rating Factors: Fair overall results on stability tests (4.2 on a scale of 0 to 10) including weak results on operational trends. Strong long-term capitalization index (10.0) based on excellent current risk adjusted capital (severe and moderate loss scenarios). Moreover, capital levels have been consistent in recent years.

Other Rating Factors: Ample reserve history (9.0) that helps to protect the company against sharp claims increases. Excellent profitability (8.7) with operating gains in each of the last five years. Excellent liquidity (8.1) with ample operational cash flow and liquid investments.

Principal Business: Medical malpractice (100%).

Principal Investments: Investment grade bonds (83%), misc. investments (13%), and cash (4%).

Investments in Affiliates: None

Group Affiliation: None

Licensed in: All states except PR

Commenced Business: September 1987

Address: 126 College Street Suite 400, Burlington, VT 05401

Phone: (800) 562-6642　　**Domicile State:** VT　　**NAIC Code:** 44105

Data Date	Rating	RACR #1	RACR #2	Loss Ratio %	Total Assets ($mil)	Capital ($mil)	Net Premium ($mil)	Net Income ($mil)
3-17	B	12.25	7.68	N/A	281.1	208.7	8.9	1.0
3-16	B	11.98	7.61	N/A	273.3	196.4	9.7	3.5
2016	B	12.62	7.95	39.4	282.0	205.8	36.5	11.2
2015	B	12.61	8.10	39.9	275.1	192.7	39.8	10.8
2014	B	12.43	8.10	8.8	268.5	182.9	41.1	19.7
2013	B	11.20	8.07	30.3	259.9	163.6	39.9	12.7
2012	B	10.21	7.63	52.3	246.0	149.5	38.8	7.5

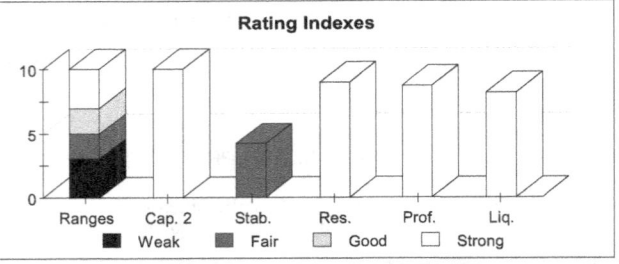

Rating Indexes

OWNERS INS CO *　　　　　　　　　　　　　　　A-　　　Excellent

Major Rating Factors: Strong long-term capitalization index (10.0 on a scale of 0 to 10) based on excellent current risk adjusted capital (severe and moderate loss scenarios). Furthermore, this high level of risk adjusted capital has been consistently maintained in previous years. Ample reserve history (8.3) that helps to protect the company against sharp claims increases.

Other Rating Factors: Excellent profitability (8.8) with operating gains in each of the last five years. Good liquidity (6.7) with sufficient resources (cash flows and marketable investments) to handle a spike in claims. Good overall results on stability tests (5.6) despite weak results on operational trends and negative cash flow from operations for 2016.

Principal Business: Auto liability (31%), commercial multiple peril (24%), auto physical damage (21%), workers compensation (8%), homeowners multiple peril (7%), other liability (5%), and other lines (4%).

Principal Investments: Investment grade bonds (84%), misc. investments (15%), and cash (1%).

Investments in Affiliates: None

Group Affiliation: Auto-Owners Group

Licensed in: AL, AZ, AR, CO, FL, GA, ID, IL, IN, IA, KS, KY, MI, MN, MS, MO, NE, NV, NM, NC, ND, OH, OR, PA, SC, SD, TN, UT, VA, WA, WI

Commenced Business: December 1975

Address: 2325 NORTH COLE STREET, Lima, OH 45801-2305

Phone: (517) 323-1200　　**Domicile State:** OH　　**NAIC Code:** 32700

Data Date	Rating	RACR #1	RACR #2	Loss Ratio %	Total Assets ($mil)	Capital ($mil)	Net Premium ($mil)	Net Income ($mil)
3-17	A-	5.74	3.83	N/A	3,948.4	1,736.5	372.3	28.3
3-16	A-	4.44	2.93	N/A	3,923.1	1,619.3	428.7	60.2
2016	A-	5.57	3.78	68.6	3,924.6	1,696.8	1,519.1	123.2
2015	A-	4.31	2.89	61.6	3,883.0	1,557.7	1,705.9	179.7
2014	A-	3.79	2.48	68.4	3,721.9	1,395.5	1,690.1	96.2
2013	A+	3.73	2.44	67.5	3,510.8	1,292.1	1,617.0	120.6
2012	A	3.48	2.08	70.3	3,191.7	1,139.3	1,518.7	92.5

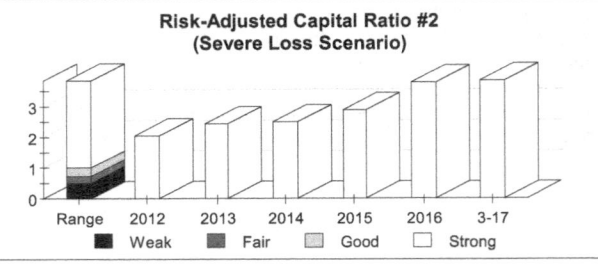

Risk-Adjusted Capital Ratio #2 (Severe Loss Scenario)

PACIFIC EMPLOYERS INS CO   B-   Good

Major Rating Factors: Fair overall results on stability tests (3.9 on a scale of 0 to 10) including potential drain of affiliation with Chubb Limited and weak results on operational trends. The largest net exposure for one risk is acceptable at 2.1% of capital. History of adequate reserve strength (6.3) as reserves have been consistently at an acceptable level.

Other Rating Factors: Good liquidity (6.9) with sufficient resources (cash flows and marketable investments) to handle a spike in claims. Strong long-term capitalization index (9.0) based on excellent current risk adjusted capital (severe and moderate loss scenarios). Moreover, capital levels have been consistent in recent years. Excellent profitability (8.4) with operating gains in each of the last five years.

Principal Business: Homeowners multiple peril (49%), inland marine (12%), other liability (10%), workers compensation (9%), auto liability (7%), auto physical damage (5%), and other lines (9%).

Principal Investments: Investment grade bonds (87%), cash (10%), and misc. investments (3%).

Investments in Affiliates: 4%

Group Affiliation: Chubb Limited

Licensed in: All states, the District of Columbia and Puerto Rico

Commenced Business: October 1923

Address: 436 WALNUT STREET, Philadelphia, PA 19106

Phone: (215) 640-1000   **Domicile State:** PA   **NAIC Code:** 22748

Data Date	Rating	RACR #1	RACR #2	Loss Ratio %	Total Assets ($mil)	Capital ($mil)	Net Premium ($mil)	Net Income ($mil)
3-17	B-	3.50	2.41	N/A	3,736.2	1,358.0	166.1	37.8
3-16	B-	3.10	2.17	N/A	3,454.9	1,256.7	164.6	16.3
2016	B-	3.41	2.36	76.5	3,774.2	1,319.9	889.3	114.6
2015	B-	3.10	2.17	72.8	3,541.6	1,240.4	846.9	69.5
2014	B-	3.12	2.20	77.6	3,390.5	1,170.2	796.9	48.4
2013	B-	3.27	2.31	72.2	3,309.0	1,141.6	774.9	89.1
2012	B-	3.27	2.27	89.9	3,329.0	1,085.8	797.6	29.4

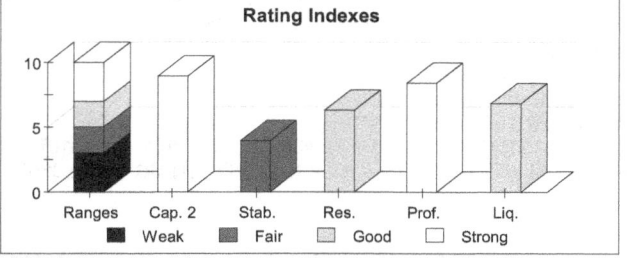

Rating Indexes

PACIFIC INDEMNITY CO   B-   Good

Major Rating Factors: Fair overall results on stability tests (3.7 on a scale of 0 to 10) including weak results on operational trends. The largest net exposure for one risk is excessive at 5.0% of capital. Good liquidity (6.9) with sufficient resources (cash flows and marketable investments) to handle a spike in claims.

Other Rating Factors: Strong long-term capitalization index (9.6) based on excellent current risk adjusted capital (severe and moderate loss scenarios), despite some fluctuation in capital levels. Ample reserve history (8.6) that helps to protect the company against sharp claims increases. Excellent profitability (7.3) with operating gains in each of the last five years. Return on equity has been good over the last five years, averaging 13.9%.

Principal Business: Homeowners multiple peril (44%), workers compensation (25%), inland marine (12%), commercial multiple peril (4%), other liability (4%), auto physical damage (3%), and other lines (6%).

Principal Investments: Investment grade bonds (96%) and misc. investments (4%).

Investments in Affiliates: 0%

Group Affiliation: Chubb Limited

Licensed in: All states except PR

Commenced Business: February 1926

Address: 330 East Kilbourn Ave Ste 1450, Milwaukee, WI 53202-3146

Phone: (908) 903-2000   **Domicile State:** WI   **NAIC Code:** 20346

Data Date	Rating	RACR #1	RACR #2	Loss Ratio %	Total Assets ($mil)	Capital ($mil)	Net Premium ($mil)	Net Income ($mil)
3-17	B-	5.70	3.65	N/A	6,782.9	2,988.7	251.9	66.9
3-16	B	4.51	2.89	N/A	6,764.2	2,873.5	338.2	173.5
2016	B-	5.52	3.53	53.2	6,555.1	2,926.6	1,074.5	417.8
2015	B	4.47	2.85	56.7	6,916.0	2,930.2	1,691.9	449.7
2014	B	4.38	2.80	56.2	6,822.4	2,922.2	1,624.5	421.6
2013	B+	4.16	2.69	52.5	6,640.5	2,771.4	1,568.7	425.6
2012	B+	3.74	2.39	66.1	6,465.8	2,496.2	1,506.1	278.8

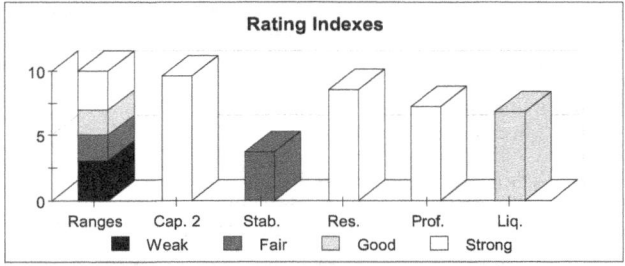

Rating Indexes

PACIFIC INS CO LTD   B   Good

Major Rating Factors: History of adequate reserve strength (5.8 on a scale of 0 to 10) as reserves have been consistently at an acceptable level. Good overall profitability index (5.3). Fair expense controls. Return on equity has been good over the last five years, averaging 10.0%.

Other Rating Factors: Good liquidity (6.8) with sufficient resources (cash flows and marketable investments) to handle a spike in claims. Good overall results on stability tests (5.8). Stability strengths include good operational trends and excellent risk diversification. Strong long-term capitalization index (9.1) based on excellent current risk adjusted capital (severe and moderate loss scenarios), despite some fluctuation in capital levels.

Principal Business: Other liability (55%), workers compensation (37%), auto liability (4%), and auto physical damage (3%).

Principal Investments: Investment grade bonds (93%) and misc. investments (7%).

Investments in Affiliates: None

Group Affiliation: Hartford Financial Services Inc

Licensed in: All states, the District of Columbia and Puerto Rico

Commenced Business: January 1995

Address: One Hartford Plaza, Hartford, CT 06155-0001

Phone: (860) 547-5000   **Domicile State:** CT   **NAIC Code:** 10046

Data Date	Rating	RACR #1	RACR #2	Loss Ratio %	Total Assets ($mil)	Capital ($mil)	Net Premium ($mil)	Net Income ($mil)
3-17	B	3.59	2.36	N/A	653.3	224.8	47.0	5.9
3-16	B	3.71	2.44	N/A	648.7	229.8	44.2	8.1
2016	B	3.62	2.40	70.4	660.7	219.2	179.1	20.4
2015	B	3.67	2.43	66.1	638.0	222.3	179.1	24.6
2014	B	3.84	2.54	67.0	635.6	227.2	174.2	28.5
2013	B	3.76	2.50	68.8	619.3	218.5	169.1	20.3
2012	B	3.86	2.57	72.7	618.7	220.2	167.4	17.2

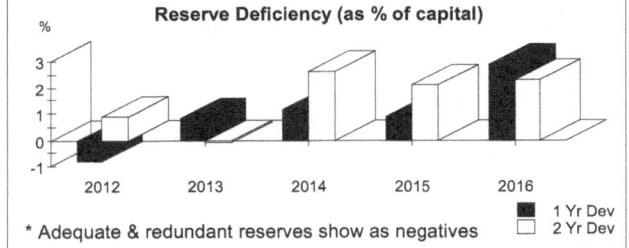

Reserve Deficiency (as % of capital)

* Adequate & redundant reserves show as negatives

PARTNER REINSURANCE CO OF THE US · C+ · Fair

Major Rating Factors: Fair overall results on stability tests (4.4 on a scale of 0 to 10) including potential drain of affiliation with Giovanni Agnelli e C Sapaz and weak results on operational trends. The largest net exposure for one risk is conservative at 1.4% of capital. Good liquidity (6.7) with sufficient resources (cash flows and marketable investments) to handle a spike in claims.

Other Rating Factors: Strong long-term capitalization index (8.0) based on excellent current risk adjusted capital (severe and moderate loss scenarios), despite some fluctuation in capital levels. Ample reserve history (9.6) that helps to protect the company against sharp claims increases. Excellent profitability (7.6) with operating gains in each of the last five years. Return on equity has been good over the last five years, averaging 11.6%.

Principal Business: (This company is a reinsurer.)

Principal Investments: Investment grade bonds (94%), misc. investments (4%), cash (1%), and non investment grade bonds (1%).

Investments in Affiliates: 3%

Group Affiliation: Giovanni Agnelli e C Sapaz

Licensed in: All states except PR

Commenced Business: May 1980

Address: 245 PARK AVE 39TH FL #39058, New York, NY 10167

Phone: (203) 485-4200 **Domicile State:** NY **NAIC Code:** 38636

Data Date	Rating	RACR #1	RACR #2	Loss Ratio %	Total Assets ($mil)	Capital ($mil)	Net Premium ($mil)	Net Income ($mil)
3-17	C+	2.54	1.60	N/A	4,720.1	1,372.1	236.1	0.8
3-16	C	1.98	1.26	N/A	4,987.8	1,420.3	267.4	15.0
2016	C+	2.73	1.73	67.2	4,822.9	1,463.8	1,188.2	71.7
2015	C	2.00	1.28	61.8	4,865.9	1,405.1	1,201.8	219.2
2014	C-	1.86	1.20	62.8	4,742.6	1,420.0	1,203.9	236.0
2013	C-	1.68	1.09	66.6	4,886.7	1,332.0	1,139.4	122.7
2012	C-	1.93	1.25	64.2	4,528.3	1,260.2	922.9	181.1

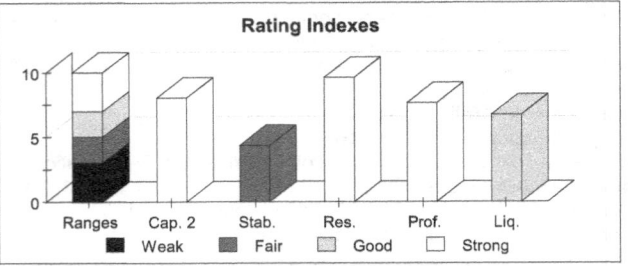

Rating Indexes
Ranges · Cap. 2 · Stab. · Res. · Prof. · Liq.
■ Weak ■ Fair □ Good □ Strong

PEERLESS INS CO · B- · Good

Major Rating Factors: Fair reserve development (4.8 on a scale of 0 to 10) as reserves have generally been sufficient to cover claims. Fair overall results on stability tests (3.9) including weak results on operational trends. The largest net exposure for one risk is excessive at 6.2% of capital.

Other Rating Factors: Good overall profitability index (6.3) despite operating losses during the first three months of 2017. Return on equity has been fair, averaging 8.6% over the past five years. Good liquidity (6.1) with sufficient resources (cash flows and marketable investments) to handle a spike in claims. Strong long-term capitalization index (7.7) based on excellent current risk adjusted capital (severe and moderate loss scenarios). Moreover, capital levels have been consistent in recent years.

Principal Business: Commercial multiple peril (27%), workers compensation (15%), auto liability (14%), inland marine (12%), other liability (10%), auto physical damage (7%), and other lines (15%).

Principal Investments: Investment grade bonds (72%), misc. investments (25%), and non investment grade bonds (5%).

Investments in Affiliates: 6%

Group Affiliation: Liberty Mutual Group

Licensed in: All states except HI, PR

Commenced Business: November 1903

Address: 62 Maple Avenue, Keene, NH 03431

Phone: (617) 357-9500 **Domicile State:** NH **NAIC Code:** 24198

Data Date	Rating	RACR #1	RACR #2	Loss Ratio %	Total Assets ($mil)	Capital ($mil)	Net Premium ($mil)	Net Income ($mil)
3-17	B-	2.18	1.53	N/A	13,521.2	3,569.9	1,308.7	-23.5
3-16	B-	2.13	1.48	N/A	13,038.7	3,387.5	1,263.4	67.1
2016	B-	2.21	1.55	69.9	13,330.8	3,538.9	5,299.8	154.3
2015	B-	2.07	1.44	68.4	13,172.4	3,316.7	5,126.4	304.6
2014	B-	1.88	1.30	70.0	12,800.9	3,058.9	5,075.4	247.2
2013	B-	1.60	1.09	73.5	13,621.2	2,786.4	5,827.5	151.5
2012	B-	1.71	1.33	66.7	7,629.8	1,887.3	2,751.4	349.4

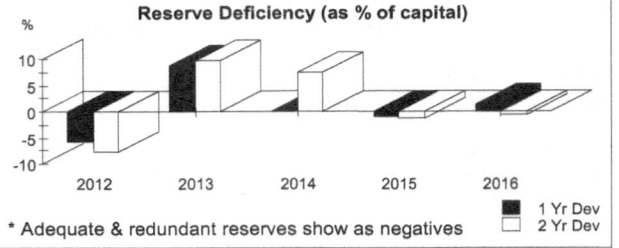

Reserve Deficiency (as % of capital)
2012 · 2013 · 2014 · 2015 · 2016
* Adequate & redundant reserves show as negatives
■ 1 Yr Dev □ 2 Yr Dev

PEKIN INS CO * · B+ · Good

Major Rating Factors: Good profitability index (5.0 on a scale of 0 to 10) despite operating losses during the first three months of 2017. Return on equity has been low, averaging 3.6% over the past five years. Good liquidity (6.6) with sufficient resources (cash flows and marketable investments) to handle a spike in claims.

Other Rating Factors: Good overall results on stability tests (5.0) despite weak results on operational trends. Strong long-term capitalization index (10.0) based on excellent current risk adjusted capital (severe and moderate loss scenarios), despite some fluctuation in capital levels. Ample reserve history (8.3) that helps to protect the company against sharp claims increases.

Principal Business: Commercial multiple peril (25%), workers compensation (20%), auto liability (20%), auto physical damage (15%), homeowners multiple peril (13%), other liability (4%), and other lines (3%).

Principal Investments: Investment grade bonds (89%) and misc. investments (11%).

Investments in Affiliates: 3%

Group Affiliation: Farmers Automobile Ins Assn

Licensed in: AZ, IL, IN, IA, MI, OH, WI

Commenced Business: July 1961

Address: 2505 COURT STREET, Pekin, IL 61558

Phone: (309) 346-1161 **Domicile State:** IL **NAIC Code:** 24228

Data Date	Rating	RACR #1	RACR #2	Loss Ratio %	Total Assets ($mil)	Capital ($mil)	Net Premium ($mil)	Net Income ($mil)
3-17	B+	4.47	3.10	N/A	306.7	127.1	29.8	-1.8
3-16	B+	4.53	3.18	N/A	302.7	126.4	29.4	1.0
2016	B+	4.62	3.27	77.7	312.2	128.3	122.8	1.2
2015	B+	4.60	3.27	71.5	295.9	125.7	120.2	5.5
2014	B+	4.63	3.29	74.3	281.2	118.7	113.8	5.5
2013	B+	4.79	3.39	75.4	281.9	117.1	107.1	4.4
2012	B+	4.80	3.43	75.1	262.7	111.6	100.5	7.6

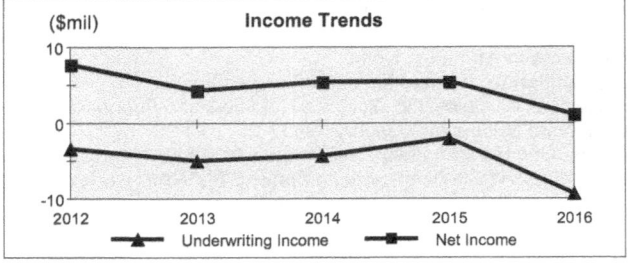

Income Trends ($mil)
2012 · 2013 · 2014 · 2015 · 2016
▲ Underwriting Income ■ Net Income

PEMCO MUTUAL INS CO   B-   Good

Major Rating Factors: Fair overall results on stability tests (4.1 on a scale of 0 to 10) including potential drain of affiliation with PEMCO Corp and weak results on operational trends. History of adequate reserve strength (6.0) as reserves have been consistently at an acceptable level.

Other Rating Factors: Good overall profitability index (5.9) despite operating losses during 2012 and 2013. Good liquidity (6.1) with sufficient resources (cash flows and marketable investments) to handle a spike in claims. Strong long-term capitalization index (8.8) based on excellent current risk adjusted capital (severe and moderate loss scenarios). Moreover, capital levels have been consistent in recent years.

Principal Business: Auto liability (47%), homeowners multiple peril (25%), auto physical damage (23%), other liability (2%), fire (2%), and inland marine (1%).

Principal Investments: Investment grade bonds (81%), real estate (11%), misc. investments (7%), and cash (1%).

Investments in Affiliates: 0%

Group Affiliation: PEMCO Corp

Licensed in: ID, OR, WA

Commenced Business: February 1949

Address: 1300 Dexter Avenue N, Seattle, WA 98109-3571

Phone: (206) 628-4290   **Domicile State:** WA   **NAIC Code:** 24341

Data Date	Rating	RACR #1	RACR #2	Loss Ratio %	Total Assets ($mil)	Capital ($mil)	Net Premium ($mil)	Net Income ($mil)
3-17	B-	2.78	2.21	N/A	735.5	282.9	104.4	0.9
3-16	B-	2.90	2.27	N/A	720.7	272.4	98.9	16.9
2016	B-	2.70	2.20	80.7	740.7	282.0	421.5	24.1
2015	B-	2.71	2.18	77.0	706.8	259.0	396.6	10.2
2014	B-	2.81	2.33	77.5	687.4	254.5	370.1	24.0
2013	B-	2.82	2.34	72.2	629.4	237.4	346.0	-3.3
2012	B-	2.77	2.23	79.3	611.4	232.7	322.6	-16.3

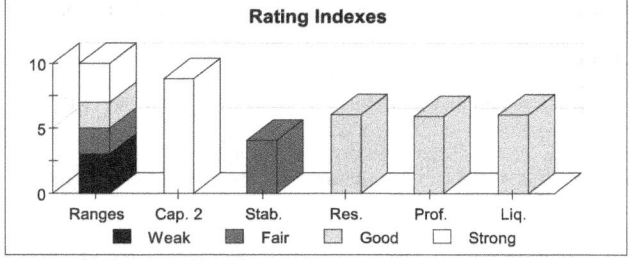

Rating Indexes

PENN NATIONAL SECURITY INS CO   B-   Good

Major Rating Factors: Fair overall results on stability tests (4.4 on a scale of 0 to 10) including potential drain of affiliation with Pennsylvania National Ins Group and weak results on operational trends. History of adequate reserve strength (6.3) as reserves have been consistently at an acceptable level.

Other Rating Factors: Good overall profitability index (6.9) with small operating losses during 2012. Return on equity has been low, averaging 4.1% over the past five years. Good liquidity (6.5) with sufficient resources (cash flows and marketable investments) to handle a spike in claims. Strong long-term capitalization index (9.3) based on excellent current risk adjusted capital (severe and moderate loss scenarios). Moreover, capital levels have been consistent in recent years.

Principal Business: Workers compensation (25%), auto liability (22%), other liability (13%), fire (13%), commercial multiple peril (10%), products liability (7%), and other lines (10%).

Principal Investments: Investment grade bonds (92%) and misc. investments (8%).

Investments in Affiliates: None

Group Affiliation: Pennsylvania National Ins Group

Licensed in: AL, DC, DE, MD, NJ, NC, PA, SC, TN, VA

Commenced Business: January 1989

Address: Two North Second Street, Harrisburg, PA 17101

Phone: (717) 234-4941   **Domicile State:** PA   **NAIC Code:** 32441

Data Date	Rating	RACR #1	RACR #2	Loss Ratio %	Total Assets ($mil)	Capital ($mil)	Net Premium ($mil)	Net Income ($mil)
3-17	B-	3.78	2.60	N/A	982.6	324.4	83.7	1.7
3-16	B-	3.51	2.44	N/A	942.6	304.0	83.9	5.5
2016	B-	3.81	2.65	64.2	950.4	320.2	336.1	22.9
2015	B-	3.56	2.50	65.0	914.5	299.7	330.9	13.3
2014	B-	3.46	2.43	64.8	894.1	287.2	326.5	18.4
2013	B-	3.04	2.07	65.5	843.2	282.1	315.8	10.3
2012	B-	2.92	2.00	77.4	804.2	254.5	309.5	-1.6

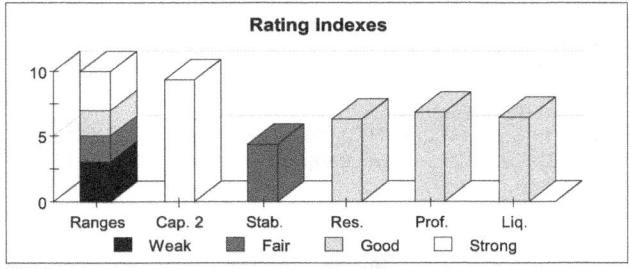

Rating Indexes

PENNSYLVANIA MANUFACTURERS ASN INS   C   Fair

Major Rating Factors: Fair overall results on stability tests (3.7 on a scale of 0 to 10). A history of deficient reserves (2.8). Underreserving can have an adverse impact on capital and profits. Deficiencies in the two year reserve development occurred in three of the previous five years and ranged between 18% and 22%.

Other Rating Factors: Good overall profitability index (6.5) with small operating losses during 2014. Return on equity has been low, averaging 2.0% over the past five years. Good liquidity (6.7) with sufficient resources (cash flows and marketable investments) to handle a spike in claims. Strong long-term capitalization index (8.1) based on excellent current risk adjusted capital (severe and moderate loss scenarios), despite some fluctuation in capital levels.

Principal Business: Workers compensation (68%), inland marine (16%), auto liability (8%), other liability (3%), commercial multiple peril (3%), and auto physical damage (1%).

Principal Investments: Investment grade bonds (76%), misc. investments (21%), and non investment grade bonds (5%).

Investments in Affiliates: None

Group Affiliation: Old Republic Group

Licensed in: All states, the District of Columbia and Puerto Rico

Commenced Business: July 1964

Address: 380 SENTRY PARKWAY, Blue Bell, PA 19422-0754

Phone: (610) 397-5000   **Domicile State:** PA   **NAIC Code:** 12262

Data Date	Rating	RACR #1	RACR #2	Loss Ratio %	Total Assets ($mil)	Capital ($mil)	Net Premium ($mil)	Net Income ($mil)
3-17	C	2.49	1.69	N/A	945.8	284.3	44.9	0.7
3-16	C	2.56	1.73	N/A	882.3	256.0	40.3	-0.9
2016	C	2.63	1.79	78.6	929.6	283.7	159.1	0.3
2015	C	2.65	1.79	83.1	821.9	251.7	134.7	6.0
2014	C	2.93	2.12	91.2	834.0	266.1	149.5	-2.1
2013	C	2.86	2.11	79.9	761.2	224.5	135.6	18.0
2012	C	2.91	2.22	79.3	730.6	225.4	143.1	1.0

Old Republic Group Composite Group Rating: B Largest Group Members	Assets ($mil)	Rating
OLD REPUB INS CO	2814	B
OLD REPUBLIC GENERAL INS CORP	2021	B
GREAT WEST CASUALTY CO	2016	B
OLD REPUBLIC SECURITY ASR CO	1057	B
PENNSYLVANIA MANUFACTURERS ASN INS	930	C

PENNSYLVANIA NTL MUTUAL CAS INS CO   B-   Good

Major Rating Factors: Fair overall results on stability tests (4.5 on a scale of 0 to 10) including potential drain of affiliation with Pennsylvania National Ins Group and weak results on operational trends. History of adequate reserve strength (6.2) as reserves have been consistently at an acceptable level.

Other Rating Factors: Good overall profitability index (6.9). Fair expense controls. Good liquidity (6.7) with sufficient resources (cash flows and marketable investments) to handle a spike in claims. Strong long-term capitalization index (7.8) based on excellent current risk adjusted capital (severe and moderate loss scenarios). Moreover, capital levels have been consistent in recent years.

Principal Business: Auto liability (24%), auto physical damage (16%), other liability (15%), homeowners multiple peril (15%), workers compensation (10%), commercial multiple peril (7%), and other lines (13%).

Principal Investments: Investment grade bonds (53%), misc. investments (45%), and cash (2%).

Investments in Affiliates: 35%

Group Affiliation: Pennsylvania National Ins Group

Licensed in: All states except CA, CT, HI, NV, NH, ND, WY, PR

Commenced Business: April 1920

Address: Two North Second Street, Harrisburg, PA 17101

Phone: (717) 234-4941   **Domicile State:** PA   **NAIC Code:** 14990

Data Date	Rating	RACR #1	RACR #2	Loss Ratio %	Total Assets ($mil)	Capital ($mil)	Net Premium ($mil)	Net Income ($mil)
3-17	B-	1.73	1.57	N/A	1,298.3	620.5	83.7	5.2
3-16	B-	1.71	1.55	N/A	1,242.7	580.9	83.9	6.5
2016	B-	1.71	1.56	64.2	1,279.7	612.0	336.1	29.4
2015	B-	1.71	1.56	65.0	1,233.6	571.4	330.9	14.6
2014	B-	1.72	1.55	64.8	1,192.6	558.8	326.5	23.8
2013	B-	1.65	1.47	65.5	1,125.8	541.2	315.8	22.4
2012	B-	1.59	1.42	77.4	1,036.8	473.7	279.4	13.9

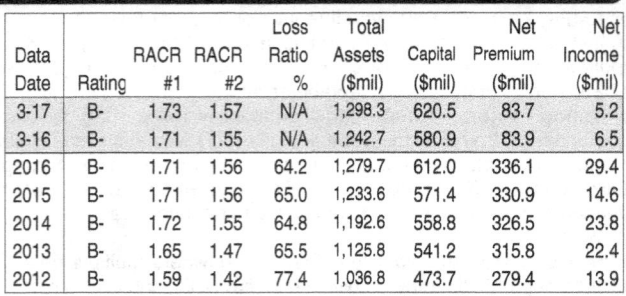

Rating Indexes

PHILADELPHIA CBSP FOR INS OF HOUSES   B-   Good

Major Rating Factors: Fair overall results on stability tests (4.1 on a scale of 0 to 10) including potential drain of affiliation with Philadelphia Contrib Group, weak results on operational trends and negative cash flow from operations for 2016. Good overall profitability index (6.6) despite modest operating losses during 2016. Return on equity has been low, averaging 1.5% over the past five years.

Other Rating Factors: Good liquidity (6.7) with sufficient resources (cash flows and marketable investments) to handle a spike in claims. Strong long-term capitalization index (7.2) based on excellent current risk adjusted capital (severe and moderate loss scenarios), despite some fluctuation in capital levels. Ample reserve history (7.3) that can protect against increases in claims costs.

Principal Business: (This company is a reinsurer.)

Principal Investments: Misc. investments (96%), investment grade bonds (2%), cash (1%), and real estate (1%).

Investments in Affiliates: 52%

Group Affiliation: Philadelphia Contrib Group

Licensed in: NJ, PA

Commenced Business: March 1753

Address: 210 SOUTH FOURTH STREET, Philadelphia, PE 19106-9232

Phone: (888) 627-1752   **Domicile State:** PA   **NAIC Code:** 17930

Data Date	Rating	RACR #1	RACR #2	Loss Ratio %	Total Assets ($mil)	Capital ($mil)	Net Premium ($mil)	Net Income ($mil)
3-17	B-	1.34	1.16	N/A	340.6	261.2	9.1	2.6
3-16	B-	1.29	1.12	N/A	307.8	229.4	9.0	-2.0
2016	B-	1.32	1.15	71.6	329.2	251.9	36.8	-0.7
2015	B-	1.31	1.14	75.1	309.5	233.1	36.6	1.1
2014	B-	1.32	1.13	85.2	326.3	245.0	37.1	8.3
2013	B-	1.30	1.10	63.0	316.6	234.8	35.8	6.0
2012	B-	1.27	1.08	87.8	266.3	187.5	33.1	1.1

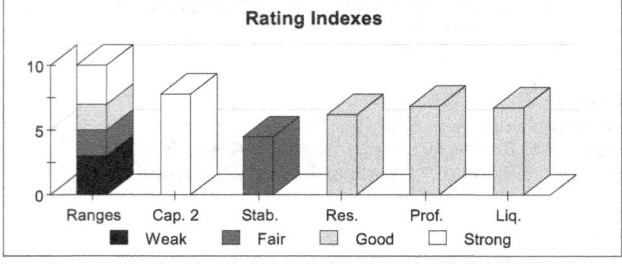

Rating Indexes

PHILADELPHIA INDEMNITY INS CO   B-   Good

Major Rating Factors: Fair overall results on stability tests (4.6 on a scale of 0 to 10) including potential drain of affiliation with Tokio Marine Holdings Inc and weak results on operational trends. Good liquidity (6.7) with sufficient resources (cash flows and marketable investments) to handle a spike in claims.

Other Rating Factors: Strong long-term capitalization index (8.3) based on excellent current risk adjusted capital (severe and moderate loss scenarios), despite some fluctuation in capital levels. Ample reserve history (7.7) that can protect against increases in claims costs. Excellent profitability (7.4) with operating gains in each of the last five years. Return on equity has been good over the last five years, averaging 13.7%.

Principal Business: Commercial multiple peril (54%), other liability (22%), auto liability (14%), auto physical damage (5%), surety (3%), and allied lines (1%).

Principal Investments: Investment grade bonds (82%), misc. investments (14%), and non investment grade bonds (4%).

Investments in Affiliates: None

Group Affiliation: Tokio Marine Holdings Inc

Licensed in: All states except PR

Commenced Business: March 1927

Address: One Bala Plaza Suite 100, Bala Cynwyd, PA 19004-1403

Phone: (610) 206-7836   **Domicile State:** PA   **NAIC Code:** 18058

Data Date	Rating	RACR #1	RACR #2	Loss Ratio %	Total Assets ($mil)	Capital ($mil)	Net Premium ($mil)	Net Income ($mil)
3-17	B-	2.51	1.87	N/A	8,309.9	2,354.2	715.0	82.4
3-16	B-	2.32	1.73	N/A	7,583.9	2,131.0	671.6	81.5
2016	B-	2.52	1.89	60.9	8,081.0	2,271.5	2,872.8	347.7
2015	B-	2.30	1.73	60.5	7,361.5	2,047.5	2,696.2	311.2
2014	B-	2.55	1.92	61.5	7,182.2	2,337.4	2,553.3	306.1
2013	B	2.66	2.02	61.0	6,526.1	2,156.7	2,351.5	293.5
2012	B	3.01	2.32	62.8	6,047.3	2,017.2	2,124.8	229.6

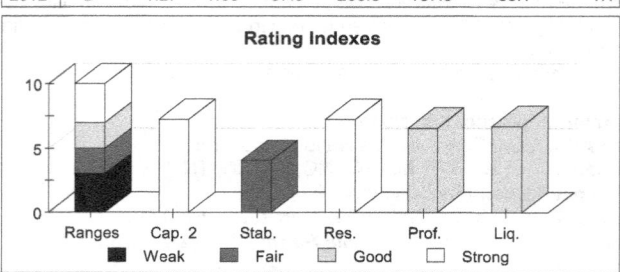

Rating Indexes

PHOENIX INS CO   B   Good

Major Rating Factors: Good liquidity (6.8 on a scale of 0 to 10) with sufficient resources (cash flows and marketable investments) to handle a spike in claims. Good overall results on stability tests (5.0) despite weak results on operational trends. Affiliation with Travelers Companies Inc is a strength.

Other Rating Factors: Strong long-term capitalization index (7.9) based on excellent current risk adjusted capital (severe and moderate loss scenarios), despite some fluctuation in capital levels. Ample reserve history (8.1) that helps to protect the company against sharp claims increases. Excellent profitability (7.4) with operating gains in each of the last five years. Return on equity has been good over the last five years, averaging 12.0%.

Principal Business: Workers compensation (35%), commercial multiple peril (26%), auto liability (12%), homeowners multiple peril (7%), other liability (7%), inland marine (5%), and other lines (7%).

Principal Investments: Investment grade bonds (69%), misc. investments (30%), and non investment grade bonds (1%).

Investments in Affiliates: 26%

Group Affiliation: Travelers Companies Inc

Licensed in: All states except CA, PR

Commenced Business: July 1850

Address: ONE TOWER SQUARE, Hartford, CT 06183

Phone: (860) 277-0111   **Domicile State:** CT   **NAIC Code:** 25623

Data Date	Rating	RACR #1	RACR #2	Loss Ratio %	Total Assets ($mil)	Capital ($mil)	Net Premium ($mil)	Net Income ($mil)
3-17	B	1.79	1.58	N/A	4,264.0	1,762.3	269.9	23.0
3-16	B	1.79	1.57	N/A	4,250.6	1,793.2	259.9	27.1
2016	B	1.77	1.57	63.4	4,184.1	1,718.4	1,088.9	215.9
2015	B	1.77	1.56	58.7	4,175.2	1,746.0	1,039.8	312.8
2014	B	1.62	1.45	60.5	4,196.2	1,739.4	1,009.4	207.8
2013	B	1.53	1.37	60.9	4,009.4	1,579.1	1,006.9	194.5
2012	B	1.43	1.27	68.4	3,860.1	1,390.6	978.0	98.5

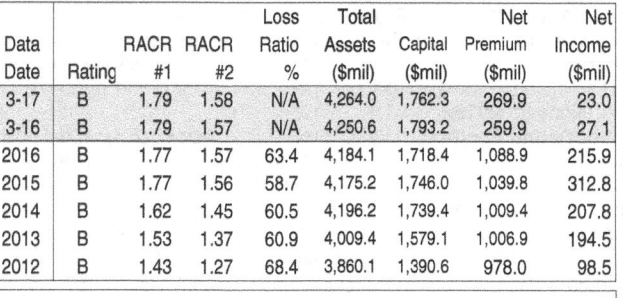

Liquidity Index

PHYSICIANS INS A MUTL CO   B-   Good

Major Rating Factors: Fair overall results on stability tests (4.1 on a scale of 0 to 10) including potential drain of affiliation with Washington State Health and weak results on operational trends. Good overall profitability index (6.8). Good expense controls.

Other Rating Factors: Strong long-term capitalization index (10.0) based on excellent current risk adjusted capital (severe and moderate loss scenarios), despite some fluctuation in capital levels. Ample reserve history (9.4) that helps to protect the company against sharp claims increases. Excellent liquidity (7.5) with ample operational cash flow and liquid investments.

Principal Business: Medical malpractice (84%), aggregate write-ins for other lines of business (16%), and other liability (1%).

Principal Investments: Investment grade bonds (76%), misc. investments (21%), and cash (3%).

Investments in Affiliates: 3%

Group Affiliation: Washington State Health

Licensed in: AK, AZ, CA, CO, GA, HI, ID, IL, MI, MT, NV, NM, OR, UT, WA, WY, PR

Commenced Business: December 1981

Address: 1301 Second Avenue Suite 2700, Seattle, WA 98101

Phone: (206) 343-7300   **Domicile State:** WA   **NAIC Code:** 40738

Data Date	Rating	RACR #1	RACR #2	Loss Ratio %	Total Assets ($mil)	Capital ($mil)	Net Premium ($mil)	Net Income ($mil)
3-17	B-	4.08	3.08	N/A	541.3	240.5	19.7	4.2
3-16	B-	4.06	3.11	N/A	508.0	224.0	19.6	4.4
2016	B-	4.07	3.12	82.2	502.3	232.1	78.2	8.1
2015	B-	4.08	3.15	84.4	471.0	220.0	76.3	6.9
2014	B-	4.08	3.16	82.1	468.3	222.6	76.7	11.6
2013	B-	4.11	3.20	85.2	454.0	211.9	72.9	5.6
2012	B-	4.03	3.21	80.1	428.5	195.4	67.8	8.2

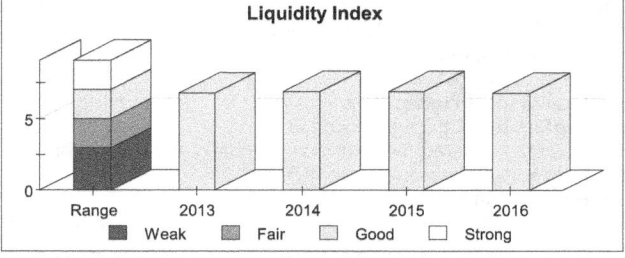

Rating Indexes

PIONEER STATE MUTUAL INS CO   B   Good

Major Rating Factors: Good liquidity (6.9 on a scale of 0 to 10) with sufficient resources (cash flows and marketable investments) to handle a spike in claims. Fair overall results on stability tests (4.7) including weak results on operational trends.

Other Rating Factors: Strong long-term capitalization index (10.0) based on excellent current risk adjusted capital (severe and moderate loss scenarios). Moreover, capital levels have been consistent in recent years. Ample reserve history (8.7) that helps to protect the company against sharp claims increases. Excellent profitability (8.8) with operating gains in each of the last five years.

Principal Business: Auto liability (37%), homeowners multiple peril (27%), auto physical damage (25%), farmowners multiple peril (5%), commercial multiple peril (3%), workers compensation (1%), and other lines (2%).

Principal Investments: Investment grade bonds (60%), misc. investments (35%), cash (3%), non investment grade bonds (1%), and real estate (1%).

Investments in Affiliates: None

Group Affiliation: None

Licensed in: IN, MI

Commenced Business: June 1908

Address: 1510 North Elms Road, Flint, MI 48532-2000

Phone: (810) 733-2300   **Domicile State:** MI   **NAIC Code:** 18309

Data Date	Rating	RACR #1	RACR #2	Loss Ratio %	Total Assets ($mil)	Capital ($mil)	Net Premium ($mil)	Net Income ($mil)
3-17	B	5.05	3.18	N/A	561.4	331.1	47.5	3.4
3-16	B	5.04	3.21	N/A	506.9	298.6	45.3	6.0
2016	B	5.12	3.24	60.1	550.7	323.5	196.7	25.7
2015	B	4.96	3.16	60.6	499.5	292.4	183.3	20.0
2014	B	4.69	2.98	66.3	472.2	277.9	174.4	16.0
2013	A	4.51	2.84	64.4	448.4	260.0	171.1	13.6
2012	A	5.03	3.25	66.2	400.9	233.1	163.7	11.8

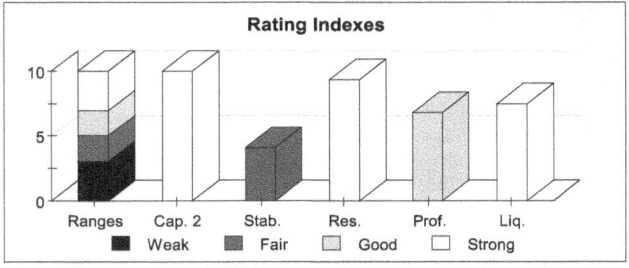

Liquidity Index

PRAETORIAN INS CO

C   **Fair**

Major Rating Factors: Fair reserve development (4.4 on a scale of 0 to 10) as reserves have generally been sufficient to cover claims. In 2013, the two year reserve development was 17% deficient. Fair overall results on stability tests (4.1) including weak results on operational trends and negative cash flow from operations for 2016.

Other Rating Factors: Weak profitability index (2.5) with operating losses during 2012, 2013 and 2014. Average return on equity over the last five years has been poor at -1.9%. Good liquidity (6.5) with sufficient resources (cash flows and marketable investments) to handle a spike in claims. Strong long-term capitalization index (8.5) based on excellent current risk adjusted capital (severe and moderate loss scenarios), despite some fluctuation in capital levels.

Principal Business: Homeowners multiple peril (27%), workers compensation (27%), auto physical damage (16%), auto liability (12%), inland marine (7%), commercial multiple peril (7%), and other liability (4%).

Principal Investments: Investment grade bonds (74%), misc. investments (18%), and cash (8%).

Investments in Affiliates: None

Group Affiliation: QBE Ins Group Ltd

Licensed in: All states, the District of Columbia and Puerto Rico

Commenced Business: August 1979

Address: 116 Pine Street Suite 320, Harrisburg, PA 17101

Phone: (608) 825-5160   **Domicile State:** PA   **NAIC Code:** 37257

Data Date	Rating	RACR #1	RACR #2	Loss Ratio %	Total Assets ($mil)	Capital ($mil)	Net Premium ($mil)	Net Income ($mil)
3-17	C	4.22	2.92	N/A	515.4	223.4	31.9	1.4
3-16	C	2.99	2.02	N/A	805.9	218.3	31.6	0.6
2016	C	4.32	3.00	58.8	492.0	226.8	61.1	5.0
2015	C	2.23	1.49	63.9	870.9	243.9	300.7	13.3
2014	C	2.08	1.43	69.2	996.8	264.9	415.5	-7.1
2013	C-	1.67	1.14	75.2	971.9	248.4	400.0	-28.2
2012	C	1.64	1.12	73.5	1,109.4	316.3	545.2	-13.5

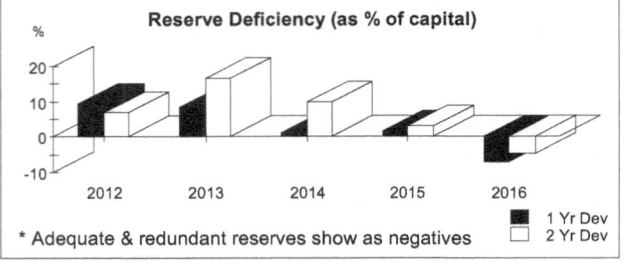

Reserve Deficiency (as % of capital)

■ 1 Yr Dev   □ 2 Yr Dev

* Adequate & redundant reserves show as negatives

PREFERRED MUTUAL INS CO

B   **Good**

Major Rating Factors: Good overall profitability index (6.2 on a scale of 0 to 10) despite operating losses during the first three months of 2017. Good liquidity (6.7) with sufficient resources (cash flows and marketable investments) to handle a spike in claims.

Other Rating Factors: Fair overall results on stability tests (4.3) including weak results on operational trends. Strong long-term capitalization index (9.9) based on excellent current risk adjusted capital (severe and moderate loss scenarios). Moreover, capital levels have been consistent in recent years. Ample reserve history (8.7) that helps to protect the company against sharp claims increases.

Principal Business: Homeowners multiple peril (42%), auto liability (18%), commercial multiple peril (18%), auto physical damage (13%), other liability (3%), fire (2%), and other lines (3%).

Principal Investments: Investment grade bonds (81%), misc. investments (12%), non investment grade bonds (8%), and real estate (1%).

Investments in Affiliates: None

Group Affiliation: None

Licensed in: CT, MA, NH, NJ, NY, NC, OH, PA, RI, SC

Commenced Business: January 1897

Address: One Preferred Way, New Berlin, NY 13411

Phone: (607) 847-6161   **Domicile State:** NY   **NAIC Code:** 15024

Data Date	Rating	RACR #1	RACR #2	Loss Ratio %	Total Assets ($mil)	Capital ($mil)	Net Premium ($mil)	Net Income ($mil)
3-17	B	4.86	3.03	N/A	531.3	234.0	53.4	-2.5
3-16	B	4.62	3.00	N/A	520.1	217.9	50.6	5.0
2016	B	4.98	3.14	60.4	539.1	234.6	213.2	16.2
2015	B	4.54	2.99	67.8	522.7	212.7	204.4	18.6
2014	B	4.38	2.89	68.2	502.3	200.1	199.9	14.3
2013	B	3.43	2.25	65.5	484.8	185.3	193.6	13.3
2012	B	3.18	2.11	66.6	456.4	166.4	182.5	11.9

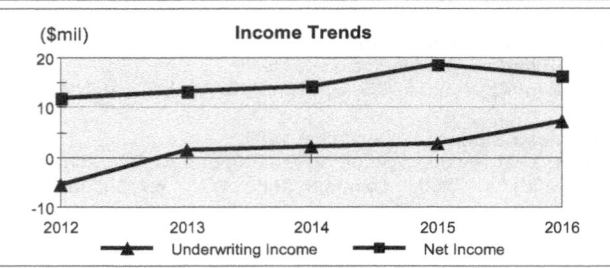

Income Trends

▲ Underwriting Income   ■ Net Income

PREMIER INS CO OF MA

B   **Good**

Major Rating Factors: History of adequate reserve strength (6.0 on a scale of 0 to 10) as reserves have been consistently at an acceptable level. Good overall profitability index (6.7). Fair expense controls. Return on equity has been fair, averaging 5.8% over the past five years.

Other Rating Factors: Fair overall results on stability tests (4.6) including weak results on operational trends and negative cash flow from operations for 2016. Strong long-term capitalization index (10.0) based on excellent current risk adjusted capital (severe and moderate loss scenarios), despite some fluctuation in capital levels. Excellent liquidity (7.0) with ample operational cash flow and liquid investments.

Principal Business: (Not applicable due to unusual reinsurance transactions.)

Principal Investments: Investment grade bonds (97%) and misc. investments (3%).

Investments in Affiliates: None

Group Affiliation: Travelers Companies Inc

Licensed in: CT, MA

Commenced Business: July 1993

Address: ONE TOWER SQUARE, Hartford, CT 06183

Phone: (860) 277-0111   **Domicile State:** CT   **NAIC Code:** 12850

Data Date	Rating	RACR #1	RACR #2	Loss Ratio %	Total Assets ($mil)	Capital ($mil)	Net Premium ($mil)	Net Income ($mil)
3-17	B	69.51	45.55	N/A	255.2	236.2	0.0	2.2
3-16	B	13.55	11.08	N/A	298.0	239.0	14.2	6.4
2016	B	57.11	42.38	46.3	259.9	234.3	-0.5	15.1
2015	B	11.11	9.56	59.7	307.2	234.0	73.8	19.7
2014	B-	7.27	6.53	69.1	350.4	227.6	112.3	13.5
2013	B	5.86	5.32	76.9	362.1	219.7	132.1	7.0
2012	B	5.06	4.61	75.6	375.0	218.6	153.4	12.2

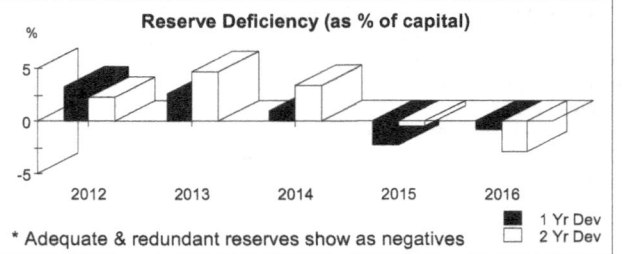

Reserve Deficiency (as % of capital)

■ 1 Yr Dev   □ 2 Yr Dev

* Adequate & redundant reserves show as negatives

PRINCETON INS CO C Fair

Major Rating Factors: Fair overall results on stability tests (3.8 on a scale of 0 to 10) including fair financial strength of affiliated Berkshire Hathaway and weak results on operational trends. Strong long-term capitalization index (10.0) based on excellent current risk adjusted capital (severe and moderate loss scenarios), despite some fluctuation in capital levels.

Other Rating Factors: Ample reserve history (9.3) that helps to protect the company against sharp claims increases. Excellent profitability (7.4) with operating gains in each of the last five years. Superior liquidity (10.0) with ample operational cash flow and liquid investments.

Principal Business: Medical malpractice (98%) and other liability (2%).

Principal Investments: Investment grade bonds (75%), misc. investments (12%), cash (11%), non investment grade bonds (1%), and real estate (1%).

Investments in Affiliates: None

Group Affiliation: Berkshire Hathaway

Licensed in: AZ, CT, DC, DE, GA, IL, IN, MD, MI, NJ, NY, NC, PA, SC, VA, WA, WV

Commenced Business: February 1982

Address: 746 Alexander Road, Princeton, NJ 08540

Phone: (609) 452-9404 **Domicile State:** NJ **NAIC Code:** 42226

Data Date	Rating	RACR #1	RACR #2	Loss Ratio %	Total Assets ($mil)	Capital ($mil)	Net Premium ($mil)	Net Income ($mil)
3-17	C	6.66	4.88	N/A	695.0	483.8	7.1	3.3
3-16	C	6.88	5.16	N/A	669.2	463.7	7.4	4.0
2016	C	6.70	4.97	65.8	689.6	475.9	29.1	18.8
2015	C	6.89	5.14	79.3	666.4	463.9	31.0	12.1
2014	C	6.60	4.76	78.1	665.0	460.7	33.1	13.9
2013	C	8.15	6.06	104.5	628.5	438.8	35.1	12.6
2012	C	10.70	7.63	99.4	585.5	412.6	-502.9	79.6

Berkshire Hathaway
Composite Group Rating: B

Largest Group Members	Assets ($mil)	Rating
NATIONAL INDEMNITY CO	178623	B
GOVERNMENT EMPLOYEES INS CO	27198	B
COLUMBIA INS CO	20707	U
BERKSHIRE HATHAWAY LIFE INS CO OF NE	17970	C+
GENERAL REINS CORP	14780	C+

PROASSURANCE CASUALTY CO B- Good

Major Rating Factors: Fair profitability index (3.2 on a scale of 0 to 10). Fair expense controls. Return on equity has been fair, averaging 14.4% over the past five years. Fair overall results on stability tests (4.5) including weak results on operational trends.

Other Rating Factors: Strong long-term capitalization index (9.1) based on excellent current risk adjusted capital (severe and moderate loss scenarios), despite some fluctuation in capital levels. Ample reserve history (9.6) that helps to protect the company against sharp claims increases. Excellent liquidity (7.3) with ample operational cash flow and liquid investments.

Principal Business: Medical malpractice (99%) and other liability (1%).

Principal Investments: Investment grade bonds (66%), misc. investments (27%), and non investment grade bonds (7%).

Investments in Affiliates: None

Group Affiliation: ProAssurance Corp

Licensed in: AL, CA, CT, DE, FL, GA, IL, IN, IA, KS, KY, MD, MA, MI, MN, MS, MO, NE, NV, NJ, NY, ND, OH, PA, SC, SD, TN, VT, VA, WV, WI

Commenced Business: June 1980

Address: 2600 PROFESSIONALS DRIVE, Okemos, MI 48864

Phone: (205) 877-4400 **Domicile State:** MI **NAIC Code:** 38954

Data Date	Rating	RACR #1	RACR #2	Loss Ratio %	Total Assets ($mil)	Capital ($mil)	Net Premium ($mil)	Net Income ($mil)
3-17	B-	3.33	2.44	N/A	1,100.5	417.9	40.0	14.4
3-16	B-	3.52	2.63	N/A	1,148.7	454.5	37.7	7.7
2016	B-	3.28	2.42	63.0	1,092.9	406.8	157.3	39.8
2015	B-	3.48	2.62	59.9	1,139.9	443.6	151.1	51.5
2014	B-	4.06	3.09	44.5	1,274.1	534.1	158.1	81.4
2013	B-	3.66	2.80	52.4	1,342.0	523.6	166.0	72.1
2012	B-	3.52	2.77	23.2	1,430.7	567.0	190.1	124.4

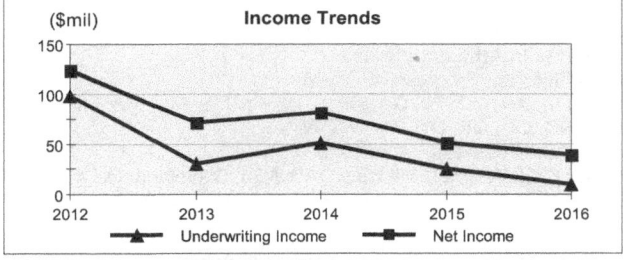

Income Trends

PROASSURANCE INDEMNTIY CO INC C Fair

Major Rating Factors: Fair overall results on stability tests (3.9 on a scale of 0 to 10) including weak results on operational trends. Weak profitability index (2.7). Good expense controls. Return on equity has been fair, averaging 18.8% over the past five years.

Other Rating Factors: Strong long-term capitalization index (8.9) based on excellent current risk adjusted capital (severe and moderate loss scenarios), despite some fluctuation in capital levels. Ample reserve history (9.6) that helps to protect the company against sharp claims increases. Excellent liquidity (7.0) with ample operational cash flow and liquid investments.

Principal Business: Medical malpractice (99%) and other liability (1%).

Principal Investments: Investment grade bonds (63%), misc. investments (29%), non investment grade bonds (6%), cash (1%), and real estate (1%).

Investments in Affiliates: 1%

Group Affiliation: ProAssurance Corp

Licensed in: All states except NY, PR

Commenced Business: April 1977

Address: 100 BROOKWOOD PLACE, Birmingham, AL 35209

Phone: (205) 877-4400 **Domicile State:** AL **NAIC Code:** 33391

Data Date	Rating	RACR #1	RACR #2	Loss Ratio %	Total Assets ($mil)	Capital ($mil)	Net Premium ($mil)	Net Income ($mil)
3-17	C	3.14	2.28	N/A	1,268.8	485.2	47.5	23.0
3-16	C+	3.84	2.91	N/A	1,386.5	575.7	49.2	17.7
2016	C	3.05	2.23	52.5	1,247.2	464.8	197.8	83.7
2015	C+	3.75	2.87	52.2	1,382.6	556.3	197.4	84.1
2014	B-	4.38	3.39	43.7	1,539.3	667.3	213.6	120.3
2013	B-	4.72	3.65	26.8	1,718.4	753.7	240.0	147.5
2012	B-	4.31	3.40	24.4	1,861.9	772.5	256.9	180.1

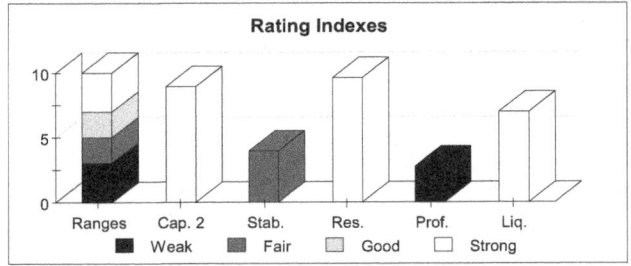

Rating Indexes

PROGRESSIVE ADVANCED INS CO | C | Fair

Major Rating Factors: Fair overall results on stability tests (3.7 on a scale of 0 to 10) including potential drain of affiliation with Progressive Group and negative cash flow from operations for 2016. Vulnerable liquidity (2.0) as a spike in claims may stretch capacity.

Other Rating Factors: Strong long-term capitalization index (8.5) based on excellent current risk adjusted capital (severe and moderate loss scenarios). Moreover, capital levels have been consistent in recent years. Ample reserve history (7.5) that can protect against increases in claims costs. Excellent profitability (8.7) with operating gains in each of the last five years.

Principal Business: Auto liability (64%), auto physical damage (35%), and inland marine (1%).

Principal Investments: Investment grade bonds (163%).

Investments in Affiliates: None

Group Affiliation: Progressive Group

Licensed in: All states except CT, MA, MI, MN, NJ, WY, PR

Commenced Business: August 1930

Address: 6300 WILSON MILLS ROAD W33, Cleveland, OH 44143-2182

Phone: (440) 461-5000 **Domicile State:** OH **NAIC Code:** 11851

Data Date	Rating	RACR #1	RACR #2	Loss Ratio %	Total Assets ($mil)	Capital ($mil)	Net Premium ($mil)	Net Income ($mil)
3-17	C	2.29	2.08	N/A	476.8	203.8	85.2	4.2
3-16	C	2.19	1.99	N/A	407.6	169.6	74.8	1.6
2016	C	2.24	2.10	76.5	467.6	199.0	328.2	9.2
2015	C	2.16	2.03	74.5	396.0	167.4	285.0	9.9
2014	C	2.11	1.98	74.3	355.3	147.2	256.3	11.0
2013	C	2.03	1.91	72.4	318.8	129.0	229.7	11.6
2012	C	1.94	1.83	74.2	296.9	117.4	219.2	7.3

Progressive Group
Composite Group Rating: C+

Largest Group Members	Assets ($mil)	Rating
PROGRESSIVE CASUALTY INS CO	6967	B-
PROGRESSIVE DIRECT INS CO	6727	C+
UNITED FINANCIAL CASUALTY CO	2897	B-
PROGRESSIVE NORTHERN INS CO	1576	C+
PROGRESSIVE NORTHWESTERN INS CO	1538	C+

PROGRESSIVE AMERICAN INS CO | C | Fair

Major Rating Factors: Fair overall results on stability tests (3.8 on a scale of 0 to 10) including potential drain of affiliation with Progressive Group, weak results on operational trends and negative cash flow from operations for 2016. History of adequate reserve strength (6.1) as reserves have been consistently at an acceptable level.

Other Rating Factors: Good liquidity (6.1) with sufficient resources (cash flows and marketable investments) to handle a spike in claims. Strong long-term capitalization index (10.0) based on excellent current risk adjusted capital (severe and moderate loss scenarios). Moreover, capital levels have been consistent in recent years. Excellent profitability (8.4) with operating gains in each of the last five years.

Principal Business: Auto liability (70%), auto physical damage (26%), inland marine (2%), and other liability (1%).

Principal Investments: Investment grade bonds (124%).

Investments in Affiliates: None

Group Affiliation: Progressive Group

Licensed in: AR, CO, FL, GA, HI, IL, IN, KY, ME, MD, MA, MI, MS, MO, MT, NM, NY, NC, ND, OH, OK, UT, VA, WA, WI

Commenced Business: April 1979

Address: 6300 WILSON MILLS ROAD W33, Cleveland, OH 44143-2182

Phone: (440) 461-5000 **Domicile State:** OH **NAIC Code:** 24252

Data Date	Rating	RACR #1	RACR #2	Loss Ratio %	Total Assets ($mil)	Capital ($mil)	Net Premium ($mil)	Net Income ($mil)
3-17	C	3.90	3.40	N/A	511.0	213.0	59.5	3.3
3-16	C	3.77	3.30	N/A	449.7	185.2	52.5	2.3
2016	C	3.86	3.49	75.3	493.8	209.3	229.2	7.4
2015	C	3.69	3.35	71.7	427.4	182.8	206.1	12.1
2014	C	3.61	3.29	71.8	416.2	175.4	199.7	12.2
2013	C	3.40	3.10	72.9	390.1	158.5	190.1	8.3
2012	C	3.19	2.91	75.1	353.4	140.9	181.5	7.6

Progressive Group
Composite Group Rating: C+

Largest Group Members	Assets ($mil)	Rating
PROGRESSIVE CASUALTY INS CO	6967	B-
PROGRESSIVE DIRECT INS CO	6727	C+
UNITED FINANCIAL CASUALTY CO	2897	B-
PROGRESSIVE NORTHERN INS CO	1576	C+
PROGRESSIVE NORTHWESTERN INS CO	1538	C+

PROGRESSIVE CASUALTY INS CO | B- | Good

Major Rating Factors: Fair overall results on stability tests (4.5 on a scale of 0 to 10) including potential drain of affiliation with Progressive Group and weak results on operational trends. The largest net exposure for one risk is conservative at 1.2% of capital. Good long-term capitalization index (6.0) based on good current risk adjusted capital (moderate loss scenario). Moreover, capital levels have been consistent over the last several years.

Other Rating Factors: History of adequate reserve strength (6.3) as reserves have been consistently at an acceptable level. Excellent profitability (9.5) with operating gains in each of the last five years. Return on equity has been excellent over the last five years averaging 27.3%. Vulnerable liquidity (1.7) as a spike in claims may stretch capacity.

Principal Business: Auto liability (66%), auto physical damage (29%), inland marine (3%), other liability (1%), and homeowners multiple peril (1%).

Principal Investments: Misc. investments (45%), investment grade bonds (41%), real estate (8%), cash (5%), and non investment grade bonds (1%).

Investments in Affiliates: 17%

Group Affiliation: Progressive Group

Licensed in: All states except PR

Commenced Business: December 1956

Address: 6300 WILSON MILLS ROAD W33, Cleveland, OH 44143-2182

Phone: (440) 461-5000 **Domicile State:** OH **NAIC Code:** 24260

Data Date	Rating	RACR #1	RACR #2	Loss Ratio %	Total Assets ($mil)	Capital ($mil)	Net Premium ($mil)	Net Income ($mil)
3-17	B-	1.14	0.93	N/A	8,195.0	2,020.5	1,457.1	83.5
3-16	B-	1.04	0.85	N/A	7,050.4	1,715.3	1,287.3	60.7
2016	B-	1.04	0.87	75.3	6,967.1	1,818.9	5,614.2	321.5
2015	B-	0.98	0.81	71.7	6,245.6	1,610.1	5,050.3	450.8
2014	C+	0.98	0.83	71.8	6,061.7	1,611.4	4,891.7	528.0
2013	C+	0.94	0.80	72.9	5,781.0	1,543.1	4,657.8	501.3
2012	C+	0.90	0.78	75.1	5,332.1	1,448.5	4,447.9	406.7

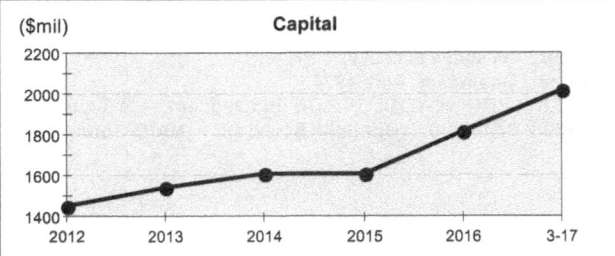

Capital ($mil)

PROGRESSIVE DIRECT INS CO   C+   Fair

Major Rating Factors: Fair overall results on stability tests (4.1 on a scale of 0 to 10) including potential drain of affiliation with Progressive Group and weak results on operational trends. The largest net exposure for one risk is conservative at 1.8% of capital. Vulnerable liquidity (1.7) as a spike in claims may stretch capacity.

Other Rating Factors: Strong long-term capitalization index (7.3) based on excellent current risk adjusted capital (severe and moderate loss scenarios). Moreover, capital levels have been consistent in recent years. Ample reserve history (7.7) that can protect against increases in claims costs. Excellent profitability (8.9) with operating gains in each of the last five years. Return on equity has been excellent over the last five years averaging 16.1%.

Principal Business: Auto liability (63%), auto physical damage (35%), and inland marine (1%).

Principal Investments: Investment grade bonds (75%), misc. investments (21%), real estate (3%), and non investment grade bonds (1%).

Investments in Affiliates: None

Group Affiliation: Progressive Group

Licensed in: All states except TX, PR

Commenced Business: January 1987

Address: 6300 WILSON MILLS ROAD W33, Cleveland, OH 44143-2182

Phone: (440) 461-5000   **Domicile State:** OH   **NAIC Code:** 16322

Data Date	Rating	RACR #1	RACR #2	Loss Ratio %	Total Assets ($mil)	Capital ($mil)	Net Premium ($mil)	Net Income ($mil)
3-17	C+	1.41	1.24	N/A	7,217.2	2,204.7	1,651.1	101.4
3-16	C	1.35	1.18	N/A	6,246.0	1,845.1	1,449.3	45.1
2016	C+	1.32	1.20	76.5	6,727.5	2,065.4	6,358.9	263.9
2015	C	1.30	1.17	74.5	5,835.3	1,783.1	5,521.8	265.6
2014	C-	1.26	1.14	74.3	5,180.2	1,571.5	4,966.6	253.6
2013	C-	1.26	1.13	72.4	4,724.2	1,433.3	4,450.2	286.3
2012	C-	1.27	1.15	74.2	4,541.6	1,363.3	4,246.7	222.7

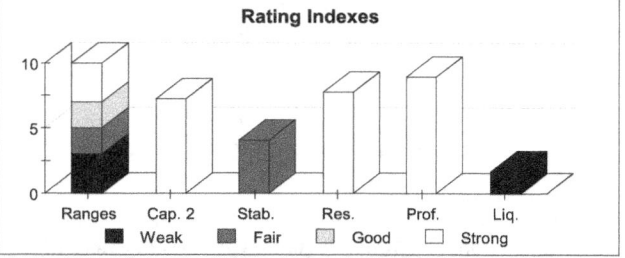

Rating Indexes

Ranges   Cap. 2   Stab.   Res.   Prof.   Liq.

■ Weak   ▨ Fair   ▥ Good   ☐ Strong

PROGRESSIVE NORTHERN INS CO   C+   Fair

Major Rating Factors: Fair overall results on stability tests (4.3 on a scale of 0 to 10) including potential drain of affiliation with Progressive Group and weak results on operational trends. The largest net exposure for one risk is conservative at 1.3% of capital. Fair liquidity (4.5) as cash resources may not be adequate to cover a spike in claims.

Other Rating Factors: History of adequate reserve strength (6.3) as reserves have been consistently at an acceptable level. Strong long-term capitalization index (7.3) based on excellent current risk adjusted capital (severe and moderate loss scenarios). Moreover, capital levels have been consistent in recent years. Excellent profitability (9.2) with operating gains in each of the last five years. Return on equity has been excellent over the last five years averaging 19.1%.

Principal Business: Auto liability (59%), auto physical damage (37%), inland marine (3%), homeowners multiple peril (1%), and other liability (1%).

Principal Investments: Investment grade bonds (84%), misc. investments (15%), and non investment grade bonds (1%).

Investments in Affiliates: None

Group Affiliation: Progressive Group

Licensed in: All states except AL, AR, CA, FL, MA, MO, NJ, ND, TN, TX, PR

Commenced Business: March 1981

Address: 8020 EXCELSIOR DRIVE, Madison, WI 53717

Phone: (440) 461-5000   **Domicile State:** WI   **NAIC Code:** 38628

Data Date	Rating	RACR #1	RACR #2	Loss Ratio %	Total Assets ($mil)	Capital ($mil)	Net Premium ($mil)	Net Income ($mil)
3-17	C+	1.44	1.22	N/A	1,676.6	475.9	356.8	22.1
3-16	C+	1.40	1.19	N/A	1,482.7	415.1	315.3	17.9
2016	C+	1.34	1.18	75.3	1,576.4	442.4	1,374.9	61.0
2015	C+	1.32	1.16	71.7	1,408.4	396.9	1,236.8	88.2
2014	C+	1.30	1.16	71.8	1,349.2	385.8	1,198.0	90.7
2013	C+	1.30	1.15	72.9	1,305.4	370.7	1,140.7	78.6
2012	C+	1.30	1.16	75.1	1,245.7	347.5	1,089.3	51.9

Progressive Group
Composite Group Rating: C+
Largest Group Members   Assets ($mil)   Rating

Largest Group Members	Assets ($mil)	Rating
PROGRESSIVE CASUALTY INS CO	6967	B-
PROGRESSIVE DIRECT INS CO	6727	C+
UNITED FINANCIAL CASUALTY CO	2897	B-
PROGRESSIVE NORTHERN INS CO	1576	C+
PROGRESSIVE NORTHWESTERN INS CO	1538	C+

PROGRESSIVE NORTHWESTERN INS CO   C+   Fair

Major Rating Factors: Fair overall results on stability tests (4.3 on a scale of 0 to 10) including potential drain of affiliation with Progressive Group and weak results on operational trends. The largest net exposure for one risk is conservative at 1.3% of capital. Fair liquidity (4.6) as cash resources may not be adequate to cover a spike in claims.

Other Rating Factors: History of adequate reserve strength (6.3) as reserves have been consistently at an acceptable level. Strong long-term capitalization index (7.3) based on excellent current risk adjusted capital (severe and moderate loss scenarios). Moreover, capital levels have been consistent in recent years. Excellent profitability (9.1) with operating gains in each of the last five years. Return on equity has been excellent over the last five years averaging 18.5%.

Principal Business: Auto liability (54%), auto physical damage (41%), inland marine (3%), and other liability (2%).

Principal Investments: Investment grade bonds (84%) and misc. investments (16%).

Investments in Affiliates: None

Group Affiliation: Progressive Group

Licensed in: All states except AL, FL, IL, MA, NH, PA, VT, WY, PR

Commenced Business: September 1983

Address: 6300 WILSON MILLS ROAD W33, Cleveland, OH 44143-2182

Phone: (440) 461-5000   **Domicile State:** OH   **NAIC Code:** 42919

Data Date	Rating	RACR #1	RACR #2	Loss Ratio %	Total Assets ($mil)	Capital ($mil)	Net Premium ($mil)	Net Income ($mil)
3-17	C+	1.43	1.21	N/A	1,622.9	473.5	356.8	21.5
3-16	C+	1.39	1.19	N/A	1,432.4	413.3	315.3	15.9
2016	C+	1.34	1.18	75.3	1,537.7	441.6	1,374.9	57.6
2015	C+	1.31	1.16	71.7	1,372.0	396.2	1,236.8	84.5
2014	C+	1.30	1.15	71.8	1,313.5	387.6	1,198.0	92.9
2013	C+	1.30	1.13	72.9	1,267.5	371.6	1,140.7	66.0
2012	C+	1.29	1.14	75.1	1,207.2	347.3	1,089.3	57.0

Progressive Group
Composite Group Rating: C+

Largest Group Members	Assets ($mil)	Rating
PROGRESSIVE CASUALTY INS CO	6967	B-
PROGRESSIVE DIRECT INS CO	6727	C+
UNITED FINANCIAL CASUALTY CO	2897	B-
PROGRESSIVE NORTHERN INS CO	1576	C+
PROGRESSIVE NORTHWESTERN INS CO	1538	C+

PROGRESSIVE PREFERRED INS CO
C   Fair

Major Rating Factors: Fair overall results on stability tests (3.9 on a scale of 0 to 10) including potential drain of affiliation with Progressive Group and weak results on operational trends. The largest net exposure for one risk is conservative at 1.3% of capital. Fair liquidity (3.0) as cash resources may not be adequate to cover a spike in claims.

Other Rating Factors: History of adequate reserve strength (6.3) as reserves have been consistently at an acceptable level. Strong long-term capitalization index (7.4) based on excellent current risk adjusted capital (severe and moderate loss scenarios). Moreover, capital levels have been consistent in recent years. Excellent profitability (9.1) with operating gains in each of the last five years. Return on equity has been excellent over the last five years averaging 18.4%.

Principal Business: Auto liability (61%), auto physical damage (36%), inland marine (2%), other liability (1%), and homeowners multiple peril (1%).

Principal Investments: Investment grade bonds (98%) and misc. investments (2%).

Investments in Affiliates: None

Group Affiliation: Progressive Group

Licensed in: AK, AZ, CO, DC, DE, GA, HI, ID, IN, IA, KY, ME, MD, MI, MN, MS, MO, MT, NE, NV, NJ, NM, NY, NC, OH, OK, OR, PA, RI, SC, SD, TN, TX, UT, VA, WA, WV

Commenced Business: April 1980

Address: 6300 WILSON MILLS ROAD W33, Cleveland, OH 44143-2182

Phone: (440) 461-5000   **Domicile State:** OH   **NAIC Code:** 37834

Data Date	Rating	RACR #1	RACR #2	Loss Ratio %	Total Assets ($mil)	Capital ($mil)	Net Premium ($mil)	Net Income ($mil)
3-17	C	1.44	1.27	N/A	839.7	233.9	178.4	10.9
3-16	C	1.42	1.25	N/A	743.2	207.5	157.6	8.0
2016	C	1.37	1.24	75.3	793.2	221.7	687.5	27.6
2015	C	1.35	1.23	71.7	705.5	198.7	618.4	43.0
2014	C	1.35	1.23	71.8	677.1	195.9	599.0	49.6
2013	C	1.32	1.20	72.9	652.5	183.7	570.3	35.4
2012	C	1.32	1.21	75.1	620.7	174.3	544.6	22.7

Progressive Group
Composite Group Rating: C+

Largest Group Members	Assets ($mil)	Rating
PROGRESSIVE CASUALTY INS CO	6967	B-
PROGRESSIVE DIRECT INS CO	6727	C+
UNITED FINANCIAL CASUALTY CO	2897	B-
PROGRESSIVE NORTHERN INS CO	1576	C+
PROGRESSIVE NORTHWESTERN INS CO	1538	C+

PROGRESSIVE SELECT INS CO
C   Fair

Major Rating Factors: Fair overall results on stability tests (3.9 on a scale of 0 to 10) including potential drain of affiliation with Progressive Group and negative cash flow from operations for 2016. Vulnerable liquidity (2.9) as a spike in claims may stretch capacity.

Other Rating Factors: History of adequate reserve strength (6.2) as reserves have been consistently at an acceptable level. Strong long-term capitalization index (10.0) based on excellent current risk adjusted capital (severe and moderate loss scenarios). Moreover, capital levels have been consistent in recent years. Excellent profitability (7.9) with operating gains in each of the last five years.

Principal Business: Auto liability (69%), auto physical damage (29%), and inland marine (1%).

Principal Investments: Investment grade bonds (119%).

Investments in Affiliates: None

Group Affiliation: Progressive Group

Licensed in: CA, FL, MD, OH

Commenced Business: July 2001

Address: 6300 WILSON MIILS ROAD W33, Cleveland, OH 44143-2182

Phone: (440) 461-5000   **Domicile State:** OH   **NAIC Code:** 10192

Data Date	Rating	RACR #1	RACR #2	Loss Ratio %	Total Assets ($mil)	Capital ($mil)	Net Premium ($mil)	Net Income ($mil)
3-17	C	4.23	3.75	N/A	732.6	200.5	40.4	1.6
3-16	C	4.06	3.61	N/A	642.1	171.1	36.0	1.3
2016	C	4.31	4.01	78.7	686.6	198.7	155.9	5.9
2015	C	4.17	3.88	77.5	595.3	169.6	135.9	4.5
2014	C	4.19	3.90	75.9	525.5	147.6	117.4	5.1
2013	C	4.08	3.82	67.7	452.5	131.8	105.4	11.1
2012	C	3.67	3.43	74.1	400.5	109.5	86.7	4.6

Progressive Group
Composite Group Rating: C+

Largest Group Members	Assets ($mil)	Rating
PROGRESSIVE CASUALTY INS CO	6967	B-
PROGRESSIVE DIRECT INS CO	6727	C+
UNITED FINANCIAL CASUALTY CO	2897	B-
PROGRESSIVE NORTHERN INS CO	1576	C+
PROGRESSIVE NORTHWESTERN INS CO	1538	C+

PROGRESSIVE SPECIALTY INS CO
C   Fair

Major Rating Factors: Fair profitability index (3.1 on a scale of 0 to 10). Good expense controls. Return on equity has been fair, averaging 18.1% over the past five years. Fair overall results on stability tests (4.0) including fair financial strength of affiliated Progressive Group and weak results on operational trends. The largest net exposure for one risk is conservative at 1.2% of capital.

Other Rating Factors: Vulnerable liquidity (2.2) as a spike in claims may stretch capacity. History of adequate reserve strength (6.3) as reserves have been consistently at an acceptable level. Strong long-term capitalization index (7.3) based on excellent current risk adjusted capital (severe and moderate loss scenarios), despite some fluctuation in capital levels.

Principal Business: Auto liability (63%), auto physical damage (35%), inland marine (1%), and homeowners multiple peril (1%).

Principal Investments: Investment grade bonds (72%) and misc. investments (28%).

Investments in Affiliates: None

Group Affiliation: Progressive Group

Licensed in: All states except LA, MA, NH, NC, WY, PR

Commenced Business: May 1976

Address: 6300 WILSON MILLS ROAD W33, Cleveland, OH 44143-2182

Phone: (440) 461-5000   **Domicile State:** OH   **NAIC Code:** 32786

Data Date	Rating	RACR #1	RACR #2	Loss Ratio %	Total Assets ($mil)	Capital ($mil)	Net Premium ($mil)	Net Income ($mil)
3-17	C	1.48	1.24	N/A	997.9	291.2	208.2	25.3
3-16	C	1.62	1.35	N/A	917.1	286.5	183.9	10.8
2016	C	1.35	1.17	75.3	943.0	263.4	802.0	38.1
2015	C	1.49	1.29	71.7	864.7	266.4	721.5	48.3
2014	C	1.78	1.54	71.8	880.2	314.1	698.8	56.9
2013	C	2.27	1.96	72.9	941.3	386.2	665.4	87.0
2012	C	2.94	2.54	75.1	994.3	467.3	635.4	60.3

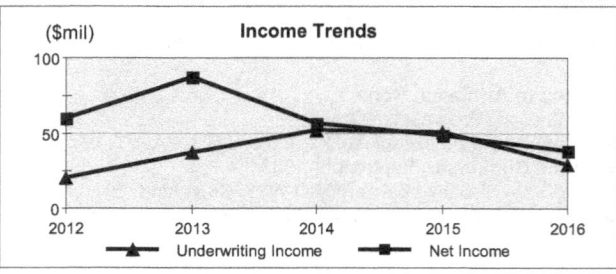

Income Trends

PROPERTY-OWNERS INS CO *   B+   Good

Major Rating Factors: History of adequate reserve strength (5.6 on a scale of 0 to 10) as reserves have been consistently at an acceptable level. Good liquidity (6.3) with sufficient resources (cash flows and marketable investments) to handle a spike in claims.

Other Rating Factors: Good overall results on stability tests (5.1) despite weak results on operational trends and excessive premium growth. Strong long-term capitalization index (7.4) based on excellent current risk adjusted capital (severe and moderate loss scenarios). Moreover, capital levels have been consistent in recent years. Excellent profitability (8.7) with operating gains in each of the last five years.

Principal Business: Homeowners multiple peril (45%), commercial multiple peril (26%), auto liability (7%), workers compensation (7%), auto physical damage (5%), inland marine (3%), and other lines (7%).

Principal Investments: Investment grade bonds (85%), misc. investments (14%), and cash (1%).

Investments in Affiliates: None

Group Affiliation: Auto-Owners Group

Licensed in: AL, AR, GA, IL, IN, IA, KY, MI, MO, NE, NV, ND, SC, SD, UT, VA, WI

Commenced Business: September 1976

Address: 3950 WEST DELPHI PIKE, Marion, IN 46952-9266

Phone: (517) 323-1200   **Domicile State:** IN   **NAIC Code:** 32905

Data Date	Rating	RACR #1	RACR #2	Loss Ratio %	Total Assets ($mil)	Capital ($mil)	Net Premium ($mil)	Net Income ($mil)
3-17	B+	2.05	1.23	N/A	289.0	129.5	29.0	5.0
3-16	B+	3.54	2.04	N/A	249.2	121.4	20.4	5.1
2016	B+	2.14	1.27	56.5	280.6	124.1	119.5	5.6
2015	B+	3.46	1.99	60.7	232.4	115.7	78.9	6.5
2014	B+	3.53	2.09	64.6	216.2	109.6	72.4	5.0
2013	A	3.83	2.21	55.5	209.7	104.5	70.0	9.0
2012	A	3.32	1.77	61.3	193.9	93.5	63.5	7.5

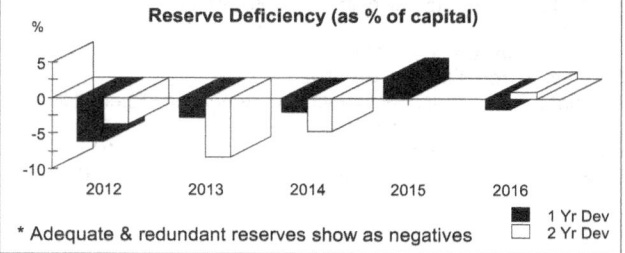

Reserve Deficiency (as % of capital)

* Adequate & redundant reserves show as negatives
■ 1 Yr Dev   □ 2 Yr Dev

PROTECTIVE INS CO *   A-   Excellent

Major Rating Factors: Strong long-term capitalization index (7.4 on a scale of 0 to 10) based on excellent current risk adjusted capital (severe and moderate loss scenarios), despite some fluctuation in capital levels. Ample reserve history (8.2) that helps to protect the company against sharp claims increases.

Other Rating Factors: Excellent profitability (7.3) with operating gains in each of the last five years. Good overall results on stability tests (6.9). Affiliation with Protective Ins Group is a strength. Good liquidity (6.8) with sufficient resources (cash flows and marketable investments) to handle a spike in claims.

Principal Business: Workers compensation (40%), other liability (20%), auto physical damage (18%), auto liability (17%), group accident & health (4%), and surety (1%).

Principal Investments: Misc. investments (56%), investment grade bonds (35%), non investment grade bonds (7%), and real estate (4%).

Investments in Affiliates: 26%

Group Affiliation: Protective Ins Group

Licensed in: All states, the District of Columbia and Puerto Rico

Commenced Business: December 1954

Address: 111 Congressional Blvd Ste 500, Carmel, IN 46032

Phone: (317) 636-9800   **Domicile State:** IN   **NAIC Code:** 12416

Data Date	Rating	RACR #1	RACR #2	Loss Ratio %	Total Assets ($mil)	Capital ($mil)	Net Premium ($mil)	Net Income ($mil)
3-17	A-	1.58	1.22	N/A	799.3	403.3	69.6	16.3
3-16	B	1.56	1.15	N/A	759.0	392.5	61.9	21.4
2016	B+	1.59	1.24	65.7	785.4	398.0	255.7	23.2
2015	B	1.54	1.13	57.4	753.5	389.4	233.2	27.1
2014	B	1.51	1.09	56.7	791.8	397.4	235.5	29.7
2013	A-	1.42	1.03	57.6	741.1	375.8	228.0	28.6
2012	A-	1.30	0.94	57.6	680.1	337.5	203.4	24.0

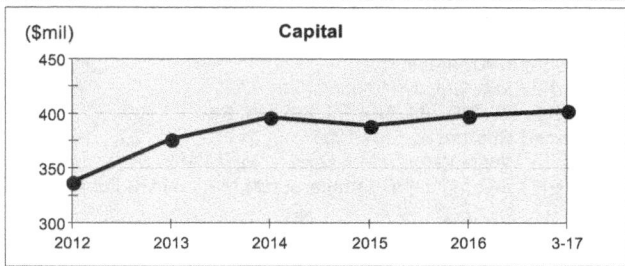

Capital

QBE INS CORP   B   Good

Major Rating Factors: Good liquidity (6.6 on a scale of 0 to 10) with sufficient resources (cash flows and marketable investments) to handle a spike in claims. Fair overall results on stability tests (4.8) including potential drain of affiliation with QBE Ins Group Ltd and weak results on operational trends.

Other Rating Factors: Fair reserve development (4.9) as reserves have generally been sufficient to cover claims. Fair profitability index (4.6) with operating losses during 2012 and 2013. Average return on equity over the last five years has been poor at -0.4%. Strong long-term capitalization index (8.1) based on excellent current risk adjusted capital (severe and moderate loss scenarios), despite some fluctuation in capital levels.

Principal Business: Commercial multiple peril (28%), group accident & health (18%), homeowners multiple peril (13%), other liability (12%), workers compensation (8%), allied lines (6%), and other lines (15%).

Principal Investments: Investment grade bonds (67%) and misc. investments (34%).

Investments in Affiliates: 10%

Group Affiliation: QBE Ins Group Ltd

Licensed in: All states except PR

Commenced Business: October 1980

Address: 116 Pine Street Suite 320, Harrisburg, PA 17101

Phone: (608) 825-5160   **Domicile State:** PA   **NAIC Code:** 39217

Data Date	Rating	RACR #1	RACR #2	Loss Ratio %	Total Assets ($mil)	Capital ($mil)	Net Premium ($mil)	Net Income ($mil)
3-17	B	2.54	1.73	N/A	2,405.5	786.7	194.1	15.5
3-16	B-	2.30	1.64	N/A	2,887.5	721.5	192.0	-0.6
2016	B	2.48	1.70	58.8	2,325.0	748.9	846.9	27.7
2015	B-	2.46	1.81	63.9	2,134.5	735.7	597.0	28.8
2014	C+	2.08	1.58	69.2	2,113.3	681.2	742.1	4.2
2013	C	1.95	1.49	75.2	2,138.2	678.7	750.5	-61.1
2012	C	2.04	1.55	73.5	2,188.1	802.4	473.1	-24.3

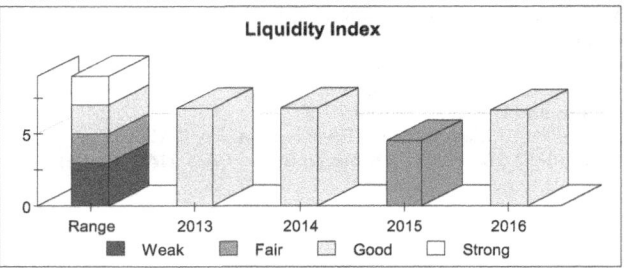

Liquidity Index

■ Weak   ■ Fair   □ Good   □ Strong

QBE REINS CORP

B   Good

Major Rating Factors: Good overall results on stability tests (5.4 on a scale of 0 to 10) despite potential drain of affiliation with QBE Ins Group Ltd and negative cash flow from operations for 2016. History of adequate reserve strength (6.0) as reserves have been consistently at an acceptable level.

Other Rating Factors: Good overall profitability index (5.5) despite modest operating losses during the first three months of 2017. Return on equity has been low, averaging 0.5% over the past five years. Good liquidity (6.5) with sufficient resources (cash flows and marketable investments) to handle a spike in claims. Strong long-term capitalization index (7.2) based on excellent current risk adjusted capital (severe and moderate loss scenarios), despite some fluctuation in capital levels.

Principal Business: (This company is a reinsurer.)

Principal Investments: Misc. investments (91%), investment grade bonds (8%), and cash (1%).

Investments in Affiliates: 71%

Group Affiliation: QBE Ins Group Ltd

Licensed in: All states, the District of Columbia and Puerto Rico

Commenced Business: October 1964

Address: 116 Pine Street Suite 320, Harrisburg, PA 17101

Phone: (608) 825-5160   **Domicile State:** PA   **NAIC Code:** 10219

Data Date	Rating	RACR #1	RACR #2	Loss Ratio %	Total Assets ($mil)	Capital ($mil)	Net Premium ($mil)	Net Income ($mil)
3-17	B	1.43	1.39	N/A	1,232.9	904.2	38.5	-0.6
3-16	B	1.36	1.33	N/A	1,218.3	829.3	38.1	-0.7
2016	B	1.39	1.36	58.8	1,171.1	863.6	147.5	1.1
2015	B	1.33	1.31	63.9	1,147.8	813.3	186.6	11.9
2014	B	1.44	1.41	69.2	1,176.1	826.8	168.3	5.0
2013	B	1.40	1.36	75.2	1,232.9	814.7	210.4	0.0
2012	B	1.33	1.28	73.5	1,545.6	943.1	333.1	5.0

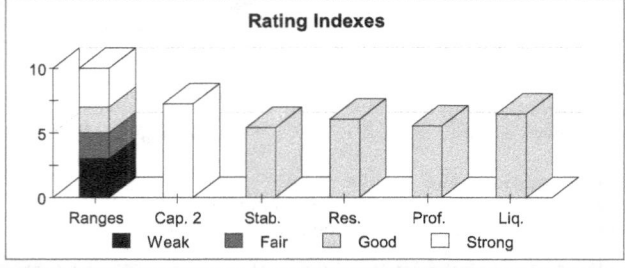

Rating Indexes

QUINCY MUTUAL FIRE INS CO

B   Good

Major Rating Factors: Good liquidity (6.9 on a scale of 0 to 10) with sufficient resources (cash flows and marketable investments) to handle a spike in claims. Fair overall results on stability tests (4.7) including potential drain of affiliation with Quincy Mutual Group and weak results on operational trends.

Other Rating Factors: Strong long-term capitalization index (9.5) based on excellent current risk adjusted capital (severe and moderate loss scenarios), despite some fluctuation in capital levels. Ample reserve history (7.9) that can protect against increases in claims costs. Excellent profitability (7.7) with operating gains in each of the last five years.

Principal Business: Homeowners multiple peril (31%), auto liability (25%), auto physical damage (20%), commercial multiple peril (19%), allied lines (3%), and fire (2%).

Principal Investments: Misc. investments (58%), investment grade bonds (37%), non investment grade bonds (3%), cash (1%), and real estate (1%).

Investments in Affiliates: 4%

Group Affiliation: Quincy Mutual Group

Licensed in: CT, ME, MA, NH, NJ, NY, PA, RI

Commenced Business: May 1851

Address: 57 Washington Street, Quincy, MA 02169

Phone: (617) 770-5100   **Domicile State:** MA   **NAIC Code:** 15067

Data Date	Rating	RACR #1	RACR #2	Loss Ratio %	Total Assets ($mil)	Capital ($mil)	Net Premium ($mil)	Net Income ($mil)
3-17	B	4.43	2.81	N/A	1,647.4	1,103.4	75.7	14.1
3-16	B	3.94	2.48	N/A	1,515.7	989.9	73.0	7.1
2016	B	4.42	2.81	52.4	1,619.5	1,079.9	307.7	62.0
2015	B	3.95	2.50	78.5	1,508.0	977.0	313.3	14.6
2014	B	3.82	2.40	45.2	1,510.5	994.7	269.3	77.0
2013	B	3.71	2.30	55.6	1,471.1	927.1	296.3	49.8
2012	B	3.72	2.36	61.7	1,310.9	796.7	284.3	47.8

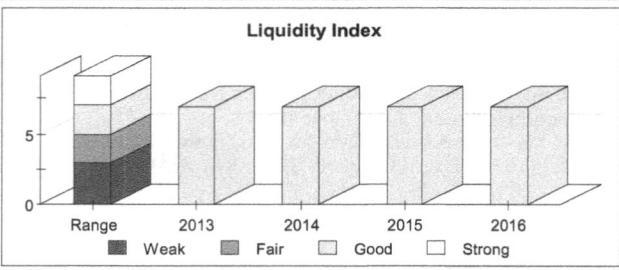

Liquidity Index

RADIAN GUARANTY INC

D+   Weak

Major Rating Factors: Weak overall results on stability tests (2.4 on a scale of 0 to 10) including weak results on operational trends. Fair reserve development (4.6) as the level of reserves has at times been insufficient to cover claims. In 2012 and 2013 the two year reserve development was 17% and 27% deficient respectively.

Other Rating Factors: Good overall profitability index (5.1) despite operating losses during 2012 and 2013. Return on equity has been good over the last five years, averaging 16.8%. Good liquidity (6.8) with sufficient resources (cash flows and marketable investments) to handle a spike in claims. Strong long-term capitalization index (7.9) based on excellent current risk adjusted capital (severe and moderate loss scenarios), despite some fluctuation in capital levels.

Principal Business: Mortgage guaranty (100%).

Principal Investments: Investment grade bonds (99%) and cash (1%).

Investments in Affiliates: None

Group Affiliation: Radian Group Inc

Licensed in: All states except PR

Commenced Business: April 1977

Address: 1601 Market Street, Philadelphia, PA 19103

Phone: (800) 523-1988   **Domicile State:** PA   **NAIC Code:** 33790

Data Date	Rating	RACR #1	RACR #2	Loss Ratio %	Total Assets ($mil)	Capital ($mil)	Net Premium ($mil)	Net Income ($mil)
3-17	D+	1.91	1.59	N/A	3,818.7	1,167.7	196.7	94.2
3-16	D+	2.17	1.83	N/A	4,074.2	1,726.2	176.8	122.7
2016	D+	2.22	1.86	22.7	3,900.1	1,349.7	628.7	480.8
2015	D+	2.04	1.73	22.2	4,009.0	1,686.5	845.7	754.8
2014	D	0.85	0.76	33.0	3,643.3	1,325.2	797.5	273.7
2013	D	0.66	0.59	81.6	3,657.5	1,317.8	814.4	-23.8
2012	D	0.45	0.38	133.2	3,872.0	926.1	686.8	-175.9

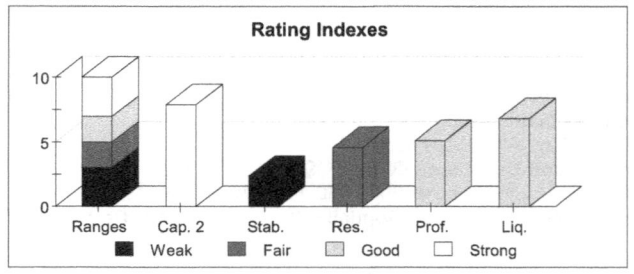

Rating Indexes

RADIAN REINS INC *   A-   Excellent

Major Rating Factors: Strong long-term capitalization index (9.5 on a scale of 0 to 10) based on excellent current risk adjusted capital (severe and moderate loss scenarios). Furthermore, this high level of risk adjusted capital has been consistently maintained in previous years. Excellent profitability (8.6) despite modest operating losses during 2015. Excellent expense controls.

Other Rating Factors: Excellent liquidity (7.2) with ample operational cash flow and liquid investments. Good overall results on stability tests (5.7) despite weak results on operational trends. Fair reserve development (3.6) as reserves have generally been sufficient to cover claims.

Principal Business: Mortgage guaranty (100%).

Principal Investments: Investment grade bonds (71%), misc. investments (27%), and cash (2%).

Investments in Affiliates: None

Group Affiliation: Radian Group Inc

(No States listed)

Data Date	Rating	RACR #1	RACR #2	Loss Ratio %	Total Assets ($mil)	Capital ($mil)	Net Premium ($mil)	Net Income ($mil)
3-17	A-	7.66	4.96	N/A	684.6	321.0	25.0	14.3
3-16	U	2.07	1.36	N/A	467.3	141.6	24.7	14.2
2016	A-	3.16	2.09	21.7	491.9	147.6	104.3	60.3
2015	U	1.95	1.33	34.9	466.6	138.7	63.9	-1.0
2014	N/A	N/A	N/A	0.0	0.0	0.0	0.0	0.0
2013	N/A	N/A	N/A	0.0	0.0	0.0	0.0	0.0
2012	N/A	N/A	N/A	0.0	0.0	0.0	0.0	0.0

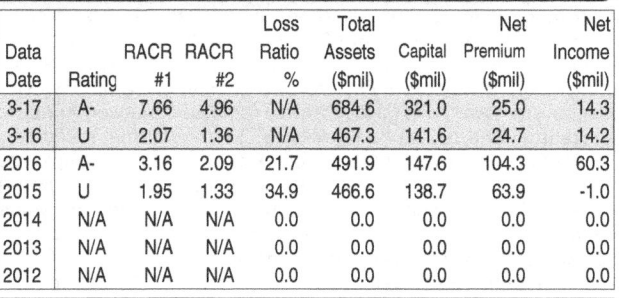

Risk-Adjusted Capital Ratio #2 (Severe Loss Scenario)

Range / 2012 / 2013 / 2014 / 2015 / 2016 / 3-17

■ Weak   ▨ Fair   ▥ Good   □ Strong

REDWOOD FIRE & CAS INS CO   C   Fair

Major Rating Factors: Fair long-term capitalization index (4.5 on a scale of 0 to 10) based on fair current risk adjusted capital (severe loss scenario). Fair overall results on stability tests (4.3) including fair risk adjusted capital in prior years.

Other Rating Factors: Ample reserve history (8.1) that helps to protect the company against sharp claims increases. Excellent profitability (8.1) with operating gains in each of the last five years. Excellent liquidity (8.6) with ample operational cash flow and liquid investments.

Principal Business: Workers compensation (85%), auto liability (11%), auto physical damage (3%), and inland marine (1%).

Principal Investments: Investment grade bonds (52%), misc. investments (36%), and cash (12%).

Investments in Affiliates: None

Group Affiliation: Berkshire-Hathaway

Licensed in: All states except FL, OR, PR

Commenced Business: January 1970

Address: 1314 Douglas Street, Omaha, NE 68102

Phone: (402) 393-7255   **Domicile State:** NE   **NAIC Code:** 11673

Data Date	Rating	RACR #1	RACR #2	Loss Ratio %	Total Assets ($mil)	Capital ($mil)	Net Premium ($mil)	Net Income ($mil)
3-17	C	0.94	0.58	N/A	1,728.1	655.7	93.1	3.7
3-16	C	0.79	0.49	N/A	1,483.8	565.2	77.1	4.5
2016	C	0.94	0.58	63.8	1,655.1	637.3	386.1	53.0
2015	C	0.78	0.49	70.2	1,428.0	552.8	401.2	46.8
2014	C	0.73	0.47	72.6	1,257.7	533.3	377.0	5.1
2013	C	0.93	0.59	66.9	1,031.3	506.0	286.9	49.2
2012	B-	1.50	0.92	53.9	761.7	426.0	97.7	3.1

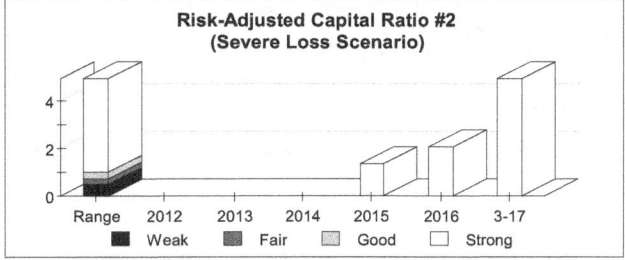

Risk-Adjusted Capital Ratio #1 (Moderate Loss Scenario)

Range / 2012 / 2013 / 2014 / 2015 / 2016 / 3-17

■ Weak   ▥ Fair   □ Good

RENAISSANCE RE US INC   B   Good

Major Rating Factors: Good profitability index (5.0 on a scale of 0 to 10). Weak expense controls. Return on equity has been good over the last five years, averaging 11.8%. Fair overall results on stability tests (4.8) including negative cash flow from operations for 2016. The largest net exposure for one risk is excessive at 5.4% of capital.

Other Rating Factors: Strong long-term capitalization index (7.9) based on excellent current risk adjusted capital (severe and moderate loss scenarios), despite some fluctuation in capital levels. Ample reserve history (9.5) that helps to protect the company against sharp claims increases. Excellent liquidity (7.1) with ample operational cash flow and liquid investments.

Principal Business: (This company is a reinsurer.)

Principal Investments: Investment grade bonds (88%), misc. investments (10%), and cash (2%).

Investments in Affiliates: None

Group Affiliation: RenaissanceRe Holdings Ltd

Licensed in: All states except PR

Commenced Business: December 1995

Address: 140 Broadway Suite 4200, New York, NY 10005

Phone: (212) 238-9600   **Domicile State:** MD   **NAIC Code:** 10357

Data Date	Rating	RACR #1	RACR #2	Loss Ratio %	Total Assets ($mil)	Capital ($mil)	Net Premium ($mil)	Net Income ($mil)
3-17	B	3.04	1.91	N/A	1,742.0	529.1	72.5	3.5
3-16	B-	2.76	1.72	N/A	1,608.4	537.8	80.3	10.1
2016	B	3.12	1.98	55.8	1,492.8	523.3	248.6	43.3
2015	B-	2.74	1.71	51.6	1,508.0	521.5	323.7	58.8
2014	B-	2.67	1.66	52.3	1,564.7	531.4	339.3	62.1
2013	B-	2.46	1.53	43.4	1,620.3	549.2	395.4	93.2
2012	B-	2.39	1.53	57.0	1,661.8	555.4	381.6	73.0

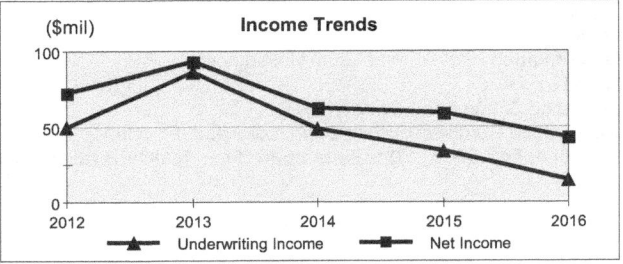

($mil) **Income Trends**

2012 / 2013 / 2014 / 2015 / 2016

▲ Underwriting Income   ■ Net Income

REPUBLIC INDEMNITY CO OF AMERICA | B- | Good

Major Rating Factors: Fair overall results on stability tests (4.7 on a scale of 0 to 10) including potential drain of affiliation with American Financial Group Inc and weak results on operational trends. Good long-term capitalization index (5.6) based on good current risk adjusted capital (moderate loss scenario). Over the last several years, capital levels have remained relatively consistent.

Other Rating Factors: Good liquidity (6.7) with sufficient resources (cash flows and marketable investments) to handle a spike in claims. Ample reserve history (9.3) that helps to protect the company against sharp claims increases. Excellent profitability (7.9) with operating gains in each of the last five years. Return on equity has been good over the last five years, averaging 11.2%.

Principal Business: Workers compensation (100%).

Principal Investments: Investment grade bonds (83%), misc. investments (15%), cash (1%), and non investment grade bonds (1%).

Investments in Affiliates: 2%

Group Affiliation: American Financial Group Inc

Licensed in: All states except CT, MA, MN, NH, NJ, NY, ND, PA, VT, WY, PR

Commenced Business: March 1973

Address: 15821 Ventura Blvd Ste 370, Encino, CA 91436

Phone: (818) 990-9860   **Domicile State:** CA   **NAIC Code:** 22179

Data Date	Rating	RACR #1	RACR #2	Loss Ratio %	Total Assets ($mil)	Capital ($mil)	Net Premium ($mil)	Net Income ($mil)
3-17	B-	1.06	0.79	N/A	2,366.6	529.7	202.8	16.5
3-16	B-	1.11	0.83	N/A	2,364.1	554.6	191.9	14.4
2016	B-	1.10	0.83	64.1	2,300.3	532.3	791.2	104.5
2015	C+	1.10	0.82	65.0	2,292.4	537.3	793.3	98.9
2014	C+	1.13	0.83	67.0	2,229.5	503.6	665.9	6.7
2013	C+	1.72	1.24	68.6	847.7	252.3	209.3	30.4
2012	B-	2.21	1.54	80.2	858.5	279.8	158.4	11.9

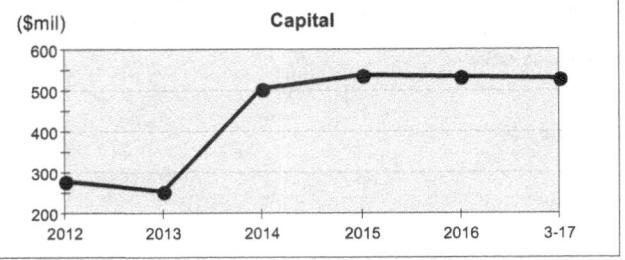

REPUBLIC UNDERWRITERS INS CO | C | Fair

Major Rating Factors: Fair reserve development (4.6 on a scale of 0 to 10) as reserves have generally been sufficient to cover claims. Fair overall results on stability tests (4.1) including weak results on operational trends and negative cash flow from operations for 2016.

Other Rating Factors: Weak profitability index (2.3) with operating losses during the first three months of 2017. Return on equity has been low, averaging 1.3% over the past five years. Good liquidity (6.7) with sufficient resources (cash flows and marketable investments) to handle a spike in claims. Strong long-term capitalization index (7.5) based on excellent current risk adjusted capital (severe and moderate loss scenarios), despite some fluctuation in capital levels.

Principal Business: Workers compensation (79%), homeowners multiple peril (7%), commercial multiple peril (5%), auto liability (4%), auto physical damage (2%), allied lines (1%), and fire (1%).

Principal Investments: Investment grade bonds (66%), misc. investments (32%), and cash (2%).

Investments in Affiliates: 13%

Group Affiliation: AmTrust Financial Services Inc

Licensed in: AZ, AR, CA, CO, CT, KS, LA, MS, NV, NM, OK, TX, UT

Commenced Business: October 1965

Address: 5525 LBJ Freeway, Dallas, TX 75240-6241

Phone: (800) 777-2249   **Domicile State:** TX   **NAIC Code:** 24538

Data Date	Rating	RACR #1	RACR #2	Loss Ratio %	Total Assets ($mil)	Capital ($mil)	Net Premium ($mil)	Net Income ($mil)
3-17	C	2.31	1.90	N/A	774.6	219.9	37.7	-1.7
3-16	C+	2.17	1.70	N/A	738.5	247.5	73.0	-7.9
2016	C	2.33	1.94	112.5	700.9	219.1	-11.7	-34.7
2015	C+	2.32	1.84	57.8	676.4	255.9	285.9	10.2
2014	C+	2.50	2.00	61.2	647.4	252.0	244.0	13.2
2013	C+	2.24	1.80	57.9	678.6	246.1	297.1	23.8
2012	C+	1.99	1.57	67.9	658.1	228.4	309.6	10.3

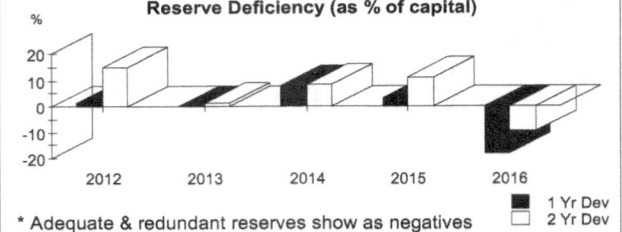

RETAILFIRST INS CO * | A- | Excellent

Major Rating Factors: Strong long-term capitalization index (8.5 on a scale of 0 to 10) based on excellent current risk adjusted capital (severe and moderate loss scenarios). Furthermore, this high level of risk adjusted capital has been consistently maintained in previous years. Excellent profitability (7.9) with operating gains in each of the last five years.

Other Rating Factors: Excellent overall results on stability tests (7.0). Stability strengths include excellent operational trends and excellent risk diversification. History of adequate reserve strength (6.6) as reserves have been consistently at an acceptable level. Good liquidity (6.6) with sufficient resources (cash flows and marketable investments) to handle a spike in claims.

Principal Business: Workers compensation (100%).

Principal Investments: Investment grade bonds (83%), misc. investments (16%), and real estate (1%).

Investments in Affiliates: None

Group Affiliation: RetailFirst Mutual Holdings Inc

Licensed in: FL

Commenced Business: January 1979

Address: 2310 Commerce Point Drive, Lakeland, FL 33801

Phone: (863) 665-6060   **Domicile State:** FL   **NAIC Code:** 10700

Data Date	Rating	RACR #1	RACR #2	Loss Ratio %	Total Assets ($mil)	Capital ($mil)	Net Premium ($mil)	Net Income ($mil)
3-17	A-	2.48	1.93	N/A	305.0	147.1	27.9	1.5
3-16	B	2.55	1.99	N/A	287.7	138.2	26.4	1.3
2016	B+	2.53	1.98	69.9	303.0	145.0	110.5	7.2
2015	B	2.64	2.07	68.0	285.5	137.1	100.0	6.9
2014	B	2.45	1.89	69.8	284.9	138.7	100.0	6.8
2013	A-	2.22	1.68	71.1	265.2	130.4	94.8	2.9
2012	A-	2.92	2.24	72.6	252.9	121.9	78.2	2.9

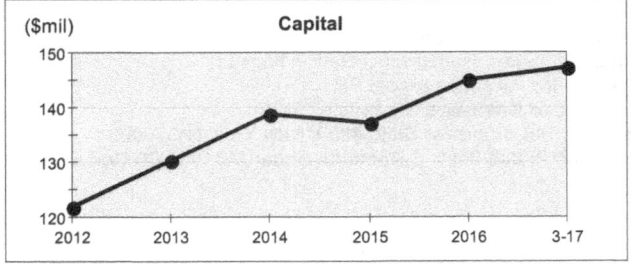

RLI INS CO   B   Good

Major Rating Factors: Good overall results on stability tests (5.7 on a scale of 0 to 10) despite potential drain of affiliation with RLI Corp. The largest net exposure for one risk is conservative at 1.1% of capital. Good liquidity (6.9) with sufficient resources (cash flows and marketable investments) to handle a spike in claims.

Other Rating Factors: Strong long-term capitalization index (7.2) based on excellent current risk adjusted capital (severe and moderate loss scenarios), despite some fluctuation in capital levels. Ample reserve history (8.0) that helps to protect the company against sharp claims increases. Excellent profitability (7.5) with operating gains in each of the last five years. Return on equity has been excellent over the last five years averaging 20.1%.

Principal Business: Other liability (37%), surety (21%), auto liability (19%), ocean marine (5%), inland marine (5%), auto physical damage (5%), and other lines (10%).

Principal Investments: Misc. investments (56%), investment grade bonds (36%), non investment grade bonds (5%), real estate (2%), and cash (1%).

Investments in Affiliates: 36%

Group Affiliation: RLI Corp

Licensed in: All states, the District of Columbia and Puerto Rico

Commenced Business: November 1960

Address: 9025 N Lindbergh Drive, Peoria, IL 61615

Phone: (309) 692-1000   **Domicile State:** IL   **NAIC Code:** 13056

Data Date	Rating	RACR #1	RACR #2	Loss Ratio %	Total Assets ($mil)	Capital ($mil)	Net Premium ($mil)	Net Income ($mil)
3-17	B	1.38	1.18	N/A	1,782.6	897.3	113.6	12.1
3-16	B	1.39	1.19	N/A	1,738.8	897.7	109.5	18.1
2016	B	1.34	1.16	52.1	1,753.4	860.0	456.3	107.3
2015	B	1.37	1.18	47.4	1,725.1	865.3	450.9	183.2
2014	B	1.31	1.14	50.6	1,707.0	849.3	437.6	238.4
2013	B	1.25	1.12	50.8	1,679.4	859.2	413.2	205.9
2012	B	1.00	0.91	53.3	1,423.9	684.1	377.2	127.2

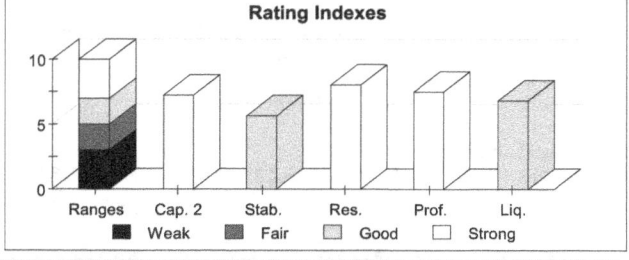

Rating Indexes

RSUI INDEMNITY CO   C+   Fair

Major Rating Factors: Good liquidity (6.9 on a scale of 0 to 10) with sufficient resources (cash flows and marketable investments) to handle a spike in claims. Weak overall results on stability tests (2.9) including potential drain of affiliation with Alleghany Corp Group and weak results on operational trends. The largest net exposure for one risk is excessive at 6.8% of capital.

Other Rating Factors: Strong long-term capitalization index (7.9) based on excellent current risk adjusted capital (severe and moderate loss scenarios), despite some fluctuation in capital levels. Ample reserve history (8.0) that helps to protect the company against sharp claims increases. Excellent profitability (7.8) with operating gains in each of the last five years. Return on equity has been good over the last five years, averaging 11.7%.

Principal Business: Other liability (74%), allied lines (14%), fire (8%), inland marine (2%), and earthquake (1%).

Principal Investments: Investment grade bonds (52%), misc. investments (42%), and non investment grade bonds (6%).

Investments in Affiliates: 9%

Group Affiliation: Alleghany Corp Group

Licensed in: All states except PR

Commenced Business: December 1977

Address: 900 Elm Street, Manchester, NH 03101

Phone: (404) 231-2366   **Domicile State:** NH   **NAIC Code:** 22314

Data Date	Rating	RACR #1	RACR #2	Loss Ratio %	Total Assets ($mil)	Capital ($mil)	Net Premium ($mil)	Net Income ($mil)
3-17	C+	2.79	2.01	N/A	3,458.4	1,574.4	169.4	57.7
3-16	C+	2.38	1.70	N/A	3,353.4	1,501.8	178.9	58.9
2016	C+	2.47	1.75	53.4	3,401.7	1,529.3	681.0	175.2
2015	C+	2.36	1.69	53.8	3,329.0	1,481.6	720.4	201.0
2014	C+	2.45	1.75	51.8	3,286.8	1,466.1	764.3	197.5
2013	C+	2.68	1.92	53.4	3,323.2	1,492.4	765.1	160.2
2012	C+	2.71	1.96	72.2	3,013.4	1,296.0	661.4	108.7

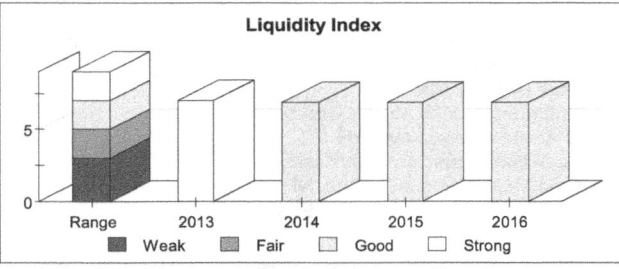

Liquidity Index

RURAL COMMUNITY INS CO   C+   Fair

Major Rating Factors: Fair overall results on stability tests (4.4 on a scale of 0 to 10) including weak results on operational trends. Strengths include potentially strong support from affiliation with Zurich Insurance Group Ltd. Weak profitability index (1.9) with small operating losses during 2012. Return on equity has been low, averaging 4.7% over the past five years.

Other Rating Factors: Vulnerable liquidity (0.0) as a spike in claims may stretch capacity. Strong long-term capitalization index (8.4) based on excellent current risk adjusted capital (severe and moderate loss scenarios), despite some fluctuation in capital levels. Ample reserve history (7.6) that can protect against increases in claims costs.

Principal Business: Allied lines (100%).

Principal Investments: Investment grade bonds (98%) and misc. investments (2%).

Investments in Affiliates: None

Group Affiliation: Zurich Insurance Group Ltd

Licensed in: All states except PR

Commenced Business: April 1980

Address: 3501 THURSTON AVENUE, Anoka, MN 55303

Phone: (847) 605-6000   **Domicile State:** MN   **NAIC Code:** 39039

Data Date	Rating	RACR #1	RACR #2	Loss Ratio %	Total Assets ($mil)	Capital ($mil)	Net Premium ($mil)	Net Income ($mil)
3-17	C+	5.99	2.99	N/A	1,821.5	267.9	0.0	0.9
3-16	B	4.91	2.51	N/A	3,260.3	246.8	5.5	-2.1
2016	C+	5.66	2.83	N/A	1,753.7	267.0	-35.3	19.2
2015	B	13.89	7.16	79.1	3,680.0	693.8	362.9	76.1
2014	B	10.11	5.84	91.2	3,758.2	618.5	380.1	21.1
2013	B	9.16	5.06	92.9	5,245.2	599.8	491.5	20.9
2012	B	11.70	6.36	100.9	5,421.1	580.3	419.4	-5.5

Zurich Insurance Group Ltd Composite Group Rating: C+ Largest Group Members	Assets ($mil)	Rating
ZURICH AMERICAN INS CO	31003	B-
ZURICH AMERICAN LIFE INS CO	12330	C
FARMERS NEW WORLD LIFE INS CO	7155	B-
CENTRE LIFE INS CO	1810	B-
RURAL COMMUNITY INS CO	1754	C+

RURAL MUTUAL INS CO

B-   **Good**

Major Rating Factors: Fair overall results on stability tests (4.1 on a scale of 0 to 10) including potential drain of affiliation with Wisconsin Farm Bureau Federation and weak results on operational trends. Good liquidity (6.7) with sufficient resources (cash flows and marketable investments) to handle a spike in claims.

Other Rating Factors: Strong long-term capitalization index (10.0) based on excellent current risk adjusted capital (severe and moderate loss scenarios). Moreover, capital levels have been consistent in recent years. Ample reserve history (8.3) that helps to protect the company against sharp claims increases. Excellent profitability (8.9) with operating gains in each of the last five years.

Principal Business: Farmowners multiple peril (33%), workers compensation (17%), commercial multiple peril (15%), auto liability (14%), auto physical damage (11%), homeowners multiple peril (9%), and allied lines (1%).

Principal Investments: Investment grade bonds (85%), misc. investments (13%), cash (1%), and non investment grade bonds (1%).

Investments in Affiliates: None

Group Affiliation: Wisconsin Farm Bureau Federation

Licensed in: IL, MN, WI

Commenced Business: June 1935

Address: 1241 JOHN Q HAMMONS DR STE 200, Madison, WI 53717-1929

Phone: (608) 836-5525   **Domicile State:** WI   **NAIC Code:** 15091

Data Date	Rating	RACR #1	RACR #2	Loss Ratio %	Total Assets ($mil)	Capital ($mil)	Net Premium ($mil)	Net Income ($mil)
3-17	B-	6.18	4.19	N/A	472.0	247.4	41.1	3.3
3-16	B-	6.16	4.26	N/A	429.7	219.1	39.5	5.6
2016	B-	6.41	4.32	57.7	460.1	241.7	171.4	24.9
2015	B-	6.18	4.19	59.9	419.9	213.5	162.6	21.3
2014	C+	5.99	4.08	59.8	385.9	194.0	152.9	20.0
2013	C+	5.74	3.93	59.7	356.6	176.5	144.7	18.1
2012	C+	5.58	3.83	60.4	324.0	156.1	136.0	8.8

Rating Indexes

SAFECO INS CO OF AMERICA

B-   **Good**

Major Rating Factors: Fair overall results on stability tests (3.9 on a scale of 0 to 10) including weak results on operational trends. The largest net exposure for one risk is high at 4.3% of capital. History of adequate reserve strength (5.9) as reserves have been consistently at an acceptable level.

Other Rating Factors: Good overall profitability index (6.6). Fair expense controls. Return on equity has been fair, averaging 10.0% over the past five years. Good liquidity (6.4) with sufficient resources (cash flows and marketable investments) to handle a spike in claims. Strong long-term capitalization index (8.2) based on excellent current risk adjusted capital (severe and moderate loss scenarios). Moreover, capital levels have been consistent in recent years.

Principal Business: Homeowners multiple peril (43%), auto liability (20%), auto physical damage (16%), allied lines (6%), fire (5%), other liability (5%), and other lines (4%).

Principal Investments: Investment grade bonds (68%), misc. investments (28%), and non investment grade bonds (5%).

Investments in Affiliates: 7%

Group Affiliation: Liberty Mutual Group

Licensed in: All states except PR

Commenced Business: October 1953

Address: 62 Maple Avenue, Keene, NH 03431

Phone: (617) 357-9500   **Domicile State:** NH   **NAIC Code:** 24740

Data Date	Rating	RACR #1	RACR #2	Loss Ratio %	Total Assets ($mil)	Capital ($mil)	Net Premium ($mil)	Net Income ($mil)
3-17	B-	2.71	1.91	N/A	4,520.7	1,523.2	392.6	1.5
3-16	B-	2.61	1.82	N/A	4,362.9	1,427.5	379.0	19.8
2016	B-	2.72	1.93	69.9	4,485.1	1,497.9	1,589.9	46.9
2015	B-	2.56	1.80	68.4	4,356.9	1,393.4	1,537.9	103.6
2014	B-	2.33	1.61	70.0	4,233.3	1,278.9	1,522.6	106.8
2013	B-	2.18	1.48	73.5	4,747.1	1,188.7	1,349.1	154.8
2012	B-	1.79	1.28	66.7	4,029.8	945.1	1,659.6	193.5

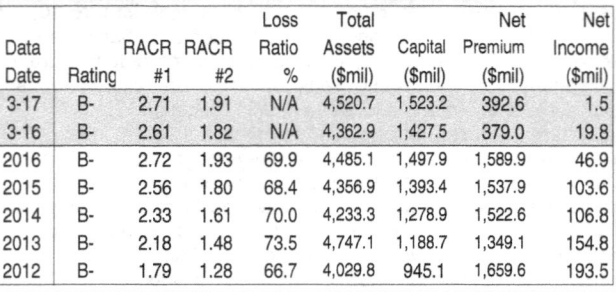

Rating Indexes

SAFETY INS CO

B-   **Good**

Major Rating Factors: Fair overall results on stability tests (4.4 on a scale of 0 to 10) including potential drain of affiliation with Safety Group and weak results on operational trends. Fair profitability index (4.4) with operating losses during 2015. Return on equity has been fair, averaging 6.6% over the past five years.

Other Rating Factors: Good liquidity (6.2) with sufficient resources (cash flows and marketable investments) to handle a spike in claims. Strong long-term capitalization index (8.9) based on excellent current risk adjusted capital (severe and moderate loss scenarios), despite some fluctuation in capital levels. Ample reserve history (8.9) that helps to protect the company against sharp claims increases.

Principal Business: Auto liability (51%), auto physical damage (35%), homeowners multiple peril (8%), commercial multiple peril (3%), other liability (1%), allied lines (1%), and fire (1%).

Principal Investments: Investment grade bonds (73%), misc. investments (18%), and non investment grade bonds (11%).

Investments in Affiliates: 6%

Group Affiliation: Safety Group

Licensed in: ME, MA, NH

Commenced Business: January 1980

Address: 20 Custom House Street, Boston, MA 02110

Phone: (617) 951-0600   **Domicile State:** MA   **NAIC Code:** 39454

Data Date	Rating	RACR #1	RACR #2	Loss Ratio %	Total Assets ($mil)	Capital ($mil)	Net Premium ($mil)	Net Income ($mil)
3-17	B-	3.21	2.21	N/A	1,470.8	603.5	170.7	11.8
3-16	B-	3.17	2.18	N/A	1,410.9	573.5	167.1	11.8
2016	B-	3.22	2.25	65.3	1,480.5	604.8	689.8	57.2
2015	B-	3.15	2.21	83.0	1,434.6	571.0	671.6	-12.2
2014	B-	3.67	2.72	66.5	1,430.1	630.0	661.4	51.2
2013	B+	3.72	2.71	65.7	1,396.8	628.0	627.8	53.1
2012	B+	3.97	2.99	65.7	1,319.7	599.0	597.5	52.4

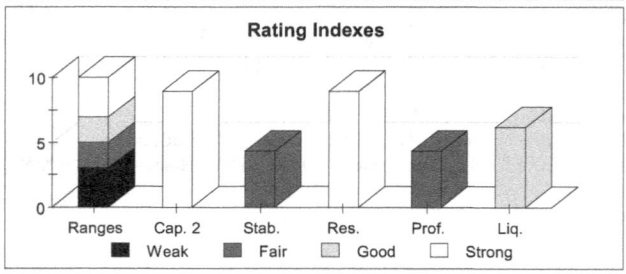

Rating Indexes

SAFETY NATIONAL CASUALTY CORP   C   Fair

Major Rating Factors: Fair overall results on stability tests (3.4 on a scale of 0 to 10) including weak results on operational trends. The largest net exposure for one risk is conservative at 1.4% of capital. A history of deficient reserves (2.5). Underreserving can have an adverse impact on capital and profits. Deficiencies in the two year reserve development occurred in three of the previous five years and ranged between 16% and 47%.

Other Rating Factors: Good overall profitability index (6.4). Good expense controls. Return on equity has been fair, averaging 8.6% over the past five years. Strong long-term capitalization index (7.2) based on excellent current risk adjusted capital (severe and moderate loss scenarios). Moreover, capital levels have been consistent in recent years. Excellent liquidity (7.4) with ample operational cash flow and liquid investments.

Principal Business: Workers compensation (24%), auto liability (4%), other liability (3%), and surety (1%).

Principal Investments: Investment grade bonds (58%), misc. investments (30%), and non investment grade bonds (12%).

Investments in Affiliates: 4%

Group Affiliation: Tokio Marine Holdings Inc

Licensed in: All states, the District of Columbia and Puerto Rico

Commenced Business: December 1942

Address: 1832 Schuetz Road, St Louis, MO 63146-3540

Phone: (314) 995-5300   **Domicile State:** MO   **NAIC Code:** 15105

Data Date	Rating	RACR #1	RACR #2	Loss Ratio %	Total Assets ($mil)	Capital ($mil)	Net Premium ($mil)	Net Income ($mil)
3-17	C	1.70	1.24	N/A	6,646.8	1,860.3	191.3	42.2
3-16	C	1.52	1.13	N/A	5,878.8	1,557.3	174.1	18.1
2016	C	1.71	1.26	84.6	6,450.4	1,812.6	778.4	175.3
2015	C	1.54	1.16	86.1	5,611.3	1,527.0	728.9	159.3
2014	C	1.46	1.10	87.8	4,985.1	1,367.6	671.2	110.2
2013	C	1.39	1.06	78.4	4,183.6	1,153.8	664.9	122.7
2012	C	1.36	1.06	101.1	3,544.1	960.8	549.0	36.8

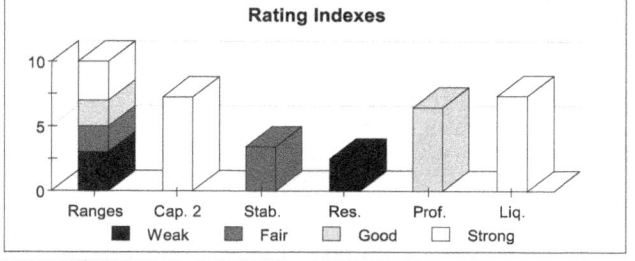

Rating Indexes

SAFEWAY INS CO   B-   Good

Major Rating Factors: Fair overall results on stability tests (4.5 on a scale of 0 to 10) including potential drain of affiliation with Safeway Ins Group and negative cash flow from operations for 2016. Fair reserve development (4.9) as reserves have generally been sufficient to cover claims.

Other Rating Factors: Fair profitability index (3.8) with operating losses during 2013 and the first three months of 2017. Return on equity has been low, averaging 2.6% over the past five years. Good liquidity (5.4) with sufficient resources (cash flows and marketable investments) to handle a spike in claims. Strong long-term capitalization index (7.6) based on excellent current risk adjusted capital (severe and moderate loss scenarios), despite some fluctuation in capital levels.

Principal Business: Auto liability (63%) and auto physical damage (37%).

Principal Investments: Misc. investments (64%), investment grade bonds (30%), cash (5%), and real estate (1%).

Investments in Affiliates: 43%

Group Affiliation: Safeway Ins Group

Licensed in: AL, AK, AZ, CA, CO, DC, DE, FL, GA, ID, IL, IN, IA, KS, LA, ME, MD, MA, MI, MN, MS, MO, MT, NE, NV, NJ, NM, ND, OK, OR, PA, SC, SD, TX, UT, WA, WV, WI, WY

Commenced Business: December 1962

Address: 790 Pasquinelli Drive, Westmont, IL 60559-1254

Phone: (630) 887-8300   **Domicile State:** IL   **NAIC Code:** 12521

Data Date	Rating	RACR #1	RACR #2	Loss Ratio %	Total Assets ($mil)	Capital ($mil)	Net Premium ($mil)	Net Income ($mil)
3-17	B-	1.54	1.38	N/A	555.5	285.4	52.1	-1.6
3-16	B-	1.64	1.49	N/A	465.6	285.3	50.5	-3.5
2016	B-	1.56	1.42	86.1	468.3	287.9	210.5	-5.5
2015	B-	1.72	1.57	82.2	463.6	302.1	204.4	33.3
2014	B-	1.53	1.41	76.0	446.1	298.8	167.5	7.3
2013	B-	1.47	1.35	79.1	417.0	279.3	156.1	-0.3
2012	B-	1.65	1.52	78.7	390.6	281.4	126.1	8.1

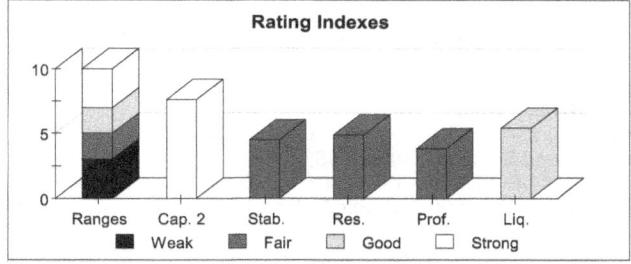

Rating Indexes

SAN FRANCISCO REINS CO   C   Fair

Major Rating Factors: Fair overall results on stability tests (3.6 on a scale of 0 to 10) including weak results on operational trends and negative cash flow from operations for 2016. Strengths include potentially strong support from affiliation with Allianz Ins Group. Fair profitability index (3.8) with operating losses during 2012, 2015 and 2016. Average return on equity over the last five years has been poor at -1.3%.

Other Rating Factors: A history of deficient reserves (0.4). Underreserving can have an adverse impact on capital and profits. Deficiencies in the two year reserve development occurred in three of the previous five years and ranged between 21% and 3048%. Strong long-term capitalization index (7.1) based on excellent current risk adjusted capital (severe and moderate loss scenarios), despite some fluctuation in capital levels. Superior liquidity (9.0) with ample operational cash flow and liquid investments.

Principal Business: (This company is a reinsurer.)

Principal Investments: Investment grade bonds (99%) and misc. investments (1%).

Investments in Affiliates: None

Group Affiliation: Allianz Ins Group

Licensed in: All states except PR

Commenced Business: August 1964

Address: 1465 N MCDOWELL BLVD STE 100, Petaluma, CA 94954

Phone: (415) 899-2000   **Domicile State:** CA   **NAIC Code:** 21911

Data Date	Rating	RACR #1	RACR #2	Loss Ratio %	Total Assets ($mil)	Capital ($mil)	Net Premium ($mil)	Net Income ($mil)
3-17	C	2.06	1.37	N/A	3,469.2	625.6	0.0	10.9
3-16	C+	1.83	1.20	N/A	3,196.0	641.4	-783.6	7.5
2016	C	2.03	1.36	76.5	3,539.8	613.9	-443.3	-22.1
2015	C+	0.75	0.54	100.0	2,931.1	655.9	2,282.7	-14.9
2014	U	18.37	5.88	0.0	98.4	74.5	0.0	1.8
2013	U	18.21	5.90	0.0	96.5	73.0	0.0	0.7
2012	U	18.78	6.11	0.0	94.3	72.1	0.0	-4.3

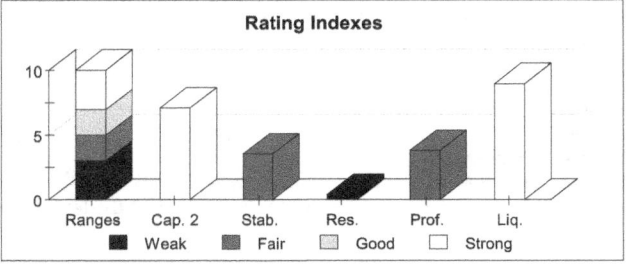

Rating Indexes

SCOR REINS CO

C Fair

Major Rating Factors: Fair overall results on stability tests (3.4 on a scale of 0 to 10) including potential drain of affiliation with SCOR Reinsurance Group and weak results on operational trends. The largest net exposure for one risk is acceptable at 2.1% of capital. History of adequate reserve strength (6.9) as reserves have been consistently at an acceptable level.

Other Rating Factors: Good overall profitability index (5.4) despite operating losses during 2012 and the first three months of 2017. Return on equity has been low, averaging 4.6% over the past five years. Good liquidity (6.9) with sufficient resources (cash flows and marketable investments) to handle a spike in claims. Strong long-term capitalization index (7.1) based on excellent current risk adjusted capital (severe and moderate loss scenarios). Moreover, capital levels have been consistent in recent years.

Principal Business: (This company is a reinsurer.)

Principal Investments: Investment grade bonds (94%), misc. investments (4%), cash (1%), and non investment grade bonds (1%).

Investments in Affiliates: None

Group Affiliation: SCOR Reinsurance Group

Licensed in: All states, the District of Columbia and Puerto Rico

Commenced Business: September 1985

Address: 199 WATER STREET SUITE 2100, New York, NY 10038-3526

Phone: (212) 480-1900   **Domicile State:** NY   **NAIC Code:** 30058

Data Date	Rating	RACR #1	RACR #2	Loss Ratio %	Total Assets ($mil)	Capital ($mil)	Net Premium ($mil)	Net Income ($mil)
3-17	C	1.79	1.06	N/A	3,212.4	1,103.1	272.2	-7.7
3-16	C-	2.03	1.32	N/A	2,801.7	978.7	219.3	4.9
2016	C	1.87	1.11	53.2	3,163.1	1,102.9	1,123.7	60.7
2015	D+	1.94	1.26	48.6	2,749.2	962.2	846.9	126.6
2014	D	1.30	0.85	54.8	2,269.6	704.3	798.2	75.1
2013	D	1.39	0.90	62.3	2,364.7	676.4	755.6	66.6
2012	D	1.04	0.69	76.6	2,247.6	618.9	709.3	-89.2

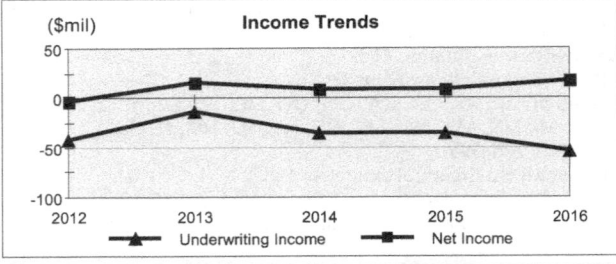

Rating Indexes

Weak   Fair   Good   Strong

SCOTTSDALE INS CO

B- Good

Major Rating Factors: Fair profitability index (4.4 on a scale of 0 to 10) with operating losses during 2012 and the first three months of 2017. Return on equity has been low, averaging 1.2% over the past five years. Fair overall results on stability tests (4.9) including weak results on operational trends.

Other Rating Factors: History of adequate reserve strength (6.0) as reserves have been consistently at an acceptable level. Good liquidity (6.0) with sufficient resources (cash flows and marketable investments) to handle a spike in claims. Strong long-term capitalization index (8.3) based on excellent current risk adjusted capital (severe and moderate loss scenarios), despite some fluctuation in capital levels.

Principal Business: Other liability (53%), commercial multiple peril (22%), allied lines (9%), homeowners multiple peril (5%), auto liability (4%), fire (3%), and other lines (4%).

Principal Investments: Investment grade bonds (78%), misc. investments (25%), and non investment grade bonds (1%).

Investments in Affiliates: 19%

Group Affiliation: Nationwide Corp

Licensed in: All states, the District of Columbia and Puerto Rico

Commenced Business: July 1982

Address: ONE WEST NATIONWIDE BLVD, Columbus, OH 43215-2220

Phone: (480) 365-4000   **Domicile State:** OH   **NAIC Code:** 41297

Data Date	Rating	RACR #1	RACR #2	Loss Ratio %	Total Assets ($mil)	Capital ($mil)	Net Premium ($mil)	Net Income ($mil)
3-17	B-	2.19	1.83	N/A	2,531.5	772.0	192.2	-3.6
3-16	B-	2.25	1.88	N/A	2,462.2	771.7	189.7	2.1
2016	B-	2.23	1.88	74.7	2,683.3	775.3	779.5	17.0
2015	B-	2.27	1.92	71.1	2,313.3	766.1	747.5	8.5
2014	B-	2.30	1.95	71.1	2,222.6	764.9	721.1	9.9
2013	B-	2.42	1.99	66.2	2,133.3	716.4	707.1	16.2
2012	B-	2.42	2.03	71.9	1,879.5	670.2	598.9	-2.3

($mil) Income Trends

Underwriting Income   Net Income

SECURA INS A MUTUAL CO

B- Good

Major Rating Factors: Fair overall results on stability tests (4.2 on a scale of 0 to 10) including potential drain of affiliation with SECURA Group and weak results on operational trends. Good liquidity (6.6) with sufficient resources (cash flows and marketable investments) to handle a spike in claims.

Other Rating Factors: Strong long-term capitalization index (8.3) based on excellent current risk adjusted capital (severe and moderate loss scenarios). Moreover, capital levels have been consistent in recent years. Ample reserve history (9.1) that helps to protect the company against sharp claims increases. Excellent profitability (8.8) with operating gains in each of the last five years.

Principal Business: Workers compensation (29%), commercial multiple peril (26%), auto liability (14%), farmowners multiple peril (10%), other liability (7%), auto physical damage (7%), and other lines (6%).

Principal Investments: Investment grade bonds (66%), misc. investments (31%), real estate (2%), and cash (1%).

Investments in Affiliates: 7%

Group Affiliation: SECURA Group

Licensed in: AZ, AR, CO, ID, IL, IN, IA, KS, KY, MI, MN, MO, MT, NE, NV, NM, ND, OH, OK, OR, PA, SD, TN, UT, WA, WI, WY

Commenced Business: May 1900

Address: 2401 S Memorial Drive, Appleton, WI 54915

Phone: (920) 739-3161   **Domicile State:** WI   **NAIC Code:** 22543

Data Date	Rating	RACR #1	RACR #2	Loss Ratio %	Total Assets ($mil)	Capital ($mil)	Net Premium ($mil)	Net Income ($mil)
3-17	B-	2.59	1.88	N/A	1,124.9	412.7	121.8	4.8
3-16	B-	2.46	1.80	N/A	1,024.8	359.3	116.2	0.2
2016	B-	2.59	1.89	59.9	1,090.1	404.2	491.3	27.7
2015	B-	2.50	1.84	60.1	1,018.7	353.1	462.5	24.7
2014	B-	2.53	1.84	62.6	940.4	332.9	424.4	37.9
2013	B-	2.58	1.87	59.4	872.1	321.7	387.1	45.3
2012	B-	1.98	1.43	64.0	797.4	273.3	344.9	22.9

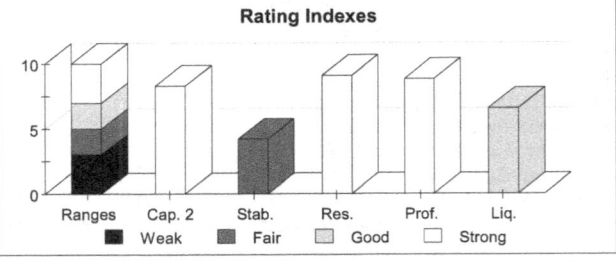

Rating Indexes

Weak   Fair   Good   Strong

SECURIAN CASUALTY CO *   A-   Excellent

Major Rating Factors: Strong long-term capitalization index (7.9 on a scale of 0 to 10) based on excellent current risk adjusted capital (severe and moderate loss scenarios). Moreover, capital levels have been consistent in recent years. Excellent profitability (8.7) with operating gains in each of the last five years.

Other Rating Factors: History of adequate reserve strength (6.3) as reserves have been consistently at an acceptable level. Good liquidity (5.8) with sufficient resources (cash flows and marketable investments) to handle a spike in claims. Good overall results on stability tests (6.9). Stability strengths include good operational trends and excellent risk diversification.

Principal Business: Inland marine (52%), other liability (42%), and credit (6%).

Principal Investments: Investment grade bonds (86%), misc. investments (9%), and cash (5%).

Investments in Affiliates: None

Group Affiliation: Securian Financial Group

Licensed in: All states except PR

Commenced Business: August 1994

Address: 400 ROBERT STREET NORTH, St Paul, MN 55101-2098

Phone: (651) 665-3500   **Domicile State:** MN   **NAIC Code:** 10054

Data Date	Rating	RACR #1	RACR #2	Loss Ratio %	Total Assets ($mil)	Capital ($mil)	Net Premium ($mil)	Net Income ($mil)
3-17	A-	2.06	1.56	N/A	288.6	122.2	57.0	1.3
3-16	B	2.43	1.86	N/A	227.3	115.5	47.4	2.1
2016	B+	2.12	1.61	55.5	275.8	120.1	231.6	4.6
2015	B	2.48	1.91	49.4	224.1	112.9	180.8	9.2
2014	B	1.83	1.37	48.1	193.3	102.6	150.1	10.8
2013	B	2.31	1.76	46.8	173.9	101.1	122.2	10.1
2012	B	2.47	2.05	47.0	155.9	90.5	105.0	9.0

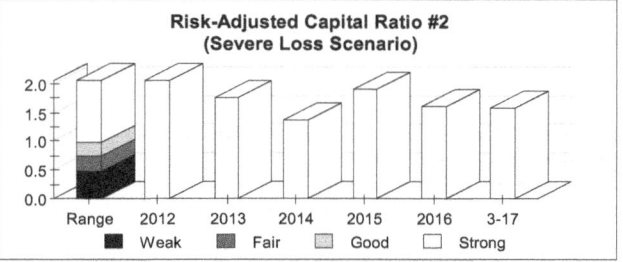

Risk-Adjusted Capital Ratio #2 (Severe Loss Scenario)

SECURITY NATIONAL INS CO   B   Good

Major Rating Factors: History of adequate reserve strength (5.6 on a scale of 0 to 10) as reserves have been consistently at an acceptable level. Good liquidity (6.8) with sufficient resources (cash flows and marketable investments) to handle a spike in claims.

Other Rating Factors: Fair overall results on stability tests (4.7) including weak results on operational trends and excessive premium growth. Affiliation with AmTrust Financial Services Inc is a strength. Strong long-term capitalization index (7.5) based on excellent current risk adjusted capital (severe and moderate loss scenarios). Moreover, capital levels have been consistent in recent years. Excellent profitability (9.4) with operating gains in each of the last five years. Return on equity has been excellent over the last five years averaging 20.6%.

Principal Business: Workers compensation (73%), other liability (12%), auto liability (5%), commercial multiple peril (2%), auto physical damage (1%), fidelity (1%), and other lines (7%).

Principal Investments: Investment grade bonds (86%), misc. investments (11%), cash (2%), and non investment grade bonds (1%).

Investments in Affiliates: 3%

Group Affiliation: AmTrust Financial Services Inc

Licensed in: All states except PR

Commenced Business: August 1924

Address: 2711 CENTERVILLE ROAD STE 400, Wilmington, DE 19808

Phone: (800) 777-2249   **Domicile State:** DE   **NAIC Code:** 19879

Data Date	Rating	RACR #1	RACR #2	Loss Ratio %	Total Assets ($mil)	Capital ($mil)	Net Premium ($mil)	Net Income ($mil)
3-17	B	1.87	1.19	N/A	1,280.4	218.6	58.7	3.1
3-16	B	1.59	1.05	N/A	1,131.5	155.1	42.0	0.2
2016	B	2.06	1.34	48.6	1,204.9	217.2	228.4	35.5
2015	B	1.79	1.19	63.5	991.4	149.5	143.4	40.5
2014	B-	4.33	2.50	69.1	703.7	125.7	63.3	30.7
2013	B-	4.73	2.61	70.5	429.0	79.8	44.7	14.4
2012	B-	4.83	2.77	71.4	232.7	51.2	28.0	10.6

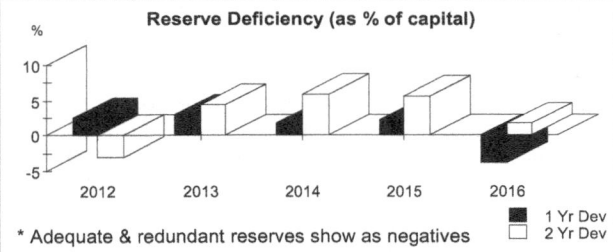

Reserve Deficiency (as % of capital)

* Adequate & redundant reserves show as negatives

SELECTIVE INS CO OF AM   B   Good

Major Rating Factors: Good overall results on stability tests (5.6 on a scale of 0 to 10) despite potential drain of affiliation with Selective Ins. Good liquidity (6.9) with sufficient resources (cash flows and marketable investments) to handle a spike in claims.

Other Rating Factors: Strong long-term capitalization index (8.3) based on excellent current risk adjusted capital (severe and moderate loss scenarios). Moreover, capital levels have been consistent in recent years. Ample reserve history (9.2) that helps to protect the company against sharp claims increases. Excellent profitability (8.3) with operating gains in each of the last five years. Return on equity has been good over the last five years, averaging 12.6%.

Principal Business: Other liability (23%), workers compensation (17%), auto liability (16%), allied lines (11%), fire (7%), auto physical damage (6%), and other lines (20%).

Principal Investments: Investment grade bonds (78%), misc. investments (16%), and non investment grade bonds (7%).

Investments in Affiliates: None

Group Affiliation: Selective Ins

Licensed in: All states except CO, FL, ID, LA, NM, OK, UT, VT, PR

Commenced Business: April 1926

Address: 40 WANTAGE AVENUE, Branchville, NJ 07890

Phone: (973) 948-3000   **Domicile State:** NJ   **NAIC Code:** 12572

Data Date	Rating	RACR #1	RACR #2	Loss Ratio %	Total Assets ($mil)	Capital ($mil)	Net Premium ($mil)	Net Income ($mil)
3-17	B	2.80	1.81	N/A	2,389.7	584.2	179.5	22.1
3-16	B	2.62	1.72	N/A	2,162.7	532.4	167.2	14.7
2016	B	2.83	1.85	57.4	2,314.2	568.6	715.9	72.2
2015	B	2.67	1.77	57.7	2,140.7	520.8	662.4	69.6
2014	B-	2.60	1.70	62.4	2,044.6	493.0	603.3	83.9
2013	B-	2.47	1.59	64.5	1,951.0	463.4	579.7	53.1
2012	C+	2.19	1.38	70.6	1,708.3	369.9	496.8	29.8

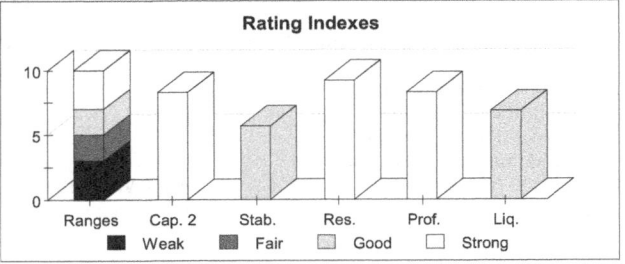

Rating Indexes

SELECTIVE WAY INS CO

B **Good**

Major Rating Factors: Good liquidity (6.6 on a scale of 0 to 10) with sufficient resources (cash flows and marketable investments) to handle a spike in claims. Fair overall results on stability tests (4.6) including weak results on operational trends.

Other Rating Factors: Strong long-term capitalization index (7.9) based on excellent current risk adjusted capital (severe and moderate loss scenarios). Moreover, capital levels have been consistent in recent years. Ample reserve history (9.3) that helps to protect the company against sharp claims increases. Excellent profitability (8.4) with operating gains in each of the last five years. Return on equity has been good over the last five years, averaging 12.0%.

Principal Business: Other liability (25%), auto liability (19%), workers compensation (16%), allied lines (8%), fire (7%), auto physical damage (7%), and other lines (18%).

Principal Investments: Investment grade bonds (91%), misc. investments (8%), and cash (1%).

Investments in Affiliates: None

Group Affiliation: Selective Ins

Licensed in: AZ, CA, DC, DE, GA, MD, MI, NH, NJ, NY, NC, PA, SC, VA

Commenced Business: November 1973

Address: 40 WANTAGE AVENUE, Branchville, NJ 07890

Phone: (973) 948-3000 **Domicile State:** NJ **NAIC Code:** 26301

Data Date	Rating	RACR #1	RACR #2	Loss Ratio %	Total Assets ($mil)	Capital ($mil)	Net Premium ($mil)	Net Income ($mil)
3-17	B	2.37	1.59	N/A	1,310.0	316.1	117.8	10.9
3-16	B	2.20	1.47	N/A	1,235.1	281.5	109.7	8.3
2016	B	2.40	1.62	57.4	1,294.2	309.5	469.8	41.2
2015	B	2.22	1.49	57.7	1,215.0	272.6	434.7	42.3
2014	B	2.07	1.38	62.4	1,167.4	250.3	395.9	37.0
2013	B	2.09	1.36	64.5	1,124.5	250.3	380.4	27.5
2012	B	2.00	1.28	70.7	1,048.0	211.2	350.0	10.1

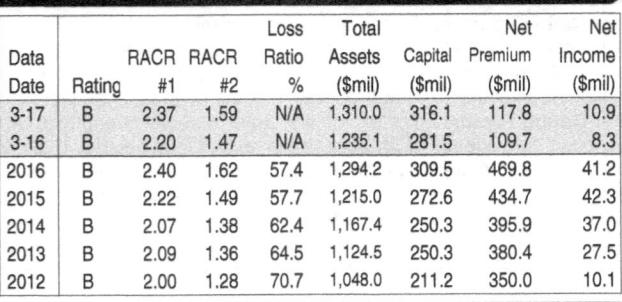

Liquidity Index

■ Weak ▨ Fair ▢ Good ▢ Strong

SENTRY INS A MUTUAL CO *

A **Excellent**

Major Rating Factors: Strong long-term capitalization index (8.7 on a scale of 0 to 10) based on excellent current risk adjusted capital (severe and moderate loss scenarios). Furthermore, this high level of risk adjusted capital has been consistently maintained in previous years. Ample reserve history (7.5) that can protect against increases in claims costs.

Other Rating Factors: Good overall profitability index (6.8). Fair expense controls. Good liquidity (6.9) with sufficient resources (cash flows and marketable investments) to handle a spike in claims. Good overall results on stability tests (6.1) despite weak results on operational trends.

Principal Business: Workers compensation (34%), auto liability (28%), other liability (9%), allied lines (8%), auto physical damage (6%), fire (5%), and other lines (9%).

Principal Investments: Misc. investments (55%), investment grade bonds (42%), non investment grade bonds (3%), and real estate (1%).

Investments in Affiliates: 22%

Group Affiliation: Sentry Ins Group

Licensed in: All states, the District of Columbia and Puerto Rico

Commenced Business: August 1914

Address: 1800 NORTH POINT DRIVE, Stevens Point, WI 54481

Phone: (715) 346-6000 **Domicile State:** WI **NAIC Code:** 24988

Data Date	Rating	RACR #1	RACR #2	Loss Ratio %	Total Assets ($mil)	Capital ($mil)	Net Premium ($mil)	Net Income ($mil)
3-17	A	2.66	2.21	N/A	7,779.6	4,846.9	269.9	52.4
3-16	A	2.50	2.10	N/A	7,335.9	4,455.7	256.8	25.3
2016	A	2.62	2.18	73.9	7,587.3	4,723.5	1,086.7	238.1
2015	A	2.49	2.10	72.7	7,214.6	4,404.3	1,014.2	297.6
2014	A	2.34	1.99	74.9	6,981.3	4,164.4	997.7	272.5
2013	A	2.34	2.01	76.3	6,632.0	4,075.3	999.7	308.4
2012	A	2.19	1.92	77.3	6,248.1	3,637.2	950.0	230.0

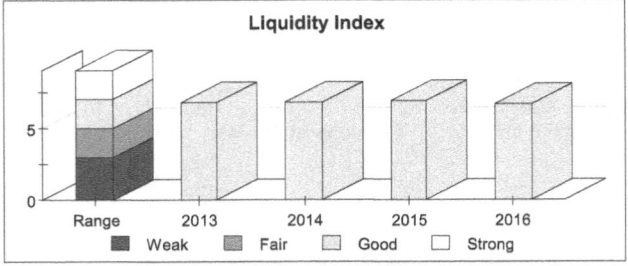

Risk-Adjusted Capital Ratio #2
(Severe Loss Scenario)

■ Weak ▨ Fair ▢ Good ▢ Strong

SENTRY SELECT INS CO *

B+ **Good**

Major Rating Factors: Good overall profitability index (5.7 on a scale of 0 to 10). Fair expense controls. Return on equity has been fair, averaging 5.7% over the past five years. Good liquidity (6.7) with sufficient resources (cash flows and marketable investments) to handle a spike in claims.

Other Rating Factors: Good overall results on stability tests (5.1) despite weak results on operational trends. The largest net exposure for one risk is conservative at 1.3% of capital. Strong long-term capitalization index (9.0) based on excellent current risk adjusted capital (severe and moderate loss scenarios), despite some fluctuation in capital levels. Ample reserve history (8.1) that helps to protect the company against sharp claims increases.

Principal Business: Auto liability (43%), auto physical damage (16%), inland marine (15%), other liability (10%), workers compensation (5%), allied lines (4%), and other lines (7%).

Principal Investments: Investment grade bonds (94%), misc. investments (5%), and non investment grade bonds (1%).

Investments in Affiliates: None

Group Affiliation: Sentry Ins Group

Licensed in: All states except PR

Commenced Business: August 1929

Address: 1800 NORTH POINT DRIVE, Stevens Point, WI 54481

Phone: (715) 346-6000 **Domicile State:** WI **NAIC Code:** 21180

Data Date	Rating	RACR #1	RACR #2	Loss Ratio %	Total Assets ($mil)	Capital ($mil)	Net Premium ($mil)	Net Income ($mil)
3-17	B+	3.57	2.26	N/A	715.6	233.9	50.0	2.6
3-16	B+	3.79	2.39	N/A	701.2	233.6	47.6	1.9
2016	B+	3.63	2.33	73.9	707.0	231.4	201.2	11.6
2015	B+	3.87	2.48	72.7	679.1	232.0	187.7	11.9
2014	B+	4.30	2.89	74.9	658.6	235.1	181.4	19.0
2013	B+	4.12	2.81	76.3	641.3	227.5	181.8	12.4
2012	B+	4.20	2.84	77.3	620.8	221.5	172.7	11.5

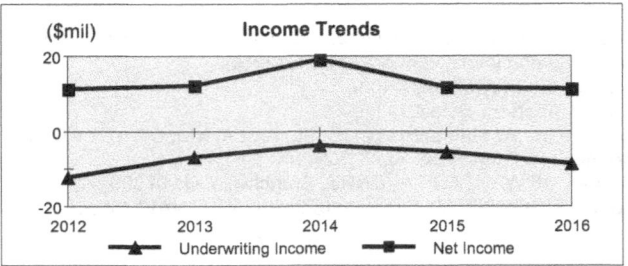

($mil) Income Trends

▲ Underwriting Income ■ Net Income

SHELTER MUTUAL INS CO

B   **Good**

Major Rating Factors: Good overall results on stability tests (5.0 on a scale of 0 to 10) despite potential drain of affiliation with Shelter Ins Companies and weak results on operational trends. Good overall profitability index (6.8). Fair expense controls.

Other Rating Factors: Good liquidity (5.8) with sufficient resources (cash flows and marketable investments) to handle a spike in claims. Strong long-term capitalization index (8.3) based on excellent current risk adjusted capital (severe and moderate loss scenarios). Moreover, capital levels have been consistent in recent years. Ample reserve history (7.6) that can protect against increases in claims costs.

Principal Business: Auto liability (31%), homeowners multiple peril (28%), auto physical damage (23%), allied lines (6%), fire (4%), farmowners multiple peril (3%), and other lines (5%).

Principal Investments: Investment grade bonds (56%), misc. investments (45%), and real estate (1%).

Investments in Affiliates: 24%

Group Affiliation: Shelter Ins Companies

Licensed in: AL, AR, CO, DE, GA, ID, IL, IN, IA, KS, KY, LA, MD, MA, MN, MS, MO, MT, NE, NV, NH, NJ, NY, NC, OH, OK, OR, PA, SC, SD, TN, TX, VT, VA, WV, WI, WY

Commenced Business: January 1946

Address: 1817 WEST BROADWAY, Columbia, MO 65218-0001

Phone: (573) 445-8441   **Domicile State:** MO   **NAIC Code:** 23388

Data Date	Rating	RACR #1	RACR #2	Loss Ratio %	Total Assets ($mil)	Capital ($mil)	Net Premium ($mil)	Net Income ($mil)
3-17	B	2.28	1.88	N/A	3,367.5	1,924.8	366.9	16.8
3-16	B	2.25	1.81	N/A	3,174.3	1,850.4	349.5	42.6
2016	B	2.25	1.86	73.9	3,305.5	1,877.1	1,449.1	46.1
2015	B	2.19	1.77	69.4	3,114.8	1,787.8	1,379.7	80.1
2014	B	2.15	1.72	69.7	2,973.8	1,682.7	1,323.6	66.8
2013	B	2.03	1.62	74.2	2,756.5	1,566.9	1,208.2	65.5
2012	B	2.06	1.60	75.1	2,490.3	1,397.9	1,144.8	70.1

Rating Indexes

(Bar chart: Ranges, Cap. 2, Stab., Res., Prof., Liq. — legend: ■ Weak, ▨ Fair, ▧ Good, ☐ Strong)

SHELTER REINS CO

B-   **Good**

Major Rating Factors: Fair overall results on stability tests (3.8 on a scale of 0 to 10) including weak results on operational trends. The largest net exposure for one risk is acceptable at 2.9% of capital. Good liquidity (6.8) with sufficient resources (cash flows and marketable investments) to handle a spike in claims.

Other Rating Factors: Strong long-term capitalization index (10.0) based on excellent current risk adjusted capital (severe and moderate loss scenarios). Moreover, capital levels have been consistent in recent years. Ample reserve history (7.0) that can protect against increases in claims costs. Excellent profitability (8.9) with operating gains in each of the last five years. Return on equity has been good over the last five years, averaging 10.9%.

Principal Business: Earthquake (100%).

Principal Investments: Investment grade bonds (93%), misc. investments (6%), and cash (1%).

Investments in Affiliates: None

Group Affiliation: Shelter Ins Companies

Licensed in: CA, IA, KS, MD, MI, MN, MO, ND, PA, SD, TN, WI, PR

Commenced Business: November 1986

Address: 1817 WEST BROADWAY, Columbia, MO 65218-0001

Phone: (573) 214-4332   **Domicile State:** MO   **NAIC Code:** 26557

Data Date	Rating	RACR #1	RACR #2	Loss Ratio %	Total Assets ($mil)	Capital ($mil)	Net Premium ($mil)	Net Income ($mil)
3-17	B-	5.49	3.55	N/A	457.1	335.7	24.8	8.3
3-16	B-	4.20	2.78	N/A	435.8	305.5	25.4	8.3
2016	B-	5.29	3.42	44.3	447.3	326.8	113.0	32.2
2015	C+	4.10	2.72	46.7	422.3	296.7	103.5	28.1
2014	C	3.51	2.30	46.1	405.7	271.0	103.4	27.2
2013	C	2.94	2.00	40.6	383.0	245.4	98.0	30.5
2012	C	1.86	1.27	54.1	321.8	165.2	102.1	21.3

Shelter Ins Companies
Composite Group Rating: B
Largest Group Members

Largest Group Members	Assets ($mil)	Rating
SHELTER MUTUAL INS CO	3306	B
SHELTER LIFE INS CO	1199	B+
SHELTER REINS CO	447	B-
SHELTER GENERAL INS CO	133	C+
HAULERS INS CO	74	B-

SIRIUS AMERICA INS CO

B-   **Good**

Major Rating Factors: Fair long-term capitalization (3.9 on a scale of 0 to 10) based on good current risk adjusted capital (moderate loss scenario) reflecting some improvement over results in 2016. Fair overall results on stability tests (3.5) including weak results on operational trends, negative cash flow from operations for 2016 and fair risk adjusted capital in prior years. The largest net exposure for one risk is high at 4.2% of capital.

Other Rating Factors: History of adequate reserve strength (6.6) as reserves have been consistently at an acceptable level. Good overall profitability index (5.2). Weak expense controls. Return on equity has been good over the last five years, averaging 10.7%. Excellent liquidity (7.4) with ample operational cash flow and liquid investments.

Principal Business: Group accident & health (99%) and commercial multiple peril (1%).

Principal Investments: Investment grade bonds (86%), misc. investments (13%), and cash (1%).

Investments in Affiliates: None

Group Affiliation: China Minsheng Investment Co Ltd

Licensed in: All states, the District of Columbia and Puerto Rico

Commenced Business: January 1980

Address: 140 BROADWAY - 32ND FLOOR, New York, NY 10005-1108

Phone: (212) 312-2500   **Domicile State:** NY   **NAIC Code:** 38776

Data Date	Rating	RACR #1	RACR #2	Loss Ratio %	Total Assets ($mil)	Capital ($mil)	Net Premium ($mil)	Net Income ($mil)
3-17	B-	1.05	0.75	N/A	1,381.3	557.7	28.5	13.4
3-16	C+	1.46	0.89	N/A	1,406.0	529.1	69.7	59.6
2016	B-	0.96	0.69	73.8	1,395.1	544.3	217.3	82.7
2015	C+	1.42	0.87	53.7	1,387.6	517.6	283.9	74.7
2014	C+	1.58	0.94	45.1	1,550.5	620.6	267.2	56.1
2013	C+	2.14	1.21	48.9	1,559.4	548.4	252.8	55.9
2012	C	1.64	1.03	76.8	1,669.7	528.3	271.2	26.2

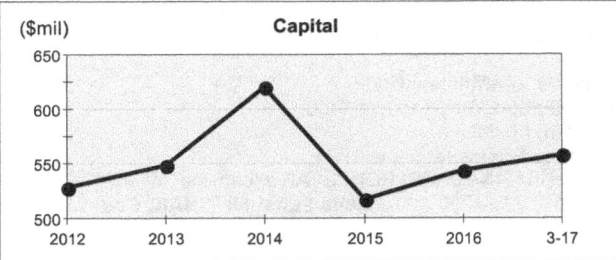

Capital ($mil) — line chart for years 2012, 2013, 2014, 2015, 2016, 3-17

SOMPO AMERICA INSURANCE CO *

A- **Excellent**

Major Rating Factors: Strong long-term capitalization index (9.8 on a scale of 0 to 10) based on excellent current risk adjusted capital (severe and moderate loss scenarios). Furthermore, this high level of risk adjusted capital has been consistently maintained in previous years. Ample reserve history (8.8) that helps to protect the company against sharp claims increases.

Other Rating Factors: Excellent liquidity (7.1) with ample operational cash flow and liquid investments. Excellent overall results on stability tests (7.0). Stability strengths include good operational trends and excellent risk diversification. Good overall profitability index (5.8). Weak expense controls. Return on equity has been low, averaging 3.8% over the past five years.

Principal Business: Workers compensation (26%), allied lines (22%), other liability (10%), ocean marine (8%), commercial multiple peril (7%), products liability (6%), and other lines (21%).

Principal Investments: Investment grade bonds (72%), misc. investments (25%), and cash (3%).

Investments in Affiliates: 1%

Group Affiliation: Sompo Holdings Inc

Licensed in: All states, the District of Columbia and Puerto Rico

Commenced Business: January 1963

Address: 777 Third Ave 24th Floor, New York, NY 10017

Phone: (704) 759-2200 **Domicile State:** NY **NAIC Code:** 11126

Data Date	Rating	RACR #1	RACR #2	Loss Ratio %	Total Assets ($mil)	Capital ($mil)	Net Premium ($mil)	Net Income ($mil)
3-17	A-	4.63	2.91	N/A	1,235.5	568.1	43.8	4.8
3-16	B	4.12	2.58	N/A	1,198.7	496.9	44.9	5.1
2016	B+	4.68	2.96	61.2	1,229.5	558.7	182.3	34.7
2015	B	4.23	2.66	64.8	1,177.6	488.7	183.0	38.1
2014	B	3.55	2.48	62.8	1,238.5	598.3	191.4	8.8
2013	B	2.44	1.86	67.7	1,187.9	555.2	197.2	1.0
2012	B	3.41	2.47	56.1	1,163.0	586.4	173.5	20.7

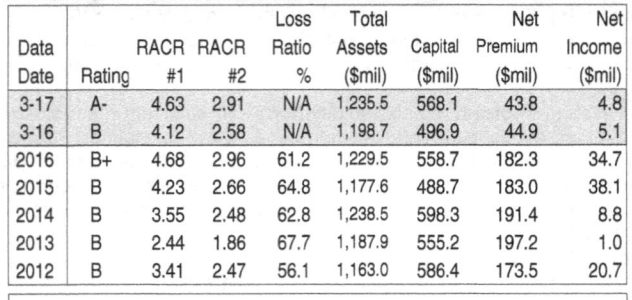

SOUTHERN FARM BUREAU CAS INS CO

B- **Good**

Major Rating Factors: Fair overall results on stability tests (4.8 on a scale of 0 to 10) including potential drain of affiliation with Southern Farm Bureau Casualty, weak results on operational trends and negative cash flow from operations for 2016. Fair profitability index (4.2) with operating losses during 2016. Return on equity has been low, averaging 2.0% over the past five years.

Other Rating Factors: Good liquidity (6.2) with sufficient resources (cash flows and marketable investments) to handle a spike in claims. Strong long-term capitalization index (8.3) based on excellent current risk adjusted capital (severe and moderate loss scenarios), despite some fluctuation in capital levels. Ample reserve history (7.8) that can protect against increases in claims costs.

Principal Business: Auto physical damage (49%), auto liability (46%), other liability (4%), and allied lines (1%).

Principal Investments: Investment grade bonds (57%), misc. investments (44%), and real estate (1%).

Investments in Affiliates: 33%

Group Affiliation: Southern Farm Bureau Casualty

Licensed in: AR, CO, FL, LA, MS, SC

Commenced Business: September 1947

Address: 1800 East County Line Road, Ridgeland, MS 39157

Phone: (601) 957-7777 **Domicile State:** MS **NAIC Code:** 18325

Data Date	Rating	RACR #1	RACR #2	Loss Ratio %	Total Assets ($mil)	Capital ($mil)	Net Premium ($mil)	Net Income ($mil)
3-17	B-	1.99	1.83	N/A	2,172.7	1,293.5	222.0	9.8
3-16	B-	2.12	1.96	N/A	2,154.7	1,312.7	208.8	-5.3
2016	B-	1.98	1.84	92.2	2,161.6	1,287.4	870.0	-50.3
2015	B-	2.13	1.98	83.9	2,150.3	1,317.8	838.3	9.8
2014	B-	2.21	2.03	79.5	2,094.5	1,275.6	841.7	50.7
2013	B-	2.29	2.09	80.3	1,998.3	1,235.9	825.8	36.4
2012	B-	2.34	2.12	74.3	1,899.2	1,161.1	803.0	70.8

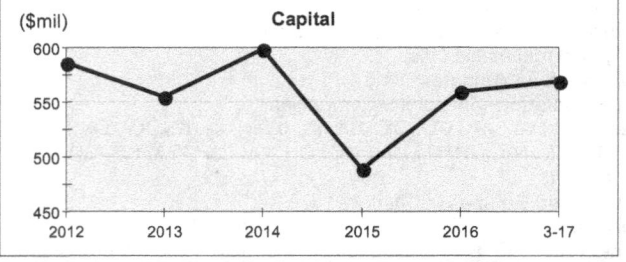

SOUTHERN-OWNERS INS CO *

A- **Excellent**

Major Rating Factors: Strong long-term capitalization index (8.4 on a scale of 0 to 10) based on excellent current risk adjusted capital (severe and moderate loss scenarios). Furthermore, this high level of risk adjusted capital has been consistently maintained in previous years. Ample reserve history (8.5) that helps to protect the company against sharp claims increases.

Other Rating Factors: Excellent profitability (7.8) with operating gains in each of the last five years. Excellent overall results on stability tests (7.3). Stability strengths include excellent operational trends and excellent risk diversification. Good liquidity (6.7) with sufficient resources (cash flows and marketable investments) to handle a spike in claims.

Principal Business: Auto liability (38%), other liability (27%), auto physical damage (14%), commercial multiple peril (13%), workers compensation (4%), homeowners multiple peril (2%), and inland marine (2%).

Principal Investments: Investment grade bonds (85%) and misc. investments (15%).

Investments in Affiliates: None

Group Affiliation: Auto-Owners Group

Licensed in: FL, MI

Commenced Business: June 1995

Address: 6101 ANACAPRI BOULEVARD, Lansing, MI 48917-3968

Phone: (517) 323-1200 **Domicile State:** MI **NAIC Code:** 10190

Data Date	Rating	RACR #1	RACR #2	Loss Ratio %	Total Assets ($mil)	Capital ($mil)	Net Premium ($mil)	Net Income ($mil)
3-17	A-	2.71	1.97	N/A	774.5	241.4	75.5	7.0
3-16	B+	2.97	2.11	N/A	688.9	228.8	68.0	8.4
2016	A-	2.66	1.96	75.5	739.3	232.2	293.2	7.2
2015	B+	2.88	2.08	65.1	665.7	219.5	266.1	24.4
2014	B+	2.64	1.93	70.9	628.8	198.2	247.1	13.1
2013	A	2.73	2.04	74.0	573.8	184.6	224.9	13.5
2012	A-	2.59	1.93	80.4	537.8	161.5	204.4	2.2

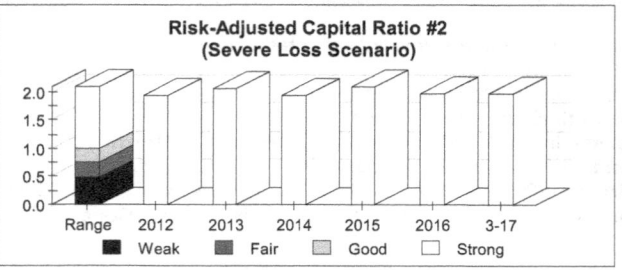

ST PAUL FIRE & MARINE INS CO | B | Good

Major Rating Factors: Good liquidity (6.8 on a scale of 0 to 10) with sufficient resources (cash flows and marketable investments) to handle a spike in claims. Good overall results on stability tests (5.1) despite weak results on operational trends.
Other Rating Factors: Fair profitability index (4.0). Fair expense controls. Return on equity has been fair, averaging 16.4% over the past five years. Strong long-term capitalization index (7.8) based on excellent current risk adjusted capital (severe and moderate loss scenarios), despite some fluctuation in capital levels. Ample reserve history (8.5) that helps to protect the company against sharp claims increases.
Principal Business: Other liability (49%), auto liability (17%), fire (9%), products liability (8%), inland marine (6%), auto physical damage (5%), and other lines (6%).
Principal Investments: Investment grade bonds (71%), misc. investments (20%), real estate (5%), and non investment grade bonds (4%).
Investments in Affiliates: 12%
Group Affiliation: Travelers Companies Inc
Licensed in: All states, the District of Columbia and Puerto Rico
Commenced Business: April 1925
Address: ONE TOWER SQUARE, Hartford, CT 06183
Phone: (860) 277-0111   **Domicile State:** CT   **NAIC Code:** 24767

Data Date	Rating	RACR #1	RACR #2	Loss Ratio %	Total Assets ($mil)	Capital ($mil)	Net Premium ($mil)	Net Income ($mil)
3-17	B	2.00	1.48	N/A	18,495.1	5,497.0	1,360.1	137.7
3-16	B	1.87	1.42	N/A	18,442.2	5,564.8	1,312.1	138.3
2016	B	2.06	1.53	63.8	18,558.7	5,558.2	5,490.5	1,199.4
2015	B	1.90	1.45	58.8	18,297.6	5,563.3	5,252.1	1,186.8
2014	B	1.58	1.28	60.3	18,917.2	5,994.1	5,123.4	933.7
2013	B	1.57	1.29	60.5	18,566.3	5,914.7	5,131.4	883.9
2012	B	1.59	1.32	67.7	18,761.8	6,000.7	5,006.4	594.8

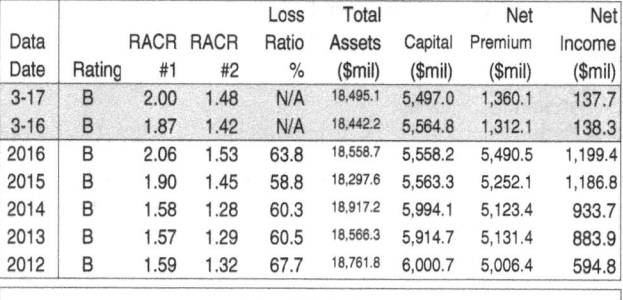

Liquidity Index

Weak   Fair   Good   Strong

ST PAUL PROTECTIVE INS CO | B- | Good

Major Rating Factors: Fair overall results on stability tests (4.6 on a scale of 0 to 10) including fair financial strength of affiliated Travelers Companies Inc and weak results on operational trends. Good overall profitability index (5.4). Fair expense controls. Return on equity has been fair, averaging 8.5% over the past five years.
Other Rating Factors: Good liquidity (6.9) with sufficient resources (cash flows and marketable investments) to handle a spike in claims. Strong long-term capitalization index (10.0) based on excellent current risk adjusted capital (severe and moderate loss scenarios), despite some fluctuation in capital levels. Ample reserve history (7.9) that can protect against increases in claims costs.
Principal Business: Auto liability (71%) and auto physical damage (29%).
Principal Investments: Investment grade bonds (99%) and misc. investments (1%).
Investments in Affiliates: None
Group Affiliation: Travelers Companies Inc
Licensed in: All states, the District of Columbia and Puerto Rico
Commenced Business: February 1932
Address: ONE TOWER SQUARE, Hartford, CT 06183
Phone: (860) 277-0111   **Domicile State:** CT   **NAIC Code:** 19224

Data Date	Rating	RACR #1	RACR #2	Loss Ratio %	Total Assets ($mil)	Capital ($mil)	Net Premium ($mil)	Net Income ($mil)
3-17	B-	4.74	3.07	N/A	521.8	226.4	31.3	3.6
3-16	B-	4.86	3.08	N/A	519.9	231.2	30.2	3.9
2016	B-	4.78	3.12	63.3	513.7	222.8	126.4	16.9
2015	B-	4.91	3.12	58.7	507.6	227.3	120.6	21.2
2014	B-	4.91	3.09	60.5	507.8	226.2	117.1	20.4
2013	B-	5.04	3.21	60.9	510.1	228.2	116.8	22.8
2012	B-	5.02	3.23	68.4	506.8	224.2	113.4	16.3

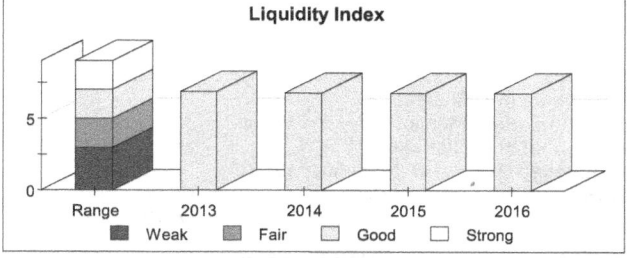

Travelers Companies Inc
Composite Group Rating: B+

Largest Group Members	Assets ($mil)	Rating
TRAVELERS INDEMNITY CO	21180	B+
ST PAUL FIRE MARINE INS CO	18559	B
TRAVELERS CASUALTY SURETY CO	16564	A-
TRAVELERS CASUALTY SURETY CO OF AM	4196	C+
PHOENIX INS CO	4184	B

STANDARD FIRE INS CO | B | Good

Major Rating Factors: Good overall profitability index (6.6 on a scale of 0 to 10). Fair expense controls. Return on equity has been excellent over the last five years averaging 16.2%. Good liquidity (6.8) with sufficient resources (cash flows and marketable investments) to handle a spike in claims.
Other Rating Factors: Good overall results on stability tests (5.0) despite weak results on operational trends. Affiliation with Travelers Companies Inc is a strength. Strong long-term capitalization index (7.8) based on excellent current risk adjusted capital (severe and moderate loss scenarios), despite some fluctuation in capital levels. Ample reserve history (8.3) that helps to protect the company against sharp claims increases.
Principal Business: Auto liability (42%), auto physical damage (25%), homeowners multiple peril (20%), workers compensation (8%), ocean marine (2%), allied lines (1%), and other lines (2%).
Principal Investments: Investment grade bonds (71%), misc. investments (27%), and non investment grade bonds (2%).
Investments in Affiliates: 17%
Group Affiliation: Travelers Companies Inc
Licensed in: All states, the District of Columbia and Puerto Rico
Commenced Business: March 1910
Address: ONE TOWER SQUARE, Hartford, CT 06183
Phone: (860) 277-0111   **Domicile State:** CT   **NAIC Code:** 19070

Data Date	Rating	RACR #1	RACR #2	Loss Ratio %	Total Assets ($mil)	Capital ($mil)	Net Premium ($mil)	Net Income ($mil)
3-17	B	1.90	1.50	N/A	3,717.4	1,195.4	261.1	24.0
3-16	B	1.85	1.45	N/A	3,627.4	1,177.6	251.5	26.0
2016	B	1.94	1.54	63.4	3,679.1	1,201.8	1,053.7	202.4
2015	B	1.90	1.49	58.7	3,583.9	1,185.5	1,005.7	204.8
2014	B	1.96	1.53	60.5	3,627.1	1,215.2	977.2	228.2
2013	B	2.02	1.60	60.9	3,605.3	1,234.8	974.8	217.9
2012	B-	1.82	1.43	68.4	3,440.2	1,057.8	946.7	130.7

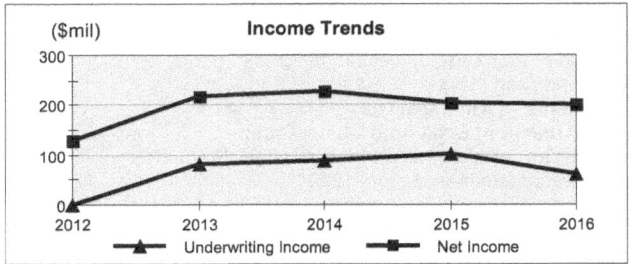

Income Trends

Underwriting Income   Net Income

STAR INS CO

C **Fair**

Major Rating Factors: Fair overall results on stability tests (3.6 on a scale of 0 to 10) including excessive premium growth and weak results on operational trends. A history of deficient reserves (2.4) that places pressure on both capital and profits. In 2013 and 2016 the two year reserve development was 19% and 33% deficient respectively.

Other Rating Factors: Good overall profitability index (6.0) despite operating losses during 2015. Return on equity has been low, averaging 3.6% over the past five years. Strong long-term capitalization index (7.1) based on excellent current risk adjusted capital (severe and moderate loss scenarios), despite some fluctuation in capital levels. Superior liquidity (9.1) with ample operational cash flow and liquid investments.

Principal Business: Workers compensation (74%), commercial multiple peril (8%), auto liability (6%), inland marine (6%), other liability (2%), auto physical damage (2%), and other lines (2%).

Principal Investments: Investment grade bonds (70%), misc. investments (25%), cash (3%), and non investment grade bonds (2%).

Investments in Affiliates: 19%

Group Affiliation: Meadowbrook Ins Group

Licensed in: All states except PR

Commenced Business: November 1985

Address: 26255 American Drive, Southfield, MI 48034

Phone: (248) 358-1100 **Domicile State:** MI **NAIC Code:** 18023

Data Date	Rating	RACR #1	RACR #2	Loss Ratio %	Total Assets ($mil)	Capital ($mil)	Net Premium ($mil)	Net Income ($mil)
3-17	C	1.29	1.02	N/A	1,819.3	520.8	141.1	56.1
3-16	C	2.14	1.74	N/A	914.4	321.1	50.9	6.0
2016	C	1.33	1.06	64.6	1,915.4	508.3	587.1	16.2
2015	C	2.13	1.74	77.1	946.4	314.1	213.0	-9.8
2014	C	2.15	1.82	66.4	963.8	324.3	211.6	14.7
2013	C	2.10	1.73	79.2	1,000.3	309.6	245.7	3.9
2012	C	1.73	1.39	79.3	956.8	263.1	285.7	5.8

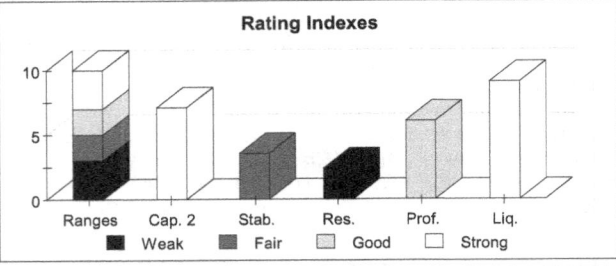

Rating Indexes

STARR INDEMNITY & LIABILITY CO

B **Good**

Major Rating Factors: Good overall profitability index (6.2 on a scale of 0 to 10). Good expense controls. Return on equity has been low, averaging 2.7% over the past five years. Good liquidity (6.8) with sufficient resources (cash flows and marketable investments) to handle a spike in claims.

Other Rating Factors: Fair reserve development (4.5) as reserves have generally been sufficient to cover claims. Fair overall results on stability tests (4.7) including weak results on operational trends. Strong long-term capitalization index (7.2) based on excellent current risk adjusted capital (severe and moderate loss scenarios), despite some fluctuation in capital levels.

Principal Business: Other liability (31%), workers compensation (29%), ocean marine (13%), aircraft (12%), auto liability (7%), commercial multiple peril (3%), and other lines (6%).

Principal Investments: Investment grade bonds (50%), misc. investments (46%), cash (3%), and non investment grade bonds (1%).

Investments in Affiliates: 34%

Group Affiliation: Starr International Co Inc

Licensed in: All states, the District of Columbia and Puerto Rico

Commenced Business: May 1919

Address: 8401 N Central Expressway #890, Dallas, TX 75225

Phone: (646) 227-6400 **Domicile State:** TX **NAIC Code:** 38318

Data Date	Rating	RACR #1	RACR #2	Loss Ratio %	Total Assets ($mil)	Capital ($mil)	Net Premium ($mil)	Net Income ($mil)
3-17	B	1.34	1.10	N/A	4,442.6	1,874.5	244.7	8.0
3-16	B	1.38	1.14	N/A	4,236.6	1,967.9	277.0	19.8
2016	B	1.37	1.14	85.9	4,442.3	1,922.5	1,003.2	98.8
2015	B	1.33	1.12	75.0	4,002.0	1,847.6	1,078.1	73.8
2014	B	1.30	1.12	78.2	3,755.1	1,832.3	1,015.8	54.6
2013	B-	1.35	1.13	81.6	3,467.4	1,865.1	847.3	13.2
2012	B-	1.38	1.22	76.7	2,904.1	1,871.3	625.3	14.9

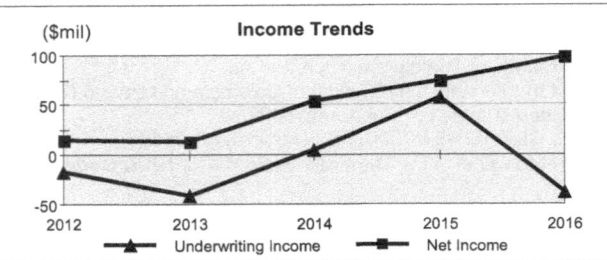

Income Trends

STATE AUTO P&C INS CO

C+ **Fair**

Major Rating Factors: Fair overall results on stability tests (4.3 on a scale of 0 to 10) including potential drain of affiliation with State Auto Mutual Group and weak results on operational trends. History of adequate reserve strength (5.7) as reserves have been consistently at an acceptable level.

Other Rating Factors: Good overall profitability index (5.3) despite operating losses during 2014. Return on equity has been low, averaging 3.1% over the past five years. Good liquidity (6.3) with sufficient resources (cash flows and marketable investments) to handle a spike in claims. Strong long-term capitalization index (7.4) based on excellent current risk adjusted capital (severe and moderate loss scenarios). Moreover, capital levels have been consistent in recent years.

Principal Business: Homeowners multiple peril (26%), auto liability (20%), commercial multiple peril (19%), auto physical damage (13%), other liability (7%), allied lines (5%), and other lines (10%).

Principal Investments: Investment grade bonds (75%), misc. investments (24%), and cash (1%).

Investments in Affiliates: None

Group Affiliation: State Auto Mutual Group

Licensed in: All states except CA, NH, NM, WA, PR

Commenced Business: April 1950

Address: 1300 Woodland Avenue, West Des Moines, IA 50265

Phone: (614) 464-5000 **Domicile State:** IA **NAIC Code:** 25127

Data Date	Rating	RACR #1	RACR #2	Loss Ratio %	Total Assets ($mil)	Capital ($mil)	Net Premium ($mil)	Net Income ($mil)
3-17	C+	2.09	1.26	N/A	2,496.9	685.3	248.9	1.0
3-16	C	2.06	1.30	N/A	2,362.7	655.3	251.0	6.6
2016	C+	2.11	1.28	73.1	2,482.6	682.5	1,014.7	19.3
2015	C	2.11	1.34	68.5	2,355.6	655.3	999.2	52.3
2014	C-	2.08	1.28	71.6	2,291.5	628.9	937.0	-13.6
2013	C-	2.19	1.40	68.5	2,066.5	607.7	833.3	39.6
2012	D+	1.92	1.26	74.8	1,889.0	505.5	828.0	3.5

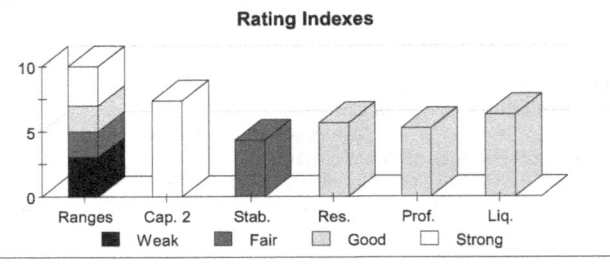

Rating Indexes

STATE AUTOMOBILE MUTUAL INS CO   C+   Fair

Major Rating Factors: Fair overall results on stability tests (4.3 on a scale of 0 to 10) including potential drain of affiliation with State Auto Mutual Group and weak results on operational trends. Fair profitability index (3.8) with operating losses during 2012, 2013, 2014 and the first three months of 2017.

Other Rating Factors: History of adequate reserve strength (5.9) as reserves have been consistently at an acceptable level. Good liquidity (6.2) with sufficient resources (cash flows and marketable investments) to handle a spike in claims. Strong long-term capitalization index (7.0) based on excellent current risk adjusted capital (severe and moderate loss scenarios), despite some fluctuation in capital levels.

Principal Business: Auto liability (20%), auto physical damage (14%), homeowners multiple peril (12%), other liability (11%), farmowners multiple peril (11%), commercial multiple peril (10%), and other lines (21%).

Principal Investments: Misc. investments (59%), investment grade bonds (37%), cash (3%), and real estate (1%).

Investments in Affiliates: 46%

Group Affiliation: State Auto Mutual Group

Licensed in: All states except PR

Commenced Business: September 1921

Address: 518 East Broad Street, Columbus, OH 43215

Phone: (614) 464-5000   **Domicile State:** OH   **NAIC Code:** 25135

Data Date	Rating	RACR #1	RACR #2	Loss Ratio %	Total Assets ($mil)	Capital ($mil)	Net Premium ($mil)	Net Income ($mil)
3-17	C+	1.14	1.01	N/A	2,488.5	826.4	168.4	-1.5
3-16	C+	1.17	1.06	N/A	2,393.0	820.1	169.8	1.3
2016	C+	1.15	1.02	73.1	2,461.1	822.6	686.4	-14.6
2015	C+	1.19	1.08	68.5	2,386.4	824.7	675.9	5.2
2014	C+	1.21	1.10	71.5	2,352.1	816.8	633.8	-17.6
2013	C+	1.33	1.22	68.5	2,205.9	866.3	563.7	-2.8
2012	C	1.28	1.17	74.6	2,093.8	748.7	552.0	-10.4

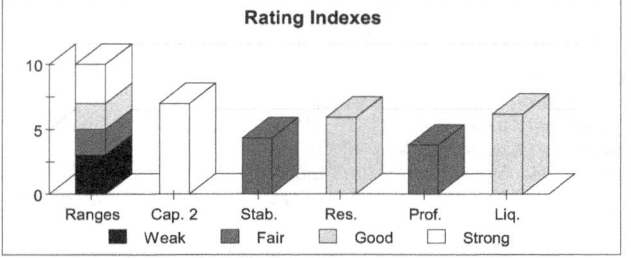

Rating Indexes

STATE FARM FIRE & CAS CO *   B+   Good

Major Rating Factors: Good overall results on stability tests (5.1 on a scale of 0 to 10) despite weak results on operational trends. Affiliation with State Farm Group is a strength. History of adequate reserve strength (6.5) as reserves have been consistently at an acceptable level.

Other Rating Factors: Good liquidity (5.5) with sufficient resources (cash flows and marketable investments) to handle a spike in claims. Strong long-term capitalization index (7.6) based on excellent current risk adjusted capital (severe and moderate loss scenarios). Moreover, capital levels have been consistent in recent years. Excellent profitability (8.3) with operating gains in each of the last five years. Return on equity has been good over the last five years, averaging 12.4%.

Principal Business: Homeowners multiple peril (71%), auto liability (9%), commercial multiple peril (6%), auto physical damage (5%), other liability (3%), inland marine (3%), and other lines (4%).

Principal Investments: Investment grade bonds (82%) and misc. investments (18%).

Investments in Affiliates: None

Group Affiliation: State Farm Group

Licensed in: All states except PR

Commenced Business: June 1935

Address: One State Farm Plaza, Bloomington, IL 61710

Phone: (309) 766-2311   **Domicile State:** IL   **NAIC Code:** 25143

Data Date	Rating	RACR #1	RACR #2	Loss Ratio %	Total Assets ($mil)	Capital ($mil)	Net Premium ($mil)	Net Income ($mil)
3-17	B+	2.74	1.71	N/A	38,866.0	16,715.8	4,034.3	244.2
3-16	B	2.52	1.57	N/A	36,507.6	15,003.2	4,042.9	705.0
2016	B+	2.71	1.67	65.2	38,352.5	16,354.7	16,167.1	1,713.6
2015	B	2.41	1.49	60.8	35,495.7	14,196.8	15,914.0	2,543.8
2014	B-	2.15	1.34	65.9	33,481.0	12,193.8	15,917.6	1,853.0
2013	B-	1.99	1.23	63.5	31,460.7	10,951.2	15,276.5	1,803.8
2012	C+	1.64	1.01	77.4	28,999.1	8,805.4	14,409.5	317.2

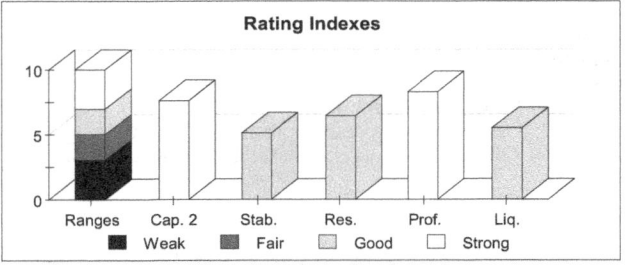

Rating Indexes

STATE FARM FLORIDA INS CO   B   Good

Major Rating Factors: Good overall results on stability tests (5.4 on a scale of 0 to 10). Stability strengths include good operational trends and excellent risk diversification. History of adequate reserve strength (6.4) as reserves have been consistently at an acceptable level.

Other Rating Factors: Good liquidity (6.7) with sufficient resources (cash flows and marketable investments) to handle a spike in claims. Strong long-term capitalization index (10.0) based on excellent current risk adjusted capital (severe and moderate loss scenarios). Moreover, capital levels have been consistent in recent years. Excellent profitability (8.9) with operating gains in each of the last five years. Return on equity has been excellent over the last five years averaging 18.0%.

Principal Business: Homeowners multiple peril (87%), other liability (5%), inland marine (5%), and commercial multiple peril (3%).

Principal Investments: Investment grade bonds (87%) and misc. investments (13%).

Investments in Affiliates: None

Group Affiliation: State Farm Group

Licensed in: FL, IL

Commenced Business: December 1998

Address: 7401 Cypress Gardens Blvd, Winter Haven, FL 33888

Phone: (863) 318-3000   **Domicile State:** FL   **NAIC Code:** 10739

Data Date	Rating	RACR #1	RACR #2	Loss Ratio %	Total Assets ($mil)	Capital ($mil)	Net Premium ($mil)	Net Income ($mil)
3-17	B	5.15	3.61	N/A	2,095.9	1,114.1	141.8	27.7
3-16	B-	4.84	3.40	N/A	2,037.9	1,078.8	144.8	45.0
2016	B	5.04	3.54	48.4	2,096.0	1,083.7	570.7	72.6
2015	C+	4.45	3.14	42.1	1,991.9	1,033.8	584.0	179.8
2014	C	3.79	2.63	36.2	1,915.6	894.5	588.7	155.1
2013	C-	1.60	1.13	40.8	1,793.7	734.6	575.4	174.5
2012	D+	1.04	0.73	53.4	1,766.2	534.5	597.3	144.5

Rating Indexes

STATE FARM GENERAL INS CO | B | Good

Major Rating Factors: History of adequate reserve strength (6.4 on a scale of 0 to 10) as reserves have been consistently at an acceptable level. Good overall profitability index (5.9) despite operating losses during the first three months of 2017. Return on equity has been fair, averaging 6.6% over the past five years.

Other Rating Factors: Good liquidity (6.7) with sufficient resources (cash flows and marketable investments) to handle a spike in claims. Fair overall results on stability tests (4.9) including weak results on operational trends. Affiliation with State Farm Group is a strength. Strong long-term capitalization index (10.0) based on excellent current risk adjusted capital (severe and moderate loss scenarios), despite some fluctuation in capital levels.

Principal Business: Homeowners multiple peril (73%), commercial multiple peril (15%), other liability (8%), inland marine (3%), earthquake (1%), and farmowners multiple peril (1%).

Principal Investments: Investment grade bonds (98%) and misc. investments (2%).

Investments in Affiliates: None

Group Affiliation: State Farm Group

Licensed in: All states except CT, MA, RI, PR

Commenced Business: May 1962

Address: One State Farm Plaza, Bloomington, IL 61710

Phone: (309) 766-2311 **Domicile State:** IL **NAIC Code:** 25151

Data Date	Rating	RACR #1	RACR #2	Loss Ratio %	Total Assets ($mil)	Capital ($mil)	Net Premium ($mil)	Net Income ($mil)
3-17	B	6.42	4.36	N/A	7,137.5	3,999.3	480.5	-70.9
3-16	B	6.63	4.45	N/A	7,035.2	4,032.6	477.2	36.8
2016	B	6.68	4.40	75.3	7,112.1	4,076.0	1,930.7	128.7
2015	B	6.66	4.33	71.5	6,918.7	3,991.2	1,904.2	174.0
2014	B	6.35	4.11	57.6	6,714.9	3,821.2	1,893.1	352.2
2013	B	5.25	3.31	55.5	6,388.1	3,452.6	1,919.0	379.9
2012	B	4.19	2.61	63.1	6,061.2	3,101.9	1,976.9	268.2

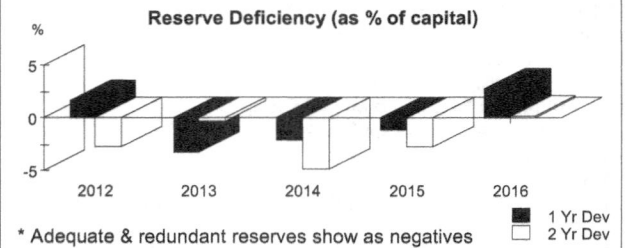

Reserve Deficiency (as % of capital)

* Adequate & redundant reserves show as negatives
■ 1 Yr Dev □ 2 Yr Dev

STATE FARM INDEMNITY CO | B | Good

Major Rating Factors: Good overall profitability index (6.6 on a scale of 0 to 10). Good expense controls. Return on equity has been fair, averaging 5.3% over the past five years. Good liquidity (6.8) with sufficient resources (cash flows and marketable investments) to handle a spike in claims.

Other Rating Factors: Good overall results on stability tests (5.0) despite weak results on operational trends. Affiliation with State Farm Group is a strength. Strong long-term capitalization index (10.0) based on excellent current risk adjusted capital (severe and moderate loss scenarios). Moreover, capital levels have been consistent in recent years. Ample reserve history (8.9) that helps to protect the company against sharp claims increases.

Principal Business: Auto liability (72%) and auto physical damage (28%).

Principal Investments: Investment grade bonds (97%) and misc. investments (3%).

Investments in Affiliates: 1%

Group Affiliation: State Farm Group

Licensed in: IL, NJ

Commenced Business: March 1991

Address: One State Farm Plaza, Bloomington, IL 61710

Phone: (973) 739-5000 **Domicile State:** IL **NAIC Code:** 43796

Data Date	Rating	RACR #1	RACR #2	Loss Ratio %	Total Assets ($mil)	Capital ($mil)	Net Premium ($mil)	Net Income ($mil)
3-17	B	5.93	5.07	N/A	2,255.2	1,230.4	159.0	10.0
3-16	B	5.79	4.97	N/A	2,237.2	1,200.0	155.4	6.5
2016	B	5.54	5.04	83.3	2,245.4	1,218.6	631.6	29.7
2015	B	5.42	4.95	82.5	2,219.7	1,194.6	621.0	78.1
2014	B-	4.95	4.36	81.1	2,158.4	1,113.6	610.1	56.0
2013	B-	4.72	4.14	75.6	2,098.9	1,061.7	603.6	74.5
2012	B-	3.97	3.45	80.2	2,047.2	965.9	597.5	56.5

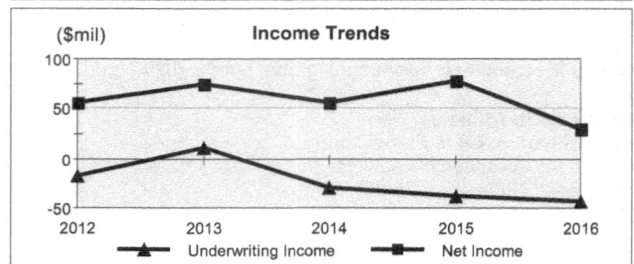

Income Trends

▲ Underwriting Income ■ Net Income

STATE FARM LLOYDS | B | Good

Major Rating Factors: Good overall results on stability tests (5.0 on a scale of 0 to 10) despite weak results on operational trends. Affiliation with State Farm Group is a strength. History of adequate reserve strength (6.6) as reserves have been consistently at an acceptable level.

Other Rating Factors: Good liquidity (6.0) with sufficient resources (cash flows and marketable investments) to handle a spike in claims. Strong long-term capitalization index (8.6) based on excellent current risk adjusted capital (severe and moderate loss scenarios), despite some fluctuation in capital levels. Excellent profitability (7.1). Return on equity has been good over the last five years, averaging 15.1%.

Principal Business: Homeowners multiple peril (93%), commercial multiple peril (5%), and farmowners multiple peril (2%).

Principal Investments: Investment grade bonds (98%) and misc. investments (4%).

Investments in Affiliates: None

Group Affiliation: State Farm Group

Licensed in: TX

Commenced Business: June 1983

Address: 1251 State Street Suite 1000, Richardson, TX 75082

Phone: (972) 732-5000 **Domicile State:** TX **NAIC Code:** 43419

Data Date	Rating	RACR #1	RACR #2	Loss Ratio %	Total Assets ($mil)	Capital ($mil)	Net Premium ($mil)	Net Income ($mil)
3-17	B	2.71	2.45	N/A	3,502.3	1,360.9	416.3	18.3
3-16	B	2.34	2.10	N/A	3,253.1	1,119.3	444.4	-23.9
2016	B	2.69	2.26	60.4	3,531.0	1,341.1	1,671.2	205.5
2015	B	2.64	2.22	63.0	3,250.8	1,213.8	1,572.6	412.2
2014	B-	1.67	1.21	51.1	3,490.8	1,039.5	1,799.7	-54.3
2013	B-	2.26	1.93	53.5	3,075.5	1,105.4	1,712.7	215.2
2012	C+	2.39	2.03	59.8	2,927.0	1,073.3	1,484.6	153.4

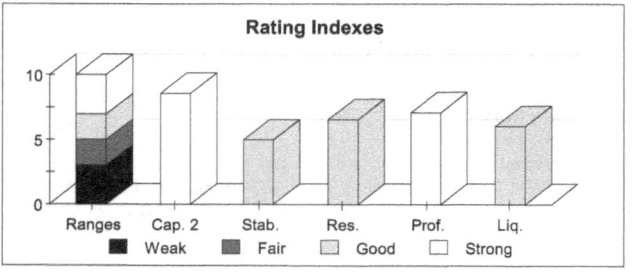

Rating Indexes

■ Weak ▨ Fair ▢ Good □ Strong

STATE FARM MUTUAL AUTOMOBILE INS CO *   B+   Good

Major Rating Factors: Good liquidity (6.5 on a scale of 0 to 10) with sufficient resources (cash flows and marketable investments) to handle a spike in claims. Good overall results on stability tests (5.3) despite weak results on operational trends and negative cash flow from operations for 2016.

Other Rating Factors: Strong long-term capitalization index (8.1) based on excellent current risk adjusted capital (severe and moderate loss scenarios). Moreover, capital levels have been consistent in recent years. Ample reserve history (7.6) that can protect against increases in claims costs. Fair profitability index (4.2) with operating losses during 2016.

Principal Business: Auto liability (58%), auto physical damage (39%), other accident & health (2%), and group accident & health (1%).

Principal Investments: Misc. investments (69%) and investment grade bonds (31%).

Investments in Affiliates: 28%

Group Affiliation: State Farm Group

Licensed in: All states except PR

Commenced Business: June 1922

Address: One State Farm Plaza, Bloomington, IL 61710

Phone: (309) 766-2311   **Domicile State:** IL   **NAIC Code:** 25178

Data Date	Rating	RACR #1	RACR #2	Loss Ratio %	Total Assets ($mil)	Capital ($mil)	Net Premium ($mil)	Net Income ($mil)
3-17	B+	2.00	1.73	N/A	150,198.0	89,522.3	10,329.4	534.4
3-16	B+	2.06	1.78	N/A	141,283.6	84,733.7	9,619.0	201.0
2016	B+	1.96	1.71	91.9	147,697.0	87,573.9	40,455.0	-2,553.8
2015	B+	2.03	1.76	84.5	138,495.0	82,630.7	37,511.4	2,137.2
2014	B+	2.10	1.79	82.2	138,798.0	79,876.9	36,928.5	1,045.8
2013	B+	2.18	1.84	79.9	129,338.0	75,678.9	35,163.3	1,836.5
2012	B+	2.14	1.81	78.1	114,933.0	65,241.9	33,697.9	1,525.0

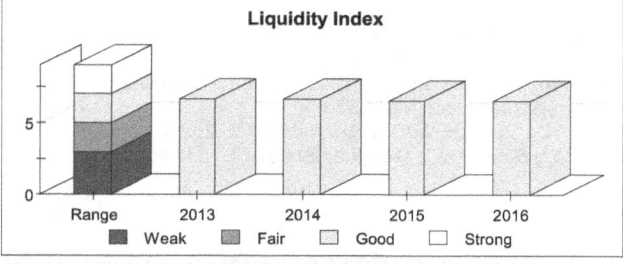

Liquidity Index

STATE NATIONAL INS CO   B-   Good

Major Rating Factors: Fair overall results on stability tests (4.8 on a scale of 0 to 10) including potential drain of affiliation with TX State National Group. History of adequate reserve strength (5.0) as reserves have been consistently at an acceptable level.

Other Rating Factors: Strong long-term capitalization index (7.8) based on excellent current risk adjusted capital (severe and moderate loss scenarios). Moreover, capital levels have been consistent in recent years. Excellent profitability (7.6) with operating gains in each of the last five years. Excellent liquidity (7.0) with ample operational cash flow and liquid investments.

Principal Business: Auto physical damage (29%), auto liability (18%), commercial multiple peril (15%), other liability (10%), workers compensation (10%), homeowners multiple peril (3%), and other lines (15%).

Principal Investments: Misc. investments (56%), investment grade bonds (35%), real estate (4%), cash (3%), and non investment grade bonds (2%).

Investments in Affiliates: 56%

Group Affiliation: TX State National Group

Licensed in: All states except PR

Commenced Business: September 1984

Address: 1900 L Don Dodson Dr, Bedford, TX 76021

Phone: (817) 265-2000   **Domicile State:** TX   **NAIC Code:** 12831

Data Date	Rating	RACR #1	RACR #2	Loss Ratio %	Total Assets ($mil)	Capital ($mil)	Net Premium ($mil)	Net Income ($mil)
3-17	B-	1.65	1.58	N/A	357.8	274.3	11.9	3.1
3-16	B-	1.94	1.82	N/A	316.3	233.6	13.5	1.3
2016	B-	1.63	1.56	47.6	369.7	269.4	62.6	6.5
2015	B-	1.92	1.81	49.1	319.3	229.8	56.2	5.6
2014	C+	1.94	1.84	42.5	290.7	215.8	52.2	3.2
2013	C+	1.94	1.81	40.3	218.8	155.6	42.0	2.5
2012	C+	1.92	1.79	39.3	206.9	147.8	30.3	4.9

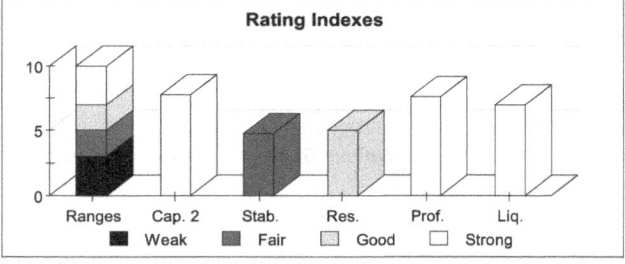

Rating Indexes

STATE VOLUNTEER MUTUAL INS CO   B   Good

Major Rating Factors: Good overall profitability index (5.4 on a scale of 0 to 10) despite operating losses during the first three months of 2017. Fair overall results on stability tests (4.9) including weak results on operational trends.

Other Rating Factors: Strong long-term capitalization index (10.0) based on excellent current risk adjusted capital (severe and moderate loss scenarios). Moreover, capital levels have been consistent in recent years. Ample reserve history (9.4) that helps to protect the company against sharp claims increases. Excellent liquidity (8.4) with ample operational cash flow and liquid investments.

Principal Business: Medical malpractice (100%).

Principal Investments: Investment grade bonds (83%), misc. investments (16%), and non investment grade bonds (1%).

Investments in Affiliates: None

Group Affiliation: None

Licensed in: AL, AR, GA, IN, KY, MS, MO, NC, TN, VA

Commenced Business: May 1976

Address: 101 Westpark Drive Suite 300, Brentwood, TN 37027

Phone: (615) 377-1999   **Domicile State:** TN   **NAIC Code:** 33049

Data Date	Rating	RACR #1	RACR #2	Loss Ratio %	Total Assets ($mil)	Capital ($mil)	Net Premium ($mil)	Net Income ($mil)
3-17	B	4.58	3.40	N/A	1,215.1	567.5	26.6	-5.4
3-16	B	4.31	3.28	N/A	1,200.4	532.2	26.9	-4.7
2016	B	4.69	3.51	79.3	1,211.1	567.0	111.8	22.4
2015	B	4.43	3.39	79.5	1,193.2	538.0	113.4	25.5
2014	B	4.03	2.96	84.6	1,199.1	516.6	114.6	21.5
2013	A+	3.65	2.76	89.0	1,186.2	496.7	122.2	17.4
2012	A+	3.54	2.71	82.6	1,169.5	464.0	154.6	26.1

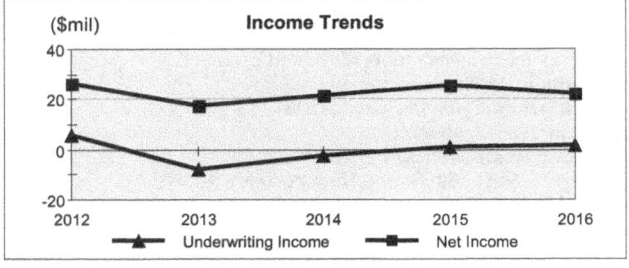

Income Trends

STEADFAST INS CO

C+ | **Fair**

Major Rating Factors: Fair overall results on stability tests (4.7 on a scale of 0 to 10) including fair financial strength of affiliated Zurich Financial Services Group and weak results on operational trends.

Other Rating Factors: Strong long-term capitalization index (9.0) based on excellent current risk adjusted capital (severe and moderate loss scenarios), despite some fluctuation in capital levels. Excellent profitability (7.3) with operating gains in each of the last five years. Excellent liquidity (7.0) with ample operational cash flow and liquid investments.

Principal Business: Other liability (56%), auto liability (15%), commercial multiple peril (9%), medical malpractice (7%), fire (5%), allied lines (3%), and other lines (5%).

Principal Investments: Investment grade bonds (58%) and misc. investments (42%).

Investments in Affiliates: 46%

Group Affiliation: Zurich Financial Services Group

Licensed in: All states, the District of Columbia and Puerto Rico

Commenced Business: May 1988

Address: 32 LOOCKERMAN SQUARE SUITE 202, Dover, DE 19904

Phone: (847) 605-6000 **Domicile State:** DE **NAIC Code:** 26387

Data Date	Rating	RACR #1	RACR #2	Loss Ratio %	Total Assets ($mil)	Capital ($mil)	Net Premium ($mil)	Net Income ($mil)
3-17	C+	2.38	2.35	N/A	577.2	500.2	0.0	0.9
3-16	C+	2.43	2.40	N/A	593.0	501.6	0.0	1.2
2016	C+	2.38	2.35	0.0	605.9	498.7	0.0	6.5
2015	C+	2.42	2.39	0.0	660.2	499.6	0.0	7.9
2014	C	3.03	2.98	0.0	528.8	436.2	0.0	9.1
2013	C	3.06	3.00	0.0	602.2	430.0	0.0	5.1
2012	C	3.21	3.15	0.0	555.4	444.4	0.0	12.7

Zurich Financial Services Group
Composite Group Rating: C+

Largest Group Members	Assets ($mil)	Rating
ZURICH AMERICAN INS CO	31003	B-
ZURICH AMERICAN LIFE INS CO	12330	C
FARMERS NEW WORLD LIFE INS CO	7155	B-
CENTRE LIFE INS CO	1810	B-
RURAL COMMUNITY INS CO	1754	C+

SWISS REINS AMERICA CORP

C- | **Fair**

Major Rating Factors: Weak overall results on stability tests (2.0 on a scale of 0 to 10) including weak results on operational trends. The largest net exposure for one risk is excessive at 14.7% of capital. Good long-term capitalization index (5.0) based on fair current risk adjusted capital (severe loss scenario), although results have slipped from the good range over the last two years.

Other Rating Factors: Fair profitability index (3.2). Fair expense controls. Return on equity has been fair, averaging 11.4% over the past five years. Ample reserve history (8.9) that helps to protect the company against sharp claims increases. Excellent liquidity (7.0) with ample operational cash flow and liquid investments.

Principal Business: (This company is a reinsurer.)

Principal Investments: Investment grade bonds (83%), misc. investments (16%), and non investment grade bonds (1%).

Investments in Affiliates: None

Group Affiliation: Swiss Reinsurance

Licensed in: All states, the District of Columbia and Puerto Rico

Commenced Business: September 1940

Address: 175 KING STREET, Armonk, NY 10504-1606

Phone: (914) 828-8000 **Domicile State:** NY **NAIC Code:** 25364

Data Date	Rating	RACR #1	RACR #2	Loss Ratio %	Total Assets ($mil)	Capital ($mil)	Net Premium ($mil)	Net Income ($mil)
3-17	C-	1.01	0.74	N/A	13,505.3	3,418.9	432.2	79.7
3-16	B-	1.07	0.78	N/A	13,832.8	3,575.8	426.8	-17.3
2016	C-	1.00	0.74	57.2	12,927.2	3,352.3	1,882.9	406.4
2015	B-	1.07	0.79	50.4	12,795.5	3,581.1	1,987.4	389.8
2014	B-	1.30	0.93	48.9	13,109.1	4,259.8	1,881.8	498.1
2013	B-	1.50	1.03	39.0	11,409.4	4,619.3	1,965.0	644.9
2012	B-	1.73	1.15	43.3	12,061.1	4,973.2	1,439.4	431.8

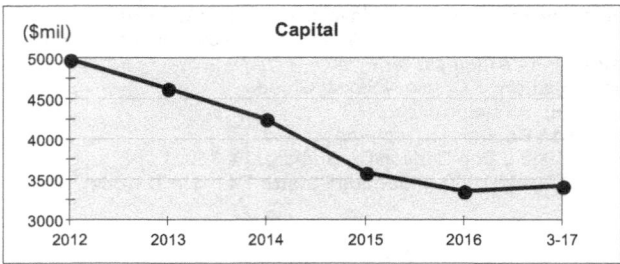

Capital ($mil)

SYNCORA CAPITAL ASR INC

E | **Very Weak**

Major Rating Factors: A history of deficient reserves (0.5 on a scale of 0 to 10) that places pressure on both capital and profits. In four of the last five years reserves (two year development) were between 17% and 165% deficient. Weak profitability index (2.8) with operating losses during 2013, 2014 and 2016. Average return on equity over the last five years has been poor at -15.8%.

Other Rating Factors: Weak overall results on stability tests (0.0) including weak results on operational trends and negative cash flow from operations for 2016. The largest net exposure for one risk is excessive at 452.3% of capital. Strong long-term capitalization index (8.9) based on excellent current risk adjusted capital (severe and moderate loss scenarios), despite some fluctuation in capital levels. Superior liquidity (9.8) with ample operational cash flow and liquid investments.

Principal Business: Financial guaranty (100%).

Principal Investments: Investment grade bonds (71%), non investment grade bonds (21%), misc. investments (7%), and cash (1%).

Investments in Affiliates: None

Group Affiliation: Syncora Holdings Ltd

Licensed in: ID, KY, MI, NY

Commenced Business: July 2009

Address: 135 West 50th Street, New York, NY 10020

Phone: (212) 478-3400 **Domicile State:** NY **NAIC Code:** 13666

Data Date	Rating	RACR #1	RACR #2	Loss Ratio %	Total Assets ($mil)	Capital ($mil)	Net Premium ($mil)	Net Income ($mil)
3-17	E	3.55	2.26	N/A	424.2	226.2	11.1	2.0
3-16	E	3.04	1.96	N/A	465.6	184.5	11.2	-11.8
2016	E	3.63	2.28	69.7	427.2	225.8	9.9	-15.5
2015	E	3.55	2.22	55.3	468.9	192.1	11.7	4.6
2014	E	3.58	2.50	82.8	495.2	164.5	15.3	-74.3
2013	E	3.45	1.91	256.8	618.7	186.5	22.2	-108.6
2012	A-	4.07	2.79	10.3	720.9	172.6	31.5	42.0

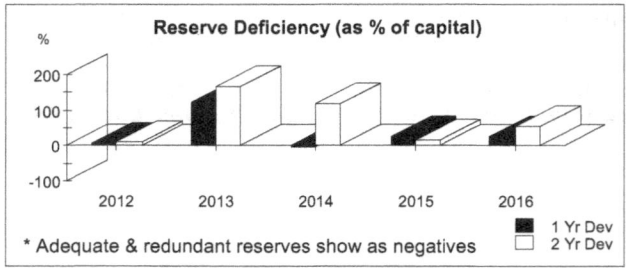

Reserve Deficiency (as % of capital)

* Adequate & redundant reserves show as negatives

■ 1 Yr Dev
□ 2 Yr Dev

SYNCORA GUARANTEE INC   E-   Very Weak

Major Rating Factors: A history of deficient reserves (1.9 on a scale of 0 to 10). Underreserving can have an adverse impact on capital and profits. Deficiencies in the two year reserve development occurred in three of the previous five years and ranged between 97% and 185%. Weak overall results on stability tests (0.0) including excessive premium growth, weak results on operational trends and negative cash flow from operations for 2016. The largest net exposure for one risk is excessive at 78.8% of capital.

Other Rating Factors: Good overall profitability index (6.1) despite operating losses during 2014 and the first three months of 2017. Return on equity has been good over the last five years, averaging 22.5%. Strong long-term capitalization index (10.0) based on excellent current risk adjusted capital (severe and moderate loss scenarios), despite some fluctuation in capital levels. Superior liquidity (10.0) with ample operational cash flow and liquid investments.

Principal Business: Financial guaranty (100%).

Principal Investments: Investment grade bonds (66%), misc. investments (24%), non investment grade bonds (9%), and cash (1%).

Investments in Affiliates: 2%

Group Affiliation: Syncora Holdings Ltd

Licensed in: All states except AK, FL, OH, TN, PR

Commenced Business: January 1872

Address: 135 West 50th Street, New York, NY 10020

Phone: (212) 478-3400   **Domicile State:** NY   **NAIC Code:** 20311

Data Date	Rating	RACR #1	RACR #2	Loss Ratio %	Total Assets ($mil)	Capital ($mil)	Net Premium ($mil)	Net Income ($mil)
3-17	E-	16.06	9.13	N/A	1,267.9	1,185.1	5.1	-8.8
3-16	E-	22.19	12.52	N/A	1,251.6	1,088.5	3.2	8.4
2016	E-	16.94	9.53	N/A	1,259.9	1,188.3	8.2	60.8
2015	E-	20.05	12.07	N/A	1,249.4	1,087.0	12.8	209.0
2014	E-	6.94	4.99	240.3	1,219.5	856.0	19.1	-52.7
2013	E-	11.39	8.21	N/A	1,034.5	973.3	23.7	391.5
2012	E-	4.15	2.98	N/A	1,099.9	510.7	27.6	307.8

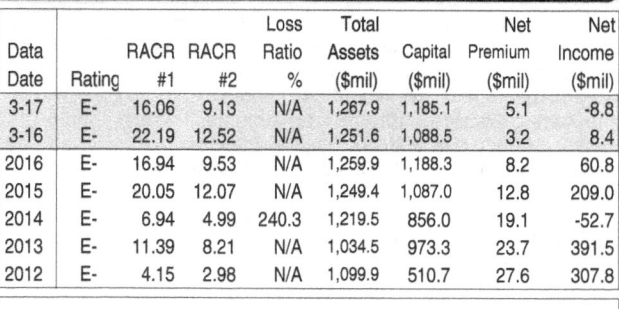

Reserve Deficiency (as % of capital)

* Adequate & redundant reserves show as negatives — ■ 1 Yr Dev □ 2 Yr Dev

TECHNOLOGY INS CO   C   Fair

Major Rating Factors: Fair reserve development (3.0 on a scale of 0 to 10) as the level of reserves has at times been insufficient to cover claims. In 2014 and 2015 the two year reserve development was 18% and 23% deficient respectively. Fair profitability index (3.7) with operating losses during 2014 and the first three months of 2017. Average return on equity over the last five years has been poor at -18.0%.

Other Rating Factors: Fair overall results on stability tests (3.6) including weak results on operational trends. Good long-term capitalization index (5.4) based on good current risk adjusted capital (moderate loss scenario). Over the last several years, capital levels have remained relatively consistent. Good liquidity (5.6) with sufficient resources (cash flows and marketable investments) to handle a spike in claims.

Principal Business: Workers compensation (83%), allied lines (5%), auto liability (4%), other liability (4%), commercial multiple peril (2%), and auto physical damage (1%).

Principal Investments: Investment grade bonds (80%), misc. investments (14%), cash (4%), and non investment grade bonds (2%).

Investments in Affiliates: 4%

Group Affiliation: AmTrust Financial Services Inc

Licensed in: All states, the District of Columbia and Puerto Rico

Commenced Business: July 1991

Address: 98 SPIT BROOK ROAD SUITE 402, Nashua, NH 03062

Phone: (212) 220-7120   **Domicile State:** DE   **NAIC Code:** 42376

Data Date	Rating	RACR #1	RACR #2	Loss Ratio %	Total Assets ($mil)	Capital ($mil)	Net Premium ($mil)	Net Income ($mil)
3-17	C	1.08	0.75	N/A	2,471.3	557.5	277.6	-16.7
3-16	C	1.04	0.74	N/A	2,326.6	486.9	251.9	4.9
2016	C	1.17	0.82	64.8	2,350.0	577.1	1,140.4	53.9
2015	C	1.08	0.78	71.0	1,981.5	478.7	985.0	0.3
2014	C	2.25	1.63	N/A	1,502.4	479.4	-250.2	-622.6
2013	C	1.62	1.11	67.1	1,132.6	236.5	485.6	16.6
2012	C	1.75	1.19	67.9	915.5	206.8	308.4	45.6

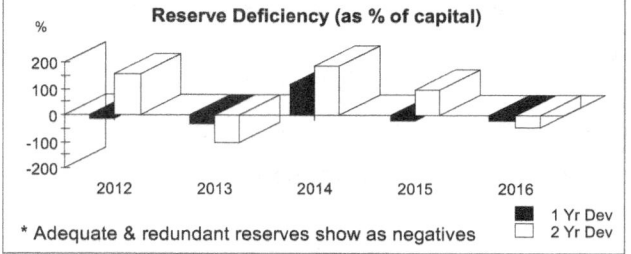

Reserve Deficiency (as % of capital)

* Adequate & redundant reserves show as negatives — ■ 1 Yr Dev □ 2 Yr Dev

TENNESSEE FARMERS ASR CO *   B+   Good

Major Rating Factors: Good liquidity (6.3 on a scale of 0 to 10) with sufficient resources (cash flows and marketable investments) to handle a spike in claims. Good overall results on stability tests (5.1) despite weak results on operational trends.

Other Rating Factors: Strong long-term capitalization index (10.0) based on excellent current risk adjusted capital (severe and moderate loss scenarios). Moreover, capital levels have been consistent in recent years. Ample reserve history (8.1) that helps to protect the company against sharp claims increases. Excellent profitability (8.6) with operating gains in each of the last five years. Return on equity has been good over the last five years, averaging 12.6%.

Principal Business: (This company is a reinsurer.)

Principal Investments: Investment grade bonds (90%) and misc. investments (10%).

Investments in Affiliates: 2%

Group Affiliation: Tennessee Farmers Mutual

Licensed in: TN

Commenced Business: August 1991

Address: 147 Bear Creek Pike, Columbia, TN 38401-2266

Phone: (931) 388-7872   **Domicile State:** TN   **NAIC Code:** 41220

Data Date	Rating	RACR #1	RACR #2	Loss Ratio %	Total Assets ($mil)	Capital ($mil)	Net Premium ($mil)	Net Income ($mil)
3-17	B+	5.87	4.05	N/A	1,442.2	994.9	148.9	4.6
3-16	B+	4.85	3.31	N/A	1,346.6	909.1	144.4	32.4
2016	B+	5.64	3.93	72.2	1,431.3	984.3	600.4	91.2
2015	B+	4.64	3.20	66.4	1,302.5	874.5	586.1	122.4
2014	B+	4.08	2.82	67.6	1,156.6	743.4	570.9	108.6
2013	B+	2.77	1.92	65.9	1,014.2	635.5	555.8	144.0
2012	B+	2.41	1.67	87.5	874.5	511.9	534.7	25.0

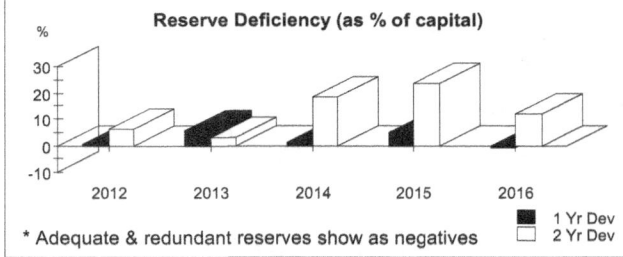

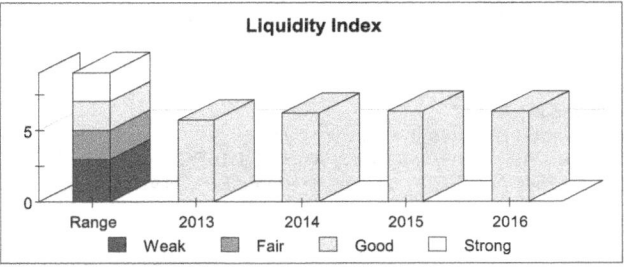

Liquidity Index

■ Weak ■ Fair □ Good □ Strong

TENNESSEE FARMERS MUTUAL INS CO *

B+ **Good**

Major Rating Factors: Good overall results on stability tests (5.1 on a scale of 0 to 10) despite weak results on operational trends. Affiliation with Tennessee Farmers Mutual is a strength. Good liquidity (6.7) with sufficient resources (cash flows and marketable investments) to handle a spike in claims.

Other Rating Factors: Strong long-term capitalization index (7.9) based on excellent current risk adjusted capital (severe and moderate loss scenarios). Moreover, capital levels have been consistent in recent years. Ample reserve history (7.6) that can protect against increases in claims costs. Excellent profitability (8.5) with operating gains in each of the last five years.

Principal Business: Homeowners multiple peril (31%), auto physical damage (26%), auto liability (25%), farmowners multiple peril (10%), fire (4%), other liability (2%), and commercial multiple peril (1%).

Principal Investments: Misc. investments (57%) and investment grade bonds (44%).

Investments in Affiliates: 49%

Group Affiliation: Tennessee Farmers Mutual

Licensed in: TN

Commenced Business: December 1952

Address: 147 Bear Creek Pike, Columbia, TN 38401-2266

Phone: (931) 388-7872 **Domicile State:** TN **NAIC Code:** 15245

Data Date	Rating	RACR #1	RACR #2	Loss Ratio %	Total Assets ($mil)	Capital ($mil)	Net Premium ($mil)	Net Income ($mil)
3-17	B+	1.84	1.74	N/A	2,919.9	2,301.8	149.6	6.8
3-16	B+	1.87	1.76	N/A	2,758.4	2,140.9	145.0	35.3
2016	B+	1.84	1.75	72.0	2,885.1	2,285.2	603.3	110.4
2015	B+	1.84	1.74	65.8	2,658.9	2,074.6	589.2	141.4
2014	B+	1.80	1.70	67.5	2,410.2	1,807.5	574.3	134.8
2013	B+	1.80	1.67	66.8	2,191.9	1,650.4	559.4	159.8
2012	B+	1.81	1.68	87.9	1,940.0	1,449.4	540.2	34.2

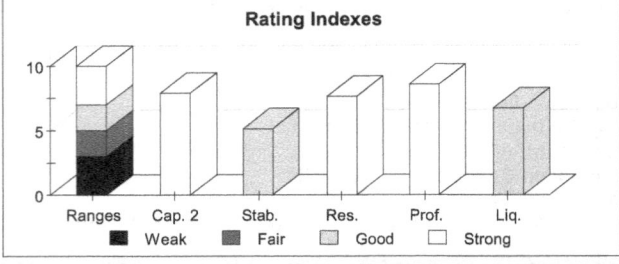

Rating Indexes

TEXAS FARM BUREAU CASUALTY INS CO *

B+ **Good**

Major Rating Factors: History of adequate reserve strength (6.1 on a scale of 0 to 10) as reserves have been consistently at an acceptable level. Good liquidity (5.5) with sufficient resources (cash flows and marketable investments) to handle a spike in claims.

Other Rating Factors: Good overall results on stability tests (6.6). Strong long-term capitalization index (10.0) based on excellent current risk adjusted capital (severe and moderate loss scenarios), despite some fluctuation in capital levels. Fair profitability index (4.2) with operating losses during 2015 and 2016. Return on equity has been low, averaging 1.9% over the past five years.

Principal Business: Auto liability (50%), auto physical damage (48%), and other liability (2%).

Principal Investments: Investment grade bonds (65%) and misc. investments (39%).

Investments in Affiliates: None

Group Affiliation: TX Farm Bureau Mutual

Licensed in: TX

Commenced Business: August 2007

Address: 7420 Fish Pond Road, Waco, TX 76710

Phone: (254) 772-3030 **Domicile State:** TX **NAIC Code:** 13004

Data Date	Rating	RACR #1	RACR #2	Loss Ratio %	Total Assets ($mil)	Capital ($mil)	Net Premium ($mil)	Net Income ($mil)
3-17	B+	4.34	3.43	N/A	1,206.1	668.2	172.5	11.2
3-16	B+	4.39	3.46	N/A	1,193.0	646.6	164.0	-2.4
2016	B+	4.21	3.42	86.9	1,230.3	653.5	687.1	-3.4
2015	B+	4.39	3.56	88.3	1,180.6	647.8	644.4	-8.6
2014	B+	4.71	3.83	82.3	1,154.8	657.1	620.8	28.4
2013	A	4.80	3.83	81.5	1,099.9	645.0	583.4	28.0
2012	A	4.65	3.60	82.5	1,048.1	606.2	546.4	8.1

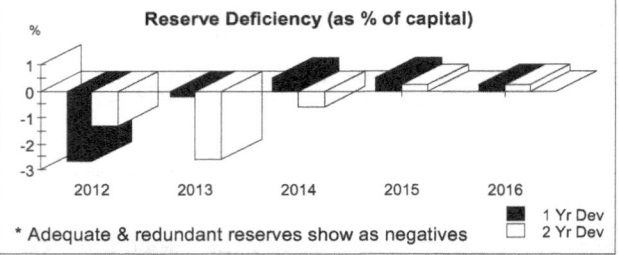

Reserve Deficiency (as % of capital)

* Adequate & redundant reserves show as negatives

TEXAS FARM BUREAU MUTUAL INS CO

C **Fair**

Major Rating Factors: Fair profitability index (4.6 on a scale of 0 to 10) with operating losses during 2012, 2013, 2014 and the first three months of 2017. Fair overall results on stability tests (4.0) including fair financial strength of affiliated TX Farm Bureau Mutual and weak results on operational trends.

Other Rating Factors: History of adequate reserve strength (6.2) as reserves have been consistently at an acceptable level. Good liquidity (5.8) with sufficient resources (cash flows and marketable investments) to handle a spike in claims. Strong long-term capitalization index (9.3) based on excellent current risk adjusted capital (severe and moderate loss scenarios), despite some fluctuation in capital levels.

Principal Business: Auto liability (36%), auto physical damage (32%), homeowners multiple peril (31%), and other liability (1%).

Principal Investments: Investment grade bonds (86%) and misc. investments (15%).

Investments in Affiliates: 1%

Group Affiliation: TX Farm Bureau Mutual

Licensed in: TX

Commenced Business: February 1950

Address: 7420 Fish Pond Road, Waco, TX 76710

Phone: (254) 772-3030 **Domicile State:** TX **NAIC Code:** 25380

Data Date	Rating	RACR #1	RACR #2	Loss Ratio %	Total Assets ($mil)	Capital ($mil)	Net Premium ($mil)	Net Income ($mil)
3-17	C	2.79	2.55	N/A	746.2	340.0	103.3	-8.1
3-16	C-	2.57	2.31	N/A	768.3	319.2	103.2	-8.5
2016	C	2.95	2.51	74.8	755.5	346.5	423.3	22.9
2015	D+	2.82	2.38	76.5	741.3	326.8	407.5	20.1
2014	D	2.81	2.36	79.7	705.1	309.8	389.1	-6.8
2013	D	3.28	2.75	82.6	659.9	313.0	343.1	-19.4
2012	B-	3.89	3.26	87.0	616.5	323.2	304.5	-39.1

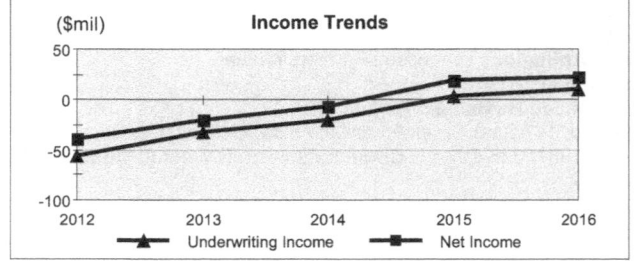

Income Trends

TIG INS CO   C   Fair

Major Rating Factors: Fair long-term capitalization index (4.0 on a scale of 0 to 10) based on fair current risk adjusted capital (severe loss scenario). Fair reserve development (3.7) as the level of reserves has at times been insufficient to cover claims. In 2016 and 2012 the two year reserve development was 18% and 19% deficient respectively.

Other Rating Factors: Fair overall results on stability tests (3.7) including excessive premium growth, weak results on operational trends, negative cash flow from operations for 2016 and fair risk adjusted capital in prior years. The largest net exposure for one risk is conservative at 1.7% of capital. Weak profitability index (2.4) with operating losses during 2012, 2013 and the first three months of 2017. Return on equity has been fair, averaging 7.2% over the past five years. Excellent liquidity (8.7) with ample operational cash flow and liquid investments.

Principal Business: Other liability (98%) and auto liability (12%).
Principal Investments: Investment grade bonds (54%), misc. investments (44%), cash (1%), and non investment grade bonds (1%).
Investments in Affiliates: 12%
Group Affiliation: Fairfax Financial
Licensed in: All states except PR
Commenced Business: April 1915
Address: 7676 HAZARD CENTER DR STE 210, San Diego, CA 92108
Phone: (603) 656-2233   **Domicile State:** CA   **NAIC Code:** 25534

Data Date	Rating	RACR #1	RACR #2	Loss Ratio %	Total Assets ($mil)	Capital ($mil)	Net Premium ($mil)	Net Income ($mil)
3-17	C	0.88	0.61	N/A	2,718.7	726.4	0.1	-43.8
3-16	U	0.77	0.48	N/A	1,863.6	548.2	0.0	43.0
2016	C	0.87	0.60	235.1	2,818.4	736.0	63.5	-46.1
2015	U	0.78	0.49	N/A	3,191.1	777.1	0.6	32.1
2014	D	0.45	0.32	N/A	3,546.0	980.3	-29.7	673.3
2013	D	0.40	0.31	N/A	2,444.8	850.0	1.0	-74.2
2012	D	0.42	0.33	N/A	2,310.1	928.1	0.1	-128.2

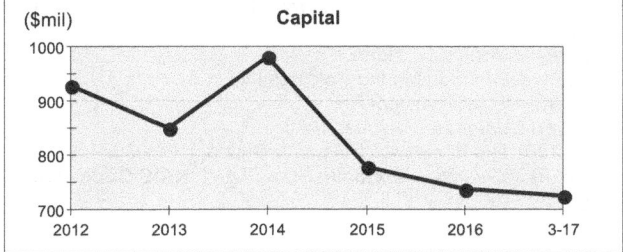

Capital

TOA REINS CO OF AMERICA *   B+   Good

Major Rating Factors: History of adequate reserve strength (6.4 on a scale of 0 to 10) as reserves have been consistently at an acceptable level. Good overall profitability index (5.7). Fair expense controls. Return on equity has been fair, averaging 7.6% over the past five years.

Other Rating Factors: Good liquidity (6.9) with sufficient resources (cash flows and marketable investments) to handle a spike in claims. Good overall results on stability tests (5.1) despite weak results on operational trends. The largest net exposure for one risk is conservative at 1.7% of capital. Strong long-term capitalization index (8.0) based on excellent current risk adjusted capital (severe and moderate loss scenarios), despite some fluctuation in capital levels.

Principal Business: (This company is a reinsurer.)
Principal Investments: Investment grade bonds (85%), misc. investments (13%), cash (1%), and non investment grade bonds (1%).
Investments in Affiliates: None
Group Affiliation: Toa Reinsurance Co Ltd Japan
Licensed in: All states except PR
Commenced Business: January 1972
Address: 2711 Centerville Road Ste 400, Wilmington, DE 19808
Phone: (973) 898-9480   **Domicile State:** DE   **NAIC Code:** 42439

Data Date	Rating	RACR #1	RACR #2	Loss Ratio %	Total Assets ($mil)	Capital ($mil)	Net Premium ($mil)	Net Income ($mil)
3-17	B+	2.42	1.58	N/A	1,749.0	640.1	101.5	12.0
3-16	B+	2.48	1.63	N/A	1,700.6	635.3	91.0	6.9
2016	B+	2.60	1.71	76.3	1,775.2	669.3	397.0	18.5
2015	B+	2.68	1.77	64.1	1,715.4	672.4	363.9	63.3
2014	B+	2.66	1.76	61.7	1,773.3	714.6	351.5	72.8
2013	B+	2.14	1.43	65.1	1,779.4	682.4	403.1	70.7
2012	B	1.84	1.23	78.3	1,670.3	599.1	391.3	32.6

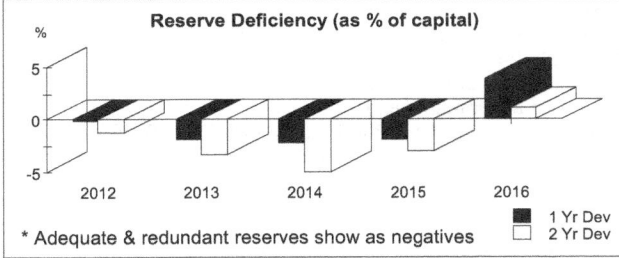

Reserve Deficiency (as % of capital)

* Adequate & redundant reserves show as negatives   ■ 1 Yr Dev   □ 2 Yr Dev

TOKIO MARINE AMERICA INS CO *   A   Excellent

Major Rating Factors: Strong long-term capitalization index (8.4 on a scale of 0 to 10) based on excellent current risk adjusted capital (severe and moderate loss scenarios). Furthermore, this high level of risk adjusted capital has been consistently maintained in previous years. Excellent overall results on stability tests (7.4). Stability strengths include excellent operational trends and excellent risk diversification.

Other Rating Factors: History of adequate reserve strength (6.9) as reserves have been consistently at an acceptable level. Good liquidity (6.8) with sufficient resources (cash flows and marketable investments) to handle a spike in claims. Fair profitability index (4.7) with modest operating losses during 2016. Return on equity has been low, averaging 2.7% over the past five years.

Principal Business: Auto liability (17%), ocean marine (13%), fire (11%), commercial multiple peril (9%), workers compensation (9%), other liability (8%), and other lines (32%).
Principal Investments: Investment grade bonds (82%), misc. investments (15%), cash (2%), and non investment grade bonds (1%).
Investments in Affiliates: 13%
Group Affiliation: Tokio Marine Holdings Inc
Licensed in: All states, the District of Columbia and Puerto Rico
Commenced Business: September 1999
Address: 230 Park Avenue, New York, NY 10169-0005
Phone: (610) 227-1253   **Domicile State:** NY   **NAIC Code:** 10945

Data Date	Rating	RACR #1	RACR #2	Loss Ratio %	Total Assets ($mil)	Capital ($mil)	Net Premium ($mil)	Net Income ($mil)
3-17	A	2.55	1.91	N/A	1,401.2	547.5	77.3	5.2
3-16	A	2.19	1.66	N/A	1,361.4	509.9	72.9	-3.1
2016	A	2.55	1.91	75.4	1,444.6	539.3	302.7	0.0
2015	A	2.27	1.73	78.0	1,360.5	510.6	308.5	17.8
2014	A	2.98	1.90	76.7	1,349.2	497.3	248.0	25.4
2013	A	2.78	1.85	73.8	1,383.5	514.4	275.0	16.0
2012	U	41.03	36.93	78.8	1,388.4	499.1	263.0	7.9

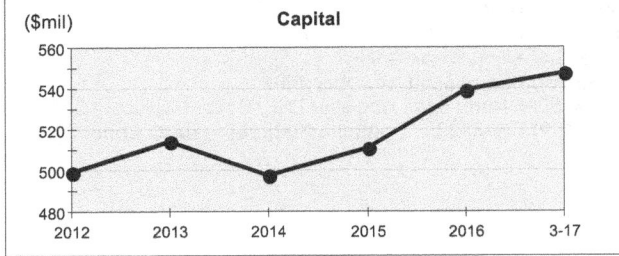

Capital

TOKIO MARINE SPECIALTY INS CO

C **Fair**

Major Rating Factors: Fair overall results on stability tests (3.9 on a scale of 0 to 10) including fair financial strength of affiliated Tokio Marine Holdings Inc and weak results on operational trends. Good liquidity (6.9) with sufficient resources (cash flows and marketable investments) to handle a spike in claims.

Other Rating Factors: Strong long-term capitalization index (9.7) based on excellent current risk adjusted capital (severe and moderate loss scenarios). Moreover, capital levels have been consistent in recent years. Ample reserve history (7.6) that can protect against increases in claims costs. Excellent profitability (8.9) with operating gains in each of the last five years. Return on equity has been good over the last five years, averaging 10.1%.

Principal Business: Other liability (69%), commercial multiple peril (11%), products liability (10%), auto physical damage (5%), and allied lines (4%).

Principal Investments: Investment grade bonds (94%), misc. investments (5%), and cash (1%).

Investments in Affiliates: None

Group Affiliation: Tokio Marine Holdings Inc

Licensed in: All states except PR

Commenced Business: October 1986

Address: 1807 North Market Street, Wilmington, DE 19802

Phone: (610) 206-7836   **Domicile State:** DE   **NAIC Code:** 23850

Data Date	Rating	RACR #1	RACR #2	Loss Ratio %	Total Assets ($mil)	Capital ($mil)	Net Premium ($mil)	Net Income ($mil)
3-17	C	3.60	2.71	N/A	583.4	201.3	37.6	4.3
3-16	C	3.71	2.79	N/A	556.2	202.7	35.3	4.9
2016	C	3.70	2.81	60.9	569.9	197.6	151.2	19.3
2015	C	3.76	2.86	60.5	517.3	197.8	141.9	19.9
2014	C	3.21	2.42	61.5	465.0	173.9	134.4	17.5
2013	C	3.26	2.47	61.0	416.1	157.3	123.8	17.3
2012	C	3.53	2.71	62.8	381.2	140.8	111.8	14.3

Tokio Marine Holdings Inc
Composite Group Rating: B

Largest Group Members	Assets ($mil)	Rating
RELIANCE STANDARD LIFE INS CO	10889	B
PHILADELPHIA INDEMNITY INS CO	8081	B-
SAFETY NATIONAL CASUALTY CORP	6450	C
HOUSTON CASUALTY CO	3330	B-
US SPECIALTY INS CO	1792	B-

TOKIO MILLENNIUM RE AG (US BRANCH)

C **Fair**

Major Rating Factors: Fair reserve development (3.6 on a scale of 0 to 10) as reserves have generally been sufficient to cover claims. Fair overall results on stability tests (3.2) including weak results on operational trends. The largest net exposure for one risk is high at 4.8% of capital.

Other Rating Factors: Weak profitability index (2.3) with operating losses during 2014, 2015 and 2016. Good overall long-term capitalization (6.1) based on good current risk adjusted capital (moderate loss scenario). However, capital levels have fluctuated somewhat during past years. Good liquidity (6.3) with sufficient resources (cash flows and marketable investments) to handle a spike in claims.

Principal Business: (This company is a reinsurer.)

Principal Investments: Investment grade bonds (93%), misc. investments (5%), and cash (2%).

Investments in Affiliates: None

Group Affiliation: Tokio Marine Holdings Inc

Licensed in: All states except PR

Commenced Business: June 2014

Address: 1177 Ave of Americas 41st Fl, New York, NY 10036

Phone: (203) 658-1900   **Domicile State:** NY   **NAIC Code:** 15529

Data Date	Rating	RACR #1	RACR #2	Loss Ratio %	Total Assets ($mil)	Capital ($mil)	Net Premium ($mil)	Net Income ($mil)
3-17	C	1.58	0.92	N/A	1,036.3	207.7	124.4	12.8
3-16	C+	1.64	0.96	N/A	882.0	231.0	108.9	13.0
2016	C	1.56	0.88	65.2	1,011.7	194.7	538.6	-23.6
2015	C+	1.91	0.97	60.0	817.3	217.9	647.4	-119.7
2014	U	5.10	2.78	60.6	222.6	102.8	121.9	-46.8
2013	N/A	N/A	N/A	0.0	0.0	0.0	0.0	0.0
2012	N/A	N/A	N/A	0.0	0.0	0.0	0.0	0.0

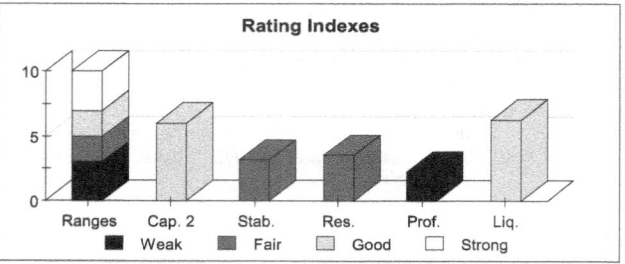

Rating Indexes

Ranges | Cap. 2 | Stab. | Res. | Prof. | Liq.
■ Weak ▦ Fair ▨ Good □ Strong

TOYOTA MOTOR INS CO

C+ **Fair**

Major Rating Factors: Fair overall results on stability tests (4.0 on a scale of 0 to 10) including potential drain of affiliation with Toyota Motor Corp, weak results on operational trends and excessive premium growth. History of adequate reserve strength (5.0) as reserves have been consistently at an acceptable level.

Other Rating Factors: Strong long-term capitalization index (10.0) based on excellent current risk adjusted capital (severe and moderate loss scenarios). Moreover, capital levels have been consistent in recent years. Excellent profitability (8.9) with operating gains in each of the last five years. Excellent liquidity (7.5) with ample operational cash flow and liquid investments.

Principal Business: Other liability (80%) and credit (4%).

Principal Investments: Investment grade bonds (91%), cash (5%), misc. investments (2%), and non investment grade bonds (2%).

Investments in Affiliates: None

Group Affiliation: Toyota Motor Corp

Licensed in: All states except PR

Commenced Business: December 1909

Address: 5005 North River Boulevard NE, Cedar Rapids, IA 52411

Phone: (469) 786-8228   **Domicile State:** IA   **NAIC Code:** 37621

Data Date	Rating	RACR #1	RACR #2	Loss Ratio %	Total Assets ($mil)	Capital ($mil)	Net Premium ($mil)	Net Income ($mil)
3-17	C+	7.06	6.07	N/A	534.8	252.3	23.5	5.3
3-16	C+	6.79	5.48	N/A	508.5	234.5	18.5	5.3
2016	C+	7.53	6.55	66.1	518.6	246.9	89.2	16.6
2015	C+	7.24	5.88	48.8	493.8	229.1	91.8	16.3
2014	C	9.12	7.65	43.3	453.0	211.4	79.7	14.9
2013	C	9.87	8.12	38.0	420.0	194.9	65.6	17.1
2012	C	11.31	9.35	34.1	411.6	177.0	52.0	20.1

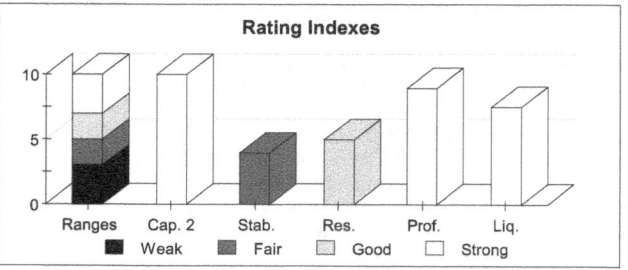

Rating Indexes

Ranges | Cap. 2 | Stab. | Res. | Prof. | Liq.
■ Weak ▦ Fair ▨ Good □ Strong

TRANSATLANTIC REINS CO   B   Good

Major Rating Factors: Good liquidity (6.8 on a scale of 0 to 10) with sufficient resources (cash flows and marketable investments) to handle a spike in claims. Fair overall results on stability tests (4.8) including weak results on operational trends. The largest net exposure for one risk is conservative at 1.2% of capital.
Other Rating Factors: Strong long-term capitalization index (7.7) based on excellent current risk adjusted capital (severe and moderate loss scenarios), despite some fluctuation in capital levels. Ample reserve history (8.9) that helps to protect the company against sharp claims increases. Excellent profitability (7.3) with operating gains in each of the last five years. Return on equity has been good over the last five years, averaging 11.5%.
Principal Business: (This company is a reinsurer.)
Principal Investments: Investment grade bonds (67%), misc. investments (27%), cash (3%), and non investment grade bonds (3%).
Investments in Affiliates: 9%
Group Affiliation: Alleghany Corp Group
Licensed in: All states, the District of Columbia and Puerto Rico
Commenced Business: January 1953
Address: ONE LIBERTY PLAZA 165 BROADWAY, New York, NY 10006
Phone: (212) 365-2200   **Domicile State:** NY   **NAIC Code:** 19453

Data Date	Rating	RACR #1	RACR #2	Loss Ratio %	Total Assets ($mil)	Capital ($mil)	Net Premium ($mil)	Net Income ($mil)
3-17	B	2.25	1.55	N/A	14,157.0	5,035.1	835.1	111.9
3-16	B	2.17	1.51	N/A	14,021.6	4,935.4	841.0	126.8
2016	B	2.15	1.48	58.2	14,019.4	4,908.7	3,574.2	541.7
2015	B	2.17	1.52	53.3	13,834.9	4,816.9	2,967.9	512.5
2014	B	2.10	1.44	55.0	14,574.6	4,770.5	2,986.8	562.1
2013	B	2.02	1.39	55.2	15,013.0	4,718.9	2,977.0	770.4
2012	B	1.92	1.28	71.2	14,661.5	4,179.1	3,074.5	345.5

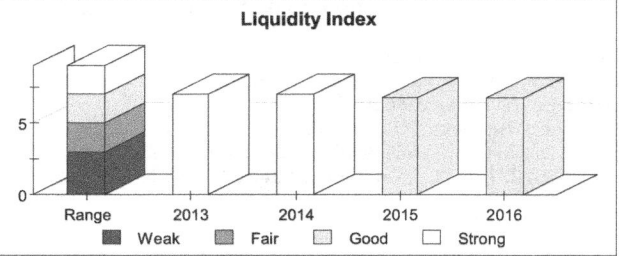

Liquidity Index

TRAVELERS CASUALTY & SURETY CO *   A-   Excellent

Major Rating Factors: Strong long-term capitalization index (7.7 on a scale of 0 to 10) based on excellent current risk adjusted capital (severe and moderate loss scenarios), despite some fluctuation in capital levels. Ample reserve history (8.1) that helps to protect the company against sharp claims increases.
Other Rating Factors: Excellent profitability (7.5) with operating gains in each of the last five years. Return on equity has been excellent over the last five years averaging 16.6%. Good liquidity (6.9) with sufficient resources (cash flows and marketable investments) to handle a spike in claims. Good overall results on stability tests (5.5) despite weak results on operational trends.
Principal Business: Workers compensation (74%), surety (15%), homeowners multiple peril (8%), other liability (1%), and fire (1%).
Principal Investments: Investment grade bonds (66%), misc. investments (33%), and non investment grade bonds (1%).
Investments in Affiliates: 26%
Group Affiliation: Travelers Companies Inc
Licensed in: All states, the District of Columbia and Puerto Rico
Commenced Business: May 1907
Address: ONE TOWER SQUARE, Hartford, CT 06183
Phone: (860) 277-0111   **Domicile State:** CT   **NAIC Code:** 19038

Data Date	Rating	RACR #1	RACR #2	Loss Ratio %	Total Assets ($mil)	Capital ($mil)	Net Premium ($mil)	Net Income ($mil)
3-17	A-	1.65	1.45	N/A	16,679.3	6,493.2	1,098.2	105.0
3-16	A-	1.62	1.41	N/A	16,349.7	6,380.0	1,057.8	78.6
2016	A-	1.68	1.49	63.4	16,564.3	6,485.8	4,432.6	1,183.9
2015	A-	1.65	1.45	58.7	16,273.6	6,376.3	4,230.7	1,259.2
2014	A-	1.63	1.43	60.5	16,436.2	6,469.5	4,111.2	1,141.3
2013	A-	1.75	1.53	60.9	16,464.4	6,558.6	4,101.0	1,165.6
2012	B+	1.58	1.36	68.3	15,137.1	5,149.5	3,983.1	610.4

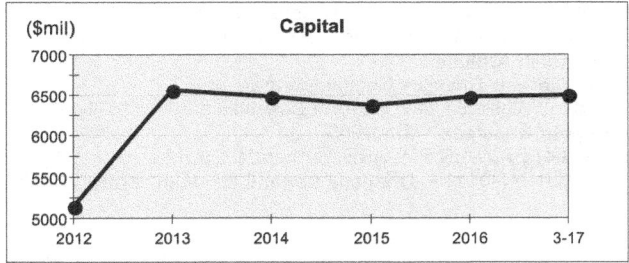

Capital

TRAVELERS CASUALTY & SURETY CO OF AM   C+   Fair

Major Rating Factors: Fair overall results on stability tests (3.0 on a scale of 0 to 10) including weak results on operational trends. The largest net exposure for one risk is excessive at 9.0% of capital. Strong long-term capitalization index (10.0) based on excellent current risk adjusted capital (severe and moderate loss scenarios), despite some fluctuation in capital levels.
Other Rating Factors: Ample reserve history (9.6) that helps to protect the company against sharp claims increases. Excellent profitability (8.0) with operating gains in each of the last five years. Return on equity has been excellent over the last five years averaging 23.9%. Excellent liquidity (7.0) with ample operational cash flow and liquid investments.
Principal Business: Other liability (48%), surety (38%), fidelity (10%), and burglary & theft (3%).
Principal Investments: Investment grade bonds (89%), misc. investments (10%), and non investment grade bonds (1%).
Investments in Affiliates: 8%
Group Affiliation: Travelers Companies Inc
Licensed in: All states, the District of Columbia and Puerto Rico
Commenced Business: July 1974
Address: ONE TOWER SQUARE, Hartford, CT 06183
Phone: (860) 277-0111   **Domicile State:** CT   **NAIC Code:** 31194

Data Date	Rating	RACR #1	RACR #2	Loss Ratio %	Total Assets ($mil)	Capital ($mil)	Net Premium ($mil)	Net Income ($mil)
3-17	C+	4.74	3.55	N/A	4,334.2	2,205.5	348.2	92.0
3-16	C+	5.24	3.78	N/A	4,331.1	2,232.1	338.6	108.6
2016	C+	4.61	3.47	20.3	4,195.8	2,088.2	1,419.8	461.9
2015	C+	5.05	3.66	20.9	4,184.9	2,103.6	1,372.9	470.0
2014	C+	4.62	3.46	9.0	4,225.2	2,114.7	1,408.3	565.8
2013	C+	4.75	3.18	13.9	4,147.5	1,881.7	1,293.9	500.5
2012	C+	3.99	2.70	26.4	4,339.6	1,780.5	1,223.0	417.0

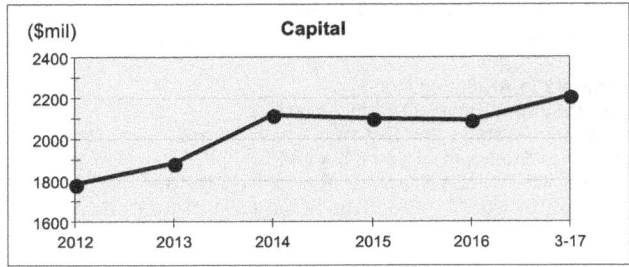

Capital

TRAVELERS CASUALTY INS CO OF AMERICA　　　　B　　　Good

Major Rating Factors: Good overall profitability index (6.3 on a scale of 0 to 10). Fair expense controls. Return on equity has been good over the last five years, averaging 14.7%. Good liquidity (6.6) with sufficient resources (cash flows and marketable investments) to handle a spike in claims.

Other Rating Factors: Fair overall results on stability tests (4.7) including weak results on operational trends. Affiliation with Travelers Companies Inc is a strength. Strong long-term capitalization index (8.0) based on excellent current risk adjusted capital (severe and moderate loss scenarios), despite some fluctuation in capital levels. Ample reserve history (8.6) that helps to protect the company against sharp claims increases.

Principal Business: Commercial multiple peril (70%), workers compensation (16%), auto liability (11%), and auto physical damage (3%).

Principal Investments: Investment grade bonds (93%) and misc. investments (7%).

Investments in Affiliates: None

Group Affiliation: Travelers Companies Inc

Licensed in: All states except PR

Commenced Business: October 1971

Address: ONE TOWER SQUARE, Hartford, CT 06183

Phone: (860) 277-0111　　**Domicile State:** CT　　**NAIC Code:** 19046

Data Date	Rating	RACR #1	RACR #2	Loss Ratio %	Total Assets ($mil)	Capital ($mil)	Net Premium ($mil)	Net Income ($mil)
3-17	B	2.60	1.69	N/A	1,971.9	574.0	147.3	16.0
3-16	B	2.74	1.74	N/A	1,957.6	601.8	141.8	16.5
2016	B	2.61	1.70	63.4	1,937.0	560.0	594.4	67.8
2015	B	2.73	1.73	58.7	1,942.2	586.0	567.3	104.2
2014	B	2.66	1.67	60.5	1,918.5	566.2	551.1	91.4
2013	B	2.62	1.66	60.9	1,893.1	549.8	549.8	91.5
2012	B	2.45	1.57	68.4	1,841.4	506.6	534.0	59.7

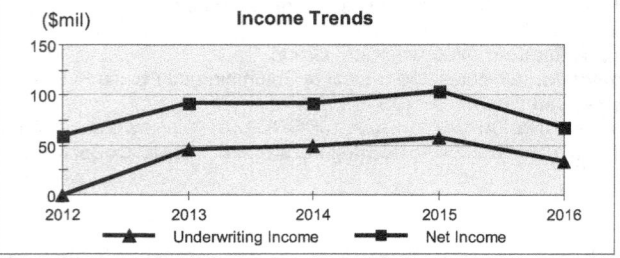

TRAVELERS INDEMNITY CO *　　　　B+　　　Good

Major Rating Factors: Good overall profitability index (6.9 on a scale of 0 to 10). Fair expense controls. Return on equity has been good over the last five years, averaging 14.5%. Good liquidity (6.9) with sufficient resources (cash flows and marketable investments) to handle a spike in claims.

Other Rating Factors: Good overall results on stability tests (5.4) despite weak results on operational trends. Strong long-term capitalization index (7.8) based on excellent current risk adjusted capital (severe and moderate loss scenarios), despite some fluctuation in capital levels. Ample reserve history (8.1) that helps to protect the company against sharp claims increases.

Principal Business: Workers compensation (22%), other liability (20%), commercial multiple peril (15%), auto liability (13%), allied lines (11%), fire (8%), and other lines (12%).

Principal Investments: Investment grade bonds (72%), misc. investments (27%), non investment grade bonds (2%), and real estate (2%).

Investments in Affiliates: 21%

Group Affiliation: Travelers Companies Inc

Licensed in: All states, the District of Columbia and Puerto Rico

Commenced Business: May 1906

Address: ONE TOWER SQUARE, Hartford, CT 06183

Phone: (860) 277-0111　　**Domicile State:** CT　　**NAIC Code:** 25658

Data Date	Rating	RACR #1	RACR #2	Loss Ratio %	Total Assets ($mil)	Capital ($mil)	Net Premium ($mil)	Net Income ($mil)
3-17	B+	1.80	1.51	N/A	21,493.8	6,957.5	1,256.3	217.9
3-16	B+	1.75	1.46	N/A	21,099.8	6,852.8	1,210.1	239.9
2016	B+	1.84	1.55	63.4	21,180.4	7,003.5	5,070.5	1,100.3
2015	B+	1.78	1.49	58.7	20,817.8	6,844.6	4,840.0	1,164.1
2014	B	1.73	1.46	60.5	20,724.5	6,633.4	4,704.2	942.2
2013	B	1.82	1.52	60.9	20,662.6	6,706.1	4,531.6	1,065.7
2012	A-	1.93	1.63	68.4	21,834.6	7,119.3	4,921.4	706.8

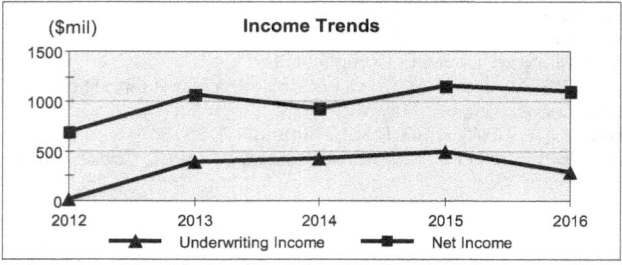

TRAVELERS INDEMNITY CO OF CT　　　　B　　　Good

Major Rating Factors: Good liquidity (6.8 on a scale of 0 to 10) with sufficient resources (cash flows and marketable investments) to handle a spike in claims. Fair profitability index (4.0). Fair expense controls. Return on equity has been fair, averaging 12.4% over the past five years.

Other Rating Factors: Fair overall results on stability tests (4.7) including weak results on operational trends. Affiliation with Travelers Companies Inc is a strength. Strong long-term capitalization index (8.6) based on excellent current risk adjusted capital (severe and moderate loss scenarios), despite some fluctuation in capital levels. Ample reserve history (8.2) that helps to protect the company against sharp claims increases.

Principal Business: Workers compensation (30%), commercial multiple peril (28%), auto liability (21%), other liability (10%), auto physical damage (6%), farmowners multiple peril (2%), and other lines (3%).

Principal Investments: Investment grade bonds (95%) and misc. investments (5%).

Investments in Affiliates: None

Group Affiliation: Travelers Companies Inc

Licensed in: All states, the District of Columbia and Puerto Rico

Commenced Business: September 1860

Address: ONE TOWER SQUARE, Hartford, CT 06183

Phone: (860) 277-0111　　**Domicile State:** CT　　**NAIC Code:** 25682

Data Date	Rating	RACR #1	RACR #2	Loss Ratio %	Total Assets ($mil)	Capital ($mil)	Net Premium ($mil)	Net Income ($mil)
3-17	B	3.15	2.05	N/A	1,108.2	354.2	73.9	9.1
3-16	B	3.23	2.05	N/A	1,099.9	361.9	71.2	8.6
2016	B	3.16	2.06	63.4	1,084.1	345.1	298.3	38.0
2015	B	3.25	2.07	58.7	1,075.7	354.4	284.7	46.2
2014	B	3.53	2.22	60.5	1,117.8	383.1	276.6	56.6
2013	B	3.43	2.18	60.9	1,082.4	365.6	275.9	51.8
2012	B	3.33	2.14	68.4	1,065.2	350.1	268.0	33.9

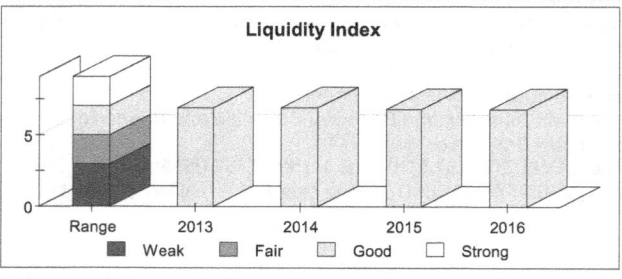

TRAVELERS PROPERTY CAS OF AMERICA · B · Good

Major Rating Factors: Fair profitability index (3.8 on a scale of 0 to 10). Fair expense controls. Return on equity has been low, averaging 3.9% over the past five years. Fair overall results on stability tests (4.7) including weak results on operational trends.

Other Rating Factors: Strong long-term capitalization index (10.0) based on excellent current risk adjusted capital (severe and moderate loss scenarios), despite some fluctuation in capital levels. Ample reserve history (7.4) that can protect against increases in claims costs. Excellent liquidity (7.6) with ample operational cash flow and liquid investments.

Principal Business: Workers compensation (33%), other liability (18%), commercial multiple peril (16%), inland marine (9%), auto liability (8%), fire (4%), and other lines (13%).

Principal Investments: Investment grade bonds (98%) and misc. investments (2%).

Investments in Affiliates: None

Group Affiliation: Travelers Companies Inc

Licensed in: All states, the District of Columbia and Puerto Rico

Commenced Business: August 1971

Address: ONE TOWER SQUARE, Hartford, CT 06183

Phone: (860) 277-0111   **Domicile State:** CT   **NAIC Code:** 25674

Data Date	Rating	RACR #1	RACR #2	Loss Ratio %	Total Assets ($mil)	Capital ($mil)	Net Premium ($mil)	Net Income ($mil)
3-17	B	13.93	8.93	N/A	863.1	440.6	19.4	3.5
3-16	B	14.12	8.88	N/A	866.3	447.8	18.7	3.7
2016	B	14.45	9.35	63.4	837.1	436.9	78.4	16.1
2015	B	14.66	9.30	58.7	848.4	443.9	74.8	19.7
2014	B	16.67	10.46	60.5	933.2	505.0	72.7	18.4
2013	B	16.40	10.35	60.9	907.0	487.0	72.5	20.2
2012	B	15.37	9.74	68.4	841.7	450.1	70.4	16.0

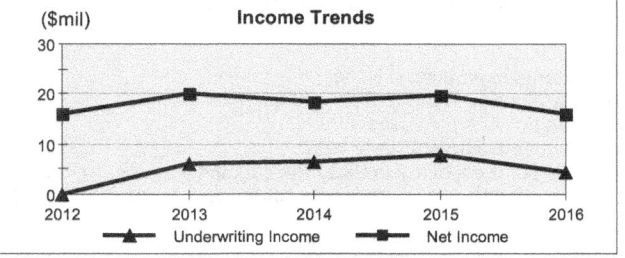

TRINITY UNIVERSAL INS CO · B · Good

Major Rating Factors: Fair profitability index (3.4 on a scale of 0 to 10) with operating losses during the first three months of 2017. Return on equity has been fair, averaging 8.6% over the past five years. Fair overall results on stability tests (4.7) including weak results on operational trends.

Other Rating Factors: Strong long-term capitalization index (7.9) based on excellent current risk adjusted capital (severe and moderate loss scenarios), despite some fluctuation in capital levels. Ample reserve history (8.9) that helps to protect the company against sharp claims increases. Vulnerable liquidity (1.5) as a spike in claims may stretch capacity.

Principal Business: Homeowners multiple peril (39%), auto liability (33%), auto physical damage (25%), other liability (2%), inland marine (1%), and fire (1%).

Principal Investments: Investment grade bonds (50%), misc. investments (44%), and non investment grade bonds (8%).

Investments in Affiliates: 15%

Group Affiliation: Kemper Corporation

Licensed in: AL, AZ, AR, CA, CO, DE, FL, GA, ID, IL, IN, IA, KS, KY, LA, MI, MN, MS, MO, MT, NE, NH, NM, NY, NC, OH, OK, OR, PA, SC, TN, TX, UT, VA, WA, WV, WI, WY

Commenced Business: February 1926

Address: 8360 LBJ FREEWAY SUITE 400, Dallas, TX 75243-1134

Phone: (904) 245-5600   **Domicile State:** TX   **NAIC Code:** 19887

Data Date	Rating	RACR #1	RACR #2	Loss Ratio %	Total Assets ($mil)	Capital ($mil)	Net Premium ($mil)	Net Income ($mil)
3-17	B	2.05	1.55	N/A	1,927.8	737.7	296.5	-20.5
3-16	B	2.19	1.65	N/A	1,986.4	824.3	298.5	12.1
2016	B	2.15	1.64	71.5	1,900.8	771.4	1,194.5	70.0
2015	B	2.16	1.64	68.4	1,964.7	817.4	1,210.9	89.7
2014	B	2.27	1.69	67.8	2,200.1	943.4	1,279.5	82.5
2013	B	2.19	1.62	66.7	2,380.9	984.1	1,435.7	138.5
2012	B	1.80	1.34	78.1	2,407.9	839.0	1,550.5	41.0

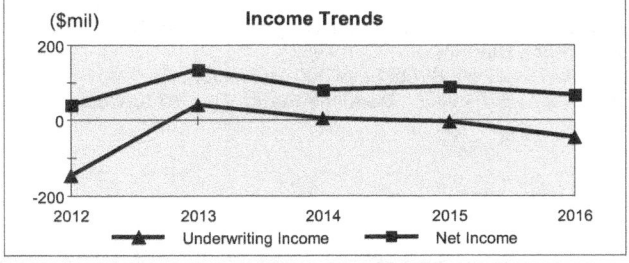

TRUCK INS EXCHANGE · C+ · Fair

Major Rating Factors: Fair profitability index (3.8 on a scale of 0 to 10) with operating losses during 2012, 2014, 2015 and 2016. Fair overall results on stability tests (4.8) including weak results on operational trends and negative cash flow from operations for 2016.

Other Rating Factors: Good overall long-term capitalization (5.2) based on good current risk adjusted capital (severe and moderate loss scenarios). However, capital levels have fluctuated somewhat during past years. History of adequate reserve strength (5.6) as reserves have been consistently at an acceptable level. Vulnerable liquidity (2.8) as a spike in claims may stretch capacity.

Principal Business: Commercial multiple peril (42%), homeowners multiple peril (19%), workers compensation (15%), other liability (11%), auto liability (9%), and auto physical damage (3%).

Principal Investments: Misc. investments (52%), investment grade bonds (49%), non investment grade bonds (1%), and real estate (1%).

Investments in Affiliates: 44%

Group Affiliation: Farmers Insurance Group of Companies

Licensed in: All states except PR

Commenced Business: February 1935

Address: 6301 OWENSMOUTH AVE, Woodland Hills, CA 91367

Phone: (323) 932-3200   **Domicile State:** CA   **NAIC Code:** 21709

Data Date	Rating	RACR #1	RACR #2	Loss Ratio %	Total Assets ($mil)	Capital ($mil)	Net Premium ($mil)	Net Income ($mil)
3-17	C+	0.85	0.78	N/A	2,234.1	612.6	278.7	7.8
3-16	C+	0.86	0.79	N/A	2,194.5	617.2	289.6	-4.3
2016	C+	0.84	0.77	72.5	2,143.6	615.7	1,144.0	-19.6
2015	C+	0.88	0.80	69.0	2,164.8	624.1	1,157.1	-6.9
2014	C+	0.90	0.83	65.8	2,077.6	618.7	1,089.8	-7.3
2013	C+	0.86	0.80	66.9	1,933.4	563.5	1,056.9	1.5
2012	C+	0.87	0.80	73.3	1,963.0	535.0	1,073.8	-29.3

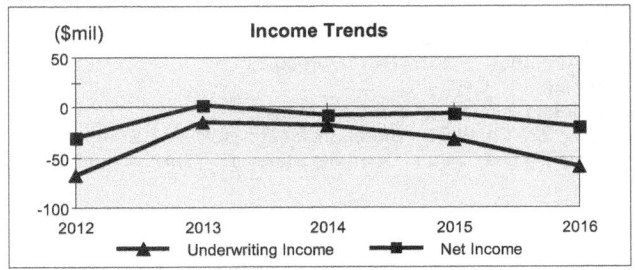

TWIN CITY FIRE INS CO   B   Good

Major Rating Factors: History of adequate reserve strength (5.9 on a scale of 0 to 10) as reserves have been consistently at an acceptable level. Good profitability index (5.0). Good expense controls. Return on equity has been fair, averaging 9.0% over the past five years.

Other Rating Factors: Good liquidity (6.8) with sufficient resources (cash flows and marketable investments) to handle a spike in claims. Fair overall results on stability tests (4.6) including weak results on operational trends. Strong long-term capitalization index (10.0) based on excellent current risk adjusted capital (severe and moderate loss scenarios), despite some fluctuation in capital levels.

Principal Business: Workers compensation (47%), other liability (21%), auto liability (12%), auto physical damage (6%), commercial multiple peril (5%), products liability (4%), and homeowners multiple peril (3%).

Principal Investments: Investment grade bonds (96%) and misc. investments (4%).

Investments in Affiliates: None

Group Affiliation: Hartford Financial Services Inc

Licensed in: All states except PR

Commenced Business: July 1987

Address: 501 Pennsylvania Pkwy Ste 400, Indianapolis, IN 46280-0014

Phone: (860) 547-5000   **Domicile State:** IN   **NAIC Code:** 29459

Data Date	Rating	RACR #1	RACR #2	Loss Ratio %	Total Assets ($mil)	Capital ($mil)	Net Premium ($mil)	Net Income ($mil)
3-17	B	5.23	3.45	N/A	680.6	287.2	41.4	6.1
3-16	B	5.47	3.60	N/A	663.5	294.7	39.0	7.9
2016	B	5.30	3.53	70.4	675.5	281.3	158.0	21.0
2015	B	5.45	3.61	66.1	653.2	286.6	158.1	27.6
2014	B	5.60	3.71	67.0	650.4	288.9	153.7	27.6
2013	B	5.67	3.77	68.8	641.7	288.1	149.2	27.7
2012	B	5.82	3.86	72.7	643.1	291.1	147.7	26.4

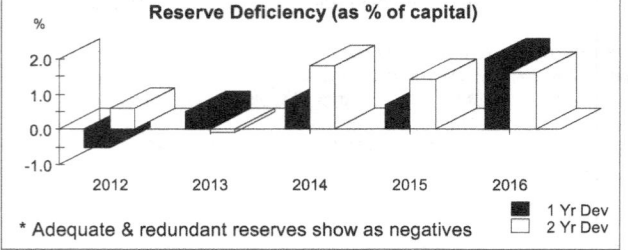

Reserve Deficiency (as % of capital)

* Adequate & redundant reserves show as negatives   ■ 1 Yr Dev   □ 2 Yr Dev

UNITED EDUCATORS INS A RECIP RRG   B   Good

Major Rating Factors: Good overall results on stability tests (6.0 on a scale of 0 to 10). The largest net exposure for one risk is acceptable at 2.7% of capital. Strong long-term capitalization index (7.3) based on excellent current risk adjusted capital (severe and moderate loss scenarios), despite some fluctuation in capital levels.

Other Rating Factors: Excellent profitability (8.0) with operating gains in each of the last five years. Excellent liquidity (7.3) with ample operational cash flow and liquid investments.

Principal Business: Other liability (100%).

Principal Investments: Investment grade bonds (82%), misc. investments (17%), and non investment grade bonds (1%).

Investments in Affiliates: None

Group Affiliation: None

Licensed in: All states, the District of Columbia and Puerto Rico

Commenced Business: March 1987

Address: 76 St Paul Street Suite 500, Burlington, VT 05401-4477

Phone: (301) 907-4908   **Domicile State:** VT   **NAIC Code:** 10020

Data Date	Rating	RACR #1	RACR #2	Loss Ratio %	Total Assets ($mil)	Capital ($mil)	Net Premium ($mil)	Net Income ($mil)
3-17	B	1.59	1.23	N/A	878.3	292.5	35.3	6.0
3-16	B-	1.68	1.35	N/A	852.8	295.1	36.1	7.5
2016	B	1.60	1.24	78.3	903.2	291.2	140.9	22.4
2015	C+	1.63	1.32	78.2	874.5	284.3	144.6	23.4
2014	C	1.74	1.41	77.3	820.4	281.8	139.0	26.1
2013	C	1.68	1.35	76.9	759.7	254.5	123.7	37.7
2012	C	1.81	1.47	83.6	727.9	253.3	110.6	19.7

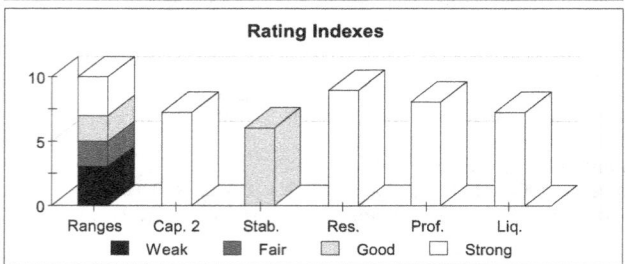

Rating Indexes

Ranges   Cap. 2   Stab.   Res.   Prof.   Liq.

■ Weak   ■ Fair   □ Good   □ Strong

UNITED FARM FAMILY MUTUAL INS CO   B   Good

Major Rating Factors: Good liquidity (5.5 on a scale of 0 to 10) with sufficient resources (cash flows and marketable investments) to handle a spike in claims. Fair profitability index (4.9) with operating losses during 2012.

Other Rating Factors: Fair overall results on stability tests (4.5) including weak results on operational trends. Strong long-term capitalization index (8.7) based on excellent current risk adjusted capital (severe and moderate loss scenarios). Moreover, capital levels have been consistent in recent years. Ample reserve history (8.2) that helps to protect the company against sharp claims increases.

Principal Business: Auto liability (24%), homeowners multiple peril (24%), auto physical damage (21%), farmowners multiple peril (15%), commercial multiple peril (8%), allied lines (3%), and other lines (4%).

Principal Investments: Investment grade bonds (78%) and misc. investments (22%).

Investments in Affiliates: 3%

Group Affiliation: Indiana Farm Bureau Inc

Licensed in: IN, OH

Commenced Business: February 1935

Address: 225 South East Street, Indianapolis, IN 46202-4056

Phone: (317) 692-7200   **Domicile State:** IN   **NAIC Code:** 15288

Data Date	Rating	RACR #1	RACR #2	Loss Ratio %	Total Assets ($mil)	Capital ($mil)	Net Premium ($mil)	Net Income ($mil)
3-17	B	3.55	2.35	N/A	1,055.2	450.5	131.5	1.9
3-16	B	3.47	2.31	N/A	1,030.7	426.5	130.7	13.3
2016	B	3.54	2.38	69.7	1,056.6	447.9	544.4	32.9
2015	B	3.40	2.30	65.9	1,015.2	414.4	536.4	55.9
2014	B-	3.18	2.18	71.5	956.8	357.1	509.6	46.9
2013	B-	2.89	2.00	72.6	915.0	323.7	503.3	35.8
2012	C+	2.02	1.35	96.9	877.5	241.4	521.2	-56.2

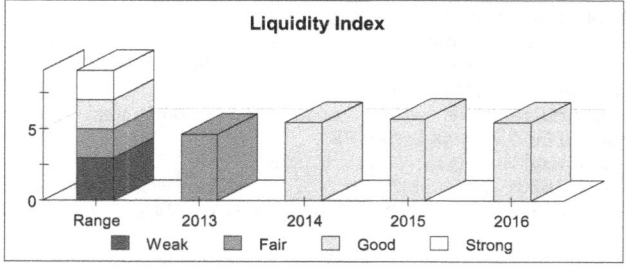

Liquidity Index

Range   2013   2014   2015   2016

■ Weak   ■ Fair   □ Good   □ Strong

UNITED FINANCIAL CASUALTY CO   B-   Good

Major Rating Factors: Fair overall results on stability tests (4.5 on a scale of 0 to 10) including potential drain of affiliation with Progressive Group. History of adequate reserve strength (6.5) as reserves have been consistently at an acceptable level.

Other Rating Factors: Good liquidity (6.0) with sufficient resources (cash flows and marketable investments) to handle a spike in claims. Strong long-term capitalization index (7.7) based on excellent current risk adjusted capital (severe and moderate loss scenarios). Moreover, capital levels have been consistent in recent years. Excellent profitability (9.4) with operating gains in each of the last five years. Return on equity has been excellent over the last five years averaging 21.1%.

Principal Business: Auto liability (64%), auto physical damage (33%), and inland marine (2%).

Principal Investments: Investment grade bonds (83%), misc. investments (16%), and non investment grade bonds (1%).

Investments in Affiliates: None

Group Affiliation: Progressive Group

Licensed in: All states except PR

Commenced Business: August 1984

Address: 6300 WILSON MILLS ROAD W33, Cleveland, OH 44143-2182

Phone: (440) 461-5000   **Domicile State:** OH   **NAIC Code:** 11770

Data Date	Rating	RACR #1	RACR #2	Loss Ratio %	Total Assets ($mil)	Capital ($mil)	Net Premium ($mil)	Net Income ($mil)
3-17	B-	2.22	1.54	N/A	2,973.9	711.6	499.0	45.4
3-16	B-	2.04	1.43	N/A	2,633.2	587.5	440.5	29.7
2016	B-	2.13	1.50	74.1	2,896.7	664.4	1,981.2	114.5
2015	B-	1.98	1.40	70.0	2,507.6	554.7	1,742.6	146.4
2014	C+	2.07	1.49	69.3	2,301.1	546.1	1,619.0	162.0
2013	C+	1.96	1.41	75.3	2,137.9	492.0	1,501.7	60.4
2012	C+	2.12	1.48	72.8	1,815.9	391.3	1,173.2	74.0

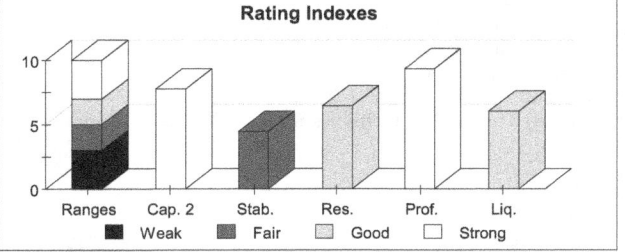

Rating Indexes

UNITED FIRE & CAS CO   B   Good

Major Rating Factors: Good overall results on stability tests (5.5 on a scale of 0 to 10) despite potential drain of affiliation with United Fire & Casualty Group. Good liquidity (6.7) with sufficient resources (cash flows and marketable investments) to handle a spike in claims.

Other Rating Factors: Strong long-term capitalization index (7.3) based on excellent current risk adjusted capital (severe and moderate loss scenarios). Moreover, capital levels have been consistent in recent years. Ample reserve history (8.3) that helps to protect the company against sharp claims increases. Excellent profitability (8.4) with operating gains in each of the last five years.

Principal Business: Other liability (20%), auto liability (19%), workers compensation (13%), auto physical damage (9%), products liability (8%), allied lines (7%), and other lines (23%).

Principal Investments: Misc. investments (57%), investment grade bonds (40%), real estate (2%), and cash (1%).

Investments in Affiliates: 34%

Group Affiliation: United Fire & Casualty Group

Licensed in: All states except DE, NH, PR

Commenced Business: January 1947

Address: 118 SECOND AVENUE SE, Cedar Rapids, IA 52401

Phone: (319) 399-5700   **Domicile State:** IA   **NAIC Code:** 13021

Data Date	Rating	RACR #1	RACR #2	Loss Ratio %	Total Assets ($mil)	Capital ($mil)	Net Premium ($mil)	Net Income ($mil)
3-17	B	1.40	1.21	N/A	1,950.1	793.5	151.3	8.3
3-16	B	1.31	1.13	N/A	1,809.8	731.9	140.9	9.1
2016	B	1.38	1.20	69.8	1,893.9	770.9	617.6	44.1
2015	B	1.31	1.13	61.2	1,777.9	722.4	564.5	37.9
2014	B	1.19	1.02	66.7	1,661.9	685.9	523.1	33.0
2013	B	1.18	1.01	63.3	1,558.7	665.8	469.8	58.9
2012	B	1.14	1.04	70.5	1,434.1	586.0	426.0	19.0

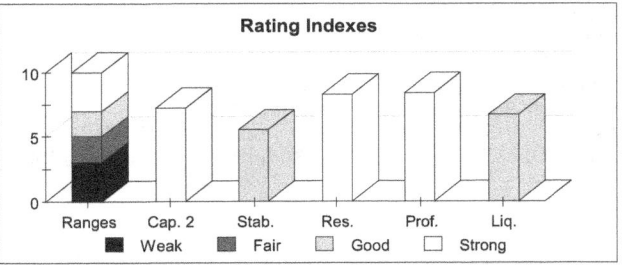

Rating Indexes

UNITED GUAR RESIDENTIAL INS CO OF NC   C+   Fair

Major Rating Factors: Fair profitability index (3.5 on a scale of 0 to 10) with operating losses during 2012. Return on equity has been fair, averaging 10.0% over the past five years. Fair overall results on stability tests (4.6) including weak results on operational trends.

Other Rating Factors: History of adequate reserve strength (5.8) as reserves have been consistently at an acceptable level. Strong long-term capitalization index (7.1) based on excellent current risk adjusted capital (severe and moderate loss scenarios), despite some fluctuation in capital levels. Superior liquidity (9.8) with ample operational cash flow and liquid investments.

Principal Business: Credit (100%).

Principal Investments: Misc. investments (94%), investment grade bonds (5%), and cash (1%).

Investments in Affiliates: 85%

Group Affiliation: American International Group

Licensed in: All states except AZ, CA, NY, WY, PR

Commenced Business: May 1963

Address: 230 NORTH ELM STREET, Greensboro, NC 27401

Phone: (336) 373-0232   **Domicile State:** NC   **NAIC Code:** 16667

Data Date	Rating	RACR #1	RACR #2	Loss Ratio %	Total Assets ($mil)	Capital ($mil)	Net Premium ($mil)	Net Income ($mil)
3-17	C+	1.29	1.28	N/A	331.6	312.8	5.7	6.4
3-16	C+	1.35	1.33	N/A	402.8	381.0	7.3	85.2
2016	C+	1.33	1.31	N/A	338.5	320.8	27.1	105.3
2015	C+	1.59	1.57	N/A	477.2	449.9	38.3	23.9
2014	C	1.48	1.46	N/A	461.1	432.3	75.6	62.6
2013	C	1.23	1.21	31.2	448.5	377.9	92.5	40.0
2012	C-	1.06	1.02	174.2	472.2	319.8	97.2	-40.4

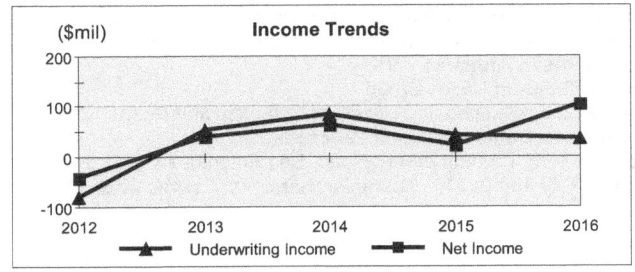

Income Trends

UNITED GUARANTY MORTGAGE INDEM CO

C+   **Fair**

Major Rating Factors: Fair profitability index (4.7 on a scale of 0 to 10) with operating losses during 2012. Return on equity has been low, averaging 0.6% over the past five years. Fair overall results on stability tests (4.6) including weak results on operational trends and negative cash flow from operations for 2016.

Other Rating Factors: History of adequate reserve strength (5.0) as reserves have been consistently at an acceptable level. Strong long-term capitalization index (10.0) based on excellent current risk adjusted capital (severe and moderate loss scenarios), despite some fluctuation in capital levels. Excellent liquidity (7.0) with ample operational cash flow and liquid investments.

Principal Business: Mortgage guaranty (100%).

Principal Investments: Investment grade bonds (99%) and misc. investments (1%).

Investments in Affiliates: None

Group Affiliation: American International Group

Licensed in: All states except IL, WY, PR

Commenced Business: July 1972

Address: 230 NORTH ELM STREET, Greensboro, NC 27401

Phone: (336) 373-0232   **Domicile State:** NC   **NAIC Code:** 26999

Data Date	Rating	RACR #1	RACR #2	Loss Ratio %	Total Assets ($mil)	Capital ($mil)	Net Premium ($mil)	Net Income ($mil)
3-17	C+	7.27	5.53	N/A	438.7	290.7	4.5	4.0
3-16	C+	6.15	4.68	N/A	434.6	289.4	3.6	7.3
2016	C+	7.65	5.82	41.8	445.2	303.7	18.5	17.9
2015	C+	5.13	3.94	47.6	439.5	283.9	29.4	15.2
2014	C+	1.65	1.29	49.3	284.1	115.1	37.7	13.9
2013	C+	1.41	1.10	71.1	283.8	113.2	44.2	5.4
2012	C+	1.54	1.15	N/A	309.8	109.4	11.4	-28.6

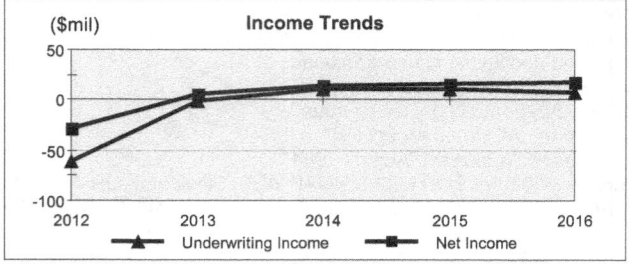

Income Trends

UNITED GUARANTY RESIDENTIAL INS CO

C+   **Fair**

Major Rating Factors: Fair reserve development (4.4 on a scale of 0 to 10) as reserves have generally been sufficient to cover claims. In 2013, the two year reserve development was 19% deficient. Fair profitability index (3.5) with operating losses during 2012. Return on equity has been fair, averaging 14.7% over the past five years.

Other Rating Factors: Fair overall results on stability tests (4.8) including weak results on operational trends. Good liquidity (6.7) with sufficient resources (cash flows and marketable investments) to handle a spike in claims. Strong long-term capitalization index (8.6) based on excellent current risk adjusted capital (severe and moderate loss scenarios), despite some fluctuation in capital levels.

Principal Business: Mortgage guaranty (100%).

Principal Investments: Investment grade bonds (81%), misc. investments (18%), and cash (1%).

Investments in Affiliates: 9%

Group Affiliation: American International Group

Licensed in: All states, the District of Columbia and Puerto Rico

Commenced Business: December 1963

Address: 230 NORTH ELM STREET, Greensboro, NC 27401

Phone: (336) 373-0232   **Domicile State:** NC   **NAIC Code:** 15873

Data Date	Rating	RACR #1	RACR #2	Loss Ratio %	Total Assets ($mil)	Capital ($mil)	Net Premium ($mil)	Net Income ($mil)
3-17	C+	2.59	2.17	N/A	3,389.7	1,192.3	135.6	104.1
3-16	C	2.22	1.79	N/A	3,112.8	1,054.1	150.5	67.5
2016	C+	2.53	2.14	17.8	3,307.9	1,186.5	548.8	335.2
2015	C	2.76	2.22	20.7	3,550.4	1,351.3	564.8	314.6
2014	C-	2.58	2.05	27.4	3,247.7	1,383.8	791.3	254.6
2013	D+	2.58	2.01	64.7	3,059.3	1,465.7	799.9	88.4
2012	D+	1.82	1.46	116.6	2,930.3	1,383.0	576.6	-100.8

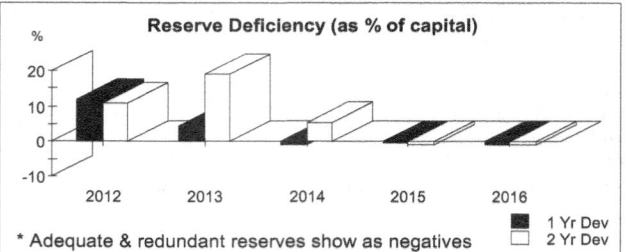

Reserve Deficiency (as % of capital)

* Adequate & redundant reserves show as negatives

UNITED SERVICES AUTOMOBILE ASN *

B+   **Good**

Major Rating Factors: Good liquidity (6.7 on a scale of 0 to 10) with sufficient resources (cash flows and marketable investments) to handle a spike in claims. Good overall results on stability tests (5.2) despite weak results on operational trends.

Other Rating Factors: Strong long-term capitalization index (7.5) based on excellent current risk adjusted capital (severe and moderate loss scenarios). Moreover, capital levels have been consistent in recent years. Ample reserve history (7.3) that can protect against increases in claims costs. Excellent profitability (7.7) with operating gains in each of the last five years.

Principal Business: Homeowners multiple peril (34%), auto liability (31%), auto physical damage (26%), allied lines (3%), other liability (2%), inland marine (2%), and fire (1%).

Principal Investments: Misc. investments (71%), investment grade bonds (26%), real estate (4%), and non investment grade bonds (1%).

Investments in Affiliates: 59%

Group Affiliation: USAA Group

Licensed in: All states, the District of Columbia and Puerto Rico

Commenced Business: June 1922

Address: 9800 Fredericksburg Road, San Antonio, TX 78288

Phone: (210) 498-2211   **Domicile State:** TX   **NAIC Code:** 25941

Data Date	Rating	RACR #1	RACR #2	Loss Ratio %	Total Assets ($mil)	Capital ($mil)	Net Premium ($mil)	Net Income ($mil)
3-17	B+	1.48	1.41	N/A	33,965.5	25,653.7	1,782.3	278.7
3-16	B+	1.49	1.42	N/A	32,311.5	24,533.9	1,743.2	-110.3
2016	B+	1.47	1.40	90.1	33,796.5	25,341.0	7,038.1	373.4
2015	A-	1.49	1.42	79.3	32,549.4	24,363.6	6,812.7	757.2
2014	A-	1.48	1.39	78.7	30,991.0	22,854.4	6,640.0	850.9
2013	A+	1.48	1.40	73.4	28,667.0	20,754.5	6,189.3	922.6
2012	A+	1.47	1.39	81.9	25,880.7	18,362.9	5,721.4	437.2

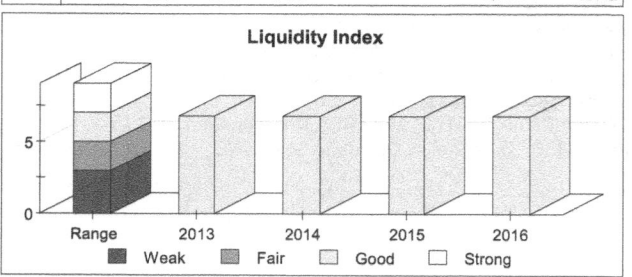

Liquidity Index

UNITED STATES FIDELITY & GUARANTY CO   C-   Fair

Major Rating Factors: Weak profitability index (1.9 on a scale of 0 to 10). Fair expense controls. Return on equity has been fair, averaging 11.5% over the past five years. Fair overall results on stability tests (3.3) including weak results on operational trends.

Other Rating Factors: Good liquidity (6.6) with sufficient resources (cash flows and marketable investments) to handle a spike in claims. Strong long-term capitalization index (8.5) based on excellent current risk adjusted capital (severe and moderate loss scenarios), despite some fluctuation in capital levels. Ample reserve history (7.7) that can protect against increases in claims costs.

Principal Business: Surety (80%) and workers compensation (19%).

Principal Investments: Investment grade bonds (94%), misc. investments (5%), and non investment grade bonds (1%).

Investments in Affiliates: 4%

Group Affiliation: Travelers Companies Inc

Licensed in: All states, the District of Columbia and Puerto Rico

Commenced Business: August 1896

Address: ONE TOWER SQUARE, Hartford, CT 06183

Phone: (860) 277-0111   **Domicile State:** CT   **NAIC Code:** 25887

Data Date	Rating	RACR #1	RACR #2	Loss Ratio %	Total Assets ($mil)	Capital ($mil)	Net Premium ($mil)	Net Income ($mil)
3-17	C-	3.01	2.01	N/A	3,291.3	1,068.3	237.9	23.7
3-16	C	4.07	2.65	N/A	3,662.4	1,439.9	229.1	29.6
2016	C-	3.01	2.02	63.4	3,252.1	1,043.3	960.1	129.7
2015	C	4.08	2.67	58.7	3,565.3	1,408.9	916.4	284.3
2014	B	7.00	4.58	60.5	4,677.4	2,466.2	890.3	206.8
2013	B	7.16	4.72	60.9	4,653.9	2,484.4	888.1	224.2
2012	B	7.64	5.08	68.4	4,797.2	2,627.5	862.6	216.7

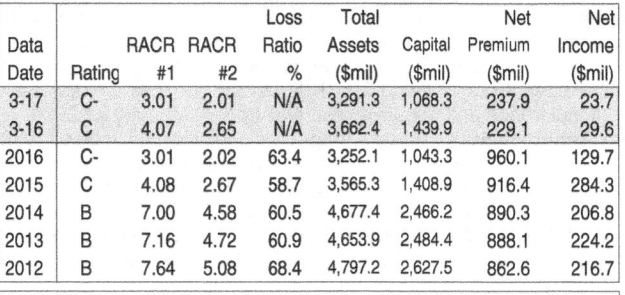

Income Trends

UNIVERSAL INS CO (PR)   B-   Good

Major Rating Factors: Fair overall results on stability tests (4.2 on a scale of 0 to 10) including potential drain of affiliation with Universal Ins Co Group and weak results on operational trends. History of adequate reserve strength (6.1) as reserves have been consistently at an acceptable level.

Other Rating Factors: Good overall profitability index (6.0). Fair expense controls. Return on equity has been fair, averaging 9.0% over the past five years. Good liquidity (6.6) with sufficient resources (cash flows and marketable investments) to handle a spike in claims. Strong long-term capitalization index (7.5) based on excellent current risk adjusted capital (severe and moderate loss scenarios), despite some fluctuation in capital levels.

Principal Business: Auto physical damage (45%), commercial multiple peril (18%), homeowners multiple peril (11%), auto liability (9%), other liability (6%), aggregate write-ins for other lines of business (4%), and other lines (7%).

Principal Investments: Investment grade bonds (50%), misc. investments (34%), real estate (8%), cash (4%), and non investment grade bonds (4%).

Investments in Affiliates: 18%

Group Affiliation: Universal Ins Co Group

Licensed in: PR

Commenced Business: January 1972

Address: Metro Office Park St 1 Lot 10, Guaynabo, PR 00968

Phone: (787) 706-7155   **Domicile State:** PR   **NAIC Code:** 31704

Data Date	Rating	RACR #1	RACR #2	Loss Ratio %	Total Assets ($mil)	Capital ($mil)	Net Premium ($mil)	Net Income ($mil)
3-17	B-	1.74	1.35	N/A	858.1	267.4	51.8	2.4
3-16	B-	1.91	1.44	N/A	806.8	261.5	49.2	3.4
2016	B-	1.74	1.36	66.2	838.5	259.4	203.7	14.7
2015	B-	1.93	1.47	64.9	770.8	251.3	194.4	17.3
2014	B-	3.20	2.13	66.4	805.5	253.1	196.3	23.4
2013	B-	3.46	2.26	69.4	802.8	253.1	202.7	38.1
2012	B-	3.56	2.32	68.4	778.3	258.9	208.5	25.2

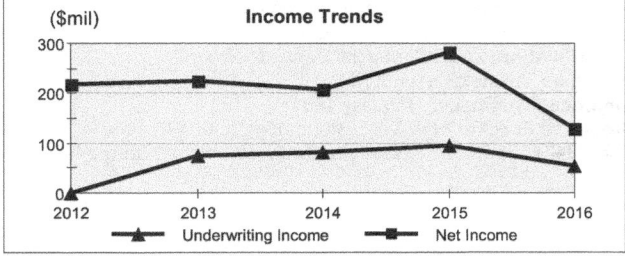

Rating Indexes

UNIVERSAL P&C INS CO   D   Weak

Major Rating Factors: Weak overall results on stability tests (2.0 on a scale of 0 to 10). History of adequate reserve strength (6.7) as reserves have been consistently at an acceptable level.

Other Rating Factors: Good overall profitability index (5.2) despite operating losses during 2012. Return on equity has been good over the last five years, averaging 11.4%. Good liquidity (6.3) with sufficient resources (cash flows and marketable investments) to handle a spike in claims. Strong long-term capitalization index (7.7) based on excellent current risk adjusted capital (severe and moderate loss scenarios). Moreover, capital levels have been consistent in recent years.

Principal Business: Homeowners multiple peril (92%), allied lines (6%), and fire (2%).

Principal Investments: Investment grade bonds (70%), cash (14%), misc. investments (13%), and real estate (3%).

Investments in Affiliates: None

Group Affiliation: Universal Insurance Holdings Inc

Licensed in: AL, DE, FL, GA, HI, IN, IA, MD, MA, MI, MN, NH, NJ, NY, NC, PA, SC, VA, WV

Commenced Business: December 1997

Address: 1110 West Commercial Boulevard, Fort Lauderdale, FL 33309

Phone: (954) 958-1200   **Domicile State:** FL   **NAIC Code:** 10861

Data Date	Rating	RACR #1	RACR #2	Loss Ratio %	Total Assets ($mil)	Capital ($mil)	Net Premium ($mil)	Net Income ($mil)
3-17	D	1.72	1.63	N/A	957.5	332.6	160.7	11.7
3-16	D	1.27	1.18	N/A	844.1	274.1	151.6	16.7
2016	D	1.63	1.40	49.9	889.3	313.8	652.3	57.7
2015	D	1.30	1.11	40.9	816.3	257.0	623.0	52.9
2014	D-	1.52	1.27	42.1	626.8	200.2	385.3	38.5
2013	E+	0.26	0.19	46.1	553.6	161.8	260.0	27.7
2012	E+	0.22	0.15	65.1	526.6	134.0	245.8	-25.5

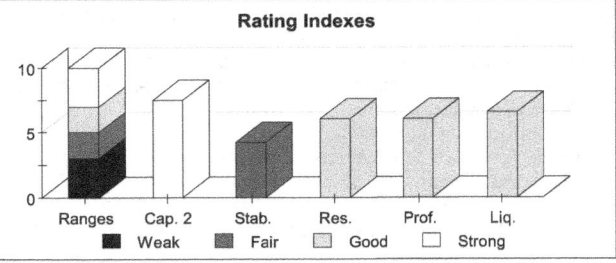

Rating Indexes

UNIVERSAL UNDERWRITERS INS CO   C+   Fair

Major Rating Factors: Fair profitability index (4.3 on a scale of 0 to 10) with operating losses during 2016. Return on equity has been low, averaging 1.8% over the past five years. Fair overall results on stability tests (4.7) including fair financial strength of affiliated Zurich Financial Services Group, weak results on operational trends and negative cash flow from operations for 2016.

Other Rating Factors: Strong long-term capitalization index (10.0) based on excellent current risk adjusted capital (severe and moderate loss scenarios), despite some fluctuation in capital levels. Excellent liquidity (7.0) with ample operational cash flow and liquid investments.

Principal Business: Auto physical damage (18%), other liability (17%), auto liability (13%), allied lines (3%), fire (2%), boiler & machinery (1%), and other lines (46%).

Principal Investments: Investment grade bonds (87%) and cash (15%).

Investments in Affiliates: 4%

Group Affiliation: Zurich Financial Services Group

Licensed in: All states except PR

Commenced Business: January 1982

Address: 1299 ZURICH WAY, Schaumburg, IL 60196-1056

Phone: (847) 605-6000   **Domicile State:** IL   **NAIC Code:** 41181

Data Date	Rating	RACR #1	RACR #2	Loss Ratio %	Total Assets ($mil)	Capital ($mil)	Net Premium ($mil)	Net Income ($mil)
3-17	C+	29.64	24.13	N/A	396.7	323.9	0.0	1.2
3-16	C+	10.06	9.09	N/A	508.6	342.9	0.0	1.4
2016	C+	30.25	25.02	0.0	328.9	322.6	0.0	-2.9
2015	C+	10.35	9.61	0.0	379.9	339.6	0.0	9.5
2014	C	10.14	8.78	0.0	363.8	338.9	0.0	8.6
2013	C	10.82	9.95	0.0	386.2	336.1	0.0	5.2
2012	C	11.63	10.69	0.0	385.4	341.7	0.0	10.4

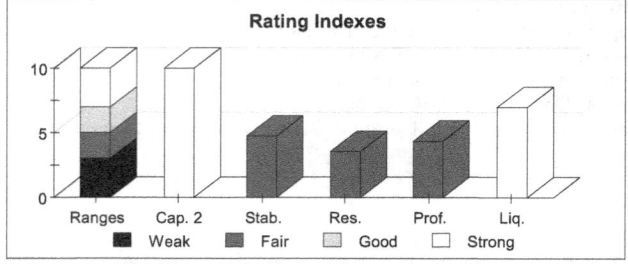

Rating Indexes

US FIRE INS CO   C   Fair

Major Rating Factors: Fair overall results on stability tests (3.7 on a scale of 0 to 10) including potential drain of affiliation with Fairfax Financial and weak results on operational trends. History of adequate reserve strength (5.8) as reserves have been consistently at an acceptable level.

Other Rating Factors: Good profitability index (5.0) despite operating losses during 2012, 2013 and the first three months of 2017. Return on equity has been low, averaging 3.0% over the past five years. Good liquidity (6.9) with sufficient resources (cash flows and marketable investments) to handle a spike in claims. Strong long-term capitalization index (7.0) based on excellent current risk adjusted capital (severe and moderate loss scenarios), despite some fluctuation in capital levels.

Principal Business: Group accident & health (30%), inland marine (20%), other liability (11%), workers compensation (11%), auto liability (9%), commercial multiple peril (6%), and other lines (14%).

Principal Investments: Investment grade bonds (54%), misc. investments (37%), cash (4%), non investment grade bonds (3%), and real estate (2%).

Investments in Affiliates: 22%

Group Affiliation: Fairfax Financial

Licensed in: All states, the District of Columbia and Puerto Rico

Commenced Business: April 1824

Address: 1209 ORANGE STREET, Wilmington, DE 19801

Phone: (973) 490-6600   **Domicile State:** DE   **NAIC Code:** 21113

Data Date	Rating	RACR #1	RACR #2	Loss Ratio %	Total Assets ($mil)	Capital ($mil)	Net Premium ($mil)	Net Income ($mil)
3-17	C	1.31	1.00	N/A	3,994.4	1,233.0	338.5	-19.5
3-16	C	1.39	1.08	N/A	3,802.6	1,158.0	321.0	72.3
2016	C	1.35	1.04	63.7	3,949.6	1,218.9	1,370.7	32.3
2015	C	1.45	1.14	64.1	3,736.1	1,178.0	1,262.9	94.5
2014	C	1.62	1.14	67.5	3,248.6	898.6	1,025.1	195.7
2013	C	1.14	0.87	71.4	3,154.5	812.1	971.7	-75.7
2012	C	1.42	1.07	81.2	2,924.1	881.7	810.0	-50.1

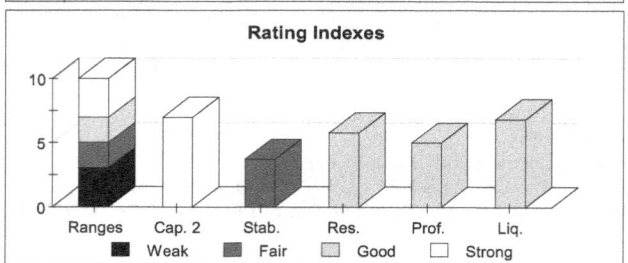

Rating Indexes

US LIABILITY INS CO   C   Fair

Major Rating Factors: Fair overall results on stability tests (4.3 on a scale of 0 to 10) including weak results on operational trends. Strong long-term capitalization index (7.1) based on excellent current risk adjusted capital (severe and moderate loss scenarios), despite some fluctuation in capital levels.

Other Rating Factors: Ample reserve history (8.7) that helps to protect the company against sharp claims increases. Excellent profitability (7.8) with operating gains in each of the last five years. Excellent liquidity (7.3) with ample operational cash flow and liquid investments.

Principal Business: Other liability (82%), fire (17%), products liability (1%), and inland marine (1%).

Principal Investments: Misc. investments (82%) and investment grade bonds (18%).

Investments in Affiliates: 54%

Group Affiliation: Berkshire-Hathaway

Licensed in: All states except ND, PR

Commenced Business: May 1951

Address: 1190 Devon Park Drive, Wayne, PA 19087

Phone: (800) 523-5545   **Domicile State:** PA   **NAIC Code:** 25895

Data Date	Rating	RACR #1	RACR #2	Loss Ratio %	Total Assets ($mil)	Capital ($mil)	Net Premium ($mil)	Net Income ($mil)
3-17	C	1.23	1.09	N/A	1,058.6	684.3	50.6	2.8
3-16	C	1.28	1.16	N/A	866.2	533.5	46.5	2.6
2016	C	1.19	1.07	38.8	1,015.3	647.3	204.3	25.2
2015	C	1.31	1.18	37.7	897.2	559.2	187.2	24.4
2014	C	1.35	1.22	51.1	885.9	563.3	169.7	4.6
2013	C	1.50	1.35	47.9	811.3	537.5	144.8	25.0
2012	C	1.52	1.31	47.2	675.5	441.1	118.5	15.7

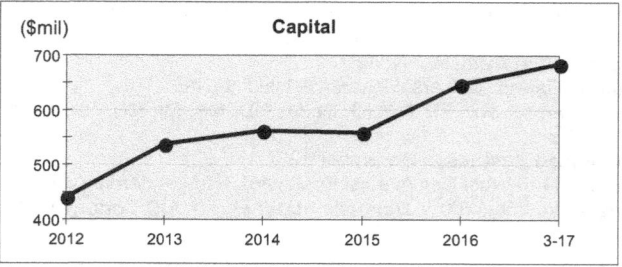

Capital

US SPECIALTY INS CO   B-   Good

Major Rating Factors: Fair profitability index (3.8 on a scale of 0 to 10). Fair expense controls. Return on equity has been fair, averaging 19.3% over the past five years. Fair overall results on stability tests (3.5) including weak results on operational trends. The largest net exposure for one risk is high at 4.9% of capital.

Other Rating Factors: History of adequate reserve strength (6.9) as reserves have been consistently at an acceptable level. Good liquidity (6.7) with sufficient resources (cash flows and marketable investments) to handle a spike in claims. Strong long-term capitalization index (7.8) based on excellent current risk adjusted capital (severe and moderate loss scenarios), despite some fluctuation in capital levels.

Principal Business: Other liability (59%), surety (12%), aircraft (8%), commercial multiple peril (7%), credit (3%), ocean marine (2%), and other lines (9%).

Principal Investments: Investment grade bonds (79%), misc. investments (11%), non investment grade bonds (9%), and cash (1%).

Investments in Affiliates: None

Group Affiliation: HCC Ins Holdings Inc

Licensed in: All states except PR

Commenced Business: April 1987

Address: 13403 Northwest Freeway, Houston, TX 77040

Phone: (713) 462-1000   **Domicile State:** TX   **NAIC Code:** 29599

Data Date	Rating	RACR #1	RACR #2	Loss Ratio %	Total Assets ($mil)	Capital ($mil)	Net Premium ($mil)	Net Income ($mil)
3-17	B-	2.46	1.58	N/A	1,826.5	547.2	113.2	28.8
3-16	B-	2.54	1.67	N/A	1,797.9	545.6	108.0	19.1
2016	B-	2.37	1.53	59.7	1,792.1	518.2	464.1	76.2
2015	B-	2.47	1.63	55.7	1,792.8	525.7	436.2	94.1
2014	B-	2.71	1.76	47.0	1,890.8	577.1	420.1	133.2
2013	B-	2.56	1.66	51.5	1,928.6	580.3	440.5	124.8
2012	B-	2.58	1.71	59.5	2,056.0	552.5	440.2	104.9

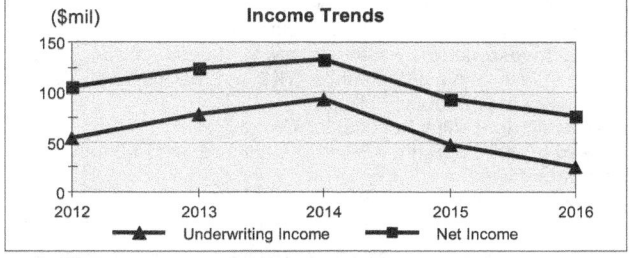
Income Trends

USAA CASUALTY INS CO *   A-   Excellent

Major Rating Factors: Strong long-term capitalization index (8.6 on a scale of 0 to 10) based on excellent current risk adjusted capital (severe and moderate loss scenarios). Furthermore, this high level of risk adjusted capital has been consistently maintained in previous years. Ample reserve history (7.7) that can protect against increases in claims costs.

Other Rating Factors: Excellent profitability (7.1) despite modest operating losses during 2016. Good liquidity (5.0) with sufficient resources (cash flows and marketable investments) to handle a spike in claims. Good overall results on stability tests (5.7) despite weak results on operational trends.

Principal Business: Auto liability (37%), homeowners multiple peril (30%), auto physical damage (28%), inland marine (2%), allied lines (2%), other liability (1%), and fire (1%).

Principal Investments: Investment grade bonds (69%), misc. investments (28%), non investment grade bonds (2%), and cash (1%).

Investments in Affiliates: 9%

Group Affiliation: USAA Group

Licensed in: All states except PR

Commenced Business: December 1990

Address: 9800 Fredericksburg Road, San Antonio, TX 78288

Phone: (210) 498-1411   **Domicile State:** TX   **NAIC Code:** 25968

Data Date	Rating	RACR #1	RACR #2	Loss Ratio %	Total Assets ($mil)	Capital ($mil)	Net Premium ($mil)	Net Income ($mil)
3-17	A-	2.72	2.06	N/A	10,235.4	4,644.9	1,600.9	61.8
3-16	A-	3.04	2.32	N/A	9,629.5	4,504.2	1,431.3	7.3
2016	A-	2.63	2.03	91.8	10,315.4	4,489.8	6,471.9	-36.6
2015	A-	2.99	2.31	86.0	9,848.0	4,451.8	5,838.6	183.3
2014	A-	2.86	2.16	81.3	8,699.0	4,392.2	4,836.8	338.4
2013	A+	2.90	2.20	77.4	8,445.8	4,168.8	4,756.9	319.9
2012	A+	2.98	2.29	83.6	7,773.4	3,673.3	4,385.4	151.9

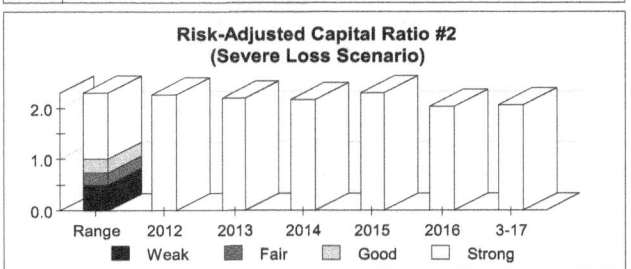
Risk-Adjusted Capital Ratio #2 (Severe Loss Scenario)

USAA GENERAL INDEMNITY CO *   B+   Good

Major Rating Factors: Good overall profitability index (6.0 on a scale of 0 to 10) despite operating losses during 2016. Return on equity has been fair, averaging 6.8% over the past five years. Good overall results on stability tests (5.0) despite weak results on operational trends and excessive premium growth.

Other Rating Factors: Strong long-term capitalization index (8.4) based on excellent current risk adjusted capital (severe and moderate loss scenarios). Moreover, capital levels have been consistent in recent years. Ample reserve history (8.6) that helps to protect the company against sharp claims increases. Vulnerable liquidity (2.7) as a spike in claims may stretch capacity.

Principal Business: Auto liability (38%), auto physical damage (33%), homeowners multiple peril (21%), allied lines (5%), inland marine (1%), and fire (1%).

Principal Investments: Investment grade bonds (73%), misc. investments (24%), and non investment grade bonds (3%).

Investments in Affiliates: None

Group Affiliation: USAA Group

Licensed in: All states, the District of Columbia and Puerto Rico

Commenced Business: August 1972

Address: 9800 Fredericksburg Road, San Antonio, TX 78288

Phone: (210) 498-1411   **Domicile State:** TX   **NAIC Code:** 18600

Data Date	Rating	RACR #1	RACR #2	Loss Ratio %	Total Assets ($mil)	Capital ($mil)	Net Premium ($mil)	Net Income ($mil)
3-17	B+	2.58	1.90	N/A	4,214.9	1,520.5	766.2	16.1
3-16	B+	2.79	2.06	N/A	3,558.6	1,317.3	610.1	2.9
2016	B+	2.58	1.95	91.7	4,001.4	1,482.0	2,752.8	-23.1
2015	B+	2.78	2.10	85.9	3,503.7	1,303.6	2,289.9	66.0
2014	B+	1.92	1.42	81.2	2,933.6	1,096.7	2,176.6	108.4
2013	B+	1.99	1.53	77.3	2,256.6	835.6	1,633.0	117.0
2012	B+	2.01	1.59	83.2	1,676.2	580.8	1,173.6	42.8

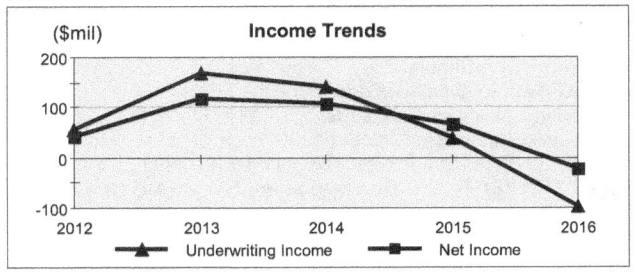
Income Trends

UTICA MUTUAL INS CO   B-   Good

Major Rating Factors: Fair overall results on stability tests (4.6 on a scale of 0 to 10) including potential drain of affiliation with Utica National Ins Group and weak results on operational trends. The largest net exposure for one risk is conservative at 1.1% of capital. History of adequate reserve strength (6.4) as reserves have been consistently at an acceptable level.

Other Rating Factors: Good overall profitability index (6.7) with small operating losses during 2012. Good liquidity (6.8) with sufficient resources (cash flows and marketable investments) to handle a spike in claims. Strong long-term capitalization index (8.2) based on excellent current risk adjusted capital (severe and moderate loss scenarios). Moreover, capital levels have been consistent in recent years.

Principal Business: Other liability (26%), workers compensation (23%), auto liability (19%), commercial multiple peril (19%), auto physical damage (8%), homeowners multiple peril (3%), and other lines (3%).

Principal Investments: Investment grade bonds (68%), misc. investments (26%), non investment grade bonds (5%), and real estate (1%).

Investments in Affiliates: 11%

Group Affiliation: Utica National Ins Group

Licensed in: All states, the District of Columbia and Puerto Rico

Commenced Business: July 1914

Address: 180 GENESEE STREET, New Hartford, NY 13413

Phone: (315) 734-2000   **Domicile State:** NY   **NAIC Code:** 25976

Data Date	Rating	RACR #1	RACR #2	Loss Ratio %	Total Assets ($mil)	Capital ($mil)	Net Premium ($mil)	Net Income ($mil)
3-17	B-	2.44	1.80	N/A	2,393.6	882.9	183.9	5.2
3-16	B-	2.27	1.69	N/A	2,358.7	818.9	173.5	-0.3
2016	B-	2.44	1.82	65.5	2,382.3	866.1	745.1	45.7
2015	B-	2.32	1.75	65.5	2,293.5	811.9	689.9	38.0
2014	B-	2.23	1.66	66.2	2,228.8	805.9	627.9	34.0
2013	B-	2.27	1.65	65.5	2,130.1	775.1	579.5	29.9
2012	B-	2.46	1.85	70.5	2,110.6	742.7	532.3	-5.9

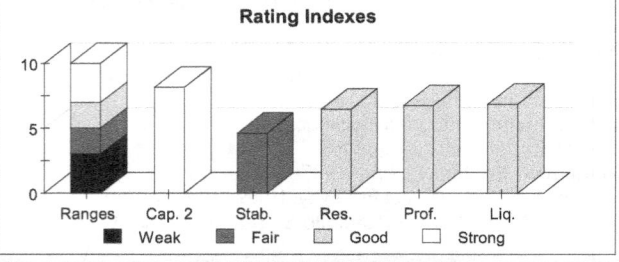

Rating Indexes

VERMONT MUTUAL INS CO   B-   Good

Major Rating Factors: Fair overall results on stability tests (4.2 on a scale of 0 to 10) including potential drain of affiliation with Vermont Mutual Group and weak results on operational trends. Good liquidity (6.7) with sufficient resources (cash flows and marketable investments) to handle a spike in claims.

Other Rating Factors: Strong long-term capitalization index (9.9) based on excellent current risk adjusted capital (severe and moderate loss scenarios). Moreover, capital levels have been consistent in recent years. Ample reserve history (8.8) that helps to protect the company against sharp claims increases. Excellent profitability (8.7) with operating gains in each of the last five years.

Principal Business: Homeowners multiple peril (42%), commercial multiple peril (23%), auto physical damage (11%), auto liability (11%), fire (5%), allied lines (4%), and other lines (4%).

Principal Investments: Investment grade bonds (75%), misc. investments (22%), cash (2%), and non investment grade bonds (1%).

Investments in Affiliates: 1%

Group Affiliation: Vermont Mutual Group

Licensed in: CT, ME, MA, NH, NY, RI, VT

Commenced Business: March 1828

Address: 89 State Street, Montpelier, VT 05602

Phone: (802) 223-2341   **Domicile State:** VT   **NAIC Code:** 26018

Data Date	Rating	RACR #1	RACR #2	Loss Ratio %	Total Assets ($mil)	Capital ($mil)	Net Premium ($mil)	Net Income ($mil)
3-17	B-	4.57	3.01	N/A	840.2	427.0	96.0	7.1
3-16	B-	4.56	3.03	N/A	771.6	382.3	88.7	5.6
2016	B-	4.61	3.00	51.1	843.3	416.0	384.0	34.3
2015	B-	4.62	3.03	64.7	753.7	376.5	358.5	13.1
2014	C+	4.49	2.91	51.1	753.1	367.8	343.3	43.2
2013	C+	4.12	2.64	54.0	690.7	328.2	313.7	25.9
2012	C+	4.19	2.77	51.0	614.2	283.8	292.3	35.0

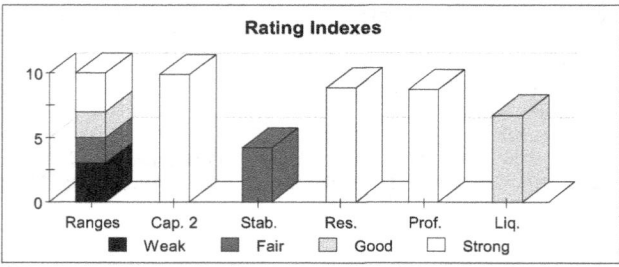

Rating Indexes

VIGILANT INS CO   B   Good

Major Rating Factors: Fair overall results on stability tests (4.6 on a scale of 0 to 10) including weak results on operational trends. The largest net exposure for one risk is conservative at 1.4% of capital. Strong long-term capitalization index (10.0) based on excellent current risk adjusted capital (severe and moderate loss scenarios). Moreover, capital levels have been consistent in recent years.

Other Rating Factors: Ample reserve history (7.6) that can protect against increases in claims costs. Excellent profitability (8.6) with operating gains in each of the last five years. Excellent liquidity (7.4) with ample operational cash flow and liquid investments.

Principal Business: Homeowners multiple peril (44%), workers compensation (17%), commercial multiple peril (14%), inland marine (7%), other liability (7%), auto physical damage (3%), and other lines (7%).

Principal Investments: Investment grade bonds (98%), misc. investments (1%), and non investment grade bonds (1%).

Investments in Affiliates: 7%

Group Affiliation: Chubb Limited

Licensed in: All states except PR

Commenced Business: October 1939

Address: 55 Water Street, New York, NY 10041-2899

Phone: (212) 827-4400   **Domicile State:** NY   **NAIC Code:** 20397

Data Date	Rating	RACR #1	RACR #2	Loss Ratio %	Total Assets ($mil)	Capital ($mil)	Net Premium ($mil)	Net Income ($mil)
3-17	B	9.16	7.13	N/A	529.7	320.3	7.4	3.1
3-16	B	8.53	6.33	N/A	527.1	307.5	9.8	4.9
2016	B	11.60	9.38	53.5	508.0	319.5	31.7	15.2
2015	B	9.88	7.48	56.5	514.8	306.2	48.9	22.0
2014	B	6.05	5.29	56.7	502.5	292.3	47.0	23.3
2013	B	5.10	4.72	52.7	467.9	264.9	45.1	16.7
2012	B	4.86	4.36	67.3	451.3	246.8	43.4	12.8

Chubb Limited Composite Group Rating: B- Largest Group Members	Assets ($mil)	Rating
FEDERAL INS CO	27371	B-
ACE AMERICAN INS CO	13036	B-
ACE PC INS CO	8192	B-
PACIFIC INDEMNITY CO	6555	B-
PACIFIC EMPLOYERS INS CO	3774	B-

VIRGINIA SURETY CO INC   B   Good

Major Rating Factors: History of adequate reserve strength (6.3 on a scale of 0 to 10) as reserves have been consistently at an acceptable level. Good liquidity (6.9) with sufficient resources (cash flows and marketable investments) to handle a spike in claims.

Other Rating Factors: Fair overall results on stability tests (4.3) including weak results on operational trends and negative cash flow from operations for 2016. Strong long-term capitalization index (10.0) based on excellent current risk adjusted capital (severe and moderate loss scenarios), despite some fluctuation in capital levels. Excellent profitability (8.2) with operating gains in each of the last five years. Return on equity has been excellent over the last five years averaging 16.7%.

Principal Business: Other liability (94%) and inland marine (1%).

Principal Investments: Investment grade bonds (83%), cash (10%), and misc. investments (7%).

Investments in Affiliates: 2%

Group Affiliation: Onex Corp

Licensed in: All states, the District of Columbia and Puerto Rico

Commenced Business: July 1982

Address: 175 W Jackson, Chicago, IL 60604

Phone: (312) 356-3000   **Domicile State:** IL   **NAIC Code:** 40827

Data Date	Rating	RACR #1	RACR #2	Loss Ratio %	Total Assets ($mil)	Capital ($mil)	Net Premium ($mil)	Net Income ($mil)
3-17	B	9.37	6.40	N/A	1,198.0	418.9	38.3	4.2
3-16	B	4.10	3.58	N/A	1,188.6	374.6	67.3	9.9
2016	B	9.25	6.42	62.8	1,169.8	410.0	45.9	64.9
2015	B	4.05	3.59	62.7	1,147.0	363.6	299.6	44.5
2014	C+	3.15	2.78	64.0	1,022.7	300.8	329.7	50.4
2013	C+	2.85	2.48	55.3	1,007.8	309.2	341.8	73.6
2012	C+	2.90	2.42	62.5	978.9	292.1	327.3	52.1

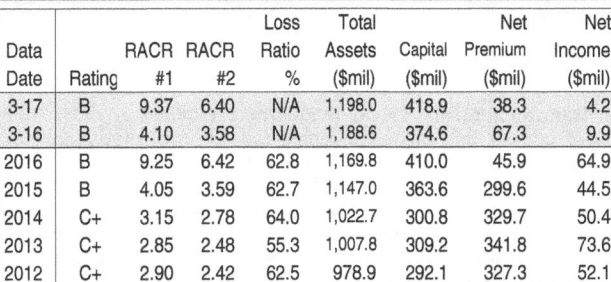

Reserve Deficiency (as % of capital)

* Adequate & redundant reserves show as negatives

■ 1 Yr Dev   □ 2 Yr Dev

WAWANESA GENERAL INS CO   B-   Good

Major Rating Factors: Fair reserve development (4.4 on a scale of 0 to 10) as reserves have generally been sufficient to cover claims. Fair profitability index (3.5) with operating losses during 2013, 2015 and 2016. Average return on equity over the last five years has been poor at -2.1%.

Other Rating Factors: Good overall results on stability tests (5.3) despite potential drain of affiliation with Wawanesa Ins Group and negative cash flow from operations for 2016. The largest net exposure for one risk is conservative at 1.5% of capital. Good liquidity (5.1) with sufficient resources (cash flows and marketable investments) to handle a spike in claims. Strong long-term capitalization index (8.2) based on excellent current risk adjusted capital (severe and moderate loss scenarios), despite some fluctuation in capital levels.

Principal Business: Auto liability (53%), auto physical damage (38%), homeowners multiple peril (8%), and earthquake (1%).

Principal Investments: Investment grade bonds (103%).

Investments in Affiliates: None

Group Affiliation: Wawanesa Ins Group

Licensed in: CA, OR

Commenced Business: January 1997

Address: 9050 FRIARS ROAD SUITE 420, San Diego, CA 92108-5865

Phone: (858) 874-5310   **Domicile State:** CA   **NAIC Code:** 10683

Data Date	Rating	RACR #1	RACR #2	Loss Ratio %	Total Assets ($mil)	Capital ($mil)	Net Premium ($mil)	Net Income ($mil)
3-17	B-	2.41	1.81	N/A	567.6	240.4	102.5	3.9
3-16	C+	1.93	1.47	N/A	593.8	194.5	91.6	-0.8
2016	B-	2.31	1.80	94.7	610.6	237.4	360.8	-6.7
2015	C+	1.89	1.50	102.5	590.3	195.5	365.9	-30.8
2014	C+	2.67	2.13	91.9	583.0	240.2	343.4	5.3
2013	C+	2.73	2.17	94.6	558.2	235.1	331.1	-1.3
2012	C+	2.86	2.27	93.8	542.9	235.8	314.4	10.2

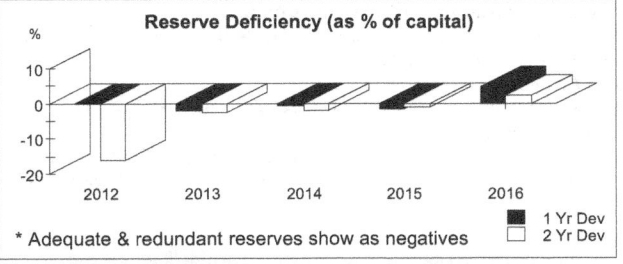

Reserve Deficiency (as % of capital)

* Adequate & redundant reserves show as negatives

■ 1 Yr Dev   □ 2 Yr Dev

WESCO INS CO   B-   Good

Major Rating Factors: Fair reserve development (4.9 on a scale of 0 to 10) as reserves have generally been sufficient to cover claims. Fair overall results on stability tests (4.7) including weak results on operational trends and excessive premium growth.

Other Rating Factors: Good long-term capitalization index (5.9) based on good current risk adjusted capital (moderate loss scenario). Moreover, capital levels have been consistent over the last several years. Good overall profitability index (5.7) despite operating losses during the first three months of 2017. Return on equity has been fair, averaging 6.1% over the past five years. Good liquidity (6.1) with sufficient resources (cash flows and marketable investments) to handle a spike in claims.

Principal Business: Workers compensation (33%), other liability (13%), auto liability (12%), commercial multiple peril (4%), fire (3%), allied lines (2%), and other lines (33%).

Principal Investments: Investment grade bonds (80%), misc. investments (18%), and non investment grade bonds (2%).

Investments in Affiliates: 7%

Group Affiliation: AmTrust Financial Services Inc

Licensed in: All states, the District of Columbia and Puerto Rico

Commenced Business: May 1963

Address: 2711 CENTERVILLE ROAD STE 400, Wilmington, DE 19808

Phone: (212) 220-7120   **Domicile State:** DE   **NAIC Code:** 25011

Data Date	Rating	RACR #1	RACR #2	Loss Ratio %	Total Assets ($mil)	Capital ($mil)	Net Premium ($mil)	Net Income ($mil)
3-17	B-	1.44	0.91	N/A	2,042.3	441.0	142.6	-5.0
3-16	B-	1.66	1.04	N/A	1,690.9	321.9	112.6	-12.3
2016	B-	1.33	0.84	67.5	1,903.7	363.5	607.0	5.9
2015	C+	1.98	1.26	64.1	1,743.4	333.5	416.8	13.1
2014	C+	4.16	2.41	72.7	1,113.6	215.5	182.6	14.2
2013	C+	5.29	3.08	63.2	804.1	166.8	114.8	21.4
2012	C+	4.38	2.58	76.6	505.2	114.5	80.7	9.3

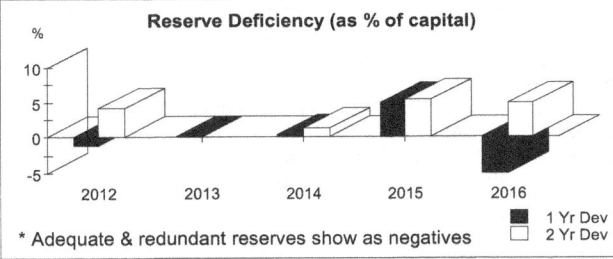

Reserve Deficiency (as % of capital)

* Adequate & redundant reserves show as negatives

■ 1 Yr Dev   □ 2 Yr Dev

WEST BEND MUTUAL INS CO *   B+   Good

Major Rating Factors: Good liquidity (6.4 on a scale of 0 to 10) with sufficient resources (cash flows and marketable investments) to handle a spike in claims. Good overall results on stability tests (5.1) despite weak results on operational trends.

Other Rating Factors: Strong long-term capitalization index (8.6) based on excellent current risk adjusted capital (severe and moderate loss scenarios). Moreover, capital levels have been consistent in recent years. Ample reserve history (8.9) that helps to protect the company against sharp claims increases. Excellent profitability (8.6) with operating gains in each of the last five years.

Principal Business: Workers compensation (24%), other liability (17%), auto liability (15%), homeowners multiple peril (12%), auto physical damage (11%), allied lines (7%), and other lines (15%).

Principal Investments: Investment grade bonds (65%), misc. investments (23%), non investment grade bonds (7%), real estate (3%), and cash (2%).

Investments in Affiliates: None

Group Affiliation: None

Licensed in: IL, IN, IA, KS, KY, MI, MN, MO, NE, OH, TN, WI

Commenced Business: May 1894

Address: 1900 South 18th Avenue, West Bend, WI 53095

Phone: (262) 334-5571   **Domicile State:** WI   **NAIC Code:** 15350

Data Date	Rating	RACR #1	RACR #2	Loss Ratio %	Total Assets ($mil)	Capital ($mil)	Net Premium ($mil)	Net Income ($mil)
3-17	B+	3.23	2.21	N/A	2,580.8	977.6	252.2	16.9
3-16	B+	3.12	2.15	N/A	2,350.0	895.5	236.5	15.4
2016	B+	3.08	2.11	65.5	2,520.9	947.0	1,016.1	40.1
2015	B+	3.18	2.20	59.3	2,329.3	878.2	960.5	44.8
2014	B+	3.48	2.24	63.6	2,171.2	823.1	895.0	57.5
2013	A-	3.27	2.11	61.1	1,975.4	690.7	814.3	62.8
2012	B+	3.34	2.20	62.3	1,786.2	613.5	726.7	60.3

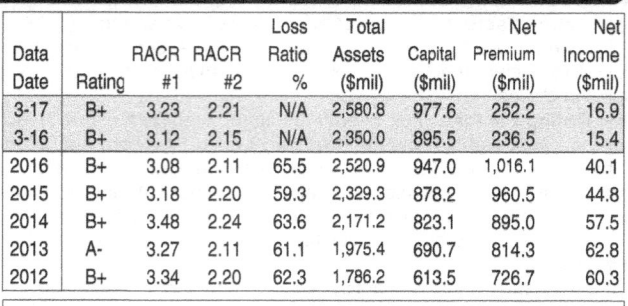

Liquidity Index

Range · 2013 · 2014 · 2015 · 2016
■ Weak ▨ Fair ▢ Good □ Strong

WESTCHESTER FIRE INS CO   C   Fair

Major Rating Factors: Fair profitability index (3.4 on a scale of 0 to 10). Fair expense controls. Return on equity has been fair, averaging 8.7% over the past five years. Weak overall results on stability tests (2.9). The largest net exposure for one risk is excessive at 10.4% of capital.

Other Rating Factors: History of adequate reserve strength (6.6) as reserves have been consistently at an acceptable level. Good liquidity (6.9) with sufficient resources (cash flows and marketable investments) to handle a spike in claims. Strong long-term capitalization index (9.3) based on excellent current risk adjusted capital (severe and moderate loss scenarios), despite some fluctuation in capital levels.

Principal Business: Other liability (58%), surety (24%), inland marine (9%), products liability (2%), fidelity (2%), auto liability (1%), and other lines (4%).

Principal Investments: Investment grade bonds (82%), non investment grade bonds (12%), misc. investments (4%), and cash (2%).

Investments in Affiliates: None

Group Affiliation: Chubb Limited

Licensed in: All states, the District of Columbia and Puerto Rico

Commenced Business: April 1967

Address: 436 WALNUT STREET, Philadelphia, PA 19106

Phone: (215) 640-1000   **Domicile State:** PA   **NAIC Code:** 10030

Data Date	Rating	RACR #1	RACR #2	Loss Ratio %	Total Assets ($mil)	Capital ($mil)	Net Premium ($mil)	Net Income ($mil)
3-17	C	3.88	2.59	N/A	1,849.8	703.3	88.5	4.1
3-16	C+	3.80	2.52	N/A	1,782.4	730.9	89.6	-7.0
2016	C	3.66	2.47	76.5	1,764.4	702.8	361.8	22.9
2015	C+	3.98	2.65	60.1	1,797.9	731.4	374.1	53.0
2014	C	4.92	3.23	56.5	2,011.9	906.1	342.6	81.9
2013	C	4.31	2.96	46.7	2,056.1	906.6	226.4	114.1
2012	C	2.05	1.25	67.2	2,119.3	813.7	389.8	103.8

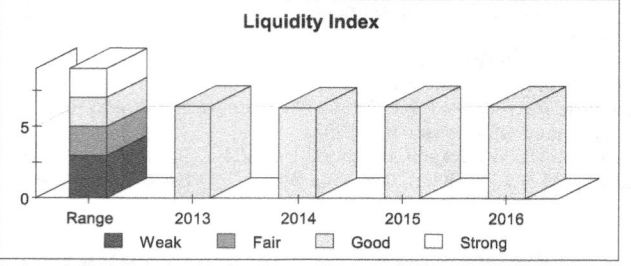

($mil)   Income Trends

2012 · 2013 · 2014 · 2015 · 2016
▲ Underwriting Income ■ Net Income

WESTERN AGRICULTURAL INS CO *   B+   Good

Major Rating Factors: Good liquidity (6.3 on a scale of 0 to 10) with sufficient resources (cash flows and marketable investments) to handle a spike in claims. Good overall results on stability tests (5.1) despite weak results on operational trends.

Other Rating Factors: Strong long-term capitalization index (10.0) based on excellent current risk adjusted capital (severe and moderate loss scenarios). Moreover, capital levels have been consistent in recent years. Ample reserve history (8.1) that helps to protect the company against sharp claims increases. Excellent profitability (8.9) with operating gains in each of the last five years. Return on equity has been good over the last five years, averaging 10.9%.

Principal Business: Allied lines (48%), homeowners multiple peril (12%), farmowners multiple peril (10%), auto liability (9%), auto physical damage (9%), commercial multiple peril (8%), and other lines (4%).

Principal Investments: Investment grade bonds (87%), misc. investments (9%), cash (3%), and non investment grade bonds (1%).

Investments in Affiliates: 2%

Group Affiliation: Iowa Farm Bureau

Licensed in: AL, AZ, AR, CO, ID, IL, IN, IA, KS, MI, MN, MO, MT, NE, NV, NM, ND, OH, OK, SC, SD, TN, TX, UT, VA, WI, WY

Commenced Business: January 1972

Address: 5400 University Avenue, West Des Moines, IA 50266-5997

Phone: (515) 225-5400   **Domicile State:** IA   **NAIC Code:** 27871

Data Date	Rating	RACR #1	RACR #2	Loss Ratio %	Total Assets ($mil)	Capital ($mil)	Net Premium ($mil)	Net Income ($mil)
3-17	B+	5.04	3.94	N/A	217.1	106.3	25.0	3.3
3-16	B+	4.59	3.58	N/A	200.0	94.7	24.6	5.5
2016	B+	4.91	3.70	59.9	211.0	103.0	105.6	13.1
2015	B+	4.33	3.25	62.3	190.4	88.9	105.1	11.1
2014	B+	4.00	3.00	70.3	182.7	77.4	101.5	5.8
2013	B+	3.93	2.92	70.2	171.2	70.7	98.1	6.4
2012	B+	3.87	2.83	71.5	163.5	63.9	91.6	7.7

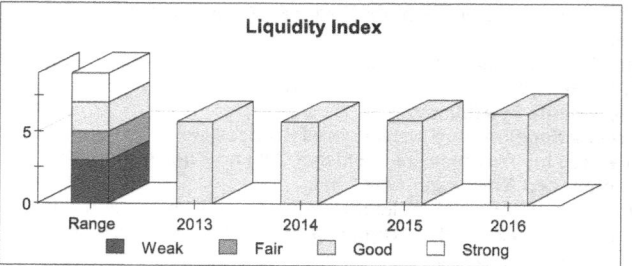

Liquidity Index

Range · 2013 · 2014 · 2015 · 2016
■ Weak ▨ Fair ▢ Good □ Strong

WESTERN NATIONAL MUTUAL INS CO   B-   Good

Major Rating Factors: Fair overall results on stability tests (4.3 on a scale of 0 to 10) including potential drain of affiliation with Western National Mutual and weak results on operational trends. Good liquidity (6.6) with sufficient resources (cash flows and marketable investments) to handle a spike in claims.

Other Rating Factors: Strong long-term capitalization index (8.6) based on excellent current risk adjusted capital (severe and moderate loss scenarios). Moreover, capital levels have been consistent in recent years. Ample reserve history (8.2) that helps to protect the company against sharp claims increases. Excellent profitability (8.6) with operating gains in each of the last five years.

Principal Business: Workers compensation (21%), auto liability (19%), homeowners multiple peril (16%), auto physical damage (15%), other liability (11%), products liability (5%), and other lines (13%).

Principal Investments: Investment grade bonds (65%), misc. investments (32%), real estate (2%), and non investment grade bonds (1%).

Investments in Affiliates: 19%

Group Affiliation: Western National Mutual

Licensed in: AK, AZ, AR, CA, CO, DE, ID, IL, IN, IA, KS, MD, MI, MN, MO, MT, NE, NV, NJ, NM, ND, OH, OK, OR, PA, RI, SD, TX, UT, WA, WI, WY

Commenced Business: June 1915

Address: 5350 WEST 78TH STREET, Edina, MN 55439

Phone: (952) 835-5350   **Domicile State:** MN   **NAIC Code:** 15377

Data Date	Rating	RACR #1	RACR #2	Loss Ratio %	Total Assets ($mil)	Capital ($mil)	Net Premium ($mil)	Net Income ($mil)
3-17	B-	2.51	2.10	N/A	996.7	447.3	94.1	5.7
3-16	B-	2.47	2.08	N/A	872.2	396.8	80.7	5.3
2016	B-	2.49	2.11	65.5	956.3	433.5	349.2	28.1
2015	B-	2.47	2.10	65.2	845.5	390.6	340.6	28.2
2014	B-	2.44	2.08	65.7	762.5	350.0	285.0	23.4
2013	B-	2.16	1.78	68.7	696.0	314.2	256.3	15.7
2012	B-	2.23	1.88	70.0	647.0	292.4	233.7	12.4

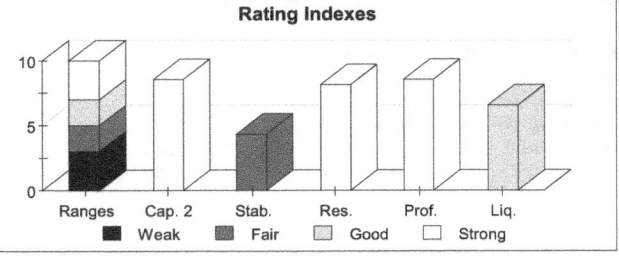

Rating Indexes

WESTERN SURETY CO   C   Fair

Major Rating Factors: Fair overall results on stability tests (3.9 on a scale of 0 to 10) including fair financial strength of affiliated CNA Financial Corp. The largest net exposure for one risk is conservative at 1.4% of capital. Strong long-term capitalization index (10.0) based on excellent current risk adjusted capital (severe and moderate loss scenarios), despite some fluctuation in capital levels.

Other Rating Factors: Ample reserve history (9.3) that helps to protect the company against sharp claims increases. Excellent profitability (8.1) with operating gains in each of the last five years. Return on equity has been good over the last five years, averaging 10.6%. Excellent liquidity (8.0) with ample operational cash flow and liquid investments.

Principal Business: Surety (92%), fidelity (7%), and other liability (1%).

Principal Investments: Investment grade bonds (97%) and misc. investments (3%).

Investments in Affiliates: 1%

Group Affiliation: CNA Financial Corp

Licensed in: All states, the District of Columbia and Puerto Rico

Commenced Business: July 1900

Address: 101 S REID STREET, Sioux Falls, SD 57103

Phone: (312) 822-5000   **Domicile State:** SD   **NAIC Code:** 13188

Data Date	Rating	RACR #1	RACR #2	Loss Ratio %	Total Assets ($mil)	Capital ($mil)	Net Premium ($mil)	Net Income ($mil)
3-17	C	7.60	5.76	N/A	2,015.0	1,439.5	81.9	17.7
3-16	C	7.16	5.56	N/A	1,873.0	1,346.4	87.6	21.5
2016	C	7.86	5.99	14.7	1,998.8	1,452.4	370.2	129.6
2015	C	7.42	5.79	21.8	1,823.7	1,323.3	295.8	116.5
2014	C	6.57	4.94	10.6	1,998.3	1,368.0	433.7	164.2
2013	C	5.67	4.30	9.2	1,856.4	1,205.6	418.4	152.7
2012	C	4.57	3.46	15.6	1,732.5	1,052.4	411.7	126.7

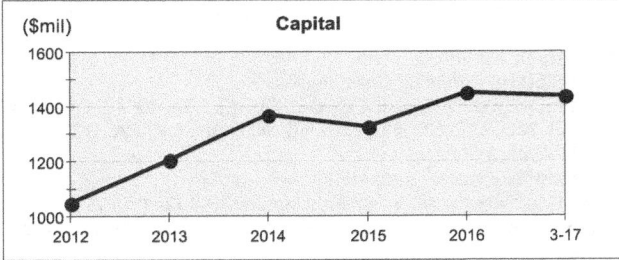

Capital

WESTERN WORLD INS CO   C   Fair

Major Rating Factors: Fair overall results on stability tests (4.1 on a scale of 0 to 10) including negative cash flow from operations for 2016. Good overall profitability index (6.0). Weak expense controls. Return on equity has been fair, averaging 8.4% over the past five years.

Other Rating Factors: Good liquidity (6.8) with sufficient resources (cash flows and marketable investments) to handle a spike in claims. Strong long-term capitalization index (7.5) based on excellent current risk adjusted capital (severe and moderate loss scenarios), despite some fluctuation in capital levels. Ample reserve history (9.5) that helps to protect the company against sharp claims increases.

Principal Business: Other liability (50%), commercial multiple peril (22%), allied lines (14%), products liability (12%), medical malpractice (2%), and inland marine (1%).

Principal Investments: Investment grade bonds (52%), misc. investments (42%), non investment grade bonds (4%), and cash (2%).

Investments in Affiliates: 35%

Group Affiliation: Western World Group

Licensed in: All states except PR

Commenced Business: April 1964

Address: 300 KIMBALL DRIVE SUITE 500, Parsippany, NJ 07054

Phone: (201) 847-8600   **Domicile State:** NH   **NAIC Code:** 13196

Data Date	Rating	RACR #1	RACR #2	Loss Ratio %	Total Assets ($mil)	Capital ($mil)	Net Premium ($mil)	Net Income ($mil)
3-17	C	1.49	1.36	N/A	836.8	387.5	30.5	63.6
3-16	C	1.67	1.51	N/A	882.2	423.0	25.4	1.7
2016	C	1.61	1.46	68.3	868.9	416.7	121.4	3.4
2015	C	1.66	1.49	72.3	916.5	421.0	96.7	22.3
2014	C	1.58	1.33	28.9	1,047.6	452.1	239.9	80.3
2013	C	1.39	1.19	69.0	1,047.0	367.7	201.7	7.8
2012	C	1.55	1.36	70.0	1,011.0	357.0	155.1	6.2

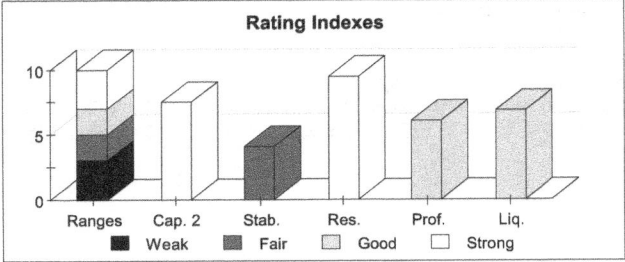

Rating Indexes

WESTFIELD INS CO   B-   Good

Major Rating Factors: Fair overall results on stability tests (4.6 on a scale of 0 to 10) including potential drain of affiliation with Westfield Companies and weak results on operational trends. Good liquidity (6.7) with sufficient resources (cash flows and marketable investments) to handle a spike in claims.

Other Rating Factors: Strong long-term capitalization index (9.7) based on excellent current risk adjusted capital (severe and moderate loss scenarios). Moreover, capital levels have been consistent in recent years. Ample reserve history (8.7) that helps to protect the company against sharp claims increases. Excellent profitability (8.6) with operating gains in each of the last five years.

Principal Business: Commercial multiple peril (28%), auto liability (23%), auto physical damage (11%), other liability (10%), homeowners multiple peril (6%), workers compensation (5%), and other lines (17%).

Principal Investments: Investment grade bonds (64%) and misc. investments (36%).

Investments in Affiliates: None
Group Affiliation: Westfield Companies
Licensed in: All states except CA, PR
Commenced Business: July 1929
Address: One Park Circle, Westfield Center, OH 44251-5001
Phone: (330) 887-0101   **Domicile State:** OH   **NAIC Code:** 24112

Data Date	Rating	RACR #1	RACR #2	Loss Ratio %	Total Assets ($mil)	Capital ($mil)	Net Premium ($mil)	Net Income ($mil)
3-17	B-	4.45	2.93	N/A	2,777.2	1,209.8	240.4	16.6
3-16	B-	4.25	2.87	N/A	2,603.8	1,121.3	238.1	18.9
2016	B-	4.46	2.96	62.3	2,739.6	1,177.3	977.1	82.3
2015	B-	4.26	2.89	62.7	2,594.4	1,092.4	955.3	70.9
2014	B-	4.14	2.78	63.5	2,536.1	1,043.0	935.9	93.3
2013	B-	3.76	2.50	59.8	2,450.5	991.2	904.7	127.7
2012	B-	3.33	2.22	64.9	2,243.1	853.6	867.8	89.6

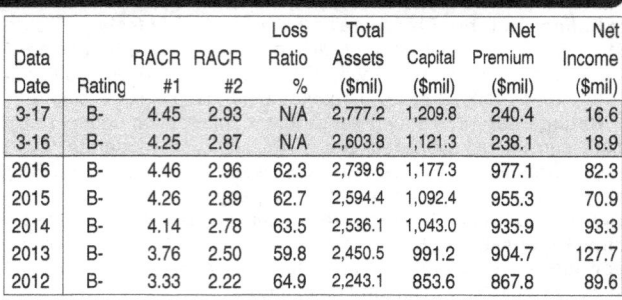

Rating Indexes

Ranges | Cap. 2 | Stab. | Res. | Prof. | Liq.
■ Weak   ■ Fair   □ Good   □ Strong

WESTFIELD NATIONAL INS CO   B-   Good

Major Rating Factors: Fair overall results on stability tests (4.6 on a scale of 0 to 10) including potential drain of affiliation with Westfield Companies and weak results on operational trends. Good liquidity (6.7) with sufficient resources (cash flows and marketable investments) to handle a spike in claims.

Other Rating Factors: Strong long-term capitalization index (9.5) based on excellent current risk adjusted capital (severe and moderate loss scenarios). Moreover, capital levels have been consistent in recent years. Ample reserve history (8.7) that helps to protect the company against sharp claims increases. Excellent profitability (8.6) with operating gains in each of the last five years.

Principal Business: Homeowners multiple peril (32%), auto liability (24%), auto physical damage (20%), commercial multiple peril (10%), workers compensation (5%), other liability (5%), and other lines (4%).

Principal Investments: Investment grade bonds (71%) and misc. investments (29%).

Investments in Affiliates: None
Group Affiliation: Westfield Companies
Licensed in: AL, AZ, AR, CA, CO, DC, DE, FL, GA, ID, IL, IN, IA, KS, KY, MD, MI, MN, MS, MO, MT, NE, NV, NM, NC, ND, OH, OK, PA, SC, SD, TN, TX, UT, VA, WA, WV, WI, WY
Commenced Business: April 1968
Address: One Park Circle, Westfield Center, OH 44251-5001
Phone: (330) 887-0101   **Domicile State:** OH   **NAIC Code:** 24120

Data Date	Rating	RACR #1	RACR #2	Loss Ratio %	Total Assets ($mil)	Capital ($mil)	Net Premium ($mil)	Net Income ($mil)
3-17	B-	4.22	2.81	N/A	664.5	305.5	57.9	4.7
3-16	B-	4.01	2.70	N/A	616.6	280.7	57.3	4.0
2016	B-	4.25	2.83	62.3	659.5	300.4	235.2	18.3
2015	B-	4.10	2.79	62.7	613.4	272.8	230.0	16.5
2014	B-	3.92	2.62	63.5	598.7	263.1	225.3	16.6
2013	B+	3.75	2.51	59.8	571.9	243.2	217.8	25.2
2012	B+	3.27	2.18	64.9	524.9	208.0	208.9	19.8

Westfield Companies
Composite Group Rating: B-
Largest Group Members

	Assets ($mil)	Rating
OHIO FARMERS INS CO	2965	B-
WESTFIELD INS CO	2740	B-
WESTFIELD NATIONAL INS CO	659	B-
OLD GUARD INS CO	453	C+
AMERICAN SELECT INS CO	255	C

WESTGUARD INS CO   B-   Good

Major Rating Factors: Fair overall results on stability tests (4.4 on a scale of 0 to 10) including weak results on operational trends, negative cash flow from operations for 2016 and excessive premium growth. Good long-term capitalization index (6.8) based on good current risk adjusted capital (moderate loss scenario). Moreover, capital levels have been consistent in recent years.

Other Rating Factors: Ample reserve history (9.2) that helps to protect the company against sharp claims increases. Excellent profitability (7.5) with operating gains in each of the last five years. Superior liquidity (10.0) with ample operational cash flow and liquid investments.

Principal Business: Workers compensation (100%).

Principal Investments: Misc. investments (82%), cash (12%), investment grade bonds (5%), and real estate (1%).

Investments in Affiliates: 65%
Group Affiliation: Berkshire-Hathaway
Licensed in: NY, PA, WV
Commenced Business: July 2004
Address: 16 SOUTH RIVER STREET, Wilkes-barre, PA 18702
Phone: (570) 825-9900   **Domicile State:** PA   **NAIC Code:** 11981

Data Date	Rating	RACR #1	RACR #2	Loss Ratio %	Total Assets ($mil)	Capital ($mil)	Net Premium ($mil)	Net Income ($mil)
3-17	B-	1.34	1.21	N/A	1,130.2	537.1	5.8	4.1
3-16	C+	1.31	1.19	N/A	832.3	435.6	4.4	2.3
2016	B-	1.30	1.19	58.9	955.0	509.2	23.0	1.6
2015	C+	1.30	1.19	60.0	780.5	430.9	19.0	0.3
2014	C+	1.09	1.06	63.2	607.1	309.1	11.9	1.2
2013	C	0.82	0.57	67.8	35.1	14.6	6.2	1.4
2012	C	1.02	0.62	N/A	42.0	13.3	3.1	1.1

Berkshire-Hathaway
Composite Group Rating: B
Largest Group Members

	Assets ($mil)	Rating
NATIONAL INDEMNITY CO	178623	B
GOVERNMENT EMPLOYEES INS CO	27198	B
COLUMBIA INS CO	20707	U
BERKSHIRE HATHAWAY LIFE INS CO OF NE	17970	C+
GENERAL REINS CORP	14780	C+

WESTPORT INS CORP   B   Good

Major Rating Factors: Fair profitability index (4.2 on a scale of 0 to 10). Weak expense controls. Return on equity has been fair, averaging 9.7% over the past five years. Fair overall results on stability tests (4.3) including weak results on operational trends and negative cash flow from operations for 2016. Affiliation with Swiss Reinsurance is a strength. The largest net exposure for one risk is conservative at 1.6% of capital.

Other Rating Factors: Strong long-term capitalization index (7.1) based on excellent current risk adjusted capital (severe and moderate loss scenarios), despite some fluctuation in capital levels. Ample reserve history (8.3) that helps to protect the company against sharp claims increases. Excellent liquidity (7.5) with ample operational cash flow and liquid investments.

Principal Business: Allied lines (34%), other liability (23%), fire (15%), group accident & health (9%), earthquake (9%), boiler & machinery (2%), and other lines (7%).

Principal Investments: Investment grade bonds (80%), misc. investments (19%), and non investment grade bonds (1%).

Investments in Affiliates: 12%

Group Affiliation: Swiss Reinsurance

Licensed in: All states, the District of Columbia and Puerto Rico

Commenced Business: September 1981

Address: 237 EAST HIGH STREET, Jefferson City, MO 65101-3206

Phone: (913) 676-5200   **Domicile State:** MO   **NAIC Code:** 39845

Data Date	Rating	RACR #1	RACR #2	Loss Ratio %	Total Assets ($mil)	Capital ($mil)	Net Premium ($mil)	Net Income ($mil)
3-17	B	1.78	1.23	N/A	4,649.0	1,562.8	80.9	21.6
3-16	B-	1.50	1.05	N/A	4,848.5	1,520.5	71.7	12.6
2016	B	1.78	1.23	80.1	4,730.1	1,558.6	287.1	189.7
2015	B-	1.48	1.03	61.5	4,693.0	1,505.3	281.6	177.3
2014	C+	1.56	1.08	67.9	5,215.7	1,630.5	135.9	160.8
2013	C+	1.25	0.85	62.2	5,454.1	1,769.4	580.1	167.8
2012	C	0.57	0.44	64.9	5,331.3	1,726.5	535.1	108.0

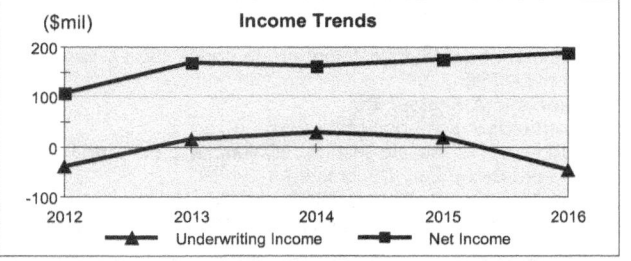

Income Trends

XL INS AMERICA INC   C   Fair

Major Rating Factors: Fair overall results on stability tests (3.7 on a scale of 0 to 10) including potential drain of affiliation with XL Group Ltd and weak results on operational trends. The largest net exposure for one risk is acceptable at 2.8% of capital. Fair profitability index (3.4). Fair expense controls. Return on equity has been fair, averaging 6.5% over the past five years.

Other Rating Factors: History of adequate reserve strength (6.3) as reserves have been consistently at an acceptable level. Strong long-term capitalization index (7.2) based on excellent current risk adjusted capital (severe and moderate loss scenarios), despite some fluctuation in capital levels. Excellent liquidity (8.3) with ample operational cash flow and liquid investments.

Principal Business: Other liability (30%), fire (15%), allied lines (15%), workers compensation (14%), earthquake (7%), inland marine (6%), and other lines (13%).

Principal Investments: Investment grade bonds (75%), misc. investments (19%), and cash (6%).

Investments in Affiliates: 18%

Group Affiliation: XL Group Ltd

Licensed in: All states, the District of Columbia and Puerto Rico

Commenced Business: December 1945

Address: 1209 Orange Street, Wilmington, DE 19801

Phone: (203) 964-5200   **Domicile State:** DE   **NAIC Code:** 24554

Data Date	Rating	RACR #1	RACR #2	Loss Ratio %	Total Assets ($mil)	Capital ($mil)	Net Premium ($mil)	Net Income ($mil)
3-17	C	1.41	1.15	N/A	724.0	196.2	31.0	3.7
3-16	C	1.53	1.24	N/A	751.1	212.6	33.9	1.9
2016	C	1.41	1.15	69.3	825.4	193.3	166.7	9.1
2015	C	1.54	1.27	71.2	678.0	211.1	132.7	6.9
2014	C	1.62	1.34	61.5	752.9	232.3	126.7	16.3
2013	C	1.35	1.07	65.3	734.2	246.8	133.1	26.0
2012	C	1.65	1.37	73.4	775.6	253.0	129.4	16.7

XL Group Ltd
Composite Group Rating: C

Largest Group Members	Assets ($mil)	Rating
XL REINS AMERICA INC	6274	C
GREENWICH INS CO	1203	C
XL SPECIALTY INS CO	920	C
XL INS AMERICA INC	825	C
CATLIN SPECIALTY INS CO	744	C+

XL REINS AMERICA INC   C   Fair

Major Rating Factors: Fair overall results on stability tests (3.8 on a scale of 0 to 10) including potential drain of affiliation with XL Group Ltd and weak results on operational trends. The largest net exposure for one risk is conservative at 1.7% of capital. Fair profitability index (4.2). Fair expense controls. Return on equity has been fair, averaging 5.8% over the past five years.

Other Rating Factors: History of adequate reserve strength (6.2) as reserves have been consistently at an acceptable level. Good liquidity (6.8) with sufficient resources (cash flows and marketable investments) to handle a spike in claims. Strong long-term capitalization index (8.4) based on excellent current risk adjusted capital (severe and moderate loss scenarios), despite some fluctuation in capital levels.

Principal Business: Other liability (95%) and group accident & health (7%).

Principal Investments: Investment grade bonds (69%), misc. investments (30%), and cash (1%).

Investments in Affiliates: 17%

Group Affiliation: XL Group Ltd

Licensed in: All states, the District of Columbia and Puerto Rico

Commenced Business: October 1929

Address: 200 LIBERTY STREET, New York, NY 10281

Phone: (203) 964-5200   **Domicile State:** NY   **NAIC Code:** 20583

Data Date	Rating	RACR #1	RACR #2	Loss Ratio %	Total Assets ($mil)	Capital ($mil)	Net Premium ($mil)	Net Income ($mil)
3-17	C	2.38	1.91	N/A	6,087.9	2,122.4	201.7	38.0
3-16	C	2.76	2.04	N/A	5,764.4	2,047.7	220.2	27.0
2016	C	2.35	1.91	69.3	6,274.1	2,076.3	1,083.7	90.9
2015	C	2.96	2.22	71.2	5,307.7	2,021.6	862.6	83.0
2014	C	3.07	2.34	61.5	5,627.6	2,233.6	823.4	219.8
2013	C	2.94	2.26	65.3	5,527.8	2,244.5	865.2	161.4
2012	C	2.93	2.25	73.4	5,413.0	2,237.8	841.2	65.5

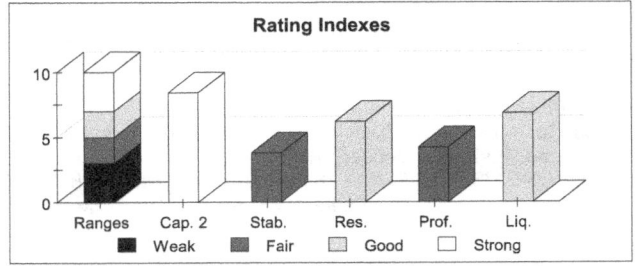

Rating Indexes

XL SPECIALTY INS CO | C | Fair

Major Rating Factors: Fair overall results on stability tests (3.8 on a scale of 0 to 10) including potential drain of affiliation with XL Group Ltd and weak results on operational trends. The largest net exposure for one risk is conservative at 1.2% of capital. History of adequate reserve strength (6.3) as reserves have been consistently at an acceptable level.

Other Rating Factors: Good profitability index (5.0) despite operating losses during 2015. Return on equity has been fair, averaging 5.3% over the past five years. Strong long-term capitalization index (9.2) based on excellent current risk adjusted capital (severe and moderate loss scenarios), despite some fluctuation in capital levels. Superior liquidity (9.8) with ample operational cash flow and liquid investments.

Principal Business: Other liability (59%), workers compensation (10%), ocean marine (9%), inland marine (7%), aircraft (6%), auto liability (1%), and other lines (7%).

Principal Investments: Investment grade bonds (65%), cash (19%), and misc. investments (16%).

Investments in Affiliates: 6%

Group Affiliation: XL Group Ltd

Licensed in: All states, the District of Columbia and Puerto Rico

Commenced Business: December 1979

Address: 1209 Orange Street, Wilmington, DE 19801

Phone: (203) 964-5200 **Domicile State:** DE **NAIC Code:** 37885

Data Date	Rating	RACR #1	RACR #2	Loss Ratio %	Total Assets ($mil)	Capital ($mil)	Net Premium ($mil)	Net Income ($mil)
3-17	C	4.27	3.13	N/A	956.4	289.3	18.6	6.5
3-16	C	4.00	2.91	N/A	813.6	262.4	20.3	7.6
2016	C	4.32	3.21	69.3	920.4	283.3	100.0	4.6
2015	C	2.14	1.59	71.2	462.2	132.7	79.6	-2.5
2014	C	2.31	1.72	61.5	432.7	143.2	76.0	9.0
2013	C	2.46	1.83	65.3	440.6	158.3	79.9	26.3
2012	C	2.12	1.67	73.4	440.7	168.7	77.6	4.7

XL Group Ltd
Composite Group Rating: C

Largest Group Members	Assets ($mil)	Rating
XL REINS AMERICA INC	6274	C
GREENWICH INS CO	1203	C
XL SPECIALTY INS CO	920	C
XL INS AMERICA INC	825	C
CATLIN SPECIALTY INS CO	744	C+

ZENITH INS CO | C+ | Fair

Major Rating Factors: Fair overall results on stability tests (4.4 on a scale of 0 to 10) including potential drain of affiliation with Fairfax Financial. Fair profitability index (4.3) with operating losses during 2012 and 2013. Return on equity has been fair, averaging 6.2% over the past five years.

Other Rating Factors: Strong long-term capitalization index (7.0) based on excellent current risk adjusted capital (severe and moderate loss scenarios), despite some fluctuation in capital levels. Ample reserve history (7.0) that can protect against increases in claims costs. Excellent liquidity (7.3) with ample operational cash flow and liquid investments.

Principal Business: Workers compensation (91%), commercial multiple peril (3%), auto liability (2%), other liability (2%), fire (1%), and auto physical damage (1%).

Principal Investments: Investment grade bonds (65%), misc. investments (30%), non investment grade bonds (2%), real estate (2%), and cash (1%).

Investments in Affiliates: 10%

Group Affiliation: Fairfax Financial

Licensed in: All states except ND, WY, PR

Commenced Business: December 1950

Address: 21255 CALIFA STREET, Woodland Hills, CA 91367

Phone: (818) 713-1000 **Domicile State:** CA **NAIC Code:** 13269

Data Date	Rating	RACR #1	RACR #2	Loss Ratio %	Total Assets ($mil)	Capital ($mil)	Net Premium ($mil)	Net Income ($mil)
3-17	C+	1.33	1.02	N/A	1,864.4	605.5	184.4	30.1
3-16	C+	1.38	1.03	N/A	1,971.7	603.7	183.6	69.8
2016	C+	1.31	1.01	44.6	1,824.6	563.6	792.7	115.2
2015	C+	1.43	1.07	46.6	1,908.8	621.7	754.9	121.0
2014	C	1.37	1.02	52.8	1,834.1	564.5	703.4	110.7
2013	C-	1.12	0.82	62.4	1,783.8	515.8	677.5	-18.1
2012	D+	1.21	0.89	77.8	1,646.3	443.7	596.7	-125.4

Fairfax Financial
Composite Group Rating: C

Largest Group Members	Assets ($mil)	Rating
ODYSSEY REINS CO	7163	C
US FIRE INS CO	3950	C
TIG INS CO	2818	C
ZENITH INS CO	1825	C+
CLEARWATER SELECT INS CO	1193	D

ZURICH AMERICAN INS CO | B- | Good

Major Rating Factors: Fair overall results on stability tests (3.5 on a scale of 0 to 10) including weak results on operational trends. The largest net exposure for one risk is high at 4.3% of capital. History of adequate reserve strength (6.0) as reserves have been consistently at an acceptable level.

Other Rating Factors: Good overall profitability index (5.9). Good expense controls. Return on equity has been good over the last five years, averaging 11.5%. Strong long-term capitalization index (7.9) based on excellent current risk adjusted capital (severe and moderate loss scenarios), despite some fluctuation in capital levels. Excellent liquidity (7.2) with ample operational cash flow and liquid investments.

Principal Business: Workers compensation (29%), other liability (22%), auto liability (11%), commercial multiple peril (7%), inland marine (6%), allied lines (6%), and other lines (19%).

Principal Investments: Investment grade bonds (70%), misc. investments (23%), non investment grade bonds (4%), and real estate (4%).

Investments in Affiliates: 8%

Group Affiliation: Zurich Financial Services Group

Licensed in: All states, the District of Columbia and Puerto Rico

Commenced Business: January 1913

Address: ONE LIBERTY PLAZA 165 BROADWAY, New York, NY 10006

Phone: (847) 605-6000 **Domicile State:** NY **NAIC Code:** 16535

Data Date	Rating	RACR #1	RACR #2	Loss Ratio %	Total Assets ($mil)	Capital ($mil)	Net Premium ($mil)	Net Income ($mil)
3-17	B-	2.34	1.63	N/A	30,708.0	7,592.2	981.1	202.4
3-16	B-	2.31	1.55	N/A	29,801.3	7,357.9	1,058.6	376.2
2016	B-	2.45	1.71	78.5	31,002.9	7,851.7	4,215.2	968.8
2015	B-	2.53	1.71	81.4	30,471.5	7,765.5	4,540.4	597.9
2014	C+	2.71	1.86	78.0	30,309.7	8,015.4	4,739.7	1,000.5
2013	C+	2.76	1.90	74.6	30,184.0	7,798.4	4,733.6	772.8
2012	C+	2.75	1.91	81.8	30,011.1	7,642.3	4,437.8	1,156.5

Rating Indexes

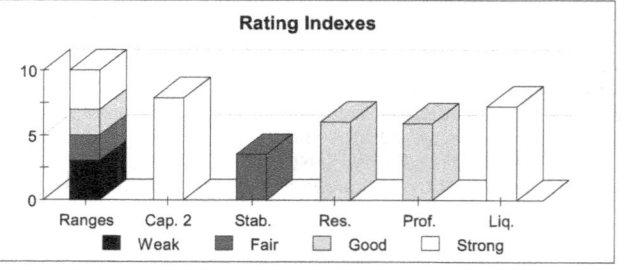

| | Weak | Fair | Good | Strong |

Ranges | Cap. 2 | Stab. | Res. | Prof. | Liq.

Section III

Weiss
Recommended Companies

A compilation of those

U.S. Property and Casualty Insurers

receiving a Weiss Safety Rating

of A+, A, A- or B+.

Companies are listed in alphabetical order.

Section III Contents

This section provides a list of recommended carriers (based strictly on financial safety) along with additional information you should have when shopping for insurance. It contains all insurers receiving a Safety Rating of A+, A, A- or B+. If an insurer is not on this list, it should not be automatically assumed that the firm is weak. Indeed, there are many firms that have not achieved a B+ or better rating but are in relatively good condition with adequate resources to cover their risk during an average recession. Not being included in this list should not be construed as a recommendation to cancel a policy.

Left Pages

1. Safety Rating

Our rating is measured on a scale from A to F and considers a wide range of factors. Highly-rated companies are, in our opinion, less likely to experience financial difficulties than lower rated firms. See *About Weiss Safety Ratings* for more information.

2. Insurance Company Name

The legally-registered name, which can sometimes differ from the name that the company uses for advertising. An insurer's name can be very similar to the name of other companies which may not be on our Recommended List, so make sure you note the exact name before contacting your agent.

3. Address

The address of the main office where you can contact the firm for additional financial data or for the location of local branches and/or registered agents.

4. Telephone Number

The number to call for additional financial data or for the phone numbers of local branches and/or registered agents.

Right Pages

The right-side pages present the percentage of the company's business that is involved in each type of insurance. Specifically, the numbers shown are the amounts of direct premium (received directly from policyholders) for each line of business as a percent of total premiums.

1. Domicile State

The state which has primary regulatory responsibility for the company. It may differ from the location of the company's corporate headquarters. You do not have to be living in the domicile state to purchase insurance from this firm, provided it is licensed to do business in your state.

2. Auto

Coverage for damage to a policyholder's own automobile and for the financial loss from auto-related bodily injury or property damage.

3. Homeowners Multiple Peril

Package policies for homeowners providing a broad spectrum of property and liability coverages.

4. Farmowners Multiple Peril

Package policies for farm or ranch owners providing a broad spectrum of property and liability coverages.

5. Commercial Multiple Peril

Package policies for businesses and other commercial establishments providing a broad spectrum of property and liability coverages.

6. Commercial Auto Liability

Coverage against financial loss because of a business auto related injuries or damages to third parties.

7. Other Liability

Encompasses all third-party liability coverages not included in other business areas. It can include among others: professional liability, environmental liability, product liability, umbrella liability, general liability.

8. Medical Malpractice

Errors and omissions liability coverages for persons engaged in the practice of medicine, surgery, dentistry, nursing, pharmacy, or other health care services. Also covers health care institutions.

9. Workers' Compensation

Liability coverage issued to employers which provides for the payment of medical care, disability income or possible additional liability amounts to employees who are injured on the job.

10. Accident and Health

This includes three categories: (1) group accident and health, which consists of medical and hospitalization insurance plans under which a number of persons and their dependents are insured under a single policy issued to an employer or a common associated entity; (2) credit accident and health, which makes certain debt payments, usually for car or home loans, in the case of accident or illness; and (3) other accident and health, issued to individuals, to pay health care benefits or loss of income due to accidental injury or death.

11. Other

Fire, allied lines, mortgage guaranty, ocean marine, inland marine, financial guaranty, product liability, aircraft, fidelity, surety, glass, burglary and theft, boiler and machinery, credit, international, reinsurance, aggregate write-ins for other lines of business and other miscellaneous types of insurance.

Weiss Safety Ratings are not deemed to be a recommendation concerning the purchase or sale of the securities of any insurance company that is publicly owned.

RATING	INSURANCE COMPANY NAME	ADDRESS	CITY	STATE	ZIP	PHONE
B+	ACUITY A MUTUAL INS CO	2800 SOUTH TAYLOR DRIVE	SHEBOYGAN	WI	53081	(920) 458-9131
B+	ALFA MUTUAL GENERAL INS CO	2108 EAST SOUTH BOULEVARD	MONTGOMERY	AL	36116	(334) 288-3900
B+	ALFA SPECIALTY INS CORP	2108 EAST SOUTH BOULEVARD	MONTGOMERY	AL	36116	(334) 288-3900
B+	ALL AMERICA INS CO	800 SOUTH WASHINGTON STREET	VAN WERT	OH	45891	(419) 238-1010
B+	ALLSTATE NJ INS CO	2775 SANDERS ROAD	NORTHBROOK	IL	60062	(908) 252-5000
B+	AMERICAN FAMILY MUTL INS CO SI	6000 AMERICAN PARKWAY	MADISON	WI	53783	(608) 249-2111
B+	AMERICAN STANDARD INS CO OF WI	6000 AMERICAN PARKWAY	MADISON	WI	53783	(608) 249-2111
B+	AMICA MUTUAL INS CO	100 AMICA WAY	LINCOLN	RI	02865	(800) 652-6422
B+	AUTO CLUB INDEMNITY CO	1225 FREEPORT PARKWAY	COPPELL	TX	75019	(714) 850-5111
A-	AUTO-OWNERS INS CO	6101 ANACAPRI BOULEVARD	LANSING	MI	48917	(517) 323-1200
A+	BERKSHIRE HATHAWAY ASR CORP	MARINE AIR TERMINAL LAGUARDIA	FLUSHING	NY	11371	(402) 916-3000
B+	BROTHERHOOD MUTUAL INS CO	6400 BROTHERHOOD WAY	FORT WAYNE	IN	46825	(260) 482-8668
A-	BUILDERS MUTUAL INS CO	5580 CENTERVIEW DRIVE	RALEIGH	NC	27606	(919) 845-1976
A-	CINCINNATI INDEMNITY CO	6200 SOUTH GILMORE ROAD	FAIRFIELD	OH	45014	(513) 870-2000
A	CINCINNATI INS CO	6200 SOUTH GILMORE ROAD	FAIRFIELD	OH	45014	(513) 870-2000
A-	CINCINNATI SPECIALTY UNDERWRITER	1807 NORTH MARKET ST	WILMINGTON	DE	19802	(513) 870-2000
A+	CITIZENS PROPERTY INS CORP	2101 MARYLAND CIRCLE	TALLAHASSEE	FL	32303	(850) 513-3700
A-	COPIC INS CO	7351 LOWRY BOULEVARD SUITE 400	DENVER	CO	80230	(720) 858-6000
A+	COPPERPOINT MUTUAL INS CO	3030 N 3RD STREET	PHOENIX	AZ	85012	(602) 631-2240
B+	COUNTRY CASUALTY INS CO	1701 N TOWANDA AVENUE	BLOOMINGTON	IL	61701	(309) 821-3000
A-	COUNTRY MUTUAL INS CO	1701 N TOWANDA AVENUE	BLOOMINGTON	IL	61701	(309) 821-3000
A-	CUMIS INS SOCIETY INC	2000 HERITAGE WAY	WAVERLY	IA	50677	(608) 238-5851
B+	DAIRYLAND INS CO	1800 NORTH POINT DRIVE	STEVENS POINT	WI	54481	(715) 346-6000
A-	EMPLOYERS COMPENSATION INS CO	500 NORTH BRAND BOULEVARD	GLENDALE	CA	91203	(775) 327-2700
A-	ENDURANCE ASR CORP	1209 ORANGE STREET	WILMINGTON	DE	19801	(914) 468-8000
A-	ESSENT GUARANTY INC	2 RADNOR CORP 100 MATSONFORD	RADNOR	PA	19087	(877) 673-8190
B+	FARM BUREAU P&C INS CO	5400 UNIVERSITY AVENUE	WEST DES MOINES	IA	50266	(515) 225-5400
B+	FARM FAMILY CASUALTY INS CO	344 ROUTE 9W	GLENMONT	NY	12077	(518) 431-5000
B+	FARMERS AUTOMOBILE INS ASN	2505 COURT STREET	PEKIN	IL	61558	(309) 346-1161
B+	GEICO CHOICE INS CO	1440 KIEWIT PLAZA	OMAHA	NE	68131	(800) 841-3000
B+	GEICO GENERAL INS CO	5260 WESTERN AVENUE	CHEVY CHASE	MD	20815	(800) 841-3000
A-	GEICO SECURE INS CO	1440 KIEWIT PLAZA	OMAHA	NE	68131	(800) 841-3000
B+	GNY CUSTOM INS CO	200 MADISON AVENUE	NEW YORK	NY	10016	(212) 683-9700
A-	HOME-OWNERS INS CO	6101 ANACAPRI BOULEVARD	LANSING	MI	48917	(517) 323-1200
B+	INTERINS EXCHANGE	3333 FAIRVIEW ROAD	COSTA MESA	CA	92626	(714) 850-5111
B+	MARKEL GLOBAL REINS CO	1209 ORANGE STREET	WILMINGTON	DE	19801	(908) 630-2700
B+	MERCURY INS CO	555 WEST IMPERIAL HIGHWAY	BREA	CA	92821	(714) 671-6600
B+	MITSUI SUMITOMO INS CO OF AMER	560 LEXINGTON AVENUE 20TH FLOO	NEW YORK	NY	10022	(908) 604-2900
A-	MOTORISTS COMMERCIAL MUTUAL INS CO	471 EAST BROAD STREET	COLUMBUS	OH	43215	(614) 225-8211
B+	MOTORISTS MUTUAL INS CO	471 EAST BROAD STREET	COLUMBUS	OH	43215	(614) 225-8211
B+	NATIONAL CASUALTY CO	8877 N GAINEY CENTER DRIVE	SCOTTSDALE	AZ	85258	(480) 365-4000
A-	NATIONAL MORTGAGE INS CORP	8040 EXCELSIOR DRIVE SUITE 200	MADISON	WI	53717	(855) 873-2584
B+	NATIONWIDE MUTUAL FIRE INS CO	ONE WEST NATIONWIDE BLVD	COLUMBUS	OH	43215	(614) 249-7111
A+	NUCLEAR ELECTRIC INS LTD	1201 MARKET ST STE 1200	WILMINGTON	DE	19801	(302) 888-3000
A+	OGLESBY REINS CO	ONE STATE FARM PLAZA	BLOOMINGTON	IL	61710	(309) 766-2311
A-	OWNERS INS CO	2325 NORTH COLE STREET	LIMA	OH	45801	(517) 323-1200
B+	PEKIN INS CO	2505 COURT STREET	PEKIN	IL	61558	(309) 346-1161
B+	PROPERTY-OWNERS INS CO	3950 WEST DELPHI PIKE	MARION	IN	46952	(517) 323-1200
A-	PROTECTIVE INS CO	111 CONGRESSIONAL BLVD STE 500	CARMEL	IN	46032	(317) 636-9800
A-	RADIAN REINS INC	1601 MARKET STREET	PHILADELPHIA	PA	19103	(800) 523-1988
A-	RETAILFIRST INS CO	2310 COMMERCE POINT DRIVE	LAKELAND	FL	33801	(863) 665-6060
A-	SECURIAN CASUALTY CO	400 ROBERT STREET NORTH	ST PAUL	MN	55101	(651) 665-3500
A	SENTRY INS A MUTUAL CO	1800 NORTH POINT DRIVE	STEVENS POINT	WI	54481	(715) 346-6000
B+	SENTRY SELECT INS CO	1800 NORTH POINT DRIVE	STEVENS POINT	WI	54481	(715) 346-6000
A-	SOMPO AMERICA INSURANCE CO	777 THIRD AVE 24TH FLOOR	NEW YORK	NY	10017	(704) 759-2200
A-	SOUTHERN-OWNERS INS CO	6101 ANACAPRI BOULEVARD	LANSING	MI	48917	(517) 323-1200

DOM. STATE	AUTO	HOME MULT. PERIL	FARM MULT. PERIL	COMM. MULT. PERIL	COMM. AUTO LIAB.	OTHER LIABILITY	MED MALPRAC.	WORK. COMP.	ACCID. & HEALTH	OTHER	INSURANCE COMPANY NAME
WI	23	10	0	11	14	9	0	23	0	9	ACUITY A MUTUAL INS CO
AL	52	47	0	0	0	1	0	0	0	0	ALFA MUTUAL GENERAL INS CO
VA	100	0	0	0	0	0	0	0	0	0	ALFA SPECIALTY INS CORP
OH	9	0	0	57	21	0	0	8	0	5	ALL AMERICA INS CO
IL	58	32	0	1	5	2	0	0	0	3	ALLSTATE NJ INS CO
WI	51	33	2	8	1	3	0	1	1	1	AMERICAN FAMILY MUTL INS CO SI
WI	100	0	0	0	0	0	0	0	0	0	AMERICAN STANDARD INS CO OF WI
RI	57	37	0	0	0	3	0	0	0	3	AMICA MUTUAL INS CO
TX	0	99	0	0	0	1	0	0	0	0	AUTO CLUB INDEMNITY CO
MI	21	34	2	9	8	6	0	6	0	14	AUTO-OWNERS INS CO
NY	0	0	0	0	0	0	0	0	0	100	BERKSHIRE HATHAWAY ASR CORP
IN	2	0	0	73	5	4	0	13	0	3	BROTHERHOOD MUTUAL INS CO
NC	0	0	0	12	2	3	0	75	0	7	BUILDERS MUTUAL INS CO
OH	6	0	0	24	13	15	1	29	0	11	CINCINNATI INDEMNITY CO
OH	20	14	0	26	9	16	1	2	0	11	CINCINNATI INS CO
DE	0	0	0	0	0	71	0	0	0	28	CINCINNATI SPECIALTY UNDERWRITER
FL	0	44	0	0	0	0	0	0	0	56	CITIZENS PROPERTY INS CORP
CO	0	0	0	0	0	4	95	0	1	0	COPIC INS CO
AZ	0	0	0	0	0	0	0	100	0	0	COPPERPOINT MUTUAL INS CO
IL	66	34	0	0	0	0	0	0	0	0	COUNTRY CASUALTY INS CO
IL	25	42	10	7	2	3	0	4	0	7	COUNTRY MUTUAL INS CO
IA	2	0	0	13	1	67	0	0	0	17	CUMIS INS SOCIETY INC
WI	100	0	0	0	0	0	0	0	0	0	DAIRYLAND INS CO
CA	0	0	0	0	0	0	0	100	0	0	EMPLOYERS COMPENSATION INS CO
DE	0	0	0	1	0	41	0	0	0	58	ENDURANCE ASR CORP
PA	0	0	0	0	0	0	0	0	0	100	ESSENT GUARANTY INC
IA	39	24	26	4	1	3	0	3	0	1	FARM BUREAU P&C INS CO
NY	16	6	0	12	12	12	0	15	0	26	FARM FAMILY CASUALTY INS CO
IL	61	33	0	0	0	0	0	0	0	6	FARMERS AUTOMOBILE INS ASN
NE	100	0	0	0	0	0	0	0	0	0	GEICO CHOICE INS CO
MD	100	0	0	0	0	0	0	0	0	0	GEICO GENERAL INS CO
NE	100	0	0	0	0	0	0	0	0	0	GEICO SECURE INS CO
AZ	0	0	0	100	0	0	0	0	0	0	GNY CUSTOM INS CO
MI	82	0	0	9	3	2	0	3	0	1	HOME-OWNERS INS CO
CA	79	19	0	0	0	1	0	0	0	1	INTERINS EXCHANGE
DE (*)	0	0	0	0	0	0	0	0	0	0	MARKEL GLOBAL REINS CO
CA	100	0	0	0	0	0	0	0	0	0	MERCURY INS CO
NY	2	0	0	24	6	10	0	29	0	28	MITSUI SUMITOMO INS CO OF AMER
OH	15	0	0	19	33	16	0	3	0	13	MOTORISTS COMMERCIAL MUTUAL INS CO
OH	31	15	0	12	14	16	0	5	0	7	MOTORISTS MUTUAL INS CO
OH	8	0	0	10	24	16	0	5	0	35	NATIONAL CASUALTY CO
WI	0	0	0	0	0	0	0	0	0	100	NATIONAL MORTGAGE INS CORP
OH	24	48	0	7	2	5	0	1	0	12	NATIONWIDE MUTUAL FIRE INS CO
DE	0	0	0	100	0	0	0	0	0	0	NUCLEAR ELECTRIC INS LTD
IL (*)	0	0	0	0	0	0	0	0	0	0	OGLESBY REINS CO
OH	40	7	1	24	12	5	0	8	0	3	OWNERS INS CO
IL	25	13	0	25	10	4	0	20	0	3	PEKIN INS CO
IN	5	45	2	26	7	3	0	7	0	5	PROPERTY-OWNERS INS CO
IN	18	0	0	0	17	20	0	40	4	1	PROTECTIVE INS CO
PA	0	0	0	0	0	0	0	0	0	100	RADIAN REINS INC
FL	0	0	0	0	0	0	0	100	0	0	RETAILFIRST INS CO
MN	0	0	0	0	0	42	0	0	0	58	SECURIAN CASUALTY CO
WI	21	0	0	2	13	9	0	34	1	20	SENTRY INS A MUTUAL CO
WI	16	0	0	0	43	10	0	5	1	25	SENTRY SELECT INS CO
NY	2	0	0	7	6	10	0	26	0	49	SOMPO AMERICA INSURANCE CO
MI	49	2	0	13	3	27	0	4	0	2	SOUTHERN-OWNERS INS CO

(*) Denotes reinsurers, companies that do not sell to consumers

RATING	INSURANCE COMPANY NAME	ADDRESS	CITY	STATE	ZIP	PHONE
B+	STATE FARM FIRE & CAS CO	ONE STATE FARM PLAZA	BLOOMINGTON	IL	61710	(309) 766-2311
B+	STATE FARM MUTUAL AUTOMOBILE INS CO	ONE STATE FARM PLAZA	BLOOMINGTON	IL	61710	(309) 766-2311
B+	TENNESSEE FARMERS ASR CO	147 BEAR CREEK PIKE	COLUMBIA	TN	38401	(931) 388-7872
B+	TENNESSEE FARMERS MUTUAL INS CO	147 BEAR CREEK PIKE	COLUMBIA	TN	38401	(931) 388-7872
B+	TEXAS FARM BUREAU CASUALTY INS CO	7420 FISH POND ROAD	WACO	TX	76710	(254) 772-3030
B+	TOA REINS CO OF AMERICA	2711 CENTERVILLE ROAD STE 400	WILMINGTON	DE	19808	(973) 898-9480
A	TOKIO MARINE AMERICA INS CO	230 PARK AVENUE	NEW YORK	NY	10169	(610) 227-1253
A-	TRAVELERS CASUALTY & SURETY CO	ONE TOWER SQUARE	HARTFORD	CT	06183	(860) 277-0111
B+	TRAVELERS INDEMNITY CO	ONE TOWER SQUARE	HARTFORD	CT	06183	(860) 277-0111
B+	UNITED SERVICES AUTOMOBILE ASN	9800 FREDERICKSBURG ROAD	SAN ANTONIO	TX	78288	(210) 498-2211
A-	USAA CASUALTY INS CO	9800 FREDERICKSBURG ROAD	SAN ANTONIO	TX	78288	(210) 498-1411
B+	USAA GENERAL INDEMNITY CO	9800 FREDERICKSBURG ROAD	SAN ANTONIO	TX	78288	(210) 498-1411
B+	WEST BEND MUTUAL INS CO	1900 SOUTH 18TH AVENUE	WEST BEND	WI	53095	(262) 334-5571
B+	WESTERN AGRICULTURAL INS CO	5400 UNIVERSITY AVENUE	WEST DES MOINES	IA	50266	(515) 225-5400

DOM. STATE	AUTO	HOME MULT. PERIL	FARM MULT. PERIL	COMM. MULT. PERIL	COMM. AUTO LIAB.	OTHER LIABILITY	MED MALPRAC.	WORK. COMP.	ACCID. & HEALTH	OTHER	INSURANCE COMPANY NAME
IL	13	71	1	6	0	3	0	1	0	4	STATE FARM FIRE & CAS CO
IL	97	0	0	0	1	0	0	0	3	0	STATE FARM MUTUAL AUTOMOBILE INS CO
TN (*)	0	0	0	0	0	0	0	0	0	0	TENNESSEE FARMERS ASR CO
TN	51	31	10	1	0	2	0	0	0	5	TENNESSEE FARMERS MUTUAL INS CO
TX	96	0	0	0	2	2	0	0	0	0	TEXAS FARM BUREAU CASUALTY INS CO
DE (*)	0	0	0	0	0	0	0	0	0	0	TOA REINS CO OF AMERICA
NY	8	2	0	9	15	8	0	9	0	47	TOKIO MARINE AMERICA INS CO
CT	0	8	0	0	0	1	0	74	0	17	TRAVELERS CASUALTY & SURETY CO
CT	4	3	1	15	12	20	0	22	0	23	TRAVELERS INDEMNITY CO
TX	57	34	0	0	0	2	0	0	0	7	UNITED SERVICES AUTOMOBILE ASN
TX	65	30	0	0	0	1	0	0	0	4	USAA CASUALTY INS CO
TX	72	21	0	0	0	0	0	0	0	7	USAA GENERAL INDEMNITY CO
WI	19	12	0	4	6	17	0	24	0	17	WEST BEND MUTUAL INS CO
IA	16	12	10	8	2	1	0	3	0	48	WESTERN AGRICULTURAL INS CO

(*) Denotes reinsurers, companies that do not sell to consumers

Section IV

Weiss Recommended Companies by Type of Business

A compilation of those

U.S. Property and Casualty Insurers

receiving a Weiss Safety Rating

of A+, A, A- or B+.

Companies are ranked by Safety Rating
in each line of business where they have received
more than $1 million in direct premiums.

Section IV Contents

This section is broken into six subsections, each presenting a list of the recommended carriers receiving at least $1 million in direct premiums from a particular line of business: Auto, Commercial Multiple Peril, Fire and Allied, Homeowners Multiple Peril, Medical Malpractice, and Workers' Compensation. Recommended companies are those insurers receiving a Safety Rating of A+, A, A- or B+. If an insurer is not on this list, it should not be automatically assumed that the firm is weak. Indeed, there are many firms that have not achieved a B+ or better rating but are in relatively good condition with adequate resources to cover their risk during an average recession. Not being included in this list should not be construed as a recommendation to cancel policies.

Companies are ranked within each line of business by their Safety Rating. However, companies with the same rating should be viewed as having the same relative financial strength regardless of their ranking in these tables. While the specific order in which they appear on the page is based upon differences in our underlying indexes, you can assume that companies with the same rating have differences that are only minor and relatively inconsequential.

The six lines of business covered in this section are defined as follows:

Auto: Coverage for auto physical damage and auto liability. Auto physical covers damage to the policyholder's own automobile. Auto liability covers against financial loss from lawsuits (and legal settlements) for auto-related bodily injuries or property damage caused by the insured.

Commercial Multiple Peril: Package policies for business and other commercial establishments providing a broad spectrum of property and liability coverages.

Fire & Allied: Coverage for losses caused by fire, lightning, sprinkler damage, windstorm, and water damage.

Homeowners Multiple Peril: Package policies for homeowners providing a broad spectrum of property and liability coverages.

Medical Malpractice: Errors and omissions liability coverages for persons engaged in the practice of medicine, surgery, dentistry, nursing, pharmacy, or other health care services. Also covers health care institutions.

Workers' Compensation: Liability coverage issued to employers which provides for the payment of medical care, certain disability income benefits and possible additional liability amounts to employees who are injured on the job.

Column definitions are as follows:

1. **Insurance Company Name**

   The legally-registered name, which can sometimes differ from the name that the company uses for advertising. An insurer's name can be very similar to the name of other companies which may not be on our Recommended List, so make sure you note the exact name before contacting your agent.

2. **Domicile State**

   The state which has primary regulatory responsibility for the company. It may differ from the location of the company's corporate headquarters. You do not have to be living in the domicile state to purchase insurance from this firm, provided it is licensed to do business in your state.

3. **Total Premiums**

   Total direct premiums received by the company during the year for all types of policies.

4. **Policy-Type Premium**

   Direct premiums received by the company for a specific type of insurance coverage, such as Auto Premiums. Companies that have less than $1,000,000 in this type of premium are not listed.

5. **Maximum Benefit**

   Conservative consumers may want to limit the size of their policy with this company to the amount shown. This figure is based on the view that a policy's maximum benefits per risk should not exceed 1% of the company's capital and surplus.

Weiss Safety Ratings are not deemed to be a recommendation concerning the purchase or sale of the securities of any insurance company that is publicly owned.

Auto

INSURANCE COMPANY NAME	DOMICILE STATE	TOTAL PREMIUM ($)	AUTO PREMIUM ($)	MAXIMUM BENEFIT ($)
Rating: **A**				
CINCINNATI INS CO	OH	3,675,892,348	1,066,346,916	50,000,000
SENTRY INS A MUTUAL CO	WI	509,963,935	174,494,107	50,000,000
TOKIO MARINE AMERICA INS CO	NY	424,537,689	99,633,323	5,000,000
Rating: **A-**				
AUTO-OWNERS INS CO	MI	3,047,950,748	867,005,202	100,000,000
BUILDERS MUTUAL INS CO	NC	255,812,971	5,906,226	3,000,000
CINCINNATI INDEMNITY CO	OH	428,448,594	83,094,967	900,000
COUNTRY MUTUAL INS CO	IL	1,548,698,580	422,447,941	20,000,000
CUMIS INS SOCIETY INC	IA	440,400,020	13,578,928	9,000,000
GEICO SECURE INS CO	NE	296,296,056	296,296,056	3,000,000
HOME-OWNERS INS CO	MI	973,399,213	821,024,427	10,000,000
MOTORISTS COMMERCIAL MUTUAL INS CO	OH	32,987,259	15,927,843	1,000,000
OWNERS INS CO	OH	1,699,528,992	885,436,453	20,000,000
PROTECTIVE INS CO	IN	367,213,000	128,289,038	4,000,000
SOMPO AMERICA INSURANCE CO	NY	343,418,512	26,325,856	5,000,000
SOUTHERN-OWNERS INS CO	MI	344,671,872	178,710,987	2,000,000
USAA CASUALTY INS CO	TX	5,791,560,846	3,750,256,587	40,000,000
Rating: **B+**				
ACUITY A MUTUAL INS CO	WI	1,376,334,520	511,642,499	20,000,000
ALFA MUTUAL GENERAL INS CO	AL	55,586,005	28,964,496	600,000
ALFA SPECIALTY INS CORP	VA	78,632,123	78,632,123	300,000
ALL AMERICA INS CO	OH	42,570,911	12,609,538	1,000,000
ALLSTATE NJ INS CO	IL	491,996,918	308,410,915	8,000,000
AMERICAN FAMILY MUTL INS CO SI	WI	5,238,090,945	2,704,209,501	70,000,000
AMERICAN STANDARD INS CO OF WI	WI	175,143,273	175,143,273	3,000,000
AMICA MUTUAL INS CO	RI	2,098,879,721	1,191,337,261	20,000,000
BROTHERHOOD MUTUAL INS CO	IN	420,923,459	30,571,630	2,000,000
COUNTRY CASUALTY INS CO	IL	39,125,915	25,716,011	700,000
DAIRYLAND INS CO	WI	133,957,714	133,957,714	5,000,000
FARM BUREAU P&C INS CO	IA	1,194,278,912	476,522,386	10,000,000
FARM FAMILY CASUALTY INS CO	NY	380,234,909	107,908,695	4,000,000
FARMERS AUTOMOBILE INS ASN	IL	241,837,452	148,207,046	5,000,000
GEICO CHOICE INS CO	NE	573,055,406	573,055,406	4,000,000
GEICO GENERAL INS CO	MD	8,605,583,249	8,605,583,248	1,000,000
INTERINS EXCHANGE	CA	2,709,139,732	2,142,263,937	60,000,000
MERCURY INS CO	CA	1,560,463,480	1,560,463,480	6,000,000
MITSUI SUMITOMO INS CO OF AMER	NY	235,181,299	19,268,493	3,000,000
MOTORISTS MUTUAL INS CO	OH	448,812,138	200,865,269	5,000,000
NATIONAL CASUALTY CO	OH	867,741,119	273,201,976	1,000,000
NATIONWIDE MUTUAL FIRE INS CO	OH	1,479,542,158	383,007,510	30,000,000
PEKIN INS CO	IL	404,990,838	141,579,417	1,000,000
PROPERTY-OWNERS INS CO	IN	155,168,711	19,403,408	1,000,000

Auto (Continued)

INSURANCE COMPANY NAME	DOMICILE STATE	TOTAL PREMIUM ($)	AUTO PREMIUM ($)	MAXIMUM BENEFIT ($)
Rating: **B+** **(Continued)**				
SENTRY SELECT INS CO	WI	516,203,001	306,178,955	2,000,000
STATE FARM FIRE & CAS CO	IL	19,397,522,500	2,628,519,925	200,000,000
STATE FARM MUTUAL AUTOMOBILE INS CO	IL	37,093,556,809	36,127,072,452	900,000,000
TENNESSEE FARMERS MUTUAL INS CO	TN	1,209,826,004	623,203,052	20,000,000
TEXAS FARM BUREAU CASUALTY INS CO	TX	239,440,573	233,683,623	6,000,000
TRAVELERS INDEMNITY CO	CT	1,829,606,390	293,014,632	70,000,000
UNITED SERVICES AUTOMOBILE ASN	TX	7,379,396,228	4,213,431,004	200,000,000
USAA GENERAL INDEMNITY CO	TX	3,383,504,509	2,430,402,636	10,000,000
WEST BEND MUTUAL INS CO	WI	1,115,054,412	286,189,138	9,000,000
WESTERN AGRICULTURAL INS CO	IA	257,857,738	47,071,751	1,000,000

Commercial Multiple Peril

INSURANCE COMPANY NAME	DOMICILE STATE	TOTAL PREMIUM ($)	COMM. MULT. PERIL PREMIUM ($)	MAXIMUM BENEFIT ($)
Rating: A+				
NUCLEAR ELECTRIC INS LTD	DE	209,773,193	209,773,193	40,000,000
Rating: A				
CINCINNATI INS CO	OH	3,675,892,348	1,556,336,705	50,000,000
SENTRY INS A MUTUAL CO	WI	509,963,935	56,721,582	50,000,000
TOKIO MARINE AMERICA INS CO	NY	424,537,689	75,898,001	5,000,000
Rating: A-				
AUTO-OWNERS INS CO	MI	3,047,950,748	473,770,948	100,000,000
BUILDERS MUTUAL INS CO	NC	255,812,971	39,116,067	3,000,000
CINCINNATI INDEMNITY CO	OH	428,448,594	168,951,368	900,000
CINCINNATI SPECIALTY UNDERWRITER	DE	198,714,015	141,812,448	4,000,000
COPIC INS CO	CO	84,657,615	3,224,282	4,000,000
COUNTRY MUTUAL INS CO	IL	1,548,698,580	150,009,894	20,000,000
CUMIS INS SOCIETY INC	IA	440,400,020	353,000,763	9,000,000
ENDURANCE ASR CORP	DE	45,261,579	19,098,967	8,000,000
HOME-OWNERS INS CO	MI	973,399,213	107,141,431	10,000,000
MOTORISTS COMMERCIAL MUTUAL INS CO	OH	32,987,259	11,605,703	1,000,000
OWNERS INS CO	OH	1,699,528,992	492,244,661	20,000,000
PROTECTIVE INS CO	IN	367,213,000	72,744,557	4,000,000
SECURIAN CASUALTY CO	MN	244,987,557	101,788,673	1,000,000
SOMPO AMERICA INSURANCE CO	NY	343,418,512	57,298,995	5,000,000
SOUTHERN-OWNERS INS CO	MI	344,671,872	136,666,136	2,000,000
TRAVELERS CASUALTY & SURETY CO	CT	315,024,322	3,129,488	60,000,000
USAA CASUALTY INS CO	TX	5,791,560,846	58,134,302	40,000,000
Rating: B+				
ACUITY A MUTUAL INS CO	WI	1,376,334,520	286,013,344	20,000,000
ALL AMERICA INS CO	OH	42,570,911	24,465,558	1,000,000
ALLSTATE NJ INS CO	IL	491,996,918	13,750,852	8,000,000
AMERICAN FAMILY MUTL INS CO SI	WI	5,238,090,945	565,719,546	70,000,000
AMICA MUTUAL INS CO	RI	2,098,879,721	58,787,264	20,000,000
BROTHERHOOD MUTUAL INS CO	IN	420,923,459	322,544,679	2,000,000
FARM BUREAU P&C INS CO	IA	1,194,278,912	81,352,153	10,000,000
FARM FAMILY CASUALTY INS CO	NY	380,234,909	94,460,110	4,000,000
INTERINS EXCHANGE	CA	2,709,139,732	14,364,074	60,000,000
MITSUI SUMITOMO INS CO OF AMER	NY	235,181,299	79,379,228	3,000,000
MOTORISTS MUTUAL INS CO	OH	448,812,138	126,371,679	5,000,000
NATIONAL CASUALTY CO	OH	867,741,119	218,578,053	1,000,000
NATIONWIDE MUTUAL FIRE INS CO	OH	1,479,542,158	183,354,104	30,000,000
PEKIN INS CO	IL	404,990,838	119,253,404	1,000,000
PROPERTY-OWNERS INS CO	IN	155,168,711	45,245,474	1,000,000
SENTRY SELECT INS CO	WI	516,203,001	50,037,822	2,000,000
STATE FARM FIRE & CAS CO	IL	19,397,522,500	1,764,644,139	200,000,000
STATE FARM MUTUAL AUTOMOBILE INS CO	IL	37,093,556,809	3,317,431	900,000,000
TENNESSEE FARMERS MUTUAL INS CO	TN	1,209,826,004	30,740,608	20,000,000
TEXAS FARM BUREAU CASUALTY INS CO	TX	239,440,573	5,756,950	6,000,000

Commercial Multiple Peril (Continued)

INSURANCE COMPANY NAME	DOMICILE STATE	TOTAL PREMIUM ($)	COMM. MULT. PERIL PREMIUM ($)	MAXIMUM BENEFIT ($)
Rating: B+ (Continued)				
TRAVELERS INDEMNITY CO	CT	1,829,606,390	634,275,511	70,000,000
UNITED SERVICES AUTOMOBILE ASN	TX	7,379,396,228	135,085,394	200,000,000
USAA GENERAL INDEMNITY CO	TX	3,383,504,509	12,459,015	10,000,000
WEST BEND MUTUAL INS CO	WI	1,115,054,412	232,551,592	9,000,000
WESTERN AGRICULTURAL INS CO	IA	257,857,738	23,465,208	1,000,000

Fire & Allied

INSURANCE COMPANY NAME	DOMICILE STATE	TOTAL PREMIUM ($)	FIRE & ALLIED PREMIUM ($)	MAXIMUM BENEFIT ($)
Rating: A+				
CITIZENS PROPERTY INS CORP	FL	973,840,305	545,116,741	70,000,000
Rating: A				
CINCINNATI INS CO	OH	3,675,892,348	163,346,814	50,000,000
SENTRY INS A MUTUAL CO	WI	509,963,935	68,292,145	50,000,000
TOKIO MARINE AMERICA INS CO	NY	424,537,689	76,665,526	5,000,000
Rating: A-				
AUTO-OWNERS INS CO	MI	3,047,950,748	338,044,909	100,000,000
CINCINNATI INDEMNITY CO	OH	428,448,594	31,722,072	900,000
CINCINNATI SPECIALTY UNDERWRITER	DE	198,714,015	26,562,357	4,000,000
COUNTRY MUTUAL INS CO	IL	1,548,698,580	99,761,054	20,000,000
CUMIS INS SOCIETY INC	IA	440,400,020	1,535,367	9,000,000
HOME-OWNERS INS CO	MI	973,399,213	2,471,462	10,000,000
OWNERS INS CO	OH	1,699,528,992	10,586,942	20,000,000
SOMPO AMERICA INSURANCE CO	NY	343,418,512	94,345,205	5,000,000
TRAVELERS CASUALTY & SURETY CO	CT	315,024,322	3,661,622	60,000,000
USAA CASUALTY INS CO	TX	5,791,560,846	133,089,513	40,000,000
Rating: B+				
ACUITY A MUTUAL INS CO	WI	1,376,334,520	73,877,668	20,000,000
ALLSTATE NJ INS CO	IL	491,996,918	9,980,054	8,000,000
AMERICAN FAMILY MUTL INS CO SI	WI	5,238,090,945	22,309,013	70,000,000
AMICA MUTUAL INS CO	RI	2,098,879,721	30,222,529	20,000,000
FARM FAMILY CASUALTY INS CO	NY	380,234,909	77,834,561	4,000,000
FARMERS AUTOMOBILE INS ASN	IL	241,837,452	11,334,385	5,000,000
INTERINS EXCHANGE	CA	2,709,139,732	21,734,159	60,000,000
MITSUI SUMITOMO INS CO OF AMER	NY	235,181,299	24,549,202	3,000,000
MOTORISTS MUTUAL INS CO	OH	448,812,138	5,311,037	5,000,000
NATIONAL CASUALTY CO	OH	867,741,119	9,309,864	1,000,000
NATIONWIDE MUTUAL FIRE INS CO	OH	1,479,542,158	145,140,547	30,000,000
PEKIN INS CO	IL	404,990,838	4,938,729	1,000,000
SENTRY SELECT INS CO	WI	516,203,001	33,684,748	2,000,000
STATE FARM FIRE & CAS CO	IL	19,397,522,500	43,542,112	200,000,000
TENNESSEE FARMERS MUTUAL INS CO	TN	1,209,826,004	64,371,846	20,000,000
TRAVELERS INDEMNITY CO	CT	1,829,606,390	336,695,969	70,000,000
UNITED SERVICES AUTOMOBILE ASN	TX	7,379,396,228	342,005,867	200,000,000
USAA GENERAL INDEMNITY CO	TX	3,383,504,509	190,633,275	10,000,000
WEST BEND MUTUAL INS CO	WI	1,115,054,412	115,337,526	9,000,000
WESTERN AGRICULTURAL INS CO	IA	257,857,738	124,056,332	1,000,000

Homeowners Multiple Peril

INSURANCE COMPANY NAME	DOMICILE STATE	TOTAL PREMIUM ($)	HOME OWNERS PREMIUM ($)	MAXIMUM BENEFIT ($)
Rating: A+				
CITIZENS PROPERTY INS CORP	FL	973,840,305	428,723,564	70,000,000
Rating: A				
CINCINNATI INS CO	OH	3,675,892,348	518,289,627	50,000,000
TOKIO MARINE AMERICA INS CO	NY	424,537,689	10,307,548	5,000,000
Rating: A-				
AUTO-OWNERS INS CO	MI	3,047,950,748	1,046,679,644	100,000,000
COUNTRY MUTUAL INS CO	IL	1,548,698,580	657,143,461	20,000,000
HOME-OWNERS INS CO	MI	973,399,213	4,604,577	10,000,000
OWNERS INS CO	OH	1,699,528,992	117,923,264	20,000,000
SOUTHERN-OWNERS INS CO	MI	344,671,872	7,943,731	2,000,000
TRAVELERS CASUALTY & SURETY CO	CT	315,024,322	26,122,423	60,000,000
USAA CASUALTY INS CO	TX	5,791,560,846	1,740,161,294	40,000,000
Rating: B+				
ACUITY A MUTUAL INS CO	WI	1,376,334,520	139,604,267	20,000,000
ALFA MUTUAL GENERAL INS CO	AL	55,586,005	26,148,114	600,000
ALLSTATE NJ INS CO	IL	491,996,918	155,081,119	8,000,000
AMERICAN FAMILY MUTL INS CO SI	WI	5,238,090,945	1,715,916,590	70,000,000
AMICA MUTUAL INS CO	RI	2,098,879,721	777,210,365	20,000,000
AUTO CLUB INDEMNITY CO	TX	113,208,535	112,210,574	50,000
COUNTRY CASUALTY INS CO	IL	39,125,915	13,374,422	700,000
FARM BUREAU P&C INS CO	IA	1,194,278,912	287,670,093	10,000,000
FARM FAMILY CASUALTY INS CO	NY	380,234,909	22,238,707	4,000,000
FARMERS AUTOMOBILE INS ASN	IL	241,837,452	79,347,812	5,000,000
INTERINS EXCHANGE	CA	2,709,139,732	525,483,847	60,000,000
MOTORISTS MUTUAL INS CO	OH	448,812,138	68,843,878	5,000,000
NATIONWIDE MUTUAL FIRE INS CO	OH	1,479,542,158	716,991,746	30,000,000
PEKIN INS CO	IL	404,990,838	51,465,520	1,000,000
PROPERTY-OWNERS INS CO	IN	155,168,711	69,423,093	1,000,000
STATE FARM FIRE & CAS CO	IL	19,397,522,500	13,688,078,880	200,000,000
TENNESSEE FARMERS MUTUAL INS CO	TN	1,209,826,004	375,248,314	20,000,000
TRAVELERS INDEMNITY CO	CT	1,829,606,390	47,164,280	70,000,000
UNITED SERVICES AUTOMOBILE ASN	TX	7,379,396,228	2,531,150,808	200,000,000
USAA GENERAL INDEMNITY CO	TX	3,383,504,509	710,252,011	10,000,000
WEST BEND MUTUAL INS CO	WI	1,115,054,412	133,323,853	9,000,000
WESTERN AGRICULTURAL INS CO	IA	257,857,738	30,774,867	1,000,000

Medical Malpractice

INSURANCE COMPANY NAME		DOMICILE STATE	TOTAL PREMIUM ($)	MEDICAL MALPRACTICE PREMIUM ($)	MAXIMUM BENEFIT ($)
Rating:	**A**				
CINCINNATI INS CO		OH	3,675,892,348	33,353,534	50,000,000
Rating:	**A-**				
CINCINNATI INDEMNITY CO		OH	428,448,594	2,199,265	900,000
COPIC INS CO		CO	84,657,615	80,331,393	4,000,000
Rating:	**B+**				
STATE FARM FIRE & CAS CO		IL	19,397,522,500	2,742,285	200,000,000

Workers' Compensation

INSURANCE COMPANY NAME	DOMICILE STATE	TOTAL PREMIUM ($)	WORKERS' COMPENSATION PREMIUM ($)	MAXIMUM BENEFIT ($)
Rating: **A+**				
COPPERPOINT MUTUAL INS CO	AZ	60,217,953	60,196,557	10,000,000
Rating: **A**				
CINCINNATI INS CO	OH	3,675,892,348	90,397,737	50,000,000
SENTRY INS A MUTUAL CO	WI	509,963,935	173,382,879	50,000,000
TOKIO MARINE AMERICA INS CO	NY	424,537,689	37,953,101	5,000,000
Rating: **A-**				
AUTO-OWNERS INS CO	MI	3,047,950,748	187,666,694	100,000,000
BUILDERS MUTUAL INS CO	NC	255,812,971	192,672,486	3,000,000
CINCINNATI INDEMNITY CO	OH	428,448,594	125,390,945	900,000
COUNTRY MUTUAL INS CO	IL	1,548,698,580	65,127,170	20,000,000
EMPLOYERS COMPENSATION INS CO	CA	49,246,365	49,246,365	3,000,000
HOME-OWNERS INS CO	MI	973,399,213	29,789,563	10,000,000
MOTORISTS COMMERCIAL MUTUAL INS CO	OH	32,987,259	1,071,366	1,000,000
OWNERS INS CO	OH	1,699,528,992	138,350,540	20,000,000
PROTECTIVE INS CO	IN	367,213,000	147,124,827	4,000,000
RETAILFIRST INS CO	FL	90,854,490	90,854,490	1,000,000
SOMPO AMERICA INSURANCE CO	NY	343,418,512	90,997,805	5,000,000
SOUTHERN-OWNERS INS CO	MI	344,671,872	14,494,645	2,000,000
TRAVELERS CASUALTY & SURETY CO	CT	315,024,322	233,316,217	60,000,000
Rating: **B+**				
ACUITY A MUTUAL INS CO	WI	1,376,334,520	312,118,060	20,000,000
ALL AMERICA INS CO	OH	42,570,911	3,537,443	1,000,000
AMERICAN FAMILY MUTL INS CO SI	WI	5,238,090,945	55,586,478	70,000,000
BROTHERHOOD MUTUAL INS CO	IN	420,923,459	54,239,042	2,000,000
FARM BUREAU P&C INS CO	IA	1,194,278,912	32,526,759	10,000,000
FARM FAMILY CASUALTY INS CO	NY	380,234,909	58,370,523	4,000,000
MITSUI SUMITOMO INS CO OF AMER	NY	235,181,299	69,006,606	3,000,000
MOTORISTS MUTUAL INS CO	OH	448,812,138	22,253,851	5,000,000
NATIONAL CASUALTY CO	OH	867,741,119	44,332,347	1,000,000
NATIONWIDE MUTUAL FIRE INS CO	OH	1,479,542,158	17,583,773	30,000,000
PEKIN INS CO	IL	404,990,838	81,797,033	1,000,000
PROPERTY-OWNERS INS CO	IN	155,168,711	10,112,938	1,000,000
SENTRY SELECT INS CO	WI	516,203,001	26,786,076	2,000,000
STATE FARM FIRE & CAS CO	IL	19,397,522,500	269,479,669	200,000,000
TRAVELERS INDEMNITY CO	CT	1,829,606,390	408,789,706	70,000,000
WEST BEND MUTUAL INS CO	WI	1,115,054,412	269,385,466	9,000,000
WESTERN AGRICULTURAL INS CO	IA	257,857,738	7,118,485	1,000,000

Section V

Weiss
Recommended Companies
by State

A compilation of those

U.S. Property and Casualty Insurers

receiving a Weiss Safety Rating

of A+, A, A- or B+.

Companies are ranked by Safety Rating
in each state where they are licensed to do business.

Section V Contents

This section provides a list of the recommended carriers licensed to do business in each state. It contains all insurers receiving a Safety Rating of A+, A, A- or B+. If an insurer is not on this list, it should not be automatically assumed that the firm is weak. Indeed, there are many firms that have not achieved a B+ or better rating but are in relatively good condition with adequate resources to cover their risk during an average recession. Not being included in this list should not be construed as a recommendation to cancel policies.

Companies are ranked within each state by their Safety Rating. However, companies with the same rating should be viewed as having the same relative safety regardless of their ranking in this table. While the specific order in which they appear on the page is based upon differences in our underlying indexes, you can assume that companies with the same rating have differences that are only minor and relatively inconsequential.

1.	**Insurance Company Name**	The legally-registered name, which can sometimes differ from the name that the company uses for advertising. An insurer's name can be very similar to the name of other companies which may not be on our Recommended List, so make sure you note the exact name before contacting your agent.
2.	**Domicile State**	The state which has primary regulatory responsibility for the company. It may differ from the location of the company's corporate headquarters. You do not have to be living in the domicile state to purchase insurance from this firm, provided it is licensed to do business in your state.
3.	**Total Assets**	All assets admitted by state insurance regulators in millions of dollars. This includes investments and current business assets such as receivables from agents and reinsurers.

Weiss Safety Ratings are not deemed to be a recommendation concerning the purchase or sale of the securities of any insurance company that is publicly owned.

Alabama

INSURANCE COMPANY NAME	DOM. STATE	TOTAL ASSETS ($MIL)
Rating:	**A+**	
BERKSHIRE HATHAWAY ASR CORP	NY	2,454.3
Rating:	**A**	
CINCINNATI INS CO	OH	12,253.3
SENTRY INS A MUTUAL CO	WI	7,779.6
TOKIO MARINE AMERICA INS CO	NY	1,401.2
Rating:	**A-**	
AUTO-OWNERS INS CO	MI	14,502.3
CINCINNATI INDEMNITY CO	OH	132.7
CINCINNATI SPECIALTY UNDERWRITER	DE	744.7
COUNTRY MUTUAL INS CO	IL	4,756.8
CUMIS INS SOCIETY INC	IA	1,894.2
EMPLOYERS COMPENSATION INS CO	CA	1,095.5
ENDURANCE ASR CORP	DE	1,824.1
ESSENT GUARANTY INC	PA	1,384.2
GEICO SECURE INS CO	NE	555.9
HOME-OWNERS INS CO	MI	2,197.5
NATIONAL MORTGAGE INS CORP	WI	645.5
OWNERS INS CO	OH	3,948.4
PROTECTIVE INS CO	IN	799.3
SECURIAN CASUALTY CO	MN	288.6
SOMPO AMERICA INSURANCE CO	NY	1,235.5
TRAVELERS CASUALTY & SURETY CO	CT	16,679.3
USAA CASUALTY INS CO	TX	10,235.4
Rating:	**B+**	
ACUITY A MUTUAL INS CO	WI	3,686.4
ALFA MUTUAL GENERAL INS CO	AL	111.8
ALFA SPECIALTY INS CORP	VA	57.1
AMICA MUTUAL INS CO	RI	5,140.7
BROTHERHOOD MUTUAL INS CO	IN	591.8
COUNTRY CASUALTY INS CO	IL	85.4
DAIRYLAND INS CO	WI	1,297.4
GEICO CHOICE INS CO	NE	919.4
GEICO GENERAL INS CO	MD	166.1
MARKEL GLOBAL REINS CO	DE	1,943.5
MITSUI SUMITOMO INS CO OF AMER	NY	958.1
MOTORISTS MUTUAL INS CO	OH	1,368.4
NATIONAL CASUALTY CO	OH	404.6
NATIONWIDE MUTUAL FIRE INS CO	OH	8,809.3
PROPERTY-OWNERS INS CO	IN	289.0
SENTRY SELECT INS CO	WI	715.6
STATE FARM FIRE & CAS CO	IL	38,866.0
STATE FARM MUTUAL AUTOMOBILE INS CO	IL	150,198.0
TOA REINS CO OF AMERICA	DE	1,749.0
TRAVELERS INDEMNITY CO	CT	21,493.8
UNITED SERVICES AUTOMOBILE ASN	TX	33,965.5
USAA GENERAL INDEMNITY CO	TX	4,214.9
WESTERN AGRICULTURAL INS CO	IA	217.1

INSURANCE COMPANY NAME	DOM. STATE	TOTAL ASSETS ($MIL)

Alaska

INSURANCE COMPANY NAME	DOM. STATE	TOTAL ASSETS ($MIL)
Rating: A+		
BERKSHIRE HATHAWAY ASR CORP	NY	2,454.3
Rating: A		
CINCINNATI INS CO	OH	12,253.3
SENTRY INS A MUTUAL CO	WI	7,779.6
TOKIO MARINE AMERICA INS CO	NY	1,401.2
Rating: A-		
CINCINNATI INDEMNITY CO	OH	132.7
CINCINNATI SPECIALTY UNDERWRITER	DE	744.7
COUNTRY MUTUAL INS CO	IL	4,756.8
CUMIS INS SOCIETY INC	IA	1,894.2
ENDURANCE ASR CORP	DE	1,824.1
ESSENT GUARANTY INC	PA	1,384.2
GEICO SECURE INS CO	NE	555.9
NATIONAL MORTGAGE INS CORP	WI	645.5
PROTECTIVE INS CO	IN	799.3
SECURIAN CASUALTY CO	MN	288.6
SOMPO AMERICA INSURANCE CO	NY	1,235.5
TRAVELERS CASUALTY & SURETY CO	CT	16,679.3
USAA CASUALTY INS CO	TX	10,235.4
Rating: B+		
AMICA MUTUAL INS CO	RI	5,140.7
BROTHERHOOD MUTUAL INS CO	IN	591.8
COUNTRY CASUALTY INS CO	IL	85.4
DAIRYLAND INS CO	WI	1,297.4
GEICO CHOICE INS CO	NE	919.4
GEICO GENERAL INS CO	MD	166.1
MARKEL GLOBAL REINS CO	DE	1,943.5
MITSUI SUMITOMO INS CO OF AMER	NY	958.1
NATIONAL CASUALTY CO	OH	404.6
NATIONWIDE MUTUAL FIRE INS CO	OH	8,809.3
SENTRY SELECT INS CO	WI	715.6
STATE FARM FIRE & CAS CO	IL	38,866.0
STATE FARM MUTUAL AUTOMOBILE INS CO	IL	150,198.0
TOA REINS CO OF AMERICA	DE	1,749.0
TRAVELERS INDEMNITY CO	CT	21,493.8
UNITED SERVICES AUTOMOBILE ASN	TX	33,965.5
USAA GENERAL INDEMNITY CO	TX	4,214.9

Arizona

INSURANCE COMPANY NAME	DOM. STATE	TOTAL ASSETS ($MIL)
Rating: A+		
BERKSHIRE HATHAWAY ASR CORP	NY	2,454.3
COPPERPOINT MUTUAL INS CO	AZ	3,655.7
Rating: A		
CINCINNATI INS CO	OH	12,253.3
SENTRY INS A MUTUAL CO	WI	7,779.6
TOKIO MARINE AMERICA INS CO	NY	1,401.2
Rating: A-		
AUTO-OWNERS INS CO	MI	14,502.3
CINCINNATI INDEMNITY CO	OH	132.7
CINCINNATI SPECIALTY UNDERWRITER	DE	744.7
COPIC INS CO	CO	716.3
COUNTRY MUTUAL INS CO	IL	4,756.8
CUMIS INS SOCIETY INC	IA	1,894.2
EMPLOYERS COMPENSATION INS CO	CA	1,095.5
ENDURANCE ASR CORP	DE	1,824.1
ESSENT GUARANTY INC	PA	1,384.2
GEICO SECURE INS CO	NE	555.9
MOTORISTS COMMERCIAL MUTUAL INS CO	OH	358.9
NATIONAL MORTGAGE INS CORP	WI	645.5
OWNERS INS CO	OH	3,948.4
PROTECTIVE INS CO	IN	799.3
SECURIAN CASUALTY CO	MN	288.6
SOMPO AMERICA INSURANCE CO	NY	1,235.5
TRAVELERS CASUALTY & SURETY CO	CT	16,679.3
USAA CASUALTY INS CO	TX	10,235.4
Rating: B+		
ACUITY A MUTUAL INS CO	WI	3,686.4
ALL AMERICA INS CO	OH	285.9
AMERICAN FAMILY MUTL INS CO SI	WI	16,206.4
AMERICAN STANDARD INS CO OF WI	WI	401.3
AMICA MUTUAL INS CO	RI	5,140.7
BROTHERHOOD MUTUAL INS CO	IN	591.8
COUNTRY CASUALTY INS CO	IL	85.4
DAIRYLAND INS CO	WI	1,297.4
FARM BUREAU P&C INS CO	IA	2,529.1
FARMERS AUTOMOBILE INS ASN	IL	1,277.1
GEICO CHOICE INS CO	NE	919.4
GEICO GENERAL INS CO	MD	166.1
GNY CUSTOM INS CO	AZ	59.3
MARKEL GLOBAL REINS CO	DE	1,943.5
MITSUI SUMITOMO INS CO OF AMER	NY	958.1
NATIONAL CASUALTY CO	OH	404.6
NATIONWIDE MUTUAL FIRE INS CO	OH	8,809.3
PEKIN INS CO	IL	306.7
SENTRY SELECT INS CO	WI	715.6
STATE FARM FIRE & CAS CO	IL	38,866.0
STATE FARM MUTUAL AUTOMOBILE INS CO	IL	150,198.0
TOA REINS CO OF AMERICA	DE	1,749.0
TRAVELERS INDEMNITY CO	CT	21,493.8
UNITED SERVICES AUTOMOBILE ASN	TX	33,965.5
USAA GENERAL INDEMNITY CO	TX	4,214.9
WESTERN AGRICULTURAL INS CO	IA	217.1

Arkansas

INSURANCE COMPANY NAME	DOM. STATE	TOTAL ASSETS ($MIL)	INSURANCE COMPANY NAME	DOM. STATE	TOTAL ASSETS ($MIL)
Rating: A+					
BERKSHIRE HATHAWAY ASR CORP	NY	2,454.3			
Rating: A					
CINCINNATI INS CO	OH	12,253.3			
SENTRY INS A MUTUAL CO	WI	7,779.6			
TOKIO MARINE AMERICA INS CO	NY	1,401.2			
Rating: A-					
AUTO-OWNERS INS CO	MI	14,502.3			
CINCINNATI INDEMNITY CO	OH	132.7			
CINCINNATI SPECIALTY UNDERWRITER	DE	744.7			
COUNTRY MUTUAL INS CO	IL	4,756.8			
CUMIS INS SOCIETY INC	IA	1,894.2			
EMPLOYERS COMPENSATION INS CO	CA	1,095.5			
ENDURANCE ASR CORP	DE	1,824.1			
ESSENT GUARANTY INC	PA	1,384.2			
GEICO SECURE INS CO	NE	555.9			
HOME-OWNERS INS CO	MI	2,197.5			
NATIONAL MORTGAGE INS CORP	WI	645.5			
OWNERS INS CO	OH	3,948.4			
PROTECTIVE INS CO	IN	799.3			
SECURIAN CASUALTY CO	MN	288.6			
SOMPO AMERICA INSURANCE CO	NY	1,235.5			
TRAVELERS CASUALTY & SURETY CO	CT	16,679.3			
USAA CASUALTY INS CO	TX	10,235.4			
Rating: B+					
ACUITY A MUTUAL INS CO	WI	3,686.4			
ALFA SPECIALTY INS CORP	VA	57.1			
ALL AMERICA INS CO	OH	285.9			
AMICA MUTUAL INS CO	RI	5,140.7			
BROTHERHOOD MUTUAL INS CO	IN	591.8			
COUNTRY CASUALTY INS CO	IL	85.4			
DAIRYLAND INS CO	WI	1,297.4			
GEICO CHOICE INS CO	NE	919.4			
GEICO GENERAL INS CO	MD	166.1			
MARKEL GLOBAL REINS CO	DE	1,943.5			
MITSUI SUMITOMO INS CO OF AMER	NY	958.1			
NATIONAL CASUALTY CO	OH	404.6			
NATIONWIDE MUTUAL FIRE INS CO	OH	8,809.3			
PROPERTY-OWNERS INS CO	IN	289.0			
SENTRY SELECT INS CO	WI	715.6			
STATE FARM FIRE & CAS CO	IL	38,866.0			
STATE FARM MUTUAL AUTOMOBILE INS CO	IL	150,198.0			
TOA REINS CO OF AMERICA	DE	1,749.0			
TRAVELERS INDEMNITY CO	CT	21,493.8			
UNITED SERVICES AUTOMOBILE ASN	TX	33,965.5			
USAA GENERAL INDEMNITY CO	TX	4,214.9			
WESTERN AGRICULTURAL INS CO	IA	217.1			

California

INSURANCE COMPANY NAME	DOM. STATE	TOTAL ASSETS ($MIL)
Rating: A+		
BERKSHIRE HATHAWAY ASR CORP	NY	2,454.3
Rating: A		
CINCINNATI INS CO	OH	12,253.3
SENTRY INS A MUTUAL CO	WI	7,779.6
TOKIO MARINE AMERICA INS CO	NY	1,401.2
Rating: A-		
CINCINNATI INDEMNITY CO	OH	132.7
CINCINNATI SPECIALTY UNDERWRITER	DE	744.7
COUNTRY MUTUAL INS CO	IL	4,756.8
CUMIS INS SOCIETY INC	IA	1,894.2
EMPLOYERS COMPENSATION INS CO	CA	1,095.5
ENDURANCE ASR CORP	DE	1,824.1
ESSENT GUARANTY INC	PA	1,384.2
MOTORISTS COMMERCIAL MUTUAL INS CO	OH	358.9
NATIONAL MORTGAGE INS CORP	WI	645.5
PROTECTIVE INS CO	IN	799.3
SECURIAN CASUALTY CO	MN	288.6
SOMPO AMERICA INSURANCE CO	NY	1,235.5
TRAVELERS CASUALTY & SURETY CO	CT	16,679.3
USAA CASUALTY INS CO	TX	10,235.4
Rating: B+		
ALL AMERICA INS CO	OH	285.9
AMICA MUTUAL INS CO	RI	5,140.7
BROTHERHOOD MUTUAL INS CO	IN	591.8
GEICO GENERAL INS CO	MD	166.1
INTERINS EXCHANGE	CA	9,670.8
MARKEL GLOBAL REINS CO	DE	1,943.5
MERCURY INS CO	CA	1,654.2
MITSUI SUMITOMO INS CO OF AMER	NY	958.1
MOTORISTS MUTUAL INS CO	OH	1,368.4
NATIONAL CASUALTY CO	OH	404.6
NATIONWIDE MUTUAL FIRE INS CO	OH	8,809.3
SENTRY SELECT INS CO	WI	715.6
STATE FARM FIRE & CAS CO	IL	38,866.0
STATE FARM MUTUAL AUTOMOBILE INS CO	IL	150,198.0
TOA REINS CO OF AMERICA	DE	1,749.0
TRAVELERS INDEMNITY CO	CT	21,493.8
UNITED SERVICES AUTOMOBILE ASN	TX	33,965.5
USAA GENERAL INDEMNITY CO	TX	4,214.9

Colorado

INSURANCE COMPANY NAME	DOM. STATE	TOTAL ASSETS ($MIL)	INSURANCE COMPANY NAME	DOM. STATE	TOTAL ASSETS ($MIL)
Rating: A+					
BERKSHIRE HATHAWAY ASR CORP	NY	2,454.3			
Rating: A					
CINCINNATI INS CO	OH	12,253.3			
SENTRY INS A MUTUAL CO	WI	7,779.6			
TOKIO MARINE AMERICA INS CO	NY	1,401.2			
Rating: A-					
AUTO-OWNERS INS CO	MI	14,502.3			
CINCINNATI INDEMNITY CO	OH	132.7			
CINCINNATI SPECIALTY UNDERWRITER	DE	744.7			
COPIC INS CO	CO	716.3			
COUNTRY MUTUAL INS CO	IL	4,756.8			
CUMIS INS SOCIETY INC	IA	1,894.2			
EMPLOYERS COMPENSATION INS CO	CA	1,095.5			
ENDURANCE ASR CORP	DE	1,824.1			
ESSENT GUARANTY INC	PA	1,384.2			
GEICO SECURE INS CO	NE	555.9			
HOME-OWNERS INS CO	MI	2,197.5			
MOTORISTS COMMERCIAL MUTUAL INS CO	OH	358.9			
NATIONAL MORTGAGE INS CORP	WI	645.5			
OWNERS INS CO	OH	3,948.4			
PROTECTIVE INS CO	IN	799.3			
SECURIAN CASUALTY CO	MN	288.6			
SOMPO AMERICA INSURANCE CO	NY	1,235.5			
TRAVELERS CASUALTY & SURETY CO	CT	16,679.3			
USAA CASUALTY INS CO	TX	10,235.4			
Rating: B+					
ACUITY A MUTUAL INS CO	WI	3,686.4			
ALL AMERICA INS CO	OH	285.9			
AMERICAN FAMILY MUTL INS CO SI	WI	16,206.4			
AMERICAN STANDARD INS CO OF WI	WI	401.3			
AMICA MUTUAL INS CO	RI	5,140.7			
BROTHERHOOD MUTUAL INS CO	IN	591.8			
COUNTRY CASUALTY INS CO	IL	85.4			
DAIRYLAND INS CO	WI	1,297.4			
GEICO CHOICE INS CO	NE	919.4			
GEICO GENERAL INS CO	MD	166.1			
MARKEL GLOBAL REINS CO	DE	1,943.5			
MITSUI SUMITOMO INS CO OF AMER	NY	958.1			
NATIONAL CASUALTY CO	OH	404.6			
NATIONWIDE MUTUAL FIRE INS CO	OH	8,809.3			
SENTRY SELECT INS CO	WI	715.6			
STATE FARM FIRE & CAS CO	IL	38,866.0			
STATE FARM MUTUAL AUTOMOBILE INS CO	IL	150,198.0			
TOA REINS CO OF AMERICA	DE	1,749.0			
TRAVELERS INDEMNITY CO	CT	21,493.8			
UNITED SERVICES AUTOMOBILE ASN	TX	33,965.5			
USAA GENERAL INDEMNITY CO	TX	4,214.9			
WESTERN AGRICULTURAL INS CO	IA	217.1			

Connecticut

INSURANCE COMPANY NAME	DOM. STATE	TOTAL ASSETS ($MIL)
Rating: A+		
BERKSHIRE HATHAWAY ASR CORP	NY	2,454.3
Rating: A		
CINCINNATI INS CO	OH	12,253.3
SENTRY INS A MUTUAL CO	WI	7,779.6
TOKIO MARINE AMERICA INS CO	NY	1,401.2
Rating: A-		
CINCINNATI INDEMNITY CO	OH	132.7
CINCINNATI SPECIALTY UNDERWRITER	DE	744.7
COUNTRY MUTUAL INS CO	IL	4,756.8
CUMIS INS SOCIETY INC	IA	1,894.2
EMPLOYERS COMPENSATION INS CO	CA	1,095.5
ENDURANCE ASR CORP	DE	1,824.1
ESSENT GUARANTY INC	PA	1,384.2
GEICO SECURE INS CO	NE	555.9
MOTORISTS COMMERCIAL MUTUAL INS CO	OH	358.9
NATIONAL MORTGAGE INS CORP	WI	645.5
PROTECTIVE INS CO	IN	799.3
SECURIAN CASUALTY CO	MN	288.6
SOMPO AMERICA INSURANCE CO	NY	1,235.5
TRAVELERS CASUALTY & SURETY CO	CT	16,679.3
USAA CASUALTY INS CO	TX	10,235.4
Rating: B+		
ALL AMERICA INS CO	OH	285.9
AMICA MUTUAL INS CO	RI	5,140.7
BROTHERHOOD MUTUAL INS CO	IN	591.8
COUNTRY CASUALTY INS CO	IL	85.4
DAIRYLAND INS CO	WI	1,297.4
FARM FAMILY CASUALTY INS CO	NY	1,188.8
GEICO CHOICE INS CO	NE	919.4
GEICO GENERAL INS CO	MD	166.1
GNY CUSTOM INS CO	AZ	59.3
MARKEL GLOBAL REINS CO	DE	1,943.5
MITSUI SUMITOMO INS CO OF AMER	NY	958.1
MOTORISTS MUTUAL INS CO	OH	1,368.4
NATIONAL CASUALTY CO	OH	404.6
NATIONWIDE MUTUAL FIRE INS CO	OH	8,809.3
SENTRY SELECT INS CO	WI	715.6
STATE FARM FIRE & CAS CO	IL	38,866.0
STATE FARM MUTUAL AUTOMOBILE INS CO	IL	150,198.0
TOA REINS CO OF AMERICA	DE	1,749.0
TRAVELERS INDEMNITY CO	CT	21,493.8
UNITED SERVICES AUTOMOBILE ASN	TX	33,965.5
USAA GENERAL INDEMNITY CO	TX	4,214.9

Delaware

INSURANCE COMPANY NAME	DOM. STATE	TOTAL ASSETS ($MIL)
Rating: A+		
BERKSHIRE HATHAWAY ASR CORP	NY	2,454.3
NUCLEAR ELECTRIC INS LTD	DE	5,050.9
Rating: A		
CINCINNATI INS CO	OH	12,253.3
SENTRY INS A MUTUAL CO	WI	7,779.6
TOKIO MARINE AMERICA INS CO	NY	1,401.2
Rating: A-		
CINCINNATI INDEMNITY CO	OH	132.7
CINCINNATI SPECIALTY UNDERWRITER	DE	744.7
COUNTRY MUTUAL INS CO	IL	4,756.8
CUMIS INS SOCIETY INC	IA	1,894.2
ENDURANCE ASR CORP	DE	1,824.1
ESSENT GUARANTY INC	PA	1,384.2
GEICO SECURE INS CO	NE	555.9
MOTORISTS COMMERCIAL MUTUAL INS CO	OH	358.9
NATIONAL MORTGAGE INS CORP	WI	645.5
PROTECTIVE INS CO	IN	799.3
SECURIAN CASUALTY CO	MN	288.6
SOMPO AMERICA INSURANCE CO	NY	1,235.5
TRAVELERS CASUALTY & SURETY CO	CT	16,679.3
USAA CASUALTY INS CO	TX	10,235.4
Rating: B+		
ACUITY A MUTUAL INS CO	WI	3,686.4
AMICA MUTUAL INS CO	RI	5,140.7
BROTHERHOOD MUTUAL INS CO	IN	591.8
COUNTRY CASUALTY INS CO	IL	85.4
DAIRYLAND INS CO	WI	1,297.4
FARM FAMILY CASUALTY INS CO	NY	1,188.8
GEICO CHOICE INS CO	NE	919.4
GEICO GENERAL INS CO	MD	166.1
GNY CUSTOM INS CO	AZ	59.3
MARKEL GLOBAL REINS CO	DE	1,943.5
MITSUI SUMITOMO INS CO OF AMER	NY	958.1
MOTORISTS MUTUAL INS CO	OH	1,368.4
NATIONAL CASUALTY CO	OH	404.6
NATIONWIDE MUTUAL FIRE INS CO	OH	8,809.3
SENTRY SELECT INS CO	WI	715.6
STATE FARM FIRE & CAS CO	IL	38,866.0
STATE FARM MUTUAL AUTOMOBILE INS CO	IL	150,198.0
TOA REINS CO OF AMERICA	DE	1,749.0
TRAVELERS INDEMNITY CO	CT	21,493.8
UNITED SERVICES AUTOMOBILE ASN	TX	33,965.5
USAA GENERAL INDEMNITY CO	TX	4,214.9

District Of Columbia

INSURANCE COMPANY NAME	DOM. STATE	TOTAL ASSETS ($MIL)
Rating: A+		
BERKSHIRE HATHAWAY ASR CORP	NY	2,454.3
Rating: A		
CINCINNATI INS CO	OH	12,253.3
SENTRY INS A MUTUAL CO	WI	7,779.6
TOKIO MARINE AMERICA INS CO	NY	1,401.2
Rating: A-		
BUILDERS MUTUAL INS CO	NC	803.9
CINCINNATI INDEMNITY CO	OH	132.7
CINCINNATI SPECIALTY UNDERWRITER	DE	744.7
CUMIS INS SOCIETY INC	IA	1,894.2
EMPLOYERS COMPENSATION INS CO	CA	1,095.5
ENDURANCE ASR CORP	DE	1,824.1
ESSENT GUARANTY INC	PA	1,384.2
GEICO SECURE INS CO	NE	555.9
MOTORISTS COMMERCIAL MUTUAL INS CO	OH	358.9
NATIONAL MORTGAGE INS CORP	WI	645.5
PROTECTIVE INS CO	IN	799.3
SECURIAN CASUALTY CO	MN	288.6
SOMPO AMERICA INSURANCE CO	NY	1,235.5
TRAVELERS CASUALTY & SURETY CO	CT	16,679.3
USAA CASUALTY INS CO	TX	10,235.4
Rating: B+		
AMICA MUTUAL INS CO	RI	5,140.7
BROTHERHOOD MUTUAL INS CO	IN	591.8
GEICO CHOICE INS CO	NE	919.4
GEICO GENERAL INS CO	MD	166.1
GNY CUSTOM INS CO	AZ	59.3
MARKEL GLOBAL REINS CO	DE	1,943.5
MITSUI SUMITOMO INS CO OF AMER	NY	958.1
NATIONAL CASUALTY CO	OH	404.6
NATIONWIDE MUTUAL FIRE INS CO	OH	8,809.3
SENTRY SELECT INS CO	WI	715.6
STATE FARM FIRE & CAS CO	IL	38,866.0
STATE FARM MUTUAL AUTOMOBILE INS CO	IL	150,198.0
TOA REINS CO OF AMERICA	DE	1,749.0
TRAVELERS INDEMNITY CO	CT	21,493.8
UNITED SERVICES AUTOMOBILE ASN	TX	33,965.5
USAA GENERAL INDEMNITY CO	TX	4,214.9

Florida

INSURANCE COMPANY NAME	DOM. STATE	TOTAL ASSETS ($MIL)	INSURANCE COMPANY NAME	DOM. STATE	TOTAL ASSETS ($MIL)
Rating: A+					
BERKSHIRE HATHAWAY ASR CORP	NY	2,454.3			
CITIZENS PROPERTY INS CORP	FL	12,268.8			
Rating: A					
CINCINNATI INS CO	OH	12,253.3			
SENTRY INS A MUTUAL CO	WI	7,779.6			
TOKIO MARINE AMERICA INS CO	NY	1,401.2			
Rating: A-					
AUTO-OWNERS INS CO	MI	14,502.3			
BUILDERS MUTUAL INS CO	NC	803.9			
CINCINNATI INDEMNITY CO	OH	132.7			
CINCINNATI SPECIALTY UNDERWRITER	DE	744.7			
CUMIS INS SOCIETY INC	IA	1,894.2			
EMPLOYERS COMPENSATION INS CO	CA	1,095.5			
ENDURANCE ASR CORP	DE	1,824.1			
ESSENT GUARANTY INC	PA	1,384.2			
NATIONAL MORTGAGE INS CORP	WI	645.5			
OWNERS INS CO	OH	3,948.4			
PROTECTIVE INS CO	IN	799.3			
RETAILFIRST INS CO	FL	305.0			
SECURIAN CASUALTY CO	MN	288.6			
SOMPO AMERICA INSURANCE CO	NY	1,235.5			
SOUTHERN-OWNERS INS CO	MI	774.5			
TRAVELERS CASUALTY & SURETY CO	CT	16,679.3			
USAA CASUALTY INS CO	TX	10,235.4			
Rating: B+					
AMERICAN FAMILY MUTL INS CO SI	WI	16,206.4			
AMICA MUTUAL INS CO	RI	5,140.7			
BROTHERHOOD MUTUAL INS CO	IN	591.8			
DAIRYLAND INS CO	WI	1,297.4			
GEICO GENERAL INS CO	MD	166.1			
INTERINS EXCHANGE	CA	9,670.8			
MARKEL GLOBAL REINS CO	DE	1,943.5			
MITSUI SUMITOMO INS CO OF AMER	NY	958.1			
NATIONAL CASUALTY CO	OH	404.6			
NATIONWIDE MUTUAL FIRE INS CO	OH	8,809.3			
SENTRY SELECT INS CO	WI	715.6			
STATE FARM FIRE & CAS CO	IL	38,866.0			
STATE FARM MUTUAL AUTOMOBILE INS CO	IL	150,198.0			
TOA REINS CO OF AMERICA	DE	1,749.0			
TRAVELERS INDEMNITY CO	CT	21,493.8			
UNITED SERVICES AUTOMOBILE ASN	TX	33,965.5			
USAA GENERAL INDEMNITY CO	TX	4,214.9			

Georgia

INSURANCE COMPANY NAME	DOM. STATE	TOTAL ASSETS ($MIL)
Rating:	**A+**	
BERKSHIRE HATHAWAY ASR CORP	NY	2,454.3
Rating:	**A**	
CINCINNATI INS CO	OH	12,253.3
SENTRY INS A MUTUAL CO	WI	7,779.6
TOKIO MARINE AMERICA INS CO	NY	1,401.2
Rating:	**A-**	
AUTO-OWNERS INS CO	MI	14,502.3
BUILDERS MUTUAL INS CO	NC	803.9
CINCINNATI INDEMNITY CO	OH	132.7
CINCINNATI SPECIALTY UNDERWRITER	DE	744.7
COPIC INS CO	CO	716.3
COUNTRY MUTUAL INS CO	IL	4,756.8
CUMIS INS SOCIETY INC	IA	1,894.2
EMPLOYERS COMPENSATION INS CO	CA	1,095.5
ENDURANCE ASR CORP	DE	1,824.1
ESSENT GUARANTY INC	PA	1,384.2
GEICO SECURE INS CO	NE	555.9
HOME-OWNERS INS CO	MI	2,197.5
MOTORISTS COMMERCIAL MUTUAL INS CO	OH	358.9
NATIONAL MORTGAGE INS CORP	WI	645.5
OWNERS INS CO	OH	3,948.4
PROTECTIVE INS CO	IN	799.3
SECURIAN CASUALTY CO	MN	288.6
SOMPO AMERICA INSURANCE CO	NY	1,235.5
TRAVELERS CASUALTY & SURETY CO	CT	16,679.3
USAA CASUALTY INS CO	TX	10,235.4
Rating:	**B+**	
ACUITY A MUTUAL INS CO	WI	3,686.4
ALFA MUTUAL GENERAL INS CO	AL	111.8
ALFA SPECIALTY INS CORP	VA	57.1
ALL AMERICA INS CO	OH	285.9
AMERICAN FAMILY MUTL INS CO SI	WI	16,206.4
AMICA MUTUAL INS CO	RI	5,140.7
BROTHERHOOD MUTUAL INS CO	IN	591.8
COUNTRY CASUALTY INS CO	IL	85.4
DAIRYLAND INS CO	WI	1,297.4
GEICO CHOICE INS CO	NE	919.4
GEICO GENERAL INS CO	MD	166.1
MARKEL GLOBAL REINS CO	DE	1,943.5
MITSUI SUMITOMO INS CO OF AMER	NY	958.1
MOTORISTS MUTUAL INS CO	OH	1,368.4
NATIONAL CASUALTY CO	OH	404.6
NATIONWIDE MUTUAL FIRE INS CO	OH	8,809.3
PROPERTY-OWNERS INS CO	IN	289.0
SENTRY SELECT INS CO	WI	715.6
STATE FARM FIRE & CAS CO	IL	38,866.0
STATE FARM MUTUAL AUTOMOBILE INS CO	IL	150,198.0
TOA REINS CO OF AMERICA	DE	1,749.0
TRAVELERS INDEMNITY CO	CT	21,493.8
UNITED SERVICES AUTOMOBILE ASN	TX	33,965.5
USAA GENERAL INDEMNITY CO	TX	4,214.9

Hawaii

INSURANCE COMPANY NAME	DOM. STATE	TOTAL ASSETS ($MIL)
Rating:	**A+**	
BERKSHIRE HATHAWAY ASR CORP	NY	2,454.3
Rating:	**A**	
CINCINNATI INS CO	OH	12,253.3
SENTRY INS A MUTUAL CO	WI	7,779.6
TOKIO MARINE AMERICA INS CO	NY	1,401.2
Rating:	**A-**	
CINCINNATI INDEMNITY CO	OH	132.7
CINCINNATI SPECIALTY UNDERWRITER	DE	744.7
CUMIS INS SOCIETY INC	IA	1,894.2
ENDURANCE ASR CORP	DE	1,824.1
ESSENT GUARANTY INC	PA	1,384.2
NATIONAL MORTGAGE INS CORP	WI	645.5
PROTECTIVE INS CO	IN	799.3
SECURIAN CASUALTY CO	MN	288.6
SOMPO AMERICA INSURANCE CO	NY	1,235.5
TRAVELERS CASUALTY & SURETY CO	CT	16,679.3
USAA CASUALTY INS CO	TX	10,235.4
Rating:	**B+**	
AMICA MUTUAL INS CO	RI	5,140.7
BROTHERHOOD MUTUAL INS CO	IN	591.8
GEICO GENERAL INS CO	MD	166.1
INTERINS EXCHANGE	CA	9,670.8
MARKEL GLOBAL REINS CO	DE	1,943.5
MITSUI SUMITOMO INS CO OF AMER	NY	958.1
NATIONAL CASUALTY CO	OH	404.6
NATIONWIDE MUTUAL FIRE INS CO	OH	8,809.3
SENTRY SELECT INS CO	WI	715.6
STATE FARM FIRE & CAS CO	IL	38,866.0
STATE FARM MUTUAL AUTOMOBILE INS CO	IL	150,198.0
TOA REINS CO OF AMERICA	DE	1,749.0
TRAVELERS INDEMNITY CO	CT	21,493.8
UNITED SERVICES AUTOMOBILE ASN	TX	33,965.5
USAA GENERAL INDEMNITY CO	TX	4,214.9

Idaho

INSURANCE COMPANY NAME	DOM. STATE	TOTAL ASSETS ($MIL)	INSURANCE COMPANY NAME	DOM. STATE	TOTAL ASSETS ($MIL)
Rating: A+					
BERKSHIRE HATHAWAY ASR CORP	NY	2,454.3			
Rating: A					
CINCINNATI INS CO	OH	12,253.3			
SENTRY INS A MUTUAL CO	WI	7,779.6			
TOKIO MARINE AMERICA INS CO	NY	1,401.2			
Rating: A-					
AUTO-OWNERS INS CO	MI	14,502.3			
CINCINNATI INDEMNITY CO	OH	132.7			
CINCINNATI SPECIALTY UNDERWRITER	DE	744.7			
COPIC INS CO	CO	716.3			
COUNTRY MUTUAL INS CO	IL	4,756.8			
CUMIS INS SOCIETY INC	IA	1,894.2			
EMPLOYERS COMPENSATION INS CO	CA	1,095.5			
ENDURANCE ASR CORP	DE	1,824.1			
ESSENT GUARANTY INC	PA	1,384.2			
GEICO SECURE INS CO	NE	555.9			
MOTORISTS COMMERCIAL MUTUAL INS CO	OH	358.9			
NATIONAL MORTGAGE INS CORP	WI	645.5			
OWNERS INS CO	OH	3,948.4			
PROTECTIVE INS CO	IN	799.3			
SECURIAN CASUALTY CO	MN	288.6			
SOMPO AMERICA INSURANCE CO	NY	1,235.5			
TRAVELERS CASUALTY & SURETY CO	CT	16,679.3			
USAA CASUALTY INS CO	TX	10,235.4			
Rating: B+					
ACUITY A MUTUAL INS CO	WI	3,686.4			
ALL AMERICA INS CO	OH	285.9			
AMERICAN FAMILY MUTL INS CO SI	WI	16,206.4			
AMERICAN STANDARD INS CO OF WI	WI	401.3			
AMICA MUTUAL INS CO	RI	5,140.7			
BROTHERHOOD MUTUAL INS CO	IN	591.8			
COUNTRY CASUALTY INS CO	IL	85.4			
DAIRYLAND INS CO	WI	1,297.4			
FARM BUREAU P&C INS CO	IA	2,529.1			
GEICO CHOICE INS CO	NE	919.4			
GEICO GENERAL INS CO	MD	166.1			
MARKEL GLOBAL REINS CO	DE	1,943.5			
MITSUI SUMITOMO INS CO OF AMER	NY	958.1			
NATIONAL CASUALTY CO	OH	404.6			
NATIONWIDE MUTUAL FIRE INS CO	OH	8,809.3			
SENTRY SELECT INS CO	WI	715.6			
STATE FARM FIRE & CAS CO	IL	38,866.0			
STATE FARM MUTUAL AUTOMOBILE INS CO	IL	150,198.0			
TOA REINS CO OF AMERICA	DE	1,749.0			
TRAVELERS INDEMNITY CO	CT	21,493.8			
UNITED SERVICES AUTOMOBILE ASN	TX	33,965.5			
USAA GENERAL INDEMNITY CO	TX	4,214.9			
WESTERN AGRICULTURAL INS CO	IA	217.1			

Illinois

INSURANCE COMPANY NAME	DOM. STATE	TOTAL ASSETS ($MIL)
Rating:		**A+**
BERKSHIRE HATHAWAY ASR CORP	NY	2,454.3
OGLESBY REINS CO	IL	4,364.9
Rating:		**A**
CINCINNATI INS CO	OH	12,253.3
SENTRY INS A MUTUAL CO	WI	7,779.6
TOKIO MARINE AMERICA INS CO	NY	1,401.2
Rating:		**A-**
AUTO-OWNERS INS CO	MI	14,502.3
CINCINNATI INDEMNITY CO	OH	132.7
CINCINNATI SPECIALTY UNDERWRITER	DE	744.7
COUNTRY MUTUAL INS CO	IL	4,756.8
CUMIS INS SOCIETY INC	IA	1,894.2
EMPLOYERS COMPENSATION INS CO	CA	1,095.5
ENDURANCE ASR CORP	DE	1,824.1
ESSENT GUARANTY INC	PA	1,384.2
GEICO SECURE INS CO	NE	555.9
HOME-OWNERS INS CO	MI	2,197.5
MOTORISTS COMMERCIAL MUTUAL INS CO	OH	358.9
NATIONAL MORTGAGE INS CORP	WI	645.5
OWNERS INS CO	OH	3,948.4
PROTECTIVE INS CO	IN	799.3
SECURIAN CASUALTY CO	MN	288.6
SOMPO AMERICA INSURANCE CO	NY	1,235.5
TRAVELERS CASUALTY & SURETY CO	CT	16,679.3
USAA CASUALTY INS CO	TX	10,235.4
Rating:		**B+**
ACUITY A MUTUAL INS CO	WI	3,686.4
ALL AMERICA INS CO	OH	285.9
ALLSTATE NJ INS CO	IL	2,557.8
AMERICAN FAMILY MUTL INS CO SI	WI	16,206.4
AMERICAN STANDARD INS CO OF WI	WI	401.3
AMICA MUTUAL INS CO	RI	5,140.7
BROTHERHOOD MUTUAL INS CO	IN	591.8
COUNTRY CASUALTY INS CO	IL	85.4
DAIRYLAND INS CO	WI	1,297.4
FARMERS AUTOMOBILE INS ASN	IL	1,277.1
GEICO CHOICE INS CO	NE	919.4
GEICO GENERAL INS CO	MD	166.1
GNY CUSTOM INS CO	AZ	59.3
MARKEL GLOBAL REINS CO	DE	1,943.5
MITSUI SUMITOMO INS CO OF AMER	NY	958.1
MOTORISTS MUTUAL INS CO	OH	1,368.4
NATIONAL CASUALTY CO	OH	404.6
NATIONWIDE MUTUAL FIRE INS CO	OH	8,809.3
PEKIN INS CO	IL	306.7
PROPERTY-OWNERS INS CO	IN	289.0
SENTRY SELECT INS CO	WI	715.6
STATE FARM FIRE & CAS CO	IL	38,866.0
STATE FARM MUTUAL AUTOMOBILE INS CO	IL	150,198.0
TOA REINS CO OF AMERICA	DE	1,749.0
TRAVELERS INDEMNITY CO	CT	21,493.8
UNITED SERVICES AUTOMOBILE ASN	TX	33,965.5
USAA GENERAL INDEMNITY CO	TX	4,214.9
WEST BEND MUTUAL INS CO	WI	2,580.8
WESTERN AGRICULTURAL INS CO	IA	217.1

Indiana

INSURANCE COMPANY NAME	DOM. STATE	TOTAL ASSETS ($MIL)
Rating: A+		
BERKSHIRE HATHAWAY ASR CORP	NY	2,454.3
Rating: A		
CINCINNATI INS CO	OH	12,253.3
SENTRY INS A MUTUAL CO	WI	7,779.6
TOKIO MARINE AMERICA INS CO	NY	1,401.2
Rating: A-		
AUTO-OWNERS INS CO	MI	14,502.3
CINCINNATI INDEMNITY CO	OH	132.7
CINCINNATI SPECIALTY UNDERWRITER	DE	744.7
COUNTRY MUTUAL INS CO	IL	4,756.8
CUMIS INS SOCIETY INC	IA	1,894.2
EMPLOYERS COMPENSATION INS CO	CA	1,095.5
ENDURANCE ASR CORP	DE	1,824.1
ESSENT GUARANTY INC	PA	1,384.2
GEICO SECURE INS CO	NE	555.9
HOME-OWNERS INS CO	MI	2,197.5
MOTORISTS COMMERCIAL MUTUAL INS CO	OH	358.9
NATIONAL MORTGAGE INS CORP	WI	645.5
OWNERS INS CO	OH	3,948.4
PROTECTIVE INS CO	IN	799.3
SECURIAN CASUALTY CO	MN	288.6
SOMPO AMERICA INSURANCE CO	NY	1,235.5
TRAVELERS CASUALTY & SURETY CO	CT	16,679.3
USAA CASUALTY INS CO	TX	10,235.4
Rating: B+		
ACUITY A MUTUAL INS CO	WI	3,686.4
ALFA SPECIALTY INS CORP	VA	57.1
ALL AMERICA INS CO	OH	285.9
AMERICAN FAMILY MUTL INS CO SI	WI	16,206.4
AMERICAN STANDARD INS CO OF WI	WI	401.3
AMICA MUTUAL INS CO	RI	5,140.7
BROTHERHOOD MUTUAL INS CO	IN	591.8
COUNTRY CASUALTY INS CO	IL	85.4
DAIRYLAND INS CO	WI	1,297.4
FARMERS AUTOMOBILE INS ASN	IL	1,277.1
GEICO CHOICE INS CO	NE	919.4
GEICO GENERAL INS CO	MD	166.1
GNY CUSTOM INS CO	AZ	59.3
MARKEL GLOBAL REINS CO	DE	1,943.5
MITSUI SUMITOMO INS CO OF AMER	NY	958.1
MOTORISTS MUTUAL INS CO	OH	1,368.4
NATIONAL CASUALTY CO	OH	404.6
NATIONWIDE MUTUAL FIRE INS CO	OH	8,809.3
PEKIN INS CO	IL	306.7
PROPERTY-OWNERS INS CO	IN	289.0
SENTRY SELECT INS CO	WI	715.6
STATE FARM FIRE & CAS CO	IL	38,866.0
STATE FARM MUTUAL AUTOMOBILE INS CO	IL	150,198.0
TOA REINS CO OF AMERICA	DE	1,749.0
TRAVELERS INDEMNITY CO	CT	21,493.8
UNITED SERVICES AUTOMOBILE ASN	TX	33,965.5
USAA GENERAL INDEMNITY CO	TX	4,214.9
WEST BEND MUTUAL INS CO	WI	2,580.8

INSURANCE COMPANY NAME	DOM. STATE	TOTAL ASSETS ($MIL)
WESTERN AGRICULTURAL INS CO	IA	217.1

Iowa

INSURANCE COMPANY NAME	DOM. STATE	TOTAL ASSETS ($MIL)
Rating: **A+**		
BERKSHIRE HATHAWAY ASR CORP	NY	2,454.3
Rating: **A**		
CINCINNATI INS CO	OH	12,253.3
SENTRY INS A MUTUAL CO	WI	7,779.6
TOKIO MARINE AMERICA INS CO	NY	1,401.2
Rating: **A-**		
AUTO-OWNERS INS CO	MI	14,502.3
CINCINNATI INDEMNITY CO	OH	132.7
CINCINNATI SPECIALTY UNDERWRITER	DE	744.7
COPIC INS CO	CO	716.3
COUNTRY MUTUAL INS CO	IL	4,756.8
CUMIS INS SOCIETY INC	IA	1,894.2
EMPLOYERS COMPENSATION INS CO	CA	1,095.5
ENDURANCE ASR CORP	DE	1,824.1
ESSENT GUARANTY INC	PA	1,384.2
GEICO SECURE INS CO	NE	555.9
HOME-OWNERS INS CO	MI	2,197.5
MOTORISTS COMMERCIAL MUTUAL INS CO	OH	358.9
NATIONAL MORTGAGE INS CORP	WI	645.5
OWNERS INS CO	OH	3,948.4
PROTECTIVE INS CO	IN	799.3
SECURIAN CASUALTY CO	MN	288.6
SOMPO AMERICA INSURANCE CO	NY	1,235.5
TRAVELERS CASUALTY & SURETY CO	CT	16,679.3
USAA CASUALTY INS CO	TX	10,235.4
Rating: **B+**		
ACUITY A MUTUAL INS CO	WI	3,686.4
ALL AMERICA INS CO	OH	285.9
AMERICAN FAMILY MUTL INS CO SI	WI	16,206.4
AMERICAN STANDARD INS CO OF WI	WI	401.3
AMICA MUTUAL INS CO	RI	5,140.7
BROTHERHOOD MUTUAL INS CO	IN	591.8
COUNTRY CASUALTY INS CO	IL	85.4
DAIRYLAND INS CO	WI	1,297.4
FARM BUREAU P&C INS CO	IA	2,529.1
FARMERS AUTOMOBILE INS ASN	IL	1,277.1
GEICO CHOICE INS CO	NE	919.4
GEICO GENERAL INS CO	MD	166.1
MARKEL GLOBAL REINS CO	DE	1,943.5
MITSUI SUMITOMO INS CO OF AMER	NY	958.1
MOTORISTS MUTUAL INS CO	OH	1,368.4
NATIONAL CASUALTY CO	OH	404.6
NATIONWIDE MUTUAL FIRE INS CO	OH	8,809.3
PEKIN INS CO	IL	306.7
PROPERTY-OWNERS INS CO	IN	289.0
SENTRY SELECT INS CO	WI	715.6
STATE FARM FIRE & CAS CO	IL	38,866.0
STATE FARM MUTUAL AUTOMOBILE INS CO	IL	150,198.0
TOA REINS CO OF AMERICA	DE	1,749.0
TRAVELERS INDEMNITY CO	CT	21,493.8
UNITED SERVICES AUTOMOBILE ASN	TX	33,965.5
USAA GENERAL INDEMNITY CO	TX	4,214.9
WEST BEND MUTUAL INS CO	WI	2,580.8

INSURANCE COMPANY NAME	DOM. STATE	TOTAL ASSETS ($MIL)
WESTERN AGRICULTURAL INS CO	IA	217.1

Kansas

INSURANCE COMPANY NAME	DOM. STATE	TOTAL ASSETS ($MIL)
Rating:	**A+**	
BERKSHIRE HATHAWAY ASR CORP	NY	2,454.3
Rating:	**A**	
CINCINNATI INS CO	OH	12,253.3
SENTRY INS A MUTUAL CO	WI	7,779.6
TOKIO MARINE AMERICA INS CO	NY	1,401.2
Rating:	**A-**	
AUTO-OWNERS INS CO	MI	14,502.3
CINCINNATI INDEMNITY CO	OH	132.7
CINCINNATI SPECIALTY UNDERWRITER	DE	744.7
COPIC INS CO	CO	716.3
COUNTRY MUTUAL INS CO	IL	4,756.8
CUMIS INS SOCIETY INC	IA	1,894.2
EMPLOYERS COMPENSATION INS CO	CA	1,095.5
ENDURANCE ASR CORP	DE	1,824.1
ESSENT GUARANTY INC	PA	1,384.2
GEICO SECURE INS CO	NE	555.9
MOTORISTS COMMERCIAL MUTUAL INS CO	OH	358.9
NATIONAL MORTGAGE INS CORP	WI	645.5
OWNERS INS CO	OH	3,948.4
PROTECTIVE INS CO	IN	799.3
SECURIAN CASUALTY CO	MN	288.6
SOMPO AMERICA INSURANCE CO	NY	1,235.5
TRAVELERS CASUALTY & SURETY CO	CT	16,679.3
USAA CASUALTY INS CO	TX	10,235.4
Rating:	**B+**	
ACUITY A MUTUAL INS CO	WI	3,686.4
AMERICAN FAMILY MUTL INS CO SI	WI	16,206.4
AMERICAN STANDARD INS CO OF WI	WI	401.3
AMICA MUTUAL INS CO	RI	5,140.7
BROTHERHOOD MUTUAL INS CO	IN	591.8
COUNTRY CASUALTY INS CO	IL	85.4
DAIRYLAND INS CO	WI	1,297.4
FARM BUREAU P&C INS CO	IA	2,529.1
GEICO CHOICE INS CO	NE	919.4
GEICO GENERAL INS CO	MD	166.1
MARKEL GLOBAL REINS CO	DE	1,943.5
MITSUI SUMITOMO INS CO OF AMER	NY	958.1
NATIONAL CASUALTY CO	OH	404.6
NATIONWIDE MUTUAL FIRE INS CO	OH	8,809.3
SENTRY SELECT INS CO	WI	715.6
STATE FARM FIRE & CAS CO	IL	38,866.0
STATE FARM MUTUAL AUTOMOBILE INS CO	IL	150,198.0
TOA REINS CO OF AMERICA	DE	1,749.0
TRAVELERS INDEMNITY CO	CT	21,493.8
UNITED SERVICES AUTOMOBILE ASN	TX	33,965.5
USAA GENERAL INDEMNITY CO	TX	4,214.9
WEST BEND MUTUAL INS CO	WI	2,580.8
WESTERN AGRICULTURAL INS CO	IA	217.1

Kentucky

INSURANCE COMPANY NAME	DOM. STATE	TOTAL ASSETS ($MIL)
Rating:	**A+**	
BERKSHIRE HATHAWAY ASR CORP	NY	2,454.3
Rating:	**A**	
CINCINNATI INS CO	OH	12,253.3
SENTRY INS A MUTUAL CO	WI	7,779.6
TOKIO MARINE AMERICA INS CO	NY	1,401.2
Rating:	**A-**	
AUTO-OWNERS INS CO	MI	14,502.3
CINCINNATI INDEMNITY CO	OH	132.7
CINCINNATI SPECIALTY UNDERWRITER	DE	744.7
COUNTRY MUTUAL INS CO	IL	4,756.8
CUMIS INS SOCIETY INC	IA	1,894.2
EMPLOYERS COMPENSATION INS CO	CA	1,095.5
ENDURANCE ASR CORP	DE	1,824.1
ESSENT GUARANTY INC	PA	1,384.2
GEICO SECURE INS CO	NE	555.9
HOME-OWNERS INS CO	MI	2,197.5
MOTORISTS COMMERCIAL MUTUAL INS CO	OH	358.9
NATIONAL MORTGAGE INS CORP	WI	645.5
OWNERS INS CO	OH	3,948.4
PROTECTIVE INS CO	IN	799.3
SECURIAN CASUALTY CO	MN	288.6
SOMPO AMERICA INSURANCE CO	NY	1,235.5
TRAVELERS CASUALTY & SURETY CO	CT	16,679.3
USAA CASUALTY INS CO	TX	10,235.4
Rating:	**B+**	
ACUITY A MUTUAL INS CO	WI	3,686.4
ALFA SPECIALTY INS CORP	VA	57.1
ALL AMERICA INS CO	OH	285.9
AMICA MUTUAL INS CO	RI	5,140.7
BROTHERHOOD MUTUAL INS CO	IN	591.8
COUNTRY CASUALTY INS CO	IL	85.4
DAIRYLAND INS CO	WI	1,297.4
GEICO CHOICE INS CO	NE	919.4
GEICO GENERAL INS CO	MD	166.1
MARKEL GLOBAL REINS CO	DE	1,943.5
MITSUI SUMITOMO INS CO OF AMER	NY	958.1
MOTORISTS MUTUAL INS CO	OH	1,368.4
NATIONAL CASUALTY CO	OH	404.6
NATIONWIDE MUTUAL FIRE INS CO	OH	8,809.3
PROPERTY-OWNERS INS CO	IN	289.0
SENTRY SELECT INS CO	WI	715.6
STATE FARM FIRE & CAS CO	IL	38,866.0
STATE FARM MUTUAL AUTOMOBILE INS CO	IL	150,198.0
TOA REINS CO OF AMERICA	DE	1,749.0
TRAVELERS INDEMNITY CO	CT	21,493.8
UNITED SERVICES AUTOMOBILE ASN	TX	33,965.5
USAA GENERAL INDEMNITY CO	TX	4,214.9
WEST BEND MUTUAL INS CO	WI	2,580.8

Louisiana

INSURANCE COMPANY NAME	DOM. STATE	TOTAL ASSETS ($MIL)
Rating: **A+**		
BERKSHIRE HATHAWAY ASR CORP	NY	2,454.3
Rating: **A**		
CINCINNATI INS CO	OH	12,253.3
SENTRY INS A MUTUAL CO	WI	7,779.6
TOKIO MARINE AMERICA INS CO	NY	1,401.2
Rating: **A-**		
CINCINNATI INDEMNITY CO	OH	132.7
CINCINNATI SPECIALTY UNDERWRITER	DE	744.7
CUMIS INS SOCIETY INC	IA	1,894.2
EMPLOYERS COMPENSATION INS CO	CA	1,095.5
ENDURANCE ASR CORP	DE	1,824.1
ESSENT GUARANTY INC	PA	1,384.2
GEICO SECURE INS CO	NE	555.9
NATIONAL MORTGAGE INS CORP	WI	645.5
PROTECTIVE INS CO	IN	799.3
SECURIAN CASUALTY CO	MN	288.6
SOMPO AMERICA INSURANCE CO	NY	1,235.5
TRAVELERS CASUALTY & SURETY CO	CT	16,679.3
USAA CASUALTY INS CO	TX	10,235.4
Rating: **B+**		
AMICA MUTUAL INS CO	RI	5,140.7
BROTHERHOOD MUTUAL INS CO	IN	591.8
GEICO CHOICE INS CO	NE	919.4
GEICO GENERAL INS CO	MD	166.1
MARKEL GLOBAL REINS CO	DE	1,943.5
MITSUI SUMITOMO INS CO OF AMER	NY	958.1
NATIONAL CASUALTY CO	OH	404.6
NATIONWIDE MUTUAL FIRE INS CO	OH	8,809.3
SENTRY SELECT INS CO	WI	715.6
STATE FARM FIRE & CAS CO	IL	38,866.0
STATE FARM MUTUAL AUTOMOBILE INS CO	IL	150,198.0
TOA REINS CO OF AMERICA	DE	1,749.0
TRAVELERS INDEMNITY CO	CT	21,493.8
UNITED SERVICES AUTOMOBILE ASN	TX	33,965.5
USAA GENERAL INDEMNITY CO	TX	4,214.9

Maine

INSURANCE COMPANY NAME	DOM. STATE	TOTAL ASSETS ($MIL)
Rating: A+		
BERKSHIRE HATHAWAY ASR CORP	NY	2,454.3
Rating: A		
CINCINNATI INS CO	OH	12,253.3
SENTRY INS A MUTUAL CO	WI	7,779.6
TOKIO MARINE AMERICA INS CO	NY	1,401.2
Rating: A-		
CINCINNATI INDEMNITY CO	OH	132.7
CINCINNATI SPECIALTY UNDERWRITER	DE	744.7
COUNTRY MUTUAL INS CO	IL	4,756.8
CUMIS INS SOCIETY INC	IA	1,894.2
ENDURANCE ASR CORP	DE	1,824.1
ESSENT GUARANTY INC	PA	1,384.2
MOTORISTS COMMERCIAL MUTUAL INS CO	OH	358.9
NATIONAL MORTGAGE INS CORP	WI	645.5
PROTECTIVE INS CO	IN	799.3
SECURIAN CASUALTY CO	MN	288.6
SOMPO AMERICA INSURANCE CO	NY	1,235.5
TRAVELERS CASUALTY & SURETY CO	CT	16,679.3
USAA CASUALTY INS CO	TX	10,235.4
Rating: B+		
ACUITY A MUTUAL INS CO	WI	3,686.4
ALL AMERICA INS CO	OH	285.9
AMICA MUTUAL INS CO	RI	5,140.7
BROTHERHOOD MUTUAL INS CO	IN	591.8
COUNTRY CASUALTY INS CO	IL	85.4
DAIRYLAND INS CO	WI	1,297.4
FARM FAMILY CASUALTY INS CO	NY	1,188.8
GEICO GENERAL INS CO	MD	166.1
INTERINS EXCHANGE	CA	9,670.8
MARKEL GLOBAL REINS CO	DE	1,943.5
MITSUI SUMITOMO INS CO OF AMER	NY	958.1
MOTORISTS MUTUAL INS CO	OH	1,368.4
NATIONAL CASUALTY CO	OH	404.6
NATIONWIDE MUTUAL FIRE INS CO	OH	8,809.3
SENTRY SELECT INS CO	WI	715.6
STATE FARM FIRE & CAS CO	IL	38,866.0
STATE FARM MUTUAL AUTOMOBILE INS CO	IL	150,198.0
TOA REINS CO OF AMERICA	DE	1,749.0
TRAVELERS INDEMNITY CO	CT	21,493.8
UNITED SERVICES AUTOMOBILE ASN	TX	33,965.5
USAA GENERAL INDEMNITY CO	TX	4,214.9

Maryland

INSURANCE COMPANY NAME	DOM. STATE	TOTAL ASSETS ($MIL)
Rating: A+		
BERKSHIRE HATHAWAY ASR CORP	NY	2,454.3
Rating: A		
CINCINNATI INS CO	OH	12,253.3
SENTRY INS A MUTUAL CO	WI	7,779.6
TOKIO MARINE AMERICA INS CO	NY	1,401.2
Rating: A-		
BUILDERS MUTUAL INS CO	NC	803.9
CINCINNATI INDEMNITY CO	OH	132.7
CINCINNATI SPECIALTY UNDERWRITER	DE	744.7
COUNTRY MUTUAL INS CO	IL	4,756.8
CUMIS INS SOCIETY INC	IA	1,894.2
EMPLOYERS COMPENSATION INS CO	CA	1,095.5
ENDURANCE ASR CORP	DE	1,824.1
ESSENT GUARANTY INC	PA	1,384.2
GEICO SECURE INS CO	NE	555.9
MOTORISTS COMMERCIAL MUTUAL INS CO	OH	358.9
NATIONAL MORTGAGE INS CORP	WI	645.5
PROTECTIVE INS CO	IN	799.3
SECURIAN CASUALTY CO	MN	288.6
SOMPO AMERICA INSURANCE CO	NY	1,235.5
TRAVELERS CASUALTY & SURETY CO	CT	16,679.3
USAA CASUALTY INS CO	TX	10,235.4
Rating: B+		
ALL AMERICA INS CO	OH	285.9
AMICA MUTUAL INS CO	RI	5,140.7
BROTHERHOOD MUTUAL INS CO	IN	591.8
COUNTRY CASUALTY INS CO	IL	85.4
DAIRYLAND INS CO	WI	1,297.4
FARM FAMILY CASUALTY INS CO	NY	1,188.8
GEICO CHOICE INS CO	NE	919.4
GEICO GENERAL INS CO	MD	166.1
GNY CUSTOM INS CO	AZ	59.3
MARKEL GLOBAL REINS CO	DE	1,943.5
MITSUI SUMITOMO INS CO OF AMER	NY	958.1
MOTORISTS MUTUAL INS CO	OH	1,368.4
NATIONAL CASUALTY CO	OH	404.6
NATIONWIDE MUTUAL FIRE INS CO	OH	8,809.3
SENTRY SELECT INS CO	WI	715.6
STATE FARM FIRE & CAS CO	IL	38,866.0
STATE FARM MUTUAL AUTOMOBILE INS CO	IL	150,198.0
TOA REINS CO OF AMERICA	DE	1,749.0
TRAVELERS INDEMNITY CO	CT	21,493.8
UNITED SERVICES AUTOMOBILE ASN	TX	33,965.5
USAA GENERAL INDEMNITY CO	TX	4,214.9

Massachusetts

INSURANCE COMPANY NAME	DOM. STATE	TOTAL ASSETS ($MIL)
Rating: A+		
BERKSHIRE HATHAWAY ASR CORP	NY	2,454.3
Rating: A		
CINCINNATI INS CO	OH	12,253.3
SENTRY INS A MUTUAL CO	WI	7,779.6
TOKIO MARINE AMERICA INS CO	NY	1,401.2
Rating: A-		
CINCINNATI INDEMNITY CO	OH	132.7
CINCINNATI SPECIALTY UNDERWRITER	DE	744.7
COUNTRY MUTUAL INS CO	IL	4,756.8
CUMIS INS SOCIETY INC	IA	1,894.2
EMPLOYERS COMPENSATION INS CO	CA	1,095.5
ENDURANCE ASR CORP	DE	1,824.1
ESSENT GUARANTY INC	PA	1,384.2
MOTORISTS COMMERCIAL MUTUAL INS CO	OH	358.9
NATIONAL MORTGAGE INS CORP	WI	645.5
PROTECTIVE INS CO	IN	799.3
SECURIAN CASUALTY CO	MN	288.6
SOMPO AMERICA INSURANCE CO	NY	1,235.5
TRAVELERS CASUALTY & SURETY CO	CT	16,679.3
USAA CASUALTY INS CO	TX	10,235.4
Rating: B+		
ALL AMERICA INS CO	OH	285.9
AMICA MUTUAL INS CO	RI	5,140.7
BROTHERHOOD MUTUAL INS CO	IN	591.8
COUNTRY CASUALTY INS CO	IL	85.4
DAIRYLAND INS CO	WI	1,297.4
FARM FAMILY CASUALTY INS CO	NY	1,188.8
GEICO GENERAL INS CO	MD	166.1
GNY CUSTOM INS CO	AZ	59.3
MARKEL GLOBAL REINS CO	DE	1,943.5
MITSUI SUMITOMO INS CO OF AMER	NY	958.1
MOTORISTS MUTUAL INS CO	OH	1,368.4
NATIONAL CASUALTY CO	OH	404.6
NATIONWIDE MUTUAL FIRE INS CO	OH	8,809.3
SENTRY SELECT INS CO	WI	715.6
STATE FARM FIRE & CAS CO	IL	38,866.0
STATE FARM MUTUAL AUTOMOBILE INS CO	IL	150,198.0
TOA REINS CO OF AMERICA	DE	1,749.0
TRAVELERS INDEMNITY CO	CT	21,493.8
UNITED SERVICES AUTOMOBILE ASN	TX	33,965.5
USAA GENERAL INDEMNITY CO	TX	4,214.9

Michigan

INSURANCE COMPANY NAME	DOM. STATE	TOTAL ASSETS ($MIL)
Rating: A+		
BERKSHIRE HATHAWAY ASR CORP	NY	2,454.3
Rating: A		
CINCINNATI INS CO	OH	12,253.3
SENTRY INS A MUTUAL CO	WI	7,779.6
TOKIO MARINE AMERICA INS CO	NY	1,401.2
Rating: A-		
AUTO-OWNERS INS CO	MI	14,502.3
CINCINNATI INDEMNITY CO	OH	132.7
CINCINNATI SPECIALTY UNDERWRITER	DE	744.7
COUNTRY MUTUAL INS CO	IL	4,756.8
CUMIS INS SOCIETY INC	IA	1,894.2
EMPLOYERS COMPENSATION INS CO	CA	1,095.5
ENDURANCE ASR CORP	DE	1,824.1
ESSENT GUARANTY INC	PA	1,384.2
HOME-OWNERS INS CO	MI	2,197.5
MOTORISTS COMMERCIAL MUTUAL INS CO	OH	358.9
NATIONAL MORTGAGE INS CORP	WI	645.5
OWNERS INS CO	OH	3,948.4
PROTECTIVE INS CO	IN	799.3
SECURIAN CASUALTY CO	MN	288.6
SOMPO AMERICA INSURANCE CO	NY	1,235.5
SOUTHERN-OWNERS INS CO	MI	774.5
TRAVELERS CASUALTY & SURETY CO	CT	16,679.3
USAA CASUALTY INS CO	TX	10,235.4
Rating: B+		
ACUITY A MUTUAL INS CO	WI	3,686.4
ALL AMERICA INS CO	OH	285.9
AMICA MUTUAL INS CO	RI	5,140.7
BROTHERHOOD MUTUAL INS CO	IN	591.8
COUNTRY CASUALTY INS CO	IL	85.4
DAIRYLAND INS CO	WI	1,297.4
FARMERS AUTOMOBILE INS ASN	IL	1,277.1
GEICO GENERAL INS CO	MD	166.1
GNY CUSTOM INS CO	AZ	59.3
INTERINS EXCHANGE	CA	9,670.8
MARKEL GLOBAL REINS CO	DE	1,943.5
MITSUI SUMITOMO INS CO OF AMER	NY	958.1
MOTORISTS MUTUAL INS CO	OH	1,368.4
NATIONAL CASUALTY CO	OH	404.6
NATIONWIDE MUTUAL FIRE INS CO	OH	8,809.3
PEKIN INS CO	IL	306.7
PROPERTY-OWNERS INS CO	IN	289.0
SENTRY SELECT INS CO	WI	715.6
STATE FARM FIRE & CAS CO	IL	38,866.0
STATE FARM MUTUAL AUTOMOBILE INS CO	IL	150,198.0
TOA REINS CO OF AMERICA	DE	1,749.0
TRAVELERS INDEMNITY CO	CT	21,493.8
UNITED SERVICES AUTOMOBILE ASN	TX	33,965.5
USAA GENERAL INDEMNITY CO	TX	4,214.9
WEST BEND MUTUAL INS CO	WI	2,580.8
WESTERN AGRICULTURAL INS CO	IA	217.1

Minnesota

INSURANCE COMPANY NAME	DOM. STATE	TOTAL ASSETS ($MIL)
Rating: A+		
BERKSHIRE HATHAWAY ASR CORP	NY	2,454.3
Rating: A		
CINCINNATI INS CO	OH	12,253.3
SENTRY INS A MUTUAL CO	WI	7,779.6
TOKIO MARINE AMERICA INS CO	NY	1,401.2
Rating: A-		
AUTO-OWNERS INS CO	MI	14,502.3
CINCINNATI INDEMNITY CO	OH	132.7
CINCINNATI SPECIALTY UNDERWRITER	DE	744.7
COPIC INS CO	CO	716.3
COUNTRY MUTUAL INS CO	IL	4,756.8
CUMIS INS SOCIETY INC	IA	1,894.2
EMPLOYERS COMPENSATION INS CO	CA	1,095.5
ENDURANCE ASR CORP	DE	1,824.1
ESSENT GUARANTY INC	PA	1,384.2
MOTORISTS COMMERCIAL MUTUAL INS CO	OH	358.9
NATIONAL MORTGAGE INS CORP	WI	645.5
OWNERS INS CO	OH	3,948.4
PROTECTIVE INS CO	IN	799.3
SECURIAN CASUALTY CO	MN	288.6
SOMPO AMERICA INSURANCE CO	NY	1,235.5
TRAVELERS CASUALTY & SURETY CO	CT	16,679.3
USAA CASUALTY INS CO	TX	10,235.4
Rating: B+		
ACUITY A MUTUAL INS CO	WI	3,686.4
ALL AMERICA INS CO	OH	285.9
AMERICAN FAMILY MUTL INS CO SI	WI	16,206.4
AMERICAN STANDARD INS CO OF WI	WI	401.3
AMICA MUTUAL INS CO	RI	5,140.7
BROTHERHOOD MUTUAL INS CO	IN	591.8
COUNTRY CASUALTY INS CO	IL	85.4
DAIRYLAND INS CO	WI	1,297.4
FARM BUREAU P&C INS CO	IA	2,529.1
GEICO GENERAL INS CO	MD	166.1
MARKEL GLOBAL REINS CO	DE	1,943.5
MITSUI SUMITOMO INS CO OF AMER	NY	958.1
NATIONAL CASUALTY CO	OH	404.6
NATIONWIDE MUTUAL FIRE INS CO	OH	8,809.3
SENTRY SELECT INS CO	WI	715.6
STATE FARM FIRE & CAS CO	IL	38,866.0
STATE FARM MUTUAL AUTOMOBILE INS CO	IL	150,198.0
TOA REINS CO OF AMERICA	DE	1,749.0
TRAVELERS INDEMNITY CO	CT	21,493.8
UNITED SERVICES AUTOMOBILE ASN	TX	33,965.5
USAA GENERAL INDEMNITY CO	TX	4,214.9
WEST BEND MUTUAL INS CO	WI	2,580.8
WESTERN AGRICULTURAL INS CO	IA	217.1

Mississippi

INSURANCE COMPANY NAME	DOM. STATE	TOTAL ASSETS ($MIL)
Rating: A+		
BERKSHIRE HATHAWAY ASR CORP	NY	2,454.3
Rating: A		
CINCINNATI INS CO	OH	12,253.3
SENTRY INS A MUTUAL CO	WI	7,779.6
TOKIO MARINE AMERICA INS CO	NY	1,401.2
Rating: A-		
AUTO-OWNERS INS CO	MI	14,502.3
BUILDERS MUTUAL INS CO	NC	803.9
CINCINNATI INDEMNITY CO	OH	132.7
CINCINNATI SPECIALTY UNDERWRITER	DE	744.7
CUMIS INS SOCIETY INC	IA	1,894.2
EMPLOYERS COMPENSATION INS CO	CA	1,095.5
ENDURANCE ASR CORP	DE	1,824.1
ESSENT GUARANTY INC	PA	1,384.2
GEICO SECURE INS CO	NE	555.9
NATIONAL MORTGAGE INS CORP	WI	645.5
OWNERS INS CO	OH	3,948.4
PROTECTIVE INS CO	IN	799.3
SECURIAN CASUALTY CO	MN	288.6
SOMPO AMERICA INSURANCE CO	NY	1,235.5
TRAVELERS CASUALTY & SURETY CO	CT	16,679.3
USAA CASUALTY INS CO	TX	10,235.4
Rating: B+		
ACUITY A MUTUAL INS CO	WI	3,686.4
ALFA MUTUAL GENERAL INS CO	AL	111.8
ALFA SPECIALTY INS CORP	VA	57.1
ALL AMERICA INS CO	OH	285.9
AMICA MUTUAL INS CO	RI	5,140.7
BROTHERHOOD MUTUAL INS CO	IN	591.8
DAIRYLAND INS CO	WI	1,297.4
GEICO CHOICE INS CO	NE	919.4
GEICO GENERAL INS CO	MD	166.1
MARKEL GLOBAL REINS CO	DE	1,943.5
MITSUI SUMITOMO INS CO OF AMER	NY	958.1
NATIONAL CASUALTY CO	OH	404.6
NATIONWIDE MUTUAL FIRE INS CO	OH	8,809.3
SENTRY SELECT INS CO	WI	715.6
STATE FARM FIRE & CAS CO	IL	38,866.0
STATE FARM MUTUAL AUTOMOBILE INS CO	IL	150,198.0
TOA REINS CO OF AMERICA	DE	1,749.0
TRAVELERS INDEMNITY CO	CT	21,493.8
UNITED SERVICES AUTOMOBILE ASN	TX	33,965.5
USAA GENERAL INDEMNITY CO	TX	4,214.9

Missouri

INSURANCE COMPANY NAME	DOM. STATE	TOTAL ASSETS ($MIL)
Rating: **A+**		
BERKSHIRE HATHAWAY ASR CORP	NY	2,454.3
Rating: **A**		
CINCINNATI INS CO	OH	12,253.3
SENTRY INS A MUTUAL CO	WI	7,779.6
TOKIO MARINE AMERICA INS CO	NY	1,401.2
Rating: **A-**		
AUTO-OWNERS INS CO	MI	14,502.3
CINCINNATI INDEMNITY CO	OH	132.7
CINCINNATI SPECIALTY UNDERWRITER	DE	744.7
COPIC INS CO	CO	716.3
COUNTRY MUTUAL INS CO	IL	4,756.8
CUMIS INS SOCIETY INC	IA	1,894.2
EMPLOYERS COMPENSATION INS CO	CA	1,095.5
ENDURANCE ASR CORP	DE	1,824.1
ESSENT GUARANTY INC	PA	1,384.2
GEICO SECURE INS CO	NE	555.9
HOME-OWNERS INS CO	MI	2,197.5
MOTORISTS COMMERCIAL MUTUAL INS CO	OH	358.9
NATIONAL MORTGAGE INS CORP	WI	645.5
OWNERS INS CO	OH	3,948.4
PROTECTIVE INS CO	IN	799.3
SECURIAN CASUALTY CO	MN	288.6
SOMPO AMERICA INSURANCE CO	NY	1,235.5
TRAVELERS CASUALTY & SURETY CO	CT	16,679.3
USAA CASUALTY INS CO	TX	10,235.4
Rating: **B+**		
ACUITY A MUTUAL INS CO	WI	3,686.4
ALFA SPECIALTY INS CORP	VA	57.1
AMERICAN FAMILY MUTL INS CO SI	WI	16,206.4
AMERICAN STANDARD INS CO OF WI	WI	401.3
AMICA MUTUAL INS CO	RI	5,140.7
BROTHERHOOD MUTUAL INS CO	IN	591.8
COUNTRY CASUALTY INS CO	IL	85.4
DAIRYLAND INS CO	WI	1,297.4
FARM BUREAU P&C INS CO	IA	2,529.1
FARM FAMILY CASUALTY INS CO	NY	1,188.8
GEICO CHOICE INS CO	NE	919.4
GEICO GENERAL INS CO	MD	166.1
INTERINS EXCHANGE	CA	9,670.8
MARKEL GLOBAL REINS CO	DE	1,943.5
MITSUI SUMITOMO INS CO OF AMER	NY	958.1
MOTORISTS MUTUAL INS CO	OH	1,368.4
NATIONAL CASUALTY CO	OH	404.6
NATIONWIDE MUTUAL FIRE INS CO	OH	8,809.3
PROPERTY-OWNERS INS CO	IN	289.0
SENTRY SELECT INS CO	WI	715.6
STATE FARM FIRE & CAS CO	IL	38,866.0
STATE FARM MUTUAL AUTOMOBILE INS CO	IL	150,198.0
TOA REINS CO OF AMERICA	DE	1,749.0
TRAVELERS INDEMNITY CO	CT	21,493.8
UNITED SERVICES AUTOMOBILE ASN	TX	33,965.5
USAA GENERAL INDEMNITY CO	TX	4,214.9
WEST BEND MUTUAL INS CO	WI	2,580.8

INSURANCE COMPANY NAME	DOM. STATE	TOTAL ASSETS ($MIL)
WESTERN AGRICULTURAL INS CO	IA	217.1

Montana

INSURANCE COMPANY NAME	DOM. STATE	TOTAL ASSETS ($MIL)
Rating: A+		
BERKSHIRE HATHAWAY ASR CORP	NY	2,454.3
Rating: A		
CINCINNATI INS CO	OH	12,253.3
SENTRY INS A MUTUAL CO	WI	7,779.6
TOKIO MARINE AMERICA INS CO	NY	1,401.2
Rating: A-		
CINCINNATI INDEMNITY CO	OH	132.7
CINCINNATI SPECIALTY UNDERWRITER	DE	744.7
COPIC INS CO	CO	716.3
COUNTRY MUTUAL INS CO	IL	4,756.8
CUMIS INS SOCIETY INC	IA	1,894.2
EMPLOYERS COMPENSATION INS CO	CA	1,095.5
ENDURANCE ASR CORP	DE	1,824.1
ESSENT GUARANTY INC	PA	1,384.2
GEICO SECURE INS CO	NE	555.9
NATIONAL MORTGAGE INS CORP	WI	645.5
PROTECTIVE INS CO	IN	799.3
SECURIAN CASUALTY CO	MN	288.6
SOMPO AMERICA INSURANCE CO	NY	1,235.5
TRAVELERS CASUALTY & SURETY CO	CT	16,679.3
USAA CASUALTY INS CO	TX	10,235.4
Rating: B+		
ACUITY A MUTUAL INS CO	WI	3,686.4
ALL AMERICA INS CO	OH	285.9
AMERICAN FAMILY MUTL INS CO SI	WI	16,206.4
AMERICAN STANDARD INS CO OF WI	WI	401.3
AMICA MUTUAL INS CO	RI	5,140.7
BROTHERHOOD MUTUAL INS CO	IN	591.8
COUNTRY CASUALTY INS CO	IL	85.4
DAIRYLAND INS CO	WI	1,297.4
GEICO CHOICE INS CO	NE	919.4
GEICO GENERAL INS CO	MD	166.1
MARKEL GLOBAL REINS CO	DE	1,943.5
MITSUI SUMITOMO INS CO OF AMER	NY	958.1
MOTORISTS MUTUAL INS CO	OH	1,368.4
NATIONAL CASUALTY CO	OH	404.6
NATIONWIDE MUTUAL FIRE INS CO	OH	8,809.3
SENTRY SELECT INS CO	WI	715.6
STATE FARM FIRE & CAS CO	IL	38,866.0
STATE FARM MUTUAL AUTOMOBILE INS CO	IL	150,198.0
TOA REINS CO OF AMERICA	DE	1,749.0
TRAVELERS INDEMNITY CO	CT	21,493.8
UNITED SERVICES AUTOMOBILE ASN	TX	33,965.5
USAA GENERAL INDEMNITY CO	TX	4,214.9
WESTERN AGRICULTURAL INS CO	IA	217.1

Nebraska

INSURANCE COMPANY NAME	DOM. STATE	TOTAL ASSETS ($MIL)
Rating: **A+**		
BERKSHIRE HATHAWAY ASR CORP	NY	2,454.3
Rating: **A**		
CINCINNATI INS CO	OH	12,253.3
SENTRY INS A MUTUAL CO	WI	7,779.6
TOKIO MARINE AMERICA INS CO	NY	1,401.2
Rating: **A-**		
AUTO-OWNERS INS CO	MI	14,502.3
CINCINNATI INDEMNITY CO	OH	132.7
CINCINNATI SPECIALTY UNDERWRITER	DE	744.7
COPIC INS CO	CO	716.3
COUNTRY MUTUAL INS CO	IL	4,756.8
CUMIS INS SOCIETY INC	IA	1,894.2
EMPLOYERS COMPENSATION INS CO	CA	1,095.5
ENDURANCE ASR CORP	DE	1,824.1
ESSENT GUARANTY INC	PA	1,384.2
GEICO SECURE INS CO	NE	555.9
HOME-OWNERS INS CO	MI	2,197.5
MOTORISTS COMMERCIAL MUTUAL INS CO	OH	358.9
NATIONAL MORTGAGE INS CORP	WI	645.5
OWNERS INS CO	OH	3,948.4
PROTECTIVE INS CO	IN	799.3
SECURIAN CASUALTY CO	MN	288.6
SOMPO AMERICA INSURANCE CO	NY	1,235.5
TRAVELERS CASUALTY & SURETY CO	CT	16,679.3
USAA CASUALTY INS CO	TX	10,235.4
Rating: **B+**		
ACUITY A MUTUAL INS CO	WI	3,686.4
AMERICAN FAMILY MUTL INS CO SI	WI	16,206.4
AMERICAN STANDARD INS CO OF WI	WI	401.3
AMICA MUTUAL INS CO	RI	5,140.7
BROTHERHOOD MUTUAL INS CO	IN	591.8
COUNTRY CASUALTY INS CO	IL	85.4
DAIRYLAND INS CO	WI	1,297.4
FARM BUREAU P&C INS CO	IA	2,529.1
GEICO CHOICE INS CO	NE	919.4
GEICO GENERAL INS CO	MD	166.1
MARKEL GLOBAL REINS CO	DE	1,943.5
MITSUI SUMITOMO INS CO OF AMER	NY	958.1
MOTORISTS MUTUAL INS CO	OH	1,368.4
NATIONAL CASUALTY CO	OH	404.6
NATIONWIDE MUTUAL FIRE INS CO	OH	8,809.3
PROPERTY-OWNERS INS CO	IN	289.0
SENTRY SELECT INS CO	WI	715.6
STATE FARM FIRE & CAS CO	IL	38,866.0
STATE FARM MUTUAL AUTOMOBILE INS CO	IL	150,198.0
TOA REINS CO OF AMERICA	DE	1,749.0
TRAVELERS INDEMNITY CO	CT	21,493.8
UNITED SERVICES AUTOMOBILE ASN	TX	33,965.5
USAA GENERAL INDEMNITY CO	TX	4,214.9
WEST BEND MUTUAL INS CO	WI	2,580.8
WESTERN AGRICULTURAL INS CO	IA	217.1

Nevada

INSURANCE COMPANY NAME	DOM. STATE	TOTAL ASSETS ($MIL)	INSURANCE COMPANY NAME	DOM. STATE	TOTAL ASSETS ($MIL)
Rating: A+					
BERKSHIRE HATHAWAY ASR CORP	NY	2,454.3			
Rating: A					
CINCINNATI INS CO	OH	12,253.3			
SENTRY INS A MUTUAL CO	WI	7,779.6			
TOKIO MARINE AMERICA INS CO	NY	1,401.2			
Rating: A-					
AUTO-OWNERS INS CO	MI	14,502.3			
CINCINNATI INDEMNITY CO	OH	132.7			
CINCINNATI SPECIALTY UNDERWRITER	DE	744.7			
COUNTRY MUTUAL INS CO	IL	4,756.8			
CUMIS INS SOCIETY INC	IA	1,894.2			
EMPLOYERS COMPENSATION INS CO	CA	1,095.5			
ENDURANCE ASR CORP	DE	1,824.1			
ESSENT GUARANTY INC	PA	1,384.2			
GEICO SECURE INS CO	NE	555.9			
HOME-OWNERS INS CO	MI	2,197.5			
MOTORISTS COMMERCIAL MUTUAL INS CO	OH	358.9			
NATIONAL MORTGAGE INS CORP	WI	645.5			
OWNERS INS CO	OH	3,948.4			
PROTECTIVE INS CO	IN	799.3			
SECURIAN CASUALTY CO	MN	288.6			
SOMPO AMERICA INSURANCE CO	NY	1,235.5			
TRAVELERS CASUALTY & SURETY CO	CT	16,679.3			
USAA CASUALTY INS CO	TX	10,235.4			
Rating: B+					
ACUITY A MUTUAL INS CO	WI	3,686.4			
ALL AMERICA INS CO	OH	285.9			
AMERICAN FAMILY MUTL INS CO SI	WI	16,206.4			
AMERICAN STANDARD INS CO OF WI	WI	401.3			
AMICA MUTUAL INS CO	RI	5,140.7			
BROTHERHOOD MUTUAL INS CO	IN	591.8			
COUNTRY CASUALTY INS CO	IL	85.4			
DAIRYLAND INS CO	WI	1,297.4			
GEICO CHOICE INS CO	NE	919.4			
GEICO GENERAL INS CO	MD	166.1			
MARKEL GLOBAL REINS CO	DE	1,943.5			
MITSUI SUMITOMO INS CO OF AMER	NY	958.1			
NATIONAL CASUALTY CO	OH	404.6			
NATIONWIDE MUTUAL FIRE INS CO	OH	8,809.3			
PROPERTY-OWNERS INS CO	IN	289.0			
SENTRY SELECT INS CO	WI	715.6			
STATE FARM FIRE & CAS CO	IL	38,866.0			
STATE FARM MUTUAL AUTOMOBILE INS CO	IL	150,198.0			
TOA REINS CO OF AMERICA	DE	1,749.0			
TRAVELERS INDEMNITY CO	CT	21,493.8			
UNITED SERVICES AUTOMOBILE ASN	TX	33,965.5			
USAA GENERAL INDEMNITY CO	TX	4,214.9			
WESTERN AGRICULTURAL INS CO	IA	217.1			

New Hampshire

INSURANCE COMPANY NAME	DOM. STATE	TOTAL ASSETS ($MIL)
Rating: A+		
BERKSHIRE HATHAWAY ASR CORP	NY	2,454.3
Rating: A		
CINCINNATI INS CO	OH	12,253.3
SENTRY INS A MUTUAL CO	WI	7,779.6
TOKIO MARINE AMERICA INS CO	NY	1,401.2
Rating: A-		
CINCINNATI INDEMNITY CO	OH	132.7
CINCINNATI SPECIALTY UNDERWRITER	DE	744.7
COUNTRY MUTUAL INS CO	IL	4,756.8
CUMIS INS SOCIETY INC	IA	1,894.2
ENDURANCE ASR CORP	DE	1,824.1
ESSENT GUARANTY INC	PA	1,384.2
GEICO SECURE INS CO	NE	555.9
MOTORISTS COMMERCIAL MUTUAL INS CO	OH	358.9
NATIONAL MORTGAGE INS CORP	WI	645.5
PROTECTIVE INS CO	IN	799.3
SECURIAN CASUALTY CO	MN	288.6
SOMPO AMERICA INSURANCE CO	NY	1,235.5
TRAVELERS CASUALTY & SURETY CO	CT	16,679.3
USAA CASUALTY INS CO	TX	10,235.4
Rating: B+		
ACUITY A MUTUAL INS CO	WI	3,686.4
ALL AMERICA INS CO	OH	285.9
AMICA MUTUAL INS CO	RI	5,140.7
BROTHERHOOD MUTUAL INS CO	IN	591.8
DAIRYLAND INS CO	WI	1,297.4
FARM FAMILY CASUALTY INS CO	NY	1,188.8
GEICO CHOICE INS CO	NE	919.4
GEICO GENERAL INS CO	MD	166.1
INTERINS EXCHANGE	CA	9,670.8
MARKEL GLOBAL REINS CO	DE	1,943.5
MITSUI SUMITOMO INS CO OF AMER	NY	958.1
MOTORISTS MUTUAL INS CO	OH	1,368.4
NATIONAL CASUALTY CO	OH	404.6
NATIONWIDE MUTUAL FIRE INS CO	OH	8,809.3
SENTRY SELECT INS CO	WI	715.6
STATE FARM FIRE & CAS CO	IL	38,866.0
STATE FARM MUTUAL AUTOMOBILE INS CO	IL	150,198.0
TOA REINS CO OF AMERICA	DE	1,749.0
TRAVELERS INDEMNITY CO	CT	21,493.8
UNITED SERVICES AUTOMOBILE ASN	TX	33,965.5
USAA GENERAL INDEMNITY CO	TX	4,214.9

New Jersey

INSURANCE COMPANY NAME	DOM. STATE	TOTAL ASSETS ($MIL)
Rating: A+		
BERKSHIRE HATHAWAY ASR CORP	NY	2,454.3
Rating: A		
CINCINNATI INS CO	OH	12,253.3
SENTRY INS A MUTUAL CO	WI	7,779.6
TOKIO MARINE AMERICA INS CO	NY	1,401.2
Rating: A-		
CINCINNATI INDEMNITY CO	OH	132.7
CINCINNATI SPECIALTY UNDERWRITER	DE	744.7
COUNTRY MUTUAL INS CO	IL	4,756.8
CUMIS INS SOCIETY INC	IA	1,894.2
EMPLOYERS COMPENSATION INS CO	CA	1,095.5
ENDURANCE ASR CORP	DE	1,824.1
ESSENT GUARANTY INC	PA	1,384.2
GEICO SECURE INS CO	NE	555.9
MOTORISTS COMMERCIAL MUTUAL INS CO	OH	358.9
NATIONAL MORTGAGE INS CORP	WI	645.5
PROTECTIVE INS CO	IN	799.3
SECURIAN CASUALTY CO	MN	288.6
SOMPO AMERICA INSURANCE CO	NY	1,235.5
TRAVELERS CASUALTY & SURETY CO	CT	16,679.3
USAA CASUALTY INS CO	TX	10,235.4
Rating: B+		
ALL AMERICA INS CO	OH	285.9
ALLSTATE NJ INS CO	IL	2,557.8
AMICA MUTUAL INS CO	RI	5,140.7
BROTHERHOOD MUTUAL INS CO	IN	591.8
FARM FAMILY CASUALTY INS CO	NY	1,188.8
GEICO CHOICE INS CO	NE	919.4
GEICO GENERAL INS CO	MD	166.1
GNY CUSTOM INS CO	AZ	59.3
MARKEL GLOBAL REINS CO	DE	1,943.5
MITSUI SUMITOMO INS CO OF AMER	NY	958.1
MOTORISTS MUTUAL INS CO	OH	1,368.4
NATIONAL CASUALTY CO	OH	404.6
NATIONWIDE MUTUAL FIRE INS CO	OH	8,809.3
SENTRY SELECT INS CO	WI	715.6
STATE FARM FIRE & CAS CO	IL	38,866.0
STATE FARM MUTUAL AUTOMOBILE INS CO	IL	150,198.0
TOA REINS CO OF AMERICA	DE	1,749.0
TRAVELERS INDEMNITY CO	CT	21,493.8
UNITED SERVICES AUTOMOBILE ASN	TX	33,965.5
USAA GENERAL INDEMNITY CO	TX	4,214.9

New Mexico

INSURANCE COMPANY NAME	DOM. STATE	TOTAL ASSETS ($MIL)
Rating:	**A+**	
BERKSHIRE HATHAWAY ASR CORP	NY	2,454.3
Rating:	**A**	
CINCINNATI INS CO	OH	12,253.3
SENTRY INS A MUTUAL CO	WI	7,779.6
TOKIO MARINE AMERICA INS CO	NY	1,401.2
Rating:	**A-**	
AUTO-OWNERS INS CO	MI	14,502.3
CINCINNATI INDEMNITY CO	OH	132.7
CINCINNATI SPECIALTY UNDERWRITER	DE	744.7
COUNTRY MUTUAL INS CO	IL	4,756.8
CUMIS INS SOCIETY INC	IA	1,894.2
EMPLOYERS COMPENSATION INS CO	CA	1,095.5
ENDURANCE ASR CORP	DE	1,824.1
ESSENT GUARANTY INC	PA	1,384.2
GEICO SECURE INS CO	NE	555.9
MOTORISTS COMMERCIAL MUTUAL INS CO	OH	358.9
NATIONAL MORTGAGE INS CORP	WI	645.5
OWNERS INS CO	OH	3,948.4
PROTECTIVE INS CO	IN	799.3
SECURIAN CASUALTY CO	MN	288.6
SOMPO AMERICA INSURANCE CO	NY	1,235.5
TRAVELERS CASUALTY & SURETY CO	CT	16,679.3
USAA CASUALTY INS CO	TX	10,235.4
Rating:	**B+**	
ACUITY A MUTUAL INS CO	WI	3,686.4
ALL AMERICA INS CO	OH	285.9
AMERICAN FAMILY MUTL INS CO SI	WI	16,206.4
AMERICAN STANDARD INS CO OF WI	WI	401.3
AMICA MUTUAL INS CO	RI	5,140.7
BROTHERHOOD MUTUAL INS CO	IN	591.8
COUNTRY CASUALTY INS CO	IL	85.4
DAIRYLAND INS CO	WI	1,297.4
FARM BUREAU P&C INS CO	IA	2,529.1
GEICO CHOICE INS CO	NE	919.4
GEICO GENERAL INS CO	MD	166.1
INTERINS EXCHANGE	CA	9,670.8
MARKEL GLOBAL REINS CO	DE	1,943.5
MITSUI SUMITOMO INS CO OF AMER	NY	958.1
NATIONAL CASUALTY CO	OH	404.6
NATIONWIDE MUTUAL FIRE INS CO	OH	8,809.3
SENTRY SELECT INS CO	WI	715.6
STATE FARM FIRE & CAS CO	IL	38,866.0
STATE FARM MUTUAL AUTOMOBILE INS CO	IL	150,198.0
TOA REINS CO OF AMERICA	DE	1,749.0
TRAVELERS INDEMNITY CO	CT	21,493.8
UNITED SERVICES AUTOMOBILE ASN	TX	33,965.5
USAA GENERAL INDEMNITY CO	TX	4,214.9
WESTERN AGRICULTURAL INS CO	IA	217.1

New York

INSURANCE COMPANY NAME	DOM. STATE	TOTAL ASSETS ($MIL)
Rating: A+		
BERKSHIRE HATHAWAY ASR CORP	NY	2,454.3
Rating: A		
CINCINNATI INS CO	OH	12,253.3
SENTRY INS A MUTUAL CO	WI	7,779.6
TOKIO MARINE AMERICA INS CO	NY	1,401.2
Rating: A-		
CINCINNATI INDEMNITY CO	OH	132.7
CINCINNATI SPECIALTY UNDERWRITER	DE	744.7
COUNTRY MUTUAL INS CO	IL	4,756.8
CUMIS INS SOCIETY INC	IA	1,894.2
EMPLOYERS COMPENSATION INS CO	CA	1,095.5
ENDURANCE ASR CORP	DE	1,824.1
ESSENT GUARANTY INC	PA	1,384.2
MOTORISTS COMMERCIAL MUTUAL INS CO	OH	358.9
NATIONAL MORTGAGE INS CORP	WI	645.5
PROTECTIVE INS CO	IN	799.3
SECURIAN CASUALTY CO	MN	288.6
SOMPO AMERICA INSURANCE CO	NY	1,235.5
TRAVELERS CASUALTY & SURETY CO	CT	16,679.3
USAA CASUALTY INS CO	TX	10,235.4
Rating: B+		
ALL AMERICA INS CO	OH	285.9
AMICA MUTUAL INS CO	RI	5,140.7
BROTHERHOOD MUTUAL INS CO	IN	591.8
DAIRYLAND INS CO	WI	1,297.4
FARM FAMILY CASUALTY INS CO	NY	1,188.8
GEICO GENERAL INS CO	MD	166.1
GNY CUSTOM INS CO	AZ	59.3
MARKEL GLOBAL REINS CO	DE	1,943.5
MITSUI SUMITOMO INS CO OF AMER	NY	958.1
MOTORISTS MUTUAL INS CO	OH	1,368.4
NATIONAL CASUALTY CO	OH	404.6
NATIONWIDE MUTUAL FIRE INS CO	OH	8,809.3
SENTRY SELECT INS CO	WI	715.6
STATE FARM FIRE & CAS CO	IL	38,866.0
STATE FARM MUTUAL AUTOMOBILE INS CO	IL	150,198.0
TOA REINS CO OF AMERICA	DE	1,749.0
TRAVELERS INDEMNITY CO	CT	21,493.8
UNITED SERVICES AUTOMOBILE ASN	TX	33,965.5
USAA GENERAL INDEMNITY CO	TX	4,214.9

North Carolina

INSURANCE COMPANY NAME	DOM. STATE	TOTAL ASSETS ($MIL)
Rating: A+		
BERKSHIRE HATHAWAY ASR CORP	NY	2,454.3
Rating: A		
CINCINNATI INS CO	OH	12,253.3
SENTRY INS A MUTUAL CO	WI	7,779.6
TOKIO MARINE AMERICA INS CO	NY	1,401.2
Rating: A-		
AUTO-OWNERS INS CO	MI	14,502.3
BUILDERS MUTUAL INS CO	NC	803.9
CINCINNATI INDEMNITY CO	OH	132.7
CINCINNATI SPECIALTY UNDERWRITER	DE	744.7
COUNTRY MUTUAL INS CO	IL	4,756.8
CUMIS INS SOCIETY INC	IA	1,894.2
ENDURANCE ASR CORP	DE	1,824.1
ESSENT GUARANTY INC	PA	1,384.2
GEICO SECURE INS CO	NE	555.9
MOTORISTS COMMERCIAL MUTUAL INS CO	OH	358.9
NATIONAL MORTGAGE INS CORP	WI	645.5
OWNERS INS CO	OH	3,948.4
PROTECTIVE INS CO	IN	799.3
SECURIAN CASUALTY CO	MN	288.6
SOMPO AMERICA INSURANCE CO	NY	1,235.5
TRAVELERS CASUALTY & SURETY CO	CT	16,679.3
USAA CASUALTY INS CO	TX	10,235.4
Rating: B+		
ALL AMERICA INS CO	OH	285.9
AMERICAN FAMILY MUTL INS CO SI	WI	16,206.4
AMERICAN STANDARD INS CO OF WI	WI	401.3
AMICA MUTUAL INS CO	RI	5,140.7
BROTHERHOOD MUTUAL INS CO	IN	591.8
DAIRYLAND INS CO	WI	1,297.4
GEICO CHOICE INS CO	NE	919.4
GEICO GENERAL INS CO	MD	166.1
GNY CUSTOM INS CO	AZ	59.3
MARKEL GLOBAL REINS CO	DE	1,943.5
MITSUI SUMITOMO INS CO OF AMER	NY	958.1
MOTORISTS MUTUAL INS CO	OH	1,368.4
NATIONAL CASUALTY CO	OH	404.6
NATIONWIDE MUTUAL FIRE INS CO	OH	8,809.3
SENTRY SELECT INS CO	WI	715.6
STATE FARM FIRE & CAS CO	IL	38,866.0
STATE FARM MUTUAL AUTOMOBILE INS CO	IL	150,198.0
TOA REINS CO OF AMERICA	DE	1,749.0
TRAVELERS INDEMNITY CO	CT	21,493.8
UNITED SERVICES AUTOMOBILE ASN	TX	33,965.5
USAA GENERAL INDEMNITY CO	TX	4,214.9

North Dakota

INSURANCE COMPANY NAME	DOM. STATE	TOTAL ASSETS ($MIL)
Rating:	**A+**	
BERKSHIRE HATHAWAY ASR CORP	NY	2,454.3
Rating:	**A**	
CINCINNATI INS CO	OH	12,253.3
SENTRY INS A MUTUAL CO	WI	7,779.6
TOKIO MARINE AMERICA INS CO	NY	1,401.2
Rating:	**A-**	
AUTO-OWNERS INS CO	MI	14,502.3
CINCINNATI INDEMNITY CO	OH	132.7
CINCINNATI SPECIALTY UNDERWRITER	DE	744.7
COUNTRY MUTUAL INS CO	IL	4,756.8
CUMIS INS SOCIETY INC	IA	1,894.2
ENDURANCE ASR CORP	DE	1,824.1
ESSENT GUARANTY INC	PA	1,384.2
HOME-OWNERS INS CO	MI	2,197.5
MOTORISTS COMMERCIAL MUTUAL INS CO	OH	358.9
NATIONAL MORTGAGE INS CORP	WI	645.5
OWNERS INS CO	OH	3,948.4
PROTECTIVE INS CO	IN	799.3
SECURIAN CASUALTY CO	MN	288.6
SOMPO AMERICA INSURANCE CO	NY	1,235.5
TRAVELERS CASUALTY & SURETY CO	CT	16,679.3
USAA CASUALTY INS CO	TX	10,235.4
Rating:	**B+**	
ACUITY A MUTUAL INS CO	WI	3,686.4
AMERICAN FAMILY MUTL INS CO SI	WI	16,206.4
AMERICAN STANDARD INS CO OF WI	WI	401.3
AMICA MUTUAL INS CO	RI	5,140.7
BROTHERHOOD MUTUAL INS CO	IN	591.8
COUNTRY CASUALTY INS CO	IL	85.4
DAIRYLAND INS CO	WI	1,297.4
GEICO GENERAL INS CO	MD	166.1
MARKEL GLOBAL REINS CO	DE	1,943.5
MITSUI SUMITOMO INS CO OF AMER	NY	958.1
MOTORISTS MUTUAL INS CO	OH	1,368.4
NATIONAL CASUALTY CO	OH	404.6
NATIONWIDE MUTUAL FIRE INS CO	OH	8,809.3
PROPERTY-OWNERS INS CO	IN	289.0
SENTRY SELECT INS CO	WI	715.6
STATE FARM FIRE & CAS CO	IL	38,866.0
STATE FARM MUTUAL AUTOMOBILE INS CO	IL	150,198.0
TOA REINS CO OF AMERICA	DE	1,749.0
TRAVELERS INDEMNITY CO	CT	21,493.8
UNITED SERVICES AUTOMOBILE ASN	TX	33,965.5
USAA GENERAL INDEMNITY CO	TX	4,214.9
WESTERN AGRICULTURAL INS CO	IA	217.1

Ohio

INSURANCE COMPANY NAME	DOM. STATE	TOTAL ASSETS ($MIL)
Rating: **A+**		
BERKSHIRE HATHAWAY ASR CORP	NY	2,454.3
Rating: **A**		
CINCINNATI INS CO	OH	12,253.3
SENTRY INS A MUTUAL CO	WI	7,779.6
TOKIO MARINE AMERICA INS CO	NY	1,401.2
Rating: **A-**		
AUTO-OWNERS INS CO	MI	14,502.3
CINCINNATI INDEMNITY CO	OH	132.7
CINCINNATI SPECIALTY UNDERWRITER	DE	744.7
COUNTRY MUTUAL INS CO	IL	4,756.8
CUMIS INS SOCIETY INC	IA	1,894.2
ENDURANCE ASR CORP	DE	1,824.1
ESSENT GUARANTY INC	PA	1,384.2
GEICO SECURE INS CO	NE	555.9
HOME-OWNERS INS CO	MI	2,197.5
MOTORISTS COMMERCIAL MUTUAL INS CO	OH	358.9
NATIONAL MORTGAGE INS CORP	WI	645.5
OWNERS INS CO	OH	3,948.4
PROTECTIVE INS CO	IN	799.3
SECURIAN CASUALTY CO	MN	288.6
SOMPO AMERICA INSURANCE CO	NY	1,235.5
TRAVELERS CASUALTY & SURETY CO	CT	16,679.3
USAA CASUALTY INS CO	TX	10,235.4
Rating: **B+**		
ACUITY A MUTUAL INS CO	WI	3,686.4
ALFA SPECIALTY INS CORP	VA	57.1
ALL AMERICA INS CO	OH	285.9
AMERICAN FAMILY MUTL INS CO SI	WI	16,206.4
AMERICAN STANDARD INS CO OF WI	WI	401.3
AMICA MUTUAL INS CO	RI	5,140.7
BROTHERHOOD MUTUAL INS CO	IN	591.8
COUNTRY CASUALTY INS CO	IL	85.4
DAIRYLAND INS CO	WI	1,297.4
FARMERS AUTOMOBILE INS ASN	IL	1,277.1
GEICO CHOICE INS CO	NE	919.4
GEICO GENERAL INS CO	MD	166.1
GNY CUSTOM INS CO	AZ	59.3
INTERINS EXCHANGE	CA	9,670.8
MARKEL GLOBAL REINS CO	DE	1,943.5
MITSUI SUMITOMO INS CO OF AMER	NY	958.1
MOTORISTS MUTUAL INS CO	OH	1,368.4
NATIONAL CASUALTY CO	OH	404.6
NATIONWIDE MUTUAL FIRE INS CO	OH	8,809.3
PEKIN INS CO	IL	306.7
SENTRY SELECT INS CO	WI	715.6
STATE FARM FIRE & CAS CO	IL	38,866.0
STATE FARM MUTUAL AUTOMOBILE INS CO	IL	150,198.0
TOA REINS CO OF AMERICA	DE	1,749.0
TRAVELERS INDEMNITY CO	CT	21,493.8
UNITED SERVICES AUTOMOBILE ASN	TX	33,965.5
USAA GENERAL INDEMNITY CO	TX	4,214.9
WEST BEND MUTUAL INS CO	WI	2,580.8
WESTERN AGRICULTURAL INS CO	IA	217.1

Oklahoma

INSURANCE COMPANY NAME	DOM. STATE	TOTAL ASSETS ($MIL)
Rating: A+		
BERKSHIRE HATHAWAY ASR CORP	NY	2,454.3
Rating: A		
CINCINNATI INS CO	OH	12,253.3
SENTRY INS A MUTUAL CO	WI	7,779.6
TOKIO MARINE AMERICA INS CO	NY	1,401.2
Rating: A-		
CINCINNATI INDEMNITY CO	OH	132.7
CINCINNATI SPECIALTY UNDERWRITER	DE	744.7
COPIC INS CO	CO	716.3
COUNTRY MUTUAL INS CO	IL	4,756.8
CUMIS INS SOCIETY INC	IA	1,894.2
EMPLOYERS COMPENSATION INS CO	CA	1,095.5
ENDURANCE ASR CORP	DE	1,824.1
ESSENT GUARANTY INC	PA	1,384.2
GEICO SECURE INS CO	NE	555.9
MOTORISTS COMMERCIAL MUTUAL INS CO	OH	358.9
NATIONAL MORTGAGE INS CORP	WI	645.5
PROTECTIVE INS CO	IN	799.3
SECURIAN CASUALTY CO	MN	288.6
SOMPO AMERICA INSURANCE CO	NY	1,235.5
TRAVELERS CASUALTY & SURETY CO	CT	16,679.3
USAA CASUALTY INS CO	TX	10,235.4
Rating: B+		
ACUITY A MUTUAL INS CO	WI	3,686.4
ALL AMERICA INS CO	OH	285.9
AMICA MUTUAL INS CO	RI	5,140.7
BROTHERHOOD MUTUAL INS CO	IN	591.8
COUNTRY CASUALTY INS CO	IL	85.4
GEICO CHOICE INS CO	NE	919.4
GEICO GENERAL INS CO	MD	166.1
MARKEL GLOBAL REINS CO	DE	1,943.5
MITSUI SUMITOMO INS CO OF AMER	NY	958.1
MOTORISTS MUTUAL INS CO	OH	1,368.4
NATIONAL CASUALTY CO	OH	404.6
NATIONWIDE MUTUAL FIRE INS CO	OH	8,809.3
SENTRY SELECT INS CO	WI	715.6
STATE FARM FIRE & CAS CO	IL	38,866.0
STATE FARM MUTUAL AUTOMOBILE INS CO	IL	150,198.0
TOA REINS CO OF AMERICA	DE	1,749.0
TRAVELERS INDEMNITY CO	CT	21,493.8
UNITED SERVICES AUTOMOBILE ASN	TX	33,965.5
USAA GENERAL INDEMNITY CO	TX	4,214.9
WESTERN AGRICULTURAL INS CO	IA	217.1

Oregon

INSURANCE COMPANY NAME	DOM. STATE	TOTAL ASSETS ($MIL)
Rating: **A+**		
BERKSHIRE HATHAWAY ASR CORP	NY	2,454.3
Rating: **A**		
CINCINNATI INS CO	OH	12,253.3
SENTRY INS A MUTUAL CO	WI	7,779.6
TOKIO MARINE AMERICA INS CO	NY	1,401.2
Rating: **A-**		
AUTO-OWNERS INS CO	MI	14,502.3
CINCINNATI INDEMNITY CO	OH	132.7
CINCINNATI SPECIALTY UNDERWRITER	DE	744.7
COUNTRY MUTUAL INS CO	IL	4,756.8
CUMIS INS SOCIETY INC	IA	1,894.2
EMPLOYERS COMPENSATION INS CO	CA	1,095.5
ENDURANCE ASR CORP	DE	1,824.1
ESSENT GUARANTY INC	PA	1,384.2
GEICO SECURE INS CO	NE	555.9
MOTORISTS COMMERCIAL MUTUAL INS CO	OH	358.9
NATIONAL MORTGAGE INS CORP	WI	645.5
OWNERS INS CO	OH	3,948.4
PROTECTIVE INS CO	IN	799.3
SECURIAN CASUALTY CO	MN	288.6
SOMPO AMERICA INSURANCE CO	NY	1,235.5
TRAVELERS CASUALTY & SURETY CO	CT	16,679.3
USAA CASUALTY INS CO	TX	10,235.4
Rating: **B+**		
ACUITY A MUTUAL INS CO	WI	3,686.4
ALL AMERICA INS CO	OH	285.9
AMERICAN FAMILY MUTL INS CO SI	WI	16,206.4
AMERICAN STANDARD INS CO OF WI	WI	401.3
AMICA MUTUAL INS CO	RI	5,140.7
BROTHERHOOD MUTUAL INS CO	IN	591.8
COUNTRY CASUALTY INS CO	IL	85.4
DAIRYLAND INS CO	WI	1,297.4
GEICO CHOICE INS CO	NE	919.4
GEICO GENERAL INS CO	MD	166.1
MARKEL GLOBAL REINS CO	DE	1,943.5
MITSUI SUMITOMO INS CO OF AMER	NY	958.1
MOTORISTS MUTUAL INS CO	OH	1,368.4
NATIONAL CASUALTY CO	OH	404.6
NATIONWIDE MUTUAL FIRE INS CO	OH	8,809.3
SENTRY SELECT INS CO	WI	715.6
STATE FARM FIRE & CAS CO	IL	38,866.0
STATE FARM MUTUAL AUTOMOBILE INS CO	IL	150,198.0
TOA REINS CO OF AMERICA	DE	1,749.0
TRAVELERS INDEMNITY CO	CT	21,493.8
UNITED SERVICES AUTOMOBILE ASN	TX	33,965.5
USAA GENERAL INDEMNITY CO	TX	4,214.9

Pennsylvania

INSURANCE COMPANY NAME	DOM. STATE	TOTAL ASSETS ($MIL)
Rating:	**A+**	
BERKSHIRE HATHAWAY ASR CORP	NY	2,454.3
Rating:	**A**	
CINCINNATI INS CO	OH	12,253.3
SENTRY INS A MUTUAL CO	WI	7,779.6
TOKIO MARINE AMERICA INS CO	NY	1,401.2
Rating:	**A-**	
AUTO-OWNERS INS CO	MI	14,502.3
CINCINNATI INDEMNITY CO	OH	132.7
CINCINNATI SPECIALTY UNDERWRITER	DE	744.7
COUNTRY MUTUAL INS CO	IL	4,756.8
CUMIS INS SOCIETY INC	IA	1,894.2
EMPLOYERS COMPENSATION INS CO	CA	1,095.5
ENDURANCE ASR CORP	DE	1,824.1
ESSENT GUARANTY INC	PA	1,384.2
GEICO SECURE INS CO	NE	555.9
HOME-OWNERS INS CO	MI	2,197.5
MOTORISTS COMMERCIAL MUTUAL INS CO	OH	358.9
NATIONAL MORTGAGE INS CORP	WI	645.5
OWNERS INS CO	OH	3,948.4
PROTECTIVE INS CO	IN	799.3
RADIAN REINS INC	PA	684.6
SECURIAN CASUALTY CO	MN	288.6
SOMPO AMERICA INSURANCE CO	NY	1,235.5
TRAVELERS CASUALTY & SURETY CO	CT	16,679.3
USAA CASUALTY INS CO	TX	10,235.4
Rating:	**B+**	
ACUITY A MUTUAL INS CO	WI	3,686.4
ALL AMERICA INS CO	OH	285.9
ALLSTATE NJ INS CO	IL	2,557.8
AMICA MUTUAL INS CO	RI	5,140.7
BROTHERHOOD MUTUAL INS CO	IN	591.8
COUNTRY CASUALTY INS CO	IL	85.4
DAIRYLAND INS CO	WI	1,297.4
FARM FAMILY CASUALTY INS CO	NY	1,188.8
GEICO CHOICE INS CO	NE	919.4
GEICO GENERAL INS CO	MD	166.1
GNY CUSTOM INS CO	AZ	59.3
INTERINS EXCHANGE	CA	9,670.8
MARKEL GLOBAL REINS CO	DE	1,943.5
MITSUI SUMITOMO INS CO OF AMER	NY	958.1
MOTORISTS MUTUAL INS CO	OH	1,368.4
NATIONAL CASUALTY CO	OH	404.6
NATIONWIDE MUTUAL FIRE INS CO	OH	8,809.3
SENTRY SELECT INS CO	WI	715.6
STATE FARM FIRE & CAS CO	IL	38,866.0
STATE FARM MUTUAL AUTOMOBILE INS CO	IL	150,198.0
TOA REINS CO OF AMERICA	DE	1,749.0
TRAVELERS INDEMNITY CO	CT	21,493.8
UNITED SERVICES AUTOMOBILE ASN	TX	33,965.5
USAA GENERAL INDEMNITY CO	TX	4,214.9

Rhode Island

INSURANCE COMPANY NAME	DOM. STATE	TOTAL ASSETS ($MIL)
Rating: A+		
BERKSHIRE HATHAWAY ASR CORP	NY	2,454.3
Rating: A		
CINCINNATI INS CO	OH	12,253.3
SENTRY INS A MUTUAL CO	WI	7,779.6
TOKIO MARINE AMERICA INS CO	NY	1,401.2
Rating: A-		
CINCINNATI INDEMNITY CO	OH	132.7
CINCINNATI SPECIALTY UNDERWRITER	DE	744.7
COUNTRY MUTUAL INS CO	IL	4,756.8
CUMIS INS SOCIETY INC	IA	1,894.2
ENDURANCE ASR CORP	DE	1,824.1
ESSENT GUARANTY INC	PA	1,384.2
GEICO SECURE INS CO	NE	555.9
MOTORISTS COMMERCIAL MUTUAL INS CO	OH	358.9
NATIONAL MORTGAGE INS CORP	WI	645.5
PROTECTIVE INS CO	IN	799.3
SECURIAN CASUALTY CO	MN	288.6
SOMPO AMERICA INSURANCE CO	NY	1,235.5
TRAVELERS CASUALTY & SURETY CO	CT	16,679.3
USAA CASUALTY INS CO	TX	10,235.4
Rating: B+		
AMICA MUTUAL INS CO	RI	5,140.7
BROTHERHOOD MUTUAL INS CO	IN	591.8
COUNTRY CASUALTY INS CO	IL	85.4
DAIRYLAND INS CO	WI	1,297.4
FARM FAMILY CASUALTY INS CO	NY	1,188.8
GEICO CHOICE INS CO	NE	919.4
GEICO GENERAL INS CO	MD	166.1
MARKEL GLOBAL REINS CO	DE	1,943.5
MITSUI SUMITOMO INS CO OF AMER	NY	958.1
MOTORISTS MUTUAL INS CO	OH	1,368.4
NATIONAL CASUALTY CO	OH	404.6
NATIONWIDE MUTUAL FIRE INS CO	OH	8,809.3
SENTRY SELECT INS CO	WI	715.6
STATE FARM FIRE & CAS CO	IL	38,866.0
STATE FARM MUTUAL AUTOMOBILE INS CO	IL	150,198.0
TOA REINS CO OF AMERICA	DE	1,749.0
TRAVELERS INDEMNITY CO	CT	21,493.8
UNITED SERVICES AUTOMOBILE ASN	TX	33,965.5
USAA GENERAL INDEMNITY CO	TX	4,214.9

South Carolina

INSURANCE COMPANY NAME	DOM. STATE	TOTAL ASSETS ($MIL)
Rating:	**A+**	
BERKSHIRE HATHAWAY ASR CORP	NY	2,454.3
Rating:	**A**	
CINCINNATI INS CO	OH	12,253.3
SENTRY INS A MUTUAL CO	WI	7,779.6
TOKIO MARINE AMERICA INS CO	NY	1,401.2
Rating:	**A-**	
AUTO-OWNERS INS CO	MI	14,502.3
BUILDERS MUTUAL INS CO	NC	803.9
CINCINNATI INDEMNITY CO	OH	132.7
CINCINNATI SPECIALTY UNDERWRITER	DE	744.7
COUNTRY MUTUAL INS CO	IL	4,756.8
CUMIS INS SOCIETY INC	IA	1,894.2
EMPLOYERS COMPENSATION INS CO	CA	1,095.5
ENDURANCE ASR CORP	DE	1,824.1
ESSENT GUARANTY INC	PA	1,384.2
GEICO SECURE INS CO	NE	555.9
HOME-OWNERS INS CO	MI	2,197.5
MOTORISTS COMMERCIAL MUTUAL INS CO	OH	358.9
NATIONAL MORTGAGE INS CORP	WI	645.5
OWNERS INS CO	OH	3,948.4
PROTECTIVE INS CO	IN	799.3
SECURIAN CASUALTY CO	MN	288.6
SOMPO AMERICA INSURANCE CO	NY	1,235.5
TRAVELERS CASUALTY & SURETY CO	CT	16,679.3
USAA CASUALTY INS CO	TX	10,235.4
Rating:	**B+**	
ALL AMERICA INS CO	OH	285.9
AMERICAN FAMILY MUTL INS CO SI	WI	16,206.4
AMERICAN STANDARD INS CO OF WI	WI	401.3
AMICA MUTUAL INS CO	RI	5,140.7
BROTHERHOOD MUTUAL INS CO	IN	591.8
DAIRYLAND INS CO	WI	1,297.4
GEICO CHOICE INS CO	NE	919.4
GEICO GENERAL INS CO	MD	166.1
MARKEL GLOBAL REINS CO	DE	1,943.5
MITSUI SUMITOMO INS CO OF AMER	NY	958.1
MOTORISTS MUTUAL INS CO	OH	1,368.4
NATIONAL CASUALTY CO	OH	404.6
NATIONWIDE MUTUAL FIRE INS CO	OH	8,809.3
PROPERTY-OWNERS INS CO	IN	289.0
SENTRY SELECT INS CO	WI	715.6
STATE FARM FIRE & CAS CO	IL	38,866.0
STATE FARM MUTUAL AUTOMOBILE INS CO	IL	150,198.0
TOA REINS CO OF AMERICA	DE	1,749.0
TRAVELERS INDEMNITY CO	CT	21,493.8
UNITED SERVICES AUTOMOBILE ASN	TX	33,965.5
USAA GENERAL INDEMNITY CO	TX	4,214.9
WESTERN AGRICULTURAL INS CO	IA	217.1

South Dakota

INSURANCE COMPANY NAME	DOM. STATE	TOTAL ASSETS ($MIL)
Rating: A+		
BERKSHIRE HATHAWAY ASR CORP	NY	2,454.3
Rating: A		
CINCINNATI INS CO	OH	12,253.3
SENTRY INS A MUTUAL CO	WI	7,779.6
TOKIO MARINE AMERICA INS CO	NY	1,401.2
Rating: A-		
AUTO-OWNERS INS CO	MI	14,502.3
CINCINNATI INDEMNITY CO	OH	132.7
CINCINNATI SPECIALTY UNDERWRITER	DE	744.7
COPIC INS CO	CO	716.3
COUNTRY MUTUAL INS CO	IL	4,756.8
CUMIS INS SOCIETY INC	IA	1,894.2
ENDURANCE ASR CORP	DE	1,824.1
ESSENT GUARANTY INC	PA	1,384.2
HOME-OWNERS INS CO	MI	2,197.5
MOTORISTS COMMERCIAL MUTUAL INS CO	OH	358.9
NATIONAL MORTGAGE INS CORP	WI	645.5
OWNERS INS CO	OH	3,948.4
PROTECTIVE INS CO	IN	799.3
SECURIAN CASUALTY CO	MN	288.6
SOMPO AMERICA INSURANCE CO	NY	1,235.5
TRAVELERS CASUALTY & SURETY CO	CT	16,679.3
USAA CASUALTY INS CO	TX	10,235.4
Rating: B+		
ACUITY A MUTUAL INS CO	WI	3,686.4
AMERICAN FAMILY MUTL INS CO SI	WI	16,206.4
AMERICAN STANDARD INS CO OF WI	WI	401.3
AMICA MUTUAL INS CO	RI	5,140.7
BROTHERHOOD MUTUAL INS CO	IN	591.8
COUNTRY CASUALTY INS CO	IL	85.4
DAIRYLAND INS CO	WI	1,297.4
FARM BUREAU P&C INS CO	IA	2,529.1
GEICO GENERAL INS CO	MD	166.1
MARKEL GLOBAL REINS CO	DE	1,943.5
MITSUI SUMITOMO INS CO OF AMER	NY	958.1
MOTORISTS MUTUAL INS CO	OH	1,368.4
NATIONAL CASUALTY CO	OH	404.6
NATIONWIDE MUTUAL FIRE INS CO	OH	8,809.3
PROPERTY-OWNERS INS CO	IN	289.0
SENTRY SELECT INS CO	WI	715.6
STATE FARM FIRE & CAS CO	IL	38,866.0
STATE FARM MUTUAL AUTOMOBILE INS CO	IL	150,198.0
TOA REINS CO OF AMERICA	DE	1,749.0
TRAVELERS INDEMNITY CO	CT	21,493.8
UNITED SERVICES AUTOMOBILE ASN	TX	33,965.5
USAA GENERAL INDEMNITY CO	TX	4,214.9
WESTERN AGRICULTURAL INS CO	IA	217.1

Tennessee

INSURANCE COMPANY NAME	DOM. STATE	TOTAL ASSETS ($MIL)
Rating: A+		
BERKSHIRE HATHAWAY ASR CORP	NY	2,454.3
Rating: A		
CINCINNATI INS CO	OH	12,253.3
SENTRY INS A MUTUAL CO	WI	7,779.6
TOKIO MARINE AMERICA INS CO	NY	1,401.2
Rating: A-		
AUTO-OWNERS INS CO	MI	14,502.3
BUILDERS MUTUAL INS CO	NC	803.9
CINCINNATI INDEMNITY CO	OH	132.7
CINCINNATI SPECIALTY UNDERWRITER	DE	744.7
COUNTRY MUTUAL INS CO	IL	4,756.8
CUMIS INS SOCIETY INC	IA	1,894.2
EMPLOYERS COMPENSATION INS CO	CA	1,095.5
ENDURANCE ASR CORP	DE	1,824.1
ESSENT GUARANTY INC	PA	1,384.2
GEICO SECURE INS CO	NE	555.9
MOTORISTS COMMERCIAL MUTUAL INS CO	OH	358.9
NATIONAL MORTGAGE INS CORP	WI	645.5
OWNERS INS CO	OH	3,948.4
PROTECTIVE INS CO	IN	799.3
SECURIAN CASUALTY CO	MN	288.6
SOMPO AMERICA INSURANCE CO	NY	1,235.5
TRAVELERS CASUALTY & SURETY CO	CT	16,679.3
USAA CASUALTY INS CO	TX	10,235.4
Rating: B+		
ACUITY A MUTUAL INS CO	WI	3,686.4
ALFA SPECIALTY INS CORP	VA	57.1
ALL AMERICA INS CO	OH	285.9
AMERICAN FAMILY MUTL INS CO SI	WI	16,206.4
AMICA MUTUAL INS CO	RI	5,140.7
BROTHERHOOD MUTUAL INS CO	IN	591.8
COUNTRY CASUALTY INS CO	IL	85.4
DAIRYLAND INS CO	WI	1,297.4
GEICO CHOICE INS CO	NE	919.4
GEICO GENERAL INS CO	MD	166.1
MARKEL GLOBAL REINS CO	DE	1,943.5
MITSUI SUMITOMO INS CO OF AMER	NY	958.1
MOTORISTS MUTUAL INS CO	OH	1,368.4
NATIONAL CASUALTY CO	OH	404.6
NATIONWIDE MUTUAL FIRE INS CO	OH	8,809.3
SENTRY SELECT INS CO	WI	715.6
STATE FARM FIRE & CAS CO	IL	38,866.0
STATE FARM MUTUAL AUTOMOBILE INS CO	IL	150,198.0
TENNESSEE FARMERS ASR CO	TN	1,442.2
TENNESSEE FARMERS MUTUAL INS CO	TN	2,919.9
TOA REINS CO OF AMERICA	DE	1,749.0
TRAVELERS INDEMNITY CO	CT	21,493.8
UNITED SERVICES AUTOMOBILE ASN	TX	33,965.5
USAA GENERAL INDEMNITY CO	TX	4,214.9
WEST BEND MUTUAL INS CO	WI	2,580.8
WESTERN AGRICULTURAL INS CO	IA	217.1

Texas

INSURANCE COMPANY NAME	DOM. STATE	TOTAL ASSETS ($MIL)	INSURANCE COMPANY NAME	DOM. STATE	TOTAL ASSETS ($MIL)
Rating:　A+					
BERKSHIRE HATHAWAY ASR CORP	NY	2,454.3			
OGLESBY REINS CO	IL	4,364.9			
Rating:　A					
CINCINNATI INS CO	OH	12,253.3			
SENTRY INS A MUTUAL CO	WI	7,779.6			
TOKIO MARINE AMERICA INS CO	NY	1,401.2			
Rating:　A-					
CINCINNATI INDEMNITY CO	OH	132.7			
CINCINNATI SPECIALTY UNDERWRITER	DE	744.7			
COUNTRY MUTUAL INS CO	IL	4,756.8			
CUMIS INS SOCIETY INC	IA	1,894.2			
EMPLOYERS COMPENSATION INS CO	CA	1,095.5			
ENDURANCE ASR CORP	DE	1,824.1			
ESSENT GUARANTY INC	PA	1,384.2			
GEICO SECURE INS CO	NE	555.9			
MOTORISTS COMMERCIAL MUTUAL INS CO	OH	358.9			
NATIONAL MORTGAGE INS CORP	WI	645.5			
PROTECTIVE INS CO	IN	799.3			
SECURIAN CASUALTY CO	MN	288.6			
SOMPO AMERICA INSURANCE CO	NY	1,235.5			
TRAVELERS CASUALTY & SURETY CO	CT	16,679.3			
USAA CASUALTY INS CO	TX	10,235.4			
Rating:　B+					
ACUITY A MUTUAL INS CO	WI	3,686.4			
ALFA SPECIALTY INS CORP	VA	57.1			
ALL AMERICA INS CO	OH	285.9			
AMERICAN FAMILY MUTL INS CO SI	WI	16,206.4			
AMICA MUTUAL INS CO	RI	5,140.7			
AUTO CLUB INDEMNITY CO	TX	25.9			
BROTHERHOOD MUTUAL INS CO	IN	591.8			
COUNTRY CASUALTY INS CO	IL	85.4			
DAIRYLAND INS CO	WI	1,297.4			
GEICO CHOICE INS CO	NE	919.4			
GEICO GENERAL INS CO	MD	166.1			
INTERINS EXCHANGE	CA	9,670.8			
MARKEL GLOBAL REINS CO	DE	1,943.5			
MITSUI SUMITOMO INS CO OF AMER	NY	958.1			
MOTORISTS MUTUAL INS CO	OH	1,368.4			
NATIONAL CASUALTY CO	OH	404.6			
NATIONWIDE MUTUAL FIRE INS CO	OH	8,809.3			
SENTRY SELECT INS CO	WI	715.6			
STATE FARM FIRE & CAS CO	IL	38,866.0			
STATE FARM MUTUAL AUTOMOBILE INS CO	IL	150,198.0			
TEXAS FARM BUREAU CASUALTY INS CO	TX	1,206.1			
TOA REINS CO OF AMERICA	DE	1,749.0			
TRAVELERS INDEMNITY CO	CT	21,493.8			
UNITED SERVICES AUTOMOBILE ASN	TX	33,965.5			
USAA GENERAL INDEMNITY CO	TX	4,214.9			
WESTERN AGRICULTURAL INS CO	IA	217.1			

Utah

INSURANCE COMPANY NAME	DOM. STATE	TOTAL ASSETS ($MIL)
Rating:	**A+**	
BERKSHIRE HATHAWAY ASR CORP	NY	2,454.3
Rating:	**A**	
CINCINNATI INS CO	OH	12,253.3
SENTRY INS A MUTUAL CO	WI	7,779.6
TOKIO MARINE AMERICA INS CO	NY	1,401.2
Rating:	**A-**	
AUTO-OWNERS INS CO	MI	14,502.3
CINCINNATI INDEMNITY CO	OH	132.7
CINCINNATI SPECIALTY UNDERWRITER	DE	744.7
COPIC INS CO	CO	716.3
COUNTRY MUTUAL INS CO	IL	4,756.8
CUMIS INS SOCIETY INC	IA	1,894.2
EMPLOYERS COMPENSATION INS CO	CA	1,095.5
ENDURANCE ASR CORP	DE	1,824.1
ESSENT GUARANTY INC	PA	1,384.2
GEICO SECURE INS CO	NE	555.9
HOME-OWNERS INS CO	MI	2,197.5
MOTORISTS COMMERCIAL MUTUAL INS CO	OH	358.9
NATIONAL MORTGAGE INS CORP	WI	645.5
OWNERS INS CO	OH	3,948.4
PROTECTIVE INS CO	IN	799.3
SECURIAN CASUALTY CO	MN	288.6
SOMPO AMERICA INSURANCE CO	NY	1,235.5
TRAVELERS CASUALTY & SURETY CO	CT	16,679.3
USAA CASUALTY INS CO	TX	10,235.4
Rating:	**B+**	
ACUITY A MUTUAL INS CO	WI	3,686.4
ALL AMERICA INS CO	OH	285.9
AMERICAN FAMILY MUTL INS CO SI	WI	16,206.4
AMERICAN STANDARD INS CO OF WI	WI	401.3
AMICA MUTUAL INS CO	RI	5,140.7
BROTHERHOOD MUTUAL INS CO	IN	591.8
DAIRYLAND INS CO	WI	1,297.4
FARM BUREAU P&C INS CO	IA	2,529.1
GEICO CHOICE INS CO	NE	919.4
GEICO GENERAL INS CO	MD	166.1
MARKEL GLOBAL REINS CO	DE	1,943.5
MITSUI SUMITOMO INS CO OF AMER	NY	958.1
MOTORISTS MUTUAL INS CO	OH	1,368.4
NATIONAL CASUALTY CO	OH	404.6
NATIONWIDE MUTUAL FIRE INS CO	OH	8,809.3
PROPERTY-OWNERS INS CO	IN	289.0
SENTRY SELECT INS CO	WI	715.6
STATE FARM FIRE & CAS CO	IL	38,866.0
STATE FARM MUTUAL AUTOMOBILE INS CO	IL	150,198.0
TOA REINS CO OF AMERICA	DE	1,749.0
TRAVELERS INDEMNITY CO	CT	21,493.8
UNITED SERVICES AUTOMOBILE ASN	TX	33,965.5
USAA GENERAL INDEMNITY CO	TX	4,214.9
WESTERN AGRICULTURAL INS CO	IA	217.1

Vermont

INSURANCE COMPANY NAME	DOM. STATE	TOTAL ASSETS ($MIL)	INSURANCE COMPANY NAME	DOM. STATE	TOTAL ASSETS ($MIL)
Rating: A+					
BERKSHIRE HATHAWAY ASR CORP	NY	2,454.3			
Rating: A					
CINCINNATI INS CO	OH	12,253.3			
SENTRY INS A MUTUAL CO	WI	7,779.6			
TOKIO MARINE AMERICA INS CO	NY	1,401.2			
Rating: A-					
CINCINNATI INDEMNITY CO	OH	132.7			
CINCINNATI SPECIALTY UNDERWRITER	DE	744.7			
COUNTRY MUTUAL INS CO	IL	4,756.8			
CUMIS INS SOCIETY INC	IA	1,894.2			
EMPLOYERS COMPENSATION INS CO	CA	1,095.5			
ENDURANCE ASR CORP	DE	1,824.1			
ESSENT GUARANTY INC	PA	1,384.2			
MOTORISTS COMMERCIAL MUTUAL INS CO	OH	358.9			
NATIONAL MORTGAGE INS CORP	WI	645.5			
PROTECTIVE INS CO	IN	799.3			
SECURIAN CASUALTY CO	MN	288.6			
SOMPO AMERICA INSURANCE CO	NY	1,235.5			
TRAVELERS CASUALTY & SURETY CO	CT	16,679.3			
USAA CASUALTY INS CO	TX	10,235.4			
Rating: B+					
ACUITY A MUTUAL INS CO	WI	3,686.4			
ALL AMERICA INS CO	OH	285.9			
AMICA MUTUAL INS CO	RI	5,140.7			
BROTHERHOOD MUTUAL INS CO	IN	591.8			
DAIRYLAND INS CO	WI	1,297.4			
FARM FAMILY CASUALTY INS CO	NY	1,188.8			
GEICO GENERAL INS CO	MD	166.1			
GNY CUSTOM INS CO	AZ	59.3			
INTERINS EXCHANGE	CA	9,670.8			
MARKEL GLOBAL REINS CO	DE	1,943.5			
MITSUI SUMITOMO INS CO OF AMER	NY	958.1			
MOTORISTS MUTUAL INS CO	OH	1,368.4			
NATIONAL CASUALTY CO	OH	404.6			
NATIONWIDE MUTUAL FIRE INS CO	OH	8,809.3			
SENTRY SELECT INS CO	WI	715.6			
STATE FARM FIRE & CAS CO	IL	38,866.0			
STATE FARM MUTUAL AUTOMOBILE INS CO	IL	150,198.0			
TOA REINS CO OF AMERICA	DE	1,749.0			
TRAVELERS INDEMNITY CO	CT	21,493.8			
UNITED SERVICES AUTOMOBILE ASN	TX	33,965.5			
USAA GENERAL INDEMNITY CO	TX	4,214.9			

Virginia

INSURANCE COMPANY NAME	DOM. STATE	TOTAL ASSETS ($MIL)
Rating: A+		
BERKSHIRE HATHAWAY ASR CORP	NY	2,454.3
Rating: A		
CINCINNATI INS CO	OH	12,253.3
SENTRY INS A MUTUAL CO	WI	7,779.6
TOKIO MARINE AMERICA INS CO	NY	1,401.2
Rating: A-		
AUTO-OWNERS INS CO	MI	14,502.3
BUILDERS MUTUAL INS CO	NC	803.9
CINCINNATI INDEMNITY CO	OH	132.7
CINCINNATI SPECIALTY UNDERWRITER	DE	744.7
COUNTRY MUTUAL INS CO	IL	4,756.8
CUMIS INS SOCIETY INC	IA	1,894.2
EMPLOYERS COMPENSATION INS CO	CA	1,095.5
ENDURANCE ASR CORP	DE	1,824.1
ESSENT GUARANTY INC	PA	1,384.2
GEICO SECURE INS CO	NE	555.9
HOME-OWNERS INS CO	MI	2,197.5
MOTORISTS COMMERCIAL MUTUAL INS CO	OH	358.9
NATIONAL MORTGAGE INS CORP	WI	645.5
OWNERS INS CO	OH	3,948.4
PROTECTIVE INS CO	IN	799.3
SECURIAN CASUALTY CO	MN	288.6
SOMPO AMERICA INSURANCE CO	NY	1,235.5
TRAVELERS CASUALTY & SURETY CO	CT	16,679.3
USAA CASUALTY INS CO	TX	10,235.4
Rating: B+		
ACUITY A MUTUAL INS CO	WI	3,686.4
ALFA SPECIALTY INS CORP	VA	57.1
ALL AMERICA INS CO	OH	285.9
AMERICAN FAMILY MUTL INS CO SI	WI	16,206.4
AMICA MUTUAL INS CO	RI	5,140.7
BROTHERHOOD MUTUAL INS CO	IN	591.8
DAIRYLAND INS CO	WI	1,297.4
FARM FAMILY CASUALTY INS CO	NY	1,188.8
GEICO CHOICE INS CO	NE	919.4
GEICO GENERAL INS CO	MD	166.1
GNY CUSTOM INS CO	AZ	59.3
INTERINS EXCHANGE	CA	9,670.8
MARKEL GLOBAL REINS CO	DE	1,943.5
MITSUI SUMITOMO INS CO OF AMER	NY	958.1
MOTORISTS MUTUAL INS CO	OH	1,368.4
NATIONAL CASUALTY CO	OH	404.6
NATIONWIDE MUTUAL FIRE INS CO	OH	8,809.3
PROPERTY-OWNERS INS CO	IN	289.0
SENTRY SELECT INS CO	WI	715.6
STATE FARM FIRE & CAS CO	IL	38,866.0
STATE FARM MUTUAL AUTOMOBILE INS CO	IL	150,198.0
TOA REINS CO OF AMERICA	DE	1,749.0
TRAVELERS INDEMNITY CO	CT	21,493.8
UNITED SERVICES AUTOMOBILE ASN	TX	33,965.5
USAA GENERAL INDEMNITY CO	TX	4,214.9
WESTERN AGRICULTURAL INS CO	IA	217.1

Washington

INSURANCE COMPANY NAME	DOM. STATE	TOTAL ASSETS ($MIL)
Rating:	**A+**	
BERKSHIRE HATHAWAY ASR CORP	NY	2,454.3
Rating:	**A**	
CINCINNATI INS CO	OH	12,253.3
SENTRY INS A MUTUAL CO	WI	7,779.6
TOKIO MARINE AMERICA INS CO	NY	1,401.2
Rating:	**A-**	
AUTO-OWNERS INS CO	MI	14,502.3
CINCINNATI INDEMNITY CO	OH	132.7
CINCINNATI SPECIALTY UNDERWRITER	DE	744.7
COUNTRY MUTUAL INS CO	IL	4,756.8
CUMIS INS SOCIETY INC	IA	1,894.2
ENDURANCE ASR CORP	DE	1,824.1
ESSENT GUARANTY INC	PA	1,384.2
GEICO SECURE INS CO	NE	555.9
MOTORISTS COMMERCIAL MUTUAL INS CO	OH	358.9
NATIONAL MORTGAGE INS CORP	WI	645.5
OWNERS INS CO	OH	3,948.4
PROTECTIVE INS CO	IN	799.3
SECURIAN CASUALTY CO	MN	288.6
SOMPO AMERICA INSURANCE CO	NY	1,235.5
TRAVELERS CASUALTY & SURETY CO	CT	16,679.3
USAA CASUALTY INS CO	TX	10,235.4
Rating:	**B+**	
ACUITY A MUTUAL INS CO	WI	3,686.4
ALL AMERICA INS CO	OH	285.9
AMERICAN FAMILY MUTL INS CO SI	WI	16,206.4
AMERICAN STANDARD INS CO OF WI	WI	401.3
AMICA MUTUAL INS CO	RI	5,140.7
BROTHERHOOD MUTUAL INS CO	IN	591.8
COUNTRY CASUALTY INS CO	IL	85.4
DAIRYLAND INS CO	WI	1,297.4
GEICO CHOICE INS CO	NE	919.4
GEICO GENERAL INS CO	MD	166.1
MARKEL GLOBAL REINS CO	DE	1,943.5
MITSUI SUMITOMO INS CO OF AMER	NY	958.1
NATIONAL CASUALTY CO	OH	404.6
NATIONWIDE MUTUAL FIRE INS CO	OH	8,809.3
SENTRY SELECT INS CO	WI	715.6
STATE FARM FIRE & CAS CO	IL	38,866.0
STATE FARM MUTUAL AUTOMOBILE INS CO	IL	150,198.0
TOA REINS CO OF AMERICA	DE	1,749.0
TRAVELERS INDEMNITY CO	CT	21,493.8
UNITED SERVICES AUTOMOBILE ASN	TX	33,965.5
USAA GENERAL INDEMNITY CO	TX	4,214.9

West Virginia

INSURANCE COMPANY NAME	DOM. STATE	TOTAL ASSETS ($MIL)	INSURANCE COMPANY NAME	DOM. STATE	TOTAL ASSETS ($MIL)
Rating: **A+**					
BERKSHIRE HATHAWAY ASR CORP	NY	2,454.3			
Rating: **A**					
CINCINNATI INS CO	OH	12,253.3			
SENTRY INS A MUTUAL CO	WI	7,779.6			
TOKIO MARINE AMERICA INS CO	NY	1,401.2			
Rating: **A-**					
CINCINNATI INDEMNITY CO	OH	132.7			
CINCINNATI SPECIALTY UNDERWRITER	DE	744.7			
COUNTRY MUTUAL INS CO	IL	4,756.8			
CUMIS INS SOCIETY INC	IA	1,894.2			
ENDURANCE ASR CORP	DE	1,824.1			
ESSENT GUARANTY INC	PA	1,384.2			
GEICO SECURE INS CO	NE	555.9			
MOTORISTS COMMERCIAL MUTUAL INS CO	OH	358.9			
NATIONAL MORTGAGE INS CORP	WI	645.5			
PROTECTIVE INS CO	IN	799.3			
SECURIAN CASUALTY CO	MN	288.6			
SOMPO AMERICA INSURANCE CO	NY	1,235.5			
TRAVELERS CASUALTY & SURETY CO	CT	16,679.3			
USAA CASUALTY INS CO	TX	10,235.4			
Rating: **B+**					
ACUITY A MUTUAL INS CO	WI	3,686.4			
AMICA MUTUAL INS CO	RI	5,140.7			
BROTHERHOOD MUTUAL INS CO	IN	591.8			
DAIRYLAND INS CO	WI	1,297.4			
FARM FAMILY CASUALTY INS CO	NY	1,188.8			
GEICO CHOICE INS CO	NE	919.4			
GEICO GENERAL INS CO	MD	166.1			
MARKEL GLOBAL REINS CO	DE	1,943.5			
MITSUI SUMITOMO INS CO OF AMER	NY	958.1			
MOTORISTS MUTUAL INS CO	OH	1,368.4			
NATIONAL CASUALTY CO	OH	404.6			
NATIONWIDE MUTUAL FIRE INS CO	OH	8,809.3			
SENTRY SELECT INS CO	WI	715.6			
STATE FARM FIRE & CAS CO	IL	38,866.0			
STATE FARM MUTUAL AUTOMOBILE INS CO	IL	150,198.0			
TOA REINS CO OF AMERICA	DE	1,749.0			
TRAVELERS INDEMNITY CO	CT	21,493.8			
UNITED SERVICES AUTOMOBILE ASN	TX	33,965.5			
USAA GENERAL INDEMNITY CO	TX	4,214.9			

Wisconsin

INSURANCE COMPANY NAME	DOM. STATE	TOTAL ASSETS ($MIL)
Rating: A+		
BERKSHIRE HATHAWAY ASR CORP	NY	2,454.3
Rating: A		
CINCINNATI INS CO	OH	12,253.3
SENTRY INS A MUTUAL CO	WI	7,779.6
TOKIO MARINE AMERICA INS CO	NY	1,401.2
Rating: A-		
AUTO-OWNERS INS CO	MI	14,502.3
BUILDERS MUTUAL INS CO	NC	803.9
CINCINNATI INDEMNITY CO	OH	132.7
CINCINNATI SPECIALTY UNDERWRITER	DE	744.7
COUNTRY MUTUAL INS CO	IL	4,756.8
CUMIS INS SOCIETY INC	IA	1,894.2
EMPLOYERS COMPENSATION INS CO	CA	1,095.5
ENDURANCE ASR CORP	DE	1,824.1
ESSENT GUARANTY INC	PA	1,384.2
GEICO SECURE INS CO	NE	555.9
HOME-OWNERS INS CO	MI	2,197.5
MOTORISTS COMMERCIAL MUTUAL INS CO	OH	358.9
NATIONAL MORTGAGE INS CORP	WI	645.5
OWNERS INS CO	OH	3,948.4
PROTECTIVE INS CO	IN	799.3
SECURIAN CASUALTY CO	MN	288.6
SOMPO AMERICA INSURANCE CO	NY	1,235.5
TRAVELERS CASUALTY & SURETY CO	CT	16,679.3
USAA CASUALTY INS CO	TX	10,235.4
Rating: B+		
ACUITY A MUTUAL INS CO	WI	3,686.4
ALL AMERICA INS CO	OH	285.9
AMERICAN FAMILY MUTL INS CO SI	WI	16,206.4
AMERICAN STANDARD INS CO OF WI	WI	401.3
AMICA MUTUAL INS CO	RI	5,140.7
BROTHERHOOD MUTUAL INS CO	IN	591.8
COUNTRY CASUALTY INS CO	IL	85.4
DAIRYLAND INS CO	WI	1,297.4
FARM BUREAU P&C INS CO	IA	2,529.1
FARMERS AUTOMOBILE INS ASN	IL	1,277.1
GEICO CHOICE INS CO	NE	919.4
GEICO GENERAL INS CO	MD	166.1
MARKEL GLOBAL REINS CO	DE	1,943.5
MITSUI SUMITOMO INS CO OF AMER	NY	958.1
MOTORISTS MUTUAL INS CO	OH	1,368.4
NATIONAL CASUALTY CO	OH	404.6
NATIONWIDE MUTUAL FIRE INS CO	OH	8,809.3
PEKIN INS CO	IL	306.7
PROPERTY-OWNERS INS CO	IN	289.0
SENTRY SELECT INS CO	WI	715.6
STATE FARM FIRE & CAS CO	IL	38,866.0
STATE FARM MUTUAL AUTOMOBILE INS CO	IL	150,198.0
TOA REINS CO OF AMERICA	DE	1,749.0
TRAVELERS INDEMNITY CO	CT	21,493.8
UNITED SERVICES AUTOMOBILE ASN	TX	33,965.5
USAA GENERAL INDEMNITY CO	TX	4,214.9
WEST BEND MUTUAL INS CO	WI	2,580.8

INSURANCE COMPANY NAME	DOM. STATE	TOTAL ASSETS ($MIL)
WESTERN AGRICULTURAL INS CO	IA	217.1

Wyoming

INSURANCE COMPANY NAME	DOM. STATE	TOTAL ASSETS ($MIL)
Rating: A+		
BERKSHIRE HATHAWAY ASR CORP	NY	2,454.3
Rating: A		
CINCINNATI INS CO	OH	12,253.3
SENTRY INS A MUTUAL CO	WI	7,779.6
TOKIO MARINE AMERICA INS CO	NY	1,401.2
Rating: A-		
CINCINNATI INDEMNITY CO	OH	132.7
CINCINNATI SPECIALTY UNDERWRITER	DE	744.7
COPIC INS CO	CO	716.3
COUNTRY MUTUAL INS CO	IL	4,756.8
CUMIS INS SOCIETY INC	IA	1,894.2
ENDURANCE ASR CORP	DE	1,824.1
ESSENT GUARANTY INC	PA	1,384.2
GEICO SECURE INS CO	NE	555.9
MOTORISTS COMMERCIAL MUTUAL INS CO	OH	358.9
NATIONAL MORTGAGE INS CORP	WI	645.5
PROTECTIVE INS CO	IN	799.3
SECURIAN CASUALTY CO	MN	288.6
SOMPO AMERICA INSURANCE CO	NY	1,235.5
TRAVELERS CASUALTY & SURETY CO	CT	16,679.3
USAA CASUALTY INS CO	TX	10,235.4
Rating: B+		
ACUITY A MUTUAL INS CO	WI	3,686.4
AMERICAN FAMILY MUTL INS CO SI	WI	16,206.4
AMERICAN STANDARD INS CO OF WI	WI	401.3
AMICA MUTUAL INS CO	RI	5,140.7
BROTHERHOOD MUTUAL INS CO	IN	591.8
COUNTRY CASUALTY INS CO	IL	85.4
DAIRYLAND INS CO	WI	1,297.4
GEICO CHOICE INS CO	NE	919.4
GEICO GENERAL INS CO	MD	166.1
MARKEL GLOBAL REINS CO	DE	1,943.5
MITSUI SUMITOMO INS CO OF AMER	NY	958.1
NATIONAL CASUALTY CO	OH	404.6
NATIONWIDE MUTUAL FIRE INS CO	OH	8,809.3
SENTRY SELECT INS CO	WI	715.6
STATE FARM FIRE & CAS CO	IL	38,866.0
STATE FARM MUTUAL AUTOMOBILE INS CO	IL	150,198.0
TOA REINS CO OF AMERICA	DE	1,749.0
TRAVELERS INDEMNITY CO	CT	21,493.8
UNITED SERVICES AUTOMOBILE ASN	TX	33,965.5
USAA GENERAL INDEMNITY CO	TX	4,214.9
WESTERN AGRICULTURAL INS CO	IA	217.1

Section VI

All Companies
Listed by Rating

A list of all rated and unrated

U.S. Property and Casualty Insurers.

Companies are ranked by Weiss Safety Rating
and then listed alphabetically within each rating category.

Section VI Contents

This section sorts all companies by their Safety Rating and then lists them alphabetically within each rating category. The purpose of this section is to provide in one place all of those companies receiving a given rating. Companies with the same rating should be viewed as having the same relative financial strength regardless of their order in this table.

1. Insurance Company Name

The legally registered name, which can sometimes differ from the name that the company uses for advertising. An insurer's name can be very similar to that of another, so verify the company's exact name and state of domicile to make sure you are looking at the correct company.

2. Domicile State

The state which has primary regulatory responsibility for the company. It may differ from the location of the company's corporate headquarters. You do not have to be living in the domicile state to purchase insurance from this firm, provided it is licensed to do business in your state.

3. Total Assets

All assets admitted by state insurance regulators in millions of dollars. This includes investments and current business assets such as receivables from agents and reinsurers.

INSURANCE COMPANY NAME	DOM. STATE	TOTAL ASSETS ($MIL)
Rating: A+		
BERKSHIRE HATHAWAY ASR CORP	NY	2,454.3
CITIZENS PROPERTY INS CORP	FL	12,268.8
COPPERPOINT MUTUAL INS CO	AZ	3,655.7
NUCLEAR ELECTRIC INS LTD	DE	5,050.9
OGLESBY REINS CO	IL	4,364.9
Rating: A		
CINCINNATI INS CO	OH	12,253.3
SENTRY INS A MUTUAL CO	WI	7,779.6
TOKIO MARINE AMERICA INS CO	NY	1,401.2
Rating: A-		
AUTO-OWNERS INS CO	MI	14,502.3
BUILDERS MUTUAL INS CO	NC	803.9
CINCINNATI INDEMNITY CO	OH	132.7
CINCINNATI SPECIALTY UNDERWRITER	DE	744.7
COPIC INS CO	CO	716.3
COUNTRY MUTUAL INS CO	IL	4,756.8
CUMIS INS SOCIETY INC	IA	1,894.2
EMPLOYERS COMPENSATION INS CO	CA	1,095.5
ENDURANCE ASR CORP	DE	1,824.1
ESSENT GUARANTY INC	PA	1,384.2
GEICO SECURE INS CO	NE	555.9
HOME-OWNERS INS CO	MI	2,197.5
MOTORISTS COMMERCIAL MUTUAL INS CO	OH	358.9
NATIONAL MORTGAGE INS CORP	WI	645.5
OWNERS INS CO	OH	3,948.4
PROTECTIVE INS CO	IN	799.3
RADIAN REINS INC	PA	684.6
RETAILFIRST INS CO	FL	305.0
SECURIAN CASUALTY CO	MN	288.6
SOMPO AMERICA INSURANCE CO	NY	1,235.5
SOUTHERN-OWNERS INS CO	MI	774.5
TRAVELERS CASUALTY & SURETY CO	CT	16,679.3
USAA CASUALTY INS CO	TX	10,235.4
Rating: B+		
ACUITY A MUTUAL INS CO	WI	3,686.4
ALFA MUTUAL GENERAL INS CO	AL	111.8
ALFA SPECIALTY INS CORP	VA	57.1
ALL AMERICA INS CO	OH	285.9
ALLSTATE NJ INS CO	IL	2,557.8
AMERICAN FAMILY MUTL INS CO SI	WI	16,206.4
AMERICAN STANDARD INS CO OF WI	WI	401.3
AMICA MUTUAL INS CO	RI	5,140.7
AUTO CLUB INDEMNITY CO	TX	25.9
BROTHERHOOD MUTUAL INS CO	IN	591.8
COUNTRY CASUALTY INS CO	IL	85.4
DAIRYLAND INS CO	WI	1,297.4
FARM BUREAU P&C INS CO	IA	2,529.1
FARM FAMILY CASUALTY INS CO	NY	1,188.8
FARMERS AUTOMOBILE INS ASN	IL	1,277.1
GEICO CHOICE INS CO	NE	919.4
GEICO GENERAL INS CO	MD	166.1
GNY CUSTOM INS CO	AZ	59.3
INTERINS EXCHANGE	CA	9,670.8

INSURANCE COMPANY NAME	DOM. STATE	TOTAL ASSETS ($MIL)
MARKEL GLOBAL REINS CO	DE	1,943.5
MERCURY INS CO	CA	1,654.2
MITSUI SUMITOMO INS CO OF AMER	NY	958.1
MOTORISTS MUTUAL INS CO	OH	1,368.4
NATIONAL CASUALTY CO	OH	404.6
NATIONWIDE MUTUAL FIRE INS CO	OH	8,809.3
PEKIN INS CO	IL	306.7
PROPERTY-OWNERS INS CO	IN	289.0
SENTRY SELECT INS CO	WI	715.6
STATE FARM FIRE & CAS CO	IL	38,866.0
STATE FARM MUTUAL AUTOMOBILE INS CO	IL	150,198.0
TENNESSEE FARMERS ASR CO	TN	1,442.2
TENNESSEE FARMERS MUTUAL INS CO	TN	2,919.9
TEXAS FARM BUREAU CASUALTY INS CO	TX	1,206.1
TOA REINS CO OF AMERICA	DE	1,749.0
TRAVELERS INDEMNITY CO	CT	21,493.4
UNITED SERVICES AUTOMOBILE ASN	TX	33,965.5
USAA GENERAL INDEMNITY CO	TX	4,214.9
WEST BEND MUTUAL INS CO	WI	2,580.8
WESTERN AGRICULTURAL INS CO	IA	217.1
Rating: B		
21ST CENTURY ADVANTAGE INS CO	MN	32.5
21ST CENTURY ASR CO	DE	73.4
21ST CENTURY CASUALTY CO	CA	14.0
21ST CENTURY CENTENNIAL INS CO	PA	611.0
21ST CENTURY INDEMNITY INS CO	PA	74.4
21ST CENTURY INS CO	CA	956.7
21ST CENTURY NATIONAL INS CO INC	NY	26.6
21ST CENTURY NORTH AMERICA INS	NY	600.1
21ST CENTURY PACIFIC INS	CO	47.6
21ST CENTURY PINNACLE INS CO	NJ	45.9
21ST CENTURY PREFERRED INS CO	PA	43.4
21ST CENTURY SECURITY INS CO	PA	222.0
ACCIDENT FUND GENERAL INS CO	MI	216.7
ACCIDENT FUND NATIONAL INS CO	MI	167.4
ALASKA NATIONAL INS CO	AK	976.4
ALFA ALLIANCE INS CORP	VA	39.0
ALFA GENERAL INS CORP	AL	100.3
ALFA INS CORP	AL	99.6
ALFA MUTUAL FIRE INS CO	AL	768.8
ALFA MUTUAL INS CO	AL	1,307.1
ALFA VISION INS CORP	VA	110.9
ALLIED P&C INS CO	IA	397.5
ALLIED WORLD SPECIALTY INS CO	DE	808.2
ALLSTATE COUNTY MUTUAL INS CO	TX	14.7
ALLSTATE INDEMNITY CO	IL	121.0
ALLSTATE INS CO	IL	46,626.9
ALLSTATE P&C INS CO	IL	257.5
ALLSTATE TEXAS LLOYDS	TX	17.4
ALLSTATE VEHICLE & PROPERTY INS CO	IL	56.5
ALPHA P&C INS CO	WI	31.4
AMERICAN AGRICULTURAL INS CO	IN	1,309.2
AMERICAN BANKERS INS CO OF FL	FL	2,070.3
AMERICAN CAPITAL ASR CORP	FL	117.4
AMERICAN CONTRACTORS INDEMNITY CO	CA	319.8

INSURANCE COMPANY NAME	DOM. STATE	TOTAL ASSETS ($MIL)	INSURANCE COMPANY NAME	DOM. STATE	TOTAL ASSETS ($MIL)
Rating: B (Continued)			CHURCH MUTUAL INS CO	WI	1,701.0
AMERICAN EQUITY SPECIALTY INS CO	CT	79.3	CINCINNATI CASUALTY CO	OH	424.0
AMERICAN FAMILY INS CO	WI	50.8	CITIZENS INS CO OF AM	MI	1,541.6
AMERICAN HALLMARK INS CO OF TX	TX	425.0	CM VANTAGE SPECIALTY INS CO	WI	58.8
AMERICAN INTERSTATE INS CO OF TEXAS	TX	70.3	COLONIAL COUNTY MUTUAL INS CO	TX	157.5
AMERICAN MERCURY INS CO	OK	349.2	CONNECTICUT MEDICAL INS CO	CT	509.6
AMERICAN MERCURY LLOYDS INS CO	TX	6.4	CONSUMERS INS USA INC	TN	71.8
AMERICAN MODERN PROPERTY & CASUALTY	OH	23.7	CONTRACTORS BONDING & INS CO	IL	217.7
AMERICAN MODERN SURPLUS LINES INS CO	OH	62.9	COUNTRY PREFERRED INS CO	IL	255.8
AMERICAN NATIONAL GENERAL INS CO	MO	103.9	COURTESY INS CO	FL	810.4
AMERICAN NATIONAL LLOYDS INS CO	TX	87.7	COVERYS SPECIALTY INS CO	NJ	63.9
AMERICAN NATIONAL PROPERTY & CAS CO	MO	1,339.7	COVINGTON SPECIALTY INS CO	NH	98.0
AMERICAN NATL COUNTY MUT INS CO	TX	24.3	CRESTBROOK INS CO	OH	143.2
AMERICAN RELIABLE INS CO	AZ	237.5	CUMIS SPECIALTY INS CO INC	IA	56.7
AMERICAN STANDARD INS CO OF OH	WI	9.6	DAIRYLAND COUNTY MUTUAL INS CO OF TX	TX	13.3
AMERICAN STATES INS CO OF TX	TX	12.9	DENTISTS INS CO	CA	325.8
AMERICAN STATES LLOYDS INS CO	TX	3.6	DRYDEN MUTUAL INS CO	NY	204.1
AMERIPRISE INS CO	WI	49.3	ECONOMY PREFERRED INS CO	IL	44.1
AMEX ASSURANCE CO	IL	244.5	ECONOMY PREMIER ASR CO	IL	82.6
ANPAC LOUISIANA INS CO	LA	126.1	ENCOMPASS INDEMNITY CO	IL	29.8
ANSUR AMERICA INS CO	MI	115.8	ERIE & NIAGARA INS ASSN	NY	213.7
ARCH MORTGAGE GUARANTY CO	WI	51.4	ERIE INS CO OF NEW YORK	NY	113.0
ARCH SPECIALTY INS CO	MO	496.9	ERIE INS EXCHANGE	PA	15,885.8
ASI ASR CORP	FL	133.1	ESSENT GUARANTY OF PA INC	PA	87.8
ASI PREFERRED INS CORP	FL	98.8	EULER HERMES NORTH AMERICA INS CO	MD	427.4
ASPEN AMERICAN INS CO	TX	791.5	FAIR AMERICAN SELECT INS CO	DE	108.0
AUTO CLUB INS ASSN	MI	4,174.1	FARM BU TOWN & COUNTRY INS CO OF MO	MO	413.9
AUTO CLUB INS CO OF FL	FL	383.4	FARM BUREAU GENERAL INS CO OF MI	MI	681.2
AUTOMOBILE INS CO OF HARTFORD CT	CT	1,021.0	FARM BUREAU INS OF NC INC	NC	9.7
AXIS INS CO	IL	1,508.9	FARM BUREAU MUTUAL INS CO OF AR	AR	404.2
BARNSTABLE COUNTY MUTUAL INS CO	MA	106.2	FARM BUREAU MUTUAL INS CO OF ID	ID	462.8
BCS INS CO	OH	286.3	FARM BUREAU MUTUAL INS CO OF MI	MI	746.2
BEAR RIVER MUTUAL INS CO	UT	263.4	FARMERS & MECH MUTUAL INS CO	PA	5.9
BERKLEY INS CO	DE	17,896.8	FARMERS INS CO OF OREGON	OR	1,693.2
BITCO GENERAL INS CORP	IL	886.0	FARMERS INS HAWAII INC	HI	101.6
BITCO NATIONAL INS CO	IL	484.1	FARMERS MUTUAL INS CO OF NE	NE	673.1
BRETHREN MUTUAL INS CO	MD	259.4	FARMINGTON CASUALTY CO	CT	1,032.4
CALIFORNIA AUTOMOBILE INS CO	CA	745.8	FARMLAND MUTUAL INS CO	IA	590.2
CALIFORNIA GENERAL UNDERWRITERS INS	CA	21.2	FBALLIANCE INS CO	IL	47.2
CALIFORNIA INS CO	CA	889.6	FEDERATED MUTUAL INS CO	MN	5,543.6
CANAL INDEMNITY CO	SC	47.8	FEDERATED RURAL ELECTRIC INS EXCH	KS	542.2
CANAL INS CO	SC	823.5	FINANCIAL PACIFIC INS CO	CA	237.6
CANOPIUS US INS INC	DE	202.1	FIRST COLONIAL INS CO	FL	338.9
CASTLE KEY INDEMNITY CO	IL	12.0	FIRST FLORIDIAN AUTO & HOME INS CO	FL	263.1
CASTLE KEY INS CO	IL	372.8	FIRST NATIONAL INS CO OF AMERICA	NH	57.3
CATERPILLAR INS CO	MO	701.1	FIRSTCOMP INS CO	NE	289.9
CENTRAL MUTUAL INS CO	OH	1,538.9	FLORIDA FAMILY INS CO	FL	107.1
CHARTER INDEMNITY CO	TX	12.4	FLORIDA FARM BUREAU GENERAL INS CO	FL	10.3
CHARTER OAK FIRE INS CO	CT	950.9	FMH AG RISK INS CO	IA	125.9
CHESAPEAKE EMPLOYERS INS CO	MD	2,252.8	FOREMOST INS CO	MI	2,309.5
CHUBB INDEMNITY INS CO	NY	379.4	FORTUITY INS CO	MI	43.0
CHUBB INS CO OF NJ	NJ	78.9	FRANKENMUTH MUTUAL INS CO	MI	1,272.5
CHUBB INS CO OF PR	PR	137.8	FRANKLIN MUTUAL INS CO	NJ	934.5
CHUBB LLOYDS INS CO OF TX	TX	51.3	FREEDOM SPECIALTY INS CO	OH	69.7
CHUBB NATIONAL INS CO	IN	379.4	GARRISON P&C INS CO	TX	2,075.2
			GEICO ADVANTAGE INS CO	NE	1,962.4

INSURANCE COMPANY NAME	DOM. STATE	TOTAL ASSETS ($MIL)	INSURANCE COMPANY NAME	DOM. STATE	TOTAL ASSETS ($MIL)
Rating: B (Continued)			LAWYERS MUTUAL INS CO	CA	329.2
			LIBERTY LLOYDS OF TX INS CO	TX	6.5
GEICO INDEMNITY CO	MD	8,771.2	LIBERTY MUTUAL INS CO	MA	44,306.8
GENWORTH MORTGAGE REINS CORP	NC	15.1	LIBERTY MUTUAL PERSONAL INS CO	MA	6.9
GEORGIA FARM BUREAU CASUALTY INS CO	GA	3.5	LION INS CO (FL)	FL	266.5
GOODVILLE MUTUAL CAS CO	PA	255.2	LOUISIANA FARM BUREAU CAS INS CO	LA	11.1
GOVERNMENT EMPLOYEES INS CO	MD	28,989.0	LOUISIANA FARM BUREAU MUTUAL INS CO	LA	223.0
GOVERNMENTAL INTERINS	IL	65.0	LUBA CASUALTY INS CO	LA	240.1
GRANGE MUTUAL CAS CO	OH	2,463.8	LYNDON SOUTHERN INS CO	DE	181.7
GREAT AMERICAN INS CO	OH	6,930.2	MEDICAL INS EXCHANGE OF CALIFORNIA	CA	425.7
GREAT MIDWEST INS CO	TX	208.8	MEDICAL LIABILITY ALLIANCE	MO	77.6
GREAT WEST CASUALTY CO	NE	2,063.9	MEDICAL MUTUAL INS CO OF MAINE	ME	292.7
GREEN MOUNTAIN INS CO	VT	12.4	MEDICAL PROTECTIVE CO	IN	3,184.7
GUARANTEE CO OF NORTH AMERICA USA	MI	223.8	MENDAKOTA INS CO	MN	12.4
GUIDEONE MUTUAL INS CO	IA	1,199.6	MERCHANTS BONDING CO (MUTUAL)	IA	183.7
GUIDEONE P&C INS CO	IA	434.6	MERCHANTS NATIONAL INS CO	NH	130.2
GUIDEONE SPECIALTY MUTUAL INS CO	IA	270.7	MERCHANTS PREFERRED INS CO	NY	72.1
HANOVER INS CO	NH	7,505.1	MERCURY CASUALTY CO	CA	1,917.0
HARTFORD ACCIDENT & INDEMNITY CO	CT	12,150.0	MERCURY COUNTY MUTUAL INS CO	TX	12.0
HARTFORD CASUALTY INS CO	IN	2,325.1	MERCURY INDEMNITY CO OF GEORGIA	GA	17.5
HARTFORD FIRE INS CO	CT	24,977.6	MERCURY INS CO OF GA	GA	22.4
HARTFORD INS CO OF IL	IL	3,906.5	MERCURY INS CO OF IL	IL	36.5
HARTFORD INS CO OF THE MIDWEST	IN	628.9	MERCURY NATIONAL INS CO	IL	16.0
HARTFORD INS CO OF THE SOUTHEAST	CT	191.5	MET LLOYDS INS CO OF TX	TX	102.8
HARTFORD LLOYDS INS CO	TX	74.1	METROPOLITAN CASUALTY INS CO	RI	199.2
HARTFORD SM BOIL INSPECTION & INS	CT	1,316.7	METROPOLITAN DIRECT PROP & CAS INS	RI	140.1
HARTFORD SM BOIL INSPECTION IC OF CT	CT	31.0	METROPOLITAN GENERAL INS CO	RI	43.9
HARTFORD UNDERWRITERS INS CO	CT	1,654.8	METROPOLITAN GROUP PROP & CAS INS CO	RI	693.9
HASTINGS MUTUAL INS CO	MI	902.9	MIAMI MUTUAL INS CO	OH	59.1
HIGH POINT P&C INS CO	NJ	390.9	MID-CENTURY INS CO	CA	4,011.1
HIGH POINT PREFERRED INS CO	NJ	276.7	MIDDLESEX INS CO	WI	725.1
HOMELAND INS CO OF DE	DE	52.3	MIDWEST BUILDERS CASUALTY MUTUAL CO	KS	86.0
HORACE MANN INS CO	IL	465.2	MILWAUKEE CASUALTY INS CO	WI	102.8
HORACE MANN P&C INS CO	IL	293.0	MINNESOTA LAWYERS MUTUAL INS CO	MN	178.1
HOUSING AUTHORITY PROP A MUTUAL CO	VT	177.5	MMG INS CO	ME	260.9
HOUSTON SPECIALTY INS CO	TX	460.3	MMIC INS INC	MN	723.2
HSB SPECIALTY INS CO	CT	54.2	MO EMPLOYERS MUTUAL INS CO	MO	683.3
HUDSON EXCESS INS CO	DE	69.7	MOTOR CLUB INS CO	RI	50.1
HYUNDAI MARINE & FIRE INS CO LTD	CA	111.0	MOUNTAIN WEST FARM BU MUTUAL INS CO	WY	362.1
ICI MUTUAL INS CO A RRG	VT	352.1	MUTUAL INS CO OF AZ	AZ	1,056.2
IMT INS CO	IA	368.3	MUTUAL OF ENUMCLAW INS CO	OR	737.9
INDIANA FARMERS MUTUAL INS CO	IN	422.8	NATIONAL BUILDERS INS CO	DE	88.3
INFINITY INS CO	IN	2,050.3	NATIONAL INDEMNITY CO	NE	194,845.0
INS CO OF ILLINOIS	IL	21.9	NATIONAL PUBLIC FINANCE GUAR CORP	NY	4,389.8
IOWA AMERICAN INS CO	IA	27.3	NATIONWIDE AFFINITY INS CO OF AMER	OH	423.7
IOWA MUTUAL INS CO	IA	101.5	NATIONWIDE LLOYDS	TX	42.2
JEWELERS MUTUAL INS CO	WI	401.1	NATIONWIDE MUTUAL INS CO	OH	35,852.6
KANSAS MEDICAL MUTUAL INS CO	KS	152.0	NAVIGATORS INS CO	NY	2,916.6
KEMPER INDEPENDENCE INS CO	IL	93.4	NCMIC INS CO	IA	732.6
KENTUCKY EMPLOYERS MUTUAL INS	KY	921.1	NEVADA CAPITAL INS CO	NV	107.8
KENTUCKY FARM BUREAU MUTUAL INS CO	KY	2,426.2	NEW ENGLAND MUTUAL INS CO	MA	44.7
KINSALE INS CO	AR	523.4	NEW JERSEY RE-INS CO	NJ	546.9
KNIGHT SPECIALTY INS CO	DE	73.9	NEW YORK SCHOOLS INS RECIPROCAL	NY	288.6
LACKAWANNA AMERICAN INS CO	PA	88.5	NJ MANUFACTURERS INS CO	NJ	7,070.7
LAMMICO	LA	416.2	NLC MUTUAL INS CO	VT	326.2
LANCER INS CO	IL	677.9	NORTH CAROLINA FARM BU MUTUAL INS CO	NC	1,935.5

INSURANCE COMPANY NAME	DOM. STATE	TOTAL ASSETS ($MIL)	INSURANCE COMPANY NAME	DOM. STATE	TOTAL ASSETS ($MIL)
Rating: B **(Continued)**			SENTRUITY CASUALTY CO	TX	196.6
NORTHLAND CASUALTY CO	CT	111.1	SENTRY CASUALTY CO	WI	311.4
NORTHLAND INS CO	CT	1,191.7	SENTRY LLOYDS OF TX	TX	7.1
OCEAN HARBOR CASUALTY INS CO	FL	277.9	SERVICE INS CO (FL)	FL	53.3
OKLAHOMA ATTORNEYS MUTUAL INS CO	OK	55.8	SFM MUTUAL INS CO	MN	585.5
OLD REPUB INS CO	PA	2,863.9	SHELTER MUTUAL INS CO	MO	3,367.5
OLD REPUB UNION INS CO	IL	62.1	SOCIETY INS A MUTUAL CO	WI	412.1
OLD REPUBLIC GENERAL INS CORP	IL	2,060.4	SOUTHERN FIDELITY INS CO	FL	199.1
OLD REPUBLIC LLOYDS OF TX	TX	2.2	SOUTHERN TRUST INS CO	GA	48.3
OLD REPUBLIC SECURITY ASR CO	IL	1,045.4	ST PAUL FIRE & MARINE INS CO	CT	18,495.1
OLD REPUBLIC SURETY CO	WI	122.7	STANDARD FIRE INS CO	CT	3,717.4
OPHTHALMIC MUTUAL INS CO RRG	VT	281.1	STARR INDEMNITY & LIABILITY CO	TX	4,442.6
OTSEGO MUTUAL FIRE INS CO	NY	122.5	STATE FARM FLORIDA INS CO	FL	2,095.9
P&C INS CO OF HARTFORD	IN	226.4	STATE FARM GENERAL INS CO	IL	7,137.5
PACIFIC INS CO LTD	CT	653.3	STATE FARM INDEMNITY CO	IL	2,255.2
PACIFIC PROPERTY & CASUALTY CO	CA	85.4	STATE FARM LLOYDS	TX	3,502.3
PATRIOT GENERAL INS CO	WI	26.0	STATE VOLUNTEER MUTUAL INS CO	TN	1,215.1
PEAK P&C INS CORP	WI	48.0	STERLING INS CO	NY	181.5
PENNSYLVANIA LUMBERMENS MUTUAL INS	PA	472.2	SUNAPEE MUTL FIRE INS CO	NH	4.5
PFD PHYSICIANS MED RRG A MUTL	MO	35.4	SURETEC INS CO	TX	228.9
PHARMACISTS MUTUAL INS CO	IA	292.9	TEACHERS INS CO	IL	350.8
PHOENIX INS CO	CT	4,264.0	TEXAS PACIFIC INDEMNITY CO	TX	7.7
PIONEER STATE MUTUAL INS CO	MI	561.4	TNUS INS CO	NY	68.1
PREFERRED MUTUAL INS CO	NY	531.3	TRANS PACIFIC INS CO	NY	71.5
PREFERRED PROFESSIONAL INS CO	NE	323.4	TRANSATLANTIC REINS CO	NY	14,157.0
PREMIER INS CO OF MA	CT	255.2	TRANSGUARD INS CO OF AMERICA INC	IL	321.4
PROGRESSIVE GARDEN STATE INS CO	NJ	382.6	TRAVCO INS CO	CT	217.8
PROTECTIVE SPECIALTY INS CO	IN	67.1	TRAVELERS CASUALTY CO OF CONNECTICUT	CT	324.9
PURE INS CO	FL	298.4	TRAVELERS CASUALTY INS CO OF AMERICA	CT	1,971.9
QBE INS CORP	PA	2,405.5	TRAVELERS COMMERCIAL CASUALTY CO	CT	333.3
QBE REINS CORP	PA	1,232.9	TRAVELERS COMMERCIAL INS CO	CT	371.1
QUINCY MUTUAL FIRE INS CO	MA	1,647.4	TRAVELERS EXCESS & SURPLUS LINES CO	CT	207.7
RADNOR SPECIALTY INS CO	NE	53.1	TRAVELERS HOME & MARINE INS CO	CT	379.1
RED SHIELD INS CO	WA	39.9	TRAVELERS INDEMNITY CO OF AMERICA	CT	647.6
RENAISSANCE RE US INC	MD	1,742.0	TRAVELERS INDEMNITY CO OF CT	CT	1,108.2
REPUBLIC MORTGAGE INS CO OF FLORIDA	FL	22.9	TRAVELERS LLOYDS INS CO	TX	20.2
RIVERPORT INS CO	IA	70.8	TRAVELERS LLOYDS OF TEXAS INS CO	TX	20.8
RLI INS CO	IL	1,782.6	TRAVELERS PERSONAL INS CO	CT	212.8
ROCKINGHAM INS CO	VA	133.7	TRAVELERS PERSONAL SECURITY INS CO	CT	212.0
SAFE AUTO INS CO	OH	440.2	TRAVELERS PROPERTY CAS OF AMERICA	CT	863.1
SAFECO INS CO OF IL	IL	193.9	TRAVELERS PROPERTY CASUALTY INS CO	CT	265.7
SAFECO INS CO OF INDIANA	IN	15.3	TRI-STATE CONSUMER INS CO	NY	102.2
SAFECO INS CO OF OREGON	OR	14.1	TRINITY UNIVERSAL INS CO	TX	1,927.8
SCOTTSDALE INDEMNITY CO	OH	85.0	TRIPLE S PROPIEDAD INC	PR	281.7
SCOTTSDALE SURPLUS LINES INS CO	AZ	50.8	TRUMBULL INS CO	CT	226.4
SECURITY NATIONAL INS CO	DE	1,280.4	TWIN CITY FIRE INS CO	IN	680.6
SELECTIVE AUTO INS CO OF NJ	NJ	368.1	UFB CASUALTY INS CO	IN	8.8
SELECTIVE CASUALTY INS CO	NJ	431.5	UMIA INS INC	OR	255.4
SELECTIVE F&C INS CO	NJ	187.6	UNION NATIONAL FIRE INS CO	LA	9.5
SELECTIVE INS CO OF AM	NJ	2,389.7	UNITED CASUALTY INS CO OF AMERICA	IL	13.5
SELECTIVE INS CO OF NY	NY	427.4	UNITED EDUCATORS INS A RECIP RRG	VT	878.3
SELECTIVE INS CO OF SC	IN	636.7	UNITED FARM FAMILY INS CO	NY	39.6
SELECTIVE INS CO OF THE SOUTHEAST	IN	497.6	UNITED FARM FAMILY MUTUAL INS CO	IN	1,055.2
SELECTIVE WAY INS CO	NJ	1,310.0	UNITED FIRE & CAS CO	IA	1,950.1
SENTINEL INS CO LTD	CT	263.7	UNITED SPECIALTY INS CO	DE	230.3
			UNITED SURETY & INDEMNITY CO	PR	102.7

INSURANCE COMPANY NAME	DOM. STATE	TOTAL ASSETS ($MIL)
Rating: B (Continued)		
UNITRIN COUNTY MUTUAL INS CO	TX	32.7
UNITRIN DIRECT INS CO	IL	12.2
UNITRIN DIRECT PROPERTY & CAS CO	IL	14.6
UNITRIN SAFEGUARD INS CO	WI	27.6
UTICA FIRST INS CO	NY	277.3
UTICA LLOYDS OF TX	TX	7.8
VALLEY P&C INS CO	OR	12.7
VANLINER INS CO	MO	427.3
VERMONT ACCIDENT INS CO	VT	9.1
VETERINARY PET INS CO	OH	238.1
VIGILANT INS CO	NY	529.7
VIRGINIA SURETY CO INC	IL	1,198.0
WATFORD SPECIALTY INS CO	NJ	70.5
WESTERN HERITAGE INS CO	AZ	134.0
WESTPORT INS CORP	MO	4,649.0
WILSON MUTUAL INS CO	WI	92.7
Rating: B-		
21ST CENTURY PREMIER INS CO	PA	302.2
360 INS CO	WY	30.6
ACCIDENT FUND INS CO OF AMERICA	MI	3,785.0
ACE AMERICAN INS CO	PA	13,190.9
ACE P&C INS CO	PA	9,120.3
ADVANTAGE WORKERS COMP INS CO	IN	497.8
AEGIS SECURITY INS CO	PA	129.4
AFFILIATES INS RECIPROCAL A RRG	VT	8.2
AGRICULTURAL WORKERS MUT AUTO INS CO	TX	83.9
AIG ASR CO	IL	38.5
AIG INS CO - PR	PR	152.2
AIX SPECIALTY INS CO	DE	55.6
ALAMANCE FARMERS MUTUAL INS CO	NC	8.5
ALLIED EASTERN INDEMNITY CO	PA	90.3
ALLIED WORLD ASR CO (US) INC	DE	335.3
ALLIED WORLD NATL ASR CO	NH	311.8
ALLSTATE NORTHBROOK INDEMNITY CO	IL	58.5
ALTERRA AMERICA INS CO	DE	424.0
AMALGAMATED CASUALTY INS CO	DC	57.7
AMERICAN COASTAL INS CO	FL	333.2
AMERICAN COMMERCE INS CO	OH	349.6
AMERICAN ECONOMY INS CO	IN	70.8
AMERICAN EUROPEAN INS CO	NH	130.3
AMERICAN FREEDOM INS CO	IL	61.4
AMERICAN INTERSTATE INS CO	NE	1,247.4
AMERICAN MINING INS CO	IA	37.4
AMERICAN MODERN INS CO OF FLORIDA	FL	32.6
AMERICAN SECURITY INS CO	DE	1,531.8
AMERICAN STATES INS CO	IN	144.6
AMERICAN STATES PREFERRED INS CO	IN	22.1
AMERIHEALTH CASUALTY INS CO	DE	322.1
AMERISURE INS CO	MI	968.8
AMERISURE MUTUAL INS CO	MI	2,397.2
AMICA P&C INS CO	RI	82.6
AMTRUST INS CO OF KANSAS INC	KS	206.3
ARAG INS CO	IA	83.1
ARCH INDEMNITY INS CO	MO	103.0

INSURANCE COMPANY NAME	DOM. STATE	TOTAL ASSETS ($MIL)
ARCH MORTGAGE INS CO	WI	550.5
ARISE BOILER INSPECT & INS CO RRG	KY	4.2
ARMED FORCES INS EXCHANGE	KS	139.0
ARROW MUTUAL LIABILITY INS CO	MA	50.7
ASI HOME INS CORP	FL	19.2
ASSOCIATED INDUSTRIES OF MA MUT INS	MA	615.2
ASURE WORLDWIDE INS CO	MI	42.4
ATLANTIC CASUALTY INS CO	NC	267.2
ATLANTIC CHARTER INS CO	MA	206.4
ATLANTIC SPECIALTY INS CO	NY	2,210.6
ATLANTIC STATES INS CO	PA	780.1
AUTO CLUB SOUTH INS CO	FL	127.0
AVATAR P&C INS CO	FL	49.2
AVEMCO INS CO	MD	83.1
BANKERS SPECIALTY INS CO	LA	59.8
BAY STATE INS CO	MA	493.9
BEAZLEY INS CO	CT	285.6
BENCHMARK INS CO	KS	296.0
BENEFIT SECURITY INS CO	IL	8.6
BONDEX INS CO	NJ	6.9
BRICKSTREET MUTUAL INS CO	WV	2,228.5
BRIDGEFIELD EMPLOYERS INS CO	FL	121.3
BUSINESSFIRST INS CO	FL	35.4
CALIFORNIA CAPITAL INS CO	CA	567.4
CAMBRIDGE MUTUAL FIRE INS CO	MA	896.4
CARING COMMUNITIES RECIP RRG	DC	96.3
CAROLINA MUTUAL INS INC	NC	93.1
CENTENNIAL CASUALTY CO	AL	118.1
CENTURION CASUALTY CO	IA	36.5
CHEROKEE INS CO	MI	523.9
CHUBB CUSTOM INS CO	NJ	370.4
CIVIL SERVICE EMPLOYEES INS CO	CA	211.6
CM REGENT INS CO	PA	179.2
CO-OPERATIVE INS COS	VT	134.1
COLONIAL SURETY CO	PA	59.6
COLUMBIA MUTUAL INS CO	MO	393.8
COMMUNITY HOSPITAL ALTERNATIVE RRG	VT	276.5
COMPWEST INS CO	CA	206.3
CONCORD GENERAL MUTUAL INS CO	NH	473.5
CONTROLLED RISK INS CO OF VT RRG	VT	152.1
CONVENTUS INTER-INS	NJ	92.4
COOPERATIVA D SEGUROS MULTIPLES D PR	PR	496.8
COPPERPOINT GENERAL INS CO	AZ	15.9
COPPERPOINT WESTERN INS CO	AZ	8.7
CRUSADER INS CO	CA	118.0
CSAA INS EXCHANGE	CA	7,009.7
CUMBERLAND INS CO	NJ	104.5
CUMBERLAND MUTUAL FIRE INS CO	NJ	275.4
DEALERS ASR CO	OH	109.4
DEPOSITORS INS CO	IA	309.2
DIAMOND STATE INS CO	IN	126.6
DOCTORS CO AN INTERINS	CA	4,272.9
DONEGAL MUTUAL INS CO	PA	462.3
DONGBU INS CO LTD US GUAM BRANCH	GU	61.8
DRIVE NEW JERSEY INS CO	NJ	209.6
EASTERN ADVANTAGE ASR CO	PA	58.4

INSURANCE COMPANY NAME	DOM. STATE	TOTAL ASSETS ($MIL)	INSURANCE COMPANY NAME	DOM. STATE	TOTAL ASSETS ($MIL)
Rating: B- (Continued)			HARCO NATIONAL INS CO	IL	480.5
EASTERN DENTISTS INS CO RRG	VT	55.0	HARFORD MUTUAL INS CO	MD	434.7
ECONOMY FIRE & CAS CO	IL	503.8	HAULERS INS CO	TN	78.0
EMC REINS CO	IA	472.2	HAWAII EMPLOYERS MUTUAL INS CO	HI	387.5
EMCASCO INS CO	IA	484.2	HAWAIIAN INS & GUARANTY CO LTD	HI	28.4
EMPIRE BONDING & INS CO	NY	3.7	HCC SPECIALTY INS CO	OK	19.6
EMPLOYERS INS OF WAUSAU	WI	5,648.8	HEALTH PROVIDERS INS RECIPROCAL RRG	HI	84.2
EMPLOYERS MUTUAL CAS CO	IA	3,269.9	HEALTHCARE UNDERWRITERS GRP MUT OH	OH	86.7
ENCOMPASS HOME & AUTO INS CO	IL	20.3	HIGH POINT SAFETY & INS CO	NJ	65.2
ENCOMPASS INDEPENDENT INS CO	IL	6.7	HM CASUALTY INS CO	PA	63.3
ENCOMPASS PROPERTY & CASUALTY CO	IL	10.8	HORACE MANN LLOYDS	TX	4.9
ENDURANCE AMERICAN INS CO	DE	1,717.5	HOUSING AUTHORITY RISK RET GROUP INC	VT	303.1
ERIE INS CO	PA	987.1	HOUSTON CASUALTY CO	TX	3,518.1
ERIE INS P&C CO	PA	102.3	IDS PROPERTY CASUALTY INS CO	WI	1,787.4
EVEREST REINS CO	DE	10,186.8	ILLINOIS EMCASCO INS CO	IA	360.0
EVERETT CASH MUTUAL INS CO	PA	126.0	ILLINOIS INS CO	IA	53.9
EXECUTIVE RISK INDEMNITY INC	DE	2,961.8	ILLINOIS NATIONAL INS CO	IL	52.9
EXECUTIVE RISK SPECIALTY INS CO	CT	295.1	INDEPENDENCE AMERICAN INS CO	DE	105.6
FACTORY MUTUAL INS CO	RI	17,343.3	INFINITY ASSURANCE INS CO	OH	7.1
FAIR AMERICAN INS & REINS CO	NY	205.5	INFINITY CASUALTY INS CO	OH	7.6
FALLS LAKE NATIONAL INS CO	OH	380.7	INFINITY SELECT INS CO	IN	7.1
FARM CREDIT SYS ASSOC CAPTIVE INS CO	CO	122.9	INTEGRITY MUTUAL INS CO	WI	106.0
FARMERS & MECHANICS MUTUAL IC OF WV	WV	66.4	INTERNATIONAL FIDELITY INS CO	NJ	223.4
FARMERS ALLIANCE MUTUAL INS CO	KS	319.0	IRONSHORE INDEMNITY INC	MN	431.9
FARMERS INS CO OF WA	WA	554.9	ISLAND INS CO LTD	HI	322.5
FARMERS MUTUAL F I C OF SALEM CTY	NJ	150.6	ISMIE MUTUAL INS CO	IL	1,443.8
FARMERS MUTUAL HAIL INS CO OF IA	IA	681.3	KESWICK GUARANTY INC	VI	5.3
FARMERS SPECIALTY INS CO	MI	61.0	KEYSTONE NATIONAL INS CO	PA	17.8
FARMERS UNION MUTUAL INS CO	ND	113.1	LACKAWANNA CASUALTY CO	PA	234.0
FEDERAL INS CO	IN	28,149.3	LACKAWANNA NATIONAL INS CO	PA	36.8
FEDERATED SERVICE INS CO	MN	433.6	LAFAYETTE INS CO	LA	207.9
FFVA MUTUAL INS CO	FL	348.5	LAWYERS MUTUAL LIAB INS CO OF NC	NC	103.9
FINANCIAL INDEMNITY CO	IL	100.3	LCTA CASUALTY INS CO	LA	79.1
FIRST GUARD INS CO	AZ	28.7	LIBERTY MUTUAL FIRE INS CO	WI	5,597.8
FLORIDA FARM BU CASUALTY INS CO	FL	562.9	LIGHTHOUSE PROPERTY INS CORP	LA	73.2
FLORIDA PENINSULA INS CO	FL	293.4	LIGHTNING ROD MUTUAL INS CO	OH	282.8
FMI INS CO	NJ	49.4	LITITZ MUTUAL INS CO	PA	280.1
FORESTRY MUTUAL INS CO	NC	61.7	LM GENERAL INS CO	IL	10.9
FORTRESS INS CO	IL	135.7	MADISON MUTUAL INS CO	IL	63.5
FRANDISCO P&C INS CO	GA	111.6	MAG MUTUAL INS CO	GA	1,840.1
GENERAL INS CO OF AM	NH	110.5	MAIDEN RE NORTH AMERICA INC	MO	1,411.2
GENERAL STAR NATIONAL INS CO	DE	239.8	MDOW INS CO	TX	22.9
GENWORTH MTG INS CORP OF NC	NC	360.3	MEDICAL MUTUAL INS CO OF NC	NC	559.8
GERMAN AMERICAN FARM MUTUAL	TX	4.4	MEDICAL MUTUAL LIAB INS SOC OF MD	MD	851.5
GERMANIA SELECT INS CO	TX	211.2	MEDICAL PROFESSIONAL MUTUAL INS CO	MA	3,165.3
GERMANTOWN MUTUAL INS CO	WI	107.2	MEDICUS INS CO	TX	54.5
GRANGE INS ASSN	WA	287.8	MEDMAL DIRECT INS CO	FL	44.5
GRANGE P&C INS CO	OH	67.0	MEMBERSELECT INS CO	MI	527.1
GRANITE STATE INS CO	IL	40.3	MEMIC CASUALTY CO	NH	52.5
GREAT NORTHERN INS CO	IN	1,694.3	MERASTAR INS CO	IL	36.3
GREATER NEW YORK MUTUAL INS CO	NY	986.2	MERCHANTS MUTUAL INS CO	NY	516.3
GRINNELL MUTUAL REINS CO	IA	1,140.1	MERRIMACK MUTUAL FIRE INS CO	MA	1,487.7
GULFSTREAM P&C INS CO	FL	112.6	METROPOLITAN P&C INS CO	RI	5,686.1
HALLMARK SPECIALTY INS CO	OK	233.5	MIDWEST FAMILY MUTUAL INS CO	IA	227.1
HAMILTON SPECIALTY INS CO	DE	101.9	MILLERS CAPITAL INS CO	PA	134.2
			MISSISSIPPI FARM BUREAU CAS INS CO	MS	435.6

INSURANCE COMPANY NAME	DOM. STATE	TOTAL ASSETS ($MIL)	INSURANCE COMPANY NAME	DOM. STATE	TOTAL ASSETS ($MIL)
Rating:	**B-**	**(Continued)**	PROASSURANCE CASUALTY CO	MI	1,100.5
MODERN USA INS CO	FL	53.5	PROFESSIONALS ADVOCATE INS CO	MD	139.6
MONARCH NATIONAL INS CO	FL	40.1	PROGRESSIVE CASUALTY INS CO	OH	8,195.0
MOUNT VERNON SPECIALTY INS CO	NE	58.3	PROGRESSIVE PROPERTY INS CO	FL	91.8
MSA INS CO	SC	18.7	PROTECTIVE P&C INS CO	MO	383.6
MUTUAL BENEFIT INS CO	PA	226.4	PROVIDENCE MUTUAL FIRE INS CO	RI	195.2
NATIONAL GENL PREMIER INS CO	CA	25.2	RAM MUTUAL INS CO	MN	110.3
NATIONAL LLOYDS INS CO	TX	229.6	RED CLAY RRG INC	SC	9.6
NATIONAL SECURITY FIRE & CAS CO	AL	75.8	REPUBLIC INDEMNITY CO OF AMERICA	CA	2,366.4
NATIONWIDE AGRIBUSINESS INS CO	IA	633.4	REPUBLIC-VANGUARD INS CO	AZ	25.1
NATIONWIDE ASR CO	OH	140.6	RESTORATION RRG INC	VT	82.4
NATIONWIDE GENERAL INS CO	OH	506.3	RETAILERS CASUALTY INS CO	LA	81.9
NATIONWIDE INS CO OF AM	OH	445.6	RURAL MUTUAL INS CO	WI	472.0
NATIONWIDE INS CO OF FL	OH	51.5	SAFE HARBOR INS CO	FL	82.7
NATIONWIDE P&C INS CO	OH	691.9	SAFECO INS CO OF AMERICA	NH	4,520.7
NAVIGATORS SPECIALTY INS CO	NY	179.9	SAFECO LLOYDS INS CO	TX	13.2
NEW HAMPSHIRE EMPLOYERS INS CO	NH	3.9	SAFECO NATIONAL INS CO	NH	15.0
NEW JERSEY CASUALTY INS CO	NJ	577.4	SAFETY INS CO	MA	1,470.8
NEW LONDON COUNTY MUTUAL INS CO	CT	117.5	SAFEWAY INS CO	IL	555.5
NEW MEXICO EMPLOYERS ASR CO	NM	6.3	SAGAMORE INS CO	IN	160.7
NEW YORK CENTRAL MUTUAL FIRE INS CO	NY	1,119.2	SCOTTSDALE INS CO	OH	2,531.5
NEW YORK MARINE & GENERAL INS CO	NY	1,351.8	SECURA INS A MUTUAL CO	WI	1,124.9
NEW YORK MUNICIPAL INS RECIPROCAL	NY	167.7	SECURITY FIRST INS CO	FL	273.9
NGM INS CO	FL	2,520.0	SEQUOIA INDEMNITY CO	NV	11.1
NODAK INS CO	ND	247.2	SERVICE LLOYDS INS CO	TX	304.6
NORCAL MUTUAL INS CO	CA	1,668.7	SHELTER REINS CO	MO	457.1
NORTH LIGHT SPECIALTY INS CO	IL	89.8	SIGMA RRG INC	DC	17.9
NORTH STAR MUTUAL INS CO	MN	712.4	SILVER OAK CASUALTY INC	NE	239.0
OASIS RECIPROCAL RRG	VT	16.6	SIMED	PR	161.0
OHIO BAR LIABILITY INS CO	OH	40.0	SIRIUS AMERICA INS CO	NY	1,381.3
OHIO FARMERS INS CO	OH	2,975.6	SOMPO AM FIRE & MARINE INS CO	NY	78.6
OHIO MUTUAL INS CO	OH	282.0	SOUTHERN FARM BUREAU CAS INS CO	MS	2,172.7
OKLAHOMA FARM BUREAU MUTUAL INS CO	OK	303.0	SOUTHERN OAK INS CO	FL	120.0
OLD AMERICAN INDEMNITY CO	KY	14.1	SPINNAKER INS CO	IL	38.6
OLD DOMINION INS CO	FL	37.6	ST PAUL MERCURY INS CO	CT	334.5
OMNI INS CO	IL	126.8	ST PAUL PROTECTIVE INS CO	CT	521.8
OMS NATIONAL INS CO RRG	IL	422.8	STANDARD GUARANTY INS CO	DE	345.2
PACIFIC EMPLOYERS INS CO	PA	3,736.2	STARR SURPLUS LINES INS CO	IL	347.2
PACIFIC INDEMNITY CO	WI	6,782.9	STATE AUTO INS CO OF WI	WI	15.9
PACIFIC SPECIALTY INS CO	CA	309.2	STATE FARM CTY MUTUAL INS CO OF TX	TX	184.3
PEERLESS INS CO	NH	13,521.2	STATE NATIONAL INS CO	TX	357.8
PEMCO MUTUAL INS CO	WA	735.5	STILLWATER INS CO	CA	377.0
PENN NATIONAL SECURITY INS CO	PA	982.6	STONETRUST COMMERCIAL INS CO	NE	161.2
PENNSYLVANIA NTL MUTUAL CAS INS CO	PA	1,298.3	STRATFORD INS CO	NH	144.3
PETROLEUM CAS CO	TX	34.7	SUNLAND RRG INC	TN	6.3
PHENIX MUTUAL FIRE INS CO	NH	67.4	TEACHERS AUTO INS CO	NJ	25.5
PHILADELPHIA CBSP FOR INS OF HOUSES	PA	340.6	TERRA INS CO (A RRG)	VT	36.0
PHILADELPHIA CONTRIBUTIONSHIP INS CO	PA	225.1	TITAN INDEMNITY CO	TX	211.1
PHILADELPHIA INDEMNITY INS CO	PA	8,309.9	TITAN INS CO	MI	132.3
PHYSICIANS INS A MUTL CO	WA	541.3	TOPA INS CO	CA	189.4
PIH INS CO A RECIP RRG	HI	21.9	TRANSAMERICA CASUALTY INS CO	OH	360.8
PLYMOUTH ROCK ASR CORP	MA	605.4	TRUSTGARD INS CO	OH	109.4
PREMIER GROUP INS CO	TN	68.1	TUSCARORA WAYNE INS CO	PA	106.4
PRIME INS CO	IL	91.1	TYPTAP INS CO	FL	26.9
PRIVILEGE UNDERWRITERS RECIP EXCH	FL	443.8	UMIALIK INS CO	AK	61.4
			UNION MUTUAL FIRE INS CO	VT	221.7

INSURANCE COMPANY NAME	DOM. STATE	TOTAL ASSETS ($MIL)	INSURANCE COMPANY NAME	DOM. STATE	TOTAL ASSETS ($MIL)
Rating: B- (Continued)			AMERICAN GUARANTEE & LIABILITY INS	NY	277.4
UNITED FINANCIAL CASUALTY CO	OH	2,973.9	AMERICAN INTEGRITY INS CO OF FL	FL	219.2
UNITED GUARANTY CREDIT INS CO	NC	25.9	AMERICAN INTER FIDELITY EXCHANGE RRG	IN	91.6
UNITED GUARANTY INS CO	NC	92.4	AMERICAN MODERN HOME INS CO	OH	1,044.3
UNITED GUARANTY MORTGAGE INS CO	NC	93.1	AMERICAN PLATINUM PROP & CAS INS CO	FL	22.8
UNITED GUARANTY MTG INS CO OF NC	NC	92.9	AMERICAN ROAD INS CO	MI	711.3
UNITED OHIO INS CO	OH	327.8	AMERICAN SOUTHERN INS CO	KS	103.6
UNITED P&C INS CO	FL	603.9	AMERICAN SUMMIT INS CO	TX	50.5
UNITED STATES SURETY CO	MD	70.5	AMERICAN TRADITIONS INS CO	FL	54.0
UNIVERSAL INS CO (PR)	PR	858.1	AMERICAN ZURICH INS CO	IL	319.1
US SPECIALTY INS CO	TX	1,826.5	AMERISURE PARTNERS INS CO	MI	93.9
UTICA MUTUAL INS CO	NY	2,393.6	ARBELLA MUTUAL INS CO	MA	1,376.4
VERLAN FIRE INS CO	NH	26.9	ARBELLA PROTECTION INS CO	MA	316.4
VERMONT MUTUAL INS CO	VT	840.2	ARCH MORTGAGE REINS CO	WI	20.2
VICTORIA AUTOMOBILE INS CO	OH	27.8	ARECA INS EXCHANGE	AK	27.6
VICTORIA SELECT INS CO	OH	21.5	AUTO CLUB GROUP INS CO	MI	361.7
VIRGINIA FARM BUREAU MUTUAL INS CO	VA	399.7	AXIS REINS CO	NY	3,236.5
WAWANESA GENERAL INS CO	CA	567.6	AXIS SURPLUS INS CO	IL	436.7
WESCO INS CO	DE	2,042.3	BADGER MUTUAL INS CO	WI	176.5
WESTERN COMMUNITY INS CO	ID	41.0	BELL UNITED INS CO	NV	35.6
WESTERN MUTUAL FIRE INS CO	MN	7.3	BERKLEY REGIONAL INS CO	DE	755.9
WESTERN NATIONAL MUTUAL INS CO	MN	996.7	BERKSHIRE HATHAWAY HOMESTATE INS	NE	2,541.9
WESTERN PACIFIC MUT INS CO RISK RET	CO	140.3	BERKSHIRE HATHAWAY SPECIALTY INS CO	NE	4,330.5
WESTERN RESERVE MUTUAL CAS CO	OH	193.5	BLOOMINGTON COMP INS CO	MN	17.7
WESTFIELD INS CO	OH	2,777.2	BRITISH AMERICAN INS CO	TX	56.3
WESTFIELD NATIONAL INS CO	OH	664.5	BROADLINE RRG INC	VT	94.0
WESTGUARD INS CO	PA	1,130.2	BUCKEYE STATE MUTUAL INS CO	OH	62.4
WINTHROP PHYSICIANS RECIP RRG	VT	2.9	BUILDERS PREMIER INS CO	NC	12.0
WISCONSIN MUTUAL INS CO	WI	154.9	BUS ALLIANCE INS CO	CA	25.0
WRIGHT NATIONAL FLOOD INS CO	TX	31.2	CA CASUALTY COMP INS CO	CA	73.0
ZURICH AMERICAN INS CO	NY	30,708.0	CALIFORNIA CASUALTY INDEMNITY EXCH	CA	581.9
Rating: C+			CALIFORNIA CASUALTY INS CO	OR	101.0
ACCREDITED SURETY & CAS CO INC	FL	48.5	CALIFORNIA HEALTHCARE INS CO INC RRG	HI	128.6
ACSTAR INS CO	IL	57.3	CALLICOON CO-OPERATIVE INS CO	NY	31.6
ADDISON INS CO	IA	123.1	CAMERON MUTUAL INS CO	MO	83.1
AGENCY INS CO OF MD INC	MD	153.6	CAMPMED CAS & INDEM CO INC OF MD	NH	21.1
AGSECURITY INS CO	OK	60.2	CAPITOL CASUALTY CO	NE	29.8
AIG SPECIALTY INS CO	IL	106.5	CAPITOL SPECIALTY INS CORP	WI	140.4
AIOI NISSAY DOWA INS CO OF AMERICA	NY	138.6	CASCO INDEMNITY CO	ME	30.8
AIU INS CO	NY	88.7	CATLIN SPECIALTY INS CO	DE	728.2
ALABAMA MUNICIPAL INS CORP	AL	121.6	CENSTAT CASUALTY CO	NE	24.8
ALLEGANY CO-OP INS CO	NY	53.6	CENTER MUTUAL INS CO	ND	53.5
ALLIANCE INDEMNITY CO	KS	10.5	CENTRAL STATES INDEMNITY CO OF OMAHA	NE	468.7
ALLIED INS CO OF AMERICA	OH	57.2	CHUNG KUO INS CO LTD GUAM BRANCH	GU	40.8
ALLMERICA FINANCIAL ALLIANCE INS CO	NH	20.4	CITATION INS CO (MA)	MA	253.1
ALLMERICA FINANCIAL BENEFIT INS CO	MI	40.8	CITIES & VILLAGES MUTUAL INS CO	WI	55.3
ALLSTATE F&C INS CO	IL	267.7	CITIZENS INS CO OF IL	IL	5.3
ALLSTATE NJ P&C INS CO	IL	75.8	CIVIC PROPERTY & CASUALTY CO INC	CA	287.4
ALPS PROPERTY & CASUALTY INS CO	MT	115.1	CLEAR BLUE SPECIALTY INS CO	NC	64.3
AMCO INS CO	IA	989.3	CMIC RRG	DC	7.1
AMERICA FIRST INS CO	NH	14.8	COLONIAL AMERICAN CAS & SURETY CO	MD	25.4
AMERICA FIRST LLOYD'S INS CO	TX	6.5	COLORADO CASUALTY INS CO	NH	25.7
AMERICAN AGRI BUSINESS INS CO	TX	1,014.4	COLUMBIA LLOYDS INS CO	TX	50.8
AMERICAN FAMILY HOME INS CO	FL	384.1	COLUMBIA NATIONAL INS CO	NE	93.3
AMERICAN FEDERATED INS CO	MS	46.8	COMMERCE INS CO	MA	2,144.7
			COMMUNITY INS CORP	WI	7.3

INSURANCE COMPANY NAME	DOM. STATE	TOTAL ASSETS ($MIL)	INSURANCE COMPANY NAME	DOM. STATE	TOTAL ASSETS ($MIL)
Rating: C+ (Continued)			FLAGSHIP CITY INS CO	PA	55.1
CONTINENTAL CASUALTY CO	IL	43,255.0	FLORIDA LAWYERS MUTUAL INS CO	FL	86.8
CONTINENTAL DIVIDE INS CO	CO	17.2	FOREMOST COUNTY MUTUAL INS CO	TX	83.9
COPPERPOINT AMERICAN INS CO	AZ	6.7	FOREMOST LLOYDS OF TEXAS	TX	63.7
COPPERPOINT CASUALTY INS CO	AZ	7.1	FOREMOST P&C INS CO	MI	63.3
CSE SAFEGUARD INS CO	CA	87.9	FOREMOST SIGNATURE INS CO	MI	65.3
CUMIS MORTGAGE REINS CO	WI	13.1	GEICO MARINE INS CO	MD	134.5
CYPRESS INS CO	CA	1,573.5	GENERAL AUTOMOBILE INS CO	OH	132.3
DAILY UNDERWRITERS OF AMERICA	PA	44.3	GENERAL CASUALTY CO OF WI	WI	970.0
DAKOTA TRUCK UNDERWRITERS	SD	115.9	GENERAL REINS CORP	DE	15,274.7
DE SMET FARM MUTUAL INS CO OF SD	SD	31.5	GERMANIA INS CO	TX	77.3
DIRECT GENERAL INS CO	IN	121.8	GERMANTOWN INS CO	PA	100.2
DIRECT NATIONAL INS CO	AR	6.9	GOLDEN BEAR INS CO	CA	144.8
DISCOVER P&C INS CO	CT	136.5	GRANITE MUTUAL INS CO	VT	4.5
DISCOVER SPECIALTY INS CO	CT	108.3	GRANITE RE INC	OK	49.8
EAGLE WEST INS CO	CA	127.4	GRAPHIC ARTS MUTUAL INS CO	NY	149.7
ELECTRIC INS CO	MA	1,577.7	GRAY INS CO	LA	284.6
EMPIRE FIRE & MARINE INS CO	NE	63.4	GREAT AMERICAN ASR CO	OH	19.8
EMPIRE INDEMNITY INS CO	OK	55.4	GREAT PLAINS CASUALTY INC	IA	21.0
ENCOMPASS INS CO	IL	9.7	GUIDEONE AMERICA INS CO	IA	12.9
ENCOMPASS INS CO OF AM	IL	20.7	GUIDEONE ELITE INS CO	IA	30.2
ENCOMPASS INS CO OF MA	MA	6.0	GUIDEONE NATIONAL INS CO	IA	55.2
ENCOMPASS INS CO OF NJ	IL	27.0	HAMILTON INS CO	DE	30.7
ENCOMPASS PROP & CAS INS CO OF NJ	IL	12.2	HANOVER LLOYDS INS CO	TX	6.1
ENDEAVOUR INS CO	MA	6.2	HERITAGE INDEMNITY CO	CA	115.6
ENDURANCE AMERICAN SPECIALTY INS CO	DE	439.6	HERITAGE P&C INS CO	FL	606.2
ENDURANCE RISK SOLUTIONS ASR CO	DE	263.6	HINGHAM MUTUAL FIRE INS CO	MA	63.4
ENUMCLAW P&C INS CO	OR	8.5	HISCOX INS CO	IL	246.0
EVEREST NATIONAL INS CO	DE	910.9	HOSPITALITY INS CO	MA	13.7
EXACT PROPERTY & CASUALTY CO INC	CA	285.7	HOUSING ENTERPRISE INS CO	VT	79.3
FAIRMONT FARMERS MUTUAL INS CO	MN	33.7	HOUSING SPECIALTY INS CO	VT	17.0
FAMILY SECURITY INS CO	HI	40.5	IL STATE BAR ASSOC MUTUAL INS CO	IL	77.6
FARMERS & MERCHANTS MUTUAL FIRE I C	MI	30.4	ILLINOIS CASUALTY CO	IL	121.4
FARMERS INS CO	KS	325.0	ILLINOIS FARMERS INS CO	IL	255.7
FARMERS INS CO OF AZ	AZ	48.4	INDEPENDENT MUTUAL FIRE INS CO	IL	47.3
FARMERS INS CO OF FLEMINGTON	NJ	66.6	INFINITY SAFEGUARD INS CO	OH	5.1
FARMERS INS CO OF IDAHO	ID	217.6	INS CO OF GREATER NY	NY	120.4
FARMERS INS OF COLUMBUS INC	OH	291.4	INTEGON NATIONAL INS CO	NC	3,052.5
FARMERS NEW CENTURY INS CO	IL	204.5	JAMES RIVER CASUALTY CO	VA	47.0
FARMERS TEXAS COUNTY MUTUAL INS CO	TX	183.4	LAKEVIEW INS CO	FL	35.9
FARMERS UNION MUTUAL INS CO	MT	62.7	LANCER INDEMNITY CO	NY	29.0
FCCI INS CO	FL	2,020.6	LANDCAR CASUALTY CO	UT	41.5
FD INS CO	FL	29.3	LE MARS INS CO	IA	64.8
FIDELITY & DEPOSIT CO OF MARYLAND	MD	211.2	LEAGUE OF WI MUNICIPALITIES MUT INS	WI	79.8
FIDELITY & GUARANTY INS	WI	153.5	LEATHERSTOCKING COOP INS CO	NY	38.1
FIDELITY & GUARANTY INS CO	IA	21.9	MADISON MUTUAL INS CO	NY	14.0
FINGER LAKES FIRE & CASUALTY CO	NY	41.6	MAISON INS CO	LA	69.7
FIRE DISTRICTS OF NY MUT INS CO INC	NY	95.2	MANUFACTURING TECHNOLOGY MUT INS CO	MI	57.7
FIRE INS EXCHANGE	CA	2,573.2	MAPFRE INS CO OF NY	NY	157.9
FIREMANS FUND INDEMNITY CORP	NJ	15.4	MARYSVILLE MUTUAL INS CO	KS	48.1
FIREMANS FUND INS CO OF HI INC	HI	11.5	MASSACHUSETTS BAY INS CO	NH	66.3
FIRST LIBERTY INS CORP	IL	22.5	MAXUM CASUALTY INS CO	CT	23.5
FIRST MEDICAL INS CO RRG	VT	98.1	MEDICAL SECURITY INS CO	NC	22.3
FIRSTLINE NATIONAL INS CO	MD	96.1	MERCED PROPERTY & CASUALTY CO	CA	23.5
FITCHBURG MUTUAL INS CO	MA	127.3	MERCER INS CO	PA	265.7
			MERCHANTS NATIONAL BONDING INC	IA	31.2

INSURANCE COMPANY NAME	DOM. STATE	TOTAL ASSETS ($MIL)	INSURANCE COMPANY NAME	DOM. STATE	TOTAL ASSETS ($MIL)
Rating: C+ (Continued)			PROGRESSIVE DIRECT INS CO	OH	7,217.2
MERCURY INS CO OF FL	FL	42.6	PROGRESSIVE NORTHERN INS CO	WI	1,676.6
MICHIGAN INS CO	MI	147.9	PROGRESSIVE NORTHWESTERN INS CO	OH	1,622.9
MICHIGAN PROFESSIONAL INS EXCHANGE	MI	107.2	RAINIER INS CO	AZ	25.6
MID-CONTINENT CAS CO	OH	515.6	RELIABLE LLOYDS INS CO	TX	16.9
MID-CONTINENT EXCESS & SURPLUS INS	DE	17.9	RELIAMAX SURETY CO	SD	61.3
MIDSTATE MUTUAL INS CO	NY	40.6	REPUBLIC-FRANKLIN INS CO	OH	109.5
MIDWEST EMPLOYERS CAS CO	DE	178.7	ROCKFORD MUTUAL INS CO	IL	79.3
MILBANK INS CO	IA	624.1	RSUI INDEMNITY CO	NH	3,458.4
MILLVILLE MUTUAL INS CO	PA	85.5	RURAL COMMUNITY INS CO	MN	1,821.5
MISSOURI HOSPITAL PLAN	MO	197.4	SAFEPOINT INS CO	FL	146.2
MITSUI SUMITOMO INS USA INC	NY	137.4	SAFETY INDEMNITY INS CO	MA	123.2
MONTEREY INS CO	CA	85.8	SAFEWAY INS CO OF LA	LA	159.8
MUNICH REINS AMERICA INC	DE	18,335.4	SECURA SUPREME INS CO	WI	139.5
MUNICIPAL MUTUAL INS CO	WV	35.4	SECURITY MUTUAL INS CO	NY	106.0
MUTUAL OF WAUSAU INS CORP	WI	24.4	SENECA SPECIALTY INS CO	DE	50.7
MUTUAL RRG INC	HI	133.2	SHEBOYGAN FALLS INS CO	WI	36.6
MUTUALAID EXCHANGE	KS	30.7	SHELTER GENERAL INS CO	MO	132.7
NAMIC INS CO	IN	53.6	SLAVONIC MUTUAL FIRE INS ASN	TX	30.1
NATIONAL AMERICAN INS CO	OK	201.0	SOUTH CAROLINA FARM BU MUTUAL INS CO	SC	106.5
NATIONAL INDEMNITY CO OF THE SOUTH	IA	398.5	SOUTHERN FIDELITY P&C INC	FL	111.0
NATIONAL INTERSTATE INS CO	OH	1,308.6	SOUTHERN INS CO OF VA	VA	150.3
NATIONAL LIABILITY & FIRE INS CO	CT	2,685.3	SOUTHERN MUTUAL CHURCH INS CO	SC	65.1
NATIONAL MORTGAGE RE INC ONE	WI	35.1	SOUTHERN MUTUAL INS CO	GA	19.1
NATIONAL SPECIALTY INS CO	TX	86.2	SOUTHERN PIONEER PROP & CAS INS CO	AR	46.9
NATIONWIDE INDEMNITY CO	OH	2,976.0	SOUTHERN STATES INS EXCHANGE	VA	38.6
NAU COUNTRY INS CO	MN	1,191.2	SOUTHWEST MARINE & GEN INS CO	AZ	128.4
NEIGHBORHOOD SPIRIT PROP & CAS CO	CA	289.5	SPARTAN PROPERTY INS CO	SC	29.3
NEW HOME WARRANTY INS CO RRG	DC	21.7	ST PAUL GUARDIAN INS CO	CT	75.1
NEW JERSEY INDEMNITY INS CO	NJ	78.7	STANDARD CASUALTY CO	TX	38.8
NEW MEXICO MUTUAL CASUALTY CO	NM	386.5	STATE AUTO P&C INS CO	IA	2,496.9
NORFOLK & DEDHAM MUTUAL FIRE INS CO	MA	413.7	STATE AUTOMOBILE MUTUAL INS CO	OH	2,488.5
NORTHERN MUTUAL INS CO	MI	35.4	STATE FARM GUARANTY INS CO	IL	36.9
NORTHFIELD INS CO	IA	390.3	STEADFAST INS CO	DE	577.2
NORTHSTONE INS CO	PA	64.7	STILLWATER P&C INS CO	NY	135.0
NOVA CASUALTY CO	NY	95.5	STONEWOOD INS CO	NC	114.1
NUTMEG INS CO	CT	766.5	SUBLIMITY INS CO	OR	40.4
OBI NATIONAL INS CO	PA	13.2	SUMMITPOINT INS CO	WV	55.6
OKLAHOMA SPECIALTY INS CO	OK	24.5	SURETEC INDEMNITY CO	CA	23.0
OLD GUARD INS CO	OH	455.6	SURETY BONDING CO OF AMERICA	SD	7.6
PACIFIC INDEMNITY INS CO	GU	34.1	SUSSEX INS CO	IL	634.7
PALMETTO CASUALTY INS CO	SC	7.1	TDC NATIONAL ASR CO	OR	318.3
PARTNER REINSURANCE CO OF THE US	NY	4,720.1	TEXAS FARMERS INS CO	TX	333.0
PARTNERRE AMERICA INS CO	DE	366.5	TEXAS LAWYERS INS EXCHANGE	TX	90.8
PEERLESS INDEMNITY INS CO	IL	198.3	TOYOTA MOTOR INS CO	IA	534.8
PENINSULA INS CO	MD	91.8	TRAVELERS CASUALTY & SURETY CO OF AM	CT	4,334.2
PENN-AMERICA INS CO	PA	133.1	TRAVELERS CASUALTY CO	CT	207.1
PENN-STAR INS CO	PA	125.2	TRAVELERS CONSTITUTION STATE INS CO	CT	209.2
PHYSICIANS PROFESSIONAL LIABILTY RRG	VT	37.8	TRI-CENTURY INS CO	PA	41.4
PINNACLEPOINT INS CO	WV	80.8	TRIANGLE INS CO	OK	88.3
PLATEAU CASUALTY INS CO	TN	43.6	TRITON INS CO	TX	412.2
PLAZA INS CO	IA	78.3	TRUCK INS EXCHANGE	CA	2,234.1
PODIATRY INS CO OF AM	IL	297.8	UNITED FIRE & INDEMNITY CO	TX	55.7
PRIME P&C INS INC	IL	33.0	UNITED FIRE LLOYDS	TX	32.1
PROFESSIONAL SECURITY INS CO	AZ	78.8	UNITED GUAR RESIDENTIAL INS CO OF NC	NC	331.6
			UNITED GUARANTY MORTGAGE INDEM CO	NC	438.7

INSURANCE COMPANY NAME	DOM. STATE	TOTAL ASSETS ($MIL)	INSURANCE COMPANY NAME	DOM. STATE	TOTAL ASSETS ($MIL)
Rating: C+ (Continued)			AMERICAN FARMERS & RANCHERS MUTUAL	OK	159.4
UNITED GUARANTY RESIDENTIAL INS CO	NC	3,389.7	AMERICAN HOME ASR CO	NY	26,144.8
UNITED WISCONSIN INS CO	WI	202.4	AMERICAN MODERN LLOYDS INS CO	TX	6.7
UNIVERSAL UNDERWRITERS INS CO	IL	396.7	AMERICAN MODERN SELECT INS CO	OH	289.4
UNIVERSAL UNDERWRITERS OF TX	IL	11.4	AMERICAN SAFETY INS CO	GA	17.6
US COASTAL P&C INS CO	FL	32.8	AMERICAN SELECT INS CO	OH	257.0
USPLATE GLASS INS CO	IL	29.8	AMERICAN SOUTHERN HOME INS CO	FL	149.3
UTICA NATIONAL INS CO OF OHIO	OH	18.8	AMERICAN STRATEGIC INS CO	FL	1,100.4
VA FARM BUREAU TOWN & COUNTRY INS CO	VA	66.9	AMERICAN SURETY CO	IN	14.1
VICTORIA FIRE & CASUALTY CO	OH	116.6	AMERICAN WEST INS CO	ND	15.9
WAYNE MUTUAL INS CO	OH	75.9	AMERICAN WESTERN HOME INS CO	OK	148.3
WEST BRANCH MUTL INS CO	PA	1.1	AMERICAS INS CO	DC	17.4
WI LAWYERS MUTUAL INS CO	WI	33.5	AMGUARD INS CO	PA	681.0
WINDSOR MOUNT JOY MUTUAL INS CO	PA	79.1	ANCHOR GENERAL INS CO	CA	103.5
WISCONSIN REINS CORP	WI	96.6	ANCHOR SPECIALTY INS CO	TX	16.5
WOLVERINE MUTUAL INS CO	MI	56.4	ANTILLES INS CO	PR	59.7
YOSEMITE INS CO	IN	166.7	APPALACHIAN INS CO	RI	330.5
ZALE INDEMNITY CO	TX	52.7	APPLIED MEDICO LEGAL SOLUTIONS RRG	AZ	136.7
ZENITH INS CO	CA	1,864.4	ARBELLA INDEMNITY INS CO	MA	51.4
ZURICH AMERICAN INS CO OF IL	IL	53.9	ARCH INS CO	MO	3,951.7
Rating: C			ARCHITECTS & ENGINEERS INS CO RRG	DE	22.0
1ST AUTO & CASUALTY INS CO	WI	28.4	ARGONAUT INS CO	IL	1,695.6
1ST CHOICE AUTO INS CO	PA	20.8	ARIZONA AUTOMOBILE INS CO	AZ	25.3
ACADIA INS CO	NH	159.5	ARTISAN & TRUCKERS CASUALTY CO	WI	320.4
ACCESS HOME INS CO	LA	37.9	ASOC DE SUSCRIPCION CONJUNTA DEL SEG	PR	159.2
ACCESS INS CO	TX	202.1	ASPEN SPECIALTY INS CO	ND	403.3
ACE FIRE UNDERWRITERS INS CO	PA	113.9	ASSN CASUALTY INS CO	TX	48.5
ACE INS CO OF THE MIDWEST	IN	98.1	ASSOCIATED EMPLOYERS INS CO	MA	5.5
ADIRONDACK INS EXCHANGE	NY	295.8	ASSOCIATED INDEMNITY CORP	CA	108.1
ADM INS CO	AZ	633.5	ASSOCIATED INDUSTRIES INS CO INC	FL	397.8
ADMIRAL INDEMNITY CO	DE	56.2	ASSOCIATED LOGGERS EXCHANGE	ID	35.5
ADMIRAL INS CO	DE	744.4	ASSOCIATED MUTUAL INS CO	NY	27.2
ADRIATIC INS CO	ND	90.4	ATAIN INS CO	TX	88.3
AFFILIATED FM INS CO	RI	2,969.7	ATAIN SPECIALTY INS CO	MI	378.4
AGENT ALLIANCE INS CO	AL	60.0	ATRADIUS TRADE CREDIT INS CO	MD	114.3
AGRI INS EXCHANGE RRG	IN	18.4	AUTO CLUB FAMILY INS CO	MO	117.4
AIG PROPERTY CASUALTY CO	PA	2,027.7	AUTO CLUB PROPERTY & CASUALTY INS CO	MI	89.2
ALASKA TIMBER INS EXCHANGE	AK	15.0	AUTOMOBILE CLUB INTERINSURANCE EXCH	MO	445.8
ALINSCO INS CO	TX	89.7	AXA ART INS CORP	NY	15.0
ALLEGHENY CASUALTY CO	NJ	36.3	BANKERS INDEPENDENT INS CO	PA	24.3
ALLIANCE INS CO	KS	25.9	BANKERS INS CO	FL	153.1
ALLIANCE OF NONPROFITS FOR INS RRG	VT	97.8	BANKERS STANDARD INS CO	PA	628.5
ALLIANCE UNITED INS CO	CA	596.6	BAR PLAN MUTUAL INS CO	MO	44.5
ALLIANZ GLOBAL RISKS US INS CO	IL	7,630.3	BAR PLAN SURETY & FIDELITY CO	MO	5.3
ALLIED WORLD INS CO	NH	1,787.4	BARNSTABLE COUNTY INS CO	MA	23.8
ALLIED WORLD SURPLUS LINES INS	AR	265.3	BATTLE CREEK MUTUAL INS CO	NE	9.0
AMERICAN ALTERNATIVE INS CORP	DE	521.1	BEARING MIDWEST CASUALTY CO	KS	6.7
AMERICAN ASSOC OF ORTHODONTIST RRG	AZ	46.1	BERKLEY NATIONAL INS CO	IA	137.0
AMERICAN AUTOMOBILE INS CO	MO	109.7	BERKLEY REGIONAL SPECIALTY INS CO	DE	62.3
AMERICAN BUILDERS INS CO	DE	137.3	BERKSHIRE HATHATWAY DIRECT INS CO	NE	135.6
AMERICAN BUS & MERCANTILE INS MUT	DE	65.9	BLUE RIDGE INDEMNITY CO	WI	6.8
AMERICAN CASUALTY CO OF READING	PA	141.1	BLUESHORE INS CO	CO	74.1
AMERICAN COUNTRY INS CO	IL	131.9	BREMEN FARMERS MUTUAL INS CO	KS	44.4
AMERICAN EMPIRE INS CO	OH	20.4	BRIAR CREEK MUTUAL INS CO	PA	14.2
AMERICAN EMPIRE SURPLUS LINES INS CO	DE	466.8	BRIDGEFIELD CASUALTY INS CO	FL	55.8
			BRISTOL WEST PREFERRED INS CO	MI	27.7

INSURANCE COMPANY NAME	DOM. STATE	TOTAL ASSETS ($MIL)
Rating: C (Continued)		
BROOME CO OPERATIVE INS CO	NY	21.7
BUILDERS INS (A MUTUAL CAPTIVE CO)	GA	592.6
BUNKER HILL INS CAS CO	MA	13.4
BUNKER HILL INS CO	MA	62.0
CALIFORNIA CAS GEN INS CO OF OREGON	OR	111.1
CALIFORNIA CASUALTY & FIRE INS CO	CA	67.6
CAMICO MUTUAL INS CO	CA	95.8
CAPITOL COUNTY MUTUAL FIRE INS CO	TX	10.5
CAPITOL INDEMNITY CORP	WI	535.5
CAPITOL PREFERRED INS CO	FL	55.5
CARIBBEAN AMERICAN PROPERTY INS CO	PR	40.5
CAROLINA CASUALTY INS CO	IA	170.5
CATLIN INDEMNITY CO	DE	144.5
CATLIN INS CO	TX	226.9
CELINA MUTUAL INS CO	OH	74.5
CENTAURI SPECIALTY INS CO	FL	134.8
CENTRAL CO-OPERATIVE INS CO	NY	17.7
CENTRAL PA PHYSICIANS RRG INC	SC	56.2
CENTURY SURETY CO	OH	172.3
CENTURY-NATIONAL INS CO	CA	544.4
CHAUTAUQUA PATRONS INS CO	NY	21.6
CHICAGO INS CO	IL	87.2
CIM INS CORP	MI	17.7
CITIZENS INS CO OF OHIO	OH	16.1
CITIZENS INS CO OF THE MIDWEST	IN	54.1
CITY NATIONAL INS CO	TX	19.5
CLARENDON NATIONAL INS CO	IL	661.5
CLEAR BLUE INS CO	IL	30.0
CLERMONT INS CO	IA	26.0
CLOISTER MUTL CAS INS CO	PA	9.7
COFACE NORTH AMERICA INS CO	MA	165.9
COLLEGE RRG INC	VT	26.0
COLONY INS CO	VA	1,554.7
COLORADO FARM BUREAU MUTUAL INS CO	CO	82.5
COLUMBIA CASUALTY CO	IL	240.6
COMMERCE & INDUSTRY INS CO	NY	403.2
COMMERCE WEST INS CO	CA	182.3
COMMERCIAL ALLIANCE INS CO	TX	85.3
COMMUNITIES OF FAITH RRG INC	SC	15.1
COMMUNITY BLOOD CENTERS EXCHANGE RRG	IN	18.5
COMPTRUST AGC MUT CAPTIVE INS CO	GA	35.7
CONEMAUGH VALLEY MUTUAL INS CO	PA	13.9
CONSOLIDATED INS CO	IN	13.4
CONSTITUTION INS CO	NY	25.2
CONTINENTAL HERITAGE INS CO	FL	21.5
CONTINENTAL INDEMNITY CO	IA	203.6
CONTINENTAL INS CO	PA	1,694.4
CONTINENTAL INS CO OF NJ	NJ	18.7
CONTINENTAL WESTERN INS CO	IA	220.3
COPPERPOINT INDEMNITY INS CO	AZ	10.7
COPPERPOINT NATIONAL INS CO	AZ	7.1
COUNTRYWAY INS CO	NY	28.1
COVENANT INS CO	CT	87.0
CROSSFIT RRG INC	MT	6.6
CSAA AFFINITY INS CO	AZ	236.4
CSAA FIRE & CASUALTY INS CO	IN	145.2
CSAA GENERAL INS CO	IN	349.8
CYPRESS P&C INS CO	FL	91.9
DAKOTA FIRE INS CO	ND	229.9
DANBURY INS CO	MA	12.2
DE SMET INS CO OF SD	SD	16.1
DENTISTS BENEFITS INS CO	OR	17.6
DOCTORS DIRECT INS INC	IL	14.3
DORCHESTER INS CO LTD	VI	21.1
DORCHESTER MUTUAL INS CO	MA	88.8
DTRIC INS CO LTD	HI	104.8
DTRIC INS UNDERWRITERS LTD	HI	12.5
DUBOIS MEDICAL RRG	DC	12.8
EAGLESTONE REINS CO	PA	6,355.1
EASTERN MUTUAL INS CO	NY	25.4
ELEPHANT INS CO	VA	236.2
EMC PROPERTY & CASUALTY CO	IA	94.3
EMERGENCY MEDICINE PROFESSIONAL ASR	NV	21.3
EMERGENCY PHYSICIANS INS RRG	VT	28.1
EMPLOYERS ASSURANCE CO	FL	482.0
EMPLOYERS PREFERRED INS CO	FL	933.6
EQUITY INS CO	TX	86.0
ESSENTIA INS CO	MO	70.4
ESURANCE INS CO	WI	179.9
ESURANCE INS CO OF NJ	WI	14.3
ESURANCE P&C INS CO	WI	97.6
EVANSTON INS CO	IL	4,551.2
EVER-GREENE MUTUAL INS CO	PA	6.1
EVEREST INDEMNITY INS CO	DE	166.5
EVEREST SECURITY INS CO	GA	36.4
EVERGREEN NATIONAL INDEMNITY CO	OH	47.7
EXCELSIOR INS CO	NH	37.5
EXCESS SHARE INS CORP	OH	52.1
EXPLORER INS CO	CA	371.6
FALLS LAKE FIRE & CASUALTY CO	CA	77.1
FALLS LAKE GENERAL INS CO	OH	13.6
FARM BUREAU CNTY MUTUAL INS CO OF TX	TX	19.9
FARM BUREAU NEW HORIZONS INS CO MO	MO	54.0
FARMERS & MECHANICS FIRE & CAS INS	WV	11.9
FARMERS FIRE INS CO	PA	28.9
FARMERS INS EXCHANGE	CA	16,534.7
FARMERS MUTUAL F I C OF OKARCHE OK	OK	19.9
FARMERS MUTUAL FIRE INS CO OF MARBLE	PA	32.1
FARMERS MUTUAL INS CO	WV	15.3
FARMERS MUTUAL OF TENNESSEE	TN	24.0
FEDERATED NATIONAL INS CO	FL	548.5
FHM INS CO	FL	78.2
FINANCIAL CASUALTY & SURETY INC	TX	28.4
FIRE DISTRICTS INS CO	NY	17.2
FIREMANS FUND INS CO	CA	2,291.0
FIREMENS INS CO OF WASHINGTON DC	DE	101.3
FIRST AMERICAN PROP & CAS INS CO	CA	100.0
FIRST AMERICAN SPECIALTY INS CO	CA	116.8
FIRST COMMUNITY INS CO	FL	101.2
FIRST DAKOTA INDEMNITY CO	SD	48.0

INSURANCE COMPANY NAME	DOM. STATE	TOTAL ASSETS ($MIL)	INSURANCE COMPANY NAME	DOM. STATE	TOTAL ASSETS ($MIL)
Rating: C (Continued)			HAWKEYE-SECURITY INS CO	WI	13.4
			HDI GLOBAL INS CO	IL	436.2
FIRST F&C INS OF HI INC	HI	9.2	HEREFORD INS CO	NY	256.7
FIRST INDEMNITY INS OF HI INC	HI	7.5	HIGHMARK CASUALTY INS CO	PA	272.8
FIRST INS CO OF HI LTD	HI	667.4	HLTHCR PROVIDERS INS CO	SC	81.2
FIRST MERCURY INS CO	DE	105.0	HOCHHEIM PRAIRIE CASUALTY INS CO	TX	78.4
FIRST NONPROFIT INS CO	DE	71.9	HOME & FARM INS CO	OH	9.9
FIRST SECURITY INS OF HI INC	HI	5.6	HOMELAND INS CO OF NY	NY	116.9
FIRST SPECIALTY INS CORP	MO	180.0	HOMEOWNERS CHOICE PROP & CAS INS CO	FL	411.8
FLORISTS INS CO	IL	6.6	HOMESITE INDEMNITY CO	WI	54.3
FOUNDERS INS CO (IL)	IL	161.3	HOMESITE INS CO	WI	156.8
FOUNDERS INS CO (NJ)	NJ	6.5	HOMESITE INS CO OF CA	CA	58.8
FRANKLIN INS CO	PA	30.8	HOMESITE INS CO OF FL	IL	14.2
GEICO CASUALTY CO	MD	3,272.5	HOMESITE INS CO OF GA	GA	30.8
GEICO COUNTY MUTUAL INS CO	TX	132.0	HOMESITE INS CO OF IL	IL	12.8
GEMINI INS CO	DE	110.0	HOMESITE INS CO OF NY	NY	37.4
GENERAL CASUALTY INS CO	WI	8.5	HOMESITE INS CO OF THE MIDWEST	WI	416.2
GENERAL STAR INDEMNITY CO	DE	862.0	HOMESITE LLOYDS OF TEXAS	TX	32.1
GENERALI - US BRANCH	NY	66.4	HOMESTEAD MUTUAL INS CO	WI	9.6
GENESIS INS CO	DE	182.4	HOOSIER INS CO	IN	8.3
GENWORTH MORTGAGE INS CORP	NC	3,038.7	HOSPITALITY MUTUAL INS CO	MA	65.3
GEORGIA CASUALTY & SURETY CO	GA	43.3	HOUSING & REDEVELOPMENT INS EXCH	PA	45.5
GEORGIA FARM BUREAU MUTUAL INS CO	GA	628.4	ID COUNTIES RISK MGMT PROGRAM UNDW	ID	70.5
GEOVERA SPECIALTY INS CO	DE	126.2	ILLINOIS UNION INS CO	IL	354.5
GERMANIA FARM MUTUAL INS ASN	TX	396.1	INDEMNITY CO OF CA	CA	22.2
GERMANIA FIRE & CASUALTY CO	TX	31.8	INDEMNITY INS CO OF NORTH AMERICA	PA	469.6
GOLDEN EAGLE INS CORP	NH	59.5	INDEMNITY NATIONAL INS CO	MS	25.0
GOTHAM INS CO	NY	242.7	INDIANA INS CO	IN	69.6
GRANGE INDEMNITY INS CO	OH	99.4	INDIANA LUMBERMENS MUTUAL INS CO	IN	55.5
GRANGE INS CO OF MI	OH	70.8	INDIANA OLD NATIONAL INS CO	VT	2,179.7
GRANWEST P&C	WA	22.6	INFINITY AUTO INS CO	OH	10.7
GRAY CASUALTY & SURETY CO	LA	17.9	INFINITY COUNTY MUTUAL INS CO	TX	62.8
GREAT AMERICAN ALLIANCE INS CO	OH	30.5	INFINITY INDEMNITY INS CO	IN	6.3
GREAT AMERICAN E & S INS CO	DE	47.3	INFINITY PREFERRED INS CO	OH	4.8
GREAT AMERICAN FIDELITY INS CO	DE	47.4	INFINITY SECURITY INS CO	IN	5.8
GREAT AMERICAN INS CO OF NEW YORK	NY	48.6	INFINITY STANDARD INS CO	IN	7.1
GREAT AMERICAN SECURITY INS CO	OH	15.4	INLAND INS CO	NE	276.0
GREAT AMERICAN SPIRIT INS CO	OH	16.9	INS CO OF NORTH AMERICA	PA	929.9
GREAT DIVIDE INS CO	ND	258.9	INS CO OF THE STATE OF PA	IL	274.5
GREENWICH INS CO	DE	1,132.8	INS CO OF THE WEST	CA	2,306.1
GREYHAWK INSURANCE CO	CO	20.2	INSURORS INDEMNITY LLOYDS	TX	5.2
GRINNELL SELECT INS CO	IA	42.0	INTEGON CASUALTY INS CO	NC	39.4
GUARDIAN INS CO	VI	28.0	INTEGON GENERAL INS CORP	NC	51.9
GULF GUARANTY INS CO	MS	4.3	INTEGON INDEMNITY CORP	NC	140.2
GUTHRIE RRG	SC	53.1	INTEGON PREFERRED INS CO	NC	81.5
HALLMARK COUNTY MUTUAL INS CO	TX	5.6	INTEGRAND ASR CO	PR	116.9
HALLMARK NATIONAL INS CO	AZ	85.0	INTREPID INS CO	IA	30.4
HAMILTON MUTUAL INS CO	IA	76.6	IRONSHORE SPECIALTY INS CO	AZ	999.7
HANOVER AMERICAN INS CO	NH	31.1	ISLAND PREMIER INS CO LTD	HI	11.5
HARLEYSVILLE INS CO	PA	163.7	JAMES RIVER INS CO	OH	600.9
HARLEYSVILLE INS CO OF NEW YORK	PA	60.6	JEFFERSON INS CO	NY	96.4
HARLEYSVILLE INS CO OF NJ	NJ	89.1	KEY RISK INS CO	IA	47.1
HARLEYSVILLE LAKE STATES INS CO	MI	57.9	KINGSTONE INS CO	NY	149.9
HARLEYSVILLE PREFERRED INS CO	PA	138.4	LANDMARK AMERICAN INS CO	NH	385.2
HARLEYSVILLE WORCESTER INS CO	PA	192.5	LAWYERS MUTUAL INS CO OF KENTUCKY	KY	23.5
HARTLAND MUTUAL INS CO	ND	12.5	LEBANON VALLEY INS CO	PA	25.2

INSURANCE COMPANY NAME	DOM. STATE	TOTAL ASSETS ($MIL)	INSURANCE COMPANY NAME	DOM. STATE	TOTAL ASSETS ($MIL)
Rating: C (Continued)			NATIONAL FIRE & MARINE INS CO	NE	9,388.5
LEXINGTON INS CO	DE	21,929.5	NATIONAL FIRE INS CO OF HARTFORD	IL	116.5
LIBERTY INS CORP	IL	252.7	NATIONAL GENERAL ASR CO	MO	39.8
LIBERTY INS UNDERWRITERS INC	IL	175.7	NATIONAL GENERAL INS CO	MO	59.8
LIBERTY MUTUAL MID ATLANTIC INS CO	MA	20.6	NATIONAL GENERAL INS ONLINE INC	MO	51.3
LIBERTY NORTHWEST INS CORP	OR	56.2	NATIONAL INDEMNITY CO OF MID-AMERICA	IA	276.9
LIBERTY PERSONAL INS CO	NH	16.7	NATIONAL INS CO OF WI	WI	13.6
LIBERTY SURPLUS INS CORP	NH	178.9	NATIONAL INTERSTATE INS CO OF HAWAII	OH	54.5
LIVINGSTON MUTUAL INS CO	PA	2.8	NATIONAL MUTUAL INS CO	OH	78.7
LM INS CORP	IL	119.7	NATIONAL SERVICE CONTRACT INS CO RRG	DC	12.5
LUTHERAN MUTUAL FIRE INS CO	IL	10.7	NATIONAL SURETY CORP	IL	136.9
MA EMPLOYERS INS CO	MA	4.3	NATIONAL TRUST INS CO	IN	36.8
MAIN STREET AMER PROTECTION INS CO	FL	15.9	NATIONAL UNION FIRE INS CO	PA	26,559.6
MAIN STREET AMERICA ASR CO	FL	68.4	NAUTILUS INS CO	AZ	265.8
MAPFRE INS CO	NJ	82.4	NCMIC RRG INC	VT	7.0
MAPFRE INS CO OF FLORIDA	FL	108.3	NETHERLANDS INS CO	NH	98.3
MAPFRE PAN AMERICAN INS CO	PR	34.5	NEW CENTURY INS CO	TX	10.7
MAPFRE PRAICO INS CO	PR	402.8	NEW HAMPSHIRE INS CO	IL	205.0
MAPLE VALLEY MUTUAL INS CO	WI	14.0	NEW MEXICO FOUNDATION INS CO	NM	23.4
MARKEL AMERICAN INS CO	VA	470.1	NEW MEXICO PREMIER INS CO	NM	3.9
MARKEL INS CO	IL	1,643.1	NEW SOUTH INS CO	NC	49.3
MAXUM INDEMNITY CO	CT	120.7	NHRMA MUTUAL INS CO	IL	37.9
MCIC VERMONT INC RRG	VT	2,024.1	NOETIC SPECIALTY INS CO	VT	124.9
MCMILLAN WARNER MUTUAL INS CO	WI	16.7	NORTH AMERICAN CAPACITY INS CO	NH	199.7
MDADVANTAGE INS CO OF NJ	NJ	345.1	NORTH AMERICAN ELITE INS CO	NH	131.3
MEDMARC CASUALTY INS CO	VT	304.0	NORTH AMERICAN SPECIALTY INS CO	NH	477.7
MEEMIC INS CO	MI	268.1	NORTH COUNTRY INS CO	NY	27.8
MEMIC INDEMNITY CO	NH	472.7	NORTH PACIFIC INS CO	OR	8.0
MENNONITE MUTUAL INS CO	OH	27.8	NORTHERN SECURITY INS CO	VT	8.5
MENTAL HEALTH RISK RETENTION GROUP	VT	30.0	NORTHWEST DENTISTS INS CO	WI	24.0
MERCER INS CO OF NJ INC	NJ	88.5	OAK RIVER INS CO	NE	693.6
MERIDIAN SECURITY INS CO	IN	123.6	ODYSSEY REINS CO	CT	7,252.6
MESA UNDERWRITERS SPECIALTY INS CO	NJ	329.1	OHIO CASUALTY INS CO	NH	5,711.1
METROMILE INS CO	DE	23.2	OHIO INDEMNITY CO	OH	150.2
MGA INS CO	TX	278.5	OKLAHOMA SURETY CO	OH	16.4
MHA INS CO	MI	600.1	OLD GLORY INS CO	TX	23.6
MIC GENERAL INS CORP	MI	44.3	OLD UNITED CAS CO	KS	625.0
MIC P&C INS CORP	MI	96.8	OLYMPUS INS CO	FL	70.5
MICHIGAN MILLERS MUTUAL INS CO	MI	177.1	OMEGA INS CO	FL	48.1
MID-CONTINENT INS CO	OH	20.4	OMEGA ONE INS CO	AL	12.0
MID-HUDSON CO-OPERTIVE INS CO	NY	26.1	OMNI INDEMNITY CO	IL	97.6
MIDSOUTH MUTUAL INS CO	TN	27.6	ONTARIO INS CO	NY	17.3
MIDWEST INS CO	IL	93.7	ONTARIO REINS CO LTD	GA	28.4
MIDWESTERN INDEMNITY CO	NH	28.2	OOIDA RISK RETENTION GROUP INC	VT	96.5
MONROE GUARANTY INS CO	IN	53.0	OREGON AUTOMOBILE INS CO	OR	8.3
MONTGOMERY MUTUAL INS CO	MA	53.5	OSWEGO COUNTY MUTUAL INS CO	NY	27.9
MOUNT VERNON FIRE INS CO	PA	668.0	PACIFIC COMPENSATION INS CO	CA	376.9
MOUNTAIN LAUREL ASR CO	OH	175.6	PACIFIC STAR INS CO	WI	14.7
MOUNTAIN STATES INDEMNITY CO	NM	50.2	PACO ASR CO INC	IL	68.4
MT HAWLEY INS CO	IL	906.2	PALISADES SAFETY & INS ASSOC	NJ	1,244.1
MT MORRIS MUTUAL INS CO	WI	37.7	PARATRANSIT INS CO A MUTUAL RRG	TN	26.9
MT WASHINGTON ASR CORP	NH	7.0	PARTNERRE INS CO OF NY	NY	122.0
NATIONAL CONTINENTAL INS CO	NY	144.6	PARTNERS MUTUAL INS CO	WI	44.2
NATIONAL FARMERS UNION PROP & CAS CO	WI	170.4	PATRIOT INS CO	ME	125.6
NATIONAL FIRE & CASUALTY CO	IL	10.2	PATRONS MUTUAL INS CO OF CT	CT	50.5
			PATRONS OXFORD INS CO	ME	21.2

INSURANCE COMPANY NAME	DOM. STATE	TOTAL ASSETS ($MIL)	INSURANCE COMPANY NAME	DOM. STATE	TOTAL ASSETS ($MIL)
Rating: C (Continued)			REPUBLIC LLOYDS	TX	12.3
			REPUBLIC MORTGAGE INS CO OF NC	NC	152.1
PENINSULA INDEMNITY CO	MD	11.0	REPUBLIC UNDERWRITERS INS CO	TX	774.6
PENN CHARTER MUTL INS CO	PA	15.5	RESPONSIVE AUTO INS CO	FL	23.5
PENN MILLERS INS CO	PA	98.5	ROCHE SURETY & CASUALTY INC	FL	23.8
PENN-PATRIOT INS CO	VA	50.1	ROCKHILL INS CO	AZ	153.4
PENNSYLVANIA INS CO	IA	66.0	ROCKINGHAM CASUALTY CO	VA	32.4
PENNSYLVANIA MANUFACTURERS ASN INS	PA	945.8	RURAL TRUST INS CO	TX	24.8
PENNSYLVANIA MANUFACTURERS IND CO	PA	218.6	RVI AMERICA INS CO	CT	105.2
PETROLEUM MARKETERS MGMT INS CO	IA	34.5	SAFETY FIRST INS CO	IL	72.8
PHYSICIANS INS PROGRAM	PA	26.6	SAFETY NATIONAL CASUALTY CORP	MO	6,646.8
PHYSICIANS REIMBURSEMENT FUND RRG	VT	31.3	SAFETY P&C INS CO	MA	45.8
PILGRIM INS CO	MA	90.4	SAFETY SPECIALTY INS CO	MO	71.4
PIONEER SPECIALTY INS CO	MN	67.7	SAFEWAY INS CO OF AL	IL	89.7
PLANS LIABILITY INS CO	OH	73.3	SAFEWAY INS CO OF GA	GA	81.2
PLATTE RIVER INS CO	NE	142.2	SAMARITAN RRG INC	SC	36.8
PLICO INC	OK	111.8	SAN FRANCISCO REINS CO	CA	3,469.2
POSITIVE PHYSICIANS INS	PA	58.7	SCOR REINS CO	NY	3,212.4
PRAETORIAN INS CO	PA	515.4	SELECT RISK INS CO	PA	43.8
PRE-PAID LEGAL CAS INC	OK	18.6	SELECTIVE INS CO OF NEW ENGLAND	NJ	188.7
PREFERRED EMPLOYERS INS CO	CA	103.5	SEQUOIA INS CO	CA	241.4
PRIMERO INS CO	NV	16.5	SEVEN SEAS INS CO	FL	24.9
PRINCETON EXCESS & SURPLUS LINES INS	DE	150.7	SONNENBERG MUTUAL INS CO	OH	26.0
PRINCETON INS CO	NJ	695.0	SOUTHERN COUNTY MUTUAL INS CO	TX	34.0
PRIORITY ONE INS CO	TX	18.6	SOUTHERN FIRE & CASUALTY CO	WI	6.8
PROASSURANCE INDEMNTIY CO INC	AL	1,268.8	SOUTHERN GUARANTY INS CO	WI	13.2
PROASSURANCE SPECIALTY INS CO INC	AL	47.2	SOUTHERN INS CO	TX	40.6
PRODUCERS AGRICULTURE INS CO	TX	515.8	SOUTHERN PILOT INS CO	WI	7.2
PRODUCERS LLOYDS INS CO	TX	6.1	SOUTHERN UNDERWRITERS INS CO	OK	5.3
PROFESSIONAL SOLUTIONS INS CO	IA	22.8	SOUTHERN VANGUARD INS CO	TX	19.9
PROGRESSIVE ADVANCED INS CO	OH	476.8	ST PAUL SURPLUS LINES INS CO	DE	636.3
PROGRESSIVE AMERICAN INS CO	OH	511.0	STANDARD P&C INS CO	IL	33.7
PROGRESSIVE BAYSIDE INS CO	OH	132.6	STAR INS CO	MI	1,819.3
PROGRESSIVE CLASSIC INS CO	WI	413.3	STARNET INS CO	DE	238.4
PROGRESSIVE EXPRESS INS CO	OH	237.6	STARSTONE NATIONAL INS CO	DE	390.8
PROGRESSIVE FREEDOM INS CO	NJ	6.6	STATE MUTUAL INS CO (ME)	ME	2.5
PROGRESSIVE GULF INS CO	OH	283.1	STATE NATIONAL FIRE INS CO	LA	3.9
PROGRESSIVE HAWAII INS CORP	OH	208.8	STRATHMORE INS CO	NY	55.0
PROGRESSIVE MARATHON INS CO	MI	552.3	SU INS CO	WI	19.8
PROGRESSIVE MAX INS CO	OH	528.9	SUTTER INS CO	CA	35.8
PROGRESSIVE MICHIGAN INS CO	MI	562.3	TANK OWNER MEMBERS INS CO	TX	28.3
PROGRESSIVE MOUNTAIN INS CO	OH	291.9	TDC SPECIALTY INS CO	DC	76.8
PROGRESSIVE PALOVERDE INS CO	IN	160.2	TECHNOLOGY INS CO	DE	2,471.3
PROGRESSIVE PREFERRED INS CO	OH	839.7	TECUMSEH HEALTH RECIPROCAL RRG	VT	55.8
PROGRESSIVE PREMIER INS CO OF IL	OH	251.8	TEXAS FARM BUREAU MUTUAL INS CO	TX	746.2
PROGRESSIVE SECURITY INS CO	LA	241.5	TEXAS FARM BUREAU UNDERWRITERS	TX	68.6
PROGRESSIVE SELECT INS CO	OH	732.6	TEXAS HERITAGE INS CO	TX	19.9
PROGRESSIVE SOUTHEASTERN INS CO	IN	191.2	TEXAS INS CO	TX	34.8
PROGRESSIVE SPECIALTY INS CO	OH	997.9	THAMES INS CO	CT	29.1
PROGRESSIVE UNIVERSAL INS CO	WI	405.9	THE INS CO	LA	206.4
PROGRESSIVE WEST INS CO	OH	127.7	TIG INS CO	CA	2,718.7
PROSELECT INS CO	NE	158.2	TITAN INS CO INC A RRG	SC	65.9
REDWOOD FIRE & CAS INS CO	NE	1,728.1	TOKIO MARINE PACIFIC INS LTD	GU	112.7
REGENT INS CO	WI	38.9	TOKIO MARINE SPECIALTY INS CO	DE	583.4
REPUBLIC FIRE & CASUALTY INS CO	OK	8.2	TOKIO MILLENNIUM RE AG (US BRANCH)	NY	1,036.3
REPUBLIC INDEMNITY OF CA	CA	33.0	TOWER HILL SELECT INS CO	FL	77.5

INSURANCE COMPANY NAME	DOM. STATE	TOTAL ASSETS ($MIL)	INSURANCE COMPANY NAME	DOM. STATE	TOTAL ASSETS ($MIL)
Rating: C (Continued)			WISCONSIN MUNICIPAL MUTUAL INS CO	WI	52.0
TOWER HILL SIGNATURE INS CO	FL	121.7	WOODLANDS INS CO	TX	28.5
TRADEWIND INS CO LTD	HI	13.8	WORTH CASUALTY CO	TX	14.8
TRANS CITY CASUALTY INS CO	AZ	18.3	XL INS AMERICA INC	DE	724.0
TRANSPORTATION INS CO	IL	77.9	XL REINS AMERICA INC	NY	6,087.9
TRI-STATE INS CO OF MN	IA	51.6	XL SPECIALTY INS CO	DE	956.4
TRIUMPHE CASUALTY CO	OH	62.2	YEL CO INS	FL	16.8
TUDOR INS CO	NH	186.6	ZEPHYR INS CO	HI	104.0
UFG SPECIALTY INS CO	IA	42.9	ZNAT INS CO	CA	70.6
UNDERWRITERS AT LLOYDS (VI)	VI	66.4	**Rating: C-**		
UNIGARD INDEMNITY CO	WI	7.5	A CENTRAL INS CO	NY	113.6
UNIGARD INS CO	WI	452.8	ACCEPTANCE INDEMNITY INS CO	NE	301.7
UNION INS CO	IA	142.3	AFFINITY MUTUAL INS CO	OH	14.0
UNION INS CO OF PROVIDENCE	IA	65.4	AGRI GENERAL INS CO	IA	130.3
UNION STANDARD LLOYDS	TX	2.5	ALAMANCE INS CO	IL	476.9
UNITED FRONTIER MUTUAL INS CO	NY	16.5	ALLIANZ UNDERWRITERS INS CO	IL	104.1
UNITED NATIONAL INS CO	PA	356.1	ALLIED PROFESSIONALS INS CO RRG	AZ	48.6
UNIVERSAL NORTH AMERICA INS CO	TX	186.6	ALLIED TRUST INS CO	TX	13.5
UNIVERSAL SURETY CO	NE	214.6	AMERICAN EXCESS INS EXCHANGE RRG	VT	305.6
UNIVERSAL SURETY OF AMERICA	SD	14.7	AMERICAN FIRE & CASUALTY CO	NH	41.5
UPLAND MUTUAL INS INC	KS	30.3	AMERICAN INS CO	OH	132.1
US FIRE INS CO	DE	3,994.4	AMERICAN MUTUAL SHARE INS CORP	OH	267.3
US LIABILITY INS CO	PA	1,058.6	AMERICAN PET INS CO	NY	61.2
US LLOYDS INS CO	TX	29.7	AMERICAN SENTINEL INS CO	PA	39.5
US UNDERWRITERS INS CO	ND	170.8	AMERIGUARD RRG INC	VT	15.1
UTICA NATIONAL ASR CO	NY	66.6	AMFED CASUALTY INS CO	MS	5.7
UTICA NATIONAL INS CO OF TX	TX	36.2	ANTHRACITE MUTUAL FIRE INS CO	PA	4.1
VALLEY FORGE INS CO	PA	71.2	APOLLO MUTUAL FIRE INS CO	PA	4.0
VERSANT CASUALTY INS CO	MS	45.5	APPLIED UNDERWRITERS CAPTIVE RISK	IA	928.7
VICTORIA SPECIALTY INSURANCE CO	OH	18.0	ARCH REINS CO	DE	2,016.7
VIKING INS CO OF WI	WI	418.5	ASI SELECT INS CORP	DE	24.3
VIRGINIA FARM BUREAU FIRE & CAS INS	VA	63.6	ASPIRE GENERAL INS CO	CA	17.4
VOYAGER INDEMNITY INS CO	GA	115.3	ASSURED GUARANTY CORP	MD	3,281.8
WADENA INS CO	IA	5.5	ATTORNEYS INS MUTUAL	DC	11.5
WASHINGTON INTL INS CO	NH	103.6	ATTORNEYS INS MUTUAL RRG	HI	15.3
WAUSAU BUSINESS INS CO	WI	36.8	AXA INS CO	NY	251.9
WAUSAU GENERAL INS CO	WI	16.1	BALBOA INS CO	CA	86.6
WAUSAU UNDERWRITERS INS CO	WI	123.7	BALDWIN MUTUAL INS CO	AL	12.4
WAYNE COOPERATIVE INS CO	NY	31.4	BEDFORD GRANGE MUTUAL INS CO	PA	10.4
WEA P&C INS CO	WI	18.4	BEDFORD PHYSICIANS RRG INC	VT	62.7
WELLINGTON INS CO	TX	33.9	BERKLEY ASR CO	IA	74.9
WEST VIRGINIA INS CO	WV	52.1	BLOOMFIELD MUTUAL INS CO	MN	12.0
WESTCHESTER FIRE INS CO	PA	1,849.8	BOND SAFEGUARD INS CO	SD	80.7
WESTCHESTER SURPLUS LINES INS CO	GA	329.9	BRIERFIELD INS CO	MS	13.3
WESTERN HOME INS CO	MN	70.3	BURLINGTON INS CO	IL	354.9
WESTERN NATIONAL ASR CO	MN	72.1	CALIFORNIA MUTUAL INS CO	CA	14.7
WESTERN PROTECTORS INS CO	OR	9.1	CAMERON NATIONAL INS CO	MO	12.5
WESTERN SELECT INS CO	IL	16.7	CARE WEST INS CO	CA	132.6
WESTERN SURETY CO	SD	2,015.0	CAREGIVERS UNITED LIAB INS CO RRG	SC	44.9
WESTERN WORLD INS CO	NH	836.8	CAROLINA FARMERS MUTUAL INS CO	NC	8.8
WESTMINSTER AMERICAN INS CO	MD	32.7	CATASTROPHE REINS CO	TX	1,886.3
WESTON INS CO	FL	78.7	CBIA COMP SERVICES INC	CT	25.2
WHITE PINE INS CO	MI	77.2	CENTURION MEDICAL LIAB PROTECT RRG	AZ	21.2
WINDHAVEN NATIONAL INS CO	TX	5.9	CENTURY MUTUAL INS CO	NC	9.8
WISCONSIN COUNTY MUTUAL INS CORP	WI	93.8	CLEARFIELD CTY GRNGE MUT FIRE INS CO	PA	2.9

INSURANCE COMPANY NAME	DOM. STATE	TOTAL ASSETS ($MIL)	INSURANCE COMPANY NAME	DOM. STATE	TOTAL ASSETS ($MIL)
Rating: C- (Continued)			INTERSTATE FIRE & CAS CO	IL	110.2
COASTAL AMERICAN INS CO	MS	8.9	KANSAS MUTUAL INS CO	KS	14.9
COLONIAL LLOYDS	TX	9.1	KENTUCKY HOSPITAL INS CO RRG	KY	20.9
CONTRACTORS INS CO OF NORTH AMER RRG	HI	37.5	LAMMICO RRG INC	DC	5.9
COREPOINTE INS CO	MI	89.1	LAUNDRY OWNERS MUTUAL LIAB INS ASN	PA	16.7
CORNERSTONE NATIONAL INS CO	MO	31.4	LEXON INS CO	TX	225.9
COVERYS RRG INC	DC	33.9	LIBERTY COUNTY MUTUAL INS CO	TX	7.2
CPA MUTL INS CO OF AM (A RRG)	VT	16.5	MANUFACTURERS ALLIANCE INS CO	PA	207.0
CSAA MID-ATLANTIC INS CO	AZ	39.2	MD RRG INC	MT	25.6
CSAA MID-ATLANTIC INS CO OF NJ	NJ	55.3	MEDPRO RRG	DC	93.8
DEALERS CHOICE MUTUAL INS INC	NC	24.7	MEMBERS INS CO	NC	31.9
DELTA FIRE & CAS INS CO	GA	7.6	MERCURY INDEMNITY CO OF AMERICA	FL	60.7
DIRECT GENERAL INS CO OF LA	LA	12.4	MFS MUTUAL INS CO	IA	3.9
DIRECT GENERAL INS CO OF MS	MS	11.9	MGIC ASSURANCE CORP	WI	18.5
DIRECT INS CO	TN	24.8	MICHIGAN COMMERCIAL INS MUTUAL	MI	74.7
DISCOVERY INS CO	NC	29.3	MIDDLE STATES INS CO	OK	5.7
DISTRICTS MUTL INS & RISK MGMT	WI	23.2	MILLVILLE INS CO OF NY	NY	2.9
DORINCO REINS CO	MI	1,538.0	MULTINATIONAL INS CO	PR	33.3
EASTERN ATLANTIC INS CO	PA	68.9	MUNICIPAL PROPERTY INS CO	WI	17.9
EMPLOYERS INS CO OF NV	NV	546.2	NARRAGANSETT BAY INS CO	RI	226.3
EXCALIBUR NATIONAL INS CO	LA	11.7	NASW RRG INC	DC	15.4
FARMERS MUTUAL F I C OF MCCANDLESS	PA	11.7	NATIONAL FIRE & INDEMNITY EXCHANGE	MO	10.8
FDM PREFERRED INS CO	NY	14.3	NATIONAL GUARDIAN RRG INC	HI	12.2
FINANCIAL AMERICAN PROP & CAS INS CO	TX	12.8	NATIONAL INDEPENDENT TRUCKERS IC RRG	SC	14.6
FIRST CHOICE CASUALTY INS CO	NV	15.1	NAZARETH MUTUAL INS CO	PA	14.5
FIRST FINANCIAL INS CO	IL	548.9	NEW JERSEY SKYLANDS INS CO	NJ	35.1
FIRST SURETY CORP	WV	40.0	NEW MEXICO ASR CO	NM	6.6
FLORIDA SPECIALTY INS CO	FL	48.3	NEW MEXICO SAFETY CASUALTY CO	NM	5.1
FLORISTS MUTUAL INS CO	IL	125.4	NEW MEXICO SOUTHWEST CASUALTY CO	NM	18.1
FRANK WINSTON CRUM INS CO	FL	86.6	NORCAL SPECIALTY INS CO	PA	63.0
FREDERICK MUTUAL INS CO	MD	44.9	NORTH CAROLINA GRANGE MUTUAL INS CO	NC	33.5
FRIENDS COVE MUTUAL INS CO	PA	5.7	NORTH POINTE INS CO	PA	19.6
GEM STATE INS CO	ID	12.1	NORTH RIVER INS CO	NJ	1,065.2
GENERAL SECURITY IND CO OF AZ	AZ	373.9	OCCIDENTAL FIRE & CAS CO OF NC	NC	624.6
GENERAL SECURITY NATIONAL INS CO	NY	390.0	OCEAN MARINE INDEMNITY INS CO	LA	11.5
GRAIN DEALERS MUTUAL INS CO	IN	11.3	OHIO SECURITY INS CO	NH	16.2
GREAT LAKES MUTUAL INS CO	MI	11.7	OLD RELIABLE CAS CO	MO	5.8
GREAT NORTHWEST INS CO	MN	19.8	OREGON MUTUAL INS CO	OR	211.9
GREENVILLE CASUALTY INS CO INC	SC	11.9	PACIFIC PIONEER INS CO	CA	22.8
GUILFORD INS CO	IL	379.3	PALOMAR SPECIALTY INS CO	OR	123.9
HEALTH CARE INDEMNITY INC	CO	366.3	PANHANDLE FARMERS MULT INS CO	WV	4.8
HEALTH CARE INDUSTRY LIAB RECIP INS	DC	44.6	PEACE CHURCH RRG INC	VT	23.6
HEALTH CARE INS RECPL	MN	30.2	PELICAN INS RRG	VT	20.2
HOME STATE COUNTY MUTUAL INS CO	TX	104.3	PERMANENT GEN ASR CORP OF OHIO	OH	249.0
HOMEOWNERS OF AMERICA INS CO	TX	47.4	PERMANENT GENERAL ASR CORP	OH	455.8
HOSPITALS INS CO	NY	1,672.5	POINT GUARD INS CO	PR	53.1
HUDSON INS CO	DE	1,035.1	PREPARED INS CO	FL	52.1
IMPERIAL F&C INS CO	LA	117.4	PREVISOR INS CO	CO	9.7
IMPERIUM INS CO	TX	375.7	PROASSURANCE AMER MUTL A RRG	DC	10.8
INDEPENDENCE CASUALTY INS CO	MA	4.7	PROCENTURY INS CO	MI	89.3
INDIAN HARBOR INS CO	DE	191.0	PROFESSIONAL CASUALTY ASSN	PA	41.3
INLAND MUTUAL INS CO	WV	6.8	QBE SPECIALTY INS CO	ND	412.8
INSPIRIEN INS CO	AL	40.5	REDPOINT COUNTY MUTUAL INS CO	TX	32.4
INSURORS INDEMNITY CO	TX	34.1	RELIAMAX INS CO	SD	17.0
INTERBORO INS CO	NY	80.9	RESIDENCE MUTUAL INS CO	CA	128.3
			RESPONSE INDEMNITY CO OF CA	CA	7.9

INSURANCE COMPANY NAME	DOM. STATE	TOTAL ASSETS ($MIL)	INSURANCE COMPANY NAME	DOM. STATE	TOTAL ASSETS ($MIL)
Rating: C- (Continued)			ACIG INS CO	IL	455.9
RESPONSE INS CO	IL	38.6	AGCS MARINE INS CO	IL	325.2
RETAILERS INS CO	MI	21.8	AIOI NISSAY DOWA INS CO LTD	GU	32.5
ROCHDALE INS CO	NY	308.5	AMERICAN ACCESS CASUALTY CO	IL	371.4
ROCKWOOD CASUALTY INS CO	PA	259.8	AMERICAN FOREST CASUALTY CO RRG	VT	8.9
RUTGERS CASUALTY INS CO	NJ	20.9	AMERICAN INDEPENDENT INS CO	PA	133.8
RUTGERS ENHANCED INS CO	NJ	11.2	AMERICAN PROPERTY INS	NJ	23.6
RVOS FARM MUTUAL INS CO	TX	87.3	AMERICAN RISK INS CO	TX	32.5
SAFE INS CO	WV	11.2	AMERICAN SAFETY RRG INC	VT	8.0
SAINT LUKES HEALTH SYSTEM RRG	SC	13.9	AMERICAN STEAMSHIP O M PROT & IND AS	NY	308.0
SAUQUOIT VALLEY INS CO	NY	4.7	AMERICAN UNDERWRITERS INS CO	AR	7.0
SAVERS P&C INS CO	MO	75.8	AMERITRUST INS CORP	MI	41.2
SERVICE INS CO (NJ)	NJ	14.9	ARGONAUT GREAT CENTRAL INS CO	IL	37.1
SFM SELECT INS CO	MN	5.0	ASI LLOYDS	TX	219.1
SOUTH CAROLINA FARM BUREAU INS	SC	3.6	ASSURANCEAMERICA INS CO	NE	74.5
SOUTHERN GENERAL INS CO	GA	54.1	ASSURED GUARANTY MUNICIPAL CORP	NY	5,395.9
SPARTAN INS CO	TX	7.4	AUTO CLUB COUNTY MUTUAL INS CO	TX	105.1
SPECIALTY RISK OF AMERICA	IL	16.3	BAR VERMONT RRG INC	VT	27.9
ST JOHNS INS CO	FL	142.6	BEDIVERE INS CO	PA	256.8
STARSTONE SPECIALTY INS CO	DE	198.0	BONDED BUILDERS INS CO RRG	NV	3.3
STATE AUTO INS CO OF OH	OH	29.0	BOSTON INDEMNITY CO INC	SD	6.7
STEADPOINT INS CO	TN	26.4	BRISTOL WEST CASUALTY INS CO	OH	17.3
SUN SURETY INS CO	SD	20.7	BRISTOL WEST INS CO	OH	153.5
SWISS REINS AMERICA CORP	NY	13,505.3	BUILD AMERICA MUTUAL ASR CO	NY	504.2
SYNERGY COMP INS CO	PA	37.2	CARE RRG INC	DC	18.5
SYNERGY INS CO	NC	68.5	CASSATT RISK RETENTION GROUP INC	VT	12.1
TEXAS HOSPITAL INS EXCHANGE	TX	36.2	CASUALTY UNDERWRITERS INS CO	UT	4.7
TEXAS MEDICAL INS CO	TX	58.2	CEM INS CO	IL	40.9
TRADERS INS CO	MO	78.4	CENTER VALLEY MUTUAL FIRE INS CO	PA	2.5
TRANSIT GENERAL INS CO	IL	32.1	CENTRE COUNTY MUTUAL FIRE INS CO	PA	6.3
UNITED CASUALTY & SURETY CO INC	MA	10.4	CENTURY CASUALTY CO	GA	4.9
UNITED HOME INS CO	AR	38.8	CLAIM PROFESSIONALS LIAB INS CO RRG	VT	4.4
UNITED INS CO	UT	46.2	COAST NATIONAL INS CO	CA	598.4
UNITED STATES FIDELITY & GUARANTY CO	CT	3,291.3	COASTAL SELECT INS CO	CA	112.6
UNITRIN ADVANTAGE INS CO	NY	3.3	COLONIAL MORTGAGE INS CO	TX	3.0
UNIVERSAL FIRE & CASUALTY INS CO	IN	15.5	COLONY SPECIALTY INS CO	OH	62.4
UNIVERSAL INS CO	NC	41.8	COLUMBIA FEDERAL INS CO	DC	3.5
UNIVERSAL INS CO OF NORTH AMERICA	FL	112.5	COMCARE PRO INS RECIPROCAL RRG	VT	5.1
UPMC WORK ALLIANCE INC	PA	6.3	COMMUNITY MUTUAL INS CO	NY	2.0
US COASTAL INS CO	NY	22.3	CONSUMER SPECIALTIES INS CO RRG	VT	4.2
USA UNDERWRITERS	MI	10.0	CRUM & FORSTER INDEMNITY CO	DE	53.2
VERTERRA INS CO	TX	75.9	CRUM & FORSTER INS CO	NJ	52.4
WARRANTY UNDERWRITERS INS CO	TX	31.5	CRUM & FORSTER SPECIALTY INS CO	DE	71.5
WEST AMERICAN INS CO	IN	51.7	DELTA LLOYDS INS CO OF HOUSTON	TX	6.5
WEST VIRGINIA FARMERS MUT INS ASSOC	WV	7.5	DOCTORS CO RRG A RECIPROCAL	DC	22.2
WEST VIRGINIA MUTUAL INS CO	WV	165.8	EAGLE POINT MUTUAL INS CO	WI	5.2
WESTERN MUTL INS CO (CA)	CA	85.2	EASTGUARD INS CO	PA	155.0
WILLIAMSBURG NATIONAL INS CO	MI	53.2	EDISON INS CO	FL	52.8
WILSHIRE INS CO	NC	301.1	ELLINGTON MUTUAL INS CO	WI	6.3
WORK FIRST CASUALTY CO	DE	43.1	ETHIO-AMERICAN INS CO	GA	10.7
XL INS CO OF NY INC	NY	227.5	FALCON INS CO	IL	37.3
YELLOWSTONE INS EXCHANGE	VT	22.5	FINIAL REINS CO	CT	1,530.0
Rating: D+			FIRST ACCEPTANCE INS CO	TX	266.4
1ST ATLANTIC SURETY CO	NC	4.0	FIRST ACCEPTANCE INS CO OF GEORGIA	GA	105.5
7710 INS CO	SC	12.9	FIRST ACCEPTANCE INS CO OF TN INC	TN	32.6
			FIRST FOUNDERS ASR CO	NJ	5.5

INSURANCE COMPANY NAME	DOM. STATE	TOTAL ASSETS ($MIL)
Rating: D+ (Continued)		
FIRST INDEMNITY OF AMERICA INS CO	NJ	10.6
FIRST MUTUAL INS CO	NC	6.7
FIRST NET INS CO	GU	20.5
FORT WAYNE MEDICAL ASR CO RRG	AZ	4.1
FRANKLIN CASUALTY INS CO RRG	VT	21.0
FREEDOM ADVANTAGE INS CO	PA	11.0
FRONTIER - MT CARROLL MUTL INS	IL	23.3
GENESEE PATRONS COOP INS	NY	9.6
GENEVA INS CO	IN	4.1
GEORGIA MUNICIPAL CAPTIVE INS CO	GA	11.2
GEOVERA INS CO	CA	85.9
GRANGE MUTUAL FIRE INS CO	PA	4.7
GREAT CENTRAL FIRE INS CO	LA	3.9
GREAT FALLS INS CO	ME	13.3
GROWERS AUTOMOBILE INS ASN	IN	7.2
HALLMARK INS CO	AZ	305.8
HANNAHSTOWN MUTUAL INS CO	PA	4.3
HANOVER FIRE & CASUALTY INS CO	PA	5.9
HARBOR INS CO	OK	12.2
HAY CREEK MUTUAL INS CO	MN	5.8
HEALTHCARE PROFESSIONAL INS CO INC	NY	231.0
HUDSON SPECIALTY INS CO	NY	356.6
INS CO OF THE SOUTH	GA	39.9
INTEGRITY P&C INS CO	WI	15.8
IU HEALTH RRG INC	SC	3.8
JUNIATA MUTUAL INS CO	PA	8.7
KENTUCKY NATIONAL INS CO	KY	31.9
LEMONADE INS CO	NY	11.3
LITTLE BLACK MUTUAL INS CO	WI	6.1
MARATHON FINANCIAL INS INC RRG	DE	4.4
MEDICAL ALLIANCE INS CO	IL	12.1
MEDICAL LIABILITY MUTUAL INS CO	NY	5,590.6
MEDICAL PROVIDERS MUTUAL INS CO RRG	DC	7.6
MENDOTA INS CO	MN	125.4
MGIC INDEMNITY CORP	WI	142.1
MIDROX INS CO	NY	8.1
MIDWESTERN EQUITY TITLE INS CO	IN	4.0
MISSOURI VALLEY MUTUAL INS CO	SD	6.3
MORTGAGE GUARANTY INS CORP	WI	4,529.7
MOUND PRAIRIE MUTUAL INS CO	MN	7.5
MOUNT BEACON INS CO	FL	20.5
MOUNTAIN STATES HEALTHCARE RECIP RRG	MT	119.3
MOWER COUNTY FARMERS MUT INS CO	MN	5.8
MUTUAL FIRE INS CO OF S BEND TOWNSHP	PA	3.6
NATIONAL ASSISTED LIVING RRG INC	DC	8.3
NATIONAL HERITAGE INS CO	IL	3.7
NATIONS INS CO	CA	48.3
NEVADA MUTUAL INS CO	NV	20.7
NEW JERSEY PHYS UNITED RECIP EXCH	NJ	31.0
NEW JERSEY SKYLANDS INS ASSN	NJ	56.9
NEW MEXICO SECURITY INS CO	NM	4.0
ONE ALLIANCE INS CORP	PR	14.0
ORANGE COUNTY MEDICAL RECIP INS RRG	AZ	6.3
PACE RRG INC	VT	4.9

INSURANCE COMPANY NAME	DOM. STATE	TOTAL ASSETS ($MIL)
PALISADES INS CO	NJ	35.1
PALLADIUM RRG INC	VT	99.9
PALMETTO SURETY CORP	SC	13.2
PATRONS MUTUAL FIRE INS CO OF IN PA	PA	2.8
PCH MUTUAL INS CO INC RRG	VT	6.8
PELEUS INS CO	VA	94.3
PERSONAL SERVICE INS CO	PA	57.9
PHYSICIANS INS CO	FL	13.7
PHYSICIANS PROACTIVE PROTECTION INC	SC	91.1
PHYSICIANS SPECIALTY LTD RRG	SC	11.5
PHYSICIANS STANDARD INS CO	KS	4.1
PIEDMONT MUTUAL INS CO	NC	4.8
PONCE DE LEON LTC RRG INC	FL	5.7
PREFERRED AUTO INS CO	TN	9.9
PRIMEONE INS CO	UT	16.1
PROFESSIONAL INS EXCHANGE MUTUAL	UT	8.1
PROGRESSIVE COUNTY MUTUAL INS CO	TX	578.4
PYMATUNING MUTUAL FIRE INS CO	PA	3.3
RADIAN GUARANTY INC	PA	3,818.7
RADIAN INS INC	PA	22.6
RANCHERS & FARMERS MUTUAL INS CO	TX	41.8
REAL LEGACY ASR CO INC	PR	131.2
REAMSTOWN MUTUAL INS CO	PA	8.3
RED ROCK RISK RETENTION GROUP INC	AZ	7.4
REPUBLIC CREDIT INDEMNITY CO	IL	64.8
REPWEST INS CO	AZ	325.7
RIDER INS CO	NJ	36.7
SAWGRASS MUTUAL INS CO	FL	32.3
SEAVIEW INS CO	CA	22.6
SECURITY NATIONAL INS CO	FL	118.2
SELECT MD RRG INC	MT	3.0
SENECA INS CO	NY	190.2
SOMERSET CASUALTY INS CO	PA	42.9
SPARTA INS CO	CT	283.6
SPIRIT MOUNTAIN INS CO RRG INC	DC	6.9
SUNDERLAND MARINE INS CO LTD	AK	10.3
TERRAFIRMA RRG LLC	VT	7.7
TITLE INDUSTRY ASR CO RRG	VT	7.3
TOWER BONDING & SURETY CO	PR	3.7
TWIN LIGHTS INS CO	NJ	8.5
UNITED EQUITABLE INS CO	IL	25.5
UNITRIN AUTO & HOME INS CO	NY	74.8
UNITRIN PREFERRED INS CO	NY	22.0
US INS CO OF AMERICA	IL	6.1
USA INS CO	MS	15.9
UV INS RRG INC	HI	1.3
VASA SPRING GARDEN MUTUAL INS CO	MN	5.4
VERTI INSURANCE CO	OH	23.9
WASHINGTON COUNTY CO-OPERATIVE INS	NY	8.2
WEST VIRGINIA NATIONAL AUTO INS CO	WV	6.5
WESTERN GENERAL INS CO	CA	90.0
WILMINGTON INS CO	DE	5.1
Rating: D		
A-ONE COMM INS RRG GROUP INC	TN	13.6
ACCC INS CO	TX	303.4

INSURANCE COMPANY NAME	DOM. STATE	TOTAL ASSETS ($MIL)	INSURANCE COMPANY NAME	DOM. STATE	TOTAL ASSETS ($MIL)
Rating: **D** **(Continued)**			DOCTORS PROF LIAB RRG INC	NC	2.4
ACCEPTANCE CASUALTY INS CO	NE	120.2	DONGBU INS CO LTD	HI	263.6
ADVANCED PHYSICIANS INS RRG INC	AZ	1.6	EASTERN ALLIANCE INS CO	PA	321.1
AEGIS HEALTHCARE RRG INC	DC	6.1	ECHELON P&C INS CO	IL	14.5
AGENTS MUTUAL INS CO	AR	4.0	ECOLE INS CO	AZ	13.9
AGRINATIONAL INS CO	VT	971.1	ELEMENTS PROPERTY INS CO	FL	49.1
ALLEGHENY SURETY CO	PA	4.3	EMERGENCY CAP MGMT LLC A RRG	VT	9.6
AMERICAN ALLIANCE CASUALTY CO	IL	30.1	EQUITABLE LIABILITY INS CO	DC	3.0
AMERICAN COMPENSATION INS CO	MN	71.3	FAIRWAY PHYSICIANS INS CO RRG	DC	13.6
AMERICAN HEARTLAND INS CO	IL	18.0	FARMERS & MECH MU I ASN OF CECIL CTY	MD	1.0
AMERICAN MILLENNIUM INS CO	NJ	34.8	FARMERS UNION MUTUAL INS CO	AR	4.5
AMERICAN RESOURCES INS CO INC	OK	26.0	FBALLIANCE INS INC	VA	4.7
AMERICAN RISK MGMT RRG INC	TN	4.0	FIRST BENEFITS INS MUTUAL INC	NC	47.2
AMERICAN SERVICE INS CO	IL	208.0	FIRST CHICAGO INS CO	IL	85.2
AMFIRST SPECIALTY INS CO	MS	2.6	FREDERICKSBURG PROFESSIONAL RISK EXC	VT	20.2
ANCHOR P&C INS CO	FL	67.2	FREMONT INS CO	MI	150.7
ARGONAUT-MIDWEST INS CO	IL	19.0	GATEWAY INS CO	MO	81.1
ARGONAUT-SOUTHWEST INS CO	IL	18.3	GEISINGER INS CORP RRG	VT	16.4
ARI INS CO	PA	99.1	GEORGIA DEALERS INS CO	GA	9.4
ARIZONA HOME INS CO	AZ	27.9	GEORGIA TRANSPORTATION CAPTIVE INS	GA	2.8
ARKANSAS MUTUAL INS CO	AR	3.4	GERMAN MUTUAL INS CO	OH	41.5
ARROWOOD INDEMNITY CO	DE	1,284.4	GLOBAL LIBERTY INS CO OF NY	NY	69.7
ASSN OF CERTIFIED MTG ORIG RRG	NV	3.1	GOAUTO INS CO	LA	60.9
ATTORNEYS LIAB ASR SOCIETY INC RRG	VT	2,203.2	GOOD SHEPHERD RECIPROCAL RRG	SC	11.2
ATTPRO RRG RECIPROCAL RRG	DC	3.2	HALIFAX MUTUAL INS CO	NC	8.2
AUSTIN MUTUAL INS CO	MN	59.4	HEALTH CARE CASUALTY RRG INC	DC	11.4
BROADWAY INS & SURETY CO	NJ	2.7	HEALTH CARE MUT CAPTIVE INS CO	GA	14.5
CAPACITY INS CO	FL	22.3	HEALTHCARE UNDERWRITING CO RRG	VT	130.9
CAPSON PHYSICIANS INS CO	TX	25.7	HEARTLAND MUTUAL INS CO	MN	8.0
CAR RRG INC	TN	1.4	HOCHHEIM PRAIRIE FARM MUT INS ASN	TX	132.7
CENTURY INS CO GUAM LTD	GU	26.9	HPIC RRG	SC	1.0
CGB INS CO	IN	378.2	HUTTERIAN BRETHREN MUTUAL INS CORP	IL	3.5
CHERRY VALLEY COOPERATIVE INS CO	NY	1.7	INTEGRA INS INC	MN	1.8
CIRCLE STAR INS CO A RRG	VT	10.4	IQS INS RRG INC	VT	1.6
CITIZENS UNITED RECIP EXCH	NJ	73.3	IRONSHORE RRG (DC) INC	DC	2.5
CLAVERACK CO-OPERATIVE INS CO	NY	2.9	ISLAND HOME INS CO	GU	23.7
CLEARWATER SELECT INS CO	CT	1,239.0	KENSINGTON INS CO	NY	15.5
COLLEGE LIAB INS CO LTD RRG	HI	14.6	KEY INS CO	KS	36.1
COMMERCIAL HIRECAR INS CO RRG	TN	4.0	KNIGHTBROOK INS CO	DE	206.6
COMMUNITY CARE RRG INC	DC	7.1	LAKE STREET RRG INC	VT	2.3
COMPASS SPCLTY INS RRG INC	TN	1.9	LOCUST MUTUAL FIRE INS CO	PA	1.2
CONSUMERS COUNTY MUTUAL INS CO	TX	228.1	LONE STAR ALLIANCE INC A RRG	DC	11.3
CONTINENTAL MUTUAL INS CO	PA	1.7	LONE STAR NATIONAL INS CO	IN	4.3
COUNTY HALL INS CO INC A RRG	NC	6.1	LOYA CASUALTY INS CO	CA	106.9
CROWN CAPTIVE INS CO	GA	2.0	LOYA INS CO	TX	272.8
CROWN CAPTIVE INS CO INC	DC	5.8	LUBA INDEMNITY INS CO	LA	5.3
CRUDEN BAY RRG INC	VT	17.3	MAKE TRANSPORTATION INS INC RRG	DE	3.9
CYPRESS TEXAS INS CO	TX	56.5	MED MAL RRG INC	TN	4.0
DAN RRG INC	SC	2.1	MEDCHOICE RRG INC	VT	2.3
DELAWARE GRANGE MUTUAL FIRE INS CO	DE	1.5	MGIC REINS CORP OF WI	WI	586.8
DELAWARE PROFESSIONAL INS CO	DE	5.1	MIDWEST INS GROUP INC RRG	VT	6.8
DELPHI CASUALTY CO	IL	2.7	MONTOUR MUTUAL INS CO	PA	1.0
DEVELOPERS SURETY & INDEMNITY CO	CA	146.1	MOTORS INS CORP	MI	2,053.7
DIAMOND INS CO	IL	49.0	MOUNTAIN LAKE RRG INC	VT	1.6
DIRECT AUTO INS CO	IL	52.7	MOUNTAIN STATES COMM INS CO	NM	1.1
			MOUNTAIN VALLEY INDEMNITY CO	NY	68.2

INSURANCE COMPANY NAME	DOM. STATE	TOTAL ASSETS ($MIL)	INSURANCE COMPANY NAME	DOM. STATE	TOTAL ASSETS ($MIL)
Rating: D (Continued)			VELOCITY INS CO A RRG	SC	2.4
MUTUAL INS CO OF LEHIGH CTY	PA	2.8	VIRGINIA PHYSICIANS RRG INC	MT	2.7
MUTUAL SAVINGS FIRE INS CO	AL	5.0	VISION INS CO	TX	29.8
NATIONAL CATHOLIC RRG	VT	65.0	WORKMENS AUTO INS CO	CA	44.7
NATIONAL DIRECT INS CO	NV	6.3	XL SELECT INS CO	DE	141.0
NATIONAL UNITY INS CO	TX	40.7	YOUNG AMERICA INS CO	TX	56.2
NATL TRANSPORTATION INS CO RRG	NC	3.0	**Rating: D-**		
NEVADA GENERAL INS CO	NV	15.7	ACADEMIC MEDICAL PROFESSIONALS RRG	VT	4.7
NEWPORT BONDING & SURETY CO	PR	4.3	AMERICAN CONTRACTORS INS CO RISK RET	TX	19.8
NORGUARD INS CO	PA	859.5	AMFED NATIONAL INS CO	MS	68.9
NORMANDY INS CO	FL	46.9	ASCENDANT COMMERCIAL INS INC	FL	62.2
NORTHWEST GF MUTUAL INS CO	SD	18.4	ATLANTIC BONDING CO	MD	7.9
OTSEGO COUNTY PATRONS CO-OP F R ASN	NY	2.1	CASUALTY CORP OF AMERICA	OK	12.2
PALISADES P&C INS CO	NJ	15.1	CONIFER INS CO	MI	95.8
PARAMOUNT INS CO	MD	11.7	COUNTRY-WIDE INS CO	NY	247.0
PEACHTREE CASUALTY INS CO	FL	20.3	FARMERS MUTUAL INS CO OF ELLINWOOD	KS	4.8
PENN RESERVE INS CO LTD	PA	2.0	FARMERS MUTUAL INS CO OF MI	MI	1.7
PEOPLES TRUST INS CO	FL	226.9	KENTUCKIANA MEDICAL RRG & INS CO INC	KY	53.8
PHYSICIANS IND RRG INC	NV	6.1	LEXINGTON NATIONAL INS CORP	FL	58.8
PIA PROFESSIONAL LIABILITY INS RRG	MT	2.1	LIGHTHOUSE CASUALTY CO	IL	27.4
PROFESSIONAL EXCHANGE ASR CO (A RRG)	HI	17.0	MACHINERY INS INC	FL	2.8
PROFESSIONALS RRG INC	MT	4.7	MIDVALE INDEMNITY CO	IL	12.1
PUERTO RICO MED DEFENSE MUT INS CO	PR	18.4	NATIONAL BUILDING MATERIAL ASR CO	IN	6.4
QBE SEGUROS	PR	56.0	OCEANUS INS CO A RRG	SC	52.9
QUALITAS INS CO	CA	66.9	PACIFIC SPECIALTY PROPERTY & CAS CO	TX	5.4
RECREATION RRG INC	VT	4.1	PHYSICIANS INS EXCHANGE RESOURCE RRG	VT	3.9
ROMULUS INS RRG INC	SC	2.3	PLATINUM TRANSPORT INS RRG INC	HI	5.5
SAFECARD SERVICES INS CO	ND	2.0	SEABRIGHT INS CO	TX	58.9
SAGE RRG INC	NV	3.7	ST CHARLES INS CO RRG	SC	16.1
SAMSUNG FIRE & MARINE INS CO LTD US	NY	249.7	STATES SELF-INSURERS RISK RET GROUP	VT	26.0
SCRUBS MUTUAL ASR CO RRG	NV	17.8	TRANSIT MUTUAL INS CORP OF WI	WI	16.0
SECURITY PLAN FIRE INS CO	LA	8.0	WASHINGTON CASUALTY CO	WA	24.9
SFM SAFE INS CO	MN	5.3	WHITECAP SURETY CO	MN	1.6
SOMPO JAPAN NIPPONKOA INS INC	GU	8.6	WINDHAVEN INS CO	FL	227.6
SOUTHWEST GENERAL INS CO	NM	2.2	**Rating: E+**		
STAR & SHIELD INS EXCHANGE	FL	9.9	ALLEGIANT INS CO INC A RRG	HI	27.2
STAR CASUALTY INS CO	FL	15.4	AMERICAN TRANSIT INS CO	NY	473.1
STERLING CASUALTY INS CO	CA	16.6	AMERICAN TRUCKING & TRANSP INS RRG	MT	36.7
STICO MUTUAL INS CO RRG	VT	23.1	ARCOA RRG INC	NV	15.8
STONEGATE INS CO	IL	22.9	CAPITOL INS CO	PA	17.7
TOWER HILL PREFERRED INS CO	FL	102.8	FAITH AFFILIATED RRG INC	VT	5.8
TOWER HILL PRIME INS CO	FL	204.3	FULMONT MUTUAL INS CO	NY	3.3
TRANSPORTATION INS SVCS RRG	SC	1.4	GOLDEN INS CO A RRG	NV	13.7
UNDERWRITERS AT LLOYDS (IL)	IL	352.1	GRANADA INS CO	FL	38.5
UNDERWRITERS AT LLOYDS (KY)	KY	171.1	GUARANTEE INS CO	FL	400.4
UNIQUE INS CO	IL	89.1	HOSPITALITY RRG INC	VT	3.9
UNITED BUS INS CO	GA	11.7	KOOKMIN BEST INS CO LTD US BR	NY	296.6
UNITED GROUP CAPTIVE INS CO	GA	1.3	LANCET IND RRG INC	NV	21.7
UNITED SECURITY HEALTH & CASUALTY	IL	2.9	MAIDSTONE INS CO	NY	54.6
UNIVERSAL P&C INS CO	FL	957.5	MAYA ASR CO	NY	18.0
UPMC HEALTH BENEFITS INC	PA	174.4	MBIA INS CORP	NY	228.8
URGENT CARE ASR CO RRG INC	NV	5.7	NEW YORK HEALTHCARE INS CO INC RRG	DC	23.0
URGENT MD RRG INC	VT	5.9	OLD AMERICAN CTY MUTUAL FIRE INS CO	TX	131.6
US LEGAL SERVICES INC	TN	3.6	ONYX INS CO INC A RRG	TN	29.1
UTAH BUSINESS INS CO	UT	21.7	STONINGTON INS CO	PA	15.1

INSURANCE COMPANY NAME	DOM. STATE	TOTAL ASSETS ($MIL)
Rating: E+ (Continued)		
UNITED HERITAGE PROP & CAS CO	ID	42.3
VICTORY INS CO	MT	12.1
WELLSPAN RRG	VT	34.0
WESTERN CATHOLIC INS CO RRG	VT	4.0
Rating: E		
ACCIDENT INS CO	NM	89.8
ALLIANCE NATIONAL INS CO	NY	48.2
ALLIED PREMIER INS A RRG	CT	3.6
ALLIED SERVICES RRG	SC	6.3
AMBAC ASSURANCE CORP	WI	5,496.2
AMERICAN LIBERTY INS CO	UT	14.5
APOLLO CASUALTY CO	IL	13.8
BUILDING INDUSTRY INS ASSN INC	VA	21.8
CALIFORNIA MEDICAL GROUP INS CO RRG	AZ	15.3
CHEROKEE GUARANTEE CO INC A RRG	AZ	23.2
COLUMBIA NATIONAL RRG INC	VT	1.9
COMMONWEALTH CASUALTY CO	AZ	25.4
CONTINUING CARE RRG INC	VT	6.3
CRYSTAL RUN RECIPROCAL RRG	VT	21.3
DIST-CO INS CO INC RRG	HI	3.8
EXCELA RECIPROCAL RRG	VT	13.2
FARMINGTON MUTUAL INS CO	WI	8.5
FINANCIAL GUARANTY INS CO	NY	2,467.9
GABLES RRG INC	VT	11.6
GOVT TECHNOLOGY INS CO RRG INC	NV	2.0
GREEN HILLS INS CO A RRG	VT	12.8
GUARDIAN INDEMNITY INC	MT	6.2
INNOVATIVE PHYSICIAN SOLUTIONS RRG	VT	4.7
KEYSTONE MUTUAL INS CO	MO	3.0
MOUNTAIN LAUREL RRG INC	VT	18.4
MUNICIPAL ASR CORP	NY	1,091.2
NOVANT HEALTH RRG INC	SC	9.8
ORISKA INS CO	NY	38.8
ORTHOFORUM INS CO	SC	22.7
PHOEBE RECIPROCAL RRG	SC	4.6
PHYSICIANS CASUALTY RRG INC	AL	13.9
PREFERRED CONTRACTORS INS CO RRG LLC	MT	96.7
PREMIER PHYSICIANS INS CO	NV	12.4
PUBLIC UTILITY MUTUAL INS CO RRG	VT	7.8
SECURITY AMERICA RRG INC	VT	4.8
SENTINEL ASR RRG INC	HI	17.2
SPIRIT COMMERCIAL AUTO RRG INC	NV	103.2
SPRING VALLEY MUTUAL INS CO	MN	4.6
ST LUKES HEALTH NETWORK INS CO RRG	VT	65.0
SUNZ INS CO	FL	140.2
SYNCORA CAPITAL ASR INC	NY	424.2
TRINITY RISK SOLUTIONS RECIP INS RRG	DC	9.1
UNITED AUTOMOBILE INS CO	FL	290.3
UNITED CENTRAL PA RRG	VT	21.8
VFH CAPTIVE INS CO	GA	5.9
WORKERS COMPENSATION EXCHANGE	ID	7.8
Rating: E-		
ACADEMIC HLTH PROFESSIONALS INS ASSO	NY	325.1

INSURANCE COMPANY NAME	DOM. STATE	TOTAL ASSETS ($MIL)
AF&L INS CO	PA	139.2
AVIATION ALLIANCE INS RRG INC	MT	3.0
ELITE TRANSPORTATION RRG INC	VT	14.4
GLOBAL HAWK INS CO RRG	VT	51.8
HEALTHCARE PROVIDERS INS EXCH	PA	37.4
INS PLACEMENT FACILITY OF PA	PA	7.5
INSUREMAX INS CO	IN	2.9
MISSOURI DOCTORS MUTUAL INS CO	MO	4.5
MISSOURI PROFESSIONALS MUTUAL INS CO	MO	15.5
NORTHWESTERN NATL INS CO SEG ACCNT	WI	22.3
PARK INS CO	NY	34.5
PHYSICIANS INS MUTUAL	MO	3.9
PHYSICIANS RECIPROCAL INSURERS	NY	1,189.6
SENIOR AMERICAN INS CO	PA	13.3
SYNCORA GUARANTEE INC	NY	1,267.9
TEXAS FAIR PLAN ASSN	TX	70.7
Rating: F		
ACCEPTANCE INS CO	NE	15.1
AFFIRMATIVE CASUALTY INS CO	LA	35.4
AFFIRMATIVE DIRECT INS CO	NY	5.1
AFFIRMATIVE INS CO OF MI	MI	9.5
ARGUS FIRE & CASUALTY INS CO	FL	3.5
CARECONCEPTS INS INC A RRG	MT	3.8
CASTLEPOINT FLORIDA INS	FL	10.0
CASTLEPOINT INS CO	NY	178.4
COMMERCIAL MUT INS CO	GA	0.0
CORNERSTONE MUTUAL INS CO	GA	0.0
DOCTORS & SURGEONS NATL RRG IC	VT	9.1
FIDUCIARY INS CO OF AMERICA	NY	38.5
FLORIDA SELECT INS CO	FL	0.0
GALEN INS CO	MO	9.3
GULF BUILDERS RRG INC	SC	0.0
HERMITAGE INS CO	NY	167.6
HIGHLANDS INS CO	TX	0.0
HOME VALUE INS CO	OH	0.0
HOSPITALITY MUT CAPT INS CO	GA	0.0
IFA INS CO	NJ	3.0
LEMIC INS CO	LA	0.0
LIBERTY FIRST RRG INS CO	UT	0.0
LUMBER MUTUAL INS CO	MA	0.0
LUMBERMENS UNDERWRITING ALLIANCE	MO	354.2
MANHATTAN RE-INS CO	DE	0.0
MASSACHUSETTS HOMELAND INS CO	MA	8.9
MILLERS CLASSIFIED INS CO	IL	2.7
MILLERS FIRST INS CO	IL	7.8
NORTH EAST INS CO	ME	35.9
NORTHWESTERN NTL INS CO MILWAUKEE	WI	22.5
PAFCO GENERAL INS CO	IN	0.0
PHOENIX FUND INC	NC	0.0
PMI INS CO	AZ	115.2
PMI MORTGAGE INS CO	AZ	926.7
PROAIR RRG INC	NV	0.5
PUBLIC SERVICE INS CO	IL	295.1
REPUB MORTGAGE INS CO	NC	638.1
SAN ANTONIO INDEMNITY CO	TX	0.0

INSURANCE COMPANY NAME	DOM. STATE	TOTAL ASSETS ($MIL)	INSURANCE COMPANY NAME	DOM. STATE	TOTAL ASSETS ($MIL)
Rating: F **(Continued)**			BUNKER HILL PREFERRED INS CO	MA	10.8
			BUNKER HILL PROPERTY INS CO	MA	10.8
SHELBY INS CO	TX	0.0	BUNKER HILL SECURITY INS CO	MA	10.8
TRIAD GUARANTY ASR CORP	IL	0.0	CAMBRIA COUNTY MUTUAL INS CO	PA	0.4
TRIAD GUARANTY INS CORP	IL	0.0	CATAWBA INS CO	SC	6.1
UNION MUTUAL INS CO	OK	5.1	CATTLEMANS INS CO A RRG	MT	0.6
VESTA INS CORP	TX	0.0	CENTRE INS CO	DE	57.3
YORK INS CO OF MAINE	ME	47.0	CENTURY INDEMNITY CO	PA	562.0
Rating: U			CHARITABLE SERVICE PROVIDERS RRG	AZ	3.5
21ST CENTURY AUTO INS CO OF NJ	NJ	25.2	CHURCH INS CO	NY	24.2
21ST CENTURY INS CO OF THE SW	TX	6.6	CINCINNATI EQUITABLE INS CO	OH	3.2
21ST CENTURY SUPERIOR INS CO	CA	33.8	CLINIC MUTUAL INS CO RRG	HI	4.1
ACA FINANCIAL GUARANTY CORP	MD	303.5	CODAN INS CO LTD	NY	2.1
AETNA INS CO OF CT	CT	16.2	COLISEUM REINS CO	DE	269.9
AFFILIATES INS CO	IN	71.3	COLUMBIA INS CO	NE	21,543.5
AGIC INC	FL	2.3	COMMERCIAL CASUALTY INS CO	IN	66.6
AIMCO MUTUAL INS CO	NC	7.6	COMMONWEALTH INS CO OF AMERICA	DE	10.8
ALEA NORTH AMERICA INS CO	NY	78.9	COMMUNITY HEALTH ALLIANCE RECIP RRG	VT	50.8
ALLSTATE NORTH AMERICAN INS CO	IL	10.8	COMPASS INS CO	NY	12.3
AMBAC ASR CORP SEGREGATED ACCT	WI	8.0	COMPUTER INS CO	RI	23.4
AMERICAN BUILDERS INS CO RRG INC	AL	0.7	CONSOLIDATED INS ASSN	TX	2.9
AMERICAN EQUITY INS CO	AZ	101.8	CONSOLIDATED LLOYDS	TX	1.6
AMERICAN FARMERS & RANCHERS INS CO	OK	8.8	CONTINENTAL RISK UNDERWRITERS RRG IN	NV	0.4
AMERICAN FEED INDUSTRY INS CO RRG	IA	1.5	COPIC A RRG	DC	0.8
AMERICAN HEALTHCARE INDEMNITY CO	OK	21.6	COPPERPOINT PREMIER INS CO	AZ	20.0
AMERICAN MEDICAL ASR CO	IL	3.2	COVENTRY INS CO	RI	1.9
AMERICAN PACIFIC INS CO	HI	11.6	CRONUS INSURANCE CO	TX	20.0
AMERICAN PHYSICIANS ASR CORP	MI	330.2	DANIELSON NATIONAL INS CO	CA	6.0
AMERICAN SPECIAL RISK INS CO	DE	0.8	EAGLE BUILDERS INS CO RRG INC	NC	1.5
AMSHIELD INS CO	MO	6.9	ELIZABETHTOWN INS CO	DE	3.9
ARCH EXCESS & SURPLUS INS CO	MO	69.1	EMPIRE INS CO	NY	23.4
ARCH MORTGAGE ASR CO	WI	15.9	EMPLOYERS FIRE INS CO	PA	12.1
ARCH STRUCTURED MRTG INS CO	NC	8.6	ENCOMPASS FLORIDIAN INDEMNITY CO	IL	4.9
ARGONAUT LTD RISK INS CO	IL	11.8	ENCOMPASS FLORIDIAN INS CO	IL	4.9
ARI CASUALTY CO	NJ	8.2	EVEREST DENALI INSURANCE CO	DE	25.4
ARROWOOD SURPLUS LINES INS CO	DE	89.0	EVEREST PREMIER INSURANCE CO	DE	25.6
ASCENT INSURANCE CO	IL	2.0	EVERGREEN USA RRG INC	VT	10.0
ASHLAND MUTUAL FIRE INS CO OF PA	PA	0.5	EVERSPAN FINANCIAL GUARANTEE CORP	WI	231.6
ASHMERE INS CO	FL	10.2	EXCALIBUR REINS CORP	PA	9.0
ASPEN SPECIALTY RRG INC	DC	0.4	EXECUTIVE INS CO	NY	1.4
ASSET PROTECTION PROGRAM RRG INC	SC	1.1	EXPLORER AMERICAN INS CO	CA	2.6
ATLANTA INTERNATIONAL INS CO	NY	24.8	FACILITY INS CORP	TX	102.6
ATRIUM INS CORP	NY	1.6	FARMERS REINS CO	CA	163.5
AUTO CLUB CASUALTY CO	TX	2.9	FB INS CO	KY	1.3
AUTO-OWNERS SPECIALTY INS CO	DE	28.4	FCCI ADVANTAGE INS CO	FL	7.3
AVIVA INS CO OF CANADA (US BR)	NY	17.1	FCCI COMMERCIAL INS CO	FL	14.8
AWBURY INS CO	DE	1.0	FEDERATED RESERVE INS CO	MN	123.3
AXIS SPECIALTY INS CO	CT	65.4	FIDELITY MOHAWK INS CO	NJ	18.1
BALTIMORE EQUITABLE SOCIETY	MD	161.9	FIRST JERSEY CASUALTY INS CO INC	NJ	5.3
BAY INS RRG INC	SC	0.8	FIRST PROFESSIONALS INS CO INC	FL	261.9
BEACONHARBOR MUTUAL RRG	ME	1.0	FIRST PROTECTIVE INS CO	FL	194.4
BLACK DIAMOND INS CO	NV	0.0	FIRST STATE INS CO	CT	135.6
BLUE HILL SPECIALTY INS CO	IL	15.5	FIRST WASHINGTON INS CO	DC	0.6
BROOKWOOD INS CO	IA	7.6	FOUNDERS INS CO OF MI	MI	6.0
BTTS INS RRG GROUP INC	SC	0.6	FRONTLINE INS UNLIMITED CO	IL	32.1
BUCKS COUNTY CONTRIBUTIONSHIP	PA	6.7	GENWORTH FINANCIAL ASR CORP	NC	8.2

INSURANCE COMPANY NAME	DOM. STATE	TOTAL ASSETS ($MIL)	INSURANCE COMPANY NAME	DOM. STATE	TOTAL ASSETS ($MIL)
Rating: U (Continued)			MIDSTATES REINS CORP	IL	78.2
GLOBAL HAWK PROPERTY CAS INS CO	DE	6.5	MISSOURI PHYSICIANS ASSOCIATES	MO	1.9
GLOBAL INS CO	GA	3.5	MLM RRG INC	DC	1.0
GLOBAL REINS CORP OF AM	NY	257.0	MMIC RRG INC	DC	0.7
GOLDSTREET INS CO	NY	5.4	MOUNTAINPOINT INS CO	AZ	12.1
GOVERNMENT ENTITIES MUTUAL INC	DC	74.0	MYCOMPASS INC	IA	5.0
GRACO RRG INC	SC	1.7	NATIONAL AMERICAN INS CO OF CA	CA	26.6
GRAY INS CO OF LOUISIANA	LA	6.0	NATIONAL BAIL & SURETY CO	FL	2.0
GREAT AMERICAN CASUALTY INS CO	OH	11.0	NATIONAL BUILDERS & CONTRACTORS INS	NV	2.9
GREAT AMERICAN CONTEMPORARY INS CO	OH	10.6	NATIONAL HOME INS CO RRG	CO	15.6
GREAT AMERICAN LLOYDS INS CO	TX	1.5	NATIONAL INS ASSN	IN	13.6
GREAT AMERICAN PROTECTION INS CO	OH	22.3	NATIONAL MEDICAL PROFESSIONAL RRG	SC	3.0
GREAT LAKES CASUALTY INS CO	MI	18.2	NEVADA DOCS MEDICAL RRG INC	NV	2.6
GREEN TREE PERPETUAL ASR CO	PA	0.2	NEW ENGLAND GUARANTY INS CO INC	VT	45.9
GUILDERLAND REINS CO	NY	3.9	NEW ENGLAND INS CO	CT	19.2
GULF STATES INS CO (LA)	LA	5.1	NEW ENGLAND REINS CORP	CT	38.2
GULF UNDERWRITERS INS CO	CT	52.7	NEW HORIZON INS CO	TX	7.0
HAMDEN ASR RRG INC	VT	92.2	NEW MEXICO PROPERTY & CASUALTY CO	NM	1.4
HANOVER NATIONAL INS CO	NH	12.6	NEW YORK TRANSPORTATION INS CORP	NY	0.0
HANOVER NJ INS CO	NH	32.7	NEWPORT INS CO	AZ	11.6
HDI SPECIALTY INSURANCE CO	IL	15.0	NORTH STAR GENERAL INS CO	MN	4.3
HERITAGE CASUALTY INS CO	KS	17.6	NW FARMERS MUTUAL INSURANCE CO	NC	5.4
HILLSTAR INS CO	IN	3.6	OAKWOOD INS CO	TN	61.0
HOME CONSTRUCTION INS CO	NV	5.3	OBI AMERICA INS CO	PA	15.4
HOMEOWNERS CHOICE ASR CO INC	AL	1.9	OBSTETRICIANS & GYNECOLOGISTS RRG	MT	0.5
HOMESHIELD FIRE & CASUALTY INS CO	OK	1.1	OHIC INS CO	OH	99.7
HOMESTEAD INS CO	PA	4.4	OKLAHOMA P&C INS CO	OK	3.4
HORIZON MIDWEST CASUALTY CO	KS	2.6	OLD ELIZABETH MUTUAL FIRE INS CO	PA	0.6
HOUSTON GENERAL INS EXCH	TX	5.2	OMAHA INDEMNITY CO	WI	14.8
HOW INS CO A RRG	VA	0.4	ONECIS INS CO	IL	22.6
INDEPENDENT SPECIALTY INS CO	DE	72.7	ORDINARY MUTUAL A RRG CORP	VT	1.6
INS CO OF THE AMERICAS	FL	6.0	P&S INS RRG INC	SC	0.8
INTEGRITY SELECT INSURANCE CO	WI	6.5	PALADIN REINS CORP	NY	1.3
ISMIE INDEMNITY CO	IL	53.6	PASSPORT INS CO	ND	2.0
JM SPECIALTY INSURANCE CO	WI	8.0	PAWTUCKET INS CO	RI	6.8
JM WOODWORTH RRG INC	NV	6.6	PENNSYLVANIA PHYSICIANS RECIP INS	PA	4.8
KAMMCO CASUALTY CO	KS	5.5	PHILADELPHIA REINS CORP	PA	6.5
KEMPER FINANCIAL INDEMNITY CO	IL	20.6	POLICYHOLDERS MUTUAL INS CO	WI	0.3
LAMORAK INS CO	PA	25.4	POTOMAC INS CO	PA	11.0
LEGAL MUTUAL LIAB INS SOCIETY OF MD	MD	0.5	PREFERRED PROFESSIONAL RRG	DC	0.8
LEON HIX INS CO	SC	3.4	PREMIER INS EXCHANGE RRG	VT	7.8
LIBERTY AMERICAN INS CO	FL	8.7	PROBUILDERS SPECIALTY INS CO RRG	DC	13.1
LIBERTY AMERICAN SELECT INS CO	FL	6.1	PROFESSIONAL QUALITY LIABILITY INS	VT	2.0
LM P&C INS CO	IN	64.2	PROGRESSIVE CHOICE INS CO	OH	6.8
LR INS INC	DE	1.7	PROGRESSIVE COMMERCIAL CASUALTY CO	OH	8.3
LVHN RRG	SC	65.0	PROSELECT NATIONAL INS CO INC	AZ	13.3
MADA INS EXCHANGE	MN	0.4	PROTECTION MUTUAL INS CO	PA	0.6
MEDSTAR LIABILITY LTD INS CO INC RRG	DC	3.7	PROTUCKET INSURANCE CO	RI	3.0
MERCHANTS PROPERTY INS CO OF IN	IN	80.0	PROVIDENCE PLANTATIONS INS CO	RI	1.2
MERITPLAN INS CO	CA	13.4	PROVIDENCE WASHINGTON INS CO	RI	178.2
MGIC CREDIT ASR CORP	WI	8.5	QUALITY CASUALTY INS CO	AL	0.8
MICA RRG INC	DC	0.8	QUEEN CITY ASR INC	VT	2,497.4
MICO INS CO	OH	11.3	R&Q REINS CO	PA	211.8
MID AMERICAN FIRE & CAS CO	NH	8.4	RADIAN GUARANTY REINS INC	PA	5.8
MID-CENTURY INS CO OF TX	TX	39.2	RADIAN INVESTOR SURETY INC	PA	4.9
			RADIAN MORTGAGE ASR INC	PA	8.8

INSURANCE COMPANY NAME	DOM. STATE	TOTAL ASSETS ($MIL)	INSURANCE COMPANY NAME	DOM. STATE	TOTAL ASSETS ($MIL)
Rating: U (Continued)					
RADIAN MORTGAGE GUARANTY INC	PA	19.7			
RADIAN MORTGAGE INS INC	PA	2.8			
RAMPART INS CO	NY	28.1			
REPUBLIC RRG	SC	1.7			
RESPONSE WORLDWIDE DIRECT AUTO INS	IL	10.3			
RESPONSE WORLDWIDE INS CO	IL	11.5			
ROOT INS CO	OH	8.1			
RPX RRG INC	HI	4.8			
SAFECO SURPLUS LINES INS CO	NH	42.1			
SALEM COUNTY MUTUAL FIRE INS CO	NJ	0.0			
SAN DIEGO INS CO	CA	70.5			
SAUCON MUTUAL INS CO	PA	20.0			
SEAWAY MUTUAL INS CO	PA	2.1			
SELECT INS CO	TX	80.2			
SELECT MARKETS INS CO	IL	16.1			
SENIORSFIRST RRG INC	NC	1.0			
SLAVONIC INS CO OF TEXAS	TX	5.0			
SOMPO JAPAN CANOPIUS RE AG	DE	25.4			
SOUTHERN FARM BUREAU PROPERTY	MS	56.7			
SOUTHLAND LLOYDS INS CO	TX	0.0			
SOUTHWEST PHYSICIANS RRG INC	SC	59.2			
SPECIALTY SURPLUS INS CO	IL	17.2			
ST CLAIR INS CO	NY	0.8			
STARR SPECIALTY INSURANCE CO	TX	20.1			
STERLING INS COOP INC	NY	0.4			
STONE VALLEY MUTUAL FIRE INS CO	PA	0.8			
SUBURBAN HEALTH ORG RRG LLC	SC	3.3			
SUECIA INS CO	NY	45.3			
TEXAS BUILDERS INS CO	TX	12.0			
THIRD COAST INS CO	WI	19.2			
TM SPECIALTY INS CO	AZ	40.0			
TRANSPORT INS CO	OH	35.8			
TRANSPORT RISK SOLUTIONS RRG	SC	1.0			
TRAVEL AIR INS CO (KS)	KS	5.1			
TRENWICK AMERICA REINSURANCE CORP	CT	54.1			
TRIDENT INSURANCE GROUP INC	MD	2.0			
TRUSTSTAR INS CO	MD	0.6			
UNITED AMERICAS INS CO	NY	5.6			
UNITED GUARANTY COML INS CO OF NC	NC	67.8			
UNITED HOME INS CO A RRG	VT	1.4			
UNITED INTERNATIONAL INS CO	NY	4.8			
UPPER HUDSON NATIONAL INS CO	NE	3.1			
USAA COUNTY MUTUAL INS CO	TX	5.4			
UTICA SPECIALTY RISK INS CO	TX	32.4			
VANTAGE CASUALTY INS CO	IN	78.1			
VANTAPRO SPECIALTY INS CO	AR	24.0			
VEHICULAR SERVICE INS CO RRG	OK	2.6			
VICTORIA NATIONAL INS CO	OH	3.6			
WALL ROSE MUTUAL INS CO	PA	1.0			
WARNER INS CO	IL	15.5			
WATFORD INS CO	NJ	22.9			
WESCAP INS CO	CO	3.6			
WESTERN PROFESSIONAL INS CO	WA	13.7			
WRM AMERICA INDEMNITY CO	NY	15.1			

Section VII

Rating Upgrades and Downgrades

A list of all

U.S. Property and Casualty Insurers

receiving a rating upgrade or downgrade
during the current quarter.

Section VII Contents

This section identifies those companies receiving a rating change since the previous edition of this publication, whether it is a rating upgrade, rating downgrade, newly rated company or the withdrawal of a rating. A rating may be withdrawn due to a merger, dissolution, or liquidation. A rating upgrade or downgrade may entail a change from one letter grade to another, or it may mean the addition or deletion of a plus or minus sign within the same letter grade previously assigned to the company. Ratings are normally updated once each quarter of the year. In some instances, however, a company's rating may be downgraded outside of the normal updates due to overriding circumstances.

Unlike other rating agencies, Weiss ratings are reviewed each and every quarter to ensure that the company's current rating reflects the most recent information available. This allows us to react more promptly and with greater flexibility to changing conditions as they occur. In addition, we are not inhibited to upgrade or downgrade a company as soon as its financial condition warrants the change. You should therefore consider the magnitude of the rating change along with the meaning of the new rating when evaluating the significance of a rating upgrade or downgrade.

1.	**Insurance Company Name**	The legally-registered name, which can sometimes differ from the name that the company uses for advertising. An insurer's name can be very similar to that of another, so verify the company's exact name and state of domicile to make sure you are looking at the correct company.
2.	**Domicile State**	The state which has primary regulatory responsibility for the company. It may differ from the location of the company's corporate headquarters. You do not have to be living in the domicile state to purchase insurance from this firm, provided it is licensed to do business in your state.
3.	**Total Assets**	All assets admitted by state insurance regulators in millions of dollars. This includes investments and current business assets such as receivables from agents and reinsurers.
4.	**New Safety Rating**	The rating assigned to the company as of the date of this Guide's publication. Our rating is measured on a scale from A to F and considers a wide range of factors. Highly-rated companies are, in our opinion, less likely to experience financial difficulties than lower-rated firms. See *About Weiss Safety Ratings* for more information.
5.	**Previous Safety Rating**	The rating assigned to the company prior to its most recent change.
6.	**Date of Change**	The date that the rating upgrade or downgrade officially occurred. Normally, all rating changes are put into effect on a single day each quarter of the year. In some instances, however, a rating may have been changed outside of this normal update.

Appearing in this Edition for the First Time

None during this quarter

Withdrawn Ratings

INSURANCE COMPANY NAME	DOM. STATE	TOTAL ASSETS ($MIL)	NEW RATING	PREVIOUS RATING	DATE OF CHANGE
AMICA TEXAS INS CO	TX	77.8	U	B	07/17/17
ATHENS FINANCIAL INS CO	OK	2.2	U	B-	07/17/17
COMPSOURCE MUTUAL INS CO	OK	0.0	U	U	07/17/17
GUIDEONE TEXAS INS CO	TX	3.3	U	B-	07/17/17
MICHIGAN AUTO INS PLACEMENT FACILITY	MI	0.0	U	U	07/17/17
MIDDLESEX MUTUAL ASR CO	CT	197.0	U	B	07/17/17
MOUNTAIN STATES MUTUAL CAS CO	NM	141.2	U	C-	07/17/17
PINE TREE INS RECIPROCAL RRG	VT	10.6	U	D-	07/17/17
SPARTA AMERICAN INS CO	CA	33.0	U	C	07/17/17
STATE INS FUND	NY	0.0	U	U	07/17/17
STATE INS FUND DISABILITY BENEFITS	NY	0.0	U	U	07/17/17

Rating Upgrades

ACADEMIC MEDICAL PROFESSIONALS RRG was upgraded to D- from E+ in July 2017 based on an increase in the stability index from a 0.50(weak) to 1.00(weak), profitability index from a 6.40(good) to 6.70(good), and capitalization index from a 6.80(good) to 6.90(excellent).

AMERICAN BUS & MERCANTILE INS MUT was upgraded to C from C- in July 2017 based on an increase in the stability index from a 2.90(fair) to 3.40(fair). Other factors: Capital and surplus increased during the period by 5.6%, from $30.6 million to $32.3 million.

AMERICAN COASTAL INS CO was upgraded to B- from C+ in July 2017 based on an increase in the capitalization index from a 9.30(excellent) to 10.00(excellent) and stability index from a 4.50(fair) to 5.00(good).

AMERICAN PET INS CO was upgraded to C- from D+ in July 2017 based on an increase in the capitalization index from a 2.50(weak) to 4.30(fair), stability index from a 2.50(weak) to 3.00(fair), and profitability index from a 8.80(excellent) to 8.90(excellent). Other factors: The company's net asset base increased during the period by 11.0%, from $55.2 million to $61.2 million.

AMERIGUARD RRG INC was upgraded to C- from D+ in July 2017 based on an increase in the stability index from a 2.50(weak) to 2.80(weak).

AMFED CASUALTY INS CO was upgraded to C- from D+ in July 2017 based on an increase in the profitability index from a 7.00(excellent) to 7.10(excellent).

AMICA P&C INS CO was upgraded to B- from C+ in July 2017 based on an increase in the stability index from a 4.50(fair) to 5.00(good).

APPOLLO CASUALTY CO was upgraded or to E from E- in July 2017 based on the overall strength of the index ratios.

APPLIED UNDERWRITERS CAPTIVE RISK was upgraded to C- from D+ in July 2017 based on an increase in the stability index from a 2.50(weak) to 3.00(fair).

ARCH MORTGAGE REINS CO was upgraded to C+ from C in July 2017 based on an increase in the stability index from a 3.10(fair) to 3.30(fair).

ASI SELECT INS CORP was upgraded to C- from D+ in July 2017 based on an increase in the stability index from a 2.50(weak) to 3.00(fair).

ATTORNEYS INS MUTUAL RRG was upgraded or to C- from D+ in July 2017 based on the overall strength of the index ratios.

BALDWIN MUTUAL INS CO was upgraded or to C- from D+ in July 2017 based on the overall strength of the index ratios.

BANKERS SPECIALTY INS CO was upgraded to B- from C+ in July 2017 based on an increase in the stability index from a 4.50(fair) to 5.00(good).

BOND SAFEGUARD INS CO was upgraded to C- from D+ in July 2017 based on an increase in the capitalization index from a 7.10(excellent) to 7.70(excellent).

BRICKSTREET MUTUAL INS CO was upgraded to B- from C+ in July 2017 based on an increase in the capitalization index from a 7.90(excellent) to 8.50(excellent) and stability index from a 4.50(fair) to 5.00(good).

BUSINESSFIRST INS CO was upgraded to B- from C+ in July 2017 based on an increase in the stability index from a 4.50(fair) to 5.00(good).

CALIFORNIA MUTUAL INS CO was upgraded or to C- from D+ in July 2017 based on the overall strength of the index ratios.

CARE WEST INS CO was upgraded to C- from D+ in July 2017 based on an increase in the capitalization index from a 4.60(fair) to 5.30(good) and stability index from a 2.50(weak) to 3.00(fair). Other factors: The company's net asset base increased during the period by 5.4%, from $125.8 million to $132.6 million.

CAREGIVERS UNITED LIAB INS CO RRG was upgraded to C- from D+ in July 2017 based on an increase in the stability index from a 2.50(weak) to 3.00(fair). Other factors: The company's net asset base increased during the period by 9.5%, from $41.0 million to $44.9 million.

CARING COMMUNITIES RECIP RRG was upgraded to B- from C+ in July 2017 based on an increase in the stability index from a 4.50(fair) to 5.00(good). Other factors: The company's net asset base increased during the period by 21.3%, from $79.4 million to $96.3 million.

CATASTROPHE REINS CO was upgraded to C- from D+ in July 2017 based on an increase in the stability index from a 2.50(weak) to 3.00(fair).

CENTURION MEDICAL LIAB PROTECT RRG was upgraded to C- from D+ in July 2017 based on an increase in the stability index from a 2.50(weak) to 3.00(fair).

CHEROKEE INS CO was upgraded to B- from C+ in July 2017 based on an increase in the stability index from a 4.50(fair) to 5.00(good). Other factors: The company's net asset base increased during the period by 5.1%, from $498.5 million to $523.9 million.

CINCINNATI SPECIALTY UNDERWRITER was upgraded to A- from B+ in July 2017 based on an increase in the stability index from a 6.50(good) to 7.00(excellent).

CM REGENT INS CO was upgraded to B- from C+ in July 2017 based on an increase in the stability index from a 4.50(fair) to 5.00(good) and capitalization index from a 8.40(excellent) to 8.90(excellent).

COLONIAL SURETY CO was upgraded to B- from C+ in July 2017 based on an increase in the stability index from a 4.50(fair) to 5.00(good) and capitalization index from a 9.90(excellent) to 10.00(excellent).

COMMUNITY HOSPITAL ALTERNATIVE RRG was upgraded to B- from C+ in July 2017 based on an increase in the stability index from a 4.50(fair) to 5.00(good). Other factors: The company's net asset base increased during the period by 15.2%, from $240.1 million to $276.5 million.

COMPWEST INS CO was upgraded to B- from C+ in July 2017 based on an increase in the stability index from a 4.50(fair) to 5.00(good) and profitability index from a 8.50(excellent) to 8.70(excellent).

CONTRACTORS INS CO OF NORTH AMER RRG was upgraded to C- from D+ in July 2017 based on an increase in the stability index from a 2.50(weak) to 3.00(fair), profitability index from a 5.30(good) to 5.50(good), and capitalization index from a 8.70(excellent) to 8.80(excellent). Other factors: Capital and surplus increased during the period by 6.6%, from $25.8 million to $27.5 million.

COPIC INS CO was upgraded to A- from B+ in July 2017 based on an increase in the stability index from a 6.50(good) to 7.00(excellent).

CUMIS INS SOCIETY INC was upgraded to A- from B+ in July 2017 based on an increase in the stability index from a 6.50(good) to 6.90(excellent).

DISTRICTS MUTL INS & RISK MGMT was upgraded to C- from D+ in July 2017 based on an increase in the stability index from a 2.50(weak) to 3.00(fair) and profitability index from a 4.60(fair) to 4.90(good).

DRIVE NEW JERSEY INS CO was upgraded to B- from C+ in July 2017 based on an increase in the stability index from a 4.50(fair) to 5.00(good) and capitalization index from a 9.60(excellent) to 9.90(excellent). Other factors: The company's net asset base increased during the period by 21.4%, from $172.6 million to $209.6 million.

EASTERN DENTISTS INS CO RRG was upgraded to B- from C+ in July 2017 based on an increase in the stability index from a 4.50(fair) to 4.90(good).

EMPLOYERS COMPENSATION INS CO was upgraded to A- from B+ in July 2017 based on an increase in the capitalization index from a 7.60(excellent) to 7.70(excellent) and stability index from a 6.40(good) to 6.50(good).

ENDURANCE ASR CORP was upgraded to A- from B+ in July 2017 based on an increase in the stability index from a 6.50(good) to 7.00(excellent), profitability index from a 5.40(good) to 5.50(good), and capitalization index from a 8.30(excellent) to 8.40(excellent).

EXCALIBUR NATIONAL INS CO was upgraded to C- from D+ in July 2017 based on an increase in the stability index from a 1.40(weak) to 2.30(weak). Other factors: The company's net asset base increased during the period by 6.7%, from $10.9 million to $11.7 million.

FFVA MUTUAL INS CO was upgraded to B- from C+ in July 2017 based on an increase in the stability index from a 4.50(fair) to 5.00(good). Other factors: The company's net asset base increased during the period by 6.2%, from $328.0 million to $348.5 million.

FIRST CHOICE CASUALTY INS CO was upgraded to C- from D+ in July 2017 based on an increase in the profitability index from a 2.90(fair) to 3.20(fair). Other factors: The company's net asset base increased during the period by 6.0%, from $14.2 million to $15.1 million.

FLORIDA PENINSULA INS CO was upgraded to B- from C+ in July 2017 based on an increase in the stability index from a 4.50(fair) to 5.00(good) and capitalization index from a 7.60(excellent) to 7.80(excellent).

FORESTRY MUTUAL INS CO was upgraded to B- from C+ in July 2017 based on an increase in the stability index from a 4.50(fair) to 4.70(fair) and capitalization index from a 7.20(excellent) to 7.30(excellent). Other factors: The company's net asset base increased during the period by 9.5%, from $56.3 million to $61.7 million.

GENERAL INS CO OF AM was upgraded or to B- from C+ in July 2017 based on the overall strength of the index ratios.

GENWORTH MTG INS CORP OF NC was upgraded to B- from C+ in July 2017 based on an increase in the capitalization index from a 8.00(excellent) to 9.20(excellent) and profitability index from a 7.80(excellent) to 8.10(excellent). Other factors: Capital and surplus increased during the period by 8.3%, from $161.5 million to $174.8 million.

HAWAII EMPLOYERS MUTUAL INS CO was upgraded to B- from C+ in July 2017 based on an increase in the stability index from a 4.50(fair) to 5.00(good).

HEALTH CARE INDUSTRY LIAB RECIP INS was upgraded to C- from D+ in July 2017 based on an increase in the stability index from a 2.50(weak) to 3.00(fair) and capitalization index from a 8.50(excellent) to 8.90(excellent).

HEALTHCARE UNDERWRITERS GRP MUT OH was upgraded to B- from C+ in July 2017 based on an increase in the stability index from a 4.50(fair) to 5.00(good) and capitalization index from a 9.90(excellent) to 10.00(excellent).

HOMEOWNERS OF AMERICA INS CO was upgraded to C- from D+ in July 2017 based on an increase in the stability index from a 2.50(weak) to 3.00(fair). Other factors: The company's net asset base increased during the period by 11.2%, from $42.7 million to $47.4 million.

HOSPITALITY RRG INC was upgraded to E+ from E in July 2017 based on an increase in the stability index from a 0.00(weak) to 0.50(weak).

ILLINOIS INS CO was upgraded to B- from C+ in July 2017 based on an increase in the profitability index from a 8.90(excellent) to 9.00(excellent) and stability index from a 3.70(fair) to 3.80(fair). Other factors: The company's net asset base increased during the period by 5.7%, from $51.0 million to $53.9 million.

INDEPENDENCE CASUALTY INS CO was upgraded to C- from D+ in July 2017 based on an increase in the stability index from a 2.50(weak) to 3.00(fair).

INSPIRIEN INS CO was upgraded to C- from D+ in July 2017 based on an increase in the stability index from a 2.50(weak) to 3.00(fair). Other factors: The company's net asset base increased during the period by 6.0%, from $38.2 million to $40.5 million.

INTERBORO INS CO was upgraded to C- from D+ in July 2017 based on an increase in the stability index from a 2.50(weak) to 3.00(fair). Other factors: Capital and surplus increased during the period by 8.6%, from $40.4 million to $43.9 million.

KENTUCKIANA MEDICAL RRG & INS CO INC was upgraded to D- from E+ in July 2017 based on an increase in the stability index from a 0.50(weak) to 1.00(weak). Other factors: The company's net asset base increased during the period by 7.9%, from $49.9 million to $53.8 million.

KENTUCKY HOSPITAL INS CO RRG was upgraded to C- from D+ in July 2017 based on an increase in the profitability index from a 2.70(weak) to 3.10(fair) and stability index from a 2.50(weak) to 2.60(weak). Other factors: The company's net asset base increased during the period by 14.3%, from $18.3 million to $20.9 million. Capital and surplus increased during the period by 10.5%, from $7.3 million to $8.1 million.

LAMMICO RRG INC was upgraded to C- from D+ in July 2017 based on an increase in the stability index from a 1.40(weak) to 1.70(weak).

MD RRG INC was upgraded to C- from D+ in July 2017 based on an increase in the stability index from a 2.50(weak) to 3.00(fair). Other factors: The company's net asset base increased during the period by 6.5%, from $24.0 million to $25.6 million. Capital and surplus increased during the period by 5.3%, from $15.7 million to $16.5 million.

Rating Upgrades (Continued)

MEMBERS INS CO was upgraded to C- from D+ in July 2017 based on an increase in the stability index from a 2.50(weak) to 3.00(fair) and profitability index from a 3.90(fair) to 4.20(fair).

MERCURY INDEMNITY CO OF AMERICA was upgraded to C- from D+ in July 2017 based on an increase in the stability index from a 2.50(weak) to 3.00(fair).

MOTORISTS COMMERCIAL MUTUAL INS CO was upgraded to A- from B+ in July 2017 based on an increase in the stability index from a 6.50(good) to 6.90(excellent).

MUNICIPAL PROPERTY INS CO was upgraded to C- from D+ in July 2017 based on an increase in the capitalization index from a 5.60(good) to 6.00(good) and profitability index from a 3.60(fair) to 3.90(fair). Other factors: The company's net asset base increased during the period by 28.1%, from $14.0 million to $17.9 million.

NARRAGANSETT BAY INS CO was upgraded to C- from D+ in July 2017 based on an increase in the capitalization index from a 8.30(excellent) to 9.00(excellent) and stability index from a 2.50(weak) to 3.00(fair). Other factors: Capital and surplus increased during the period by 5.4%, from $89.4 million to $94.2 million.

NASW RRG INC was upgraded to C- from D+ in July 2017 based on an increase in the stability index from a 2.10(weak) to 2.30(weak) and profitability index from a 4.00(fair) to 4.10(fair). Other factors: The company's net asset base increased during the period by 10.8%, from $13.9 million to $15.4 million.

NEW MEXICO SAFETY CASUALTY CO was upgraded to C- from D+ in July 2017 based on an increase in the stability index from a 2.10(weak) to 2.30(weak).

NORTH CAROLINA GRANGE MUTUAL INS CO was upgraded to C- from D+ in July 2017 based on an increase in the stability index from a 2.50(weak) to 2.60(weak). Other factors: Capital and surplus increased during the period by 14.4%, from $15.1 million to $17.2 million.

NUTMEG INS CO was upgraded to C+ from C in July 2017 based on an increase in the stability index from a 3.90(fair) to 4.40(fair).

PACIFIC PIONEER INS CO was upgraded to C- from D+ in July 2017 based on an increase in the capitalization index from a 4.60(fair) to 5.30(good) and stability index from a 2.20(weak) to 2.30(weak).

PACIFIC SPECIALTY PROPERTY & CAS CO was upgraded to D- from E+ in July 2017 based on an increase in the stability index from a 0.50(weak) to 1.00(weak).

PEACE CHURCH RRG INC was upgraded to C- from D+ in July 2017 based on an increase in the stability index from a 2.50(weak) to 3.00(fair). Other factors: The company's net asset base increased during the period by 13.1%, from $20.9 million to $23.6 million.

PELICAN INS RRG was upgraded to C- from D+ in July 2017 based on an increase in the stability index from a 2.50(weak) to 3.00(fair) and capitalization index from a 7.90(excellent) to 8.00(excellent). Other factors: The company's net asset base increased during the period by 18.9%, from $17.0 million to $20.2 million.

PETROLEUM CAS CO was upgraded to B- from C+ in July 2017 based on an increase in the stability index from a 4.50(fair) to 4.90(good).

PREMIER GROUP INS CO was upgraded to B- from C+ in July 2017 based on an increase in the stability index from a 4.50(fair) to 5.00(good) and capitalization index from a 9.40(excellent) to 9.50(excellent). Other factors: The company's net asset base increased during the period by 22.8%, from $55.4 million to $68.1 million.

PREVISOR INS CO was upgraded or to C- from D+ in July 2017 based on the overall strength of the index ratios.

PRIME INS CO was upgraded to B- from C+ in July 2017 based on an increase in the stability index from a 4.50(fair) to 5.00(good) and capitalization index from a 7.40(excellent) to 7.70(excellent). Other factors: The company's net asset base increased during the period by 10.7%, from $82.3 million to $91.1 million.

PROGRESSIVE PROPERTY INS CO was upgraded to B- from C+ in July 2017 based on an increase in the stability index from a 4.50(fair) to 5.00(good) and capitalization index from a 7.30(excellent) to 7.40(excellent).

Rating Upgrades (Continued)

PROTECTIVE INS CO was upgraded to A- from B+ in July 2017 based on an increase in the stability index from a 6.50(good) to 6.90(excellent) and capitalization index from a 7.20(excellent) to 7.40(excellent).

RELIAMAX INS CO was upgraded to C- from D+ in July 2017 based on an increase in the capitalization index from a 3.90(fair) to 5.00(good) and stability index from a 2.50(weak) to 3.00(fair).

REPUBLIC MORTGAGE INS CO OF FLORIDA was upgraded to B from B- in July 2017 based on an increase in the stability index from a 3.70(fair) to 4.20(fair) and capitalization index from a 6.80(good) to 7.10(excellent).

REPUBLIC MORTGAGE INS CO OF NC was upgraded to C from C- in July 2017 based on an increase in the capitalization index from a 1.60(weak) to 2.20(weak) and stability index from a 2.90(fair) to 3.40(fair).

RESTORATION RRG INC was upgraded to B- from C+ in July 2017 based on an increase in the stability index from a 4.50(fair) to 5.00(good) and capitalization index from a 6.90(excellent) to 7.20(excellent).

RETAILERS CASUALTY INS CO was upgraded to B- from C+ in July 2017 based on an increase in the stability index from a 4.50(fair) to 5.00(good) and capitalization index from a 8.20(excellent) to 8.50(excellent).

RETAILERS INS CO was upgraded to C- from D+ in July 2017 based on an increase in the stability index from a 2.50(weak) to 3.00(fair) and capitalization index from a 7.20(excellent) to 7.50(excellent).

RETAILFIRST INS CO was upgraded to A- from B+ in July 2017 based on an increase in the stability index from a 6.50(good) to 7.00(excellent) and capitalization index from a 8.40(excellent) to 8.50(excellent).

RVOS FARM MUTUAL INS CO was upgraded to C- from D+ in July 2017 based on an increase in the stability index from a 2.50(weak) to 3.00(fair) and capitalization index from a 6.80(good) to 7.10(excellent).

SAFE HARBOR INS CO was upgraded to B- from C+ in July 2017 based on an increase in the capitalization index from a 5.90(good) to 7.00(excellent) and stability index from a 4.50(fair) to 5.00(good). Other factors: The company's net asset base increased during the period by 5.2%, from $78.6 million to $82.7 million.

SAFE INS CO was upgraded or to C- from D+ in July 2017 based on the overall strength of the index ratios.

SECURIAN CASUALTY CO was upgraded to A- from B+ in July 2017 based on an increase in the stability index from a 6.50(good) to 6.90(excellent).

SERVICE INS CO (NJ) was upgraded or to C- from D+ in July 2017 based on the overall strength of the index ratios.

SFM SELECT INS CO was upgraded or to C- from D+ in July 2017 based on the overall strength of the index ratios.

SIMED was upgraded to B- from C+ in July 2017 based on an increase in the stability index from a 4.50(fair) to 5.00(good) and profitability index from a 7.90(excellent) to 8.10(excellent).

SOMPO AM FIRE & MARINE INS CO was upgraded or to B- from C+ in July 2017 based on the overall strength of the index ratios.

SOMPO AMERICA INSURANCE CO was upgraded to A- from B+ in July 2017 based on an increase in the stability index from a 6.50(good) to 7.00(excellent) and capitalization index from a 9.40(excellent) to 9.80(excellent).

SOUTH CAROLINA FARM BUREAU INS was upgraded or to C- from D+ in July 2017 based on the overall strength of the index ratios.

SOUTHERN GENERAL INS CO was upgraded to C- from D+ in July 2017 based on an increase in the capitalization index from a 6.10(good) to 6.70(good) and stability index from a 2.50(weak) to 2.80(weak). Other factors: The company's net asset base increased during the period by 7.6%, from $50.3 million to $54.1 million.

SOUTHERN OAK INS CO was upgraded to B- from C+ in July 2017 based on an increase in the stability index from a 4.50(fair) to 5.00(good) and capitalization index from a 8.20(excellent) to 8.30(excellent).

ST CHARLES INS CO RRG was upgraded to D- from E+ in July 2017 based on an increase in the stability index from a 0.50(weak) to 1.00(weak).

STONETRUST COMMERCIAL INS CO was upgraded to B- from C+ in July 2017 based on an increase in the stability index from a 4.50(fair) to 4.90(good) and profitability index from a 4.40(fair) to 4.50(fair). Other factors: The company's net asset base increased during the period by 5.2%, from $153.2 million to $161.2 million. Capital and surplus increased during the period by 7.8%, from $56.2 million to $60.6 million.

SYNERGY COMP INS CO was upgraded to C- from D+ in July 2017 based on an increase in the capitalization index from a 5.10(good) to 6.60(good) and stability index from a 2.50(weak) to 3.00(fair). Other factors: The company's net asset base increased during the period by 5.7%, from $35.2 million to $37.2 million.

TEXAS MEDICAL INS CO was upgraded to C- from D+ in July 2017 based on an increase in the stability index from a 2.50(weak) to 3.00(fair) and capitalization index from a 7.80(excellent) to 8.00(excellent). Other factors: The company's net asset base increased during the period by 7.2%, from $54.3 million to $58.2 million.

TRADERS INS CO was upgraded to C- from D+ in July 2017 based on an increase in the capitalization index from a 2.80(weak) to 3.20(fair) and stability index from a 2.80(weak) to 3.00(fair). Other factors: The company's net asset base increased during the period by 10.3%, from $71.1 million to $78.4 million.

TRANSIT GENERAL INS CO was upgraded to C- from D+ in July 2017 based on an increase in the capitalization index from a 3.30(fair) to 5.40(good) and stability index from a 2.10(weak) to 2.20(weak). Other factors: The company's net asset base increased during the period by 50.6%, from $21.3 million to $32.1 million.

UNITED CASUALTY & SURETY CO INC was upgraded or to C- from D+ in July 2017 based on the overall strength of the index ratios.

UNITED HOME INS CO was upgraded to C- from D+ in July 2017 based on an increase in the capitalization index from a 3.40(fair) to 4.10(fair) and stability index from a 2.40(weak) to 2.50(weak).

UNITRIN ADVANTAGE INS CO was upgraded to C- from D+ in July 2017 based on an increase in the stability index from a 2.50(weak) to 3.00(fair) and profitability index from a 7.50(excellent) to 7.60(excellent).

UNIVERSAL INS CO was upgraded to C- from D+ in July 2017 based on an increase in the stability index from a 2.50(weak) to 2.70(weak) and profitability index from a 3.40(fair) to 3.50(fair). Other factors: The company's net asset base increased during the period by 7.4%, from $38.9 million to $41.8 million.

UPMC WORK ALLIANCE INC was upgraded to C- from D+ in July 2017 based on an increase in the profitability index from a 2.50(weak) to 2.70(weak) and stability index from a 2.10(weak) to 2.20(weak). Other factors: The company's net asset base increased during the period by 22.7%, from $5.1 million to $6.3 million. Capital and surplus increased during the period by 14.3%, from $2.0 million to $2.3 million.

US COASTAL INS CO was upgraded to C- from D+ in July 2017 based on an increase in the stability index from a 2.50(weak) to 2.70(weak).

WASHINGTON CASUALTY CO was upgraded to D- from E+ in July 2017 based on an increase in the stability index from a 0.50(weak) to 1.00(weak). Other factors: The company's net asset base increased during the period by 8.2%, from $23.0 million to $24.9 million.

WEST VIRGINIA MUTUAL INS CO was upgraded to C- from D+ in July 2017 based on an increase in the stability index from a 2.50(weak) to 3.00(fair).

WINDHAVEN INS CO was upgraded to D- from E+ in July 2017 based on an increase in the capitalization index from a 0.80(weak) to 1.20(weak), stability index from a 0.60(weak) to 0.90(weak), and profitability index from a 5.40(good) to 5.50(good). Other factors: The company's net asset base increased during the period by 13.4%, from $200.7 million to $227.6 million. Capital and surplus increased during the period by 8.9%, from $46.2 million to $50.3 million.

WORK FIRST CASUALTY CO was upgraded to C- from D+ in July 2017 based on an increase in the capitalization index from a 2.60(weak) to 3.90(fair) and stability index from a 2.40(weak) to 2.50(weak).

WRIGHT NATIONAL FLOOD INS CO was upgraded to B- from C+ in July 2017 based on an increase in the stability index from a 3.70(fair) to 4.80(fair).

YELLOWSTONE INS EXCHANGE was upgraded to C- from D+ in July 2017 based on an increase in the capitalization index from a 8.10(excellent) to 8.50(excellent) and stability index from a 2.50(weak) to 2.90(fair). Other factors: The company's net asset base increased during the period by 48.5%, from $15.1 million to $22.5 million.

AMERICAN INDEPENDENT INS CO was downgraded to D+ from C- in July 2017 based on a decrease in the stability index from a 2.90(fair) to 2.40(weak), capitalization index from a 5.60(good) to 5.10(good), and profitability index from a 1.30(weak) to 1.20(weak). Other factors: Capital and surplus decreased during the period by 28.7%, from $11.6 million to $9.0 million.

ATLANTIC BONDING CO was downgraded to D- from D in July 2017 based on a decrease in the stability index from a 1.40(weak) to 0.80(weak). Other factors: The company's net asset base decreased during the period by 24.3%, from $9.8 million to $7.9 million. Capital and surplus decreased during the period by 21.6%, from $9.1 million to $7.4 million.

AVIATION ALLIANCE INS RRG INC was downgraded to E- from E in July 2017 based on a decrease in the profitability index from a 1.50(weak) to 1.30(weak). Other factors: The company's net asset base decreased during the period by 7.2%, from $3.2 million to $3.0 million. Capital and surplus decreased during the period by 26.2%, from $1.0 million to $0.8 million.

CASTLEPOINT FLORIDA INS was downgraded to F having been placed into liquidation by the state insurance regulator in July 2016.

CASTLEPOINT INS CO was downgraded to F having been placed into liquidation by the state insurance regulator in July 2016.

DEVELOPERS SURETY & INDEMNITY CO was downgraded to D from C- in July 2017 based on a decrease in the capitalization index from a 2.90(fair) to 1.60(weak) and stability index from a 3.20(fair) to 2.10(weak).

FIDUCIARY INS CO OF AMERICA was downgraded to F following an order for liquidation being filed by the state insurance regulator in May 2017.

FULMONT MUTUAL INS CO was downgraded to E+ from D in July 2017 based on a decrease in the capitalization index from a 4.50(fair) to 3.30(fair), stability index from a 1.10(weak) to 0.40(weak), and profitability index from a 1.70(weak) to 1.60(weak). Other factors: The company's net asset base decreased during the period by 13.2%, from $3.8 million to $3.3 million. Capital and surplus decreased during the period by 24.8%, from $1.2 million to $0.9 million.

GALEN INS CO was downgraded to F having been placed into liquidation by the state insurance regulator in May 2017.

GOVT TECHNOLOGY INS CO RRG INC was downgraded to E from B- in July 2017 based on a decrease in the stability index from a 3.50(fair) to 0.00(weak), profitability index from a 7.20(excellent) to 3.90(fair), and capitalization index from a 6.20(good) to 3.80(fair). Other factors: Capital and surplus decreased during the period by 35.3%, from $0.8 million to $0.6 million.

HERMITAGE INS CO was downgraded to F having been placed into liquidation by the state insurance regulator in July 2016.

LEAGUE OF WI MUNICIPALITIES MUT INS was downgraded to C+ from B- in July 2017 based on a decrease in the profitability index from a 8.90(excellent) to 2.90(fair) and stability index from a 5.10(good) to 4.40(fair). Other factors: Capital and surplus decreased during the period by 14.7%, from $34.0 million to $29.6 million.

MANUFACTURING TECHNOLOGY MUT INS CO was downgraded to C+ from B- in July 2017 based on a decrease in the profitability index from a 8.90(excellent) to 3.00(fair) and stability index from a 4.80(fair) to 4.40(fair). Other factors: Capital and surplus decreased during the period by 10.2%, from $27.7 million to $25.2 million.

MASSACHUSETTS HOMELAND INS CO was downgraded to F having been placed into liquidation by the state insurance regulator in July 2016.

NEW MEXICO PREMIER INS CO was downgraded to C from C+ in July 2017 based on a decrease in the stability index from a 3.20(fair) to 2.80(weak).

NORTH EAST INS CO was downgraded to F having been placed into liquidation by the state insurance regulator in July 2016.

PARK INS CO was downgraded to E- from E in July 2017 based on a decrease in the profitability index from a 1.90(weak) to 1.50(weak). Other factors: Capital and surplus decreased during the period by 29.2%, from $2.7 million to $2.1 million.

PHOEBE RECIPROCAL RRG was downgraded to E from E+ in July 2017 based on a decrease in the profitability index from a 8.70(excellent) to 7.00(excellent), stability index from a 0.50(weak) to 0.00(weak), and capitalization index from a 9.00(excellent) to 8.80(excellent). Other factors: The company's net asset base decreased during the period by 35.0%, from $6.2 million to $4.6 million. Capital and surplus decreased during the period by 63.6%, from $4.9 million to $3.0 million.

PHYSICIANS INS MUTUAL was downgraded to E- from D- in July 2017 based on a decrease in the stability index from a 1.00(weak) to 0.10(weak), capitalization index from a 4.60(fair) to 4.20(fair), and profitability index from a 1.80(weak) to 1.50(weak). Other factors: The company's net asset base decreased during the period by 14.8%, from $4.5 million to $3.9 million. Capital and surplus decreased during the period by 66.7%, from $1.0 million to $0.6 million.

PLATINUM TRANSPORT INS RRG INC was downgraded to D- from D in July 2017 based on a decrease in the stability index from a 1.10(weak) to 0.70(weak), capitalization index from a 3.00(fair) to 2.70(weak), and profitability index from a 2.30(weak) to 2.20(weak). Other factors: Capital and surplus decreased during the period by 52.4%, from $1.6 million to $1.1 million.

SEAVIEW INS CO was downgraded to D+ from C- in July 2017 based on a decrease in the profitability index from a 8.60(excellent) to 7.90(excellent) and stability index from a 2.00(weak) to 1.60(weak). Other factors: Capital and surplus decreased during the period by 18.2%, from $13.3 million to $11.2 million.

UNITED HERITAGE PROP & CAS CO was downgraded to E+ from D+ in July 2017 based on a decrease in the profitability index from a 6.00(good) to 3.40(fair) and stability index from a 1.40(weak) to 0.60(weak). Other factors: Capital and surplus decreased during the period by 8.1%, from $17.0 million to $15.7 million.

UPMC HEALTH BENEFITS INC was downgraded to D from D+ in July 2017 based on a decrease in the stability index from a 2.60(weak) to 2.30(weak), capitalization index from a 1.80(weak) to 1.60(weak), and profitability index from a 3.80(fair) to 3.70(fair).

VIRGINIA PHYSICIANS RRG INC was downgraded to D from D+ in July 2017 based on a decrease in the profitability index from a 4.10(fair) to 3.00(fair), stability index from a 1.40(weak) to 1.00(weak), and capitalization index from a 8.00(excellent) to 7.90(excellent).

WELLSPAN RRG was downgraded to E+ from D in July 2017 based on a decrease in the profitability index from a 8.50(excellent) to 7.20(excellent), stability index from a 1.40(weak) to 0.50(weak), and capitalization index from a 7.30(excellent) to 7.20(excellent). Other factors: Capital and surplus decreased during the period by 44.7%, from $9.2 million to $6.4 million.

YORK INS CO OF MAINE was downgraded to F having been placed into liquidation by the state insurance regulator in July 2016.

Appendix

State Guaranty Associations

The states have established insurance guaranty associations to help pay claims to policyholders of failed insurance companies. However, there are several cautions which you must be aware of with respect to this coverage:

1. Most of the guaranty associations do not set aside funds in advance. Rather, states assess contributions from other insurance companies after an insolvency occurs.

2. There can be an unacceptably long delay before claims are paid.

3. Each state has different levels and types of coverage, often governed by legislation unique to that state that can sometimes conflict with coverage of other states. Generally speaking, most property and casualty lines of business written by licensed insurers are covered by guaranty associations subject to the conditions and limitations set forth in the various acts. The Guaranty Funds do not cover non-admitted carriers (except in the state of New Jersey). Most state guaranty funds will not cover title, surety, credit, mortgage guarantee or ocean marine insurance.

The table on the following page is designed to help you sort out these issues. However, it is not intended to handle all of them. If your carrier has failed and you need a complete answer, we recommend you contact your State Insurance Official.

Following is a brief explanation of each of the columns in the table.

1.	**Maximum Per Claim**	The maximum amount payable by the State Guaranty Fund on a single covered claim, with the exception of workers' compensation claims, which are paid in full in most states.
2.	**Workers' Comp. Paid in Full**	"Yes" indicates that there is no cap on the amount paid for workers' compensation claims.
3.	**Net Worth Provision**	A net worth provision gives the association the right to seek reimbursement from an insured if the insured's net worth exceeds $50 million, essentially excluding certain large organizations from coverage by the guaranty association. Roughly half of the states have a net worth provision. If a state has a provision, marked "yes", there are other conditions applicable; contact your local department of insurance for further information.
4.	**Guaranty Fund Trigger**	The action that triggers the guaranty fund process.

COVERAGE OF STATE GUARANTY FUNDS

STATE	MAXIMUM PER CLAIM	WORKERS' COMP. PAID IN FULL	NET WORTH PROVISION	GUARANTY FUND TRIGGER		
				FINAL ORDER OF LIQUIDATION WITH FINDING OF INSOLVENCY	FINDING OF INSOLVENCY ONLY	OTHER
Alabama	$150,000	Yes	Yes	X		(16)
Alaska	$500,000	Yes	None	X		
Arizona	$300,000	(8)	None	X		(16)
Arkansas	$300,000	(9)	Yes		X	
California	$500,000	Yes	None	X		
Colorado	$300,000	Yes	Yes	X		(16)
Connecticut	$400,000	Yes	Yes		X	
Delaware	$300,000	Yes	Yes	X		(16)
Dist. of Colombia	$300,000	Yes	Yes	X		(16)
Florida	$300,000 (1)	(10)	None	X		(17)
Georgia	$300,000	Yes	Yes	X		(16)
Hawaii	$300,000	Yes	Yes	X		
Idaho	$300,000	Yes	None	X		
Illinois	$500,000	Yes	Yes	X		(17)
Indiana	$300,000	Yes	Yes	X		(17)
Iowa	$500,000	Yes	yes (15)	X		
Kansas	$300,000	Yes	None	X		
Kentucky	$300,000	Yes	Yes	X		
Louisiana	$500,000	Yes	Yes	X		(18)
Maine	$300,000	Yes	Yes	X		
Maryland	$300,000 (2)	Yes	Yes	X		
Massachusetts	$300,000	Yes	Yes		X	
Michigan	(3)	Yes	Yes	X		(19)
Minnesota	$300,000	Yes	Yes	X		
Mississippi	$300,000	Yes	None	X		(16)
Missouri	$300,000	Yes	Yes	X		(16)
Montana	$300,000	Yes	Yes	X		
Nebraska	$300,000	Yes	None	X		
Nevada	$300,000	Yes	Yes	X		(20)
New Hampshire	$300,000	Yes	Yes	X		(21)
New Jersey	$300,000 (2)	(10)	Yes			(22)
New Mexico	$100,000	Yes	None	X		(16)
New York	$1,000,000 (4)	(10)	None			(23)
North Carolina	$300,000	Yes	Yes	X		(16)
North Dakota	$300,000	(11)	Yes	X		
Ohio	$300,000	(11)	Yes			(24)
Oklahoma	$150,000 (6)	Yes	Yes	X		
Oregon	$300,000	Yes	Yes	X		
Pennsylvania	$300,000	(10)	Yes	X		
Puerto Rico	$300,000	(12)	None	X		(16)
Rhode Island	$500,000	Yes	Yes	X		
South Carolina	$300,000	Yes	Yes		X	(25)
South Dakota	$300,000	Yes	Yes	X		
Tennessee	$100,000	Yes	Yes	X		
Texas	$300,000	Yes	Yes		X	(26)
Utah	$300,000	Yes	Yes			(22)
Vermont	$500,000	Yes	None	X		
Virgin Island	$50,000	(9)	None		X	
Virginia	$300,000	Yes	Yes			(22)
Washington	$300,000	(13)	None			(24)
West Virginia	$300,000	Yes	None			(24)
Wisconsin	$300,000 (5)	(12)	yes			(24)
Wyoming	$300,000 (2)	Yes	None	X		

NOTES

1. Limit of $100,000 per residential unit for policies covering condominium associations or homeowners' associations. Policies providing coverage for homeowner's insurance shall provide for an additional 200,000 for the portion of covered claim which relates only to the damage to the structure and contents.

2. Maximum claim per occurrence is $300,000.

3. $5,000,000 – Subject to Consumer Price Index.

4. $100,000 – Per claim or claimant

5. $1,000,000/Claim; $5,000,000/Policy (non residents)

6. $150,000 limit per claimant for each covered claim.

7. $300,000 is the limit on a sinlge risk, loss or life.

8. Workers' compensation claims of insolvent insurers paid by Arizona's state fund.

9. Workers' compensation payments subject only to maximu claim amount.

10. Workers' compensation not covered, workers' compensation claims covered by a separate workers' compensation security fund.

11. Workers' compensation insurance written exclusively through monopolistic state fund.

12. Workers' compensation payments subject to both deductible and maximum claim amount.

13. Workers compensation not covered except Longshore Harbor workers'. Workers' compensation insurance written exclusively through monopolistic state fund.

14. Covered clain does not include any claim that would otherwise be a covered clain under this part that has been rejected by any other state guaranty fund on the grounds that an insured's net worth is greater than that allowed under that state's guaranty fund law.

15. Iowa does not cover claim of person whose net worth is greater than that allowed by guaranty fund law of his or her state of residence.

16. Order not stayed or subject to supersedeas.

17. Liquidation order not final until there is no further right of appeal.

18. Associated also obligatd to pay claims of an insurer in rehabilitation upon joint motion of association and receiver; order not stayed or subject to supersedeas.

19. All appeals exhausted

20. Also triggered if the insolvent insurer is involved in a court proceeding to determine its status of solvency, rehabilitation or liquidation, and the court has prohibited the insurer from paying claims for more than thirty days.

21. A new act (NH Act of 2004) was enacted for insolvencies occurring after 8-6-2004 and defines an insolvent insurer as a licensed insurer against whom a final order of liquidation has been entered with a finding of insolvency by a court of competent jurisdiction in the insurer's state of domicile. The prior act requires a finding of insolvency only.

22. Order of liquidation with finding of insolvency.

23. Insolvency of Insurer.

24. Triggered by finding of insolvency and liquidation order.

25. Fails to meet obligation to policyholders and state.

26. Requires separate impairment order.

Although the NCIGF has made every effort to produce the most complete, up-to-date and accurate law summaries possible, this work is meant to be used for reference purposes only. It is not meant as a substitute for an official version of a state statue or for legal advice.

Information provided in the Coverage of State Guaranty Funds chart was obtained from the National Conference of Insurance Guaranty Funds (NCIGF).

State Insurance Commissioners'
Website and Departmental Phone Numbers

State	Official's Title	Website Address	Phone Number
Alabama	Commissioner	www.aldoi.org	(334) 269-3550
Alaska	Director	https://www.commerce.alaska.gov/web/ins/	(800) 467-8725
Arizona	Director	https://insurance.az.gov/	(602) 364-2499
Arkansas	Commissioner	www.insurance.arkansas.gov	(800) 282-9134
California	Commissioner	www.insurance.ca.gov	(800) 927-4357
Colorado	Commissioner	https://www.colorado.gov/dora/division-insurance	(800) 886-7675
Connecticut	Commissioner	http://www.ct.gov/cid/site/default.asp	(800) 203-3447
Delaware	Commissioner	http://delawareinsurance.gov/	(800) 282-8611
Dist. of Columbia	Commissioner	http://disb.dc.gov/	(202) 727-8000
Florida	Commissioner	www.floir.com/	(850) 413-3140
Georgia	Commissioner	www.oci.ga.gov/	(800) 656-2298
Hawaii	Commissioner	http://cca.hawaii.gov/ins/	(808) 586-2790
Idaho	Director	www.doi.idaho.gov	(800) 721-3272
Illinois	Director	www.insurance.illinois.gov/	(866) 445-5364
Indiana	Commissioner	www.in.gov/idoi/	(317) 232-2385
Iowa	Commissioner	www.iid.state.ia.us	(877) 955-1212
Kansas	Commissioner	www.ksinsurance.org	(800) 432-2484
Kentucky	Commissioner	http://insurance.ky.gov/	(800) 595-6053
Louisiana	Commissioner	www.ldi.la.gov/	(800) 259-5300
Maine	Superintendent	www.maine.gov/pfr/insurance/	(800) 300-5000
Maryland	Commissioner	http://insurance.maryland.gov/Pages/default.aspx	(800) 492-6116
Massachusetts	Commissioner	www.mass.gov/ocabr/government/oca-agencies/doi-lp/	(877) 563-4467
Michigan	Director	http://www.michigan.gov/difs	(877) 999-6442
Minnesota	Commissioner	http://mn.gov/commerce/	(651) 539-1500
Mississippi	Commissioner	http://www.mid.ms.gov/	(601) 359-3569
Missouri	Director	www.insurance.mo.gov	(800) 726-7390
Montana	Commissioner	http://csimt.gov/	(800) 332-6148
Nebraska	Director	www.doi.nebraska.gov/	(402) 471-2201
Nevada	Commissioner	www.doi.nv.gov/	(888) 872-3234
New Hampshire	Commissioner	www.nh.gov/insurance/	(800) 852-3416
New Jersey	Commissioner	www.state.nj.us/dobi/	(800) 446-7467
New Mexico	Superintendent	www.osi.state.nm.us/	(855) 427-5674
New York	Superintendent	www.dfs.ny.gov/	(800) 342-3736
North Carolina	Commissioner	www.ncdoi.com	(800) 546-5664
North Dakota	Commissioner	www.nd.gov/ndins/	(800) 247-0560
Ohio	Lieutenant Governor	www.insurance.ohio.gov/	(800) 686-1526
Oklahoma	Commissioner	www.ok.gov/oid/	(800) 522-0071
Oregon	Insurance Commissioner	www.oregon.gov/dcbs/insurance/Pages/index.aspx	(888) 877-4894
Pennsylvania	Commissioner	www.insurance.pa.gov/	(877) 881-6388
Puerto Rico	Commissioner	www.ocs.gobierno.pr	(787) 304-8686
Rhode Island	Superintendent	www.dbr.state.ri.us/divisions/insurance/	(401) 462-9500
South Carolina	Director	www.doi.sc.gov	(803) 737-6160
South Dakota	Director	http://dlr.sd.gov/insurance/default.aspx	(605) 773-3563
Tennessee	Commissioner	www.tn.gov/insurance/	(615) 741-2241
Texas	Commissioner	www.tdi.texas.gov/	(800) 252-3439
Utah	Commissioner	www.insurance.utah.gov	(800) 439-3805
Vermont	Commissioner	www.dfr.vermont.gov/	(802) 828-3301
Virgin Islands	Lieutenant Governor	http://ltg.gov.vi/division-of-banking-and-insurance.html	(340) 774-7166
Virginia	Commissioner	www.scc.virginia.gov/boi/	(804) 371-9741
Washington	Commissioner	www.insurance.wa.gov	(800) 562-6900
West Virginia	Commissioner	www.wvinsurance.gov	(888) 879-9842
Wisconsin	Commissioner	oci.wi.gov	(800) 236-8517
Wyoming	Commissioner	http://doi.wyo.gov/	(800) 438-5768

Risk-Adjusted Capital for Property and Casualty Insurers in Weiss Rating Model

Among the most important indicators used in the analysis of an individual company are our two risk-adjusted capital ratios, which are useful tools in determining exposure to investment, liquidity and insurance risk in relation to the capital the company has to cover those risks.

The first risk-adjusted capital ratio evaluates the company's ability to withstand a moderate loss scenario. The second ratio evaluates the company's ability to withstand a severe loss scenario.

In order to calculate these Risk-Adjusted Capital Ratios, we follow these steps:

1. Capital Resources	First, we find out how much capital a company actually has by adding the company's resources which could be used to cover unexpected losses. These resources are primarily composed of stock issued by the company (capital) and accumulated funds from prior year profits (retained earnings or surplus). Additional credit can also be given for conservative reserving practices and other "hidden capital" where applicable.
	Conservative policy reserves can be an important source of capital and can contribute significantly to the financial strength of a company. Companies that set aside more than is necessary in their reserves year after year are less likely to be over run with claims and forced to dip into capital to pay them. Conversely, a company that understates its reserves year after year will be forced to routinely withdraw from capital to pay claims. Accordingly, we give companies credit for consistent over- reserving and penalize companies for consistent under-reserving.
2. Target Capital	Next, we determine how much capital the company should have to cover moderate losses based upon the company's level of risk in both its insurance business and its investment portfolio. We examine each of the company's risk areas and determine how much capital is needed for each area, based on how risky it is and how much exposure it has in that area. Then we combine these amounts to arrive at a total risk figure.
	Credit is given for the company's diversification, since it is unlikely that "the worst" will happen in all areas at once.
3. Risk-Adjusted Capital Ratio #1	We compare the results of Step 1 with those of Step 2. Specifically, we divide the "capital resources" by the "target capital" and express it in terms of a ratio. This ratio is called RACR #1.
	If a company has a Risk-Adjusted Capital Ratio of 1.0 or more, it means the company has all of the capital we believe it requires to withstand potential losses which could be inflicted by a moderate economic decline. If the company has a ratio of less than 1.0, it does not currently have all of the capital resources we think it needs. During times of financial distress, companies often have access to additional capital through contributions from a parent or holding company, current profits or reductions in dividends. Therefore, we make an allowance for firms with Risk-Adjusted Capital Ratios of somewhat less than 1.0.

4. Risk-Adjusted Capital Ratio #2	We repeat Steps 2 and 3 but now assume a severe loss scenario. This ratio is called RACR #2.	
5. Risk-Adjusted Capital Index	We convert RACR #1 and #2 into an index. It is measured on a scale of zero to ten, with ten being the best and seven or better considered strong. A company whose capital resources exactly equal its target capital will have a Risk-Adjusted Capital Ratio of 1.0 and a Risk-Adjusted Capital Index of 7.0.	

How We Determine Target Capital

The basic procedure for determining target capital is to identify the risk areas where the company is exposed to loss such as: (1) the risk of receiving more claims than expected; (2) the risk of not being able to collect from reinsurers or others who owe the company money; (3) the risk of losses on investments and (4) the risk of having inadequate reserves. Then we ask questions, such as:

- What is the breakdown of the company's investment portfolio? What types of policies does the company offer? Who owes the company money and how likely are they to pay? What losses has the company experienced on its underwriting (when claims and expenses exceeded premiums)? How accurate have reserve estimates been? What exposure does the company have to catastrophic property losses, such as Hurricane Andrew or the Los Angeles earthquake? What exposure does the company have to catastrophic liability losses such as asbestos pollution?

- For each category, what are the potential losses which could be incurred in both a moderate loss and a severe loss scenario?

- In order to cover those potential losses, how much in capital resources does the company need? It stands to reason that more capital is needed as a cushion for losses on high-risk investments, such as junk bonds, than on low-risk investments, such as AAA-rated utility bonds.

Amounts from each separate risk area are added together and adjustments are made to take into account the low likelihood that all risk areas would suffer severe losses at the same time. Finally, target capital is adjusted for the company's spread of risk in the diversification of its investment portfolio, the size and number of the policies it writes and the diversification of its business.

Table 1 on the next page shows target capital percentages used in Weiss Ratings Risk-Adjusted Capital Ratios #1 and #2 (RACR #1 and RACR #2).

The percentages shown in the table answer the question: How much should the firm hold in capital resources for every $100 it has committed to each category? Several of the items in Table 1 are expressed as ranges. The actual percentages used in the calculation of target capital for an individual company are determined by the levels of risk in the operations, investments or policy obligations of that specific company.

Table 1. Target Capital Percentages

Invested Asset Risk	Weiss Ratings	
	RACR#	RACR#2
Bonds	(%)	(%)
Government guarantee bonds	0	0
Class 1	.5-.75	1-1.5
Class 2	2	5
Class 3	5	15
Class 4	10	30
Class 5	20	60
Class 6	20	60
Preferred Stock	7	9.1
Common Stock		
Unaffiliated	25	33
Affiliated	25-100	33-100
Mortgages	5	15
Real Estate	10	33
Short-term investment	0.5	1
Collateral loans	2	5
Other invested assets	5	10
Credit Risk		
Agents' Balances	0.5	1
Premium Notes	2	5
Receivable Investment Income	2	3
Misc. Non-invested Assets	5	10
Reinsurance Recov. Current	1	1.5
30 to 90 Days Overdue	2	3
90 to 180 Days Overdue	5	7.5
More Than 180 Days Overdue	10	15
Rein Recov on Unpaid Losses	5	7.5
Rein Recov on IBNR	10	15
Rein Recov on UEP	5	7.5
Off Balance Sheet RBC		
Noncontrolled assets	1	2
Guarantee for affiliates	2	5
Contingent Liabilities	2	5
Reserve Risk*		
Homeowner Reserves	19-152	22-176
Private Auto Reserves	10-80	14-108
Commercial Auto Reserves	11-88	14-108
Worker's Comp Reserves	8-60	21-168
Commercial Multiple Peril Res.	19-152	22-176
Medical Malpractice Res.	26-208	39-312
Special Liability Res.	13-100	15-120
Other Liability Res.	24-192	26-208
International Reserves	16-128	19-152
Product Liability Reserves	24-192	39-312
Health Lines Reserves	15-116	23-180
Other Lines Reserves	20-156	25-196
Premium Risk*		
Homeowners NPW	29-260	43-260
Auto Liability NPW	34-304	35-319
Worker's Comp NPW	34-303	40-363
Commercial Multiperil NPW	30-272	39-347
Medical Malpractice NPW	53-478	79-478
Special Liabilities NPW	29-266	32-281
Other Liabilities NPW	38-342	49-441
International NPW	41-373	43-388
Product Liabilities NPW	41-365	52-464
Other Lines NPW	24-220	26-234

* All numbers are shown for illustrative purposes. Figures actually used in the formula vary annually based on industry experience.

Investment Class		**Description**
Government guaranteed bonds		Guaranteed bonds issued by U.S. and other governments which receive the top rating of state insurance commissioners
Bonds	Class 1	Investment grade bonds rated AAA, AA or A by Moody's or Standard & Poor's or deemed AAA - A equivalent by state insurance regulators
	Class 2	Investment grade bonds with some speculative elements rated BBB or equivalent
	Class 3	Noninvestment grade bonds, rated BB or equivalent
	Class 4	Noninvestment grade bonds, rated B or equivalent
	Class 5	Noninvestment grade bonds, rated CCC, C, C- or equivalent
	Class 6	Noninvestment grade bonds, in or near default
Preferred Stock		
Common Stock		Unaffiliated common stock Affiliated common stock
Mortgages		
Real Estate		Company occupied and other investment properties
Short-term Investments		All investments whose maturities at the time of acquisition were one year or less
Collateral Loans		Loans made to a company or individual where the underlying security is in the form of bonds, stocks or other marketable securities
Other Invested Assets		Any invested assets that do not fit under the main categories above

Credit Risk

Agents' Balances	Amounts which have been booked as written and billed to agents
Premium Notes	Loans to policyholders for payments of premiums
Receivable Interest Income	Interest income due but not yet received
Misc. Non-invested Income	Misc. income that is not related to invested assets
Reinsurance Recov. Current	Current receivables from reinsurers for their portion of the recorded losses
30 to 90 Days Overdue	Receivables from reinsurers 30 - 90 days overdue
90 to 180 Days Overdue	Receivables from reinsurers 90 - 180 days overdue
More Than 180 Days Overdue	Receivables from reinsurers more than 180 days overdue
Rein. Recov. on Unpaid Losses	Receivables from reinsurers for unpaid losses
Rein. Recov. on IBNR	Receivables from reinsurers for incurred but not reported losses
Rein. Recov. on UEP	Receivables from reinsurers for unearned premium

Off Balance Sheet Risk

Noncontrolled Assets	Assets not subject to complete insurer control
Guarantee for Affiliates	Guarantees on behalf of affiliates
Contingent Liabilities	Liabilities that are likely to happen but are not certain

Table 2. Bond Default Rates - potential losses as a percent of bond portfolio

Bond Rating	(1) Moody's 15 Yr Rate (%)	(2) Moody's 12 Yr Rate (%)	(3) Worst Year (%)	(4) 3 Cum. Recession Years (%)	(5) Weiss 15 Year Rate (%)	(6) Assumed Loss Rate (%)	(7) Losses as % of Holdings (%)	(8) RACR #2 Rate (%)
Aaa	0.73	0.55	0.08	0.24	0.79	50	0.95	1.00
Aa	1.39	1.04	0.13	0.39	1.43	50	1.09	1.00
A	4.05	2.96	0.35	1.05	4.02	55	2.02	1.00
Baa	7.27	5.29	0.67	2.02	7.31	60	5.15	5.00
Ba	23.93	19.57	2.04	6.11	25.68	65	23.71	15.00
B	43.37	39.30	4.99	14.96	54.26	70	43.57	30.00

Comments on Target Capital Percentages

The factors in the RACR calculations can be grouped into five categories: (1) Investment Risks; (2) Credit Risks; (3) Off Balance Sheet Risks; (4) Reserve Risks and (5) Premium Risks. Each of these has numerous subcomponents. The five categories are discussed below along with specific comments on some of the most important subcomponents.

Investment Risks:

Bonds

Target capital percentages for bonds are derived from a model that factors in historical cumulative bond default rates from the last 45 years and the additional loss potential during a prolonged economic decline.

Table 2 shows how this was done for each bond rating classification. A 15-year cumulative default rate is used (column 1). These are historical default rates for 1970-2015 for each bond class, taken from Moody's Annual Default Study. To factor in the additional loss potential of a severe three-year-long economic decline, we reduced the base to Moody's 12-year rate (column 2), determined the worst single year experience (column 3), extended that experience over three years (column 4) and added the historical 12-year rate to the 3-year projection to derive Weiss Ratings 15-year default rate (column 5). The next step was to determine the losses that could be expected from these defaults. This would be equivalent to the capital a company should have to cover those losses. Loss rates were assigned for each bond class (column 6), based on the fact that higher rated issues generally carry less debt and the fact that the debt is also better secured, leading to higher recovery rates upon default.

Column 7 shows losses as a percent of holdings for each bond class. Column 8 shows the target capital percentages that are used in RACR #2 (Table 1, RACR #2 column, Bonds -classes 1 to 6).

Regulations limiting junk bond holdings of insurers to a set percent of assets are a tacit acknowledgement that the reserve requirements used by State Insurance Commissioners are inadequate. If the figure adequately represented full loss potential, there would be no need to limit holdings through legislation since an adequate loss reserve would provide sufficient capital to absorb potential losses.

| **Affiliate Common Stock** | These stocks are often only "paper" assets, difficult to sell, and not truly available to pay insurance claims. The appropriate value of the stock may also be difficult to determine unless the stock is publicly traded. |

The target capital rate on affiliate common stock for RACR #2 can vary between 33% and 100% (Table 1, RACR #2 column, Common stock — Affiliated), depending on the financial strength of the affiliate and the prospects for obtaining capital from the affiliate should the need arise.

| **Credit Risk** | This category refers to the financial risk faced if the company cannot collect funds it is owed. These include funds owed to the company by its agents and reinsurers. |

| **Off Balance Sheet Risk** | A miscellaneous category of risk that is developed from data not found on the company's balance sheet. It includes risks associated with rapid premium growth, unsettled lawsuits against the company, guarantees to affiliates and investment risks such as interest rate swaps. |

| **Reserve Risk** | The risk that reserve estimates are too low to pay all outstanding claims. Target capital percentages used for each line of business are based on the historical experience of both the company and industry, for that line. |

Rather than basing our figures solely on the company's average experience over the last nine years, we factor in the company's worst results over the same period. We believe that this gives a more realistic appraisal of the company's loss potential. Of two companies with identical averages, one may have greater ups and downs than the other.

Target capital requirements have been reduced for each line of business in order to reflect the time value of money. As claims are generally paid months or years after premiums are received, insurers invest those premium funds, accumulating investment income until the claims must be paid. The discount given varies from 9% for private auto liability, a "short-tail" line where claims are paid shortly after receipt of premiums, to 21% for medical malpractice, a "long-tail" line where claims are generally paid many years after receipt of premiums.

| **Premium Risk** | The risk that premium levels are not sufficient to pay claims and related expenses. Individual target capital percentages are used for each line of business based on the riskiness of the line and the company's own experience with reserve risk. Target capital requirements are reduced to account for the time value of money, using a technique similar to that used for reserve risk. |

| **Risky Lines of Business and Catastrophic Losses** | These include fire, earthquake, multiple peril (including storm damage) and similar personal and commercial property coverages. Even excluding Hurricane Andrew, and other major storms since then, the insured losses from natural disasters since 1989 have been far greater than in previous decades. Yet, too many insurance companies are basing their risk calculations on the assumption that losses will return to more normal levels. They are not ready for the possibility that the pattern of increasing disasters might be a real, continuing trend. |

Also considered high risk lines are medical malpractice, general liability, product liability and other similar liability coverages. Court awards for damages often run into the millions. These settlement amounts can be very difficult to predict. This uncertainty hinders an insurer's ability to accurately assess how much to charge policyholders and how much to set aside to pay claims. Of special concern are large, unexpected liabilities related to environmental damages such as asbestos. Similar risk may lie hidden in coverage for medical equipment and procedures, industrial wastes, carcinogens and other substances found in products previously viewed as benign.

RECENT INDUSTRY FAILURES

2017

Institution	Headquarters	Industry	Date of Failure	At Date of Failure Total Assets ($Mil)	Safety Rating
IFA Ins Co	New Jersey	P&C	03/07/17	8.4	E (Very Weak)
Public Service Ins Co	New York	P&C	03/16/17	278.5	E (Very Weak)
Zoom Health Plan Inc	Oregon	Health	04/26/17	6.0	U (Unrated)
Galen Insurance Co	Missouri	P&C	05/31/17	10.0	E- (Very Weak)

2016

Institution	Headquarters	Industry	Date of Failure	At Date of Failure	
				Total Assets ($Mil)	Safety Rating
Consumers Choice Health Ins Co	South Carolina	Health	01/06/16	92.4	D (Weak)
Moda Health Plan Inc	Oregon	Health	01/28/16	445.5	D+ (Weak)
Family Health Hawaii MBS	Hawaii	Health	04/07/16	5.5	D (Weak)
Health Republic Ins of NY Corp	New York	Health	04/22/16	525.3	D (Weak)
Coordinated Health Mutual Inc	Ohio	Health	05/26/16	94.9	E (Very Weak)
HealthyCT Inc	Connecticut	Health	07/01/16	112.3	D+ (Weak)
Oregons Health Co-Op	Oregon	Health	07/11/16	46.6	D (Weak)
Land of Lincoln Mut Health Ins Co	Illinois	Health	07/14/16	107.8	D+ (Weak)
Excalibur Reins Corp	Pennsylvania	P&C	07/18/16	9.0	U (Unrated)
Castlepoint Florida Ins	Florida	P&C	07/28/16	100.0	D (Weak)
Castlepoint Insurance Co	New York	P&C	07/28/16	178.4	E (Very Weak)
Castlepoint National Ins Co	California	P&C	07/28/16	355.1	C- (Fair)
Hermitage Insurance Co	New York	P&C	07/28/16	167.6	E+ (Very Weak)
Massachusetts Homeland Ins Co	Massachusetts	P&C	07/28/16	8.9	C (Fair)
North East Insurance Co	Maine	P&C	07/28/16	35.9	D (Weak)
York Ins Co of Maine	Maine	P&C	07/28/16	47.0	C (Fair)
Careconcepts Ins Inc A RRG	Montana	P&C	08/08/16	3.8	E (Very Weak)
Freelancers Consumer Operated	New Jersey	Health	09/12/16	135.3	D+ (Weak)
Doctors & Surgeons Natl RRG IC	Kentucky	P&C	10/07/16	9.1	E+ (Very Weak)
American Medical & Life Ins Co	New York	L&H	12/28/16	4.4	U (Unrated)

2015

Institution	Headquarters	Industry	Date of Failure	At Date of Failure	
				Total Assets ($Mil)	Safety Rating
Millers Classified Ins Co	Illinois	P&C	01/20/15	2.7	E (Very Weak)
Eveready Ins Co	New York	P&C	01/29/15	10.6	E- (Very Weak)
Jordan Funeral and Ins Co, Inc	Alabama	L&H	02/17/15	1.1	U (Unrated)
Drivers Insurance Co	New York	P&C	03/12/15	3.0	E- (Very Weak)
Lumbermens Underwriting Alliance	Missouri	P&C	05/19/15	354.3	E- (Very Weak)
Pinelands Ins Co RRG, Inc	District of Columbia	P&C	08/25/15	4.9	E (Very Weak)
Louisiana Health Cooperative, Inc	Louisiana	Health	09/01/15	59.5	E (Very Weak)
Affirmative Ins Co	Illinois	P&C	09/16/15	181.2	E (Very Weak)
Affirmative Casualty Ins Co	Louisiana	P&C	10/05/15	32.6	D+ (Weak)
Affirmative Direct Ins Co	New York	P&C	10/05/15	5.3	U (Unrated)
Nevada Health Co-op	Nevada	Health	10/14/15	47.9	E- (Very Weak)
WINHealth Partners	Wyoming	Health	10/21/15	34.0	D (Weak)
Kentucky Health Cooperative Inc	Kentucky	Health	10/29/15	189.5	D+ (Weak)
Meritus Mutual Health Partners	Arizona	Health	10/30/15	45.8	D (Weak)
Meritus Health Partners	Arizona	Health	10/30/15	43.0	D+ (Weak)
Regis Ins Co	Pennsylvania	P&C	10/30/15	.6	E- (Very Weak)
Arches Mutual Ins Co	Utah	Health	11/02/15	77.2	D (Weak)
Lincoln General Ins Co	Pennsylvania	P&C	11/05/15	65.6	E- (Very Weak)
Advantage Health Solutions Inc	Indiana	Health	11/06/15	64.2	E (Very Weak)
Colorado Health Ins Coop Inc	Colorado	Health	11/10/15	108.7	D+ (Weak)
Consumers Mutual Ins of Michigan	Michigan	Health	11/13/15	60.4	E- (Very Weak)

2014

Institution	Headquarters	Industry	Date of Failure	At Date of Failure Total Assets ($Mil)	Safety Rating
Union Mutual Ins Co	Oklahoma	P&C	01/24/14	5.1	E+ (Very Weak)
Commonwealth Ins Co	Pennsylvania	P&C	03/20/14	1.1	E (Very Weak)
LEMIC Ins Co	Louisiana	P&C	03/31/14	51.6	D (Weak)
Interstate Bankers Casualty Co	Illinois	P&C	04/16/14	16.2	D+ (Weak)
Freestone Ins Co	Delaware	P&C	04/28/14	421.2	D- (Weak)
Alameda Alliance For Health	California	Health	05/05/14	176.3	D (Weak)
Sunshine State Ins Co	Florida	P&C	06/03/14	22.9	E+ (Very Weak)
Physicians United Plan Inc	Florida	Health	06/09/14	110.7	E (Very Weak)
Red Rock Ins Co	Oklahoma	P&C	08/01/14	28.5	E+ (Very Weak)
DLE Life Ins co	Louisiana	L&H	10/02/14	39.3	D+ (Weak)
Mothe Life Ins Co	Louisiana	L&H	10/02/14	15.2	E- (Very Weak)
First Keystone RRG Inc	South Carolina	P&C	10/21/14	13.6	E+ (Very Weak)
SeeChange Health Ins Co	California	Health	11/19/14	23.4	D (Weak)
PROAIR Risk Retention Grp Inc	Nevada	P&C	11/12/14	0.5	U (Unrated)
Florida Healthcare Plus, Inc	Florida	Health	12/10/14	11.1	U (Unrated)
CoOportunity Health, Inc	Iowa	Health	12/23/14	195.7	U (Unrated)

2013

Institution	Headquarters	Industry	Date of Failure	Total Assets ($Mil)	Safety Rating
				At Date of Failure	
Partnership Health Plan Inc	Wisconsin	Health	01/18/13	27.1	D (Weak)
Driver's Insurance Co	Oklahoma	P&C	02/21/13	33.1	D+ (Weak)
Lewis & Clark LTC RRG	Nevada	P&C	02/28/13	16.4	E (Very Weak)
Pride National Ins Co	Oklahoma	P&C	03/08/13	17.1	E+ (Very Weak)
Santa Fe Auto	Texas	P&C	03/08/13	22.9	E (Very Weak)
Ullico Casualty Co	Delaware	P&C	03/11/13	327.7	D (Weak)
Builders Ins Co Inc	Nevada	P&C	03/15/13	15.0	U (Unrated)
Nevada Contractors Ins Co Inc	Nevada	P&C	03/15/13	49.0	U (Unrated)
Universal Health Care Ins Co Inc	Florida	Health	03/22/13	106.1	C (Fair)
Universal Health Care Inc	Florida	Health	03/25/13	109.0	D (Weak)
Universal HMO of Texas	Texas	Health	04/18/13	15.3	C- (Fair)
Universal Health Care of NV Inc	Nevada	Health	06/03/13	1.9	D+ (Weak)
Liberty First RRG Ins Co	Utah	P&C	08/06/13	2.5	E (Very Weak)
United Contrs Ins Co Inc, RRG	Delaware	P&C	08/22/13	17.0	E (Very Weak)
Advance Physicians Ins RRG, Inc	Arizona	P&C	08/29/13	1.9	D (Weak)
Georgia Mutual Ins Co	Georgia	P&C	09/10/13	3.3	D (Weak)
Ocean Risk Retention Group	D.C.	P&C	09/06/13	7.9	E (Very Weak)
Gertrude Geddes Willis Life Ins Co	Louisiana	L&H	10/24/13	4.9	U (Unrated)
San Antonio Indemnity Co	Texas	P&C	10/31/13	2.8	E+ (Very Weak)
Higginbotham Burial Ins Co	Arkansas	L&H	11/04/13	1.3	U (Unrated)
Indemnity Ins Corp RRG	Delaware	P&C	11/07/13	83.2	D- (Weak)
Concert Health Plan Ins Co	Illinois	L&H	12/10/13	1.8	D- (Weak)
ICM Insurance Co	New York	P&C	12/23/13	5.0	E+ (Very Weak)

2012

Institution	Headquarters	Industry	Date of Failure	At Date of Failure Total Assets ($Mil)	Safety Rating
Autoglass Ins Co	New York	P&C	01/09/12	29.7	E+ (Very Weak)
Hlth Facilities of CA Mut I C RRG	Nevada	P&C	01/10/12	1.9	U (Unrated)
Republic Mortgage Ins Co	North Carolina	P&C	01/19/12	1.41	E (Very Weak)
CAGC Ins Co	North Carolina	P&C	01/26/12	11.8	U (Unrated)
First Sealord Surety Inc	Pennsylvania	P&C	02/08/12	15.2	U (Unrated)
Scaffold Industry Ins Co RRG Inc	D.C.	P&C	05/01/12	5.1	E+ (Very Weak)
Financial Guaranty Ins Co	New York	P&C	06/11/12	2054.0	E- (Very Weak)
Global Health Plan & Ins Co	Puerto Rico	Health	06/13/12	1.1	U (Unrated)
Garden State Indemnity Co, Inc	New Jersey	P&C	06/22/12	2.93	E- (Very Weak)
AvaHealth Inc	Florida	HMO	06/27/12	3.3	E (Very Weak)
American Manufacturers Mutual	Illinois	P&C	07/02/12	10.3	E+ (Very Weak)
Lumbermens Mutual Casualty Co	Illinois	P&C	07/02/12	789.4	E (Very Weak)
Millers First Ins Co	Illinois	P&C	07/24/12	23.0	E (Very Weak)
American Motorists Ins Co	Illinois	P&C	08/16/12	19.7	D (Weak)
Home Value Ins Co	Ohio	P&C	08/31/12	3.5	U (Unrated)
Northern Plains Ins Co	South Dakota	P&C	09/18/12	1.4	D (Weak)
Jamestown Ins Co RRG	South Carolina	P&C	09/24/12	5.9	E+ (Very Weak)
Interstate Auto Ins Co	Maryland	P&C	10/11/12	4.6	D (Weak)
Regional Health Ins Co, RRG	D.C.	P&C	10/18/12	0.6	U (Unrated)
DC Chartered Health Plan Inc	D.C.	HMO	10/19/12	65.4	E- (Very Weak)
American Fellowship Mut Ins Co	Michigan	P&C	10/29/20	50.0	D (Weak)
Gramercy Ins Co	Texas	P&C	12/04/12	41.8	D (Weak)
Triad Guaranty Ins Corp	Illinois	P&C	12/11/12	766.7	E (Very Weak)
Triad Guaranty ASR Corp	Illinois	P&C	12/11/12	16.1	B (Good)

Glossary

This glossary contains the most important terms used in this publication.

Admitted Assets	The total of all investments and business interests which are acceptable under statutory accounting rules.
Asset/Liability Matching	Management of cash flows so that investments pay interest or mature at just the right time to meet the need for cash to pay claims and expenses.
Average Recession	A recession involving a decline in real GDP which is approximately equivalent to the average of the postwar recessions of 1957-58, 1960, 1970, 1974-75, 1980, 1981-82, 1990-1991, 2001, and 2007-2009. It is assumed, however, that in today's market, the financial losses suffered from a recession of that magnitude would be greater than those experienced in previous decades. (See also "Severe Recession.")
Capital	Strictly speaking, capital refers to funds raised through the sale of common and preferred stock. Mutual companies have capital in the form of retained earnings. In a more general sense, the term capital is commonly used to refer to a company's equity or net worth, that is, the difference between assets and liabilities (i.e., capital and surplus as shown on the balance sheet).
Capital Resources	The sum of various resources which serve as a capital cushion to losses, including capital and surplus.
Cash and Demand Deposits	Includes cash on hand and on deposit. A negative figure indicates that the company has more checks outstanding than current funds to cover those checks. This is not an unusual situation for an insurance company.
Common and Preferred Stocks	See "Stocks".
Direct Premiums Written	Premiums derived from policies issued directly by the company. This figure excludes the impact of reinsurance.
Safety Rating	Weiss Safety Ratings grade insurers on a scale from A (Excellent) to F (Failed). Ratings for property and casualty insurers are based on five major factors: liquidity, reserve adequacy, capitalization, profitability, and stability of operations.
Five-Year Profitability Index	See "Profitability Index".

Government Securities	Securities issued and/or guaranteed by U.S. and foreign governments which are rated as highest quality (class 1) by state insurance commissioners. Included in this category are bonds issued by governmental agencies and guaranteed with the full faith and credit of the government. Regardless of the issuing entity, they are viewed as being relatively safer than the other investment categories.
Interest Rate Risk	The risk that, due to changes in interest rates, investment income will not meet the needs of policy commitments. This risk can be reduced by effective asset/liability matching.
Invested Assets	The total size of the firm's investment portfolio.
Investments in Affiliates	Includes bonds, preferred stocks and common stocks, as well as other vehicles which many insurance companies use to invest in— and establish a corporate link with—affiliated companies.
Line of Business	Types of insurance coverage such as fire, inland marine, group accident and health, auto physical damage and auto liability. Statutory accounting uses over 30 different lines of business. A particular insurer may write coverage in any or all of these lines.
Liquidity Index	An index, expressed on a scale of zero to ten, with seven or higher considered excellent, that measures a company's ability to raise the necessary cash to settle claims. It is possible for a company to have the resources to pay claims on paper, but be unable to raise the cash. This can occur when a company is owed a great deal of money by its agents or reinsurers, or when it cannot sell its investments at the anticipated price.
	Our liquidity tests examine how the company might fare under various cash flow scenarios.
Long/Short-Tail Lines	Time periods over which claims are paid out. For example, auto physical damage is considered a short-tail line, since claims are generally paid within one year of an accident. On the other hand, medical malpractice is considered a long-tail line as claims are typically paid five years or more after the occurrence of the incident giving rise to the claim.
	For the insurer, the risks associated with long-tail lines are greater than with short-tail lines because the period of uncertainty in which unexpected claims can arise is longer.
Moderate Loss Scenario	Possible future events that would result in loss levels comparable to those experienced in recent history. (Compare with "Severe Loss Scenario.")
Net Premiums Written	The dollar volume of premiums retained by the company. This figure is equal to direct premiums written, plus reinsurance assumed, less reinsurance ceded to other companies.

Noninvestment Grade Bonds	Low-rated issues, commonly known as "junk bonds," which carry a high risk as defined by the state insurance commissioners. These include bond classes 3 - 6.
Other Investments	Items not included in any of the other categories, such as premium notes, collateral loans, short-term investments and other miscellaneous items.
Premium Risk	The risk that, for a particular group of policies, premiums will not be sufficient to meet the level of claims and related expenses.
Profitability Index	An index, expressed on a scale of zero to ten, with seven or higher considered excellent, that measures the soundness of the company's operations and the contribution of profits to the company's fiscal strength. The Profitability Index is a composite of five factors: (1) gain or loss on underwriting (core insurance business); (2) gain or loss on overall operations; (3) consistency of operating results; (4) impact of operating results on surplus and (5) expenses in relation to industry averages for the types of policies that the company offers.
Real Estate	Direct real estate investments, including property (a) occupied by the company; (b) acquired through foreclosure of a mortgage and (c) purchased as an investment.
Reinsurance Assumed	Insurance risk acquired by taking on partial or full responsibility for claims on policies written by other companies. (See "Reinsurance Ceded.")
Reinsurance Ceded	Insurance risk sold to another company. When there is a claim on a reinsured policy, the original company generally pays the claim and then is reimbursed by its reinsurer.
Reserve Adequacy Index	An index, expressed on a scale of zero to ten with seven or higher considered excellent, that measures the adequacy of the company's reserves over the last five years. Companies that have a history of inadequate reserves will receive a low score. Reserves are company estimates of unsettled claims in each year, including both claims that have been received but not yet settled, as well as claims that the company expects to receive. A company that underestimates its claims inflates profits and capital. Additionally, chronically deficient reserves call into question the company's ability to manage its policy risk effectively.
Risk-Adjusted Capital	The capital resources that would be needed to deal with unexpected claims or other adverse developments (same as "Target Capital").
Risk-Adjusted Capital Ratio #1	The capital resources which a company currently has, expressed as a ratio, to the resources that would be needed to deal with a moderate loss scenario. (See "Moderate Loss Scenario.")

Risk-Adjusted Capital Ratio #2	The capital resources which a company currently has, expressed as a ratio, to the resources that would be needed to deal with a severe loss scenario. (See "Severe Loss Scenario.")
Severe Loss Scenario	Possible future events that could result in loss levels that are somewhat higher than recent experience. These levels are developed from examination of current trends. (Compare with "Moderate Loss Scenario.")
Severe Recession	A prolonged economic slowdown in which the single worst year of the postwar period is extended for a period of three years. (See also "Average Recession.")
Short-Tail Lines	See "Long/Short-Tail Lines".
Stability Index	An index, measured on a scale of zero to ten, integrating a wide variety of factors that reflect the company's stability and diversification of risk.
State of Domicile	Although most insurance companies are licensed to do business in many states, they have only one state of domicile. This is the state which has primary regulatory responsibility for the company. Use the state of domicile to make absolutely sure that you have the correct company. Bear in mind, however, that this need not be the state where the company's main offices are located.
State Guaranty Funds	Funds that are designed to raise cash from existing insurance carriers to cover policy claims of bankrupt insurance companies.
Stocks	Common and preferred equities, including stocks in affiliates.
Surplus	Accumulated funds from prior years' profits (retained earnings) plus additional amounts paid-in by a parent or other corporation. The term "surplus" is also sometimes used broadly to include capital such as common stock.
Target Capital	See "Risk-Adjusted Capital."
Total Assets	Total admitted assets, including investments and other business assets. (See "Admitted Assets.")